Financial Accounting Standards Board

"CURRENT TEXT"

1995/96 EDITION

ACCOUNTING STANDARDS

AS OF JUNE 1, 1995

VOLUME I

GENERAL STANDARDS
TOPICAL INDEX

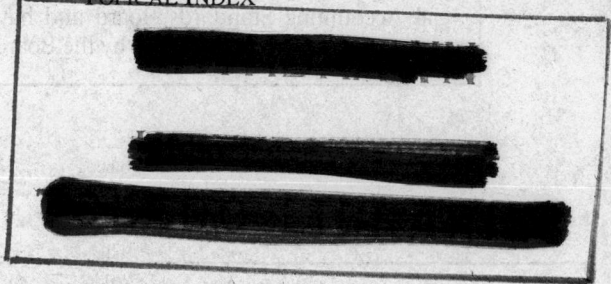

JOHN WILEY & SONS, INC.

New York • Chichester • Brisbane • Toronto • Singapore

y the
Standards Board

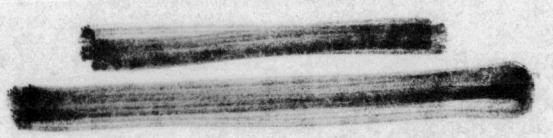

NOTICE TO USERS OF THE *CURRENT TEXT*

This year's edition of the Financial Accounting Standards Board's (FASB) *Current Text* has been updated to include revisions from the following new pronouncements:

FAS 118: Accounting by Creditors for Impairment of a Loan—Income Recognition and Disclosures

Section I08, "Impairment," has been revised to reflect the issuance of Statement 118. The Statement amends FASB Statement 114, *Accounting by Creditors for Impairment of a Loan,* to allow a creditor to use existing methods for recognizing interest income on an impaired loan. Statement 118 eliminates the provisions in Statement 114 that describe how a creditor should report income on an impaired loan. In addition, Statement 118 amends the disclosure requirements in Statement 114 to require information about the recorded investment in certain impaired loans and about how a creditor recognizes interest income related to those impaired loans.

FAS 119: Disclosure about Derivative Financial Instruments and Fair Value of Financial Instruments

Section F25, "Financial Instruments: Disclosure," has been revised to reflect the issuance of Statement 119. The Statement requires disclosures about derivative financial instruments—futures, forward, swap, and option contracts, and other financial instruments with similar characteristics. Statement 119 also amends existing disclosure requirements of FASB Statements 105, *Disclosure of Information about Financial Instruments with Off-Balance-Sheet Risk and Financial Instruments with Concentrations of Credit Risk,* and 107, *Disclosures about Fair Value of Financial Instruments.*

Statement 119 requires disclosures about the amounts, nature, and terms of derivative financial instruments that are not within the scope of Statement 105. It requires that a distinction be made between financial instruments held or issued for trading purposes and financial instruments held or issued for purposes other than trading.

FAS 120: Accounting and Reporting by Mutual Life Insurance Enterprises and by Insurance Enterprises for Certain Long-Duration Participating Contracts

Section In6, "Insurance Industry," has been revised to reflect the issuance of Statement 120. The Statement extends the requirements of FASB Statements 60, *Accounting and Reporting by Insurance Enterprises;* 97, *Accounting and Reporting by Insurance Enterprises for Certain Long-Duration Contracts and for Realized Gains and Losses from the Sale of Investments;* and 113, *Accounting and Reporting for Reinsurance of*

Short-Duration and Long-Duration Contracts, to mutual life insurance enterprises, assessment enterprises, and fraternal benefit societies. Statement 120 also provides that the provisions of AICPA Statement of Position 95-1, *Accounting for Certain Insurance Activities of Mutual Life Insurance Enterprises,* shall be applied to those participating life insurance contracts of mutual life insurance enterprises that meet the conditions specified in the Statement and that the SOP *may* be applied by stock life insurance enterprises to those participating contracts that meet those specified conditions.

FAS 121: Accounting for the Impairment of Long-Lived Assets and for Long-Lived Assets to Be Disposed Of

Section I08, "Impairment," has been revised to reflect the issuance of Statement 121. That Statement addresses accounting for the impairment of long-lived assets that will be held and used, including certain identifiable intangibles, and the goodwill related to those assets. The Statement also addresses the accounting for long-lived assets and certain identifiable assets to be disposed of.

Statement 121 requires that assets to be held and used be reviewed for impairment whenever events or changes in circumstances indicate that the carrying amount of the asset in question may not be recoverable. The Statement provides guidance for determining whether there is an impairment loss and requires the loss to be measured as the difference between the asset's fair value and its carrying amount. An asset to be disposed of, with certain exceptions, would be reported at the lower of carrying amount or fair value less the cost to sell the asset.

Many other sections in the General Standards and Industry Standards have been revised to reflect the provisions of Statement 121.

FAS 122: Accounting for Mortgage Servicing Rights

Section Mo4, "Mortgage Servicing Rights," has been revised to reflect the issuance of Statement 122. The Statement amends FASB Statement 65, *Accounting for Certain Mortgage Banking Activities,* to require mortgage servicers to recognize as separate assets rights to service mortgage loans, no matter how the rights were acquired. Statement 122 requires that mortgage servicers that sell or securitize loans and retain the servicing rights allocate the total cost of the mortgage loans to the servicing rights and loans based on fair value if practicable to estimate. If not practicable, the cost of acquiring the loans should be allocated to the mortgage loans only. The Statement also requires that mortgage banking enterprises assess their capitalized mortgage servicing rights for impairment based on the fair value of the rights.

FIN 41: Offsetting of Amounts Related to Certain Repurchase and Reverse Repurchase Agreements

Section B10, "Balance Sheet Display: Offsetting," has been revised to reflect the issuance of Interpretation 41. The Interpretation permits offsetting on the balance sheet of receivables and payables that represent repurchase and reverse repurchase agreements provided certain conditions are met.

Acknowledgments

Judith A. Noë, FASB project manager, compiled the *Current Text* with the assistance of Deborah L. Monroe, FASB assistant project manager. Eileen C. Mishley provided production assistance in the preparation of these volumes.

Norwalk, Connecticut

June 1995

Timothy S. Lucas
Director of Research and
Technical Activities

AN INTRODUCTION TO THE CURRENT TEXT

Material Disclosed in the *Current Text*

The FASB *Current Text* is an integration of currently effective accounting and reporting standards. Material in the *Current Text* is drawn from AICPA Accounting Research Bulletins, APB Opinions, FASB Statements of Financial Accounting Standards, and FASB Interpretations. Those pronouncements are covered by Rule 203 of the AICPA Code of Professional Conduct, which states:

> *Rule 203—Accounting principles.* A member shall not (1) express an opinion or state affirmatively that the financial statements or other financial data of any entity are presented in conformity with generally accepted accounting principles or (2) state that he or she is not aware of any material modifications that should be made to such statements or data in order for them to be in conformity with generally accepted accounting principles, if such statements or data contain any departure from an accounting principle promulgated by bodies designated by Council to establish such principles that has a material effect on the statements or data taken as a whole. If, however, the statements or data contain such a departure and the member can demonstrate that due to unusual circumstances the financial statements or data would otherwise have been misleading, the member can comply with the rule by describing the departure, its approximate effects, if practicable, and the reasons why compliance with the principle would result in a misleading statement.

Interpretation No. 2 of Rule 203 states:

> *Status of FASB interpretations.* Council is authorized under Rule 203 to designate a body to establish accounting principles and has designated the Financial Accounting Standards Board as such body. Council also has resolved that FASB Statements of Financial Accounting Standards, together with those Accounting Research Bulletins and APB Opinions which are not superseded by action of the FASB, constitute accounting principles as contemplated in Rule 203.
>
> In determining the existence of a departure from an accounting principle established by a Statement of Financial Accounting Standards, Accounting Research Bulletin or APB Opinion encompassed by Rule 203, the division of professional ethics will construe such Statement, Bulletin or Opinion in the light of any interpretations thereof issued by the FASB.

The *Current Text* also incorporates the supplemental guidance provided by FASB Technical Bulletins and AICPA Accounting Interpretations.

The *Current Text* does not in any way supersede, change, or otherwise affect the pronouncements from which it is drawn. Although edited by the FASB staff, the abridged text has not been subjected to the FASB's due process procedures used for issuing FASB Statements. The authority of the *Current Text* is derived from the underlying pronouncements, which remain in force.

Material Excluded from the *Current Text*

The *Current Text* does not include FASB Statements of Financial Accounting Concepts, issues discussed by the FASB Emerging Issues Task Force (EITF), or FASB Special Reports in question-and-answer format (Q&As). The concepts Statements may be found in *Original Pronouncements,* the companion publication to the *Current Text,* and *Statements of Financial Accounting Concepts.* The EITF issues are contained in the FASB's *EITF Abstracts* and the Q&As are available individually. (See the introduction to the topical index, page T-3, for order information.) References to all of the accounting literature referred to above are included in the *Current Text* topical index.

The *Current Text* also does not include AICPA audit and accounting Guides, Statements of Position, or Practice Bulletins, except as specialized principles in them have been extracted and issued in FASB Statements. Nor are Statements of International Accounting Standards included. All of those documents, however, are available from the American Institute of Certified Public Accountants, Order Department, P.O. Box 2209, Jersey City, NJ 07303-2209.

The *Current Text* is a condensed version of original pronouncements. Descriptive material, such as information about Exposure Drafts, respondents' comments, background information, and reasons for conclusions and dissents, is generally excluded. However, certain material contained in other than the standards section of an original pronouncement is included to help the reader understand or implement the *Current Text*. Readers wishing to better understand the rationale behind a pronouncement or seeking background information should refer to the original pronouncement from which the related *Current Text* material is drawn. This is easy to do because each paragraph in the *Current Text* contains a source reference to the original pronouncement.

Organization of Text

The *Current Text* integrates financial accounting and reporting standards according to the major subject areas to which they apply. The subjects are arranged alphabetically in sections that are grouped into two volumes. Volume I (General Standards) contains those standards that are generally applicable to all enterprises; Volume II (Industry Standards) contains specialized standards that are applicable to not-for-profit organizations and enterprises operating in specific industries. A comprehensive topical index is included in both Volumes I and II and various appendixes appear at the end of Volume II. (Refer to the introduction to the topical index for detailed information about the contents and use of the index.) The *Current Text* includes an appendix (G) showing where material from each paragraph of each original pronouncement is located in the *Current Text* or the reason why it is not included.

Each **section** is identified by an alpha-numeric code. (The numeric part has been arbitrarily selected to allow space for future additions.) The alpha-numeric code in the General Standards volume follows an alpha-numeric-numeric pattern (for example, A99), and the code in the Industry Standards volume follows an alpha-alpha-numeric pattern (for example, Aa9).

Paragraphs within each section are numbered consecutively, according to the following numeric format:

> Paragraphs .101 - .399: Standards
> Paragraphs .401 - .499: Glossary
> Paragraphs .501 - .999: Supplemental guidance (not covered by Rule 203)

All **section-paragraph references** are made in the following form: B05.127 or In6.102. For example, B05.127 refers to Section B05, "Balance Sheet Classification: Current Assets and Current Liabilities," paragraph .127, and In6.102 refers to Section In6, "Insurance Industry," paragraph .102.

Terms defined in the **Glossary** for a section are in boldface type the first time they appear in that section.

Source references are provided to indicate the original pronouncements from which material in each paragraph and footnote is derived. They appear in brackets and use the following abbreviations:

FAS	FASB Statement of Financial Accounting Standards
FIN	FASB Interpretation
FTB	FASB Technical Bulletin
CON	FASB Statement of Financial Accounting Concepts
APB	AICPA Accounting Principles Board Opinion
ARB	AICPA Accounting Research Bulletin
AIN	AICPA Accounting Interpretation
ch	chapter
fn	footnote

For example, the source reference [FIN21, ¶15, fn3] indicates footnote 3 to paragraph 15 of FASB Interpretation No. 21, *Accounting for Leases in a Business Combination*. Similarly, the source reference [AIN-APB15, #27] indicates the twenty-seventh AICPA Accounting Interpretation of APB Opinion No. 15, *Earnings per Share*.

Transitional language and editorial changes that *add* wording to an original pronouncement to maintain a consistent editorial style within the volumes appear in brackets. If an original pronouncement *deletes* wording from a previous pronouncement and it does not provide substitute wording, the amending pronouncement is not included in the source reference described in the preceding paragraph. Only the source reference for the earlier pronouncement is noted. However, Appendix B identifies the sources for all such deletions. Certain editorial deletions have been made to original pronouncements either to maintain a consistent editorial style or for clarity. Those deletions also are not noted. However, in such cases the deletions have not affected the substance of the text. Other changes, which are not presented in brackets, have been made to conform format (for example, "iii" may have been changed to "c"), to provide paragraph and exhibit headings, or to conform terminology, as follows:

Term in *Original Pronouncement*	Term in *Current Text*
should (meaning *must*)	shall
see (in making a reference)	refer to
which (in a restrictive clause)	that
where (not location)	if
when (not specific timing)	if
entity (if used broadly)	enterprise
company	enterprise
corporation	enterprise
earned surplus	retained earnings
capital surplus	additional paid-in capital
additional paid-in surplus	additional paid-in capital

Effective Dates and Transition Provisions of Underlying Pronouncements

The effective dates of FASB Statements of Financial Accounting Standards, FASB Interpretations, APB Opinions, and Accounting Research Bulletins, and the issue dates of AICPA Accounting Interpretations and FASB Technical Bulletins are summarized in Appendix C. That appendix also presents the transition paragraphs of more recent pronouncements whose effective dates and transition provisions are such that they might be initially applied in annual financial statements issued on or after June 1, 1995.

If an entire section of the *Current Text* is superseded by a recently issued pronouncement that has a significantly delayed effective date (for example, FASB Statement No. 106, *Employers' Accounting for Postretirement Benefits Other Than Pensions*), that superseded section is retained in the *Current Text* in a separate appendix (E) for the benefit of those enterprises that have not yet adopted the new standard. Appendix E also includes a topical index. To indicate that its material is superseded, the entire appendix is shaded.

Users may need to refer to Appendix C to determine if the requirements of recently issued pronouncements that do not affect entire sections are effective in their particular circumstances. Users concerned with accounting and reporting standards for financial statements of prior years also may need to refer to the original pronouncements that were effective for those years. Appendix B lists changes to original pronouncements as the result of subsequent pronouncements.

FASB Emerging Issues Task Force

The Emerging Issues Task Force (EITF) was established in 1984 to aid the FASB in identifying implementation and emerging issues that may ultimately require action by the FASB. Make-up of the Task Force is designed to include persons in a position to be aware of emerging issues before they become widespread and before divergent practices regarding them become entrenched. After discussing the issues and the relevant accounting pronouncements, the group sometimes can reach a consensus on an issue, in which case no action by the FASB is usually needed. Because the application of EITF consensuses is mandatory under AICPA Statement on Auditing Standards (SAS) No. 69 (see Appendix A), a listing of all issues discussed to date and their current status is presented in Appendix D and references to those issues are included in the comprehensive topical index.

The FASB publishes a summary of the proceedings of the Task Force in a loose-leaf service, *EITF Abstracts*. A separate Abstract is presented for each issue considered by the Task Force since its inception in 1984. A comprehensive topical index is included to facilitate quick identification of relevant issues that have been addressed by the Task Force. *EITF Abstracts* is also published annually in a bound version.

Copies of *EITF Abstracts,* the Issue Summary packages, and related meeting minutes can be obtained from the FASB Order Department. For information on prices and discounts, call (203) 847-0700.

Volume I

GENERAL STANDARDS
TABLE OF CONTENTS

		Page
Notice to Users of the Current Text		i
An Introduction to the Current Text		v

Section

A06	—Accounting Changes	251
A10	—Accounting Policies	421
A31	—Additional Paid-in Capital	1303
A35	—Adjustments of Financial Statements for Prior Periods	1471
B05	—Balance Sheet Classification: Current Assets and Current Liabilities	4471
B10	—Balance Sheet Display: Offsetting	4521
B50	—Business Combinations	4801
C08	—Capital Stock: Capital Transactions	5329
C11	—Capital Stock: Dividends-in-Kind	5529
C16	—Capital Stock: Preferred Stock	5859
C20	—Capital Stock: Stock Dividends and Stock Splits	5923
C23	—Capital Stock: Treasury Stock	6125
C25	—Cash Flows Statement	6251
C28	—Changing Prices: Reporting Their Effects in Financial Reports	6601
C30	—Collateralized Mortgage Obligations	6961
C32	—Commitments: Long-Term Obligations	6985
C38	—Compensation to Employees: Deferred Compensation Agreements	7081
C44	—Compensation to Employees: Paid Absences	7477
C47	—Compensation to Employees: Stock Purchase and Option Plans	7675
C51	—Consolidation	7873
C59	—Contingencies	8301
C67	—Contributions	9051
D10	—Debt: Convertible Debt, Conversion of Convertible Debt, and Debt with Stock Purchase Warrants	11421
D14	—Debt: Extinguishments	11589

Table of Contents

Section		Page
D18	—Debt: Product Financing Arrangements	11657
D22	—Debt: Restructurings	11825
D40	—Depreciation	12607
E09	—Earnings per Share	14127
F25	—Financial Instruments: Disclosure	16501
F43	—Financial Statements: Comparative Financial Statements	18351
F60	—Foreign Currency Translation	19251
F65	—Foreign Operations	19501
F80	—Futures Contracts	19801
I08	—Impairment	23701
I13	—Income Statement Presentation: Discontinued Operations	24275
I17	—Income Statement Presentation: Extraordinary Items	24467
I22	—Income Statement Presentation: Unusual or Infrequent Items	24667
I27	—Income Taxes	25331
I50	—Insurance Costs	26155
I60	—Intangible Assets	26635
I67	—Interest: Capitalization of Interest Costs	26971
I69	—Interest: Imputation of an Interest Cost	27087
I73	—Interim Financial Reporting	27279
I78	—Inventory	27519
I80	—Investments: Debt and Equity Securities	27631
I82	—Investments: Equity Method	27715
L10	—Leases	29141
L20	—Lending Activities	30101
N35	—Nonmonetary Transactions	31981
P16	—Pension Costs	34201
P32	—Postemployment Benefits	34851
P40	—Postretirement Benefits Other Than Pensions	35011
Q15	—Quasi Reorganizations	37647
R10	—Real Estate	38295
R20	—Receivables Sold with Recourse	38335
R36	—Related Parties	38345

Table of Contents

Section		Page
R50	—Research and Development	38847
R55	—Research and Development Arrangements	38887
R70	—Retained Earnings	39567
R75	—Revenue Recognition	39747
S20	—Segment of Business Reporting	41727
T10	—Taxes: Real and Personal Property Taxes	42687
V18	—Valuation: Use of Valuation Allowances	44703

Topical Index T-1

(Refer to Volume II for the appendixes.)

Table of Contents

Volume II

INDUSTRY STANDARDS
TABLE OF CONTENTS
(A Companion Volume)

Section		Page
Br5	—Broadcasting Industry	51503
Bt7	—Banking and Thrift Industries	51601
Ca4	—Cable Television Industry	51701
Co2	—Computer Software to Be Sold, Leased, or Otherwise Marketed	52401
Co4	—Contractor Accounting: Construction-Type Contracts	52605
Co5	—Contractor Accounting: Government Contracts	52905
De4	—Development Stage Enterprises	54507
Fi4	—Finance Companies	56307
Fr3	—Franchising: Accounting by Franchisors	57007
In6	—Insurance Industry	58007
In8	—Investment Companies	59007
Mo4	—Mortgage Banking Activities	61451
Mo6	—Motion Picture Industry	61507
No5	—Not-for-Profit Organizations	62307
Oi5	—Oil and Gas Producing Activities	62507
Pe5	—Pension Funds: Accounting and Reporting by Defined Benefit Pension Plans	63107
Re1	—Real Estate: Sales	64507
Re2	—Real Estate: Accounting for Costs and Initial Rental Operations of Real Estate Projects	64607
Re4	—Record and Music Industry	66107
Re6	—Regulated Operations	67107
Ti7	—Title Plant	75151

Table of Contents

Appendixes

Appendix A—Schedule of AICPA Practice Bulletins, Audit and
Accounting Guides, and Statements of Position A-1

Appendix B—Schedule of Amended and Superseded
Accounting Pronouncements B-1

Appendix C—Effective Dates of Pronouncements C-1

Appendix D—Issues Discussed by the FASB Emerging Issues Task Force . . .   D-1

Appendix E—Current Text Sections That Are Superseded by
Pronouncements with Delayed Effective Dates E-1

   P50 —Postretirement Health Care and Life Insurance Benefits E-207

   Appendix E Index E-217

Appendix F—Schedule of AICPA and FASB Original Pronouncements . . .   F-1

Appendix G—Cross-Reference—Original Pronouncements to
Current Text Paragraphs G-1

Topical Index T-1

Sources: APB Opinion 20; FASB Statement 63; FASB Statement 73;
FASB Statement 95; FASB Statement 111; FASB Interpretation 1;
FASB Interpretation 20

Summary

There is a presumption in preparing financial statements that an accounting principle once adopted should not be changed in accounting for events and transactions of a similar type. That presumption may be overcome only if the enterprise justifies the use of an alternative acceptable accounting principle on the basis that it is preferable.

Except for changes in certain specified accounting principles that are made by retroactive restatement, the cumulative effect of a change in an accounting principle shall be included in net income of the period of the change and presented in the income statement net of related tax effects after extraordinary items.

A change in accounting estimate shall be accounted for in the period of change if the change affects that period only or in the period of change and future periods if the change affects both. The change shall not be accounted for by restating amounts reported in financial statements of prior periods or by reporting pro forma amounts for prior periods. This section does not apply to accounting changes made in conformity with FASB Statements, Interpretations, and Technical Bulletins, AICPA Accounting Research Bulletins, APB Opinions, Industry Guides, Statements of Position, and Practice Bulletins, or EITF consensuses issued in the past or in the future.

Applicability and Scope

.101 This section defines various types of **accounting changes** and establishes guides for determining the manner of reporting each type. [APB20, ¶2]

.102 This section applies to financial statements that purport to present financial position, [APB20, ¶3] cash flows, [FAS95, ¶152] and results of operations in conformity with generally accepted accounting principles. The guides in this section also may be appropriate in presenting financial information in other forms or for special purposes. [APB20, ¶3]

.103 Each FASB Statement and Interpretation, APB Opinion, and AICPA Accounting Research Bulletin specifies its effective date and manner of reporting a change to conform with the conclusions of that pronouncement. Other pronouncements of the FASB or other designated bodies as described in categories *(b)-(d)* of AICPA Statement on Auditing Standards (SAS) No. 69, *The Meaning of "Present Fairly in Conformity with Generally Accepted Accounting Principles" in the Independent Auditor's Report,* may also prescribe the manner of reporting a change in accounting principle. [FAS111, ¶7] [Refer to Appendix A for a current list of AICPA documents in categories *(b)-(d)* and for a more detailed explanation of SAS 69.] This section does not apply to [accounting] changes made in conformity with such pronouncements issued in the past or in the future. [APB20, ¶4]

Types of Accounting Changes

.104 The term *accounting change* in this section means a change in (a) an **accounting principle,** (b) an accounting estimate, or (c) the reporting enterprise (which is a special type of change in accounting principle [discussed in Section A35, "Adjustments of Financial Statements for Prior Periods," paragraphs .112 and .113]). The correction of an error in previously issued financial statements is not deemed to be an accounting change. [APB20, ¶6]

Change in Accounting Principle

.105 A change in accounting principle results from adoption of a generally accepted accounting principle different from the one used previously for reporting purposes. The term *accounting principle* includes not only accounting principles and practices but also the methods of applying them. [APB20, ¶7]

.106 A characteristic of a change in accounting principle is that it concerns a choice from among two or more generally accepted accounting principles. However, neither (a) initial adoption of an accounting principle in recognition of events or transactions occurring for the first time or that previously were immaterial in their effect, nor (b) adoption or modification of an accounting principle necessitated by transactions or events that are clearly different in substance from those previously occurring is a change in accounting principle. [APB20, ¶8]

.107 Changes in accounting principle are numerous and varied. They include, for example, a change in the method of inventory pricing, such as from the last-in, first-out (LIFO) method to the first-in, first-out (FIFO) method; a change in depreciation method for previously recorded assets, such as from the double-declining-balance method to the straight-line method;[1] and a change in the method of accounting for long-term construction-type contracts, such as from the completed-contract method to the percentage-of-completion method. (Paragraph .110 covers a change in accounting principle to effect a change in estimate.) [APB20, ¶9]

.108 A change in composition of the elements of costs included in inventory also is an accounting change. An enterprise that makes such a change for financial reporting shall conform to the requirements of this section, including justifying the change on the basis of preferability as specified by paragraph .112. In applying this section, preferability among accounting principles shall be determined on the basis of whether the new principle constitutes an improvement in financial reporting and not on the basis of the income tax effect alone. [FIN1, ¶5]

Change in Accounting Estimate

.109 Changes in estimates used in accounting are necessary consequences of periodic presentations of financial statements. Preparing financial statements requires estimating the effects of future events. Examples of items for which estimates are necessary are uncollectible receivables, inventory obsolescence, service lives and salvage values of depreciable assets, warranty costs, periods benefited by a deferred cost, and recoverable mineral reserves. Future events and their effects cannot be perceived with certainty; estimating, therefore, requires the exercise of judgment. Thus, accounting estimates change as new events occur, as more experience is acquired, or as additional information is obtained. [APB20, ¶10]

Change in Estimate Effected by a Change in Accounting Principle

.110 Distinguishing between a change in an accounting principle and a change in an accounting estimate is sometimes difficult. For example, an enterprise may change from deferring and amortizing a cost to recording it as an expense when incurred because future benefits of the cost have become doubtful. The new accounting method is adopted, therefore, in partial or complete recognition of the change in estimated future benefits. The effect of the change in accounting principle is inseparable from the effect of the change in accounting estimate. Changes of this type are often related to the continuing process of obtaining additional information and revising estimates and are therefore considered as changes in estimates for purposes of applying this section. [APB20, ¶11]

---

[1] A change to the straight-line method at a specific point in the service life of an asset may be planned at the time the accelerated depreciation method is adopted to fully depreciate the cost over the estimated life of the asset. Consistent application of such a policy does not constitute a change in accounting principle for purposes of applying this section. [APB20, ¶9, fn3]

Justification for a Change in Accounting Principle

.111 In the preparation of financial statements, there is a presumption that an accounting principle once adopted should not be changed in accounting for events and transactions of a similar type. Consistent use of accounting principles from one accounting period to another enhances the utility of financial statements to users by facilitating analysis and understanding of comparative accounting data. [APB20, ¶15]

.112 The presumption that an enterprise should not change an accounting principle may be overcome only if the enterprise justifies the use of an alternative acceptable accounting principle on the basis that it is preferable. However, a method of accounting that was previously adopted for a type of transaction or event that is being terminated or that was a single, nonrecurring event in the past shall not be changed. For example, the method of accounting shall not be changed for a tax or tax credit that is being discontinued or for preoperating costs relating to a specific plant. [That is not intended] to imply, however, that a change in the estimated period to be benefited for a deferred cost (if justified by the facts) should not be recognized as a change in accounting estimate. [APB20, ¶16] The issuance of a new pronouncement by the FASB or by other designated bodies as described in categories *(a)-(d)* of SAS 69 that creates a new accounting principle, interprets an existing principle, expresses a preference for an accounting principle, or rejects a specific principle *may require* an entity to adopt a change in accounting principle. The issuance of such a pronouncement is considered to constitute sufficient support for making a change in accounting principle provided that the hierarchy established by SAS 69 is followed. [FAS111, ¶7(b)] [SAS 69 requires that] if there is a conflict between accounting principles relevant to the circumstances from one or more sources in category *(b)*, *(c)*, or *(d)*, the enterprise should follow the treatment specified by the source in the higher category—for example, follow category *(b)* treatment over category *(c)*. [FAS111, ¶17] The burden of justifying other changes rests with the enterprise proposing the change. [APB20, ¶16]

Exhibit 112A

[Deleted 11/92 because of FASB Statement 111, *Rescission of FASB Statement No. 32 and Technical Corrections.*]

General Disclosure—A Change in Accounting Principle

.113 The nature of and justification for a change in accounting principle and its effect on income shall be disclosed in the financial statements of the period in which the change is

---

[[1a]Deleted 2/92 because of FASB Statement 109, *Accounting for Income Taxes.*]

[[1b through 1d]Deleted 11/92 because of Statement 111.]

made. The justification for the change shall explain clearly why the newly adopted accounting principle is preferable. [APB20, ¶17]

Reporting a Change in Accounting Principle

.114 Although they conflict, both (a) the potential dilution of public confidence in financial statements resulting from restating financial statements of prior periods and (b) consistent application of accounting principles in comparative statements are important factors in reporting a change in accounting principles. Most changes in accounting shall be recognized by including the cumulative effect, based on a retroactive computation, of changing to a new accounting principle in net income of the period of the change (refer to paragraphs .115 through .122) but a few specific changes in accounting principles shall be reported by restating the financial statements of prior periods (refer to paragraphs .123 through .126 and to Section A35, paragraphs .112 and .113, regarding a change in entity). [APB20, ¶18]

.115 For all changes in accounting principle except those described in paragraphs .123 through .128 and Section A35, paragraphs .112 and .113, regarding a change in entity:

a. Financial statements for prior periods included for comparative purposes shall be presented as previously reported.
b. The cumulative effect of changing to a new accounting principle on the amount of retained earnings at the beginning of the period in which the change is made shall be included in net income of the period of the change (refer to paragraph .116).
c. The effect of adopting the new accounting principle on income before extraordinary items and on net income (and on the related per share amounts) of the period of the change shall be disclosed.
d. Income before extraordinary items and net income computed on a pro forma basis[2] shall be shown on the face of the income statements for all periods presented as if the newly adopted accounting principle had been applied during all periods affected (refer to paragraph .117).

---

[2]The pro forma amounts include both (a) the direct effects of a change and (b) nondiscretionary adjustments in items based on income before taxes or net income, such as profit sharing expense and certain royalties, that would have been recognized if the newly adopted accounting principle had been followed in prior periods: related income tax effects shall be recognized for both (a) and (b). Direct effects are limited to those adjustments that would have been recorded to restate the financial statements of prior periods to apply the change retroactively. The nondiscretionary adjustments described in (b) shall not therefore be recognized in computing the adjustment for the cumulative effect of the change described in paragraph .116 unless nondiscretionary adjustments of the prior periods are actually recorded. [APB20, ¶19, fn6]

Thus, income before extraordinary items and net income (exclusive of the cumulative adjustment) for the period of the change shall be reported on the basis of the newly adopted accounting principle. The conclusions in this paragraph are modified for various special situations that are described in paragraphs .119 through .128. [APB20, ¶19]

Cumulative Effect of a Change in Accounting Principle

.116 The amount shown in the income statement for the cumulative effect of changing to a new accounting principle is the difference between (a) the amount of retained earnings at the beginning of the period of a change and (b) the amount of retained earnings that would have been reported at that date if the new accounting principle had been applied retroactively for all prior periods that would have been affected and by recognizing only the direct effects of the change and related income tax effect.[3] The amount of the cumulative effect shall be shown in the income statement between the captions "extraordinary items" and "net income." The cumulative effect is not an extraordinary item but shall be reported in a manner similar to an extraordinary item. The per share information shown on the face of the income statement shall include the per share amount of the cumulative effect of the accounting change. [APB20, ¶20]

Pro Forma Effects of Retroactive Application

.117 Pro forma effects of retroactive application (refer to paragraph .115(d) including footnote 2) shall be shown on the face of the income statement for income before extraordinary items and net income. The earnings per share amounts (primary and fully diluted, as appropriate under Section E09, "Earnings per Share") for income before extraordinary items and net income computed on a pro forma basis shall be shown on the face of the income statement. If space does not permit, such per share amounts may be disclosed prominently in a separate schedule or in tabular form in the notes to the financial statements with appropriate cross-reference; if this is done, the actual per share amounts shall be repeated for comparative purposes. Pro forma amounts shall be shown in both current and future reports for all periods presented that are prior to the change and that would have been affected. Paragraphs .135 through .138 illustrate the manner of reporting a change in accounting principle. If an income statement is presented for the current period only, the actual and the pro forma amounts (and related per share data) for the immediately preceding period shall be disclosed. [APB20, ¶21]

---

[3]Refer to footnote 2. [APB20, ¶20, fn7]

.118 The principal steps in computing and reporting the cumulative effect and the pro forma amounts of a change in accounting principle may be illustrated by a change in depreciation method for previously recorded assets as follows:

a. The class or classes of depreciable assets to which the change applies shall be identified. (A *class of assets* relates to general physical characteristics.)
b. The amount of accumulated depreciation on recorded assets at the beginning of the period of the change shall be recomputed on the basis of applying retroactively the new depreciation method. Accumulated depreciation shall be adjusted for the difference between the recomputed amount and the recorded amount. Deferred taxes shall be adjusted for the related income tax effects.
c. The cumulative effect on the amount of retained earnings at the beginning of the period of the change resulting from the adjustments referred to in (b) above shall be shown in the income statement of the period of the change.
d. The pro forma amounts shall give effect to the pro forma provisions for depreciation of each prior period presented and to the pro forma adjustments of nondiscretionary items,[4] computed on the assumption of retroactive application of the newly adopted method to all prior periods and adjusted for the related income tax effects.

[APB20, ¶22]

Change in Method of Amortization and Related Disclosure

.119 Accounting for the costs of long-lived assets requires adopting a systematic pattern of charging those costs to expense. Those patterns are referred to as depreciation, depletion, or amortization methods (all of which are referred to in this section as *methods of amortization*). Various patterns of charging costs to expenses are acceptable for depreciable assets; fewer patterns are acceptable for other long-lived assets. [APB20, ¶23]

.120 Various factors are considered in selecting an amortization method for identifiable assets, and those factors may change, even for similar assets. For example, an enterprise may adopt a new method of amortization for newly acquired, identifiable, long-lived assets and use that method for all additional new assets of the same class but continue to use the previous method for existing balances of previously recorded assets of that class. For that type of change in accounting principle, there is no adjustment of the type outlined in paragraphs .115 through .118, but a description of the nature of the change in method and its effect on income before extraordinary items and net income of the period of the change, together with the related per share amounts, shall be disclosed. If the new

---

[4]Refer to footnote 2. [APB20, ¶22, fn8]

method of amortization is, however, applied to previously recorded assets of that class, the change in accounting principle requires an adjustment for the cumulative effect of the change and the provisions of paragraphs .111 through .118 shall be applied. [APB20, ¶24]

Pro Forma Amounts Not Determinable

.121 In rare situations, the pro forma amounts described in paragraph .117 cannot be computed or reasonably estimated for individual prior periods, although the cumulative effect on retained earnings at the beginning of the period of change can be determined. The cumulative effect shall then be reported in the income statement of the period of change in the manner described in paragraph .116. The reason for not showing the pro forma amounts by periods shall be explained because disclosing those amounts is otherwise required and is expected by users of financial statements. [APB20, ¶25]

Cumulative Effect Not Determinable

.122 Computing the effect on retained earnings at the beginning of the period in which a change in accounting principle is made may sometimes be impossible. In those rare situations, disclosure will be limited to showing the effect of the change on the results of operations of the period of change (including per share data) and to explaining the reason for omitting accounting for the cumulative effect and disclosure of pro forma amounts for prior years. The principle example of this type of accounting change is a change in inventory pricing method from FIFO to LIFO. [APB20, ¶26]

Special Changes in Accounting Principle Reported by Applying Retroactively the New Method in Restatements of Prior Periods

.123 Certain changes in accounting principle are such that the advantages of retroactive treatment in prior period reports outweigh the disadvantages. Accordingly, for those few changes, the financial statements of all prior periods presented shall be restated. The changes that shall be accorded that treatment are: (a) a change from the LIFO method of inventory pricing to another method, (b) a change in the method of accounting for long-term construction-type contracts, and (c) a change to or from the *full cost* method of accounting that is used in the extractive industries [APB20, ¶27] , [and] (d) a change from retirement-replacement-betterment accounting[5] to depreciation accounting. [FAS73, ¶2]

.124 The nature of and justification for a change in accounting principle described in paragraph .123 shall be disclosed in the financial statements for the period the change was adopted. In addition, the effect of the change on income before extraordinary items, net income, and the related per share amounts shall be disclosed for all periods presented. That disclosure may be on the face of the income statement or in the notes. Paragraphs .139 through .142 illustrate the manner of reporting a change in accounting principle retroactively by restating the statements of those prior periods affected. Financial statements of subsequent periods need not repeat the disclosures. [APB20, ¶28]

Special Exemption for an Initial Public Distribution

.125 In one specific situation, the application of the foregoing provisions of this section may result in financial statement presentations of results of operations that are not of maximum usefulness to intended users. For example, an enterprise owned by a few individuals may decide to change from one acceptable accounting principle to another acceptable principle in connection with a forthcoming public offering of shares of its equity securities. The potential investors may be better served by statements of income for a period of years reflecting the use of the newly adopted accounting principles because they will be the same as those expected to be used in future periods. In recognition of that situation, financial statements for all prior periods presented may be restated retroactively when an enterprise first issues its financial statements for any one of the following purposes: (a) obtaining additional equity capital from investors, (b) effecting a business combination, or (c) registering securities. This exemption is available only once for changes made at thetime an enterprise's financial statements are first used for any of those purposes and is not available to enterprises whose securities currently are widely held. [APB20, ¶29]

---

[5]On February 17, 1983, the Interstate Commerce Commission (ICC) ruled that railroads must use depreciation accounting for railroad track structures in reports to the ICC. The ruling is effective for 1983 annual filings, 1984 quarterly filings, and all filings thereafter with the ICC. The ICC previously had required RRB [(retirement-replacement-betterment)] for railroad track structures in reports to the ICC. [FAS73, ¶5] Under RRB, the initial costs of installing track are capitalized, not depreciated, and remain capitalized until the track is retired. The costs of replacing track are expensed unless a betterment (for example, replacing a 110-lb. rail with a 132-lb. rail) occurs. In that case, the amount by which the cost of the new part exceeds the current cost of the part replaced is considered a betterment and is capitalized but not depreciated, and the current cost of the part replaced is expensed. Railroads generally have used RRB for financial reporting. [FAS73, ¶6] The ICC ruling does not apply to financial reporting by railroads, but [if a] railroad adopts depreciation accounting for financial reporting, [the] change from RRB to depreciation accounting would be a change in accounting principle under this section. [FAS73, ¶7]

.126 The enterprise shall disclose in financial statements issued under the circumstances described in paragraph .125 the nature of the change in accounting principle and the justification for it (refer to paragraph .113). [APB20, ¶30]

Reporting Accounting Changes under AICPA Statements of Position and Practice Bulletins, FASB Technical Bulletins, or EITF Consensuses

.127 For purposes of applying this section, an enterprise making a change in accounting principle to conform with the recommendations of an AICPA statement of position [FIN20, ¶5] or practice bulletin, an FASB technical bulletin, or a consensus of the FASB Emerging Issues Task Force (EITF) [FAS111, ¶10] shall report the change as specified in the [FIN20, ¶5] pronouncement. If the pronouncement does not specify the manner of reporting a change in accounting principle to conform with its recommendations, an enterprise making a change in accounting principle to conform with the recommendations of the pronouncement shall report the change as specified by this section, except that EITF consensuses may be applied prospectively to future transactions unless otherwise stated.[6] [FAS111, ¶10]

.128 [Deleted 12/90 because of FASB Statement 106, *Employers' Accounting for Postretirement Benefits Other Than Pensions*.]

Reporting Accounting Changes in Interim Financial Statements

.129 [The reporting of accounting changes in interim financial statements is indicated in Section I73, "Interim Financial Reporting," paragraphs .131 through .142.]

Reporting a Change in Accounting Estimate

.130 The effect of a change in accounting estimate shall be accounted for in (a) the period of change if the change affects that period only or (b) the period of change and future periods if the change affects both. A change in an estimate shall not be accounted for by restating amounts reported in financial statements of prior periods or by reporting pro forma amounts for prior periods. [APB20, ¶31]

.131 A change in accounting estimate that is recognized in whole or in part by a change in accounting principle shall be reported as a change in an estimate because the cumulative effect attributable to the change in accounting principle cannot be separated from the current or future effects of the change in estimate (refer to paragraph .110). Although that type of accounting change is somewhat similar to a change in method of amortiza-

---

[6]Unless a consensus specifies the manner of reporting a change in accounting principle, an enterprise making a change in accounting principle to conform with an EITF consensus may apply the consensus prospectively to future transactions or may apply the provisions of this section to prior transactions. [FAS111, ¶27]

tion (refer to paragraphs .119 and .120), the accounting effect of a change in a method of amortization can be separated from the effect of a change in the estimate of periods of benefit or service and residual values of assets. A change in method of amortization for previously recorded assets therefore shall be treated as a change in accounting principle, whereas a change in the estimated period of benefit or residual value shall be treated as a change in accounting estimate. [APB20, ¶32]

Disclosure

.132 The effect on income before extraordinary items, net income and related per share amounts of the current period shall be disclosed for a change in estimate that affects several future periods, such as a change in service lives of depreciable assets or actuarial assumptions affecting pension costs. Disclosure of the effect on those income statement amounts is not necessary for estimates made each period in the ordinary course of accounting for items such as uncollectible accounts or inventory obsolescence; however, disclosure is recommended if the effect of a change in the estimate is material. [APB20, ¶33]

Materiality

.133 A number of factors are relevant to the materiality of accounting changes contemplated in this section in determining both the accounting treatment of those items and the necessity for disclosure. Materiality shall be considered in relation to both the effects of each change separately and the combined effect of all changes. If a change has a material effect on income before extraordinary items or on net income of the current period before the effect of the change, the treatments and disclosures described in this section shall be followed. Furthermore, if a change has a material effect on the trend of earnings, the same treatments and disclosures are required. A change that does not have a material effect in the period of change but is reasonably certain to have a material effect in later periods shall be disclosed whenever the financial statements of the period of change are presented. [APB20, ¶38]

Historical Summaries of Financial Information

.134 Summaries of financial information for a number of periods are commonly included in financial reports. The summaries often show condensed income statements, including related earnings per share amounts, for five years or more. In many annual reports to stockholders, the financial highlights present similar information in capsule form. That information shall be prepared in the same manner (including the presentation of pro forma amounts) as that prescribed in this section for primary financial statements (refer to paragraphs .111 through .128 and .130 through .133) because the summaries include financial data based on the primary financial statements. In a summary of financial information that includes an accounting period in which a change in accounting principle was made, the amount of the cumulative effect of the change that was included in net income of the period of the change shall be shown separately along with the net income and related per share amounts of that period and shall not be disclosed only by a note or parenthetical notation. [APB20, ¶39]

An Illustration of Reporting a Change in Accounting Principle

.135 ABC Company decides in 19X5 to adopt the straight-line method of depreciation for plant equipment. The straight-line method will be used for new acquisitions as well as for previously acquired plant equipment for which depreciation had been provided on an accelerated method. [APB20, ¶41]

.136 This illustration assumes that the direct effects are limited to the effect on depreciation and related income tax provisions and that the direct effect on inventories is not material. The pro forma amounts have been adjusted for the hypothetical effects of the change in the provisions for incentive compensation. The per share amounts are computed assuming that 1,000,000 shares of common stock are issued and outstanding, that 100,000 additional shares would be issued if all outstanding bonds (which are not common stock equivalents) are converted, and that the annual interest expense, less taxes, for the convertible bonds is $25,000. Other data assumed for this illustration are as follows:

Year	Excess of Accelerated Depreciation over Straight-Line Depreciation	Effects of Change Direct, Less Tax Effect	Pro Forma (Note A)
Prior to 19X1	$ 20,000	$ 10,000	$ 9,000
19X1	80,000	40,000	36,000
19X2	70,000	35,000	31,500
19X3	50,000	25,000	22,500
19X4	30,000	15,000	13,500
Total at beginning of 19X5	$250,000	$125,000	$112,500

[APB20, ¶42]

.137 The manner of reporting the change in two-year comparative statements is [presented in Exhibit 137A]. [APB20, ¶43]

Exhibit 137A

Two-Year Illustration of Reporting a Change in Accounting Principle

	19X5	19X4
Income before extraordinary item and cumulative effect of a change in accounting principle	$1,200,000	$1,100,000
Extraordinary item (description)	(35,000)	100,000
Cumulative effect on prior years (to December 31, 19X4) of changing to a different depreciation method (Note A)	125,000	
Net income	$1,290,000	$1,200,000
Per share amounts:		
Earnings per common share—assuming no dilution:		
Income before extraordinary item and cumulative effect of a change in accounting principle	$1.20	$1.10
Extraordinary item	(0.04)	0.10
Cumulative effect on prior years (to December 31, 19X4) of changing to a different depreciation method	0.13	
Net income	$1.29	$1.20
Earnings per common share—assuming full dilution:		
Income before extraordinary item and cumulative effect of a change in accounting principle	$1.11	$1.02
Extraordinary item	(0.03)	0.09
Cumulative effect on prior years (to December 31, 19X4) of changing to a different depreciation method	0.11	
Net income	$1.19	$1.11
Pro forma amounts assuming the new depreciation method is applied retroactively:		
Income before extraordinary item	$1,200,000	$1,113,500
Earnings per common share—assuming no dilution	$1.20	$1.11
Earnings per common share—assuming full dilution	$1.11	$1.04
Net income	$1,165,000	$1,213,500
Earnings per common share—assuming no dilution	$1.16	$1.21
Earnings per common share—assuming full dilution	$1.08	$1.13

(Refer to accompanying note to the financial statements.)

Exhibit 137A (continued)

Note A—Change in Depreciation Method for Plant Equipment

Depreciation of plant equipment has been computed by the straight-line method in 19X5. Depreciation of plant equipment in prior years, beginning in 19WW, was computed by the sum-of-the-years' digits method. The new method of depreciation was adopted to recognize . . . (state justification for change of depreciation method) . . . and has been applied retroactively to equipment acquisitions of prior years. The effect of the change in 19X5 was to increase income before extraordinary item by approximately $10,000 (or 1 cent per share). The adjustment of $125,000 (after reduction for income taxes of $125,000) to apply retroactively the new method is included in income of 19X5. The pro forma amounts shown on the income statement have been adjusted for the effect of retroactive application on depreciation, the change in provisions for incentive compensation that would have been made had the new method been in effect, and the related income taxes. [APB20, ¶43]

.138 The manner of reporting the change in five-year comparative statements is [presented in Exhibit 138A] .

(This page intentionally left blank.)

Exhibit 138A

Five-Year Illustration of Reporting a Change in Accounting Principle

	19X5	19X4	19X3	19X2	19X1
Income before extraordinary item and cumulative effect of a change in accounting principle	$1,200,000	$1,100,000	$1,300,000	$1,000,000	$800,000
Extraordinary item	(35,000)	100,000		40,000	
Cumulative effect on prior years (to December 31, 19X4) of changing to a different depreciation method (Note A)	125,000				
Net income	$1,290,000	$1,200,000	$1,300,000	$1,040,000	$800,000
Earnings per common share—assuming no dilution:					
Income before extraordinary item and cumulative effect of change in accounting principle	$1.20	$1.10	$1.30	$1.00	$0.80
Extraordinary item	(0.04)	0.10		0.04	
Cumulative effect on prior years (to December 31, 19X4) of changing to a different depreciation method	0.13				
Net income	$1.29	$1.20	$1.30	$1.04	$0.80

Earnings per common share—assuming full dilution:					
Income before extraordinary item and cumulative effect of change in accounting principle	$1.11	$1.02	$1.20	$0.93	$0.75
Extraordinary item	(0.03)	0.09		0.04	
Cumulative effect on prior years (to December 31, 19X4) of changing to a different depreciation method	0.11				
Net income	$1.19	$1.11	$1.20	$0.97	$0.75
Pro forma amounts assuming the new depreciation method is applied retroactively:					
Income before extraordinary item	$1,200,000	$1,113,500	$1,322,500	$1,031,500	$836,000
Earnings per common share—assuming no dilution	$1.20	$1.11	$1.32	$1.03	$0.84
Earnings per common share—assuming full dilution	$1.11	$1.04	$1.23	$0.96	$0.78
Net income	$1,165,000	$1,213,500	$1,322,500	$1,071,500	$836,000
Earnings per common share—assuming no dilution	$1.16	$1.21	$1.32	$1.07	$0.84
Earnings per common share—assuming full dilution	$1.08	$1.13	$1.23	$1.00	$0.78

A note similar to Note A of Exhibit 137A shall accompany the five-year comparative income statement. [APB20, ¶44]

An Illustration of Reporting a Special Change in Accounting Principle by Restating Prior Period Financial Statements

.139 XYZ Company decides in 19X5 to adopt the percentage-of-completion method in accounting for all of its long-term construction contracts. The enterprise had used in prior years the completed-contract method and had maintained records that are adequate to apply retroactively the percentage-of-completion method. The change in accounting principle is to be reported in the manner described in paragraphs .123 and .124. [APB20, ¶45]

.140 The direct effect of the change in accounting principle and other data assumed for this illustration are as follows:

Year	Pretax Income Reported by Percentage-of-Completion Method	Completed-Contract Method	Difference in Income Direct	Less Tax Effect
Prior to 19X1	$1,800,000	$1,300,000	$ 500,000	$ 250,000
19X1	900,000	800,000	100,000	50,000
19X2	700,000	1,000,000	(300,000)	(150,000)
19X3	800,000	600,000	200,000	100,000
19X4	1,000,000	1,100,000	(100,000)	(50,000)
Total at beginning of 19X5	5,200,000	4,800,000	400,000	200,000
19X5	1,100,000	900,000	200,000	100,000
Total	$6,300,000	$5,700,000	$ 600,000	$ 300,000

The per share amounts are computed assuming that 1,000,000 shares of common stock are issued and outstanding, that 100,000 additional shares would be issued if all outstanding bonds (that are not common stock equivalents) are converted, and that the annual interest expense, less taxes, for the convertible bonds is $25,000. [APB20, ¶46]

.141 The manner of reporting the change in two-year comparative statements is presented in Exhibit 141A. [APB20, ¶47]

Exhibit 141A

Two-Year Illustration of an Accounting Change with Restatement of Prior Period Financial Statements

	19X5	19X4 as adjusted (Note A)
Income Statement		
Income before extraordinary item	$ 550,000	$ 500,000
Extraordinary item (description)		(80,000)
Net income	$ 550,000	$ 420,000
Per share amounts:		
Earnings per common share—assuming no dilution:		
Income before extraordinary item	$0.55	$0.50
Extraordinary item		(.08)
Net income	$0.55	$0.42
Earnings per common share—assuming full dilution:		
Income before extraordinary item	$0.52	$0.47
Extraordinary item		(.07)
Net income	$0.52	$0.40
Statement of Retained Earnings		
Balance at beginning of year, as previously reported	$17,800,000	$17,330,000
Add adjustment for the cumulative effect on prior years of applying retroactively the new method of accounting for long-term contracts (Note A)	200,000	250,000
Balance at beginning of year, as adjusted	18,000,000	17,580,000
Net income	550,000	420,000
Balance at end of year	$18,550,000	$18,000,000

(Refer to accompanying note to the financial statements.)

Note A—Change in Method of Accounting for Long-Term Contracts

The enterprise has accounted for revenue and costs for long-term construction contracts by the percentage-of-completion method in 19X5, whereas in all prior years revenue and costs were determined by the completed-contract method. The new method of accounting for long-term contracts was adopted to recognize . . . (state justification for change in accounting principle) . . . and financial statements of prior years have been restated to apply the new method retroactively. For income tax purposes, the completed-

contract method has been continued. The effect of the accounting change on income of 19X5 and on income as previously reported for 19X4 is—

	Increase 19X5	(Decrease) 19X4
Effect on—		
Income before extraordinary item and net income	$100,000	$(50,000)
Earnings per common share—assuming no dilution	$ 0.10	$ (0.05)
Earnings per common share—assuming full dilution	$ 0.09	$ (0.05)

The balances of retained earnings for 19X4 and 19X5 have been adjusted for the effect (net of income taxes) of applying retroactively the new method of accounting. [APB20, ¶47]

.142 A note to a five-year summary of financial statements should disclose the effect of the change on net income and related per share amounts for the periods affected in the manner illustrated in Exhibit 142A. [APB20, ¶48]

Exhibit 142A

Illustrative Note for a Five-Year Illustration of an Accounting Change with Restatement of Prior Period Financial Statements

Note A—Change in Method of Accounting for Long-Term Contracts

The enterprise has accounted for revenue and costs for long-term construction contracts by the percentage-of-completion method in 19X5, whereas in all prior years revenue and costs were determined by the completed-contract method. The new method of accounting for long-term contracts was adopted to recognize . . . (state justification for change in accounting principle) . . . and financial statements of prior years have been restated to apply the new method retroactively. For income tax purposes, the completed-

Exhibit 142A (continued)

contract method has been continued. The effect of the accounting change on net income as previously reported for 19X4 and prior years is:

	19X4	19X3	19X2	19X1
Net income as previously reported	$470,000	$300,000	$ 500,000	$ 400,00
Adjustment for effect of a change in accounting principle that is applied retroactively	(50,000)	100,000	(150,000)	50,000
Net income as adjusted	$420,000	$500,000	$ 350,000	$450,000
Per share amounts:				
Earnings per common share— assuming no dilution:				
Net income as previously reported	$0.47	$0.30	$0.50	$0.40
Adjustment for effect of a change in accounting principle that is applied retroactively	(0.05)	0.10	0.15	0.05
Net income as adjusted	$0.42	$0.40	$0.35	$0.45
Earnings per common share— assuming full dilution:				
Net income as previously reported	$0.45	$0.30	$0.47	$0.38
Adjustment for effect of a change in accounting principle that is applied retroactively	(0.05)	0.09	(0.13)	0.05
Net income as adjusted	$0.40	$0.39	$0.34	$0.43

[APB20, ¶48]

Glossary

.401 **Accounting change.** A change in (a) an accounting principle, (b) an accounting estimate, or (c) the reporting enterprise (which is a special type of change in accounting principle [discussed in Section A35, paragraphs .112 and .113]). The correction of an error in previously issued financial statements is not deemed to be an accounting change. [APB20, ¶6]

.402 **Accounting principle.** The term includes not only accounting principles and practices but also the methods of applying them. [APB20, ¶7]

(The next page is 421.)

Sources: APB Opinion 22; FASB Statement 95; FASB Interpretation 40

Summary

All significant accounting policies followed by an enterprise shall be disclosed in its financial statements. The format and the location of the disclosure are flexible, although preference is given to the use of a separate summary preceding the notes to the financial statements or to presentation as the first note.

.101 The **accounting policies** of a reporting enterprise are the specific accounting principles and the methods of applying those principles that are judged by the management of the enterprise to be the most appropriate in the circumstances to present fairly financial position, [APB22, ¶6] cash flows, [FAS95, ¶152] and results of operations in accordance with generally accepted accounting principles and that accordingly have been adopted for preparing the financial statements. [APB22, ¶6]

Applicability

.102 Information about the accounting policies adopted by a reporting enterprise is essential for financial statement users. When financial statements are issued purporting to present fairly financial position, [APB22, ¶8] cash flows, [FAS95, ¶152] and results of operations in accordance with generally accepted accounting principles, a description of all significant accounting policies of the reporting enterprise shall be included as an integral part of the financial statements. If one or more of the basic financial statements [are issued] without the others and purport to present fairly the information given in accordance with generally accepted accounting principles, the statements so presented shall also include disclosure of the pertinent accounting policies. [APB22, ¶8]

.102A All business enterprises are required to provide disclosures about significant accounting policies used to prepare financial statements that are intended to be in conformity with generally accepted accounting principles. This section provides guidance on the content of those disclosures, which shall include [those described in paragraph .105]. [FIN40, ¶5]

.103 Information about the accounting policies adopted and followed by not-for-profit enterprises shall be presented as an integral part of their financial statements. [APB22, ¶9]

.104 The provisions of paragraphs .102 and .103 are not intended to apply to unaudited financial statements issued as of a date between annual reporting dates (for example, each quarter) if the reporting enterprise has not changed its accounting policies since the end of its preceding fiscal year.[1] [APB22, ¶10]

Disclosure

.105 Disclosure of accounting policies shall identify and describe the accounting principles followed by the reporting enterprise and the methods of applying those principles that materially affect the determination of financial position, [APB22, ¶12] cash flows, [FAS95, ¶152] or results of operations. In general, the disclosure shall encompass important judgments as to appropriateness of principles relating to recognition of revenue and allocation of asset costs to current and future periods; in particular, it shall encompass those accounting principles and methods that involve any of the following:

a. A selection from existing acceptable alternatives;
b. Principles and methods peculiar to the industry in which the reporting enterprise operates, even if such principles and methods are predominantly followed in that industry;
c. Unusual or innovative applications of generally accepted accounting principles (and, as applicable, of principles and methods peculiar to the industry in which the reporting enterprise operates). [APB22, ¶12]

.106 Examples of disclosures by a business enterprise commonly required with respect to accounting policies include those relating to basis of consolidation, depreciation methods, amortization of intangibles, inventory pricing, and recognition of profit on long-term construction-type contracts. This list of examples is not all-inclusive. [APB22, ¶13]

.107 Financial statement disclosure of accounting policies shall not duplicate details (for example, composition of inventories or of plant assets) presented elsewhere as part of the financial statements. In some cases, the disclosure of accounting policies shall refer to related details presented elsewhere as part of the financial statements; for example, changes in accounting policies during the period shall be described with cross-reference to the disclosure required by Section A06, "Accounting Changes," of the current effect of the change and of the pro forma effect of retroactive application. [APB22, ¶14]

---

[1]It may be appropriate to omit disclosure of accounting policies in some other circumstances; for example, from certain special reports in which incomplete or no financial presentations are made. [APB22, ¶10, fn2]

Presentation

.108 Provided that the enterprise identifies and describes its significant accounting policies as an integral part of its financial statements in accordance with paragraph .105, [the format (including location) for disclosing those policies is flexible. Preference is given to disclosing accounting policies] in a separate "Summary of Significant Accounting Policies" [or a similar title] preceding the notes to financial statements or as the initial note. [APB22, ¶15]

(The next page is 1303.)

Glossary

.401 **Accounting policies.** The specific accounting principles and the methods of applying those principles that are judged by the management of the enterprise to be the most appropriate in the circumstances. [APB22, ¶6]

(The next page is 1303.)

Source: ARB 43, Chapter 1A

Summary

Items that would normally be charged to expense in the current or future years should not be charged against additional paid-in capital. The only exception to this rule may occur when an enterprise undergoes a reorganization or a quasi reorganization, in which the shareholders have been fully informed and have approved the action.

.101 Additional paid-in capital, however created, shall not be used to relieve income of the current or future years of charges which would otherwise be made against [income]. This rule might be subject to the exception that where, upon reorganization, a reorganized enterprise would be relieved of charges that would be made against income if the existing enterprise were continued, it might be regarded as permissible to accomplish the same result without reorganization provided the facts were as fully revealed to and the action as formally approved by the shareholders as in reorganization. [ARB43, ch1A, ¶2] [For discussion of quasi reorganizations including disclosure requirements, refer to Section Q15, "Quasi Reorganizations."]

.102 [Section C08, "Capital Stock: Capital Transactions," paragraph .102, requires disclosure of changes in the separate accounts, such as additional paid-in capital, comprising stockholders' equity.]

(The next page is 1471.)

ADJUSTMENTS OF FINANCIAL STATEMENTS FOR PRIOR PERIODS

Sources: APB Opinion 9; APB Opinion 20; FASB Statement 16; FASB Statement 58; FASB Statement 73; FASB Statement 109; FASB Statement 111

Summary

Adjustments of previously issued financial statements are required if there is a correction of an error in the financial statements of a prior period, a change in certain accounting principles, or an adjustment related to prior interim statements of the current fiscal period or if an enterprise realizes the income tax benefits of a preacquisition loss carryforward of a purchased subsidiary. All other revenues, expenses, gains, and losses recognized during a period shall be included in the net income of that period.

Applicability

.101 This section does not affect the manner of reporting accounting changes required or permitted by other sections.[1] [FAS16, ¶12]

Prior-Period Adjustments

.102 Except as specified in paragraph .103 and in paragraphs .109 and .110 with respect to prior interim periods of the current year, all items of profit and loss recognized during a period,[2] including accruals of estimated losses from loss contingencies, shall be included in the determination of net income for that period. [FAS16, ¶10]

.103 An item of profit and loss related to the correction of an error in the financial statements of a prior period [(as discussed in paragraph .104)] shall be accounted for and reported as a prior-period adjustment [(as described in paragraphs .106 and .107)] and excluded from the determination of net income for the current period. [FAS109, ¶288(n)]

---

[1] Accounting changes resulting in restatement of previously issued financial statements of prior periods include a change in accounting method permitted by Section B50, "Business Combinations," paragraph .111. [FAS16, ¶12, fn6]

[2] As used in this section, the term *period* refers to both annual and interim reporting periods. [FAS16, ¶10, fn1]

[3] [Deleted 2/92 because of FASB Statement 109, *Accounting for Income Taxes.*]

.104 Errors[4] in financial statements result from mathematical mistakes, mistakes in the application of accounting principles, or oversight or misuse of facts that existed at the time the financial statements were prepared. In contrast, a change in accounting estimate results from new information or subsequent developments and accordingly from better insight or improved judgment. Thus, an error is distinguishable from a change in estimate. A change from an accounting principle that is not generally accepted to one that is generally accepted is a correction of an error for purposes of applying this section. [APB20, ¶13]

.105 The nature of an error in previously issued financial statements and the effect of its correction on income before extraordinary items, net income, and the related per share amounts shall be disclosed in the period in which the error was discovered and corrected. Financial statements of subsequent periods need not repeat the disclosures. [APB20, ¶37]

.106 Those items that are reported as prior-period adjustments shall, in single period statements, be reflected as adjustments of the opening balance of retained earnings. [FAS16, ¶16(a)] When comparative statements are presented, corresponding adjustments shall be made of the amounts of net income, its components, retained earnings balances, and other affected balances for all of the periods presented to reflect the retroactive application of the prior-period adjustments. [APB9, ¶18]

.107 If prior-period adjustments are recorded, the resulting effects (both gross and net of applicable income tax) on the net income of prior periods shall be disclosed in the annual report for the year in which the adjustments are made. If financial statements for a single period only are presented, this disclosure shall indicate the effects of such restatement on the balance of retained earnings at the beginning of the period and on the net income of the immediately preceding period. If financial statements for more than one period are presented, which is ordinarily the preferable procedure,[5] the disclosure shall include the effects for each of the periods included in the statements. Such disclosures shall include the amounts of income tax applicable to the prior-period adjustments. Disclosure of restatements in annual reports issued subsequent to the first such postrevision disclosure would ordinarily not be required. [APB9, ¶26]

---

[4]Section 561 of Statement on Auditing Standards No. 1, *Codification of Auditing Standards and Procedures,* [FAS111, ¶9(a)] discusses other aspects of errors in previously issued financial statements. [APB20, ¶13, fn4]

[5]Refer to Section F43, "Financial Statements: Comparative Financial Statements." [APB9, ¶26, fn4]

Historical Summaries of Financial Data

.108 It has become customary for business enterprises to present historical statistical-type summaries of financial data for a number of periods—commonly 5 or 10 years. [If] prior-period adjustments have been recorded during any of the periods [presented], the reported amounts of net income, its components, and other affected items, shall be appropriately restated, with disclosure, in the first summary published after the adjustments. [APB9, ¶27]

Adjustments Related to Prior Interim Periods of the Current Fiscal Year

.109 For purposes of this section, an *adjustment related to prior interim periods of the current fiscal year* is an adjustment or settlement of litigation or similar claims, of income taxes [FAS16, ¶13] (except for the effects of retroactive tax legislation) [FAS109, ¶288(n)], of renegotiation proceedings, or of utility revenue under rate-making processes provided that the adjustment or settlement meets each of the following criteria:

a. The effect of the adjustment or settlement is material in relation to income from continuing operations of the current fiscal year or in relation to the trend of income from continuing operations or is material by other appropriate criteria.
b. All or part of the adjustment or settlement can be specifically identified with and is directly related to business activities of specific prior interim periods of the current fiscal year.
c. The amount of the adjustment or settlement could not be reasonably estimated prior to the current interim period but becomes reasonably estimable in the current interim period.

Criterion (b) above is not met solely because of incidental effects such as interest on a settlement. Criterion (c) would be met by the occurrence of an event with currently measurable effects such as a final decision on a rate order. Treatment as adjustments related to prior interim periods of the current fiscal year shall not be applied to the normal recurring corrections and adjustments that are the result of the use of estimates inherent in the accounting process. Changes in provisions for doubtful accounts shall not be considered to be adjustments related to prior interim periods of the current fiscal year even though the changes result from litigation or similar claims. [FAS16, ¶13]

.110 If an item of profit or loss occurs in *other than the first* interim period of the enterprise's fiscal year and all or a part of the item of profit or loss is an adjustment related to prior interim periods of the current fiscal year,[5a] as defined in paragraph .109, the item shall be reported as follows:

a. The portion of the item that is directly related to business activities of the enterprise during the current interim period, if any, shall be included in the determination of net income for that period.
b. Prior interim periods of the current fiscal year shall be restated to include the portion of the item that is directly related to business activities of the enterprise during each prior interim period in the determination of net income for that period.
c. The portion of the item that is directly related to business activities of the enterprise during prior fiscal years, if any, shall be included in the determination of net income of the first interim period of the current fiscal year. [FAS16, ¶14]

.111 The following disclosures shall be made in interim financial reports about an adjustment related to prior interim periods of the current fiscal year. In financial reports for the interim period in which the adjustment occurs, disclosure shall be made of (a) the effect on income from continuing operations, net income, and related per share amounts for each prior interim period of the current fiscal year and (b) income from continuing operations, net income, and related per share amounts for each prior interim period restated in accordance with paragraph .110. [FAS16, ¶15]

Changes in Accounting Principles

Change in Reporting Entity

.112 Accounting changes that result in financial statements that are in effect the statements of a different reporting entity shall be reported by restating the financial statements of all prior periods presented in order to show financial information for the new reporting entity for all periods.[6] [APB20, ¶34] This type [of accounting change] is limited mainly to (a) presenting consolidated or combined statements in place of statements of individual enterprises, (b) changing specific subsidiaries comprising the group of enterprises for which consolidated financial statements are presented, and (c) changing the enterprises included in combined financial statements. A different group of entities comprise the reporting entity after each change. A business combination accounted for by the pooling-of-interests method also results in a different reporting entity. [APB20, ¶12]

[5a]Deleted 2/92 because of FASB Statement 109.]

[6]The amount of interest cost capitalized through application of Section I67, "Interest: Capitalization of Interest Costs," shall not be changed when restating financial statements of prior periods [for a change in the reporting entity]. [FAS58, ¶8]

.113 The financial statements of the period of a change in reporting entity shall describe the nature of the change and the reason for it. In addition, the effect of the change on income before extraordinary items, net income, and related per share amounts shall be disclosed for all periods presented. Financial statements of subsequent periods need not repeat the disclosures. (Section B50, paragraphs .115 through .124 and .162 through .165 describe the manner of reporting and the disclosures required for a change in reporting entity that occurs because of a business combination.) [APB20, ¶35]

Other Changes in Accounting Principles

.114 Certain changes in accounting principle are such that the advantages of retroactive treatment in prior period reports outweigh the disadvantages. Accordingly, for those few changes, the financial statements of all prior periods presented shall be restated. The changes that shall be accorded this treatment are:

a. A change from the LIFO method of inventory pricing to another method
b. A change in the method of accounting for long-term construction-type contracts
c. A change to or from the "full cost" method of accounting that is used in the extractive industries [APB20, ¶27]
d. A change from retirement-replacement-betterment accounting[7] to depreciation accounting. [FAS73, ¶2]

[This treatment also can be used for] a change from one acceptable accounting principle to another acceptable principle in connection with a forthcoming public offering when an enterprise first issues its financial statements for any one of the following purposes: (1) obtaining additional equity capital from investors, (2) effecting a business combination, [or] (3) registering securities. [Such restatement is a special exemption (refer to Section A06, "Accounting Changes," paragraph .125) that] is available only once for changes made at the time an enterprise's financial statements are first used for any of those purposes and is not available to enterprises whose securities currently are widely held. [APB20, ¶29]

---

[7]On February 17, 1983, the Interstate Commerce Commission (ICC) ruled that railroads must use depreciation accounting for railroad track structures in reports to the ICC. The ruling is effective for 1983 annual filings, 1984 quarterly filings, and all filings thereafter with the ICC. The ICC previously had required RRB [(retirement-replacement-betterment)] for railroad track structures in reports to the ICC. [FAS73, ¶5] Under RRB, the initial costs of installing track are capitalized, not depreciated, and remain capitalized until the track is retired. The costs of replacing track are expensed unless a betterment (for example, replacing a 110-lb. rail with a 132-lb. rail) occurs. In that case, the amount by which the cost of the new part exceeds the current cost of the part replaced is considered a betterment and is capitalized but not depreciated, and the current cost of the part replaced is expensed. Railroads generally have used RRB for financial reporting. [FAS73, ¶6] The ICC ruling does not apply to financial reporting by railroads, but [if a] railroad adopts depreciation accounting for financial reporting, [the] change from RRB to depreciation accounting would be a change in accounting principle under this section. [FAS73, ¶7]

.115 The nature of and justification for a change in accounting principle described in paragraph .114 shall be disclosed in the financial statements for the period the change was adopted. In addition, [for accounting changes described in subparagraphs .114(a) through .114(c),] the effect of the change on income before extraordinary items, net income, and the related per share amounts shall be disclosed for all periods presented. This disclosure may be on the face of the income statement or in the notes. Paragraphs .116 through .119 illustrate the manner of reporting a change in accounting principle retroactively by restating the statements of those prior periods affected. Financial statements of subsequent periods need not repeat the disclosures. [APB20, ¶28]

An Illustration of Reporting a Special Change in Accounting Principle by Restating Prior Period Financial Statements

.116 XYZ Company decides in 19X5 to adopt the percentage-of-completion method in accounting for all of its long-term construction contracts. The enterprise had used the completed-contract method in prior years and had maintained records that are adequate to apply retroactively the percentage-of-completion method. The change in accounting principle is to be reported in the manner described in paragraphs .114 and .115. [APB20, ¶45]

.117 The direct effect of the change in accounting principle and other data assumed for this illustration are:

| Year | Pretax Income Reported by | | Difference in Income | |
	Percentage-of-Completion Method	Completed-Contract Method	Direct	Less Tax Effect
Prior to 19X1	$1,800,000	$1,300,000	$ 500,000	$ 250,000
19X1	900,000	800,000	100,000	50,000
19X2	700,000	1,000,000	(300,000)	(150,000)
19X3	800,000	600,000	200,000	100,000
19X4	1,000,000	1,100,000	(100,000)	(50,000)
Total at beginning of 19X5	5,200,000	4,800,000	400,000	200,000
19X5	1,100,000	900,000	200,000	100,000
Total	$6,300,000	$5,700,000	$ 600,000	$ 300,000

The per share amounts are computed assuming that 1,000,000 shares of common stock are issued and outstanding, that 100,000 additional shares would be issued if all outstanding bonds (that are not common stock equivalents) are converted, and that the annual interest expense, less taxes, for the convertible bonds is $25,000. [APB20, ¶46]

.118 The manner of reporting the change in two-year comparative statements is [presented in Exhibit 118A]. [APB20, ¶47]

Exhibit 118A

Two-Year Illustration of an Accounting Change
with Restatement of Prior Period Financial Statements

Income Statement

	19X5	19X4 as adjusted (Note A)
Income before extraordinary item	$550,000	$500,000
Extraordinary item (description)		(80,000)
Net income	$550,000	$420,000
Per share amounts:		
Earnings per common share—assuming no dilution:		
Income before extraordinary item	$ 0.55	$ 0.50
Extraordinary item		(.08)
Net income	$ 0.55	$ 0.42
Earnings per common share—assuming full dilution:		
Income before extraordinary item	$ 0.52	$ 0.47
Extraordinary item		(.07)
Net income	$ 0.52	$ 0.40

Statement of Retained Earnings

	19X5	19X4 as adjusted (Note A)
Balance at beginning of year, as previously reported	$17,800,000	$17,330,000
Add adjustment for the cumulative effect on prior years of applying retroactively the new method of accounting for long-term contracts (Note A)	200,000	250,000
Balance at beginning of year, as adjusted	$18,000,000	$17,580,000
Net income	550,000	420,000
Balance at end of year	$18,550,000	$18,000,000

(Refer to accompanying note to the financial statements.)

Note A—Change in Method of Accounting for Long-Term Contracts

The enterprise has accounted for revenue and costs for long-term construction contracts by the percentage-of-completion method in 19X5, whereas in all prior years revenue and costs were determined by the completed-contract method. The new method of accounting for long-term contracts was adopted to recognize . . . (state justification for change in accounting principle) . . . and financial statements of prior years have been restated to apply the new method retroactively. For income tax purposes, the completed-contract method has been continued. The effect of the accounting change on income of 19X5 and on income as previously reported for 19X4 is:

	Increase 19X5	(Decrease) 19X4
Effect on:		
Income before extraordinary item and net income	$100,000	$(50,000)
Earnings per common share—assuming no dilution	$ 0.10	$ (0.05)
Earnings per common share—assuming full dilution	$ 0.09	$ (0.05)

The balances of retained earnings for 19X4 and 19X5 have been adjusted for the effect (net of income taxes) of applying retroactively the new method of accounting. [APB20, ¶47]

.119 A note to a five-year summary of financial statements should disclose the effect of the change on net income and related per share amounts for the periods affected in the manner [illustrated in Exhibit 119A].

Exhibit 119A

Illustrative Note for a Five-Year Illustration of an Accounting Change with Restatement of Prior Period Financial Statements

Note A—Change in Method of Accounting for Long-Term Contracts

The enterprise has accounted for revenue and costs for long-term construction contracts by the percentage-of-completion method in 19X5, whereas in all prior years revenue and costs were determined by the completed-contract method. The new method of accounting for long-term contracts was adopted to recognize . . . (state justification for change in accounting principle) . . . and financial statements of prior years have been restated to apply the new method retroactively. For income tax purposes, the completed-

Exhibit 119A (continued)

contract method has been continued. The effect of the accounting change on net income as previously reported for 19X4 and prior years is:

	19X4	19X3	19X2	19X1
Net income as previously reported	$470,000	$300,000	$ 500,000	$400,000
Adjustment for effect of a change in accounting principle that is applied retroactively	(50,000)	100,000	(150,000)	50,000
Net income as adjusted	$420,000	$400,000	$ 350,000	$450,000
Per share amounts:				
Earnings per common share— assuming no dilution:				
Net income as previously reported	$ 0.47	$ 0.30	$ 0.50	$ 0.40
Adjustment for effect of a change in accounting principle that is applied retroactively	(0.05)	0.10	(0.15)	0.05
Net income as adjusted	$ 0.42	$ 0.40	$ 0.35	$ 0.45
Earnings per common share— assuming full dilution:				
Net income as previously reported	$ 0.45	$ 0.30	$ 0.47	$ 0.38
Adjustment for effect of a change in accounting principle that is applied retroactively	(0.05)	0.09	(0.13)	0.05
Net income as adjusted	$ 0.40	$ 0.39	$ 0.34	$ 0.43

[APB20, ¶48]

(The next page is 4471.)

BALANCE SHEET CLASSIFICATION: CURRENT ASSETS AND CURRENT LIABILITIES

Sources: ARB 43, Chapter 3A; APB Opinion 6; FASB Statement 6;
FASB Statement 78; FASB Statement 115; FASB Interpretation 8;
FASB Technical Bulletin 79-3

Summary

An enterprise preparing a classified balance sheet shall segregate current assets and current liabilities separately from other assets and liabilities. The current classification applies to those assets which will be realized in cash, sold or consumed within one year (or operating cycle, if longer), and those liabilities that will be discharged by use of current assets or the creation of other current liabilities within one year (or operating cycle, if longer). The current liability classification is also intended to include obligations that, by their terms, are due on demand or will be due on demand within one year (or operating cycle, if longer) from the balance sheet date, even though liquidation may not be expected within that period. It is also intended to include long-term obligations that are or will be callable by the creditor either because the debtor's violation of a provision of the debt agreement at the balance sheet date makes the obligation callable or because the violation, if not cured within a specified grace period, will make the obligation callable. Such callable obligations are to be classified as current liabilities unless one of the following conditions is met:

a. The creditor has waived or subsequently lost the right to demand repayment for more than one year (or operating cycle, if longer) from the balance sheet date.
b. For long-term obligations containing a grace period within which the debtor may cure the violation, it is probable that the violation will be cured within that period, thus preventing the obligation from becoming callable.

Short-term obligations expected to be refinanced on a long-term basis, including those callable obligations discussed above, shall be excluded from current liabilities only if the enterprise intends to refinance the obligation on a long-term basis and has the demonstrated ability to consummate the refinancing.

.101 [Editorial deletion.]

.102 The balance sheets of most enterprises show separate classifications of **current assets** and **current liabilities** (commonly referred to as classified balance sheets) permitting ready determination of **working capital.** Enterprises in several specialized industries (including broker-dealers and finance, real estate, and stock life insurance enterprises) for which the current/noncurrent distinction is deemed in practice to have little or no relevance prepare unclassified balance sheets. The standards established in paragraphs .110 through .137 apply only when an enterprise is preparing a classified balance sheet for financial accounting and reporting purposes. [FAS6, ¶7]

.103 Financial statements of a going concern are prepared on the assumption that the enterprise will continue in business. Accordingly, this section represents a departure from any narrow definition or strict *one-year* interpretation of either current assets or current liabilities; the objective is to relate the criteria developed to the **operating cycle** of a business. [ARB43, ch3A, ¶2]

.104 Financial position is revealed in a presentation of the assets and liabilities of the enterprise. Generally [these assets and liabilities] are classified and segregated; summations or totals of the current assets and current liabilities will permit the ready determination of *working capital. Working capital,* sometimes called *net working capital,* is represented by the excess of current assets over current liabilities and identifies the relatively liquid portion of total enterprise capital that constitutes a margin or buffer for meeting obligations within the ordinary operating cycle of the business. It is recognized that there may be exceptions, in special cases, to certain of the inclusions and exclusions as set forth in this section. When such exceptions occur they should be accorded the treatment merited in the particular circumstances under the general principles outlined herein. [ARB43, ch3A, ¶3]

Current Assets

.105 For accounting purposes, the term *current assets* is used to designate cash and other assets or resources commonly identified as those that are reasonably expected to be realized in cash or sold or consumed during the normal operating cycle of the business. Thus the term comprehends in general such resources as (a) cash available for current operations and items that are the equivalent of cash; (b) inventories of merchandise, raw materials, goods in process, finished goods, operating supplies, and ordinary maintenance material and parts; (c) trade accounts, notes, and acceptances receivable; (d) receivables from officers, employees, affiliates, and others, if collectible in the ordinary course of business within a year; (e) installment or deferred accounts and notes receivable if they conform generally to normal trade practices and terms within the business;

(f) marketable securities representing the investment of cash available for current operations [ARB43, ch3A, ¶4], including investments in debt and equity securities classified as trading securities under Section I80, "Investments: Debt and Equity Securities"; [FAS115, ¶125] and (g) prepaid expenses such as insurance, interest, rents, taxes, unused royalties, current paid advertising service not yet received, and operating supplies. Prepaid expenses are current assets not in the sense that they will be converted into cash but in the sense that, if not paid in advance, they would require the use of current assets during the operating cycle. [ARB43, ch3A, ¶4]

.106 The ordinary operations of a business involve a circulation of capital within the current asset group. Cash is expended for materials, finished parts, operating supplies, labor, and other factory services, and such expenditures are accumulated as inventory cost. Inventory costs, upon sale of the products to which such costs attach, are converted into trade receivables and ultimately into cash again. The average time intervening between the acquisition of materials or services entering this process and the final cash realization constitutes an *operating cycle*. A one-year time period is to be used as a basis for the segregation of current assets in cases where there are several operating cycles occurring within a year. However, where the period of the operating cycle is more than 12 months, as in, for instance, the tobacco, distillery, and lumber businesses, the longer period shall be used. Where a particular business has no clearly defined operating cycle, the one-year rule shall govern.[1] [ARB43, ch3A, ¶5]

.107 This concept of the nature of current assets contemplates the exclusion from that classification of such resources as: (a) cash and claims to cash that are restricted as to withdrawal or use for other than current operations, are designated for expenditure in the acquisition or construction of noncurrent assets, or are segregated[2] for the liquidation of long-term debts; (b) investments in securities (whether marketable or not) or advances that have been made for the purposes of control, affiliation, or other continuing business advantage; (c) receivables arising from unusual transactions (such as the sale of capital assets, or loans or advances to affiliates, officers, or employees) that are not expected to be collected within 12 months; (d) cash surrender value of life insurance policies; (e) land and other natural resources; (f) depreciable assets; and (g) long-term prepayments that are fairly chargeable to the operations of several years, or deferred charges

---

[1] The criteria for classifying deferred income tax assets as current assets are described in Section I27, "Income Taxes," paragraph .140.]

[2] Even though not actually set aside in special accounts, funds that are clearly to be used in the near future for the liquidation of long-term debts, payments to sinking funds, or for similar purposes should also, under this concept, be excluded from current assets. However, where such funds are considered to offset maturing debt that has properly been set up as a current liability, they may be included within the current asset classification. [ARB43, ch3A, ¶6, fn1]

such as bonus payments under a long-term lease, costs of rearrangement of factory layout, or removal to a new location. [ARB43, ch3A, ¶6]

.107A The amounts at which various current assets are carried do not always represent their present realizable cash values. Accounts receivable net of allowances for uncollectible accounts, and for unearned discounts where unearned discounts are considered, are effectively stated at the amount of cash estimated as realizable.[3] [ARB43, ch3A, ¶9] [Refer to Section I78, "Inventory," for disclosure requirements for inventory.]

Current Liabilities

.108 The term *current liabilities* is used principally to designate obligations whose liquidation is reasonably expected to require the use of existing resources properly classifiable as current assets, or the creation of other current liabilities. As a balance sheet category, the classification is intended to include obligations for items that have entered into the operating cycle, such as payables incurred in the acquisition of materials and supplies to be used in the production of goods or in providing services to be offered for sale; collections received in advance of the delivery of goods or performance of services;[4] and debts that arise from operations directly related to the operating cycle, such as accruals for wages, salaries, commissions, rentals, royalties, and income and other taxes. Other liabilities whose regular and ordinary liquidation is expected to occur within a relatively short period of time, usually 12 months, are also intended for inclusion,[5] such as short-term debts arising from the acquisition of capital assets, serial maturities of **long-term obligations,** amounts required to be expended within 1 year under sinking

---

[3]Unearned discounts (other than cash or quantity discounts and the like), finance charges, and interest included in the face amount of receivables shall be shown as a deduction from the related receivables. [APB6, ¶14]

[4]Examples of such current liabilities are obligations resulting from advance collections on ticket sales, which will normally be liquidated in the ordinary course of business by the delivery of services. On the contrary, obligations representing long-term deferments of the delivery of goods or services would not be shown as current liabilities. Examples of the latter are the issuance of a long-term warranty or the advance receipt by a lessor of rental for the final period of a 10-year [operating] lease as a condition to execution of the lease agreement. [ARB43, ch3A, ¶7, fn2]

[5]The criteria for classifying deferred income tax liabilities as current liabilities are described in Section I27, paragraph .140.]

fund provisions, and agency obligations arising from the collection or acceptance of cash or other assets for the account of third persons.[6] [ARB43, ch3A, ¶7]

.109 This concept of current liabilities would include estimated or accrued amounts that are expected to be required to cover expenditures within the year for known obligations (a) the amount of which can be determined only approximately (as in the case of provisions for accruing bonus payments) or (b) where the specific person or persons to whom payment will be made cannot as yet be designated (as in the case of estimated costs to be incurred in connection with guaranteed servicing or repair of products already sold). The current liability classification, however, is not intended to include debts to be liquidated by funds that have been accumulated in accounts of a type not properly classified as current assets, or long-term obligations incurred to provide increased amounts of working capital for long periods. When the amounts of the periodic payments of an obligation are, by contract, measured by current transactions, as for example by rents or revenues received in the case of equipment trust certificates or by the depletion of natural resources in the case of property obligations, the portion of the total obligation to be included as a current liability shall be that representing the amount accrued at the balance sheet date. [ARB43, ch3A, ¶8]

.109A The current liability classification is also intended to include obligations that, by their terms, are due on demand or will be due on demand within one year (or operating cycle, if longer) from the balance sheet date, even though liquidation may not be expected within that period. It is also intended to include long-term obligations that are or will be **callable** by the creditor either because the debtor's violation of a provision[6a] of the debt agreement at the balance sheet date makes the obligation callable or because the

---

[6]Loans accompanied by pledge of life insurance policies would be classified as current liabilities when, by their terms or by intent, they are to be repaid within 12 months. The pledging of life insurance policies does not affect the classification of the asset any more than does the pledging of receivables, inventories, real estate, or other assets as collateral for a short-term loan. However, when a loan on a life insurance policy is obtained from the insurance enterprise with the intent that it will not be paid but will be liquidated by deduction from the proceeds of the policy upon maturity or cancellation, the obligation shall be excluded from current liabilities. [ARB43, ch3A, ¶7, fn3]

[6a]A *violation of a provision* is the failure to meet a condition in a debt agreement or a breach of a provision in the agreement for which compliance is objectively determinable, whether or not a grace period is allowed or the creditor is required to give notice of its intention to demand repayment. [FAS78, ¶1, fn2] Drawing a distinction between significant violations of critical conditions and technical violations is not practicable. A violation that a debtor considers to be technical may be considered critical by the creditor. Furthermore, a creditor may choose to use a technical violation as a means to withdraw from its lending relationship with the debtor. If the violation is considered insignificant by the creditor, then the debtor should be able to obtain a waiver as discussed in (a) of this paragraph. [FAS78, ¶16] The effect of a violation of a debt agreement that occurs between the balance sheet date and the date the financial statements are issued [is not addressed by paragraph .109A]. [FAS78, ¶17]

violation, if not cured within a specified grace period, will make the obligation callable. Accordingly, such callable obligations shall be classified as current liabilities unless one of the following conditions is met:

a. The creditor has waived[6b] or subsequently lost[6c] the right to demand repayment for more than one year (or operating cycle, if longer) from the balance sheet date.
b. For long-term obligations containing a grace period within which the debtor may cure the violation, it is probable[6d] that the violation will be cured within that period, thus preventing the obligation from becoming callable.

Short-term obligations that are expected to be refinanced on a long-term basis, including those callable obligations discussed herein, shall be classified in accordance with paragraphs .110 through .118 of this section. [FAS78, ¶5]

.109B [The] general principle [underlying paragraph .109A is that] classification of debt in a debtor's balance sheet should be based on facts existing at the balance sheet date rather than on expectations. If the creditor has at that date, or will have within one year (or operating cycle, if longer) from that date, the unilateral right to demand immediate repayment of the debt under any provision of the debt agreement, the obligation shall be classified as a current liability unless (a) one of the conditions in paragraph .109A is met or (b) the obligation is expected to be refinanced on a long-term basis and the provisions of paragraphs .110 through .118 are met. [FAS78, ¶13]

Classification of Short-Term Obligations Expected to Be Refinanced

.110 Some **short-term obligations** are expected to be refinanced on a long-term basis and, therefore, are not expected to require the use of enterprise working capital during the ensuing fiscal year. Examples include commercial paper, construction loans, and the currently maturing portion of long-term debt. [FAS6, ¶1]

.111 For purposes of this section, *short-term obligations* are those that are scheduled to mature within one year after the date of an enterprise's balance sheet or, for those enterprises that use the operating cycle concept of working capital described in paragraphs .106 and .108, within an enterprise's operating cycle that is longer than one year.

[6b]If the obligation is callable because of violations of certain provisions of the debt agreement, the creditor needs to waive its right with regard only to those violations. [FAS78, ¶5, fn*]

[6c]For example, the debtor has cured the violation after the balance sheet date and the obligation is not callable at the time the financial statements are issued. [FAS78, ¶5, fn†]

[6d]*Probable* is defined in Section C59, "Contingencies," paragraph .104(a), as "likely to occur" and is used in the same sense in this paragraph. [FAS78, ¶5, fn‡]

Long-term obligations are those scheduled to mature beyond one year (or the operating cycle, if applicable) from the date of an enterprise's balance sheet. *Refinancing a short-term obligation on a long-term basis* means either replacing it with a long-term obligation or with equity securities or renewing, extending, or replacing it with short-term obligations for an uninterrupted period extending beyond one year (or the operating cycle, if applicable) from the date of an enterprise's balance sheet. Accordingly, despite the fact the short-term obligation is scheduled to mature during the ensuing fiscal year (or the operating cycle, if applicable), it will not require the use of working capital during that period. [FAS6, ¶2]

.112 Short-term obligations arising from transactions in the normal course of business that are due in customary terms [(refer to paragraph .108)[7]] shall be classified as current liabilities. [FAS6, ¶8]

.113 A short-term obligation other than one classified as a current liability in accordance with paragraph .112 shall be excluded from current liabilities only if[8] [FAS6, ¶9] the enterprise intends to *refinance the obligation on a long-term basis* (refer to paragraph .111) [FAS6, ¶10] [and such] intent is supported by an ability to consummate the refinancing demonstrated in either of the following ways:

a. *Post-balance-sheet-date issuance of a long-term obligation or equity securities.* After the date of an enterprise's balance sheet but before that balance sheet is issued, a long-term obligation or equity securities[9] have been issued for the purpose of refinancing the short-term obligation on a long-term basis.

---

[7]Paragraph .112 does not apply to] short-term obligations arising from the acquisition or construction of noncurrent assets [or to those] not directly related to the operating cycle (for example, a note given to a supplier to replace an account payable that originally arose in the normal course of business and had been due in customary terms) [(refer to paragraph .113)]. [FAS6, ¶20]

[8]Paragraph .109 describes a circumstance, unaffected by paragraph .113, in which obligations maturing within one year would be excluded from current liabilities as follows: "The current liability classification, however, is not intended to include debts to be liquidated by funds that have been accumulated in accounts of a type not properly classified as current assets. . . ." Footnote 2 describes another circumstance, also unaffected by paragraph .113: ". . . Funds that are clearly to be used in the near future for the liquidation of long-term debts, payments to sinking funds, or for similar purposes should also . . . be excluded from current assets. However, if such funds are considered to offset maturing debt that has properly been set up as a current liability, they may be included within the current asset classification." Accordingly, funds obtained on a long-term basis prior to the balance sheet date would be excluded from current assets if the obligation to be liquidated is excluded from current liabilities. [FAS6, ¶9, fn1]

[9]If equity securities have been issued, the short-term obligation, although excluded from current liabilities, shall not be included in owners' equity. [FAS6, ¶11, fn2]

b. *Financing agreement.* Before the balance sheet is issued, the enterprise has entered into a financing agreement that clearly permits the enterprise to refinance the short-term obligation on a long-term basis on terms that are readily determinable, and all of the following conditions are met:

(1) The agreement does not expire within one year (or operating cycle—refer to paragraph .111) from the date of the enterprise's balance sheet and during that period the agreement is not cancelable by the lender or the prospective lender or investor (and obligations incurred under the agreement are not callable during that period) except for violation of a provision[10] with which compliance is objectively[11] determinable or measurable.[12]

(2) No violation of any provision in the financing agreement exists at the balance sheet date and no available information indicates that a violation has occurred thereafter but prior to the issuance of the balance sheet, or, if one exists at the balance sheet date or has occurred thereafter, a waiver has been obtained.

(3) The lender or the prospective lender or investor with which the enterprise has entered into the financing agreement is expected to be financially capable of honoring the agreement. [FAS6, ¶11]

.114 If an enterprise's ability to consummate an intended refinancing of a short-term obligation on a long-term basis is demonstrated by post-balance-sheet-date issuance of a long-term obligation or equity securities (refer to paragraph .113(a)), the amount of the short-term obligation to be excluded from current liabilities shall not exceed the proceeds of the new long-term obligation or the equity securities issued. If ability to refinance is demonstrated by the existence of a financing agreement (refer to paragraph .113(b)), the amount of the short-term obligation to be excluded from current liabilities shall be reduced to the amount available for refinancing under the agreement when the amount available is less than the amount of the short-term obligation. The amount to be excluded shall be reduced further if information (such as restrictions in other agreements or restrictions as to transferability of funds) indicates that funds obtainable under the agreement will not be available to liquidate the short-term obligation. Further, if amounts that could be obtained under the financing agreement fluctuate (for example, in relation to the enterprise's needs, in proportion to the value of collateral, or in accordance with other terms of the agreement), the amount to be excluded from current liabilities shall be

---

[10]For purposes of this section, *violation of a provision* means failure to meet a condition set forth in the agreement or breach or violation of a provision such as a restrictive covenant, representation, or warranty, whether or not a grace period is allowed or the lender is required to give notice. [FAS6, ¶11, fn3]

[11]Refer to paragraphs .501 through .503 for guidance regarding classification of long-term debt agreements with **subjective acceleration clauses.**]

[12]Financing agreements cancelable for violation of a provision that can be evaluated differently by the parties to the agreement (such as *a material adverse change* or *failure to maintain satisfactory operations*) do not comply with this condition. [FAS6, ¶11, fn4]

limited to a reasonable estimate of the minimum amount expected to be available at any date from the scheduled maturity of the short-term obligation to the end of the fiscal year (or operating cycle—refer to paragraph .111). If no reasonable estimate can be made, the entire outstanding short-term obligation shall be included in current liabilities. [FAS6, ¶12]

.115 The enterprise may intend to seek an alternative source of financing rather than to exercise its rights under the existing agreement when the short-term obligation becomes due. The enterprise must intend to exercise its rights under the existing agreement, however, if that other source does not become available.[13] [FAS6, ¶13]

.116 Replacement of a short-term obligation with another short-term obligation after the date of the balance sheet but before the balance sheet is issued is not, by itself, sufficient to demonstrate an enterprise's ability to refinance the short-term obligation on a long-term basis. If, for example, the replacement is made under the terms of a revolving credit agreement that provides for renewal or extension of the short-term obligation for an uninterrupted period extending beyond one year (or operating cycle—refer to paragraph .111) from the date of the balance sheet, the revolving credit agreement must meet the conditions in paragraph .113(b) to justify excluding the short-term obligation from current liabilities. Similarly, if the replacement is a rollover of commercial paper accompanied by a *standby* credit agreement, the standby agreement must meet the conditions in paragraph .113(b) to justify excluding the short-term obligation from current liabilities. [FAS6, ¶14]

.117 Repayment of a short-term obligation *before* funds are obtained through a long-term refinancing requires the use of current assets. Therefore, if a short-term obligation is repaid after the balance sheet date and subsequently a long-term obligation or equity securities are issued whose proceeds are used to replenish current assets before the balance sheet is issued, the short-term obligation shall not be excluded from current liabilities at the balance sheet date. [(Refer to paragraphs .138 and .139 for an example of applying this paragraph.)] [FIN8, ¶3]

Disclosure

.118 A total of current liabilities[13a] shall be presented in classified balance sheets. If a short-term obligation is excluded from current liabilities pursuant to the provisions of

---

[13]The intent to exercise may not be present if the terms of the agreement contain conditions or permit the prospective lender or investor to establish conditions, such as interest rates or collateral requirements, that are unreasonable to the enterprise. [FAS6, ¶13, fn5]

[13a]B05.104 addresses the need to present a total of current assets.]

this section, the notes to the financial statements shall include a general description of the financing agreement and the terms of any new obligation incurred or expected to be incurred or equity securities issued or expected to be issued as a result of a refinancing. [FAS6, ¶15] If an obligation under paragraph .109A(b) is classified as a long-term liability (or, in the case of an unclassified balance sheet, is included as a long-term liability in the disclosure of debt maturities), the circumstances shall be disclosed. [The requirements of Section C32, "Commitments: Long-Term Obligations," may also apply.] [FAS78, ¶5]

Examples of Classifying Obligations

.119 The following examples provide guidance for applying this section. It should be recognized that these examples do not comprehend all possible circumstances and do not include all the disclosures that would typically be made regarding long-term debt or current liabilities. [FAS6, ¶32]

General Assumptions

.120 The assumptions on which examples [1 through 7] are based are:

a. ABC Company's fiscal year-end is December 31, 19X5.
b. The date of issuance of the December 31, 19X5 financial statements is March 31, 19X6; the Company's practice is to issue a classified balance sheet.
c. At December 31, 19X5, short-term obligations include $5,000,000 representing the portion of 6 percent long-term debt maturing in February 19X6 and $3,000,000 of 9 percent notes payable issued in November 19X5 and maturing in July 19X6.
d. The Company intends to refinance on a long-term basis both the current maturity of long-term debt and the 9 percent notes payable.
e. Accounts other than the long-term debt maturing in February 19X6 and the notes payable maturing in July 19X6 are:

Current assets	$30,000,000
Other assets	$50,000,000
Accounts payable and accruals	$10,000,000
Other long-term debt	$25,000,000
Shareholders' equity	$37,000,000

f. Unless otherwise indicated, the examples also assume that the lender or prospective lender is expected to be capable of honoring the agreement, that there is no evidence of a violation of any provision, and that the terms of borrowings available under the agreement are readily determinable. [FAS6, ¶33]

Example 1—Financing Agreement Used to Refinance Existing Obligation

.121 The Company negotiates a financing agreement with a commercial bank in December 19X5 for a maximum borrowing of $8,000,000 at any time through 19X7 with the following terms:

a. Borrowings are available at ABC Company's request for such purposes as it deems appropriate and will mature three years from the date of borrowing.
b. Amounts borrowed will bear interest at the bank's prime rate.
c. An annual commitment fee of ½ of 1 percent is payable on the difference between the amount borrowed and $8,000,000.
d. The agreement is cancelable by the lender only if:
   (1) The Company's working capital, excluding borrowings under the agreement, falls below $10,000,000.
   (2) The Company becomes obligated under lease agreements to pay an annual rental in excess of $1,000,000.
   (3) Treasury stock is acquired without the prior approval of the prospective lender.
   (4) The Company guarantees indebtedness of unaffiliated persons in excess of $500,000. [FAS6, ¶34]

.122 The enterprise's intention to refinance meets the condition specified by paragraph .113. Compliance with the provisions listed in paragraph .121(d) is objectively determinable or measurable; therefore, the condition specified by paragraph .113(b)(1) is met. The proceeds of borrowings under the agreement are clearly available for the liquidation of the 9 percent notes payable and the long-term debt maturing in February 19X6. Both obligations, therefore, would be classified as other than current liabilities. [FAS6, ¶35]

.123 Following are the liability section of ABC Company's balance sheet at December 31, 19X5 and the related footnote disclosures required by this section, based on the information in paragraphs .120 and .121. Because the balance sheet is issued subsequent to the February 19X6 maturity of the long-term debt, the footnote describes the refinancing of that obligation.

	December 31, 19X5
Current Liabilities:	
Accounts payable and accruals	$10,000,000
Total Current Liabilities	10,000,000
Long-Term Debt:	
9% notes payable (Note A)	3,000,000*
6% debt due February 19X6 (Note A)	5,000,000*
Other long-term debt	25,000,000
Total Long-Term Debt	33,000,000
Total Liabilities	$43,000,000

---

*These obligations may also be shown in captions distinct from both current liabilities and long-term debt, such as "Interim Debt," "Short-Term Debt Expected to Be Refinanced," and "Intermediate Debt."

Note A—The Company has entered into a financing agreement with a commercial bank that permits the Company to borrow at any time through 19X7 up to $8,000,000 at the bank's prime rate of interest. The Company must pay an annual commitment fee of ½ of 1 percent of the unused portion of the commitment. Borrowings under the financing agreement mature three years after the date of the loan. Among other things, the agreement prohibits the acquisition of treasury stock without prior approval by the bank, requires maintenance of working capital of $10,000,000 exclusive of borrowings under the agreement, and limits the annual rental under lease agreements to $1,000,000. In February 19X6, the Company borrowed $5,000,000 at 8 percent and liquidated the 6 percent long-term debt, and it intends to borrow additional funds available under the agreement to refinance the 9 percent notes payable maturing in July 19X6. [FAS6, ¶36]

Example 2—Effect of Restriction on Transferring Funds to Be Obtained from Financing Agreement by Foreign Subsidiary

.124 A foreign subsidiary of the enterprise negotiates a financing agreement with its local bank in December 19X5. Funds are available to the subsidiary for its unrestricted use, including loans to affiliated companies; other terms are identical to those cited in paragraph .121. Local laws prohibit the transfer of funds outside the country. [FAS6, ¶37]

.125 The requirement of paragraph .113(b)(1) is met because compliance with the provisions of the agreement is objectively determinable or measurable. Because of the laws prohibiting the transfer of funds, however, the proceeds from borrowings under the agreement are not available for liquidation of the debt maturing in February and July 19X6. Accordingly, both the 6 percent debt maturing in February 19X6 and the 9 percent notes payable maturing in July 19X6 would be classified as current liabilities. [FAS6, ¶38]

Example 3—Refinancing through Post-Balance-Sheet-Date Issuance of Long-Term Obligations or Equity Securities

.126 Assume that instead of utilizing the agreement cited in paragraph .121, the Company issues $8,000,000 of 10-year debentures to the public in January 19X6. The Company intends to use the proceeds to liquidate the $5,000,000 debt maturing February 19X6 and the $3,000,000 of 9 percent notes payable maturing July 19X6. In addition, assume the debt maturing February 19X6 is paid prior to the issuance of the balance sheet, and the remaining proceeds from the sale of debentures are invested in a U.S. Treasury note maturing the same day as the 9 percent notes payable. [FAS6, ¶39]

.127 Since the Company refinanced the long-term debt maturing in February 19X6 in a manner that meets the conditions set forth in paragraph .113, that obligation would be excluded from current liabilities. In addition, the 9 percent notes payable maturing in July 19X6 would also be excluded because the Company has obtained funds expressly intended to be used to liquidate those notes and not intended to be used in current operations. In balance sheets after the date of sale of the debentures and before the maturity date of the notes payable, the Company would exclude the notes payable from current liabilities if the U.S. Treasury note is excluded from current assets (refer to paragraph .107). [FAS6, ¶40]

.128 If the debentures had been sold prior to January 1, 19X6, the $8,000,000 of obligations to be paid would be excluded from current liabilities in the balance sheet at that date if the $8,000,000 in funds were excluded from current assets. [FAS6, ¶41]

.129 If, instead of issuing the 10-year debentures, the Company had issued $8,000,000 of equity securities and all other facts in this example remained unchanged, both the 6 percent debt due February 19X6 and the 9 percent notes payable due July 19X6 would be classified as liabilities other than current liabilities, such as "Indebtedness Due in 19X6 Refinanced in January 19X6." [FAS6, ¶42]

Example 4—Use of Revolving Credit Agreement

.130 In December 19X5 the Company negotiates a revolving credit agreement providing for unrestricted borrowings up to $10,000,000. Borrowings will bear interest at 1 percent over the prevailing prime rate of the bank with which the agreement is arranged but in any event not less than 8 percent, will have stated maturities of 90 days, and will be continuously renewable for 90-day periods at the Company's option for 3 years provided there is compliance with the terms of the agreement. Provisions of the agreement are similar to those cited in paragraph .121(d). Further, the enterprise intends to renew obligations incurred under the agreement for a period extending beyond one year from the balance sheet date. There are no outstanding borrowings under the agreement at December 31, 19X5. [FAS6, ¶43]

.131 In this instance, the long-term debt maturing in February 19X6 and the 9 percent notes payable maturing in July 19X6 would be excluded from current liabilities because the Company consummated a financing agreement meeting the conditions set forth in paragraph .113(b) prior to the issuance of the balance sheet. [FAS6, ¶44]

Example 5—Financing Agreement with Fluctuating Maximum Borrowings

.132 Assume that the agreement cited in Example 4 above included an additional provision limiting the amount to be borrowed by the Company to the amount of its inventory, which is pledged as collateral and is expected to range between a high of $8,000,000 during the second quarter of 19X6 and a low of $4,000,000 during the fourth quarter of 19X6. [FAS6, ¶45]

.133 The terms of the agreement comply with the conditions required by this section; however, because the minimum amount expected to be available from February to December 19X6 is $4,000,000, only that amount of short-term obligations can be excluded from current liabilities (refer to paragraph .114). Whether the obligation to be excluded is a portion of the currently maturing long-term debt or some portions of both it and the 9 percent notes payable depends on the intended timing of the borrowing. [FAS6, ¶46]

.134 If the Company intended to refinance only the 9 percent notes payable due July 19X6 and the amount of its inventory is expected to reach a low of approximately $2,000,000 during the second quarter of 19X6 but be at least $3,000,000 in July 19X6 and thereafter during 19X6, the $3,000,000 [of] 9 percent notes payable would be excluded from current liabilities at December 31, 19X5 (refer to paragraph .114). [FAS6, ¶47]

Example 6—Classifying Obligations Related to Acquisition of Noncurrent Assets

.135 In lieu of the facts given in paragraphs .120(c) and .120(d), assume that during 19X5 the Company entered into a contract to have a warehouse built. The warehouse is expected to be financed by issuance of the Company's commercial paper. In addition, the Company negotiated a standby agreement with a commercial bank that provides for maximum borrowings equal to the expected cost of the warehouse, which will be pledged as collateral. The agreement also requires that the proceeds from the sale of commercial paper be used to pay construction costs. Borrowings may be made under the agreement only if the Company is unable to issue new commercial paper. The proceeds of borrowings must be used to retire outstanding commercial paper and to liquidate additional liabilities incurred in the construction of the warehouse. At December 31, 19X5 the Company has $7,000,000 of commercial paper outstanding and $1,000,000 of unpaid construction costs resulting from a progress billing through December 31. [FAS6, ¶48]

.136 Because the commercial paper will be refinanced on a long-term basis, either by uninterrupted renewal or, failing that, by a borrowing under the agreement, the commercial paper would be excluded from current liabilities. The $1,000,000 liability for the unpaid progress billing results from the construction of a noncurrent asset and will be refinanced on the same basis as the commercial paper and, therefore, it would also be excluded from current liabilities (refer to footnote 7 of this section). [FAS6, ¶49]

Example 7—Reporting Obligations That Are Expected to Be Refinanced But Do Not Meet Criteria in Paragraph .113

.137 Following are two methods of presenting liabilities in ABC Company's balance sheet at December 31, 19X5 assuming the Company intends to refinance the 6 percent debt maturing in February 19X6 and the 9 percent notes payable maturing in July 19X6 but has not met the conditions required by this section to exclude those obligations from current liabilities.

Alternative 1

	December 31, 19X5
Current Liabilities:	
Accounts payable and accruals	$10,000,000
Notes payable due July 19X6	3,000,000
6% debt due February 19X6	5,000,000
Total Current Liabilities	18,000,000
Long-Term Debt	25,000,000
Total Liabilities	$43,000,000

Alternative 2

		December 31, 19X5
Current Liabilities:		
Accounts payable and accruals		$10,000,000
Short-term debt expected to be refinanced:		
Notes payable due July 19X6	$3,000,000	
6% debt due February 19X6	5,000,000	8,000,000
Total Current Liabilities		18,000,000
Long-Term Debt		25,000,000
Total Liabilities		$43,000,000

[FAS6, ¶50]

Example 8—Classifying Short-Term Obligations Repaid Prior to Being Replaced by a Long-Term Security

.138 Assume that an enterprise has issued $3,000,000 of short-term commercial paper during the year to finance construction of a plant. At June 30, 19X6, the enterprise's fiscal year-end, the enterprise intends to refinance the commercial paper by issuing long-term debt. However, because the enterprise temporarily has excess cash, in July 19X6 it liquidates $1,000,000 of the commercial paper as the paper matures. In August 19X6, the enterprise completes a $6,000,000 long-term debt offering. Later during the month of August, it issues its June 30, 19X6 financial statements. The proceeds of the long-term debt offering are to be used to replenish $1,000,000 in working capital, to pay $2,000,000 of commercial paper as it matures in September 19X6, and to pay $3,000,000 of construction costs expected to be incurred later that year to complete the plant. [FIN8, ¶2]

.139 In the example described in paragraph .138, the $1,000,000 of commercial paper liquidated in July would be classified as a current liability in the enterprise's balance sheet at June 30, 19X6. The $2,000,000 of commercial paper liquidated in September 19X6 but refinanced by the long-term debt offering in August 19X6 would be excluded from current liabilities in balance sheets at the end of June 19X6, July 19X6, and August 19X6.[14] It should be noted that the existence of a financing agreement at the date of issuance of the financial statements rather than a completed financing at that date would not change these classifications. [FIN8, ¶4]

---

[14]At the end of August 19X6, $2,000,000 of cash would be excluded from current assets or if included in current assets, a like amount of debt would be classified as a current liability [(refer to footnote 8 and paragraph .127)]. [FIN8, ¶4, fn1]

Glossary

.400 Callable. An obligation is *callable* at a given date if the creditor has the right at that date to demand, or to give notice of its intention to demand, repayment of the obligation owed to it by the debtor. [FAS78, ¶1, fn1]

.401 Current assets. [Those assets that] are reasonably expected to be realized in cash or sold or consumed during the normal operating cycle of the business. [ARB43, ch3A, ¶4]

.402 Current liabilities. [Those] obligations whose liquidation is reasonably expected to require the use of existing resources properly classifiable as current assets or the creation of other current liabilities. [ARB43, ch3A, ¶7]

.403 Long-term obligations. Those [obligations] scheduled to mature beyond one year (or the operating cycle, if applicable) from the date of an enterprise's balance sheet. [FAS6, ¶2]

.404 Operating cycle. The average time intervening between the acquisition of materials or services and the final cash realization [from the sale of products or services (refer to paragraph .106)]. [ARB43, ch3A, ¶5]

.405 Short-term obligations. Those [obligations] that are scheduled to mature within one year after the date of an enterprise's balance sheet or, for those enterprises that use the operating cycle concept of working capital, within an enterprise's operating cycle that is longer than one year. [FAS6, ¶2]

.405A Subjective acceleration clause. A provision in a debt agreement that states that the creditor may accelerate the scheduled maturities of the obligation under conditions that are not objectively determinable (for example, "if the debtor fails to maintain satisfactory operations" or "if a material adverse change occurs"). [FAS78, ¶10, fn3]

.406 Working capital. The excess of current assets over current liabilities. [ARB43, ch3A, ¶3]

Supplemental Guidance

Subjective Acceleration Clauses in Long-Term Debt Agreements

.501 *Question*—Should long-term debt be classified as a current liability if the long-term debt agreement contains a subjective clause that may accelerate the due date? [FTB79-3, ¶1]

.502 *Background*—Paragraph .113 indicates that a subjective acceleration clause contained in a financing agreement that would otherwise permit a short-term obligation to be refinanced on a long-term basis would preclude that short-term obligation from being classified as long-term. That paragraph does not address financing agreements other than those related to short-term obligations. [FTB79-3, ¶2]

.503 *Response*—In some situations, the circumstances (for example, recurring losses or liquidity problems) would indicate that long-term debt subject to a subjective acceleration clause should be classified as a current liability. Other situations would indicate only disclosure of the existence of such clauses. It would seem that neither reclassification nor disclosure would be required if the likelihood of the acceleration of the due date were remote, such as when the lender historically has not accelerated due dates of loans containing similar clauses and the financial condition of the borrower is strong and its prospects bright. [The requirements of this paragraph are not modified by the requirements of paragraphs .109A and .109B.] [FTB79-3, ¶3]

(The next page is 4521.)

Sources: APB Opinion 10; FASB Interpretation 39; FASB Interpretation 41

Summary

The offsetting of related assets and liabilities in the statement of financial position (balance sheet) is permitted only when there is a right of setoff. This section presents the criteria for determining when a right of setoff exists.

The offset of cash or other assets against the tax liability or other amounts owing to governmental bodies is not acceptable except in limited circumstances described in this section. This section also addresses the applicability of the general principle on offsetting to forward, interest rate swap, currency swap, option, and other conditional or exchange contracts and clarifies the circumstances in which it is appropriate to offset amounts recognized for those contracts in the statement of financial position. The conditions required to offset payables and receivables that represent repurchase agreements and reverse repurchase agreements are also described in this section.

General Principle on Offsetting

.101 It is a general principle of accounting that the offsetting of assets and liabilities in the [statement of financial position] is improper except when a **right of setoff** exists. [APB10, ¶7(1)]

.101A A *right of setoff* is a debtor's legal right, by contract or otherwise, to discharge all or a portion of the debt owed to another party by applying against the debt an amount that the other party owes to the debtor.[1] A right of setoff exists when all of the following conditions are met:

a. Each of *two* parties[2] owes the other determinable amounts.[3]

---

[1]For purposes of this section, cash on deposit at a financial institution is to be considered by the depositor as cash rather than as an amount owed to the depositor. [FIN39, ¶5, fn2]

[2]A right of setoff involves only two parties. [FIN39, ¶43]

[3]If the parties meet the other criteria specified in the definition, [it] is unnecessary [that] those amounts be in the same currency and bear the same interest rate. However, if maturities differ, only the party with the nearer maturity could offset because the party with the longer term maturity must settle in the manner that the other party selects at the earlier maturity date. [FIN39, ¶44]

b. The reporting party has the right to set off the amount owed with the amount owed by the other party.
c. The reporting party intends to set off.[4]
d. The right of setoff is enforceable at law. [5]

A debtor having a valid right of setoff may offset the related asset and liability and report the net amount.[6] [FIN39, ¶5]

.101B Generally, debts may be set off if they exist between mutual debtors each acting in its capacity as both debtor and creditor. In particular cases, however, state laws about the right of setoff may provide results different from those normally provided by contract or as a matter of common law. Similarly, the U.S. Bankruptcy Code imposes restrictions on or prohibitions against the right of setoff in bankruptcy under certain circumstances. Legal constraints shall be considered to determine whether the right of setoff is enforceable. [FIN39, ¶6]

Offsetting Securities against Taxes Payable

.102 The offset of cash or other assets against the tax liability or other amounts owing to governmental bodies is not acceptable except in the circumstances described in paragraph .103. [APB10, ¶7(1)] Most securities now issued by governments are not by their terms designed specifically for the payment of taxes and, accordingly, shall not be deducted from taxes payable on the [statement of financial position]. [APB10, ¶7(2)]

.103 [Regarding the offsetting of assets against the tax liability] the only exception to the general principle [in paragraph .101] occurs when it is clear that a purchase of securities (acceptable for the payment of taxes) is in substance an advance payment of taxes that will be payable in the relatively near future, so that in the special circumstances the purchase is tantamount to the prepayment of taxes. This occurs at times, for example, as an accommodation to a local government and in some instances when governments

---

[4]Acknowledgment of the intent to set off by the reporting party and, if applicable, demonstration of the execution of the setoff in similar situations meet the criterion of intent. [FIN39, ¶45]

[5][The phrase] *enforceable at law* includes those situations in which the right of setoff is enforceable because of regulatory procedures or as part of normal business practice [even if] not specifically included in contractual agreements. [FIN39, ¶47]

[6]This section does not address derecognition or nonrecognition of assets and liabilities. Derecognition by sale of an asset or extinguishment of a liability results in removal of a recognized asset or liability and generally results in the recognition of gain or loss. Although conceptually different, offsetting that results in a net amount of zero and derecognition with no gain or loss are indistinguishable in their effects on the statement of financial position. Likewise, not recognizing assets and liabilities of the same amount in financial statements achieves similar reported results. [FIN39, ¶5, fn3]

issue securities that are specifically designated as being acceptable for the payment of taxes of those governments. [APB10, ¶7(3)]

Offsetting Forward, Interest Rate Swap, Currency Swap, Option, and Other Conditional or Exchange Contracts

.104 Unless the conditions in paragraph .101A are met, the *fair value* of [**conditional or exchange] contracts**[7] in a loss position shall not be offset against the fair value of contracts in a gain position. [Refer to paragraph .115A of Section F25, "Financial Instruments: Disclosure," for the definition of fair value.] Similarly, amounts recognized as accrued receivables shall not be offset against amounts recognized as accrued payables unless a right of setoff exists. [FIN39, ¶8]

.105 When fair value or an amount receivable or payable related to conditional or exchange contracts of the reporting entity are recognized in the statement of financial position, the amount recognized represents an asset or a liability. The fair value of a contract in a gain position or an amount accrued as a receivable represents a probable future economic benefit controlled by the reporting entity under the contract. The fair value of a contract in a loss position or an amount accrued as a payable represents a probable future sacrifice of economic benefits arising from the reporting entity's present obligations to transfer assets under the contract. [FIN39, ¶9]

.106 Without regard to the condition in paragraph .101A(c), fair value amounts[8],[9] recognized for forward, interest rate swap, currency swap, option, and other conditional or exchange contracts executed with the same counterparty under a **master netting arrangement** may be offset. The reporting entity's choice to offset or not must be

---

[7]*Conditional contracts* are those whose obligations or rights depend on the occurrence of some specified future event that is not certain to occur and that could change the timing of the amounts or of the instruments to be received, delivered, or exchanged. *Exchange contracts* are those that require a future exchange of assets or liabilities rather than a one-way transfer of assets. [FIN39, ¶3]

[8]The fair value recognized for some contracts may include an accrual component for the periodic unconditional receivables and payables that result from the contract; the accrual component included therein may also be offset for contracts executed with the same counterparty under a master netting arrangement. [FIN39, ¶10, fn4]

[9]This paragraph applies only to fair value amounts recognized for conditional or exchange contracts executed with the same counterparty under a master netting arrangement. It does not apply to other amounts recognized for other types of contracts executed under a master netting arrangement; however, those amounts could otherwise meet the conditions of paragraph .101A for a right of setoff. For example, unless the conditions in paragraph .101A are met, the amount recognized under a repurchase agreement may not be offset against the amount recognized under a reverse repurchase agreement solely because the agreements are executed with the same counterparty under a master netting arrangement, nor may an accrued receivable be offset against an accrued payable on interest rate swaps that are not recognized at fair value solely because the swaps are executed with the same counterparty under a master netting arrangement. [FIN39, ¶22]

applied consistently. A master netting arrangement exists if the reporting entity has multiple contracts, whether for the same type of conditional or exchange contract or for different types of contracts, with a single counterparty that are subject to a contractual agreement that provides for the net settlement of all contracts through a single payment in a single currency in the event of default on or termination of any one contract. Offsetting the fair values recognized for forward, interest rate swap, currency swap, option, and other conditional or exchange contracts outstanding with a single counterparty results in the net fair value of the position between the two counterparties being reported as an asset or a liability in the statement of financial position. [FIN39, ¶10]

Offsetting Payables and Receivables under Repurchase and Reverse Repurchase Agreements

.106A Notwithstanding the condition in paragraph .101A(c), an enterprise may, but is not required to, offset amounts recognized as payables under **repurchase agreements**[10] and amounts recognized as receivables under **reverse repurchase agreements**[11] if all of the following conditions are met:[12]

a. The repurchase and reverse repurchase agreements are executed with the same counterparty.
b. The repurchase and reverse repurchase agreements have the same explicit settlement date specified at the inception of the agreement.
c. The repurchase and reverse repurchase agreements are executed in accordance with a master netting arrangement. [Refer to paragraph .106.]

---

[10]For purposes of this section, a repurchase agreement (repo) refers to a transaction that is accounted for as a collateralized borrowing in which a seller-borrower of securities sells those securities to a buyer-lender with an agreement to repurchase them at a stated price plus interest at a specified date or in specified circumstances. The "payable" under a repurchase agreement refers to the amount of the seller-borrower's obligation recognized for the future repurchase of the securities from the buyer-lender. In certain industries, the terminology is reversed; that is, entities in those industries refer to this type of agreement as a "reverse repo." [FIN41, ¶1, fn1]

[11]For purposes of this section, a reverse repurchase agreement (reverse repo) refers to a transaction that is accounted for as a collateralized lending in which a buyer-lender buys securities with an agreement to resell them to the seller-borrower at a stated price plus interest at a specified date or in specified circumstances. The "receivable" under a reverse repurchase agreement refers to the amount due from the seller-borrower for the repurchase of the securities from the buyer-lender. In certain industries, the terminology is reversed; that is, entities in those industries refer to this type of agreement as a "repo." [FIN41, ¶1, fn2]

[12]Paragraph .106A does not apply to amounts recognized for other types of repurchase and reverse repurchase agreements executed under a master netting arrangement; however, those amounts could otherwise meet the conditions of paragraph .101A for a right of setoff. Therefore, unless all conditions in paragraph .101A are met, the amount recognized under a repurchase agreement that does not settle in accordance with the conditions of paragraphs .106A and .106B may not be offset against the amount recognized under a reverse repurchase agreement merely because the agreements are executed with the same counterparty under a master netting arrangement. [FIN41, ¶14]

d. The securities underlying the repurchase and reverse repurchase agreements exist in "book entry" form and can be transferred only by means of entries in the records of the transfer system operator or securities custodian.[13]

e. The repurchase and reverse repurchase agreements will be settled on a securities transfer system that operates in the manner described in paragraph .106B, and the enterprise must have associated banking arrangements in place as described in paragraph .106B. Cash settlements for securities transferred are made under established banking arrangements that provide that the enterprise will need available cash on deposit only for any net amounts that are due at the end of the business day. It must be *probable*[14] that the associated banking arrangements will provide sufficient **daylight overdraft or other intraday credit**[15] at the settlement date for each of the parties.

f. The enterprise intends to use the same account at the clearing bank or other financial institution at the settlement date in transacting both (1) the cash inflows resulting from the settlement of the reverse repurchase agreement and (2) the cash outflows in settlement of the offsetting repurchase agreement.

The enterprise's choice to offset or not must be applied consistently. Net receivables resulting from the application of this section should not be offset against net payables resulting from the application of this section in the statement of financial position. [FIN41, ¶3]

.106B   In a securities transfer system for repurchase and reverse repurchase agreements that meets the requirements of paragraph .106A(e), cash transfers are initiated by notification from the owner of record of the securities to its securities custodian[16] to transfer those securities to the counterparty to the agreement. Under associated banking arrange-

---

[13]**"Book entry" securities** meeting the criterion in paragraph .106A(d) exist only as items in accounting records maintained by a transfer system operator. This requirement does not preclude offsetting of securities held in "book entry" form solely because other securities of the same issue exist in other forms. [FIN41, ¶3, fn4]

[14]The term *probable* is used in this section consistent with its use in paragraph .104(a) of Section C59, "Contingencies," to mean that a transaction or event is likely to occur. [FIN41, ¶3, fn5]

[15]*Daylight overdraft or other intraday credit* refers to the accommodation in the banking arrangements that allows transactions to be completed even if there is insufficient cash on deposit during the day provided there is sufficient cash to cover the net cash requirement at the end of the day. That accommodation may be through a credit facility, including a credit facility for which a fee is charged, or from a deposit of collateral. [FIN41, ¶3, fn6]

[16]The securities custodian for a securities transfer system may be the bank or financial institution that executes securities transfers over the securities transfer system, and "book entry" securities exist only in electronic form on the records of the transfer system operator for each entity that has a security account with the transfer system operator. "Book entry" securities exist only as items of account on the "controlling" records of the transfer system operator. Banks or other financial institutions may maintain "subsidiary" records of "book entry" securities. "Book entry" securities may be transferred on the subsidiary records of a bank or financial institution but, for entities that have a security account with the transfer system operator, may be transferred from the account of such an entity only through the transfer system operator. [FIN41, ¶4, fn7]

ments, each party to a same-day settlement of both a repurchase agreement and a reverse repurchase agreement would be obligated to pay a gross amount of cash for the securities transferred from its counterparty but would be able to reduce that gross obligation by notifying its securities custodian to transfer other securities to that counterparty the same day. Thus, each party is responsible for maintaining available cash on deposit only for the amount of any net payable unless it fails to instruct its securities custodian to transfer securities to its counterparty.[17] If both parties transfer the appropriate securities in settlement of the repurchase and reverse repurchase agreements, the party with a net receivable will not need any cash to facilitate the settlement, while the party with a net payable will need only to have available the required net amount due at the end of the business day. [FIN41, ¶4]

Special Applications

.107 Various other sections and AICPA Audit and Accounting Guides, Industry Audit Guides, and Statements of Position specify accounting treatments in circumstances that result in offsetting or in a presentation in a statement of financial position that is similar to the effect of offsetting. This section does not modify the accounting treatment in the particular circumstances prescribed by any other sections or AICPA Guides or Statements of Position. Examples of those other sections and AICPA Guides are:

a. Section L10, "Leases" (leveraged leases, paragraphs .144 through .149)
b. [Deleted 12/92 because of FASB Statement 113, *Accounting and Reporting for Reinsurance of Short-Duration and Long-Duration Contracts.*]
c. Section P16, "Pension Costs" (accounting for pension plan assets and liabilities)
d. Section P40, "Postretirement Benefits Other Than Pensions" (accounting for plan assets and liabilities)
e. Section I27, "Income Taxes" (net tax asset or liability amounts reported)
f. Section I13, "Income Statement Presentation: Discontinued Operations" (reporting of discontinued operations)
g. AICPA Audit and Accounting Guides, *Audits of Brokers and Dealers in Securities* (trade date accounting for trading portfolio positions), and *Construction Contractors* and *Audits of Federal Government Contractors* (advances received on construction contracts)
h. AICPA Industry Audit Guide, *Audits of Banks* (reciprocal balances with other banks).

[FIN39, ¶7]

---

[17]Failure by either party to instruct its securities custodian to transfer securities owned of record would result in that party's failing to receive cash from the counterparty and, thereby, would require that party to have available cash on deposit for the gross payable due for securities transferred to it. The failure also should be an event of default under the master netting arrangement required by paragraph .106A(c). The event of default, in turn, should entitle the other party to terminate the arrangement and demand the immediate net settlement of all contracts. [FIN41, ¶4, fn8]

Glossary

.401 **"Book entry" securities.** Exist only as items in accounting records maintained by a [securities] transfer system operator. [FIN41, ¶3, fn4]

.402 **Conditional contracts.** Those [contracts] whose obligations or rights depend on the occurrence of some specified future event that is not certain to occur and that could change the timing of the amounts or of the instruments to be received, delivered, or exchanged. [FIN39, ¶3]

.403 **Daylight overdraft or other intraday credit.** Refers to the accommodation in banking arrangements that allows transactions to be completed even if there is insufficient cash on deposit during the day provided there is sufficient cash to cover the net cash requirement at the end of the day. [FIN41, ¶3, fn6]

.404 **Exchange contracts.** Those [contracts] that require a future exchange of assets or liabilities rather than a one-way transfer of assets. [FIN39, ¶3]

.405 **Master netting arrangement.** Exists if the reporting entity has multiple contracts, whether for the same type of conditional or exchange contract or for different types of contracts, with a single counterparty that are subject to a contractual agreement that provides for the net settlement of all contracts through a single payment in a single currency in the event of default on or termination of any one contract. [FIN39, ¶10]

.406 **Repurchase agreement (repo).** Refers to a transaction that is accounted for as a collateralized borrowing in which a seller-borrower of securities sells those securities to a buyer-lender with an agreement to repurchase them at a stated price plus interest at a specified date or in specified circumstances. [FIN41, ¶1, fn1]

.407 **Reverse repurchase agreement (reverse repo).** Refers to a transaction that is accounted for as a collateralized lending in which a buyer-lender buys securities with an agreement to resell them to the seller-borrower at a stated price plus interest at a specified date or in specified circumstances. [FIN41, ¶1, fn2]

.408 **Right of setoff.** A debtor's legal right, by contract or otherwise, to discharge all or a portion of the debt owed to another party by applying against the debt an amount that the other party owes to the debtor. [FIN39, ¶5]

Supplemental Guidance

.501-.504 [Deleted 3/92 because of FASB Interpretation 39, *Offsetting of Amounts Related to Certain Contracts.*]

(The next page is 4801.)

501-505[Deleted 3/92 because of FASB Interpretation 39.]

Sources: ARB 43, Chapter 1A; ARB 51; APB Opinion 16;
AICPA Interpretations of APB Opinion 16;
FASB Statement 10; FASB Statement 38; FASB Statement 72;
FASB Statement 79; FASB Statement 87; FASB Statement 106;
FASB Statement 109; FASB Statement 111; FASB Statement 121;
FASB Interpretation 4; FASB Interpretation 9; FASB Technical Bulletin 85-5

Summary

A business combination occurs when a corporation and one or more incorporated or unincorporated businesses are brought together into one accounting entity. The single entity carries on the activities of the previously separate, independent enterprises. The purchase method and the pooling-of-interests method are both acceptable in accounting for business combinations, although not as alternatives in accounting for the same business combination. This section provides that a business combination shall be accounted for as a pooling of interests if it meets certain specified criteria. Business combinations that do not meet all of the specified criteria shall be accounted for as purchases.

The criteria for the pooling method relate to the attributes of the combining enterprises before the combination, the manner of combining the enterprises, and the absence of certain planned transactions after the combination. The pooling-of-interests method accounts for a business combination as the uniting of the ownership interests of two or more companies by exchange of equity securities. No acquisition is recognized because the combination is accomplished without disbursing resources of the constituents. Ownership interests continue and the former bases of accounting shall be retained. The recorded assets and liabilities of the constituents shall be carried forward to the combined corporation at their recorded amounts. Income of the combined corporation shall include income of the constituents for the entire fiscal period in which the combination occurs. The reported income of the constituents for prior periods shall be combined and restated as income of the combined corporation.

The purchase method accounts for a business combination as the acquisition of one enterprise by another. The acquiring corporation shall record at its cost the acquired assets less liabilities assumed. A difference between the cost of an acquired enterprise and the sum of the fair values of tangible and identifiable intangible assets less liabilities assumed shall be recorded as goodwill. The reported income of an acquiring corporation shall include the operations of the acquired enterprise after acquisition, based on the cost to the acquiring corporation.

Scope

.101 This section covers the combination of a corporation and one or more incorporated or unincorporated enterprises. The conclusions of this section apply equally to business combinations in which one or more enterprises become subsidiaries, one enterprise transfers its net assets to another, and each enterprise transfers its net assets to a newly formed enterprise. The acquisition of some or all of the stock held by minority stockholders of a subsidiary is not a business combination, but paragraph .102 specifies the applicable method of accounting. The term *business combination* excludes a transfer by an enterprise of its net assets to a newly formed substitute corporate entity chartered by the existing enterprise and a transfer of net assets or exchange of shares between enterprises under common control (control is described in Section C51, "Consolidation," paragraph .102), such as between a parent and its subsidiary or between two subsidiaries of the same parent.[1] This section does not specifically discuss the combination of a corporation and one or more unincorporated enterprises or of two or more unincorporated enterprises, but its provisions shall be applied as a general guide. [APB16, ¶5]

Applicability of Accounting Methods

.102 Some business combinations shall be accounted for by the **purchase method** and other combinations shall be accounted for by the **pooling-of-interests method**.[2] [APB 16, ¶42] The two methods are not alternatives in accounting for the same business combination. A single method shall be applied to an entire combination; the practice known as part-purchase, part-pooling is not acceptable. The acquisition of some or all of the

---

[1][Refer to paragraphs .521 through .527, .597 through .605, and .645 through .648 for supplemental guidance as to the application of this paragraph.]

[2]This section refers to the *purchase method of accounting* for a business combination because the term is widely used and generally understood. However, the more inclusive terms *acquire* (to come into possession of) and *acquisition* are generally used to describe transactions rather than the more narrow term *purchase* (to acquire by the payment of money or its equivalent). The broader terms clearly encompass obtaining assets by issuing stock as well as by disbursing cash and thus avoid the confusion that results from describing a stock transaction as a *purchase*. This section does not describe a business combination accounted for by the pooling-of-interests method as an *acquisition* because the meaning of the word is inconsistent with the method of accounting. [APB16, ¶11, fn2]

stock held by minority stockholders of a subsidiary—whether acquired by the parent, the subsidiary itself, or another affiliate—shall be accounted for by the purchase method rather than by the pooling-of-interests method. [APB16, ¶43]

.103 The distinctive conditions that require pooling-of-interest accounting are described in paragraphs .104 through .107 and combinations involving all of those conditions shall be accounted for as described in paragraphs .109 through .124.[3] All other business combinations shall be treated as the acquisition of one enterprise by another and accounted for by the purchase method as described in paragraphs .125 through .166.[4] [APB16, ¶44]

Conditions for Pooling-of-Interests Method

.104 The pooling-of-interests method of accounting is intended to present as a single interest two or more common stockholder interests that were previously independent and the combined rights and risks represented by those interests. That method shows that stockholder groups neither withdraw nor invest assets but in effect exchange voting common stock in a ratio that determines their respective interests in the combined enterprise. Some business combinations have those features. A business combination that meets *all* of the conditions specified and explained in paragraphs .105 through .107 shall be accounted for by the pooling-of-interests method. The conditions are classified by (a) attributes of the combining enterprises, (b) manner of combining interests, and (c) absence of planned transactions. [APB16, ¶45]

Combining Enterprises

.105 Certain attributes of combining enterprises indicate that independent ownership interests are combined in their entirety to continue previously separate operations. Combining virtually all of existing common stock interests avoids combining only selected assets, operations, or ownership interests, any of which is more akin to disposing of and acquiring interests than to sharing risks and rights. It also avoids combining interests that are already related by substantial intercorporate investments. The two conditions in this paragraph define essential attributes of combining enterprises. [APB16, ¶46]

a. Each of the combining enterprises is autonomous and has not been a subsidiary or division of another enterprise within two years before the plan of combination is initiated.

---

[3][Refer to paragraphs .501 through .520, .528 through .631, and .635 through .644 for supplemental guidance as to the application of paragraphs .104 through .124.]

[4][Refer to paragraphs .521 through .527, .593 through .596, .627 through .629, .632 through .634, and .649 and .650 for supplemental guidance as to the application of paragraphs .125 through .165.]

(1) A plan of combination is initiated on the earlier of (i) the date that the major terms of a plan, including the ratio of exchange of stock, are announced publicly or otherwise formally made known to the stockholders of any one of the combining enterprises or (ii) the date that stockholders of a combining enterprise are notified in writing of an exchange offer. Therefore, a plan of combination is often initiated even though consummation is subject to the approval of stockholders and others.

(2) A new enterprise incorporated within the preceding two years meets this condition unless the enterprise is successor to a part of an enterprise or to an enterprise that is otherwise not autonomous for this condition. A wholly owned subsidiary that distributes voting common stock of its parent to effect the combination is also considered an autonomous enterprise provided the parent would have met all conditions in paragraphs .105 through .107 had the parent issued its stock directly to effect the combination.

(3) Divestiture of assets to comply with an order of a governmental authority or judicial body results in an exception to the terms of this condition. Either a subsidiary divested under an order or a new enterprise that acquires assets disposed of under an order is therefore autonomous for this condition. [APB16, ¶46(a)]

b. Each of the combining enterprises is independent of the other combining enterprises.

(1) This condition means that at the date the plan of combination is initiated and consummated the combining enterprises hold as intercorporate investments no more than 10 percent in total of the outstanding voting common stock of any combining enterprise.[5] For the percentage computation, intercorporate investments exclude voting common stock that is acquired after the date the plan of combination is initiated in exchange for the voting common stock issued to effect the combination. Investments of 10 percent or less are explained in paragraph .106(b). [APB16, ¶46(b)]

Combining of Interests

.106   The combining of existing voting common stock interests by the exchange of stock is the essence of a business combination accounted for by the pooling-of-interests method. The separate stockholder interests lose their identities and all share mutually in the combined risks and rights. Exchanges of common stock that alter relative voting rights, that result in preferential claims to distributions of profits or assets for some common stockholder groups, or that leave significant minority interests in combining enterprises are incompatible with the idea of mutual sharing. Similarly, acquisitions of common stock for assets or debt, reacquisitions of outstanding stock for the purpose of exchanging it in a business combination, and other transactions that reduce the common stock interests

---

[5]An exception for common stock held on October 31, 1970 is explained in paragraph .167. [APB16, ¶46(b), fn4]

are contrary to the idea of combining existing stockholder interests. The seven conditions in this paragraph relate to the exchange to effect the combination. [APB16, ¶47]

a. The combination is effected in a single transaction or is completed in accordance with a specific plan within one year after the plan is initiated.

   (1) Altering the terms of exchange of stock constitutes initiation of a new plan of combination unless earlier exchanges of stock are adjusted to the new terms.

   (2) A business combination completed in more than one year from the date the plan is initiated meets this condition if the delay is beyond the control of the combining enterprises because proceedings of a governmental authority or litigation prevents completing the combination. [APB16, ¶47(a)]

b. An enterprise offers and issues only common stock with rights identical to those of the majority of its outstanding voting common stock[6] in exchange for substantially all of the voting common stock interest of another enterprise at the date the plan of combination is consummated.

   (1) The plan to issue voting common stock in exchange for voting common stock may include, within limits, provisions to distribute cash or other consideration for fractional shares, for shares held by dissenting stockholders, and the like, but may not include a pro rata distribution of cash or other consideration.

   (2) Substantially all of the voting common stock means 90 percent or more for this condition. That is, after the date the plan of combination is initiated, one of the combining enterprises (issuing enterprise) issues voting common stock in exchange for at least 90 percent of the voting common stock of another combining enterprise that is outstanding at the date the combination is consummated. The number of shares exchanged therefore excludes those shares of the combining enterprise (a) acquired before and held by the issuing enterprise and its subsidiaries at the date the plan of combination is initiated, regardless of the form of consideration;[7] (b) acquired by the issuing enterprise and its subsidiaries after the date the plan of combination is initiated other than by issuing its own voting common stock; and (c) outstanding after the date the combination is consummated.

   (3) *An investment in stock of the issuing enterprise* held by a combining enterprise may prevent a combination from meeting this condition even though the investment of the combining enterprise is not more than 10 percent of the outstanding stock of the issuing enterprise (refer to paragraph .105(b)). An investment in stock of the issuing enterprise by another combining enterprise is the same in a mutual exchange as an investment by the issuing enterprise in stock of the other combin-

---

[6]A class of stock that has voting control of an enterprise is the majority class. [APB16, ¶47(b), fn6]

[7]An exception for common stock held on October 31, 1970 is explained in paragraph .167. [APB16, ¶47(b), fn7]

ing enterprise—the choice of issuing enterprise is essentially a matter of convenience. An investment in stock of the issuing enterprise must be expressed as an equivalent number of shares of the investor combining enterprise because the measure of percent of shares exchanged is in terms of shares of stock of the investor enterprise. An investment in 10 percent or less of the outstanding voting common stock of the issuing enterprise affects the measure of percent of shares exchanged in the combination as follows:

(a) The number of shares of voting common stock of the issuing enterprise held by the investor combining enterprise at the date the plan is initiated plus shares it acquired after that date are restated as an equivalent number of shares of voting common stock of the investor combining enterprise based on the ratio of exchange of stock in the combination.

(b) The equivalent number of shares is deducted from the number of shares of voting common stock of the investor combining enterprise exchanged for voting common stock of the issuing enterprise as part of the plan of combination.

(c) The reduced number of shares is considered the number exchanged and is compared with 90 percent of the outstanding voting common stock of the investor combining enterprise at the date the plan is consummated to determine whether the terms of condition .106(b) are met.

(4) Since the number of shares of voting common stock exchanged is reduced for an intercorporate investment in voting common stock of the issuing enterprise, the terms of condition .106(b) may not be met even though 90 percent or more of the outstanding common stock of a combining enterprise is exchanged to effect a combination.

(5) *A combination of more than two enterprises* is evaluated essentially the same as a combination of two enterprises. The percent of voting common stock exchanged is measured separately for each combining enterprise, and condition .106(b) is met if 90 percent or more of the voting common stock for each of the several combining enterprises is exchanged for voting common stock of the issuing enterprise. The number of shares exchanged for stock of the issuing enterprise includes only shares exchanged by stockholders other than the several combining enterprises themselves. Thus, intercorporate investments in combining enterprises are included in the number of shares of stock outstanding but are excluded from the number of shares of stock exchanged to effect the combination.

(6) *A new enterprise formed to issue its stock* to effect the combination of two or more enterprises meets condition .106(b) if (i) the number of shares of each enterprise exchanged to effect the combination is not less than 90 percent of its voting commmon stock outstanding at the date the combination is consummated and (ii) condition .106(b) would have been met had any one of the combining enterprises issued its stock to effect the combination on essentially the same basis.

(7) *Condition .106(b) relates to issuing common stock for the common stock interests in another enterprise.* Hence, an enterprise issuing stock to effect the combination may assume the debt securities of the other enterprise or may exchange substantially identical securities or voting common stock for other outstanding equity and debt securities of the other combining enterprise. An issuing enterprise may also distribute cash to holders of debt and equity securities that either are callable or redeemable and may retire those securities. However, the issuing enterprise may exchange only voting common stock for outstanding equity and debt securities of the other combining enterprise that have been issued in exchange for voting common stock of that enterprise during a period beginning two years preceding the date the combination is initiated.

(8) *A transfer of the net assets of a combining enterprise* to effect a business combination satisfies condition .106(b) provided all net assets of the enterprise at the date the plan is consummated are transferred in exchange for stock of the issuing enterprise. However, the combining enterprise may temporarily retain cash, receivables, or marketable securities to settle liabilities, contingencies, or items in dispute if the plan provides that the assets remaining after settlement are to be transferred to the enterprise issuing the stock to effect the combination.

(9) Only voting common stock may be issued to effect the combination unless both voting common stock and other stock of the other combining enterprise are outstanding at the date the plan is consummated. The combination may then be effected by issuing all voting common stock or by issuing voting common and other stock in the same proportions as the outstanding voting common and other stock of the other combining enterprise. An investment in 10 percent or less of the outstanding voting common stock of a combining enterprise held by another combining enterprise requires special computations to evaluate condition .106(b). The computations and comparisons are in terms of the voting common stock of the issuing enterprise and involve:

    (a) *Stock issued for common stock interest.* The total number of shares of voting common stock issued for all of the assets[8] is divided between those applicable to outstanding voting common stock and those applicable to other outstanding stock, if any, of the combining enterprise that transfers assets (transferor enterprise).

    (b) *Reduction for intercorporate investments.* The number of issued shares of voting common stock applicable to the voting common stock interest of the transferor combining enterprise is reduced by the sum of (i) the number of shares of voting stock of the issuing enterprise held by the transferor combining enterprise at the date the plan of combination is initiated plus shares it acquired

---

[8]Including (for this computation) stock of the issuing enterprise held by the transferor combining enterprise. [APB16, ¶47(b), fn8]

after that date and (ii) the number of shares of voting common stock of the transferor combining enterprise held by the issuing enterprise at the date the plan of combination is initiated plus shares it acquired after that date. The shares of the transferor combining enterprise are restated as the equivalent number of shares of voting common stock of the issuing enterprise for this purpose. Restatement is based on the ratio of the number of shares of voting common stock of the transferor combining enterprise that are outstanding at the date the plan is consummated to the number of issued shares of voting common stock applicable to the voting common stock interests.

(c) *Comparison with 90 percent.* The reduced number of shares of stock issued is compared with 90 percent of the issued number of shares of voting common stock applicable to voting common stock interests to determine if the transfer of assets meets the terms of condition .106(b). [APB16, ¶47(b)]

c. None of the combining enterprises changes the equity interest of the voting common stock in contemplation of effecting the combination either within two years before the plan of combination is initiated or between the dates the combination is initiated and consummated; changes in contemplation of effecting the combination may include distributions to stockholders and additional issuances, exchanges and retirements of securities.

(1) Distributions to stockholders that are no greater than normal dividends are not changes for this condition. Normality of dividends is determined in relation to earnings during the period and to the previous dividend policy and record. Dividend distributions on stock of a combining enterprise that are equivalent to normal dividends on the stock to be issued in exchange in the combination are considered normal for this condition. [APB16, ¶47(c)]

d. Each of the combining enterprises reacquires shares of voting common stock only for purposes other than business combinations, and no enterprise reacquires more than a normal number of shares between the dates the plan of combination is initiated and consummated.

(1) Treasury stock acquired for purposes other than business combinations includes shares for stock option and compensation plans and other recurring distributions provided a systematic pattern of reacquisitions is established at least two years before the plan of combination is initiated. A systematic pattern of reacquisitions may be established for less than two years if it coincides with the adoption of a new stock option or compensation plan. The normal number of shares of voting common stock reacquired is determined by the pattern of reacquisitions of stock before the plan of combination is initiated.

(2) Acquisitions by other combining enterprises of voting common stock of the issuing enterprise after the date the plan of combination is initiated are essentially the same as if the issuing enterprise reacquired its own common stock. [APB16, ¶47(d)]

e. The ratio of the interest of an individual common stockholder to those of other common stockholders in a combining enterprise remains the same as a result of the exchange of stock to effect the combination.

  (1) This condition means that each individual common stockholder who exchanges stock receives a voting common stock interest exactly in proportion to its relative voting common stock interest before the combination is effected. Thus, no common stockholder is denied or surrenders its potential share of a voting common stock interest in a combined enterprise. [APB16, ¶47(e)]

f. The voting rights to which the common stock ownership interests in the resulting combined enterprise are entitled are exercisable by the stockholders; the stockholders are neither deprived of nor restricted in exercising those rights for a period.

  (1) This condition is not met, for example, if shares of common stock issued to effect the combination are transferred to a voting trust. [APB16, ¶47(f)]

g. The combination is resolved at the date the plan is consummated and no provisions of the plan relating to the issue of securities or other consideration are pending.

  (1) This condition means that (a) the combined enterprise does not agree to contingently issue additional shares of stock or distribute other consideration at a later date to the former stockholders of a combining enterprise or (b) the combined enterprise does not issue or distribute to an escrow agent common stock or other consideration that is to be either transferred to common stockholders or returned to the enterprise at the time the contingency is resolved.

  (2) An agreement may provide, however, that the number of shares of common stock issued to effect the combination may be revised for the later settlement of a contingency at a different amount than that recorded by a combining enterprise. [APB16, ¶47(g)]

Absence of Planned Transactions

.107 Some transactions after a combination is consummated are inconsistent with the combining of entire existing interests of common stockholders. Including those transactions in the negotiations and terms of the combination, either explicitly or by intent, counteracts the effect of combining stockholder interests. The three conditions in this paragraph relate to certain future transactions. [APB16, ¶48]

a. The combined enterprise does not agree directly or indirectly to retire or reacquire all or part of the common stock issued to effect the combination. [APB16, ¶48(a)]

b. The combined enterprise does not enter into other financial arrangements for the benefit of the former stockholders of a combining enterprise, such as a guaranty of loans secured by stock issued in the combination, that in effect negates the exchange of equity securities. [APB16, ¶48(b)]

c. The combined enterprise does not intend or plan to dispose of a significant part of the assets of the combining enterprises within two years after the combination other than disposals in the ordinary course of business of the formerly separate enterprises and to eliminate duplicate facilities or excess capacity. [APB16, ¶48(c)]

Subsidiary Enterprise

.108 Dissolution of a combining enterprise is not a condition for applying the pooling-of-interests method of accounting for a business combination. One or more combining enterprises may be subsidiaries of the issuing enterprise after the combination is consummated if the other conditions are met. [APB16, ¶49]

Application of Pooling-of-Interests Method

.109 A business combination that meets all of the conditions in paragraphs .104 through .107 shall be accounted for by the pooling-of-interests method. Appropriate procedures are described in paragraphs .110 through .124. [APB16, ¶50]

Assets and Liabilities Combined

.110 The recorded assets and liabilities of the separate enterprises generally become the recorded assets and liabilities of the combined enterprise. The combined enterprise therefore recognizes those assets and liabilities recorded in conformity with generally accepted accounting principles by the separate enterprises at the date the combination is consummated. [APB16, ¶51]

.111 The combined enterprise records the historical cost-based amounts of the assets and liabilities of the separate enterprises because the existing basis of accounting continues. However, the separate enterprises may have recorded assets and liabilities under differing methods of accounting and the amounts may be adjusted to the same basis of accounting if the change would otherwise have been appropriate for the separate enterprise. A change in accounting method to conform the individual methods shall be applied retroactively, and financial statements presented for prior periods shall be restated. [APB16, ¶52]

Stockholders' Equity Combined

.112 The stockholders' equities of the separate enterprises are also combined as a part of the pooling-of-interests method of accounting. The combined enterprise records as capital the capital stock and capital in excess of par or stated value of outstanding stock of the separate enterprises. Similarly, retained earnings or deficits of the separate enterprises are combined and recognized as retained earnings of the combined enterprise (refer to paragraph .115). The amount of outstanding shares of stock of the combined enterprise at par or stated value may exceed the total amount of capital stock of the separate combining enterprises; the excess shall be deducted first from the combined other contributed capital and then from the combined retained earnings. The combined retained earnings could be misleading if shortly before or as a part of the combination transaction one or more of the combining enterprises adjusted the elements of stockholders' equity to eliminate a deficit; therefore, the elements of equity before the adjustment shall be combined. [APB16, ¶53]

.113 An enterprise that effects a combination accounted for by the pooling-of-interests method by distributing stock previously acquired as treasury stock (refer to paragraph .106(d)) shall first account for those shares of stock as though retired. The issuance of the shares for the common stock interests of the combining enterprise is then accounted for like the issuance of previously unissued shares. [APB16, ¶54]

.114 Accounting for common stock of one of the combining enterprises that is held by another combining enterprise at the date a combination is consummated depends on whether the stock is the same as that issued to effect the combination or is the same as the stock that is exchanged in the combination. An investment of a combining enterprise in the common stock of the issuing enterprise is in effect returned to the resulting combined enterprise in the combination. The combined enterprise shall account for the investment as treasury stock. In contrast, an investment in the common stock of other combining enterprises (not the one issuing stock in the combination) is an investment in stock that is exchanged in the combination for the common stock issued. The stock in that type of intercorporate investment is in effect eliminated in the combination. The combined enterprise shall account for that investment as stock retired as part of the combination. [APB16, ¶55]

Reporting Combined Operations

.115 An enterprise that applies the pooling-of-interests method of accounting to a combination shall report results of operations for the period in which the combination occurs as though the enterprises had been combined as of the beginning of the period. Results of operations for that period thus comprise those of the separate enterprises combined from the beginning of the period to the date the combination is consummated and those of the combined operations from that date to the end of the period. Eliminating the effects of intercompany transactions from operations before the date of combination reports operations before and after the date of combination on substantially the same basis. The effects of intercompany transactions on current assets, current liabilities, revenue, and cost of sales for periods presented and on retained earnings at the beginning of the periods presented shall be eliminated to the extent possible. The nature of and effects on earnings per share of nonrecurring intercompany transactions involving long-term assets and liabilities need not be eliminated but shall be disclosed. A combined enterprise shall disclose in notes to financial statements the revenue, extraordinary items, and net income of each of the separate enterprises from the beginning of the period to the date the combination is consummated (refer to paragraph .123(d)). The information relating to the separate enterprises may be as of the end of the interim period nearest the date that the combination is consummated. [APB16, ¶56]

.116 Similarly, balance sheets and other financial information of the separate enterprises as of the beginning of the period shall be presented as though the enterprises had been combined at that date. Financial statements and financial information of the separate enterprises presented for prior years shall also be restated on a combined basis to furnish comparative information. All restated financial statements and financial summaries shall indicate clearly that financial data of the previously separate enterprises are combined. [APB16, ¶57]

Expenses Related to Combination

.117 The pooling-of-interests method records neither the acquiring of assets nor the obtaining of capital. Therefore, costs incurred to effect a combination accounted for by that method and to integrate the continuing operations are expenses of the combined enterprise rather than additions to assets or direct reductions of stockholders' equity. Accordingly, all expenses related to effecting a business combination accounted for by the pooling-of-interests method shall be deducted in determining the net income of the resulting combined enterprise for the period in which the expenses are incurred. Those expenses include, for example, registration fees, costs of furnishing information to stockholders, fees of finders and consultants, salaries and other expenses related to services of employees, and costs and losses of combining operations of the previously separate enterprises and instituting efficiencies. [APB16, ¶58]

Disposition of Assets after Combination

.118 A combined enterprise may dispose of those assets of the separate enterprises that are duplicate facilities or excess capacity in the combined operations. Losses or estimated losses on disposal of specifically identified duplicate or excess facilities shall be deducted in determining the net income of the resulting combined enterprise. However, a loss estimated and recorded while a facility remains in service shall not include the portion of the cost that is properly allocable to anticipated future service of the facility. [APB16, ¶59]

.119 Profit or loss on other dispositions of assets of the previously separate enterprises may require special disclosure unless the disposals are part of customary business activities of the combined enterprise. Specific treatment of a profit or loss on those dispositions is warranted because the pooling-of-interests method of accounting would have been inappropriate (refer to paragraph .107(c)) if the combined enterprise were committed or planned to dispose of a significant part of the assets of one of the combining enterprises. A combined enterprise shall disclose separately a profit or loss resulting from the disposal of a significant part of the assets or a separable segment of the previously separate enterprises, provided (a) the profit or loss is material in relation to the net income of the combined enterprise and (b) the disposition is within two years after the combination is consummated. The disclosed profit or loss, less applicable income tax effect, shall be classified as an extraordinary item [(refer to Section I17, "Income Statement Presentation: Extraordinary Items")]. [APB16, ¶60]

Date of Recording Combination

.120 A business combination accounted for by the pooling-of-interests method shall be recorded as of the date the combination is consummated. Therefore, even though a business combination is consummated before one or more of the combining enterprises first issues its financial statements as of an earlier date, the financial statements issued shall be those of the combining enterprise and not those of the resulting combined enterprise. A combining enterprise shall, however, disclose as supplemental information, in notes to financial statements or otherwise, the substance of a combination consummated before financial statements are issued and the effects of the combination on reported financial position and results of operations (refer to paragraph .124). Comparative financial statements presented in reports of the resulting combined enterprise after a combination is consummated shall combine earlier financial statements of the separate enterprises. [APB16, ¶61]

.121 An enterprise may be reasonably assured that a business combination that has been initiated but not consummated as of the date of financial statements will meet the conditions requiring the pooling-of-interests method of accounting. The enterprise shall record, as an investment, common stock of the other combining enterprise acquired before the statement date. Common stock acquired by disbursing cash or other assets or by incurring liabilities shall be recorded at cost. Stock acquired in exchange for common stock of the issuing enterprise shall, however, be recorded at the proportionate share of underlying net assets at the date acquired as recorded by the other enterprise. Until the pooling-of-interests method of accounting for the combination is known to be appropriate, the investment and net income of the investor enterprise shall include the proportionate share of earnings or losses of the other enterprise after the date of acquisition of the stock. The investor enterprise shall also disclose results of operations for all prior periods presented as well as the entire current period as they will be reported if the combination is later accounted for by the pooling-of-interests method. After the combination is consummated and the applicable method of accounting is known, financial statements issued previously shall be restated as necessary to include the other combining enterprise. [APB16, ¶62]

Disclosure of a Combination

.122 A combined enterprise shall disclose in its financial statements that a combination accounted for by the pooling-of-interests method has occurred during the period. The basis of current presentation and restatements of prior periods may be disclosed in the financial statements by captions or by references to notes. [APB16, ¶63]

.123 Notes to financial statements of a combined enterprise shall disclose the following for the period in which a business combination occurs and is accounted for by the pooling-of-interests method:

a. Name and brief description of the enterprises combined, except an enterprise whose name is carried forward to the combined enterprise.
b. Method of accounting for the combination—that is, by the pooling-of-interests method.
c. Description and number of shares of stock issued in the business combination.
d. Details of the results of operations of the previously separate enterprises for the period before the combination is consummated that are included in the current combined net income (refer to paragraph .115). The details shall include revenue, extraordinary items, net income, other changes in stockholders' equity, and amount of and manner of accounting for intercompany transactions.
e. Descriptions of the nature of adjustments of net assets of the combining enterprises to adopt the same accounting practices and of the effects of the changes on net income reported previously by the separate enterprises and now presented in comparative financial statements (refer to paragraph .111).
f. Details of an increase or decrease in retained earnings from changing the fiscal year of a combining enterprise. The details shall include at least revenue, expenses, extraordinary items, net income, and other changes in stockholders' equity for the period excluded from the reported results of operations.
g. Reconciliations of amounts of revenue and earnings previously reported by the enterprise that issues the stock to effect the combination with the combined amounts currently presented in financial statements and summaries. A new enterprise formed to effect a combination may instead disclose the earnings of the separate enterprises that comprise combined earnings for prior periods.

The information disclosed in notes to financial statements shall also be furnished on a pro forma basis in information on a proposed business combination that is given to stockholders of combining enterprises. [APB16, ¶64]

.124 Notes to the financial statements shall disclose details of the effects of a business combination consummated before the financial statements are issued but that is either incomplete as of the date of the financial statements or initiated after that date (refer to paragraph .120). The details shall include revenue, net income, earnings per share, and the effects of anticipated changes in accounting methods as if the combination had been consummated at the date of the financial statements (refer to paragraph .111). [APB16, ¶65]

Application of Purchase Method

Principles of Historical Cost Accounting

Acquiring Assets

.125 The general principles to apply the historical cost[9] basis of accounting to an acquisition of an asset depend on the nature of the transaction:

a. An asset acquired by exchanging cash or other assets is recorded at cost—that is, at the amount of cash disbursed or the fair value of other assets distributed.
b. An asset acquired by incurring liabilities is recorded at cost—that is, at the present value of the amounts to be paid.
c. An asset acquired by issuing shares of stock of the acquiring enterprise is recorded at the fair value of the asset[10]—that is, shares of stock issued are recorded at the fair value of the consideration received for the stock.

The general principles must be supplemented to apply them in certain transactions. For example, the fair value of an asset received for stock issued may not be reliably determinable, or the fair value of an asset acquired in an exchange may be more reliably determinable than the fair value of a noncash asset given up. Restraints on measurement have led to the practical rule that assets acquired for other than cash, including shares of stock issued, should be stated at "cost" when they are acquired and "cost" may be determined either by the fair value of the consideration given or by the fair value of the property acquired, whichever is the more clearly evident.[11] "Cost" in accounting often means the amount at which an enterprise records an asset at the date it is acquired whatever its manner of acquisition, and that cost forms the basis for historical cost accounting. [APB16, ¶67]

---

[9] Accounting for a business combination by the purchase method follows principles normally applicable under historical cost accounting to recording acquisitions of assets and issuances of stock and to accounting for assets and liabilities after acquisition. [APB16, ¶66]

[10] An asset acquired may be an entire enterprise which may have intangible assets, including **goodwill.** [APB16, ¶67, fn9]

[11] [Refer to] ARB No. 24, *Accounting for Intangible Assets;* the substance was retained in slightly different words in Chapter 5 of ARB 43 and ARB 48. [APB16, ¶67, fn10]

Allocating Cost

.126 Acquiring assets in groups requires not only ascertaining the cost of the assets as a group but also allocating the cost to the individual assets that comprise the group. The cost of a group is determined by the principles described in paragraph .125. A portion of the total cost is then assigned to each individual asset acquired on the basis of its fair value. A difference between the sum of the assigned costs of the tangible and identifiable intangible assets acquired less liabilities assumed and the cost of the group is evidence of unspecified intangible values. [APB16, ¶68]

Accounting after Acquisition

.127 The nature of an asset and not the manner of its acquisition determines an acquirer's subsequent accounting for the cost of that asset. The basis for measuring the cost of an asset—whether amount of cash paid, fair value of an asset received or given up, amount of a liability incurred, or fair value of stock issued—has no effect on the subsequent accounting for that cost, which is retained as an asset, depreciated, amortized, or otherwise matched with revenue. [APB16, ¶69]

Acquiring Enterprise

.128 An enterprise that distributes cash or other assets or incurs liabilities to obtain the assets or stock of another enterprise is clearly the acquirer. The identities of the acquirer and the acquired enterprise are usually evident in a business combination effected by the issue of stock. The acquiring enterprise normally issues the stock and commonly is the larger enterprise. The acquired enterprise may, however, survive as the corporate enterprise, and the nature of the negotiations sometimes clearly indicates that a smaller enterprise acquires a larger enterprise. Presumptive evidence of the acquiring enterprise in combinations effected by an exchange of stock is obtained by identifying the former common stockholder interests of a combining enterprise that either retain or receive the larger portion of the voting rights in the combined enterprise. That enterprise shall be treated as the acquirer unless other evidence clearly indicates that another enterprise is the acquirer. For example, a substantial investment of one enterprise in common stock of another before the combination may be evidence that the investor is the acquiring enterprise. [APB16, ¶70]

.129 If a new enterprise is formed to issue stock to effect a business combination to be accounted for by the purchase method, one of the existing combining enterprises shall be considered the acquirer on the basis of the evidence available. [APB16, ¶71]

Determining Cost of an Acquired Enterprise

.130 The same accounting principles apply to determining the cost of assets acquired individually, those acquired in a group, and those acquired in a business combination. A cash payment by an enterprise measures the cost of acquired assets less liabilities assumed. Similarly, the fair values of other assets distributed, such as marketable securities or properties, and the fair value of liabilities incurred by an acquiring enterprise measure the cost of an acquired enterprise. The present value of a debt security represents the fair value of the liability, and a premium or discount shall be recorded for a debt security issued with an interest rate fixed materially above or below the effective rate or current yield for an otherwise comparable security. [APB16, ¶72]

.131 The distinctive attributes of preferred stocks make some issues similar to a debt security while others possess common stock characteristics, with many gradations between the extremes. Determining cost of an acquired enterprise may be affected by those characteristics. For example, the fair value of a nonvoting, nonconvertible preferred stock that lacks characteristics of common stock may be determined by comparing the specified dividend and redemption terms with comparable securities and by assessing market factors. Thus, although the principle of recording the fair value of consideration received for stock issued applies to all equity securities, senior as well as common stock, the cost of an enterprise acquired by issuing senior equity securities may be determined in practice on the same basis as for debt securities. [APB16, ¶73]

.132 The fair value of securities traded in the market is normally more clearly evident than the fair value of an acquired enterprise (refer to paragraph .125). Thus, the quoted market price of an equity security issued to effect a business combination may usually be used to approximate the fair value of an acquired enterprise after recognizing possible effects of price fluctuations, quantities traded, issue costs, and the like. The market price for a reasonable period before and after the date the terms of the acquisition are agreed to and announced shall be considered in determining the fair value of securities issued. [APB16, ¶74]

.133 If the quoted market price is not the fair value of stock, either preferred or common, the consideration received shall be estimated even though measuring directly the fair values of assets received is difficult. Both the consideration received, including *goodwill,* and the extent of the adjustment of the quoted market price of the stock issued shall be weighed to determine the amount to be recorded. All aspects of the acquisition, including the negotiations, shall be studied, and independent appraisals may be used as an aid in determining the fair value of securities issued. Consideration other than stock distributed to effect an acquisition may provide evidence of the total fair value received. [APB16, ¶75]

Costs of Acquisition

.134 The cost of an enterprise acquired in a business combination accounted for by the purchase method includes the direct costs of acquisition. Costs of registering and issuing equity securities are a reduction of the otherwise determinable fair value of the securities. However, indirect and general expenses related to acquisitions are deducted as incurred in determining net income. [APB16, ¶76]

Contingent Consideration

.135 A business combination agreement may provide for the issuance of additional shares of a security or the transfer of cash or other consideration contingent on specified events or transactions in the future. Some agreements provide that a portion of the consideration be placed in escrow to be distributed or to be returned to the transferor when specified events occur. Either debt or equity securities may be placed in escrow, and amounts equal to interest or dividends on the securities during the contingency period may be paid to the escrow agent or to the potential security holder. [APB16, ¶77]

.136 Cash and other assets distributed and securities issued unconditionally and amounts of **contingent consideration** that are determinable at the date of acquisition shall be included in determining the cost of an acquired enterprise and recorded at that date. Consideration that is issued or issuable at the expiration of the contingency period or that is held in escrow pending the outcome of the contingency shall be disclosed but not recorded as a liability or shown as outstanding securities unless the outcome of the contingency is determinable beyond reasonable doubt. [APB16, ¶78]

.137 Contingent consideration shall usually be recorded when the contingency is resolved and consideration is issued or becomes issuable. In general, the issue of additional securities or distribution of other consideration at resolution of contingencies based on earnings shall result in an additional element of cost of an acquired enterprise. In contrast, the issue of additional securities or distribution of other consideration at resolution of contingencies based on security prices shall not change the recorded cost of an acquired enterprise. [APB16, ¶79]

Contingency Based on Earnings

.138 Additional consideration may be contingent on maintaining or achieving specified earnings levels in future periods. When the contingency is resolved and additional consideration is distributable, the acquiring enterprise shall record the current fair value of the consideration issued or issuable as additional cost of the acquired enterprise. The additional costs of affected assets, usually goodwill, shall be amortized over the remaining life of the asset. [APB16, ¶80]

Contingency Based on Security Prices

.139 Additional consideration may be contingent on the market price of a specified security issued to effect a business combination. Unless the price of the security at least equals the specified amount on a specified date or dates, the acquiring enterprise is required to issue additional equity or debt securities or transfer cash or other assets sufficient to make the current value of the total consideration equal to the specified amount. The securities issued unconditionally at the date the combination is consummated shall be recorded at that date at the specified amount. [APB16, ¶81]

.140 The cost of an acquired enterprise recorded at the date of acquisition represents the entire payment, including contingent consideration. Therefore, the issuance of additional securities or distribution of other consideration does not affect the cost of the acquired enterprise, regardless of whether the amount specified is a security price to be maintained or a higher security price to be achieved. On a later date when the contingency is resolved and additional consideration is distributable, the acquiring enterprise shall record the current fair value of the additional consideration issued or issuable. However, the amount previously recorded for securities issued at the date of acquisition shall simultaneously be reduced to the lower current value of those securities. Reducing the value of debt securities previously issued to their later fair value results in recording a discount on debt securities. The discount shall be amortized from the date the additional securities are issued. [APB16, ¶82]

.141 Accounting for contingent consideration based on conditions other than those described shall be inferred from the procedures outlined. For example, if the consideration contingently issuable depends on both future earnings and future security prices, additional cost of the acquired enterprise shall be recorded for the additional consideration contingent on earnings, and previously recorded consideration shall be reduced to current value of the consideration contingent on security prices. Similarly, if the consideration contingently issuable depends on later settlement of a contingency, an increase in the cost of acquired assets, if any, shall be amortized over the remaining life of the assets. [APB16, ¶83]

Interest or Dividends during Contingency Period

.142 Amounts paid to an escrow agent representing interest and dividends on securities held in escrow shall be accounted for according to the accounting for the securities. That is, until the disposition of the securities in escrow is resolved, payments to the escrow agent shall not be recorded as interest expense or dividend distributions. An amount equal to interest and dividends later distributed by the escrow agent to the former stockholders shall be added to the cost of the acquired assets at the date distributed and amortized over the remaining life of the assets. [APB16, ¶84]

Tax Effect of Imputed Interest

.143 A tax reduction resulting from imputed interest on contingently issuable stock reduces the fair value recorded for contingent consideration based on earnings and increases additional capital recorded for contingent consideration based on security prices. [APB16, ¶85]

Compensation in Contingent Agreements

.144 The substance of some agreements for contingent consideration is to provide compensation for services or use of property or profit sharing, and the additional consideration given shall be accounted for as expenses of the appropriate periods. [APB16, ¶86]

Recording Assets Acquired and Liabilities Assumed

.145 An acquiring enterprise shall allocate the cost of an acquired enterprise to the assets acquired and liabilities assumed. Allocation shall follow the principles described in paragraph .126.

a. First, all identifiable assets acquired, either individually or by type, and liabilities assumed in a business combination, whether or not shown in the financial statements of the acquired enterprise, shall be assigned a portion of the cost of the acquired enterprise, normally equal to their fair values at date of acquisition.
b. Second, the excess of the cost of the acquired enterprise over the sum of the amounts assigned to identifiable assets acquired less liabilities assumed shall be recorded as goodwill. The sum of the market or appraisal values of identifiable assets acquired less liabilities assumed may sometimes exceed the cost of the acquired enterprise. If so, the values otherwise assignable to noncurrent assets acquired (except long-term investments in marketable securities) shall be reduced by a proportionate part of the excess to determine the assigned values. A deferred credit for an excess of assigned value of identifiable assets over cost of an acquired enterprise (sometimes called **negative goodwill**) shall not be recorded unless those assets are reduced to zero value.

Independent appraisals may be used as an aid in determining the fair values of some assets and liabilities. Subsequent sales of assets may also provide evidence of values. [APB16, ¶87] The tax basis of an asset or liability shall not be a factor in determining its fair value. [FAS109, ¶288(d)]

.146 General guides for assigning amounts to the individual assets acquired and liabilities assumed, except goodwill, are:

a. Marketable securities at current net realizable values
b. Receivables at present values of amounts to be received determined at appropriate current interest rates, less allowances for uncollectibility and collection costs, if necessary
c. Inventories:
   (1) Finished goods and merchandise at estimated selling prices less the sum of (a) costs of disposal and (b) a reasonable profit allowance for the selling effort of the acquiring enterprise
   (2) Work in process at estimated selling prices of finished goods less the sum of (a) costs to complete, (b) costs of disposal, and (c) a reasonable profit allowance for the completing and selling effort of the acquiring enterprise based on profit for similar finished goods
   (3) Raw materials at current replacement costs [APB16, ¶88]
d. Plant and equipment:
   (1) To be used, at the current replacement cost for similar capacity[12] unless the expected future use of the assets indicates a lower value to the acquirer
   (2) To be sold, at fair value less cost to sell [FAS121, ¶20]
e. Intangible assets that can be identified and named, including contracts, patents, franchises, customer and supplier lists, and favorable leases, at appraised values[13]
f. Other assets, including land, natural resources, and nonmarketable securities, at appraised values
g. Accounts and notes payable, long-term debt, and other claims payable at present values of amounts to be paid determined at appropriate current interest rates
h. Liabilities and accruals—for example, accruals for warranties, vacation pay, deferred compensation—at present values of amounts to be paid determined at appropriate current interest rates

---

[12]Replacement cost may be determined directly if a used asset market exists for the assets acquired. Otherwise, the replacement cost shall be approximated from replacement cost new less estimated accumulated depreciation. [APB16, ¶88, fn11]

[13]Fair values shall be ascribed to specific assets; identifiable assets shall not be included in goodwill. [APB16, ¶88, fn12]

[14][Deleted 12/85 because of FASB Statement 87, *Employers' Accounting for Pensions*.]

i. Other liabilities and commitments, including unfavorable leases, contracts, and commitments and plant closing expense incident to the acquisition, at present values of amounts to be paid determined at appropriate current interest rates [APB16, ¶88]

[j.] [For an] employer [that] sponsors a single-employer defined benefit pension plan, the assignment of the purchase price to individual assets acquired and liabilities assumed shall include a liability for the projected benefit obligation in excess of plan assets or an asset for plan assets in excess of the projected benefit obligation, thereby eliminating any previously existing unrecognized net gain or loss, unrecognized prior service cost, or unrecognized net obligation or net asset existing at the date of initial application of Section P16, "Pension Costs." Subsequently, to the extent that those amounts are considered in determining the amounts of contributions, differences between the purchaser's net pension cost and amounts contributed will reduce the liability or asset recognized at the date of the combination. If it is expected that the plan will be terminated or curtailed, the effects of those actions shall be considered in measuring the projected benefit obligation. [FAS87, ¶74]

[k.] [For] an employer that sponsors a single-employer defined benefit postretirement plan [other than a pension plan], the assignment of the purchase price to individual assets acquired and liabilities assumed shall include a liability for the accumulated postretirement benefit obligation in excess of the fair value of the plan assets or an asset for the fair value of the plan assets in excess of the accumulated postretirement benefit obligation. The accumulated postretirement benefit obligation assumed shall be measured based on the benefits attributed by the acquired entity to employee service prior to the date the business combination is consummated, adjusted to reflect (a) any changes in assumptions based on the purchaser's assessment of relevant future events (as discussed in paragraphs .116 through .135 of Section P40, "Postretirement Benefits Other Than Pensions") and (b) the terms of the substantive plan (as discussed in paragraphs .116 through .121 of Section P40) to be provided by the purchaser to the extent they differ from the terms of the acquired entity's substantive plan. [FAS106, ¶86]

   If the postretirement benefit plan of the acquired entity is amended as a condition of the business combination (for example, if the change is required by the seller as part of the consummation of the acquisition), the effects of any improvements attributed to services rendered by the participants of the acquired entity's plan prior to the date of the business combination shall be accounted for as part of the accumulated postretirement benefit obligation of the acquired entity. Otherwise, if improvements to the postretirement benefit plan of the acquired entity are not a condition of the business combination, credit granted for prior service shall be recognized as a plan amendment. If it is expected that the plan will be terminated or curtailed, the effects of those actions shall be considered in measuring the accumulated postretirement benefit obligation. Otherwise, no future changes to the plan shall be anticipated. [FAS106, ¶87] [(Refer to Appendix C, "Effective Dates of Pronouncements" for paragraphs 108 and 111 of FASB Statement 106, *Employers' Accounting for Post-retirement Benefits Other Than Pensions.*)] Subsequently, to the extent that the net obligation assumed or net assets acquired are considered in determining the amounts of contributions to the plan, differences between the purchaser's net periodic post-retirement benefit cost and amounts it contributes will reduce the liability or asset recognized at the date of the combination. [FAS106, ¶88]

[l.] [For an employer that participates in a multi-employer pension plan]no recognition of [a] withdrawal liability [is] required unless withdrawal under conditions that would result in a liability is probable. [FAS87, ¶253] [Similarly, for an employer that participates in a multi-employer postretirement benefit plan] no recognition of [an] additional liability [is] required under this section unless conditions exist that make an additional liability probable. [FAS106, ¶387]

An acquiring enterprise shall record periodically as a part of income the accrual of interest on assets and liabilities recorded at acquisition date at the discounted values of amounts to be received or paid. An acquiring enterprise shall not record as a separate asset the goodwill previously recorded by an acquired enterprise and shall not record deferred income taxes recorded by an acquired enterprise before its acquisition. [APB16, ¶88] Paragraph .129 of Section I27, "Income Taxes," addresses accounting for the deferred tax consequences of the differences between the assigned values and the tax bases of assets and liabilities of an enterprise acquired in a purchase business combination. [FAS109, ¶288(d)]

.147 [Deleted 2/92 because of FASB Statement 109, *Accounting for Income Taxes.*]

.147A [Deleted 2/92 because of FASB Statement 109.]

Accounting for Preacquisition Contingencies

.147B [Paragraphs .148 through .150 do] not apply to potential income tax [FAS38, ¶2] effects of (a) temporary differences and carryforwards of the acquired enterprise that exist at the acquisition date and (b) income tax uncertainties related to the acquisition (for example, an uncertainty related to the tax basis of an acquired asset that will ultimately be agreed to by the taxing authority) [FAS109, ¶288(q)] or adjustments that result from realization of those benefits [or other effects]. [FAS38, ¶2]

.148 A **preacquisition contingency**[15] other than the potential [FAS38, ¶5] income tax effects referred to in paragraph .147B[16] [FAS109, ¶288(q)] shall be included in the purchase allocation based on an amount determined as follows:

a. If the fair value of the preacquisition contingency can be determined during the **allocation period,** that preacquisition contingency shall be included in the allocation of the purchase price based on that fair value.[17]

b. If the fair value of the preacquisition contingency cannot be determined during the allocation period, that preacquisition contingency shall be included in the allocation of the purchase price based on an amount determined in accordance with the following criteria:

  (1) Information available prior to the end of the allocation period indicates that it is probable that an asset existed, a liability had been incurred, or an asset had been impaired at the consummation of the business combination. It is implicit in this condition that it must be probable that one or more future events will occur confirming the existence of the asset, liability, or impairment.

  (2) The amount of the asset or liability can be reasonably estimated.

  The criteria of this subparagraph shall be applied using the guidance provided in Section C59, "Contingencies," for application of the similar criteria of Section C59, paragraph .105. [FAS38, ¶5]

.149 After the end of the allocation period, an adjustment that results from a preacquisition contingency other than a loss carryforward (refer to footnote 16 of this section) shall be included in the determination of net income in the period in which the adjustment is determined. [FAS38, ¶6]

.150 Contingencies that arise from the acquisition and did not exist prior to the acquisition (examples [are] litigation over the acquisition and the tax effect of the purchase) are the acquiring enterprise's contingencies, rather than preacquisition contingencies of the acquired enterprise. [FAS38, ¶23]

---

[15]Paragraphs .148 through .150 apply to all preacquisition contingencies assumed in business combinations for which the allocation period has *not* ended at the initial application of FASB Statement 38, *Accounting for Preacquisition Contingencies of Purchased Enterprises.* If the enterprise so elects they can be applied to *all other* unresolved preacquisition contingencies at the date of initial application. [FAS38, ¶9] [If the enterprise does not make that election, special disclosures are required by paragraph .166.]

[16]Those potential income tax effects shall be accounted for in accordance with the provisions of Section I27. [FAS109, ¶288(q)]

[17]For example, if it can be demonstrated that the parties to a business combination agreed to adjust the total consideration by an amount as a result of a newly discovered contingency, that amount would be a determined fair value of that contingency. [FAS38, ¶5, fn3]

Research and Development Costs Acquired

.151 Costs shall be assigned to all identifiable tangible and intangible assets, including any *resulting from* research and development activities of the acquired enterprise or *to be used in* research and development activities of the combined enterprise. Identifiable assets *resulting from* research and development activities of the acquired enterprise might include, for example, patents received or applied for, blueprints, formulas, and specifications or designs for new products or processes. Identifiable assets *to be used in* research and development activities of the combined enterprise might include, for example, materials and supplies, equipment and facilities, and perhaps even a specific research project in process. In either case, the costs to be assigned are determined from the amount paid by the acquiring enterprise and *not* from the original cost to the acquired enterprise. [FIN4, ¶4]

.152 The subsequent accounting by the combined enterprise for the costs allocated to assets *to be used in* research and development activities shall be determined by reference to Section R50, "Research and Development." Accordingly, costs assigned to assets to be used in a particular research and development project and that have no alternative future use (refer to Section R50, paragraph .107) shall be charged to expense at the date of consummation of the combination. [FIN4, ¶5]

.153-.154 [Deleted 2/92 because of FASB Statement 109.]

Acquisition of a Banking or Thrift Institution

.155 [In applying this section to] the acquisition of a [banking or thrift institution][19] in a business combination accounted for by the purchase method, [FIN9, ¶1] the net-spread

---

[18][Deleted 2/92 because of FASB Statement 109.]

[19]Paragraphs .156 through .158F apply not only in the case of the acquisition of a savings and loan association but also in the case of the acquisition of a savings and loan association holding company, [FIN9, ¶1, fn1] a commercial bank, a mutual savings bank, a credit union, [or] other depository institutions having assets and liabilities of the same types as those institutions, and branches of such enterprises. [FAS72, ¶2]

method[20] [is inappropriate] because [that] method ignores fair value of individual assets and liabilities or types of assets and liabilities. [FIN9, ¶4]

.156 Ascertaining appropriate current interest rates and the periods over which the receivables (refer to paragraph .146(b)) are to be discounted requires an analysis of the many factors that determine the fair values of the portfolio of loans acquired. [FIN9, ¶5]

.157 [The] present value of savings deposits due on demand (refer to paragraph .146(g)) is their face amount plus interest accrued or accruable as of the date of acquisition. [The] present value for other liabilities assumed, for example, time savings deposits, borrowings from a Federal Home Loan Bank, or other borrowings, shall be determined by using prevailing interest rates for similar liabilities at the acquisition date. [FIN9, ¶7]

.158 The purchase price paid for a [banking or thrift institution] may include an amount for one or more factors, such as the following:

a. Capacity of existing savings accounts and loan accounts to generate future income
b. Capacity of existing savings accounts and loan accounts to generate additional business or new business
c. Nature of territory served. [FIN9, ¶8]

In a business combination accounted for by the purchase method involving the acquisition of a banking or thrift institution, intangible assets acquired that can be separately identified shall be assigned a portion of the total cost of the acquired enterprise if the fair values of those assets can be reliably[21] determined. [FAS72, ¶4] The amount paid for [a] separately identified intangible shall be recorded as the cost of the intangible and amortized over [its] estimated life as specified by Section I60, "Intangible Assets," [paragraphs .108 through .112]. Any portion of the purchase price that cannot be assigned to specifically identifiable tangible and intangible assets acquired (refer to paragraph .146(e) and footnote 13 of this section) less liabilities assumed shall be assigned to goodwill.

---

[20]Under the net-spread method, the acquisition of a savings and loan association is viewed as the acquisition of a leveraged whole rather than the acquisition of the separate assets and liabilities of the association. Therefore, if the spread between the rates of interest received on mortgage loans and the rates of interest (often called *dividends* in the industry) paid on savings accounts is normal for the particular market area, the acquired savings and loan association's principal assets and liabilities, i.e., its mortgage loan portfolio and savings accounts, are brought forward at the carrying amounts shown in the financial statements of the acquired association. [FIN9, ¶2] In contrast, under the separate-valuation method, each of the identifiable assets and liabilities [assumed] of the acquired savings and loan association is accounted for in the consolidated financial statements at an amount based on fair value at the date of acquisition, either individually or by types of assets and types of liabilities. [FIN9, ¶3]

[21]Reliability embodies the characteristics of representational faithfulness and verifiability, as discussed in FASB Concepts Statement No. 2, *Qualitative Characteristics of Accounting Information.* [FAS72, ¶4, fn1]

[FIN9, ¶8] The fair values of [identifiable intangible] assets that relate to depositor or borrower relationships (refer to (a) and (b) [above]) shall be based on the estimated benefits attributable to the relationships that *exist* at the date of acquisition without regard to new depositors or borrowers that may replace them. Those identified intangible assets shall be amortized over the estimated lives of those existing relationships. [FAS72, ¶4]

Unidentifiable Intangible Asset

.158A If, in a combination [involving a banking or thrift institution], the fair value of liabilities assumed exceeds the fair value of tangible and identified intangible assets acquired, that excess constitutes an unidentifiable intangible asset. [FAS72, ¶5] [Section I60, paragraphs .133 and .134 describe appropriate accounting for such intangible assets.]

Regulatory-Assisted Combinations

.158B The provisions of paragraphs .158C through .158F, which relate to the reporting of regulatory financial assistance, apply to all acquisitions of banking or thrift institutions. [It is] understood that regulatory financial assistance agreements are not standardized and that the conditions under which assistance will be granted vary widely. As a result, this section does not specifically address all forms of regulatory financial assistance, but its provisions should serve as a general guide. [FAS72, ¶3]

.158C In connection with a business combination [involving a banking or thrift institution], a regulatory authority may agree to pay amounts by which future interest received or receivable on the interest-bearing assets acquired is less than the interest cost of carrying those assets for a period by a stated margin. In such a case, the projected assistance, computed as of the date of acquisition based on the interest-rate margin existing at that date, shall be considered as additional interest on the interest-bearing assets acquired in determining their fair values for purposes of applying the purchase method (refer to paragraphs .145 and .146). The carrying amount of those interest-bearing assets shall not be adjusted for subsequent changes in the estimated amount of assistance to be received. Actual assistance shall be reported in income of the period in which it accrues. Notwithstanding the above provisions, if an enterprise intends to sell all or a portion of the interest-bearing assets acquired, those assets shall not be stated at amounts in excess of their current market values. [FAS72, ¶8]

.158D Other forms of financial assistance may be granted to a combining enterprise or the combined enterprise by a regulatory authority in connection with a business combination accounted for by the purchase method. If receipt of the assistance is probable and the amount is reasonably estimable, that portion of the cost of the acquired enterprise shall be assigned to such assistance. Assets and liabilities that have been or will be transferred to or assumed by a regulatory authority shall not be recognized in the acquisition. If receipt of the assistance is not probable or the amount is not reasonably estimable, any assistance subsequently recognized in the financial statements shall be reported as a reduction of the unidentifiable intangible asset, described in paragraph .158A, that was recognized in the acquisition. Subsequent amortization shall be adjusted proportionally. Assistance recognized in excess of that intangible asset shall be reported in income. [FAS72, ¶9]

.158E Under certain forms of assistance granted in connection with a business combination, the combined enterprise may agree to repay all or a portion of the assistance if certain criteria related to the level of future revenues, expenses, or profits are met. Such a repayment obligation shall be recognized as a liability and as a charge to income at the time the conditions in Section C59, paragraph .105, are met. This paragraph does not address repayments of assistance granted in exchange for debt or equity instruments. [FAS72, ¶10]

Disclosures

.158F The nature and amounts of any regulatory financial assistance granted to or recognized by an enterprise during a period in connection with the acquisition of a banking or thrift institution shall be disclosed. [FAS72, ¶11]

Amortization of Goodwill

.159 Goodwill recorded in a business combination accounted for by the purchase method shall be amortized in accordance with the provisions in paragraphs .108 through .112 of Section I60. [APB16, ¶90]

Excess of Acquired Net Assets over Cost

.160 The value assigned to net assets acquired should not exceed the cost of an acquired company because the general assumption in historical cost-based accounting is that net assets acquired should be recorded at not more than cost. The total market or appraisal values of identifiable assets acquired less liabilities assumed in a few business combinations may exceed the cost of the acquired company. An excess over cost should be allocated to reduce proportionately the values assigned to noncurrent assets (except long-term investments in marketable securities) in determining their fair values. If the allocation [in paragraph .145] reduces the noncurrent assets to zero value, the remainder of the excess over cost shall be classified as a deferred credit and shall be amortized systematically to income over the period estimated to be benefited but not in excess of 40 years. The method and period of amortization shall be disclosed. [APB16, ¶91]

.161 No part of the excess of acquired net assets over cost shall be added directly to stockholders' equity at the date of acquisition. [APB16, ¶92]

Acquisition Date

.162 The date of acquisition of an enterprise shall ordinarily be the date assets are received and other assets are given or securities are issued. However, the parties may, for convenience, designate as the effective date the end of an accounting period between the dates a business combination is initiated and consummated. The designated date shall ordinarily be the date of acquisition for accounting purposes if a written agreement provides that effective control of the acquired enterprise is transferred to the acquiring enterprise on that date without restrictions except those required to protect the stockholders or other owners of the acquired enterprise—for example, restrictions on significant changes in the operations, permission to pay dividends equal to those regularly paid before the effective date, and the like. Designating an effective date other than the date assets or securities are transferred requires adjusting the cost of an acquired enterprise and net income otherwise reported to compensate for recognizing income before consideration is transferred. The cost of an acquired enterprise and net income shall therefore be reduced by imputed interest at an appropriate current rate on assets given, liabilities incurred, or preferred stock distributed as of the transfer date to acquire the enterprise. [APB16, ¶93]

.163 The values assigned to assets acquired and liabilities assumed shall be determined as of the date of acquisition. The statement of income of an acquiring enterprise for the period in which a business combination occurs shall include income of the acquired enterprise after the date of acquisition by including the revenue and expenses of the acquired operations based on the cost to the acquiring enterprise. [APB16, ¶94] Any dividend declared out of [an acquired enterprise's retained earnings created prior to acquisition shall not be included in income of the acquiring enterprise]. [ARB43, ch1A, ¶3] The retained earnings or deficit of an [acquired enterprise] at the date of acquisition shall not be included in consolidated retained earnings [if the business combination was accounted for under the purchase method]. [ARB51, ¶9]

Disclosure in Financial Statements

.164 Notes to the financial statements of an acquiring enterprise shall disclose the following for the period in which a business combination occurs and is accounted for by the purchase method:

a. Name and a brief description of the acquired enterprise
b. Method of accounting for the combination—that is, by the purchase method
c. Period for which results of operations of the acquired enterprise are included in the income statement of the acquiring enterprise
d. Cost of the acquired enterprise and, if applicable, the number of shares of stock issued or issuable and the amount assigned to the issued and issuable shares
e. Description of the plan for amortization of acquired goodwill, the amortization method, and period (refer to Section I60, paragraphs .108 through .112)
f. Contingent payments, options, or commitments specified in the acquisition agreement and their proposed accounting treatment.

Information relating to several relatively minor acquisitions may be combined for disclosure. [APB16, ¶95]

.165 Notes to the financial statements of the acquiring enterprise for the period in which a business combination occurs and is accounted for by the purchase method shall include as supplemental information the following results of operations on a pro forma basis:

a. Results of operations for the current period as though the enterprises had combined at the beginning of the period, unless the acquisition was at or near the beginning of the period
b. Results of operations for the immediately preceding period as though the enterprises had combined at the beginning of that period if comparative financial statements are presented.

The supplemental pro forma information shall as a minimum disclose revenue, income before extraordinary items, net income, and earnings per share. To present pro forma information, income taxes, interest expense, preferred stock dividends, depreciation, and amortization of assets, including goodwill, shall be adjusted to their accounting bases recognized in recording the combination. Pro forma presentation of results of operations of periods prior to the combination transaction shall be limited to the immediately preceding period. [APB16, ¶96] The disclosures [required by] this paragraph are not required in the financial statements of **nonpublic enterprises.** [FAS79, ¶6]

.166 If the [enterprise does not elect to apply paragraphs .148 through .150 to all other unresolved preacquisition contingencies (as discussed in footnote 15)], financial statements for periods ending after December 15, 1980 shall include disclosure of the amount and nature of adjustments determined after December 15, 1980 that result from preacquisition contingencies and that are reported other than as specified in paragraph .149. The disclosure shall include a description of how those adjustments are reported and the effect of the adjustments on current or expected future cash flows of the enterprise. [FAS38, ¶10]

Transitional Matters

.167 If an enterprise holds as an investment on October 31, 1970 a minority interest in or exactly 50 percent of the common stock of another enterprise and the enterprise initiates after October 31, 1970 a plan of combination with that enterprise, the resulting business combination may be accounted for by the pooling-of-interests method provided the combination meets all conditions specified in paragraphs .104 through .107, except that:

a. The minority interest in the voting common stock of the combining enterprise held on October 31, 1970 may exceed 10 percent of the outstanding voting common stock of the combining enterprise (refer to paragraph .105(b)).
b. The enterprise that effects the combination issues voting common stock for at least 90 percent of the outstanding voting common stock interest, as described in paragraph .106(b), of the other combining enterprise not already held on October 31, 1970 (rather than 90 percent of all the common stock interest of the combining enterprise). [APB16, ¶99]

.168 The investment in common stock held on October 31, 1970 shall not be accounted for as treasury stock or retired stock at the date of the combination. Instead, the excess of cost over the investor enterprise's proportionate equity in the net assets of the combining enterprise at or near the date the stock investment was acquired shall be allocated to identifiable assets of the combining enterprise at the date the combination is consummated on the basis of the fair values of those assets at the combination date. The unallocated portion of the excess shall be assigned to an unidentified intangible asset (goodwill) and shall be accounted for according to applicable previous pronouncements. The cost of goodwill shall not be amortized retroactively but may be amortized prospectively under the provisions of Section I60, paragraph .102(b). If the cost of the investment is less than the investor's equity in the net assets of the combining enterprise, that difference shall reduce proportionately the recorded amounts of noncurrent assets (except long-term investments in marketable securities) of the combining enterprise. [APB16, ¶99]

Glossary

.401 Allocation period. The period that is required to identify and quantify the assets acquired and the liabilities assumed [in a business combination accounted for by the purchase method]. The allocation period ends when the acquiring enterprise is no longer waiting for information that it has arranged to obtain and that is known to be available or obtainable. Thus, the existence of a preacquisition contingency for which an asset, a liability, or an impairment of an asset cannot be estimated does not, of itself, extend the allocation period. Although the time required will vary with circumstances, the allocation period should usually not exceed one year from the consummation of a business combination. [FAS38, ¶4(b)]

.402 Contingent consideration. Consideration that is issued or issuable at the expiration of the contingency period or that is held in escrow pending the outcome of the contingency. [APB16, ¶78] [(Refer to paragraphs .135 through .144.)]

.403 Goodwill. The excess of the cost of the acquired enterprise over the sum of the amounts assigned to identifiable assets acquired less liabilities assumed. [APB16, ¶87]

.404 Negative goodwill. The excess of assigned value of identifiable assets [acquired] over the cost of an acquired enterprise. [APB16, ¶87]

.404A Nonpublic enterprise. An enterprise other than one (a) whose debt or equity securities are traded in a public market, including those traded on a stock exchange or in the over-the-counter market (including securities quoted only locally or regionally), or (b) whose financial statements are filed with a regulatory agency in preparation for the sale of any class of securities. [FAS79, ¶5] [This] definition [does not] exclude mutual and cooperative organizations whose financial statements are broadly distributed. [FAS79, ¶16]

.405 Pooling-of-interests method. [This] method of accounting is intended to present as a single interest two or more common shareholder interests that were previously independent and the combined rights and risks represented by those interests. [APB16, ¶45] [(Refer to paragraphs .104 through .124.)]

.406 Preacquisition contingency. A contingency (defined in Section C59) of an enterprise that is acquired in a business combination accounted for by the purchase method and that is in existence before the consummation of the combination. A preacquisition contingency can be a contingent asset, a contingent liability, or a contingent impairment of an asset. [FAS38, ¶4(a)]

.407 **Purchase method.** [A method of accounting for] the acquisition of one enterprise by another. [APB16, ¶44] [This method is applied to all business combinations not meeting the criteria for a pooling-of-interests. (Refer to paragraphs .103 and .125 through .166.)]

Supplemental Guidance

Contents

	Paragraph Numbers
Ratio of Exchange	.501–.504
Notification to Stockholders	.505–.508
Intercorporate Investment Exceeding 10 Percent Limit	.509–.510
Consummation Date for a Business Combination	.511–.515
Pooling Not Completed within One Year	.516–.518
Registered Stock Exchanged for Restricted Stock	.519–.520
Applying Purchase Accounting	.521–.527
Effect of Terminating a Plan of Combination	.528–.529
Use of Restricted Stock to Effect a Business Combination	.530–.533
Warrants May Defeat Pooling	.534–.538
Two-Class Common for Pooling	.539–.541
Identical Common Shares for a Pooling of Interests	.541A–.541B
Contingent Shares Defeat Pooling	.542–.544
Paragraph .167 Is Not Mandatory	.545–.548
Changes in Intercorporate Investments	.549–.551
Intercorporate Investment at October 31, 1970	.552–.555
Wholly Owned Subsidiary	.556–.559
Equity and Debt Issued for Common Stock before Pooling	.560–.561
Treasury Stock Allowed with Pooling	.562–.568
Pooling with Bail-out	.569–.571
Disposition of Assets to Comply with an Order	.572–.574
Retroactive Disclosure of Pooling	.575–.579
Grandfather for Subsidiaries	.580–.583
All Shares Must Be Exchanged to Pool	.584–.592
Acquisition of Minority Interest	.593–.596
Stock Transactions between Enterprises under Common Control	.596A–.596D
Downstream Mergers	.596E–.596F
Enterprises under Common Control in a Business Combination	.597–.605
Pooling by Subsidiary of Personal Holding Enterprise	.606–.608
Option May Initiate Combination	.609–.612
Representations in a Pooling	.613–.619
Employment Contingencies in a Pooling	.620–.623
Stock Options in a Pooling	.624–.626
Costs of Maintaining an Acquisitions Department	.627–.629

Forced Sale of Stock... .630–.631
Registration Costs in a Purchase.. .632–.634
No Pooling with Wholly Owned Subsidiary .... .635–.637
Combination Contingent on Bail-out .... .638–.640
Several Enterprises in a Single Business Combination..................... .641–.644
Transfers and Exchanges between Enterprises under Common
  Control... .645–.648
Accounting for Unused Investment Tax Credits Acquired in a Business
  Combination Accounted for by the Purchase Method..................... .649–.650
Costs of Closing Duplicate Facilities of an Acquirer........................ .651–.652
Pooling of Interests by Mutual and Cooperative Enterprises.............. .653–.655

Supplemental Guidance

Ratio of Exchange

.501 *Question*—Paragraph .105(a) defines the initiation date for a business combination as the earlier of (a) the date the major terms of a plan, including the ratio of exchange of stock, are announced publicly or otherwise formally made known to the stockholders of any one of the combining enterprises or (b) the date that stockholders of a combining enterprise are notified in writing of an exchange offer. Does the announcement of a formula by which the ratio of exchange will be determined in the future constitute the initiation of a plan of combination? [AIN-APB16, #1]

.502 *Interpretation*—Yes, the actual exchange ratio (1 for 1, 2 for 1, etc.) need not be known to constitute initiation of a business combination so long as the ratio of exchange is absolutely determinable by objective means in the future. A formula would usually provide such a determination. [AIN-APB16, #1]

.503 A formula to determine the exchange ratio might include factors such as earnings for some period of time, market prices of stock at a particular date, average market prices for some period of time, appraised valuations, etc. The formula may include upper or lower limits or both for the exchange ratio and the limits may provide for adjustments based upon appraised valuations, audit of the financial statements, etc. Also, the formula must be announced or communicated to stockholders as specified by paragraph .105(a) to constitute initiation. [AIN-APB16, #1]

.504 If a formula is used to initiate a business combination that is intended to be accounted for by the pooling-of-interests method, the actual exchange ratio would have to be determined by the consummation date and therefore no later than one year after the initiation date to meet the conditions of paragraph .106(a). [AIN-APB16, #1]

Notification to Stockholders

.505 *Question*—Paragraph .105(a) specifies that a business combination is initiated on the earlier of (a) the date major terms of a plan are formally announced or (b) the date that stockholders of a combining enterprise are notified in writing of an exchange offer. Does communication in writing to an enterprise's own stockholders that the enterprise plans a future exchange offer to another enterprise without disclosure of the terms constitute initiation of a business combination? [AIN-APB16, #2]

.506 *Interpretation*—No, paragraph .105(a) defines *initiation* in terms of two dates. The first date is for the announcement of an exchange offer negotiated between representatives of two (or more) enterprises. The second date is for a tender offer made by an enterprise directly or by newspaper advertisement to the stockholders of another enterprise. It is implicit in the circumstances of a tender offer that the plan is not initiated until the stockholders of the other enterprise have been informed as to the offer and its major terms, including the ratio of exchange. [AIN-APB16, #2]

.507 Therefore, in the second date specified for initiation in paragraph .105(a), *a combining enterprise* refers to the enterprise whose stockholders will tender their shares to the issuing enterprise. *An exchange offer* means the major terms of a plan including the ratio of exchange (or a formula to objectively determine the ratio). [AIN-APB16, #2]

.508 An enterprise may communicate to its own stockholders its intent to make a tender offer or to negotiate on the terms of a proposed business combination with another enterprise. However, intent to tender or to negotiate does not constitute *initiation*. A business combination is not initiated until the major terms are set and announced publicly or formally communicated to stockholders. [AIN-APB16, #2]

Intercorporate Investment Exceeding 10 Percent Limit

.509 *Question*—Paragraph .105(b) (the *independence* condition) states that the pooling-of-interests method of accounting for a business combination may not be applied if *at* the dates the plan of combination is initiated and consummated the combining enterprises hold as intercorporate investments more than 10 percent in total of the outstanding voting common stock of any combining enterprise. Would an intercorporate investment of 10 percent or less *at* the initiation and consummation dates but exceeding 10 percent *between* these dates (for example, through a cash purchase and subsequent sale of the voting common stock of a combining enterprise) prohibit accounting for a business combination under the pooling-of-interests method? [AIN-APB16, #3]

.510 *Interpretation*—Paragraph .105(b) would not be met if *between* the initiation and consummation dates combining enterprises hold as intercorporate investments more than 10 percent of the outstanding voting common stock of any combining enterprise even though the intercorporate investments do not exceed 10 percent *at* either the initiation or consummation date. Although paragraph .105(b) mentions only the initiation and consummation dates, intercorporate investments exceeding 10 percent in the interim would violate the spirit of the independence condition and the business combination would be an acquisition accounted for under the purchase method. For the 10 percent computation, however, intercorporate investments exclude voting common stock that is acquired after the date the plan of combination is initiated in exchange for the voting common stock issued to effect the combination. [AIN-APB16, #3]

Consummation Date for a Business Combination

.511 *Question*—Paragraphs .105 through .107 specify certain conditions that require a business combination to be accounted for by the pooling-of-interests method. Among these conditions in paragraphs .105(b) and .106(b) are quantitative measurements that are to be made on the consummation date. When does the consummation date occur for a business combination? [AIN-APB16, #4]

.512 *Interpretation*—A plan of combination is consummated on the date the combination is completed, that is, the date assets are transferred to the issuing enterprise. The quantitative measurements specified in paragraphs .105(b) and .106(b) are, therefore, made on the date the combination is completed. If they and all of the other conditions specified in paragraphs .105 through .107 are met on that date, the combination must be accounted for by the pooling-of-interests method. [AIN-APB16, #4]

.513 It should not be overlooked that paragraph .106(a) states the plan of combination must be *completed* in accordance with a specific plan within one year after it is initiated unless delay is beyond the control of the combining enterprises as described in that paragraph. Therefore, ownership of the issuing enterprise's common stock must pass to combining stockholders and assets must be transferred from the combining enterprise to the issuing enterprise within one year after the initiation date (unless the described delay exists) if the business combination is to be accounted for by the pooling-of-interests method. Physical transfer of stock certificates need not be accomplished on the consummation date so long as the transfer is in process. [AIN-APB16, #4]

.514 If any of the conditions specified in paragraphs .105 through .107 are not met, a business combination is an acquisition that must be accounted for by the purchase method. Paragraph .162 specifies that the date of acquisition should ordinarily be the date assets are received and other assets are given or securities are issued, that is, the consummation date. However, this paragraph allows the parties for convenience to designate the end of an accounting period falling between the initiation and consummation dates as the effective date for the combination. [AIN-APB16, #4]

.515 The designated effective date is not a substitute for the consummation date in determining whether the purchase or pooling-of-interests method of accounting applies to the combination. In designating an effective date as some date prior to the consummation date, the parties would automatically be anticipating that the business combination would be accounted for as a purchase since paragraphs .110 and .120 specify that a business combination accounted for by the pooling-of-interests method must be recorded as of the date the combination is consummated. [AIN-APB16, #4]

Pooling Not Completed within One Year

.516 *Question*—Paragraph .106(a) specifies that a condition for a business combination to be accounted for by the pooling-of-interests method is for the combination to be completed in accordance with a specific plan within one year after the plan is initiated unless delay is beyond the control of the combining enterprises. This paragraph also indicates that new terms may be offered if earlier exchanges of stock are adjusted to the new terms. If completion of a business combination is delayed beyond one year, would the offering of new terms during the delay period meet the condition of paragraph .106(a) for a business combination to be accounted for by the pooling-of-interests method? [AIN-APB16, #5]

.517 *Interpretation*—New terms may be offered under the conditions of paragraph .106(a) more than one year after the initiation date if delay in completion is beyond the control of the combining enterprises because of certain circumstances and earlier exchanges of stock are adjusted to the new terms. However, the only delays permitted under paragraph .106(a) are proceedings of a governmental authority and litigation. [AIN-APB16, #5]

.518 Proceedings of a governmental authority for this purpose include deliberations by a federal or state regulatory agency on whether to approve or disapprove a combination where the combination cannot be effected without approval. They do *not* include registration of the securities with the SEC or a state securities commission. Litigation for this purpose means, for example, an antitrust suit filed by the Justice Department or a suit filed by a dissenting minority stockholder to prohibit a combination. [AIN-APB16, #5]

Registered Stock Exchanged for Restricted Stock

.519 *Question*—The pooling-of-interests method of accounting for a business combination is required if the conditions specified in paragraphs .105 through .107 are met showing that stockholder groups have combined their rights and risks. Would the exchange of unrestricted voting common stock of the issuing enterprise for the shares owned by a substantial common stockholder of a combining enterprise whose stock was restricted as to voting or public sale indicate the conditions were not met if the stock issued could be sold immediately? [AIN-APB16, #6]

.520 *Interpretation*—Stockholder groups have combined their rights and risks so long as stockholders holding substantially all classes of the voting common stock in the combining enterprise receive shares of the majority class of voting common stock of the issuing enterprise exactly in proportion to their relative voting common stock interest before the combination was effected. The fact that unrestricted voting common stock is exchanged for stock previously held in a voting trust would not negate accounting for a business combination by the pooling-of-interests method. Likewise, the fact that *registered* voting common stock of the issuing enterprise is exchanged for *restricted* voting common stock of the combining enterprise also would not negate accounting for a business combination by the pooling-of-interests method. [AIN-APB16, #6]

Applying Purchase Accounting

.521 *Question*—This section clearly applies when one enterprise obtains at least 90 percent of the voting common stock of another enterprise, whether through a purchase or a pooling of interests. Does this section also apply when one enterprise acquires less than 90 percent of the voting common stock of another enterprise? [AIN-APB16, #8]

.522 *Interpretation*—Paragraph .106(b) discusses a 90 percent cut-off only as one of the conditions to be met to account for a business combination by the pooling-of-interests method. If this condition—or any other condition in paragraphs .105 through .107— is not met, a business combination must be accounted for by the purchase method. [AIN-APB16, #8]

.523 This section does not create new rules for purchase accounting. Paragraphs .125 through .147 [and .160 through .166] merely discuss valuation techniques in much greater detail than [previously] given. Thus, this section provides more guidance for the application of purchase accounting, whether the item purchased is an entire enterprise, a major portion of the stock of an enterprise or a manufacturing plant and regardless of whether the consideration given is cash, other assets, debt, common or preferred stock, or a combination of these. [AIN-APB16, #8]

.524 An investment by an enterprise in the voting common stock of another enterprise that does not meet the 90 percent condition must be accounted for as a purchase. The purchase method of accounting applies even though the investment is acquired through an exchange of the voting common stock of the enterprises. [AIN-APB16, #8]

.525 The acquisition by an enterprise of voting control over another enterprise creates a parent-subsidiary relationship. Generally, domestic subsidiaries either are consolidated or are included in consolidated financial statements under the equity method of accounting (refer to Section C51). [AIN-APB16, #8]

.526 Since a controlling interest is usually considered to be more than 50 percent of the outstanding voting stock in another enterprise, the fair value of the assets and liabilities of the subsidiary would be determined when control is acquired if the resulting subsidiary is either consolidated in the financial statements or included under the equity method of accounting. Also, Section I60 specifies the appropriate accounting for intangible assets, if any, recognized for these cases. [AIN-APB16, #8]

.527 In addition, the subsequent acquisition of some or all of the stock held by minority stockholders of a subsidiary is accounted for by the purchase method (refer to paragraphs .101 and .102). Thus, after a business combination has been completed or a controlling interest in a subsidiary has been obtained, the acquisition of some or all of the remaining minority interest is accounted for by the purchase method. The purchase method applies even though the minority interest is acquired through an exchange of common stock for common stock, including the acquisition of a minority interest remaining after the completion of a business combination accounted for by the pooling-of-interests method. [AIN-APB16, #8]

Effect of Terminating a Plan of Combination

.528 *Question*—Paragraph .105(a) defines the initiation of a plan of combination as the date the major terms of an exchange offer are announced publicly or communicated to stockholders even though the plan is still subject to approval of stockholders and others. What is the effect of termination of a plan of combination prior to approval by stockholders and the subsequent resumption of negotiations between the parties? [AIN-APB16, #10]

.529 *Interpretation*—Paragraph .106(a) specifies that a combination must be completed in accordance with a *specific plan*. Therefore, if negotiations are formally terminated after a plan has been initiated (as defined in paragraph .105(a)), the subsequent resumption of negotiations always constitutes a new plan. Formal announcement of the major terms of the new plan constitutes a new initiation, even if the terms are the same as the terms of the old plan. Any shares of stock exchanged under the old plan become subject to the conditions of paragraphs .105(b) and .106(b) (the 10 percent and 90 percent tests) upon initiation of the new plan. [AIN-APB16, #10]

Use of Restricted Stock to Effect a Business Combination

.530 *Question*—Paragraph .106(b) states as a condition for accounting for a business combination by the pooling-of-interests method that an enterprise may issue only common stock with rights *identical* to those of the majority of its outstanding voting common stock in exchange for the voting common stock of another enterprise. Would restrictions on the sale of the shares of common stock issued result in different rights for these shares? [AIN-APB16, #11]

.531 *Interpretation*—The *rights* pertinent to paragraph .106(b) are those involving relationships between stockholders and the enterprise rather than between the stockholders and other parties. The *rights* therefore pertain to voting, dividends, liquidation, etc., and not necessarily to a stockholder's right to sell stock. Restrictions imposed on the sale of the stock to the public in compliance with governmental regulations do not ordinarily cause the *rights* to be different, but other restrictions may create different rights. [AIN-APB16, #11]

.532 For example, voting common stock issued by a publicly held enterprise to effect a business combination may be restricted as to public sale until a registration with the SEC or a state securities commission becomes effective. If a registration were in process or the issuing enterprise agreed to register the stock subsequent to the combination, the rights of the stock would not be different because of the restriction. [AIN-APB16, #11]

.533 However, a restriction imposed by the issuing enterprise upon the sale of the stock in the absence of a governmental regulation would probably create different rights between previously outstanding and newly issued stock. Such a restriction might also indicate the previously separate stockholder groups would not be sharing the same risks in the business combination (refer to paragraph .104 and introductory statements in paragraphs .105 and .106). Likewise, a restriction upon the sale of the stock to anyone other than the issuing enterprise or an affiliate would not meet the "absence of planned transactions" condition specified in paragraph .107(a). [AIN-APB16, #11]

Warrants May Defeat Pooling

.534 *Question*—May a business combination be accounted for by the pooling-of-interests method if the issuing enterprise exchanges voting common stock *and* warrants for the voting common stock of a combining enterprise? [AIN-APB16, #12]

.535 *Interpretation*—Paragraph .106(b) specifies that in a business combination accounted for by the pooling-of-interests method an enterprise may issue *only* common stock in exchange for at least 90 percent of the common stock of another enterprise. Therefore, a pro rata distribution of warrants of the issuing enterprise to all stockholders of a combining enterprise would not meet this condition and the business combination would be accounted for as a purchase. [AIN-APB16, #12]

.536 In some cases, however, warrants may be used in a business combination accounted for by the pooling-of-interests method. Warrants (as well as cash or debt) could be used, for example, to acquire up to 10 percent of the common stock of a combining enterprise under paragraph .106(b) and the combination could still qualify as a pooling so long as the common stock acquired plus other intercorporate investments plus any remaining minority interest would allow the 90 percent test to be met. [AIN-APB16, #12]

.537 Warrants may be issued in exchange for the combining enterprise's outstanding preferred stock or debt. [AIN-APB16, #12]

.538 The issuing enterprise may exchange its warrants for the combining enterprise's outstanding warrants. Any warrants issued could not provide for the purchase of a greater number of shares than could be obtained if the warrants were exercised. For example, if the issuing enterprise will exchange three of its common shares for each of the combining enterprise's common shares outstanding and the combining enterprise has warrants outstanding allowing the holders to purchase two common shares per warrant, each warrant issued in exchange for the outstanding warrants could provide for the purchase of no more than six of the issuing enterprise's common shares. (Warrants issued by either enterprise in contemplation of effecting the combination might not meet the conditions referred to in paragraph .106(c).) [AIN-APB16, #12]

Two-Class Common for Pooling

.539 *Question*—Paragraph .106(b) specifies that an enterprise must issue common stock "with rights identical to those of the majority class of its outstanding voting common stock" in a business combination that is to be accounted for by the pooling-of-interests method. Could the common stock issued be designated as a class of stock different from the majority class (for example, Class A if the majority class has no class designation) and meet this condition? [AIN-APB16, #13]

.540 *Interpretation*—Paragraph .106(b) does not prohibit designating the common stock issued as a different class if it has *rights identical* to those of the majority class of outstanding voting common stock. Thus, the different class must have the same voting, dividend, liquidation, preemptive, etc., rights as the majority class with the stipulation that these rights cannot be changed unless a corresponding change is made in the rights of the majority class. [AIN-APB16, #13]

.541 Issuing a different class of common stock with rights identical to other common stock would generally serve no useful purpose. It would be suspected that the parties might have secretly agreed that they would in the future change the rights of the different class to restrict voting; grant a preference in liquidation; or increase, guarantee, or limit dividends. [AIN-APB16, #13]

Identical Common Shares for a Pooling of Interests

.541A *Question*—Does the issuance in a business combination of common shares that are identical to other outstanding common shares, except that the issuer retains a right of first refusal to repurchase the shares issued in certain specific circumstances, preclude the issuer from accounting for the business combination as a pooling of interests? [FTB85-5, ¶16]

.541B *Response*—Yes. Paragraph .106(b) states that the shares that are issued by a combining enterprise to effect a business combination must have "rights identical to those of the majority of its outstanding voting common stock" in order for the combination to meet the requirements for pooling. [FTB85-5, ¶17] [See] paragraphs .530 through .533 [FTB85-5, ¶19] [, and] .539 through .541. [FTB85-5, ¶18]

Contingent Shares Defeat Pooling

.542 *Question*—Paragraph .106(g) specifies that in a business combination to be accounted for by the pooling-of-interests method an enterprise may not (a) agree to issue additional shares of stock at a later date or (b) issue to an escrow agent shares that will later be transferred to stockholders or returned to the enterprise. Would this condition be met if the enterprise issued some maximum number of shares to stockholders of the combining enterprise under an agreement that part of the shares would be returned if future earnings are below a certain amount or the future market price of the stock is above a stipulated price? [AIN-APB16, #14]

.543 *Interpretation*—No, contingent shares based on earnings, market prices, and the like require a business combination to be accounted for as a purchase. Paragraph .106(g) states that the combination must be "resolved at the date the plan is consummated." [AIN-APB16, #14]

.544 The only contingent arrangement permitted under paragraph .106(g) is for settlement of a contingency pending at consummation, such as the later settlement of a lawsuit. A contingent arrangement would also be permitted for an additional income tax liability resulting from the examination of open income tax returns. [AIN-APB16, #14]

Paragraph .167 Is Not Mandatory

.545 *Question*—This section requires business combinations meeting the conditions of paragraphs .105 through .107 to be accounted for by the pooling-of-interests method and all other business combinations to be accounted for by the purchase method. However, paragraph .167 provides a *grandfather clause* permitting certain exceptions to the pooling conditions for business combinations that meet the conditions of that paragraph. Under paragraph .167, the accounting treatment is: (a) the excess of cost of the investment in common stock acquired prior to November 1, 1970 over equity in net assets when the stock investment was acquired is allocated to identifiable assets and goodwill regardless of the percentage of ownership on October 31, 1970 and (b) the pooling-of-interests method is applied for the common stock issued in the combination if the combination meets the conditions for accounting by the pooling-of-interests method. That is, the combination is accounted for as a *part-purchase, part-pooling*. Is the application of paragraph .167 mandatory for a business combination meeting the conditions of that paragraph? [AIN-APB16, #15]

.546 *Interpretation*—No, the accounting described in paragraph .167 is an election available to an issuing enterprise to apply the pooling-of-interests method to account for a business combination not otherwise meeting the conditions of paragraphs .105(b) and .106(b). Paragraph .167 specifies "the resulting business combination *may* [emphasis added] be accounted for by the pooling-of-interests method provided. . . ." [AIN-APB16, #15]

.547 Paragraph .167 applies only for intercorporate investments held at October 31, 1970. The provision was inserted to avoid retroactivity by allowing pooling-of-interest accounting for a combination that would not have met the conditions of paragraphs .105(b) and .106(b) because an intercorporate investment held at October 31, 1970 then was near or exceeded 10 percent of the outstanding voting common stock of the combining enterprise. [AIN-APB16, #15]

.548 A business combination meeting all of the conditions of paragraphs .105 through .107 as well as the conditions of paragraph .167 would be accounted for by the pooling-of-interests method. Paragraph .167 would not apply and the intercorporate investment would be accounted for as described in paragraph .114. A business combination meeting the conditions of paragraph .167 but not otherwise meeting the conditions of paragraphs .105(b) and .106(b) may either be accounted for as a *part-purchase, part-pooling* as described in paragraph .167 or as a purchase. [AIN-APB16, #15]

Changes in Intercorporate Investments

.549 *Question*—How do sales of investments in another enterprise's voting common stock owned at October 31, 1970 and acquisitions of additional investment of the same class of stock after that date affect computations under the *grandfather clause* in paragraph .167? [AIN-APB16, #16]

.550 *Interpretation*—Sales after October 31, 1970 of investments in another enterprise's voting common stock that were owned at that date are always considered as reductions of the common stock to which the *grandfather clause* in paragraph .167 applies, in other words, on a first-in, first-out basis. This reduction is made even though the common stock sold is identified as having been acquired after October 31, 1970. [AIN-APB16, #16]

.551 The *grandfather clause* in paragraph .167 does not apply to acquisitions after October 31, 1970 of voting common stock of the same class as was owned at that date. Any stock so acquired is therefore subject to the conditions of paragraphs .105(b) and .106(b). [AIN-APB16, #16]

Intercorporate Investment at October 31, 1970

.552 *Question*—Paragraph .167 contains a *grandfather clause* that exempts minority interests held on October 31, 1970 from certain provisions of this section in business combinations initiated after that date. The paragraph is written in terms of an intercorporate investment owned by the enterprise that effects the combination by issuing voting common stock. Does this paragraph also apply to stock of the issuing enterprise that is owned by the other combining enterprise on October 31, 1970? [AIN-APB16, #17]

.553 *Interpretation*—Paragraph .167 was intended to exempt intercorporate investments owned on October 31, 1970 by all of the parties to the business combination in the circumstances described. Thus, stock of the issuing enterprise that is owned by the other combining enterprise on October 31, 1970 may be ignored in computing the 90 percent condition described in paragraph .106(b). [AIN-APB16, #17]

.554 For example, assume that on October 31, 1970 Baker Company owned 500,000 of the 3,000,000 shares of the voting common stock of Adam Corporation. Subsequently, Adam Corporation initiated a business combination by offering the stockholders of Baker Company one share of Adam common for each share of Baker common outstanding. The combination was consummated in a single transaction within one year after initiation. Of the 1,000,000 Baker common shares outstanding at initiation and consummation, 950,000 shares were tendered to Adam Corporation. Assume also that the combination meets all of the conditions of paragraphs .105 through .107 to be accounted for by the pooling-of-interests method except the conditions of paragraph .105(b) (no more than 10 percent intercorporate investments) and paragraph .106(b) (the 90 percent condition). [AIN-APB16, #17]

.555 Under paragraph .167, the business combination may be accounted for by the pooling-of-interests method since the 500,000 Adam shares owned by Baker Company need not be considered in applying the conditions of paragraphs .105(b) and .106(b). Under the pooling-of-interests method, the 500,000 Adam shares would become treasury stock of Adam Corporation as specified by paragraph .114. [AIN-APB16, #17]

Wholly Owned Subsidiary

.556 *Question*—Paragraph .105(a) states that a wholly owned subsidiary may distribute voting common stock of its parent enterprise in a *pooling* combination if its parent would have met all of the conditions in paragraphs .105 through .107 had the parent issued its stock directly to effect the combination. As a practical matter, a parent may be unable to own all of a subsidiary's stock. State laws generally require a certain number of the directors of an enterprise to own some of the enterprise's shares, so a parent would not legally own a few *qualifying directors' shares* registered in the names of *inside* directors. Also, even though a parent attempts to purchase all of a subsidiary's shares owned by outsiders, a few shareholders may never be located and others may refuse to sell their shares for a reasonable amount. If a parent enterprise owns *substantially all* of the outstanding voting stock of a subsidiary, will the subsidiary be considered *wholly* owned for purposes of applying paragraph .105(a)? [AIN-APB16, #18]

.557 *Interpretation*—Yes, a subsidiary is considered *wholly owned* under paragraph .105(a) if its parent owns substantially all of the subsidiary's outstanding voting stock. The subsidiary may therefore *pool* with another enterprise by distributing the parent enterprise's voting common stock if the parent would have met the conditions of paragraphs .105 through .107 in a direct issuance. [AIN-APB16, #18]

.558 What constitutes *substantially all* of a subsidiary's voting stock will vary according to circumstances. Generally, the shares not owned by the parent would be expected to be an insignificant number, such as qualifying directors' shares. A parent might also be considered as owning *substantially all* of a subsidiary's voting stock if the parent had attempted to buy all of the stock but some owners either could not be located or refused to sell a small number of shares at a reasonable price. In no case, however, would less than 90 percent be considered *substantially all* (refer to paragraph .106(b)) and generally the percentage would be expected to be much higher. [AIN-APB16, #18]

.559 The reason for using the subsidiary as the combining enterprise would also be important in determining if *substantially all* of its voting stock is owned by the parent. A parent would be expected to own all but a few of its subsidiary's shares, other than qualifying directors' shares, in a combination in which either the parent or subsidiary could engage if the parent is to be considered as owning *substantially all* of its subsidiary's voting stock. A somewhat greater percentage of outside ownership would be acceptable in a combination between a subsidiary authorized to operate in a state where the parent is not authorized to operate and another enterprise operating in that state. An even larger outside ownership (but not more than 10 percent) would be acceptable in a regulated industry (where a subsidiary in the industry—but not its parent outside the industry—could combine with another enterprise in the industry) if a subsidiary engages in a combination that its parent could not undertake directly. [AIN-APB16, #18]

Equity and Debt Issued for Common Stock before Pooling

.560 *Question*—Paragraph .106(b) states that the issuing enterprise may exchange only voting common stock for outstanding equity and debt securities of the other combining enterprise that have been issued in exchange for voting common stock of that enterprise during a period beginning two years preceding the date a *pooling* combination is initiated. What is the purpose of this provision? [AIN-APB16, #19]

.561 *Interpretation*—Paragraph .106(c) prohibits accounting for a business combination by the pooling-of-interests method if equity or debt securities or both have been issued by a combining enterprise in exchange for or to retire its voting common stock in contemplation of effecting the combination within two years before the plan of combination was initiated or between the dates of initiation and consummation. In paragraph .106(b) there is an implied presumption that all such transactions of the other combining enterprise were made in contemplation of effecting a combination, thereby violating the condition of paragraph .106(c). However, the issuance of voting common stock of the issuing enterprise to the holders of such equity and debt securities of the other combining enterprise in exactly the same ratio as their former holdings of voting common stock of the other combining enterprise will restore the holders of the securities to their former position and, hence, will cure the violation of the condition of paragraph .106(c). [AIN-APB16, #19]

Treasury Stock Allowed with Pooling

.562 *Question*—Paragraph .106(d) states as a condition for *pooling* that each of the combining enterprises may reacquire shares of voting common stock (as treasury stock) only for purposes other than business combinations. Also, paragraphs .106(c) and .106(d) include provisions related to the reacquisition of treasury stock within two years prior to initiation and between initiation and consummation of a business combination that is planned to be accounted for by the pooling-of-interests method. For what purposes may treasury stock be reacquired during this period? [AIN-APB16, #20]

.563 *Interpretation*—The statement *for purposes other than business combinations* means combinations initiated under this section that are to be accounted for by the pooling-of-interests method. Therefore, acquisitions of treasury stock for specific purposes that are not related to a particular business combination that is planned to be accounted for by the pooling-of-interests method are not prohibited by the conditions of either paragraph .106(c) or .106(d). [AIN-APB16, #20]

.564 In the absence of persuasive evidence to the contrary, however, it should be presumed that all acquisitions of treasury stock during the two years preceding the date a plan of combination is initiated and between initiation and consummation were made in contemplation of effecting business combinations to be accounted for as a pooling of interests. Thus, lacking such evidence, this combination would be accounted for by the purchase method regardless of whether treasury stock or unissued shares or both are issued in the combination. [AIN-APB16, #20]

.565 The specific purposes for which treasury shares may be reacquired prior to consummation of a *pooling* include shares granted under stock option or compensation plans, stock dividends declared (or to be declared as a recurring distribution), and recurring distributions as provided in paragraph .106(d). Likewise, treasury shares reacquired for issuance in a specific *purchase* or to resolve an existing contingent share agreement from a prior business combination would not invalidate a concurrent *pooling*. Treasury shares reacquired for these purposes should be either reissued prior to consummation or specifically reserved for these purposes existing at consummation. [AIN-APB16, #20]

.566 To the extent that treasury shares reacquired within two years prior to initiation or between initiation and consummation have not been reissued or specifically reserved, an equivalent number of shares of treasury stock may be sold prior to consummation to *cure* the presumed violation of paragraphs .106(c) and .106(d). If the number of shares not reserved or disposed of prior to consummation of a combination is material in relation to the number of shares *to be issued* to effect the combination, the combination should be accounted for by the purchase method. [AIN-APB16, #20]

.567 Treasury shares reacquired more than two years prior to initiation may be reissued in a pooling. Also, *tainted* treasury shares purchased within two years prior to initiation or between initiation and consummation and not disposed of or reserved may be reissued in a pooling if not material in relation to the total number of shares issued to effect the combination. Treasury shares reissued in a pooling should be accounted for as specified in paragraph .113. [AIN-APB16, #20]

.568 It should be noted that earnings and market price contingencies were permitted in both *purchases* and *poolings* under *old rules*. These contingencies in a combination consummated under this section require the combination to be accounted for as a purchase. Although *liability-type* contingencies may exist in a pooling as specified in paragraph .106(g), treasury stock may not be reacquired to satisfy such a contingency. [AIN-APB16, #20]

Pooling with Bailout

.569 *Question*—Paragraph .107(a) specifies that a combined enterprise may not agree to directly or indirectly retire or reacquire all or part of the common stock issued to effect a business combination and paragraph .107(b) specifies that a combined enterprise may not enter into financial arrangements for the benefit of the former stockholders of a combining enterprise if a business combination is to be accounted for by the pooling-of-interests method. Would an arrangement whereby a third party buys all or part of the voting common stock issued to stockholders of a combining enterprise immediately after consummation of a business combination cause the combination to not meet these conditions? [AIN-APB16, #21]

.570 *Interpretation*—The fact that stockholders of a combining enterprise sell voting common stock received in a business combination to a third party would not indicate failure to meet the conditions of paragraphs .107(a) and .107(b). *Continuity of ownership interests* is *not* a condition to account for a business combination by the pooling-of-interests method under this section. The critical factor in meeting the conditions of paragraphs .107(a) and .107(b) is that the voting common stock issued to effect a business combination remains outstanding outside the combined enterprise without arrangements on the part of any of the enterprises involving the use of their financial resources to bail out former stockholders of a combining enterprise or to induce others to do so. [AIN-APB16, #21]

.571 Either the combined enterprise or one of the combining enterprises may assist the former stockholders in locating an unrelated buyer for their shares (such as by introduction to underwriters) so long as compensation or other financial inducements from the enterprise are not in some way involved in the arrangement. If unregistered stock is issued, the combined enterprise may also agree to pay the costs of initial registration. [AIN-APB16, #21]

Disposition of Assets to Comply with an Order

.572 *Question*—As a condition to account for a business combination by the pooling-of-interests method, paragraph .107(c) prohibits the planned disposal of a significant part of the assets of the combining enterprises within two years after the consummation date other than disposals in the ordinary course of business and eliminations of duplicate facilities or excess capacity. Likewise, paragraph .106(c) prohibits a change in the equity interests of the voting common stock—such as through the spin-off of a division or a subsidiary—in contemplation of effecting a pooling combination either within two years before initiation or between initiation and consummation. Does a prior or a planned disposition of a significant part of the assets of a combining enterprise to comply with an order of governmental authority or judicial body constitute a violation of this condition? [AIN-APB16, #22]

.573 *Interpretation*—No, the prior or planned disposition of a significant part of the assets of a combining enterprise (even though in contemplation of effecting or planned subsequent to a combination) does not negate accounting for a business combination as a pooling if the disposition is undertaken to comply with an order of a governmental authority or judicial body or to avoid circumstances that, on the basis of available evidence, would result in the issuance of such an order. This is generally consistent with paragraph .105(a) (autonomy of combining enterprises) that permits subsidiaries disposed of in compliance with an order of a governmental authority or judicial body to be considered autonomous for purposes of that condition. [AIN-APB16, #22]

.574 Any gain or loss resulting from a disposal within two years after consummation of a pooling of interests should be accounted for in accordance with paragraphs .118 and .119. [AIN-APB16, #22]

Retroactive Disclosure of Pooling

.575 *Question*—Paragraph .120 specifies that a business combination accounted for by the pooling-of-interests method should be recorded as of the date the combination is consummated. This paragraph prohibits a combining enterprise from retroactively reflecting in the financial statements for the current year a combination consummated after the close of the year but before financial statements are issued. However, this paragraph requires an enterprise to disclose *as supplemental information, in notes to financial statements or otherwise, the substance of a combination consummated before financial statements are issued and the effects of the combination on reported financial position and results of operations.* Could this disclosure be in the form of a statement with side-by-side columns reporting financial data for (a) the issuing enterprise, (b) the combined enterprises, and, perhaps, (c) the other combining enterprise? [AIN-APB16, #23]

.576 *Interpretation*—This section does not prohibit the side-by-side columnar format described above, nor, alternatively, does it prohibit an above-and-below columnar format. The term *or otherwise* included in paragraph .120 is sufficiently broad to permit disclosure of the information on the face of the financial statements in either side-by-side or above-and-below columns. [AIN-APB16, #23]

.577 Because this section prohibits retroactive pooling for a combination completed after the close of the year but before the financial statements are issued, however, the individual columns in the presentation should be separately identified as primary or supplemental information. That is, data for the issuing enterprise would be identified as the primary financial statements and data for the combined enterprise would be identified as supplemental information. If presented, data for the combining enterprise would also be identified as supplemental information. [AIN-APB16, #23]

.578 It might be noted that a side-by-side presentation will disclose information in greater detail than is required by paragraph .124 (which requires that only revenue, net income, earnings per share, and the effects of anticipated changes in accounting methods be disclosed as if the combination had been consummated at the date of the financial statements). Although both paragraphs .120 and .124 specify disclosure in *notes* to the financial statements and paragraph .124 specifies only *note* disclosure without the *or otherwise* provision, this paragraph refers back to paragraph .120 so the columnar format is not prohibited by paragraph .124 as long as the information is properly identified as primary and supplemental. [AIN-APB16, #23]

.579 Information for the combined enterprise identified as supplemental information (as described above) would be reported as primary information in statements for the following period when the combination was consummated if comparative financial statements are presented. Reporting and disclosure requirements for the period when a business combination is consummated and for prior periods are contained in paragraphs .110 through .117 and .122 and .123. [AIN-APB16, #23]

Grandfather for Subsidiaries

.580 *Question*—Paragraph .105(a) prohibits use of pooling accounting for a business combination initiated after October 31, 1970 (the effective date of this section) that involves an enterprise that was a "subsidiary." However, this section is not intended to be retroactive. Paragraph .105(a) appears to impose a retroactive effect on subsidiaries with significant minority interests that may have been considering engaging in pooling combinations. Was this intended? [AIN-APB16, #24]

.581 *Interpretation*—Paragraph .105(a) was not intended to have the retroactive effect described above. Subsidiaries that had a *significant* outstanding minority interest at October 31, 1970 may take part in a pooling combination providing the significant minority also exists at the initiation of the combination. In addition, the combination must meet all of the other pooling conditions specified in paragraphs .105 through .107 both directly and indirectly (that is, the parent company cannot take actions on behalf of the subsidiary that the subsidiary could not take itself). [AIN-APB16, #24]

.582 For purposes of [paragraphs .580 through .583] , a significant minority means that at least 20 percent of the voting common stock of the subsidiary is owned by persons not affiliated with the parent company. [AIN-APB16, #24]

.583 This *grandfathering* is consistent with paragraph .167 and applies both to combi-- nations where the subsidary with a significant minority interest is the issuing enterprise and those where it is the other combining enterprise. However, it does not permit a pooling between a subsidiary and its parent. [AIN-APB16, #24]

All Shares Must Be Exchanged to Pool

.584 *Question*—Paragraph .106(b) specifies that an issuing enterprise must exchange only voting common stock for at least 90 percent of the voting common stock interest of a combining enterprise to account for the combination as a pooling of interests. The paragraph permits cash or other consideration to be exchanged for the remaining shares or they may continue outstanding as a minority interest. Under paragraph .106(b), assuming the issuing enterprise exchanges common stock for at least 90 percent of the common stock of the combining enterprise, may an individual common shareholder of the combining enterprise exchange some of its shares for shares of the issuing enterprise and either retain the balance of its shares or sell the shares to the issuing enterprise for cash? [AIN-APB16, #25]

.585 *Interpretation*—If a business combination is to be accounted for as a pooling of interests, each common shareholder of the combining enterprise must either agree to exchange *all* of its shares for common shares of the issuing enterprise or refuse to exchange *any* of its shares. [AIN-APB16, #25]

.586 It would be contrary to the pooling concept expressed in this section for an individual shareholder of a combining enterprise to exchange some of its shares and keep some of its shares in a pooling of interests or for the issuing enterprise to exchange common stock for some of an individual shareholder's shares and pay cash for some of its shares. The pooling concept would be violated in these cases even though the issuing enterprise exchanged its common stock for at least 90 percent of the common stock of the combining enterprise as required by paragraph .106(b). [AIN-APB16, #25]

.587 Theoretically two or more *entire* common stockholder groups join together as a single enterprise in a pooling of interests to share the combined risks and rights represented by the previously independent interests without the distribution of corporate assets to *any* of the common stockholders (refer to paragraph .104). Paragraph .105 states as an attribute of pooling that independent ownership interests are combined in their entirety. That paragraph indicates that combining only selected assets or ownership interests would be more akin to disposing of or acquiring interests than to sharing rights and risks. Paragraph .106 states that acquisitions of common stock for assets or debt and other transactions that reduce the common stock interest are contrary to the idea of combining existing stockholder interests. [AIN-APB16, #25]

.588 This section permits the theoretical concept of pooling to be modified only within strict limits to accommodate practical obstacles that may be encountered in many combinations. Thus, the 90 percent test in paragraph .106(b) recognizes that, as a practical matter, some shareholders of a combining enterprise may refuse to exchange their shares even though most shareholders agree to a combination. [AIN-APB16, #25]

.589 Paragraph .106(b) permits cash or other consideration to be distributed by the issuing enterprise for shares held by these dissenting shareholders of the combining enterprise. However, a shareholder who assents to exchange part of its shares can hardly be considered a dissenting shareholder. [AIN-APB16, #25]

.590 In addition, the exchange by an individual shareholder of a combining enterprise of only part of its shares for common stock of the issuing enterprise would not meet paragraph .106(e). That paragraph states that each individual shareholder who exchanges its stock must receive a voting common stock interest in proportion to its relative voting common stock interest in the combining enterprise before the combination. [AIN-APB16, #25]

.591 Usually the determination of whether a shareholder of a combining enterprise is exchanging all of its shares for common stock of the issuing enterprise will be made at consummation. However, transactions prior to consummation between the issuing enterprise and a shareholder of a combining enterprise who exchanges shares at consummation may also preclude a pooling. In the absence of persuasive evidence to the contrary, it should be presumed that the purchase was made in contemplation of effecting the combination (refer to paragraph .106(c)) if the issuing enterprise purchased shares of a combining enterprise within two years prior to initiation and before consummation from a shareholder who also exchanges shares at consummation. [AIN-APB16, #25]

.592 To overcome another purely practical problem, paragraph .106(b) also allows cash or other consideration to be distributed by the issuing enterprise in lieu of fractional shares. There is no essential difference between the payment of cash to a common shareholder for a fraction of a share and the payment of cash for some of its shares. Therefore, the payment of more than a reasonable amount of cash to a shareholder for a fractional share would also be contrary to the pooling concept expressed in this section. Thus, the payment for fractional shares among shareholders must be reasonable in amount and shall be proportional to each shareholder's fractional share interest. [AIN-APB16, #25]

Acquisition of Minority Interest

.593 *Question*—How should an enterprise account for the acquisition of all or part of the minority interest of a subsidiary? [AIN-APB16, #26]

.594 *Interpretation*—Paragraph .101 states, "the acquisition of some or all of the stock held by minority shareholders of a subsidiary is not a business combination, but paragraph .102 specifies the applicable method of accounting." Paragraph .102 states that the acquisition of some or all of the stock held by minority stockholders of a subsidiary—whether acquired by the parent, the subsidiary itself, or another affiliate—shall be accounted for by the purchase method. Thus, purchase accounting applies when (a) a parent exchanges its common stock, assets, or debt for common stock held by minority shareholders of its subsidiary; (b) the subsidiary buys as treasury stock the common stock held by minority shareholders; or (c) another subsidiary of the parent exchanges its common stock or assets or debt for common stock held by the minority shareholders of an affiliated subsidiary. [AIN-APB16, #26]

.595 In addition, paragraph .105(b) precludes pooling when the combining enterprises hold as intercorporate investments more than 10 percent of the outstanding voting common stock of any combining enterprise (except when paragraph .167 applies, as discussed in paragraph .596). Therefore, pooling is precluded in the exchange by a subsidiary of its common stock for the outstanding voting common stock of its parent (usually referred to as a *downstream merger*). Instead, purchase accounting applies and the transaction should be accounted for as if the parent had exchanged its common stock for common stock held by minority shareholders of its subsidiary. (Whether a parent acquires the minority or a subsidiary acquires its parent, the end result is a single shareholder group, including the former minority shareholders, owning the consolidated net assets.) The same would be true if a new enterprise exchanged its common stock for the common stock of the parent and the common stock of the subsidiary held by minority shareholders. [AIN-APB16, #26]

.596 An exception to the requirement for purchase accounting in the acquisition of a minority interest may exist in some rare cases under paragraph .167. This paragraph permits pooling accounting to be elected on a grandfather basis under certain conditions, one condition being a combination in which one enterprise owns no more than 50 percent of the voting *common* stock of the other combining enterprise. Since a parent enterprise may control a subsidiary even though the parent owns less than 50 percent of the subsidiary's voting common stock (for example, by owning voting preferred stock in addition to voting common stock—refer to Section C51, paragraph .102), the exchange by the parent of its voting common stock for the voting common stock of the subsidiary owned by outsiders could qualify for pooling accounting. However, it should be noted that paragraph .167 would require the parent to allocate the excess of the cost of its previously existing investment over its proportionate equity in the subsidiary's net assets to the subsidiary's identifiable assets (and to goodwill, if any) based on fair values at the consummation date. [AIN-APB16, #26]

Stock Transactions between Enterprises under Common Control

.596A *Question*—How should a parent enterprise account for minority interest in an exchange of stock between two of its subsidiaries if one or both of the subsidiaries are partially owned? [FTB85-5, ¶5]

.596B *Response*—The accounting depends on whether the minority shareholders are party to the exchange of shares. If some or all of the shares owned by minority shareholders are exchanged for shares of ownership in another subsidiary of the parent (or a new subsidiary formed by combining two or more subsidiaries of the parent), then the transaction is recognized by the parent enterprise as the acquisition of shares from the minority interest, which according to paragraph .102 should be accounted for by the purchase method, that is, based on fair value. The original minority interest effectively is purchased, and a new minority interest in a different subsidiary is created. However, if the exchange lacks substance, it is not a purchase event and should be accounted for based on existing carrying amounts. That is, if the minority interest does not change and if in substance the only assets of the combined entity after the exchange are those of the partially owned subsidiary prior to the exchange, a change in ownership has not taken place, and the exchange should be accounted for based on the carrying amounts of the partially owned subsidiary's assets and liabilities. [FTB85-5, ¶6]

.596C If, however, minority shareholders are not party to an exchange of shares between two subsidiaries of the same parent (a partially owned subsidiary issues its shares in exchange for shares of another subsidiary previously owned by the same parent), the minority interest in the issuing subsidiary remains outstanding, and the transaction is an exchange of stock between enterprises under common control. In contrast to the acquisition of a minority interest, this transaction leaves all of the issuing subsidiary's minority interest outstanding, although the minority stockholders' interest in the net assets has changed in each case. Paragraphs .645 through .648 of this section indicate that the assets and liabilities transferred in such an exchange of shares should be accounted for at existing carrying amounts. [FTB85-5, ¶7]

.596D Some transactions involve both an effective acquisition of a minority interest and an exchange of stock between enterprises under common control, which usually are accounted for differently. In those cases, the accounting depends on whether the minority shareholders are party to the exchange of shares. In transactions described in paragraphs .593 through .596, an exchange takes place involving the minority shareholders. In transactions described in paragraphs .645 through .648, an effective change in the equity interest of the minority shareholders arises, but no exchange takes place. The accounting for the above types of transactions depends on the nature of the exchange that takes place, not the apparent similarity of the results of different transactions. [FTB85-5, ¶12]

Downstream Mergers

.596E   *Question*—Are there circumstances in which an exchange by a partially owned subsidiary of its common stock for the outstanding voting common stock of its parent (a "downstream merger") can be accounted for like a pooling of interests? [FTB85-5, ¶13]

.596F   *Response*—No. Accounting for this transaction is specifically addressed in paragraphs .593 through .596. [FTB85-5, ¶14]

Enterprises under Common Control in a Business Combination

.597   *Question*—Paragraph .101 states that the provisions of this section shall be applied as a general guide in a business combination involving one or more unincorporated enterprises. Paragraph .105(a) requires that each enterprise in a pooling be autonomous and have not been a subsidiary or division for two years prior to initiation. How does this section apply to a combination involving one enterprise controlled by one or a few individuals who control several other enterprises? [AIN-APB16, #27]

.598   *Interpretation*—A proprietorship or a partnership may be a party to a business combination accounted for under this section as stated in the first sentence of paragraph .101. Many of these enterprises are very similar, except for legal form of organization, to a closely held corporation. Often, a single individual may own one or more proprietorships and also may own the controlling interest in one or more corporations and in addition may have an interest in one or more partnerships. [AIN-APB16, #27]

.599   Considerable judgment will usually be required to determine the substance of a combination involving one (or more) of several enterprises under common control. For example, it may be necessary to look beyond the form of the legal organizations to determine substance when an unincorporated enterprise or a closely held corporation owned by one or a few individuals who also control other entities is involved since the dividing lines may not be as sharp as they would be in publicly held enterprises with wide ownership interests. [AIN-APB16, #27]

.600 An individual who owns two separate enterprises organized as corporations theoretically is a parent with two subsidiaries. The same would be true if the enterprises were organized as two proprietorships or as one proprietorship and one corporation. To apply paragraph .105(a) to a combination involving one of these enterprises, however, the relationship between the two enterprises is more important than the fact that each enterprise is theoretically a subsidiary, because paragraph .105(a) precludes fragmenting an enterprise and pooling only a part of the enterprise. The following examples demonstrate these points. [AIN-APB16, #27]

.601 If both enterprises are grocery stores, a combination involving only *one* enterprise should presumably be accounted for as a purchase because the two stores presumably are part of a single kind of business and the two separate legal organizations should be ignored. [AIN-APB16, #27]

.602 On the other hand, if one enterprise is a grocery store and the other is an automobile dealership, a combination involving only one enterprise would be accounted for as a pooling of interests if all other conditions of paragraphs .105 through .107 are met because the individual is operating two unrelated businesses. In these examples, a *line of business* is an indicator of a single business. [AIN-APB16, #27]

.603 Also, a combination involving two or more enterprises owned by one individual must be accounted for by a single method. For example, if both the grocery store and the automobile dealership are to be combined with another unrelated enterprise, one could *not* be a purchase and the other a pooling. (Paragraph .106(b) discusses a combination of more than two enterprises and paragraph .102 states the two methods are not alternatives in accounting for the same combination.) [AIN-APB16, #27]

.604 In general, the same guidelines apply to an enterprise with a few owners rather than an individual owner. They would apply, for example, to two partnerships having the same partners, two closely held corporations having the same stockholders, or to a partnership and a closely held corporation whose stockholders are the partners in the partnership. If the various individuals are all members of one family, the effect may be the same (but is not always the same) as if there were only an individual owner rather than several partners or several stockholders. [AIN-APB16, #27]

.605 Because the ratios of ownership of the different enterprises may differ or the ownership groups may overlap but be different, however, several owners of different enterprises create complexities that are not present if there is a single owner. Because of the diversity of the situations that might be encountered in practice, stating guidelines beyond those given above is impossible. [AIN-APB16, #27]

Pooling by Subsidiary of Personal Holding Enterprise

.606 *Question*—A single individual may control other enterprises (for federal income tax reasons) through a personal holding enterprise. Paragraph .105(a) requires that each enterprise in a pooling be autonomous and not have been a subsidiary or division for two years prior to the initiation of a combination. Does this preclude a pooling by an enterprise that is controlled by a personal holding enterprise? [AIN-APB16, #28]

.607 *Interpretation*—The legal form may sometimes be ignored in a combination involving a subsidiary of a personal holding enterprise. Under paragraph .105(a) a personal holding enterprise is technically a parent company and the enterprises it controls are technically subsidiaries. In many cases, a parent-subsidiary relationship does in fact exist and should be considered as such in applying paragraph .105(a) if the personal holding enterprise or any of its subsidiaries is involved in a business combination. [AIN-APB16, #28]

.608 In other cases, a personal holding enterprise is a convenience established for federal income tax reasons and the various subsidiaries are in fact operated by the owners as if the personal holding enterprise did not exist. In a combination involving such a subsidiary, the personal holding enterprise may be disregarded and the various subsidiaries considered autonomous in applying paragraph .105(a). However, the guidelines described in paragraphs .597 through .605 should be applied in determining the appropriate method of accounting for the combination and all other conditions of paragraphs .105 through .107 must be met in a pooling. [AIN-APB16, #28]

Option May Initiate Combination

.609 *Question*—Paragraph .105(a) specifies the requirements for initiation of a business combination. Does an option to exchange substantially all of their shares at a future date (for example, three years hence) granted by the shareholders of a closely held enterprise to another enterprise constitute the initiation of a business combination? [AIN-APB16, #29]

.610 *Interpretation*—An option that *requires* unilateral performance by either party or bilateral performance by both parties constitutes initiation. Thus, if one enterprise is required to issue stock upon the tendering of shares by the shareholders of another enterprise or if the shareholders are required to tender their shares upon demand, the date the option is granted is the initiation date. The combination must be consummated within one year thereafter to be accounted for by the pooling-of-interests method (refer to paragraph .106(a)). [AIN-APB16, #29]

.611 However, an agreement that grants only the right of first refusal does not constitute initiation. This would be the case, for example, if the stockholders of a closely held enterprise agree to negotiate with one enterprise before negotiating with any other enterprise if the shareholders should in the future decide to consider entering into a business combination. Neither party may be obligated to perform, however, or to pay damages in the absence of performance. [AIN-APB16, #29]

.612 The payment of cash or other consideration by either enterprise for a first refusal agreement would also be contrary to the pooling concept expressed in this section. Individual shareholders, however, may pay cash to obtain the agreement so long as enterprise resources are not directly or indirectly involved. [AIN-APB16, #29]

Representations in a Pooling

.613 *Question*—Paragraph .106(g) specifies that in a business combination accounted for as a pooling of interests there can be no agreement to contingently issue additional shares of stock or other consideration at a later date and no escrowing of shares until a contingency is resolved. This paragraph allows, however, revision of the number of shares issued upon the settlement of a contingency at an amount different from that recorded by a combining enterprise. May an issuing enterprise reserve or escrow some shares against the representations of the management of a combining enterprise in a pooling? [AIN-APB16, #30]

.614 *Interpretation*—Paragraph .106(g) is intended to require purchase accounting if an earnings or market price contingency agreement is present in a business combination. However, this paragraph does not prohibit certain kinds of contingency agreements in a pooling so long as they provide for the sharing of rights and risks arising after consummation and are not in effect earnings or market price contingency agreements. [AIN-APB16, #30]

.615 A contingency agreement that is not prohibited in a pooling may provide for the reservation by the issuing enterprise of a portion of the shares being issued, the issuance of additional shares, the return of shares by former shareholders of the combining enterprise, or the issuance of shares to an escrow agent who will subsequently transfer them to the former shareholders of the combining enterprise or return them to the issuing enterprise. (Note that the former shareholders of the combining enterprise must be able to vote any shares issued, reserved, or escrowed to meet the condition of paragraph .106(f).) [AIN-APB16, #30]

.616 The most common type of contingency agreement *not* prohibited in a pooling by paragraph .106(g) is the *general management representation* that is present in nearly all business combinations. In such a representation, management of a combining enterprise typically warrants that the assets exist and are worth specified amounts and that all liabilities and their amounts have been disclosed. The contingency agreement usually calls for an adjustment in the total number of shares exchanged up to a relatively small percentage (normally about 10 percent) for variations from the amounts represented, but actual adjustments of the number of shares are rare. [AIN-APB16, #30]

.617 A contingency agreement for a *general management representation* does not violate paragraph .106(g) if it provides for a substantial sharing of rights and risks beginning with consummation and the complete sharing within a reasonable period of time. In this light, the contingency agreement is merely a device to provide time for the issuing enterprise to determine that the representations are accurate so it does not share risks arising prior to consummation. Although the time required will vary with circumstances, these determinations should be completed within a few months following consummation of the combination. In any case, the maximum time should not extend beyond the issuance of the first independent audit report on the enterprise making the representations following consummation of the combination. Thereafter, the combined shareholder interests share the risks of inventory obsolescence, collection of receivables, etc. However, if the complete sharing of risks is unduly delayed or if the risk sharing is not substantial at consummation, a *general management representation* may in effect indicate an earnings contingency agreement. [AIN-APB16, #30]

.618 Paragraph .106(g) specifically allows certain contingency agreements in a pooling to cover specific situations whose outcome cannot be reasonably determined at consummation and perhaps even for several years thereafter. (Contingencies of this type are described [AIN-APB16, #30] [in paragraphs .148 and .402 and] in Section C59, paragraphs [.101 and] .104(b).) [FAS111, ¶8(o)] Although management of a combining enterprise may make specific representations as to these contingencies that are known at the consummation of a pooling and as to those that may arise within a reasonable period thereafter, the combined shareholder interests are expected to share the risks and rights of all other contingencies if paragraph .106(g) is to be met. Likewise, the former shareholders of a combining enterprise must be able to vote any shares issued, reserved, or escrowed for a specific contingency until it is finally resolved if paragraph .106(f) is to be met. The contingency agreement may provide, however, that any dividends during the contingency period on contingent shares follow the shares when the contingency is resolved. [AIN-APB16, #30]

.619 It should also be noted that any change in the number of shares (as originally recorded for a pooling of interests) upon the final resolution of either a general or a specific representation contingency is recorded as an adjustment to stockholders' equity (refer to paragraph .112). The effect of the resolution of a contingency involving an asset or liability, whether or not previously recorded, is reflected currently in net income or as a prior period adjustment in accordance with Section A35, "Adjustments of Financial Statements for Prior Periods." In no case may a contingency agreement for either a general or a specific representation in a pooling be used as a means of relieving current or prior net income of an amount that should be reflected therein. [AIN-APB16, #30]

Employment Contingencies in a Pooling

.620 *Question*—Paragraph .106(g) stipulates that in a business combination accounted for as a pooling of interests there can be no agreement for contingent issuance of additional shares of stock or distribution of other consideration to the former stockholders of a combining enterprise. Would the granting of an employment contract or a deferred compensation plan by the combined enterprise to former stockholders of a combining enterprise cause this condition not to be met? [AIN-APB16, #31]

.621 *Interpretation*—An employment contract or a deferred compensation plan granted by the combined enterprise to former stockholders of a combining enterprise would not automatically constitute failure of paragraph .106(g). The critical factors would be the reasonableness of the arrangement and restriction of the arrangement to continuing management personnel. Generally, reasonable contracts or plans entered into for valid enterprise purposes would meet paragraph .106(g). Substance, however, is more important than form. [AIN-APB16, #31]

.622 As an example, the granting of employment contracts to former stockholders of a combining enterprise who were active in its management and who will be active in management of the combined enterprise would meet paragraph .106(g) if the contracts are reasonable in relation to existing contracts granted by the issuing enterprise to its management. However, the granting of employment contracts to former stockholders of a combining enterprise who were not or will not be active in management probably indicates a contingent payout arrangement. Likewise, *consultant* contracts for former stockholders might also indicate a contingent payout arrangement. [AIN-APB16, #31]

.623 Employment contracts and deferred compensation plans entered into by a combining enterprise between the initiation and consummation dates may also cause a business combination not to meet [the requirements of] paragraph .106(g). For example, a combining enterprise may not enter into a *contingency-type* compensation agreement *in contemplation* of the combination and meet [the requirements of] paragraph .106(g) if the issuing enterprise could not also enter into the same agreement under the paragraph. [AIN-APB16, #31]

Stock Options in a Pooling

.624 *Question*—Paragraph .106(g) states that in a business combination accounted for as a pooling of interests, the combined enterprise may not agree to contingently issue additional shares of stock to the former stockholders of a combining enterprise. Would this condition be violated if the combined enterprise granted stock options to these stockholders? [AIN-APB16, #32]

.625 *Interpretation*—Generally, stock options granted by the combined enterprise as current compensation to former stockholders of a combining enterprise would not violate [the conditions of] paragraph .106(g). That is, the former stockholders of a combining enterprise who are employees or directors of the combined enterprise may participate in a stock option plan adopted by the combined enterprise for its employees or directors or both. [AIN-APB16, #32]

.626 Paragraph .106(g) would be violated, however, if the stock option plan in reality is an arrangement to issue additional shares of stock at a relatively low cost to these former stockholders of the combining enterprise to satisfy a contingency agreement. Also, a stock option plan to accomplish the same result adopted by the combining enterprise prior to consummation but *in contemplation* of the combination would not meet [the requirements of] paragraphs .106(c) and .106(g). [AIN-APB16, #32]

Costs of Maintaining an Acquisitions Department

.627 *Question*—An enterprise maintains an acquisitions department to find, evaluate, and negotiate with possible merger candidates. The president of the enterprise also spends a considerable amount of time negotiating business combinations. Cost records are excellent and the total cost is determined for each investigation and negotiation, whether it is successful or unsuccessful. What accounting is specified by this section for these costs? [AIN-APB16, #33]

.628 *Interpretation*—All *internal* costs associated with a business combination are deducted *as incurred* in determining net income under this section. This answer applies to costs incurred for both *poolings* (refer to paragraph .117) and *purchases* (refer to paragraph .134). Naturally, costs incurred in unsuccessful negotiations are also deducted as incurred. [AIN-APB16, #33]

.629 Paragraph .134 specifies that in a business combination accounted for by the purchase method the cost of an enterprise acquired includes the *direct* cost of acquisition. These direct costs, however, are *out-of-pocket* or incremental costs rather than recurring internal costs that may be directly related to an acquisition. The direct costs that are capitalized in a purchase therefore include, for example, a finder's fee and fees paid to outside consultants for accounting, legal, or engineering investigations or for appraisals, etc. All costs related to effecting a pooling of interests, including the direct costs listed above, are charged to expense as specified in paragraph .117. [AIN-APB16, #33]

Forced Sale of Stock

.630 *Question*—A publicly held enterprise wants to effect a business combination with a large closely held enterprise and to account for the combination as a pooling of interests. Because management of the publicly held enterprise prefers not to have a single stockholder owning a large block of its stock, the agreement to combine requires the majority stockholder of the closely held enterprise to sell 25 percent of the voting common stock [that stockholder] receives immediately following consummation and to sell another 25 percent within one year thereafter. The stock is to be sold in public offerings and all of the shares will remain outstanding outside the combined enterprise. Since this section does not have the "continuity of ownership interests" criterion of ARB No. 48, *Business Combinations,* as a condition for pooling, should this combination be accounted for as a pooling of interests or as a purchase? [AIN-APB16, #34]

.631 *Interpretation*—The combination is a purchase because of the *requirement* imposed on a shareholder to sell some of the voting common stock received. Any requirement imposed on a stockholder (other than by a governmental authority) either *to sell* or *to not sell* stock received in a business combination is contrary to the pooling concept of the sharing of rights and risks by the previously independent stockholder interests. While such a requirement does not violate any specific condition for pooling described in paragraphs .105 through .107, it violates the whole pooling concept of this section. [AIN-APB16, #34]

Registration Costs in a Purchase

.632 *Question*—If an enterprise issues previously *registered* equity securities in a business combination accounted for by the purchase method, the fair value of the securities issued is credited to the capital accounts of the issuing enterprise. However, if the securities issued have not been previously registered, paragraph .134 specifies that the costs of registering and issuing equity securities are a reduction of the otherwise determinable fair value of the securities. How should an enterprise account for the costs of a registration that will not be undertaken until after the securities are issued? [AIN-APB16, #35]

.633 *Interpretation*—A publicly held enterprise issuing *un*registered equity securities in an acquisition with an agreement for subsequent registration shall credit the fair value of securities (the otherwise determinable fair value less registration costs) to its capital accounts. The present value of the estimated costs of registration should be accrued as a liability at the date of acquisition (refer to paragraph .146(h)) with an immediate charge to the assets acquired (in most cases, to goodwill). Any difference between the actual costs of registration and the amount accrued at the payment date (original accrual plus imputed interest) would be an adjustment to the recorded goodwill. Total assets (including goodwill) and total capital will thereby be recorded at the same amounts as if previously registered securities had been issued except for any difference in fair value ascribed to restrictions prohibiting sale of the securities at time of issuance. [AIN-APB16, #35]

.634 Agreements for the subsequent registration of unregistered securities issued in business combinations often specify that the securities will be registered *piggyback* (that is, included in the registration of a planned future offering of other securities). In such a case, only the incremental costs of registering the equity securities issued in the acquisition would be accrued or subsequently charged to goodwill as described above and amortized prospectively over the remaining term of the period of amortization of the initial goodwill. [AIN-APB16, #35]

No Pooling with Wholly Owned Subsidiary

.635 *Question*—Company A initiated a combination by making a tender offer for Company B which was at the time an independent enterprise. Company C, which owned a large interest in but not control of Company B, subsequently and without Company A's knowledge purchased all of the remaining outstanding voting common stock of Company B and operated Company B as a wholly owned subsidiary. Within one year of the date Company A made the tender offer, Company C tendered all of the voting common stock of Company B to Company A in exchange for voting common stock of Company A at the ratio of exchange of the tender offer. Paragraph .105(a) generally precludes accounting for a business combination by the pooling-of-interests method if one of the combining enterprises has been a subsidiary of another enterprise within two years prior to initiation of the combination. Does the fact that Company B became a wholly owned subsidiary of Company C following initiation of the combination by Company A preclude pooling in this case? [AIN-APB16, #36]

.636 *Interpretation*—Yes, pooling is precluded and Company A shall account for the combination as a purchase. (Company C, in effect, sold its wholly owned subsidiary B to Company A.) Paragraph .105(a) provides that a wholly owned subsidiary may pool only by distributing the stock of its parent enterprise. [AIN-APB16, #36]

.637 Although paragraph .105(a) refers to not being a subsidiary "within two years before the plan of combination is initiated," the intent of the paragraph is that a combining enterprise in a pooling has not been a subsidiary during a period beginning two years prior to initiation and ending at consummation of a combination. [AIN-APB16, #36]

Combination Contingent on Bail-out

.638 *Question*—Paragraphs .569 through .571 indicate that former shareholders of a combining enterprise may sell voting common stock received in a business combination accounted for as a pooling of interests. Would the accounting for a combination be affected by the fact that its consummation is contingent upon the purchase by a third party or parties of all or part of the voting common stock to be issued in the combination? [AIN-APB16, #37]

.639 *Interpretation*—Yes, a business combination should be accounted for as a purchase if its consummation is contingent upon the purchase by a third party or parties of *any* of the voting common stock to be issued. This would be the case, for example, if the parties to the combination have agreed that consummation of the combination will not occur until there is a commitment by a third party for a private purchase, a firm public offering, or some other form of a guaranteed market for all or part of the shares to be issued. Including such a contingency in the arrangements of the combination, either explicitly or by intent, would be considered a financial arrangement that is precluded in a pooling by paragraph .107(b). [AIN-APB16, #37]

.640 Paragraphs .638 through .640 do not modify paragraphs .569 through .571 that state that shareholders may sell stock received in a pooling and that the enterprise may assist them in locating an unrelated buyer for their shares. Although shareholders may sell stock received in a pooling, consummation of the business combination must first occur without regard to such a sale and cannot be contingent upon a firm commitment by the potential purchaser of the shares to be issued. [AIN-APB16, #37]

Several Enterprises in a Single Business Combination

.641 *Question*—How does this section apply if more than two enterprises are involved in a single business combination? [AIN-APB16, #38]

.642 *Interpretation*—If more than two enterprises negotiate a combination that is contingent upon the mutual agreement by the several enterprises to the terms, the resulting combination is deemed a single business combination regardless of the number of enterprises involved. Each enterprise must meet all of the conditions of paragraphs .105 through .107 if the combination is to be accounted for by the pooling-of-interests method. In particular, paragraphs .105(b) and .106(b) specify how the 10 percent and 90 percent tests should be made when more than two enterprises are involved in a single combination. [AIN-APB16, #38]

.643 Paragraph .102 specifies that a single method should be applied to account for an entire combination. Therefore, if any condition in paragraphs .105 through .107 is not met by any enterprise, the entire combination would be accounted for by the purchase method. [AIN-APB16, #38]

.644 However, it should be noted that an enterprise may be involved in more than one business combination at the same time and that different methods of accounting may apply to the different combinations. [AIN-APB16, #38]

Transfers and Exchanges between Enterprises under Common Control

.645 *Question*—Paragraph .101 states that this section does not apply to a transfer of net assets or to an exchange of shares between enterprises under common control. What are some examples of the types of transactions excluded from this section by this provision and what accounting should be applied? [AIN-APB16, #39]

.646 *Interpretation*—In general, paragraph .101 excludes transfers and exchanges that do not involve outsiders. For example, a parent company may transfer the net assets of a wholly owned subsidiary into the parent company and liquidate the subsidiary, which is a change in legal organization but not a change in the enterprise. Likewise, a parent may transfer its interest in several partially owned subsidiaries to a new wholly owned subsidiary, which is again a change in legal organization but not in the enterprise. Also, a parent may exchange its ownership or the net assets of a wholly owned subsidiary for additional shares issued by the parent's partially owned subsidiary, thereby increasing the parent's percentage of ownership in the partially owned subsidiary but leaving all of the existing minority interest outstanding. [AIN-APB16, #39]

.647 None of the above transfers or exchanges is covered by this section. The assets and liabilities so transferred would be accounted for at historical cost in a manner similar to that in pooling-of-interests accounting. [AIN-APB16, #39]

.648 It should be noted, however, that purchase accounting applies when the effect of a transfer or exchange is to acquire all or part of the outstanding shares held by the minority interest of a subsidiary (refer to paragraph .102). The acquisition of all or part of a minority interest, however acquired, is never considered a transfer or exchange by enterprises under common control (refer to paragraphs .594 through .596). [AIN-APB16, #39]

.649-.650 [Deleted 2/92 because of FASB Statement 109.]

Costs of Closing Duplicate Facilities of an Acquirer

.651 *Question*—Are the costs incurred to close duplicate facilities of an acquiring enterprise recognized as part of the cost of acquisition in a business combination accounted for by the purchase method? [FTB85-5, ¶1]

.652 *Response*—No. Only the direct costs of an acquisition should be included in the cost of a purchased enterprise in a business combination accounted for by the purchase method. Indirect expenses of an acquiring enterprise, including costs incurred when the acquiring enterprise closes some of its facilities because they duplicate facilities acquired in a purchase business combination, should be charged to expense in determining net income. Therefore, the disposition of the acquiring enterprise's assets do not affect the accounting for assets acquired and liabilities assumed of the acquired enterprise, and any gain or loss on disposal or other cost associated with the disposition of an existing asset of the acquiring enterprise should be charged to income. [Refer also to paragraph .134.] [FTB85-5, ¶2]

Pooling of Interests by Mutual and Cooperative Enterprises

.653 *Question*—Does the conversion of a mutual or cooperative enterprise to stock ownership within two years before a plan of combination is initiated or between the dates a combination is initiated and consummated preclude accounting for the combination as a pooling of interests? [FTB85-5, ¶21]

.654 *Response*—No. The changes in the equity interests of the combining enterprises that are proscribed in a pooling of interests are those that might be used to circumvent the intent of this section—that the combination is effected through an exchange of voting interests. In the case of a conversion from mutual ownership to stock ownership, the change to stock ownership may be a necessary step to effect a combination, in which case it should not preclude accounting for a combination as a pooling. [FTB85-5, ¶22] [Refer to] paragraph .106(c). [FTB85-5, ¶23]

.655 Combinations of mutuals and cooperative enterprises [are] not specifically addressed in this section, although paragraph .101 indicates that this section should be applied to a combination of two or more unincorporated businesses. The requirements of paragraph .106(c) were included to ensure that other provisions of this section would not be circumvented. In the special case of a mutual or cooperative enterprise that converts to stock ownership for purposes of effecting a business combination, the conversion is not a shift of equity ownership from one group of equity owners to another. It is a shift from a form of organization that has no substantive equity ownership to one that has. This would not preclude accounting for the transaction as a pooling of interests. This exception to paragraph .106(c) applies exclusively to mutual and cooperative enterprises, which must meet all of the other requirements of this section in order to qualify for a pooling of interests. [FTB85-5, ¶24]

(The next page is 5329.)

Sources: ARB 43, Chapter 1A; APB Opinion 9; APB Opinion 12;
APB Opinion 14

Summary

Capital transactions shall generally be excluded from the determination of income but shall be adequately disclosed in the financial statements.

Capital Transactions Are Excluded from Income

.101 The following [capital transactions] shall be excluded from the determination of net income or the results of operations under all circumstances:

a. Adjustments or charges or credits resulting from transactions in the enterprise's own capital stock [(refer to Section C23, "Capital Stock: Treasury Stock," paragraphs .102 through .104)]
b. Transfers to and from accounts properly designated as appropriated retained earnings (such as general purpose contingency reserves or provisions for replacement costs of fixed assets) [(refer to Section C59, "Contingencies," paragraph .117)]
c. Adjustments made pursuant to a quasi reorganization [(refer to Section Q15, "Quasi Reorganizations," paragraphs .104 through .109)][APB9, ¶28]

Disclosure of Changes in Capital Accounts

.102 When both financial position and results of operations are presented, disclosure of changes in the separate accounts comprising stockholders' equity (in addition to re-tained earnings) and of the changes in the number of shares of equity securities during at least the most recent annual fiscal period and any subsequent interim period presented is required. Disclosure of such changes may take the form of separate statements or may be made in the basic financial statements or notes thereto. [APB12, ¶10]

Stock Issued for Property and Subsequently Contributed Back to Enterprise

.103 If capital stock is issued nominally for the acquisition of property and it appears that at about the same time, and pursuant to a previous agreement or understanding, some portion of the stock so issued is donated to the enterprise, the par value of the stock nominally issued for the property [shall not be treated] as the cost of that property. If stock so donated is subsequently sold, the proceeds [shall not be treated] as a credit to additional paid-in capital of the enterprise. [ARB43, ch1A, ¶6]

Detachable Stock Purchase Warrants Issued in Connection with Debt

.104 The portion of the proceeds of debt securities issued with detachable stock purchase warrants that is allocable to the warrants shall be accounted for as additional paid-in capital. [(For further information refer to Section D10, "Debt: Convertible Debt, Conversion of Convertible Debt, and Debt with Stock Purchase Warrants," paragraphs .104 through .106.)] [APB14, ¶16]

(The next page is 5529.)

Source: APB Opinion 29

Summary

Dividends-in-kind are recorded at the fair value of the assets transferred.

.101 [This section does not apply to] a transfer of nonmonetary assets solely between enterprises or persons under common control, such as between a parent company and its subsidiaries or between two subsidiary corporations of the same parent, or between a corporate joint venture and its owners. [APB29, ¶4(b)] [The distribution of nonmonetary assets, other than an enterprise's own capital stock, to stockholders as dividends is generally referred to as a *dividend-in-kind,* and is considered a nonreciprocal transfer. A dividend-in-kind] shall be recorded at the fair value of the asset transferred, and a gain or loss shall be recognized [by the enterprise] on the disposition of the asset. [APB29, ¶18]

.102 [The issuer of a dividend-in-kind] shall disclose in financial statements for the period the nature of the transaction, the basis of accounting for the assets transferred, and the gains and losses recognized. [APB29, ¶28] Paragraph .113 of Section C51, "Consolidation," includes additional disclosures that are preferred if a parent company disposes of a subsidiary during the year. [APB29, ¶28, fn7]

(The next page is 5859.)

Sources: APB Opinion 10; APB Opinion 15

Summary

Enterprises shall disclose the aggregate liquidation preference of its outstanding preferred stock and the price at which the preferred stock may be called or redeemed. Enterprises shall also disclose the aggregate and per share amounts of cumulative preferred dividends in arrears.

.101 Enterprises [can] issue preferred (or other senior) stock that has a preference in involuntary liquidation considerably in excess of the par or stated value of the shares. The liquidation preference of the stock shall be disclosed in the equity section of the balance sheet in the aggregate, either parenthetically or "in short," rather than on a per share basis or by disclosure in notes. [APB10, ¶10]

.102 In addition, the financial statements shall disclose, either on the face of the balance sheet or in notes pertaining thereto:

a. The aggregate or per share amounts at which preferred shares may be called or are subject to redemption through sinking fund operations or otherwise [APB10, ¶11]
b. The per share and aggregate amounts of cumulative preferred dividends in arrears. [APB15, ¶50, fn16]

(The next page is 5923.)

CAPITAL STOCK: STOCK DIVIDENDS AND STOCK SPLITS

Sources: ARB 43, Chapter 7B; ARB 51

Summary

An enterprise issuing a stock dividend shall capitalize retained earnings in an amount equal to the fair value of the additional shares issued. On the other hand, an enterpise effecting a stock split shall capitalize retained earnings only to the extent required by law. Stock distributions involving issuance of additional shares of more than 25 percent of the number previously outstanding are generally accounted for as stock splits.

.101 [This section presents the accounting for **stock dividends** and **stock splits** (also called stock split-ups).] It is not concerned with the accounting for a distribution or issuance to shareholders of (a) shares of another enterprise theretofore held as an investment or (b) shares of a different class or (c) rights to subscribe for additional shares or (d) shares of the same class in cases where each shareholder is given an election to receive cash or shares. [ARB43, ch7B, ¶3]

Accounting by the Recipient

.102 Since a shareholder's interest in the enterprise remains unchanged by a stock dividend or split except as to the number of share units constituting such interest, the cost of the shares previously held shall be allocated equitably to the total shares held after receipt of the stock dividend or split. When any shares are later disposed of, a gain or loss shall be determined on the basis of the adjusted cost per share. [ARB43, ch7B, ¶9]

Accounting by the Issuer

Stock Dividends

.103 A stock dividend does not give rise to any change in either the enterprise's assets or its respective shareholders' proportionate interests therein. However, merely as a consequence of the expressed purpose of the transaction and its characterization as a *dividend* in related notices to shareholders and the public at large, many recipients of stock dividends look upon them as distributions of corporate earnings and usually in an amount equivalent to the fair value of the additional shares received. Furthermore, when issuances [of stock dividends] are small in comparison with the shares previously outstanding, they do not have any apparent effect upon the share market value. Therefore, where these circumstances exist, the enterprise shall account for [stock dividends] by transferring from retained earnings to the category of permanent capitalization (represented by the capital stock and additional paid-in capital accounts) an amount equal to the fair value of the additional shares issued. [ARB43, ch7B, ¶10]

.104 When the number of additional shares issued as a stock dividend is so great that it has, or may reasonably be expected to have, the effect of materially reducing the share market value, the transaction partakes of the nature of a stock split. Consequently, under such circumstances there is no need to capitalize retained earnings, other than to the extent occasioned by legal requirements. It is recommended, however, that in such instances every effort be made to avoid the use of the word *dividend* in related corporate resolutions, notices, and announcements and that, in those cases where because of legal requirements this cannot be done, the transaction be described, for example, as a *[stock] split effected in the form of a dividend.* [ARB43, ch7B, ¶11]

.105 In closely held enterprises, the intimate knowledge of the enterprises' affairs possessed by their shareholders would preclude implications [that the stock dividends are distributions of corporate earnings]. In such cases, there is no need to capitalize retained earnings other than to meet legal requirements. [ARB43, ch7B, ¶12]

.106 The point at which the relative size of the additional shares issued becomes large enough to materially influence the unit market price of the stock will vary with individual enterprises and under differing market conditions and, hence, no single percentage can be laid down as a standard for determining when capitalization of retained earnings in excess of legal requirements is called for and when it is not. However, it would appear that there would be few instances involving the issuance of additional shares of less than, say, 20 percent or 25 percent of the number previously outstanding where the effect would not be such as to call for the procedure referred to in paragraph .103, [that is, the capitalization of retained earnings in an amount equal to the fair value of the shares issued]. [ARB43, ch7B, ¶13]

.107 The accounting recommended in paragraph .103 will in many cases, probably the majority, result in the capitalization of retained earnings in an amount in excess of that called for by the laws of the state of incorporation; such laws generally require the capitalization only of the par value of the shares issued, or, in the case of shares without par value, an amount usually within the discretion of the board of directors. However, these legal requirements are, in effect, minimum requirements and do not prevent the capitalization of a larger amount per share. [ARB43, ch7B, ¶14]

Stock Splits

.108 When a stock split is clearly for the purpose of effecting a reduction in the unit market price of shares of the class issued and, thus, of obtaining wider distribution and improved marketability of the shares, no transfer from retained earnings to the additional paid-in capital or capital stock account is called for, other than to the extent occasioned by legal requirements. However, few cases will arise where the aforementioned purpose can be accomplished through an issuance of shares which is less than, say, 20 percent or 25 percent of the previously outstanding shares. [ARB43, ch7B, ¶15]

.109 An enterprise's representations to its shareholders as to the nature of the issuance is one of the principal considerations in determining whether it should be recorded as a stock dividend or a [stock] split. Nevertheless, the issuance of new shares in ratios of less than, say, 20 percent or 25 percent of the previously outstanding shares, or the frequent recurrence of issuances of shares, would destroy the presumption that transactions represented to be [stock] splits should be recorded as [stock] splits. [ARB43, ch7B, ¶16]

Stock Dividends of Subsidiaries

.110 Occasionally, subsidiary enterprises capitalize retained earnings arising since acquisition, by means of a stock dividend or otherwise. This does not require a transfer to additional paid-in capital on consolidation, inasmuch as the retained earnings in the consolidated financial statements should reflect the accumulated earnings of the consolidated group not distributed to the shareholders of, or capitalized by, the parent company. [ARB51, ¶18]

Glossary

.401 **Stock dividend.** An issuance by an enterprise of its own common shares to its common shareholders without consideration and under conditions indicating that such action is prompted mainly by a desire to give the recipient shareholders some ostensibly separate evidence of a part of their respective interests in accumulated corporate earnings without distribution of cash or other property which the board of directors deems necessary or desirable to retain in the business. [ARB43, ch7B, ¶1]

.402 **Stock split.** An issuance by an enterprise of its own common shares to its common shareholders without consideration and under conditions indicating that such action is prompted mainly by a desire to increase the number of outstanding shares for the purpose of effecting a reduction in their unit market price, and, thereby, of obtaining wider distribution and improved marketability of the shares. [ARB43, ch7B, ¶2]

(The next page is 6125.)

CAPITAL STOCK: TREASURY STOCK SECTION C23

Sources: ARB 43, Chapters 1A and 1B; APB Opinion 6;
FASB Technical Bulletin 85-6

Summary

If an enterprise acquires shares of its own capital stock, the cost of the acquired shares shall generally be shown as a deduction from capital. Dividends on such shares held in the enterprise's treasury (treasury stock) shall not be credited to income. Gains and losses on sales of treasury stock shall be accounted for as adjustments to capital and not as part of income.

If the price paid for the shares is significantly in excess of current market price, that may indicate that the price paid may include consideration for other factors such as stated or unstated rights, privileges, or agreements in addition to the capital stock. In such cases, the excess should be attributed to the other factors.

Dividends on Treasury Stock

.101 The dividends on [treasury] stock shall not be treated as a credit to the income account of the enterprise. [ARB43, ch1A, ¶4]

Retirement of Treasury Stock

.102 If an enterprise's [capital] stock is retired, or purchased for constructive retirement (with or without an intention to retire the stock formally in accordance with applicable laws):[a]

a. *An excess of purchase price over par or stated value* may be allocated between additional paid-in capital and retained earnings. The portion of the excess allocated to additional paid-in capital shall be limited to the sum of (1) all additional paid-in capital arising from previous retirements and net "gains" on sales of treasury stock of the same issue and (2) the pro rata portion of additional paid-in capital, voluntary transfers of retained earnings, capitalization of stock dividends, etc., on the same issue.

[aRefer to paragraphs .501 through .503 for guidance regarding accounting for a purchase of treasury shares at a price significantly in excess of the current market price of the shares.]

For this purpose, any remaining additional paid-in capital applicable to issues fully retired (formal or constructive) is deemed to be applicable pro rata to shares of common stock. Alternatively, the excess may be charged entirely to retained earnings in recognition of the fact that an enterprise can always capitalize or allocate retained earnings for such purposes [APB6, ¶12(a)] or may be reflected [entirely as a deduction from] additional paid-in capital. [ARB43, ch1B, ¶7]

b. *An excess of par or stated value over purchase price* shall be credited to additional paid-in capital. [APB6, ¶12(a)]

.103 If an enterprise's stock is acquired for purposes other than retirement (formal or constructive), or if ultimate disposition has not yet been decided, the cost[1] of acquired stock may be shown separately as a deduction from the total of capital stock, additional paid-in capital, and retained earnings, or may be accorded the accounting treatment appropriate for retired stock, [APB6, ¶12(b)] or in some circumstances may be shown as an asset, if adequately disclosed. [ARB43, ch1A, ¶4] "Gains" on sales of treasury stock not previously accounted for as constructively retired shall be credited to additional paid-in capital;[2] "losses" may be charged to additional paid-in capital to the extent that previous net "gains" from sales or retirements of the same class of stock are included therein, otherwise to retained earnings.[3] [APB6, ¶12(b)]

.104 Laws of some states govern the circumstances under which an enterprise may acquire its own stock and prescribe the accounting treatment therefor. If such requirements are at variance with paragraphs .102 and .103, the accounting shall conform to the applicable law. If state laws relating to acquisition of stock restrict the availability of retained earnings for payment of dividends or have other effects of a significant nature, these facts shall be disclosed. [APB6, ¶13]

---

[1]Refer to Section N35, "Nonmonetary Transactions," paragraph .105, for guidance regarding the cost of stock acquired in a nonmonetary transaction.]

[2]Although there may be cases where the transactions involved are so inconsequential as to be immaterial, [ARB43, ch1B, ¶10] [accounting treatment different from that specified in paragraph .102] shall not be applied to any transaction that, although in itself inconsiderable in amount, is a part of a series of transactions that in the aggregate are of substantial importance. [ARB43, ch1B, ¶11]

[3]Refer to paragraphs .501 through .503 for guidance regarding accounting for a purchase of treasury shares at a stated price significantly in excess of the current market price of the shares.]

Supplemental Guidance

Accounting for a Purchase of Treasury Shares at a Price Significantly in Excess of the Current Market Price of the Shares

.501 *Question*—How should an enterprise account for a purchase of treasury shares at a stated price significantly in excess of the current market price of the shares? [FTB85-6, ¶1]

.502 *Response*—An agreement to purchase shares from a shareholder may also involve the receipt or payment of consideration in exchange for stated or unstated rights or privileges that should be identified to allocate properly the purchase price. [FTB85-6, ¶2]

.503 An enterprise offering to repurchase shares only from a specific shareholder (or group of shareholders) suggests that the repurchase may involve more than the purchase of treasury shares. [FTB85-6, ¶14] [Also,] a purchase of shares at a price significantly in excess of the current market price creates a presumption that the purchase price includes amounts attributable to items other than the shares purchased. For example, the selling shareholder may agree to abandon certain acquisition plans, forego other planned trans- actions, settle litigation, settle employment contracts, or restrict voluntarily the ability to purchase shares of the enterprise or its affiliates within a stated time period. If the pur- chase of treasury shares includes the receipt of stated or unstated rights, privileges, or agreements in addition to the capital stock, only the amount representing the fair value of the treasury shares at the date the major terms of the agreement to purchase the shares are reached should be accounted for as the cost of the shares acquired. The price paid in excess of the amount accounted for as the cost of treasury shares should be attributed to the other elements of the transaction and accounted for according to their substance. If the fair value of those other elements of the transaction is more clearly evident, for ex- ample, because an enterprise's shares are not publicly traded, that amount should be assigned to those elements and the difference recorded as the cost of treasury shares. If no stated or unstated consideration in addition to the capital stock can be identified, the entire purchase price should be accounted for as the cost of treasury shares. The alloca- tion of amounts paid and the accounting treatment for such amounts should be dis- closed. [FTB85-6, ¶3] The allocation of amounts described in this paragraph requires significant judgment and consideration of many factors that can significantly affect amounts recognized in the financial statements. [FTB85-6, ¶16]

.504 Transactions do arise, however, in which an acquisition of an enterprise's stock may take place at prices different from routine transactions in the open market. For ex- ample, to obtain the desired number of shares in a tender offer to all or most share- holders, the offer may need to be at a price in excess of the current market price. In addition, a block of shares representing a controlling interest will generally trade at a price in excess of market, and a large block of shares may trade at a price above or below the current market price depending on whether the buyer or seller initiates the transaction. An enterprise's acquisition of its shares in those circumstances is solely a treasury stock transaction properly accounted for at the purchase price of the treasury shares. Therefore, in the absence of the receipt of stated or unstated consideration in addition to the capital stock, the entire purchase price should be accounted for as the cost of treasury shares. [FTB85-6, ¶15]

(The next page is 6251.)

Sources: FASB Statement 95; FASB Statement 102; FASB Statement 104; FASB Statement 115; FASB Statement 117

Summary

This section presents standards for cash flow reporting. A statement of cash flows is required as part of a full set of financial statements for all business enterprises and not-for-profit organizations other than defined benefit pension plans and certain other employee benefit plans and highly liquid investment companies that meet specified conditions.

A statement of cash flows shall classify cash receipts and payments according to whether they stem from operating, investing, or financing activities. This section provides definitions of each category.

Generally, cash flow information about the gross amounts of cash receipts and cash payments during a period is more relevant than information about net amounts of cash receipts and payments. However, because the net amount of related receipts and payments provides sufficient information when the turnover is quick, the amounts are large, and the maturities are short, the reporting of net cash flows for certain items with those characteristics is permitted. Additionally, certain investing and financing activities of banks, savings institutions, and credit unions may be reported as net cash flows.

Enterprises are encouraged to report cash flows from operating activities directly by showing major classes of operating cash receipts and payments (the direct method). Enterprises that choose not to show operating cash receipts and payments are required to report the same amount of net cash flow from operating activities indirectly by adjusting net income of a business enterprise or change in net assets of a not-for-profit organization to reconcile it to net cash flow from operating activities (the indirect or reconciliation method). If the direct method is used, a reconciliation of net income of a business enterprise or change in net assets of a not-for-profit organization and net cash flow from operating activities is required to be provided in a separate schedule.

A statement of cash flows shall report the reporting currency equivalent of foreign currency cash flows, using the current exchange rate at the time of the cash flows. The effect of the exchange rate changes on cash held in foreign currencies is reported as a separate item in the reconciliation of beginning and ending balances of cash and cash equivalents.

Information about investing and financing activities not resulting in cash receipts or payments in the period shall be provided separately.

Scope

.101 This section [presents] standards for providing a statement of cash flows in general-purpose financial statements. [FAS95, ¶1] A business enterprise [FAS95, ¶3] or not-for-profit organization [FAS117, ¶30(a)] that provides a set of financial statements that reports both financial position and results of operations shall also provide a statement of cash flows for each period for which results of operations are provided. [FAS95, ¶3] In this section, *enterprise* encompasses both business enterprises and not-for-profit organizations, and the phrase *investors, creditors, and others* encompasses donors. The terms *income statement* and *net income* apply to a business enterprise; the terms *statement of activities* and *change in net assets* apply to a not-for-profit organization. [FAS117, ¶30(b)] [However,] a statement of cash flows is not required for defined benefit pension plans and certain other employee benefit plans or for certain investment companies as provided by paragraphs .135A through .135C. [FAS102, ¶10(a)]

Purpose of a Statement of Cash Flows

.102 The primary purpose of a statement of cash flows is to provide relevant information about the cash receipts and cash payments of an enterprise during a period. [FAS95, ¶4]

.103 The information provided in a statement of cash flows, if used with related disclosures and information in the other financial statements, should help investors, creditors, and others to (a) assess the enterprise's ability to generate positive future net cash flows; (b) assess the enterprise's ability to meet its obligations, its ability to pay dividends, and its needs for external financing; (c) assess the reasons for differences between net income and associated cash receipts and payments; and (d) assess the effects on an enterprise's financial position of both its cash and noncash investing and financing transactions during the period. [FAS95, ¶5]

[1 Editorial deletion, 6/93.]

.104 To achieve its purpose of providing information to help investors, creditors, and others in making those assessments, a statement of cash flows should report the cash effects during a period of an enterprise's operations, its investing transactions, and its financing transactions. Related disclosures should report the effects of investing and financing transactions that affect an enterprise's financial position but do not directly affect cash flows during the period. A reconciliation of net income and net cash flow from operating activities, which generally provides information about the net effects of operating transactions and other events that affect net income and operating cash flows in different periods, also should be provided. [FAS95, ¶6]

Focus on Cash and Cash Equivalents

.105 A statement of cash flows shall explain the change during the period in cash[2] and cash equivalents. The statement shall use descriptive terms such as *cash* or *cash and cash equivalents* rather than ambiguous terms such as *funds*. The total amounts of cash and cash equivalents at the beginning and end of the period shown in the statement of cash flows shall be the same amounts as similarly titled line items or subtotals shown in the statements of financial position as of those dates. [FAS95, ¶7]

.106 For purposes of this section, cash equivalents are short-term, highly liquid investments that are both:

a. Readily convertible to known amounts of cash
b. So near their maturity that they present insignificant risk of changes in value because of changes in interest rates.

Generally, only investments with original maturities[3] of three months or less qualify under that definition. [FAS95, ¶8]

---

[2]Consistent with common usage, *cash* includes not only currency on hand but demand deposits with banks or other financial institutions. *Cash* also includes other kinds of accounts that have the general characteristics of demand deposits in that the customer may deposit additional funds at any time and also effectively may withdraw funds at any time without prior notice or penalty. All charges and credits to those accounts are cash receipts or payments to both the entity owning the account and the bank holding it. For example, a bank's granting of a loan by crediting the proceeds to a customer's demand deposit account is a cash payment by the bank and a cash receipt of the customer when the entry is made. [FAS95, ¶7, fn1]

[3]*Original maturity* [in this paragraph] means original maturity to the entity holding the investment. For example, both a three-month U.S. Treasury bill and a three-year Treasury note purchased three months from maturity qualify as cash equivalents. However, a Treasury note purchased three years ago does not become a cash equivalent when its remaining maturity is three months. [FAS95, ¶8, fn2]

.107 Examples of items commonly considered to be cash equivalents are Treasury bills, commercial paper, money market funds, and federal funds sold (for an enterprise with banking operations). Cash purchases and sales of those investments generally are part of the enterprise's cash management activities rather than part of its operating, investing, and financing activities, and details of those transactions need not be reported in a statement of cash flows. [FAS95, ¶9]

.108 Not all investments that qualify [as cash equivalents under paragraph .106] are required to be treated as cash equivalents [in the statement of cash flows]. An enterprise shall establish a policy concerning which short-term, highly liquid investments that satisfy the definition in paragraph .106 are treated as cash equivalents. For example, an enterprise having banking operations might decide that all investments that qualify except for those purchased for its trading account will be treated as cash equivalents, while an enterprise whose operations consist largely of investing in short-term, highly liquid investments might decide that all those items will be treated as investments rather than cash equivalents. An enterprise shall disclose its policy for determining which items are treated as cash equivalents [in the statement of cash flows]. Any change to that policy is a change in accounting principle that shall be effected by restating financial statements for earlier years presented for comparative purposes. [FAS95, ¶10]

Gross and Net Cash Flows

.109 Generally, information about the gross amounts of cash receipts and cash payments during a period is more relevant than information about the net amounts of cash receipts and payments. However, the net amount of related receipts and payments provides sufficient information not only for cash equivalents, as noted in paragraph .107, but also for certain other classes of cash flows specified in paragraphs .110, .111, [.111A], and .126. [FAS95, ¶11]

.110 For certain items, the turnover is quick, the amounts are large, and the maturities are short. For certain other items, such as demand deposits of a bank and customer accounts payable of a broker-dealer, the enterprise is substantively holding or disbursing cash on behalf of its customers. Only the net changes during the period in assets and liabilities with those characteristics need be reported because knowledge of the gross cash receipts and payments related to them may not be necessary to understand the enterprise's operating, investing, and financing activities. [FAS95, ¶12]

.111 Items that qualify for net reporting because their turnover is quick, their amounts are large, and their maturities are short are cash receipts and payments pertaining to

(a) investments (other than cash equivalents), (b) loans receivable, and (c) debt, providing that the original maturity of the asset or liability is three months or less.[4] [FAS95, ¶13]

.111A Banks, savings institutions, and credit unions are not required to report gross amounts of cash receipts and cash payments for (a) deposits placed with other financial institutions and withdrawals of deposits, (b) time deposits accepted and repayments of deposits, and (c) loans made to customers and principal collections of loans. When those enterprises constitute part of a consolidated enterprise, net amounts of cash receipts and cash payments for deposit or lending activities of those enterprises shall be reported separate from gross amounts of cash receipts and cash payments for other investing and financing activities of the consolidated enterprise, including those of a subsidiary of a bank, savings institution, or credit union that is not itself a bank, savings institution, or credit union. [FAS104, ¶7(a)]

Classification of Cash Receipts and Cash Payments

.112 A statement of cash flows shall classify cash receipts and cash payments as resulting from investing, financing, or operating activities.[5] [FAS95, ¶14]

Cash Flows from Investing Activities

.113 Investing activities include making and collecting loans and acquiring and disposing of debt or equity instruments and property, plant, and equipment and other productive assets, that is, assets held for or used in the production of goods or services by the enterprise (other than materials that are part of the enterprise's inventory). [FAS95, ¶15]

---

[4]For this purpose, amounts due on demand are considered to have maturities of three months or less. For convenience, credit card receivables of financial services operations—generally, receivables resulting from cardholder charges that may, at the cardholder's option, be paid in full when first billed, usually within one month, without incurring interest charges and that do not stem from the enterprise's sale of goods or services— also are considered to be loans with original maturities of three months or less. [FAS95, ¶13, fn3]

[5]Generally, each cash receipt or payment is to be classified according to its nature without regard to whether it stems from an item intended as a hedge of another item. For example, the proceeds of a borrowing are a financing cash inflow even though the debt is intended as a hedge of an investment, and the purchase or sale of a futures contract is an investing activity even though the contract is intended as a hedge of a firm commitment to purchase inventory. However, cash flows from futures contracts, forward contracts, option contracts, or swap contracts that are accounted for as hedges of identifiable transactions or events (for example, a cash payment from a futures contract that hedges a purchase or sale of inventory), including anticipatory hedges, may be classified in the same category as the cash flows from the items being hedged provided that accounting policy is disclosed. If for any reason hedge accounting for an instrument that hedges an identifiable transaction or event is discontinued, then any cash flows subsequent to the date of discontinuance shall be classified consistent with the nature of the instrument. [FAS104, ¶7(b)]

Investing activities exclude acquiring and disposing of certain loans or other debt or equity instruments that are acquired specifically for resale, as discussed in paragraphs .122A through .122B. [FAS102, ¶10(b)]

.114 Cash inflows from investing activities are:[6]

a. Receipts from collections or sales of loans made by the enterprise and of other entities' debt instruments [FAS95, ¶16] (other than cash equivalents and certain debt instruments that are acquired specifically for resale) [FAS102, ¶10(c)] that were purchased by the enterprise
b. Receipts from sales of equity instruments of other enterprises [FAS95, ¶16] (other than certain equity instruments carried in a trading account) [FAS102, ¶10(d)] and from returns *of* investment in those instruments
c. Receipts from sales of property, plant, and equipment and other productive assets. [FAS95, ¶16]

.115 Cash outflows for investing activities are:

a. Disbursements for loans made by the enterprise and payments to acquire debt instruments of other entities [FAS95, ¶17] (other than cash equivalents and certain debt instruments that are acquired specifically for resale) [FAS102, ¶10(c)]
b. Payments to acquire equity instruments of other enterprises [FAS95, ¶17] (other than certain equity instruments carried in a trading account) [FAS102, ¶10(d)]
c. Payments at the time of purchase or soon before or after purchase[7] to acquire property, plant, and equipment and other productive assets.[8] [FAS95, ¶17]

Cash Flows from Financing Activities

.116 Financing activities include obtaining resources from owners and providing them with a return on, and a return of, their investment; [FAS95, ¶18] receiving restricted re-

---

[6]Receipts from disposing of loans, debt or equity instruments, or property, plant, and equipment include directly related proceeds of insurance settlements, such as the proceeds of insurance on a building that is damaged or destroyed. [FAS95, ¶16, fn5]

[7]Generally, only advance payments, the down payment, or other amounts paid at the time of purchase or soon before or after purchase of property, plant, and equipment and other productive assets are investing cash outflows. Incurring directly related debt [payable] to the seller is a financing transaction, and subsequent payments of principal on that debt thus are financing cash outflows. [FAS95, ¶17, fn6]

[8]Enterprises [are not] required to distinguish between expenditures for maintenance and those for expansion. [FAS95, ¶99] Payments to acquire productive assets include interest capitalized as part of the cost of those assets. [FAS95, ¶17, fn7]

sources that by donor stipulation must be used for long-term purposes; [FAS117, ¶30(c)] borrowing money and repaying amounts borrowed, or otherwise settling the obligation; and obtaining and paying for other resources obtained from creditors on long-term credit. [FAS95, ¶18]

.117 Cash inflows from financing activities are:

a. Proceeds from issuing equity instruments
b. Proceeds from issuing bonds, mortgages, notes, and from other short- or long-term borrowing [FAS95, ¶19]
c. Receipts from contributions and investment income that by donor stipulation are restricted for the purposes of acquiring, constructing, or improving property, plant, equipment, or other long-lived assets or establishing or increasing a permanent endowment or term endowment. [FAS117, ¶30(d)]

.118 Cash outflows for financing activities are:

a. Payments of dividends or other distributions to owners, including outlays to reacquire the enterprise's equity instruments
b. Repayments of amounts borrowed
c. Other principal payments to creditors who have extended long-term credit.[9] [FAS95, ¶20]

Cash Flows from Operating Activities

.119 Operating activities include all transactions and other events that are not defined as investing or financing activities in paragraphs .113 through .118. Operating activities generally involve producing and delivering goods and providing services. Cash flows from operating activities are generally the cash effects of transactions and other events that enter into the determination of net income. [Refer to paragraphs .122A and .122B for guidance on reporting cash flows from assets in trading accounts and from loans acquired for resale.] [FAS95, ¶21]

---

[9]Refer to footnote 7, which indicates that most principal payments on seller-financed debt directly related to a purchase of property, plant, and equipment or other productive assets are financing cash outflows. [FAS95, ¶20, fn8]

.120 Cash inflows from operating activities are:

a. Cash receipts from sales of goods[9a] or services, including receipts from collection or sale of accounts and both short- and long-term notes receivable from customers arising from those sales
b. Cash receipts from returns *on* loans, other debt instruments of other entities, and equity securities—interest and dividends
c. All other cash receipts that do not stem from transactions defined as investing or financing activities, such as amounts received to settle lawsuits; proceeds of insurance settlements except for those that are directly related to investing or financing activities, such as from destruction of a building; and refunds from suppliers. [FAS95, ¶22]

.121 Cash outflows for operating activities are:

a. Cash payments to acquire materials for manufacture or goods[9b] for resale, including principal payments on accounts and both short- and long-term notes payable to suppliers for those materials or goods
b. Cash payments to other suppliers and employees for other goods or services
c. Cash payments to governments for taxes, duties, fines, and other fees or penalties
d. Cash payments to lenders and other creditors for interest
e. All other cash payments that do not stem from transactions defined as investing or financing activities, such as payments to settle lawsuits, cash contributions to charities, and cash refunds to customers. [FAS95, ¶23]

.122 Certain cash receipts and payments may have aspects of more than one class of cash flows. For example, a cash payment may pertain to an item that could be considered either inventory or a productive asset. If so, the appropriate classification shall depend on the activity that is likely to be the predominant source of cash flows for the item. For example, the acquisition and sale of equipment to be used by the enterprise or rented to others generally are investing activities. However, equipment sometimes is acquired or produced to be used by the enterprise or rented to others for a short period and then sold. In those circumstances, the acquisition or production and subsequent sale of those assets shall be considered operating activities. [FAS95, ¶24] [Similarly,] real estate generally is considered a productive asset, and a cash payment to purchase real estate generally is an investing cash outflow. However, if real estate is acquired by a real estate developer to be subdivided, improved, and sold in individual lots, then the cash payment

---

[9a]The term *goods* includes certain loans and other debt and equity instruments of other enterprises that are acquired specifically for resale, as discussed in paragraph .122B. [FAS102, ¶10(e)]

[9b][Refer to footnote 9a.] [FAS102, ¶10(e)]

to purchase that real estate would be classified as an operating cash flow because the real estate is acquired specifically for resale and is similar to inventory in other businesses. [FAS102, ¶25]

Classification of Cash Flows from Acquisitions and Sales of Certain Securities and Other Assets

.122A Banks, brokers and dealers in securities, and other enterprises may carry securities and other assets in a trading account.[9c] Cash receipts and cash payments resulting from purchases and sales of securities and other assets shall be classified as operating cash flows if those assets are acquired specifically for resale and are carried at market value in a trading account. [FAS102, ¶8] Cash flows from purchases, sales, and maturities of available-for-sale securities shall be classified as cash flows from investing activities and reported gross in the statement of cash flows. [FAS115, ¶132(a)]

.122B Some loans are similar to securities in a trading account in that they are originated or purchased specifically for resale and are held for short periods of time. Cash receipts and cash payments resulting from acquisitions and sales of loans also shall be classified as operating cash flows if those loans are acquired specifically for resale and are carried at market value or at the lower of cost or market value.[9d] Cash receipts resulting from sales of loans that were not specifically acquired for resale shall be classified as investing cash inflows. That is, if loans were acquired as investments, cash receipts from sales of those loans shall be classified as investing cash inflows regardless of a change in the purpose for holding those loans. [FAS102, ¶9]

Foreign Currency Cash Flows

.123 A statement of cash flows of an enterprise with foreign currency transactions or foreign operations shall report the reporting currency equivalent of foreign currency cash flows using the exchange rates in effect at the time of the cash flows. An appropriately weighted average exchange rate for the period may be used for translation if the result is substantially the same as if the rates at the dates of the cash flows were used.[10] The state-

---

[9c]Characteristics of trading account activities are described in Section C28, "Changing Prices: Reporting Their Effects in Financial Reporting," paragraphs .192 and .193, and in the AICPA Industry Audit Guide, *Audits of Banks,* and Audit and Accounting Guide, *Audits of Brokers and Dealers in Securities.* [FAS102, ¶8, fn3]

[9d]Mortgage loans held for sale are required to be reported at the lower of cost or market value in accordance with Section Mo4, "Mortgage Banking Activities," paragraph .105. [FAS102, ¶9, fn4]

[10]Paragraph .118 of Section F60, "Foreign Currency Translation," recognizes the general impracticality of translating revenues, expenses, gains, and losses at the exchange rates on dates they are recognized and permits an appropriately weighted average exchange rate for the period to be used to translate those elements. This section applies that provision to cash receipts and cash payments. [FAS95, ¶25, fn9]

ment shall report the effect of exchange rate changes on cash balances held in foreign currencies as a separate part of the reconciliation of the change in cash and cash equivalents during the period. [FAS95, ¶25]

Content and Form of the Statement of Cash Flows

.124 A statement of cash flows for a period shall report net cash provided or used by operating, investing, and financing activities[11] and the net effect of those flows on cash and cash equivalents during the period in a manner that reconciles beginning and ending cash and cash equivalents. [FAS95, ¶26]

.125 In reporting cash flows from operating activities, enterprises are encouraged to report major classes of gross cash receipts and gross cash payments and their arithmetic sum—the net cash flow from operating activities (the direct method). Enterprises that do so should, at a minimum, separately report the following classes of operating cash receipts and payments:[12]

a. Cash collected from customers, including lessees, licensees, and the like
b. Interest and dividends received[12a]
c. Other operating cash receipts, if any
d. Cash paid to employees and other suppliers of goods or services, including suppliers of insurance, advertising, and the like
e. Interest paid
f. Income taxes paid
g. Other operating cash payments, if any.

Enterprises are encouraged to provide further breakdowns of operating cash receipts and payments that they consider meaningful and feasible. For example, a retailer or manufacturer might decide to further divide cash paid to employees and suppliers (category (d) above) into payments for costs of inventory and payments for selling, general, and administrative expenses. [FAS95, ¶27]

---

[11]Separate disclosure of cash flows pertaining to extraordinary items or discontinued operations reflected in those categories is not required. An enterprise that nevertheless chooses to report separately operating cash flows of discontinued operations shall do so consistently for all periods affected, which may include periods long after sale or liquidation of the operation. [FAS95, ¶26, fn10]

[12]Paragraphs .130 through .133 and paragraph .141, respectively, discuss and illustrate a method by which those major classes of gross operating cash receipts and payments generally may be determined indirectly. [FAS95, ¶27, fn11]

[12a]Interest and dividends that are donor restricted for long-term purposes as noted in paragraphs .116 and .117(c) are not part of operating cash receipts. [FAS117, ¶30(e)]

.126 Enterprises that choose not to provide information about major classes of operating cash receipts and payments by the direct method as encouraged in paragraph .125 shall determine and report the same amount for net cash flow from operating activities indirectly by adjusting net income [FAS95, ¶28] of a business enterprise or change in net assets of a not-for-profit organization [FAS117, ¶30(f)] to reconcile it to net cash flow from operating activities (the indirect or reconciliation method). That requires adjusting net income [FAS95, ¶28] of a business enterprise or change in net assets of a not-for-profit organization [FAS117, ¶30(f)] to remove (a) the effects of all deferrals of past operating cash receipts and payments, such as changes during the period in inventory, deferred income, and the like, and all accruals of expected future operating cash receipts and payments, such as changes during the period in receivables and payables,[13] and (b) the effects of all items whose cash effects are investing or financing cash flows, such as depreciation, amortization of goodwill, and gains or losses on sales of property, plant, and equipment and discontinued operations (which relate to investing activities), and gains or losses on extinguishment of debt (which is a financing activity). [FAS95, ¶28]

.127 The reconciliation of net income [FAS95, ¶29] of a business enterprise or change in net assets of a not-for-profit orgnization [FAS117, ¶30(f)] to net cash flow from operating activities described in paragraph .126 shall be provided regardless of whether the direct or indirect method of reporting net cash flow from operating activities is used. That reconciliation shall separately report all major classes of reconciling items. For example, major classes of deferrals of past operating cash receipts and payments and accruals of expected future operating cash receipts and payments, including at a minimum changes during the period in receivables pertaining to operating activities, in inventory, and in payables pertaining to operating activities, shall be separately reported. Enterprises are encouraged to provide further breakdowns of those categories that they consider meaningful. For example, changes in receivables from customers for an enterprise's sale of goods or services might be reported separately from changes in other operating receivables. In addition, if the indirect method is used, amounts of interest paid (net of amounts capitalized) and income taxes paid during the period shall be provided in related disclosures. [FAS95, ¶29]

---

[13]Adjustments to net income [FAS95, ¶28, fn12] of a business enterprise or change in net assets of a not-for-profit organization [FAS117, ¶30(f)] to determine net cash flow from operating activities shall reflect accruals for interest earned but not received and interest incurred but not paid. Those accruals may be reflected in the statement of financial position in changes in assets and liabilities that relate to investing or financing activities, such as loans or deposits. However, interest credited directly to a deposit account that has the general characteristics described in paragraph .105, footnote 2, is a cash outflow of the payor and a cash inflow of the payee when the entry is made. [FAS95, ¶28, fn12]

.128 If the direct method of reporting net cash flow from operating activities is used, the reconciliation of net income [FAS95, ¶30] of a business enterprise or change in net assets of a not-for-profit orgnization [FAS117, ¶30(f)] to net cash flow from operating activities shall be provided in a separate schedule. If the indirect method is used, the reconciliation may be either reported within the statement of cash flows or provided in a separate schedule, with the statement of cash flows reporting only the net cash flow from operating activities. If the reconciliation is presented in the statement of cash flows, all adjustments to net income [FAS95, ¶30] of a business enterprise or change in net assets of a not-for-profit organization [FAS117, ¶30(f)] to determine net cash flow from operating activities shall be clearly identified as reconciling items. [FAS95, ¶30]

.129 Except for items described in paragraphs .110 and .111, both investing cash inflows and outflows and financing cash inflows and outflows shall be reported separately in a statement of cash flows—for example, outlays for acquisitions of property, plant, and equipment shall be reported separately from proceeds from sales of property, plant, and equipment; proceeds of borrowings shall be reported separately from repayments of debt; and proceeds from issuing stock shall be reported separately from outlays to reaquire the enterprise's stock. [FAS95, ¶31]

Indirectly Determining Amounts of Operating Cash Receipts and Payments

.130 Given sufficiently detailed information, major classes of operating cash receipts and payments may be determined indirectly by adjusting revenue and expense amounts for the change during the period in related asset and liability accounts. For example, cash collected from customers may be determined indirectly by adjusting sales for the change during the period in receivables from customers for the enterprise's delivery of goods or services. Likewise, cash paid to suppliers and employees may be determined indirectly by adjusting cost of sales and expenses (exclusive of depreciation, interest, and income taxes) for the change during the period in inventories and payables for operating items. That procedure, of course, requires the availability of information concerning the change during the period in the appropriate classes of receivables and payables.[14] The more detailed the categories of operating cash receipts and payments to be reported, the more complex the procedure for determining them. [FAS95, ¶115]

.131 It seems likely that amounts of operating cash receipts and payments at the minimum level of detail specified in paragraph .125 often may be determined indirectly with-

---

[14]For the resulting operating cash receipts and payments to be accurate, the effects of all noncash entries to accounts receivable and payable, inventory, and other balance sheet accounts used in the calculation must be eliminated. For example, the change in accounts receivable would have to be determined exclusive of any bad debt write-offs and other noncash charges and credits to customer accounts during the period. [FAS95, ¶115, fn17]

out incurring unduly burdensome costs over those involved in appropriately applying the indirect method. For example, determining net cash flow from operating activities by the indirect method requires the availability of the total amount of operating receivables. That is, any receivables for investing or financing items must be segregated. Within the total amount of operating receivables, information on receivables from customers for an enterprise's delivery of goods or services may well be available separately from those for interest and dividends. Thus, it may be possible to determine indirectly cash collected from customers and interest and dividends received using much the same information needed to determine net cash flow from operating activities using the indirect method. [FAS95, ¶116]

.132 The same procedure may be used to determine cash paid to suppliers and employees. Determining net cash flow from operating activities by the direct method requires the availability of the total amount of payables pertaining to operating activities. Within that amount, payables to suppliers and employees may well be available separately from those for interest and taxes. [FAS95, ¶117]

.133 Many enterprises may well be able to determine amounts of operating cash receipts and payments at the minimum level of detail that this section encourages (refer to paragraph .125) indirectly at reasonable cost by the procedure discussed in the foregoing paragraphs. The degree of difficulty encountered in applying it undoubtedly would vary depending on the nature of an enterprise's operations and the features of its current accounting system. [FAS95, ¶118]

Information about Noncash Investing and Financing Activities

.134 Information about all investing and financing activities of an enterprise during a period that affect recognized assets or liabilities but that do not result in cash receipts or cash payments in the period shall be reported in related disclosures. Those disclosures may be either narrative or summarized in a schedule. [FAS95, ¶32] If there are only a few such transactions, it may be convenient to include them on the same page as the statement of cash flows. Otherwise, the transactions may be reported elsewhere in the financial statements, clearly referenced to the statement of cash flows. [FAS95, ¶74] [The disclosures] shall clearly relate the cash and noncash aspects of transactions involving similar items. Examples of noncash investing and financing transactions are converting debt to equity; acquiring assets by assuming directly related liabilities, such as purchasing a building by incurring a mortgage to the seller; obtaining an asset by entering into a capital lease; [FAS95, ¶32] obtaining a building or investment asset by receiving a gift; [FAS117, ¶30(g)] and exchanging noncash assets or liabilities for other noncash assets or liabilities. Some transactions are part cash and part noncash; only the cash portion shall be reported in the statement of cash flows. [FAS95, ¶32]

Cash Flow per Share

.135 Financial statements shall not report an amount of cash flow per share. Neither cash flow nor any component of it is an alternative to net income as an indicator of an enterprise's performance, as reporting per share amounts might imply.[15] [FAS95, ¶33]

Exemptions from the Requirement to Provide a Statement of Cash Flows

Employee Benefit Plans

.135A A statement of cash flows is not required to be provided by a defined benefit pension plan that presents financial information in accordance with the provisions of Section Pe5, "Pension Funds: Accounting and Reporting by Defined Benefit Pension Plans."[16] Other employee benefit plans that present financial information similar to that required by Section Pe5 (including the presentation of plan investments at fair value) also are not required to provide a statement of cash flows. Employee benefit plans are encouraged to include a statement of cash flows with their annual financial statements when that statement would provide relevant information about the ability of the plan to meet future obligations (for example, when the plan invests in assets that are not highly liquid or obtains financing for investments). [FAS102, ¶5]

Investment Companies

.135B Provided that the conditions in paragraph .135C are met, a statement of cash flows is not required to be provided by (a) an investment company that is subject to the registration and regulatory requirements of the Investment Company Act of 1940 (1940 Act),[17] (b) an investment enterprise that has essentially the same characteristics

---

[15]Reporting a contractually determined per unit amount, [such as a] per unit amount of cash flow distributable under the terms of a partnership agreement or other agreement between an enterprise and its owners, is not the same as reporting a cash flow per share amount intended to provide information useful to all investors and creditors and thus is not precluded by this section. [FAS95, ¶125]

[16]Paragraph .105 of Section Pe5 presents a comprehensive list of the basic financial statements that defined benefit pension plans are required to provide, although additional financial information may be provided. This section [does not] modify the reporting requirements for [defined benefit pension] plans. [FAS102, ¶15]

[17]Investment companies that are subject to the reporting requirements of the 1940 Act are required to provide a statement of changes in net assets. Net assets and changes in those net assets are relevant because net asset value per share is used by many investment companies to determine the price of shares redeemed and sold. [FAS102, ¶21]

as those subject to the 1940 Act,[18] or (c) a common trust fund, variable annuity account, or similar fund maintained by a bank, insurance company, or other enterprise in its capacity as a trustee, administrator, or guardian for the collective investment and reinvestment of moneys. [FAS102, ¶6]

.135C For an investment enterprise specified in paragraph .135B to be exempt from the requirement to provide a statement of cash flows, all of the following conditions must be met:

a. During the period, substantially all of the enterprise's investments were highly liquid (for example, marketable securities and other assets for which a market is readily available).[19]
b. Substantially all of the enterprise's investments are carried at market value.[20]
c. The enterprise had little or no debt, based on average debt outstanding[21] during the period, in relation to average total assets.
d. The enterprise provides a statement of changes in net assets.[22] [FAS102, ¶7]

Illustrative Examples

.136 Paragraphs .137 through .155 provide illustrations for the preparation of statements of cash flows [FAS95, ¶130] of business enterprises. Paragraph .136 of Section No5, "Not-for-Profit Organizations," provides illustrations for the preparation of statements of cash flows for a not-for-profit organization. [FAS117, ¶ 30(h)] Example 1 (para-

---

[18]Certain investment enterprises have essentially the same characteristics as investment companies that are subject to the requirements of the 1940 Act [but] may not be subject to the registration requirements of the 1940 Act either because the number of stockholders is limited or because they are otherwise exempted from the 1940 Act (for example, offshore funds, commodity pools, certain common trust funds of banks, or variable annuity accounts of life insurance companies). [FAS102, ¶22]

[19]For highly liquid investment companies that do not finance investments with debt, the financial statements other than a statement of cash flows generally provide sufficient information for users to assess the enterprises' liquidity, financial flexibility, profitability, and risk. [FAS102, ¶20]

[20]Securities for which market value is determined using matrix pricing techniques, which are described in the AICPA Audit and Accounting Guide, *Audits of Investment Companies* [3d ed. (1987)], would meet this condition. Other securities for which market value is not readily determinable and for which fair value must be determined in good faith by the board of directors would not. [FAS102, ¶7, fn1]

[21]For the purpose of determining average debt outstanding, obligations resulting from redemptions of shares by the enterprise, from unsettled purchases of securities or similar assets, or from covered options written generally may be excluded. However, any extension of credit by the seller that is not in accordance with standard industry practices for redeeming shares or for settling purchases of investments shall be included in average debt outstanding. [FAS102, ¶7, fn2]

[22]Although the purpose and format of a statement of changes in net assets are different from those of a statement of cash flows, much of the information contained in those statements is similar. [FAS102, ¶21]

graphs .137 through .141) illustrates a statement of cash flows under both the direct method and the indirect method for a domestic manufacturing company. Example 2 (paragraphs .142 through .152) illustrates a statement of cash flows under the direct method for a manufacturing company with foreign operations. Example 3 (paragraphs .153 through .155) illustrates a statement of cash flows under the direct method for a financial institution. These illustrations are intended as examples only. Also, the illustrations of the reconciliation of net income to net cash provided by operating activities may provide detailed information in excess of that required for a meaningful presentation. Other formats or levels of detail may be appropriate for particular circumstances. [FAS95, ¶130]

Example 1

.137 [Exhibits 137A, 137B, and 137C] present a statement of cash flows [and related schedule and disclosures] for the year ended December 31, 19X1 for Company M, a U.S. corporation engaged principally in manufacturing activities. This statement of cash flows illustrates the direct method of presenting cash flows from operating activities, as encouraged in paragraph .125 of this section. [FAS95, ¶131]

(This page intentionally left blank.)

Exhibit 137A

Company M
Consolidated Statement of Cash Flows
For the Year Ended December 31, 19X1

Cash flows from operating activities:		
Cash received from customers	$ 13,850	
Cash paid to suppliers and employees	(12,000)	
Dividend received from affiliate	20	
Interest received	55	
Interest paid (net of amount capitalized)	(220)	
Income taxes paid	(325)	
Insurance proceeds received	15	
Cash paid to settle lawsuit for patent infringement	(30)	
Net cash provided by operating activities		$ 1,365
Cash flows from investing activities:		
Proceeds from sale of facility	600	
Payment received on note for sale of plant	150	
Capital expenditures	(1,000)	
Payment for purchase of Company S, net of cash acquired	(925)	
Net cash used in investing activities		(1,175)
Cash flows from financing activities:		
Net borrowings under line-of-credit agreement	300	
Principal payments under capital lease obligation	(125)	
Proceeds from issuance of long-term debt	400	
Proceeds from issuance of common stock	500	
Dividends paid	(200)	
Net cash provided by financing activities		875
Net increase in cash and cash equivalents		1,065
Cash and cash equivalents at beginning of year		600
Cash and cash equivalents at end of year		$ 1,665

[FAS95, ¶131]

Exhibit 137B

Reconciliation of Net Income to Net Cash
Provided by Operating Activities

Net income		$ 760
Adjustments to reconcile net income to net cash provided by operating activities:		
Depreciation and amortization	$ 445	
Provision for losses on accounts receivable	200	
Gain on sale of facility	(80)	
Undistributed earnings of affiliate	(25)	
Payment received on installment note receivable for sale of inventory	100	
Change in assets and liabilities net of effects from purchase of Company S:		
Increase in accounts receivable	(215)	
Decrease in inventory	205	
Increase in prepaid expenses	(25)	
Decrease in accounts payable and accrued expenses	(250)	
Increase in interest and income taxes payable	50	
Increase in deferred taxes	150	
Increase in other liabilities	50	
Total adjustments		605
Net cash provided by operating activities		$1,365

[FAS95, ¶131]

Exhibit 137C

Disclosures in Financial Statements

Supplemental Schedule of Noncash Investing and Financing Activities

The Company purchased all of the capital stock of Company S for $950. In conjunction with the acquisition, liabilities were assumed as follows:

Fair value of assets acquired	$1,580
Cash paid for the capital stock	(950)
Liabilities assumed	$ 630

A capital lease obligation of $850 was incurred when the Company entered into a lease for new equipment.

Additional common stock was issued upon the conversion of $500 of long-term debt.

Disclosure of Accounting Policy

For purposes of the statement of cash flows, the Company considers all highly liquid debt instruments purchased with a maturity of three months or less to be cash equivalents.

[FAS95, ¶131]

.138 [Exhibits 138A and 138B] present Company M's statement of cash flows [and the related disclosures] for the year ended December 31, 19X1 prepared using the indirect method, as described in paragraph .126 of this section. [FAS95, ¶132]

.139 [Exhibits 139A and 139B] summarize financial information for the current year for Company M, which provides the basis for the statements of cash flows presented in Exhibits 137A and 138A. [FAS95, ¶133]

Exhibit 138A

Company M
Consolidated Statement of Cash Flows
For the Year Ended December 31, 19X1

Cash flows from operating activities:

Net income		$ 760
Adjustments to reconcile net income to net cash provided by operating activities:		
Depreciation and amortization	$ 445	
Provision for losses on accounts receivable	200	
Gain on sale of facility	(80)	
Undistributed earnings of affiliate	(25)	
Payment received on installment note receivable for sale of inventory	100	
Change in assets and liabilities net of effects from purchase of Company S:		
Increase in accounts receivable	(215)	
Decrease in inventory	205	
Increase in prepaid expenses	(25)	
Decrease in accounts payable and accrued expenses	(250)	
Increase in interest and income taxes payable	50	
Increase in deferred taxes	150	
Increase in other liabilities	50	
Total adjustments		605
Net cash provided by operating activities		1,365
Cash flows from investing activities:		
Proceeds from sale of facility	600	
Payment received on note for sale of plant	150	
Capital expenditures	(1,000)	
Payment for purchase of Company S, net of cash acquired	(925)	
Net cash used in investing activities		(1,175)
Cash flows from financing activities:		
Net borrowings under line-of-credit agreement	300	
Principal payments under capital lease obligation	(125)	
Proceeds from issuance of long-term debt	400	
Proceeds from issuance of common stock	500	
Dividends paid	(200)	
Net cash provided by financing activities		875
Net increase in cash and cash equivalents		1,065
Cash and cash equivalents at beginning of year		600
Cash and cash equivalents at end of year		$ 1,665

[FAS95, ¶132]

Exhibit 138B

<h3 style="text-align:center">Disclosures in Financial Statements</h3>

<h3 style="text-align:center">Supplemental Disclosures of Cash Flow Information</h3>

Cash paid during the year for:

Interest (net of amount capitalized)	$220
Income taxes	325

<h3 style="text-align:center">Supplemental Schedule of Noncash Investing and Financing Activities</h3>

The Company purchased all of the capital stock of Company S for $950. In conjunction with the acquisition, liabilities were assumed as follows:

Fair value of assets acquired	$1,580
Cash paid for the capital stock	(950)
Liabilities assumed	$ 630

A capital lease obligation of $850 was incurred when the Company entered into a lease for new equipment.

Additional common stock was issued upon the conversion of $500 of long-term debt.

<h3 style="text-align:center">Disclosure of Accounting Policy</h3>

For purposes of the statement of cash flows, the Company considers all highly liquid debt instruments purchased with a maturity of three months or less to be cash equivalents.

[FAS95, ¶132]

Exhibit 139A

Company M
[Comparative] Consolidated Statements of Financial Position
[January 1 and December 31, 19X1]

	1/1/X1	12/31/X1	Change
Assets:			
Cash and cash equivalents	$ 600	$ 1,665	$1,065
Accounts receivable (net of allowance for losses			
of $600 and $450)	1,770	1,940	170
Notes receivable	400	150	(250)
Inventory	1,230	1,375	145
Prepaid expenses	110	135	25
Investments	250	275	25
Property, plant, and equipment:			
Cost	6,460	8,460	2,000
Accumulated depreciation	(2,100)	(2,300)	(200)
Property, plant, and equipment, net	4,360	6,160	1,800
Intangible assets	40	175	135
Total assets	$ 8,760	$11,875	$3,115
Liabilities:			
Accounts payable and accrued expenses	$ 1,085	$ 1,090	$ 5
Interest payable	30	45	15
Income taxes payable	50	85	35
Short-term debt	450	750	300
Lease obligation	–	725	725
Long-term debt	2,150	2,425	275
Deferred taxes	375	525	150
Other liabilities	225	275	50
Total liabilities	4,365	5,920	1,555
Stockholders' equity:			
Capital stock	2,000	3,000	1,000
Retained earnings	2,395	2,955	560
Total stockholders' equity	4,395	5,955	1,560
Total liabilities and stockholders' equity	$ 8,760	$11,875	$3,115

[FAS95, ¶133]

Exhibit 139B

Company M
Consolidated Statement of Income
For the Year Ended December 31, 19X1

Sales	$ 13,965
Cost of sales	(10,290)
Depreciation and amortization	(445)
Selling, general, and administrative expenses	(1,890)
Interest expense	(235)
Equity in earnings of affiliate	45
Gain on sale of facility	80
Interest income	55
Insurance proceeds	15
Loss from patent infringement lawsuit	(30)
Income before income taxes	1,270
Provision for income taxes	(510)
Net income	$ 760

[FAS95, ¶133]

.140 The following transactions were entered into by Company M during 19X1 and are reflected in the above financial statements:

a. Company M wrote off $350 of accounts receivable when a customer filed for bankruptcy. A provision for losses on accounts receivable of $200 was included in Company M's selling, general, and administrative expenses.

b. Company M collected the third and final annual installment payment of $100 on a note receivable for the sale of inventory and collected the third of four annual installment payments of $150 each on a note receivable for the sale of a plant. Interest on these notes through December 31 totaling $55 was also collected.

c. Company M received a dividend of $20 from an affiliate accounted for under the equity method of accounting.

d. Company M sold a facility with a book value of $520 and an original cost of $750 for $600 cash.

e. Company M constructed a new facility for its own use and placed it in service. Accumulated expenditures during the year of $1,000 included capitalized interest of $10.

f. Company M entered into a capital lease for new equipment with a fair value of $850. Principal payments under the lease obligation totaled $125.

g. Company M purchased all of the capital stock of Company S for $950. The acquisition was recorded under the purchase method of accounting. The fair values of Company S's assets and liabilities at the date of acquisition are presented below:

Cash	$ 25
Accounts receivable	155
Inventory	350
Property, plant, and equipment	900
Patents	80
Goodwill	70
Accounts payable and accrued expenses	(255)
Long-term note payable	(375)
Net assets acquired	$ 950

h. Company M borrowed and repaid various amounts under a line-of-credit agreement in which borrowings are payable 30 days after demand. The net increase during the year in the amount borrowed against the line-of-credit totaled $300.

i. Company M issued $400 of long-term debt securities.

j. Company M's provision for income taxes included a deferred provision of $150.

k. Company M's depreciation totaled $430, and amortization of intangible assets totaled $15.

l. Company M's selling, general, and administrative expenses included an accrual for incentive compensation of $50 that has been deferred by executives until their retirement. The related obligation was included in other liabilities.

m. Company M collected insurance proceeds of $15 from a business interruption claim that resulted when a storm precluded shipment of inventory for one week.

n. Company M paid $30 to settle a lawsuit for patent infringement.

o. Company M issued $1,000 of additional common stock of which $500 was issued for cash and $500 was issued upon conversion of long-term debt.

p. Company M paid dividends of $200. [FAS95, ¶134]

.141 Based on the financial data from the preceding example, the following computations [in Exhibit 141A] illustrate a method of indirectly determining cash received from customers and cash paid to suppliers and employees for use in a statement of cash flows under the direct method. [FAS95, ¶135]

Exhibit 141A

Computation of Cash Received from Customers and Cash Paid to Suppliers and Employees

Cash received from customers during the year:

Customer sales		$13,965
Collection of installment payment for sale of inventory		100
Gross accounts receivable at beginning of year	$ 2,370	
Accounts receivable acquired in purchase of Company S	155	
Accounts receivable written off	(350)	
Gross accounts receivable at end of year	(2,390)	
Excess of new accounts receivable over collections from customers		(215)
Cash received from customers during the year		$13,850

Exhibit 141A (continued)

Cash paid to suppliers and employees during the year:

Cost of sales			$10,290
General and administrative expenses		$ 1,890	
Expenses not requiring cash outlay (provision for uncollectible accounts receivable)		(200)	
Net expenses requiring cash payments			1,690
Inventory at beginning of year		(1,230)	
Inventory acquired in purchase of Company S		(350)	
Inventory at end of year		1,375	
Net decrease in inventory from Company M's operations			(205)
Adjustments for changes in related accruals:			
Account balances at beginning of year:			
Accounts payable and accrued expenses	$1,085		
Other liabilities	225		
Prepaid expenses	(110)		
Total		1,200	
Accounts payable and accrued expenses acquired in purchase of Company S		255	
Account balances at end of year:			
Accounts payable and accrued expenses	1,090		
Other liabilities	275		
Prepaid expenses	(135)		
Total		(1,230)	
Additional cash payments not included in expense			225
Cash paid to suppliers and employees during the year			$12,000

[FAS95, ¶135]

Example 2

.142 [Exhibits 142A, 142B, and 142C] present a consolidating statement of cash flows [and the related disclosures] for the year ended December 31, 19X1 for Company F, a multinational U.S. corporation engaged principally in manufacturing activities, which has two wholly owned foreign subsidiaries—Subsidiary A and Subsidiary B. For Subsidiary A, the local currency is the functional currency. For Subsidiary B, which operates in a highly inflationary economy, the U.S. dollar is the functional currency. [FAS95, ¶136]

Exhibit 142A

Company F
Consolidating Statement of Cash Flows
For the Year Ended December 31, 19X1

	Parent Company	Subsidiary A	Subsidiary B	Eliminations	Consolidated
Cash flows from operating activities:					
Cash received from customers	$ 4,610[a]	$ 888[a]	$ 561[a]	$(430)	$ 5,629
Cash paid to suppliers and employees	(3,756)[a]	(806)[a]	(370)[a]	430	(4,502)
Interest paid	(170)	(86)	(135)	–	(391)
Income taxes paid	(158)	(25)	(21)	–	(204)
Interest and dividends received	57	–	–	(22)	35
Miscellaneous cash received (paid)	–	45	(5)		40
Net cash provided by operating activities	583	16	30	(22)	607
Cash flows from investing activities:					
Proceeds from sale of equipment	150	116	14		280
Payments for purchase of equipment	(450)	(258)	(15)		(723)
Net cash used in investing activities	(300)	(142)	(1)		(443)

Cash flows from financing activities:				
Proceeds from issuance of short-term debt	20	75	–	–	95
Intercompany loan	(15)	–	15	–	–
Proceeds from issuance of long-term debt	–	165	–	–	165
Repayment of long-term debt	(200)	(105)	(35)	–	(340)
Payment of dividends	(120)	(22)	–	22	(120)
Net cash provided by (used in) financing activities	(315)	113	(20)	22	(200)
Effect of exchange rate changes on cash	–	9^b	$(5)^b$	–	4
Net change in cash and cash equivalents	(32)	(4)	4	–	(32)
Cash and cash equivalents at beginning of year	255	15	5	–	275
Cash and cash equivalents at end of year	$ 223	$ 11	$ 9	$ –	$ 243

---

[a] The computation of this amount is provided in paragraph .151.
[b] The computation of this amount is provided in paragraph .152.

[FAS95, ¶136]

Exhibit 142B

Reconciliation of Net Income to Net Cash Provided by Operating Activities

	Parent Company	Subsidiary A	Subsidiary B	Eliminations	Consolidated
Net income	$ 417	$ 50	$ (66)	$(37)	$ 364
Adjustment to reconcile net income to net cash provided by operating activities:					
Depreciation and amortization	350	85	90	–	525
(Gain) loss on sale of equipment	(115)	–	25	–	(90)
Writedown of facility to net realizable value	50	–	–	–	50
Exchange gain	–	–	(115)	–	(115)
Provision for deferred taxes	90	–	–	–	90
Increase in accounts receivable	(85)	(37)	(9)	–	(131)
(Increase) decrease in inventory	(80)	(97)	107	15	(55)
Increase (decrease) in accounts payable and accrued expenses	(41)	16	(6)	–	(31)
Increase (decrease) in interest and taxes payable	(3)	(1)	4	–	–
Net cash provided by operating activities	$ 583	$ 16	$ 30	$(22)	$ 607

[FAS95, ¶136]

Exhibit 142C

Disclosure of Accounting Policy

Cash in excess of daily requirements is invested in marketable securities consisting of Treasury bills with maturities of three months or less. Such investments are deemed to be cash equivalents for purposes of the statement of cash flows.

[FAS95, ¶136]

.143 [Exhibits 143A and 143B] summarize financial information for the current year for Company F, which provides the basis for the statement of cash flows presented in paragraph .142. [FAS95, ¶137]

.144 The U.S. dollar equivalents of one unit of local currency applicable to Subsidiary A and to Subsidiary B are as follows:

	Subsidiary A	Subsidiary B
1/1/X1	.40	.05
Weighted average	.43	.03
12/31/X1	.45	.02

The computation of the weighted-average exchange rate for Subsidiary A excludes the effect of Subsidiary A's sale of inventory to the parent company at the beginning of the year discussed in paragraph .148(a). [FAS95, ¶138]

.145 Comparative statements of financial position for the parent company and for each of the foreign subsidiaries are presented [in Exhibit 145A]. [FAS95, ¶139]

Exhibit 143A

Company F
Consolidating Statement of Financial Position
December 31, 19X1

	Parent Company	Subsidiary A	Subsidiary B	Eliminations	Consolidated
Assets:					
Cash and cash equivalents	$ 223	$ 11	$ 9	$ –	$ 243
Accounts receivable	725	95	20	–	840
Intercompany loan receivable	15	–	–	(15)	–
Inventory	630	281	96	(15)	992
Investments	730	–	–	(730)	–
Property, plant, and equipment, net	3,305	1,441	816	–	5,562
Other assets	160	11	–	–	171
Total assets	$5,788	$1,839	$941	$(760)	$7,808
Liabilities:					
Accounts payable and accrued expenses	$ 529	$ 135	$ 38	$ –	$ 702
Interest payable	35	11	4	–	50
Taxes payable	45	5	2	–	52
Short-term debt	160	135	–	–	295
Intercompany debt	–	–	15	(15)	–
Long-term debt	1,100	315	40	–	1,455
Deferred taxes	342	–	–	–	342
Total liabilities	2,211	601	99	(15)	2,896
Stockholders' equity:					
Capital stock	550	455	275	(730)	550
Retained earnings	3,027	554	567	(15)	4,133
Cumulative translation adjustment	–	229	–	–	229
Total stockholders' equity	3,577	1,238	842	(745)	4,912
Total liabilities and stockholders' equity	$5,788	$1,839	$941	$(760)	$7,808

[FAS95, ¶137]

Exhibit 143B

Company F
Consolidating Statement of Income
For the Year Ended December 31, 19X1

	Parent Company	Subsidiary A	Subsidiary B	Eliminations	Consolidated
Revenues	$ 4,695	$ 925	$ 570	$(430)	$ 5,760
Cost of sales	(3,210)	(615)	(406)	415	(3,816)
Depreciation and amortization	(350)	(85)	(90)	–	(525)
General and administrative expenses	(425)	(110)	(65)	–	(600)
Interest expense	(165)	(90)	(135)	–	(390)
Interest and dividend income	57	–	–	(22)	35
Gain (loss) on sale of equipment	115	–	(25)	–	90
Miscellaneous income (expense)	(50)	45	(5)	–	(10)
Exchange gain	–	–	115	–	115
Income before income taxes	667	70	(41)	(37)	659
Provision for income taxes	(250)	(20)	(25)	–	(295)
Net income	$ 417	$ 50	$ (66)	$ (37)	$ 364

[FAS95, ¶137]

Exhibit 145A

Comparative Statements of Financial Position

	Parent Company			Subsidiary A Local Currency		
	1/1/X1	12/31/X1	Change	1/1/X1	12/31/X1	Change
Assets:						
Cash and cash equivalents	$ 255	$ 223	$ (32)	LC 38	LC 25	LC (13)
Accounts receivables	640	725	85	125	210	85
Intercompany loan receivable	–	15	15	–	–	–
Inventory	550	630	80	400	625	225
Investments	730	730	–	–	–	–
Property, plant, and equipment, net	3,280	3,305	25	3,075	3,202	127
Other assets	170	160	(10)	25	25	–
Total assets	$5,625	$5,788	$ 163	LC3,663	LC4,087	LC 424
Liabilities:						
Accounts payable and accrued expenses	$ 570	$ 529	$ (41)	LC 263	LC 300	LC 37
Interest payable	40	35	(5)	15	24	9
Taxes payable	43	45	2	25	12	(13)
Short-term debt	140	160	20	125	300	175
Intercompany debt	–	–	–	–	–	–
Long-term debt	1,300	1,100	(200)	550	700	150
Deferred taxes	252	342	90	–	–	–
Total liabilities	2,345	2,211	(134)	978	1,336	358
Stockholders' equity:						
Capital stock	550	550	–	1,300	1,300	–
Retained earnings	2,730	3,027	297	1,385	1,451	66
Cumulative translation adjustment	–	–	–	–	–	–
Total stockholders' equity	3,280	3,577	297	2,685	2,751	66
Total liabilities and stockholders' equity	$5,625	$5,788	$ 163	LC3,663	LC4,087	LC 424

[FAS95, ¶139]

	Subsidiary A U.S. Dollars			Subsidiary B Local Currency			Subsidiary B U.S. Dollars		
	1/1/X1	12/31/X1	Change	1/1/X1	12/31/X1	Change	1/1/X1	12/31/X1	Change
	$ 15	$ 11	$ (4)	LC 100	LC 449	LC 349	$ 5	$ 9	$ 4
	50	95	45	700	1,000	300	35	20	(15)
	–	–	–	–	–	–	–	–	–
	160	281	121	2,900	3,200	300	203	96	(107)
	–	–	–	–	–	–	–	–	–
	1,230	1,441	211	6,200	5,900	(300)	930	816	(114)
	10	11	1	–	–	–	–	–	–
	$1,465	$1,839	$374	LC9,900	LC10,549	LC 649	$1,173	$941	$(232)
	$ 105	$ 135	$ 30	LC2,100	LC 1,900	LC (200)	$ 105	$ 38	$ (67)
	6	11	5	200	200	–	10	4	(6)
	10	5	(5)	–	120	120	–	2	2
	50	135	85	–	–	–	–	–	–
	–	–	–	–	500	500	–	15	15
	220	315	95	3,000	2,000	(1,000)	150	40	(110)
	–	–	–	–	–	–	–	–	–
	391	601	210	5,300	4,720	(580)	265	99	(166)
	455	455	–	1,375	1,375	–	275	275	–
	526	554	28	3,225	4,454	1,229	633	567	(66)
	93	229	136	–	–	–	–	–	–
	1,074	1,238	164	4,600	5,829	1,229	908	842	(66)
	$1,465	$1,839	$374	LC9,900	LC10,549	LC 649	$1,173	$941	$(232)

.146 Statements of income in local currency and U.S. dollars for each of the foreign subsidiaries are presented [in Exhibit 146A]. [FAS95, ¶140]

Exhibit 146A

Statements of Income
For the Year Ended December 31, 19X1

	Subsidiary A		Subsidiary B	
	Local Currency	U.S. Dollars	Local Currency	U.S. Dollars
Revenues	LC2,179	$ 925[a]	LC19,000	$ 570
Cost of sales	(1,458)	(615)[b]	(9,667)	(406)
Depreciation and amortization	(198)	(85)	(600)	(90)
General and administrative expenses	(256)	(110)	(2,167)	(65)
Interest expense	(209)	(90)	(4,500)	(135)
Gain (loss) on sale of equipment	–	–	150	(25)
Miscellaneous income (expense)	105	45	(167)	(5)
Exchange gain	–	–	–	115
Income before income taxes	163	70	2,049	(41)
Provision for income taxes	(47)	(20)	(820)	(25)
Net income	LC 116	$ 50	LC 1,229	$ (66)

[a]This amount was computed as follows:

Sale to parent company at beginning of year	LC 400 @ .40	=	$160
Sales to customers	LC1,779 @ .43	=	765
Total sales in U.S. dollars			$925

[b]This amount was computed as follows:

Cost of sale to parent company at beginning of year	LC 400 @ .40	=	$160
Cost of sales to customers	LC1,058 @ .43	=	455
Total cost of sales in U.S. dollars			$615

[FAS95, ¶140]

.147 The following transactions were entered into during the year by the parent company and are reflected in the above financial statements:

a. The parent company invested cash in excess of daily requirements in Treasury bills. Interest earned on such investments totaled $35.
b. The parent company sold excess property with a net book value of $35 for $150.
c. The parent company's capital expenditures totaled $450.
d. The parent company wrote down to its estimated net realizable value of $25 a facility with a net book value of $75.
e. The parent company's short-term debt consisted of commercial paper with maturities not exceeding 60 days.
f. The parent company repaid long-term notes of $200.
g. The parent company's depreciation totaled $340, and amortization of intangible assets totaled $10.
h. The parent company's provision for income taxes included deferred taxes of $90.
i. Because of a change in product design, the parent company purchased all of Subsidiary A's beginning inventory for its book value of $160. All of the inventory was subsequently sold by the parent company.
j. The parent company received a dividend of $22 from Subsidiary A. The dividend was credited to the parent company's income.
k. The parent company purchased from Subsidiary B $270 of merchandise of which $45 remained in the parent company's inventory at year-end. Intercompany profit on the remaining inventory totaled $15.
l. The parent company loaned $15, payable in U.S. dollars, to Subsidiary B.
m. Company F paid dividends totaling $120 to shareholders. [FAS95, ¶141]

.148 The following transactions were entered into during the year by Subsidiary A and are reflected in the above financial statements. The U.S. dollar equivalent of the local currency amount based on the exchange rate at the date of each transaction is included. Except for the sale of inventory to the parent company (transaction (a) below), Subsidiary A's sales and purchases and operating cash receipts and payments occurred evenly throughout the year.

a. Because of a change in product design, Subsidiary A sold all of its beginning inventory to the parent company for its book value of LC400 ($160).
b. Subsidiary A sold equipment for its book value of LC275 ($116) and purchased new equipment at a cost of LC600 ($258).
c. Subsidiary A issued an additional LC175 ($75) of 30-day notes and renewed the notes at each maturity date.
d. Subsidiary A issued long-term debt of LC400 ($165) and repaid long-term debt of LC250 ($105).
e. Subsidiary A paid a dividend to the parent company of LC50 ($22). [FAS95, ¶142]

.149 The following transactions were entered into during the year by Subsidiary B and are reflected in the above financial statements. The U.S. dollar equivalent of the local currency amount based on the exchange rate at the date of each transaction is included. Subsidiary B's sales and operating cash receipts and payments occurred evenly throughout the year. For convenience, all purchases of inventory were based on the weighted-average exchange rate for the year. Subsidiary B uses the FIFO method of inventory valuation.

a. Subsidiary B had sales to the parent company as follows:

	Local Currency	U.S. Dollars
Intercompany sales	LC 9,000	$ 270
Cost of sales	(4,500)	(180)
Gross profit	LC 4,500	$ 90

b. Subsidiary B sold equipment with a net book value of LC200 ($39) for LC350 ($14). New equipment was purchased at a cost of LC500 ($15).
c. Subsidiary B borrowed $15 (LC500), payable in U.S. dollars, from the parent company.
d. Subsidiary B repaid LC1,000 ($35) of long-term debt. [FAS95, ¶143]

.150 Statements of cash flows in the local currency and in U.S. dollars for Subsidiary A and Subsidiary B, [and related reconciliation of net cash provided by operating activities,] are presented [in Exhibits 150A and 150B]. [FAS95, ¶144]

(This page intentionally left blank.)

Exhibit 150A

Statement of Cash Flows
For the Year Ended December 31, 19X1

	Subsidiary A		Subsidiary B	
	Local Currency	U.S. Dollars	Local Currency	U.S. Dollars
Cash flows from operating activities:				
Cash received from customers	LC2,094[a]	$ 888[a]	LC18,700[a]	$ 561[a]
Cash paid to suppliers and employees	(1,902)[a]	(806)[a]	(12,334)[a]	(370)[a]
Interest paid	(200)	(86)[b]	(4,500)	(135)[b]
Income taxes paid	(60)	(25)[b]	(700)	(21)[b]
Miscellaneous receipts (payments)	105	45[b]	(167)	(5)[b]
Net cash provided by operating activities	37	16	999	30
Cash flows from investing activities:				
Proceeds from sale of equipment	275	116[c]	350	14[c]
Payments for purchase of equipment	(600)	(258)[c]	(500)	(15)[c]
Net cash used in investing activities	(325)	(142)	(150)	(1)
Cash flows from financing activities:				
Net increase in short-term debt	175	75[c]	–	–
Proceeds from intercompany loan	–	–	500	15[c]
Proceeds from issuance of long-term debt	400	165[c]	–	–
Repayment of long-term debt	(250)	(105)[c]	(1,000)	(35)[c]
Payment of dividends	(50)	(22)[c]	–	–
Net cash provided by (used in) financing activities	275	113	(500)	(20)
Effect of exchange rate changes on cash	–	9[d]	–	(5)[d]
Net increase (decrease) in cash	(13)	(4)	349	4
Cash at beginning of year	38	15	100	5
Cash at end of year	LC 25	$ 11	LC 449	$ 9

[a]The computation of this amount is provided in paragraph .151.

[b]This amount represents the U.S. dollar equivalent of the foreign currency cash flow based on the weighted-average exchange rate for the year.

[c]This amount represents the U.S. dollar equivalent of the foreign currency cash flow based on the exchange rate in effect at the time of the cash flow.

[d]The computation of this amount is provided in paragraph .152.

[FAS95, ¶144]

Exhibit 150B

Reconciliation of Net Income to Net Cash Provided by Operating Activities

	Subsidiary A		Subsidiary B	
	Local Currency	U.S. Dollars	Local Currency	U.S. Dollars
Net income	LC116	$ 50	LC1,229	$ (66)
Adjustments to reconcile net income to net cash provided by operating activities:				
Depreciation and amortization	198	85[a]	600	90[b]
(Gain) loss on sale of equipment	–	–	(150)	25[b]
Exchange gain	–	–	–	(115)[c]
Increase in accounts receivable	(85)	(37)[a]	(300)	(9)[a]
(Increase) decrease in inventory	(225)	(97)[a]	(300)	107[d]
Increase (decrease) in accounts payable and accrued expenses	37	16[a]	(200)	(6)[a]
Increase (decrease) in interest and taxes payable	(4)	(1)[a]	120	4[a]
Net cash provided by operating activities	LC 37	$ 16	LC 999	$ 30

[a]This amount represents the U.S. dollar equivalent of the foreign currency amount based on the weighted-average exchange rate for the year.

[b]This amount represents the U.S. dollar equivalent of the foreign currency amount based on historical exchange rates.

[c]This amount represents the exchange gain included in net income as a result of remeasuring Subsidiary B's financial statements from the local currency to U.S. dollars.

[d]This amount represents the difference between beginning and ending inventory after remeasurement into U.S. dollars based on historical exchange rates.

[FAS95, ¶144]

.151 Exhibit 151A presents the computation of cash received from customers and cash paid to suppliers and employees as reported in the consolidating statement of cash flows for Company F appearing in paragraph .142. [FAS95, ¶145]

.152 [Exhibit 152A] presents the computation of the effect of exchange rate changes on cash for Subsidiary A and Subsidiary B. [FAS95, ¶146]

Exhibit 151A

Computation of Cash Received from Customers and Cash Paid to Suppliers and Employees

	Parent Company	Subsidiary A		Subsidiary B	
		Local Currency	U.S. Dollars	Local Currency	U.S. Dollars
Cash received from customers during the year:					
Revenues	$4,695	LC2,179	$925	LC19,000	$ 570
Increase in accounts receivable	(85)	(85)	(37)	(300)	(9)
Cash received from customers	$4,610	LC2,094	$888	LC18,700	$ 561
Cash paid to suppliers and employees during the year:					
Cost of sales	$3,210	LC1,458	$615	L C9,667	$ 406
Effect of exchange rate changes on cost of sales	–	–	–	–	(116)a
General and administrative expenses	425	256	110	2,167	65
Total operating expenses requiring cash payments	3,635	1,714	725	11,834	355
Increase in inventory	80	225	97	300	9
Decrease (increase) in accounts payable and accrued expenses	41	(37)	(16)	200	6
Cash paid to suppliers and employees	$3,756	LC1,902	$806	LC12,334	$ 370

---

aThis adjustment represents the difference between cost of sales remeasured at historical exchange rates ($406) and cost of sales translated based on the weighted-average exchange rate for the year ($290). The adjustment is necessary because cash payments for inventory, which were made evenly throughout the year, were based on the weighted-average exchange rate for the year.

[FAS95, ¶145]

Exhibit 152A

Computation of the Effect of Exchange Rate Changes on Cash

	Subsidiary A		Subsidiary B	
Effect on beginning cash balance:				
Beginning cash balance in local currency	LC 38		LC 100	
Net change in exchange rate during the year	× .05		× (.03)	
Effect on beginning cash balance		$ 2		$ (3)
Effect from operating activities during the year:				
Cash provided by operating activities in local currency	LC 37		LC 999	
Year-end exchange rate	× 45		× .02	
Operating cash flows based on year-end exchange rate	$ 16[a]		$ 20	
Operating cash flows reported in the statement of cash flows	16		30	
Effect from operating activities during the year		0		(10)
Effect from investing activities during the year:				
Cash used in investing activities in local currency	LC(325)		LC(150)	
Year-end exchange rate	× .45		× .02	
Investing cash flows based on year-end exchange rate	$ (146)		$ (3)	
Investing cash flows reported in the statement of cash flows	(142)		(1)	
Effect from investing activities during the year		(4)		(2)
Effect from financing activities during the year:				
Cash provided by (used in) financing activities in local currency	LC 275		LC(500)	
Year-end exchange rate	× .45		× .02	
Financing cash flows based on year-end exchange rate	$ 124		$ (10)	
Financing cash flows reported in the statement of cash flows	113		(20)	
Effect from financing activities during the year		11		10
Effect of exchange rate changes on cash		$ 9		$ (5)

---

[a]This amount includes the effect of rounding.

[FAS95, ¶146]

Example 3

.153 [Exhibits 153A, 153B, and 153C] present a statement of cash flows [and related schedule and disclosures] for Financial Institution, Inc., a U.S. corporation that provides a broad range of financial services. This statement of cash flows illustrates the direct method of presenting cash flows from operating activities, as encouraged in paragraph .125 of this section. [FAS95, ¶147]

.154 [Exhibits 154A and 154B] summarize financial information for the current year for Financial Institution, Inc., which provides the basis for the statement of cash flows presented in paragraph .153. [FAS95, ¶148]

(This page intentionally left blank.)

Exhibit 153A

Financial Institution, Inc.
Statement of Cash Flows
For the Year Ended December 31, 19X1

Cash flows from operating activities:		
Interest received	$ 5,350	
Fees and commissions received	1,320	
Proceeds from sales of trading securities	20,550	
Purchase of trading securities	(21,075)	
Financing revenue received under leases	60	
Interest paid	(3,925)	
Cash paid to suppliers and employees	(795)	
Income taxes paid	(471)	
Net cash provided by operating activities		$ 1,014
Cash flows from investing activities:		
Proceeds from sales of investment securities	2,225	
Purchase of investment securities	(4,000)	
Net increase in credit card receivables	(1,300)	
Net decrease in customer loans with maturities of		
3 months or less	2,250	
Principal collected on longer term loans	26,550	
Longer term loans made to customers	(36,300)	
Purchase of assets to be leased	(1,500)	
Principal payments received under leases	107	
Capital expenditures	(450)	
Proceeds from sale of property, plant, and equipment	260	
Net cash used in investing activities		(12,158)
Cash flows from financing activities:		
Net increase in demand deposits, NOW accounts, and		
savings accounts	3,000	
Proceeds from sales of certificates of deposit	63,000	
Payments for maturing certificates of deposit	(61,000)	
Net increase in federal funds purchased	4,500	
Net increase in 90-day borrowings	50	
Proceeds from issuance of nonrecourse debt	600	
Principal payment on nonrecourse debt	(20)	
Proceeds from issuance of 6-month note	100	
Proceeds from issuance of long-term debt	1,000	
Repayment of long-term debt	(200)	
Proceeds from issuance of common stock	350	
Payments to acquire treasury stock	(175)	
Dividends paid	(240)	
Net cash provided by financing activities		10,965
Net decrease in cash and cash equivalents		(179)
Cash and cash equivalents at beginning of year		6,700
Cash and cash equivalents at end of year		$ 6,521

[FAS102, ¶30]

Exhibit 153B

Reconciliation of Net Income
to Net Cash Provided by Operating Activities

Net income		$1,056
Adjustments to reconcile net income to net cash provided by operating activities:		
Depreciation	$ 100	
Provision for probable credit losses	300	
Provision for deferred taxes	58	
Loss on sales of investment securities	75	
Gain on sale of equipment	(50)	
Increase in trading securities (including unrealized appreciation of $25)	(700)	
Increase in taxes payable	175	
Increase in interest receivable	(150)	
Increase in interest payable	75	
Decrease in fees and commissions receivable	20	
Increase in accrued expenses	55	
Total adjustments		(42)
Net cash provided by operating activities		$1,014

[FAS102, ¶30]

Exhibit 153C

Disclosures in Financial Statements

Supplemental Schedule of Noncash Investing and Financing Activities

Conversion of long-term debt to common stock	$500

Disclosure of Accounting Policy

For purposes of reporting cash flows, cash and cash equivalents include cash on hand, amounts due from banks, and federal funds sold. Generally, federal funds are purchased and sold for one-day periods. [FAS95, ¶147]

Exhibit 154A

Financial Institution, Inc.
[Comparative] Statements of Financial Position
[January 1 and December 31, 19X1]

	1/1/X1	12/31/X1	Change
Assets:			
Cash and due from banks	$ 4,400	$ 3,121	$ (1,279)
Federal funds sold	2,300	3,400	1,100
Total cash and cash equivalents	6,700	6,521	(179)
Trading securities	4,000	4,700	700
Investment securities	5,000	6,700	1,700
Credit card receivables	8,500	9,800	1,300
Loans	28,000	35,250	7,250
Allowance for credit losses	(800)	(850)	(50)
Interest receivable	600	750	150
Fees and commissions receivable	60	40	(20)
Investment in direct financing lease	–	421	421
Investment in leveraged lease	–	392	392
Property, plant, and equipment, net	525	665	140
Total assets	$52,585	$64,389	$11,804
Liabilities:			
Deposits	$38,000	$43,000	$ 5,000
Federal funds purchased	7,500	12,000	4,500
Short-term borrowings	1,200	1,350	150
Interest payable	350	425	75
Accrued expenses	275	330	55
Taxes payable	75	250	175
Dividends payable	–	80	80
Long-term debt	2,000	2,300	300
Deferred taxes	–	58	58
Total liabilities	49,400	59,793	10,393
Stockholders' equity:			
Common stock	1,250	2,100	850
Treasury stock	–	(175)	(175)
Retained earnings	1,935	2,671	736
Total stockholders' equity	3,185	4,596	1,411
Total liabilities and stockholders' equity	$52,585	$64,389	$11,804

[FAS102, ¶31]

Exhibit 154B

Financial Institution, Inc.
Statement of Income
For the Year Ended December 31, 19X1

Revenues:
Interest income	$5,500	
Fees and commissions	1,300	
Net gain on sales of trading and investment securities	75	
Unrealized appreciation of trading securities	25	
Lease income	60	
Gain on sale of equipment	50	
Total revenues		$7,010

Expenses:
Interest expense	4,000	
Provision for probable credit losses	300	
Operating expenses	850	
Depreciation	100	
Total expenses		5,250
Income before income taxes		1,760
Provision for income taxes		704
Net income		$1,056

[FAS102, ¶31]

.155 The following transactions were entered into by Financial Institution, Inc., during 19X1 and are reflected in the above financial statements [FAS95, ¶149]:

a. Financial Institution sold trading securities with a carrying value of $20,400 for $20,550 and purchased trading securities for $21,075. Financial Institution recorded unrealized appreciation of trading securities of $25. Financial Institution also sold investment securities with a carrying value of $2,300 for $2,225 and purchased investment securities for $4,000. [FAS102, ¶32]

b. Financial Institution had a net decrease in short-term loans receivable (those with original maturities of 3 months or less) of $2,250. Financial Institution made longer term loans of $36,300 and collected $26,550 on those loans. Financial Institution wrote off $250 of loans as uncollectible.

c. Financial Institution purchased property for $500 to be leased under a direct financing lease. The first annual rental payment of $131 was collected. The portion of the rental payment representing interest income totaled $52.

d. Financial Institution purchased equipment for $1,000 to be leased under a leveraged lease. The cost of the leased asset was financed by an equity investment of $400 and a long-term nonrecourse bank loan of $600. The first annual rental payment of $90, of which $28 represented principal, was collected and the first annual loan installment of $74, of which $20 represented principal, was paid. Pretax income of $8 was recorded.

e. Financial Institution purchased new property, plant, and equipment for $450 and sold property, plant, and equipment with a book value of $210 for $260.

f. Customer deposits with Financial Institution consisted of the following:

	1/1/X1	12/31/X1	Increase
Demand deposits	$ 8,000	$ 8,600	$ 600
NOW accounts and savings accounts	15,200	17,600	2,400
Certificates of deposit	14,800	16,800	2,000
Total deposits	$38,000	$43,000	$5,000

Sales of certificates of deposit during the year totaled $63,000; certificates of deposit with principal amounts totaling $61,000 matured. For presentation in the statement of cash flows, Financial Institution chose to report gross cash receipts and payments for both certificates of deposit with maturities of three months or less and those with maturities of more than three months.

g. Short-term borrowing activity for Financial Institution consisted of repayment of a $200 90-day note and issuance of a 90-day note for $250 and a 6-month note for $100.

h. Financial Institution repaid $200 of long-term debt and issued 5-year notes for $600 and 10-year notes for $400.

i. Financial Institution issued $850 of common stock, $500 of which was issued upon conversion of long-term debt and $350 of which was issued for cash.

j. Financial Institution acquired $175 of treasury stock.

k. Financial Institution declared dividends of $320. The fourth quarter dividend of $80 was payable the following January.

l. Financial Institution's provision for income taxes included a deferred provision of $58.

m. In accordance with paragraph .105, footnote 2, of this section, interest paid includes amounts credited directly to demand deposit, NOW, and savings accounts. [FAS95, ¶149]

(The next page is 6601.)

CHANGING PRICES: REPORTING THEIR EFFECTS IN FINANCIAL REPORTS

Sources: FASB Statement 89; FASB Statement 109

Summary

This section encourages supplementary disclosure of current cost/constant purchasing power information.

Disclosure

.101 A business enterprise that prepares its financial statements in U.S. dollars and in accordance with U.S. generally accepted accounting principles is encouraged, but not required, to disclose supplementary information on the effects of changing prices. This section provides measurement and presentation guidelines for disclosure. Entities are not discouraged from experimenting with other forms of disclosure. [FAS89, ¶3]

.102 [The following paragraphs present guidance for the presentation and measurement of supplementary information on effects of changing prices:]

	Paragraph Numbers
Presentation	.103–.111
Five-Year Summary of Selected Financial Data	.103–.106
Additional Disclosures for the Current Year	.107–.109
Additional Disclosures by Enterprises with Mineral Resource Assets	.110–.111
Measurement	.112–.139
Inventory and Property, Plant, and Equipment	.112–.118
Specialized Assets	.119–.122
Net Assets	.123–.124
Recoverable Amount	.125–.127
Income from Continuing Operations	.128–.129
Increase or Decrease in the Current Cost Amounts of Inventory and Property, Plant, and Equipment, Net of Inflation	.130–.131
Restatement of Current Cost Information into Units of Constant Purchasing Power	.132–.133
Translation Adjustment	.134–.135
Purchasing Power Gain or Loss on Net Monetary Items	.136–.139

Illustrations of Disclosures .... .140

Illustrative Calculations of Current Cost/Constant Purchasing Power
Information .... .141–.190

  Introduction.. .141–.148

  Parent Company Information .... .149–.153

  Parent Company Calculations .... .154–.167

    Step 1: Analysis of Inventory and Cost of Goods Sold .... .155

    Step 2: Current Cost of Inventory and Cost of Goods Sold 156–.157

    Step 3: Analysis of Property, Plant, and Equipment and Depreciation ... .158

    Step 4: Current Cost of Property, Plant, and Equipment and
    Depreciation.. .159

    Step 5: Identification of Net Monetary Items .... .160

    Step 6: Computation of the Purchasing Power Gain or Loss on Net
    Monetary Items... .161

    Step 7: Computation of the Change in Current Cost of Inventory and
    Property, Plant, and Equipment and the Effect of General Price-
    Level Changes .... .162–.165

    Summary of Increase in Current Cost Amounts .... .166

    Check of Calculations.. .167

  Sub Company Information .... .168–.173

  Sub Company Calculations: Translate-Restate Method .... .174–.180

    Current Cost Depreciation and Income from Continuing Operations..... .175–.176

    Excess of Increase in Specific Prices over Increase in General Price
    Level .... .177

    Purchasing Power Gain or Loss on Net Monetary Items .... .178

    Check of Calculations.. .179

    Translation Adjustment.. .180

  Consolidation: Translate-Restate Method.. .181–.182

  Sub Company Calculations: Restate-Translate Method .... .183–.190

    Current Cost Depreciation and Income from Continuing Operations..... .184

    Purchasing Power Gain or Loss on Net Monetary Items .... .185

    Excess of Increase in Specific Prices over Increase in General Price
    Level .... .186

    Check of Calculations.. .187–.188

    Translation Adjustment.. .189

    Parity Adjustment .... .190

Monetary and Nonmonetary Items.. .191–.203

[Consumer Price Index .... .204]

Glossary .... .401–.419

[FAS89, Appendix A]

Presentation

Five-Year Summary of Selected Financial Data

.103 An enterprise shall[1] disclose the following information[2] for each of the five most recent years[3] (paragraphs .132 and .133):

a. Net sales and other operating revenues
b. **Income from continuing operations** on a current cost basis (paragraphs .128 and .129)
c. **Purchasing power gain or loss** on net monetary items (paragraphs .136 through .139)
d. Increase or decrease in the current cost or lower **recoverable amount** of inventory and property, plant, and equipment,[4] net of inflation (paragraphs .130 and .131)
e. The aggregate foreign currency **translation adjustment** on a current cost basis, if applicable (paragraphs .105, .134, and .135)
f. Net assets at year-end on a current cost basis (paragraphs .123 and .124)
g. Income per common share from continuing operations on a current cost basis
h. Cash dividends declared per common share
i. Market price per common share at year-end.

[FAS89, ¶7]

---

[1]This section uses the word] "shall" even though the presentations and measurements described are now voluntary. [FAS89, ¶5, fn1]

[2]An enterprise that presents consolidated financial statements shall present the information required by this section on the same consolidated basis. The information required by this section need not be presented for a parent company, an investee company, or other enterprise in a financial report that includes the results for that enterprise in consolidated financial statements. [FAS89, ¶7, fn2]

[3]The information required by this section shall be presented as supplementary information in any published annual report that contains the primary financial statements of the enterprise except that the information need not be presented in an interim financial report. The information required by this section need not be presented for segments of a business enterprise although such presentations are encouraged. [FAS89, ¶7, fn3]

[4]For the purposes of this section, except where otherwise provided, "inventory" and "property, plant, and equipment" shall include land and other natural resources and capitalized leasehold interests but *not* goodwill or other intangible assets. [FAS89, ¶7, fn5]

.104 The information presented in the five-year summary shall be stated as either of the following:

a. In average-for-the-year or end-of-year units of constant purchasing power
b. In dollars[5] having a purchasing power equal to that of dollars of the base period used by the Bureau of Labor Statistics in calculating the Consumer Price Index for All Urban Consumers (CPI-U)[6] (currently 1967).

An enterprise shall disclose the level of the CPI-U used for each of the five most recent years. [FAS89, ¶8]

.105 If the enterprise has a significant foreign operation measured in a functional currency other than the U.S. dollar (dollar), it shall disclose whether adjustments to the current cost information to reflect the effects of general inflation are based on the U.S. general price level index (the **translate-restate** method, paragraph .134) or on a functional currency general price level index (the **restate-translate** method, paragraph .135). [FAS89, ¶9]

.106 The enterprise shall provide an explanation of the disclosures required by this section and a discussion of their significance in the circumstances of the enterprise. Disclosure and discussion of additional information to help users of the financial report understand the effects of changing prices on the activities of the enterprise are encouraged. [FAS89, ¶10]

Additional Disclosures for the Current Year

.107 In addition to the information required by paragraphs .103 through .106, an enterprise shall provide the information specified in paragraphs .108 and .109 if income from continuing operations on a **current cost/constant purchasing power** basis would differ significantly from income from continuing operations in the primary financial statements. [FAS89, ¶11]

---

[5]As a practical matter, this option is not available to enterprises that measure a significant part of their operations in one or more functional currencies other than the U.S. dollar and that elect to use the restate-translate method (paragraph .135) for measuring inflation-adjusted current cost information. [FAS89, ¶8, fn6]

[6][Refer to paragraph .204.] The index is published in *Monthly Labor Review*. Those desiring prompt and direct information may subscribe to the Consumer Price Index press release mailing list of the Department of Labor. If the level of the Consumer Price Index at the end of the year and the data required to compute the average level of the index over the year have not been published in time for preparation of the annual report, they may be estimated by referring to published forecasts based on economic statistics or by extrapolation based on recently reported changes in the index. [FAS89, ¶8, fn7]

.108 An enterprise shall disclose certain components of income from continuing operations for the current year on a current cost basis (paragraphs .128 and .129) applying the same constant purchasing power option used for presentation of the five-year summary. The information may be presented in a *statement format* (disclosing revenues, expenses, gains, and losses), in a *reconciliation format* (disclosing adjustments to the income from continuing operations that is shown in the primary income statement), or in notes to the five-year summary required by paragraph .103. Formats for presenting the supplementary information are illustrated in paragraph .140. Whichever format is used, the presentation shall disclose (for example, in a reconciliation format) or allow the reader to determine (for example, in a statement format) the difference between the amount in the primary statements and the current cost amount of the following items: cost of goods sold and depreciation, depletion, and amortization expense. If depreciation has been allocated among various expense categories in the supplementary computations of income from continuing operations (for example, among cost of goods sold and other functional expenses), the aggregate amount of depreciation on a current cost basis shall be included in the notes to the supplementary information. In addition to information about income from continuing operations, the enterprise may include the following items in a schedule of current year information: (a) the purchasing power gain or loss on net monetary items, (b) the increase or decrease in the current cost or lower recoverable amount of inventory and property, plant, and equipment, net of inflation, and (c) the translation adjustment. As illustrated in paragraph .140 and defined in the glossary in paragraph .405, income from continuing operations does not include items (a), (b), or (c). [FAS89, ¶12]

.109 An enterprise shall also disclose:

a. Separate amounts for the current cost or lower recoverable amount at the end of the current year of inventory and property, plant, and equipment (paragraphs .112 through .122 and .125 through .127)

b. The increase or decrease in current cost or lower recoverable amount before and after adjusting for the effects of inflation of inventory and property, plant, and equipment for the current year (paragraphs .130 and .131)

c. The principal types of information used to calculate the current cost of inventory; property, plant, and equipment; cost of goods sold; and depreciation, depletion, and amortization expense (paragraphs .115 through .122)

d. Any differences between (1) the depreciation methods, estimates of useful lives, and salvage values of assets used for calculations of current cost/constant purchasing power depreciation and (2) the methods and estimates used for calculations of depreciation in the primary financial statements (paragraph .118).

[FAS89, ¶13]

Additional Disclosures by Enterprises with Mineral Resource Assets

.110 For its mineral reserves other than oil and gas, an enterprise shall disclose the following additional information for each of its five most recent fiscal years:

a. Estimates of significant quantities of **proved mineral reserves** or proved and **probable mineral reserves** (whichever is used for cost amortization purposes) at the end of the year or at the most recent date during the year for which estimates can be made (If estimates are not made as of the end of the year, the disclosures shall indicate the dates of the estimates.)
b. The estimated quantity, expressed in physical units or in percentages of reserves, of each mineral product that is recoverable in significant commercial quantities if the mineral reserves included under subparagraph (a) include deposits containing one or more significant mineral products
c. The quantities of each significant mineral produced during the year (If the mineral reserves included under subparagraph (a) are ones that are milled or similarly processed, the quantity of each significant mineral product produced by the milling or similar process shall also be disclosed.)
d. The quantity of significant proved, or proved and probable, mineral reserves purchased or sold in place during the year
e. For each significant mineral product, the average market price or, for mineral products transferred within the enterprise, the equivalent market price prior to use in a manufacturing process.

[FAS89, ¶14]

.111 In determining the quantities to be reported in conformity with paragraph .110:

a. If the enterprise issues consolidated financial statements, 100 percent of the quantities attributable to the parent company and 100 percent of the quantities attributable to its consolidated subsidiaries (whether or not wholly owned) shall be included.
b. If the enterprise's financial statements include investments that are proportionately consolidated, the enterprise's quantities shall include its proportionate share of the investee's quantities.
c. If the enterprise's financial statements include investments that are accounted for by the equity method, the investee's quantities shall not be included in the disclosures of the enterprise's quantities. However, the enterprise's (investor's) share of the investee's quantities of reserves shall be reported separately, if significant.

[FAS89, ¶15]

Measurement

Inventory and Property, Plant, and Equipment

.112 Current cost amounts of inventory and property, plant, and equipment are measured as follows:

a. Inventory at current cost or lower recoverable amount at the measurement date
b. Property, plant, and equipment at the current cost or lower recoverable amount of the assets' remaining service potential at the measurement date
c. Resources used on a partly completed contract at current cost or lower recoverable amount at the date of use on or commitment to the contract.

[FAS89, ¶16]

.113 The current cost of inventory owned by an enterprise is the current cost of purchasing the goods concerned or the current cost of the resources required to produce the goods concerned (including an allowance for the current overhead costs according to the allocation bases used under generally accepted accounting principles), whichever would be applicable in the circumstances of the enterprise. [FAS89, ¶17]

.114 The current cost of property, plant, and equipment owned by an enterprise is the current cost of acquiring the same service potential (indicated by operating costs and physical output capacity) as embodied by the asset owned; the information used to measure current cost reflects whatever method of acquisition would currently be appropriate in the circumstances of the enterprise. The current cost of a used asset may be calculated:

a. By measuring the current cost of a new asset that has the same service potential as the used asset had when it was new (the current cost of the asset as if it were new) and deducting an allowance for depreciation
b. By measuring the current cost of a used asset of the same age and in the same condition as the asset owned
c. By measuring the current cost of a new asset with a different service potential and adjusting that cost for the value of the difference in service potential due to differences in life, output capacity, nature of service, and operating costs.

[FAS89, ¶18]

.115 Various types of information may be used in the measurement methods described in paragraphs .113 and .114 to determine the current cost of inventory; property, plant, and equipment; cost of goods sold;[7] and depreciation, depletion, and amortization expense. The information may be applied to single items or broad categories, as appropriate in the circumstances. The following types of information are listed as examples of the information that may be used but are *not* listed in any order of preferability. The enterprise is expected to select types of information appropriate to its particular circumstances, giving due consideration to their availability, reliability, and cost:

a. Indexation
   (1) Externally generated price indexes for the class of goods or services being measured
   (2) Internally generated price indexes for the class of goods or services being measured
b. Direct pricing
   (1) Current invoice prices
   (2) Vendors' price lists or other quotations or estimates
   (3) Standard manufacturing costs that reflect current costs.

[FAS89, ¶19]

.116 An enterprise may substitute **historical cost** amounts adjusted by an externally generated price index of a broad-based measure of general purchasing power (that is, **historical cost/constant purchasing power** amounts) for current cost amounts if that substitution would not result in a significantly different number for income from continuing operations than other means of estimating current cost amounts described in this section. For example, an enterprise with small amounts of inventory and property, plant, and equipment apart from certain specialized assets (paragraphs .119 through .122) may be able to report historical cost/constant purchasing power information. In such circumstances, disclosure of the increase or decrease in the current cost or lower recoverable amount of inventory and property, plant, and equipment, net of inflation (paragraphs .103(d) and .109(b)), is not required, but the discussions described in paragraphs .106 and .109(a), (c), and (d) are required. [FAS89, ¶20]

.117 Current cost measurements are to be based on production or purchase of the asset in whatever location or market would minimize total cost including transportation cost. For a U.S. operation, either (a) the purchase would be made in the United States and current cost would be estimated directly in dollars or (b) the purchase would be made in

---

[7]If turnover is rapid and material amounts of depreciation are not allocated to inventory, cost of goods sold measured on a Last-In, First-Out (LIFO) basis may provide an acceptable approximation of cost of goods sold, measured at current cost, provided that the effect of any LIFO inventory liquidations (that is, any decreases in earlier years' LIFO layers) is excluded. [FAS89, ¶19, fn8]

a foreign market and the current cost in that market would be translated into dollars at the current exchange rate. An enterprise may need to measure the current cost of inventory and property, plant, and equipment located outside the United States. That may be difficult depending upon the availability of information in the country concerned, and, accordingly, reasonable approximations are acceptable. If a foreign operation first measures current cost in a currency other than its functional currency, that amount is then translated into the functional currency at the current exchange rate. [FAS89, ¶21]

.118 There is a presumption that depreciation methods, estimates of useful lives, and salvage values of assets for purposes of the supplementary information are the same as the methods and estimates used for calculations in the primary financial statements. However, if the primary financial statements are based on methods and estimates that partly allow for price changes, different methods and estimates may be used for purposes of the supplementary information. [FAS89, ¶22]

Specialized Assets

.119 The current cost of **mineral resource assets** is determined by current market buying prices or by the current cost of finding and developing mineral reserves. [It is recognized] that no generally accepted approach exists for measuring the current finding cost of mineral reserves. To indicate the effects of changes in current costs, it may be impracticable to do more than adjust historical costs by an index of the changes in specific prices of the inputs concerned. That approach may fail to yield a close approximation of the current cost of finding and developing new reserves. In recognition of that difficulty, the requirements of this section are flexible regarding the approach used to measure current cost of mineral resource assets. The approach may include use of specific price indexes, direct information about market buying prices, and other statistical evidence of the cost of acquisitions. [FAS89, ¶23]

.120 Because Section Oi5, "Oil and Gas Producing Activities," requires an enterprise to disclose a standardized measure of discounted future net cash flows relating to proved oil and gas reserve quantities, the enterprise may follow the approach in paragraph .119 or in paragraph .121 for its oil and gas mineral resource assets. Paragraph .109(c) requires disclosure of the types of information that have been used to measure current costs. [FAS89, ¶24]

.121 Timberlands and growing timber, **income-producing real estate,** and **motion picture films** have certain special features that raise doubts about the applicability of the current cost measurement methods required for other assets. Accordingly, an enterprise may disclose historical cost amounts adjusted by an externally generated index of a broad-based measure of general purchasing power as substitutes for current cost amounts for such assets and their related expenses. [FAS89, ¶25]

.122 If an enterprise estimates the current cost of growing timber and timber harvested by adjusting historical cost for the changes in specific prices, those historical costs may either (a) be limited to the costs that are capitalized in the primary financial statements or (b) include all costs that are directly related to reforestation and forest management, such as planting, fertilization, fire protection, property taxes, and nursery stock, whether or not those costs are capitalized in the primary financial statements. [FAS89, ¶26]

Net Assets

.123 If the enterprise presents the minimum information required by this section, the amount of net assets (that is, shareholders' equity) is the amount of net assets reported in the primary financial statements, adjusted for the difference between the historical cost amounts and the current cost or lower recoverable amounts of inventory and property, plant, and equipment. [FAS89, ¶27]

.124 If the enterprise elects to present comprehensive current cost/constant purchasing power financial statements as supplementary information, the amount of net assets in the five-year summary is the amount reported in the supplementary balance sheet. [FAS89, ¶28]

Recoverable Amount

.125 Recoverable amount is the current worth of the net amount of cash expected to be recoverable from the use or sale of an asset. It may be measured by considering the **value in use** or **current market value** of the asset concerned. Value in use is used to determine recoverable amount of an asset if immediate sale of the asset is not intended. Current market value is used to determine recoverable amount only if the asset is about to be sold. [FAS89, ¶29]

.126 If the recoverable amount for a group of assets is judged to be materially and permanently lower than the current cost amount, the *recoverable amount* is used as a measure of the assets and of the expense associated with the use or sale of the assets. Decisions on the measurement of assets at their recoverable amounts need not be made by considering assets individually unless they are used independently of other assets. [FAS89, ¶30]

.127 An enterprise that is subject to rate regulation or another form of price control may be limited to a maximum recovery through its selling prices, based on the nominal currency amount of the historical cost of its assets. In that situation, historical costs measured in nominal currency may represent an appropriate basis for the measurement of the recoverable amounts associated with those assets. Recoverable amounts may also be lower than historical costs. Nevertheless, cost of goods sold and depreciation, depletion, and amortization expense are to be measured at current cost/constant purchasing power amounts provided that replacement of the service potential of the related assets would be undertaken, if necessary, in current economic conditions; if replacement would not be undertaken, those expenses are to be measured at recoverable amounts. [FAS89, ¶31]

Income from Continuing Operations

.128 An enterprise that presents the minimum information required by this section shall measure income from continuing operations on a current cost basis as follows:

a. Cost of goods sold at current cost or lower recoverable amount at the date of sale or at the date on which resources are used on or committed to a specific contract
b. Depreciation, depletion, and amortization expense of property, plant, and equipment on the basis of the average current cost of the assets' service potential or lower recoverable amount during the period of use.

Other revenues, expenses, gains, and losses may be measured at the amounts included in the primary income statement. (Refer to paragraphs .112 through .122 and .125 through .127 for discussions of current cost or lower recoverable amount measurements.) [FAS89, ¶32]

.129 The amount of income tax expense in computations of current cost/constant purchasing power income from continuing operations is the same as the amount of income tax expense charged against income from continuing operations in the primary financial statements. No adjustments are to be made to income tax expense for any [FAS89, ¶33] temporary differences [FAS109, ¶287] that might be deemed to arise as a result of the use of current cost accounting methods. Income tax expense is not to be allocated between income from continuing operations and the increases or decreases in current cost amounts of inventory and property, plant, and equipment. [FAS89, ¶33]

Increase or Decrease in the Current Cost Amounts of Inventory and Property, Plant, and Equipment, Net of Inflation

.130 The increase or decrease in the current cost amounts of inventory and property, plant, and equipment represents the difference between the measures of the assets at their *entry dates* for the year and the measures of the assets at their *exit dates* for the year. *Entry dates* means the beginning of the year or the dates of acquisition, whichever is applicable; *exit dates* means the end of the year or the dates of use, sale, or commitment to a specific contract, whichever is applicable. For the purposes of this paragraph, assets are measured in accordance with the provisions of paragraphs .112 through .122 and .125 through .127. [FAS89, ¶34]

.131 For the current year, the increase or decrease in current cost amounts of inventory and property, plant, and equipment is reported both before and after eliminating the effects of general inflation (paragraph .109(b)). In the five-year summary, the increase or decrease is reported after elimination of the effects of each year's general inflation (paragraph .103(d)). An acceptable approximate method of calculating the increase or decrease in current cost amounts and the inflation adjustment is illustrated in paragraphs .162 through .165. [FAS89, ¶35]

Restatement of Current Cost Information into Units of Constant Purchasing Power

.132 Enterprises that do not have significant foreign operations or that use the dollar as the functional currency for all significant foreign operations are to use the CPI-U to restate current costs into units of constant purchasing power. Acceptable approximate methods are illustrated in paragraph .177. [FAS89, ¶36]

.133 The effects of general inflation on current cost information for operations measured in a foreign functional currency are measured either (a) after translation and based upon the CPI-U (the translate-restate method) or (b) before translation and based on a broad-based measure of the change in the general purchasing power of the functional currency (the restate-translate method).[8] The same method is to be used for all operations measured in functional currencies other than the dollar and for all periods presented. Acceptable approximate methods are illustrated in paragraphs .177, .178, .185, and .186. [FAS89, ¶37]

Translation Adjustment

.134 If current cost information for operations measured in functional currencies other than the dollar is based on the translate-restate method, the aggregate translation adjustment on the current cost basis is stated net of any income taxes allocated to the aggregate translation adjustment in the primary financial statements (Section F60, "Foreign Currency Translation," paragraph .141(c)). [FAS89, ¶38]

---

[8]The choice of a measure of functional currency purchasing power should take into account the availability, reliability, and timeliness of a general price level index and the frequency with which it is adjusted. It is anticipated that an appropriate index of the change in the general price level will be available for most functional currencies. Indexes are published in most countries, and some indexes are published periodically by organizations such as the International Monetary Fund, the Organisation for Economic Co-Operation and Development, and the United Nations. However, in some cases indexes may not be available on a timely basis or may not be sufficiently reliable. In those circumstances, management should estimate the change in the general price level. [FAS89, ¶37, fn9]

.135 If current cost information for operations measured in functional currencies other than the dollar is based on the restate-translate method, the aggregate translation adjustment on the current cost basis is stated net of both any income taxes allocated to the aggregate translation adjustment in the primary financial statements and the aggregate **parity adjustment.** The parity adjustment is the amount needed to measure end-of-year net assets in (a) average-for-the-year dollars, if income from continuing operations is measured in average-for-the-year functional currency units, or (b) end-of-year dollars, if income from continuing operations is measured in end-of-year functional currency units. [FAS89, ¶39]

Purchasing Power Gain or Loss on Net Monetary Items

.136 The purchasing power gain or loss on net monetary items is the net gain or loss determined by restating in units of constant purchasing power the opening and closing balances of, and transactions in, **monetary assets** and **monetary liabilities.** Acceptable approximate methods of calculating the purchasing power gain or loss on net monetary items are illustrated in paragraphs .161, .178, and .185. [FAS89, ¶40]

.137 The economic significance of monetary assets and liabilities depends heavily on the general purchasing power of money, although other factors, such as creditworthiness of debtors, may affect their significance. The economic significance of nonmonetary items depends heavily on the value of specific goods and services. Nonmonetary assets include (a) goods held primarily for resale or assets held primarily for direct use in providing services for the business of the enterprise, (b) claims to cash in amounts dependent on future prices of specific goods or services, and (c) residual rights such as goodwill or equity interests. Nonmonetary liabilities include (a) obligations to furnish goods or services in quantities that are fixed or determinable without reference to changes in prices and (b) obligations to pay cash in amounts dependent on future prices of specific goods or services. Guidance on the classification of balance sheet items as monetary or nonmonetary is set forth in paragraphs .191 through .203. [FAS89, ¶41]

.138 If inflation-adjusted current cost information is based on the translate-restate method, the purchasing power gain or loss on net monetary items is equal to the net gain or loss determined by restating the opening and closing balances of, and transactions in, monetary assets and liabilities in units of constant purchasing power as measured by the CPI-U. [FAS89, ¶42]

.139 If inflation-adjusted current cost information is based on the restate-translate method, the purchasing power gain or loss on net monetary items is equal to the net gain or loss determined by restating the opening and closing balances of, and transactions in, monetary assets and liabilities in units of constant purchasing power as measured by the change in the general purchasing power of the functional currency. The purchasing power gain or loss computed in that manner is translated into its dollar equivalent at the average exchange rate for the period. [FAS89, ¶43]

Illustrations of Disclosures

.140 This paragraph illustrates formats that may be used to disclose the information required by this section for a manufacturing enterprise. An enterprise may choose to disclose the information required by paragraphs .103 through .109 of this section (a) in a schedule of annual information (for example, Exhibit 140A or Exhibit 140B), in a five-year summary (for example, Exhibit 140C or Exhibit 140D), and notes to those schedules or (b) in a five-year summary and notes to that summary (for example, Exhibit 140E). Many enterprises have included amounts reported in the primary statements alongside current cost/constant purchasing power amounts in the five-year summary. Enterprises [are encouraged] to continue to adapt the disclosure formats to enhance such comparisons. Exhibit 140D illustrates a five-year summary with comparative data from the primary financial statements. Enterprises [also are encouraged] to provide more detailed discussions than the illustrative notes in this paragraph—especially discussion of the significance of the information in the circumstances of the enterprise (required by paragraph .106) and the principal types of information used to calculate current cost amounts (required by paragraph .109(c)). Illustrative calculations are given in paragraphs .141 through .190. In the exhibits that follow, the CPI-U is expressed in average dollars. [FAS89, ¶45]

Exhibit 140A

Statement of Income from Continuing Operations Adjusted for Changing Prices[a]

For the Year Ended December 31, 19X6
In Thousands of Average 19X6 Dollars

Income from continuing operations, as reported in the primary income statement	$22,995
Adjustments to reflect current costs	
Cost of goods sold	(8,408)
Depreciation expense	(9,748)
Income from continuing operations adjusted for changes in specific prices	$ 4,839
Gain from decline in purchasing power of net amounts owed[b]	$ 2,449
Increase in specific prices (current cost) of inventory and property, plant, and equipment held during the year[c]	$25,846
Effect of increase in general price level	5,388
Excess of increase in specific prices over increase in the general price level	$20,458
Foreign currency translation adjustment[d]	$ (624)

[a]The condensed financial information in this exhibit compares selected information from the primary financial statements with information that reflects effects of changes in the specific prices (current cost) of inventory and property, plant, and equipment expressed in units of constant purchasing power. The current cost amounts for inventory and cost of goods sold reflect actual manufacturing costs incurred in 19X6. The current cost amounts for major components of property, plant, and equipment were determined by applying specific price indexes to the applicable historical costs. For assets used in U.S. operations, Producer Price Indexes and Factory Mutual Building Indexes were used; for assets used in foreign operations, appropriate indexes for each country were used. The current cost information is expressed in average 19X6 dollars as measured by the CPI-U.

[b]The purchasing power gain on net amounts owed is an economic benefit to the enterprise that results from being able to repay those amounts with cheaper dollars.

[c]During 19X6, the specific prices (current cost) of inventory increased by $9,108 and of property, plant, and equipment by $16,738. The total increase of $25,846 exceeded the increase necessary to keep pace with general inflation. At December 31, 19X6, the current cost of inventory was $65,700 and of property, plant, and equipment, net of accumulated depreciation, was $89,335 (both measured in December 31, 19X6 units of purchasing power). Those amounts are higher than the amounts in the primary statements of $63,000 for inventory and $45,750 for property, plant, and equipment, net of accumulated depreciation; therefore, it is reasonable to expect income from continuing operations on a current cost basis for 19X7 to remain significantly below that reported in the primary statements.

[d]Current cost amounts for foreign operations are measured in their functional currencies, translated into dollar equivalents using the average exchange rate for the year, and restated into constant units of purchasing power using the CPI-U. Essentially, the foreign currency translation adjustment is the effect of changes in exchange rates during the year on shareholders' equity. The negative translation adjustment indicates that, overall, the dollar has increased in value relative to the functional currencies used to measure the foreign operations of the enterprise.

[FAS89, ¶45]

Exhibit 140B

Statement of Income from Continuing Operations
Adjusted for Changing Prices[a]

For the Year Ended December 31, 19X6
In Thousands of Dollars

	As Reported in the Primary Statements	Adjusted for Changes in Specific Prices (Current Cost)
Net sales and other operating revenues	$275,500	$275,500
Cost of goods sold	197,000	205,408
Depreciation expense	10,275	20,023
Other operating expenses	14,685	14,685
Interest expense	7,550	7,550
Income tax expense	22,995	22,995
[Total expenses]	252,505	270,661
Income from continuing operations	$ 22,995	$ 4,839
Gain from decline in purchasing power of net amounts owed[b]		$ 2,449
Increase in specific prices (current cost) of inventory and property, plant, and equipment held during the year[c]		$ 25,846
Effect of increase in general price level		5,388
Excess of increase in specific prices over increase in the general price level		$ 20,458
Foreign currency translation adjustment[d]	$ (295)	$ (624)

(Footnotes are on the following page.)

---

[a]The condensed financial information in this exhibit compares selected information from the primary financial statements with information that reflects effects of changes in the specific prices (current cost) of inventory and property, plant, and equipment expressed in units of constant purchasing power. The current cost amounts for inventory and cost of goods sold reflect actual manufacturing costs incurred in 19X6. The current cost amounts for major components of property, plant, and equipment were determined by applying specific price indexes to the applicable historical costs. For assets used in U.S. operations, Producer Price Indexes and Factory Mutual Building Indexes were used; for assets used in foreign operations, appropriate indexes for each country were used. The current cost information is expressed in average 19X6 dollars as measured by the CPI-U.

[b]The purchasing power gain on net amounts owed is an economic benefit to the enterprise that results from being able to repay those amounts with cheaper dollars.

[c]During 19X6, the specific prices (current cost) of inventory increased by $9,108 and of property, plant, and equipment by $16,738. The total increase of $25,846 exceeded the increase necessary to keep pace with general inflation. At December 31, 19X6, the current cost of inventory was $65,700 and of property, plant, and equipment, net of accumulated depreciation, was $89,335 (both measured in December 31, 19X6 units of purchasing power). Those amounts are higher than the amounts in the primary statements of $63,000 for inventory and $45,750 for property, plant, and equipment, net of accumulated depreciation; therefore, it is reasonable to expect income from continuing operations on a current cost basis for 19X7 to remain significantly below that reported in the primary statements.

[d]Current cost amounts for foreign operations are measured in their functional currencies, translated into dollar equivalents using the average exchange rate for the year, and restated into constant units of purchasing power using the CPI-U. Essentially, the foreign currency translation adjustment is the effect of changes in exchange rates during the year on shareholders' equity. The negative translation adjustment indicates that, overall, the dollar has increased in value relative to the functional currencies used to measure the foreign operations of the enterprise.

[FAS89, ¶45]

Exhibit 140C

Five-Year Comparison of Selected
Financial Data Adjusted for Effects of Changing Prices
In Thousands of Average 19X6 Dollars,
except for Per Share Amounts

	Year Ended December 31,				
	19X6	19X5	19X4	19X3	19X2
Net sales and other operating revenues	$275,500	$247,500	$240,000	$235,500	$265,000
Income (loss) from continuing operations	4,839	1,660	(2,102)	(4,663)	1,261
Gain from decline in purchasing power of net amounts owed	2,449	7,027	5,432	1,247	6,375
Excess of increase in specific prices of inventory and property, plant, and equipment over increase in the general price level	20,458	2,292	3,853	8,597	3,777
Foreign currency translation adjustment	(624)	(386)	(454)	(293)	127
Net assets at year-end[a]	92,027	67,905	60,409	56,966	55,705
Per share information:					
Income (loss) from continuing operations	$ 3.23	$ 1.11	$ (1.40)	$ (3.11)	$ .84
Cash dividends declared	2.00	2.06	2.19	2.42	2.75
Market price at year-end	35	39	43	27	32
Average consumer price index[b]	298.4	289.1	272.4	246.8	217.4

aNet assets include inventory and property, plant, and equipment at current cost and all other items as they are reported in the primary financial statements. No adjustment has been made for the lower tax basis applicable to the current cost amounts included in net assets.

bFor purposes of this exhibit, although the years for which information has been provided are nonspecific, the actual 1979-1983 average index numbers have been applied.

[FAS89, ¶45]

Exhibit 140D

Five-Year Comparison of Selected Financial Data

**In Thousands of Dollars,
except for Per Share Amounts**

	Year Ended December 31,				
	19X6	19X5	19X4	19X3	19X2
Total revenue					
As reported	$275,500	$239,800	$219,100	$194,800	$193,100
Adjusted for general inflation[a]	275,500	247,500	240,000	235,500	265,000
Income (loss) from operations					
As reported	22,995	11,097	4,756	9,977	11,847
Adjusted for specific price changes[a]	4,839	1,660	(2,102)	(4,663)	1,261
Purchasing power gain from holding net monetary liabilities[a]	2,449	7,027	5,432	1,247	6,375
Excess of increase in specific prices of assets over increase in the general price level[a]	20,458	2,292	3,853	8,597	3,777
Foreign currency translation adjustment					
As reported	(295)	(276)	(396)	(138)	76
Adjusted for specific price changes[a]	(624)	(386)	(454)	(293)	127
Net assets at year-end					
As reported	47,700	28,000	20,179	18,819	11,980
Adjusted for specific price changes[b]	92,027	67,905	60,409	56,966	55,705

Per share information:

Income (loss) from operations:					
As reported	$15.33	$ 7.40	$ 3.17	$ 6.65	$ 7.90
Adjusted for specific price changes[a]	3.23	1.11	(1.40)	(3.11)	.84
Cash dividends declared					
As reported	2.00	2.00	2.00	2.00	2.00
Adjusted for general inflation[a]	2.00	2.06	2.19	2.42	2.75
Market price at year-end					
As reported	36	38	41	23	25
Adjusted for general inflation[a]	35	39	43	27	32
Average consumer price index[c]	298.4	289.1	272.4	246.8	217.4

[a] In average 19X6 dollars.

[b] Net assets adjusted for specific price changes include inventory and property, plant, and equipment at current cost and all other items as they are reported in the primary financial statements. No adjustment has been made for the lower tax basis applicable to the current cost amounts included in net assets.

[c] For purposes of this exhibit, although the years for which information has been provided are nonspecific, the actual 1979-1983 average index numbers have been applied.

[FAS89, ¶45]

Exhibit 140E

Five-Year Comparison of Selected
Financial Data Adjusted for Effects of Changing Prices[a]

In Thousands of Average 19X6 Dollars,
except for Per Share Amounts

	Year Ended December 31,				
	19X6	19X5	19X4	19X3	19X2
Net sales and other operating revenues	$275,500	$247,500	$240,000	$235,500	$265,000
Income (loss) from continuing operations[b]	4,839	1,660	(2,102)	(4,663)	1,261
Gain from decline in purchasing power of net amounts owed[c]	2,449	7,027	5,432	1,247	6,375
Increase in specific prices of inventory and property, plant, and equipment[d]	20,458	2,292	3,853	8,597	3,777
Foreign currency translation adjustment[e]	(624)	(386)	(454)	(293)	127
Net assets at year-end[d]	92,027	67,905	60,409	56,966	55,705
Per share information:					
Income (loss) from continuing operations	$ 3.23	$ 1.11	$ (1.40)	$ (3.11)	$ .84
Cash dividends declared	2.00	2.06	2.19	2.42	2.75
Market price at year-end	35	39	43	27	32
Average consumer price index[f]	298.4	289.1	272.4	246.8	217.4

[a]The condensed financial information in this exhibit presents selected information that reflects effects of changes in the specific prices (current cost) of inventory and property, plant, and equipment expressed in units of constant purchasing power. The current cost amounts for inventory and cost of goods sold reflect actual manufacturing costs incurred in 19X6. The current cost amounts for major components of property, plant, and equipment were determined by applying specific price indexes to the applicable historical costs. For assets used in U.S. operations, Producer Price Indexes and Factory Mutual Building Indexes were used; for assets used in foreign operations, appropriate indexes for each country were used. The current cost information is expressed in average 19X6 dollars as measured by the CPI-U.

[b]Income from continuing operations reported in the primary financial statements was $22,995 for 19X6. Current cost income reported in the five-year summary was only $4,839 because depreciation expense on a current cost basis exceeded depreciation expense in the primary statements by $9,748 and current cost of goods sold was $8,408 greater than the amount reported in the primary statements.

[c]The purchasing power gain on net amounts owed is an economic benefit that results from being able to repay those amounts with cheaper dollars.

[d]During 19X6, the specific prices (current cost) of inventory increased by $9,108 and of property, plant, and equipment by $16,738. The total increase exceeded the increase necessary to keep pace with general inflation by $20,458. Net assets include inventory and property, plant, and equipment at current cost and all other items as reported in the primary financial statements (restated into average-for-19X6 dollars). No adjustment has been made for the lower tax basis applicable to the current cost amounts included in net assets. At December 31, 19X6, the current cost of inventory was $65,700 and of property, plant, and equipment, net of accumulated depreciation, was $89,335 (both measured in December 31, 19X6 units of purchasing power). Those amounts are higher than the amounts in the primary statements of $63,000 for inventory and $45,750 for property, plant, and equipment, net of accumulated depreciation; therefore, it is reasonable to expect income from continuing operations on a current cost basis for 19X7 to remain significantly below that reported in the primary statements.

[e]Current cost amounts for foreign operations are measured in their functional currencies, translated into dollar equivalents using the average exchange rate for the year, and restated into constant units of purchasing power using the CPI-U. Essentially, the foreign currency translation adjustment is the effect of changes in exchange rates during the year on shareholders' equity. A negative (positive) translation adjustment indicates that, overall, the dollar increased (decreased) in value relative to the functional currencies used to measure the foreign operations of the enterprise.

[f]For purposes of this exhibit, although the years for which information has been provided are nonspecific, the actual 1979-1983 average index numbers have been applied.

[FAS89, ¶45]

Illustrative Calculations of Current Cost/Constant Purchasing Power Information

Introduction

.141 Paragraphs .142 through .190 illustrate the methodology that might be used in calculating the disclosures in paragraph .140. [FAS89, ¶46]

.142 Computation of current cost information should be based on a detailed analysis of all transactions; however, the costs of preparing the information can be reduced with little loss of usefulness by simplifying the methods of calculation. Therefore, only cost of sales and depreciation expense need to be adjusted from the amounts shown in the primary income statement. Revenues, other expenses, and gains and losses need not be adjusted. Approximate methods of computation are acceptable for adjusting cost of sales and depreciation expense. The *measurement* of current cost is not illustrated. [FAS89, ¶47]

.143 The objective in making these calculations is to obtain a *reasonable degree* of accuracy—complete precision is not required. Preparers are encouraged to devise short-cut methods of calculation, appropriate to their individual circumstances. [FAS89, ¶48]

.144 If inventories and cost of sales are accounted for under the LIFO method in the primary financial statements, the only adjustment normally required in computing income from continuing operations would be to eliminate the effect of changing prices on any prior-period LIFO layer liquidation. [FAS89, ¶49]

.145 Seven basic steps to restate historical cost information into current cost/constant purchasing power information are illustrated in paragraphs .142 through .190:

a. Analyze inventory (at the beginning and end of the year) and cost of goods sold to determine when the costs were incurred
b. Restate inventory and cost of goods sold into current cost
c. Analyze property, plant, and equipment to determine when the related assets were acquired
d. Restate property, plant, and equipment and depreciation, depletion, and amortization expense into current cost
e. Identify the amount of net monetary items (paragraphs .191 through .203) at the beginning and end of the period and changes during the period
f. Compute the purchasing power gain or loss on net monetary items
g. Compute the change in current cost of inventory and property, plant, and equipment and the related effect of the increase in the general price level.

[FAS89, ¶50]

.146 The methodology illustrated in paragraphs .142 through .190 has been developed for the hypothetical enterprise, Parent Company. Parent Company has a wholly owned foreign subsidiary, Sub Company. Sub Company measures its operations in a functional currency other than the dollar. The changing prices disclosures for Parent Company and Sub Company are developed separately. Merging the amounts calculated for each entity results in a consolidated disclosure:

a. Paragraphs .154 through .166 illustrate the minimum recommended calculations for the domestic operations of Parent Company. A method of checking the arithmetic accuracy of the calculations is included in paragraph .167.
b. Paragraphs .174 through .181 illustrate the translate-restate method for Sub Company, a foreign subsidiary that does not use the dollar as a functional currency. A method of checking the arithmetic accuracy of the calculations is included in paragraph .179.
c. The results of the calculations described in (a) and (b) are summarized in paragraph .182 and are reflected in the illustrative disclosures in paragraph .140.

[FAS89, ¶51]

.147 Paragraphs .183 through .190 illustrate the restate-translate method for Sub Company. A method of checking the arithmetic accuracy of the calculations is included in paragraphs .187 and .188. [FAS89, ¶52]

.148 Throughout this section, $ indicates nominal dollars, C$ indicates average 19X6 constant dollars, FC indicates nominal functional currency, C$E indicates dollar equivalents of FC amounts using the translate-restate method, CFC indicates average 19X6 constant functional currency, and CFC$ indicates the translated dollar equivalents of CFC amounts using the restate-translate method. [FAS89, ¶53]

Parent Company Information

.149 The historical cost/nominal dollar financial statements [are presented below]:

Parent Company
Balance Sheet (Unconsolidated)
As of December 31, 19X6 and 19X5
(000s)

	19X6	19X5
Current assets:		
Cash	$ 1,000	$ 2,000
Accounts receivable	36,000	16,500
Inventories, at FIFO cost	63,000	56,000
Total current assets	100,000	74,500
Property, plant, and equipment, at cost	100,000	85,000
Less accumulated depreciation	56,000	46,000
	44,000	39,000
Investment in Sub Company*	1,500	1,500
	$145,500	$115,000

	19X6	19X5
Current liabilities:		
Accounts payable and accrued expenses	$ 47,000	$ 32,000
Income taxes payable	6,000	6,000
Current portion of long-term debt	5,000	5,000
Total current liabilities	58,000	43,000
Deferred income taxes	6,000	5,000
Long-term debt	34,000	39,000
Total liabilities	98,000	87,000
Capital stock†	10,000	10,000
Retained earnings	37,500	18,000
	$145,500	$115,000

* Investment in Sub Company is recorded at cost and is eliminated in consolidation. Parent Company does not issue separate unconsolidated statements.

†1,500,000 shares outstanding.

[FAS89, ¶55]

Parent Company (Unconsolidated)
Statement of Earnings and Retained Earnings
For the Year Ended December 31, 19X6

	(000s)
Sales	$270,000
Cost of goods sold, exclusive of depreciation	197,000
Selling, general, and administrative expenses	10,835
Depreciation	10,000
Interest	7,165
[Total expenses]	225,000
Earnings before taxes	45,000
Income taxes	22,500
Net income	22,500
Retained earnings at beginning of year	18,000
	40,500
Dividends	3,000
Retained earnings at end of year	$ 37,500
Net income per share	$ 15

[FAS89, ¶54]

.150 Inventory and production [information is as follows]:

a. Inventory is accounted for on a first-in, first-out (FIFO) basis and turns over four times per year. There is no significant amount of work in progress or raw materials.
b. At December 31, 19X6 and 19X5 inventory consisted of 900,000 units and 1,000,000 units respectively—representing production of the immediately preceding quarter. Management has measured the current cost of inventory at $73 per unit at December 31, 19X6 ($65,700,000) and $58 per unit at December 31, 19X5 ($58,000,000).
c. Costs were incurred and goods produced as follows:

	19X5	19X6				
	4th	1st	2nd	3rd	4th	Total
Historical costs	$56,000	$39,560	$59,400	$42,040	$63,000	$204,000
Units produced	1,000	618	900	618	900	3,036
Units sold		1,000	618	900	618	3,136

d. At December 31, 19X6 the selling price per unit was $85.
e. There were no write-downs or disposals of inventory.

[FAS89, ¶55]

.151 Property, plant, and equipment [information is as follows]:

a. Details of fixed assets at December 31, 19X6 are as follows:

		(000s)	
Date Acquired	Percent Depreciated	Historical Cost	Accumulated Depreciation
19W9	80	$ 50,000	$40,000
19X0	70	5,000	3,500
19X1	60	5,000	3,000
19X2	50	5,000	2,500
19X3	40	5,000	2,000
19X4	30	5,000	1,500
19X5	20	10,000	2,000
19X6	10	15,000	1,500
		$100,000	$56,000

b. Depreciation is calculated at 10 percent per annum, straight line. A full year's depreciation is charged in the year of acquisition.
c. There were no disposals.
d. Management has measured the current cost of property, plant, and equipment at December 31, 19X6 and 19X5 as follows:

	(000s)			
	December 31, 19X6		December 31, 19X5	
Date Acquired	Current Cost	Accumulated Depreciation	Current Cost	Accumulated Depreciation
19W9	$120,000	$ 96,000	$110,000	$77,000
19X0	10,000	7,000	6,000	3,600
19X1	15,000	9,000	7,000	3,500
19X2	18,000	9,000	12,000	4,800
19X3	12,000	4,800	10,000	3,000
19X4	17,000	5,100	15,000	3,000
19X5	12,000	2,400	10,000	1,000
19X6	16,000	1,600	—	—
	220,000	$134,900	170,000	$95,900
Accumulated depreciation	134,900		95,900	
Net current cost	$ 85,100		$ 74,100	

e. The recoverable amount has been determined by management to be in excess of current cost, net of accumulated depreciation.

[FAS89, ¶56]

.152 Dividends were paid at the rate of $750,000 per quarter. [FAS89, ¶57]

.153 Consumer Price Index for All Urban Consumers (from the *Survey of Current Business*, U.S. Department of Commerce, Bureau of Economic Analysis) [is as follows]:

December 19X5	292.4
Average 19X6	298.4
December 19X6	303.5

[FAS89, ¶58]

Parent Company Calculations

.154 The objective is to express the supplementary information in average 19X6 dollars. As indicated in paragraph .123, nominal dollar measurements may be used for all elements of net assets other than inventory and property, plant, and equipment. As indicated in paragraph .128, nominal dollar measurements may be used for all elements of income from continuing operations other than cost of sales and depreciation. [FAS89, ¶59]

Step 1: Analysis of Inventory and Cost of Goods Sold

.155 Inventory is assumed to turn over four times per year. Therefore, inventory with a historical cost of $63,000,000 at December 31, 19X6 is assumed to have been acquired during the fourth quarter of 19X6, and inventory with a historical cost of $56,000,000 at December 31, 19X5 is assumed to have been acquired in the fourth quarter of 19X5. [FAS89, ¶60]

Step 2: Current Cost of Inventory and Cost of Goods Sold

.156 Cost of goods sold, current cost, [data is as follows]:

Current cost at the beginning of year	$	58/unit
Current cost at the end of year		73/unit
	$	131/unit
Average current cost ($131 ÷ 2)	$	65.5/unit
Units sold during the year (000s) (par. .150(c))		× 3,136
Average current cost of goods sold (000s)	$205,408	

[FAS89, ¶61]

.157 The current cost amounts should be compared with the recoverable amount. This is illustrated below:

Market price per unit at end of year	$85
Current cost per unit of inventory on hand at end of year	73
Excess—no write-down required	$12

[FAS89, ¶62]

Step 3: Analysis of Property, Plant, and Equipment and Depreciation

.158 An analysis of property, plant, and equipment was given in paragraph .151. [FAS89, ¶63]

Step 4: Current Cost of Property, Plant, and Equipment and Depreciation

.159 It will usually be appropriate to calculate current cost depreciation, depletion, and amortization expense by reference to average current cost of the related assets (current cost of assets at beginning of year + current cost of assets at end of year ÷ 2).

	(000s) Current Cost
Current cost—12/31/X5 (par. .151(d))	$170,000
Current cost—12/31/X6 (par. .151(d))	220,000
	390,000
	÷ 2
Average current cost	$195,000
Current cost depreciation: 10%, straight line	$ 19,500

In this example, management has determined that the recoverable amount is greater than net current cost of property, plant, and equipment and there is no write-down. [FAS89, ¶64]

Step 5: Identification of Net Monetary Items

.160 Net monetary items (refer to paragraph .149) [are as follows]:

	(000s)	
	Dec. 31, 19X6	**Dec. 31, 19X5**
Cash	$ 1,000	$ 2,000
Accounts receivable	36,000	16,500
Accounts payable and accrued expenses	(47,000)	(32,000)
Income taxes payable	(6,000)	(6,000)
Current portion of long-term debt	(5,000)	(5,000)
Deferred income taxes	(6,000)	(5,000)
Long-term debt	(34,000)	(39,000)
Net monetary liabilities	$(61,000)	$(68,500)

[FAS89, ¶65]

Step 6: Computation of the Purchasing Power Gain or Loss on Net Monetary Items

.161 The amount of net monetary items at the beginning of the year, changes in the net monetary items, and the amount at the end of the year are restated into average 19X6 dollars. The purchasing power gain or loss on net monetary items is then the balancing item as illustrated below:

	(000s) Nominal Dollars	Conversion Factor	(000s) Avg. 19X6 Dollars
Balance—1/1/X6	$68,500	298.4 (avg. 19X6) 292.4 (Dec. 19X5)	C$69,906
Decrease in net monetary liabilities during the year	(7,500)	*	(7,500)
Balance—12/31/X6	$61,000	298.4 (avg. 19X6) 303.5 (Dec. 19X6)	(59,975)
Purchasing power gain on net monetary items			C$ 2,431

---

*Assumed to be in average 19X6 dollars.

[FAS89, ¶66]

Step 7: Computation of the Change in Current Cost of Inventory and Property, Plant, and Equipment and the Effect of General Price-Level Changes

.162 The increase in current cost of inventories [is as follows]:

	(000s) Current Cost/ Nominal Dollars	Conversion Factor	(000s) Current Cost/ Average 19X6 Dollars
Balance—1/1/X6		298.4 (avg. 19X6)	
(par. .150(b))	$ 58,000	292.4 (Dec. 19X5)	C$59,190
Production (par. .150(c))	204,000	*	204,000
Cost of goods sold (par. .156)	(205,408)	*	(205,408)
Balance—12/31/X6		298.4 (avg. 19X6)	
(par. .150(b))	(65,700)	303.5 (Dec. 19X6)	(64,596)
Increase in current cost of inventories	$ 9,108		C$ 6,814

---

*Assumed to be in average 19X6 dollars.

[FAS89, ¶67]

.163 The inflation component of the increase in current cost amount is the difference between the nominal dollar and constant dollar measures. Using the numbers from paragraph .162, [the inflation component is]:

	(000s)
Increase in current cost (nominal dollars)	$9,108
Increase in current cost (constant dollars)	C$6,814
Inflation component	2,294

[FAS89, ¶68]

.164 The increase in current cost of property, plant, and equipment [is as follows]:

	(000s) Current Cost/ Nominal Dollars	Conversion Factor	(000s) Current Cost/ Average 19X6 Dollars
Balance—1/1/X6		298.4 (avg. 19X6)	
(par. .151(d))	$ 74,100	292.4 (Dec. 19X5)	C$75,621
Additions (par. .151(a))	15,000	*	15,000
Depreciation (par. .159)	(19,500)	*	(19,500)
Balance—12/31/X6		298.4 (avg. 19X6)	
(par. .151(d))	(85,100)	303.5 (Dec. 19X6)	(83,670)
Increase in current cost of property, plant, and equipment	$ 15,500		C$12,549

---

*Assumed to be in average 19X6 dollars.

[FAS89, ¶69]

.165 The inflation component of the increase in current cost amount is the difference between the nominal dollar and constant dollar measures. Using the numbers from paragraph .164, [the inflation component is]:

	(000s)
Increase in current cost (nominal dollars)	$15,500
Increase in current cost (constant dollars)	C$12,549
Inflation component	2,951

[FAS89, ¶70]

Summary of Increase in Current Cost Amounts

.166 [The following summarizes] paragraphs .163 and .165 above:

	Increase in Current Cost (000s)	Inflation Component	Increase Net of Inflation
Inventory	$ 9,108	2,294	C$ 6,814
Property, plant, and equipment	15,500	2,951	12,549
Total	$24,608	5,245	C$19,363

[FAS89, ¶71]

Check of Calculations

.167 A reconciliation of shareholders' equity[9] (net assets) on a current cost/constant purchasing power basis acts as a check on the arithmetic accuracy of the calculations. Changes in shareholders' equity during 19X6 in average 19X6 dollars appear below:

	Source Paragraph	(000s) Current Cost/ Average 19X6 Dollars
Equity at January 1, 19X6		
Inventory	.162	C$59,190
Property, plant, and equipment—net	.164	75,621
Net monetary items	.161	(69,906)
		64,905
Income from continuing operations	.182	4,592
Dividends	.152	(3,000)
Gain from decline in purchasing power of net monetary liabilities	.161	2,431
Excess of increase in specific prices over increase in the general price level	.166	19,363
		C$88,291
Equity at December 31, 19X6		
Inventory	.162	C$64,596
Property, plant, and equipment—net	.164	83,670
Net monetary items	.161	(59,975)
		C$88,291

[FAS89, ¶72]

---

[9]To facilitate the illustration of consolidated amounts in paragraph .182, investment in Sub Company has been excluded from net assets of Parent Company in this paragraph. [FAS89, ¶72, fn10]

Sub Company Information

.168 The functional currency financial statements of Sub Company[10] [are presented] below:

Sub Company
Historical Cost/Nominal FC Balance Sheets
As of December 31, 19X6 and 19X5
(000s)

	19X6	19X5
Cash	FC2,550	FC1,250
Equipment	2,500	2,500
Accumulated depreciation	750	500
Net equipment	1,750	2,000
Total assets	FC4,300	FC3,250
Accounts payable	FC 600	FC 500
Long-term debt	2,000	1,500
Total liabilities	2,600	2,000
Capital stock	500	500
Retained earnings	1,200	750
Total equity	1,700	1,250
Total liabilities and equity	FC4,300	FC3,250

Sub Company
Historical Cost/Nominal FC Statement of Income and Retained Earnings
For the Year Ended December 31, 19X6

	(000s)
Revenue	FC5,000
General and administrative expenses	3,500
Depreciation	250
Interest	350
[Total expenses]	4,100
Income before taxes	900
Income taxes	450
Net income	450
Retained earnings—beginning of year	750
Retained earnings—end of year	FC1,200

[FAS89, ¶73]

---

[10]For simplicity, Sub Company is assumed to have a fixed asset but no inventory. The mechanics of restating inventory and cost of goods sold on a current cost basis are essentially the same as those illustrated for property, plant, and equipment. [FAS89, ¶73, fn11]

.169 The fixed asset was acquired on December 31, 19X4. It is depreciated on a straight-line basis over 10 years and is expected to have no salvage value. There were no acquisitions or disposals of assets during the year. [FAS89, ¶74]

.170 Exchange rates between the functional currency and the dollar are:

December 31, 19X5	FC1 = $1.20
Average 19X6	FC1 = $1.10
December 31, 19X6	FC1 = $1.00

[FAS89, ¶75]

.171 Management has measured the current cost of equipment at December 31, 19X6 and 19X5 as follows:

	(000s)	
	19X6	**19X5**
Current cost	FC5,500	FC4,000
Accumulated depreciation	(1,650)	(800)
Net current cost	FC3,850	FC3,200

The recoverable amount has been determined to be in excess of net current cost at both dates. [FAS89, ¶76]

.172 Current cost equity in nominal FC at the beginning and end of the year may be computed by adding net monetary items and net property, plant, and equipment at current cost. To determine current cost equity in nominal dollars, those FC amounts are translated at the appropriate exchange rate:

	December 31,					
	19X6			**19X5**		
	(000s) FC	Exchange Rate	(000s) $	(000s) FC	Exchange Rate	(000s) $
Monetary items (par. .168):						
Cash	FC2,550	$1	$ 2,550	FC1,250	$1.20	$ 1,500
Current liabilities	(600)	$1	(600)	(500)	$1.20	(600)
Long-term debt	(2,000)	$1	(2,000)	(1,500)	$1.20	(1,800)
Net monetary liabilities	FC (50)		$ (50)	FC (750)		$ (900)
Equipment—net (par. .171)	FC3,850	$1	$ 3,850	FC3,200	$1.20	$ 3,840
Equity at current cost	FC3,800		$ 3,800	FC2,450		$ 2,940

[FAS89, ¶177]

.173 The U.S. and local general price level indexes are:

	Local	U.S.
December 19X5	144	292.4
Average 19X6	158	298.4
December 19X6	173	303.5

[FAS89, ¶78]

Sub Company Calculations: Translate-Restate Method

.174 To apply the translate-restate method, amounts measured in nominal FC are first translated into their dollar equivalents. Changes in those dollar equivalent amounts are then restated to reflect the effects of U.S. inflation. [FAS89, ¶79]

Current Cost Depreciation and Income from Continuing Operations

.175 The first step is to determine current cost depreciation for the year as follows:

	(000s)
Current cost—beginning of year (par. .171)	FC4,000
Current cost—end of year (par. .171)	5,500
	9,500
	÷ 2
Average current cost, gross	FC4,750

Current cost depreciation expense for the year is FC475,000 (FC4,750,000 × 10%). Computation of current cost depreciation and income from continuing operations does not involve use of a general price level index if measurements are made in average-for-the-year currency units. Accordingly, reported current cost depreciation under the translate-restate method is C$E523,000 (FC475,000 × $1.10). [FAS89, ¶80]

.176 Income from continuing operations on a current cost basis is computed by simply replacing historical cost depreciation in income from continuing operations in the primary financial statements with the current cost amount. Accordingly, current cost income from continuing operations is:

Net income + historical cost depreciation – current cost depreciation
= FC450,000 (par. .168) + FC250,000 (par. .168) – FC475,000
(par. .175) = FC225,000.

Reported current cost income from continuing operations under the translate-restate method is C$E247,000[11] (FC225,000 × $1.10). [FAS89, ¶81]

---

[11]Current cost income has been rounded down from $247,500 to $247,000. This is necessary because current cost depreciation was rounded up to $523,000 from $522,500 and current cost income is a remainder of this number. [FAS89, ¶81, fn12]

Excess of Increase in Specific Prices over Increase in General Price Level

.177 The second step is to compute the change in the current cost of equipment and the effect of the increase in the general price level. To measure the increase in current cost of equipment in nominal FC dollar equivalents, the effect of the exchange rate change must be excluded. One way to accomplish this is to translate the December 31, 19X5 and 19X6 FC current cost amounts to dollar equivalents at the average exchange rate and then restate those dollar amounts to average 19X6 constant dollar equivalents:

	(000s) Current Cost/FC	Exchange Rate	(000s) Current Cost/$	Conversion Factor	(000s) Current Cost/C$E
Current cost, net—12/31/X5 (par. .171)	FC3,200	$1.10	$ 3,520	298.4 (avg. 19X6) / 292.4 (Dec. 19X5)	C$E3,592
Depreciation (par. .175)	(475)	$1.10	(523)	*	(523)
Current cost, net—12/31/X6 (par. .171)	(3,850)	$1.10	(4,235)	298.4 (avg. 19X6) / 303.5 (Dec. 19X6)	(4,164)
Increase in current cost	FC1,125		$ 1,238		C$E1,095

* Assumed to be in average 19X6 C$E.

The inflation component of the increase in current cost amount is the difference between the nominal dollar and the constant dollar equivalent amounts:

	(000s)
Increase in current cost (nominal dollars)	$1,238
Increase in current cost (constant dollars)	C$E1,095
Inflation component	143

[FAS89, ¶82]

Purchasing Power Gain or Loss on Net Monetary Items

.178 The third step is to compute the purchasing power gain or loss on net monetary items. Under the translate-restate method, the translated beginning and ending net monetary liabilities are restated to average 19X6 dollars. The U.S. purchasing power gain is then the balancing amount:

	(000s) **FC**	**Exchange** **Rate**	**(000s)** **$**
Net monetary liabilities—12/31/X5 (par. .172)	FC750	$1.20	$900
Net monetary liabilities—12/31/X6 (par. .172)	50	$1.00	50
Decrease during the year	FC700		$850

	(000s) **$**	**Conversion** **Factor**	**(000s)** **C$E**
Net monetary liabilities—12/31/X5	$ 900	298.4 (avg. 19X6) 292.4 (Dec. 19X5)	C$E918
Decrease during the year	(850)	*	(850)
Net monetary liabilities—12/31/X6	$ 50	298.4 (avg. 19X6) 303.5 (Dec. 19X6)	(49)
Purchasing power gain			C$E 19

---

*Assumed to be in average 19X6 C$E.

In some circumstances, the above procedure will include a part of the effect of exchange rate changes on net monetary items in the purchasing power gain or loss. A more precise computation that would completely exclude the effect of exchange rate changes would be to compute a separate purchasing power gain or loss for each functional currency operation in a manner similar to that illustrated in paragraph .177 for the increase in specific prices. For Sub Company, that alternative method produces a purchasing power gain of C$E18:

	FC (000s)	Average Exchange Rate	$ (000s)	Conversion Factor	C$E (000s)
Net monetary liabilities—12/31/X5 (par. .172)	FC750	$1.10	$ 825	298.4 (avg. 19X6)/292.4 (Dec. 19X5)	C$E842
Decrease during the year	(700)	$1.10	(770)	*	(770)
Net monetary liabilities—12/31/X6 (par. .172)	FC50	$1.10	$ 55	298.4 (avg. 19X6)/303.5 (Dec. 19X6)	(54)
Purchasing power gain					C$E 18

* Assumed to be in average 19X6 C$E.

The first procedure illustrated is less costly because it can be applied on a consolidated basis, and it generally provides a reasonable approximation. Accordingly, that method is acceptable. For this exercise, the more precise computation is used. [FAS89, ¶83]

Check of Calculations

.179 A reconciliation of equity serves as a check of the calculations and is a convenient way to compute the translation adjustment:

		(000s)
Equity at 12/31/X5 in average 19X6 C$—$2,940		
(par. .172) × 298.4/292.4		C$3,000
Income from continuing operations (par. .176)	C$E247	
Purchasing power gain (par. .178)	18	
Excess of increase in specific prices over increase		
in general price level (par. .177)	1095	
Translation adjustment (par. .180)	(624)	
Increase in equity in terms of U.S. purchasing power		736
		C$3,736
Equity at 12/31/X6 in average 19X6 C$—$3,800		
(par. .172) × 298.4/303.5		C$3,736

[FAS89, ¶84]

Translation Adjustment

.180 The preceding paragraph shows that the translation adjustment is the amount needed to balance the reconciliation of equity. The translation adjustment may be checked by computing the effect of changes in the exchange rate on beginning-of-year equity and on the increase or decrease in equity during the year. To check the translation adjustment determined under the translate-restate method: (a) translate the beginning- and end-of-year equity on a C$basis into FC amounts and (b) use those FC amounts to compute the effect on equity of changes in the exchange rate.

	(000s) C$	Exchange Rate	(000s) FC
Equity at 12/31/X5 in average 19X6 C$ (par. .179)	C$3,000	$0.833*	FC2,499
Equity at 12/31/X6 in average 19X6 C$ (par. .179)	3,736	$ 1.00	3,736
Increase in equity	C$ 736		FC1,237

	(000s)	
Beginning-of-year equity	FC2,499	
Exchange rate change during 19X6 ($1.20 – $1.00)	× (.20)	$(500)
Increase in equity	FC1,237	
Difference between ending exchange rate and average rate for 19X6 ($1.10 – $1.00)	× (.10)	
		$(124)
Translation adjustment		$(624)

---

*FC1 – $1.20 = $0.833

If the short-cut method for determining the purchasing power gain or loss described in paragraph .178 were followed, the translation adjustment would be $(625). [FAS89, ¶85]

Consolidation: Translate-Restate Method

.181 Parent Company prepares its changing prices disclosures on a consolidated basis and complies with the minimum requirements in determining current cost income from continuing operations (paragraph .128). Accordingly, revenue, general and administrative expenses, interest, and income taxes (paragraph .129) are shown at amounts reported in the historical cost financial statements. For Sub Company, those amounts are translated into dollars as follows:

	(000s) FC Amount (Par. .168)	Exchange Rate	(000s) U.S. Dollars
Revenue	FC5,000	1.10	$5,500
General and administrative expenses	FC3,500	1.10	$3,850
Interest	FC 350	1.10	$ 385
Income taxes	FC 450	1.10	$ 495

[FAS89, ¶86]

.182 The "Total" column of the following schedule provides the figures in Exhibit 140B, "Illustrations of Disclosures."

	Source Par.	(000s) Parent Company	Source Par.	(000s) Sub Company	Total
Average 19X6 Units of Purchasing Power					
Net sales & other revenues	.149	$270,000	.181	$5,500	$275,500
Cost of goods sold	.156	205,408			205,408
Depreciation expense	.159	19,500	.175	523	20,023
Selling, general, and administrative expenses	.149	10,835	.181	3,850	14,685
Interest expense	.149	7,165	.181	385	7,550
Provision for taxes	.149	22,500	.181	495	22,995
		265,408		5,253	270,661
Income (loss) from operations		$ 4,592		$ 247	$ 4,839
Purchasing power gain (loss)	.161	$ 2,431	.178	$ 18	$ 2,449
Increase in specific prices					
Inventory	.166	$ 9,108			$ 9,108
Property, plant, and equipment	.166	15,500	.177	$1,238	16,738
		24,608		1,238	25,846
Effect of increase in general price level	.166	5,245	.177	143	$ 5,388
Increase in specific prices— net of inflation	.166	$ 19,363	.177	$1,095	$ 20,458
Translation adjustment			.180	$ (624)	$ (624)
Net assets	.167	$ 88,291	.179	$3,736	$ 92,027
December 31, 19X6 Units of Purchasing Power					
Inventory	.150	$ 65,700			$ 65,700
Property, plant, and equipment—net of accumulated depreciation	.151(d)	$ 85,100	.177	$4,235	$ 89,335

[FAS89, ¶87]

Sub Company Calculations: Restate-Translate Method

.183 To apply the restate-translate method, the steps illustrated in paragraphs .174 through .180 are followed except that all restatements to reflect the effects of general inflation are made using the local general price level index before translation to dollar equivalents. [FAS89, ¶88]

Current Cost Depreciation and Income from Continuing Operations

.184 Current cost depreciation and income from continuing operations are FC475,000 and FC225,000, respectively, as determined in paragraphs .175 and .176. [FAS89, ¶89]

Purchasing Power Gain or Loss on Net Monetary Items

.185 To apply the restate-translate method, the FC amount of net monetary items at the beginning of the year, changes in the net monetary items, and the amount at the end of the year are restated into average 19X6 CFC. The purchasing power gain or loss on net monetary items is then the balancing item:

	(000s) FC	Conversion Factor	(000s) CFC
Net monetary liabilities— 12/31/X5 (par. .172)	FC750	158 (avg. 19X6) 144 (Dec. 19X5)	CFC823
Decrease during the year	(700)	*	(700)
Net monetary liabilities— 12/31/X6 (par. .172)	FC 50	158 (avg. 19X6) 173 (Dec. 19X6)	(46)
Purchasing power gain			CFC 77

---

*Assumed to be in average 19X6 C$E.

[FAS89, ¶90]

Excess of Increase in Specific Prices over Increase in General Price Level

.186 Under the restate-translate method, the local index is used to restate the beginning and ending current cost FC amounts into average 19X6 CFC:

	(000s) Current Cost/FC	Conversion Factor	(000s) Current Cost/CFC
Current cost, net— 12/31/X5 (par. .171)	FC3,200	158 (avg. 19X6) 144 (Dec. 19X5)	CFC3,511
Depreciation (par. .184)	(475)	*	(475)
Current cost, net— 12/31/X6 (par. 171)	(3,850)	158 (avg. 19X6) 173 (Dec. 19X6)	(3,516)
Increase in current cost	FC1,125		CFC 480

---

*Assumed to be in average 19X6 C$E.

The inflation component of the increase in current cost amount is the difference between the nominal functional currency and constant functional currency amounts:

	(000s)
Increase in current cost (FC)	FC1,125
Increase in current cost (CFC)	CFC 480
Inflation component	645

[FAS89, ¶91]

Check of Calculations

.187 As with the translate-restate method, a reconciliation of equity acts as a check of the calculations. A reconciliation of equity also is a convenient point at which to translate the functional currency amounts determined in the preceding paragraphs into dollar equivalents and is a convenient way to compute the translation and parity adjustments. [FAS89, ¶92]

.188 If beginning and ending equity are restated to average 19X6 CFC using the local
index, the reconciliation of equity under the restate-translate method would be:

	(000s) CFC	Exchange Rate	(000s) CFC$
Equity at 12/31/X5 in average 19X6 CFC			
(FC2,450 (par. .172) × 158/144)	CFC2,688	1.20	CFC$3,226
Income from continuing operations (par. .184)	225	1.10	247
Purchasing power gain (par. .185)	77	1.10	85
Excess of increase in specific prices over			
increase in general price level (par. .186)	480	1.10	528
Translation adjustment (par. .189)			(616)
	CFC3,470		CFC$3,470
Equity at 12/31/X6 in average 19X6 CFC			
(FC3,800 (par. .172) × 158/173)	CFC3,470	1.00	CFC$3,470

[FAS89, ¶93]

Translation Adjustment

.189 The translation adjustment is the amount needed to balance the CFC$ reconciliation
of equity. The adjustment may be computed as (a) the change in exchange rates during the
period multiplied by the restated amount of net assets at the beginning of the period plus
(b) the difference between the average exchange rate for the period and the end-of-period
exchange rate multiplied by the increase or decrease in restated net assets for the period.
Accordingly, the translation adjustment under the restate-translate method is:

	(000s)
Beginning-of-year equity (par. .188)	CFC2,688
Exchange rate change during 19X6 ($1.20 – $1.00)	× .20
	$(538)
Increase in equity (3,470 – 2,688)	CFC 782
Difference between ending exchange rate and	
average rate for 19X6 ($1.10 – $1.00)	× .10
	(78)
Translation adjustment	$(616)

[FAS89, ¶94]

Parity Adjustment

.190 The reconciliation of equity in paragraph .188, in which beginning-of-year and end-of-year equity are stated in average 19X6 CFC, is needed to calculate the translation adjustment in CFC$. However, beginning- and end-of-year equity and the increase in equity must be stated in average 19X6 constant dollars in the supplementary current cost information. Beginning- and end-of-year equity in average 19X6 constant dollars are C$3,000,000 and C$3,736,000, respectively, as computed in paragraph .179. Thus, the overall increase in U.S. purchasing power for the year is C$3,736,000 – C$3,000,000 = C$736,000. However, the reconciliation of equity in paragraph .188 indicates that the increase in equity for the year is CFC$244,000 (CFC$3,470,000 – CFC$3,226,000). The difference between C$736,000 and CFC$244,000 is the parity adjustment needed to adjust the ending net investment and the increase in the net investment to measures in average 19X6 constant dollars. Accordingly, the parity adjustment is C$736,000 – CFC$244,000 = $492,000. That amount represents (a) the effect of the difference between local and U.S. inflation from December 31, 19X5 average for 19X6 on the restatement of opening equity to average units plus (b) the effect of the difference between local and U.S. inflation from average for 19X6 to December 31, 19X6 the restatement of ending nominal dollar equity to average units:

		(000s)
Beginning-of-year equity (par. .172)	$	2,940
Difference between local and U.S. inflation from		
12/31/X5 to average 19X6 (158/144 – 298.4/292.4)		× 0.0767
		$225
Equity at 12/31/X6 (par. .172)		3,800
Difference between local and U.S. inflation from		
average 19X6 to 12/31/X6 (158/173 – 298.4/303.5)		× 0.0699
		266
		491
Rounding difference		1
Parity adjustment		$492

For display purposes, the parity adjustment [is]combined with the $(616,000) translation adjustment (paragraph .189). Accordingly, the net translation adjustment disclosed in the supplementary current cost information prepared using the restate-translate method would be $(616,000) + $492,000 = $(124,000). The components of current cost information based on the restate-translate method thus would be:

		(000s)
Beginning-of-year equity—		
$2,940 (par. .172) × 298.4/292.4		C$3,000
Income from continuing operations—		
CFC225 (par. .184) × 1.10	CFC$ 247	
Purchasing power gain— CFC77 (par. .185) × 1.10	85	
Excess of increase in specific prices over increase in general price level—CFC480 (par. .186) × 1.10	528	
Translation and parity adjustments	(124)	
Increase in equity in terms of U.S. purchasing power		736
End-of-year equity—$3,800 (par. .172) × 298.4/303.5		C$3,736

[FAS89, ¶95]

Monetary and Nonmonetary Items

.191 Paragraphs .191 through .203 provide guidance on the interpretation of paragraphs .136 through .139 for the classification of certain asset and liability items as monetary or nonmonetary. The following table illustrates the application of the definitions to common cases under typical circumstances. In other circumstances the classification should be resolved by reference to the definitions. Paragraphs .191 through .203 are not intended to provide answers that should be followed regardless of the circumstances of the case. (Footnote reference is at the end of the table.)

	Monetary	Nonmonetary
Assets		
Cash on hand and demand bank deposits (dollars)	X	
Time deposits (dollars)	X	
Foreign currency on hand and claims to foreign currency[a]	X	
Securities:		
Common stocks (not accounted for on the equity method)		X
Common stocks represent residual interests in the underlying net assets and earnings of the issuer.		

	Monetary	Nonmonetary
Assets		
Preferred stock (convertible or participating)		Circumstances may indicate that such stock is either monetary or nonmonetary. Refer to convertible bonds.
Preferred stock (nonconvertible, nonparticipating) Future cash receipts are likely to be substantially unaffected by changes in specific prices.	X	
Convertible bonds		If the market values the security primarily as a bond, it is monetary, if it values the security primarily as stock, it is nonmonetary.
Bonds (other than convertibles)	X	
Trading account investments in fixed-income securities owned by banks, investment brokers, and others (paragraphs .192 and .193)		X
Accounts and notes receivable	X	
Allowance for doubtful accounts and notes receivable	X	
Variable-rate mortgage loans The terms of such loans do not link them directly to the rate of inflation. Also, there are practical reasons for classifying all loans as monetary.	X	
Inventories used on contracts		They are, in substance, rights to receive sums of money if the future cash receipts on the contracts will not vary due to future changes in specific prices. Goods used on contracts to be priced at market upon delivery are nonmonetary.

	Monetary	Nonmonetary

Assets

Inventories (other than inventories used on contracts) and commodity inventories (other than those described below)

| | | X |

Commodity inventories whose values are hedged by futures contracts whose contract amounts have not been recorded in the financial statements

Refer to paragraphs .194 and .195.

Loans to employees

| X | |

Prepaid insurance, advertising, rent, and other prepayments

Claims to future services are non-monetary. Prepayments that are deposits, advance payments, or receivables are monetary because the prepayment does not obtain a given quantity of future services, but rather is a fixed-money offset.

Long-term receivables

| X | |

Refundable deposits

| X | |

Advances to unconsolidated subsidiaries

| X | |

Equity investment in unconsolidated subsidiaries or other investees

| | X |

Pension, sinking, and other funds under an enterprise's control

The specific assets in the fund should be classified as monetary or nonmonetary. Refer to listings under securities above.

Property, plant, and equipment

| | X |

Accumulated depreciation of property, plant, and equipment

| | X |

The unguaranteed residual value of property owned by a lessor and leased under direct financing, sales-type, and leveraged leases

Refer to paragraphs .196 and .197.

	Monetary	Nonmonetary
Assets		
Investment tax credits that are deferred by a lessor as part of the unearned income of a leveraged lease	Refer to paragraphs .198 and .199.	
Portion of the carrying amount of lessors' assets leased under noncancellable operating leases that represent claims to fixed sums of money (paragraphs .200 and .201)		X
Cash surrender value of life insurance	X	
Purchase commitments—portion paid on fixed-price contracts		X
An advance on a fixed-price contract is the portion of the purchaser's claim to non-monetary goods or services that is recognized in the accounts; it is not a right to receive money.		
Advances to supplier—not on a fixed-price contract	X	
Such advances are rights to receive credit for a sum of money, not claims to a specified quantity of goods or services. [FAS89, ¶96]		
Deferred tax assets[a] [FAS109, ¶288w]	X	
Patents, trademarks, licenses, and formulas		X
Goodwill		X
Deferred life insurance policy acquisition costs[a]	X	
Such costs represent the portion of future cash receipts for premiums that is recognized in the accounts and are sometimes viewed as an offset to the policy reserve.		
Deferred property and casualty insurance policy acquisition costs related to unearned premiums		X
Other intangible assets and deferred charges		X

	Monetary	Nonmonetary
Liabilities		
Accounts and notes payable	X	
Accrued expenses payable (wages and so forth)	X	
Accrued vacation pay		If to be paid at the wage rates as of the vacation dates and if those rates may vary, accrued vacation pay is nonmonetary.
Cash dividends payable	X	
Obligations payable in foreign currency	X	
Sales commitments—portion collected on fixed-price contracts An advance received on a fixed- price contract is the portion of the seller's obligation to deliver goods or services that is recognized in the accounts; it is not an obligation to pay money.		X
Advances from customers—not on a fixed-price contract Such advances are equivalent to loans from customers and are not obligations to furnish specified quantities of goods or services.	X	
Accrued losses on firm purchase commitments In essence, these are accounts payable.	X	
Deferred revenue		If an obligation to furnish goods or services is involved, deferred revenue is nonmonetary. Certain "deferred income" items of savings and loan associations are monetary.
Refundable deposits	X	
Bonds payable and other long-term debt	X	

	Monetary	Nonmonetary
Liabilities		
Unamortized premium or discount and prepaid interest on bonds or notes payable Such items are inseparable from the debt to which they relate—a monetary item.	X	
Convertible bonds payable Until converted, these are obligations to pay sums of money.	X	
Accrued pension obligations		Fixed amounts payable to a fund are monetary; all other amounts are nonmonetary.
Obligations under warranties These are nonmonetary because they oblige the enterprise to furnish goods or services or their future price. [FAS89, ¶96]		X
Deferred tax liabilities[a] [FAS109, ¶288w]	X	
Deferred investment tax credits These are not to be settled by payment of cash and are related to nonmonetary assets.		X
Life insurance policy reserves These represent portions of policies' face values that are now deemed liabilities.	X	
Property and casualty insurance loss reserves	X	
Unearned property and casualty insurance premiums These are nonmonetary because they are principally obligations to furnish insurance coverage. The dollar amount of payments to be made under that coverage might vary materially due to changes in specific prices.		X
Deposit liabilities of financial institutions	X	
Minority interests in consolidated subsidiaries (paragraph .202)		X

	Monetary	**Nonmonetary**
Equity		
Capital stock of the enterprise or of its consolidated subsidiaries subject to mandatory redemption at fixed amounts (paragraph .203)	X	

---

[a]Although classification of this item as nonmonetary may be technically preferable, the monetary classification provides a more practical solution for the purposes of computing the purchasing power gain or loss on a consolidated basis.

[FAS89, ¶96]

.192 *Trading account investments in fixed-income securities owned by banks, investment brokers, and others.* Trading account securities are securities of all types carried in a dealer trading account that are held principally for resale to customers. The predominant practice by banks is to carry these securities at market value. Trading account investments include both fixed-income securities (for example, nonconvertible preferred stock, convertible bonds, and other bonds) and other securities (for example, common stock). Usually, trading account securities are held for extremely short periods of time—sometimes for only a few hours. Frequently, the enterprise buys and sells the securities expecting to make a profit on the difference between dealer and retail, or bid and ask, prices rather than on price changes during the period securities are held. However, the prices of the securities change with market forces. [FAS89, ¶97]

.193 Trading account investments in fixed-income securities are not claims to receive sums of money that are fixed or determinable. The market prices of the securities might and frequently do change while the securities are held. Generally, nonconvertible and nonparticipating preferred stock, convertible bonds that the market values primarily as bonds rather than as stocks, and nonconvertible bonds should be classified as monetary items. However, those classifications are based, in part, on the assumption that those securities would be held for long periods, if not to maturity. Trading account investments, on the other hand, are held for shorter periods and their value depends much less heavily on the general purchasing power of money and more on the specific values of the securities. Therefore, trading account investments in fixed-income securities should be classified as nonmonetary. [FAS89, ¶98]

.194 *Commodity inventories whose values are hedged by futures contracts.* Many enterprises hedge commodity inventories (such as grain or metals). *Short hedges* are designed to provide a degree of assurance that a decline in the price of the commodity would be offset by an increase in the value of the hedge contract. Short hedges thus tend to reduce the effects of price changes on the inventory that is hedged. [FAS89, ¶99]

.195 There are certain similarities between inventories that are hedged and inventories that are used on or committed to a fixed-price contract. In each case, the risk of gain or loss due to price changes before the inventory is sold is largely or entirely eliminated. To the extent that hedges fix the value of an inventory in dollars (or units of foreign functional currency, if appropriate), the inventory effectively becomes a monetary item. [FAS89, ¶100]

.196 *The unguaranteed residual value of property owned by a lessor and leased under direct financing, sales-type, and leveraged leases.* The unguaranteed residual value is included with the minimum lease payments, at present value, in the net investment in the lease. [FAS89, ¶101]

.197 The minimum lease payments are monetary items because they are claims to fixed sums of money. The residual value is not a claim to a fixed sum of money, so it is a nonmonetary item. Some assets and liabilities, of which the net investment in the lease is a good example, are combinations of claims to (or obligations of) fixed amounts and claims to (or obligations of) variable amounts. Ideally, those claims should be separated for purposes of classifying them as monetary and nonmonetary. However, if the information necessary to make the separation is not available or is impracticable to obtain, such items need not be divided into monetary and nonmonetary components and would be classified according to their dominant element. If the net investment in leases is principally claims to fixed amounts, it would be classified as monetary; it would be classified as nonmonetary if it is principally claims to residuals. [FAS89, ¶102]

.198 *Investment tax credits that are deferred by a lessor as part of the unearned income of a leveraged lease.* Under Section L10, "Leases," the deferred investment tax credit related to the leased asset is subtracted from rentals receivable and estimated residual value as part of the calculation of the lessor's investment in the leveraged lease. The investment, including the deferred investment tax credit related to the leveraged lease, is presented as one amount in the balance sheet. As indicated in paragraph .197, the investment in a leveraged lease would be classified as monetary or nonmonetary according to its dominant element. [FAS89, ¶103]

.199 As indicated in the table in paragraph .191, a deferred investment tax credit should be classified as nonmonetary but, if it is part of an investment in a leveraged lease and if the information necessary to separate its elements is not available or is impracticable to obtain, the investment would be classified according to its dominant element. [FAS89, ¶104]

.200 *Portion of the carrying amount of lessors' assets leased under noncancellable operating leases that represent claims to fixed sums of money.* These assets are carried at

depreciated historical cost under generally accepted accounting principles and are classified with or near property, plant, and equipment, which are nonmonetary. [FAS89, ¶105]

.201 The classification of a lease as an operating lease under Section L10 indicates that
the lease has not transferred substantially all of the benefits and risks incident to ownership to the lessee. Thus, the economic significance of the asset continues to depend heavily
on the value of the future lease rentals, residual values, and associated costs. Therefore,
an asset subject to an operating lease should be classified as nonmonetary. [FAS89, ¶106]

.202 *Minority interests in consolidated subsidiaries.* The interests of minority shareholders in the earnings and equity of subsidiaries are, from the consolidated entity's point
of view, claims that are not fixed. Rather, they are residuals that will vary based on the
subsidiary's earnings, dividends, and other transactions affecting its equity and so are
nonmonetary. (Refer to paragraph .203 as to classification of capital stock of the enterprise or of its consolidated subsidiaries subject to mandatory redemption at fixed amounts.)
[FAS89, ¶107]

.203 *Capital stock of the enterprise or of its consolidated subsidiaries subject to mandatory redemption at fixed amounts.* Such securities are claims of the stockholders to a
fixed sum of money and therefore are monetary. Classification as a monetary item called
for in paragraphs .191 through .203 is only for purposes of determining a purchasing
power gain or loss. Paragraphs .191 through .203 do not address how such securities
should be classified in balance sheets or the accounting for dividends on those securities.
[FAS89, ¶108]

The Consumer Price Index

.204 [The table in Exhibit 204A is the offical Department of Labor Consumer Price Index—
CPI(U), U.S. City Average, All Items (1967 = 100). This table includes monthly indexes
and the average index for the year from 1913. Monthly updates to the table are published
in the United States Department of Labor, Bureau of Labor Statistics, *News.*]

[Exhibit 204A]

Consumer Price Index
All Urban Consumers—(CPI-U)
U.S. City Average
All Items
(1967 = 100)

Year	Jan.	Feb.	Mar.	Apr.	May	June	July	Aug.	Sept.	Oct.	Nov.	Dec.	Avg.
1913	29.4	29.3	29.3	29.4	29.2	29.3	29.6	29.8	29.9	30.1	30.2	30.1	29.7
1914	30.1	29.8	29.7	29.4	29.6	29.8	30.1	30.5	30.6	30.4	30.5	30.4	30.1
1915	30.3	30.1	29.8	30.1	30.2	30.3	30.3	30.3	30.4	30.7	30.9	31.0	30.4
1916	31.3	31.3	31.6	31.9	32.0	32.4	32.4	32.8	33.4	33.8	34.4	34.6	32.7
1917	35.0	35.8	36.0	37.6	38.4	38.8	38.4	39.0	39.7	40.4	40.5	41.0	38.4
1918	41.8	42.2	42.0	42.5	43.3	44.1	45.2	46.0	47.1	47.9	48.7	49.4	45.1
1919	49.5	48.4	49.0	49.9	50.6	50.7	52.1	53.0	53.3	54.2	55.5	56.7	51.8
1920	57.8	58.5	59.1	60.8	61.8	62.7	62.3	60.7	60.0	59.7	59.3	58.0	60.0
1921	57.0	55.2	54.8	54.1	53.1	52.8	52.9	53.1	52.5	52.4	52.1	51.8	53.6
1922	50.7	50.6	50.0	50.0	50.0	50.1	50.2	49.7	49.8	50.1	50.3	50.5	50.2
1923	50.3	50.2	50.4	50.6	50.7	51.0	51.5	51.3	51.6	51.7	51.8	51.8	51.1
1924	51.7	51.5	51.2	51.0	51.0	51.0	51.1	51.0	51.2	51.4	51.6	51.7	51.2
1925	51.8	51.6	51.7	51.6	51.8	52.4	53.1	53.1	52.9	53.1	54.0	53.7	52.5
1926	53.7	53.5	53.2	53.7	53.4	53.0	52.5	52.2	52.5	52.7	52.9	52.9	53.0
1927	52.5	52.1	51.8	51.8	52.2	52.7	51.7	51.4	51.7	52.0	51.9	51.8	52.0
1928	51.7	51.2	51.2	51.3	51.6	51.2	51.2	51.3	51.7	51.6	51.5	51.3	51.3
1929	51.2	51.1	50.9	50.7	51.0	51.2	51.7	51.9	51.8	51.8	51.7	51.4	51.3
1930	51.2	51.0	50.7	51.0	50.7	50.4	49.7	49.4	49.7	49.4	49.0	48.3	50.0

Year													
1931	45.6	43.7	44.1	44.6	44.9	45.1	45.2	45.3	45.8	46.3	46.6	46.9	47.6
1932	40.9	39.2	39.6	39.8	40.1	40.3	40.8	40.8	41.1	41.7	42.0	42.2	42.8
1933	38.8	39.4	39.6	39.6	39.6	39.6	39.2	38.1	37.7	37.6	37.7	38.0	38.6
1934	40.1	40.2	40.3	40.4	40.7	40.1	40.0	40.0	39.9	39.8	39.9	39.9	39.6
1935	41.1	41.4	41.3	41.1	41.1	40.9	40.9	41.1	41.2	41.4	41.0	41.1	40.8
1936	41.5	41.9	41.9	41.9	42.0	41.9	41.6	41.4	41.0	41.0	41.0	41.2	41.4
1937	43.0	43.2	43.3	43.6	43.8	43.4	43.3	43.1	43.0	42.8	42.6	42.3	42.2
1938	42.2	42.0	41.9	42.0	42.2	42.2	42.3	42.2	42.2	42.4	42.2	42.2	42.6
1939	41.6	41.8	42.0	42.0	42.2	41.4	41.4	41.4	41.4	41.4	41.5	41.6	41.8
1940	42.0	42.2	42.0	42.0	42.0	41.9	42.0	42.1	42.0	41.9	41.9	42.0	41.7
1941	44.1	46.3	46.2	45.8	45.3	44.5	44.1	43.9	43.1	42.8	42.4	42.2	42.2
1942	48.8	50.6	50.2	49.9	49.4	49.3	49.0	48.8	48.7	48.2	47.9	47.3	46.9
1943	51.8	52.2	52.1	52.2	52.0	51.8	52.0	52.4	52.5	52.1	51.5	50.7	50.6
1944	52.7	53.3	53.1	53.1	53.1	53.1	52.9	52.6	52.5	52.3	52.0	52.0	52.1
1945	53.9	54.5	54.3	54.1	54.1	54.3	54.3	54.2	53.7	53.3	53.2	53.2	53.3
1946	58.5	64.4	63.9	62.4	61.2	60.5	59.2	55.9	55.3	55.0	54.7	54.3	54.5
1947	66.9	70.2	69.3	68.9	68.9	67.3	66.6	66.0	65.5	65.7	65.7	64.3	64.4
1948	72.1	72.1	72.6	73.1	73.4	73.4	73.1	72.2	71.7	71.2	70.2	70.4	71.0
1949	71.4	70.8	71.2	71.1	71.5	71.2	71.0	71.5	71.4	71.5	71.4	71.2	72.0
1950	72.1	74.9	73.9	73.6	73.2	72.7	72.1	71.4	71.0	70.7	70.6	70.3	70.5

Exhibit 204A (continued)

Year	Jan.	Feb.	Mar.	Apr.	May	June	July	Aug.	Sept.	Oct.	Nov.	Dec.	Avg.
1951	76.1	77.0	77.3	77.4	77.7	77.6	77.7	77.7	78.2	78.6	79.0	79.3	77.8
1952	79.3	78.8	78.8	79.1	79.2	79.4	80.0	80.1	80.0	80.1	80.1	80.0	79.5
1953	79.8	79.4	79.6	79.7	79.9	80.2	80.4	80.6	80.7	80.9	80.6	80.5	80.1
1954	80.7	80.6	80.5	80.3	80.6	80.7	80.7	80.6	80.4	80.2	80.3	80.1	80.5
1955	80.1	80.1	80.1	80.1	80.1	80.1	80.4	80.2	80.5	80.5	80.6	80.4	80.2
1956	80.3	80.3	80.4	80.5	80.9	81.4	82.0	81.9	82.0	82.5	82.5	82.7	81.4
1957	82.8	83.1	83.3	83.6	83.8	84.3	84.7	84.8	84.9	84.9	85.2	85.2	84.3
1958	85.7	85.8	86.4	86.6	86.6	86.7	86.8	86.7	86.7	86.7	86.8	86.7	86.6
1959	86.8	86.7	86.7	86.8	86.9	87.3	87.5	87.4	87.7	88.0	88.0	88.0	87.3
1960	87.9	88.0	88.0	88.5	88.5	88.7	88.7	88.7	88.8	89.2	89.3	89.3	88.7
1961	89.3	89.3	89.3	89.3	89.3	89.4	89.8	89.7	89.9	89.9	89.9	89.9	89.6
1962	89.9	90.1	90.3	90.5	90.5	90.5	90.7	90.7	91.2	91.1	91.1	91.0	90.6
1963	91.1	91.2	91.3	91.3	91.3	91.7	92.1	92.1	92.1	92.2	92.3	92.5	91.7
1964	92.6	92.5	92.6	92.7	92.7	92.9	93.1	93.0	93.2	93.3	93.5	93.6	92.9
1965	93.6	93.6	93.7	94.0	94.2	94.7	94.8	94.6	94.8	94.9	95.1	95.4	94.5
1966	95.4	96.0	96.3	96.7	96.8	97.1	97.4	97.9	98.1	98.5	98.5	98.6	97.2
1967	98.6	98.7	98.9	99.1	99.4	99.7	100.2	100.5	100.7	101.0	101.3	101.6	100.0
1968	102.0	102.3	102.8	103.1	103.4	104.0	104.5	104.8	105.1	105.7	106.1	106.4	104.2
1969	106.7	107.1	108.0	108.7	109.0	109.7	110.2	110.7	111.2	111.6	112.2	112.9	109.8
1970	113.3	113.9	114.5	115.2	115.7	116.3	116.7	116.9	117.5	118.1	118.5	119.1	116.3

Year													
1971	119.2	119.4	119.8	120.2	120.8	121.5	121.8	122.1	122.2	122.4	122.6	123.1	121.3
1972	123.2	123.8	124.0	124.3	124.7	125.0	125.5	125.7	126.2	126.6	126.9	127.3	125.3
1973	127.7	128.6	129.8	130.7	131.5	132.4	132.7	135.1	135.5	136.6	137.6	138.5	133.1
1974	139.7	141.5	143.1	143.9	145.5	146.9	148.0	149.9	151.7	153.0	154.3	155.4	147.7
1975	156.1	157.2	157.8	158.6	159.3	160.6	162.3	162.8	163.6	164.6	165.6	166.3	161.2
1976	166.7	167.1	167.5	168.2	169.2	170.1	171.1	171.9	172.6	173.3	173.8	174.3	170.5
1977	175.3	177.1	178.2	179.6	180.6	181.8	182.6	183.3	184.0	184.5	185.4	186.1	181.5
1978	187.2	188.4	189.8	191.5	193.3	195.3	196.7	197.8	199.3	200.9	202.0	202.9	195.4
1979	204.7	207.1	209.1	211.5	214.1	216.6	218.9	221.1	223.4	225.4	227.5	229.9	217.4
1980	233.2	236.4	239.8	242.5	244.9	247.6	247.8	249.4	251.7	253.9	256.2	258.4	246.8
1981	260.5	263.2	265.1	266.8	269.0	271.3	274.4	276.5	279.3	279.9	280.7	281.5	272.4
1982	282.5	283.4	283.1	284.3	287.1	290.6	292.2	292.8	293.3	294.1	293.6	292.4	289.1
1983	293.1	293.2	293.4	295.5	297.1	298.1	299.3	300.3	301.8	302.6	303.1	303.5	298.4
1984	305.2	306.6	307.3	308.8	309.7	310.7	311.7	313.0	314.5	315.3	315.3	315.5	311.1
1985	316.1	317.4	318.8	320.1	321.3	322.3	322.8	323.5	324.5	325.5	326.6	327.4	322.2
1986	328.4	327.5	326.0	325.3	326.3	327.9	328.0	328.6	330.2	330.5	330.8	331.1	328.4
1987	333.1	334.4	335.9	337.7	338.7	340.1	340.8	342.7	344.4	345.3	345.8	345.7	340.4
1988	346.7	347.4	349.0	350.8	352.0	353.5	354.9	356.6	358.9	360.1	360.5	360.9	354.3
1989	362.7	364.1	366.2	368.8	370.8	371.7	372.7	373.1	374.6	376.2	377.0	377.6	371.3
1990	381.5	383.3	385.5	386.2	386.9	389.1	390.7	394.1	397.5	400.0	400.7	400.9	391.4

Exhibit 204A (continued)

Year	Jan.	Feb.	Mar.	Apr.	May	June	July	Aug.	Sept.	Oct.	Nov.	Dec.	Avg.
1991	403.1	403.8	404.3	405.1	406.3	407.3	408.0	409.2	411.1	411.5	412.7	413.0	408.0
1992	413.8	415.2	417.2	417.9	418.6	419.9	420.8	422.0	423.2	424.7	425.3	425.2	420.3
1993	427.0	428.7	430.1	431.2	432.0	432.4	432.6	433.9	434.7	436.4	436.9	436.8	432.7
1994	437.8	439.3	441.1	441.4	441.9	443.3	444.4	446.4	447.5	448.0	448.6	448.4	444.0
1995	450.3	452.0	453.5	455.0	455.8								

Source: U.S. Department of Labor, Room 1539, Bureau of Labor Statistics, Washington, D.C. 20212. The CPI Detailed Report may be ordered from the Superintendent of Documents, U.S. Government Printing Office, Washington, D.C. 20402. The Library of Congress Catalog number is 74-647019.]

Glossary

.401 Current cost/constant purchasing power accounting. A method of accounting based on measures of current cost or lower recoverable amount in units of currency, each of which has the same general purchasing power. For operations in which the dollar is the functional currency, the general purchasing power of the dollar is used and the CPI-U is the required measure of purchasing power (paragraph .132). For operations in which the functional currency is other than the dollar, the general purchasing power of either the dollar or the functional currency is used (paragraph .133). [FAS89, ¶44]

.402 Current market value. The amount of cash, or its equivalent, expected to be derived from the sale of an asset net of costs required to be incurred as a result of the sale. [FAS89, ¶44]

.403 Historical cost accounting. The generally accepted method of accounting used in the primary financial statements that is based on measures of historical prices without restatement into units, each of which has the same general purchasing power. [FAS89, ¶44]

.404 Historical cost/constant purchasing power accounting. A method of accounting based on measures of historical prices in units of a currency, each of which has the same general purchasing power. [FAS89, ¶44]

.405 Income from continuing operations. Income after applicable income taxes but excluding the results of discontinued operations, extraordinary items, the cumulative effect of accounting changes, translation adjustments, purchasing power gains and losses on monetary items, and increases and decreases in the current cost or lower recoverable amount of nonmonetary assets and liabilities. [FAS89, ¶44]

.406 Income-producing real estate. Properties that meet all of the following criteria:

a. Cash flows can be directly associated with a long-term leasing agreement with unaffiliated parties.
b. The property is being operated. (It is not in a construction phase.)
c. Future cash flows from the property are reasonably estimable.
d. Ancillary services are not a significant part of the lease agreement.

Hotels, which have occupancy rates and related cash flows that may fluctuate to a relatively large extent, do not meet the criteria for income-producing real estate. [FAS89, ¶44]

.407 **Mineral resource assets.** Assets that are directly associated with and derive value from all minerals that are extracted from the earth. Such minerals include oil and gas, ores containing ferrous and nonferrous metals, coal, shale, geothermal steam, sulphur, salt, stone, phosphate, sand, and gravel. Mineral resource assets include mineral interests in properties, completed and uncompleted wells, and related equipment and facilities and other facilities required for purposes of extraction (Section Oi5, paragraph .103). This definition does not cover support equipment because that equipment is included in the property, plant, and equipment for which current cost measurements are required by this section. [FAS89, ¶44]

.408 **Monetary asset.** Money or a claim to receive a sum of money the amount of which is fixed or determinable without reference to future prices of specific goods or services. [FAS89, ¶44]

.409 **Monetary liability.** An obligation to pay a sum of money the amount of which is fixed or determinable without reference to future prices of specific goods and services. [FAS89, ¶44]

.410 **Motion picture films.** All types of films and videotapes and disks, including features, television specials, series, and cartoons that meet one of the following criteria:

a. Exhibited in theaters
b. Licensed for exhibition by individual television stations, groups of stations, networks, cable television systems, or other means
c. Licensed for commercial reproduction (for example, for the home viewing market).

[FAS89, ¶44]

.411 **Parity adjustment.** The effect of the difference between local and U.S. inflation for the year on net assets (that is, shareholders' equity) measured in nominal dollars. If only the differential rates of U.S. and local inflation are reflected in the exchange rates (parity), the parity adjustment and the translation adjustment net to zero. Therefore, the sum of the parity adjustment and the translation adjustment represents the effect of exchange rate changes in excess of (or less than) that needed to maintain purchasing power parity between the functional currency and the dollar. [FAS89, ¶44]

.412 **Probable mineral reserves.** In extractive industries other than oil and gas, the estimated quantities of commercially recoverable reserves that are less well defined than proved. [FAS89, ¶44]

.413 **Proved mineral reserves.** In extractive industries other than oil and gas, the estimated quantities of commercially recoverable reserves that, on the basis of geological, geophysical, and engineering data, can be demonstrated with a reasonably high degree of certainty to be recoverable in the future from known mineral deposits by either primary or improved recovery methods. [FAS89, ¶44]

.414 **Purchasing power gain or loss** on net monetary items. The net gain or loss determined by restating in units of constant purchasing power the opening and closing balances of, and transactions in, monetary assets and liabilities. [FAS89, ¶44]

.415 **Recoverable amount.** Current worth of the net amount of cash expected to be recoverable from the use or sale of an asset (paragraphs .125 through .127). [FAS89, ¶44]

.416 **Restate-translate.** An approach to converting current cost/nominal functional currency data of a foreign operation into units of constant purchasing power expressed in dollars. Using this approach, the current cost/nominal functional currency data are restated into units of constant purchasing power using a general price index for the foreign currency. After restatement into units of constant functional currency purchasing power, the current cost data are translated into dollars. This approach often necessitates a parity adjustment. [FAS89, ¶44]

.417 **Translate-restate.** An approach to converting current cost/nominal functional currency data of a foreign operation into units of constant purchasing power expressed in dollars. Using this approach, the current cost/nominal functional currency data are first translated into dollars and then restated into units of constant purchasing power using the CPI-U. [FAS89, ¶44]

.418 **Translation adjustment.** The effect that results from the process of translating an entity's financial statements from its functional currency into the dollar (paragraphs .134 and .135). [FAS89, ¶44]

.419 **Value in use.** The amount determined by discounting the future cash flows (including the ultimate proceeds of disposal) expected to be derived from the use of an asset at an appropriate rate that allows for the risk of the activities concerned. [FAS89, ¶44]

(The next page is 6961.)

COLLATERALIZED MORTGAGE OBLIGATIONS   SECTION C30

Source: FASB Technical Bulletin 85-2

Supplemental Guidance

.501 *Question*—Certain types of bonds secured by mortgage-backed securities[501] or mortgage loans are structured so that all or substantially all of the collections of principal and interest from the underlying collateral are paid through to the holders of the bonds. The bonds are typically issued with two or more maturity classes; the actual maturity of each bond class will vary depending upon the timing of the cash receipts from the underlying collateral. These bonds are issued by a minimally capitalized special-purpose corporation (issuer) established by a sponsoring parent corporation and are commonly referred to as "collateralized mortgage obligations," or CMOs. The mortgage-backed securities or mortgage loans securing the obligation are acquired by the special-purpose corporation and then pledged to an independent trustee until the issuer's obligation under the bond indenture has been fully satisfied. The investor can look only to the issuer's assets (primarily the trusteed assets) or third parties (such as insurers or guarantors) for repayment of the obligation. As a result, the sponsor and its other affiliates have no financial obligation under the instrument, although one of those entities may retain the responsibility for servicing the underlying mortgage loans. How should the special-purpose issuer account for this transaction? [FTB85-2, ¶1]

.502 *Response*—CMOs should be presumed to be borrowings that are reported as liabilities in the financial statements of the issuer unless all but a nominal[502] portion of the future economic benefits inherent in the associated collateral have been irrevocably passed to the investor and no affiliate[503] of the issuer can be required to make future payments with respect to the obligation. The existence of all of the following conditions

---

[501]The term *mortgage-backed securities* is defined in Section Mo4, "Mortgage Banking Activities," as securities issued by a governmental agency or corporation (for example, the Government National Mortgage Association or the Federal Home Loan Mortgage Corporation) or by private issuers (for example, the Federal National Mortgage Association, banks, and mortgage banking enterprises). Mortgage-backed securities generally are referred to as mortgage participation certificates or pass-through certificates (PCs). A PC represents an undivided interest in a pool of specific mortgage loans. [FTB85-2, ¶1, fn1]

[502]The term *nominal* is used in this section to mean insignificantly small or trifling (The American Heritage Dictionary, 2d college ed. [Boston: Houghton Mifflin Company, 1982], p. 845) and implies a lower amount than that normally associated with materiality as defined in FASB Concepts Statement 2, *Qualitative Characteristics of Accounting Information.* [FTB85-2, ¶2, fn2]

[503]The term *affiliate* is defined in Section R36, "Related Parties," as "a party that, directly or indirectly through one or more intermediaries, controls, is controlled by, or is under common control with an enterprise" and is used in the same sense in this section. [FTB85-2, ¶2, fn3]

at the date of issuance of the CMO would generally indicate that the borrowing presumption has been overcome, that the associated collateral should be eliminated from the issuer's financial statements, and that gain or loss should be recognized:

a. The issuer and its affiliates surrender the future economic benefits embodied in the collateral securing the obligation.
   (1) Neither the issuer nor its affiliates have the right or obligation to substitute collateral or obtain it by calling the obligation.[504]
   (2) The expected residual interest,[505] if any, in the collateral is nominal.[506]
b. No affiliate of the issuer can be required to make any future payments with respect to the obligation.[507]
   (1) The investor can look only to the issuer's assets or third parties (such as insurers or guarantors) for repayment of both principal and interest on the obligation, and neither the sponsor of the issuer nor its other affiliates are secondarily liable.
   (2) Neither the issuer nor its affiliates can be required to redeem the obligation prior to its stated maturity other than through the normal pay-through of collections from the collateral.

If the associated collateral is eliminated from the financial statements because all of the above conditions are met, any expected residual interest in the collateral should not be recognized as an asset. Rather, such residual interest should be recorded as it accrues to the benefit of the issuer or its affiliates. If servicing rights are retained by an affiliate of the issuer and the stated servicing fee rate is less than a current (normal) servicing fee rate,[508] the CMO proceeds should be adjusted to provide for a normal servicing fee in each subsequent servicing period. [(Refer to Section Mo4, "Mortgage Banking Activi-

---

[504]Some CMOs require or permit the issuer to call the obligation when the amount of the outstanding bonds is minor to keep the cost of servicing the underlying mortgage loans relative to their remaining outstanding balances from becoming unreasonable. If the amount of reacquired collateral is expected to be minor, the existence of this type of call provision alone does not preclude the collateral from being eliminated from the financial statements. [FTB85-2, ¶2, fn4]

[505]The expected residual interest in the collateral should be computed using the present value of all amounts expected to revert to the issuer or its affiliates (including reinvestment earnings). Excess (above-normal) servicing fees should be considered to be part of the expected residual interest. [FTB85-2, ¶2, fn5]

[506]This condition would not be met if an affiliate of the issuer retained a partial ownership interest in the mortgage-backed securities or mortgage loans securing the obligation. [FTB85-2, ¶2, fn6]

[507]The retention of servicing rights by an affiliate of the issuer does not, in itself, preclude the associated collateral from being eliminated from the financial statements. [FTB85-2, ¶2, fn7]

[508]The term *current (normal) servicing fee rate* is defined in Section Mo4, "Mortgage Banking Activities," as "a servicing fee rate that is representative of servicing fee rates most commonly used in comparable servicing agreements covering similar types of mortgage loans" and is used in the same sense in this section. [FTB85-2, ¶2, fn8]

ties," paragraphs .501 through .507 for further guidance on determining a normal servicing fee rate.)] All transaction costs associated with the offering should be charged to expense when the associated collateral is eliminated from the financial statements. [FTB85-2, ¶2]

.503 Because a majority-owned entity formed to issue the CMO is merely a conduit for the sponsor, the financial statements of that entity should be consolidated with those of its sponsor.[509] [FTB85-2, ¶3]

.504 For CMOs recorded as liabilities, the pledging of collateral against the related liability is not tantamount to prepayment as it was contemplated by Section B10, "Balance Sheet Display: Offsetting," paragraphs .101 through .103. Therefore, CMOs are not an exception to the general principle of accounting stated in Section B10, paragraphs .101 through .103, and offsetting the collateral against the related liability in the balance sheet is not appropriate. [FTB85-2, ¶4]

(The next page is 6985.)

---

[509][Deleted 11/87 because of FASB Statement 94, *Consolidation of All Majority-Owned Subsidiaries* and FASB Statement 111, *Rescission of FASB Statement No. 32 and Technical Corrections.*]

Source: FASB Statement 47

Summary

An enterprise shall disclose its commitments under unconditional purchase obligations that are associated with suppliers' financing arrangements. Such obligations often are in the form of take-or-pay contracts and throughput contracts. Future payments on long-term borrowings and redeemable stock also shall be disclosed. For long-term unconditional purchase obligations that are associated with suppliers' financing and are not recognized on purchasers' balance sheets, the disclosures include the nature of the obligation, the amount of the fixed and determinable obligation in the aggregate and for each of the next five years, a description of any portion of the obligation that is variable, and the purchases in each year for which an income statement is presented. For long-term unconditional purchase obligations that are associated with suppliers' financing and are recognized on purchasers' balance sheets, payments for each of the next five years shall be disclosed. For long-term borrowings and redeemable stock, the disclosures include maturities and sinking fund requirements (if any) for each of the next five years and redemption requirements for each of the next five years, respectively.

Definition and Scope

.101 [This section specifies disclosures relating to] unconditional purchase obligations typically associated with **project financing arrangements.** [FAS47, ¶1] An unconditional purchase obligation is an obligation to transfer funds in the future for fixed or minimum amounts or quantities of goods or services at fixed or minimum prices (for example, as in **take-or-pay contracts** or **throughput contracts**). An unconditional purchase obligation that has all of the following characteristics shall be disclosed in accordance with paragraph .102 (if not recorded on the purchaser's balance sheet) or in accordance with paragraph .105(a) (if recorded on the purchaser's balance sheet):

a. Is noncancelable, or cancelable only
   (1) Upon the occurrence of some remote contingency or
   (2) With the permission of the other party or

　　(3) If a replacement agreement is signed between the same parties or

　　(4) Upon payment of a penalty in an amount such that continuation of the agreement appears reasonably assured

　b. Was negotiated as part of arranging financing for the facilities that will provide the contracted goods or services or for costs related to those goods or services (for example, carrying costs for contracted goods)[1]

　c. Has a remaining term in excess of one year.

Future minimum lease payments under leases that have those characteristics need not be disclosed in accordance with this section if they are disclosed in accordance with Section L10, "Leases." [FAS47, ¶6]

Unrecorded Obligations

.102　A purchaser shall disclose unconditional purchase obligations that meet the criteria of paragraph .101 and that have not been recognized on its balance sheet. The disclosures shall include:

　a. The nature and term of the obligation(s)

　b. The amount of the fixed and determinable portion of the obligation(s) as of the date of the latest balance sheet presented in the aggregate and, if determinable, for each of the five succeeding fiscal years (refer to paragraph .103)

　c. The nature of any variable components of the obligation(s)

　d. The amounts purchased under the obligation(s) (for example, the take-or-pay or through-put contract) for each period for which an income statement is presented.

Disclosures of similar or related unconditional purchase obligations may be combined. Those disclosures may be omitted only if the aggregate commitment for all such obligations not disclosed is immaterial. [Disclosures about unconditional purchase obligations that are not subject to the requirements of this section may be required by the provisions in Section F25, "Financial Instruments: Disclosure."] [FAS47, ¶7]

.103　Disclosure of the amount of imputed interest necessary to reduce the unconditional purchase obligation(s) to present value is encouraged but not required. The discount rate shall be the effective initial interest rate of the borrowings that financed the facility (or facilities) that will provide the contracted goods or services, if known by the purchaser. If not, the discount rate shall be the **purchaser's incremental borrowing rate** at the date the obligation is entered into. [FAS47, ¶8]

---

[1]A purchaser [is not required] to investigate whether a supplier used an unconditional purchase obligation to help secure financing, if the purchaser would otherwise be unaware of that fact. [FAS47, ¶17]

Recorded Obligations and Redeemable Stock

.104 Certain unconditional purchase obligations are presently recorded as liabilities on purchasers' balance sheets with the related assets also recognized. This section does not alter that accounting treatment or the treatment of future unconditional purchase obligations that are substantially the same as those obligations already recorded as liabilities with related assets, nor does it suggest that disclosure is an appropriate substitute for accounting recognition if the substance of an arrangement is the acquisition of an asset and incurrence of a liability. [FAS47, ¶9]

.105 The following information shall be disclosed for each of the five years following the date of the latest balance sheet presented:

a. The aggregate amount of payments for unconditional purchase obligations that meet the criteria of paragraph .101 and that have been recognized on the purchaser's balance sheet
b. The combined aggregate amount of maturities and sinking fund requirements for all long-term borrowings
c. The amount of redemption requirements for all issues of capital stock that are redeemable at fixed or determinable prices on fixed or determinable dates, separately by issue or combined. [FAS47, ¶10]

Illustrations of the Application of This Section to Common Arrangements

Example 1

.106 B Company has entered into a throughput agreement with a manufacturing plant providing that B will submit specified quantities of a chemical (representing a portion of plant capacity) for processing through the plant each period while the debt used to finance the plant remains outstanding. B's processing charges are intended to be sufficient to cover a proportional share of fixed and variable operating expenses and debt service of the plant. If, however, the processing charges do not cover such operating expenses and debt service, B must advance additional funds to cover a specified percentage of operating expenses and debt service. Such additional funds are considered advance payments for future throughput. [FAS47, ¶24]

.107 B's unconditional obligation to pay a specified percentage of the plant's fixed operating expenses and debt service is fixed and determinable, while the amount of variable operating expenses that B is obligated to pay will vary depending on plant operations and economic conditions. [FAS47, ¶25]

.108 B's disclosure might be as follows:

> To secure access to facilities to process chemical X, the company has signed a processing agreement with a chemical company allowing B Company to submit 100,000 tons for processing annually for 20 years. Under the terms of the agreement, B Company may be required to advance funds against future processing charges if the chemical company is unable to meet its financial obligations. The aggregate amount of required payments at December 31, 19X1 is as follows (in thousands):

19X2	$ 10,000
19X3	10,000
19X4	9,000
19X5	8,000
19X6	8,000
Later years	100,000
Total	145,000
Less: Amount representing interest	(45,000)
Total at present value	$100,000

> In addition, the company is required to pay a proportional share of the variable operating expenses of the plant. The company's total processing charges under the agreement in each of the past 3 years have been $12 million. [FAS47, ¶26]

Example 2

.109 C Company has entered into a throughput agreement with a natural gas pipeline providing that C will provide specified quantities of natural gas (representing a portion of capacity) for transportation through the pipeline each period while the debt used to finance the pipeline remains outstanding. The tariff approved by the Federal Energy Regulatory Commission contains two portions, a demand charge and a commodity charge. The demand charge is computed to cover debt service, depreciation, and certain expected expenses. The commodity charge is intended to cover other expenses and provide a return on the pipeline enterprise's investment. C Company must pay the demand charge based on the contracted quantity regardless of actual quantities shipped, while the commodity charge is applied to actual quantities shipped. Accordingly, the demand charge multiplied by the contracted quantity represents a fixed and determinable payment. [FAS47, ¶27]

.110 C's disclosure might be as follows:

> C Company has signed an agreement providing for the availability of needed pipeline transportation capacity through 1990. Under that agreement, the enterprise must make specified minimum payments monthly. The aggregate amount of such required payments at December 31, 19X1 is as follows (in thousands):

19X2	$ 5,000
19X3	5,000
19X4	5,000
19X5	4,000
19X6	4,000
Later years	26,000
Total	49,000
Less: Amount representing interest	(9,000)
Total at present value	$40,000

> In addition, the enterprise is required to pay additional amounts depending on actual quantities shipped under the agreement. The enterprise's total payments under the agreement were (in thousands) $6,000 in 19W9 and $5,500 both in 19X0 and in 19X1. [FAS47, ¶28]

Example 3

.111 A subsidiary of F Company has entered into a take-or-pay contract with an ammonia plant. F's subsidiary is obligated to purchase 50 percent of the planned capacity production of the plant each period while the debt used to finance the plant remains outstanding. The monthly payment equals the sum of 50 percent of raw material costs, operating expenses, depreciation, interest on the debt used to finance the plant, and a return on the owner's equity investment. [FAS47, ¶29]

.112 F's disclosure might be as follows:

> To assure a long-term supply, one of the enterprise's subsidiaries has contracted to purchase half the output of an ammonia plant through the year

2005 and to make minimum annual payments as follows, whether or not it is able to take delivery (in thousands):

19X2 through 19X6 ($6,000 per annum)	$ 30,000
Later years	120,000
Total	150,000
Less: Amount representing interest	(65,000)
Total at present value	$ 85,000

In addition, the subsidiary must reimburse the owner of the plant for a pro-portional share of raw material costs and operating expenses of the plant. The subsidiary's total purchases under the agreement were (in thousands) $7,000, $7,100, and $7,200 in 19W9, 19X0, and 19X1, respectively. [FAS47, ¶30]

Example 4

.113 D Company has outstanding two long-term borrowings and one issue of preferred stock with mandatory redemption requirements. The first borrowing is a $100 million sinking fund debenture with annual sinking fund payments of $10 million in 19X2, 19X3, and 19X4, $15 million in 19X5 and 19X6, and $20 million in 19X7 and 19X8. The second borrowing is a $50 million note due in 19X5. The $30 million issue of preferred stock requires a 5 percent annual cumulative sinking fund payment of $1.5 million until retired. [FAS47, ¶31]

.114 D's disclosures might be as follows:

Maturities and sinking fund requirements on long-term debt and sinking fund requirements on preferred stock subject to mandatory redemption are as follows (in thousands):

	Long-Term Debt	Preferred Stock
19X2	$10,000	$1,500
19X3	10,000	1,500
19X4	10,000	1,500
19X5	65,000	1,500
19X6	15,000	1,500

[FAS47, ¶32]

Glossary

.401 Project financing arrangement. The financing of a major capital project in which the lender looks principally to the cash flows and earnings of the project as the source of funds for repayment and to the assets of the project as collateral for the loan. The general credit of the project entity is usually not a significant factor, either because the entity is an enterprise without other assets or because the financing is without direct recourse to the owner(s) of the enterprise. [FAS47, ¶23]

.402 Purchaser's incremental borrowing rate. The rate that, at the inception of an unconditional purchase obligation, the purchaser would have incurred to borrow over a similar term the funds necessary to discharge the obligation. [FAS47, ¶23]

.403 Take-or-pay contract. An agreement between a purchaser and a seller that provides for the purchaser to pay specified amounts periodically in return for products or services. The purchaser must make specified minimum payments even if it does not take delivery of the contracted products or services. [FAS47, ¶23]

.404 Throughput contract. An agreement between a shipper (processor) and the owner of a transportation facility (such as an oil or natural gas pipeline or a ship) or a manufacturing facility that provides for the shipper (processor) to pay specified amounts periodically in return for the transportation (processing) of a product. The shipper (processor) is obligated to provide specified minimum quantities to be transported (processed) in each period and is required to make cash payments even if it does not provide the contracted quantities. [FAS47, ¶23]

(The next page is 7081.)

Sources: APB Opinion 12; FASB Statement 106; FASB Statement 111

Summary

Estimated amounts to be paid under a deferred compensation contract that is not equivalent to a pension plan or a postretirement health or welfare benefit plan shall be accrued over the period of an employee's active employment from the time the contract is signed to the employee's full eligibility date.

.101 Section P16, "Pension Costs," or Section P40, "Postretirement Benefits Other Than Pensions," applies to deferred compensation contracts with individual employees if those contracts, taken together, are equivalent to a postretirement income plan or a postretirement health or welfare benefit plan, respectively. [FAS106, ¶13]

Individual Deferred Compensation Contracts

.101A Deferred compensation contracts shall be accounted for individually on an accrual basis in accordance with the terms of the underlying contract. To the extent the terms of the contract attribute all or a portion of the expected future benefits to an individual year of the employee's service, the cost of those benefits shall be recognized in that year. To the extent the terms of the contract attribute all or a portion of the expected future benefits to a period of service greater than one year, the cost of those benefits shall be accrued over that period of the employee's service in a systematic and rational manner. At the end of that period the aggregate amount accrued shall equal the then present value of the benefits expected to be provided to the employee, any beneficiaries, and covered dependents in exchange for the employee's service to that date.[1] [FAS106, ¶13] If elements of both current and future services are present, only the portion applicable to the current services shall be accrued. [APB12, ¶6]

.102 Some deferred compensation contracts provide for periodic payments to employees or their surviving spouses for life with provisions for a minimum lump-sum settle-

---

[1]The amounts to be accrued periodically shall result in an accrued amount at the full eligibility date (as defined in Section P40) equal to the then present value of all of the future benefits expected to be paid. Paragraphs [.104] through .106 illustrate application of this paragraph. [FAS106, ¶13]

ment in the event of the early death of one or all of the beneficiaries. The estimated amount[1a] of future payments to be made under those contracts shall be accrued over the period of active employment from the time the contract is entered into. The estimated amount shall be based on the life expectancy of each individual concerned (based on the most recent mortality tables available) or on the estimated cost of an annuity contract rather than on the minimum payable in the event of early death. [APB12, ¶7]

Illustrations

.103 Paragraphs .104 through .106 illustrate the application of paragraph .101A for individual deferred compensation contracts. [FAS106, ¶413]

Contract Provides Only Prospective Benefits

.104 A company enters into a deferred compensation contract with an employee at the date of hire. The contract provides for a payment of $150,000 upon termination of employment following a minimum 3-year service period. The contract provides for a compensation adjustment for each year of service after the third year determined by multiplying $150,000 by the company's return on equity for the year. Also, each year after the third year of service, interest at 10 percent per year is credited on the amount due under the contract at the beginning of that year. Accordingly, a liability of $150,000 is accrued in a systematic and rational manner over the employee's first 3 years of service. Following the third year of service, the accrued liability is adjusted annually for accrued interest and the increased or decreased compensation based on the company's return on equity for that year. At the end of the third year and each subsequent year of the employee's service, the amount accrued equals the then present value of the benefit expected to be paid in exchange for the employee's service rendered to that date. [FAS106, ¶414]

Contract Provides Retroactive Benefits

.105 A company enters into a contract with a 55-year-old employee who has worked 5 years for the company. The contract states that in exchange for past and future services and for serving as a consultant for 2 years after the employee retires, the company will pay an annual pension of $20,000 to the employee, commencing immediately upon the employee's retirement. It is expected that the future benefits to the employer from the consulting services will be minimal. Consequently, the actuarial present value of a lifetime annuity of $20,000 that begins at the employee's expected retirement date is accrued at the date the contract is entered into because the employee is fully eligible for the pension benefit at that date. [FAS106, ¶415]

[1a][Refer to footnote 1.] [FAS111, ¶8(f)]

.106 If the terms of the contract described in paragraph .105 had stated that the employee is entitled to the pension benefit only if the sum of the employee's age and years of service equal 70 or more at the date of retirement, the employee would be fully eligible for the pension benefit at age 60, after rendering 5 more years of service. The actuarial present value of a lifetime annuity of $20,000 that begins at the expected retirement date would be accrued in a systematic and rational manner over the 5-year period from the date the contract is entered into to the date the employee is fully eligible for the pension benefit. [FAS106, ¶416]

(The next page is 7477.)

COMPENSATION TO EMPLOYEES: PAID ABSENCES

SECTION C44

Sources: FASB Statement 43; FASB Statement 112

Summary

An employer is required to accrue a liability for employees' rights to receive compensation for future absences and for postemployment benefits provided to former or inactive employees, their beneficiaries, and covered dependents when certain conditions are met. For example, a liability shall be accrued for vacation benefits that employees have earned but have not yet taken and for benefits provided as a result of disability or layoff; however, a liability is generally not required to be accrued for future sick pay benefits, holidays, and similar compensated absences until employees are actually absent.

.101 [This section describes the conditions under which an employer is required to accrue a liability for **compensated absences.** Compensated absences are defined, for purposes of this section, as] employee absences, such as vacation, illness, and holidays, for which it is expected that employees will be paid. [FAS43, ¶1] This section also applies to all forms of postemployment benefits as defined in Section P32, "Postemployment Benefits," that meet the conditions in paragraph .104, except as noted in paragraph .102. Postemployment benefits that do not meet the conditions in paragraph .104 shall be accounted for in accordance with Section C59, "Contingencies." This section does not address the accounting for benefits paid to active employees other than compensated absences. [FAS112, ¶8]

.102 This section does not apply to:

a. Postemployment benefits provided through a pension or postretirement benefit plan (Sections P16, "Pensions," and P40, "Postretirement Benefits Other Than Pensions," specify the accounting for those costs.)
b. Individual deferred compensation arrangements that are addressed by Section C38, "Compensation to Employees: Deferred Compensation Agreements"
c. Special or contractual termination benefits covered by Sections P16 and P40
d. Stock compensation plans that are addressed by Section C47, "Compensation to Employees: Stock Purchase and Option Plans."

This section does not address the allocation of costs of compensated absences to interim periods. The cost of postemployment benefits as determined under this section that is directly related to the disposal of a segment of a business or a portion of a line of business shall be recognized pursuant to the requirements of Section I13, "Income Statement Presentation: Discontinued Operations," and included in determining the gain or loss associated with that event. [FAS112, ¶9]

.103 [This section does not present standards for] how an employer should estimate its liability for compensated absences. [Guidance is not provided on measurement issues such as] (a) whether the liability should be based on current or on future rates of pay, (b) whether it should be discounted, and (c) when the effect of scheduled increases should be accrued. [FAS43, ¶20]

Conditions for Accrual

.104 An employer shall accrue a liability for employees' compensation for future absences if *all* of the following conditions are met:[1]

a. The employer's obligation relating to employees' rights to receive compensation for future absences is attributable to employees' services already rendered.
b. The obligation relates to rights that [eventually] vest[2] or accumulate.[3]
c. Payment of the compensation is probable.
d. The amount can be reasonably estimated.

If an employer meets conditions (a), (b), and (c) and does not accrue a liability because condition (d) is not met, that fact shall be disclosed. [FAS43, ¶6]

.105 [The belief] that a liability for amounts to be paid as a result of employees' rights to compensated absences should be accrued, considering anticipated forfeitures, in the year in which earned [is based on the definition of a liability in FASB Concepts Statement No. 6, *Elements of Financial Statements,* paragraph 35.] For example, if new employees receive vested rights to two weeks' paid vacation at the beginning of their second year of employment with no pro rata payment in the event of termination during the first year, the two weeks' vacation would be considered to be earned by work performed

---

[1]An exemption to this requirement is discussed in paragraph .108.]

[2]In this section, *vested rights* are those for which the employer has an obligation to make payment even if an employee terminates; thus, they are not contingent on an employee's future service. [FAS43, ¶6, fn1]

[3]For purposes of this section, *accumulate* means that earned but unused rights to compensated absences may be carried forward to one or more periods subsequent to that in which they are earned, even though there may be a limit to the amount that can be carried forward. [FAS43, ¶6, fn2]

in the first year and an accrual for vacation pay would be required for new employees during their first year of service, allowing for estimated forfeitures due to turnover. [FAS43, ¶12]

.106 Furthermore, the definition of a liability [in Concepts Statement 6] does not limit an employer's liability for compensated absences solely to rights to compensation for those absences that eventually vest. The definition also encompasses a constructive obligation for reasonably estimable compensation for past services that, based on the employer's past practices, probably will be paid and can be reasonably estimated. Individual facts and circumstances must be considered in determining when nonvesting rights to compensated absences are earned by services rendered. [FAS43,¶12] [For example,] the appropriate accounting for a sabbatical leave depends on the purpose of the leave. If a sabbatical leave is granted only to perform research or public service to enhance the reputation of or otherwise benefit the employer, the compensation is not attributable to services already rendered (refer to paragraph .104(a)); a liability should not be accrued in advance of the employee's service during such leave. If the leave is granted to provide compensated unrestricted time off for past service and the other conditions for accrual are met, a liability for sabbatical leave should be accrued. [FAS43, ¶18]

.107 The requirement to accrue a liability for nonvesting rights to compensated absences [also] depends on whether the unused rights (a) expire at the end of the year in which earned or (b) accumulate and are carried forward to succeeding years, thereby increasing the benefits that would otherwise be available in those later years. If the rights expire, a liability for future absences should not be accrued at year-end because the benefits to be paid in subsequent years would not be attributable to employee services rendered in prior years. (Jury duty and military leave benefits generally do not accumulate if unused and, unless they accumulate, a liability for those benefits would not be accrued at year-end.) On the other hand, if unused rights do accumulate and increase the benefits otherwise available in subsequent years, a liability should be accrued at year-end to the extent that it is probable that employees will be paid in subsequent years for the increased benefits attributable to the accumulated rights and the amount can be reasonably estimated. [FAS43, ¶13]

.108 Notwithstanding the conditions specified in paragraph .104, an employer is not required to accrue a liability for nonvesting accumulating rights to receive sick pay benefits (that is, compensation for an employee's absence due to illness). [FAS43, ¶7] On the other hand, this section does not prohibit an employer from accruing a liability for such nonvesting accumulating sick pay benefits, providing the criteria of paragraph .104 are met. [FAS43, ¶15]

.109 In accounting for compensated absences, the form of an employer's policy for compensated absences should not prevail over actual practices. For example, if employees are customarily paid "sick pay" benefits even though their absences from work are not actually the result of illness or if employees are routinely allowed to take compensated "terminal leave" for [nonvesting] accumulated unused sick pay benefits prior to retirement, such benefits shall not be considered sick pay benefits for purposes of applying the provisions of paragraph .108 but rather should be accounted for in accordance with paragraph .104. [FAS43, ¶7, fn3]

Glossary

.401 **Compensated absences.** Employee absences, such as vacation, illness, and holidays, for which it is expected that [active] employees will be paid. [FAS43, ¶1]

(The next page is 7675.)

COMPENSATION TO EMPLOYEES:
STOCK PURCHASE AND OPTION PLANS

Sources: ARB 43, Chapter 13B; APB Opinion 25;
AICPA Interpretation of APB Opinion 25; FASB Statement 109;
FASB Interpretation 28; FASB Interpretation 38;
FASB Technical Bulletin 82-2

Summary

An employer shall recognize compensation costs for stock issued through nonvariable employee stock option, purchase, and award plans as the difference between the quoted market price of the stock at the measurement date (ordinarily the date of grant or award) less the amount, if any, the employee is required to pay. That cost shall be charged to expense over the periods in which the employee performs the related services. Some plans, referred to as noncompensatory plans, involve no compensation expense because the employees' purchase price is not set lower than would reasonably be required in an offer of shares to all shareholders for the purpose of raising an equivalent amount of capital.

The measurement date for stock appreciation rights and other variable stock option and award plans typically is not the date of grant or award. Compensation relating to such variable plans shall be measured at the end of each period as the amount by which the quoted market value of the shares of the employer's stock covered by a grant exceeds the option price or value specified under the plan and shall be charged to expense over the periods the employee performs the related services.

The measurement date for grants under stock option, purchase, and award plans involving junior stock is the first date on which are known both the number of shares of the employer's regular common stock that an employee is entitled to receive in exchange for the junior stock and the option or purchase price, if any. Generally, total compensation cost shall be the amount by which the market price at the measurement date of the employer's regular common stock that an employee is entitled to receive exceeds the amount that the employee paid or will pay for the junior stock. If the performance goals to which the junior stock award relates will probably be achieved, compensation cost shall be charged to expense over the periods the employee performs the related services.

Changes in the quoted market value shall be reflected as an adjustment of accrued compensation and compensation expense in the periods in which the changes occur until the date the number of shares and purchase price, if any, are both known.

Applicability and Scope

.101 Many employers have adopted various **plans,** contracts, and agreements to compensate officers and other employees by issuing to them stock of the employer. Under traditional stock option and stock purchase plans an employer grants options to purchase a fixed number of shares of stock of the employer at a stated price during a specified period or grants rights to purchase shares of stock of the employer at a stated price, often at a discount from the market price of the stock at the date the rights are granted. Stock options and purchase rights are normally granted for future services of employees. [APB25, ¶1]

.102 Some employers have replaced or supplemented traditional plans with more complex plans, contracts, and agreements for issuing stock. [Those latter] arrangements may be based on variable factors that depend on future events; for example, an employer may award a variable number of shares of stock or may grant a stock option with a variable option price. Other arrangements combine the characteristics of two or more types of plans, and some give an employee an election. [APB25, ¶2]

.103 Paragraphs .106 through .118 [discuss] some aspects of accounting for stock issued to employees through both noncompensatory and compensatory plans. [Those paragraphs discuss] (a) plans in which the number of shares of stock that may be acquired by or awarded to an employee and the option or purchase price, if any, are known or determinable at the date of grant or award, (b) plans in which either the number of shares of stock or the option or purchase price depends on future events, and (c) income tax benefits related to stock issued to employees through stock option, purchase, and award plans. Paragraphs .124 through .137 illustrate measuring and accounting for compensation under typical plans. [Paragraphs .119 through .122 provide further guidance in accounting for **stock appreciation rights** and other **variable stock option, purchase, and award plans.** Paragraphs .138 through .144 illustrate accounting for those plans. Paragraphs .135A through .135E provide guidance in accounting for stock option, purchase, and award plans involving **junior stock.**] [APB25, ¶4]

Noncompensatory Plans

.104 Stock option plans in many cases may be intended not primarily as a special form of compensation but rather as an important means of raising capital, or as an inducement to obtain greater or more widespread ownership of the employer's stock among its officers and other employees. In general, the terms under which stock options are granted, including any conditions as to exercise of the options or disposal of the stock acquired, are the most significant evidence ordinarily available as to the nature and purpose of a particular stock option or stock option plan. It is often apparent that a particular option or plan involves elements of two or more of the above purposes. If the inducements are not larger per share than would reasonably be required in an offer of shares to all shareholders for the purpose of raising an equivalent amount of capital, those plans shall be considered noncompensatory. [ARB43, ch13B, ¶4]

.105 Stock purchase plans also are frequently an integral part of an employer's program to secure equity capital or to obtain widespread ownership among employees, or both. Those [plans shall be considered noncompensatory] if the purchase price is not lower than is reasonably required to interest employees generally or to secure the contemplated funds. [ARB43, ch13B, ¶5]

.106 An employer shall recognize no compensation [expense] for services in [accounting for] consideration received for stock that is issued through noncompensatory plans. Four characteristics are essential in a noncompensatory plan: (a) substantially all full-time employees meeting limited employment qualifications may participate (employees owning a specified percent of the outstanding stock and executives may be excluded), (b) stock is offered to eligible employees equally or based on a uniform percentage of salary or wages (the plan may limit the number of shares of stock that an employee may purchase through the plan), (c) the time permitted for exercise of an option or purchase right is limited to a reasonable period, and (d) the discount from the market price of the stock is no greater than would be reasonable in an offer of stock to stockholders or others. [APB25, ¶7]

Compensatory Plans

.107 Stock options involving an element of compensation usually arise out of an offer or agreement by an employer to issue shares of its capital stock to one or more officers or other employees (referred to in this section as *grantees*) at a stated price. The grantees are accorded the right to require issuance of the shares either at a specified time or during some determinable period. In some cases, the grantees' options are exercisable only if at the time of exercise certain conditions exist, such as that the grantee is then or until a specified date has been an employee. In other cases, the grantees may have undertaken certain obligations, such as to remain in the employment of the employer for at least a specified period, or to take the shares only for investment purposes and not for resale. [ARB43, ch13B, ¶3]

.108 Plans that do not possess the four characteristics of noncompensatory plans [described in paragraph .106] are classified as compensatory plans. Classification as a compensatory plan does not necessarily require that compensation cost be recognized.[1] [APB25, ¶8]

Services as Consideration for Stock Issued

.109 The consideration that an employer receives for stock issued through a stock option, purchase, or award plan consists of cash or other assets, if any, plus services received from the employee. [APB25, ¶9] On exercise of an option, the sum of the cash received and the amount of compensation charged to income shall be accounted for as the consideration received on the issuance of the stock. [ARB43, ch13B, ¶14]

Measuring Compensation for Services

.110 Compensation for services that an employer receives as consideration for stock issued through employee stock option, purchase, and award plans shall be measured by the quoted market price of the stock at the **measurement date** less the amount, if any, that the employee is required to pay.

a. The unadjusted *quoted market price* of a share of stock of the same class that trades freely in an established market shall be used in measuring compensation. If a quoted market price is unavailable, the best estimate of the market value of the stock shall be used to measure compensation.

b. The *measurement date* for determining compensation cost in stock option, purchase, and award plans is the first date on which are known both (1) the number of shares that an individual employee is entitled to receive and (2) the option or purchase price, if any. That date for many or most plans is the date an option or purchase right is granted or stock is awarded to an individual employee. However, the measurement date may be later than the date of grant or award in plans with variable terms that depend on events after date of grant or award.

Thus, an employer recognizes compensation cost for stock issued through compensatory plans unless the employee pays an amount that is at least equal to the quoted market price of the stock at the measurement date. [APB25, ¶10]

---

[1] All compensation arrangements involving stock, regardless of the name given, shall be accounted for according to their substance. For example, an arrangement in which the consideration for stock issued to an employee is a nonrecourse note secured by the stock issued may be in substance the same as the grant of a stock option and shall be accounted for accordingly. The note shall be classified as a reduction of stockholders' equity rather than as an asset. [APB25, ¶8, fn2]

Applying the Measurement Principle

.111   The following supplements paragraph .110 for special situations in some plans:

a. Measuring compensation by the cost to an employer of reacquired (treasury) stock that is distributed through a stock option, purchase, or award plan is not acceptable practice. The only exception is that compensation costs under a plan with all the provisions described in paragraph .111(c) may be measured by the cost of stock that the employer (1) reacquires during the fiscal period for which the stock is to be awarded and (2) awards shortly thereafter to employees for services during that period.

b. The measurement date is not changed from the grant or award date to a later date solely by provisions that termination of employment reduces the number of shares of stock that may be issued to an employee.

c. The measurement date of an award of stock for current service may be the end of the fiscal period, which is normally the effective date of the award, instead of the date that the award to an employee is determined if (1) the award is provided for by the terms of an established formal plan; (2) the plan designates the factors that determine the total dollar amount of awards to employees for the period (for example, a percentage of income), although the total amount or the individual awards may not be known at the end of the period; and (3) the award pertains to current service of the employee for the period.

d. Renewing a stock option or purchase right or extending its period establishes a new measurement date as if the right were newly granted.

e. Transferring stock or assets to a trustee, agent, or other third party for distribution of stock to employees under the terms of an option, purchase, or award plan does not change the measurement date from a later date to the date of transfer unless the terms of the transfer provide that the stock (1) will not revert to the employer, (2) will not be granted or awarded later to the same employee on terms different from or for services other than those specified in the original grant or award, and (3) will not be granted or awarded later to another employee.

f. The measurement date for a grant or award of convertible stock (or stock that is otherwise exchangeable for other securities of the employer) is the date on which the ratio of conversion (or exchange) is known unless other terms are variable at that date (refer to paragraph .110(b)). The higher of the quoted market price at the measurement date of (1) the convertible stock granted or awarded or (2) the securities into which the original grant or award is convertible shall be used to measure compensation. [Refer to paragraphs .135A through .135E for guidance on accounting for stock option, purchase, and award plans involving junior stock.]

g. Cash paid to an employee to settle an earlier award of stock or to settle a grant of option to the employee shall determine compensation cost. If the cash payment differs from the earlier measure of the award of stock or grant of option, compensation cost shall be adjusted (refer to paragraph .115). The amount that an employer pays to an employee to purchase stock previously issued to the employee through a compensation plan is *cash paid to an employee to settle an earlier award of stock or to settle a grant of option* if stock is reacquired shortly after issuance. Cash proceeds that an employer receives from sale of awarded stock or stock issued on exercise of an option and remits to the taxing authorities to cover required withholding of income taxes on an award is not *cash paid to an employee to settle an earlier award of stock or to settle a grant of option* in measuring compensation cost.

h. Some plans are a combination of two or more types of plans. An employer may need to measure compensation for the separate parts. Compensation cost for a combination plan permitting an employee to elect one part shall be measured according to the terms that an employee is most likely to elect based on the facts available each period.

[APB25, ¶11]

Accruing Compensation Cost

.112 Compensation cost in stock option, purchase, and award plans shall be recognized as an expense of one or more periods in which an employee performs services and also as part or all of the consideration received for stock issued to the employee through a plan. The grant or award may specify the period or periods during which the employee performs services, or the period or periods may be inferred from the terms or from the past pattern of grants or awards (refer to Section C38, "Compensation to Employees: Deferred Compensation Agreements," paragraph .101). [APB25, ¶12]

.113 An employee may perform services in several periods before an employer issues stock to him for those services. The employer shall accrue compensation expense in each period in which the services are performed. If the measurement date is later than the date of grant or award, an employer shall record the compensation expense each period from date of grant or award to date of measurement based on the quoted market price of the stock at the end of each period. [APB25, ¶13]

.114 If stock is issued in a plan before some or all of the services are performed,[2] part of the consideration recorded for the stock issued is unearned compensation and shall be shown as a separate reduction of stockholders' equity. The unearned compensation shall be accounted for as expense of the period or periods in which the employee performs service. [APB25, ¶14]

---

[2]State law governs the issuance of an employer's stock including the acceptability of issuing stock for future services. [APB25, ¶14, fn3]

.115 Accruing compensation expense may require estimates, and adjustment of those estimates in later periods may be necessary (refer to Section A06, "Accounting Changes," paragraphs .130 through .132). For example, if a stock option is not exercised (or awarded stock is returned to the employer) because an employee fails to fulfill an obligation, the estimate of compensation expense recorded in previous periods shall be adjusted by decreasing compensation expense in the period of forfeiture. [APB25, ¶15]

Accounting for Income Tax Benefits

.116 An employer may obtain an income tax benefit related to stock issued to an employee through a stock option, purchase, or award plan. An employer is usually entitled to a deduction for income tax purposes of the amount that an employee reports as ordinary income, and the deduction is allowable to the employer in the year in which the amount is includable in the gross income of the employee. Thus, a deduction for income tax purposes may differ from the related compensation expense that the employer recognizes,[3] and the deduction may be allowable in a period that differs from the one in which the employer recognizes compensation expense in measuring net income. [APB25, ¶16]

.117 An employer shall reduce income tax expense for a period by no more of a tax reduction under a stock option, purchase, or award plan than the proportion of the tax reduction that is related to the compensation expense for the period. Compensation expenses that are deductible in a tax return in a period different from the one in which they are reported as expenses in measuring net income [APB25, ¶17] result in temporary differences [FAS109, ¶288(g)], and deferred taxes shall be recorded [APB25, ¶17] in accordance with the provisions of Section I27. [FAS109, ¶288(g)] The remainder of the tax reduction, if any, is related to an amount that is deductible for income tax purposes but does not affect net income. The remainder of the tax reduction shall not be included in income but shall be added to capital in addition to par or stated value of capital stock in the period of the tax reduction. Conversely, a tax reduction may be less than if recorded compensation expenses were deductible for income tax purposes. If so, the employer may deduct the difference from additional capital in the period of the tax reduction to the extent that tax reductions under the same or similar compensatory stock option, purchase, or award plans have been included in additional capital. [APB25, ¶17]

.118 An employer may, either by cash payment or otherwise—for example, by allowing a reduction in the purchase price of stock—reimburse an employee for his action related to a stock option, purchase, or award plan that results in a reduction of income taxes of the employer. The employer shall include the reimbursement in income as an expense. [APB25, ¶18]

---

[3] An employer may be entitled to a deduction for income tax purposes even though it recognizes no compensation expense in measuring net income. [APB25, ¶16, fn4]

Stock Appreciation Rights and Other Variable Stock Option or Award Plans

.119 When stock appreciation rights[4] or other variable plan awards[5] are granted, an employer shall measure compensation as the amount by which the quoted market value of the shares of the employer's stock covered by the grant exceeds the option price or value specified, by reference to a market price or otherwise, subject to any appreciation limitations under the plan. Changes, either increases or decreases, in the quoted market value of those shares between the date of grant and the measurement date result in a change in the measure of compensation for the right or award. [FIN28, ¶2]

.120 Compensation determined in accordance with paragraph .119 shall be accrued as a charge to expense over the period or periods the employee performs the related services (referred to in this section as the **service period**). If the stock appreciation rights or other variable plan awards are granted for past services, compensation shall be accrued as a charge to expense of the period in which the rights or awards are granted. If the service period is not defined in the plan or some other agreement, such as an employment agreement, as a shorter or previous period, the service period shall be presumed to be the vesting period.[6] [FIN28, ¶3]

---

[4]Stock appreciation rights are awards entitling employees to receive cash, stock, or a combination of cash and stock in an amount equivalent to any excess of the market value of a stated number of shares of the employer's stock over a stated price. The form of payment may be specified when the rights are granted or may be determined when they are exercised; in some plans the employee may choose the form of payment. [FIN28, ¶9]

[5]Plans for which (a) the number of shares of stock that may be acquired by or awarded to an employee or (b) the price or (c) both are not specified or determinable until after the date of grant or award are referred to in this section as *variable plan* awards. However, plans described in paragraph .111(c) and book value stock option, purchase, or award plans are not covered by paragraphs .119 through .122. Plans under which an employee may receive cash in lieu of stock or additional cash upon the exercise of a stock option are variable plans for purposes of this section if the amount is contingent on the occurrence of future events. [FIN28, ¶2, fn1] Even though junior stock possesses certain features of equity securities, the substance of junior stock plans is that they are compensation plans with the junior stock being a means for an employee ultimately to acquire regular common stock. Because the conversion of junior stock to regular common stock is contingent on certain performance goals being achieved or on certain transactions occurring, the number of shares of regular common stock that an employee is entitled to receive is not known until those future events occur. The number of shares of regular common stock that an employee is entitled to receive depends on events occurring after the date of grant of junior stock, thereby causing the plan to be variable under the provisions of paragraph .110(b). [FIN38, ¶22]

[6]For purposes of this section, stock appreciation rights and other variable plan awards become vested when the employee's right to receive or retain shares or cash under the rights or awards is not contingent upon the performance of additional services. Frequently, the vesting period is the period from the date of grant to the date the rights or awards become exercisable. [FIN28, ¶3, fn3]

.121 Compensation accrued during the service period in accordance with paragraph .120 shall be adjusted in subsequent periods up to the measurement date for changes, either increases or decreases, in the quoted market value of the shares of the employer's stock covered by the grant but shall not be adjusted below zero. The offsetting adjustment shall be made to compensation expense of the period in which changes in the market value occur. Except as provided in paragraph .122, the accrued compensation for a right that is forfeited or canceled shall be adjusted by decreasing compensation expense in the period of forfeiture in accordance with paragraph .115. [FIN28, ¶4]

.122 For purposes of applying paragraph .111(h), compensation expense for a combination plan[7] involving stock appreciation rights or other variable plan awards (including those that are granted after the date of grant of related stock options) shall be measured according to the terms the employee is most likely to elect based on the facts available each period. An employer shall presume that the employee will elect to exercise the stock appreciation rights or other variable plan awards, but the presumption may be overcome if past experience or the terms of a combination plan that limit the market appreciation available to the employee in the stock appreciation rights or other variable plan awards provide evidence that the employee will elect to exercise the related stock option. If an employer has been accruing compensation for a stock appreciation right or other variable plan award and a change in circumstances provides evidence that the employee will likely elect to exercise the related stock option, accrued compensation recorded for the right or award shall *not* be adjusted.[8] If the employee elects to exercise the stock option, the accrued compensation recorded for the right or award shall be recognized as a consideration for the stock issue. If all parts of the grant or award (for example, both the option and the right or award) are forfeited or canceled, accrued compensation shall be adjusted by decreasing compensation expense in that period. [FIN28, ¶5]

---

[7]Stock appreciation rights are usually granted in combination with compensatory stock options but also may be granted separately. Combination plans usually provide that the rights are exercisable for the same period as the companion stock options and that the exercise of either cancels the other. In some combination plans, the employer may grant stock appreciation rights either when the options are granted or at a later date. In some cases, the holder of stock options may apply to receive share appreciation in cash or stock with the approval of the employer in lieu of exercising the options. [FIN28, ¶10]

[8]A change in the circumstances may be indicated by market appreciation in excess of any appreciation limitations under the plan or the cancellation or forfeiture of the stock appreciation right or other variable plan award without a concurrent cancellation or forfeiture of the related stock option. A subsequent decrease in market value that reduces the appreciation to a level below the limitations under the plan would require adjustment of accrued compensation in accordance with paragraph .121 if evidence then indicates that the employee will elect to exercise the stock appreciation right or other variable plan award. [FIN28, ¶5, fn7]

Disclosure

.123 Disclosure shall be made as to the status of the option or plan at the end of the period of report, including the number of shares under option, the option price, and the number of shares as to which options were exercisable. As to options exercised during the period, disclosure shall be made of the number of shares involved and the option price of the shares.[8a] [ARB43, ch13B, ¶15]

Measuring and Accounting for Compensation under Typical Plans

.124 Enterprises issue stock to officers and other employees through plans with a variety of names and a multiplicity of terms. Plans in which employees pay cash, either directly or through payroll withholding, as all or a significant part of the consideration for stock they receive, are commonly designated by names such as stock option, stock purchase, or stock thrift or savings plans. Plans in which employees receive stock for current or future services without paying cash (or with a nominal payment) are commonly designated by names such as stock bonus or stock award plans. Stock bonus and award plans are invariably compensatory. Stock thrift and savings plans are compensatory to the extent of contributions of an employer. Stock option and purchase plans may be either compensatory or noncompensatory. The combination of terms in some plans tend to make various types of plans shade into one another, and an assigned name may not describe the nature of a plan. [APB25, ¶21]

.125 Paragraphs .126 through .137 are organized according to the most vital distinction in this section—compensatory plans are divided between plans in which the cost of compensation is measured at the date of grant or award and those in which the cost of compensation depends on events after the date of grant or award. Combination plans are also described briefly. [APB25, ¶22]

Compensation Cost Measured at Date of Grant or Award

Accounting

.126 Total compensation cost is measured by the difference between the quoted market price of the stock at the date of grant or award and the price, if any, to be paid by an employee and is recognized as expense over the period the employee performs related services. The sum of compensation and cash paid by the employee is the consideration received for the stock issued. Compensation cost related to an award of stock may be adjusted for a later cash settlement (refer to paragraph .111(g)). [APB25, ¶23]

[8a]Other disclosure requirements are in Regulation S-[K] for financial statements filed with the Securities and Exchange Commission and in listing agreements of the stock exchanges for financial statements included in annual reports to shareholders. [APB25, ¶19, fn5]

Typical Plans with Fixed and Determinable Terms

.127 The characteristic that identifies plans in this group is that the terms fix and provide means for determining at the date of grant or award both the number of shares of stock that may be acquired by or awarded to an employee and the cash, if any, to be paid by the employee. Plans usually presume or provide that the employee perform current or future services. The right to transfer stock received is sometimes restricted for a specified period. [APB25, ¶24]

Stock Option and Stock Purchase Plans

.128 Typical terms provide for an employer to grant to an employee the right to purchase a fixed number of shares of stock of the employer at a stated price during a specified period. [APB25, ¶25]

Stock Bonus or Award Plans

.129 Typical terms provide for an employer to award to an employee a fixed number of shares of stock of the employer without a cash payment (or with a nominal cash payment) by the employee. Often the award is specified as a fixed dollar amount but is distributable in stock with the number of shares determined by the quoted market price of the stock at the date of award, the effective date of award (refer to paragraph .111(c)), or the date treasury stock is acquired (refer to paragraph .111(a)). [APB25, ¶26]

Compensation Cost Measured at Other Than Date of Grant or Award

Accounting

.130 Compensation cost is accounted for the same as for plans in the first group with one exception. The quoted market price used in the measurement is not the price at date of grant or award but the price at the date on which both the number of shares of stock that may be acquired by or awarded to an individual employee and the option or purchase price are known. Total compensation cost is measured by the difference between that quoted market price of the stock and the amount, if any, to be paid by an employee and is recognized as expense over the period the employee performs related services. The sum of compensation and cash paid by the employee is the consideration received for the stock issued. Compensation cost related to an award of stock may be adjusted for a later cash settlement (refer to paragraph .111(g)). [APB25, ¶27]

.131 Estimates of compensation cost are recorded before the measurement date based on the quoted market price of the stock at intervening dates. Recorded compensation expense between the date of grant or award and the measurement date may either increase or decrease because changes in quoted market price of the stock require recomputations of the estimated compensation cost. [APB25, ¶28]

Typical Plans with Variable Terms

.132 The characteristic that identifies plans in this group is that the terms prevent determining at the date of grant or award either the number of shares of stock that may be acquired by or awarded to an employee or the price to be paid by the employee, or both. The indeterminate factors usually depend on events that are not known or determinable at the date of grant or award. Plans usually presume or provide that the employee perform current or future services. The right to transfer stock received is sometimes restricted for a specified period. [APB25, ¶29]

Stock Option and Stock Purchase Plans

.133 Some terms provide for an employer to grant to an employee the right to purchase shares of stock of the employer during a specified period. The number of shares of stock, the option or purchase price, or both may vary depending on various factors during a specified period, such as market performance of the stock, equivalents of dividends distributed, or level of earnings of the employer. [APB25, ¶30]

Stock Bonus or Award Plans

.134 Some terms provide for an employer to award to an employee the right to receive shares of stock of the employer but the number of shares is not determinable at the date of award. Often the award is specified as a fixed dollar amount but is distributable in stock with the number of shares of stock determined by the market price of the stock at the date distributed, or the award may be of an undesignated number of shares of stock and that number is to be determined by variable factors during a specified period. [APB25, ¶31]

.135 The terms of some plans, often called *phantom stock* or *shadow stock* plans, base the obligations for compensation on increases in market price of or dividends distributed on a specified or variable number of shares of stock of the employer but provide for settlement of the obligation to the employee in cash, in stock of the employer, or a combination of cash and stock. [APB25, ¶32]

Stock Option, Purchase, and Award Plans Involving Junior Stock

.135A Stock option, purchase, and award plans involving junior stock are designed to provide that an employer ultimately will issue shares of regular common stock to employees. Those plans are variable plans because the number of shares of regular common stock that an individual employee is entitled to receive is not known until certain performance goals are achieved or certain transactions occur. For purposes of measuring compensation cost, the measurement date for grants under stock option, purchase, and award plans involving junior stock is the first date on which are known both the number of shares of the employer's regular common stock that an employee is entitled to receive in exchange for the junior stock and the option or purchase price, if any. [FIN38, ¶2]

.135B Paragraph .111(f) of this section indicates that the measurement date for a grant or award of convertible stock is the date on which the ratio of conversion is known, unless other terms are variable at that date. Because conversion of junior stock to regular common stock generally is contingent on achieving certain performance goals or on certain transactions occurring, the conversion ratio[9] is not known with certainty until those future events occur. After those goals are achieved or those transactions occur, the conversion ratio is determinable and, accordingly, the number of shares of regular common stock that an individual is entitled to receive is known. [FIN38, ¶3]

.135C Compensation cost for stock option, purchase, and award plans involving junior stock shall be accrued according to the provisions of paragraphs .119 through .121 and paragraph .111. However, the provisions of paragraph .119 shall be applied only when it becomes probable[10] that certain performance goals will be achieved or certain transactions will occur; that probability may or may not be present at the date junior stock is issued. [FIN38, ¶4]

.135D Stock option, purchase, and award plans involving junior stock generally are based on certain performance goals being achieved or certain transactions occurring within specific periods. Some plans, however, do not specify a period during which those future events must occur. If it is probable that the future event will occur at some time, compensation cost shall be charged to expense over the period from the date the future event becomes probable to the date the future event is most likely to occur or the end of any required service period. Other plans provide for different ratios of conversion of junior stock to regular common stock within a specific period based on variable performance goals. If achieving more than one performance goal is probable, compensation cost shall be based on the highest ratio of conversion of junior stock to regular common stock attributable to those goals whose achievement is probable. However, the final measure of

---

[9]If junior stock becomes convertible only to an equal number of shares of regular common stock upon achieving certain performance goals, the conversion ratio is either one-to-zero or one-to-one; some junior stock plans provide for different ratios of conversion depending on the level of performance attained. [FIN38, ¶3, fn2]

[10]*Probable* is used here, consistent with its use in Section C59, "Contingencies," to mean that it is likely that certain performance goals will be achieved or certain transactions will occur. [FIN38, ¶4, fn3]

compensation cost shall be based on the ratio of conversion attributable to the performance goal achieved at the measurement date. For all plans, total compensation shall be based on the market price of the regular common stock as of the date compensation cost is determined. [FIN38, ¶5]

.135E Total compensation cost shall be the amount by which the market price at the measurement date of the employer's regular common stock that an employee is entitled to receive exceeds the amount that the employee paid or will pay for the junior stock. If vesting provisions cause junior stock to become convertible to regular common stock after the measurement date, compensation cost shall be recognized during the period from (a) the first date that it becomes probable that the future events will occur or the date the events have occurred to (b) the date that junior stock becomes convertible or the end of the service period, whichever occurs first. If junior stock does not become convertible to regular common stock but cash is paid to an employee to purchase previously issued junior stock, total compensation cost is the amount by which cash paid to the employee exceeds the amount initially paid by the employee for the junior stock. [FIN38, ¶6]

Combination and Elective Plans

Accounting

.136 In general, compensation is measured for the separate parts of combination or elective plans. Compensation expense is the sum of the parts that apply. An employer may need to measure compensation at various dates as the terms of separate parts become known. For example, if an employee is entitled to dividend equivalents, compensation cost is the sum of the costs measured at the dates the dividends are credited to the employee in accordance with the terms of the plan. If an employee may choose between alternatives, compensation expense is accrued for the alternative that the employee is most likely to elect based on the facts available at the date of accrual. [APB25, ¶33]

Typical Combination and Elective Plans

.137 Some plans provide for an employer to grant or award to an employee rights with more than one set of terms. Often an employee may elect the right to be exercised. The combination of rights may be granted or awarded simultaneously or an employee who holds a right may subsequently be granted or awarded a second but different right. The rights may run concurrently or for different periods. An illustration is: An employee holding an option to purchase a fixed number of shares of stock at a fixed price during a specified period is granted an alternative option to purchase the same number of shares at a different price or during a different specified period. Instead of a second option, the award may be the right to elect to receive cash or shares of stock without paying cash.

Often the election to acquire or receive stock under either right decreases the other right. Plans combining rights are often called *tandem stock* or *alternate stock* plans; the second right may be of the type that is sometimes called a *phantom stock* plan. [APB25, ¶34]

Illustrations of the Accounting for Stock Appreciation Rights and Other Variable Stock Option or Award Plans

.138 Paragraphs .139 through .144 illustrate applications of this section in accounting for stock appreciation rights and other variable stock option or award plans when the service period is presumed to be the vesting period. The examples do not comprehend all possible combinations of circumstances nor do the examples illustrate the computation of deferred income taxes. [FIN28, ¶19]

Example 1

.139 Provisions of the agreements [are as follows]:

Stock appreciation rights are granted in tandem with stock options for market value appreciation in excess of the option price. Exercise of the rights cancels the option for an equal number of shares and vice versa. Share appreciation is payable in stock, cash, or a combination of stock and cash at the employer's election.

Date of grant	January 1, 19X9
Expiration date	December 31, 19Y8
Vesting	100% at the end of 19Y2
Number of shares under option	1,000
Option price	$10 per share
Quoted market price at date of grant	$10 per share

[FIN28, ¶20]

.140 Market price assumptions [are as follows]:

Quoted market price per share at December 31 of subsequent years:

19X9	–$11
19Y0	– 12
19Y1	– 15
19Y2	– 14
19Y3	– 15
19Y4	– 18

[FIN28, ¶21]

.141 Exhibit 141A illustrates the annual computation of compensation expense for the above described stock appreciation right plan. [FIN28, ¶22]

Exhibit 141A

Illustration of Compensation Expense by Year
For a Stock Appreciation Right Plan with Complete Vesting at End of Four-Year Period

Date	Market Price	Per Share	Compensation Aggregate (1)	Percentage Accrued (2)	Compensation Accrued to Date	19X9	19Y0	19Y1	19Y2	19Y3	19Y4
12/31/X9	$11	$1	$1,000	25%	$ 250	$250					
12/31/Y0	12	2	2,000	50	750 / 1,000		$750				
12/31/Y1	15	5	5,000	75	2,750 / 3,750			$2,750			
12/31/Y2	14	4	4,000	100	250 / 4,000				$250		
12/31/Y3	15	5	5,000	100	1,000 / 5,000					$1,000	
12/31/Y4	18	8	8,000	100	3,000 / $8,000						$3,000

Notes:

(1) Aggregate compensation for unexercised shares to be allocated to periods service performed.

(2) The percentage accrued is based upon the four-year vesting period.

(3) A similar computation would be made for interim reporting periods.

[FIN28, ¶22]

Example 2

.142 If the stock appreciation rights vested 25 percent per year commencing in 19X9, the computation of compensation expense in the preceding example would change as illustrated in the following paragraphs. [FIN28, ¶23]

.143 Because 25 percent of the rights vest each year commencing in 19X9, the service period over which compensation is accrued as a charge to expense is determined separately for each 25 percent portion. For example, the services for the 25 percent portion of the rights vesting in 19Y0 are performed in both 19X9 and 19Y0 and the related compensation is accrued proportionately as a charge to expense in each year. Similarly, compensation for rights vesting in 19Y1 is proportionately accrued as a charge to expense in 19X9, 19Y0, and 19Y1. In this way, compensation related to the portion of the rights vesting in 19X9 is recognized in 19X9, compensation related to the portion of the rights vesting in 19Y0 is recognized in 19X9 and 19Y0, and so forth. The following schedule indicates the service period for each 25 percent portion of the rights and the computation of the aggregate percentage of compensation accrued by the end of each year of service (the vesting period). A similar computation would be made for interim reporting periods.

For Rights Vesting in	Service Period	Aggregate Percentage of Compensation Accrued by the End of Each Year of Service			
		19X9	**19Y0**	**19Y1**	**19Y2**
19X9	1 year	25.00%	25.00%	25.00%	25%
19Y0	2 years	12.50	25.00	25.00	25
19Y1	3 years	8.33	16.67	25.00	25
19Y2	4 years	6.25	12.50	18.75	25
Aggregate percentage accrued at the end of each year		52.08%	79.17%	93.75%	100%
Rounded for purposes of Examples 2 and 3		52%	79%	94%	100%

For periods ending after 19Y2, 100 percent of the aggregate compensation shall be accrued. [FIN28, ¶24]

.144 Additional assumptions [are as follows]:

a. On December 31, 19Y1, the employee exercises the right to receive share appreciation on 300 shares.

b. On March 15, 19Y2, the employee exercises the right to receive share appreciation on 100 shares; quoted market price $15 per share.

c. On June 15, 19Y3, the employee exercises the right to receive share appreciation on 100 shares; quoted market price $16 per share.

d. On December 31, 19Y3, the employee exercises the right to receive share appreciation on 300 shares.

e. On December 31, 19Y4, the employee exercises the right to receive share appreciation on 200 shares.

[FIN28, ¶25]

[Exhibit 144A illustrates the annual computation of compensation expense for the above described stock appreciation right plan.]

Exhibit 144A

Illustration of Compensation Expense by Year
For a Stock Appreciation Right Plan with Progressive Vesting over a Four-Year Period

Date	Transaction	Number of Shares	Market Price	Per Share	Compensation Aggregate (1)	Percentage Accrued (2)	Compensation Accrued to Date	19X9	19Y0	19Y1	19Y2	19Y3	19Y4
										Accrual of Expense by Year (3)			
12/31/X9	A		$11	$1	$1,000	52%	$ 520	$520					
12/31/Y0	A		12	2	2,000	79	1,580		$1,060				
12/31/Y1	A		15	5	5,000	94	4,700						
12/31/Y1	E	300	15	5	(1,500)	–	3,200			$3,120			
3/15/Y2	E	100	15	5	(500)	–	2,700						
12/31/Y2	A		14	4	2,400	100	2,400				$(300)		
6/15/Y3	E	100	16	6	(600)	–	2,000					$200	
12/31/Y3	A		15	5	2,500	100	2,500					500	
12/31/Y3	E	300	15	5	(1,500)	–	1,000						
12/31/Y4	A		18	8	1,600	100	1,600						$600
12/31/Y4	E	200	18	8	(1,600)	–	$ –						

Transaction Codes:

A—Adjustment for changes in the market price of stock.
E—Exercise of a stock appreciation right.

Notes:

(1) Aggregate compensation for unexercised shares to be allocated to periods service performed.
(2) Refer to the schedule in paragraph .143.
(3) A similar computation would be made for interim reporting periods.

[FIN28, ¶25]

Example 3

.145 If the plan limits the amount of share appreciation that the employee can receive to $5, the computation of compensation expense in Example 2 would change as illustrated in Exhibit 145A. [FIN28, ¶26]

.146 When the quoted market price exceeds the appreciation limitation, the employee is more likely to exercise the related stock option rather than the stock appreciation right. Therefore, accrued compensation is *not* adjusted for changes in the quoted market price of the stock. The assumptions stated in paragraph .144 are changed to the extent that on June 15, 19Y3 and December 31, 19Y4 the employee exercises the related stock option instead of the stock appreciation right. Accordingly, accrued compensation for the equivalent number of rights is recognized as part or all of the consideration for the stock issued in accordance with paragraph .122. [FIN28, ¶27]

Exhibit 145A

Illustration of Compensation Expense by Year
For a Stock Appreciation Right Plan That Limits Appreciation per Share

Date	Transaction	Number of Shares	Market Price	Compensation Per Share	Compensation Aggregate (1)	Percentage Accrued (2)	Compensation Accrued to Date	Accrual of Expense by Year (3) 19X9	19Y0	19Y1	19Y2	19Y3	19Y4
12/31/X9	A		$11	$1	$ 1,000	52%	$ 520	$520					
12/31/Y0	A		12	2	2,000	79	1,060		$1,060				
							1,580						
12/31/Y1	A		15	5	5,000	94	3,120			$3,120			
							4,700						
12/31/Y1	E	300	15	5	(1,500)	—	(1,500)						
							3,200						
3/15/Y2	E	100	15	5	(500)	—	(500)						
							2,700						
12/31/Y2	A		14	4	2,400	100	(300)				$(300)		
							2,400						
6/15/Y3	O	100	16	5	(500)	—	(400)					$100	
							2,000						
12/31/Y3	A		15	5	2,500	100	500					500	
							2,500						
12/31/Y3	E	300	15	5	(1,500)	—	(1,500)						
							1,000						
12/31/Y4	NA		18	5	1,000	100	—						$ —
							1,000						
12/31/Y4	O	200	18	5	(1,000)	—	(1,000)						
							$ —						

Transaction Codes:
A—Adjustment for changes in the market price of stock.
NA—No adjustment required because the market price exceeds the appreciation limitation.
E—Exercise of a stock appreciation right.
O—Exercise of the related stock option.

Notes:
(1) Aggregate compensation for unexercised shares to be allocated to periods service performed.
(2) Refer to the schedule in paragraph .143.
(3) A similar computation would be made for interim reporting periods.

[FIN28, ¶27]

Glossary

.400 Junior stock. A specific type of stock issued to employees that generally is subordinate to an employer's regular common stock with respect to voting, liquidation, and dividend rights and is convertible into regular common stock if certain performance goals are achieved or if certain transactions occur. Junior stock generally is not transferable, except back to the issuing enterprise, and has a fair value lower than regular common stock because of its subordinate rights and the uncertainty of conversion to regular common stock. [FIN38, ¶1] Junior stock that is not convertible per se but that has restrictions that lapse (such as restrictions that lapse when certain performance goals are achieved) so that it ultimately becomes regular common stock is considered to be convertible. [FIN38, ¶1, fn1]

.401 Measurement date. The first date on which are known both (a) the number of shares that an individual employee is entitled to receive and (b) the option or purchase price, if any [(refer to paragraphs .110 and .111)]. [APB25, ¶10]

.402 Plan. Any arrangement to issue stock to officers and employees, as a group or individually. [APB25, ¶4]

.402A Service period. The period or periods the employee performs the related services. If the service period is not defined in the plan or some other agreement, such as an employment agreement, as a shorter or previous period, the service period shall be presumed to be the vesting period [of the plan]. [FIN28, ¶3]

.403 Stock appreciation rights. Awards entitling employees to receive cash, stock, or a combination of cash and stock in an amount equivalent to any excess of the market value of a stated number of shares of the employer's stock over a stated price. The form of payment may be specified when the rights are granted or may be determined when they are exercised; in some plans the employee may choose the form of payment. [FIN28, ¶9]

.404 [Editorial Deletion.]

.405 [Variable stock option, purchase, and award plans.] The characteristic that identifies [these] plans is that the terms prevent determining at the date of grant or award either the number of shares of stock that may be acquired by or awarded to an employee or the price to be paid by the employee, or both. [APB25, ¶29]

Supplemental Guidance

Stock Plans Established by a Principal Stockholder

.501 *Question*—Accounting for compensatory and noncompensatory stock option, purchase, and award plans adopted by an employer is discussed in this section. Should an employer account for plans or transactions *(plans),* if they have characteristics otherwise similar to compensatory plans adopted by employers, that are established or financed by a principal stockholder (that is, one who either owns 10 percent or more of the employer's common stock or has the ability, directly or indirectly, to control or significantly influence the employer)? [AIN-APB25]

.502 *Interpretation*—It is difficult to evaluate a principal stockholder's intent when he establishes or finances a plan with characteristics otherwise similar to compensatory plans generally adopted by employers. A principal stockholder may be satisfying his generous nature, settling a moral obligation, or attempting to increase or maintain the value of his own investment. If a principal stockholder's intention is to enhance or maintain the value of his investment by entering into such an arrangement, the employer is implicitly benefiting from the plan by retention of, and possibly improved performance by, the employee. In that case, the benefits to a principal stockholder and to the employer are generally impossible to separate. Similarly, it is virtually impossible to separate a principal stockholder's personal satisfaction from the benefit to the employer. APB Statement No. 4, *Basic Concepts and Accounting Principles Underlying Financial Statements of Business Enterprises,* paragraph 127, states that "Financial accounting emphasizes the economic substance of events even though the legal form may differ from the economic substance and suggest different treatment." [AIN-APB25]

.503 The economic substance of this type of plan is substantially the same for the employer and the employee, whether the plan is adopted by the employer or a principal stockholder. Consequently, the employer should account for this type of plan when one is established or financed by a principal stockholder unless (a) the relationship between the stockholder and the employer's employee is one that would normally result in generosity (that is, an immediate family relationship), (b) the stockholder has an obligation to the employee that is completely unrelated to the latter's employment (for example, the stockholder transfers shares to the employee because of personal business relationships in the past, unrelated to the present employment situation), or (c) the employer clearly does not benefit from the transaction (for example, the stockholder transfers shares to a minor employee with whom he has had a close relationship over a number of years). [AIN-APB25]

.504 This type of plan should be treated as a contribution to capital by the principal stockholder with the offsetting charge accounted for in the same manner as compensatory plans adopted by employers. [AIN-APB25]

.505 Compensation cost should be recognized as an expense of one or more periods in accordance with the provisions of paragraphs .112 through .115. [AIN-APB25]

.506 The employer should account for tax benefits, if any, from this type of plan in accordance with the provisions of paragraphs .116 through .118. If the employer receives no tax benefit from this type of plan, but would have received the benefit had the plan been adopted by the employer, the absence of the tax benefit is one of the variables in estimating the plan's cost to the employer. [AIN-APB25]

Conversion of Stock Options into Incentive Stock Options as a Result of the Economic Recovery Tax Act of 1981

.507 *Question*—What are the accounting implications for enterprises that convert previously issued stock options into incentive stock options (ISOs) as a result of the Economic Recovery Tax Act of 1981 (Act)? [FTB82-2, ¶1]

.508 *Background*—The Act includes provisions that grant favorable tax treatment to individuals who own incentive stock options. Enterprises can provide individuals with ISOs in two ways, by issuing new ISOs and by converting previously issued options into ISOs through changes to conform those options to the requirements of the Act. Accounting issues arise for enterprises with respect to plan modifications that are undertaken to convert existing options into ISOs. [FTB82-2, ¶2]

.509 One ISO requirement is that the option price must either equal or exceed the fair market value of the stock either at the date of grant or, if the option has been modified or renewed, at the date of the most recent amendment providing benefits to the option holder. This is commonly referred to as the "repricing" requirement of the Act. Enterprises electing to convert existing options into ISOs may be forced to raise option prices to meet the repricing requirement. [FTB82-2, ¶3]

.510 The Act allows enterprises to limit or eliminate the need to raise option prices by canceling certain prior plan amendments. For example, assume the option price and stock price at date of grant are $8 and $10, respectively, for a nonqualified plan and that a plan amendment is later introduced when the stock price is $17. By canceling the amendment, the option can be repriced at $10, resulting in $2 of additional cost to the employee; if the amendment is not canceled, the repricing is at $17 and the employee's additional cost is $9. In recent years, several stock option plans have been amended to add a tandem stock appreciation right (SAR). Therefore, if they are converting the underlying stock option into an ISO, some enterprises may elect to cancel SARs that were previously added through plan amendments. [FTB82-2, ¶4]

Repricing

.511 *Response*—This section requires an enterprise [to] record compensation for services it receives for stock issued to employees through a stock option plan. That compensation is equal to the quoted market price of the stock on the measurement date less the amount the employee is required to pay. The compensation cost is charged to expense over the periods in which the employee performs the related services. Increasing the option price to meet the repricing requirement described in paragraph .509 results in the enterprise's recapturing the compensation cost that arose when the option was granted. In recognition of that recapture, enterprises should reverse, in the period in which the option price is increased, the portion of total compensation cost that arose when the option was granted and has been charged to expense in subsequent periods. [FTB82-2, ¶8]

.512 A variable plan is a plan that has variable terms at its inception, as described in paragraph .132. A variable plan therefore differs from a plan with terms that are fixed at inception, modified once to increase the option price to conform to the Act, and remain fixed thereafter. A stock option plan that has fixed terms does not become a variable plan simply because the option price is raised to meet the repricing requirements of the Act. Accordingly, the increase in the option price to 100 percent of the fair market value to qualify an option under the Act does not result in a new measurement date. [FTB82-2, ¶9]

Tandem Plans

.513 *Presumption as to Exercise.* Paragraphs .119 through .123 clarify how compensation expense shall be recorded in connection with a combination or tandem stock option and SAR plan. Paragraph .122 states that ". . . compensation expense . . . shall be measured according to the terms an employee is most likely to elect based on the facts available each period. An enterprise shall presume that the employee will elect to exercise the stock appreciation rights or other variable plan awards, but the presumption may be overcome. . . ." The fact that the Act grants more favorable tax treatment to holders of stock options does not invalidate the presumption that the SAR will be exercised. However, it may be an important factor in evaluating what the employee is most likely to elect. [FTB82-2, ¶10]

.514 *Cancellation of SAR Only.* Paragraphs .119 through .123 also discuss accounting for the cancellation of the SAR in a tandem SAR and stock option plan. Paragraph .122 and footnote 8 state that accrued compensation recorded for a SAR shall not be adjusted if cancellation or forfeiture of the SAR occurs without a concurrent cancellation or forfeiture of the related stock option. Enterprises that cancel SARs under the circumstances described in paragraph .510 should look to paragraph .122 and footnote 8 for guidance. Paragraph .122 also includes guidance concerning the ultimate disposition of the accrued compensation amount if the option is exercised, canceled, or forfeited. [FTB82-2, ¶11]

Combination of Circumstances

.515 A combination of certain of the circumstances described in the preceding paragraphs may exist. For example, the cancellation of a tandem SAR may be combined with the repricing of the underlying option. If that happens, the portion of total accrued compensation that relates to the repricing should be reversed as described in paragraph .511; the balance of accrued compensation relates to the cancellation of the SAR and should be accounted for under the provisions of paragraph .514. As an illustration, assume the following: (a) a nonqualified option for $110 was granted when the market value of the stock was $130, (b) a tandem SAR was subsequently introduced through a plan amendment, (c) all compensation costs for the option and SAR relate to prior periods and have been charged to expense, and (d) the enterprise decides to cancel the SAR and reprice the stock option to a $130 option price when the market value of the stock is $180. The accounting result is that $20 of accrued compensation (computed $130 – $110) is reversed in the current period and the remaining $50 (computed $180 – $130) is retained as accrued compensation. [FTB82-2, ¶12]

Taxes

.516 Certain of the guidance in this section involves adjustments to compensation expense. For accounting purposes, the tax effects of those adjustments should be determined in accordance with the general guidance concerning accounting for income tax benefits under stock option plans found in paragraph .117. For example, a reversal of compensation expense in connection with a repricing as described in paragraph .511 results in a corresponding reversal of the related deferred tax benefits. Likewise, if a tandem SAR is canceled as described in paragraph .514, the tax benefit is not adjusted, but is retained along with the accrued compensation that gave rise to it. Ultimately, depending on the employee's actions, the compensation and tax benefit are disposed of in the same manner—together, they are either reversed or applied to additional paid-in capital. [FTB82-2, ¶13]

(The next page is 7873.)

Sources: ARB 51; FASB Statement 13; FASB Statement 58; FASB Statement 94; FASB Statement 109

Summary

Consolidated financial statements present the results of operations, financial position, and cash flows of a parent and its subsidiaries as if the group were a single enterprise. This section provides that consolidated financial statements generally shall include enterprises in which the parent has a controlling financial interest (usually, majority voting interest). This section also describes consolidation accounting procedures, such as elimination of intercompany profit and treatment of minority interests, and requires certain disclosures for unconsolidated subsidiaries accounted for by the cost method.

Consolidation Policy

.101 The purpose of **consolidated statements** is to present, primarily for the benefit of the shareholders and creditors of the parent company, the results of operations and the financial position of a parent company and its subsidiaries essentially as if the group were a single enterprise with one or more branches or divisions. There is a presumption that consolidated statements are more meaningful than separate statements and that they are usually necessary for a fair presentation when one of the enterprises in the group directly or indirectly has a controlling financial interest in the other enterprises. [ARB51, ¶1] If an enterprise has one or more subsidiaries, consolidated [statements] rather than parent-company financial statements are the appropriate general-purpose financial statements. [FAS94, ¶61]

.102 The usual condition for a controlling financial interest is ownership of a majority voting interest, and, therefore, as a general rule ownership by one enterprise, directly or indirectly, of over fifty percent of the outstanding voting shares of another enterprise is a condition pointing toward consolidation. However, there are exceptions to this general rule.[a] A majority-owned subsidiary shall not be consolidated if control is likely to be temporary or if it does not rest with the majority owner (as, for instance, if the subsidiary is in legal reorganization or in bankruptcy or operates under

---

[aThese exceptions] relate to the concept of control and its place in consolidation policy [and] are part of a broader FASB project on the reporting entity, including consolidations and the equity method. Similarly, consolidation of subsidiaries controlled by means other than ownership of a majority voting interest—control by significant minority ownership, by contract, lease, or agreement with other stockholders, by court decree, or otherwise—[is also] part of the project on the reporting entity. [FAS94, ¶10]

foreign exchange restrictions, controls, or other governmentally imposed uncertainties so severe that they cast significant doubt on the parent's ability to control the subsidiary). [FAS94, ¶13]

.103 All majority-owned subsidiaries—all companies in which a parent has a controlling financial interest through direct or indirect ownership of a majority voting interest— shall be consolidated except those described in the last sentence of paragraph .102. [FAS94, ¶13]

.104-.106 [Deleted 11/87 because of FASB Statement 94, *Consolidation of All Majority-Owned Subsidiaries.*]

.107 A difference in fiscal periods of a parent and subsidiary does not of itself justify the exclusion of the subsidiary from consolidation. It ordinarily is feasible for the subsidiary to prepare, for consolidation purposes, statements for a period that corresponds with or closely approaches the fiscal period of the parent. However, if the difference is not more than about three months, it usually is acceptable to use, for consolidation purposes, the subsidiary's statements for its fiscal period; when this is done, recognition shall be given by disclosure or otherwise to the effect of intervening events that materially affect the financial position or results of operations.[2] [ARB51, ¶4]

Disclosure

.108 Consolidated statements shall disclose the consolidation policy that is being followed. In most cases this can be made apparent by the headings or other information in the statements, but in other cases a footnote is required. [ARB51, ¶5]

.108A An entity that is a member of a group that files a consolidated tax return shall disclose in its separately issued financial statements:

a. The aggregate amount of current and deferred tax expense for each statement of earnings presented and the amount of any tax-related balances due to or from affiliates as of the date of each statement of financial position presented

---

[1][Deleted 11/87 because of FASB Statement 94.]

[2Editorial deletion, 5/93.]

b. The principal provisions of the method by which the consolidated amount of current and deferred tax expense is allocated to members of the group and the nature and effect of any changes in that method (and in determining related balances to or from affiliates) during the years for which the disclosures in (a) above are presented. [FAS109, ¶49]

Consolidation Procedure Generally

.109 In the preparation of consolidated statements, intercompany balances and transactions shall be eliminated. This includes intercompany open account balances, security holdings, sales and purchases, interest, dividends, etc. As consolidated statements are based on the assumption that they represent the financial position and operating results of a single business enterprise, such statements shall not include gain or loss on transactions among the enterprises in the group. Accordingly, any intercompany profit or loss on assets remaining within the group shall be eliminated; the concept usually applied for this purpose is gross profit or loss (refer to paragraph .110). [ARB51, ¶6]

.110 If income taxes have been paid on intercompany profits on assets remaining within the group, such taxes should be deferred or the intercompany profits to be eliminated in consolidation should be appropriately reduced. [ARB51, ¶17]

.111 If one enterprise purchases two or more blocks of stock of another enterprise at various dates and eventually obtains control of the other enterprise, the date of acquisition (for the purpose of preparing consolidated statements) depends on the circumstances. If two or more purchases are made over a period of time, the retained earnings of the subsidiary at acquisition shall generally be determined on a step-by-step basis; however, if small purchases are made over a period of time and then a purchase is made that results in control, the date of the latest purchase, as a matter of convenience, may be considered as the date of acquisition. Thus, there would generally be included in consolidated income for the year in which control is obtained the postacquisition income for that year, and in consolidated retained earnings the postacquisition income of prior years attributable to each block previously acquired [if not previously recognized by accounting for the investment by the equity method]. For example, if a 45 percent interest was acquired on October 1, 19X7 and a further 30 percent interest was acquired on April 1, 19X8, it would be appropriate to include in consolidated income for the year ended December 31, 19X8, 45 percent of the earnings of the subsidiary for the 3 months ended March 31, and 75 percent of the earnings for the 9 months ended December 31, and to credit consolidated retained earnings in 19X8 with 45 percent of the undistributed earnings of the subsidiary for the 3

2a[Deleted 2/92 because of FASB Statement 109, *Accounting for Income Taxes.*]

months ended December 31, 19X7 [if the investor's equity in those undistributed earnings had not been recognized previously].[3] [ARB51, ¶10]

.112 If a subsidiary is purchased during the year, there are alternative ways of dealing with the results of its operations in the consolidated income statement. One method, which usually is preferable, especially if there are several dates of acquisition of blocks of shares, is to include the subsidiary in the consolidation as though it had been acquired at the beginning of the year, and to deduct at the bottom of the consolidated income statement the preacquisition earnings applicable to each block of stock. This method presents results that are more indicative of the current status of the group, and facilitates future comparison with subsequent years. Another method of prorating income is to include in the consolidated statement only the subsidiary's revenue and expenses subsequent to the date of acquisition. [ARB51, ¶11]

.113 If the investment in a subsidiary is disposed of during the year, it may be preferable to omit the details of operations of the subsidiary from the consolidated income statement, and to show the equity of the parent in the earnings of the subsidiary prior to disposal as a separate item in the statement. [ARB51, ¶12]

.114 Shares of the parent held by a subsidiary shall not be treated as outstanding stock in the consolidated balance sheet. [ARB51, ¶13]

Minority Interests

.115 The amount of intercompany profit or loss to be eliminated in accordance with paragraph .109 is not affected by the existence of a minority interest. The complete elimination of the intercompany profit or loss is consistent with the underlying assumption that consolidated statements represent the financial position and operating results of a single business enterprise. The elimination of the intercompany profit or loss may be allocated proportionately between the majority and minority interests. [ARB51, ¶14]

.116 In the unusual case in which losses applicable to the minority interest in a subsidiary exceed the minority interest in the equity capital of the subsidiary, such excess and any further losses applicable to the minority interest shall be charged against the majority interest, as there is no obligation of the minority interest to make good such losses. However, if future earnings do materialize, the majority interest shall be credited to the extent of such losses previously absorbed. [ARB51, ¶15]

---

[3]The amount of interest cost capitalized through application of Section 167, "Interest: Capitalization of Interest Costs," shall not be changed when restating financial statements of prior periods [to account for acquiring a subsidiary on a step-by-step basis]. [FAS58, ¶8]

Stock Dividends of Subsidiaries

.117 Occasionally, subsidiary enterprises capitalize retained earnings arising since acquisition, by means of a stock dividend or otherwise. This does not require a transfer to capital surplus on consolidation, inasmuch as the retained earnings in the consolidated financial statements shall reflect the accumulated earnings of the consolidated group not distributed to the shareholders of, or capitalized by, the parent company. [ARB51, ¶18]

Unconsolidated Subsidiaries in Consolidated Statements

.118 [Section I82, "Investments: Equity Method," describes when investments in unconsolidated subsidiaries shall be accounted for by the equity method in consolidated financial statements. The limitations on consolidation described in paragraphs .102 and .103 of this section also are limitations on use of the equity method; a subsidiary affected by those limitations shall be accounted for by the cost method.]

.119-.120 [Deleted 11/87 because of FASB Statement 94.]

Disclosure About Formerly Unconsolidated Majority-Owned Subsidiaries

.120A Information that was disclosed under Section I82, paragraph .110(c), about majority-owned subsidiaries that were unconsolidated in financial statements for fiscal years 1986 or 1987 shall continue to be disclosed for them after they are consolidated pursuant to the provisions of this section. That is, summarized information about the assets, liabilities, and results of operations (or separate statements) shall be provided for those subsidiaries, either individually or in groups, as appropriate, in the consolidated financial statements or notes.[3a] [FAS94, ¶14]

Combined Statements

.121 To justify the preparation of consolidated statements, the controlling financial interest shall rest directly or indirectly in one of the enterprises included in the consolidation. There are circumstances, however, where combined financial statements (as distinguished from consolidated statements) of commonly controlled enterprises are likely to be more meaningful than their separate statements. For example, combined

---

[3a]The FASB project [referred to in footnote a] on the reporting entity, including consolidations and the equity method, will consider what disaggregated information should be disclosed with consolidated financial statements. To prevent loss in the meantime of information about [previously] unconsolidated subsidiaries, paragraph .120A requires continued disclosure of that information for subsidiaries that are [now] consolidated. [FAS94, ¶11] The time [before the] issuance [of a Statement on that project] provides an opportunity for business enterprises to explore ways to provide additional information that is useful to investors, creditors, and others in understanding and assessing the effects of the differing risks and returns of various activities. [FAS94, ¶12]

financial statements would be useful if one individual owns a controlling interest in several enterprises that are related in their operations. Combined statements also would be used to present the financial position and the results of operations of a group of unconsolidated subsidiaries. [(Refer to paragraph .102 for rules requiring consolidation of majority-owned subsidiaries.)] They also might be used to combine the financial statements of enterprises under common management. [ARB51, ¶22]

.122 If combined statements are prepared for a group of related enterprises, such as a group of unconsolidated subsidiaries [(refer to paragraph .102 for rules requiring consolidation of majority-owned subsidiaries)] or a group of commonly controlled enterprises, intercompany transactions and profits or losses shall be eliminated, and if there are problems in connection with such matters as minority interests, foreign operations, different fiscal periods, or income taxes, they shall be treated in the same manner as in consolidated statements. [ARB51, ¶23]

Parent Company Statements

.123 In some cases parent company statements may be needed, in addition to consolidated statements, to indicate adequately the position of bondholders and other creditors or preferred stockholders of the parent. Consolidated statements, in which one column is used for the parent company and other columns for particular subsidiaries or groups of subsidiaries, often are an effective means of presenting the pertinent information. [ARB51, ¶24]

Glossary

.401 **Consolidated statements.** Consolidated statements present, primarily for the benefit of the shareholders and creditors of the parent company, the results of operations and the financial position of a parent company and its subsidiaries essentially as if the group were a single enterprise with one or more branches or divisions. [ARB51, ¶1]

(The next page is 8301.)

Sources: APB Opinion 16; FASB Statement 5; FASB Statement 16;
FASB Statement 38; FASB Statement 87; FASB Statement 109;
FASB Statement 112; FASB Statement 113; FASB Statement 114;
FASB Interpretation 14; FASB Interpretation 34

Summary

An estimated loss from a loss contingency shall be charged to income if (a) it is probable that an asset had been impaired or a liability had been incurred at the date of the financial statements and (b) the amount of the loss can be reasonably estimated. Disclosure is required for loss contingencies not meeting both those conditions if there is a reasonable possibility that a loss may have been incurred. Gain contingencies shall not be credited to income because to do so would recognize income prior to realization.

.101 For purposes of this section, a **contingency** is defined as an existing condition, situation, or set of circumstances involving uncertainty as to possible gain (hereinafter a *gain contingency*) or loss (hereinafter a *loss contingency*) to an enterprise that will ultimately be resolved when one or more future events occur or fail to occur.[1] Resolution of the uncertainty may confirm the acquisition of an asset or the reduction of a liability or the loss or impairment of an asset or the incurrence of a liability. [FAS5, ¶1] The term *loss* is used in this section to include many charges against income that are commonly referred to as *expenses* and others that are commonly referred to as *losses*. [FAS5, ¶1, fn1]

Scope

.102 This section [presents] standards of financial accounting and reporting for loss contingencies and gain contingencies. [FAS5, ¶6] [However, accounting for pension costs, for vacation pay,] and for deferred compensation contracts and stock issued to employees are excluded from the scope of this section. Those matters are covered [in Section P16, "Pension Costs"; Section C44, "Compensation to Employees: Paid Absences"; and Section C47, "Compensation to Employees: Stock Purchase and Option Plans," respectively.] [FAS5, ¶7] Accounting for other employment-related costs is also excluded from the scope of this section except for postemployment benefits that become subject to [the provisions of] this section through application of paragraph .103 of Section P32, "Postemployment

---

[1] Refer to paragraphs .121 and .122 for further discussion and examples of loss contingencies.]

Benefits." [FAS112, ¶10] [Further,] this section does not change [prescribed] accounting practices for life insurance enterprises [FAS5, ¶102] [in Section In6, "Insurance Industry." As discussed in paragraph .137, this section does not address the question of whether] it is appropriate to write down the carrying amount of an operating asset to an amount expected to be recoverable through future operations. [FAS5, ¶31]

.103 Examples of application of the conditions for accrual of loss contingencies in paragraph .105 and the disclosure requirements in paragraphs .108 through .114 are presented in paragraphs .124 through .151. [FAS5, ¶16]

Probability Classifications for Loss Contingencies

.104 When a loss contingency exists, the likelihood that the future event or events will confirm the loss or impairment of an asset or the incurrence of a liability can range from probable to remote. This section uses the terms **probable, reasonably possible,** and **remote** to identify three areas within that range, as follows:

a. *Probable.* The future event or events are likely to occur.
b. *Reasonably possible.* The chance of the future event or events occurring is more than remote but less than likely.
c. *Remote.* The chance of the future event or events occurring is slight. [FAS5, ¶3]

Accrual of Loss Contingencies

.105 An estimated loss from a loss contingency (as defined in paragraph .101) shall be accrued by a charge to income if *both* of the following conditions are met:

a. Information available prior to issuance of the financial statements indicates that it is probable[2] that an asset had been impaired or a liability had been incurred at the date of the financial statements.[3] It is implicit in this condition that it must be probable that one or more future events will occur confirming the fact of the loss.
b. The amount of loss can be reasonably estimated.[4] [FAS5, ¶8]

.106 Condition (b) in paragraph .105 does not delay accrual of a loss until only a

---

[2]Virtual certainty [is not required] before a loss is accrued. [FAS5, ¶84]

[3]*Date of the financial statements* means the end of the most recent accounting period for which financial statements are being presented. [FAS5, ¶8, fn4]

[4]If a loss cannot be accrued in the period when it is probable that an asset had been impaired or a liability had been incurred because the amount of loss cannot be reasonably estimated, the loss shall be charged to the income [of the period] when the amount of the loss can be reasonably estimated [and not] be charged retroactively to an earlier period. [FAS16, ¶37] [Refer to Section A35, "Adjustments of Financial Statements for Prior Periods," paragraph .102.]

single amount can be reasonably estimated. To the contrary, if condition (a) in paragraph .105 is met and information available indicates that the estimated amount of loss is within a range of amounts, it follows that some amount of loss has occurred and can be reasonably estimated. [FIN14, ¶2]

.107 If condition (a) in paragraph .105 is met with respect to a particular loss contingency and the reasonable estimate of the loss is a range, condition (b) in paragraph .105 is met and an amount shall be accrued for the loss. If some amount within the range appears at the time to be a better estimate than any other amount within the range, that amount shall be accrued. If no amount within the range is a better estimate than any other amount, however, the minimum amount in the range shall be accrued. [FIN14, ¶3] (Even though the minimum amount in the range is not necessarily the amount of loss that will be ultimately determined, it is not likely that the ultimate loss will be less than the minimum amount.) [FIN14, ¶3, fn1]

Disclosure of Loss Contingencies

.108 Disclosure of the nature of an accrual made pursuant to the provisions of paragraph .105, and in some circumstances the amount accrued, may be necessary for the financial statements not to be misleading. [FAS5, ¶9] (Terminology used shall be descriptive of the nature of the accrual.) [FAS5, ¶9, fn5]

.109 If no accrual is made for a loss contingency because one or both of the conditions in paragraph .105 are not met, or if an exposure to loss exists in excess of the amount accrued pursuant to the provisions of paragraph .105, disclosure of the contingency shall be made when there is at least a reasonable possibility that a loss or an additional loss may have been incurred. The disclosure shall indicate the nature of the contingency and shall give an estimate of the possible loss or range of loss or state that such an estimate cannot be made.[5] [FAS5, ¶10]

.110 For example, disclosure shall be made of any loss contingency that meets the condition in paragraph .105(a) but that is not accrued because the amount of loss cannot be reasonably estimated (refer to paragraph .105(b)). Disclosure is also required of some loss contingencies that do not meet the condition in paragraph .105(a)— namely, those contingencies for which there is a *reasonable possibility* that a loss may have been incurred even though information may not indicate that it is *probable* that an asset had been impaired or a liability had been incurred at the date of the financial statements. [FAS5, ¶10, fn6]

.111 Disclosure is not required of a loss contingency involving an unasserted claim or assessment if there has been no manifestation by a potential claimant of an awareness

---

[5]Disclosure is not required for uninsured risks. However, disclosure in appropriate circumstances is not discouraged. [FAS5, ¶103]

of a possible claim or assessment unless it is considered probable that a claim will be asserted and there is a reasonable possibility that the outcome will be unfavorable. [FAS5, ¶10]

.112 After the date of an enterprise's financial statements but before those financial statements are issued, information may become available indicating that an asset was impaired or a liability was incurred after the date of the financial statements or that there is at least a reasonable possibility that an asset was impaired or a liability was incurred after that date. The information may relate to a loss contingency that existed at the date of the financial statements, that is, an asset that was not insured at the date of the financial statements. On the other hand, the information may relate to a loss contingency that did not exist at the date of the financial statements, that is, threat of expropriation of assets after the date of financial statements or the filing for bankruptcy by an enterprise whose debt was guaranteed after the date of the financial statements. In none of the cases cited in this paragraph was an asset impaired or a liability incurred at the date of the financial statements, and the condition for accrual in paragraph .105(a) is, therefore, not met. Disclosure of those kinds of losses or loss contingencies may be necessary, however, to keep the financial statements from being misleading. If disclosure is deemed necessary, the financial statements shall indicate the nature of the loss or loss contingency and give an estimate of the amount or range of loss or possible loss or state that such an estimate cannot be made. Occasionally, in the case of a loss arising after the date of the financial statements where the amount of asset impairment or liability incurrence can be reasonably estimated, disclosure may best be made by supplementing the historical financial statements with pro forma financial data giving effect to the loss as if it had occurred at the date of the financial statements. It may be desirable to present pro forma statements, usually a balance sheet only, in columnar form on the face of the historical financial statements. [FAS5, ¶11]

.113 Certain loss contingencies are presently being disclosed in financial statements even though the possibility of loss may be remote. The common characteristic of those contingencies is a guarantee, normally with a right to proceed against an outside party in the event that the guarantor is called upon to satisfy the guarantee. Examples include (a) guarantees of indebtedness of others, (b) obligations of commercial banks under standby letters of credit, and (c) guarantees to repurchase receivables (or, in some cases, to repurchase the related property) that have been sold or otherwise assigned. Disclosure of those loss contingencies, and others that in substance have the same characteristic, shall be continued. The disclosure shall include the nature and amount of the guarantee. Consideration should be given to disclosing, if estimable, the value of any recovery that could be expected to result, such as from the guarantor's right to proceed against an outside party. [FAS5, ¶12]

.114 The term *guarantees of indebtedness of others* in paragraph .113 includes

indirect guarantees of indebtedness of others. [FIN34, ¶3] An indirect guarantee of another arises under an agreement that obligates one enterprise to transfer funds to a second enterprise upon occurrence of specified events, under conditions whereby (a) the funds are legally available to creditors of the second enterprise and (b) those creditors may enforce the second enterprise's claims against the first enterprise under the agreement. Examples of indirect guarantees include agreements to advance funds if a second enterprise's income, coverage of fixed charges, or working capital falls below a specified minimum.[6] [FIN34, ¶2]

.115 [Deleted 12/82 because of FASB Statement 71, *Accounting for the Effects of Certain Types of Regulation.*]

General or Unspecified Business Risks

.116 Some enterprises have in the past accrued so-called reserves for general contingencies. General or unspecified business risks do not meet the conditions for accrual in paragraph .105 and no accrual for loss shall be made. No disclosure about them is required by this section. [FAS5, ¶14]

Appropriation of Retained Earnings

.117 Some enterprises have classified a portion of retained earnings as *appropriated* for loss contingencies. In some cases, the appropriation has been shown outside the stockholders' equity section of the balance sheet. Appropriation of retained earnings is not prohibited by this section provided that it is shown within the stockholders' equity section of the balance sheet and is clearly identified as an appropriation of retained earnings. Costs or losses shall not be charged to an appropriation of retained earnings, and no part of the appropriation shall be transferred to income. [FAS5, ¶15]

Gain Contingencies

.118 Contingencies that might result in gains usually are not reflected in the accounts since to do so might be to recognize revenue prior to its realization. Adequate disclosure shall be made of contingencies that might result in gains, but care shall be exercised to avoid misleading implications as to the likelihood of realization. [FAS5, ¶17]

Contingencies Related to Business Combinations

.119 A business combination agreement may provide for the issuance of additional shares of a security or the transfer of cash or other consideration contingent on specified events or transactions in the future. [APB16, ¶77] [The accounting for such contingent consideration is discussed in Section B50, "Business Combinations,"

---

[6]Disclosure of an indirect guarantee is not required if it is otherwise disclosed in an entity's financial statements. [FIN34, ¶2, fn1]

paragraphs .135 through .144. Similarly, Section B50, paragraphs .148 through .150, discusses the accounting for preacquisition contingencies.] A preacquisition contingency [is] a contingency of an enterprise that is acquired in a business combination accounted for by the purchase method and that is in existence before the consummation of the combination. A preacquisition contingency can be a contingent asset, a contingent liability, or a contingent impairment of an asset. [FAS38, ¶4a]

Other Disclosures

.120 Unused letters of credit, assets pledged as security for loans, and commitments, such as those for plant acquisition or an obligation to reduce debts, maintain working capital, or restrict dividends, [FAS5, ¶18] shall be disclosed in financial statements. This section does not alter the present disclosure requirements with respect to those items. [Refer to Section F25, "Financial Instruments: Disclosure," for guidance on possible additional disclosure requirements.] [FAS5, ¶19]

Examples of Loss Contingencies

.121 Not all uncertainties[6a] inherent in the accounting process give rise to *contingencies* as that term is used in this section. Estimates are required in financial statements for many ongoing and recurring activities of an enterprise. The mere fact that an estimate is involved does not of itself constitute the type of uncertainty referred to in the definition in paragraph .101. For example, the fact that estimates are used to allocate the known cost of a depreciable asset over the period of use by an enterprise does not make depreciation a contingency; the eventual expiration of the utility of the asset is not uncertain. Thus, depreciation of assets is not a contingency as defined in paragraph .101, nor are such matters as recurring repairs, maintenance, and overhauls, which interrelate with depreciation. Also, amounts owed for services received, such as advertising and utilities, are not contingencies even though the accrued amounts may have been estimated; there is nothing uncertain about the fact that those obligations have been incurred. [FAS5, ¶2]

.122 Examples of loss contingencies include:

a. Collectibility of receivables
b. Obligations related to product warranties and product defects
c. Risk of loss or damage of enterprise property by fire, explosion, or other hazards
d. Threat of expropriation of assets
e. Pending or threatened litigation
f. Actual or possible claims and assessments
g. Risk of loss from catastrophes assumed by property and casualty insurance enterprises including reinsurance enterprises
h. Guarantees of indebtedness of others

[6a]The possibility of a change in the tax law in some future year is not an *uncertainty* as that term is used in this section. [FAS109, ¶172]

i. Obligations of commercial banks under standby letters of credit[7]
j. Agreements to repurchase receivables (or to repurchase the related property) that have been sold [FAS5, ¶4]
[k. Withdrawal from a multiemployer plan.[7a]]

Examples of Application of the Conditions for Accrual and Disclosure of Loss Contingencies

.123 Paragraphs .124 through .151 contain examples of application of the conditions for accrual of loss contingencies in paragraph .105 and of the disclosure requirements in paragraphs .108 through .114. It should be recognized that no set of examples can encompass all possible contingencies or circumstances. Accordingly, accrual and disclosure of loss contingencies should be based on an evaluation of the facts in each particular case. [FAS5, ¶21]

Estimation of a Loss within a Range of Amounts

.124 Assume that an enterprise is involved in litigation at the close of its fiscal year ending December 31, 19X6 and information available indicates that an unfavorable outcome is probable. Subsequently, after a trial on the issues, a verdict unfavorable to the enterprise is handed down, but the amount of damages remains unresolved at the time the financial statements are issued. Although the enterprise is unable to estimate the exact amount of loss, its reasonable estimate at the time is that the judgment will be for not less than $3 million or more than $9 million. No amount in that range appears at the time to be a better estimate than any other amount. This section requires accrual of the $3 million at December 31, 19X6, disclosure of the nature of the contingency and the exposure to an additional amount of loss of up to $6 million, and possibly disclosure of the amount of the accrual. [FIN14, ¶4]

.125 The same answer would result under the example in paragraph .124 if it is prob-

---

[7]As defined by the Federal Reserve Board, *standby letters of credit* include "every letter of credit (or similar arrangement however named or designated) which represents an obligation to the beneficiary on the part of the issuer (1) to repay money borrowed by or advanced to or for the account of the account party or (2) to make payment on account of any evidence of indebtedness undertaken by the account party or (3) to make payment on account of any default by the account party in the performance of an obligation." A note to that definition states that "as defined, 'standby letters of credit' would not include (1) commercial letters of credit and similar instruments where the issuing bank expects the beneficiary to draw upon the issuer and which do not 'guaranty' payment of a money obligation or (2) a guaranty or similar obligation issued by a foreign branch in accordance with the subject to the limitations of Regulation M [of the Federal Reserve Board]." Regulations of the Comptroller of the Currency and the Federal Deposit Insurance Corporation contain similar definitions. [FAS5, ¶4, fn2]

[7a]In some situations, withdrawal from a multiemployer plan may result in an employer's having an obligation to the plan for a portion of its unfunded benefit obligations. If withdrawal under circumstances that would give rise to an obligation is either probable or reasonably possible, the provisions of this section shall apply. [FAS87, ¶70]

able that a verdict will be unfavorable even though the trial has not been completed before the financial statements are issued. In that situation, condition (a) in paragraph .105 would be met because information available to the enterprise indicates that an unfavorable verdict is probable. An assessment that the range of loss is between $3 million and $9 million would meet condition (b) in paragraph .105. If no single amount in that range is a better estimate than any other amount, this section requires accrual of $3 million at December 31, 19X6, disclosure of the nature of the contingency and the exposure to an additional amount of loss of up to $6 million, and possibly disclosure of the amount of the accrual. Note, however, that if the enterprise had assessed the verdict differently (that is, that an unfavorable verdict was *not* probable but was only reasonably possible), condition (a) in paragraph .105 would not have been met and no amount of loss would be accrued but the nature of the contingency and any amount of loss that is reasonably possible would be disclosed. [FIN14, ¶5]

.126 Assume that in the examples given in paragraphs .124 and .125 condition (a) in paragraph .105 has been met and a reasonable estimate of loss is a range between $3 million and $9 million but a loss of $4 million is a better estimate than any other amount in that range. In that situation, this section requires accrual of $4 million, disclosure of the nature of the contingency and the exposure to an additional amount of loss of up to $5 million, and possibly disclosure of the amount of the accrual. [FIN14, ¶6]

.127 As a further example, assume that at December 31, 19X6 an enterprise has an investment of $1,000,000 in the securities of another enterprise that has declared bankruptcy, and there is no quoted market price for the securities. Condition (a) in paragraph .105 has been met because information available indicates that the value of the investment has been impaired, and a reasonable estimate of loss is a range between $300,000 and $600,000. No amount of loss in that range appears at the time to be a better estimate of loss than any other amount. This section requires accrual of the $300,000 loss at December 31, 19X6, disclosure of the nature of the contingency and the exposure to an additional amount of loss of up to $300,000, and possibly disclosure of the amount of the accrual. [FIN14, ¶7]

Collectibility of Receivables

.128 The assets of an enterprise may include receivables that arose from credit sales, loans, or other transactions. The conditions under which receivables exist usually involve some degree of uncertainty about their collectibility, in which case a contingency exists as defined in paragraph .101. Losses from uncollectible receivables shall be accrued when both conditions in paragraph .105 are met. Those conditions may be considered in relation to individual receivables or in relation to groups of similar types of receivables. If the conditions are met, accrual shall be made even though the particular receivables that are uncollectible may not be identifiable. [FAS5, ¶22]

.129 If, based on current information and events, it is probable that the enterprise will be unable to collect all amounts due according to the contractual terms of the receivable, the condition in paragraph .105(a) is met. As used here, *all amounts due according to the contractual terms* means that both the contractual interest payments and the contractual principal payments will be collected as scheduled according to the receivable's contractual terms. However, a creditor need not consider an insignificant delay or insignificant shortfall in amount of payments as meeting the condition in paragraph .105(a). [FAS114, ¶21] Whether the amount of loss can be reasonably estimated (the condition in paragraph .105(b)) will normally depend on, among other things, the experience of the enterprise, information about the ability of individual debtors to pay, and appraisal of the receivables in light of the current economic environment. In the case of an enterprise that has no experience of its own, reference to the experience of other enterprises in the same business may be appropriate. Inability to make a reasonable estimate of the amount of loss from uncollectible receivables (that is, failure to satisfy the condition in paragraph .105(b)) precludes accrual and may, if there is significant uncertainty as to collection, suggest that the installment method, the cost recovery method, or some other method of revenue recognition be used [(refer to Section R75, "Revenue Recognition")]; in addition, the disclosures called for by paragraph .109 should be made. [FAS5, ¶23]

Obligations Related to Product Warranties and Product Defects

.130 A warranty is an obligation incurred in connection with the sale of goods or services that may require further performance by the seller after the sale has taken place. Because of the uncertainty surrounding claims that may be made under warranties, warranty obligations fall within the definition of a contingency in paragraph .101. Losses from warranty obligations shall be accrued when the conditions in paragraph .105 are met. Those conditions may be considered in relation to individual sales made with warranties or in relation to groups of similar types of sales made with warranties. If the conditions are met, accrual shall be made even though the particular parties that will make claims under warranties may not be identifiable. [FAS5, ¶24] [Refer to Section R75, paragraphs .501 through .505, for guidance on recognition of revenues and costs from separately priced extended warranty and product maintenance contracts.]

.131 If, based on available information, it is probable that customers will make claims under warranties relating to goods or services that have been sold, the condition in paragraph .105(a) is met at the date of an enterprise's financial statements because it is probable that a liability has been incurred. Satisfaction of the condition in paragraph .105(b) will normally depend on the experience of an enterprise or other information. In the case of an enterprise that has no experience of its own, reference to the experience of other enterprises in the same business may be appropriate. Inability to make a reasonable estimate of the amount of a warranty obligation at the time of sale because of significant uncertainty about possible claims (that is, failure to satisfy the condition in paragraph .105(b)) precludes accrual and, if the range of possible loss is wide, may raise a question about whether a sale should be recorded prior to expiration of the warranty period or until sufficient experience has been gained to permit a reasonable estimate of the obligation; in addition, the disclosures called for by paragraph .109 should be made. [FAS5, ¶25]

.132 Obligations other than warranties may arise with respect to products or services that have been sold, for example, claims resulting from injury or damage caused by product defects. If it is probable that claims will arise with respect to products or services that have been sold, accrual for losses may be appropriate. The condition in paragraph .105(a) would be met, for instance, with respect to a drug product or toys that have been sold if a health or safety hazard related to those products is discovered and as a result it is considered probable that liabilities have been incurred. The condition in paragraph .105(b) would be met if experience or other information enables the enterprise to make a reasonable estimate of the loss with respect to the drug product or the toys. [FAS5, ¶26]

Risk of Loss or Damage of Enterprise Property

.133 At the date of an enterprise's financial statements, it may not be insured against risk of future loss or damage to its property by fire, explosion, or other hazards. The absence of insurance against losses from risks of those types constitutes an existing condition involving uncertainty about the amount and timing of any losses that may occur, in which case a contingency exists as defined in paragraph .101. Uninsured risks may arise in a number of ways, including (a) noninsurance of certain risks or coinsurance or deductible clauses in an insurance contract or (b) insurance through a subsidiary or investee[8] to the extent not reinsured with an independent insurer. Some risks, for all practical purposes, may be noninsurable, and the self-assumption of those risks is mandatory. [FAS5, ¶27]

.134 The absence of insurance does not mean that an asset has been impaired or a liability has been incurred at the date of an enterprise's financial statements. Fires, explosions, and other similar events that may cause loss or damage of an enterprise's property are random in their occurrence.[9] With respect to events of that type, the condition for accrual in paragraph .105(a) is not satisfied prior to the occurrence of the event because until that time there is no diminution in the value of the property. There is no relationship of those events to the activities of the enterprise prior to their occurrence, and no asset is impaired prior to their occurrence. Further, unlike an insurance enterprise, which has a contractual obligation under policies in force to reimburse insureds for losses, an enterprise can have no such obligation to itself and, hence, no liability. [FAS5, ¶28]

---

[8]The effects of transactions between a parent or other investor and a subsidiary or investee insurance enterprise shall be eliminated from an enterprise's financial statements (refer to Section C51, "Consolidation," and Section I82, "Investments: Equity Method"). [FAS5, ¶27, fn7]

[9]Experience regarding loss or damage to depreciable assets is in some cases one of the factors considered in estimating the depreciable lives of a group of depreciable assets, along with such other factors as wear and tear, obsolescence, and maintenance and replacement policies. This section is not intended to alter present depreciation practices (refer to paragraph .121). [FAS5, ¶28, fn8]

Risk of Loss from Future Injury to Others, Damage to the Property of Others, and Business Interruption

.135 An enterprise may choose not to purchase insurance against risk of loss that may result from injury to others, damage to the property of others, or interruption of its business operations.[10] Exposure to risks of those types constitutes an existing condition involving uncertainty about the amount and timing of any losses that may occur, in which case a contingency exists as defined in paragraph .101. [FAS5, ¶29]

.136 Mere exposure to risks of those types, however, does not mean that an asset has been impaired or a liability has been incurred. The condition for accrual in paragraph .105(a) is not met with respect to loss that may result from injury to others, damage to the property of others, or business interruption that may occur after the date of an enterprise's financial statements. Losses of those types do not relate to the current or a prior period but rather to the *future* period in which they occur. Thus, for example, an enterprise with a fleet of vehicles should not accrue for injury to others or damage to the property of others that may be caused by those vehicles in the future even if the amount of those losses may be reasonably estimable. On the other hand, the conditions in paragraph .105 would be met with respect to uninsured losses resulting from injury to others or damage to the property of others that took place prior to the date of the financial statements, even though the enterprise may not become aware of those matters until after that date, if the experience of the enterprise or other information enables it to make a reasonable estimate of the loss that was incurred prior to the date of its financial statements. [FAS5, ¶30]

Write-Down of Operating Assets

.137 In some cases, the carrying amount of an operating asset not intended for disposal may exceed the amount expected to be recoverable through future use of that asset even though there has been no physical loss or damage of the asset or threat of such loss or damage. For example, changed economic conditions may have made recovery of the carrying amount of a productive facility doubtful. The question of whether, in those cases, it is appropriate to write down the carrying amount of the asset to an amount expected to be recoverable through future operations is not covered by this section. [FAS5, ¶31]

Threat of Expropriation

.138 The threat of expropriation of assets is a contingency within the definition of paragraph .101 because of the uncertainty about its outcome and effect. If information indicates that expropriation is imminent and compensation will be less than the carrying amount of the assets, the condition for accrual in paragraph .105(a) is met.

---

[10] As to injury or damage resulting from products that have been sold, refer to paragraph .132. [FAS5, ¶29, fn9]

Imminence may be indicated, for example, by public or private declarations of intent by a government to expropriate assets of the enterprise or actual expropriation of assets of other enterprises. Paragraph .105(b) requires that accrual be made only if the amount of loss can be reasonably estimated. If the conditions for accrual are not met, the disclosures specified in paragraph .109 would be made when there is at least a reasonable possibility that an asset has been impaired. [FAS5, ¶32]

Litigation, Claims, and Assessments

.139 The following factors, among others, must be considered in determining whether accrual and disclosure, or both, are required with respect to pending or threatened litigation and actual or possible claims and assessments:

a. The period in which the underlying cause (that is, the cause for action) of the pending or threatened litigation or of the actual or possible claim or assessment occurred
b. The degree of probability of an unfavorable outcome
c. The ability to make a reasonable estimate of the amount of loss [FAS5, ¶33]

.140 As a condition for accrual of a loss contingency, paragraph .105(a) requires that information available prior to the issuance of financial statements indicates that it is probable that an asset had been impaired or a liability had been incurred at the date of the financial statements. Accordingly, accrual would clearly be inappropriate for litigation, claims, or assessments whose underlying cause is an event or condition occurring after the date of financial statements but before those financial statements are issued, for example, a suit for damages alleged to have been suffered as a result of an accident that occurred after the date of the financial statements. Disclosure may be required, however, by paragraph .112.
[FAS5, ¶34]

.141 On the other hand, accrual may be appropriate for litigation, claims, or assessments whose underlying cause is an event occurring on or before the date of an enterprise's financial statements even if the enterprise does not become aware of the existence or possibility of the lawsuit, claim, or assessment until after the date of the financial statements. If those financial statements have not been issued, accrual of a loss related to the litigation, claim, or assessment would be required if the probability of loss is such that the condition in paragraph .105(a) is met and the amount of loss can be reasonably estimated. [FAS5, ¶35]

.142 If the underlying cause of the litigation, claim, or assessment is an event occurring before the date of an enterprise's financial statements, the probability of an outcome unfavorable to the enterprise must be assessed to determine whether the condition in paragraph .105(a) is met. Among the factors that should be considered are the nature of the litigation, claim, or assessment; the progress of the case (including progress after the date of the financial statements but before those statements are issued); the opinions or views of legal counsel and other advisers; the experience of the enterprise in similar cases; the experience of other enterprises; and any decision of the enterprise's management as to how the enterprise intends to respond to the lawsuit, claim, or assessment (for example, a decision to contest the case vigorously or a decision to seek an out-of-court settlement). The fact that legal counsel is unable to express an opinion that the outcome will be favorable to the enterprise should not necessarily be interpreted to mean that the condition for accrual of a loss in paragraph .105(a) is met. [FAS5, ¶36]

.143 The filing of a suit or formal assertion of a claim or assessment does not automatically indicate that accrual of a loss may be appropriate. The degree of probability of an unfavorable outcome must be assessed. The condition for accrual in paragraph .105(a) would be met if an unfavorable outcome is determined to be probable. If an unfavorable outcome is determined to be reasonably possible but not probable, or if the amount of loss cannot be reasonably estimated, accrual would be inappropriate, but disclosure would be required by paragraph .109. [FAS5, ¶37]

.144 With respect to unasserted claims and assessments, an enterprise must determine the degree of probability that a suit may be filed or a claim or assessment may be asserted and the possibility of an unfavorable outcome. For example, a catastrophe, accident, or other similar physical occurrence predictably engenders claims for redress, and in such circumstances their assertion may be probable; similarly, an investigation of an enterprise by a governmental agency, if enforcement proceedings have been or are likely to be instituted, is often followed by private claims for redress, and the probability of their assertion and the possibility of loss should be considered in each case. By way of further example, an enterprise may believe there is a possibility that it has infringed on another enterprise's patent rights, but the enterprise owning the patent rights has not indicated an intention to take any action and has not even indicated an awareness of the possible infringement. In that case, a judgment must first be made as to whether the assertion of a claim is probable. If the judgment is that assertion is not probable, no accrual or disclosure would be required. On the other hand, if the judgment is that assertion is probable, then a second judgment must be made as to the degree of probability of an unfavorable outcome. If an unfavorable outcome is probable and the amount of loss can be reasonably estimated, accrual of a loss is required by paragraph .105. If an unfavorable outcome is probable but the amount of loss cannot be reasonably estimated, accrual would not be appropriate, but disclosure would be required by paragraph .109. If an unfavorable outcome is reasonably possible but not probable, disclosure would be required by paragraph .109. [FAS5, ¶38]

.145 As a condition for accrual of a loss contingency, paragraph .105(b) requires that the amount of loss can be reasonably estimated. In some cases, it may be determined that a loss was incurred because an unfavorable outcome of the litigation, claim, or assessment is probable (thus satisfying the condition in paragraph .105(a)), but the range of possible loss is wide. For example, an enterprise may be litigating an income tax matter. In preparation for the trial, it may determine that, based on recent decisions involving one aspect of the litigation, it is probable that it will have to pay additional taxes of $2 million. Another aspect of the litigation may, however, be open to considerable interpretation, and depending on the interpretation by the court the enterprise may have to pay taxes of $8 million over and above the $2 million. In that case, paragraph .105 requires accrual of the $2 million if that is considered a reasonable estimate of the loss. Paragraph .109 requires disclosure of the additional exposure to loss if there is a reasonable possibility that additional taxes will be paid. Depending on the circumstances, paragraph .108 may require disclosure of the $2 million that was accrued. [FAS5, ¶39]

Catastrophe Losses of Property and Casualty Insurance Enterprises

.146 At the time that a property and casualty insurance enterprise or reinsurance enterprise issues an insurance policy covering risk of loss from catastrophes, a contingency arises. The contingency is the risk of loss *assumed* by the insurance enterprise, that is, the risk of loss from catastrophes that may occur *during the term of the policy.* The insurance enterprise has not assumed risk of loss for catastrophes that may occur *beyond* the term of the policy. Clearly, therefore, no asset has been impaired or liability incurred with respect to catastrophes that may occur beyond the terms of policies in force. [FAS5, ¶40]

.147 The conditions in paragraph .105 should be considered with respect to the risk of loss assumed by an insurance enterprise for catastrophes that may occur during the terms of policies in force to determine whether accrual of a loss is appropriate. To satisfy the condition in paragraph .105(a) that it be probable that a liability has been incurred to existing policyholders, the occurrence of catastrophes (that is, the confirming future events) would have to be reasonably predictable within the terms of policies in force. Further, to satisfy the condition in paragraph .105(b), the amounts of losses therefrom would have to be reasonably estimable. Actuarial techniques are employed by insurance enterprises to predict the rate of occurrence of and amounts of losses from catastrophes over long periods of time for insurance rate-setting purposes. Predictions over relatively short periods of time, such as an individual accounting period or the terms of a large number of existing insurance policies in force, are subject to substantial deviations. Consequently, assumption of risk of loss from catastrophes by property and casualty insurance enterprises and reinsurance enterprises fails to satisfy the conditions for accrual in paragraph .105. [FAS5, ¶41]

.148 Although some property and casualty insurance enterprises have accrued an estimated amount for catastrophe losses, other insurance enterprises have accomplished the same objective by deferring a portion of the premium income. Deferral of any portion of premium income *beyond the terms of policies in force* is, in substance, similar to premature accrual of catastrophe losses and, therefore, also does not meet the conditions of paragraph .105. [FAS5, ¶42]

.149 The conditions for accrual in paragraph .105 do not prohibit a property and casualty insurance enterprise from accruing probable catastrophe losses that have been incurred on or before the date of its financial statements but that have not been reported by its policyholders as of that date. If the amount of loss can be reasonably estimated, paragraph .105 requires accrual of those incurred-but-not-reported losses. [FAS5, ¶43]

Payments to Insurance Enterprises That May Not Involve Transfer of Risk

.150 To the extent that an insurance contract or reinsurance contract does not, despite its form, provide for indemnification of the insured or the ceding enterprise by the insurer or reinsurer against loss or liability, the premium paid less the amount of the premium to be retained by the insurer or reinsurer shall be accounted for as a deposit by the insured or the ceding enterprise. Those contracts may be structured in various ways, but if, regardless of form, their substance is that all or part of the premium paid by the insured or the ceding enterprise is a deposit, it shall be accounted for as such.[11] [FAS5, ¶44]

.151 Operations in certain industries may be subject to such high risks that insurance is unavailable or is available only at what is considered to be a prohibitively high cost. Some enterprises in those industries have "pooled" their risks by forming a mutual insurance enterprise in which they retain an equity interest and to which they pay insurance premiums. For example, some electric enterprises have formed such a mutual insurance enterprise to insure risks related to nuclear power plants, and some oil enterprises have formed an enterprise to insure against risks associated with petroleum exploration and production. Whether the premium paid represents a payment for the transfer of risk or whether it represents merely a deposit will depend on the circumstances surrounding each enterprise's interest in and insurance arrangement with the mutual insurance enterprise. An analysis of the contract is required to determine whether risk has been transferred and to what extent. [FAS5, ¶45]

---

[11]Paragraphs .171 through .177 of Section In6 identify conditions that are required for a reinsurance contract to indemnify the ceding enterprise against loss or liability and to be accounted for as reinsurance. Any transaction between enterprises to which Section In6 applies must meet those conditions to be accounted for as reinsurance. [FAS113, ¶30]

Glossary

.401 **Contingency.** An existing condition, situation, or set of circumstances involving uncertainty as to possible gain (a *gain contingency*) or loss (a *loss contingency*) to an enterprise that will ultimately be resolved when one or more future events occur or fail to occur. [FAS5, ¶1]

.402 **Indirect guarantee of indebtedness of others.** A guarantee under an agreement that obligates one enterprise to transfer funds to a second enterprise upon occurrence of specified events under conditions whereby (a) the funds are legally available to creditors of the second enterprise and (b) those creditors may enforce the second enterprise's claims against the first enterprise under the agreement. [FIN34, ¶2]

.403 **Probable.** [A probability classification for loss contingencies—when] the future event or events are likely to occur. [FAS5, ¶3]

.404 **Reasonably possible.** [A probability classification for loss contingencies—when] the chance of the future event or events occurring is more than remote but less than likely. [FAS5, ¶3]

.405 **Remote.** [A probability classification for loss contingencies—when] the chance of the future event or events occurring is slight. [FAS5, ¶3]

(The next page is 9051.)

Source: FASB Statement 116

Summary

This section presents standards for contributions and applies to all entities that receive or make contributions. Generally, contributions received, including unconditional promises to give, are recognized as revenues in the period received at their fair values. Contributions made, including unconditional promises to give, are recognized as expenses in the period made at their fair values. Conditional promises to give, whether received or made, are recognized when they become unconditional, that is, when the conditions are substantially met.

Certain exceptions are allowed for contributions of services and works of art, historical treasures, and similar assets. Contributions of services are recognized only if the services received (a) create or enhance nonfinancial assets or (b) require specialized skills, are provided by individuals possessing those skills, and would typically need to be purchased if not provided by donation. Contributions of works of art, historical treasures, and similar assets need not be recognized as revenues and capitalized if the donated items are added to collections held for public exhibition, education, or research in furtherance of public service rather than financial gain. Certain disclosures are required for collection items not capitalized and for receipts of contributed services and promises to give.

[**Note:** Not-for-profit organizations should refer to Section No5, "Not-for-Profit Organizations," for guidance on reporting information about donor-imposed restrictions on contributions received and recognition of the expiration of those restrictions.]

.101 This section establishes standards of financial accounting and reporting for **contributions** received and contributions made. Accounting for contributions is an issue primarily for **not-for-profit organizations** because contributions are a significant source of revenues for many of those organizations. However, this section applies to all entities (not-for-profit organizations and business enterprises) that receive or make contributions. [Not-for-profit organizations should refer to paragraphs .143 through .147 of Section No5, "Not-for-Profit Organizations," for guidance on reporting information about donor-imposed restrictions on contributions received and recognition of the expiration of those restrictions.] This section also establishes standards for accounting for **collections** of works of art, historical treasures, and similar assets acquired by contribution or by other means. [FAS116, ¶1]

Scope

.102 This section applies to contributions[1] of cash and other assets, including **promises to give.** It does not apply to transfers of assets that are in substance purchases of goods or services—exchange transactions in which each party receives and sacrifices commensurate value. However, if an entity voluntarily transfers assets to another or performs services for another in exchange for assets of substantially lower value and no unstated rights or privileges are involved, the contribution inherent in that transaction is within the scope of this section. [FAS116, ¶3] Because some exchange transactions may appear to be much like contributions, a careful assessment of the characteristics of the transaction is required to determine whether the recipient of a transfer of assets has given up an asset or incurred a liability of commensurate value. Assessing the characteristics of transactions from the perspectives of both the resource provider and the recipient [may be] necessary to determine whether a contribution has occurred.[2] [FAS116, ¶49]

.103 This section does not apply to transfers of assets in which the reporting entity acts as an agent, trustee, or intermediary, rather than as a donor or donee.[3] It also does not apply to tax exemptions, tax incentives, or tax abatements, or to transfers of assets from governmental units to business enterprises. [FAS116, ¶4]

---

[1]This section also uses terms such as *gift* and *donation* to refer to a contribution; however, it generally avoids terms such as *awards, grants, sponsorships,* and *appropriations* that often are more broadly used to refer not only to contributions but also to assets transferred in exchange transactions in which the *grantor, sponsor,* or *appropriator* expects to receive commensurate value. [FAS116, ¶3, fn3]

[2]For example, a resource provider may sponsor research and development activities at a research university and retain proprietary rights or other privileges, such as patents, copyrights, or advance and exclusive knowledge of the research outcomes. The research outcomes may be intangible, uncertain, or difficult to measure, and may be perceived by the university as a sacrifice of little or no value; however, their value often is commensurate with the value that a resource provider expects in exchange. Similarly, a resource provider may sponsor research and development activities and specify the protocol of the testing so the research outcomes are particularly valuable to the resource provider. Those transactions are not contributions if their potential public benefits are secondary to the potential proprietary benefits to the resource providers. [FAS116, ¶50] Moreover, a single transaction may be in part an exchange and in part a contribution. For example, if a donor transfers a building to an entity at a price significantly lower than its market value and no unstated rights or privileges are involved, the transaction is in part an exchange of assets and in part a contribution to be accounted for as required by this section. [FAS116, ¶51]

[3]The recipient of assets who is an agent or trustee has little or no discretion in determining how the assets transferred will be used. For example, if a recipient receives cash that it must disburse to *any* who meet guidelines specified by a resource provider or return the cash, those receipts may be deposits held by the recipient as an agent rather than contributions received as a donee. Similarly, if a recipient receives cash that it must disburse to individuals identified by the resource provider or return the cash, neither the receipt nor the disbursement is a contribution for the agent, trustee, or intermediary. [FAS116, ¶53] In contrast, if the resource provider allows the recipient to establish, define, and carry out the programs that disburse the cash, products, or services to the recipient's beneficiaries, the recipient generally is involved in receiving and making contributions. [FAS116, ¶54]

Definitions

.104 A contribution is an unconditional transfer of cash or other assets to an entity or a settlement or cancellation of its liabilities in a voluntary **nonreciprocal transfer** by another entity acting other than as an owner. Other assets include securities, land, buildings, use of facilities or utilities, materials and supplies, intangible assets, services, and **unconditional promises to give** those items in the future. [FAS116, ¶5]

.105 A promise to give is a written or oral agreement to contribute cash or other assets to another entity; however, to be recognized in financial statements there must be sufficient evidence in the form of verifiable documentation that a promise was made and received. A communication that does not indicate clearly whether it is a promise is considered an unconditional promise to give if it indicates an unconditional intention to give that is legally enforceable.[4] [FAS116, ¶6]

.106 A **donor-imposed condition** on a transfer of assets or a promise to give specifies a future and uncertain event whose occurrence or failure to occur gives the promisor a right of return of the assets transferred or releases the promisor from its obligation to transfer assets promised. [FAS116, ¶7] Imposing a condition creates a barrier that must be overcome before the recipient of the transferred assets has an unconditional right to retain those promised assets. For example, a transfer of cash with a promise to contribute that cash if a like amount of new gifts are raised from others within 30 days and a provision that the cash be returned if the gifts are not raised imposes a condition on which a promised gift depends. [FAS116, ¶60]

.107 In contrast, a **donor-imposed restriction** limits the use of contributed assets; it specifies a use that is more specific than broad limits resulting from the nature of the organization, the environment in which it operates, and the purposes specified in its articles of incorporation or bylaws or comparable documents for an unincorporated association. [FAS116, ¶7] Failures to comply with donors' restrictions, although rare, do occur, sometimes as a result of events occurring subsequent to receiving a contribution. [FAS116, ¶65] [Refer to] Section C59, "Contingencies," paragraph .105 if a subsequent event raises the possibility that an organization may not satisfy a restriction. [FAS116, ¶66]

Contributions Received

.108 Except as provided in paragraphs .109 and .111, contributions received shall be recognized as revenues or gains in the period received and as assets, decreases of liabilities, or expenses depending on the form of the benefits received. Contributions received shall be measured at their fair values. Contributions received by not-for-profit

---

[4]Legal enforceability refers to] the *availability* of legal remedies, [not] the intent to use them. [FAS116, ¶108]

organizations shall be reported as **restricted support** or **unrestricted support** as provided in Section No5, paragraphs .143 through .145. [FAS116, ¶8]

Contributed Services

.109 Contributions of services shall be recognized if the services received (a) create or enhance nonfinancial assets or (b) require specialized skills, are provided by individuals possessing those skills, and would typically need to be purchased if not provided by donation. Services requiring specialized skills are provided by accountants, architects, carpenters, doctors, electricians, lawyers, nurses, plumbers, teachers, and other professionals and craftsmen. Contributed services and promises to give services that do not meet the above criteria shall not be recognized. [FAS116, ¶9]

.110 An entity that receives contributed services shall describe the programs or activities for which those services were used, including the nature and extent[5] of contributed services received for the period and the amount recognized as revenues for the period. Entities are encouraged to disclose the fair value of contributed services received but not recognized as revenues if that is practicable. [FAS116, ¶10]

Contributed Collection Items

.111 An entity need not recognize contributions of works of art, historical treasures, and similar assets if the donated items are added to collections[6] that meet all of the following conditions:

a. Are held for public exhibition, education, or research in furtherance of public service rather than financial gain
b. Are protected, kept unencumbered, cared for, and preserved
c. Are subject to an organizational policy that requires the proceeds from sales of collection items to be used to acquire other items for collections. [FAS116, ¶11]

.112 Works of art, historical treasures, and similar items that are not part of a collection shall be recognized as assets in financial statements. Some entities that hold these items do not espouse the mission of public education, exhibition, and research and the attendant responsibilities to protect, keep unencumbered, care for, and preserve the items, and some entities that do maintain collections have some items that are not part of their collections [and, thus, are not exempted from recognition as assets.] [FAS116, ¶135]

---

[5]The nature and extent can be described by] nonmonetary information, such as the number and trends of donated hours received or service outputs provided by volunteer efforts, [or] other monetary information such as the dollar amount of contributions raised by volunteers. [FAS116, ¶123]

[6]Collections, as used in this section, generally are held by museums, botanical gardens, libraries, aquariums, arboretums, historic sites, planetariums, zoos, art galleries, nature, science and technology centers, and similar educational, research, and public service organizations that have those divisions; however, the definition is not limited to those entities nor does it apply to all items held by those entities. [FAS116, ¶128]

.113 Contributed collection items shall be recognized as revenues or gains if collections are capitalized and shall not be recognized as revenues or gains if collections are not capitalized. An entity that does not recognize and capitalize its collections or that capitalizes collections prospectively [Refer to Appendix C, "Effective Dates of Pronouncements," for options for entities that choose to capitalize collections.] shall disclose the additional information required by paragraphs .123 and .124. [FAS116, ¶13] Capitalization of selected collections or items is precluded. [FAS116, ¶12]

Contributions Made

.114 Contributions made shall be recognized as expenses in the period made and as decreases of assets or increases of liabilities depending on the form of the benefits given. For example, gifts of items from inventory held for sale are recognized as decreases of inventory[7] and contribution expenses, and unconditional promises to give cash are recognized as payables and contribution expenses. Contributions made shall be measured at the fair values of the assets given or, if made in the form of a settlement or cancellation of a donee's liabilities, at the fair value of the liabilities canceled. [FAS116, ¶18]

Measurement at Fair Value

.115 Quoted market prices, if available, are the best evidence of the fair value of monetary and nonmonetary assets, including services. If quoted market prices are not available, fair value may be estimated based on quoted market prices for similar assets, independent appraisals, or valuation techniques, such as the present value of estimated future cash flows. Contributions of services that create or enhance nonfinancial assets may be measured by referring to either the fair value of the services received or the fair value of the asset or of the asset enhancement resulting from the services. A major uncertainty about the existence of value may indicate that an item received or given should not be recognized.[8] [FAS116, ¶19]

---

[7]If the fair value of an asset transferred differs from its carrying amount, a gain or loss shall be recognized on the disposition of the asset. (Refer to Section N35, "Nonmonetary Transactions," paragraph .105.) [FAS116, ¶18, fn6]

[8]Contributed tangible property worth accepting generally possesses the common characteristic of all assets—future economic benefit or service potential. The future economic benefit or service potential of a tangible item usually can be obtained by exchanging it for cash or by using it to produce goods or services. However, if an item is accepted solely to be saved for its potential future use in scientific or educational research and has no alternative use, it may have uncertain value, or perhaps no value, and should not be recognized. [FAS116, ¶19, fn7]

.116 The present value of estimated future cash flows using a discount rate commensurate with the risks involved is an appropriate measure of fair value of unconditional promises to give cash.[9] Subsequent accruals of the interest element shall be accounted for as contribution income by donees and contribution expense by donors. [FAS116, ¶20]

.117 Unconditional promises to give that are expected to be collected or paid in less than one year may be measured at net realizable value (net settlement value) because that amount, although not equivalent to the present value of estimated future cash flows, results in a reasonable estimate of fair value. [FAS116, ¶21]

Conditional Promises to Give

.118 **Conditional promises to give,** which depend on the occurrence of a specified future and uncertain event to bind the promisor, shall be recognized when the conditions on which they depend are substantially met, that is, when the conditional promise becomes unconditional. A conditional promise to give is considered unconditional if the possibility that the condition will not be met is remote. For example, a stipulation that an annual report must be provided by the donee to receive subsequent annual payments on a multiyear promise is not a condition if the possibility of not meeting that administrative requirement is remote. [FAS116, ¶22]

.119 A transfer of assets with a conditional promise to contribute them shall be accounted for as a refundable advance until the conditions have been substantially met. [FAS116, ¶22] [Some entities] transfer cash or other assets with both donor-imposed restrictions and stipulations that impose a condition on which a gift depends. If a restriction and a condition exist, the transfer shall be accounted for as a refundable advance until the condition on which it depends is substantially met.[10] [FAS116, ¶63]

.120 Determining whether a promise is conditional or unconditional can be difficult if it contains donor stipulations that do not clearly state whether the right to receive payment or delivery of the promised assets depends on meeting those stipulations. It may be difficult to determine whether those stipulations are conditions or restrictions. In cases of ambiguous donor stipulations, a promise containing stipulations that are not clearly unconditional shall be presumed to be a conditional promise. [FAS116, ¶23]

---

[9]An entity may estimate the future cash flows of a portfolio of short-term promises resulting from a mass fund-raising appeal by using experience it gained from similar appeals. [FAS116, ¶20, fn8]

[10]A change in the original conditions of the agreement between promisor and promisee shall not be implied without an explicit waiver. A transfer of assets after a conditional promise to give is made and before the conditions are met is the same as a transfer of assets with a conditional promise to contribute those assets. [FAS116, ¶81]

Disclosures of Promises to Give

.121 Recipients of unconditional promises to give shall disclose the following:

a. The amounts of promises receivable in less than one year, in one to five years, and in more than five years
b. The amount of the allowance for uncollectible promises receivable. [FAS116, ¶24]

.122 Recipients of conditional promises to give shall disclose the following:

a. The total of the amounts promised
b. A description and amount for each group of promises having similar characteristics, such as amounts of promises conditioned on establishing new programs, completing a new building, and raising matching gifts by a specified date.[11] [FAS116, ¶25]

Financial Statement Presentation and Disclosure for Collections

.123 An entity that does not recognize and capitalize its collections shall report the following on the face of its statement of activities [or income statement for business enterprises], separately from revenues, expenses, gains, and losses:

a. Costs of collection items purchased as a decrease in the appropriate class of net assets [or equity]
b. Proceeds from sale of collection items as an increase in the appropriate class of net assets [or equity]
c. Proceeds from insurance recoveries of lost or destroyed collection items as an increase in the appropriate class of net assets [or equity].

Similarly, an entity that capitalizes its collections prospectively shall report proceeds from sales and insurance recoveries of items not previously capitalized separately from revenues, expenses, gains, and losses. [FAS116, ¶26] [Not-for-profit organizations should refer to paragraph .142, Exhibit 142A of Section No5 for an example of a possible format for these disclosures.]

.124 An entity that does not recognize and capitalize its collections or that capitalizes collections prospectively shall describe its collections, including their relative significance, and its accounting and stewardship policies for collections. If collection items not capitalized are deaccessed during the period, it also shall (a) describe the items given away, damaged, destroyed, lost, or otherwise deaccessed during the period or (b) disclose their fair value. In addition, a line item shall be shown on the face of the statement of financial position that refers to the disclosures required by this paragraph. That line item shall be dated if collections are capitalized prospectively, for example, "Collections acquired since January 1, 1995 (Note X)." [FAS116, ¶27]

---

[11]This section neither requires nor precludes disclosures for intentions to give. [FAS116, ¶117]

Examples of the Application of This Section to Specific Situations

.125   Paragraphs .126 through .160 provide additional discussion and examples that illustrate application of this section to some specific situations. The examples do not address all possible applications of this section and assume that all items addressed are material. [FAS116, ¶173]

	Paragraph Numbers
Scope and Definition	.126–.133
Example 1—Receipt of Resources in an Exchange	.128
Example 2—Receipt of Resources Partially in Exchange and Partially as a Contribution	.129–.130
Example 3—Receipt of Resources as an Agent Rather Than as a Donee	.131
Example 4—Intermediary between Donor and Donee	.132
Example 5—Intermediary between Government Provider and Its Beneficiary	.133
Contributions Received	.134–.160
Example 6—Contribution of Real Property	.135–.136
Example 7—Contribution of a Work of Art	.137–.139
Example 8—Contribution of Historical Objects	.140–.141
Example 9—Contribution of Utilities	.142–.143
Example 10—Contribution of Use of Property	.144–.146
Example 11—Contribution of Services	.147–.149
Example 12—Contribution of Services	.150–.152
Example 13—Contribution of Services	.153–.154
Example 14—Contribution of Services	.155–.156
Example 15—Contribution of Services	.157–.158
Example 16—Contribution of an Interest in an Estate	.159–.160

Scope and Definition

.126   Some transfers of assets that are exchange transactions may appear to be contributions if the services or other assets given in exchange are perceived to be a sacrifice of little value and the exchanges are compatible with the recipient's mission. Furthermore, a single transaction may be in part an exchange and in part a contribution. A careful assessment of the characteristics of the transaction, from the perspectives of both the resource provider and the recipient, is necessary to determine whether a contribution has occurred. Examples 1 and 2 illustrate the need to assess the relevant facts and circumstances to distinguish between the receipt of resources in an exchange and the receipt of resources in a contribution. [FAS116, ¶174]

.127 A transfer of assets also may appear to be a contribution when a donor uses an agent, a trustee, or an intermediary to transfer assets to a donee. Receipts of resources as an agent, trustee, or intermediary of a donor are not contributions received to the agent. Deliveries of resources as an agent, trustee, or intermediary of a donor are not contributions made by the agent. Similarly, contributions of services (time, skills, or expertise) between donors and donees that are facilitated by an intermediary are not contributions received or contributions made by the intermediary. Examples 3 through 5 illustrate the need to assess the relevant facts and circumstances to distinguish between the receipt of resources as a donee and the receipt of resources as an agent, a trustee, or an intermediary organization. [FAS116, ¶175]

Example 1—Receipt of Resources in an Exchange

.128 University A, a large research university with a cancer research center, regularly conducts research to discover more effective methods of treating cancer and often receives contributions to support its efforts. University A receives resources from a pharmaceutical company to finance the costs of a clinical trial of an experimental cancer drug the company developed. The pharmaceutical company specifies the protocol of the testing, including the number of participants to be tested, the dosages to be administered, and the frequency and nature of follow-up examinations. The pharmaceutical company requires a detailed report of the test outcome within two months of the test's conclusion. Because the results of the clinical trial have particular commercial value for the pharmaceutical company, receipt of the resources is not a contribution received by University A, nor is the disbursement of the resources a contribution made by the pharmaceutical company. [FAS116, ¶176]

Example 2—Receipt of Resources Partially in Exchange and Partially as a Contribution

.129 Organization B receives $100,000 in cash from a donor under a charitable remainder annuity trust agreement designating Organization B as the trustee and charitable remainder beneficiary—a donee. The terms of the trust agreement require that Organization B, as trustee, invest the trust assets and pay $5,000 each year to an annuitant (an income beneficiary specified by the donor) for the remainder of the annuitant's life. Upon death of the annuitant, Organization B may use its remainder interest for any purpose consistent with its mission. [FAS116, ¶177]

.130 Organization B, as a donee, would recognize the contribution received as revenue in the period the trust is established. The transfer is partially an exchange transaction—an agreement for annuity payments to a beneficiary over time—and partially a contribution. The contribution received by Organization B is the unconditional right to receive the remainder interest of the annuity trust. The amount of the contribution received by Organization B is the fair value of the trust assets ($100,000 cash transferred) less the fair value of the estimated annuity payments (the present value of $5,000 to be paid annually over the expected life of the annuitant). Because

Organization B must invest the underlying donated assets until the annuitant's death, [if Organization B is a not-for-profit organization,] the revenue recognized [is] temporarily restricted support [and] shall be distinguished from revenues from gifts that are either unrestricted or permanently restricted (paragraph .143 of Section No5). The death of the annuitant determines when the required annuity payments cease and when the trust expires and effectively removes all restrictions on the net assets of Organization B. If [Organization B is a not-for-profit organization and] the terms of this agreement had specified that upon death of the annuitant Organization B is to use its remainder interest to establish a permanent endowment, the revenue would be recognized as permanently restricted support rather than temporarily restricted support. [FAS116, ¶178]

Example 3—Receipt of Resources as an Agent Rather Than as a Donee

.131 Organization C receives relief supplies from Individual D with instructions to deliver the supplies to specified third-party beneficiaries. Organization C accepts responsibility for delivering those supplies because it has a distribution network and a mutual interest in serving the needs of the specified beneficiaries. Organization C has no discretion in determining the parties to be benefited; it must deliver the resources to the specified beneficiaries. Receipt of those goods is not a contribution received to Organization C, nor is the delivery of those goods to the beneficiaries a contribution made by Organization C. Rather, a contribution of goods is made by Individual D and received by the third-party beneficiaries. [FAS116, ¶179]

Example 4—Intermediary between Donor and Donee

.132 Organization E develops and maintains a list of lawyers and law firms that are interested in providing services without charge to charitable organizations and certain individuals. Organization E encourages individuals in need of free legal services to contact Organization E for referral to lawyers in the individual's community that may be willing to serve them. The decision about whether and how to serve a specific individual rests with the lawyer. Under those circumstances, Organization E merely acts as an intermediary in bringing together a willing donor and donee. The free legal services are not a contribution received by Organization E. [FAS116, ¶180]

Example 5—Intermediary between Government Provider and Its Beneficiary

.133 Hospital F provides health care services to patients that are entitled to Medicaid assistance under a joint federal and state program. The program sets forth various administrative and technical requirements covering provider participation, payment mechanisms, and individual eligibility and benefit provisions. Medicaid payments made to Hospital F on behalf of the program beneficiaries are third-party payments for patient services rendered. Hospital F provides patient care for a fee—an exchange transaction—and acts as an intermediary between the government provider of assistance and the eligible beneficiary. The Medicaid payments are not contributions to Hospital F. [FAS116, ¶181]

Contributions Received

.134 Contributions are received in several different forms. Most often the item contributed is an asset, but it also can be forgiveness of a liability. The types of assets commonly contributed include cash, marketable securities, land, buildings, use of facilities or utilities, materials and supplies, other goods or services, and unconditional promises to give those items in the future. This section requires entities receiving contributions to recognize them at the fair values of the assets received. However, recognition of contributions of works of art, historical treasures, and similar assets is not required if the donated items are added to collections (paragraph .111). Recognition of contributions of services is required for those contributed services received that meet one of the specified conditions of paragraph .109 of this section and is precluded for contributed services that do not. Examples 6 through 16 illustrate application of the recognition and measurement principles in this section. [FAS116, ¶182]

Example 6—Contribution of Real Property

.135 Organization G receives a building (including the land on which it was constructed) as a gift from a local corporation with the understanding that the building will be used principally as an education and training center for organization members or for any other purpose consistent with the organization's mission. Educating and training its members is an important activity of the organization. [FAS116, ¶183]

.136 Organization G would recognize the contributed property as an asset and as support and measure that property at its fair value (paragraph .108). Information necessary to estimate the fair value of that property could be obtained from various sources, including (a) amounts recently paid for similar properties in the locality, (b) estimates of the market value of the property by local appraisers or real estate brokers, (c) an estimate of the fair value of the property by the local tax assessor's office, or (d) estimates of its replacement cost (paragraph .115). [If Organization G is a not-for-profit organization,] this contribution is unrestricted support because the donated assets may be used for any purpose and Organization G does not have a policy of implying time restrictions on gifts of long-lived assets (paragraph .145 of Section No5). If Organization G's policy is to imply a time restriction, the contribution is temporarily restricted support and the restriction expires over the useful life of the building. [FAS116, ¶184]

Example 7—Contribution of a Work of Art

.137 Museum H, which preserves its collections as described in paragraph .111, receives a gift of a valuable painting from a donor. The donor obtained an independent appraisal of the fair value of the painting for tax purposes and furnished a copy to the museum. The museum staff evaluated the painting to determine its authenticity and worthiness for addition to the museum's collection. The staff recommended that the gift be accepted, adding that it was not aware of any evidence contradicting the fair value provided by the donor and the donor's appraiser. [FAS116, ¶185]

.138 If Museum H capitalizes its collections, Museum H would recognize the fair value of the contributed work of art received as revenue and capitalize it as an asset at its fair value (paragraphs .113 and .115). The staff of Museum H is qualified to estimate the fair value of the contributed painting and evidence of its fair value exists. If Museum H does not capitalize its collections, Museum H is precluded from recognizing the contribution (paragraph .113) and would provide the information required by paragraphs .123 and .124. [FAS116, ¶186]

.139 If Museum H [is a not-for-profit organization and] accepted the painting with the donor's understanding that it would be sold rather than added to its collection, Museum H would recognize the contribution of the painting received as unrestricted revenue and as an asset at its fair value (paragraph .108 and paragraph .145 of Section No5). [FAS116, ¶187]

Example 8—Contribution of Historical Objects

.140 Historical Society I receives several old photographs as a gift from a long-time local resident. The photographs depict a particular area as it was 75 years ago. After evaluating whether the photographs were worthy of addition to the historical society's collection, the staff concluded the photographs should be accepted solely because of their potential historical and educational use; that is, the photographs may be of interest to future researchers, historians, or others interested in studying the area. The photographs are not suitable for display and no alternative use exists. [FAS116, ¶188]

.141 Regardless of whether Historical Society I capitalizes its collections, Historical Society I would not recognize the contributed photographs in this example as assets because there is major uncertainty about the existence of value and no alternative use exists (paragraph .115). [FAS116, ¶189]

Example 9—Contribution of Utilities

.142 Organization J operates from a building it owns in City K. The holding company of a local utility has been contributing electricity on a continuous basis subject to the donor's cancellation. [FAS116, ¶190]

.143 The simultaneous receipt and use of electricity or other utilities is a form of contributed assets and not services. Organization J would recognize the fair value of the contributed electricity as both revenue and expense in the period it is received and used (paragraph .108). Organization J could estimate the fair value of the electricity received by using rates normally charged to a consumer of similar usage requirements. [FAS116, ¶191]

Example 10—Contribution of Use of Property

.144 Organization L receives the free use of 10,000 square feet of prime office space provided by a local company. The local company has informed Organization L that it intends to continue providing the space as long as it is available, and although it expects it would be able to give the organization 30 days advance notice, it may discontinue providing the space at any time. The local company normally rents similar space for $14 to $16 annually per square foot, the going market rate for office space in the area. Organization L decides to accept this gift—the free use of office space—to conduct its daily central administrative activities. [FAS116, ¶192]

.145 The simultaneous receipt and use of facilities is a form of contributed assets and not services. Organization L would recognize the fair value of the contributed use of facilities as both revenue and expense in the period it is received and used (paragraph .108). [FAS116, ¶193]

.146 If the local company explicitly and unconditionally promises the use of the facility for a specified period of time (for example, five years), the promise would be an unconditional promise to give. In that case, Organization L would recognize the receipt of the unconditional promise as a receivable and [if Organization L is a not-for-profit organization it would recognize the unconditional promise] as restricted support at its fair value. The donor would recognize the unconditional promise when made as a payable and an expense at its fair value (paragraph .114). [FAS116, ¶194]

Example 11—Contribution of Services

.147 Organization M decides to construct a building on its property. It obtains the necessary architectural plans and specifications and purchases the necessary continuing architectural services, materials, permits, and so forth at a total cost of $400,000. A local construction company contributes the necessary labor and equipment. An independent appraisal of the building (exclusive of land), obtained for insurance purposes, estimates its fair value at $725,000. [FAS116, ¶195]

.148 Organization M would recognize the services contributed by the construction company because the contributed services received meet condition (a)—the services received create or enhance nonfinancial assets—or because the services meet condition (b)—the services require specialized skills, are provided by individuals possessing those skills, and would typically need to be purchased if not provided by donation (paragraph .109). Contributions of services that create or enhance nonfinancial assets may be measured by referring to either the fair value of the services received or the fair value of the asset or of the asset enhancement resulting from the services (paragraph .115). In this example, the fair value of the contributed services received could be determined by subtracting the cost of the purchased services, materials, and permits ($400,000) from the fair value of the asset created ($725,000), which results in contributed services received of $325,000.

Alternatively, the amount the construction company would have charged could be used if more readily available. [FAS116, ¶196]

.149 If some of the labor did not require specialized skills and was provided by volunteers, those services still would be recognized because they meet condition (a). [FAS116, ¶197]

Example 12—Contribution of Services

.150 Faculty salaries are a major expense of University N. The faculty includes both compensated faculty members (approximately 80 percent) and uncompensated faculty members (approximately 20 percent) who are associated with religious orders and contribute their services to the university. The performance of both compensated and uncompensated faculty members is regularly and similarly evaluated; both must meet the university's standards and both provide services in the same way. [FAS116, ¶198]

.151 University N would recognize both revenue and expense for the services contributed by the uncompensated faculty members because the contribution meets condition (b) of paragraph .109. Teaching requires specialized skills; the religious personnel are qualified and trained to provide those skills; and University N typically would hire paid instructors if the religious personnel did not donate their services. University N could refer to the salaries it pays similarly qualified compensated faculty members to determine fair value of the services received. [FAS116, ¶199]

.152 Similarly, if the uncompensated faculty members in this example were given a nominal stipend to help defray certain of their out-of-pocket expenses, University N still would recognize both revenue and expense for the services contributed. The contribution received would be measured at the fair value of the services received less the amount of the nominal stipend paid. [FAS116, ¶200]

Example 13—Contribution of Services

.153 A member of the Board of Trustees of Organization O is a lawyer and from time to time in the capacity of a trustee provides advice on general business matters, including questions about business opportunities and risks and ethical, moral, and legal matters. The advice provided on legal matters is provided as a trustee in the role of a trustee, not as a lawyer, and the opinions generally are limited to routine matters. Generally, the lawyer suggests that Organization O seek the opinion of its attorneys on substantive or complex legal questions. All of the organization's trustees serve without compensation, and most trustees have specialized expertise (for example, a chief executive officer, a minister, a physician, a professor, and a public accountant) that makes their advice valuable to Organization O. The trustee-lawyer also serves without compensation as a trustee for two other organizations. [FAS116, ¶201]

.154 Organization O would be precluded from recognizing the contributed services it receives from its trustee-lawyer or its other trustees because the services contributed do not meet either of the conditions of paragraph .109. Condition (a) is not relevant. The trustee-lawyer's services do not meet condition (b) because the substantive or complex legal questions that require the specialized skills of a lawyer are referred to the organization's attorneys or because the advice provided by trustees typically would not be purchased if not provided by donation. [FAS116, ¶202]

Example 14—Contribution of Services

.155 Hospital P provides short-term inpatient and outpatient care and also provides long-term care for the elderly. As part of the long-term care program, the hospital has organized a program whereby local high school students may contribute a minimum of 10 hours a week, from 3:00 p.m. to 6:00 p.m., to the hospital. These students are assigned various duties, such as visiting and talking with the patients, distributing books and magazines, reading, playing chess, and similar activities. The hospital does not pay for these services or similar services. The services are accepted as a way of enhancing or supplementing the quality of care and comfort provided to the elderly long-term care patients. [FAS116, ¶203]

.156 Hospital P would be precluded from recognizing the contributed services because the services contributed do not meet either of the conditions of paragraph .109. Condition (a) is not relevant. Condition (b) has not been met because the services the students provide do not require specialized skills nor would they typically need to be purchased if not provided by donation. [FAS116, ¶204]

Example 15—Contribution of Services

.157 School Q conducts an annual fund-raising campaign to solicit contributions from its alumni. In prior years, School Q recruited unpaid student volunteers to make phone calls to its alumni. This year, a telemarketing company, whose president is an alumnus of School Q, contributed its services to School Q for the annual alumni fund-raising campaign. The company normally provides telemarketing services to a variety of clients on a fee basis. School Q provided the company with a list of 10,000 alumni, several copies of a typed appeal to be read over the phone, and blank contribution forms to record pledges received. The company contacted most of the 10,000 alumni. [FAS116, ¶205]

.158 School Q would be precluded from recognizing the contributed services of the telemarketing company. Condition (a) of paragraph .109 is not relevant. Condition (b) has not been met because the services do not require specialized skills or because School Q typically would not need to purchase the services if they were not provided by donation. School Q normally conducts its campaign with untrained students in a manner similar to the manner used by the telemarketing firm. [FAS116, ¶206]

Example 16—Contribution of an Interest in an Estate

.159 In 19X0, Individual R notifies Organization S that she has remembered the organization in her will and provides a written copy of the will. In 19X5, Individual R dies. In 19X6, Individual R's last will and testament enters probate and the probate court declares the will valid. The executor informs Organization S that the will has been declared valid and that it will receive 10 percent of Individual R's estate, after satisfying the estate's liabilities and certain specific bequests. The executor provides an estimate of the estate's assets and liabilities and the expected amount and time for payment of Organization S's interest in the estate. [FAS116, ¶207]

.160 The 19X0 communication between Individual R and Organization S specified an intention to give. The ability to modify a will at any time prior to death is well established; thus, in 19X0 Organization S did not receive a promise to give and did not recognize a contribution received. When the probate court declares the will valid, Organization S would recognize a receivable and revenue for an unconditional promise to give at the fair value of its interest in the estate (paragraphs .108 and .115 through .117). If the promise to give contained in the valid will was instead conditioned on a future and uncertain event, Organization S would recognize the contribution when the condition was substantially met. A conditional promise in a valid will would be disclosed in notes to financial statements (paragraph .122). [FAS116, ¶208]

[Note: Additional guidance with respect to implementing Section C67 is presented in FASB Highlights, "Time for a Change—Implementing FASB Statements 116 and 117," in FASB *Status Report,* January 6, 1995. The article addresses 18 questions and was written by FASB staff member Karen F. Berk. This publication is available from the Order Department, Financial Accounting Standards Board, 401 Merritt 7, P.O. Box 5116, Norwalk, CT 06856-5116, telephone (203) 847-0700, extension 555.]

Glossary

.401 Collections. Works of art, historical treasures, or similar assets that are (a) held for public exhibition, education, or research in furtherance of public service rather than financial gain, (b) protected, kept unencumbered, cared for, and preserved, and (c) subject to an organizational policy that requires the proceeds of items that are sold to be used to acquire other items for collections. [FAS116, ¶209]

.402 Conditional promise to give. A promise to give that depends on the occurrence of a specified future and uncertain event to bind the promisor. [FAS116, ¶209]

.403 Contribution. An unconditional transfer of cash or other assets to an entity or a settlement or cancellation of its liabilities in a voluntary nonreciprocal transfer by another entity acting other than as an owner. [FAS116, ¶209]

.404 Donor-imposed condition. A donor stipulation that specifies a future and uncertain event whose occurrence or failure to occur gives the promisor a right of return of the assets it has transferred or releases the promisor from its obligation to transfer its assets. [FAS116, ¶209]

.405 Donor-imposed restriction. A donor stipulation that specifies a use for the contributed asset that is more specific than broad limits resulting from the nature of the organization, the environment in which it operates, and the purposes specified in its articles of incorporation or bylaws or comparable documents for an unincorporated association. A restriction on an organization's use of the asset contributed may be temporary or permanent. [FAS116, ¶209]

.406 Nonreciprocal transfer. A transaction in which an entity incurs a liability or transfers an asset to another entity (or receives an asset or cancellation of a liability) without directly receiving (or giving) value in exchange. [FAS116, ¶209]

.407 Not-for-profit organization. An entity that possesses the following characteristics that distinguish it from a business enterprise: (a) contributions of significant amounts of resources from resource providers who do not expect commensurate or proportionate pecuniary return, (b) operating purposes other than to provide goods or services at a profit, and (c) absence of ownership interests like those of business enterprises. Not-for-profit organizations have those characteristics in varying degrees (FASB Concepts Statement 4, *Objectives of Financial Reporting by Nonbusiness Organizations,* paragraph 6). Organizations that clearly fall outside this definition include all investor-owned enterprises and entities that provide dividends, lower costs, or other economic benefits directly and proportionately to their owners, members, or participants, such as mutual insurance companies, credit unions, farm and rural electric cooperatives, and employee benefit plans (Concepts Statement 4, paragraph 7). [FAS116, ¶209]

.408 **Promise to give.** A written or oral agreement to contribute cash or other assets to another entity. A promise to give may be either conditional or unconditional. [FAS116, ¶209]

.409 **Restricted support.** Donor-restricted revenues or gains from contributions that increase either temporarily restricted net assets or permanently restricted net assets. Also refer to **Unrestricted support.** [FAS116, ¶209]

.410 **Unconditional promise to give.** A promise to give that depends only on passage of time or demand by the promisee for performance. [FAS116, ¶209]

.411 **Unrestricted support.** Revenues or gains from contributions that are not restricted by donors. Also refer to **Restricted support.** [FAS116, ¶209]

(The next page is 11421.)

Sources: APB Opinion 14; AICPA Interpretation of APB Opinion 26;
FASB Statement 84

Summary

The proceeds from issuance of debt securities with detachable warrants shall be allocated between the warrants and the debt securities based on their relative fair values at time of issuance; the portion allocable to the warrants shall be accounted for as additional paid-in capital. No similar allocation shall be made for the issuance of either convertible debt or debt securities with nondetachable warrants.

When a debtor induces conversion of convertible debt by issuing additional securities or paying other consideration to convertible debt holders, there shall be recognition of an expense equal to the fair value of the additional securities or other consideration issued to induce conversion.

Convertible Debt

.101 Convertible debt securities discussed in this section are those debt securities that are convertible into common stock of the issuer or an affiliated enterprise at a specified price at the option of the holder and that are sold at a price or have a value at issuance not significantly in excess of the face amount. The terms of such securities generally include (a) an interest rate that is lower than the issuer could establish for nonconvertible debt, (b) an initial conversion price that is greater than the market value of the common stock at time of issuance, and (c) a conversion price that does not decrease except pursuant to antidilution provisions. In most cases such securities also are callable at the option of the issuer and are subordinated to nonconvertible debt. [APB14, ¶3]

.102 A convertible debt security is an instrument bearing an option, the alternative choices of which are mutually exclusive; they cannot both be consummated. Thus, the security will either be converted into common stock or be redeemed for cash. The holder cannot exercise the option to convert unless he foregoes the right to redemption, and vice versa. [APB14, ¶7] If the market value of the underlying common stock increases sufficiently in the future, the issuer [of a convertible debt security] can [effectively] force conversion of the convertible debt into common stock by calling the issue for redemption. [APB14, ¶4]

.103 No portion of the proceeds from the issuance of convertible debt securities shall be accounted for as attributable to the conversion feature. [APB14, ¶12]

Conversion of Debt

Scope

.103A [Paragraphs .103A through .103D] apply to conversions[1] of convertible debt to equity securities pursuant to terms that reflect changes made by the debtor to the conversion privileges provided in the terms of the debt at issuance (including changes that involve the payment of consideration) for the purpose of inducing conversion. [The paragraphs apply] only to conversions[2] that both (a) occur pursuant to changed conversion privileges that are exercisable only for a limited period of time and (b) include the issuance of all of the equity securities issuable pursuant to conversion privileges included in the terms of the debt at issuance for each debt instrument that is converted.[3] The changed terms may involve reduction of the original conversion price thereby resulting in the issuance of additional shares of stock, issuance of warrants or other securities not provided for in the original conversion terms, or payment of cash or other consideration to those debt holders who convert during the specified time period. [Paragraphs .103A through .103D do] not apply to conversions pursuant to other changes in conversion privileges or to changes in terms of convertible debt instruments that are different from those described in this paragraph. [FAS84, ¶2]

.103B [Paragraphs .103A through .103D] require no recognition of gain or loss with respect to the shares issuable pursuant to the original conversion privileges of the convertible debt when additional securities or assets are transferred to a debt holder to induce

---

[1] A conversion includes an exchange of a convertible debt instrument for equity securities or a combination of equity securities and other consideration, whether or not the exchange involves legal exercise of the contractual conversion privileges included in terms of debt. [FAS84, ¶2, fn2]

[2] Some convertible debt instruments include provisions allowing the debtor to alter terms of the debt to the benefit of debt holders in a manner similar to transactions described in this paragraph. Such provisions may be general in nature, permitting the debtor or trustee to take actions to protect the interests of the debt holders, or they may be specific, for example, specifically authorizing the debtor to temporarily reduce the conversion price for the purpose of inducing conversion. Conversions pursuant to amended or altered conversion privileges on such instruments, even though they are literally "provided in the terms of the debt at issuance," should be included within the scope of [paragraphs .103A through .103D]. [FAS84, ¶29]

[3] A transaction that does not include the issuance of all of the equity securities issuable pursuant to the conversion privileges should not be characterized as a conversion transaction. [FAS84, ¶33]

prompt conversion of the debt to equity securities. [FAS84, ¶22] In a conversion pursuant to original conversion terms, debt is extinguished in exchange for equity pursuant to a preexisting contract that is already recognized in the financial statements, and no gain or loss is recognized upon conversion. [FAS84, ¶23]

Recognition of Expense upon Conversion

.103C When convertible debt is converted to equity securities of the debtor pursuant to an inducement offer described in paragraph .103A, the debtor enterprise shall recognize an expense equal to the fair value of all securities and other consideration transferred in the transaction in excess of the fair value of securities issuable pursuant to the original conversion terms. The expense shall not be reported as an extraordinary item. [FAS84, ¶3]

.103D The fair value of the securities or other consideration shall be measured as of the date the inducement offer is accepted by the convertible debt holder. Normally this will be the date the debt holder converts the convertible debt into equity securities or enters into a binding agreement to do so. [FAS84, ¶4] The transaction should not be recognized until the inducement offer has been accepted by the debt holder. [FAS84, ¶30]

Debt with Stock Purchase Warrants

.104 Unlike convertible debt, debt with detachable warrants to purchase stock is usually issued with the expectation that the debt will be repaid when it matures. Detachable warrants often trade separately from the debt instrument. Thus, the two elements of the security exist independently and may be treated as separate securities. [APB14, ¶13]

.105 The portion of the proceeds of debt securities issued with detachable stock purchase warrants that is allocable to the warrants shall be accounted for as additional paid-in capital. The allocation shall be based on the relative fair values of the two securities at time of issuance.[4] Any resulting discount or premium on the debt securities shall be accounted for as such.[5] The same accounting treatment applies to issues of debt securities (issued with detachable warrants) that may be surrendered in settlement of the exercise price of the warrant. However, if stock purchase warrants are not detachable from the debt and the debt security must be surrendered in order to exercise the warrant, the two

---

[4]The time of issuance generally is the date when agreement as to terms has been reached and announced, even though the agreement is subject to certain further actions, such as directors' or stockholders' approval. [APB14, ¶16, fn2]

[5][Refer to Section I69, "Interest: Imputation of an Interest Cost," paragraph .108, footnote 4, for guidance regarding the amortization of debt discount and premium.]

securities taken together are substantially equivalent to convertible debt and the accounting specified in paragraph .103 shall apply. [APB14, ¶16]

.106 If detachable warrants are issued in conjunction with debt as consideration in purchase transactions, the amounts attributable to each class of security issued shall be determined separately, based on values at the time of issuance.[6] The debt discount or premium is obtained by comparing the value attributed to the debt securities with the face amount thereof. [APB14, ¶17]

Other Types of Debt Securities

.107 It is not practicable in this section to discuss all possible types of debt with conversion features, debt issued with stock purchase warrants, or debt securities with a combination of such features. Securities not explicitly discussed in this section shall be dealt with in accordance with the substance of the transaction. For example, when convertible debt is issued at a substantial premium, there is a presumption that such premium represents additional paid-in capital. [APB14, ¶18]

Examples of Accounting for Conversion of Debt

.108 Paragraphs .109 to .114 present examples that illustrate application of [the requirements of paragraphs .103A through .103D]. The facts assumed are illustrative only and are not intended to modify or limit in any way the provisions of [these paragraphs]. For simplicity, the face amount of each security is assumed to be equal to its carrying amount in the financial statements (that is, no original issue premium or discount exists). [FAS84, ¶7]

Example 1

.109 On January 1, 19X4, Company A issues a $1,000 face amount 10 percent convertible bond maturing December 31, 20X3. The carrying amount of the bond in the financial statements of Company A is $1,000, and it is convertible into common shares of Company A at a conversion price of $25 per share. On January 1, 19X6, the convertible bond has a market value of $1,700. To induce convertible bondholders to convert their bonds promptly, Company A reduces the conversion price to $20 for bondholders who convert prior to February 29, 19X6 (within 60 days). [FAS84, ¶8]

---

[6][See footnote 4.]

.110 Assuming the market price of Company A's common stock on the date of conversion is $40 per share, the fair value of the incremental consideration paid by Company A upon conversion is calculated as follows for each $1,000 bond that is converted prior to February 29, 19X6:

Value of securities issued[a]	$2,000
Value of securities issuable pursuant to original conversion privileges[b]	$1,600
Fair value of incremental consideration	$ 400

---

[a]Value of securities issued to debt holders is computed as follows:

Face amount	$1,000	
÷ New conversion price	÷ $ 20	per share
Number of common shares issued upon conversion	50	shares
× Price per common share	× $ 40	per share
Value of securities issued	$2,000	

[b]Value of securities issuable pursuant to original conversion privileges is computed as follows:

Face amount	$1,000	
÷ Original conversion price	÷ $ 25	per share
Number of common shares issuable pursuant to original conversion privileges	40	shares
× Price per common share	× $ 40	per share
Value of securities issuable pursuant to original conversion privileges	$1,600	

[FAS84, ¶9]

.111 Therefore, Company A records debt conversion expense equal to the fair value of the incremental consideration paid as follows:

	Debit	Credit
Convertible debt	1,000	
Debt conversion expense	400	
Common stock		1,400

[FAS84, ¶10]

Example 2

.112 On January 1, 19X1, Company B issues a $1,000 face amount 4 percent convertible bond maturing December 31, 20X0. The carrying amount of the bond in the financial statements of Company B is $1,000, and it is convertible into common shares of Company B at a conversion price of $25. On June 1, 19X4, the convertible bond has a market value of $500. To induce convertible bondholders to convert their bonds promptly, Company B reduces the conversion price to $20 for bondholders who convert prior to July 1, 19X4 (within 30 days). [FAS84, ¶11]

.113 Assuming the market price of Company B's common stock on the date of conversion is $12 per share, the fair value of the incremental consideration paid by Company B upon conversion is calculated as follows for each $1,000 bond that is converted prior to July 1, 19X4:

Value of securities issued[a]	$600
Value of securities issuable pursuant to original conversion privileges[b]	$480
Fair value of incremental consideration	$120

---

[a]Value of securities issued to debt holders is computed as follows:

Face amount	$1,000	
÷ New conversion price	÷ $ 20	per share
Number of common shares issued upon conversion	50	shares
× Price per common share	× $ 12	per share
Value of securities issued	$ 600	

[b]Value of securities issuable pursuant to original conversion privileges is computed as follows:

Face amount	$1,000	
÷ Original conversion price	÷ $ 25	per share
Number of common shares issuable pursuant to original conversion privileges	40	shares
× Price per common share	× $ 12	per share
Value of securities issuable pursuant to original conversion privileges	$ 480	

[FAS84, ¶12]

.114 Therefore, Company B records debt conversion expense equal to the fair value of the incremental consideration paid as follows:

	Debit	Credit
Convertible debt	1,000	
Debt conversion expense	120	
Common stock		1,120

The same accounting would apply if, instead of reducing the conversion price, Company B issued shares pursuant to a tender offer of 50 shares of its common stock for each $1,000 bond surrendered to the company before July 1, 19X4. Refer to paragraph .103A of this section. [FAS84, ¶13]

Supplemental Guidance

Accounting for the Conversion of Debt Pursuant to Original Conversion Terms

.501 In practice, the carrying amount of the debt, including any unamortized premium or discount, is credited to the capital accounts upon conversion to reflect the stock issued and no gain or loss is recognized. [AIN-APB26, #1]

(The next page is 11589.)

DEBT: EXTINGUISHMENTS

Sources: APB Opinion 26; AICPA Interpretation of APB Opinion 26;
FASB Statement 4; FASB Statement 64; FASB Statement 76;
FASB Statement 84; FASB Statement 111;
FASB Technical Bulletin 80-1; FASB Technical Bulletin 84-4

Summary

This section applies to all extinguishments of debt, whether early or not, other than debt conversions and troubled debt restructurings.

Debt is considered extinguished for financial reporting purposes when the debtor pays the creditor and is relieved of all its obligations with respect to that debt, or the debtor is legally released from being the primary obligor under the debt either judicially or by the creditor and it is probable that the debtor will not be required to make future payments with respect to that debt under any guarantees, or the debtor irrevocably places cash or other assets in a trust to be used solely for satisfying scheduled payments of both interest and principal of a specific obligation and the possibility that the debtor will be required to make future payments with respect to that debt is remote.

The difference between the amount paid to extinguish the debt and the net carrying amount of the debt shall be recognized currently in income and, if material, generally shall be classified as an extraordinary item whether the extinguishment is early or at scheduled maturity date or later.

Scope

.101 This section applies to all extinguishments of debt, whether early or not, except debt that is extinguished through a troubled debt restructuring [refer to Section D22, "Debt: Restructurings"]; debt that is converted to equity securities of the debtor pursuant to conversion privileges provided in terms of the debt at issuance; [FAS76, ¶7] [and] conversions of convertible debt when conversion privileges included in terms at issuance are changed, or additional consideration is paid, to induce conversion of the debt to equity securities [as described in Section D10, "Debt: Convertible Debt, Conversion of Convertible Debt, and Debt with Stock Purchase Warrants."] [FAS84, ¶5] This section does not address the accounting for redeemable preferred stock. [Refer to Section C16, "Capital Stock: Preferred Stock."] [FAS76, ¶1]

.102 All extinguishments of debt are fundamentally alike. The accounting for such transactions shall be the same regardless of the means used to achieve the extinguishment. [APB26, ¶19]

Circumstances for an Extinguishment of Debt

.102A A debtor shall consider debt to be extinguished for financial reporting purposes in the following circumstances:

a. The debtor pays the creditor and is relieved of all its obligations with respect to the debt. This includes the debtor's reacquisition of its outstanding debt securities in the public securities markets, regardless of whether the securities are cancelled or held as so-called treasury bonds.

b. The debtor is legally[1] released[2] from being the primary obligor under the debt either judicially or by the creditor and it is probable[3] that the debtor will not be required to make future payments with respect to that debt under any guarantees.[4]

c. The debtor irrevocably places cash or other assets in a trust to be used solely for satisfying scheduled payments of both interest and principal of a specific obligation and the possibility that the debtor will be required to make future payments with respect to that debt is remote.[5] In this circumstance, debt is extinguished even though the debtor is not legally released from being the primary obligor under the debt obligation.[6] [FAS76, ¶3]

---

[1]*Defeasance* connotes the debtor's release from legal liability. [FAS76, ¶14, fn6]

[2]If nonrecourse debt (such as certain mortgages) is assumed by a third party in conjunction with the sale of an asset that serves as the sole collateral for that debt, the sale and related assumption effectively accomplish a legal release of the seller/debtor for purposes of applying this section. [FAS76, ¶3, fn1]

[3]*Probable* is used here, consistent with its use in Section C59, "Contingencies," to mean that it is likely that no payments will be required. [FAS76, ¶3, fn2]

[4]The circumstances for an extinguishment of debt described in paragraph .102A(b) do not apply to debt that [remains] convertible into the debtor's equity securities. [FAS76, ¶1]

[5]The term *remote* [establishes a] high threshold for **in-substance defeasance** transactions. [FAS76, ¶25] [The requirement] that the possibility be remote that the debtor will be required to make future payments with respect to the debt [necessitates] an assessment of the circumstances at the date of the in-substance defeasance transaction regarding the likelihood of the debtor's being required to make such future payments. A requirement for such future payments by the debtor could arise due to an inadequacy of trust assets attributable not only to a failure to realize scheduled cash flows from trust assets but also to an acceleration of the debt's maturity due to a violation of a covenant of the debt issue being extinguished or, if cross-default provisions exist, of a covenant of another debt issue. [FAS76, ¶26]

[6]The circumstances for an extinguishment of debt [in an in-substance defeasance] described in paragraph .102A(c) do not apply to debt that is convertible into the debtor's equity securities. Furthermore, the circumstances described in paragraph .102A(c) apply only to debt with specified maturities and fixed payment schedules; consequently, those circumstances do not apply to debt with variable terms that do not permit advance determination of debt service requirements, such as debt with a floating interest rate. [FAS76, ¶1] [Paragraphs .507 through .510 describe a special circumstance that is not eligible for an extinguishment through an in-substance defeasance as described in paragraph .102A(c). Paragraphs .515 through .518 discuss the in-substance defeasance of callable debt.] However, the provisions for in-substance defeasance generally apply to capitalized lease obligations if the lease obligation has a specified maturity and a fixed payment schedule. [FAS76, ¶37]

Restrictions on the Nature of Assets in Trust

.102B The following requirements regarding the nature of the assets held by the trust shall be met to effect an extinguishment of debt under paragraph .102A(c):

a. The trust shall be restricted to owning only monetary assets[7] that are *essentially risk free* as to the amount, timing, and collection of interest and principal. The monetary assets shall be denominated in the currency in which the debt is payable.[8] For debt denominated in U.S. dollars, essentially risk-free monetary assets shall be limited to:
   (1) Direct obligations of the U.S. government
   (2) Obligations guaranteed by the U.S. government
   (3) Securities that are backed by U.S. government obligations as collateral under an arrangement by which the interest and principal payments on the collateral generally flow immediately through to the holder of the security [FAS76, ¶4], for example, as in a closed trust. [FAS76, ¶31]
   However, some securities described in the previous sentence can be paid prior to scheduled maturity and so are not essentially risk free as to the *timing* of the collection of interest and principal; thus, they do not qualify for ownership by the trust.
b. The monetary assets held by the trust shall provide cash flows (from interest and maturity of those assets) that approximately coincide, as to timing and amount, with the scheduled interest and principal payments on the debt that is being extinguished.[9] [FAS76, ¶4]

Costs Related to Placing Assets in Trust

.102C If, in conjunction with placing assets in trust to effect an extinguishment of debt, it is expected that trust assets will be used to pay related costs, such as trustee fees, as well as to satisfy scheduled interest and principal payments of a specific debt, those costs shall be considered in determining the amount of funds required by the trust. On the other hand, if the debtor incurs an obligation to pay any related costs, the debtor shall accrue a liability for those probable future payments in the period that the debt is recognized as extinguished. [FAS76, ¶5]

---

[7]A monetary asset is money or a claim to receive a sum of money that is fixed or determinable without reference to future prices of specific goods or services. [FAS76, ¶4, fn3]

[8]Neither U.S. government obligations nor forward contracts would be essentially risk-free monetary assets to defease debt denominated in foreign currencies. The level of assurance with respect to the collection of interest and principal, and the timing of such collections, from monetary assets denominated in foreign currencies should be equivalent to that required for the in-substance defeasance of debt denominated in U.S. dollars. [FAS76, ¶32] [Paragraphs .511 through .514 discuss when an assessment of remoteness can be used in applying this paragraph for determining whether assets are essentially risk free.]

[9]This requirement] will serve to minimize significant reinvestment earnings. [FAS76, ¶35]

Partial [In-Substance] Defeasances

.102D In a partial in-substance defeasance, the debt considered extinguished will be either (a) a pro rata portion of all remaining interest and principal repayment obligations of the debt issue or (b) the principal and interest payments for a specific debt instrument (such as a serial bond with a specific scheduled maturity). Thus, the debtor cannot recognize a partial defeasance of the obligation for only the interest payments or for only the principal repayment. [FAS76, ¶36]

Accounting for Extinguishment of Debt

.103 The difference between the **reacquisition price** and the **net carrying amount** of the extinguished debt shall be recognized currently in income of the period of extinguishment as [a] loss or gain and identified as a separate item [refer to paragraph .105 below].[10] Gains and losses shall not be amortized to future periods. [APB26, ¶20]

.104 The extinguishment of convertible debt does not change the character of the security as between debt and equity at that time. Therefore, a difference between the cash acquisition price of the debt and its net carrying amount shall be recognized currently in income in the period of extinguishment as a loss or gain. [APB26, ¶21]

Income Statement Classification of Debt Extinguishments

.105 Gains and losses from extinguishment[s] of debt that are included in the determination of net income shall be aggregated and, if material,[11] classified as an extraordinary item, net of related income tax effect. That conclusion shall apply whether an extinguishment is early or at scheduled maturity date or later. [FAS4, ¶8] The conclusion does not apply, however, to gains or losses from extinguishments of debt made to satisfy sinking-fund requirements that an enterprise must meet within one year of the date of the extinguishment.[12] [FAS64, ¶4] Those gains and losses shall be aggregated and the amount shall be identified as a separate item. [FAS4, ¶8]

---

[10]If upon extinguishment of debt, the parties also exchange unstated (or stated) rights or privileges, the portion of the consideration exchanged allocable to such unstated (or stated) rights or privileges should be given appropriate accounting recognition. Moreover, extinguishment transactions between related enterprises may be in essence capital transactions. [APB26, ¶20, fn1]

[11]Refer to the first sentence of Section 117, "Income Statement Presentation: Extraordinary Items," paragraph .118. [FAS4, ¶8, fn1]

[12]Some obligations to acquire debt have the essential characteristics of sinking-fund requirements, and resulting gains or losses are not required to be classified as extraordinary items if the obligations must be met within one year of the date of the extinguishment. [FAS64, ¶4, fn2] For example, if an enterprise is required each year to purchase a certain percentage of its outstanding bonds before their scheduled maturity, the gain or loss from such purchase is not required to be classified as an extraordinary item. Debt maturing serially, however, does not have the characteristics of sinking-fund requirements, and gain or loss from extinguishment of serial debt shall be classified as an extraordinary item. [FAS4, ¶8, fn2]

.106 Classification of gains or losses from extinguishment[s] of debt as extraordinary item[s] pursuant to the first two sentences of paragraph .105 shall be made without regard to the criteria in Section I17, "Income Statement Presentation: Extraordinary Items," paragraph .107. [FAS4, ¶10]

Reacquired Debt Previously Extinguished in an In-Substance Defeasance

.106A If a debtor purchases its own debt securities that have previously been recognized as extinguished in an in-substance defeasance, the debtor is making an investment in the future cash flows from the trust and should report its investment as an asset in its balance sheet. The debtor [is] not considered to be reextinguishing its debt. Thus, no gain or loss [is] recognized from such purchase of those debt securities. [FAS76, ¶33]

Disclosure

.107 Gains or losses from extinguishment[s] of debt that are classified as extraordinary items should be described sufficiently to enable users of financial statements to evaluate their significance. Accordingly, the following information, to the extent not shown separately on the face of the income statement, shall be disclosed in a single note to the financial statements or adequately cross-referenced if in more than one note:

a. A description of the extinguishment transactions, including the sources of any funds used to extinguish debt if it is practicable to identify the sources
b. The income tax effect in the period of extinguishment
c. The per share amount of the aggregate gain or loss net of related income tax effect. [FAS4, ¶9]

.108 If debt is considered to be extinguished [in an in-substance defeasance] under the provisions of paragraph .102A(c), a general description of the transaction and the amount of debt that is considered extinguished at the end of the period shall be disclosed so long as that debt remains outstanding. [FAS76, ¶6]

Glossary

.401 [Deleted 12/83 because of FASB Statement 76, *Extinguishment of Debt*.]

.401A **Instantaneous in-substance defeasance.** Certain structured transactions [in which it is suggested that] assets be irrevocably placed in trust to effect an in-substance defeasance of newly issued debt. [The transaction is typically suggested when,] due to differences in interest rates in different markets, the opportunity exists for an enterprise to borrow at one interest rate and concurrently invest in "essentially risk-free" assets that yield a higher interest rate. [In that situation, an in-substance defeasance, if permitted, would involve] immediately recognizing a gain related to the concurrent differences in interest rates. [FTB84-4, ¶2]

.401B **In-substance defeasance.** In-substance defeasance [transactions] involve placing assets in trust and irrevocably restricting their use solely to satisfy specific debt. [FAS76, ¶14] Because settlement in cash is not always feasible and the effect of an in-substance defeasance is essentially the same [as extinguishment of debt], in certain circumstances, debt [is] considered extinguished for financial reporting purposes even though the debtor is not legally released from being the primary obligor under the debt obligation. [FAS76, ¶22]

.402 **Net carrying amount [of debt].** The amount due at maturity, adjusted for unamortized premium, discount, and cost of issuance. [APB26, ¶3]

.403 **Reacquisition price [of debt].** The amount paid on extinguishment, including a call premium and miscellaneous costs of reacquisition. If extinguishment is achieved by a direct exchange of new securities, the reacquisition price is the total present value of the new securities. [APB26, ¶3]

Supplemental Guidance

Extinguishment of Debt through Exchange for Common or Preferred Stock

.501 *Question*—Does this section apply to extinguishments of debt effected by issuance of common or preferred stock, including redeemable and fixed-maturity preferred stock? [FTB80-1, ¶1]

.502 *Background*—The conversion of debt to common or preferred stock is not an extinguishment if the conversion represents the exercise of a conversion right contained in the terms of the debt issue. Other exchanges of common or preferred stock for debt would constitute extinguishment. [FTB80-l, ¶2]

.503 *Response*—All extinguishments of debt must be accounted for in accordance with either [FTB80-1, ¶3] Section D10, [FAS111, ¶8(bb)] Section D22, or this section. [Section D10 applies to conversion of convertible debt,] Section D22 applies to extinguishments effected in a troubled debt restructuring, [and] this section applies to all other extinguishments of debt. [FTB80-l, ¶3]

.504 This section applies to all extinguishments of debt effected by issuance of common or preferred stock, including redeemable and fixed maturity preferred stock, unless the extinguishment is a troubled debt restructuring or [FTB80-1, ¶4] a conversion of debt to equity securities of the debtor (a) pursuant to conversion privileges provided in the terms of the debt at issuance or (b) when conversion privileges provided in the terms of the debt at issuance are changed (including changes that involve payment of consideration) to induce conversion of the debt to security equities in accordance with paragraph .103A of Section D10. [FAS111, ¶8(bb)] The reacquisition price of the extinguished debt is to be determined by the value of the common or preferred stock issued or the value of the debt—whichever is more clearly evident. [FTB80-1, ¶4]

Debt Tendered to Exercise Warrants

.505 *Question*—This section stipulates that gain or loss should be recognized currently in income when any form of debt security is reacquired by the issuer except through conversion by the holder. Does this section apply to debt tendered to exercise warrants that were originally issued with that debt but which were detachable? [AIN-APB26, #1]

.506 *Response*—This section does not apply to debt tendered to exercise detachable warrants that were originally issued with that debt if the debt is permitted to be tendered towards the exercise price of the warrants under the terms of the securities at issuance. The tendering of the debt in such a case would be a conversion [pursuant to conversion privileges provided in the terms of the debt at issuance]. [AIN-APB26, #1]

Instantaneous In-Substance Defeasance

.507 *Question*—May debt be extinguished through an in-substance defeasance (under paragraph .102A(c) of this section) if the debtor irrevocably places in trust assets that were acquired at about the time that the debt was incurred? [FTB84-4, ¶1]

.508 *Response*—No. Debt may not be extinguished through an in-substance defeasance if the assets that the debtor irrevocably places in trust were acquired at about the time that the debt was incurred or were acquired as part of a series of investment activities (for example, purchasing assets or entering into a purchase agreement or futures contract) initiated at about the time that the debt was incurred. Similarly, debt may not be extinguished through an in-substance defeasance if the debt was incurred pursuant to a forward contract entered into at about the time the debtor acquired the assets being irrevocably placed in trust. [FTB84-4, ¶3]

.509 Although the conceptual basis for recognizing an in-substance defeasance as an extinguishment of debt does not impose special conditions, such as restrictions on how the borrowed funds are used or on when the debtor acquires the assets being placed in the trust, certain structured transactions warrant special consideration in determining whether debt is extinguished under this section. [FTB84-4, ¶4]

.510 Enterprises that borrow funds and concurrently purchase higher-yielding securities to be used in an in-substance defeasance, thereby recognizing a gain on the extinguishment, are essentially engaging in borrow-and-invest activities. The proximity of the borrowing and the acquisition of securities suggest a structured transaction in which the enterprise borrowed with the intent of executing an in-substance defeasance. [Statement 76 states that] "in general, recognizing the effect of in-substance defeasance transactions as extinguishing debt is reasonable because settlement in cash is not always feasible and the *effect of an in-substance defeasance is essentially the same.*" (Emphasis added.) [However,] the effect of considering [those] structured borrow-and-invest transactions as extinguishments is substantively different from the effect of considering in-substance defeasances of previously outstanding debt as extinguishments. Such borrow-and-invest activities, in effect, hedge the debtor against the risk of changes in interest rates. Any gain or loss on extinguishing previously outstanding debt reflects in large measure the effect of past changes in interest rates for the debtor, whereas the gain or loss related to borrow-and-invest activities reflects principally the concurrent differences in interest rates when the debt was issued. [FTB84-4, ¶5]

Assessing Remoteness of Risk of Trust Assets

.511 *Question*—In determining whether an in-substance defeasance transaction meets the requirement in paragraph .102B(a) of this section that the cash inflows to the trust from its assets be essentially risk free, may a debtor use an assessment of the remoteness of the related risks? [FTB84-4, ¶6]

.512 *Background*—For an in-substance defeasance, paragraph .102A(c) of this section requires that "the debtor irrevocably places cash or other assets in a trust to be used solely for satisfying scheduled payments of both interest and principal of a specific obligation and [that] the possibility that the debtor will be required to make future payments with respect to that debt is remote." Paragraph .102B addresses the nature of the assets that the debtor irrevocably places in trust and requires, among other things, that those assets be monetary assets "that are *essentially risk free* as to the amount, timing, and collection of interest and principal." [FTB 84-4, ¶7]

.513 *Response*—No, in some circumstances; yes, in others. In requiring that the cash inflows to the trust in an in-substance defeasance be essentially risk free, this section establishes specific criteria with respect to certain aspects of the transaction but requires the use of judgment in assessing remoteness in other areas. The specified criteria focus principally on the nature of the monetary assets placed in trust rather than on possible external events. For example, the following [are required]:

a. The monetary assets placed in the trust must be denominated in the currency in which the debt is payable. (Refer to paragraph .102B(a) and footnote 8.)
b. The monetary assets placed in the trust must be direct obligations of the sovereign government in whose currency the debt is payable or must be obligations collateralized by such government securities or guaranteed by that government. (Refer to paragraph .102B(a) and footnote 8.)
c. Monetary assets that are callable (that is, can be prepaid) are not essentially risk free as to the timing of the interest and principal payments to be received by the trust and thus do not qualify for ownership by the trust. (Refer to paragraph .102B(a).)

This section does not permit variations from those requirements on the basis that any related risks are remote. Thus, a debtor may not justify use of assets denominated in differing currencies in combination with a forward exchange contract on the basis that the likelihood of default on the forward contract is remote. Similarly, a debtor may not use securities issued by a sovereign government but denominated in a currency other than its own (for example, French government securities denominated in Swiss francs used to defease Swiss franc debt) on the basis that the likelihood of the French government's being unable to obtain sufficient Swiss francs to make timely payments is remote. Likewise, securities that are callable may not be used in the trust on the basis that the likelihood is remote that the call provision will introduce any risk that the trust could have insufficient funds. [FTB84-4, ¶8]

.514 However, for areas not specifically covered, this section requires the debtor to assess the remoteness of various contingencies in determining whether the cash inflows to the trust from its assets are essentially risk free. For example, since any default by a sovereign government on its obligations held by the trust would cause the trust assets to be insufficient to pay the defeased debt (thereby requiring the debtor to make up the deficiency), this section implicitly requires the debtor to conclude that the likelihood of a default by the sovereign government on its direct obligations is remote. Similarly, the likely resolution of other uncertainties that could affect the cash flows to the trust, such as the imposition of currency controls or withholding taxes through future legislation, needs to be assessed to determine whether it is remote that the debtor will be required to make further payments with respect to the debt. [FTB84-4, ¶9]

In-Substance Defeasance of Callable Debt

.515 *Question*—May a debt be extinguished through an in-substance defeasance if it is callable by the debtor? [FTB84-4, ¶10]

.516 *Response*—Yes. Debt that is callable by the debtor can be extinguished through an in-substance defeasance. The debtor's retention of an option to purchase the debt through a call provision is not, in itself, an impediment to an in-substance defeasance; the mere existence of the option creates no risk that the debtor will be required to make further payments with respect to the debt because exercise of the option is at the debtor's discretion. Furthermore, the existence of the call option does not mitigate the debtor's previous surrender of control over the assets that were irrevocably placed in trust. [FTB84-4, ¶12]

.517 If exercise of the call option by the debtor prior to the debt's scheduled maturity is not remote, the debtor ordinarily would not be able to extinguish the debt through an in-substance defeasance because the possibility of future payments with respect to the debt would also not be remote, as required by paragraph .102A(c) of this section. However, if the debtor plans to exercise the call option at a specific date and takes the necessary action currently to effect the call irrevocably for that future date (thereby giving the debt a new, earlier maturity date), extinguishment through an in-substance defeasance is possible provided the assets in the trust are structured to meet the cash flow requirements of the revised payment schedule and new maturity date. [FTB84-4, ¶13]

.518 Paragraph .106A of this section states that "if a debtor purchases its own debt securities that have previously been recognized as extinguished in an in-substance defeasance, the debtor is making an investment in the future cash flows from the trust and should report its investment as an asset in its balance sheet." Whether such debt securities are purchased in the open market or acquired through exercise of a call option, it is appropriate to account for them as an investment in the future cash flows to be distributed by the trust as originally scheduled. However, because the assets in the trust must "be used *solely* for satisfying *scheduled* payments of both interest and principal" (paragraph .102A(c); emphasis added), the debtor could not use funds from the trust to purchase its debt securities; rather, the debtor would need to use other funds to acquire the debt securities as an investment. Exercise of the call option would not negate compliance with the requirement in this section that the assets be irrevocably placed in trust because the call option should not enable the debtor to invade the trust and reacquire those assets prematurely. [FTB84-4, ¶14]

(The next page is 11657.)

DEBT: PRODUCT FINANCING ARRANGEMENTS   SECTION D18

Source: FASB Statement 49

Summary

A product financing arrangement is a transaction in which an enterprise sells and agrees to repurchase inventory with the repurchase price equal to the original sale price plus carrying and financing costs, or other similar transactions. This section specifies criteria for determining when an arrangement involving the sale of inventory is in substance a financing arrangement. A product financing arrangement shall be accounted for as a borrowing rather than as a sale.

Applicability and Scope

.101 **Product financing arrangements** include agreements in which a sponsor (the enterprise seeking to finance product pending its future use or resale) either:

a. Sells the product to another enterprise (the enterprise through which the financing flows), and in a related transaction agrees to repurchase the product (or a substantially identical product)

b. Arranges for another enterprise to purchase the product on the sponsor's behalf and, in a related transaction, agrees to purchase the product from the other enterprise

c. Controls the disposition of the product that has been purchased by another enterprise in accordance with the arrangements described in either (a) or (b) above.

In all of the foregoing cases, the sponsor agrees to purchase the product, or processed goods of which the product is a component, from the other enterprise at specified prices over specified periods or, to the extent that it does not do so, guarantees resale prices to third parties (refer to paragraph .103(a)(1)). Paragraphs .108 through .114 illustrate each of the types of arrangements described in (a) and (b) above. [FAS49, ¶3]

.102 Other characteristics that commonly exist in product financing arrangements but that are not necessarily present in all such arrangements are:

a. The enterprise that purchases the product from the sponsor or purchases it directly from a third party on behalf of the sponsor was established expressly for that purpose or is an existing trust, nonbusiness organization, or credit grantor.

b. The product covered by the financing arrangement is to be used or sold by the sponsor, although a portion may be sold by the other enterprise directly to third parties.
c. The product covered by the financing arrangement is stored on the sponsor's premises.
d. The debt of the enterprise that purchases the product being financed is guaranteed by the sponsor. [FAS49, ¶4]

.103 This section applies to product financing arrangements for products[1] that have been produced by or were originally purchased by the sponsor or purchased by another enterprise on behalf of the sponsor and have both of the following characteristics:

a. The financing arrangement requires the sponsor to purchase the product, a substantially identical product, or processed goods of which the product is a component at specified prices. The specified prices are not subject to change except for fluctuations due to finance and holding costs. This characteristic of predetermined prices also is present if any of the following circumstances exists:
  (1) The specified prices in the financing arrangement are in the form of resale price guarantees under which the sponsor agrees to make up any difference between the specified price and the resale price for products sold to third parties.
  (2) The sponsor is not required to purchase the product but has an option to purchase the product, the economic effect of which compels the sponsor to purchase the product; for example, an option arrangement that provides for a significant penalty if the sponsor does not exercise the option to purchase.
  (3) The sponsor is not required by the agreement to purchase the product but the other enterprise has an option whereby it can require the sponsor to purchase the product.
b. The payments that the other enterprise will receive on the transaction are established by the financing arrangement, and the amounts to be paid by the sponsor will be adjusted, as necessary, to cover substantially all fluctuations in costs incurred by the other enterprise in purchasing and holding the product (including interest).[2] [FAS49, ¶5]

---

[1]Unmined or unharvested natural resources and financial instruments are not considered to be a product for purposes of this section. [FAS49, ¶5, fn2]

[2]The characteristic described in paragraph .103(b) ordinarily is not present in [FAS49, ¶5, fn3] (a) ordinary purchase commitments in which the risks and rewards of ownership are retained by the seller (for example, a manufacturer or other supplier) until the product is transferred to a purchaser or (b) typical contractor-subcontractor relationships in which the contractor is not in substance the owner of product held by the subcontractor and the obligation of the contractor is contingent on substantial performance on the part of the subcontractor. [FAS49, ¶18]

.104 This section does not modify any of the provisions of Section R75, "Revenue Recognition," paragraphs .105 through .109, and does not apply to transactions for which sales revenue is recognized currently in accordance with those provisions of that section. [FAS49, ¶6]

.105 The accounting for product financing arrangements specified by this section differs from the accounting for long-term unconditional purchase obligations (for example, take-or-pay contracts) specified by Section C32, "Commitments: Long-Term Obligations." [FAS49, ¶20] This section concludes that, [in a product financing arrangement that has the characteristics described in paragraph .103,] the sponsor is in substance the owner of the product and that the sponsor should, therefore, report the product as an asset and the related obligation as a liability. At the time a take-or-pay contract is entered into, by contrast, either the product does not yet exist (for example, electricity) or the product exists in a form unsuitable to the purchaser (for example, unmined coal); the purchaser has a right to receive future product but is not the substantive owner of existing product. [FAS49, ¶22]

Accounting for Product Financing Arrangements

.106 Product and obligations under product financing arrangements that have both of the characteristics described in paragraph .103 shall be accounted for by the sponsor as follows:

a If a sponsor sells a product to another enterprise and, in a related transaction, agrees to repurchase the product (or a substantially identical product) or processed goods of which the product is a component, the sponsor shall record a liability at the time the proceeds are received from the other enterprise to the extent that the product is covered by the financing arrangement. The sponsor shall not record the transaction as a sale and shall not remove the covered product from its balance sheet.

b. If the sponsor is a party to an arrangement whereby another enterprise purchases a product on the sponsor's behalf and, in a related transaction, the sponsor agrees to purchase the product or processed goods of which the product is a component from the enterprise, the sponsor shall record the asset and the related liability when the product is purchased by the other enterprise. [FAS49, ¶8]

.107 Costs of the product, excluding processing costs, in excess of the sponsor's original production or purchase costs or the other enterprise's purchase costs represent financing and holding costs. The sponsor shall account for such costs in accordance with the sponsor's accounting policies applicable to financing and holding costs as those costs are incurred by the other enterprise. For example, if insurance costs ordinarily are accounted for as period costs by the sponsor, similar costs associated with the product covered by financing arrangements shall be expensed by the sponsor as those costs are incurred by the other enterprise. Interest costs associated with the product covered by financing arrangements shall be identified separately and accounted for by the sponsor in accordance with Section I67, "Interest: Capitalization of Interest Costs," as those costs are incurred by the other enterprise. [FAS49, ¶9]

Illustrations of the Application of This Section to Common Product Financing Arrangements

.108 Paragraphs .109 through .114 illustrate how this section applies to two common product financing arrangements. The facts assumed in the examples are illustrative only and are not intended to modify or limit in any way the provisions of this section. The facts assumed in each case could vary in one or more respects without altering the application of the provisions of this section. [FAS49, ¶25]

Example 1

.109 An enterprise (sponsor) sells a portion of its inventory to another enterprise (the enterprise through which the financing flows), and in a related transaction agrees to repurchase the inventory (refer to paragraph .101(a)). [FAS49, ¶26]

Assumptions and Provisions of the Financing Arrangement

.110 The sponsor arranges for the other enterprise to acquire a portion of the sponsor's inventory. The other enterprise's sole asset is the transferred inventory that is, in turn, used as collateral for bank financing. The proceeds of the bank financing are then remitted to the sponsor. The debt of the other enterprise is guaranteed by the sponsor. The inventory is stored in a public warehouse during the holding period. The sponsor, in connection with the "sale" (legal title passes to the enterprise), enters into a financing arrangement under which:

a. The sponsor agrees to pay all costs of the other enterprise associated with the inventory, including holding and storage costs.
b. The sponsor agrees to pay the other enterprise interest on the purchase price of the inventory equivalent to the interest and fees incurred in connection with the bank financing.
c. The sponsor agrees to repurchase the inventory from the other enterprise at a specified future date for the same price originally paid by the enterprise to purchase the inventory irrespective of changes in market prices during the holding period.
d. The other enterprise agrees not to assign or otherwise encumber the inventory during its ownership period, except to the extent of providing collateral for the bank financing. [FAS49, ¶27]

Application of the Provisions of This Section

.111 In the product financing arrangement outlined above, both of the characteristics in paragraph .103 are present; accordingly, the sponsor neither records the transaction as a sale of inventory nor removes the inventory from its balance sheet. The sponsor recognizes a liability when the proceeds are received from the other enterprise. Financing and holding costs are accrued by the sponsor as incurred by the other enterprise and accounted for in accordance with the sponsor's accounting policies for such costs. Interest costs are separately identified and accounted for in accordance with Section I67. [FAS49, ¶28]

Example 2

.112 A sponsor arranges for another enterprise to buy product on the sponsor's behalf with a related agreement to purchase the product from the other enterprise (refer to paragraph .101(b)). [FAS49, ¶29]

Assumptions and Provisions of the Financing Arrangement

.113 The sponsor arranges for the other enterprise to purchase on its behalf an existing supply of fuel. In a related agreement, the sponsor agrees to purchase the fuel from the other enterprise over a specified period and at specified prices. The prices established are adequate to cover all financing and holding costs of the other enterprise. The other enterprise finances the purchase of fuel using the fuel and the agreement as collateral. [FAS49, ¶30]

Application of the Provisions of This Section

.114 In the product financing arrangement described above, both of the characteristics in paragraph .103 are present; accordingly, the sponsor reports the asset (fuel) and the related liability on its balance sheet when the fuel is acquired by the other enterprise. Financing and holding costs are accrued by the sponsor as incurred by the other enterprise and accounted for in accordance with the sponsor's accounting policies for financing and holding costs. Interest costs are separately identified and accounted for in accordance with Section I67. [FAS49, ¶31]

Glossary

.401 **Product financing arrangements.** Includes agreements in which a sponsor (the enterprise seeking to finance product pending its future use or resale):

a. Sells the product to another enterprise (the enterprise through which the financing flows), and in a related transaction agrees to repurchase the product (or a substantially identical product)
b. Arranges for another enterprise to purchase the product on the sponsor's behalf and, in a related transaction, agrees to purchase the product from the other enterprise
c. Controls the disposition of the product that has been purchased by another enterprise in accordance with the arrangements described in either (a) or (b) above.

In all of the foregoing cases, the sponsor agrees to purchase the product, or processed goods of which the product is a component, from the other enterprise at specified prices over specified periods or, to the extent that it does not do so, guarantees resale to third parties [(refer to paragraphs .101 through .103)]. [FAS49, ¶3]

(The next page is 11825.)

DEBT: RESTRUCTURINGS

Sources: FASB Statement 15; FASB Statement 91; FASB Statement 114;
FASB Statement 121; FASB Technical Bulletin 80-2;
FASB Technical Bulletin 81-6

Summary

This section presents standards of financial accounting and reporting by debtors and creditors for a troubled debt restructuring. A restructuring of debt constitutes a troubled debt restructuring if the creditor, for reasons related to the debtor's financial difficulties, grants a concession to the debtor that it would not otherwise consider. This section does not apply to routine changes in debt terms.

The accounting for a troubled debt restructuring is based on the type of the restructuring, and this section identifies two primary types of restructurings: (a) a transfer of assets (or equity interest) from a debtor to a creditor in full settlement of a debt and (b) a modification of terms.

If a debtor satisfies a debt in full by transferring assets, or by granting an equity interest, to a creditor and the fair market value of the assets transferred or equity interest granted is less than the carrying value of the debt (or, in the case of the creditor, is less than the recorded investment in the debt) the difference generally is an extraordinary gain to the debtor and ordinary loss to the creditor. Also, the debtor must recognize a gain or loss for any difference between the carrying value of the assets transferred and their fair value. Subsequent accounting for assets received in a troubled debt restructuring is the same as if the assets were acquired for cash.

If a creditor receives assets or an equity interest in the debtor in full satisfaction of a receivable, the creditor accounts for those assets at their fair value at the time of the restructuring and accounts for those assets received the same as if the assets had been acquired for cash.

For a creditor in a troubled debt restructuring in fiscal years beginning before December 16, 1994 involving only a modification of terms, the effects of the restructuring shall be accounted for prospectively from the time of restructuring, as long as the loan is not impaired based on the terms of the restructuring agreement. No gain or loss shall be recorded at the time of restructuring unless the carrying amount of the debt (or, in the case of the creditor, the recorded investment in the debt) exceeds the total future cash payments (or receipts) specified by the new terms. A creditor in a troubled debt restructuring in fiscal years beginning after December 15, 1994 involving a modification of terms or in a troubled debt restructuring in fiscal years beginning before December 16, 1994 that becomes impaired after that date based on the terms of the restructuring agreement shall account for the restructured loan in accordance with the provisions of Section I08, "Impairment."

Scope

.101 This section [presents] standards of financial accounting and reporting by the debtor and by the creditor for a troubled **debt** restructuring. [FAS15, ¶1]

.101A A creditor in a troubled debt restructuring involving a modification of terms shall account for the restructured loan in accordance with [paragraphs .139 through .146 and] the provisions of paragraphs .102 through .119 of Section I08, "Impairment," except that a troubled debt restructuring involving a modification of terms in fiscal years beginning before December 16, 1994[a] may continue to be accounted for and disclosed in accordance with this section [(paragraphs .126 through .138)] as long as the restructured loan [(a)] is not impaired based on the terms of the restructuring agreement. [FAS114, ¶22(a)] [and (b) is not a *security* as defined in paragraph .406 of Section I80, "Investments: Debt and Equity Securities." Also refer to paragraphs .503 and .504 of Section I80 for further guidance on that section's applicability to loans restructured in a troubled debt restructuring.]

.102 For purposes of this section, **troubled debt restructurings** do not include changes in lease agreements (the accounting [for which] is prescribed by Section L10, "Leases") or employment-related agreements (for example, pension plans and deferred compensation contracts). Nor do troubled debt restructurings include debtors' failures to pay trade accounts according to their terms or creditors' delays in taking legal action to collect overdue amounts of interest and principal, unless they involve an agreement between debtor and creditor to restructure. [FAS15, ¶8]

[aRestructurings in those fiscal years are before the required effective date for the provisions of Section I08, paragraphs .102 through .119. If a creditor initially applies Section I08, paragraphs .102 through .119 earlier than the required effective date (fiscal years beginning after December 15, 1994), the provisions described in paragraph .123(b)(1) become effective at that time.]

.103 This section shall be applied to troubled debt restructurings consummated under reorganization, arrangement, or other provisions of the Federal Bankruptcy Act or other federal statutes related thereto.[1] [FAS15, ¶10]

Troubled Debt Restructuring

.104 A restructuring of debt constitutes a *troubled debt restructuring*, for purposes of this section, if the creditor for economic or legal reasons related to the debtor's financial difficulties grants a concession to the debtor that it would not otherwise consider. That concession either stems from an agreement between the creditor and the debtor or is imposed by law or a court. For example, a creditor may restructure the terms of a debt to alleviate the burden of the debtor's near-term cash requirements, and many troubled debt restructurings involve modifying terms to reduce or defer cash payments required of the debtor in the near future to help the debtor attempt to improve its financial condition and eventually be able to pay the creditor. Or, for example, the creditor may accept cash, other assets, or an equity interest in the debtor in satisfaction of the debt though the value received is less than the amount of the debt because the creditor concludes that step will maximize recovery of its investment.[2] [FAS15, ¶2]

.105 A troubled debt restructuring may include, but is not necessarily limited to, one or a combination of the following:

a. Transfer from the debtor to the creditor of receivables from third parties, real estate, or other assets to satisfy fully or partially a debt (including a transfer resulting from foreclosure or repossession)
b. Issuance or other granting of an equity interest to the creditor by the debtor to satisfy fully or partially a debt unless the equity interest is granted pursuant to existing terms for converting the debt into an equity interest
c. Modification of terms of a debt, such as one or a combination of:
   (1) Reduction (absolute or contingent) of the stated interest rate for the remaining original life of the debt
   (2) Extension of the maturity date or dates at a stated interest rate lower than the current market rate for new debt with similar risk

---

[1]The section does not apply, however, if under provisions of those federal statutes or in a quasi reorganization or corporate readjustment (refer to Section Q15, "Quasi Reorganizations") with which a troubled debt restructuring coincides, the debtor restates its liabilities generally. [FAS15, ¶10, fn4] [Refer to paragraphs .509 through .513 for guidance regarding a general restatement of a debtor's liabilities in bankruptcy situations.]

[2]Although troubled debt that is fully satisfied by foreclosure, repossession, or other transfer of assets or by grant of equity securities by the debtor is, in a technical sense, not restructured, that kind of event is included in the term *troubled debt restructuring* in this section. [FAS15, ¶2, fn1]

(3) Reduction (absolute or contingent) of the face amount or maturity amount of the debt as stated in the instrument or other agreement

(4) Reduction (absolute or contingent) of accrued interest.

[FAS15, ¶5]

.106 Whatever the form of concession granted by the creditor to the debtor in a troubled debt restructuring, the creditor's objective is to make the best of a difficult situation. That is, the creditor expects to obtain more cash or other value from the debtor, or to increase the probability of receipt, by granting the concession than by not granting it. [FAS15, ¶3]

.107 A debt restructuring is not necessarily a troubled debt restructuring, for purposes of this section, even if the debtor is experiencing some financial difficulties. For example, a troubled debt restructuring is not involved if (a) the fair value of cash, other assets, or an equity interest accepted by a creditor from a debtor in full satisfaction of its receivable at least equals the creditor's **recorded investment in the receivable;**[3] (b) the fair value of cash, other assets, or an equity interest transferred by a debtor to a creditor in full settlement of its payable at least equals the debtor's **carrying amount of the payable;** (c) the creditor reduces the effective interest rate on the debt primarily to reflect a decrease in market interest rates in general or a decrease in the risk so as to maintain a relationship with a debtor that can readily obtain funds from other sources at the current market interest rate; or (d) the debtor issues in exchange for its debt new marketable debt having an effective interest rate based on its market price that is at or near the current market interest rates of debt with similar maturity dates and stated interest rates issued by nontroubled debtors. In general, a debtor that can obtain funds from sources other than the existing creditor at market interest rates at or near those for nontroubled debt is not involved in a troubled debt restructuring. A debtor in a troubled debt restructuring can obtain funds from sources other than the existing creditor in the troubled debt restructuring, if at all, only at effective interest rates (based on market prices) so high that it cannot afford to pay them. [FAS15, ¶7]

Accounting by Debtors

.108 A debtor shall account for a troubled debt restructuring according to the type of the restructuring as prescribed in paragraphs .109 through .122. [FAS15, ¶12]

---

[3][Refer to paragraphs .506 through .508 for further guidance regarding when a debt restructuring can be a troubled debt restructuring for the debtor but not for the creditor.]

Transfer of Assets in Full Settlement

.109 A debtor that transfers its receivables from third parties, real estate, or other assets to a creditor to settle fully a payable shall recognize a gain on restructuring of payables (refer to paragraph .117). The gain shall be measured by the excess of (a) the carrying amount of the payable settled over (b) the fair value of the assets transferred to the creditor.[4] The fair value of the assets transferred is the amount that the debtor could reasonably expect to receive for them in a current sale between a willing buyer and a willing seller, that is, other than in a forced or liquidation sale. Fair value of assets shall be measured by their market value if an active market for them exists. If no active market exists for the assets transferred but exists for similar assets, the selling prices in that market may be helpful in estimating the fair value of the assets transferred. If no market price is available, a forecast of expected cash flows may aid in estimating the fair value of assets transferred, provided the expected cash flows are discounted at a rate commensurate with the risk involved.[5] [FAS15, ¶13]

.110 A difference between the fair value and the carrying amount of assets transferred to a creditor to settle a payable is a gain or loss on transfer of assets.[6] The debtor shall include that gain or loss in measuring net income for the period of transfer, reported as provided in Section I17, "Income Statement Presentation: Extraordinary Items," or Section I22, "Income Statement Presentation: Unusual or Infrequent Items." [FAS15, ¶14]

---

[4]Paragraphs .109, .111, and .115 indicate that the fair value of assets transferred or the fair value of an equity interest granted shall be used in accounting for a settlement of a payable in a troubled debt restructuring. That guidance is not intended to preclude using the fair value of the payable settled if more clearly evident than the fair value of the assets transferred or of the equity interest granted in a full settlement of a payable (refer to paragraphs .109 and .111). (Refer to Section B50, "Business Combinations," paragraph .125.) However, in a partial settlement of a payable (refer to paragraph .115), the fair value of the assets transferred or of the equity interest granted shall be used in all cases to avoid the need to allocate the fair value of the payable between the part settled and the part still outstanding. [FAS15, ¶13, fn5]

[5]Some factors that may be relevant in estimating the fair value of various kinds of assets are described in Section B50, paragraph .146, Section I69, "Interest: Imputation of an Interest Cost," paragraphs .105 through .107, and Section N35, "Nonmonetary Transactions," paragraph .111. [FAS15, ¶13, fn6]

[6]The carrying amount of a receivable encompasses not only unamortized premium, discount, acquisition costs, and the like but also an allowance for uncollectible amounts and other *valuation* accounts, if any. A loss on transferring receivables to creditors may therefore have been wholly or partially recognized in measuring net income before the transfer and be wholly or partly a reduction of a valuation account rather than a gain or loss in measuring net income for the period of the transfer. [FAS15, ¶14, fn7]

Grant of Equity Interest in Full Settlement

.111 A debtor that issues or otherwise grants an equity interest to a creditor to settle fully a payable shall account for the equity interest at its fair value.[7] The difference between the fair value of the equity interest granted and the carrying amount of the payable settled shall be recognized as a gain on restructuring of payables (refer to paragraph .117). [FAS15, ¶15]

Modification of Terms

.112 A debtor in a troubled debt restructuring involving only modification of terms of a payable—that is, not involving a transfer of assets or grant of an equity interest—shall account for the effects of the restructuring prospectively from the **time of restructuring,** and shall not change the carrying amount of the payable at the time of the restructuring unless the carrying amount exceeds the total future cash payments specified by the new terms.[8] That is, the effects of changes in the amounts or timing (or both) of future cash payments designated as either interest or face amount shall be reflected in future periods.[9] Interest expense shall be computed in a way that a constant effective interest rate is applied to the carrying amount of the payable at the beginning of each period between restructuring and maturity (in substance the *interest* method prescribed by Section I69, "Interest: Imputation of an Interest Cost," paragraph .108). The new effective interest rate shall be the discount rate that equates the present value of the future cash payments specified by the new terms (excluding amounts contingently payable) with the carrying amount of the payable. [FAS15, ¶16]

.113 If, however, the total future cash payments specified by the new terms of a payable, including both payments designated as interest and those designated as face amount, are less than the carrying amount of the payable, the debtor shall reduce the carrying amount to an amount equal to the total future cash payments specified by the new terms and shall recognize a gain on restructuring of payables equal to the amount of the reduction

---

[7]Refer to footnote 4. [FAS15, ¶15, fn8]

[8]In this section, *total future cash payments* includes related accrued interest, if any, at the time of the restructuring that continues to be payable under the new terms. [FAS15, ¶16, fn9]

[9]All or a portion of the carrying amount of the payable at the time of the restructuring may need to be reclassified in the balance sheet because of changes in the terms, for example, a change in the amount of the payable due within one year after the date of the debtor's balance sheet. A troubled debt restructuring of a short-term obligation after the date of a debtor's balance sheet but before that balance sheet is issued may affect the classification of that obligation in accordance with Section B05, "Balance Sheet Classification: Current Assets and Current Liabilities." [FAS15, ¶16, fn10]

(refer to paragraph .117).[10] Thereafter, all cash payments under the terms of the payable shall be accounted for as reductions of the carrying amount of the payable, and no interest expense shall be recognized on the payable for any period between the restructuring and maturity of the payable.[11] [FAS15, ¶17]

.114 A debtor shall not recognize a gain on a restructured payable involving indeterminate future cash payments as long as the maximum total future cash payments may exceed the carrying amount of the payable. Amounts designated either as interest or as face amount by the new terms may be payable contingent on a specified event or circumstance (for example, the debtor may be required to pay specified amounts if its financial condition improves to a specified degree within a specified period). To determine whether the debtor shall recognize a gain according to the provisions of paragraphs .111 and .112, those contingent amounts shall be included in the *total future cash payments specified by the new terms* to the extent necessary to prevent recognizing a gain at the time of restructuring that may be offset by future interest expense. Thus, the debtor shall apply [the provisions of] Section C59, "Contingencies," paragraph .118, in which probability of occurrence of a gain contingency is not a factor, and shall assume that contingent future payments will have to be paid. The same principle applies to amounts of future cash payments that must sometimes be estimated to apply the provisions of paragraphs .112 and .113. For example, if the number of future interest payments is flexible because the face amount and accrued interest is payable on demand or becomes payable on demand, estimates of total future cash payments shall be based on the maximum number of periods possible under the restructured terms. [FAS15, ¶18]

Combination of Types

.115 A troubled debt restructuring may involve partial settlement of a payable by the debtor's transferring assets or granting an equity interest (or both) to the creditor and modification of terms of the remaining payable.[12] A debtor shall account for a troubled debt restructuring involving a partial settlement and a modification of terms as prescribed in paragraphs .112 through .114 except that, first, assets transferred or an equity

---

[10]If the carrying amount of the payable comprises several accounts (for example, face amount, accrued interest, and unamortized premium, discount, finance charges, and issue costs) that are to be continued after the restructuring, some possibly being combined, the reduction in carrying amount may need to be allocated among the remaining accounts in proportion to the previous balances. However, the debtor may choose to carry the amount designated as face amount by the new terms in a separate account and adjust another account accordingly. [FAS15, ¶17, fn11]

[11]The only exception is to recognize interest expense according to paragraph .118. [FAS15, ¶17, fn12]

[12]Even if the stated terms of the remaining payable, for example, the stated interest rate and the maturity date or dates, are not changed in connection with the transfer of assets or grant of an equity interest, the restructuring shall be accounted for as prescribed by paragraph .115. [FAS15, ¶19, fn13]

interest granted in that partial settlement shall be measured as prescribed in paragraphs .109 and .111, respectively, and the carrying amount of the payable shall be reduced by the total fair value of those assets or equity interest.[13] A difference between the fair value and the carrying amount of assets transferred to the creditor shall be recognized as a gain or loss on transfer of assets. No gain on restructuring of payables shall be recognized unless the remaining carrying amount of the payable exceeds the total future cash payments (including amounts contingently payable) specified by the terms of the debt remaining unsettled after the restructuring. Future interest expense, if any, shall be determined according to the provisions of paragraphs .112 through .114. [FAS15, ¶19]

Related Matters

.116 A troubled debt restructuring that is in substance a repossession or foreclosure by the creditor or other transfer of assets to the creditor shall be accounted for according to the provisions of paragraphs .109, .110, and .115. [FAS15, ¶20]

.117 Gains on restructuring of payables determined by applying the provisions of paragraphs .109 through .116 of this section shall be aggregated, included in measuring net income for the period of restructuring, and, if material, classified as an extraordinary item, net of related income tax effect, in accordance with Section D14, "Debt: Extinguishments," paragraph .105. [FAS15, ¶21]

.118 If a troubled debt restructuring involves amounts contingently payable, those contingent amounts shall be recognized as a payable and as interest expense in future periods in accordance with Section C59. Thus, in general, interest expense for contingent payments shall be recognized in each period in which (a) it is probable that a liability has been incurred and (b) the amount of that liability can be reasonably estimated. Before recognizing a payable and interest expense for amounts contingently payable, however, accrual or payment of those amounts shall be deducted from the carrying amount of the restructured payable to the extent that contingent payments included in *total future cash payments specified by the new terms* prevented recognition of a gain at the time of restructuring (refer to paragraph .114). [FAS15, ¶22]

.119 If amounts of future cash payments must be estimated to apply the provisions of paragraphs .112 through .114 because future interest payments are expected to fluctuate—for example, the restructured terms may specify the stated interest rate to be the prime interest rate increased by a specified amount or proportion—estimates of maximum total future payments shall be based on the interest rate in effect at the time of the restructur-

---

[13]If cash is paid in partial settlement of a payable in a troubled debt restructuring, the carrying amount of the payable shall be reduced by the amount of cash paid. [FAS15, ¶19, fn14]

ing. Fluctuations in the effective interest rate after the restructuring from changes in the prime rate or other causes shall be accounted for as changes in estimates in the periods the changes occur. However, the accounting for those fluctuations shall not result in recognizing a gain on restructuring that may be offset by future cash payments (refer to paragraphs .114 and .118). Rather, the carrying amount of the restructured payable shall remain unchanged, and future cash payments shall reduce the carrying amount until the time that any gain recognized cannot be offset by future cash payments. [FAS15, ¶23]

.120 Legal fees and other direct costs that a debtor incurs in granting an equity interest to a creditor in a troubled debt restructuring shall reduce the amount otherwise recorded for that equity interest according to paragraphs .111 and .115. All other direct costs that a debtor incurs to effect a troubled debt restructuring shall be deducted in measuring gain on restructuring of payables or shall be included in expense for the period if no gain on restructuring is recognized. [FAS15, ¶24]

Disclosure by Debtors

.121 A debtor shall disclose, either in the body of the financial statements or in the accompanying notes, the following information about troubled debt restructurings that have occurred during a period for which financial statements are presented:

a. For each restructuring:[14] a description of the principal changes in terms, the major features of settlement, or both
b. Aggregate gain on restructuring of payables and the related income tax effect (refer to paragraph .117)
c. Aggregate net gain or loss on transfers of assets recognized during the period (refer to paragraphs .110 and .115)
d. Per share amount of the aggregate gain on restructuring of payables, net of related income tax effect.

[FAS15, ¶25]

.122 A debtor shall disclose in financial statements for periods after a troubled debt restructuring the extent to which amounts contingently payable are included in the carrying amount of restructured payables pursuant to the provisions of paragraph .114. If required by Section C59, a debtor shall also disclose in those financial statements total amounts that are contingently payable on restructured payables and the conditions under

---

[14]Separate restructurings within a fiscal period for the same category of payables (for example, accounts payable or subordinated debentures) may be grouped for disclosure purposes. [FAS15, ¶25, fn15]

which those amounts would become payable or would be forgiven. [Refer to Section F25, "Financial Instruments: Disclosure," for guidance on possible additional disclosure requirements.] [FAS15, ¶26]

Accounting by Creditors

.123 A creditor shall account for a troubled debt restructuring according to the type of the restructuring as prescribed in the following paragraphs: [FAS15, ¶27]

[a. A restructuring where there is a receipt of assets in full satisfaction of the loan is accounted for in accordance with paragraphs .124 and .125.

b. A restructuring where there is only a modification of terms or a restructuring where there is a combination of types (that is, both a receipt of assets and a modification of terms) is accounted for as follows:

  (1) *Restructurings in fiscal years beginning before December 16, 1994*[14a]

    (a) A troubled debt restructuring involving a modification of terms which *is not* impaired based on the terms of the restructuring agreement may be accounted for in accordance with paragraphs .126 through .138.

    (b) A troubled debt restructuring involving a modification of terms which *is* impaired based on the terms of the restructuring agreement is accounted for in accordance with paragraphs .139 through .146 and Section I08, paragraphs .102 through .119.

  (2) *Restructurings in fiscal years beginning after December 15, 1994*[14b]

    A troubled debt restructuring involving a modification of terms is accounted for in accordance with the provisions of paragraphs .139 through .146 and Section I08, paragraphs .102 through .119.]

Paragraphs .124 through [.146] do not apply to a receivable that the creditor is accounting for at market value in accordance with specialized industry practice (for example, a marketable debt security accounted for at market value by a mutual fund). Estimated cash expected to be received less estimated costs expected to be incurred is not market value in accordance with specialized industry practice as that term is used in this paragraph. [FAS15, ¶27]

[14a]Restructurings in those fiscal years are before the required effective date for the provisions of Section I08, paragraphs .102 through .119. If a creditor initially applies Section I08, paragraphs .102 through .119 earlier than the required effective date (fiscal years beginning after December 15, 1994), the provisions described in paragraph .123(b)(2) above should be applied to all loans restructured on or after that date of initial application.]

[14b]Restructurings in those fiscal years are after the required effective date for the provisions of Section I08, paragraphs .102 through .119. If a creditor initially applies Section I08, paragraphs .102 through .119 earlier than the required effective date (fiscal years beginning after December 15, 1994), the provisions described in .123(b)(2) above become effective at that time.]

Receipt of Assets in Full Satisfaction

.124 A creditor that receives from a debtor in full satisfaction of a receivable either (a) receivables from third parties, real estate, or other assets or (b) shares of stock or other evidence of an equity interest in the debtor, or both, shall account for those assets (including an equity interest) at their fair value at the time of the restructuring (refer to paragraph .109 for how to measure fair value).[15] [FAS15, ¶28] A creditor that receives long-lived assets that will be sold from a debtor in full satisfaction of a receivable shall account for those assets at their fair value less cost to sell, as that term is used in paragraphs .134 through .136 of Section I08. [FAS121, ¶24(a)] The excess of (a) the recorded investment in the receivable satisfied over (b) the fair value of assets received (less cost to sell, if required above) is a loss to be recognized. For purposes of this paragraph, losses, to the extent they are not offset against allowances for uncollectible amounts or other valuation accounts, shall be included in measuring net income for the period. [FAS121, ¶24(b)]

.125 After a troubled debt restructuring, a creditor shall account for assets received in satisfaction of a receivable the same as if the assets had been acquired for cash. [FAS15, ¶29]

Restructurings in Fiscal Years Beginning before December 16, 1994[15a]

Modification of Terms

.126 A creditor in a troubled debt restructuring involving only modification of terms of a receivable—that is, not involving receipt of assets (including an equity interest in the debtor)—shall account for the effects of the restructuring prospectively and shall not change the recorded investment in the receivable at the time of the restructuring unless that amount exceeds the *total future cash receipts specified by the new terms.*[16] That is, the effects of

---

[15]Paragraphs .124 and .129 indicate that the fair value of assets received shall be used in accounting for satisfaction of a receivable in a troubled debt restructuring. That guidance is not intended to preclude using the fair value of the receivable satisfied if more clearly evident than the fair value of the assets received in full satisfaction of a receivable (refer to paragraph .124). (Refer to Section B50, paragraph .125.) However, in a partial satisfaction of a receivable (refer to paragraph .129), the fair value of the assets received shall be used in all cases to avoid the need to allocate the fair value of the receivable between the part satisfied and the part still outstanding. [FAS15, ¶28, fn16]

[15a] Refer to footnote 14a.]

[16]In this section, *total future cash receipts* include related accrued interest, if any, at the time of the restructuring that continues to be receivable under the new terms. Uncertainty of collection of noncontingent amounts specified by the new terms (refer to paragraph .128 for inclusion of contingent amounts) is not a factor in applying paragraphs .126 through .128 but should, of course, be considered in accounting for allowances for uncollectible amounts. [FAS15, ¶30, fn18]

changes in the amounts or timing (or both) of future cash receipts designated either as interest or as face amount shall be reflected in future periods.[17] Interest income shall be computed in a way that a constant effective interest rate is applied to the recorded investment in the receivable at the beginning of each period between restructuring and maturity (in substance the *interest* method prescribed by Section I69, paragraph .108[18]). The new effective interest rate shall be the discount rate that equates the present value of the future cash receipts specified by the new terms (excluding amounts contingently receivable) with the recorded investment in the receivable. [FAS15, ¶30]

.127 If, however, the total future cash receipts specified by the new terms of the receivable, including both receipts designated as interest and those designated as face amount, are less than the recorded investment in the receivable before restructuring, the creditor shall reduce the recorded investment in the receivable to an amount equal to the total future cash receipts specified by the new terms. The amount of the reduction is a loss to be recognized according to paragraph .131. Thereafter, all cash receipts by the creditor under the terms of the restructured receivable, whether designated as interest or as face amount, shall be accounted for as recovery of the recorded investment in the receivable, and no interest income shall be recognized on the receivable for any period between the restructuring and maturity of the receivable.[19] [FAS15, ¶31]

.128 A creditor shall recognize a loss on a restructured receivable involving indeterminate future cash receipts unless the minimum future cash receipts specified by the new terms at least equal the recorded investment in the receivable. Amounts designated either as interest or as face amount that are receivable from the debtor may be contingent on a specified event or circumstance (for example, specified amounts may be receivable from the debtor if the debtor's financial condition improves to a specified degree within a specified period). To determine whether the creditor shall recognize a loss according to the provisions of paragraphs .126 and .127, those contingent amounts shall be included in the *total future cash receipts specified by the new terms* only if at the time of restructuring those amounts meet the conditions that would be applied under the provisions of Section C59, in accruing a loss. That is, a creditor shall recognize a loss unless contingent future cash receipts needed to make total future cash receipts specified by the new terms at least equal to the recorded investment in the receivable both are probable and can be reasonably estimated. The same principle applies to amounts of future cash receipts that must sometimes be estimated to apply the provisions of paragraphs .126 and .127. For

---

[17]All or a portion of the recorded investment in the receivable at the time of restructuring may need to be reclassified in the balance sheet because of changes in the terms. [FAS15, ¶30, fn19]

[18][Deleted 11/92 because of FASB Statement 111, *Rescission of FASB Statement No. 32 and Technical Corrections.*]

[19]The only exception is to recognize interest income according to paragraph .132. [FAS15, ¶31, fn21]

example, if the number of interest receipts is flexible because the face amount and accrued interest is collectible on demand or becomes collectible on demand after a specified period, estimates of total future cash receipts should be based on the minimum number of periods possible under the restructured terms. [FAS15, ¶32]

Combination of Types

.129 A troubled debt restructuring may involve receipt of assets (including an equity interest in the debtor) in partial satisfaction of a receivable and a modification of terms of the remaining receivable.[20] A creditor shall account for a troubled debt restructuring involving a partial satisfaction and modification of terms as prescribed in paragraphs .126 through .128 except that, first, the assets received shall be accounted for as prescribed in paragraph .124 and the recorded investment in the receivable shall be reduced by the fair value [FAS15, ¶33] less cost to sell [FAS121, ¶24(c)] of the assets received.[21] No loss on the restructuring shall be recognized unless the remaining recorded investment in the receivable exceeds the total future cash receipts specified by the terms of the receivable remaining unsatisfied after the restructuring. Future interest income, if any, shall be determined according to the provisions of paragraphs .126 through .128. [FAS15, ¶33]

.129A Fees received in connection with a modification of terms of a troubled debt restructuring as defined in this section shall be applied as a reduction of the recorded investment in the loan. [FAS91, ¶14]

Related Matters

.130 A troubled debt restructuring that is in substance a repossession or foreclosure by the creditor, or in which the creditor otherwise obtains one or more of the debtor's assets in place of all or part of the receivable, shall be accounted for according to the provisions of paragraphs .124 and .129 and, if appropriate, .135. [FAS15, ¶34]

.131 Losses determined by applying the provisions of paragraphs .124 through .130 of this section shall, to the extent that they are not offset against allowances for uncollectible amounts or other valuation accounts, be included in measuring net income for the period of restructuring and reported according to Section I17. Although this section does not address questions concerning estimating uncollectible amounts or accounting for the

---

[20]Even if the stated terms of the remaining receivable, for example, the stated interest rate and the maturity date or dates, are not changed in connection with the receipt of assets (including an equity interest in the debtor), the restructuring shall be accounted for as prescribed by paragraph .129. [FAS15, ¶33, fn22]

[21]If cash is received in a partial satisfaction of a receivable, the recorded investment in the receivable shall be reduced by the amount of cash received. [FAS15, ¶33, fn23]

related valuation allowance (refer to paragraph .101), it recognizes that creditors use allowances for uncollectible amounts. Thus, a loss from reducing the recorded investment in a receivable may have been recognized before the restructuring by deducting an estimate of uncollectible amounts in measuring net income and increasing an appropriate valuation allowance. If so, a reduction in the recorded investment in the receivable in a troubled debt restructuring is a deduction from the valuation allowance rather than a loss in measuring net income for the period of restructuring. A valuation allowance can also be used to recognize a loss determined by applying paragraphs .124 through .130 that has not been previously recognized in measuring income. For example, a creditor with an allowance for uncollectible amounts pertaining to a group of receivables that includes the restructured receivable may deduct from the allowance the reduction of recorded investment in the restructured receivable and recognize the loss in measuring net income for the period of restructuring by estimating the appropriate allowance for remaining receivables, including the restructured receivable. [FAS15, ¶35]

.132 If a troubled debt restructuring involves amounts contingently receivable, those contingent amounts shall not be recognized as interest income in future periods before they become receivable—that is, they shall not be recognized as interest income before both the contingency has been removed and the interest has been earned.[22] Before recognizing those amounts as interest income, however, they shall be deducted from the recorded investment in the restructured receivable to the extent that contingent receipts included in *total future cash receipts specified by the new terms* avoided recognition of a loss at the time of restructuring (refer to paragraph .128). [FAS15, ¶36]

.133 If amounts of future cash receipts must be estimated to apply the provisions of paragraphs .126 through .128 because future interest receipts are expected to fluctuate—for example, the restructured terms may specify the stated interest rate to be the prime interest rate increased by a specified amount or proportion—estimates of the minimum total future receipts shall be based on the interest rate in effect at the time of restructuring. Fluctuations in the effective interest rate after the restructuring from changes in the prime rate or other causes shall be accounted for as changes in estimates in the periods the changes occur except that a creditor shall recognize a loss and reduce the recorded investment in a restructured receivable if the interest rate decreases to an extent that the minimum total future cash receipts determined using that interest rate fall below the recorded investment in the receivable at that time. [FAS15, ¶37]

---

[22]Section C59, paragraph .118, states, in part: "Contingencies that might result in gains usually are not reflected in the accounts since to do so might be to recognize revenue prior to its realization." [FAS15, ¶36, fn24]

.134 Legal fees and other direct costs [FAS15, ¶38] including direct loan origination costs [FAS91, ¶14] incurred by a creditor to effect a troubled debt restructuring shall be included in expense when incurred. [FAS15, ¶38]

.135 A receivable from the sale of assets previously obtained in a troubled debt restructuring shall be accounted for according to Section I69, regardless of whether the assets were obtained in satisfaction (full or partial) of a receivable to which that section was not intended to apply. A difference, if any, between the amount of the new receivable and the carrying amount of the assets sold is a gain or loss on sale of assets. [FAS15, ¶39]

Disclosures by Creditors

.136 A creditor shall disclose, either in the body of the financial statements or in the accompanying notes, the following information about troubled debt restructurings as of the date of each balance sheet presented:

a. For outstanding receivables whose terms have been modified in troubled debt restructurings, by major category:[23] (1) the aggregate recorded investment; (2) the gross interest income that would have been recorded in the period then ended if those receivables had been current in accordance with their original terms and had been outstanding throughout the period or since origination, if held for part of the period; and (3) the amount of interest income on those receivables that was included in net income for the period. A receivable whose terms have been modified need not be included in that disclosure if, subsequent to restructuring, its effective interest rate (refer to paragraph .126) had been equal to or greater than the rate that the creditor was willing to accept for a new receivable with comparable risk.
b. The amount of commitments, if any, to lend additional funds to debtors owing receivables whose terms have been modified in troubled debt restructurings. [Refer to Section F25 for guidance on possible additional disclosure requirements.]

[FAS15, ¶40]

.137 A financial institution, or other creditor, may appropriately disclose the information prescribed by paragraph .136, by major category, for the aggregate of outstanding reduced-earning and nonearning receivables rather than separately for outstanding receivables whose terms have been modified in troubled debt restructurings. [FAS15, ¶41]

---

[23]The appropriate major categories depend on various factors, including the industry or industries in which the creditor is involved. For example, for a commercial banking enterprise, at a minimum, the appropriate categories are investments in debt securities and loans. Information need not be disclosed, however, for noninterest-bearing trade receivables; loans to individuals for household, family, and other personal expenditures; and real estate loans secured by one-to-four family residential properties. [FAS15, ¶40, fn25]

Substitution or Addition of Debtors

.138 A troubled debt restructuring may involve substituting debt of another business enterprise, individual, or governmental unit[24] for that of the troubled debtor or adding another debtor (for example, as a joint debtor). That kind of restructuring should be accounted for according to its substance. For example, a restructuring in which, after the restructuring, the substitute or additional debtor controls, is controlled by, or is under common control[25] with the original debtor is an example of one that shall be accounted for by the creditor according to the provisions of paragraphs .126 through .128. Those paragraphs also shall apply to a restructuring in which the substitute or additional debtor and original debtor are related after the restructuring by an agency, trust, or other relationship that in substance earmarks certain of the original debtor's funds or funds flows for the creditor although payments to the creditor may be made by the substitute or additional debtor. In contrast, a restructuring in which the substitute or additional debtor and the original debtor do not have any of the relationships described above after the restructuring shall be accounted for by the creditor according to the provisions of paragraphs .124 and .129. [FAS15, ¶42]

Restructurings in Fiscal Years Beginning after December 15, 1994[26]

Modification of Terms

.139 A creditor in a troubled debt restructuring involving only a modification of terms of a receivable—that is, not involving receipt of assets (including an equity interest in the debtor)—shall account for the troubled debt restructuring in accordance with the provisions of Section I08, paragraphs .102 through .119. [FAS114, ¶22(b)]

Combination of Types

.140 A troubled debt restructuring may involve receipt of assets (including an equity interest in the debtor) in partial satisfaction of a receivable and a modification of terms

---

[24]Governmental units include, but are not limited to, states, counties, townships, municipalities, school districts, authorities, and commissions. [FAS15, ¶42, fn26]

[25]*Control* in this paragraph has the meaning described in Section I82, "Investments: Equity Method," paragraph .408: "The usual condition for control is ownership of a majority (over 50 percent) of the outstanding voting stock. The power to control may also exist with a lesser percentage of ownership, for example, by contract, lease, agreement with other stockholders, or by court decree." [FAS15, ¶42, fn27]

[[26]Refer to footnote 14b.]

of the remaining receivable.[27] A creditor shall account for a troubled debt restructuring involving a partial satisfaction and modification of terms as prescribed in [FAS15, ¶33] Section I08, paragraphs .102 through .119, [FAS114, ¶22(c)] except that, first, the assets received shall be accounted for as prescribed in paragraph .124 and the recorded investment in the receivable shall be reduced by the fair value [FAS15, ¶33] less cost to sell [FAS121, ¶24(c)] of the assets received.[28] [FAS15, ¶33]

.141 Fees received in connection with a modification of terms of a troubled debt restructuring as defined in this section shall be applied as a reduction of the recorded investment in the loan. [FAS91, ¶14]

Related Matters

.142 A troubled debt restructuring that is in substance a repossession or foreclosure by the creditor, [FAS15, ¶34] that is, the creditor receives physical possession of the debtor's assets regardless of whether formal foreclosure proceedings take place, [FAS114, ¶22(d)] or in which the creditor otherwise obtains one or more of the debtor's assets in place of all or part of the receivable, shall be accounted for according to the provisions of paragraphs .124 and .140 and, if appropriate, .144. [FAS15, ¶34]

.143 Legal fees and other direct costs [FAS15, ¶38] including direct loan origination costs [FAS91, ¶14] incurred by a creditor to effect a troubled debt restructuring shall be included in expense when incurred. [FAS15, ¶38]

.144 A receivable from the sale of assets previously obtained in a troubled debt restructuring shall be accounted for according to Section I69, regardless of whether the assets were obtained in satisfaction (full or partial) of a receivable to which that section was not intended to apply. A difference, if any, between the amount of the new receivable and the carrying amount of the assets sold is a gain or loss on sale of assets. [FAS15, ¶39]

Disclosures by Creditors

.145 A creditor shall disclose, either in the body of the financial statements or in the accompanying notes, the amount of commitments, if any, to lend additional funds to debtors owing receivables whose terms have been modified in troubled debt restructurings,

---

[27]Even if the stated terms of the remaining receivable, for example, the stated interest rate and the maturity date or dates, are not changed in connection with the receipt of assets (including an equity interest in the debtor), the restructuring shall be accounted for as prescribed by paragraph .129. [FAS15, ¶33, fn22]

[28]If cash is received in a partial satisfaction of a receivable, the recorded investment in the receivable shall be reduced by the amount of cash received. [FAS15, ¶33, fn23]

as of the date of each balance sheet presented. [FAS15, ¶40] [Refer to Section F25 and Section I08 for guidance on additional disclosure requirements.]

Substitution or Addition of Debtors

.146 A troubled debt restructuring may involve substituting debt of another business enterprise, individual, or governmental unit[29] for that of the troubled debtor or adding another debtor (for example, as a joint debtor). That kind of restructuring should be accounted for according to its substance. For example, a restructuring in which, after the restructuring, the substitute or additional debtor controls, is controlled by, or is under common control[30] with the original debtor is an example of one that shall be accounted for by the creditor [FAS15, ¶42] as prescribed in Section I08, paragraphs .102 through .119. That section [FAS114, ¶22(e)] also shall apply to a restructuring in which the substitute or additional debtor and original debtor are related after the restructuring by an agency, trust, or other relationship that in substance earmarks certain of the original debtor's funds or funds flows for the creditor although payments to the creditor may be made by the substitute or additional debtor. In contrast, a restructuring in which the substitute or additional debtor and the original debtor do not have any of the relationships described above after the restructuring shall be accounted for by the creditor according to the provisions of paragraphs .124 and .140. [FAS15, ¶42]

---

[29]Governmental units include, but are not limited to, states, counties, townships, municipalities, school districts, authorities, and commissions. [FAS15, ¶42, fn26]

[30]*Control* in this paragraph has the meaning described in Section I82, "Investments: Equity Method," paragraph .408: "The usual condition for control is ownership of a majority (over 50 percent) of the outstanding voting stock. The power to control may also exist with a lesser percentage of ownership, for example, by contract, lease, agreement with other stockholders, or by court decree." [FAS15, ¶42, fn27]

Glossary

.401 **Carrying amount of the payable.** Face amount increased or decreased by applicable accrued interest and applicable unamortized premium, discount, finance charges, or issue costs. [FAS15, ¶13]

.402 **Debt.** A *receivable* or *payable* (collectively referred to as *debt*) represents a contractual right to receive money or a contractual obligation to pay money on demand or on fixed or determinable dates that is already included as an asset or liability in the creditor's or debtor's balance sheet at the time of the restructuring. Receivables or payables that may be involved in troubled debt restructurings commonly result from lending or borrowing of cash, investing in debt securities that were previously issued, or selling or purchasing goods or services on credit. Examples are accounts receivable or payable, notes, debentures and bonds (whether those receivables or payables are secured or unsecured and whether thay are convertible or nonconvertible), and related accrued interest, if any. Typically, each receivable or payable is negotiated separately, but sometimes two or more receivables or payables are negotiated together. For example, a debtor may negotiate with a group of creditors but sign separate debt instruments with each creditor. For purposes of this section, restructuring of each receivable or payable, including those negotiated and restructured jointly, shall be accounted for individually. The substance rather than the form of the receivable or payable shall govern. For example, to a debtor, a bond constitutes one payable even though there are many bondholders. [FAS15, ¶4]

.403 **Recorded investment in the receivable.** Face amount increased or decreased by applicable accrued interest and unamortized premium, discount, finance charges, or acquisition costs. The recorded investment in the receivable may reflect a previous direct write-down of the investment [but differs from the *carrying amount of receivable* in that] the latter is net of an allowance for estimated uncollectible amounts or other valuation account, if any. [FAS15, ¶28, fn17]

.404 **Time of restructuring.** Troubled debt restructurings may occur before, at, or after the stated maturity of debt, and time may elapse between the agreement, court order, etc., and the transfer of assets or equity interest, the effective date of new terms, or the occurrence of another event that constitutes consummation of the restructuring. The date of consummation is the time of the restructuring. [FAS15, ¶6]

.405 **Troubled debt restructuring.** The creditor for economic or legal reasons related to the debtor's financial difficulties grants a concession to the debtor that it would not otherwise consider. [Refer to paragraphs .104 through .107 for examples and clarification.] [FAS15, ¶2]

Supplemental Guidance

.501-.505 [Deleted 5/93 because of FASB Statement 114, *Accounting by Creditors for Impairment of a Loan.*]

Classification of Debt Restructurings by Debtors and Creditors

.506 *Question*—In applying this section can a debt restructuring be a troubled debt restructuring for a debtor but not for the creditor? [FTB80-2, ¶1]

.507 *Response*—Yes, a debtor may have a troubled debt restructuring even though the related creditor does not have a troubled debt restructuring. The debtor and creditor must individually apply this section to the specific facts and circumstances to determine whether a troubled debt restructuring has occurred. Example (a) in paragraph .107 identifies a type of debt restructuring that is *not* a troubled debt restructuring for the creditor; similarly, example (b) in paragraph .107 identifies a type of debt restructuring that is *not* a troubled debt restructuring for the debtor. This section establishes tests for applicability that are not symmetrical as between the debtor and the creditor when the debtor's carrying amount and the creditor's recorded investment differ. [FTB80-2, ¶3]

.508 *Illustration*—Creditor A makes a $10,000 interest-bearing loan to Debtor X and, when Debtor X later encounters financial difficulties, sells its receivable from Debtor X to Creditor B for $4,000 on a nonrecourse basis. Following the sale, the carrying amount of the loan payable by Debtor X would still be $10,000 and the recorded investment of the loan by Creditor B would be $4,000. If Debtor X subsequently transfers to Creditor B assets with a fair value of $5,500 in full settlement of the loan, that transaction would be a troubled debt restructuring for Debtor X because the fair value of the assets is less than the carrying amount of the loan, whereas Creditor B would not have a troubled debt restructuring because the fair value of the assets received exceeds its recorded investment in the loan. [FTB80-2, ¶4]

Applicability to Debtors in Bankruptcy Situations

.509 *Question*—Does this section apply to troubled debt restructurings of debtors involved in bankruptcy proceedings? [FTB81-6, ¶1]

.510 *Background*—Some confusion has arisen about the interaction of paragraph .104 and footnote 1. Paragraph .103 indicates that this section applies to troubled debt restructurings consummated under reorganization, arrangement, or other provisions of the Federal Bankruptcy Act or other federal statutes related thereto. However, footnote 1 to that paragraph states that this section does not apply ". . . if, under provisions of those federal statutes or in a quasi reorganization or corporate readjustment [(refer to Section Q15, "Quasi Reorganizations")] with which a troubled debt restructuring coincides, the debtor restates its liabilities generally." [FTB81-6, ¶2]

.511 *Response*—This section does not apply to debtors who, in connection with bankruptcy proceedings, enter into troubled debt restructurings that result in a general restatement of the debtor's liabilities, that is, when such restructurings or modifications accomplished under purview of the bankruptcy court encompass most of the amount of the debtor's liabilities. [FTB81-6, ¶3]

.512 For example, enterprises involved with Chapter XI bankruptcy proceedings frequently reduce all or most of their indebtedness with the approval of their creditors and the court in order to provide an opportunity for the enterprise to have a fresh start. Such reductions are usually by a stated percentage so that, for example, the debtor owes only 60 cents on the dollar. Because the debtor would be restating its liabilities generally, this section would not apply to the debtor's accounting for such reduction of liabilities. [FTB81-6, ¶4]

.513 On the other hand, this section would apply to an isolated troubled debt restructuring by a debtor involved in bankruptcy proceedings if such restructuring did not result in a general restatement of the debtor's liabilities. [FTB81-6, ¶5]

(The next page is 12607.)

DEPRECIATION

SECTION D40

Sources: ARB 43, Chapter 9C; APB Opinion 6; APB Opinion 12;
FASB Statement 92; FASB Statement 93; FASB Statement 109

Summary

Depreciation is the method of allocating the cost of a tangible capital asset, less salvage (if any), over the estimated useful life of the asset in a systematic and rational manner. Except when an enterprise is undergoing a reorganization, capital assets shall not be depreciated at appraisal, market, or current values that are above cost to the enterprise.

This section applies to both business enterprises and not-for-profit organizations.

Basic Principle

.101 The cost of an [asset] is one of the costs of the services it renders during its useful economic life. Generally accepted accounting principles require that this cost be spread over the expected useful life of the [asset] in such a way as to allocate it as equitably as possible to the periods during which services are obtained from the use of the [asset]. This procedure is known as **depreciation accounting,** a system of accounting that aims to distribute the cost or other basic value of tangible capital assets, less salvage (if any), over the estimated useful life of the unit (which may be a group of assets) in a systematic and rational manner. It is a process of allocation, not of valuation. [ARB43, ch9C, ¶5] Not-for-profit organizations[a] [also] shall recognize the cost of using up the future economic benefits or service potentials of their long-lived tangible assets [as] depreciation. [FAS93, ¶5]

---

[a]The term *not-for-profit organizations* in this section encompasses all entities described by FASB Concepts Statement 4, *Objectives of Financial Reporting by Nonbusiness Organizations,* as possessing characteristics that distinguish them from business enterprises. Concepts Statement 4, paragraph 6, lists as the distinguishing characteristics of not-for-profit organizations (a) contributions of significant amounts of resources from resource providers who do not expect commensurate or proportionate pecuniary return, (b) operating purposes other than to provide goods or services at a profit, and (c) absence of ownership interests like those of business enterprises. Not-for-profit organizations have those characteristics in varying degrees. The term not-for-profit organizations encompasses the kinds of organizations covered by the AICPA specialized industry pronouncements: *[Audits of Providers of Health Care Services], Audits of Colleges and Universities, Audits of Voluntary Health and Welfare Organizations,* and Statement of Position 78-10, *Accounting Principles and Reporting Practices for Certain Nonprofit Organizations.* [FAS93, ¶1, fn1]

.101A Consistent with the accepted practice for land used as a building site,[b] depreciation need not be recognized on individual works of art or historical treasures whose economic benefit or service potential is used up so slowly that their estimated useful lives are extraordinarily long. A work of art or historical treasure shall be deemed to have that characteristic only if verifiable[c] evidence exists demonstrating that (a) the asset individually has cultural, aesthetic, or historical value that is worth preserving perpetually and (b) the holder has the technological and financial ability to protect and preserve essentially undiminished the service potential of the asset and is doing that. [FAS93, ¶6] [A] recognized cultural, aesthetic, or historical value and, generally, [an] already long existence have established each [work of art and historical treasure] as a member of a group of rare works with that characteristic. Most of them are acquired by purchase, gift, or discovery with that characteristic already having been demonstrated, and the holder or acquirer usually takes steps to protect and preserve it, for example, by keeping a work of art in a protective environment and limiting its use solely to display. While that characteristic is not limited to assets with an already long existence, an asset that has come into existence relatively recently cannot be assumed to have it in the absence of the verifiable evidence described above. For example, to put a painting in a protective environment is not by itself evidence of cultural, aesthetic, or historical value that is worth preserving perpetually. [FAS93, ¶36]

.101B The future economic benefits or service potentials of individual items comprising "collections" and of buildings and other structures—including those designated as landmarks, monuments, cathedrals, or historical treasures—are used up not only by wear and tear in intended uses but also by the continuous destructive effects of pollutants, vibrations, and so forth. The cultural, aesthetic, or historical values of those assets can be preserved, if at all, only by periodic major efforts to protect, clean, and restore them, usually at significant cost. Thus, depreciation of those assets [shall] be recognized. [FAS93, ¶35]

.101C Depreciation should be recognized, of course, on any capitalized costs of major preservation or restoration devices or efforts, which provide future economic benefits or

---

[b]The process of using up the future economic benefit or service potential of land often takes place over a period so long that its occurrence is imperceptible—land used as a building site is perhaps the most common example. In contrast, however, that process also sometimes occurs much more rapidly—land used as a site for toxic waste, as a source of gravel or ore, or for farming under conditions in which fertility dissipates relatively quickly and cannot be restored economically are examples. [FAS93, ¶34]

[c]*Verifiability* means that several measurers or observers are likely to obtain essentially the same measure or conclude that a description of an item faithfully represents what it purports to represent. (Refer to FASB Concepts Statement 2, *Qualitative Characteristics of Accounting Information,* paragraphs 81 through 89.) [FAS93, ¶6, fn2]

service potentials until the next expected preservation or restoration, regardless of whether depreciation is recognized on the asset being protected or restored. [FAS93, ¶37]

.102 Property, plant, and equipment shall not be written up by an enterprise to reflect appraisal, market, or current values which are above cost to the enterprise. This section is not intended to change accounting practices followed in connection with quasi reorganizations[1] or reorganizations. This section may not apply to foreign operations under unusual conditions such as serious inflation or currency devaluation. However, when the accounts of an enterprise with foreign operations are translated into U.S. currency for consolidation, such write-ups normally are eliminated. Whenever appreciation has been recorded on the books, income shall be charged with depreciation computed on the written-up amounts. [APB6, ¶17]

Application

.103 [Deleted 2/92 because of FASB Statement 109, *Accounting for Income Taxes*.]

.104 The declining-balance method is one that meets the requirements of being systematic and rational.[3] If the expected productivity or revenue-earning power of the asset is relatively greater during the earlier years of its life, or where maintenance charges tend to increase during later years, the declining-balance method may provide the most satisfactory allocation of cost. That conclusion also applies to other methods, including the sum-of-the-years'-digits method, that produce substantially similar results. [FAS109, ¶288(a)] Annuity methods of depreciation are not acceptable under generally accepted accounting principles applicable to enterprises in general. [FAS92, ¶37]

Disclosure

.105 Because of the significant effects on financial position and results of operations of the depreciation method or methods used, the following disclosures shall be made in the financial statements or in notes thereto:

a. Depreciation expense for the period
b. Balances of major classes of depreciable assets, by nature or function, at the balance sheet date
c. Accumulated depreciation, either by major classes of depreciable assets or in total, at the balance sheet date

---

[1]Refer to Section Q15, "Quasi Reorganizations." [APB6, ¶17, fn6]

[[2]Deleted 12/87 because guidance is no longer applicable.]

[3]Accounting Terminology Bulletin No. 1, *Review and Résumé*, paragraph 56. [FAS109, ¶288(a)]

d. A general description of the method or methods used in computing depreciation with respect to major classes of depreciable assets.

[APB12, ¶5]

.106 [Deleted 12/82 because of FASB Statement 71, *Accounting for the Effects of Certain Types of Regulation.*]

.107 [Deleted 12/86 because of FASB Statement 89, *Financial Reporting and Changing Prices.*]

Glossary

.401 **Depreciation accounting.** A system of accounting that aims to distribute the cost or other basic value of tangible capital assets, less salvage (if any), over the estimated useful life of the unit (which may be a group of assets) in a systematic and rational manner. It is a process of allocation, not of valuation. [ARB43, ch9C, ¶5]

(The next page is 14127.)

Sources: APB Opinion 15; APB Opinion 30;
AICPA Interpretations of APB Opinion 15;
AICPA Interpretations of APB Opinion 20;
FASB Statement 21; FASB Statement 85; FASB Statement 95;
FASB Statement 109; FASB Statement 111; FASB Interpretation 28;
FASB Interpretation 31; FASB Interpretation 38;
FASB Technical Bulletin 79-8

Summary

This section includes standards for determining and presenting earnings per share data in general purpose financial statements. It requires earnings per share data for income before extraordinary items and net income to be shown on the face of the income statement for all periods presented.

This section does not apply to mutual enterprises, registered investment enterprises, government-owned enterprises, nonprofit enterprises, parent company financial statements accompanied by consolidated financial statements, statements of wholly owned subsidiaries, or special purpose statements. In addition, it need not be applied by nonpublic enterprises as defined by this section.

Enterprises with simple capital structures (only common stock or no potentially dilutive securities) shall make a single presentation of earnings per share data on the face of the income statement. The single presentation (*earnings per common share*) shall be based on weighted average common stock outstanding during the period.

Enterprises with complex capital structures shall present two types of earnings per share data with equal prominence on the face of the income statement. The first presentation, *primary earnings per share* shall be based on weighted average common stock outstanding during the period and common stock assumed to be outstanding to reflect the dilutive effect of *common stock equivalents*. The second, fully diluted *earnings per share,* shall be based on weighted average common stock outstanding and additional common stock assumed to be outstanding to reflect the dilutive effect of common stock equivalents and all other potentially dilutive securities. Fully diluted earnings per share need not be reported if potentially dilutive securities, in the aggregate, dilute earnings per share by less than 3 percent.

Securities that enable their holders to obtain common stock are classified as either common stock equivalents or as other potentially dilutive securities solely for purposes of determining earnings per share. That classification is made at the time of issuance and generally does not change thereafter.

A common stock equivalent is a security that, because of its terms or the circumstances under which it was issued, is in substance equivalent to common stock. Stock options and warrants, including stock appreciation rights and other variable plan awards, are classified as common stock equivalents. From April 1, 1985, convertible securities that have an effective yield of less than two-thirds of the average Aa corporate bond yield at the time of issuance are also classified as common stock equivalents. The yield test to determine common stock equivalency for convertible securities for the period March 1, 1982 through March 31, 1985 was based on a cash yield of less than $66^2/_3$ percent of the average Aa corporate bond yield. The yield test for convertible securities issued after May 31, 1969 but prior to March 1, 1982 was based on a cash yield of less than $66^2/_3$ percent of the then current bank prime interest rate.

Stock options and warrants and their equivalents enter earnings per share computations under the treasury stock method. Under that method, exercise of options or warrants is assumed at the beginning of the period (or time of issuance, if later) and proceeds from the exercise are assumed to be used to repurchase common stock for the treasury. Common stock outstanding is assumed to increase by the difference between the number of shares issued and the number of shares purchased.

Convertible securities are included in earnings per share computations under the if-converted method. Under that method, the security is assumed to have been converted into common stock at the beginning of the period (or at issuance, if later). Interest deductions, net of related income taxes, relating to convertible debt and dividends on convertible preferred stock shall be taken into consideration in determining income applicable to common stock.

Applicability and Scope

.101 This section applies to financial presentations that purport to present results of operations of enterprises in conformity with generally accepted accounting principles and to summaries of those presentations, except as excluded in paragraph .102. Thus, it applies to enterprises whose capital structures include only **common stock** or common stock and **senior securities** and to those whose capital structures also include securities that should be considered the equivalent of common stock[1] in computing **earnings per share** data. [APB15, ¶5]

---

[1]In this section, the term **common stock equivalents** [is used to describe] those securities other than common stock that should be dealt with as common stock in the determination of earnings per share. [APB15, ¶5, fn1]

.102 This section does not apply to mutual enterprises that do not have outstanding common stock or common stock equivalents (for example, mutual savings banks, cooperatives, credit unions, and similar enterprises), to registered investment enterprises, to government-owned enterprises, or to nonprofit enterprises. This section also does not apply to parent company statements accompanied by consolidated financial statements, to statements of wholly owned subsidiaries, or to special purpose statements. [APB15, ¶6] [In addition,] the provisions of this section need not be applied by a **nonpublic enterprise** pending further action by the FASB.[2] [FAS21, ¶15] [Accordingly,] the information specified by this section [need not be disclosed] in a complete set of separately issued financial statements of a subsidiary, corporate joint venture, or other investee that is a nonpublic enterprise. [FAS21, ¶12] Although the presentation of earnings per share information is not required in the financial statements of nonpublic enterprises, any such information that is presented in the financial statements shall be consistent with the requirements of this section. [FAS21, ¶14]

Presentation on Face of Income Statement

.103 Earnings per share or net loss per share data shall be shown on the face of the income statement. [APB15, ¶12] The extent of the data to be presented and the captions used will vary with the complexity of the enterprise's capital structure, as discussed in the following paragraphs. [APB15, ¶12]

.104 Earnings per share amounts shall be presented for (a) income from continuing operations, [APB30, ¶9] (b) income before extraordinary items, [APB15, ¶13] (c) the cumulative effect of a change in accounting principle, [APB20, ¶20] and (d) net income. It may also be desirable to present earnings per share amounts for extraordinary items, if any. [APB15, ¶13] [Also], per share data for the results of discontinued operations and gain or loss from disposal of the business segment may be included on the face of the income statement or in a related note. [APB30, ¶9] [Refer to Section A06, "Accounting Changes," for additional guidance on disclosure of earnings per share information if there are changes in accounting principles.]

Simple Capital Structures

.105 The capital structures of many enterprises are relatively simple—that is, they either consist of only common stock or include no potentially **dilutive** convertible securities, **options, warrants,** or other rights that on conversion or exercise could

---

[2]This provision does not modify other generally accepted accounting principles or practices (such as those specified in Section C47, "Compensation to Employees: Stock Purchase and Option Plans," paragraph .123, and Section C16, "Capital Stock: Preferred Stock," paragraphs .101 and .102, that require disclosure of information concerning the capital structure of an enterprise). [FAS21, ¶12, fn3]

in the aggregate dilute[3] earnings per common share. In those cases, a single presentation expressed in terms such as *earnings per common share* on the face of the income statement (based on common shares outstanding and computed in accordance with the provisions of paragraphs .138 through .141) is the appropriate presentation of earnings per share data. [APB15, ¶14]

Complex Capital Structures

.106 Enterprises with capital structures other than those described in the preceding paragraph shall present two types of earnings per share data (**dual presentation**) with equal prominence on the face of the income statement. The first presentation is based on the outstanding common shares and those securities that are in substance equivalent to common shares and have a dilutive effect. The second is a pro forma presentation that reflects the dilution of earnings per share that would have occurred if *all* **contingent issuances** of common stock that would individually reduce earnings per share had taken place at the beginning of the period (or **time of issuance** of the convertible **security,** etc., if later). For convenience in this section, those two presentations are referred to as **primary earnings per share** and **fully diluted earnings per share,** respectively, and would, in certain circumstances discussed in paragraphs .110 through .114 be supplemented by other disclosures and other earnings per share data. [APB15, ¶15]

Dual Presentation

.107 If dual presentation of earnings per share data is required, the primary and fully diluted earnings per share amounts shall be presented with equal prominence on the face of the income statement. The difference between the primary and fully diluted earnings per share amounts shows the maximum extent of potential dilution of current earnings that conversions of securities that are not common stock equivalents could create. If the capital structure contains no common stock equivalents, the first may be designated "earnings per common share—assuming no dilution" and the second "earnings per common share—assuming full dilution." If common stock equivalents are present and dilutive, the primary amount may be designated "earnings per common and common equivalent share." Precise designations [are] not prescribed; enterprises [are] free to designate those dual presentations in a manner that best fits the circumstances provided they are in accord with the substance of this section. The term *earnings per common share* shall not be used without appropriate qualification except under the conditions discussed in paragraph .105. [APB15, ¶16]

---

[3]Any reduction of less than 3 percent in the aggregate need not be considered dilution in the computation and presentation of earnings per share data discussed throughout this section. In applying this test, only issues that reduce earnings per share shall be considered. [That] guideline [does not] imply that a similar measure should be applied in any circumstances other than the computation and presentation of earnings per share data under this section. [APB15, ¶15, fn2]

Periods Presented

.108 Earnings per share data shall be presented for all periods covered by the statement of income or summary of earnings. If potential dilution exists in any of the periods presented, the dual presentation of primary earnings per share and fully diluted earnings per share data shall be made for all periods presented. This information together with other disclosures required (refer to paragraphs .110 through .114) will give the reader an understanding of the extent and trend of the potential dilution. [APB15, ¶17]

.109 If results of operations of a prior period included in the statement of income or summary of earnings have been restated as a result of a prior period adjustment, earnings per share data given for the prior period shall be restated [refer to Section A35, "Adjustments of Financial Statements for Prior Periods"]. The effect of the restatement, expressed in per share terms, shall be disclosed in the year of restatement. [APB15, ¶18]

Additional Disclosures

Capital Structure

.110 The use of complex securities complicates earnings per share computations and makes additional disclosures necessary. Financial statements shall include a description, in summary form, sufficient to explain the pertinent rights and privileges of the various securities outstanding. Examples of information that shall be disclosed are dividend and liquidation preferences, participation rights, **call prices** and dates, **conversion** or **exercise prices** or rates and pertinent dates, sinking fund requirements, unusual voting rights, etc. [APB15, ¶19]

Dual Earnings per Share Data

.111 A schedule or note relating to the earnings per share data shall explain the bases on which both primary and fully diluted earnings per share are calculated. That information shall include identification of any issues regarded as common stock equivalents in the computation of primary earnings per share and the securities included in the computation of fully diluted earnings per share. It shall describe all assumptions and any resulting adjustments used in deriving the earnings per share data.[4] There shall also be disclosed the number of shares issued on conversion, exercise, or satisfaction of required conditions, etc., during at least the most recent annual fiscal period and any subsequent interim period presented.[5] [APB15, ¶20]

---

[4]Those computations shall give effect to all adjustments that would result from conversion: for example, dividends paid on convertible preferred stocks shall not be deducted from net income; interest and related expenses on convertible debt, less applicable income tax, shall be added to net income, and any other adjustments affecting net income because of those assumptions shall also be made (refer to paragraph .143). [APB15, ¶20, fn4]

[5]Refer to Section C08, "Capital Stock: Capital Transactions," paragraph .102. [APB15, ¶20, fn5]

.112 Computations or reconciliations may sometimes be desirable to provide a clear understanding of the manner in which the earnings per share amounts were obtained. That information may include data on each issue of securities entering into the computation of the primary and fully diluted earnings per share. It shall not, however, be shown on the face of the income statement or otherwise furnished in a manner implying that an earnings per share amount that ignores the effect of common stock equivalents (that is, earnings per share based on outstanding common shares only) constitutes an acceptable presentation of primary earnings per share. [APB15, ¶21]

Supplementary Earnings per Share Data

.113 Primary earnings per share shall be related to the capital structures existing during each of the various periods presented.[6] Although conversions ordinarily do not alter substantially the amount of capital employed in the business, they can significantly affect the trend in earnings per share data. Therefore, if conversions during the current period would have affected (either dilutively or incrementally) primary earnings per share if they had taken place at the beginning of the period, supplementary information shall be furnished (preferably in a note) for the latest period showing what primary earnings per share would have been if such conversions had taken place at the beginning of that period (or date of issuance of the security, if within the period). Similar supplementary per share earnings shall be furnished if conversions occur after the close of the period but before completion of the financial report. It may also be desirable to furnish supplementary per share data for each period presented, giving the cumulative retroactive effect of all such conversions or changes. However, primary earnings per share data shall not be adjusted retroactively for conversions. [APB15, ¶22]

.114 Occasionally a sale of common stock or common stock equivalents for cash occurs during the latest period presented or shortly after its close but before completion of the financial report. When a portion or all of the proceeds of such a sale have been used to retire preferred stock or debt, or are to be used for that purpose, supplementary earnings per share data shall be furnished (preferably in a note) to show what the earnings would have been for the latest fiscal year and any subsequent interim period presented if the retirement had taken place at the beginning of the respective period (or date of issuance of the retired security, if later). The number of shares of common stock whose proceeds are to be used to retire the preferred stock or debt shall be included in this computation. The bases of those supplementary computations shall be disclosed.[7] [APB15, ¶23]

---

[6]Refer to paragraphs .139, .140, and .153 through .155 for exceptions to that general rule. [APB15, ¶22, fn6]

[7]There may be other forms of recapitalization that should be reflected in a similar manner. [APB15, ¶23, fn7]

Primary Earnings per Share

.115 If an enterprise's capital structure is complex and either does not include common stock equivalents or includes common stock equivalents that do not have a dilutive effect, the primary earnings per share figures shall be based on the **weighted average number of shares** of common stock outstanding during the period. In those cases, potential dilutive effects of contingent issuances would be reflected in the fully diluted earnings per share amounts. Certain securities, however, are considered to be the equivalent of outstanding common stock and shall be recognized in the computation of primary earnings per share if they have a dilutive effect. [APB15, ¶24]

Nature of Common Stock Equivalents

.116 A common stock equivalent is a security that is not, in form, a common stock but that usually contains provisions to enable its holder to become a common stockholder and that, because of its terms and the circumstances under which it was issued, is in substance equivalent to a common stock. The holders of those securities can expect to participate in the appreciation of the value of the common stock resulting principally from the earnings and earnings potential of the issuing enterprise. That participation is essentially the same as that of a common stockholder except that the security may carry a specified dividend or interest rate yielding a return different from that received by a common stockholder. The attractiveness of this type of security to investors is often based principally on this potential right to share in increases in the earnings potential of the issuing enterprise rather than on its fixed return or other senior security characteristics. With respect to a convertible security, any difference in yield between it and the underlying common stock as well as any other senior characteristics of the convertible security become secondary. The value of a common stock equivalent is derived in large part from the value of the common stock to which it is related, and changes in its value tend to reflect changes in the value of the common stock. Neither conversion nor the imminence of conversion is necessary to cause a security to be a common stock equivalent. [APB15, ¶25]

.117 Outstanding convertible securities that have the foregoing characteristics and that meet the criteria set forth in this section for the determination of common stock equivalents at the time they are issued shall be considered the equivalent of common stock in computing primary earnings per share if the effect is dilutive. The recognition of common stock equivalents in the computation of primary earnings per share avoids the misleading implication that would otherwise result from the use of common stock only; use of the latter basis would place form over substance. [APB15, ¶26]

.118 In addition to convertible debt and convertible preferred stocks, the following types of securities are or may be considered as common stock equivalents:

14133

a. *Stock options and warrants (and their equivalents) and stock purchase contracts*—shall always be considered common stock equivalents (refer to paragraphs .124 through .127).

b. *Participating securities and two-class common stocks*—if their participation features enable their holders to share in the earnings potential of the issuing enterprise on substantially the same basis as common stock even though the securities may not give the holder the right to exchange its shares for common stock (refer to paragraphs .150 and .151).

c. *Contingent shares*—if shares are to be issued in the future on the mere passage of time (or are held in escrow pending the satisfaction of conditions unrelated to earnings or market value) they shall be considered as outstanding for the computation of earnings per share. If additional shares of stock are issuable for little or no consideration upon the satisfaction of certain conditions, they shall be considered as outstanding when the conditions are met (refer to paragraphs .152 through .155). [APB15, ¶27]

Determination of Common Stock Equivalents at Issuance

.119 Determination of whether a convertible security is a common stock equivalent shall be made only at the time of issuance and shall not be changed thereafter so long as the security remains outstanding. However, convertible securities outstanding or subsequently issued with the same terms as those of a common stock equivalent also shall be classified as common stock equivalents. However, dilutive effect of any convertible securities that were not common stock equivalents at time of their issuance shall be included only in the fully diluted earnings per share amount. [APB15, ¶28]

.120 Various factors shall be considered in determining the appropriate *time of issuance* in evaluating whether a security is substantially equivalent to a common stock. The time of issuance generally is the date when agreement as to terms has been reached and announced, even though subject to certain further actions, such as directors' or stockholders' approval. [APB15, ¶29] [Refer to paragraph .128 for guidance in determining whether stock appreciation rights or other variable plan awards are common stock equivalents.]

No Antidilution

.121 Computations of primary earnings per share shall not give effect to common stock equivalents or other contingent issuance for any period in which their inclusion would have the effect of increasing the earnings per share amount or decreasing the loss per share amount otherwise computed.[8] Consequently, while a security once determined to be a common stock equivalent retains that status, it may enter into the computation of primary earnings per share in one period and not in another. [APB15, ¶30]

Test of Common Stock Equivalent Status

Convertible Securities

.122 A convertible security that at the time of issuance has terms that make it for all practical purposes substantially equivalent to a common stock shall be regarded as a common stock equivalent. The complexity of convertible securities makes it impractical to establish definitive guidelines to encompass all the varying terms that might bear on this determination. [APB15, ¶31]

.123 [Deleted 3/85 because of FASB Statement 85, *Yield Test for Determining whether a Convertible Security Is a Common Stock Equivalent.*]

.123A A convertible security shall be considered a common stock equivalent if, at the time of issuance, it has an effective yield[9a] of less than $66^{2}/_{3}$ percent of the then current average Aa^{10} corporate bond yield.[10a] The effective yield[10b] shall be based on the security's stated annual interest or dividend payments,[10c] any original issuance pre-

---

[8]The presence of a common stock equivalent or other dilutive securities together with income from continuing operations and extraordinary items may result in diluting one of the per share amounts that is required to be disclosed on the face of the income statement, that is, income from continuing operations, income before extraordinary items and before the cumulative effect of accounting changes, if any, and net income—while increasing another. In [those circumstances], the common stock equivalent or other dilutive securities shall be recognized for all computations even though they have an antidilutive effect on one of the per share amounts. [APB30, ¶9, fn3]

[9][Deleted 3/85 because of FASB Statement 85.]

[9a]In computing effective yield, interest shall be compounded on the same basis as publicly traded bonds in the country that the convertible securities are sold or issued. In the United States, interest is generally compounded on a semiannual basis. [FAS85, ¶3, fn*]

[10]The designation Aa refers to the quality of the individual bonds that make up the yield applied in the yield test. In the context of this section, Aa [is intended] to refer to bonds of equal quality to those rated Aa by either *Moody's* or *Standard & Poor's*. Those two organizations define Aa bonds as being of high quality and as having a very strong capacity to pay interest and repay principal. Bond yield information is widely and regularly published by a number of financial institutions and investor information services.

For purposes of applying the yield test, the *average* bond yield shall be based on bond yields for a brief period of time, for example, one week, including or immediately preceding the date of issuance of the security being tested. [FAS85, ¶3, fn†]

[10a]If convertible securities are sold or issued outside the United States, the most comparable long-term yield in the foreign country should be used for this test. [FAS85, ¶3, fn‡]

[10b]Effective yield for a security that does not have a stated maturity date shall be computed as the ratio of the security's stated annual interest or dividend payments to its market price at issuance. [FAS85, ¶3, fn§]

[10c]If the security's stated annual interest or dividend payments are adjustable, effective yield shall be computed based on scheduled formula adjustments and formula information at issuance. [FAS85, ¶3, fn#]

mium or discount, and any call premium or discount and shall be the lowest of the yield to maturity and the yields to all call dates. The computation of effective yield does not include considerations of put options or changing conversion rates. [FAS85, ¶3]

Options, Warrants, and Their Equivalents

.124 Options, warrants, and similar arrangements usually have no yield and derive their value from their right to obtain common stock at specified prices for an extended period. Therefore, those securities shall be regarded as common stock equivalents at all times. Other securities, usually having a low yield, require the payment of cash on conversion and shall be considered the equivalents of warrants for the purposes of this section. Accordingly, they shall also be regarded as common stock equivalents at all times. Primary earnings per share shall reflect the dilution that would result from exercise or conversion of those securities and use of the funds, if any, obtained. Options and warrants (and their equivalents) shall, therefore, be treated as if they had been exercised and earnings per share data shall be computed as described in the following paragraphs. The computation of earnings per share shall not, however, reflect exercise or conversion of any such security[11] if its effect on earnings per share is antidilutive (refer to paragraph .121) except as indicated in paragraph .127. [APB15, ¶35]

.125 Except as indicated in this paragraph and in paragraphs .126 and .127, the amount of dilution to be reflected in earnings per share data shall be computed by application of the **treasury stock method.** Under that method, earnings per share data are computed as if the options and warrants were exercised at the beginning of the period (or at time of issuance, if later) and as if the funds obtained thereby were used to purchase common stock at the average market price during the period.[12] As a practical matter, [it is recommended] that assumption of exercise not be reflected in earnings per share data until the market price of the common stock obtainable has been in excess of the exercise price for substantially all of three consecutive months ending with the last month of the period to which earnings per share data relate. Under the treasury stock method, options and warrants have a dilutive effect (and are, therefore, reflected in earnings per share computations) only when the average market price of the common stock obtainable on exercise during the period exceeds the exercise price of the options or warrants. Previously reported earnings per share amounts shall not be retroactively adjusted, in the case of options and warrants, as a result of

---

[11]Reasonable grouping of like securities may be appropriate. [APB15, ¶35, fn11]

[12]For example, if an enterprise has 10,000 warrants outstanding, exercisable at $54, and the average market price of the common stock during the reporting period is $60, the $540,000 that would be realized from exercise of the warrants and issuance of 10,000 shares would be an amount sufficient to acquire 9,000 shares; thus, 1,000 shares would be added to the outstanding common shares in computing primary earnings per share for the period. [APB15, ¶36, fn12]

changes in market prices of common stock. Funds obtained by issuers from the exercise of options and warrants are used in many ways with a wide variety of results that cannot be anticipated. Application of the treasury stock method in earnings per share computations is not based on an assumption that the funds will or could actually be used in that manner. In the usual case, it represents a practical approach to reflecting the dilutive effect that would result from the issuance of common stock under option and warrant agreements at an effective price below the current market price. However, the treasury stock method is inappropriate, or shall be modified, in certain cases described in paragraphs .126 and .127. [APB15, ¶36]

.126 Some warrants contain provisions that permit, or require, the tendering of debt (usually at face amount) or other securities of the issuer in payment for all or a portion of the exercise price. The terms of some debt securities issued with warrants require that the proceeds of the exercise of the related warrants be applied toward retirement of the debt. As indicated in paragraph .124, some convertible securities require cash payments on conversion and are, therefore, considered to be the equivalent of warrants. In all of those cases, the **if-converted method** (refer to paragraph .142) shall be applied as if retirement or conversion of the securities had occurred and as if the excess proceeds, if any, had been applied to the purchase of common stock under the treasury-stock method. However, exercise of the options and warrants shall not be reflected in the computation unless for the period specified in paragraph .125 either (a) the market price of the related common stock exceeds the exercise price or (b) the security that may be (or must be) tendered is selling at a price below that at which it may be tendered under the option or warrant agreement and the resulting discount is sufficient to establish an effective exercise price below the market price of the common stock that can be obtained upon exercise. Similar treatment shall be followed for preferred stock bearing similar provisions or other securities having conversion options permitting payment of cash for a more favorable **conversion rate** from the standpoint of the investor. [APB15, ¶37]

.127 The treasury stock method of reflecting use of proceeds from options and warrants may not adequately reflect potential dilution if options or warrants to acquire a substantial number of common shares are outstanding. Accordingly, if the number of shares of common stock obtainable on exercise of outstanding options and warrants in the aggregate exceeds 20 percent of the number of common shares outstanding at the end of the period for which the computation is being made, the treasury stock method shall be modified in determining the dilutive effect of the options and warrants on earnings per share data. In those circumstances, all the options and warrants shall be assumed to have been exercised and the aggregate proceeds therefrom to have been applied in two steps:

a. [First,] as if the funds obtained were first applied to the repurchase of outstanding common shares at the average market price during the period (treasury stock method) but not to exceed 20 percent of the outstanding shares

b. [Second,] as if the balance of the funds were applied first to reduce any short-term or long-term borrowings and any remaining funds were invested in U.S. government securities or commercial paper, with appropriate recognition of any income tax effect

The results of steps (a) and (b) of the computation (whether dilutive or antidilutive) shall be aggregated and, if the net effect is dilutive, shall enter into the earnings per share computation.[13] [APB15, ¶38]

Treatment of Stock Compensation Plans in EPS Computations

.128 Stock appreciation rights and other variable plan awards are common stock equivalents to the extent payable in stock for purposes of applying this section. Stock appreciation rights and other variable plan awards payable only in cash are

---

[13]The following are examples of the application of paragraph .127:

	Case 1	Case 2
Assumptions:		
Net income for year	$ 4,000,000	$ 2,000,000
Common shares outstanding	3,000,000	3,000,000
Options and warrants outstanding to purchase		
equivalent shares	1,000,000	1,000,000
20% limitation on assumed repurchase	600,000	600,000
Exercise price per share	$15	$15
Average and year-end market value per common		
share to be used (refer to paragraph .135)	$20	$12
Computations:		
Application of assumed proceeds ($15,000,000):		
Toward repurchase of outstanding common		
shares at applicable market value	$12,000,000	$ 7,200,000
Reduction of debt	3,000,000	7,800,000
	$15,000,000	$15,000,000
Adjustment of net income:		
Actual net income	$ 4,000,000	$ 2,000,000
Interest reduction (6%) less 50% tax effect	90,000	234,000
Adjusted net income (A)	$ 4,090,000	$ 2,234,000
Adjustment of shares outstanding:		
Actual outstanding	3,000,000	3,000,000
Net additional shares issuable (1,000,000 − 600,000)	400,000	400,000
Adjusted shares outstanding (B)	3,400,000	3,400,000
Earnings per share:		
Before adjustment	$1.33	$.67
After adjustment (A ÷ B)	$1.20	$.66

[APB15, ¶38, fn13]

not common stock equivalents for the computation of earnings per share under this section. [FIN28, ¶6] If stock appreciation rights or other variable plan awards are payable in stock or in cash at the election of the enterprise or the employee, the decision of whether those rights or awards are common stock equivalents shall be made according to the terms most likely to be elected based on the facts available each period. It shall be presumed that those rights or awards will be paid in stock, but that presumption may be overcome if past experience or a stated policy provides a reasonable basis to believe that the rights or awards will be paid partially or wholly in cash. [FIN31, ¶6] Paragraphs .128 through .131 do not alter the treatment of shares issuable contingent on certain conditions being met, as discussed in paragraphs .152 through .155. [FIN31, ¶2] [The application of paragraphs .128 through .131 is illustrated in paragraphs .169 through .175.]

.129 In applying the treasury-stock method of paragraph .125 to stock options, including stock appreciation rights and other variable plan awards, the exercise proceeds of the options are the sum of the amount the employee must pay, the amount of measurable compensation ascribed to future services and not yet charged to expense (whether or not accrued), and the amount of any *windfall* tax benefit[14] to be credited[15] to capital. Exercise proceeds shall not include compensation ascribed to past services. [FIN31, ¶3]

.130 The dilutive effect of stock appreciation rights and other variable plan awards on primary earnings per share shall be computed using the average aggregate compensation and average market price for the period. The market price of an enterprise's stock and the resulting aggregate compensation used to compute the dilutive effect of stock appreciation rights and other variable plan awards in fully diluted earnings per share computations shall be the more dilutive of the market price and aggregate compensation at the close of the period being reported on or the average market price and average aggregate compensation for that period.[16] [FIN31, ¶4]

.130A Junior stock plans are variable plans for purposes of computing earnings per share under the provisions of this section. Paragraph .128 provides that variable plan awards are common stock equivalents to the extent payable in stock. Paragraphs .128

---

[14]The *windfall* tax benefit is the tax credit resulting from a tax deduction for compensation in excess of compensation expense recognized for financial reporting purposes. That credit arises from an increase in the market price of the stock under option between the measurement date (as defined in Section C47) and the date at which the compensation deduction for income tax purposes is determinable. The amount of the windfall tax benefit shall be determined by a with-and-without computation. [FIN31, ¶3, fn1]

[15]Section C47, paragraph .117, states that there may be instances when the tax deduction for compensation is less than the compensation expense recognized for financial reporting purposes. If the resulting difference in income tax will be deducted from capital in accordance with that paragraph, such taxes to be deducted from capital shall be treated as a reduction of exercise proceeds. [FIN31, ¶3, fn2]

[16]If the rights or awards were granted during the period, the shares issuable must be weighted to reflect the portion of the period during which the rights or awards were outstanding. [FIN31, ¶4, fn3]

through .131 and .169 through .176 provide guidance in applying the treasury stock method to variable plan awards. [FIN38, ¶7]

.131 If an enterprise has a combination plan allowing the enterprise or the employee to make an election involving stock appreciation rights or other variable plan awards, earnings per share for a period shall be computed based on the terms used in the computation of compensation for that period. [FIN31, ¶5]

Nonrecognition of Common Stock Equivalents in Financial Statements

.132 The designation of securities as common stock equivalents in this section is solely for the purpose of determining primary earnings per share. No changes from present practices are recommended in the accounting for such securities, in their presentation within the financial statements or in the manner of determining net assets per common share. Information is available in the financial statements and elsewhere for readers to make judgments as to the present and potential status of the various securities outstanding. [APB15, ¶39]

Fully Diluted Earnings per Share

No Antidilution

.133 The purpose of the fully diluted earnings per share presentation is to show the maximum potential dilution of current earnings per share on a prospective basis. Consequently, computations of fully diluted earnings per share for each period shall exclude those securities whose conversion, exercise, or other contingent issuance would have the effect of increasing the earnings per share amount or decreasing the loss per share amount[17] for the period. [APB15, ¶40]

When Required

.134 Fully diluted earnings per share data shall be presented on the face of the statement of income for each period presented if shares of common stock (a) were issued during the period on conversions, exercise, etc., or (b) were contingently issuable at the close of any period presented and if primary earnings per share for such period would have been affected (either dilutively or incrementally) had the actual issuances taken place at the beginning of the period or would have been reduced had the contingent issuances taken place at the beginning of the period. The above contingencies may result from the existence of (a) senior stock or debt that is convertible into common shares but is not a common stock equivalent, (b) options or warrants, or (c) agreements for the issuance of common shares upon the satisfaction of certain conditions (for example, the attainment of specified higher levels of earnings following a business combination). The computation shall be based on the assumption that all those issued and issuable shares were outstanding from the beginning of the period (or from the time the contingency

---

[17]Refer to paragraph .121, footnote 8. [APB15, ¶40, fn14]

arose, if after the beginning of the period). Previously reported fully diluted earnings per share amounts shall not be retroactively adjusted for subsequent conversions or subsequent changes in the market prices of the common stock. [APB15, ¶41]

.135 The methods described in paragraphs .125 through .127 shall be used to compute fully diluted earnings per share if dilution results from outstanding options and warrants; however, to reflect maximum potential dilution, the market price at the close of the period reported on shall be used to determine the number of shares that would be assumed to be repurchased (under the treasury stock method) if that market price is higher than the average price used in computing primary earnings per share (refer to paragraph .121). Common shares issued on exercise of options or warrants during each period shall be included in fully diluted earnings per share from the beginning of the period or date of issuance of the options or warrants if later; the computation for the portion of the period prior to the date of exercise shall be based on market prices of the common stock when exercised. [APB15, ¶42]

Situations Not Covered in This Section

.136 It is impracticable to cover all possible conditions and circumstances that may be encountered in computing earnings per share. If situations not expressly covered in this section occur, however, they shall be dealt with in accordance with their substance, giving cognizance to the guidelines and criteria outlined in this section. [APB15, ¶43]

Computational Guidelines

.137 The determination of earnings per share data required under this section reflects the complexities of the capital structures of some enterprises. The calculations shall give effect to matters such as stock dividends and splits, business combinations, changes in conversion rates, etc. Guidelines that shall be used in dealing with some of the more common computational matters are set forth in paragraphs .138 through .161. [APB15, ¶44]

Weighted Average

.138 Computations of earnings per share data shall be based on the weighted average number of common shares and common share equivalents outstanding during each period presented. Use of a weighted average is necessary so that the effect of increases or decreases in outstanding shares on earnings per share data is related to the portion of the period during which the related consideration affected operations. Reacquired shares shall be excluded from date of their acquisition. [APB15, ¶47]

Stock Dividends or Splits

.139 If the number of common shares outstanding increases as a result of a stock dividend or stock split[18] or decreases as a result of a reverse split, the computations shall give retroactive recognition to an appropriate equivalent change in capital structure for all periods presented. If changes in common stock resulting from stock dividends or stock splits or reverse splits have been consummated after the close of the period but before completion of the financial report, the per share computations shall be based on the new number of shares because the readers' primary interest is presumed to be related to the current capitalization. If per share computations reflect those changes in the number of shares after the close of the period, that fact shall be disclosed. [APB15, ¶48]

Business Combinations and Reorganization

.140 If shares are issued to acquire a business in a transaction accounted for as a purchase, the computation of earnings per share shall give recognition to the existence of the new shares only from the date the acquisition took place. If a business combination is accounted for as a pooling of interests, the computation shall be based on the aggregate of the weighted average outstanding shares of the constituent enterprises, adjusted to equivalent shares of the surviving enterprise for all periods presented. This difference in treatment reflects the fact that in a purchase the results of operations of the acquired enterprise are included in the statement of income only from the date of acquisition, whereas in a pooling of interests the results of operations are combined for all periods presented. In reorganizations, the computations shall be based on analysis of the particular transaction according to the criteria in this section. [APB15, ¶49]

Claims of Senior Securities

.141 The claims of senior securities on earnings of a period shall be deducted from net income (and also from income before extraordinary items if an amount therefor appears in the statement) before computing earnings per share. Dividends on cumulative preferred senior securities, whether or not earned, shall be deducted from net income.[19] If there is a net loss, the amount of the loss shall be increased by any cumulative dividends for the period on those preferred stocks. If interest or preferred dividends are cumulative only if earned, no adjustment of this type is required, except to the extent of income available therefor. If interest or preferred dividends are not cumulative, only the interest accruable or dividends declared shall be deducted. In all cases, the effect that has been given to rights of senior securities in arriving at the earnings per share shall be disclosed. [APB15, ¶50]

---

[18]Refer to Section C20, "Capital Stock: Stock Dividends and Stock Splits." [APB15, ¶48, fn15]

[19]The per share and aggregate amounts of cumulative preferred dividends in arrears shall be disclosed. [APB15, ¶50, fn16]

Use of If-Converted Method of Computation

.142 If convertible securities are deemed to be common stock equivalents for the purpose of computing primary earnings per share, or are assumed to have been converted for the purpose of computing fully diluted earnings per share, the securities shall be assumed to have been converted at the beginning of the earliest period reported (or at time of issuance, if later). Interest charges applicable to convertible securities and nondiscretionary adjustments that would have been made to items based on net income or income before taxes, such as profit-sharing expense, certain royalties, and investment credit, or preferred dividends applicable to the convertible securities shall be taken into account in determining the balance of income applicable to common stock. As to primary earnings per share, that amount shall be divided by the total of the average outstanding common shares and the number of shares that would have been issued on conversion or exercise of common stock equivalents.[20] As to fully diluted earnings per share, that amount shall be divided by the total of the average outstanding common shares plus the number of shares applicable to conversions during the period from the beginning of the period to the date of conversion and the number of shares that would have been issued on conversion or exercise of any other security that might dilute earnings. [APB15, ¶51]

.143 The if-converted method recognizes the fact that the holders of convertible securities cannot share in distributions of earnings applicable to the common stock unless they relinquish their right to senior distributions. Conversion is assumed and earnings applicable to common stock and common stock equivalents are determined before distributions to holders of those securities. [APB15, ¶52]

.144 The if-converted method also recognizes the fact that a convertible issue can participate in earnings, through dividends or interest, either as a senior security or as a common stock, but not both. The **two-class method** (refer to paragraph .146) does not recognize that limitation and may attribute to common stock an amount of earnings per share less than if the convertible security had actually been converted. The amount of earnings per share on common stock as computed under the two-class method is affected by the amount of dividends declared on the common stock. [APB15, ¶53]

Use of Two-Class Method of Computation

.145 Although the two-class method is considered inappropriate with respect to the securities described in paragraph .142, its use may be necessary in the case of participating securities and two-class common stock. (Refer to paragraphs .150 and .151 for discussion of those securities.) That is the case, for example, when those securities are not convertible into common stock. [APB15, ¶54]

---

[20]Determined as to options and warrants by application of the method described in paragraphs .125 through .127. [APB15, ¶51, fn17]

.146 Under the two-class method, common stock equivalents are treated as common stock with a dividend rate different from the dividend rate on the common stock and, therefore, conversion of convertible securities is not assumed. No use of proceeds is assumed. Distributions to holders of senior securities, common stock equivalents, and common stock are first deducted from net income. The remaining amount (the undistributed earnings) is divided by the total of common shares and common share equivalents. Per share distributions to the common stockholders are added to that per share amount to arrive at primary earnings per share. [APB15, ¶55]

Delayed Effectiveness and Changing Conversion Rates or Exercise Prices

.147 In some cases, a conversion option does not become effective until a future date; in others, conversion becomes more (or less) advantageous to the security holder at some later date as the conversion rate increases (or decreases), generally over an extended period. For example, an issue may be convertible into 1 share of common stock in the first year, 1.10 shares in the second year, 1.20 shares in the third year, and so forth. Frequently, those securities receive little or no cash dividends. Hence, under those circumstances, their value is derived principally from their conversion or exercise option and they would be deemed to be common stock equivalents under the yield test previously described (refer to paragraph .123A).[21] Similarly, the right to exercise options or warrants may be deferred or the exercise price may increase or decrease. [APB15, ¶56]

Conversion Rate or Exercise Price to Be Used

Primary Earnings per Share

.148 The conversion rate or exercise price of a common stock equivalent in effect during each period presented shall be used in computing primary earnings per share, with the exceptions stated in this paragraph. Prior period primary earnings per share shall not be restated for changes in the conversion ratio or exercise price. If options, warrants, or other common stock equivalents are not immediately exercisable or convertible, the earliest effective exercise price or conversion rate if any during the succeeding five years shall be used. If a convertible security having an increasing conversion rate is issued in exchange for another class of security of the issuing enterprise and is convertible back into the same or a similar security, and if a conversion rate equal to or greater than the original exchange rate becomes effective during the period of convertibility, the conversion rate used in the computation shall not result in a reduction in the number of common shares (or common share equivalents) existing before the original exchange took place until a greater rate becomes effective. [APB15, ¶57]

---

[21]An increasing conversion rate shall not be accounted for as a stock dividend. [APB15, ¶56, fn18]

Fully Diluted Earnings per Share

.149 Fully diluted earnings per share computations shall be based on the most advantageous (from the standpoint of the security holder) conversion or exercise rights that become effective within 10 years following the closing date of the period being reported on.[22] Conversion or exercise options that are not effective until after 10 or more years may be expected to be of limited significance because (a) investors' decisions are not likely to be influenced substantially by events beyond 10 years, and (b) it is questionable whether they are relevant to current operating results. [APB15, ¶58]

Participating Securities and Two-Class Common

.150 The capital structures of some enterprises include:

a.   Securities that may participate in dividends with common stocks according to a predetermined formula (for example, two for one) with, at times, an upper limit on the extent of participation (for example, up to but not beyond a specified amount per share)
b.   A class of common stock with different dividend rates or voting rights from those of another class of common stock, but without prior or senior rights

Additionally, some of those securities are convertible into common stock. Earnings per share computations relating to certain types of participating securities may require the use of the two-class method (refer to paragraphs .145 and .146). [APB15, ¶59]

.151 Because of the variety of features that those securities possess, frequently representing combinations of the features referred to above, it is not practicable to set out specific guidelines as to whether they should be considered common stock equivalents. Dividend participation does not per se make a security a common stock equivalent. A determination of the status of one of those securities shall be based on an analysis of all the characteristics of the security, including the ability to share in the earnings potential of the issuing enterprise on substantially the same basis as the common stock. [APB15, ¶60]

Issuance Contingent on Certain Conditions

.152 At times, agreements call for the issuance of additional shares contingent on certain conditions being met. Frequently those conditions are either:

---

[22]The conversion rate shall also reflect the cumulative effect of any stock dividends on the preferred stock that the enterprise has contracted or otherwise committed itself to issue within the next 10 years. [APB15, ¶58, fn19]

a. The maintenance of current earnings levels
b. The attainment of specified increased earnings

Alternatively, agreements sometimes provide for immediate issuance of the maximum number of shares issuable in the transaction with some to be placed in escrow and later returned to the issuer if specified conditions are not met. For purposes of computing earnings per share, contingently returnable shares placed in escrow shall be treated in the same manner as contingently issuable shares. [APB15, ¶61]

.153 If attainment or maintenance of a level of earnings is the condition, and if that level is currently being attained, the additional shares shall be considered as outstanding for the purpose of computing both primary and fully diluted earnings per share. If attainment of increased earnings reasonably above the present level or maintenance of increased earnings above the present level over a period of years is the condition, the additional shares shall be considered as outstanding only for the purpose of computing fully diluted earnings per share (but only if dilution is the result); for that computation, earnings shall be adjusted to give effect to the increase in earnings specified by the particular agreements (if different levels of earnings are specified, the level that would result in the largest potential dilution shall be used). Previously reported earnings per share data shall not be restated to give retroactive effect to shares subsequently issued as a result of attainment of specified increased earnings levels. If on expiration of the term of the agreement providing for contingent issuance of additional shares the conditions have not been met, the shares shall not be considered outstanding in that year. Previously reported earnings per share data shall then be restated to give retroactive effect to the removal of the contingency. [APB15, ¶62]

.154 The number of shares contingently issuable may depend on the market price of the stock at a future date. In that case, computations of earnings per share shall reflect the number of shares that would be issuable based on the market price at the close of the period being reported on. Prior period earnings per share shall be restated if the number of shares issued or contingently issuable subsequently changes because the market price changes. [APB15, ¶63]

.155 In some cases, the number of shares contingently issuable may depend on both future earnings and future prices of the shares. In that case, the number of shares that would be issuable shall be based on both conditions, that is, market prices and earnings to date as they exist at the end of each period being reported on. (For example, if (a) a certain number of shares will be issued at the end of three years following an acquisition if earnings of the acquired enterprise increase during those three years by a specified amount and (b) a stipulated number of additional shares will be issued if the value of the shares issued in the acquisition is not at least a designated amount at the end of the three-year period, the number of shares to be included in the earnings per share for each period shall be determined by reference to the cumulative earnings of the acquired enterprise and the value of the shares at the end of the latest period.) Prior period earnings per share shall be restated if the number of shares issued or contingently issuable subsequently changes from the number of shares previously included in the earnings per share computation. [APB15, ¶64]

Securities of Subsidiaries

.156 At times, subsidiaries issue securities that should be considered common stock equivalents from the standpoint of consolidated and parent company financial statements for the purpose of computing earnings per share. This could occur when convertible securities, options, warrants, or common stock issued by the subsidiary are in the hands of the public and the subsidiary's results of operations are either consolidated or reflected in the equity method. Circumstances in which conversion or exercise of a subsidiary's securities shall be assumed for the purpose of computing the consolidated and parent company earnings per share, or that would otherwise require recognition in the computation of earnings per share data, include those in which:

a.   *As to the subsidiary:*
  (1) Certain of the subsidiary's securities are common stock equivalents in relation to its own common stock.
  (2) Other of the subsidiary's convertible securities, although not common stock equivalents in relation to its own common stock, would enter into the computation of its fully diluted earnings per share.
b.   *As to the parent:*
  (1) The subsidiary's securities are convertible into the parent company's common stock.
  (2) The subsidiary issues options and warrants to purchase the parent company's common stock.

The treatment of those securities for the purpose of consolidated and parent company reporting of earnings per share is discussed in paragraphs .157 through .160. [APB15, ¶65]

.157 If a subsidiary has dilutive warrants or options outstanding or dilutive convertible securities that are common stock equivalents from the standpoint of the subsidiary, consolidated and parent company primary earnings per share shall include the portion of the subsidiary's income that would be applicable to the consolidated group based on its holdings and the subsidiary's primary earnings per share (refer to paragraph .132). [APB15, ¶66]

.158 If a subsidiary's convertible securities are not common stock equivalents from the standpoint of the subsidiary, only the portion of the subsidiary's income that would be applicable to the consolidated group based on its holdings and the fully diluted earnings per share of the subsidiary shall be included in consolidated and parent company fully diluted earnings per share (refer to paragraph .133). [APB15, ¶67]

.159 If a subsidiary's securities are convertible into its parent company's stock, they shall be considered among the common stock equivalents of the parent company for the purpose of computing consolidated and parent company primary and fully diluted earnings per share if the conditions set forth in paragraph .123A exist. If those conditions do not exist, the subsidiary's convertible securities shall be included in the computation of the consolidated and parent company fully diluted earnings per share only. [APB15, ¶68]

.160 If a subsidiary issues options or warrants to purchase stock of the parent company, they shall be considered common stock equivalents by the parent in computing consolidated and parent company primary and fully diluted earnings per share. [APB15, ¶69]

Dividends per Share

.161 Dividends constitute historical facts and usually are so reported. However, in certain cases, such as those affected by stock dividends or splits or reverse splits, the presentation of dividends per share shall be made in terms of the current equivalent of the number of common shares outstanding at the time of the dividend. A disclosure problem exists in presenting data as to dividends per share following a pooling of interests. In those cases, it is usually preferable to disclose the dividends declared per share by the principal constituent and to disclose, in addition, either the amount per equivalent or the total amount for each period for the other constituent, with appropriate explanation of the circumstances. If dividends per share are presented on other than an historical basis, the basis of presentation shall be disclosed. [APB15, ¶70]

Illustrative Statements

.162 The following illustrates the disclosure of earnings per share data. The format of the disclosure is illustrative only, and does not necessarily reflect a preference. [APB15, Appendix C]

Earnings per Share for a Simple Capital Structure

.163 Exhibit 163A illustrates the disclosure of earnings per share data for an enterprise with a simple capital structure (refer to paragraph .105). The facts assumed for Exhibit 163A are as follows:

	Number of Shares	
	19X8	**19X7**
Common stock outstanding:		
Beginning of year	3,300,000	3,300,000
End of year	3,300,000	3,300,000
Issued or acquired during year	None	None
Common stock reserved under		
employee stock options granted	7,200	7,200
Weighted average number of shares	3,300,000	3,300,000

Note: Shares issuable under employee stock options are excluded from the weighted average number of shares on the assumption that their effect is not dilutive (refer to paragraph .105). [APB15, Appendix C]

Exhibit 163A

**Disclosure of Earnings per Share
with a Simple Capital Structure**

	Thousands Except per share data	
(Bottom of Income Statement)	**19X8**	**19X7**
Income before extraordinary item	$ 9,150	$ 7,650
Extraordinary item—[description of		
transaction] less applicable income taxes	900	—
Net Income	$10,050	$ 7,650
Earnings per common share:		
Income before extraordinary item	$ 2.77	$ 2.32
Extraordinary item	.28	—
Net Income	$ 3.05	$ 2.32

[APB15, Appendix C]

Earnings per Share for Complex Capital Structure

.164 Exhibit 167A illustrates the disclosure of earnings per share data for an enterprise with a complex capital structure (refer to paragraph .106). The facts assumed for Exhibit 167A are as follows:

a. *Market Price of Common Stock*—The market price of the common stock was as follows:

	19X8	**19X7**	**19X6**
Average Price:			
First quarter	50	45	40
Second quarter	60	52	41
Third quarter	70	50	40
Fourth quarter	70	50	45
December 31 closing price	72	51	44

b. *Cash Dividends*—Cash dividends of $0.125 per common share were declared and paid for each quarter of 19X6 and 19X7. Cash dividends of $0.25 per common share were declared and paid for each quarter of 19X8.

c. *Convertible Debentures*—Four-percent, [20-year] convertible debentures with a principal amount of $10,000,000 were sold for cash at a price of 100 in the last quarter of 19X6. Each $100 debenture was convertible into 2 shares of common stock. No debentures were converted during 19X6 or 19X7. The entire issue was converted at the beginning of the third quarter of 19X8 because the issue was called by the enterprise. Those convertible debentures were not common stock equivalents under the terms of this section. [APB15, Appendix C] The average Aa corporate bond yield as defined in paragraph .123A [FAS111, ¶8(g)] at the time the debentures were sold in the last quarter of 19X6 was 6 percent. The debentures carried a coupon interest rate of 4 percent and had a market value of $100 at issuance. The [effective] yield of 4 percent was not less than $66\,2/3$ percent of the [APB15, Appendix C] average Aa corporate bond yield as defined in paragraph .123A. [FAS111, ¶8(g)] [Effective] yield is the same as the coupon interest rate in this case only because the market value at issuance was $100.

d. *Convertible Preferred Stock*—Six hundred thousand shares of convertible preferred stock were issued for assets in a purchase transaction at the beginning of the second quarter of 19X7. The annual dividend on each share of the convertible preferred stock is $0.20. Each share is convertible into one share of common stock. The convertible stock had a market value of $53 at the time of issuance and was therefore a common stock equivalent under the terms of this section at the time of its issuance because the [effective] yield was only 0.4 percent and the [APB15, Appendix C] average Aa corporate bond yield as defined in paragraph .123A [FAS111, ¶8(g)] was 5.5 percent. Holders of 500,000 shares of this convertible preferred stock converted their preferred stock into common stock during 19X8 because the cash dividend on the common stock exceeded the cash dividend on the preferred stock.

e. *Warrants*—Warrants to buy 500,000 shares of common stock at $60 per share for a period of 5 years were issued along with the convertible preferred stock mentioned above. No warrants have been exercised. (Note that the number of shares issuable on exercise of the warrants is less than 20 percent of outstanding common shares; hence paragraph .127 is not applicable.) The number of common shares represented by the warrants (refer to paragraph .125) was 71,428 for each of the third and fourth quarters of 19X8 ($60 exercise price × 500,000 warrants = $30,000,000; $30,000,000 ÷ $70 share market price = 428,572 shares; 500,000 shares − 428,572 shares = 71,428 shares). No shares were deemed to be represented by the warrants for the second quarter of 19X8 or for any preceding quarter (refer to paragraph .125) because the market price of the stock did not exceed the exercise price for substantially all of three consecutive months until the third quarter of 19X8.

f. *Common Stock*—The number of shares of common stock outstanding were as follows:

	19X8	19X7
Beginning of year	3,300,000	3,300,000
Conversion of preferred stock	500,000	—
Conversion of debentures	200,000	—
End of year	4,000,000	3,300,000

[APB15, Appendix C]

Weighted Average Number of Shares

.165 The weighted average number of shares of common stock and common stock equivalents was determined as follows:

	19X8	19X7
Common stock:		
Shares outstanding from beginning of period	3,300,000	3,300,000
500,000 shares issued on conversion of preferred stock; assume issuance evenly during year	250,000	—
200,000 shares issued on conversion of convertible debentures at beginning of third quarter of 19X8	100,000	—
	3,650,000	3,300,000
Common stock equivalents:		
600,000 shares convertible preferred stock issued at the beginning of the second quarter of 19X7, excluding 250,000 shares included under common stock in 19X8	350,000	450,000
Warrants: 71,428 common share equivalents outstanding for third and fourth quarters of 19X8, that is, 1/2 year	35,714	—
	385,714	450,000
Weighted average number of shares	4,035,714	3,750,000

[APB15, Appendix C]

.166 The weighted average number of shares would be adjusted to calculate fully diluted earnings per share as follows:

	19X8	19X7
Weighted average number of shares	4,035,714	3,750,000
Shares applicable to convertible debentures converted at the beginning of the third quarter of 19X8, excluding 100,000 shares included under common stock for 19X8	100,000	200,000
Shares applicable to warrants included above	(35,714)	—
Shares applicable to warrants based on year-end price of $72 (refer to paragraph .135)	83,333	—
Total	4,183,333	3,950,000

[APB15, Appendix C]

Adjustment of Income for Interest Expense

.167 Income before extraordinary item and net income would be adjusted for interest expense on the debentures in calculating fully diluted earnings per share as follows:

	Thousands		
	Before Adjustment	Interest, Net of Tax Effect	After Adjustment
19X7:			
Net income	$10,300	$208	$10,508
19X8:			
Income before extraordinary item	12,900	94	12,994
Net income	13,800	94	13,894

Notes: (a) Taxes in 19X7 were 48 percent; in 19X8 they were 52.8 percent.
(b) Net income is before dividends on preferred stock.

[APB15, Appendix C]

Exhibit 167A

Disclosure of Earnings per Share: Complex Capital Structure

(Bottom of Income Statement)	Thousands Except per share data	
	19X8	**19X7**
Income before extraordinary item	$12,900	$10,300
Extraordinary item—[description of		
transaction] less applicable income taxes	900	—
Net Income	$13,800	$10,300
Earnings per common share and		
common equivalent share (Note X):		
Income before extraordinary item	$ 3.20	$ 2.75
Extraordinary item	.22	—
Net Income	$ 3.42	$ 2.75
Earnings per common share—		
assuming full dilution (Note X):		
Income before extraordinary item	$ 3.11	$ 2.66
Extraordinary item	.21	—
Net Income	$ 3.32	$ 2.66
[APB15, Appendix C]		

Footnote Disclosure for Earnings per Share for a Complex Capital Structure

.168 [Exhibit 168A presents an example of the footnote disclosures to Exhibit 167A, based on the following assumed] disclosures in the December 31, 19X8 balance sheet:

Exhibit 168A

	19X8	19X7
Long-term debt:		
4% convertible debentures, due 19Z6	—	$10,000,000
Stockholders' equity (Note X):		
Convertible voting preferred stock of		
$1 par value, $0.20 cumulative		
dividend. Authorized 600,000		
shares; issued and outstanding		
100,000 shares (600,000 in 19X7)	$ 100,000	$ 600,000
(Liquidation value $22 per share,		
aggregating $2,200,000 in 19X8		
and $13,200,000 in 19X7)		
Common stock of $1 par value per		
share. Authorized 5,000,000 shares;		
issued and outstanding 4,000,000		
shares (3,300,000 in 19X7)	4,000,000	3,300,000
Additional paid-in capital	XXX	XXX
Retained earnings	XXX	XXX
	$ XXX	$ XXX

[APB15, Appendix C]

Example of Note X to Exhibit 167A

The $0.20 convertible preferred stock is callable by the enterprise after March 31, 19Y2 at $53 per share. Each share is convertible into one share of common stock.

During 19X8, 700,000 shares of common stock were issued on conversions: 500,000 shares on conversion of preferred stock and 200,000 on conversion of all the 4 percent convertible debentures.

Warrants to acquire 500,000 shares of the enterprise's stock at $60 per share were outstanding at the end of 19X8 and 19X7. These warrants expire March 31, 19Y2.

Earnings per common share and common equivalent share were computed by dividing net income by the weighted average number of shares of common stock and common stock equivalents outstanding during the year. The convertible preferred stock has been considered to be the equivalent of common stock from the time of its issuance in 19X7. The number of shares issuable on conversion of preferred stock was added to the number of common shares. The number of common shares was also increased by the number of shares issuable on the exercise of warrants when the market price of the common stock exceeds the exercise price of the warrants. This increase in the number of common shares was reduced by the number of common shares that are

Exhibit 168A (continued)

assumed to have been purchased with the proceeds from the exercise of the warrants; those purchases were assumed to have been made at the average price of the common stock during that part of the year when the market price of the common stock exceeded the exercise price of the warrants.

Earnings per common share and common equivalent share for 19X8 would have been $3.36 for net income and $3.14 for income before extraordinary item had the 4-percent [20-year] convertible debentures been converted on January 1, 19X8. (Those debentures were called for redemption as of July 1, 19X8 and all were converted into common shares.)

Earnings per common share—assuming full dilution for 19X8 were determined on the assumptions that the convertible debentures were converted and the warrants were exercised on January 1, 19X8. As to the debentures, net earnings were adjusted for the interest net of its tax effect. As to the warrants, outstanding shares were increased as described above except that purchases of common stock are assumed to have been made at the year-end price of $72.

Earnings per common share—assuming full dilution for 19X7 were determined on the assumption that the convertible debentures were converted on January 1, 19X7. The outstanding warrants had no effect on the earnings per share data for 19X7, as the exercise price was in excess of the market price of the common stock. [APB15, Appendix C]

Illustration of the Application of the Treasury Stock Method for Stock Appreciation Rights and Other Variable Stock Option Award Plans

.169 Paragraphs .170 through .175 illustrate applications of this section in computing the dilutive effect on earnings per share of stock appreciation rights and other variable stock option or award plans when the service period is presumed to be the vesting period. The examples do not comprehend all possible combinations of circumstances. Amounts and quantities have been rounded down to whole units for simplicity. [FIN31, ¶14]

.170 Provisions of the agreements [are as follows:]

Stock appreciation rights are granted in tandem with stock options for market value appreciation in excess of the option price. Exercise of the rights cancels the option for an equal number of shares and vice versa. Share appreciation is payable in stock, cash, or a combination of stock and cash at the enterprise's election.

Date of grant	January 1, 19X9
Expiration date	December 31, 19Y8
Vesting	100% at the end of 19Y2
Number of shares under option	1,000
Option price	$10 per share
Quoted market price at date of grant	$10 per share

[FIN31, ¶15]

.171 Assumptions [are as follows:]

a. There are no circumstances in these three examples that would overcome the presumption that the rights are payable in stock.
b. The tax deduction for compensation will equal the compensation recognized for financial reporting purposes.
c. Quoted market price per share at December 31 of subsequent years:

19X9 — $11
19Y0 — 12
19Y1 — 15
19Y2 — 14
19Y3 — 15
19Y4 — 18

[FIN31, ¶16]

Example 1

.172 Exhibit 172A illustrates the annual computation of incremental shares for the above described stock appreciation right plan. A single annual computation is shown for simplicity in this and the following examples. Normally, a computation would be done monthly or quarterly. [FIN31, ¶17]

Exhibit 172A

Computation of Incremental Shares Outstanding for Use in Earnings per Share Calculations

		COMPENSATION							FOR PRIMARY EARNINGS PER SHARE			FOR FULLY DILUTED EARNINGS PER SHARE		
Date	Market Price	Per Share	Aggregate (a)	Percentage Accrued (b)	Compensation Accrued to Date	Measurable Compensation Ascribed to Future Periods (c)	Amount to Be Paid by Employee	Exercise Proceeds	Shares Issuable (d)	Treasury Shares Assumed Repurchased (e)]	Incremental Shares	Shares Issuable (f)	Treasury Shares Assumed Repurchased (g)	Incremental Shares
12/31/X9	$11	$1	$1,000	25%	$ 250	$ 750	—	$ 750	47	35	12	90	68	22
12/31/Y0	12	2	2,000	50	1,000	1,000	—	1,000	130	76	54	166	83	83
12/31/Y1	15	5	5,000	75	3,750	1,250	—	1,250	259	83	176	333	83	250
12/31/Y2	14	4	4,000	100	4,000	—	—	—	310	43	267	285	—	285
12/31/Y3	15	5	5,000	100	5,000	—	—	—	310	—	310	333	—	333
12/31/Y4	18	8	8,000	100	8,000	—	—	—	393	—	393	444	—	444

Notes

(a) Aggregate compensation for unexercised shares to be allocated to periods service performed.
(b) The percentage accrued is based upon the four-year vesting period.
(c) Unaccrued compensation in this example.
(d) Average aggregate compensation divided by average market price.*
(e) Average exercise proceeds divided by average market price.*
(f) End-of-year aggregate compensation divided by market price as of year-end.
(g) End-of-year exercise proceeds divided by market price as of year-end.

Illustration of computation for one year (19Y2)

Date	Market Price	Aggregate Compensation	Exercise Proceeds	Shares Issuable	Treasury Shares Assumed Repurchased	Incremental Shares
12/31/Y1 (beginning of year)	$15	$5000	$1250	N/A	N/A	N/A
12/31/Y2 (end of year)	14	4000	—	285	—	285
Average	14.50	4500	625	310	43	267

If average incremental shares were higher than end-of-year incremental shares, average incremental shares would be used for both primary and fully diluted earnings per share computations.

*These computations could also be done using other methods of averaging.

[FIN31, ¶17]

Example 2

.173 If the stock appreciation rights vested 25 percent per year commencing in 19X9, the annual computation of incremental shares for primary earnings per share in the preceding example would change as illustrated in Exhibit 174A. Similar computations would be made for fully diluted earnings per share. The computation of compensation expense is explained in Section C47. [FIN31, ¶18]

.174 Additional assumptions [for Exhibit 174A are as follows:]

a. On December 31, 19Y1, the employee exercises the right to receive share appreciation on 300 shares.
b. On March 15, 19Y2, the employee exercises the right to receive share appreciation on 100 shares; quoted market price $15 per share.
c. On June 15, 19Y3, the employee exercises the right to receive share appreciation on 100 shares; quoted market price $16 per share.
d. On December 31, 19Y3, the employee exercises the right to receive share appreciation on 300 shares.
e. On December 31, 19Y4, the employee exercises the right to receive share appreciation on 200 shares. [FIN31, ¶19]

Exhibit 174A

Computation of Incremental Shares Outstanding for Use in Earnings per Share Calculations

| | | | COMPENSATION | | | | | | | ADDITIONAL SHARES FOR PRIMARY EARNINGS PER SHARE | | | | | |
Date	Transaction	Number of Shares	Market Price	Per Share	Aggregate (a)	Percentage Accrued (b)	Compensation Accrued to Date	Measurable Compensation Ascribed to Future Periods (c)	Amount to Be Paid by Employee	Exercise Proceeds	Shares Issuable (d)	Treasury Shares Assumed Repurchased (e)	Incremental Shares	Weighted Average Shares Outstanding (f)	Total Shares
12/31/X9			$11	$1	$1,000	52%	$ 520	$480	–	$ 480	47	22	25	–	25
12/31/Y0			12	2	2,000	79	1,580	420	–	420	130	39	91	–	91
12/31/Y1			15	5	5,000	94	4,700	300	–	300	259	26	233	–	233
12/31/Y1	E	300	15	5	(1,500)	–									
3/15/Y2	E	100	15	5	(500)	–									
12/31/Y2			14	4	2,400	100	2,400	–	–	–	193	10	183	126	309
6/15/Y3	E	100	16	6	(600)	–									
12/31/Y3			15	5	2,500	100	2,500	–	–	–	170	–	170	153	323
12/31/Y3	E	300	15	5	(1,500)	–									
12/31/Y4			18	8	1,600	100	1,600	–	–	–	78	–	78	270	348
12/31/Y4	E	200	18	8	(1,600)	–									

Transaction Code
E—Exercise of a stock appreciation right.

Notes

(a) Aggregate compensation for unexercised shares to be allocated to periods service performed.

(b) Refer to the schedule in Section C47, paragraph .143.

(c) Unaccrued compensation in this example.

(d) Average aggregate compensation divided by average market price, weighted for proportion of period during which rights were unexercised.

(e) Average exercise proceeds divided by average market price.

(f) Shares issued upon exercise of stock appreciation rights and stock options. These would be included in the enterprise's total weighted average shares outstanding.

Illustration of Computation for One Year (1Y2)

	Number of Shares	Average Market Price	Average Aggregate Compensation	Aggregate Shares Issuable	Weighting Factor	Shares Issuable
Rights outstanding entire year	600	$14.50	$2700	186	12/12	186
Rights outstanding 1/1-3/15	100	15.00	500	33	2.5/12	7
						193

[FIN31, ¶19]

Example 3

.175 If the plan limits the amount of share appreciation that the employee can receive to $5, the computation of additional shares in Exhibit 174A would change as illustrated in Exhibit 176A. [FIN31, ¶20]

.176 When the quoted market price exceeds the appreciation limitations, the employee is more likely to exercise the related stock option rather than the stock appreciation right. Therefore, accrued compensation is not adjusted for changes in the quoted market price of the stock. The assumptions stated in paragraph .174 are changed to the extent that on June 15, 19Y3 and December 31, 19Y4 the employee exercises the related stock option instead of the stock appreciation right. In addition, it is assumed that the market price does not exceed $15 for substantially all of a 3-month period until 19Y4. Therefore, for earnings per share purposes the incremental shares are computed based on assumed exercise of the stock appreciation rights prior to 19Y4 and on assumed exercise of the stock options in 19Y4. [FIN31, ¶21]

Exhibit 176A

Computation of Incremental Shares Outstanding for Use in Earnings per Share Calculations

Date	Transaction	Number of Shares	Market Price	COMPENSATION Per Share	Aggregate (a)	Percentage Accrued (b)	Compensation Accrued to Date	Measurable Compensation Ascribed to Future Periods (c)	Amount to Be Paid by Employee	Exercise Proceeds	ADDITIONAL SHARES FOR PRIMARY EARNINGS PER SHARE (f) Shares Issuable (d)	Treasury Shares Assumed Repurchased (e)	Incremental Shares	Weighted Average Shares Outstanding (g)	Total Shares
12/31/X9			$11	$1	$1,000	52%	$ 520	$480	—	$ 480	47	22	25	—	25
12/31/Y0			12	2	2,000	79	1,580	420	—	420	130	39	91	—	91
12/31/Y1			15	5	5,000	94	4,700	300	—	300	259	26	233	—	233
12/31/Y1	E	300	15	5	(1,500)	—									
3/15/Y2	E	100	15	5	(500)	—									
12/31/Y2			14	4	2,400	100	2,400	—	—	—	193	10	183	126	309
6/15/Y3	O	100	16	5	(500)	—									
12/31/Y3			15	5	2,500	100	2,500	—	—	—	170	—	170	187	357
12/31/Y3	E	300	15	5	(1,500)	—									
12/31/Y4			18	5	1,000	100	1,000	—	$2,000	2,000	200	121	79	333	412
12/31/Y4	O	200	18	5	(1,000)	—									

Transaction Codes
E—Exercise of a stock appreciation right.
O—Exercise of the related stock option.

Notes
(a) Aggregate compensation for unexercised shares to be allocated to periods service performed.
(b) Refer to the schedule in Section C47, paragraph .143.
(c) Unaccrued compensation in this example.
(d) Average aggregate compensation divided by average market price, weighted for proportion of period during which options or rights were unexercised.
(e) Average exercise proceeds divided by average market price.
(f) Similar computations would be made for fully diluted earnings per share.
(g) Shares issued upon exercise of stock appreciation rights and stock options. These would be included in the enterprise's total weighted average shares outstanding.

[FIN31, ¶21]

Glossary

.401 **Call price.** The amount at which a security may be redeemed by the issuer at the issuer's option. [APB15, Appendix D]

.402 [Deleted 3/85 because of FASB Statement 85.]

.403 **Common stock.** A stock that is subordinate to all other stocks of the issuer. [APB15, Appendix D]

.404 **Common stock equivalent.** A security that, because of its terms or the circumstances under which it was issued, is in substance equivalent to common stock. [APB15, Appendix D]

.405 **Contingent issuance.** A possible issuance of shares of common stock that is dependent on the exercise of conversion rights, options, or warrants, the satisfaction of certain conditions, or similar arrangements. [APB15, Appendix D]

.406 **Conversion price.** The price that determines the number of shares of common stock into which a security is convertible. For example, $100 face value of debt convertible into 5 shares of common stock would be stated to have a conversion price of $20. [APB15, Appendix D]

.407 **Conversion rate.** The ratio of (a) the number of common shares issuable on conversion to (b) a unit of a convertible security. For example, a preferred stock may be convertible at the rate of three shares of common stock for each share of preferred stock. [APB15, Appendix D]

.408 **Conversion value.** The current market value of the common shares obtainable on conversion of a convertible security, after deducting any cash payment required on conversion. [APB15, Appendix D]

.409 **Dilution (dilutive).** A reduction in earnings per share resulting from the assumption that convertible securities have been converted or that options and warrants have been exercised or other shares have been issued upon the fulfillment of certain conditions (refer to footnote 3). [APB15, Appendix D]

.410 **Dual presentation.** The presentation with equal prominence of two types of earnings per share amounts on the face of the income statement—one is primary earnings per share; the other is fully diluted earnings per share. [APB15, Appendix D]

.411 **Earnings per share.** The amount of earnings attributable to each share of common stock. For convenience, the term is used in this section to refer to either net income (earnings) per share or to net loss per share. It shall be used without qualifying language only when no potentially dilutive convertible securities, options, warrants, or other agreements providing for contingent issuances of common stock are outstanding. [APB15, Appendix D]

.412 **Exercise price.** The amount that must be paid for a share of common stock on exercise of a stock option or warrant. [APB15, Appendix D]

.413 **Fully diluted earnings per share.** The amount of current earnings per share reflecting the maximum dilution that would have resulted from conversions, exercises, and other contingent issuances that individually would have decreased earnings per share and in the aggregate would have had a dilutive effect. All those issuances are assumed to have taken place at the beginning of the period (or at the time the contingency arose, if later). [APB15, Appendix D]

.414 **If-converted method.** A method of computing earnings per share data that assumes conversion of convertible securities as of the beginning of the earliest period reported (or at time of issuance, if later). [APB15, Appendix D]

.415 **Investment value.** The price at which it is estimated a convertible security would sell if it were not convertible, based on its stipulated preferred dividend or interest rate and its other senior security characteristics. [APB15, Appendix D]

.416 **Market parity.** A market price relationship in which the market price of a convertible security and its conversion value are approximately equal. [APB15, Appendix D]

.417 **Nonpublic enterprise.** An enterprise other than one (a) whose debt or equity securities trade in a public market on a foreign or domestic stock exchange or in the over-the-counter market (including securities quoted only locally or regionally) or (b) that is required to file financial statements with the Securities and Exchange Commission. An enterprise is no longer considered a nonpublic enterprise when its financial statements are issued in preparation for the sale of any class of securities in a public market. [FAS21, ¶13]

.418 **Option.** The right to purchase shares of common stock in accordance with an agreement, upon payment of a specified amount. As used in this section, options include but are not limited to options granted to and stock purchase agreements entered into with employees. Options are considered securities in this section. [APB15, Appendix D]

.419 Primary earnings per share. The amount of earnings attributable to each share of common stock outstanding, including common stock equivalents. [APB15, Appendix D]

.420 Redemption price. The amount at which a security is required to be redeemed at maturity or under a sinking fund arrangement. [APB15, Appendix D]

.421 Security. The evidence of a debt or ownership or related right. For purposes of this section, it includes stock options and warrants, as well as debt and stock. [APB15, Appendix D]

.422 Senior security. A security having preferential rights and that is not a common stock or common stock equivalent, for example, nonconvertible preferred stock. [APB15, Appendix D]

.423 Supplementary earnings per share. A computation of earnings per share, other than primary or fully diluted earnings per share, that gives effect to conversions, etc., that took place during the period or shortly thereafter as though they had occurred at the beginning of the period (or date of issuance, if later). [APB15, Appendix D]

.424 Time of issuance. The time of issuance generally is the date when agreement as to terms has been reached and announced, even though the agreement is subject to certain further actions, such as directors' or stockholders' approval. [APB15, Appendix D]

.425 Treasury-stock method. A method of recognizing the use of proceeds that would be obtained on exercise of options and warrants in computing earnings per share. It assumes that any proceeds would be used to purchase common stock at current market prices (refer to paragraphs .125 through .127). [APB15, Appendix D]

.426 Two-class method. A method of computing primary earnings per share that treats common stock equivalents as though they were common stocks with different dividend rates from that of the common stock. [APB15, Appendix D]

.427 Warrant. A security giving the holder the right to purchase shares of common stock in accordance with the terms of the instrument, usually on payment of a specified amount. [APB15, Appendix D]

.428 Weighted average number of shares. The number of shares determined by relating (a) the portion of time within a reporting period that a particular number of shares of a certain security has been outstanding to (b) the total time in that period. Thus, for example, if 100 shares of a certain security were outstanding during the first quarter of a fiscal year and 300 shares were outstanding during the balance of the year, the weighted average number of outstanding shares would be 250. [APB15, Appendix D]

Supplemental Guidance

Contents

	Paragraph Numbers
Applicablity to Certain Brokers and Dealers in Securities	.501–.502
Restatement of Earnings per Share for Accounting Changes	.503–.510
EPS for Catch-Up Adjustment	.511–.514
Classification of Securities	.515–.517
Antidilutive Securities	.518
Convertible Securities	.519–.520
Options and Warrants	.521–.524
Restatement of Previously Reported Data	.525–.526
Definitional Interpretations	.527–.542
Security	.527
Common Stock Equivalents	.528
Other Potentially Dilutive Securities	.529–.530
Dilution—Dilutive Security	.531–.532
Antidilution—Antidilutive Security	.533–.535
Dual Presentation	.536–.538
Primary Earnings per Share	.539–.540
Fully Diluted Earnings per Share	.541–.542
Applicability of This Section	.543–.563
Enterprises and Financial Presentations Excepted	.543–.547
Closely Held Enterprises	.548–.549
Dilution Less Than Three Percent	.550–.553
Three-Percent Test	.554–.559
Subchapter S Corporations	.560–.561
Unaudited Financial Statements	.562–.563
Earnings per Share Presentation	.564–.589
Reporting Loss per Share	.564–.565
EPS for Extraordinary Items	.566–.568
Simple Capital Structure	.569–.570
Complex Capital Structure	.571–.573
EPS for Simple and Complex Capital Structures	.574–.576
Dual Presentation for Enterprises with Simple Capital Structures	.577–.580
Primary versus Fully Diluted EPS	.581–.583
Captions for Earnings per Share Presentations	.584–.586
Captions in Comparative Statements	.587–.589
Computing Earnings per Share	.590–.601
Earnings Applicable to Common Stock	.590–.594
Weighted Average of Shares Outstanding	.595–.601

Paragraph Numbers

Convertible Securities .... .602–.665
  Classification and Assumed Conversion...................... .602–.607
  Time of Issuance .... .608–.612
  Classification and Computation Not Always the Same........... .613–.618
  Change of Classification of Convertible Security.............. .619–.622
  Change of Classification Is Mandatory .... .623–.626
  Definition of Same Terms .... .627–.628
  Issue Price Is Not a Term................................... .629–.630
  Sale of Treasury Securities Is a New Issue.................... .631–.632
  Effective Yield of Convertible Security in a Package.......... .637–.638
  Property Included in Effective Yield......................... .639–.641
  Benchmark Used in Yield Test................................ .642–.643
  Original Issue Premium or Discount on Convertible Securities..... .644–.645
  No Antidilution from Convertible Preferred Stock .... .646–.648
  No Antidilution from Convertible Debt .... .649–.651
  Conversion Assumed for Primary Only .... .652–.656
  If-Converted Method at Actual Conversion.................... .657–.660
  Securities Convertible into Other Convertible Securities .... .661–.665
Options and Warrants and Their Equivalents...................... .666–.835
  Classification of Options and Warrants .... .666–.667
  No Antidilution from Options and Warrants................... .668–.671
  Equivalents of Options and Warrants......................... .672–.673
  Grouping Options and Warrants.............................. .674–.678
  Methods Used for Options and Warrants...................... .679–.683
  Treasury-Stock Method Reflects Dilution of Options and Warrants. .684–.688
  Market Prices Used for Treasury-Stock Method .... .689–.695
  How Many Market Prices? .... .696–.699
  What Market Price to Use?.................................. .700–.703
  Over-the-Counter and Listed Stocks Not Traded .... .704–.707
  Fair Value Used If No Market Price .... .708–.713
  Options and Warrants Outstanding Part of a Period............. .714–.722
  What Is a Period? .... .723–.726
  Share Averaging... .727–.729
  Applying Ending and Average Market Prices .... .730–.736
  Treasury-Stock Method at Exercise.......................... .737–.744
  Antidilutive Exercise .... .745–.754
  Substantially All of Three Months .... .755–.760
  Total of Quarters May Not Equal Annual EPS .... .761–.764
  Unusual Warrants and Their Equivalents...................... .765–.766
  Securities Subject to Paragraph .126 Tests .... .767–.772
  Market Prices Used in Paragraph .126 Tests................... .773–.777
  Computations for Warrants Requiring the Tendering of Debt ..... .778–.779

	Paragraph Numbers

Computations for Warrants Allowing Tendering of Debt .... .780–.785
Computations for Warrants Whose Proceeds Are Applied to
  Retire Debt .... .786–.789
Treasury-Stock Method for Convertibles .... .790–.794
Antidilutive Options and Warrants Included .... .795–.796
No Order for Exercise .... .797–.798
Explanation of 20-Percent Provision .... .799–.805
Original Issue Premium or Discount............................ .806–.807
Redemption Premium or Discount .... .808–.811
Debt Purchased under Paragraph .127 .... .812–.814
Compensating Balances Excluded.............................. .815–.816
Investments under Paragraph .127 .... .817–.819
Debt Eligible Only While Outstanding .... .820–.821
Computations May Differ for Primary and Fully Diluted
  If Paragraph .127 Applies .... .822–.825
Stock Subscriptions Are Warrants............................. .826–.829
Options or Warrants to Purchase Convertible Securities .... .830–.835
Two-Class Common Stock and Participating Securities .... .836–.851
EPS Treatment of Two-Class and Participating Securities......... .836–.841
Two-Class Method for Nonconvertible Securities .... .842–.846
Two-Class Method for Convertible Securities .... .847–.851
Securities Issuable upon Satisfaction of Specified Conditions........ .852–.882
Contingent Shares .... .852–.857
Time of Issuance for Contingent Issuances .... .858–.859
Market Price Conditions .... .860–.868
Earnings Conditions .... .869–.877
Convertible Securities Contingently Issuable .... .878–.882
Parent and Consolidated Financial Statements .... .883–.888
Securities Issued by Subsidiaries .... .883–.888
Effects of Scheduled Changes .... .889–.892
Changing Exercise Prices and Conversion Rates .... .889–.892
Election to Classify Outstanding Securities .... .893–.899
Effect of New Issue of Common Stock Equivalents .... .893–.894
No Change for Options and Warrants .... .895–.897
Is Prior Period Restatement Permitted? .... .898–.899
Disclosure... .900–.905
Required Disclosure... .900–.901
Supplementary Data .... .902–.905
Examples of Computing Average Market Prices .... .906–.909
Application of the Treasury-Stock Method for Options and Warrants. .910
Two-Class Method for Warrants Issued by REITs................. .911–.916

Supplemental Guidance

Applicability to Certain Brokers and Dealers in Securities

.501 *Question*—[Paragraph .102 indicates that this section need not be applied by a nonpublic enterprise.] Should closely held brokers or dealers in securities that file financial statements with the SEC be considered nonpublic enterprises for purposes of applying [the provisions of] this section? [FTB79-8, ¶1]

.502 *Response*—Closely held broker-dealers that are required to file financial statements with the SEC only for use by its Division of Market Regulation [should be considered nonpublic enterprises for purposes of applying the provisions of this section], principally because the broker-dealer can cause a significant portion of those financial statements (that is, the income statement and [FTB79-8, ¶6] statement of cash flows [FAS111, ¶8(aa)]) to be unavailable for public inspection by requesting confidential treatment. [FTB79-8, ¶6]

Restatement of Earnings per Share for Accounting Changes

.503 *Question*—Section A06 specifies that certain accounting changes shall be reported by retroactively restating all prior periods presented. It also requires that the effect of those changes on the prior periods' earnings per share amounts be disclosed. The antidilution prohibitions of paragraphs .121 and .133 require the exclusion from earnings per share computations of securities whose conversion, exercise, or other contingent issuance would have the effect of increasing the earnings per share amount or decreasing the loss per share amount. If those securities were originally included in the earnings per share computations in a prior period but would have been excluded if the retroactively restated amount had been reported in the prior period, should the securities be included or excluded when computing the restated earnings per share amount? [AIN-APB20, #1]

.504 *Answer*—A retroactively restated earnings per share amount should always be computed as if the restated income or loss had been originally reported in the prior period. Common stock assumed to be issued for exercise, conversion, etc., and included in the original earnings per share denominator should, therefore, in circumstances such as those described below be excluded from the denominator in computing the restated earnings per share amount. [AIN-APB20, #1]

.505 For example, assume that an enterprise that reported $200,000 net income in the immediately preceding year changes its methods or accounting for long-term construction-type contracts from the completed-contract method to the percentage-of-completion method. In applying this change retroactively (refer to Section A06, paragraph .123) the net income originally reported for the immediately preceding year is decreased $290,000 and restated as a net loss of $90,000. Further assume that in the prior year the enterprise had 900,000 shares of common stock and 150,000 warrants outstanding for the entire year. Each warrant could be exercised to purchase 1 share of common stock for $10 while the market price of common was $30 throughout the year. Earnings per share were originally reported as $.20 based on $200,000 net income divided by a denominator of 1,000,000 common shares (900,000 shares outstanding plus 100,000 shares for warrants computed under the treasury stock method). The assumption of exercise of warrants is antidilutive when there is a loss, so the restated amount would be reported as a net loss of $.10 per share based on $90,000 net loss divided by a denominator of 900,000 common shares outstanding. [AIN-APB20, #1]

.506 Note that retroactive restatement could also cause securities originally determined to be antidilutive to become dilutive. For example, assume the same facts as given in the preceding illustration except a $90,000 net loss was originally reported and is restated as $200,000 net income. Exercise of the warrants would not have been assumed in the original per share computation because the result would have been antidilutive but would be assumed in computing the restated earnings per share because the result is dilutive. [AIN-APB20, #1]

.507 Retroactive restatement may also cause the earnings per share numerator to change by an amount different from the amount of the retroactive adjustment. For example, assume that an enterprise changes from the LIFO method of inventory pricing to the FIFO method, retroactively increasing net income for the immediately preceding year by $400,000 (refer to Section A06, paragraph .123). Further assume that the enterprise originally reported a net income of $800,000 in the prior year and had 800,000 shares of common stock outstanding. In addition, 200,000 shares of preferred stock were outstanding that were convertible into common stock on a 1-for-1 basis. The preferred stock is a common stock equivalent and paid a dividend of $1 per share. Earnings per share were originally reported as $.75 based on an earnings per share numerator of $600,000 ($800,000 net income less $200,000 preferred dividends) and a denominator of 800,000 common shares. The assumption of conversion in the original computation of earnings per share is $1.20 based on a numerator of $1,200,000 and a denominator of 1,000,000 shares (800,000 common shares outstanding plus 200,000 common shares for the assumed conversion of preferred stock). Although restatement increased net income and, therefore, the earnings per share numerator $400,000 in this case, the assumed conversion of the preferred stock increased the earnings per share numerator by another $200,000. [AIN-APB20, #1]

.508 In addition to a retroactive adjustment for a change in accounting principle, the guidelines given in paragraphs .503 through .507 apply to (a) retroactive restatement, (b) restatement of prior periods for a change in the reporting entity, (c) the correction of an error in previously issued financial statements (refer to descriptions in Section A06), and (d) a prior period adjustment (refer to Section A35). Those guidelines will likewise apply if an accounting standard requires that it be applied retroactively, including those that may be issued in the future. Also, those guidelines should be applied in computing the pro forma earnings per share amounts for the types of changes in accounting principle described in Section A06, paragraph .115. Although those types of changes in accounting principle are not applied retroactively, paragraphs .115(d) and .117 of Section A06 require that the pro forma effects of retroactive application be disclosed. [AIN-APB20, #1]

.509 A change in the earnings per share denominator (and perhaps numerator) from that originally used in the computation may create certain complications in reporting the effect of a retroactive change. Those complications may be illustrated by considering the data in the [following] table, given for the examples presented in paragraphs .505 through .507:

	Warrant Example	Convertible Preferred Stock Example
Net income as previously reported	$ 200,000	$ 800,000
Adjustment for retroactive change	(290,000)	400,000
Net income (loss) as adjusted	$ (90,000)	$1,200,000
Earnings per share amounts:		
As previously reported	$ .20 (a)	$ .75 (c)
Effect of retroactive change	(.30)	.45
As adjusted	$ (.10)(b)	$ 1.20 (d)

Computational Notes:

(a) $200,000 ÷ (900,000 + 100,000) shares
(b) $90,000 ÷ 900,000 shares
(c) ($800,000 − $200,000) ÷ 800,000 shares
(d) $1,200,000 ÷ (800,000 + 200,000) shares

[AIN-APB20, #1]

.510 In both of the above examples, the earnings per share amounts shown for "effect of retroactive change" are computed by subtracting the previously reported amounts from the adjusted amounts. Determining the per share amount of the change by subtraction comprehends the effects of any necessary changes in the denominator and the numerator by reason of retroactive application. [AIN-APB20, #1]

EPS for Catch-Up Adjustment

.511 *Question*—Section A06, paragraph .116, requires the per share amount of the cumulative effect of most accounting changes (refer to Section A06, paragraphs .114 and .115) to be shown on the face of the income statement similar to the manner in which an extraordinary item would be shown. Footnote 8, giving an exception to the antidilution prohibition in primary earnings per share computations, states that if an extraordinary item is present and a common stock equivalent results in dilution of either income before extraordinary items or net income on a per share basis, the common stock equivalent shall be recognized for all computations. Footnote 17 gives a similar reference for fully diluted computations. How does reporting the cumulative effect of an accounting change in a manner similar to an extraordinary item affect the application of those two footnotes in computing earnings per share? [AIN-APB20, #2]

.512 *Answer*—The cumulative effect of an accounting change (sometimes referred to as a *catch-up* adjustment) is considered the same as an extraordinary item, whether or not extraordinary items are present, in computing earnings per share. Therefore, a common stock equivalent that has a dilutive effect on the primary earnings per share computation for either (a) income before extraordinary items (if any) and the cumulative effect of a change in accounting principle or (b) net income should be recognized in all computations of primary earnings per share for the period. Likewise, a common stock equivalent or other potentially dilutive security that has a dilutive effect on the fully diluted earnings per share computation for either (a) income before extraordinary items (if any) and cumulative effect of a change in accounting principle or (b) net income should be recognized in all computations of fully diluted earnings per share for the period. Note that, under these exceptions to the antidilution prohibitions of this section, a common stock equivalent or other potentially dilutive security may have an antidilutive effect on either (a) or (b) but not on both. The per share amount of an extraordinary item or a catch-up adjustment is always computed by using the same denominator used to compute both the (a) and (b) earnings per share amounts. [AIN-APB20, #2]

.513 However, the exceptions to the antidilution prohibitions do not permit an assumed exercise, conversion, etc., to cause fully diluted net income (loss) per share to be antidilutive in relation to primary net income (loss) per share. That is, the assumed exercise, conversion, etc., of a security may have an antidilutive effect within primary earnings per share or within fully diluted earnings per share, but the assumed exercise, conversion, etc., should not have the effect of increasing (decreasing) the fully diluted net income (loss) per share amount to more (less) than the primary net income (loss) per share amount. [AIN-APB20, #2]

.514 Although the catch-up adjustment is considered the same as an extraordinary item in computing earnings per share, the earnings per share reporting requirement for the two items is different. This section does not require that per share amounts be reported for extraordinary items, although this presentation may generally be desirable. Section A06, paragraph .116, does require per share data for a catch-up adjustment to be shown on the face of the income statement. Preferably, when both an extraordinary item and a catch-up adjustment are reflected in net income for a period, per share data for both should be presented on the face of the income statement. [AIN-APB20, #2]

Classification of Securities

.515 The advent of securities that are not common stock in form but that enable their holders to obtain common stock modifies some of the traditional relationships among securities. While common stock is regarded as the basic equity security and nonconvertible preferred stock and nonconvertible debt are regarded as senior securities, those securities that enable their holders to obtain common stock are classified as either *common stock equivalents* or as *other potentially dilutive securities* for earnings per share computations. That classification is made at time of issuance and does not change thereafter.[501] [AIN-APB15, Part 1]

.516 A security is classified solely for purposes of determining earnings per share. The accounting for securities, their presentation in the financial statements, and the determination of book value per share are not affected by the classification of securities for earnings per share computations. [AIN-APB15, Part 1]

.517 Common stock equivalents are included in both primary and fully diluted earnings per share computations. Other potentially dilutive securities are included only in fully diluted earnings per share computations. However, common stock equivalents and other potentially dilutive securities are included in the *computations* only if their effect is dilutive. Both are excluded from the *computations* whenever their effect is antidilutive except in the situations described in the following paragraph. Thus, a security retains its status as a common stock equivalent or as another potentially dilutive security after its classification has been determined, but it may enter earnings per share computations in one period and not in another period. [AIN-APB15, Part 1]

Antidilutive Securities

.518 Antidilutive securities are excluded from earnings per share computations unless (a) common stock was issued during the period on an antidilutive exercise or conversion or (b) a security is antidilutive in earnings per share for income before extraordinary items but is dilutive in earnings per share for net income or vice

---

[501]Except as explained in paragraphs .619 through .626. [AIN-APB15, Part 1, fn4]

versa[502] or (c) an aggregate computation is required that has a net dilutive effect but that may include antidilutive securities or antidilutive computations.[503] All other antidilutive securities are excluded from earnings per share computations even if some antidilutive securities are included in the computation because of one or more of the above exceptions. In an aggregate computation, only if the net result is dilutive may antidilutive securities be included in the earnings per share computations. [AIN-APB15, Part 1]

Convertible Securities

.519 Convertible securities that *require* the payment of cash at conversion are considered the equivalent of warrants for computational purposes. Both the treasury-stock method and the if-converted method must be applied. Convertible securities that *permit* the payment of cash as an alternative at conversion are also considered the equivalent of warrants. But if conversion without the payment of cash would be more advantageous to the holder with this alternative, only the if-converted method is applied. No proceeds would be received to which the treasury stock method could be applied. [AIN-APB15, Part 1]

.520 If conversion is not assumed because the result would be antidilutive, dividends declared for the period (or accumulated for the period even though not declared) are deducted from net income to determine earnings applicable to common stock. [AIN-APB15, Part 1]

Options and Warrants

.521 Some warrants require or permit the tendering of debt or other securities in payment of all or part of the exercise price. On the assumed exercise of those warrants, the debt or other securities are assumed to be tendered (unless tendering cash would be more advantageous to the warrant holder if permitted and the treasury-stock method is applied). Interest, net of income tax, on any debt tendered is added back to net income. The treasury-stock method is applied for proceeds assumed to be received in cash. [AIN-APB15, Part 1]

---

[502]Note that either primary earnings per share for net income or primary earnings per share for income before extraordinary items may be antidilutive if common stock equivalents are present together with extraordinary items. The common stock equivalents may have an antidilutive effect on either of those amounts so long as the effect is dilutive on the other amount. The same type of antidilution may be reflected *within* fully diluted earnings per share if common stock equivalents and other potentially dilutive securities are present together with extraordinary items. However, fully diluted earnings per share for net income would not be antidilutive with respect to primary earnings per share for net income unless the antidilution is caused by actual exercises or conversions. [AIN-APB15, Part 1, fn5]

[503]For example, an aggregate computation is required by paragraph .127 if the number of common shares issuable upon the exercise of all options, warrants, and their equivalents exceeds 20 percent of the number of common shares outstanding at the end of the period for which the computation is being made. An aggregate computation would also be made for an antidilutive option that must be exercised before a dilutive option may be exercised (refer to paragraphs .674 through .678). [AIN-APB15, Part 1, fn6]

.522 The proceeds from the exercise of some warrants must be applied to retire debt under the terms of the debt. On the assumed exercise of those warrants, the proceeds are applied to purchase the debt at its market price rather than to purchase common stock under the treasury-stock method. The treasury-stock method is applied, however, for excess proceeds from the assumed exercise. Interest, net of income tax, on any debt assumed to be purchased is added back to net income. [AIN-APB15, Part 1]

.523 Some convertible securities require or permit the payment of cash on conversion and are considered the equivalent of warrants. The treasury-stock method must be applied to purchase common stock from proceeds assumed to be received. The if-converted method must also be applied for the convertible security. [AIN-APB15, Part 1]

.524 The application of the treasury-stock method is modified if the number of common shares that would be issued if all outstanding options and warrants and their equivalents were exercised exceeds 20 percent of the number of common shares outstanding at the end of the period. This 20-percent test is based only on common shares actually outstanding, not considering any assumed conversion and contingently issuable shares. [AIN-APB15, Part 1]

Restatement of Previously Reported Data

.525 Earnings per share amounts reported in a prior period generally will be reported at the same amounts when that prior period is included in a later comparative income statement. This section specifically prohibits retroactive restatement (a) for changes in market prices of common stock if the treasury-stock method has been applied for options and warrants, (b) if conversion rates of convertible securities or exercise prices of options or warrants change, (c) if convertible securities are actually converted, and (d) for primary earnings per share, if the number of shares issued on the attainment of increased earnings levels differs from the number of shares previously considered outstanding. [AIN-APB15, Part 1]

.526 This section requires retroactive restatement (a) to give effect to prior period adjustments,[504] (b) to give effect to stock dividends, stock splits, and reverse splits, including those occurring after the close of the period being reported on, (c) to give to a pooling of interests, (d) to give effect to changes in the number of shares contingently issuable or issued if such changes are caused by changes in market prices of the stock, and (e) to give effect to a reduction in the number of shares contingently issuable if the term of an agreement to issue additional shares expires and the conditions have not been met.[505] [AIN-APB15, Part 1]

---

[504]Refer to Section A35. [AIN-APB15, Part 1, fn7]

[505]But note that restatement is prohibited for primary earnings per share if increased earnings levels are attained and shares are issued that were not previously considered outstanding for prior primary computations (refer to paragraph .525(d), and paragraph .153). [AIN-APB15, Part 1, fn8]

Definitional Interpretations

Security

.527 The term *security* is used in this section in a broad context to include instruments not usually considered to be securities. Securities are usually thought of as being common stocks, preferred stocks (both nonconvertible and convertible), bonds (both ordinary and convertible), and warrants. In a broad context, the term *security* also includes all debt instruments, options to purchase stock (or other securities), stock purchase contracts, stock subscriptions, and agreements to issue stock (or other securities) at a future date. Several securities may be included in a single instrument, that may or may not be separable. [AIN-APB15, #1]

Common Stock Equivalents

.528 A common stock equivalent is defined in this section as: "a security that, because of its terms or the circumstances under which it was issued, is in substance equivalent to common stock." A common stock equivalent is not common stock in form but rather derives a large portion of its value from its common stock characteristics or conversion privileges. Such a security typically contains provisions enabling its holder to become a common stockholder. Its value tends to change with changes in the value of the common stock to which it is related. Examples of common stock equivalents are: options and warrants, preferred stock or debt convertible into common stock if the stock or debt [AIN-APB15, #2] has an effective [FAS85, ¶3] yield of less than $66^2/_3$ percent of the [AIN-APB15, #2] average Aa corporate bond yield as defined in paragraph .123A [FAS111, ¶8(n)] at time of issuance, and agreements to issue common stock with the passage of time as the only condition to issuance. [AIN-APB15, #2]

Other Potentially Dilutive Securities

.529 *Other potentially dilutive securities* is a term used in this supplemental guidance to designate a classification of securities that are similar to common stock equivalents but that for one reason or another do not meet the tests for common stock equivalents.[506] Other potentially dilutive securities are included only in fully diluted earnings per share computations while common stock equivalents are, in effect, included in both primary and fully diluted earnings per share computations. [AIN-APB15, #3]

---

[506]The term is not used in paragraphs .101 through .176 of this section in that strict context. *Potentially dilutive securities,* as that term is used in those paragraphs, includes common stock equivalents (for example, refer to paragraph .105). Those paragraphs discuss senior securities that are not common stock equivalents and other contingent issuances that are not common stock equivalents. Securities that are *not* common stock equivalents but that enable their holders to obtain common stock are described in this supplemental guidance as *other potentially dilutive securities.* Therefore, convertible senior securities described in paragraphs .101 through .176 are classified as *other potentially dilutive securities* in this supplemental guidance. [AIN-APB15, #3, fn13]

.530 Examples of other potentially dilutive securities are convertible senior securities (convertible preferred stock and convertible debt) and options or warrants [issued prior to June 1, 1969 that were not classified as common stock equivalents under the transition requirements of APB Opinion No. 9, *Reporting the Results of Operations*]. [AIN-APB15, #3]

Dilution—Dilutive Security

.531 *Dilution,* as used in this section, is a reduction of the amount that would otherwise be reported as earnings per share. A dilutive security is a security that results in a decrease in the amount reported as earnings per share. As explained in paragraphs .533 through .535 and .564 and .565, there is no dilution of net loss per share if an enterprise reports a net loss on its income statement. [AIN-APB15, #4]

.532 A dilutive security increases the number of common shares that are considered to be outstanding during the period for which the earnings per share computation is being made. Thus, a dilutive security increases the denominator used in the earnings per share computation. Earnings applicable to common stock, the numerator in the computation, may also increase. But so long as the numerator increase per additional denominator share is less than earnings per outstanding share, the security will be dilutive. [AIN-APB15, #4]

Antidilution—Antidilutive Security

.533 *Antidilution* is an increase in the amount that would otherwise be reported as earnings per share or a decrease in the amount of the net loss per share. Antidilution therefore has an incremental effect on earnings per share data. An antidilutive security is a security that would result in an increase in the amount reported as earnings per share or a decrease in the amount reported as net loss per share. [AIN-APB15, #5]

.534 If net income is reported, an antidilutive option or warrant under the treasury-stock method reduces the number of common shares considered outstanding during a period. Those options or warrants, if permitted to enter the computation, would increase earnings per share by reducing the denominator used. Antidilutive convertible debt would increase the denominator. However, its interest adjustment would increase earnings applicable to common stock, the numerator used in the computation, by a greater amount per additional share than earnings per share computed without assuming conversion. Any numerator increase per additional denominator share that is greater than earnings per share computed without assuming conversion would have an incremental effect on earnings per share and would be antidilutive. Convertible preferred stock is antidilutive if its dividend per common share obtainable on conversion exceeds earnings per share computed without assuming conversion. [AIN-APB15, #5]

.535 If a net loss is reported, exercise or conversion is not assumed.[507] Any computation is antidilutive that increases the number of shares considered outstanding during a period for which a net loss is reported. Exercise of options and warrants is not assumed since this would increase the number of shares considered outstanding. Likewise, conversion would increase the number of shares considered outstanding. In addition, the if-converted adjustments for convertible debt would decrease the amount of the loss. Not deducting dividends on convertible preferred stock would also decrease the amount of the loss applicable to common stock. [AIN-APB15, #5]

Dual Presentation

.536 The dual presentation has two groups of earnings per share data; one is primary earnings per share data and the other is fully diluted earnings per share data. Both must be presented with equal prominence on the face of the income statement. [AIN-APB15, #6]

.537 The dual presentation of primary and fully diluted earnings per share data should not be confused with the two earnings per share amounts that must be presented if an enterprise reports extraordinary items on its income statement. Even if the dual presentation is not required, an enterprise reporting extraordinary items must report (a) earnings per share for income before extraordinary items and (b) earnings per share for net income. If the dual presentation is required, an enterprise reporting extraordinary items must report both amounts for primary earnings per share and both amounts for fully diluted earnings per share. [AIN-APB15, #6]

.538 An enterprise with no [discontinued operations, cumulative effects of accounting changes, or] extraordinary items on its income statement would report only earnings per share for net income. But this must be reported for both primary and fully diluted earnings per share by an enterprise if dual presentation is required. [AIN-APB15, #6]

Primary Earnings per Share

.539 Primary earnings per share is the amount of earnings attributable to each share of common stock outstanding and common stock assumed to be outstanding to reflect the dilutive effect of common stock equivalents. Primary earnings per share data include an earnings per share amount for [income from continuing operations,] income before extraordinary items, [the cumulative effects of accounting changes,] and net income. Those data may also include an earnings per share amount for extraordinary items, [discontinued operations, and gain or loss on disposal of a segment]. [AIN-APB15, #7]

---

[507]Refer to footnote 502. [AIN-APB15, #5, fn15]

.540 Primary earnings per share is used in this section as a convenient means of designating the presentation of those data that must appear on the face of an income statement of an enterprise if the dual presentation is required. Thus, *primary* is a communication tool used merely to identify this group of earnings per share data to be presented and is not suggested as a caption to be used on the income statement. The term *primary* is not intended in any way to attribute greater significance to this group of data than is attributed to the fully diluted data. [AIN-APB15, #7]

Fully Diluted Earnings per Share

.541 Fully diluted earnings per share is the amount of earnings attributable to each share of common stock outstanding and common stock assumed outstanding to reflect the dilutive effect of common stock equivalents and other potentially dilutive securities. Fully diluted earnings per share data include an earnings per share amount for [income from continuing operations,] income before extraordinary items, [the cumulative effects of accounting changes,] and net income. Those data may also include an earnings per share amount for extraordinary items, [discontinued operations, and gain or loss on disposal of a segment]. [AIN-APB15, #8]

.542 *Fully diluted earnings per share* is used in this section as a convenient means of designating the presentation of those data that must appear on the face of an income statement of an enterprise if the dual presentation is required. Thus, *fully diluted* is a communication tool used merely to identify this group of earnings per share data to be presented and is not suggested as a caption to be used on the income statement. [AIN-APB15, #8]

Applicability of This Section

Enterprises and Financial Presentations Excepted

.543 *Question*—Does this section require all enterprises to present earnings per share on all income statements? [AIN-APB15, #9]

.544 *Answer*—All enterprises that are not specifically excepted by this section must present earnings per share on the face of any income statement or summary of [operations]. [AIN-APB15, #9]

.545 The only enterprises excepted from the provisions of this section are:

a. Mutual enterprises without common stock or common stock equivalents outstanding (for example, mutual savings banks, cooperatives, credit unions, etc.)
b. Enterprises registered under the Investment Company Act of 1940

c. Enterprises owned by political subdivisions or municipal, county, state, federal, or foreign governments
d. Not-for-profit enterprises (for example, colleges, universities, medical or scientific research entities, trade and professional associations, religious organizations, etc., that are incorporated) [AIN-APB15, #9]
e. [Nonpublic enterprises] [FAS21, ¶15]

.546 This section applies to all financial presentations that purport to present results of operations in conformity with generally accepted accounting principles and to summaries of those presentations for all enterprises except those listed above. However, the following financial presentations are also excepted from the provisions of this section:

a. Parent company statements accompanying consolidated financial statements
b. Statements of wholly owned subsidiaries
c. Special purpose statements [AIN-APB15, #9]

.547 Special purpose statements (as described in Section 621 of Statements on Auditing Standards) by definition are not prepared in accordance with generally accepted accounting principles. Special purpose statements are not, however, merely those prepared for specific purposes if they purport to present results of operations in conformity with generally accepted accounting principles. [AIN-APB15, #9]

.548-.549 [Deleted 11/92 because of FASB Statement 111, *Rescission of FASB Statement No. 32 and Technical Corrections.*]

Dilution Less Than Three Percent

.550 *Question*—Must an enterprise with a few dilutive securities outstanding make the dual presentation? May that enterprise ignore the dilutive securities and report earnings per share based on common shares outstanding? [AIN-APB15, #11]

.551 *Answer*—The required reporting of earnings per share data depends on the materiality of the amount of dilution produced by securities that enable their holders to obtain common stock in the future. Aggregate dilution from all those securities that is less than three percent of earnings per common share outstanding need not be reported for either primary or fully diluted earnings per share, since that dilution is not considered to be material. Thus, if both the primary and fully diluted amounts are more than 97 percent of earnings per common share outstanding, earnings per share may be based on only common shares outstanding. [AIN-APB15, #11]

.552 The three-percent provision applies to fully diluted earnings per share compared to earnings per common share outstanding, not compared to primary earnings per share. Antidilutive securities are not dilutive by definition and should be excluded in computing aggregate dilution. The three-percent provision also applies to the reporting of any other earnings per share information, such as supplementary data. Aggregate dilution of less than three percent generally should be reported if it is anticipated that earnings per share data for a period when the provision applies might subsequently be included in a comparative income statement in that the following period reflects dilution of three percent or more. Otherwise, dilution in the following period would appear greater than it in fact was. [AIN-APB15, #11]

.553 The three-percent provision [is intended] to provide relief from complex computations to enterprises that would have insignificant dilution if all obligations to issue common stock in the future were fulfilled currently. This would be the case, for example, for an enterprise that has no obligations to issue common stock except for a small amount of stock under options granted to its executives. [AIN-APB15, #11]

Three-Percent Test

.554 *Question*—Is there a simple test that can be applied to determine if dilution would be at least three percent? [AIN-APB15, #12]

.555 *Answer*—Yes. As a rule of thumb, make both the primary and fully diluted computations if the number of additional common shares that must be assumed to be issued exceeds three percent[508] of the number of outstanding common shares. If the dilution produced by either computation is at least three percent, the dual presentation is required. [AIN-APB15, #12]

.556 Dilutive options and warrants are included in earnings per share computations under the treasury-stock method that produces incremental shares (as explained in

---

[508]Actually, the number of additional shares must be at least 3/97 (or 3.09 + percent) of the number of outstanding common shares. If earnings applicable to common stock includes an if-converted adjustment, a greater number of additional shares would be required to produce dilution of at least three percent. Thus, although the number of additional shares is not the only determinant of dilution, common shares assumed outstanding must increase more than three percent to produce dilution of at least three percent. [AIN-APB15, #12, fn16]

paragraphs .684 through .688). The number of incremental shares the treasury-stock method will produce can be approximated by applying a simple formula. Since stock options are the only obligations of many closely held enterprises to issue common stock, the formula is useful if the test described above is to be applied and only options or warrants are considered. [AIN-APB15, #12]

.557 The following formula[509] will approximate the number of incremental shares that will result from applying the treasury-stock method for options or warrants:

$$I = \frac{M - E}{M} (N)$$

Where:

   I   is the number of incremental shares that would be produced by the treasury stock method.

   M is the market price (or fair value) per share of common stock.

   E is the exercise price of the option or warrant per common share obtainable upon exercise.

   N is the total number of shares obtainable on exercise.

Subject to the constraint[510] that M is greater than E. [AIN-APB15, #12]

.558 An example of the application of the formula follows. Assume that an enterprise has granted options to its officers to purchase 10,000 shares of common stock at $6 per share and the common stock has a market price (or fair value) of $10 per share. [AIN-APB15, #12]

.559 Applying the formula for the information given, the amounts to be substituted for the letters are:

$$
\begin{aligned}
I &= \text{unknown} \\
M &= \$10 \\
E &= \$6 \\
N &= 10{,}000
\end{aligned}
$$

Therefore:

$$I = \frac{\$10 - \$6}{\$10} (10{,}000)$$

$$I = .4 \, (10{,}000)$$

$$I = 4{,}000$$

---

[509] The formula should not be used if paragraph .127 applies, that is, if the number of common shares obtainable on the exercise of all options and warrants and their equivalents exceeds 20 percent of the number of common shares outstanding. [AIN-APB15, #12, fn17]

[510] The formula would not be used unless the market price is greater than the exercise price since the result could be antidilutive. [AIN-APB15, #12, fn18]

If the 4,000 incremental shares exceeds 3 percent of the number of outstanding common shares, actual dilution would be computed to determine if dilution is at least 3 percent. [AIN-APB15, #12]

.560-.561 [Deleted 2/92 because of FASB Statement 109, *Accounting for Income Taxes.*]

Unaudited Financial Statements

.562 *Question*—Does this section apply to unaudited financial statements? [AIN-APB15, #14]

.563 *Answer*—Yes. [AIN-APB15, #14]

Earnings per Share Presentation

Reporting Loss per Share

.564 *Question*—Must net loss per share be reported? [AIN-APB15, #15]

.565 *Answer*—Yes, net loss per share must be reported under the same requirements that earnings per share must be reported. Net loss per share, however, is based on outstanding common shares. Assuming exercise of options and warrants or conversion of convertible securities would be anti-dilutive because an increase in the number of shares assumed to be outstanding would reduce the amount of the loss per share.[511] The amount of the loss is increased by any dividends declared (or cumulative even though not declared) for the period on preferred stocks. [AIN-APB15, #15]

.566-.568 [Deleted 2/92 because of FASB Statement 109.]

Simple Capital Structure

.569 *Question*—What is a simple capital structure for purposes of computing earnings per share? [AIN-APB15, #17]

.570 *Answer*—An enterprise has a simple capital structure for purposes of computing earnings per share if during the period it had no securities outstanding (or agreements to issue securities) that in the aggregate dilute earnings per outstanding common share. [AIN-APB15, #17]

---

[511]Refer to footnote 502. [AIN-APB15, #15, fn19]

Complex Capital Structure

.571 *Question*—What is a complex capital structure for purposes of computing earnings per share? [AIN-APB15, #18]

.572 *Answer*—An enterprise has a complex capital structure for purposes of computing earnings per share if it has issued, in addition to common stock, securities that have a dilutive effect on earnings per outstanding common share. Among the securities that may have a dilutive effect are convertible preferred stock, convertible debt, options, warrants, participating securities, different classes of common stock, and agreements to issue those securities or shares of common stock in the future. [AIN-APB15, #18]

.573 As explained in paragraphs .550 through .553, if the aggregate dilution for the period produced by all those securities that are dilutive does not reduce earnings per outstanding common share by at least three percent, an enterprise may be considered as having a simple capital structure for purposes of computing earnings per share. It may be desirable, however, to report the actual dilution in that case, particularly if the period being reported on might later be included in a comparative income statement that includes one or more periods with dilution of three percent or more. [AIN-APB15, #18]

EPS for Simple and Complex Capital Structures

.574 *Question*—How does the reporting of earnings per share data differ for enterprises with simple capital structures and enterprises with complex capital structures? [AIN-APB15, #19]

.575 *Answer*—An enterprise with a simple capital structure is required to have a single presentation of "earnings per common share" on the face of its income statement. An enterprise with a complex capital structure is required to have a dual presentation of both primary and fully diluted earnings per share on the face of its income statement. [AIN-APB15, #19]

.576 Exceptions that apply to enterprises with simple capital structures are explained in paragraphs .577 through .580. An exception that applies to enterprises with complex capital structures is explained in paragraphs .571 through .573. [AIN-APB15, #19]

Dual Presentation for Enterprises with Simple Capital Structures

.577 *Question*—Is an enterprise with a simple capital structure ever required to have the dual presentation? [AIN-APB15, #20]

.578 *Answer*—Yes, the dual presentation is required if common stock was issued during the period on exercise, conversion, etc., and primary earnings per share would have increased or decreased if the issuance had taken place at the beginning of the period. [AIN-APB15, #20]

.579 An enterprise has a simple capital structure if it has no dilutive securities outstanding. If outstanding antidilutive securities are exercised or converted, however, that enterprise would be required to have the dual presentation if primary earnings per share would have been affected as described in paragraph .578. Thus, the dual presentation may be required for an enterprise with a simple capital structure to report the incremental effect of an antidilutive exercise or conversion. [AIN-APB15, #20]

.580 Also, the dual presentation is required for all periods presented in a comparative income statement if it is required for any period. The dual presentation may therefore be required for one or more periods in a comparative income statement if the enterprise had a simple capital structure. [AIN-APB15, #20]

Primary versus Fully Diluted EPS

.581 *Question*—How do fully diluted earnings per share differ from primary earnings per share? [AIN-APB15, #21]

.582 *Answer*—Primary earnings per share computations include only common stock and dilutive common stock equivalents. Fully diluted earnings per share computations include common stock and dilutive common stock equivalents together with other potentially dilutive securities. Fully diluted earnings per share also include those exercises or conversions for which common stock was issued during the period whether their effect is dilutive or antidilutive. [AIN-APB15, #21]

.583 Fully diluted earnings per share show the maximum potential dilution of all dilutive contractual obligations to issue common stock and their effect on current earnings per share on a prospective basis. The difference between primary and fully diluted earnings per share shows (a) the maximum extent of potential dilution of current earnings that would occur from the conversions of securities that are not common stock equivalents or the contingent issuance of common stock not included in the computation of primary earnings per share and (b) the effect of all issuances of common stock on exercises or conversions during the year as if the issuance had occurred at the beginning of the year. [AIN-APB15, #21]

Captions for Earnings per Share Presentations

.584 *Question*—What captions should be used for reporting earnings per share amounts in the dual presentation? [AIN-APB15, #22]

.585 *Answer*—Precise designations are not prescribed by this section except that the term *earnings per common share* should not be used unless an enterprise has a simple capital structure or the term is appropriately qualified. The qualification is determined by whether the enterprise has only common stock equivalents or also has other potentially dilutive securities. [AIN-APB15, #22]

.586 Listed below are five captions that may be used to designate earnings per share amounts. Following the captions is a table indicating the captions an enterprise may use if it has various combinations of securities outstanding. The first two columns of the table indicate the combinations of securities an enterprise might have. The numbers in the other three columns refer to the numbers listed beside the captions that may be used to designate the earnings per share amounts. For example, an enterprise having both dilutive common stock equivalents and other potentially dilutive securities outstanding could designate the primary amounts "earnings per common and common equivalent share" and could designate the fully diluted amounts "earnings per common share—assuming full dilution."

a.   Suggested earnings per share captions:
   (1) "Earnings per common share."
   (2) "Earnings per common share—assuming no dilution."
   (3) "Earnings per common share—assuming full dilution."
   (4) "Earnings per common and common equivalent share." (If both dilutive and antidilutive common stock equivalents are present, the caption may be: "Earnings per common and dilutive common equivalent share.")
   (5) "Earnings per common share—assuming issuance of all dilutive contingent shares."

b.   Table indicating use of EPS captions:

Common Stock Equivalents Present	Other Potentially Dilutive Securities Present	Caption for Single Presentation	Dual Presentation	
			Primary Caption	Fully Diluted Caption
No (a)	No (a)	1		
No (a)	Dilutive		2	3
No (a)	Antidilutive	1 (b)		
Dilutive	No		4	3 (c)
Dilutive	Dilutive		4	3
Dilutive	Antidilutive		4	5 (b)(c)
Antidilutive	No (a)	1 (b)		
Antidilutive	Dilutive		2 (b)	5 (b)
Antidilutive	Antidilutive	1 (b)		

Notes: (a) Or dilution is less than three percent if those securities are present.
     (b) In a note, disclose the existence of the antidilutive securities.
     (c) Primary and fully diluted amounts will be the same.
[AIN-APB15, #22]

Captions in Comparative Statements

.587 *Question*—What presentation is required in a comparative income statement if an enterprise has a simple capital structure in one period and a complex capital structure in another period? [AIN-APB15, #23]

.588 *Answer*—The dual presentation is required for all periods presented if it is required for any period presented. Since the enterprise had a complex capital structure in one period presented, the dual presentation is required for that period and for all other periods presented in the comparative income statement. [AIN-APB15, #23]

.589 In a comparative income statement the captions used should be appropriate for the most dilutive presentation. For example, if there were no common stock equivalents in one period, antidilutive common stock equivalents in one period, and dilutive common stock equivalents in another period in a comparative income statement, the primary amounts could have a designation such as "earnings per common and dilutive common equivalent share." Explanatory disclosure in a note may also be appropriate. [AIN-APB15, #23]

Computing Earnings per Share

Earnings Applicable to Common Stock

.590 *Question*—How are *earnings applicable to common stock* determined for earnings per share computations? [AIN-APB15, #24]

.591 *Answer*—For an enterprise with a simple capital structure, earnings applicable to common stock are net income reduced by dividends declared or paid for the period to preferred stock. Cumulative preferred dividends for the current period not paid or declared also are deducted from net income in determining earnings applicable to common stock. However, preferred dividends that are cumulative only if earned are deducted only to the extent they are earned. Interest on debt need not be adjusted in determining earnings applicable to common stock since it was deducted in arriving at net income. [AIN-APB15, #24]

.592 For example, assume that an enterprise has a net income of $6,000 and has 1,000 shares of common stock outstanding. Also outstanding are 1,000 shares of nonconvertible noncumulative preferred stock and $10,000 of 6-percent nonconvertible bonds. The enterprise has a simple capital structure. If no dividends were paid on preferred stock, earnings applicable to common stock would be $6,000. Earnings per common share would be $6 per share ($6,000 net income divided by 1,000 common shares). The declaration of a dividend of $1 per share on preferred stock would result in earnings applicable to common stock of $5,000 ($6,000 net income less $1,000 for preferred dividends) and earnings per common share of $5 per share. The same result would be obtained if the dividend were cumulative and had not been declared. The same result would also be obtained whether or not the enterprise paid (or declared) a dividend on common stock. [AIN-APB15, #24]

.593 For an enterprise with a complex capital structure, net income is reduced by dividends on nonconvertible preferred stock as described above. If the if-converted method is applied for outstanding convertible securities, however, dividends on convertible preferred stock are not deducted from net income but other adjustments may be necessary. Under the if-converted method, convertible dividends are not deducted if conversion is assumed, and interest (less applicable income tax) is added back to net income if convertible debt is assumed to be converted. [AIN-APB15, #24]

.594 For example, assume that an enterprise has a net income of $6,000 and has 1,000 shares of common stock outstanding. Also outstanding are 1,000 shares of common stock equivalent convertible preferred stock (convertible at 1 common share for each preferred share) and $10,000 of 6-percent convertible bonds (convertible at 3 common shares for each $100 bond) that are not common stock equivalents. The enterprise has a complex capital structure. Assume also that the enterprise paid a $1 per share dividend on both common and preferred stock and the income tax rate is 22 percent. For primary earnings per share, earnings applicable to common stock is $6,000 and earnings per common and common equivalent share is $3 per share ($6,000 divided by 2,000 shares, composed of 1,000 common shares and 1,000 common equivalent shares from the assumed conversion of the convertible preferred stock). For fully diluted earnings per share, earnings applicable to common stock is $6,468 ($6,000 net income plus $600 interest less $132 additional tax payable if the interest had not reduced net income). Earnings per common share assuming full dilution is $2.81 per share ($6,468 divided by 2,300 shares; composed of 1,000 common shares, 1,000 common equivalent shares, and 300 shares from the assumed conversion of the convertible bonds). [AIN-APB15, #24]

Weighted Average of Shares Outstanding

.595 *Question*—What is the effect on earnings per share computations of issuing common stock or other securities that may be converted or exercised to obtain common stock or of reacquiring common stock or those securities during a period? [AIN-APB15, #25]

.596 *Answer*—Those issuances or reacquisitions of common stock or other securities during a period require that a weighted average of shares be computed for the denominator to be used in the earnings per share computations. A weighted average gives due consideration to all shares outstanding and assumed to have been outstanding during a period. Shares issued or retired during a period are weighted by the fraction of the period they were outstanding. The weighted number of shares is added to the number of shares outstanding for the entire period to obtain the weighted average number of shares outstanding during the period. [AIN-APB15, #25]

.597 For example, assume that an enterprise had 100,000 common shares outstanding on January 1 and issued 6,000 additional common shares on March 1. The weighted average would be 102,000 shares for the quarter ending March 31 (100,000 + 1/3(6,000) = 102,000), or 104,000 shares for the 6 months ending June 30 (100,000 + 4/6(6,000) = 104,000), or 105,000 shares for the year ending December 31 (100,000 + 10/12(6,000) = 105,000). The same answers would result if the 6,000 shares issued on March 1 were merely assumed to have been issued to reflect the dilutive effect of common stock equivalents issued on March 1. It should be noted that the number of shares in the weighted average for the quarter and for the year are different. [AIN-APB15, #25]

.598 Reacquired shares are included in the weighted average only for the time they were outstanding. For example, assume that an enterprise had 100,000 shares outstanding on January 1 and reacquired 6,000 shares on March 1. The weighted average would be 98,000 shares for the quarter ending March 31, 96,000 shares for the 6 months ending June 30, and 95,000 shares for the year ending December 31.

Computational Notes:

$100,000 - 6,000 = 94,000$
$94,000 + 2/3\ (6,000) = 98,000$
$94,000 + 2/6\ (6,000) = 96,000$
$94,000 + 2/12\ (6,000) = 95,000$

The same answers would result if the 100,000 shares had included common stock equivalents and the enterprise had reacquired 100 dilutive common stock equivalent convertible bonds (convertible at 60 common shares for 1 bond) on March 1. [AIN-APB15, #25]

.599 More complex methods for computing a weighted average could be used if the number of shares involved changes frequently, such as computing an average weighted by days. [AIN-APB15, #25]

.600 The weighted average discussed in this section is technically an arithmetical mean average of shares outstanding and assumed to be outstanding for earnings per share computations. The most precise average would be the sum of the shares determined on a daily basis divided by the number of days in the period. Less precise averaging methods may be used, however, as illustrated above, if they produce reasonable results. But methods that introduce artificial weighting are not acceptable for computing a weighted average of shares for earnings per share computations. For example, the "Rule of 78" method, that weights shares for the first month of the year by 12 and weights shares for the last month of the year by 1, is not an acceptable method. [AIN-APB15, #25]

.601 Retroactive recognition is given for all periods presented to any stock dividend, stock split, or reverse split, including those occurring after the end of the period for which the computation is being made but before the statements are issued. [AIN-APB15, #25]

Convertible Securities

Classification and Assumed Conversion

.602 *Question*—Which convertible securities are assumed to be converted for primary earnings per share computations and which are assumed to be converted for fully diluted earnings per share computations? [AIN-APB15, #26]

.603 *Answer*—Convertible securities that are classified as common stock equivalents are assumed to be converted for both primary and fully diluted earnings per share computations. Convertible securities that are not common stock equivalents are classified as other potentially dilutive securities and are assumed to be converted only for fully diluted earnings per share computations. [AIN-APB15, #26]

.604 Conversion is assumed for either computation only if the result is dilutive unless (a) the security is included in an aggregate computation that has a net dilutive effect or (b) for fully diluted earnings per share, common stock was issued during the period on an antidilutive conversion, that is, a conversion that would have had the effect of increasing earnings per share if it had occurred at the beginning of the period. If conversion is assumed, the if-converted method is applied.[512] If conversion is not assumed because the result would be antidilutive, interest or dividends on the securities reduce the amount of earnings or increase the amount of loss otherwise applicable to common stock. [AIN-APB15, #26]

.605 Most convertible securities are classified on the basis of their [AIN-APB15, #26] effective [FAS85, ¶3] yield at time of issuance. (The exceptions are discussed in paragraphs .606 and .607.) Under the yield test, convertible securities that [AIN-APB15, #26] have an effective [FAS85, ¶3] yield less than $66^2/_3$ percent of the [AIN-APB15, #26] average Aa corporate bond yield as defined in paragraph .123A [FAS111, ¶8(g)] at time of issuance are common stock equivalents; those yielding at least $66^2/_3$ percent of the [AIN-APB15, #26] average Aa corporate bond yield as defined in paragraph .123A [FAS111, ¶8(n)] are other potentially dilutive securities. [AIN-APB15, #26]

.606 A convertible security that would not otherwise be a common stock equivalent at time of issuance is classified as a common stock equivalent if it is issued with the same terms as those of an outstanding convertible security that is a common stock equivalent. [AIN-APB15, #26] [Convertible securities issued before June 1, 1969 were classified as common stock equivalents or as other potentially dilutive securities based on the transition requirements of APB Opinion No. 15, *Earnings per Share.* The yield test to determine common stock equivalency for convertible securities issued after May 31, 1969 but prior to March 1, 1982 was based on a cash yield of less than $66^2/_3$ percent of the then *current bank prime interest rate.]*

.607 Convertible securities that require or permit the payment of cash on conversion are considered the equivalents of warrants and are classified as common stock equivalents. (Refer to paragraphs .790 through .794 for the treatment of those securities.) A few convertible participating securities are common stock equivalents for which the two-class method may be applied. (Refer to paragraphs .847 through .851 for the treatment of those securities.) The if-converted method is applied if any convertible security is assumed to be converted except for unusual cases when the two-class method is applied. [AIN-APB15, #26]

Time of Issuance

.608 *Question*—What is the *time of issuance* of a convertible security? [AIN-APB15, #27]

[512]Refer to paragraph .142 for a description of the if-converted method. [AIN-APB15, #26, fn20]

.609 *Answer—Time of issuance* is *generally* the date when agreement as to terms has been reached and announced even though subject to further actions, such as directors' or stockholders' approval. In this context, time of issuance is often referred to in financial jargon as the *handshake date*. Thus, time of issuance will usually precede the actual date of issuance of a security by some period that might be as long as several months or as short as a few hours. [AIN-APB15, #27]

.610 *Agreement as to terms* means that all of the terms have been set, not merely that the parties have reached an agreement in principle but the number of securities to be issued or the issue price is still to be determined at a later date. Agreement as to terms is reached when the parties are obligated to complete the transaction if it is ratified by the directors or stockholders, that is, neither party may legally terminate the agreement except for failure to receive approval from the directors or stockholders. The fact that the agreement is subject to a *favorable* ruling from the Treasury Department or a regulatory agency does not affect time of issuance so long as all of the terms of the agreement have been set. [AIN-APB15, #27]

.611 The classification of a convertible security is determined at time of issuance and does not change when the security is actually issued except as discussed in paragraphs .619 through .622. [AIN-APB15, #27]

.612 If time of issuance occurs before a year-end but the agreement has not been approved by either the directors or stockholders before the financial statements are issued, the securities are not considered outstanding in the financial statements being issued or in earnings per share computations. (The securities are similar to a contingent issuance whose conditions are not currently being met.) [AIN-APB15, #27]

Classification and Computation Not Always the Same

.613 *Question*—Are convertible securities included in earnings per share computations at time of issuance? [AIN-APB15, #28]

.614 *Answer*—Convertible securities are classified at time of issuance. Generally they are assumed to be converted for earnings per share computations from that date also. Although a convertible security is classified at time of issuance, in some cases it is not assumed to be converted for earnings per share computations until a later date. [AIN-APB15, #28]

.615 If the conversion privilege is not effective during the period being reported on, the length of time before the privilege becomes effective determines when the security is eligible for assumed conversion in earnings per share computations. Conversion is not assumed for either primary or fully diluted computations if the conversion privilege is not effective within 10 years from the end of the period being reported on. Conversion is assumed only for fully diluted computations if the conversion privilege is effective after five years but within ten years from the end of the period being reported upon. Conversion is assumed as if the security were immediately convertible if the conversion privilege is effective within five years from the end of the period being reported on. [AIN-APB15, #28]

.616 For example, assume that an enterprise issued a debt security at the end of its 1979 reporting year that may be converted into common stock after 12 years (at the end of 1991). The security's yield at time of issuance requires that it be classified as a common stock equivalent. Conversion would not be assumed for 1979 and 1980 earnings per share computations (interest would reduce net income in 1980, however). Conversion would be assumed if the effect is dilutive for fully diluted computations beginning in 1981 and for both primary and fully diluted computations beginning in 1986. Thus, the security is classified at time of issuance but conversion is not assumed for earnings per share computations until later. [AIN-APB15, #28]

.617 Time of issuance and classification of a convertible security may precede the obligation to issue and actual issuance by as much as several months, but a convertible security is not considered outstanding in the interim until there is a valid obligation to issue the security. For example, assume that agreement as to terms for a business combination is reached and announced on December 1, 19X1. Final approval by stockholders occurs on February 16, 19X2 and a convertible security is to be issued March 2, 19X2. Classification of the security is determined at December 1, 19X1. The security would be omitted from 19X1 earnings per share computations if the financial statements are issued before February 16, 19X2, but the impending issuance would be disclosed. [AIN-APB15, #28]

.618 If the business combination is accounted for as a purchase, the security would be considered outstanding from the date of the acquisition in 19X2 earnings per share computations if the stockholders in fact ratify the agreement. If the business combination is accounted for as a pooling of interests, prior periods' earnings per share data would be retroactively restated in comparative income statements issued subsequently to reflect the security as outstanding for all periods presented. [AIN-APB15, #28]

Change of Classification of Convertible Security

.619 *Question*—When does the classification of a convertible security change? [AIN-APB15, #29]

.620 *Answer*—A convertible security's classification is generally determined only at time of issuance and does not change thereafter. However, a change of classification (usually from other potentially dilutive security status to common stock equivalent status) may be required in two situations. Those are if (a) an incorrect estimate of the security's value at time of issuance was made in the absence of a market price or (b) a common stock equivalent convertible security is issued with the same terms as an already outstanding convertible security that is not a common stock equivalent (refer to paragraphs .623 through .626). [AIN-APB15, #29]

.621 If a convertible security does not have a market price at time of issuance, an estimate must be made of the security's fair value to apply the yield test. If the estimate of the security's value is too low, a convertible security that should be classified as a common stock equivalent might not be so classified. In that case, the security would have to be reclassified as a common stock equivalent at actual issuance. Typically, an obviously incorrect estimate would be evidenced by materially higher market transactions for the security at actual issuance shortly after the time of issuance. [AIN-APB15, #29]

.622 A change of the classification of the security would not be appropriate in that case, however, if the higher market prices resulted from an external change over which the issuer had no control. (A general increase in the market prices of other securities might indicate an external change.) A change of the classification would also not be appropriate if convertible securities were sold for cash and the gross proceeds to the issuer were substantially equal to the total amount of the original fair value estimate for the securities. In that case, the total of the net amount received by the issuer plus brokerage commissions paid is approximately equal to the original estimate of fair value of the securities. [AIN-APB15, #29]

Change of Classification Is Mandatory

.623 *Question*—Would convertible securities issued prior to June 1, 1969 [the effective date of this section with regard to classification of outstanding securities] and classified as other potentially dilutive securities become common stock equivalents if another convertible security is issued with the same terms after May 31, 1969 and is classified as a common stock equivalent? [AIN-APB15, #30]

.624 *Answer*—Yes, a change in classification is required by the second sentence of paragraph .119 for any outstanding convertible security that is not a common stock equivalent but that has the same terms as those of another convertible security being issued that is classified as a common stock equivalent at time of issuance. Thus, an outstanding convertible security that is not a common stock equivalent would be reclassified as a common stock equivalent if another convertible security is issued with the same terms and is classified as a common stock equivalent at time of issuance. [AIN-APB15, #30]

.625 Although that reclassification is an exception to the general rule that securities do not change status subsequent to time of issuance, reclassification is mandatory. All of an enterprise's convertible securities issued with the same terms therefore are classified the same for earnings per share computations. [AIN-APB15, #30]

.626 For example, assume that convertible securities were issued with the same terms on May 2, June 2, and July 2, 1969. Only the July 2 issue is a common stock equivalent if classification is based on yield at time of issuance because of an increase in

[AIN-APB15, #30] the average Aa corporate bond yield as defined in paragraph .123A. [FAS111, ¶8(n)] Under paragraph .119, however, both the May 2 and June 2 issues become common stock equivalents also. [AIN-APB15, #30]

Definition of Same Terms

.627 *Question*—What are the *same terms* (as used in the second sentence of paragraph .119) for the subsequent issuance of a convertible security? [AIN-APB15, #31]

.628 *Answer*—The *same terms* are identical terms, not merely similar terms. Thus, any change in dividend or interest rates, conversion rates, call prices or dates, preferences in liquidation, etc., is a change in terms. Market price or issue price is not considered a *term* (refer to paragraphs .629 and .630). [AIN-APB15, #31]

Issue Price Is Not a Term

.629 *Question*—Do different issue prices for different issuances of convertible securities constitute a change in *terms* if all other terms for the securities are the same? [AIN-APB15, #32]

.630 *Answer*—No, different issue prices for convertible securities with the same terms otherwise is not a change in terms. Thus, two convertible securities issued at different prices but with the same stated dividend or interest rates, conversion rates, call prices and dates, preferences in liquidation, etc., have the same terms. [AIN-APB15, #32]

Sale of Treasury Securities Is a New Issue

.631 *Question*—Are convertible securities sold by an issuer from securities held as treasury securities to be classified as a new issue or as part of the original issue under the provisions of the second sentence of paragraph .119? [AIN-APB15, #33]

.632 *Answer*—If convertible securities are acquired by the issuing enterprise and subsequently reissued, they constitute a new issue with the same terms as the existing outstanding convertible security. The *new* issue's status (as a common stock equivalent or not) should be determined under both the common stock equivalent test and the provisions of the second sentence of paragraph .119. If deemed a common stock equivalent, the *new* issue could also affect the status of outstanding securities with the same terms as described in the second sentence of paragraph .119. For example, if the outstanding securities are not common stock equivalents and the reissued securities are common stock equivalents under the yield test (because of a change in market prices or the [AIN-APB15, #33] average Aa corporate bond yield as defined in paragraph .123A), [FAS111, ¶8(n)] the outstanding securities also become common stock equivalents. [AIN-APB15, #33]

.633-.636 [Deleted 3/85 because of FASB Statement 85.]

Effective Yield of Convertible Security in a Package

.637 *Question*—How is the [AIN-APB15, #36] effective [FAS85, ¶3] yield determined for a convertible security issued in a *package*, that is, a convertible security is one of two or more securities issued as a unit? [AIN-APB15, #36]

.638 *Answer*—If two or more securities are issued as a unit, the unit price at time of issuance should be allocated to each security based on the relative fair values of the securities at time of issuance. For example, assume that a *package* consisting of 1 share of common stock, 1 share of convertible preferred stock, and 1 nonconvertible $100 bond with a detachable warrant is sold as a unit for a total price of $200. At time of issuance, fair values were $42.00 per share of common stock, $63.00 per share of convertible preferred stock, $99.75 per bond, and $5.25 per warrant. The $200 unit amount would be allocated to each security as follows:

	Fair Value at Issuance	Percentage of Total	Allocated Amount of $200
Common stock	$ 42.00	20.0%	$ 40.00
Preferred stock	63.00	30.0%	60.00
Bond	99.75	47.5%	95.00
Warrant	5.25	2.5%	5.00
Totals	$210.00	100.0%	$200.00

If the convertible preferred stock is scheduled to pay a dividend of $3.15 per share each year, it would yield 5.25 percent (computed $\frac{\$ 3.15}{\$60.00} \times 100$). [AIN-APB15, #36]

---

[513][Deleted 3/85 because of FASB Statement 85.]

Property Included in Effective Yield

.639 *Question*—May the fair value of property to be paid as dividends or interest be included in computing [AIN-APB15, #37] effective [FAS85, ¶3] yield since this section specifically states only cash? [AIN-APB15, #37]

.640 *Answer*—Yes, the fair value to be paid in lieu of cash may be included in computing the [AIN-APB15, #37] effective [FAS85, ¶3] yield of a convertible security. The property so treated may include nonconvertible senior securities of the same enterprise. But it may not include the same issue for which common stock equivalency is being determined. And it may not include securities of the issuer or its parent or subsidiary that are currently or potentially dilutive and enter into the computation of either primary or fully diluted earnings per share. [AIN-APB15, #37]

.641 For example, any common stock or common stock equivalent of the issuer and securities such as those described in paragraphs .150, .151, and .156 through .160 would not be considered property for this purpose. Also, *extra* dividends to be paid on convertible stock on a nonrecurring basis would not be considered in computing [AIN-APB15, #37] effective [FAS85, ¶3] yield. [AIN-APB15, #37]

.642-.643 [Deleted 11/92 because of FASB Statement 111.]

514[Deleted 11/92 because of FASB Statement 111.]

Original Issue Premium or Discount on Convertible Securities

.644 *Question*—What happens to original issue premium or discount if convertible securities are assumed to be converted and common stock is assumed to be issued for earnings per share computations? [AIN-APB15, #40]

.645 *Answer*—Any original issue premium or discount amortized during the period (to compute the effective interest deducted from net income for a debt security) is eliminated from net income in arriving at earnings applicable to common stock. The unamortized original issue premium or discount balance at the date of assumed conversion (the ending balance plus the amount amortized during the period) is then ignored for earnings per share computations. The if-converted method only assumes conversion of the securities; it does not assume retirement. The converted securities are assumed to be held by the issuer as treasury securities during the period being reported on and balance sheet accounts related to those securities are not affected by the assumed conversion. Note that those assumptions are made only for earnings per share computations; the issuer's balance sheet and net income for the period are not affected in any way by the assumptions made for earnings per share computations. [AIN-APB15, #40]

No Antidilution from Convertible Preferred Stock

.646 *Question*—When is convertible preferred stock antidilutive and therefore not assumed to be converted for earnings per share computations? [AIN-APB15, #41]

.647 *Answer*—Convertible preferred stock is antidilutive and conversion is not assumed[515] if the amount of the dividend paid or declared for the current period (or accumulated if not paid) per common share obtainable on conversion exceeds the earnings per share amount computed without assuming conversion. [AIN-APB15, #41]

---

[515]Refer to paragraphs .657 through .660 for an exception if actual conversion occurs. [AIN-APB15, #41, fn23]

.648 For example, assume that an enterprise had a net income of $1,500 and had 1,000 shares of common stock outstanding. Also outstanding were 1,000 shares of preferred stock convertible on a 1-for-1 basis and classified as a common stock equivalent. A $1.00 per share dividend was paid to the convertible shareholders. Assumption of conversion would be antidilutive in this case since earnings per outstanding common share is $.50 per share. (Earnings per common and common equivalent share would be $.75 per share if conversion were assumed.) Conversion would not be assumed, but rather the preferred dividend would be deducted to compute earnings applicable to common stock. Earnings per share would be computed on the basis of actual common stock outstanding. The same result would be obtained if the dividend were cumulative and not paid. [AIN-APB15, #41]

No Antidilution from Convertible Debt

.649 *Question*—When is convertible debt antidilutive and therefore not assumed to be converted for earnings per share computations? [AIN-APB15, #42]

.650 *Answer*—Convertible debt is antidilutive and conversion is not assumed[516] if its interest (net of tax) per common share obtainable on conversion exceeds the earnings per share computed without assuming conversion. [AIN-APB15, #42]

.651 For example, assume that an enterprise has a net income of $500 and had 1,000 shares of common stock outstanding. Also outstanding were 1,000 convertible bonds with a par value of $100 each paying interest at 3 percent per annum and convertible into 1 share of common stock each. Assume the bonds are classified as common stock equivalents and that the effective income tax rate is 50 percent. The earnings per common share outstanding (ignoring conversion of the bonds) is $.50 per share. Assuming conversion, $3,000 of interest would be added back less $1,500 of additional income tax, resulting in a net increase of $1,500 and earnings applicable to common stock of $2,000. The $1.00 earnings per share for the 2,000 common and common equivalent shares would be antidilutive and conversion would therefore not be assumed. [AIN-APB15, #42]

Conversion Assumed for Primary Only

.652 *Question*—If a common stock equivalent convertible security is assumed to be converted for primary earnings per share computations, must it also be assumed to be converted for fully diluted earnings per share computations? [AIN-APB15, #43]

.653 *Answer*—Generally, a common stock equivalent convertible security is assumed to be converted for both computations. However, if fully diluted earnings

---

[516]Refer to paragraphs .657 through .660 for an exception if actual conversion occurs. [AIN-APB15, #42, fn24]

per share would be increased by the assumed conversion, conversion would be assumed only for the primary earnings per share computation. That situation could occur if two convertible securities were outstanding and the dividend on one classified as a common stock equivalent exceeds fully diluted earnings per share but not primary earnings per share. [AIN-APB15, #43]

.654 For example, assume that an enterprise had a net income of $9,500 and had 2,000 shares of common stock outstanding. Also outstanding were 1,000 shares of Class A convertible preferred stock that was a common stock equivalent and 1,500 shares of Class B convertible preferred stock that was not a common stock equivalent. The Class A paid a dividend of $2.50 per share and the Class B paid a dividend of $1.00 per share. Both are convertible into common on a one-for-one basis. [AIN-APB15, #43]

.655 Primary earnings per share is $2.67 per share assuming conversion of the Class A convertible preferred ($9,500 - $1,500 = $8,000 earnings applicable to common divided by 3,000 shares). Fully diluted earnings per share would be $2.11 per share if conversion were assumed for both the Class A and Class B convertible preferred ($9,000 ÷ 4,500 shares). However, fully diluted earnings per share is $2.00 per share if conversion is assumed for only the Class B ($9,500 - $2,500 = $7,000 earnings applicable to common divided by 3,500 shares). The difference between $2.11 and $2.00 is caused by the incremental effect of assuming conversion of the Class A. Since the Class A dividend per common share obtainable on conversion exceeds fully diluted earnings per share computed without assuming conversion, conversion would be antidilutive (refer to paragraphs .646 through .648). Therefore, primary earnings per share is reported at $2.67 per share and fully diluted earnings per share is reported at $2.00 per share since this is the maximum dilutive amount. [AIN-APB15, #43]

.656 This example illustrates the fact that earnings per share amounts may be affected by changes either in the numerator or in the denominator used in the computation. Naturally, in some cases, both change. [AIN-APB15, #43]

If-Converted Method at Actual Conversion

.657 *Question*—Is the if-converted method applied differently for primary and fully diluted earnings per share computations if actual conversion occurs? [AIN-APB15, #44]

.658 *Answer*—If a common stock equivalent convertible security is converted during a period, the if-converted method is applied from the beginning of the period[517] to the date of conversion for both primary and fully diluted earnings per share computations if the result is dilutive. [AIN-APB15, #44]

---

[517]For convertible securities issued and converted during the period, conversion is assumed only from time of issuance rather than from the beginning of the period. [AIN-APB15, #44, fn25]

.659 If the result is antidilutive, however, conversion is not assumed for the primary computation. But if an actual conversion occurs during a period, conversion is assumed at the beginning of the period for the fully diluted computation and the if-converted method is applied, regardless of whether the result is dilutive or antidilutive. [AIN-APB15, #44]

.660 On actual conversion, common stock issued is included in the weighted average of shares outstanding in both the primary and fully diluted computations from the date of conversion. The securities tendered by the holder for conversion are thereafter considered to be retired. [AIN-APB15, #44]

Securities Convertible into Other Convertible Securities

.661 *Question*—How is a convertible security that is convertible into another convertible security included in earnings per share computations? [AIN-APB15, #45]

.662 *Answer*—Those convertible securities enter earnings per share computations according to their provisions and their characteristics. [AIN-APB15, #45]

.663 A convertible security issued by a subsidiary that is convertible only into a parent company's convertible security is a senior security from the standpoint of the subsidiary, that is, the yield test does not apply. For consolidated earnings per share computations, however, the subsidiary's security would be assumed to be converted into the parent's security. The parent's security would then be assumed to be converted under the if-converted method (if the net result is dilutive). If the parent's convertible security is not a common stock equivalent, conversion of the parent's security would be assumed only for fully diluted computations. If it is a common stock equivalent, conversion of the parent's security would be assumed for both primary and fully diluted computations (refer to paragraphs .883 through .888). [AIN-APB15, #45]

.664 Convertible securities that are convertible at the option of the holder into either another convertible security or a nonconvertible security are assumed to be converted into the security that would be more advantageous for the holder (but not if the result is antidilutive). If conversion is assumed into the other convertible security, that security is then assumed to be converted into common stock for earnings per share computations (but not if the net result is antidilutive). If conversion is assumed into the nonconvertible security, dividends that would have been applicable to the nonconvertible security, as if it had been outstanding, are deducted in determining earnings applicable to common stock. If converted, adjustments may also be applicable. The classification (determined under the yield test) as a common stock equivalent or other potentially dilutive security of convertible securities that are convertible at the option of the holder as discussed in this paragraph determines whether conversion is assumed for both primary and fully diluted computations or only for fully diluted computations. [AIN-APB15, #45]

.665 In some cases, the security that would be more advantageous for assumed conversion cannot be determined. That might be the case, for example, if the non-convertible security pays a high dividend and the second convertible security has good prospects for an increase in its market price. If the more advantageous security to the holders cannot be determined, the computation should give effect to the greater earnings per share dilution. [AIN-APB15, #45]

Options and Warrants and Their Equivalents

Classification of Options and Warrants

.666 *Question*—How are options, warrants, and their equivalents classified for earnings per share computations? [AIN-APB15, #46]

.667 *Answer*—Options, warrants, and their equivalents are always common stock equivalents unless they were issued prior to June 1, 1969 *and* the issuer [made an election under the transition requirements of this section to exclude them from common stock equivalents.][518] All other options, warrants, and their equivalents are included in both primary and fully diluted earnings per share computations. [AIN-APB15, #46]

No Antidilution from Options and Warrants

.668 *Question*—When are options and warrants antidilutive under the treasury-stock method? [AIN-APB15, #47]

.669 *Answer*—Generally, options and warrants are antidilutive if their exercise price exceeds the market price of the common stock obtainable on exercise. This is because application of the treasury-stock method in that case would reduce the number of common shares included in the computation and would increase the earnings per share amount. [AIN-APB15, #47]

.670 The prohibition against antidilution in applying the treasury-stock method recognizes the economic fact that an option or warrant would not be exercised when the exercise price was above the market price because the stock could be purchased in the market for less than it could be purchased by exercising the option or warrant. However, if for some reason options or warrants are exercised when the market price is below the exercise price, the market price at the exercise date is applied in the fully diluted computation for the exercised options or warrants for the period they were outstanding (refer to paragraphs .745 through .754). However, antidilution is not reflected in the primary computation prior to exercise. [AIN-APB15, #47]

---

[518]Those options and warrants would be common stock equivalents except for the fact that they were issued before [June 1, 1969]. This section provides that they be classified as common stock equivalents only if the issuer [previously] elected to so classify them. [AIN-APB15, #46, fn26]

.671 In special cases for which other methods are applied (refer to paragraphs .126 and .127), the factors that cause dilution or antidilution are, of course, different. Those special cases are discussed in paragraphs .679 through .683 and .765 through .794. [AIN-APB15, #47]

Equivalents of Options and Warrants

.672 *Question*—What kinds of securities are considered the equivalents of options and warrants and therefore always classified as common stock equivalents? [AIN-APB15, #48]

.673 *Answer*—Stock purchase contracts, stock subscriptions not fully paid, deferred compensation plans providing for the issuance of common stock, and convertible debt and convertible preferred stock allowing or requiring the payment of cash at conversion (regardless of the yield of those convertible securities at time of issuance) are considered the equivalents of options or warrants. The treasury-stock method should be applied for all of those securities unless their terms or the provisions of paragraphs .126 and .127 require that another method be applied for the computation of earnings per share. [AIN-APB15, #48]

Grouping Options and Warrants

.674 *Question*—May antidilutive options and warrants be grouped with dilutive options and warrants in applying the treasury-stock method? [AIN-APB15, #49]

.675 *Answer*—No, except in the special situations discussed below. [AIN-APB15, #49]

.676 Footnote 11 allows reasonable grouping of like securities, that is, options and warrants with the same exercise prices per common share to be issued. For example, it would be appropriate to group an option to purchase 1 share of common stock for $20 with a warrant to purchase 2 shares of common stock for $40. Assuming a market price of $15 per share for common stock, those options and warrants would not be grouped with a warrant to purchase 1 share of common stock for $10. [AIN-APB15, #49]

.677 If an aggregate computation is required, however, antidilutive and dilutive securities must be included in the same computation. Paragraph .127 provides for an aggregate computation, for example. An antidilutive option that must be exercised before a dilutive option may be exercised must also be included in an aggregate computation. [AIN-APB15, #49]

.678 For example, assume an option is exercisable at $30 to purchase 1 share of common stock and a second option is exercisable at $10 to purchase 1 share of common stock *after* the first option is exercised. The 2 options would be grouped and considered as a *2-step* option to buy 2 shares of common stock for $40. Their aggregate effect would be dilutive if the market price of common stock exceeds $20 per share. An aggregate computation would not be made for a dilutive option that must be exercised before an antidilutive option may be exercised, because the anti-dilutive option would not be exercised in that situation. [AIN-APB15, #49]

Methods Used for Options and Warrants

.679 *Question*—Since different methods are described for the treatment of options and warrants in this section, in what order should the different methods be applied? [AIN-APB15, #50]

.680 *Answer*—In determining the effect of options and warrants and their equivalents in earnings per share computations, apply paragraphs in the following order (to the extent that each is pertinent): paragraph .126, [then] paragraph .127, [then] paragraph .125. [AIN-APB15, #50]

.681 Paragraph .126 applies to options and warrants or their equivalents (a) that either allow or require the tendering of debt at exercise or (b) whose proceeds from exercise must be applied to retire debt or other securities under the terms of those securities. Paragraph .126 also applies to convertible securities that either allow or permit the payment of cash at conversion. Those convertibles are considered the equivalents of warrants. [AIN-APB15, #50]

.682 Paragraph .127 applies only if the number of common shares obtainable on exercise of all outstanding options and warrants and their equivalents exceed 20 percent of the number of common shares outstanding at the end of the period. [AIN-APB15, #50]

.683 Paragraph .125 (the treasury-stock method) applies to all other options and warrants and their equivalents. [AIN-APB15, #50]

Treasury-Stock Method Reflects Dilution of Options and Warrants

.684 *Question*—How does the treasury-stock method reflect the dilutive effect of options and warrants? [AIN-APB15, #51]

.685 *Answer*—The treasury-stock method increases the number of shares assumed to be outstanding if the exercise price of an option or warrant is below the market price of common stock obtainable on exercise. The dilutive effect of the treasury-stock method is demonstrated in the following example. [AIN-APB15, #51]

.686 Assume that an enterprise earned $125,000 during a period when it had 60,000 shares of common stock outstanding. The common stock sold at an average market price of $20 per share during the period. Also outstanding were 10,000 warrants that could be exercised to purchase 1 share of common stock for $15 for each warrant exercised. Earnings per common share *outstanding* would be $2.08 per share ($125,000 ÷ 60,000 shares). [AIN-APB15, #51]

.687 Applying the treasury-stock method, the 10,000 warrants would be assumed to have been exercised by their holders at the beginning of the period. On exercise, 10,000 shares of common stock would be assumed to have been issued by the enterprise to the holders. The $150,000 proceeds (10,000 warrants at an exercise price of $15 per share) would be assumed to have been used by the enterprise to purchase 7,500 shares ($150,000 ÷ $20 per share average market price) of common stock in the market on the exercise date. Common stock would therefore increase [by] 2,500 shares.[519] (The 10,000 shares issued less 7,500 shares purchased results in 2,500 *incremental* shares.) A total of 62,500 shares would be considered as outstanding for the entire period. The amount to be reported as primary earnings per share would be $2.00 per share ($125,000 ÷ 62,500 shares), or dilution of $.08 per share. [AIN-APB15, #51]

.688 Fully diluted earnings per share would also be $2.00 per share if the ending market price of the common stock were $20 per share or less. But an ending market price above $20 per share would cause more dilution to be reflected in fully diluted earnings per share. For example, an ending market price of $25 per share would produce 4,000 incremental common shares[520] that would result in fully diluted earnings per share of $1.95 per share. Dilution would be $.13 per share from earnings per outstanding share and $.05 per share from primary earnings per share. [AIN-APB15, #51]

Market Prices Used for Treasury-Stock Method

.689 *Question*—What market prices of common stock are used in applying the treasury-stock method for options and warrants? [AIN-APB15, #52]

.690 *Answer*—The average market price of common stock during each three-month quarter included in the period being reported on is used to determine the number of incremental shares included in primary earnings per share computations. If a period of less than three months is being reported on, the average market price during that period is used. [AIN-APB15, #52]

---

[519]The incremental number of shares may be more simply computed $\frac{\$20 - \$15}{\$20} \times 10,000 = 2,500$ using the formula given in paragraph .557. [AIN-APB15, #51, fn27]

[520]For fully diluted incremental shares, the computation would be $\frac{\$25 - \$15}{\$25} \times 10,000 = 4,000$. [AIN-APB15, #51, fn28]

.691 The average market price during each three-month quarter included in the period being reported on is also used to determine the number of incremental shares included in fully diluted earnings per share computations *unless* (a) the ending market price for the quarter is higher than the average market price or (b) options or warrants were exercised during the quarter. [AIN-APB15, #52]

.692 A higher ending market price for the quarter is used in fully diluted computations rather than the average market price. For the fully diluted year-to-date computation, the number of incremental shares produced by applying the ending market price is compared to the number of shares determined by computing a year-to-date weighted average of incremental shares included in the quarterly fully diluted computations. The number of incremental shares used in the fully diluted year-to-date computation is the greater of the number of incremental shares determined from the ending market price or from the weighted average of quarters (refer to paragraphs .730 through .736 for examples). [AIN-APB15, #52]

.693 If options or warrants are exercised, the market price on the exercise date is applied for the exercised options or warrants from the beginning of the year to the exercise date for fully diluted computations. Thus, the incremental share computations for quarters prior to the exercise date use the market price at the exercise date rather than the ending or average market price (refer to paragraphs .737 through .754 for examples). [AIN-APB15, #52]

.694 In accordance with the antidilution provisions of this section, exercise of options or warrants is not assumed for any quarter if the exercise price is higher than the market price determined for the computation (as described above) except if options or warrants have in fact been exercised. However, antidilutive options or warrants would be included in an aggregate computation resulting in a net dilutive effect. [AIN-APB15, #52]

.695 Thus, options and warrants may be included in the computations in some quarters but not in other quarters. Also, options and warrants may be included in fully diluted earnings per share computations for the quarter because the average market price is below the exercise price. [AIN-APB15, #52]

How Many Market Prices?

.696 *Question*—How many market prices should be used to determine the average market price of common stock if applying the treasury-stock method? [AIN-APB15, #53]

.697 *Answer*—As many market prices as are needed to compute a meaningful average would be used. [AIN-APB15, #53]

.698 Theoretically, every market transaction for an enterprise's common stock (both the number of shares and the price per share) could be included in determining the average market price. For example, consider 4 transactions of: 100 shares at $10 per share, 60 shares at $11 per share, 30 shares at $12 per share, and 10 shares at $13 per share. The average of the 4 prices would be $11.50 (a simple average) but the average price for the 200 shares would be $10.75 per share (a weighted average). [AIN-APB15, #53]

.699 As a practical matter, however, a simple average of monthly prices is adequate so long as prices do not fluctuate significantly. If prices fluctuate greatly, weekly or daily prices probably would be used. Only if volume of common shares traded and prices at which trades occurred both fluctuated significantly would it be necessary to compute a weighted average to obtain a meaningful average market price. [AIN-APB15, #53]

What Market Price to Use?

.700 *Question*—Should the market price used in computing the average described in paragraphs .696 through .699 be the high, low, close, or an average of high and low prices? [AIN-APB15, #54]

.701 *Answer*—Generally, closing market prices would be adequate for use in computing the average market price. If prices fluctuate widely, however, an average of the high and low prices for the period the price represents (whether a month, week, or day) would usually produce a more representative price to be used. [AIN-APB15, #54]

.702 Perhaps more important than the price selected is that the particular price selected be used consistently unless it is no longer representative because of changed conditions. For example, an enterprise using the closing price during several years of relatively stable market prices could change to an average of high and low prices if prices started fluctuating greatly and the closing market price would no longer produce a representative average market price. Likewise, an enterprise using an average of high and low prices during several years of relatively stable volume could use an average weighted by the number of shares included in market transactions during the period if both prices and volume started fluctuating greatly and the simple average of high and low prices would no longer produce a representative average market price. Shorter periods would be more appropriate than longer periods in that case also, as noted in paragraphs .696 through .699. [AIN-APB15, #54]

.703 The price, period, or method used in computing the average market price would only be changed if it becomes obvious that a representative average market price would not be obtained if the change were not made. In the absence of changed conditions, a change would not be made. [AIN-APB15, #54]

Over-the-Counter and Listed Stocks Not Traded

.704 *Question*—What price should be used if applying the treasury-stock method for an over-the-counter stock or a listed stock not traded? [AIN-APB15, #55]

.705 *Answer*—If available, market prices at which trades occur would be used in applying the treasury-stock method. For stocks traded over the counter, the actual trade prices may not be known. Bid and asked quotations generally are available, however, for both over-the-counter stocks and listed stocks not traded. [AIN-APB15, #55]

.706 The price that will be representative of the market price may have to be computed from the information available. An average of the bid and asked quotations might produce a representative price. In some cases, an average of quotations from several dealers could be used. Generally, the method selected would be used consistently in the absence of actual market prices. [AIN-APB15, #55]

.707 It should be noted that although bid quotations produce a conservative estimate of a stock's market value, asked quotations are more conservative for earnings per share computations. This is because a higher market price produces more incremental shares under the treasury-stock method than does a lower price. Therefore, to obtain a conservative answer, the asked quotation would be used in applying the treasury-stock method for listed common stocks not traded and for common stocks traded over the counter. [AIN-APB15, #55]

Fair Value Used If No Market Price

.708 *Question*—How should the average market price be determined, to apply the treasury-stock method for options and warrants, if an enterprise's common stock is not traded (for example, for a closely held enterprise with only options outstanding)? [AIN-APB15, #56]

.709 *Answer*—If an enterprise's common stock is not traded and market prices are therefore not available, the fair value per share of its common stock is used to apply the treasury-stock method for options and warrants. [AIN-APB15, #56]

.710 Estimating the fair value of a share of common stock that is seldom, if ever, traded is often difficult. Various methods of valuation may be appropriate under different circumstances. While book value or liquidation value per share may provide some indication of fair value, those amounts usually would not be used without adjustment. Estimations based on replacement value or capitalized earnings value, however, might be used in determining fair value. [AIN-APB15, #56]

.711 In some cases, documents may be used as a basis for estimating the fair value of an enterprise's common stock. Personal financial statements of stockholders may present the estimated value of their stock ownership in the enterprise. Buy and sell agreements contain provisions for determining the value of a stockholder's interest in an enterprise in the event of death or retirement or withdrawal from participation in the enterprise's activities. Estate tax valuations established for recently deceased stockholders may provide a basis for estimating the current value of an enterprise's stock. Merger or sales negotiations entered into by the enterprise and valuations or appraisals obtained by a stockholder or the enterprise for credit purposes may provide established values appropriate for use in estimating the fair value of an enterprise's stock. A fair value estimate of the stock might also be projected currently from the relationship at the time of issuance of the warrant or option to earnings (on a per share basis) or to the book value of the common stock. [AIN-APB15, #56]

.712 External sources may also be used to obtain a fair value estimate for an enterprise's stock. Traded securities of other enterprises in the same industry, their price-earnings ratios, dividend yields, and the relationship of their market prices to book values per share may provide guidance for estimating the value of a stock that is not traded. In addition to the methods suggested above, articles in professional publications may suggest other valuation methods and provide more specific guidance for applying selected techniques (for example, refer to the *Journal of Accountancy,* August 1969, pages 35-47, and March 1966, pages 47-55). In some instances, enterprises have engaged investment bankers to estimate the value of the common stock if management believed a fair value could not be obtained any other way. [AIN-APB15, #56]

.713 If a fair estimate is used in the absence of market prices for an enterprise's common stock, that fact and the method used to estimate the fair value would be disclosed as required by paragraph .111. The disclosure would usually be contained in a note to the earnings per share amounts presented (refer to Exhibit 168A for an example). [AIN-APB15, #56]

Options and Warrants Outstanding Part of a Period

.714 *Question*—How should dilutive options or warrants that are outstanding for only part of a period be treated for earnings per share computations? [AIN-APB15, #57]

.715 *Answer*—Dilutive options or warrants that are issued during a period or that expire or are canceled during a period are reflected in both primary and fully diluted earnings per share computations for the time they were outstanding during the period being reported on. The common equivalent shares to be considered enter earnings per share computations as a weighted average as described in paragraph .138. [AIN-APB15, #57]

.716 For example, assume that an enterprise whose financial reporting year ends on December 31 issued 100,000 warrants for 1 share each on October 8, 19X1 with an exercise price of $10. Assume also an average market price for common stock during the intervening 12-week period of $12 per share. Applying the treasury-stock method for primary earnings per share computations for the fourth quarter, the 16,667 incremental shares computed $\frac{\$12 - \$10}{\$12}$ x 100,000 = 16,667 would be weighted 12/13, since they were outstanding for only 12 of the 13 weeks during the quarter, and would represent 15,385 common shares (16,667 x 12/13) in the fourth quarter of 19X1. In the annual earnings per share computation for 19X1, those warrants would represent 3,846 common shares (15,385 ÷ 4). [AIN-APB15, #57]

.717 If the market price at December 31, 19X1 for common stock exceeded the $12 average market price, the higher market price would be used in computing fully diluted earnings per share to reflect maximum potential dilution as specified in paragraph .135. For a market price of common stock on December 31 of $12.50 per share, the shares to be added for the fourth quarter fully diluted earnings per share would be computed as follows:

$$\frac{\$12.50 - \$10}{12.50} \text{ x } 100,000 = 20,000$$

$$12/13 \text{ x } 20,000 = 18,462 \text{ shares}$$

[AIN-APB15, #57]

.718 The shares to be added for 19X1 annual fully diluted earnings per share in this case would be 4,615. [AIN-APB15, #57]

.719 If the warrants described in the above example expired or were canceled on March 25, 19X2 and we assume an average market price for common stock during the 12 weeks then ended of $12, the same results as above would be obtained for primary earnings per share computations for the first quarter of 19X2. That is, assumed exercise of the 100,000 warrants would produce 16,667 incremental shares weighted 12/13 and would represent 15,385 common shares in the first quarter of 19X2. In the annual earnings per share computations for 19X2, those warrants would represent 3,846 common shares. [AIN-APB15, #57]

.720 If the market price of common stock on the *last day the warrants were outstanding* (March 25, 19X2) exceeded the $12 average market price for the 12-week period, the higher market price would be used in computing fully diluted earnings per share to reflect maximum dilution. For a market price of $12.50 on March 25, 19X2 in this example, 18,462 shares would be added for the first quarter computations and 4,615 shares would be added for the 19X2 annual computations in computing fully diluted earnings per share. [AIN-APB15, #57]

.721 Generally, options or warrants that expire or are canceled will not affect earnings per share computations. The above examples are included only for those rare cases when they do. Most dilutive options and warrants will be exercised prior to expiration or cancellation. Antidilutive options and warrants do not enter earnings per share computations,[521] since they would not be exercised if common stock could be purchased for less in the market than through exercise. [AIN-APB15, #57]

.722 If dilutive options or warrants expire or are canceled during a period, it may also be desirable to furnish supplementary earnings per share data as described in paragraph .113, but previously reported earnings per share data would not be retroactively adjusted for expirations or cancellations of warrants or options. [AIN-APB15, #57]

What Is a Period?

.723 *Question*—What is a *period* as the term is used in this section? [AIN-APB15, #58]

.724 *Answer*—A *period* is the time for which net income is reported and earnings per share are computed. [AIN-APB15, #58]

.725 However, if the treasury-stock method or any method[522] requiring the computation of an average market price is used and the reporting period is longer than three months, a separate computation is made for each three-month period. [AIN-APB15, #58]

.726 If a period of less than a quarter is being reported on, the average market price of common stock during the period encompassed by the income statement is used in applying the treasury-stock methods. Other methods requiring the use of average market prices also use the prices in effect during this shorter period. [AIN-APB15, #58]

Share Averaging

.727 *Question*—If the reporting period is longer than three months and the treasury-stock method is applied, how is the weighted average of shares computed for the reported period? [AIN-APB15, #59]

---

[521] Except in the unusual situations described in paragraph .127 and in footnote 503. [AIN-APB15, #57, fn29]

[522] For example, refer to paragraphs .773 through .777, .786 through .789, .812 through .814, and .817 through .819. [AIN-APB15, #58, fn30]

.728 *Answer*—A weighted average of shares is computed based on the average market prices during each three months included in the reporting period. Thus, if the period being reported on is six months, nine months, or one year, a weighted average[523] of shares is computed for each quarter. The weighted averages for all quarters are then added together, and the resulting total is divided by the number of quarters to determine the weighted average for the period. [AIN-APB15, #59]

.729 Assume, for example, that an enterprise had 25,000 shares of common stock outstanding during a year and also had granted options that resulted in the following incremental shares computed using the treasury-stock method: 500 in the first quarter, none in the second quarter because they would have been antidilutive, 1,400 in the third quarter, and 1,000 in the fourth quarter. The weighted average of shares for the year could be computed either:

$$25,500 + 25,000 + 26,400 + 26,000 = 102,900$$

$$102,900 \div 4 = 25,725$$

or

$$\frac{500}{4} + \frac{1,400}{4} + \frac{1,000}{4} = 725$$

$$725 + 25,000 = 25,725$$

[AIN-APB15, #59]

Applying Ending and Average Market Prices

.730 *Question*—How do the computations of primary and fully diluted earnings per share differ if the treasury-stock method is applied for options and warrants and the ending market price of common stock is different from the average market price? [AIN-APB15, #60]

.731 *Answer*—If the ending market price of common stock is higher than the average market price for the period, the ending market price is used for the fully diluted computation to reflect maximum potential dilution. The use of different market prices for primary and fully diluted earnings per share computations naturally results in different numbers of shares for the two computations. The use of a higher ending market price for fully diluted computations may also result in the assumption of exercise for fully diluted earnings per share but not for primary earnings per share. Year-to-date computations for fully diluted earnings per share may also be more complex if market prices of common stock increase and then decrease during

---

[523]Refer to paragraphs .595 through .601 and .906 through .909 for examples of computing a weighted average. [AIN-APB15, #59, fn31]

the year, since the share computation is then made two ways and the greater number of shares is used in computing year-to-date fully diluted earnings per share. The above situations are illustrated in the following example. [AIN-APB15, #60]

.732 Assume stock options are outstanding to obtain 5,000 shares of common stock at an exercise price of $10 per share. Assume also the following average and ending market prices of common stock during the calendar year:

	Average Market Price	Ending Market Price
First quarter	$11.11	$12.00
Second quarter	9.75	11.00
Third quarter	13.89	14.00
Fourth quarter	12.50	13.00

[AIN-APB15, #60]

.733 For primary earnings per share, the treasury-stock method would produce the following number of *incremental* shares to reflect the dilutive effect of the options:

	Primary Incremental Shares	
	Quarterly EPS	Year-to-Date EPS
First quarter	500 (a)	500
Second quarter	0	250 (b)
Third quarter	1,400 (c)	633 (d)
Fourth quarter	1,000 (e)	725 (f)

[AIN-APB15, #60]

Computational Notes:

(a) $\dfrac{\$11.11 - \$10}{\$11.11} \times 5,000 = 500$

(b) $500 + 0 = 500$ $500 \div 2 = 250$

(c) $\dfrac{\$13.89 - \$10}{\$13.89} \times 5,000 = 1,400$

(d) $500 + 0 + 1,400 = 1,900$ $1,900 \div 3 = 633$

(e) $\dfrac{\$12.50 - \$10}{\$12.50} \times 5,000 = 1,000$

(f) $500 + 0 + 1,400 + 1,000 = 2,900$ $2,900 \div 4 = 725$

[AIN-APB15, #60]

.734 For fully diluted earnings per share, the treasury-stock method would produce the following number of incremental shares to reflect the maximum dilutive effect of the options:

	Fully Diluted Incremental Shares	
	Quarterly EPS (a)	Year-to-Date EPS
First quarter	833	833
Second quarter	455 (b)	644 (c)
Third quarter	1,429	1,429 (d)
Fourth quarter	1,154	1,154 (e)

Computational Notes:

(a) Based on ending market price for each quarter.

(b) Note that the *average* market price for this quarter was antidilutive, so the computation is made only for fully diluted earnings per share.

(c) $833 + 455 = 1,288$. $1,288 \div 2 = 644$
Use 644 weighted average since 644 is greater than 455 incremental shares based on ending market price.

(d) $833 + 455 + 1,429 = 2,717$. $2,717 \div 3 = 906$
Use 1,429 incremental shares based on the ending market price since 1,429 is greater than 906.

(e) $833 + 455 + 1,429 + 1,154 = 3,871$. $3,871 \div 4 = 968$
Use 1,154 incremental shares based on the ending market price since 1,154 is greater than 968. [AIN-APB15, #60]

.735 Note that the two computations made for year-to-date fully diluted incremental shares may in some cases cause different market prices to be applied for the quarterly and year-to-date fully diluted computations. For example, assume that in the above illustration the average market price in the fourth quarter was $13.00 and the ending market price was $12.50. The $13 average market price would produce 1,154 incremental shares in the fourth quarter for both primary and fully diluted computations. In the annual fully diluted computation, however, the $12.50 ending market price would produce 1,000 incremental shares while the average number of shares for the four quarters would be only 968 (refer to computational note (e) above under fully diluted). Therefore, the average market price would be used for the fourth quarter fully diluted computation and the ending market price would be used for the annual fully diluted computation. [AIN-APB15, #60]

.736 A more comprehensive example of those points appears in paragraph .910. [AIN-APB15, #60]

Treasury-Stock Method at Exercise

.737 *Question*—How is the treasury-stock method applied for options and warrants that are exercised? [AIN-APB15, #61]

.738 *Answer*—Common stock issued on the exercise of options or warrants is included in the weighted average of outstanding shares from the exercise date. The treasury-stock method is applied for exercised options or warrants from the beginning of the period to the exercise date. For primary earnings per share, the computation for the period prior to exercise is based on the average market price of common stock during the period the exercised options or warrants were outstanding (if the result is dilutive). Incremental shares are weighted for the period the options or warrants were outstanding and shares issued are weighted for the period the shares were outstanding. For fully diluted earnings per share, however, the computation for the period prior to exercise is based on the market price of common stock when the options or warrants were exercised regardless of whether the result is dilutive or antidilutive. Incremental shares are weighted for the period the options or warrants were outstanding and shares issued are weighted for the period the shares are outstanding. Those situations are illustrated in paragraphs .739 through .744. [AIN-APB15, #61]

.739 Assume stock options are outstanding to obtain 5,000 shares of common stock at an exercise price of $10 per share. Assume also the following average and ending market prices of common stock during the calendar year:

	Average Market Price	Ending Market Price
First quarter	$11.11	$12.00
Second quarter	9.75	11.00
Third quarter	13.89	14.00
Fourth quarter	12.50	13.00

[AIN-APB15, #61]

.740 Also assume that 1,000 options were exercised May 1 when the market price of common stock was $10.50 per share and another 1,000 options were exercised

September 1 when the market price of common stock was $15.00 per share. The average market price from April 1 to May 1 was $11.25 and from July 1 to September 1 was $13.00. [AIN-APB15, #61]

.741 For primary earnings per share, the treasury-stock method would produce the following number of *incremental* shares to reflect the dilutive effect of the options:

	Primary Incremental Shares	
	Quarterly EPS	Year-to-Date EPS
First quarter	500	500
Second quarter	37 (a)	269 (b)
Third quarter	994 (c)	510 (d)
Fourth quarter	600	533 (e)

Computational Notes:

(a) 1/3 of 111 incremental shares for 1,000 options exercised May 1 (using $11.25 average market price for the period the options were outstanding). Remaining options are antidilutive.

(b) 500 + 37 = 537.   537 ÷ 2 = 269

(c) 840 incremental shares for 3,000 options outstanding all of the quarter (exercise assumed at $13.89 average market price for the quarter) plus 2/3 of the 231 incremental shares for 1,000 options outstanding for 2 months of the quarter (exercise assumed at $13 average market price for the period the options were outstanding).   840 + 154 = 994

(d) 500 + 37 + 994 = 1,531.   1,531 ÷ 3 = 510

(e) 500 + 37 + 994 + 600 = 2,131.   2,131 ÷ 4 = 533

[AIN-APB15, #61]

.742 In addition, outstanding shares would increase as follows to reflect options *exercised* May 1 and September 1:

	Increase in Outstanding Shares	
	Quarterly EPS	Year-to-Date EPS
First quarter	0	0
Second quarter	667 (a)	333 (b)
Third quarter	1,333 (c)	667 (d)
Fourth quarter	2,000 (e)	1,000 (f)

Computational Notes:

(a) 2/3 of 1,000 shares issued May 1 and outstanding for 2 months.
(b) $0 + 667 = 667$. $667 \div 2 = 333$
(c) 1,000 shares issued May 1 plus 1/3 of 1,000 shares issued September 1.
(d) $667 + 1,333 = 2,000$. $2,000 \div 3 = 667$
(e) 1,000 shares issued May 1 plus 1,000 shares issued September 1.
(f) $0 + 667 + 1,333 + 2,000 = 4,000$. $4,000 \div 4 = 1,000$

[AIN-APB15, #61]

.743 For fully diluted earnings per share, the treasury-stock method would produce the following number of *incremental* shares to reflect the maximum dilutive
effect of the options:

| | Fully Diluted Incremental Shares | |
	Quarterly EPS	Year-to-Date EPS
First quarter	833	833
Second quarter	380 (a)	548 (b)
Third quarter	1,079 (c)	1,174 (d)
Fourth quarter	692 (e)	930 (f)

Computational Notes:

(a) 364 incremental shares for 4,000 options outstanding all of the quarter
(using $11.00 ending market price) plus 1/3 of 48 incremental shares for
1,000 options exercised May 1 (using $10.50 market price at exercise date).
(b) $(667 + 48) + 380 = 1,095$. $1,095 \div 2 = 548$. For the first quarter, 667 incremental shares for 4,000 options (using $12 ending market price) plus 48 incre-
mental shares for 1,000 options exercised May 1 (using $10.50 market price at
exercise date). Refer to computational Note (a) for second quarter. The incremental shares for the two quarters are then weighted.
(c) 857 incremental shares for 3,000 options outstanding all of the quarter plus
$2/3 (333) = 222$ incremental shares for 1,000 options exercised September 1
and outstanding 2 months.
(d) 857 incremental shares for 3,000 options outstanding for all of the 3 quarters
based on $14 higher ending market price applied for all of the 3 quarters plus
$4/9 (48) = 21$ for the May 1 exercise plus $8/9 (333) = 296$ for the September
1 exercise.
(e) Based on $13 market price and 3,000 options.
(f) $500 + 273 + 857 + 692 = 2,322$. $2,322 \div 4 = 581$ incremental shares for
3,000 options outstanding for 4 quarters using market prices of $12, $11,
$14, and $13 for the respective quarters for computing the weighted average

of incremental shares. Since 692 incremental shares determined by applying the ending market price is greater than 581 weighted incremental shares, 692 is used. The 692 is increased by 4/12 (48) = 16 shares for the May 1 exercise plus 8/12 (333) = 222 for the September 1 exercise. 692 + 16 + 222 = 930. [AIN-APB15, #61]

.744 In addition, outstanding shares would increase by the same number of shares as illustrated for the primary earnings per share computation for the options *exercised* on May 1 and September 1; that is, 667 shares in the second quarter, 1,333 in the third quarter, 2,000 in the fourth quarter, 333 for the first 6 months, 667 for the first 9 months, and 1,000 for the year. [AIN-APB15, #61]

Antidilutive Exercise

.745 *Question*—Is the treasury-stock method applied for options and warrants that are exercised when the market price is below the exercise price? [AIN-APB15, #62]

.746 *Answer*—Options or warrants usually would not be exercised in that situation. The common stock obtainable on exercise could be purchased in the market for less than the exercise price. However, in those rare cases where that exercise does occur, the treasury-stock method is applied from the beginning of the year to the exercise date for fully diluted computations using the market price at the exercise date. The result will be antidilutive. [AIN-APB15, #62]

.747 For primary computations, the average market price from the beginning of the quarter to the exercise date is used, but only if the result is dilutive. Thus, if the average market price is less than the exercise price while the exercised options or warrants were outstanding, the exercised options or warrants are omitted from primary computations. [AIN-APB15, #62]

.748 Common stock issued on exercise is included in the weighted average of outstanding shares from the exercise date for both primary and fully diluted computations. Shares produced by the treasury-stock method are included in the weighted average of outstanding shares for the time the exercised options or warrants were outstanding. [AIN-APB15, #62]

.749 For example, assume stock options are outstanding to obtain 5,000 shares of common stock at an exercise price of $10 per share. Assume also the following average and ending market prices of common stock during the calendar year:

	Average Market Price	Ending Market Price
First quarter	$11.11	$12.00
Second quarter	9.75	11.00
Third quarter	13.89	14.00
Fourth quarter	12.50	13.00

[AIN-APB15, #62]

.750 On June 1, 1,000 options were exercised when the market price of common stock was $9.50 per share. The average market price from April 1 to June 1 was $9.65 per share. [AIN-APB15, #62]

.751 For primary earnings per share, the treasury-stock method would produce the following number of *incremental* shares to reflect the dilutive effect of the options:

	Primary Incremental Shares	
	Quarterly EPS	Year-to-Date EPS
First quarter	500	500
Second quarter	0 (a)	250
Third quarter	1,120 (b)	540 (c)
Fourth quarter	800	605 (d)

Computational Notes:

(a) Average market prices for both outstanding options and exercised options are antidilutive.

(b) 1,120 incremental shares for 4,000 options outstanding all of the quarter.

(c) $500 + 0 + 1,120 = 1,620$. $1,620 \div 3 = 540$

(d) $500 + 0 + 1,120 + 800 = 2,420$. $2,420 \div 4 = 605$

[AIN-APB15, #62]

.752 In addition, outstanding shares would increase as follows to reflect options exercised June 1:

| | Increase in Outstanding Shares | |
	Quarterly EPS	Year-to-Date EPS
First quarter	0	0
Second quarter	333 (a)	167 (b)
Third quarter	1,000 (c)	444 (d)
Fourth quarter	1,000 (e)	583 (f)

Computational Notes:

(a) 1/3 of 1,000 shares issued June 1 and outstanding for 1 month.
(b) 0 + 333 = 333.   333 ÷ 2 = 167
(c) 1,000 shares issued June 1.
(d) 0 + 333 + 1,000 = 1,333.   1,333 ÷ 3 = 444
(e) 1,000 shares issued June 1.
(f) 0 + 333 + 1,000 + 1,000 = 2,333.   2,333 ÷ 4 = 583

[AIN-APB15, #62]

.753 For fully diluted earnings per share, the treasury-stock method would produce the following number of *incremental* shares to reflect the maximum dilutive effect of the options:

| | Fully Diluted Incremental Shares | |
	Quarterly EPS	Year-to-Date EPS
First quarter	833	833
Second quarter	329 (a)	472 (b)
Third quarter	1,143 (c)	1,114 (d)
Fourth quarter	923 (e)	901 (f)

Computational Notes:

(a) 364 incremental shares for 4,000 options outstanding all of the quarter less 2/3 (1,000 - 1,053) = -35 to reflect the antidilutive effect of the exercise of 1,000 options outstanding 2 months during the quarter.   364 - 35 = 329
(b) (667 - 53) + (364 - 35) = 943.   943 ÷ 2 = 472. Refer to Note 1. For the first quarter, 667 incremental shares for 4,000 options are reduced by 53 antidilutive shares for 1,000 options exercised June 1. The net incremental shares for the two quarters are then weighted.
(c) 1,143 incremental shares for 4,000 options outstanding all of the quarter.
(d) 1,143 incremental shares for 4,000 options outstanding for all of the 3 quarters based on $14 higher ending market price applied for all of the 3 quarters less 5/9 (53) = -29 for the June 1 antidilutive exercise.

(e)   Based on $13 market price and 4,000 options.

(f)   667 + 364 + 1,143 + 923 = 3,097.   3,097 ÷ 4 = 774 incremental shares for 4,000 options outstanding for 4 quarters using market prices of $12, $11, $14, and $13 for the respective quarters for computing the weighted average of incremental shares. Since 923 incremental shares determined by applying the ending market price is greater than 774 weighted incremental shares, 923 is used. The 923 is decreased by 5/12 (-53) = -22 for the June 1 antidilutive exercise.   923 - 22 = 901. [AIN-APB15, #62]

.754 In addition, outstanding shares would increase by the same number of shares as illustrated for the primary earnings per share computation for the options *exercised* on June 1, that is, 333 shares in the second quarter, 1,000 shares in the third and fourth quarters, 167 shares for the first 6 months, 444 shares for the first 9 months, and 583 shares for the year. [AIN-APB15, #62]

Substantially All of Three Months

.755 *Question*—How long is substantially all of a three-month period and why should exercise of options and warrants not be assumed in applying the treasury-stock method *until* the market price has exceeded the exercise price for that period? [AIN-APB15, #63]

.756 *Answer*—*Substantially all* is not defined in this section. Following the recommendations[524] not to assume exercise before the three-month test is met (a) eliminates the need to make the computation until the market price has exceeded the exercise price for a significant period and (b) reduces "flip-flop" of options and warrants in and out of the computation because of the common stock's market price fluctuations above and below the exercise price. [AIN-APB15, #63]

.757 Presumably, 11 weeks would be substantially all of a 13-week quarter. Therefore, the computation would be made for any quarter after the market price has been above the exercise price for any 11 weeks during a quarter. [AIN-APB15, #63]

.758 Note that this is a one-time test. Exercise need not be assumed for the computations *until* the test has been met, not *unless* the test is met in a particular quarter. Thus, once the test is met, the average market price would be computed thereafter unless the market prices are clearly antidilutive. [AIN-APB15, #63]

.759 The test applies for both primary and fully diluted computations. But after the test has once been met, an ending market price that is above the exercise price

---

[524][It is recommended] that exercise of options and warrants not be assumed for earnings per share data *until* the market price has been above the exercise price for *substantially all* of the three months ending with the month for which the computation is being made. [AIN-APB15, #63, fn32]

is used for the fully diluted computation even though the average market price is below the exercise price. [AIN-APB15, #63]

.760 This recommendation also applies to earnings per share computations for income statements prepared for periods that are less than a quarter. If applied to shorter periods, however, virtually all market prices in the shorter period should be above the exercise price or exercise need not be assumed. For a one-month statement, for example, the market price during that month and for most of the two preceding months should be above the exercise price. [AIN-APB15, #63]

Total of Quarters May Not Equal Annual EPS

.761 *Question*—Are previously reported earnings per share data ever retroactively adjusted or restated for changes in the incremental number of shares computed using the treasury-stock method? [AIN-APB15, #64]

.762 *Answer*—No. Retroactive adjustment or restatement of previously reported earnings per share data are not made if the incremental number of shares determined by applying the treasury-stock method changes. [AIN-APB15, #64]

.763 The total of four quarters' earnings per share might not equal the earnings per share for the year if market prices change and the treasury-stock method is applied. [AIN-APB15, #64]

.764 Computations for each quarter or other period are independent. Earnings per share data would be neither restated retroactively nor adjusted currently to obtain quarterly (or other period) amounts to equal the amount computed for the year or year to date. [AIN-APB15, #64]

Unusual Warrants and Their Equivalents

.765 *Question*—To what kinds of securities does paragraph .126 apply? [AIN-APB15, #65]

.766 *Answer*—Paragraph .126 must be applied for earnings per share computations for the following kinds of securities, all of which are classified as common stock equivalents:

a. Warrants that *require* the tendering of debt or other securities of the issuer or its parent or its subsidiary in full or partial payment of the exercise price.
b. Warrants that *permit* as an alternative the tendering of debt or other securities of the issuer or its parent or its subsidiary in full or partial payment of the exercise price.
c. Warrants whose proceeds from exercise must be applied toward the retirement of debt or other securities of the issuer. That debt or other securities would

have been issued with the warrants and the requirement to apply any proceeds toward retirement would usually be written into an indenture, making the requirement a contractual obligation.

d. Convertible securities that *require* the payment of cash on conversion (regardless of their yield at time of issuance).

e. Convertible securities that *permit* the payment of cash as an alternative on conversion, for example, to obtain a greater number of common shares than could be obtained from straight conversion (regardless of their yield at time of issuance). [AIN-APB15, #65]

Securities Subject to Paragraph .126 Tests

.767 *Question*—Are all of the securities listed in paragraph .766 subject to the two tests described in paragraph .126? [AIN-APB15, #66]

.768 *Answer*—The two tests described in paragraph .126 [under (a) and (b)] are tests to determine whether certain warrants are dilutive or antidilutive. The (a) test is the usual test to determine if a warrant is dilutive. The (b) test is applied if securities can be tendered in lieu of cash to exercise a warrant. The computations to be made if either or both tests are met are described in paragraphs .773 through .789. [AIN-APB15, #66]

.769 The (a) test (the market price of the related common stock must exceed the exercise price of the warrant or the convertible security considered the equivalent of a warrant) applies to warrants (1) that require the tendering of debt, (2) that permit the tendering of debt, and (3) whose proceeds must be used to retire debt. [AIN-APB15, #66]

.770 The (b) test (the security to be tendered is selling at enough discount to establish an effective exercise price below the market price of the common stock obtainable) applies only to the debt or other securities that must or may be tendered toward the exercise price of the warrant (the debt listed in paragraphs .766(a) and .766(b)). The (b) test gives recognition to the possibility that a warrant holder could purchase debt in the market at a discount and exercise a warrant by tendering the debt at its face amount, thereby effecting the purchase of the common stock for less than its market price. [AIN-APB15, #66]

.771 Those tests are demonstrated in the following example. Assume that a warrant may be exercised to purchase 2 shares of common stock by tendering either $100 cash or a $100 face value debenture when market prices are $48 per common share, $94 per debenture, and $6 per warrant. The (a) test is not met (2 x $48 = $96 market price of common does not exceed the exercise price of $100 cash). The (b) test is met. (The $94 market price of the debenture is below the $96 market price for 2 shares of common. This may also be computed:

$$\frac{\$94 \text{ market price of debenture}}{\$100 \text{ tender value of debenture}} \times \$50 \text{ exercise price per share} = \$47 \text{ effective exer-}$$

cise price per share.) Note that the market price of the warrant is not considered in either test. [AIN-APB15, #66]

.772 The (a) and (b) tests apply to securities on an individual basis. However, if paragraph .127 applies (refer to paragraphs .795 through .805), the securities subject to those tests are included in the aggregate computation required by that paragraph whether their individual effect is dilutive or antidilutive. [AIN-APB15, #66]

Market Prices Used in Paragraph .126 Tests

.773 *Question*—What market prices are used for the two tests described in paragraph .126? [AIN-APB15, #67]

.774 *Answer*—The market prices used for those two tests and for the computations if the tests are met correspond to the market prices used for the treasury-stock method (refer to paragraphs .689 through .713). Therefore, the computations are made for each quarter and the shares for the quarters are averaged for annual primary computations. [AIN-APB15, #67]

.775 The market price of common stock for both tests is the average market price during each three-month quarter included in the period being reported on. The ending market price of common stock is used, however, for fully diluted earnings per share if the ending price is *higher* than the average price. [AIN-APB15, #67]

.776 For the (b) test, the average market price of the debt or other security during each three-month quarter included in the period being reported on is used. The ending market price of the debt or other security is used, however, for fully diluted earnings per share if the ending price is *lower* than the average price. [AIN-APB15, #67]

.777 Usually, only one test will be met. In some cases, however, both tests will be met. Also, different tests may be met for primary and fully diluted computations. The computations to be made in those situations are explained in paragraphs .778 through .785. If neither test is met, those securities are not included in earnings per share computations unless paragraph .127 applies. [AIN-APB15, #67]

Computations for Warrants Requiring the Tendering of Debt

.778 *Question*—What computations are made under the (a) and (b) tests specified in paragraph .126 for warrants that require that debt or other securities be tendered on exercise? [AIN-APB15, #68]

.779 *Answer*—If either the (a) or (b) test described in paragraphs .767 through .777 is met if debt or other securities *must* be tendered toward the exercise price, exercise of the warrants is assumed. The debt or other security is tendered at the amount it must be tendered (usually face amount). Interest, net of tax, on the debt is added back to net income in determining earnings applicable to common stock. Common stock is assumed to be issued on the exercise date. The treasury-stock method is applied for any cash proceeds if cash is also to be tendered with the debt. The fact that both tests may sometimes be met does not affect the computations. [AIN-APB15, #68]

Computations for Warrants Allowing Tendering of Debt

.780 *Question*—What computations are made under the (a) and (b) tests specified in paragraph .126 for warrants that permit the tendering of debt or other securities on exercise? [AIN-APB15, #69]

.781 *Answer*—The computations depend on the test met. If both tests are met, the computations depend on the alternatives available since some warrants and their equivalents provide two or more exercise or conversion alternatives to the holder. For example, a warrant may be exercisable by paying $60 cash to obtain 1 share of common stock or by tendering $100 face value debt to obtain 2 shares of common stock. In that case, debt *may* be tendered but is not required to be tendered. [AIN-APB15, #69]

.782 If only the (a) test is met (because the debt or other security is selling for more than the amount for which it may be tendered), the treasury-stock method is applied since the debt or other security would not be tendered toward exercise of the warrant or its equivalent. [AIN-APB15, #69]

.783 If only the (b) test is met (the debt or other security that may be tendered is selling at enough discount to create an effective exercise price below the market price of the common stock), the procedures described in paragraphs .778 and .779 (for when debt or other securities *must* be tendered) are applied. [AIN-APB15, #69]

.784 If *both* the (a) and (b) tests described above are met when debt or other securities *may* be tendered toward the exercise price or if two or more exercise or conversion alternatives meet one test (whether or not both tests are met), the computation should be based on the alternative that meets the test and is more (or most) advantageous to the holder of the warrant or its equivalent. [AIN-APB15, #69]

.785 The (a) and (b) tests are applied for each quarter using the market prices specified in paragraphs .773 through .777. If either test is met, the computations are made for that quarter. Different tests may apply for different quarters in the period. The shares determined for each quarter are averaged for year-to-date primary computations. In fully diluted year-to-date computations, the greater of the average number of shares included in the fully diluted quarterly computations or the number of shares determined by applying ending market prices is used. [AIN-APB15, #69]

Computations for Warrants Whose Proceeds Are Applied to Retire Debt

.786 *Question*—How are warrants whose proceeds must be used to retire debt or other securities included in earnings per share computations? [AIN-APB15, #70]

.787 *Answer*—If debt or other securities of the issuer require that the proceeds from the exercise of warrants or their equivalents be applied toward retirement of those securities, exercise of the warrants is assumed at the beginning of the period (or time of issuance, if later). The proceeds from exercise are assumed to have been used to purchase the securities to be retired at the date of assumed exercise. [AIN-APB15, #70]

.788 Those computations are made on a quarterly basis. The shares determined for each quarter are averaged for annual earnings per share computations. The purchase price to be used is the average market price during each three-month quarter for the securities assumed to have been purchased. To reflect maximum potential dilution, the purchase price for the computation of fully diluted earnings per share is the market price of the securities to be retired at the end of the period if this price is *higher* than the average market price. [AIN-APB15, #70]

.789 Exercise of the warrants is not assumed for either primary or fully diluted earnings per share unless the market price of the related common stock exceeds the exercise price of the warrants.[525] If exercise is assumed and the proceeds from exercise are used to purchase securities to be retired, interest (net of tax) on any debt retired must be added back to net income in determining earnings applicable to common stock. Any excess amount from the assumed exercise of the warrants above the amount needed for the purchase of securities is used to purchase common stock under the treasury-stock method. [AIN-APB15, #70]

Treasury-Stock Method for Convertibles

.790 *Question*—How are convertible securities that require or permit the payment of cash at conversion included in earnings per share computations? [AIN-APB15, #71]

---

[525]Exercise may be assumed, however, if paragraph .127 applies (refer to paragraphs .795 through .805). [AIN-APB15, #70, fn33]

.791 *Answer*—Convertible securities that require or permit the payment of cash at conversion are considered the equivalents of warrants and are therefore always[526] common stock equivalents. [AIN-APB15, #71]

.792 Convertible securities requiring the payment of cash are assumed to be converted at the beginning of the period (or time of issuance, if later) and the if-converted method is applied. Proceeds from conversion are used to purchase common stock under the treasury-stock method. Thus, the incremental number of shares assumed to be outstanding is the difference between the number of shares issued on assumed conversion and the number of shares assumed purchased under the treasury-stock method. If the net result of the aggregate computation of applying both the if-converted method and the treasury-stock method is dilutive, those computations are concluded in both primary and fully diluted earnings per share. The computations are not included, however, if the net result is antidilutive.[527] [AIN-APB15, #71]

.793 Some convertible securities permit the payment of cash at conversion to obtain a more favorable conversion rate. The procedures described in the preceding paragraph are applied for those securities except that no proceeds are assumed to be received on conversion if the amount of cash to be paid exceeds the market value of the additional shares obtainable. The treasury-stock method, therefore, cannot be applied if this condition exists and only the if-converted method is applied (if the result is dilutive).[528] [AIN-APB15, #71]

.794 If several conversion alternatives exist (for example, permitting the payment of different amounts of cash for different conversion rates), the computation shall give effect to the alternative that is most advantageous to the holder of the convertible security. [AIN-APB15, #71]

Antidilutive Options and Warrants Included

.795 *Question*—If paragraph .127 applies (the number of common shares obtainable on exercise of all options and warrants exceeds 20 percent of the number of common shares outstanding at the end of the period), are antidilutive options and warrants assumed to be exercised as well as dilutive options and warrants? [AIN-APB15, #72]

.796 *Answer*—Yes, if paragraph .127 applies, all options and warrants and their equivalents are assumed to be exercised (or converted) whether they are dilutive or

---

[526]Unless issued before June 1, 1969 and [the issuer made an election under the transition requirements of this section to exclude them from common stock equivalents.] [AIN-APB15, #71, fn34]

[527]Conversion may be assumed even if the result is antidilutive if paragraph .127 applies (refer to paragraphs .124 and .127 and paragraphs .795 through .805). [AIN-APB15, #71, fn35]

[528][Refer to footnote 527.]

antidilutive. Under this exception to the general rule that computations should not give effect to antidilution, all of the computations specified in paragraphs .125 through .127 are made and aggregated. If the net result is dilutive, all are included. If the net result is antidilutive, all are excluded. [AIN-APB15, #72]

No Order for Exercise

.797 *Question*—If paragraph .127 applies and several issues of options and warrants with different exercise prices are outstanding, which options and warrants should be assumed to be exercised to obtain common stock under the treasury-stock method, that is, may antidilutive options and warrants be used in applying the treasury-stock method applicable only for dilutive options and warrants? [AIN-APB15, #73]

.798 *Answer*—All options and warrants are assumed to be exercised if paragraph .127 applies without regard to whether the proceeds will be applied to purchase common stock under the treasury-stock method or will be applied to the retirement of debt. Specific options or warrants are not to be allocated for the treasury-stock method, but rather all options and warrants are assumed to be exercised and the number of common shares assumed to be repurchased under the treasury-stock method may not exceed 20 percent of the number of common shares outstanding at the end of the period. [AIN-APB15, #73]

Explanation of 20-Percent Provision

.799 *Question*—How is the 20-percent provision described in paragraph .127 applied? [AIN-APB15, #74]

.800 *Answer*—Twenty percent is used in two ways in paragraph .127. First, a 20-percent *test* is applied[529] to outstanding common shares. If the 20-percent test is met, an aggregate computation is required and all options and warrants and their equivalents are assumed to be exercised. Then a 20-percent *limitation* is applied to the number of common shares purchased under the treasury-stock method. [AIN-APB15, #74]

.801 Even though the 20-percent test is met, the number of shares purchased under the treasury-stock method may be below the 20-percent limitation if the market price is high relative to the exercise price. For example, if 1,000,000 common shares and warrants to obtain 500,000 shares were outstanding, the 20-percent test would be met and the 20-percent limitation for the treasury-stock

---

[529][An enterprise that has elected not to consider securities issued before June 1, 1969 as common stock equivalents] would apply this test for both primary and fully diluted earnings per share computations, since the number of shares obtainable from options and warrants may differ for the two computations as described in paragraphs .822 through .825. [AIN-APB15, #74, fn36]

method would be 200,000 shares. At an exercise price of $10 and a market price of $50, however, only 100,000 shares could be purchased under the treasury-stock method. [AIN-APB15, #74]

.802 Note that the 20-percent limitation applies only to shares assumed *purchased* under the treasury-stock method. It does not apply to the number of incremental shares that results from the computation. In the above example, 400,000 incremental shares resulted from the assumed issuance of 500,000 shares upon exercise and the assumed purchase of 100,000 shares under the treasury-stock method. [AIN-APB15, #74]

.803 In addition, some warrants and their equivalents for which the treasury-stock method may not be applicable result in the assumed issuance of common stock. They are, therefore, included in applying the 20-percent test and are included in the aggregate computation if the test is met. For example, warrants whose proceeds must be used to retire debt are included in applying the 20-percent test and in the aggregate computation if the test is met. Only the proceeds in excess of the amount required for debt retirement would be eligible for the treasury-stock method, however. Warrants assumed to be exercised by tendering debt or other securities would also be included in applying the 20-percent test and in the aggregate computation if the test is met. But only if both cash and debt or other securities were assumed tendered would there be any proceeds eligible for the treasury-stock method. Convertible securities that require or permit the payment of cash at conversion are considered the equivalent of warrants. Those convertible securities would be included in applying the 20-percent test and in the aggregate computations if the test is met. [AIN-APB15, #74]

.804 Most convertible securities, however, (those that do *not* require or permit the payment of cash at conversion) are *not* included in applying the 20-percent test. Nor are other securities that are not options or warrants or their equivalents included in the 20-percent test. For example, the usual participating securities, 2-class common stocks and common stock issuable if specified conditions are met, are not included in the 20-percent test. [AIN-APB15, #74]

.805 Securities that are not included in the 20-percent test are not included in the aggregate computation[530] described in paragraph .127. Thus, even if the net result of the aggregate computation is antidilutive and therefore not included in the earnings per share computation, other securities not included in the aggregate computation would be included in the earnings per share computation if they are dilutive. [AIN-APB15, #74]

---

[530]However, convertible debt assumed to be retired with proceeds from exercise in excess of the amount required for applying the treasury-stock method would be included in the aggregate computation and its interest would be eliminated as described in paragraph .142. [AIN-APB15, #74, fn37]

Original Issue Premium or Discount

.806 *Question*—What treatment is accorded to any original issue premium or discount if debt is assumed acquired under the provisions of paragraphs .126 and .127? [AIN-APB15, #75]

.807 *Answer*—Original issue premium or discount is treated as specified in paragraphs .644 and .645, that is, applicable premium or discount amortized during the period is eliminated from net income. Unamortized premium or discount is not included in earnings applicable to common stock and does not affect earnings per share. [AIN-APB15, #75]

Redemption Premium or Discount

.808 *Question*—What treatment is accorded to any redemption premium or discount if debt is assumed acquired under the provisions of paragraphs .126 and .127? [AIN-APB15, #76]

.809 *Answer*—Redemption premium or discount, that is the difference between the purchase price and the *book* carrying amount of debt, is ignored for earnings per share computations. [AIN-APB15, #76]

.810 Redemption premium or discount could occur only if the proceeds from the assumed exercise of options and warrants are applied to purchase debt at the market price under the provisions of either paragraph .126 or .127. Redemption premium or discount is not included in earnings applicable to common stock and does not affect earnings per share. [AIN-APB15, #76]

.811 Common shares are, of course, assumed to be issued for all options and warrants assumed to be exercised. [AIN-APB15, #76]

Debt Purchased under Paragraph .127

.812 *Question*—What debt may the issuer assume is purchased if the provisions of paragraph .127 apply? [AIN-APB15, #77]

.813 *Answer*—The issuer may select any debt that is eligible to be retired for assumed purchase if the provisions of paragraph .127 apply. That includes convertible debt (both common stock equivalents and other potentially dilutive securities) except that convertible debt may not be assumed purchased if the purchase would be antidilutive (that is, would result in less dilution). Debt is eligible to be retired if it either may be called or is trading and could be purchased in the market. [AIN-APB15, #77]

.814 The same debt is assumed purchased for both primary and fully diluted earnings per share computations. Different amounts of debt may be assumed purchased, however, since different market prices may have to be used for the primary and fully diluted computations for the treasury-stock method. The average market price of the debt during each quarter for which the computations are made is used for both the primary and fully diluted computations under paragraph .127. [AIN-APB15, #77]

Compensating Balances Excluded

.815 *Question*—If paragraph .127 applies and a loan is assumed to be paid, what treatment is accorded to any compensating balance maintained for the loan? [AIN-APB15, #78]

.816 *Answer*—A compensating balance maintained for a loan assumed to be paid is excluded from consideration in applying paragraph .127. Although a compensating balance increases the effective interest rate on a loan to the borrower, only the actual interest paid or accrued (less applicable income tax) is adjusted against net income for earnings per share computations. [AIN-APB15, #78]

Investments under Paragraph .127

.817 *Question*—What securities are eligible for assumed purchase as investments if the provisions of paragraph .127 apply? [AIN-APB15, #79]

.818 *Answer*—Only U.S. government securities and commercial paper are eligible for assumed purchase as investments if the provisions of paragraph .127 apply. Tax-exempt securities of state and local governments are not eligible. The same securities are assumed purchased as investments for both primary and fully diluted earnings per share computations. Different amounts may have to be assumed invested for primary and fully diluted computations, however. [AIN-APB15, #79]

.819 U.S. government securities, in the context of paragraph .127, are securities issued by the federal government, not merely securities guaranteed by the federal government. Typically, the securities to be considered would be short-term securities, such as Treasury bills. [AIN-APB15, #79]

Debt Eligible Only While Outstanding

.820 *Question*—If paragraph .127 applies and debt assumed purchased was actually outstanding only part of the period, may the assumed purchase apply for the entire period? [AIN-APB15, #80]

.821 *Answer*—No. Debt issued or retired during the period may be assumed purchased at its average market price under paragraph .127 only for the time the debt was actually outstanding. Since all computations under this paragraph are made on a quarterly basis, the issue or retirement typically affects only one quarter. An investment in U.S. government securities or commercial paper must be assumed for the time when debt was not outstanding and therefore could not be purchased. Any difference in interest (net of tax) between the debt and the investment naturally is reflected in earnings applicable to common stock. [AIN-APB15, #80]

Computations May Differ for Primary and Fully Diluted If Paragraph .127 Applies

.822 *Question*—Will paragraph .127 always apply for both primary and fully diluted computations if it applies to either? [AIN-APB15, #81]

.823 *Answer*—No, in some cases paragraph .127 may apply for fully diluted computations but not for primary computations. This could occur if an issuer has [elected not to treat options and warrants issued before June 1, 1969 as common stock equivalents under the transition requirements for this section] and the common shares obtainable on exercise of options and warrants issued before June 1, 1969 exceed 20 percent of the common shares outstanding. Paragraph .127 applies in that case for fully diluted but not for primary computations because the options and warrants issued before June 1, 1969 are included only in fully diluted computations. [AIN-APB15, #81]

.824 Even if the common shares obtainable on exercise of options and warrants issued before June 1, 1969 do not exceed 20 percent of the outstanding common shares if the election [described in paragraph .823] is met, the subsequent issuance of additional options or warrants could cause paragraph .127 to apply for fully diluted but not for primary computations. In that case, paragraph .127 would be applied only for fully diluted computations because options and warrants issued before June 1, 1969 would not be included in primary computations. [AIN-APB15, #81]

.825 The computation of primary and fully diluted earnings per share would also differ if paragraph .127 applied for both computations, but the net result in primary is antidilutive and is dilutive in fully diluted. This could occur if the ending market price is above the exercise price but the average market price is below the exercise price. In that case, the computations would be included only for determining fully diluted earnings per share. [AIN-APB15, #81]

Stock Subscriptions Are Warrants

.826 *Question*—How are stock subscriptions included in earnings per share computations? [AIN-APB15, #83]

.827 *Answer*—Fully paid stock subscriptions are considered outstanding stock whether or not the shares have actually been issued. Partially paid stock subscriptions are considered the equivalents of warrants and are, therefore, always[531] common stock equivalents. The unpaid balance is assumed to be proceeds used to purchase stock under the treasury-stock method. [AIN-APB15, #83]

.828 The number of shares included in earnings per share computations for partially paid stock subscriptions is the difference between the number of shares subscribed and the number of shares assumed to be purchased under the treasury-stock method. [AIN-APB15, #83]

.829 The procedures described above are used for subscriptions to purchase convertible securities as well as for subscriptions to purchase common stock. Any incremental convertible securities resulting are then assumed to be converted into common stock if the result is dilutive (refer to paragraphs .830 through .835). [AIN-APB15, #83]

Options or Warrants to Purchase Convertible Securities

.830 *Question*—What treatment is accorded options or warrants to purchase convertible securities? [AIN-APB15, #84]

.831 *Answer*—Options or warrants to purchase convertible securities are assumed to be exercised to purchase the *convertible* security if the market price of both the convertible security and the common stock obtainable upon conversion are above the exercise price of the warrant. However, exercise is not assumed unless conversion of the *outstanding* convertible securities is also assumed. The treasury-stock method is applied to determine the incremental number of convertible securities that are assumed to be issued and immediately converted into common stock. The if-converted adjustments that would be applicable to the incremental convertible securities are ignored since the adjustment would be self-canceling, that is, any interest or dividends imputed to the incremental convertible securities would be canceled in applying the if-converted method. [AIN-APB15, #84]

.832 For example, assume that an enterprise issued 10,000 warrants exercisable to obtain its $100 par value 5-percent convertible debt. Each warrant may be exercised at $90 to obtain 1 convertible bond. Each bond is convertible into two shares of common stock. The market prices of the securities are $46 per common share and $95 per convertible bond. The warrants are dilutive (2 x $46 = $92 which is greater than the $90 exercise price). [AIN-APB15, #84]

---

[531]Unless subscribed before June 1, 1969 and [the enterprise elects not to consider them common stock equivalents]. [AIN-APB15, #83, fn43]

.833 Assumption of exercise would produce $900,000 proceeds, which would be used to purchase 9,474 convertible bonds, resulting in 526 incremental bonds. Conversion would be assumed and 1,052 shares of common (2 x 526 = 1,052) would be issued to replace the 526 convertible bonds. [AIN-APB15, #84]

.834 If the market price of common were $45 per share or less, exercise would not be assumed (for example, at $42 per share, 2 x $42 = $84 which is less than $90). [AIN-APB15, #84]

.835 The classification of the convertible security as a common stock equivalent or other potentially dilutive security determines whether the incremental number of common shares enters primary and fully diluted or enters only fully diluted earnings per share computations. [AIN-APB15, #84]

Two-Class Common Stock and Participating Securities

EPS Treatment of Two-Class and Participating Securities

.836 *Question*—How are two-class common stocks and participating securities treated for earnings per share computations? [AIN-APB15, #85]

.837 *Answer—Two-class common* is a term applied if an enterprise has issued more than one class of common stock (for example, Class A and Class B). A participating security is a security eligible to participate in dividends with common stock; often a fixed amount is guaranteed to the participating security, then common is paid a dividend at the same rate, and the security participates with common on a reduced ratio thereafter. Classes of common stock other than *ordinary* common stock and the participating securities may be convertible into ordinary common stock or may be nonconvertible and may or may not be senior to common stock. [AIN-APB15, #85]

.838 For example, some stocks may be designated as common stock (that is, Class B Common), but their terms and conditions are equivalent to preferred stock (by limiting their voting rights or the amount of dividends they may receive and by giving them preferences in liquidation). If dividends are guaranteed in some way but limited in participation to a maximum amount for a particular class of common stock, that common stock is considered the equivalent of a senior security to the extent it is to share in earnings. [AIN-APB15, #85]

.839 If dividend participation for a particular class of common stock is not limited but the participation is at a rate different from the ordinary common stock (for example, participating equally to some amount per share and partially participating thereafter), the two-class method is used. The two-class method is also used for participating preferred stock that is not limited as to participation in dividends with common stock. The two-class method is modified, however, if it is applied for a convertible security (refer to paragraphs .847 through .857). To be applied for a convertible security, the two-class method must result in greater dilution than would result from application of the if-converted method. [AIN-APB15, #85]

.840 A determination of the status of a two-class common stock or other participating security as a common stock equivalent or as another potentially dilutive security is based on an analysis of all the characteristics of the security, including the ability to share in the earnings potential of the issuing enterprise on substantially the same basis as the common stock. Dividend participation per se does not make that security a common stock equivalent. [AIN-APB15, #85]

.841 The two-class method of computation for nonconvertible securities is discussed in paragraphs .842 through .846. The two-class method of computation for convertible securities is discussed in paragraphs .847 through .851. [AIN-APB15, #85]

Two-Class Method for Nonconvertible Securities

.842 *Question*—How is the two-class method applied for nonconvertible securities? [AIN-APB15, #86]

.843 *Answer*—The two-class method for nonconvertible securities is an earnings allocation formula that determines earnings per share for each class of common stock and participating security according to dividends paid and participation rights in undistributed earnings. [AIN-APB15, #86]

.844 Under the two-class method, net income is first reduced by the amount of dividends actually paid for the period of each class of stock and by the contractual amount of any dividends (or interest on participating income bonds) that must be paid (for example, unpaid cumulative dividends or dividends declared during the period and paid during the following period). The remaining unencumbered undistributed earnings is secondly allocated to common stock and participating securities to the extent each security may share in earnings. The total earnings allocated to each security is determined by adding together the amount allocated for dividends and the amount allocated for a participation feature. [AIN-APB15, #86]

.845 That amount is divided by the number of outstanding shares of the security to which the earnings are allocated to determine the earnings per share for the security. For this computation, outstanding common stock (the *ordinary* class of common stock) includes the usual common stock equivalent securities assumed to be converted or exercised for primary computations and includes those securities and all other potentially dilutive securities assumed to be converted or exercised for fully diluted computations. Although reporting earnings per share for each class of security may be desirable, earnings per share must be reported for the *ordinary* class of common stock. [AIN-APB15, #86]

.846 The application of the two-class method for a nonconvertible security is illustrated in the following example. Assume that an enterprise had 5,000 shares of $100 par value nonconvertible preferred stock and 10,000 shares of $50 par value common stock outstanding during 19X9 and had a net income of $65,000. The preferred stock is entitled to a noncumulative annual dividend of $5 per share before any dividend is paid on common. After common has been paid a dividend of $2 per share, the preferred stock then participates in any additional dividends on a 40:60 *per share* ratio with common. That is, after preferred and common have been paid dividends of $5 and $2 per share respectively, preferred participates in any additional dividends at a rate of 2/3 of the additional amount paid to common on a per share basis. Also assume that for 19X9 preferred shareholders have been paid $27,000 (or $5.40 per share) and common shareholders have been paid $26,000 (or $2.60 per share). Earnings per share for 19X9 would be computed as follows under the two-class method for nonconvertible securities:

Net income		$65,000
Less dividends paid:		
Preferred	$27,000	
Common	26,000	53,000
Undistributed 19X9 earnings		$12,000

Allocation of undistributed earnings:
  To preferred:

$$\frac{.4(5,000)}{.4(5,000) + .6(10,000)} \quad \text{x} \quad \$12,000 = \$3,000$$

$$\$3,000 \div 5,000 \text{ shares} = \$.60 \text{ per share}$$

  To common:

$$\frac{.6(10,000)}{.4(5,000) + .6(10,000)} \quad \text{x} \quad \$12,000 = \$9,000$$

$$\$9,000 \div 10,000 \text{ shares} = \$.90 \text{ per share}$$

Earnings per share amounts:

	Preferred Stock	Common Stock
Distributed earnings	$5.40	$2.60
Undistributed earnings	.60	.90
Totals	$6.00	$3.50

[AIN-APB15, #86]

Two-Class Method for Convertible Securities

.847 *Question*—How is the two-class method applied for convertible securities? [AIN-APB15, #87]

.848 *Answer*—Most convertible two-class common stocks and other convertible participating securities are assumed to be converted and the if-converted method is applied for earnings per share computations. The two-class method is rarely appropriate for those convertible securities and may be applied only if it results in greater dilution than would result from the if-converted method. [AIN-APB15, #87]

.849 If the two-class method is used for a convertible two-class common or other convertible participating security, net income is first allocated under the procedure described in paragraphs .842 through .846 for dividends for the current period that were paid or declared or are cumulative if not paid or declared. Conversions of the converted method are *not* made. Unencumbered undistributed earnings is divided by the total of all common shares outstanding and assumed outstanding from conversions and exercise. The resulting amount per share is added to the amount of the dividends per share allocated to each class of security to determine the earnings per share for each class of security. Although reporting earnings per share for each class of security may be desirable, earnings per share must be reported for the *ordinary* class of common stock. [AIN-APB15, #87]

.850 The application of the two-class method for a convertible security is illustrated in the following example. Assume that an enterprise had 10,000 shares of Class A common stock (the *ordinary* common) and 5,000 shares of Class B common stock outstanding during 19X9 and had a net income of $65,000. Each share of Class B is convertible into two shares of Class A. The Class B is entitled to a noncumulative annual dividend of $5 per share. After Class A has been paid a dividend of $2 per share, Class B then participates in any additional dividends on a 40:60 *per share* ratio with Class A. For 19X9, the Class A shareholders have been paid $26,000 (or $2.60 per share) and the Class B shareholders have been paid $27,000 (or $5.40 per share). Earnings per share for 19X9 would be computed as follows:

Under the if-converted method:

$$\frac{\$65,000}{20,000 \text{ shares*}} = \$3.25 \text{ per share}$$

*Conversion of Class B is assumed.

Under the two-class method for convertible securities:

Net income		$65,000
Less dividends paid:		
Class A common	$26,000	
Class B common	27,000	53,000
Undistributed 19X9 earnings		$12,000

Allocation of undistributed earnings:

$$\frac{\$12,000}{20,000 \text{ shares}} = \$.60 \text{ per share}$$

$$2(.60) = \$1.20 \text{ per Class B share}$$

Earnings per share amounts:

	Class A	Class B
Distributed earnings	$2.60	$5.40
Undistributed earnings	.60	1.20
Totals	$3.20	$6.60

[AIN-APB15, #87]

.851 The two-class method may be used in this case since it results in greater dilution than the if-converted method. [AIN-APB15, #87]

Securities Issuable upon Satisfaction of Specified Conditions

Contingent Shares

.852 *Question*—How is common stock contingently issuable or subject to recall classified and treated in earnings per share computations? [AIN-APB15, #88]

.853 *Answer*—Common stock contingently issuable or subject to contingent recall is always[532] classified as a common stock equivalent unless it will be issued on the

---

[532]Unless their time of issuance (refer to paragraphs .858 and .859) is prior to June 1, 1969 *and* the issuer [elects not to treat them as common stock equivalents]. Contingent shares meeting those conditions are other potentially dilutive securities. [AIN-APB15, #88, fn44]

mere passage of time and is therefore considered to be outstanding for both primary and fully diluted computations. Whether (a) the stock will be issued in the future on the satisfaction of specified conditions, (b) the stock has been placed in escrow and part must be returned if specified conditions are not met, or (c) the stock has been issued but the holder must return part if specified conditions are not met does not affect the classification of contingent shares. [AIN-APB15, #88]

.854 If certain conditions are not met, however, contingent shares are omitted from primary or from primary and fully diluted earnings per share computations. Typical examples of the conditions to be met for contingent shares are (a) the passage of time along with other conditions, (b) the maintenance of some level of earnings, (c) the attainment of some level of earnings, and (d) changes in market prices that modify the number of shares to be issued. [AIN-APB15, #88]

.855 Contingent shares are included in both primary and fully diluted computations if the conditions for their issuance are currently being met. If additional shares would be contingently issuable if a higher earnings level were being attained currently, the additional shares are included only in fully diluted computations (giving effect to the higher earnings level) but only if dilution results. Contingent shares based on (a) the attainment of increased earnings levels above the present earnings level or (b) the maintenance of increased earnings above the present level of earnings over a period of years is included only in fully diluted computations (giving effect to the higher earnings level) but only if dilution results. [AIN-APB15, #88]

.856 If contingent shares have been included in an earnings per share computation, they continue to be included in the computations in following periods until the expiration of the term of the agreement providing for the contingent issuance of additional shares. However, contingent shares are excluded from the computations if their effect would be antidilutive. [AIN-APB15, #88]

.857 Prior period primary and fully diluted earnings per share should be retroactively restated if the number of shares issued or contingently issuable changes from the number of shares originally included in the computation. However, prior period earnings per share data are not retroactively restated for shares actually issued if the condition was the attainment of specified increased earnings levels and the shares were not previously considered outstanding. [AIN-APB15, #88]

Time of Issuance for Contingent Issuances

.858 *Question*—What is the time of issuance of a contingently issuable security? [AIN-APB15, #89]

.859 *Answer*—The time of issuance of a contingently issuable security is the date when agreement to terms has been reached and announced even though subject to further actions, such as directors' or stockholders' approval. But, contingently issuable common stock is considered outstanding for earnings per share computations only if the terms become binding (refer to paragraphs .608 through .618). [AIN-APB15, #89]

Market Price Conditions

.860 *Question*—How do market price conditions affect the number of contingent shares included in earnings per share computations? [AIN-APB15, #90]

.861 *Answer*—The number of contingently issuable shares may depend on market prices for an issuer's common stock. Generally, those market price conditions for contingent shares may be classified as (a) maximum future market price guarantees, (b) market prices for base number of shares to be determined, and (c) minimum future market price guarantees. Additionally, some agreements based on market prices for an issuer's common stock specify that no less than some minimum number of shares or no more than some maximum number of shares will be issued regardless of market prices. [AIN-APB15, #90]

.862 Conditions that guarantee a maximum future price provide *upside* assurance. That is, the issuer guarantees that the market price per share will increase to some stated amount within some time period. To the extent that the market price does not increase as guaranteed, the issuer agrees to issue additional shares or pay cash to make up the difference. That guarantee may extend to shares already issued as well as shares to be issued. [AIN-APB15, #90]

.863 Conditions for market prices to determine the base number of shares to be issued may relate to periodic prices (such as the end of each year), an average of prices over some period, or some final price (such as the end of five years). The conditions may also specify maximum or minimum market price guarantees. [AIN-APB15, #90]

.864 Conditions that guarantee a minimum future price provide *downside* protection. That is, the issuer guarantees that the market price per share will not decrease below some stated amount within some time period. To the extent that the market price goes below that amount, the issuer agrees to issue additional shares or pay cash to make up the difference. That guarantee may extend to shares already issued as well as to shares to be issued. [AIN-APB15, #90]

.865 If the number of contingently issuable shares depends on the future market price of an issuer's common stock, earnings per share computations reflect the number of shares that would be issuable based on the market price at the close of the period being reported on. If a minimum or maximum number of shares, or both, is also specified, the number of shares determined from the market price at the close of the period would, if necessary, be adjusted to not less than the minimum nor more than the maximum number of shares so specified. [AIN-APB15, #90]

.866 If additional shares are to be issued for an upside or a downside guarantee and the market price at the close of the period is less than the guaranteed price, earnings per share computations should give effect to the additional shares that would be issued. [AIN-APB15, #90]

.867 The number of contingently issuable shares may differ for primary and fully diluted computations based on earnings levels. But market price conditions do not cause different numbers of contingently issuable shares to be included in primary and fully diluted computations. Specifically, more shares are not included in fully diluted than in primary computations because of market price guarantees. A market price guarantee has the same effect on both computations. [AIN-APB15, #90]

.868 Prior period earnings per share would be retroactively restated if the number of shares issued or contingently issuable subsequently changes because of market price changes. [AIN-APB15, #90]

Earnings Conditions

.869 *Question*—How does an earnings condition affect the number of contingent shares included in earnings per share computations? [AIN-APB15, #91]

.870 *Answer*—Earnings conditions for the contingent issuance of common stock vary. Some earnings conditions determine the *total* number of shares to be issued, for example, 1 share for each $100 earned (a) each year for 5 years or (b) based on a formula, such as 10 times the average annual earnings for 5 years. [AIN-APB15, #91]

.871 Other earnings conditions determine the *additional* number of shares to be issued. Typically, additional shares are to be issued based on either (a) the *maintenance* of (1) present level of earnings or (2) a higher level of earnings or (b) the *attainment* of (1) a higher level of earnings or (2) successively higher levels of earnings. [AIN-APB15, #91]

.872 Earnings conditions may specify a minimum or a maximum number of shares to be issued regardless of earnings. Shares may be issued each year or only at the end of several years. Earnings conditions may apply to each year individually or may apply to all years on some cumulative or average basis. Various combinations of the earnings conditions described above may be contained in an agreement. [AIN-APB15, #91]

.873 Some maximum number of shares may be issued initially (or placed in escrow) with the stipulation that unearned shares are to be returned to the issuer. Those plans specifying that shares are returnable are treated the same as contingently issuable shares for earnings per share computations. [AIN-APB15, #91]

.874 Because of the diversity of earnings conditions, stating general guidelines that will apply to all agreements is difficult. The number of shares included in earnings per share computations for an earnings agreement should conform to the provisions of paragraphs .153 and .155 and to the guidelines given below. [AIN-APB15, #91]

.875 If shares would at some time be issuable based on the present level of earnings, the shares issuable based on that level of earnings projected to the end of the agreement are considered outstanding for both primary and fully diluted computations. If shares previously considered outstanding become unissuable (for example, because of a decline in earnings), previously reported earnings per share data would be retroactively restated if the term of the condition expires and it is determined that the shares will not be issued. [AIN-APB15, #91]

.876 If additional shares would at some time be issuable if a level of earnings higher than the present level were attained, the additional shares issuable based on the higher level (or levels) projected to the end of the agreement are considered outstanding only for the fully diluted computation, giving effect to the higher earnings level. If different levels of earnings are specified, the level that results in the greatest dilution is used. If additional shares previously considered outstanding become unissuable (for example, because the higher earnings level is not maintained), previously reported earnings per share data would be retroactively restated if it is determined that the shares will not be issued. If in giving effect to the higher earnings level dilution does not result, the additional shares are not included in the computation. If such additional shares were not included in prior earnings per share computations but are subsequently issued (for example, because the higher earnings level was actually attained), previously reported earnings per share data are *not* retroactively restated. [AIN-APB15, #91]

.877 If an earnings condition specifies a minimum or a maximum number of shares to be issued, no less than the minimum nor no more than the maximum number specified would be included in the earnings per share computations. If shares are issued each year and a total minimum or maximum number is specified, the minimum or maximum would be reduced by the number of shares issued. [AIN-APB15, #91]

Convertible Securities Contingently Issuable

.878 *Question*—How are contingently issuable convertible securities treated for earnings per share computations? [AIN-APB15, #92]

.879 *Answer*—Contingently issuable convertible securities are included in earnings per share computations under the guidelines described for convertible securities and the guidelines described for contingently issuable common stock. That is, additional convertible securities are assumed to be issued in conformity with the conditions specified for their issuance. (Refer to paragraphs .852 through .877 for an explanation of how conditions affect the number of securities outstanding.) [AIN-APB15, #92]

.880 Time of issuance of the contingently issuable convertible securities is the date when agreement as to terms has been reached and announced. The classification of the contingently issuable convertible security as a common stock equivalent or other potentially dilutive security is determined at time of issuance based on its [AIN-APB15, #92] effective [FAS85, ¶3] yield at that time[533] and does not change if the security is actually issued. A change in the [AIN-APB15, #92] average Aa corporate bond yield as defined in paragraph .123A [FAS111, ¶8(n)] or the market price of the security between the time of issuance and actual issuance of a contingently issuable convertible security has no effect on its classification.[534] [AIN-APB15, #92]

.881 Those contingently issuable convertible securities classified as common stock equivalents are included in both primary and fully diluted computations. However, those common stock equivalents based on the attainment or maintenance of earnings above the present level are included only in fully diluted computations. Contingently issuable convertible securities classified as other potentially dilutive securities are included in fully diluted computations. [AIN-APB15, #92]

.882 If contingently issuable convertible securities are to be included in earnings per share computations, conversion of the additional securities is assumed. However, conversion is not assumed for the additional securities unless conversion is also assumed for their counterpart outstanding convertible securities. Interest or dividends are not computed for the additional contingently issuable convertible securities since any imputed amount would be reversed by the if-converted adjustments for assumed conversion. [AIN-APB15, #92]

Parent and Consolidated Financial Statements

Securities Issued by Subsidiaries

.883 *Question*—How do convertible securities and options and warrants issued by a subsidiary affect parent or consolidated earnings per share? [AIN-APB15, #93]

---

[533]Unless it has the same terms as the terms of an outstanding convertible security that is a common stock equivalent. A convertible security contingently issuable at May 31, 1969 would be classified under [the] original transition requirements for this section. [AIN-APB15, #92, fn45]

[534]Except in the situations described in paragraphs .619 through .626. [AIN-APB15, #92, fn46]

.884 *Answer*—The effect of options and warrants and convertible securities issued by a subsidiary on consolidated earnings per share (or parent company earnings per share if parent company statements are prepared as the primary financial statements using the equity method) depends on whether the securities issued by the subsidiary to the public enable their holders to obtain common stock of the subsidiary or common stock of the parent. [AIN-APB15, #93]

.885 Securities issued by a subsidiary that enable their holders to obtain the subsidiary's common stock are included in computing the subsidiary's earnings per share data. Those earnings per share data are then included in the parent or consolidated earnings per share computations based on the consolidated group's holdings of the subsidiary's securities. [AIN-APB15, #93]

.886 Options and warrants issued by a subsidiary that enable their holders to purchase parent company common stock are common stock equivalents[535] for parent or consolidated earnings per share computations. Securities of a subsidiary convertible into parent company common stock are classified as common stock equivalents or other potentially dilutive securities for parent or consolidated earnings per share computations under the yield test.[536] [AIN-APB15, #93]

.887 Exhibits 887A and 887B illustrate the earnings per share computations for a subsidiary's securities that enable their holders to obtain the subsidiary's common stock. Assume that a parent company had a net income of $10,000 from operations (excluding any dividends paid by the subsidiary), had 10,000 shares of common stock outstanding, and had not issued any other securities. The parent company owned 900 of the common shares of a domestic subsidiary and also owned 40 warrants and 100 shares of convertible preferred stock issued by the subsidiary. The subsidiary had a net income of $3,600 and had outstanding 1,000 shares of common stock, 200 warrants exercisable to purchase 200 shares of its common at $10 per share (assume $20 average and ending market price for common), and 200 shares of preferred stock convertible into 2 of its common shares for each preferred share. The convertible preferred paid a dividend of $1.50 per share and is not a common stock equivalent. Assume that no intercompany eliminations or adjustments are necessary except for dividends. (Income taxes have been ignored in the following computations for simplicity.) [AIN-APB15, #93]

---

[535]Unless issued prior to June 1, 1969 and the parent company [elects not to consider them as common stock equivalents]. [AIN-APB15, #93, fn47]
[536]Refer to paragraphs .661 through .665 for a description of the treatment of a subsidiary security convertible into a parent company's convertible security. [AIN-APB15, #93, fn48]

Exhibit 887A

Earnings per Share for the Subsidiary

Primary earnings per share $3.00

Computed:

$$\frac{\$3,600(a) - \$300\ (b)}{1,000(c) + 100(d)}$$

(a) Subsidiary's net income.
(b) Dividends paid by subsidiary on convertible preferred stock.
(c) Shares of subsidiary's common stock outstanding.
(d) Incremental shares of subsidiary's common stock assumed outstanding applying the treasury-stock method for warrants (computed $\frac{\$20 - \$10}{\$20}$ x 200).

Fully diluted earnings per share $2.40

Computed:

$$\frac{\$3,600(e)}{1,000 + 100 + 400(f)}$$

(e) Subsidiary's earnings applicable to common stock applying the if-converted method for convertible preferred stock.
(f) Shares of subsidiary's common stock assumed outstanding from conversion of convertible preferred stock. [AIN-APB15, #93]

Exhibit 887B

Parent or Consolidated Earnings per Share

Primary earnings per share $1.29

Computed:

$$\frac{\$10,000(a) + \$150(b) + \$2,700(c) + \$60(d)}{10,000(e)}$$

Exhibit 887B (continued)

(a) Parent's net income.
(b) Dividends received by parent on subsidiary's convertible preferred stock.
(c) Parent's proportionate interest in subsidiary's earnings attributable to common stock, computed: $\frac{900}{1,000}$ (1,000 shares x $3 per share).
(d) Parent's proportionate interest in subsidiary's earnings attributable to warrants, $\frac{40}{200}$ (100 incremental shares x $3 per share).
(e) Shares of parent's common stock outstanding.

Fully diluted earnings per share $1.27

Computed:

$$\frac{\$10,000 + \$2,160(f) + \$48(g) + \$480(h)}{10,000}$$

(f) Parent's proportionate interest in subsidiary's earnings attributable to common stock, computed: $\frac{900}{1,000}$ (1,000 shares x $3 per share).
(g) Parent's proportionate interest in subsidiary's earnings attributable to warrants, computed: $\frac{400}{200}$ (100 incremental shares x $2.40 per share).
(h) Parent's proportionate interest in subsidiary's earnings attributable to convertible preferred stock, computed: $\frac{100}{200}$ (400 shares from conversion x $2.40 per share).

The above computations apply only to earnings per share data. Parent or consolidated net income is determined in the usual manner as follows:

Parent net income from operations			$10,000
Subsidiary net income		$3,600	
Less minority interest:			
Preferred	$150 (i)		
Common	330 (j)	480	3,120
Parent or consolidated net income			$13,120

Computed:

(i) 50% (200 preferred shares x $1.50 dividend per share).
(j) 10% ($3,600 net income - $300 preferred dividends).

Note that parent or consolidated net income in Exhibit 887B is not the basis for parent or consolidated earnings per share compensations. [AIN-APB15, #93]

.888 Those computations would be different if the subsidiary's securities could be exercised or converted only to obtain the parent company's common stock. For example, assume the same facts as were given in the preceding illustration except (a) the warrants and convertible securities are all owned by outsiders, (b) the subsidiary's warrants are exercisable only to obtain parent company common stock, and (3) the subsidiary's preferred stock is convertible only into parent company common stock. [Exhibits 888A and 888B illustrate the effect of the change in assumptions.] [AIN-APB15, #93]

Exhibit 888A

Earnings per Share for the Subsidiary

Primary earnings per share $3.30

Computed:

$$\frac{\$3,600 - \$300}{1,000}$$

Fully diluted earnings per share $3.30

Computed:

$$\frac{\$3,600 - \$300}{1,000}$$

[AIN-APB15, #93]

Exhibit 888B

Parent or Consolidated Earnings per Share

Primary earnings per share $1.28

Computed:

$$\frac{\$10,000(a) + \$2,970(b)}{10,000(c) + 100(d)}$$

(a) Parent's net income.
(b) Parent's proportionate interest in subsidiary's earnings attributable to common stock
    Computed:

$$\frac{900}{1,000} (1,000) \text{ shares x \$3.30 per share.}$$

Exhibit 888B (continued)

(c) Shares of parent's common stock outstanding.

(d) Incremental shares of parent's common stock assumed outstanding applying the treasury-stock method for warrants issued by subsidiary exercisable to obtain parent's common stock (computed: $\frac{\$20-\$10}{\$20} \times 200$).

Fully diluted earnings per share $1.26

Computed:

$$\frac{\$10,000 + \$2,970 + \$300(e)}{10,000 + 100 + 400(f)}$$

(e) Dividends paid by subsidiary on convertible preferred stock that would not have been received by outsiders if the subsidiary's preferred stock had been converted into parent's common stock at the beginning of the period.

(f) Shares of parent's common stock assumed outstanding from conversion of subsidiary's preferred stock convertible into parent's common stock.

Parent or consolidated net income would be determined as follows:

Parent net income from operations		$10,000
Subsidiary net income	$3,600	
Less: Dividends on preferred stock	$300	
Minority common interest (10%)	330	630	2,970
Parent or consolidated net income		$12,970

Note that parent or consolidated net income is not the basis for parent or consolidated earnings per share computations. [AIN-APB15, #93]

Effects of Scheduled Changes

Changing Exercise Prices and Conversion Rates

.889 *Question*—How do changes that may occur in exercise prices or conversion rates affect earnings per share computations? [AIN-APB15, #94]

.890 *Answer*—Except as discussed in the next paragraph, if an exercise price or conversion rate is in effect during a period, that exercise price or conversion rate is used for primary computations. If no exercise price or conversion rate is in effect during a period, the earliest effective exercise price or conversion rate during the following five years is used for primary computations. The most advantageous exercise price or conversion rate available to the holder within 10 years is always used for fully diluted computations. Previously reported earnings per share data are not restated for subsequent changes in the conversion rate or exercise price. [AIN-APB15, #94]

.891 If a convertible security having an increasing conversion rate is issued in exchange for another class of security of the issuing enterprise and is at some time convertible back into as many of the same or a similar security as was exchanged, the conversion rate used in the computation does not result in a reduction of the number of common shares (or common stock equivalents) existing before the exchange. [AIN-APB15, #94]

.892 For example, assume that an enterprise issued 100,000 shares of convertible preferred to officers and principal stockholders in exchange for 300,000 shares of common stock and each preferred share is convertible back into 1 common share the first year, 2 common shares the second year, 3 common shares the third year, and 4 common shares the fourth year and thereafter. The convertible preferred would be included as 300,000 common equivalent shares for primary earnings per share computations and 400,000 common equivalent shares for fully diluted earnings per share computations for the first 3 years and 400,000 common equivalent shares thereafter for both computations. [AIN-APB15, #94]

Election to Classify Outstanding Securities

Effect of New Issue of Common Stock Equivalents

.893 *Question*—[If securities issued prior to June 1, 1969 were not considered to be common stock equivalents under the original transition requirements of this section,] can the classifications of those securities change in the future? [AIN-APB15, #96]

.894 *Answer*—Generally, the classification of a security does not change after that election is made. However, convertible securities issued before June 1, 1969 would change from other potentially dilutive security status to common stock equivalent status if another convertible security is issued with the same terms which is a common stock equivalent as specified by the second sentence of paragraph .119 (refer to paragraphs .623 through .626). [AIN-APB15, #96]

No Change for Options and Warrants

.895 *Question*—Would outstanding options or warrants issued prior to June 1, 1969 [not considered to be common stock equivalents] become common stock equivalents under the second sentence of paragraph .119 if another option or warrant were issued with the same terms after May 31, 1969? [AIN-APB15, #97]

.896 *Answer*—No, that change of classification applies only to convertible securities. Although this creates a difference of treatment between convertible securities and options and warrants, this section is explicit in naming only convertible securities. [AIN-APB15, #97]

.897 Because warrants are often traded, identification of a warrant being exercised as having been issued *before* or *after* may be impossible. If an exercised warrant cannot definitely be identified as having been issued after May 31, 1969, exercise is assumed on a FIFO basis. That is, the first warrants issued are assumed to be the first exercised if specific identification is impossible. The same treatment applies for options, except options usually are not transferable and the specific option being exercised can usually be identified. [AIN-APB15, #97]

Is Prior Period Restatement Permitted?

.898 *Question*—May prior period earnings per share amounts be retroactively restated other than if restatement is required, for example, for changes in the number of shares computed under the treasury-stock method or if a convertible security being issued is determined to be a common stock equivalent and causes outstanding convertible securities with the same terms that were not common stock equivalents at issuance to also become common stock equivalents? [AIN-APB15, #99]

.899 *Answer*—No, previously reported earnings per share amounts generally are retroactively restated only if restatement is required. Earnings per share data are not restated because of changes in the number of shares computed under the treasury-stock method. Nor should primary earnings per share data be restated if a convertible security's classification changes because of the subsequent issuance of another convertible security with the same terms. [AIN-APB15, #99]

Disclosure

Required Disclosure

.900 *Question*—What information related to earnings per share is required to be disclosed in addition to earnings per share data? [AIN-APB15, #100]

.901 *Answer*—This section requires disclosure of the following information:

a. Restatement for a prior period adjustment.
b. Dividend preferences.
c. Liquidation preferences.
d. Participation rights.
e. Call prices and dates.
f. Conversion rates and dates.
g. Exercise prices and dates.

h. Sinking fund requirements.
i. Unusual voting rights.
j. Bases on which primary and fully diluted earnings per share were calculated. (The computations would not, however, appear on the face of the income statement.)
k. Issues that are common stock equivalents.
l. Issues that are other potentially dilutive securities.
m. Assumptions and adjustments made for earnings per share data.
n. Shares issued on conversion, exercise, and conditions met for contingent issuances.
o. Recapitalization occurring during the period or before the statements are issued.
p. Stock dividends, stock splits, or reverse splits occurring after the close of the period before the statements are issued.
q. Claims of senior securities entering earnings per share computations.
r. Dividends declared by the constituents in a pooling.
s. Basis of presentation of dividends in a pooling on other than a historical basis.
t. Per share and aggregate amount of cumulative preferred dividends in arrears.
[AIN-APB15, #100]

Supplementary Data

.902 *Question*—When must supplementary earnings per share data be furnished? [AIN-APB15, #101]

.903 *Answer*—Supplementary earnings per share data must be furnished for the latest period if common stock is issued on conversion during the period or after the close of the period before the report is issued if primary earnings per share would have increased or decreased at least 3 percent if the issuance had occurred at the beginning of the period. It may also be desirable to furnish supplementary earnings per share data for each period presented giving the cumulative retroactive effect of all such issuances, but primary earnings per share as reported in those periods should not be retroactively adjusted. [AIN-APB15, #101]

.904 Supplementary earnings per share data generally would also be furnished if common stock or common stock equivalents have been sold for cash and the proceeds have been or are to be used to retire preferred stock or debt. The supplementary data would be furnished even though the sale occurred shortly after the close of the period but before completion of the financial report. [AIN-APB15, #101]

.905 If the issuance of a convertible security classified as a common stock equivalent causes outstanding convertible securities with the same terms classified as other potentially dilutive securities to be reclassified as common stock equivalents; supplementary earnings per share data may be useful to explain the change in classification. The supplementary data would show what previously reported primary earnings per share would have been if the convertible securities had been classified as common stock equivalents since issuance and thus reconstruct the primary earnings trend. Previously reported primary earnings per share would not be retroactively restated for prior periods in a comparative income statement because of that change in classification. [AIN-APB15, #101]

Examples of Computing Average Market Prices

.906 An average market price may be computed various ways in applying the treasury-stock method for options and warrants. In first applying the treasury-stock method, the computation depends on the stability of the market price of the common stock. [AIN-APB15, Exhibit 3]

.907 In the following example, an average market price has been computed eight different ways for one quarter. [In Exhibit 909A,] the computation is based on weekly prices. The weekly prices are then averaged to determine a monthly average, that is then averaged to determine a quarterly average. (Although not illustrated, a quarterly average could also be computed by adding weekly prices and dividing by 13, thereby eliminating the computation of a monthly average.) In Exhibit 909B, the computation is based on monthly prices. [AIN-APB15, Exhibit 3]

.908 The *high-low* computation is based on an average of the high and low prices for the week or month. In the weighted averages, the market prices are weighted by the number of shares involved in the transactions. [AIN-APB15, Exhibit 3]

.909 Assume the following market transactions for a corporation's common stock during a three-month period:

Week	High	Low	Close	Shares Traded
1	21	19	20	300
2	24	20	23	700
3	24	22	22	500
4	23	21	21	500
5	26	22	23	1,000
6	27	23	26	1,200
7	29	27	28	1,500
8	31	29	31	2,000
9	28	26	26	2,500
10	26	22	23	1,500
11	24	22	22	1,000
12	22	20	21	800
13	20	20	20	500

[AIN-APB15, Exhibit 3]

Exhibit 909A

Quarterly Average Market Prices
from Monthly Averages Based on Weekly Prices

Week	Simple Averages			Weighted Averages		
	High-Low	Close		Shares	High-Low	Close
1	20	20		300	6,000	6,000
2	22	23		700	15,400	16,100
3	23	22		500	11,500	11,000
4	22	21		500	11,000	10,500
Month 1 totals	87	86		2,000	43,900	43,600
Divide by	4				2,000	2,000
Month 1 averages	21.75	21.50			21.95	21.80
5	24	23		1,000	24,000	23,000
6	25	26		1,200	30,000	31,200
7	28	28		1,500	42,000	42,000
8	30	31		2,000	60,000	62,000
Month 2 totals	107	108		5,700	156,000	158,200
Divide by	4	4			5,700	5,700
Month 2 averages	26.75	27.00			27.37	27.75
9	27	26		2,500	67,500	65,000
10	24	23		1,500	36,000	34,500
11	23	22		1,000	23,000	22,000
12	21	21		800	16,800	16,800
13	20	20		500	10,000	10,000
Month 3 totals	115	112		6,300	153,300	148,300
Divide by	5	5			6,300	6,300
Month 3 averages	23.00	22.40			24.33	23.54
Three-month total	71.50	70.90			73.65	73.09
Divide by	3	3			3	3
Three-month average	23.83	23.63			24.55	24.36

[AIN-APB15, Exhibit 3]

Exhibit 909B

Quarterly Average Market Prices from Monthly Prices

	Simple Averages		Weighted Averages		
	High-Low	Close	Shares	High-Low	Close
Month 1	21.50	21.00	2,000	43,000	42,000
Month 2	26.50	31.00	5,700	151,050	176,700
Month 3	24.00	20.00	6,300	151,200	126,000
Quarterly total	72.00	72.00	14,000	345,250	344,700
Divided by	3	3		14,000	14,000
Quarterly average	24.00	24.00		24.66	24.62

Assuming an exercise price of $20 for options or warrants to purchase 10,000 shares, the above average market prices would produce the following incremental shares:

	Simple Averages		Weighted Averages	
	High-Low	Close	High-Low	Close
Weekly prices	1,607	1,536	1,853	1,790
Monthly prices	1,667	1,667	1,890	1,877

Note: Computed $10{,}000 - \dfrac{\$20 \times 10{,}000}{\text{average price}}$ = incremental shares

[AIN-APB15, Exhibit 3]

Application of the Treasury-Stock Method for Options and Warrants

.910 [Exhibits 910A and 910B illustrate the computation of incremental shares for purposes of applying the treasury-stock method for options and warrants.] Assume 100,000 common shares are outstanding and 10,000 warrants are outstanding that are exercisable at $20 per share to obtain 10,000 common shares. Assume also the following market prices for common stock during a three-year period:

	Market Prices per Share of Common Stock					
	Year 1		Year 2		Year 3	
Quarter	Average	Ending	Average	Ending	Average	Ending
1	$18*	$22	$24	$25	$20	$18
2	20*	21	22	21	18	22
3	22	19	20	19	24	21
4	24	23	18	17	22	25

*Assume market prices had been more than $20 for substantially all of a previous quarter.

[AIN-APB15, Exhibit 4]

Exhibit 910A

Computation of Number of Incremental Shares by Quarters

Primary Earnings per Share (a)

Quarter	Year 1	Year 2	Year 3
1	0	1,667	0
2	0	909	0
3	909	0	1,667
4	1,667	0	909

Fully Diluted Earnings per Share

Quarter	Year 1	Year 2	Year 3
1	909 (b)	2,000 (b)	0
2	476 (b)	909 (a)	909 (b)
3	909 (a)	0	1,667 (a)
4	1,667 (a)	0	2,000 (b)

(a) Based on average market price.
(b) Based on ending market price.

Computed: $\frac{\text{Market Price} - \text{Exercise Price}}{\text{Market Price}} \times 10{,}000 = $ Incremental Shares

[AIN-APB15, Exhibit 4]

Exhibit 910B

**Number of Incremental Shares Included in Year-to-Date
Weighted Average**

Primary Earnings per Share (a)

	Year 1	Year 2	Year 3
First quarter	0	1,667	0
6 months	0	1,288	0
9 months	303	859	556
Year	644	644	644

Fully Diluted Earnings per Share

	Year 1	Year 2	Year 3
First quarter	909 (a)	2,000 (a)	0 (a)
6 months	693 (a)	1,455 (a)	909 (b)
9 months	765 (a)	970 (a)	859 (a)
Year	1,304 (b)	727 (a)	2,000 (b)

(a) Computed by adding incremental shares of each quarter included and dividing by number of quarters included in the year to date.

(b) Incremental shares for all quarters included based on ending market price.

[AIN-APB15, Exhibit 4]

Two-Class Method for Warrants Issued by REITs

.911 *Question*—The capitalization of a real estate investment trust (REIT) includes shares of beneficial interest (common stock) and an equal number of warrants. This REIT is not subject to federal income tax with respect to the income it distributes to its shareholders because it distributes at least 90 percent of its annual taxable income (as defined by the *Internal Revenue Code*) and elects not to be taxed on the income distributed. How should this entity treat warrants in computing earnings per share under this section? [AIN-APB15, #102]

.912 *Interpretation*—The "two-class" method of computing primary earnings per share should be used by any REIT that elects under the *Internal Revenue Code* not to be subject to tax on income distributed and that pays dividends equal to 90 percent or more of its taxable income. Under this method, dividends are deducted from net income and the remaining amount (the undistributed earnings) is allocated to the total of common shares and common share equivalents with use of warrant proceeds applied as described in paragraph .125 or .127. Per share distributions to common shareholders (total dividends divided by the weighted average of common shares outstanding) are added to that per share amount to determine primary earnings per share. [AIN-APB15, #102]

.913 For example, the REIT described in the question above should compute primary earnings per share under the "two-class" method in conjunction with paragraph .127. Assume that this REIT has a net income of $1,000,000 and distributes $900,000 in dividends on 1,000,000 common shares outstanding. Warrants exercisable at $5 per share for 1,000,000 common shares are also outstanding. Assuming a market price of $23 per share for common and a 3 percent interest rate for debt and/or investments in commercial paper or U.S. government securities, primary earnings per share would be determined applying the two-class method and paragraph .127 as follows:

Net income		$1,000,000
Less dividends		900,000
Undistributed earnings		100,000
Proceeds from the exercise of warrants:		
1,000,000 × $5	$5,000,000	
Purchase of treasury stock under paragraph .127(a)		
200,000 shares × $23	4,600,000	
Balance to retire debt under paragraph .127(b)	400,000	
Interest rate on debt retired	.03	
Interest adjustment		12,000
Adjusted undistributed earnings		$ 112,000
Common shares outstanding		1,000,000
Common shares assumed issued for warrants	1,000,000	
Less treasury stock purchased	200,000	
Incremental shares for warrants		800,000
Common and common equivalent shares		1,800,000
Primary earnings per share:		
Distributed earnings ($900,000 ÷ 1,000,000)		$ .90
Undistributed earnings ($112,000 ÷ 1,800,000)		.06
Total earnings per common and common equivalent share		$ .96

[AIN-APB15, #102]

.914 If the per share amount computed in paragraph .913 above had exceeded earnings per outstanding common share of $1.00 (computed: $1,000,000 ÷ 1,000,000 shares), the result would be anti-dilutive and primary earnings per share would be reported as $1.00 in accordance with paragraph .121. [AIN-APB15, #102]

.915 The two-class method should not be used by a REIT in computing fully diluted earnings per share in order to reflect maximum potential dilution. Therefore, fully diluted earnings per share computed for the example in paragraph .913 would be $.56 (computed: $1,012,000 ÷ 1,800,000 shares) applying only paragraph .127. [AIN-APB15, #102]

.916 Although dividends declared after the close of the taxable year may be included in meeting the 90 percent requirement for federal income tax purposes, only dividends paid or declared during the period for which the computation is being made should be considered in applying the two-class method. However, a dividend declaration (or official company policy in lieu of actual declaration) before the close of the period stated as a percentage of taxable earnings (the amount to be determined after the close of the period) will be considered as being declared during the period if the dividend is paid by the date the financial statements are issued. [AIN-APB15, #102]

(The next page is 16501.)

Sources: FASB Statement 105; FASB Statement 107; FASB Statement 111; FASB Statement 112; FASB Statement 113; FASB Statement 119

Summary

This section presents requirements for all entities to disclose certain information about their financial instruments. Certain specified financial instruments are exempt from the disclosure requirements of this section.

All entities are required to disclose the following information about financial instruments with off-balance-sheet risk of accounting loss disaggregated by class of financial instrument, business activity, risk, or other category that is consistent with an entity's management of those instruments:

- The face, contract, or notional principal amount
- The nature and terms of the instruments and a discussion of their credit and market risk, cash requirements, and related accounting policies
- The *accounting loss* the entity would incur if any party to the financial instrument failed completely to perform according to the terms of the contract and the collateral or other security, if any, for the amount due proved to be of no value to the entity
- The entity's policy for requiring collateral or other security on financial instruments it accepts and a description of collateral on instruments presently held.

Disclosure of information about significant concentrations of credit risk from an individual counterparty or groups of counterparties for all financial instruments is also required.

In addition, all entities are required to disclose the fair value of financial instruments, both assets and liabilities recognized and not recognized in the statement of financial position, for which it is practicable to estimate fair value. If estimating fair value is not practicable, this section requires disclosure of descriptive information pertinent to estimating the value of a financial instrument.

This section also requires disclosures by all entities about derivative financial instruments—futures, forward, swap, and option contracts, and other financial instruments with similar characteristics.

This section requires disclosures about amounts, nature, and terms
of derivative financial instruments that do not result in off-balance-
sheet risk of accounting loss. It requires that a distinction be made
between financial instruments held or issued for trading purposes (including dealing and other trading activities measured at fair value with
gains and losses recognized in earnings) and financial instruments
held or issued for purposes other than trading.

This section also encourages, but does not require, quantitative
information about market risks of derivative financial instruments,
and also of other assets and liabilities, that is consistent with the way
the entity manages or adjusts those risks.

Applicability and Scope

Financial Instruments with Off-Balance-Sheet Risk and Concentrations of Credit Risk

.101 [The provisions of] paragraphs .112 through .115 require disclosure of information
about **financial instruments** that have off-balance-sheet risk[1] and about financial instruments with concentrations of **credit risk** except as specifically modified by paragraphs .104 and .105. [They do] not change any requirements for recognition, measurement, or classification of financial instruments in financial statements. [FAS105, ¶12]

.102 Generally accepted accounting principles contain specific requirements to disclose
information about the financial instruments noted in paragraphs .104 and .105, and this
section does not change those requirements. For all other financial instruments, the requirements in this section are in addition to other disclosure requirements prescribed by
generally accepted accounting principles. [FAS105, ¶16]

.103 Examples of financial instruments with off-balance-sheet risk that are included within
the scope of paragraphs .112 through .115 are outstanding loan commitments written,[2]
standby and commercial letters of credit written, financial guarantees written, options
written, interest rate caps and floors written, recourse obligations on receivables sold,
obligations to repurchase securities sold, outstanding commitments to purchase or sell
financial instruments at predetermined prices, futures contracts, interest rate and foreign

---

[1]In this section, off-balance-sheet risk is used to refer to off-balance-sheet **risk of accounting loss.**
[FAS105, ¶9, fn7] [Refer to paragraph .107 for the definition of risk of accounting loss.]

[2]The off-balance-sheet risk from a commitment to lend cash at a floating interest rate is the exposure to
credit loss arising from the obligation to fund a loan in accordance with the terms of the commitment.
[FAS105, ¶13, fn8]

currency swaps, and obligations arising from financial instruments sold short. Paragraphs .133 through .134 provide additional examples of financial instruments that have and do not have off-balance-sheet risk. [FAS105, ¶13]

.104 The requirements of paragraphs .112, .113, and .115 do not apply to the following financial instruments, whether written or held:

a. Insurance contracts, other than financial guarantees and investment contracts, as discussed in Section In6, "Insurance Industry" [FAS105, ¶14] (Concentrations of credit risk associated with reinsurance receivables and prepaid reinsurance premiums must, however, be disclosed under the requirements of paragraph .115 as required in paragraph .192 of Section In6.) [FAS113, ¶28]

b. Unconditional purchase obligations subject to the disclosure requirements of Section C32, "Commitments: Long-Term Obligations"[3]

c. Employers' and plans' obligations for pension benefits, postretirement health care and life insurance benefits, employee stock option and stock purchase plans, and other forms of deferred compensation arrangements, as defined in Sections Pe5, "Pension Funds: Accounting and Reporting by Defined Benefit Pension Plans," P16, "Pension Costs," [FAS105, ¶14] P40, "Postretirement Benefits Other Than Pensions," [FAS111, ¶8(y)] C47, "Compensation to Employees: Stock Purchase and Option Plans," C44, "Compensation to Employees: Paid Absences," and C38, "Compensation to Employees: Deferred Compensation Agreements"

d. Financial instruments of a pension plan, including plan assets, if subject to the accounting and reporting requirements of Section P16[4]

e. Substantively extinguished debt subject to the disclosure requirements of paragraph .108 of Section D14, "Debt: Extinguishments," and any assets held in trust in connection with an in-substance defeasance of that debt. [FAS105, ¶14]

---

[3]Unconditional purchase obligations not subject to the requirements of Section C32 are included in the scope of paragraphs .112 through .115. That is, unconditional purchase obligations that require the purchaser to make payment without regard to delivery of the goods or receipt of benefit of the services specified by the contract and are not within the scope of Section C32 (because they were not negotiated as part of a financing arrangement, for example) are included in the scope of paragraphs .112 through .115. [FAS105, ¶14, fn9]

[4]Financial instruments of a pension plan, other than the obligations for pension benefits, if subject to the accounting and reporting requirements of Section Pe5 *are included* in the scope of this section. [FAS105, ¶14, fn10]

.105 The requirements of paragraphs .112 and .113 do not apply to the following instruments:

a. Lease contracts[5] as defined in Section L10, "Leases"
b. Accounts and notes payable and other financial instrument obligations that result in accruals or other amounts that are denominated in foreign currencies and are included at translated or remeasured amounts in the statement of financial position in accordance with Section F60, "Foreign Currency Translation," except (1) obligations under financial instruments that have off-balance-sheet risk from other risks in addition to foreign exchange risk and (2) obligations under foreign currency exchange contracts. Examples of the first exception include a commitment to lend foreign currency and an option written to exchange foreign currency for a bond (whether or not denominated in a foreign currency). Examples of the second exception include a forward exchange contract, a currency swap, a foreign currency futures contract, and an option to exchange currencies.

The requirements of paragraph .115 of this section [regarding disclosure of concentrations of credit risk] do apply to the items described in subparagraphs (a) and (b) above. [FAS105, ¶15]

.105A-.105C [Deleted 10/94 and renumbered as .105G through .105I.]

Derivative Financial Instruments

.105D [This section also requires disclosures about] *derivative financial instruments,* [which are defined as] futures, forward, swap, or option contracts, or other financial instruments with similar characteristics. [FAS119, ¶5] The information required to be disclosed by paragraph .115N(b) shall be included for each [date after December 15, 1994] for which an income statement is presented [, even if presented only] for comparative purposes. All other information required to be disclosed by paragraphs .115L through .115O shall be included for each [date after December 15, 1994] for which a statement of financial position is presented [, even if presented only] for comparative purposes. [FAS119, ¶17]

.105E Examples of other financial instruments with characteristics similar to option contracts include interest rate caps or floors and fixed-rate loan commitments. Those instruments have characteristics similar to options in that they provide the holder with benefits of favorable movements in the price of an underlying asset or index with limited or no exposure to losses from unfavorable price movements, generally in return for a premium paid at inception by the holder to the issuer. Variable-rate loan commitments and other

---

[5]A contingent obligation arising out of a cancelled lease contract and a guarantee of a third-party lease obligation are not lease contracts and are included in the scope of this section. [FAS105, ¶15, fn11]

variable-rate financial instruments also may have characteristics similar to option contracts. For example, contract rate adjustments may lag changes in market rates or be subject to caps or floors. Examples of other financial instruments with characteristics similar to forward contracts include various kinds of commitments to purchase stocks or bonds, forward interest rate agreements, and interest rate collars. Those instruments are similar to forwards in that they provide benefits of favorable movements in the price of an underlying asset or index and exposure to losses from unfavorable price movements, generally with no payments at inception. [FAS119, ¶6]

.105F The definition of *derivative financial instrument* in paragraph .105D excludes all on-balance-sheet receivables and payables, including those that "derive" their values or contractually required cash flows from the price of some other security or index, such as mortgage-backed securities, interest-only and principal-only obligations, and indexed debt instruments. It also excludes optional features that are embedded within an on-balance-sheet receivable or payable, for example, the conversion feature and call provisions embedded in convertible bonds. [FAS119, ¶7]

All Financial Instruments

.105G This section [also] requires disclosures about **fair value** for all financial instruments, whether recognized or not recognized in the statement of financial position, except for those specifically listed in paragraph .105H. It applies to all entities. It does not change any requirements for recognition, measurement, or classification of financial instruments in financial statements. [FAS107, ¶7]

.105H The disclosures about fair value prescribed in paragraphs .115C through .115F, .115I, and .115J are not required for the following:

a. Employers' and plans' obligations for pension benefits, other postretirement benefits including health care and life insurance benefits, [FAS107, ¶8] postemployment benefits, [FAS112, ¶11] employee stock option and stock purchase plans, and other forms of deferred compensation arrangements, as defined in Sections Pe5, P16, P40, [FAS107, ¶8] P32, "Postemployment Benefits," [FAS112, ¶11] C44, C47, and C38
b. Substantively extinguished debt subject to the disclosure requirements of paragraph .108 of Section D14, and assets held in trust in connection with an in-substance defeasance of that debt
c. Insurance contracts, other than financial guarantees and investment contracts, as discussed in Section In6
d. Lease contracts as defined in Section L10, (a contingent obligation arising out of a cancelled lease and a guarantee of a third-party lease obligation are not lease contracts and are included in the scope of this section)
e. Warranty obligations and rights

f. Unconditional purchase obligations as defined in paragraph .101 of Section C32
g. Investments accounted for under the equity method in accordance with the requirements of Section I82, "Investments: Equity Method"
h. Minority interests in consolidated subsidiaries
i. Equity investments in consolidated subsidiaries
j. Equity instruments issued by the entity and classified in stockholders' equity in the statement of financial position. [FAS107, ¶8]

.105I Generally accepted accounting principles already require disclosure of or subsequent measurement at fair value for many classes of financial instruments. Although the definitions or the methods of estimation of fair value vary to some extent, and various terms such as market value, current value, or mark-to-market are used, the amounts computed under those requirements satisfy the requirements of this section and those requirements are not superseded or modified by this section. [FAS107, ¶9]

Definition of a Financial Instrument

.106 A financial instrument is [FAS105, ¶6] defined as [FAS107, ¶3] cash, evidence of an ownership interest in an entity, or a contract that both:

a. Imposes on one entity a contractual obligation[6] (1) to deliver cash or another financial instrument[7] to a second entity or (2) to exchange [FAS105, ¶6] other [FAS107, ¶3] financial instruments on potentially unfavorable terms with the second entity
b. Conveys to that second entity a contractual right[8] (1) to receive cash or another financial instrument from the first entity or (2) to exchange other financial instruments on potentially favorable terms with the first entity. [FAS105, ¶6]

---

[6] *Contractual obligations* encompass both those that are conditioned on the occurrence of a specified event and those that are not. All contractual obligations that are financial instruments meet the definition of *liability* set forth in FASB Concepts Statement No. 6, *Elements of Financial Statements,* although some may not be recognized as liabilities in financial statements—may be "off-balance-sheet"—because they fail to meet some other criterion for recognition. For some financial instruments, the obligation is owed to or by a group of entities rather than a single entity. [FAS105, ¶6, fn1]

[7]The use of the term *financial instrument* in this definition is recursive (because the term *financial instrument* is included in it), [FAS105, ¶6, fn2] though [FAS107, ¶3, fn2] it is not circular. [FAS105, ¶6, fn2] The definition [FAS107, ¶3, fn2] requires a chain of contractual obligations that ends with the delivery of cash or an ownership interest in an entity. Any number of obligations to deliver financial instruments can be links in a chain that qualifies a particular contract as a financial instrument. [FAS105, ¶6, fn2]

[8]*Contractual rights* encompass both those that are conditioned on the occurrence of a specified event and those that are not. All contractual rights that are financial instruments meet the definition of *asset* set forth in Concepts Statement 6, although some may not be recognized as assets in financial statements—may be "off-balance-sheet"—because they fail to meet some other criterion for recognition. For some financial instruments, the [FAS105, ¶6, fn3] right [FAS107, ¶3, fn3] is held by or [FAS105, ¶6, fn3] the obligation is [FAS107, ¶3, fn3] due from a group of entities rather than a single entity. [FAS105, ¶6, fn3]

.106A Paragraphs .117 through .132 provide examples of instruments that are included in and excluded from the definition of a financial instrument. [FAS107, ¶4]

Financial Instruments with Risk of Accounting Loss

.107 The risk of accounting loss[9] from a financial instrument includes (a) the possibility that a loss may occur from the failure of another party to perform according to the terms of a contract (credit risk), (b) the possibility that future changes in market prices may make a financial instrument less valuable or more onerous (**market risk**),[10] and (c) the risk of theft or physical loss. Paragraphs .108 through .115 address credit and market risk only. [FAS105, ¶7]

.108 Some financial instruments are recognized as assets, and the amount recognized reflects the risk of accounting loss to the entity. A receivable that is recognized and measured at the present value of future cash inflows, discounted at the historical interest rate (often termed *amortized cost*), is an example: the accounting loss that might arise from that account receivable cannot exceed the amount recognized as an asset in the statement of financial position.[11] [FAS105, ¶8]

.109 Some financial instruments that are recognized as assets entail conditional rights and obligations that expose the entity to a risk of accounting loss that may exceed the amount recognized in the statement of financial position; for example, an interest rate swap contract providing for net settlement of cash receipts and payments that conveys a right to receive cash at current interest rates may impose an obligation to deliver cash if interest rates change in the future. Those financial instruments have off-balance-sheet risk. [FAS105, ¶9]

.110 Some financial instruments are recognized as liabilities, and the possible sacrifice needed to settle the obligation under the terms of the financial instrument cannot exceed the amount recognized in the statement of financial position. However, other financial instruments that are recognized as liabilities expose the entity to a risk of accounting loss because the ultimate obligation may exceed the amount that is recognized in the state-

---

[9]Accounting loss refers to the loss that may have to be recognized due to credit and market risk as a direct result of the rights and obligations of a financial instrument. [FAS105, ¶7, fn4]

[10]A change in market price may occur (for example, for interest-bearing financial instruments) because of changes in general interest rates (interest rate risk), changes in the relationship between general and specific market interest rates (an aspect of credit risk), or changes in the rates of exchange between currencies (foreign exchange risk). [FAS105, ¶7, fn5]

[11]It is possible that an economic loss could exceed that amount if, for example, the current market value of an asset was higher than the amount recognized in the statement of financial position. Paragraphs .107 through .115, however, do not address that economic loss. [FAS105, ¶8, fn6]

ment of financial position; for example, the ultimate obligation under a financial guarantee may exceed the amount that has been recognized as a liability. Those financial instruments have off-balance-sheet risk. [FAS105, ¶10]

.111 Still other financial instruments may not be recognized either as assets or as liabilities, yet may expose the entity to a risk of accounting loss; for example, a forward interest rate agreement that, unless a loss has been incurred, is not recognized until settlement. Those financial instruments also have off-balance-sheet risk. [FAS105, ¶11]

Disclosure of Extent, Nature, and Terms of Financial Instruments with Off-Balance-Sheet Risk of Accounting Loss

.112 For financial instruments with off-balance-sheet risk[11a], except as noted in paragraphs .104 and .105, an entity shall disclose either in the body of the financial statements or in the accompanying notes[12] the following information by [FAS105, ¶17] category [FAS119, ¶14(b)] of financial instrument:[13]

a. The face or contract amount (or notional principal amount if there is no face or contract amount)
b. The nature and terms, including, at a minimum, a discussion of (1) the credit and market risk of those instruments, (2) the cash requirements of those instruments, and (3) the related accounting policy pursuant to the requirements of Section A10, "Accounting Policies."[14] [FAS105, ¶17]

.112A The disclosures required in paragraph .112 shall distinguish between financial instruments with off-balance-sheet risk held or issued for trading purposes, including dealing and other trading activities measured at fair value with gains and losses recognized in earnings, and financial instruments with off-balance-sheet risk held or issued for purposes other than trading. [FAS119, ¶14(d)]

[11a]Similar disclosures are required for derivative financial instruments without off-balance-sheet risk in paragraph .115L. [FAS119, ¶14(a)]

[[12]The] incorporation of information by reference [is sufficient] as long as that information is included elsewhere in the document containing the financial statements. [FAS105, ¶122]

[13]In this section, *category of financial instrument* refers to class of financial instrument, business activity, risk, or other category that is consistent with the management of those instruments. If disaggregation of financial instruments is other than by class, the entity also shall describe for each category the classes of financial instruments included in that category. [FAS119, ¶14(c)]

Practices for grouping and separately identifying—classifying—similar financial instruments in statements of financial position, in notes to financial statements, and in various regulatory reports have developed and become generally accepted, largely without being codified in authoritative literature. In this section, *class of financial instrument* refers to those classifications. [FAS105, ¶17, fn12]

[14][Refer to] paragraph .105 of Section A10. [FAS105, ¶17, fn13]

Disclosure of Credit Risk of Financial Instruments with Off-Balance-Sheet Credit Risk

.113 For financial instruments with off-balance-sheet credit risk, except as noted in paragraphs .104 and .105, an entity shall disclose either in the body of the financial statements or in the accompanying notes the following information by [FAS105, ¶18] category [FAS119, ¶14(b)] of financial instrument:

a. The amount of accounting loss the entity would incur if any party to the financial instrument failed completely to perform according to the terms of the contract and the collateral or other security, if any, for the amount due proved to be of no value to the entity

b. The entity's policy of requiring collateral or other security to support financial instruments subject to credit risk, information about the entity's access to that collateral or other security, and the nature and a brief description of the collateral or other security supporting those financial instruments. [FAS105, ¶18]

.114 An entity may find that disclosing additional information about the extent of collateral or other security for the underlying instrument indicates better the extent of credit risk. Disclosure of that additional information in those circumstances is encouraged. [FAS105, ¶19]

Disclosure of Concentrations of Credit Risk of All Financial Instruments

.115 Except as noted in paragraph .104, an entity shall disclose all significant[15] concentrations[16] of credit risk arising from *all* financial instruments, whether from an individual counterparty or groups of counterparties. *Group concentrations* of credit risk exist if a number of counterparties are engaged in similar activities [FAS105, ¶20] or activities in the same region or [FAS105, ¶101] have similar economic characteristics that would cause their ability to meet contractual obligations to be similarly affected by

---

[15]A threshold [for determining whether a concentration is significant is not specified] because "significance" depends, to a great extent, on individual circumstances. [FAS105, ¶101]

[16]Industry or regional concentrations often may be disclosed adequately by a description of the entity's principal activities, which may greatly reduce the cost of determining whether significant concentrations exist and of reporting their existence. For example, a local retail store may be able to disclose concentrations of credit risk adequately by describing its business, location, and the related granting of credit to local customers. In a similar manner, an entity whose principal activity consists of supplying parts to the computer industry may adequately disclose concentrations of credit risk by describing its principal activity and the related granting of credit to computer manufacturers. However, in other cases, a description of the principal activities may not provide sufficient information about concentrations of credit risk. [FAS105, ¶103]

changes in economic or other conditions [FAS105, ¶20], for example, concentrations of credit risk resulting from loans to highly leveraged entities. [FAS105, ¶101] The following shall be disclosed about each significant concentration:

a. Information about the (shared) activity, region, or economic characteristic that identifies the concentration
b. The amount of the accounting loss due to credit risk the entity would incur if parties to the financial instruments that make up the concentration failed completely to perform according to the terms of the contracts and the collateral or other security, if any, for the amount due proved to be of no value to the entity
c. The entity's policy of requiring collateral or other security to support financial instruments subject to credit risk, information about the entity's access to that collateral or other security, and the nature and a brief description of the collateral or other security supporting those financial instruments. [FAS105, ¶20]

Fair Value of Financial Instruments

.115A For purposes of this section, the fair value of a financial instrument is the amount at which the instrument could be exchanged in a current transaction between willing parties, other than in a forced or liquidation sale. If a quoted market price is available for an instrument, the fair value to be disclosed for that instrument is the product of the number of trading units of the instrument times that market price. [FAS107, ¶5]

.115B Under the definition of fair value in paragraph .115A, the quoted price for a single trading unit in the most active market is the basis for determining market price and reporting fair value. This is the case even if placing orders to sell all of an entity's holdings of an asset or to buy back all of a liability might affect the price, or if a market's normal volume for one day might not be sufficient to absorb the quantity held or owed by an entity. [FAS107, ¶6]

Disclosures about Fair Value of Financial Instruments

.115C An entity shall disclose, either in the body of the financial statements or in the accompanying notes,[16a] the fair value of financial instruments for which it is practicable to estimate that value. [FAS107, ¶10] Fair value disclosed in the notes shall be presented together with the related carrying amount in a form that makes it clear whether the fair value and carrying amount represent assets or liabilities and how the carrying amounts relate to what is reported in the statement of financial position. [FAS119, ¶15(b)]

[16a]If disclosed in more than a single note, one of the notes shall include a summary table. The summary table shall contain the fair value and related carrying amounts and cross-references to the location(s) of the remaining disclosures required by this section. [FAS119, ¶15(a)]

An entity also shall disclose the method(s) and significant assumptions used to estimate the fair value of financial instruments. [FAS107, ¶10] The disclosures shall distinguish between financial instruments held or issued for trading purposes, including dealing and other trading activities measured at fair value with gains and losses recognized in earnings, and financial instruments held or issued for purposes other than trading. [FAS119, ¶15(c)]

.115D Quoted market prices, if available, are the best evidence of the fair value of financial instruments. If quoted market prices are not available, management's best estimate of fair value may be based on the quoted market price of a financial instrument with similar characteristics or on valuation techniques (for example, the present value of estimated future cash flows using a discount rate commensurate with the risks involved, option pricing models, or matrix pricing models). Paragraphs .141 through .152 contain examples of procedures for estimating fair value. [FAS107, ¶11]

.115E In estimating the fair value of deposit liabilities, a financial entity shall not take into account the value of its long-term relationships with depositors, commonly known as core deposit intangibles, which are separate intangible assets, not financial instruments. For deposit liabilities with no defined maturities, the fair value to be disclosed under this section is the amount payable on demand at the reporting date. This section does not prohibit an entity from disclosing separately the estimated fair value of any of its nonfinancial intangible and tangible assets and nonfinancial liabilities. [FAS107, ¶12]

.115F For trade receivables and payables, no disclosure is required under paragraph .115C if the carrying amount approximates fair value. [FAS107, ¶13]

.115G-.115H [Deleted 10/94 and renumbered as paragraphs .115J and .115K.]

.115I In disclosing the fair value of a derivative financial instrument,[16b] an entity shall not (a) combine, aggregate, or net that fair value with the fair value of nonderivative financial instruments or (b) net that fair value with the fair value of other derivative financial instruments—even if those nonderivative or derivative financial instruments are considered to be related, for example, by a risk management strategy—except to the extent that the offsetting of carrying amounts in the statement of financial position is permitted under the general principle in paragraphs .101A and .101B of Section B10, "Balance Sheet Display: Offsetting," or the exception for master netting arrangements in paragraph .106 of Section B10.[16c] [FAS119, ¶15(d)]

[16b]*Derivative financial instrument* is used [here] in the same sense as [it is used] in paragraph .105D. [FAS119, ¶15(d)]

[16c]If some entities believe that additional disclosures are necessary to prevent the disaggregated fair value amounts from being misleading, this section would not prohibit those disclosures. [FAS119, ¶90]

.115J If it is not practicable for an entity to estimate the fair value of a financial instrument or a class of financial instruments, the following shall be disclosed:

a. Information pertinent to estimating the fair value of that financial instrument or class of financial instruments, such as the carrying amount, effective interest rate, and maturity
b. The reasons why it is not practicable to estimate fair value. [FAS107, ¶14]

.115K In the context of paragraphs .115C through .115F and .115J, *practicable* means that an estimate of fair value can be made without incurring excessive costs. It is a dynamic concept: what is practicable for one entity might not be for another; what is not practicable in one year might be in another. For example, it might not be practicable for an entity to estimate the fair value of a class of financial instruments for which a quoted market price is not available because it has not yet obtained or developed the valuation model necessary to make the estimate, and the cost of obtaining an independent valuation appears excessive considering the materiality of the instruments to the entity. Practicability, that is, cost considerations, also may affect the required precision of the estimate; for example, while in many cases it might seem impracticable to estimate fair value on an individual instrument basis, it may be practicable for a class of financial instruments in a portfolio or on a portfolio basis. In those cases, the fair value of that class or of the portfolio shall be disclosed. Finally, it might be practicable for an entity to estimate the fair value only of a subset of a class of financial instruments; the fair value of that subset shall be disclosed. [FAS107, ¶15]

Disclosure about All Derivative Financial Instruments

.115L For many derivative financial instruments, information about their amounts, nature, and terms is required to be disclosed because those instruments are included in the scope of paragraphs .101 through .105. For options held and other derivative financial instruments not included in the scope of paragraphs .101 through .105 (because they do not have *off-balance-sheet risk of accounting loss,* as defined in paragraph .107), an entity shall disclose either in the body of the financial statements or in the accompanying notes the following information by *category of financial instrument:*[16d]

a. The face or contract amount (or notional principal amount if there is no face or contract amount)[16e]

[16d][Refer to footnote 13.]

[16e]Disclosure of the face or contract amount of financial instruments, including those within the scope of paragraphs .101 through .105, may be misleading when the instruments are leveraged and the leverage features are not adequately disclosed. For example, the notional amounts of an interest rate swap may be misleading if the contract's settlement payments are based on a formula that multiplies the effect of interest rate changes. Disclosure of the nature and terms of those instruments requires a discussion of the leverage features and their general effects on (a) the credit and market risk, (b) the cash requirements, and (c) the related accounting policy. [FAS119, ¶8, fn2]

b. The nature and terms, including, at a minimum, a discussion of (1) the credit and market risk of those instruments, (2) the cash requirements of those instruments, and (3) the related accounting policy pursuant to the requirements of Section A10. [FAS119, ¶8]

Disclosure about Purposes for Which Derivative Financial Instruments Are Held or Issued

.115M The disclosures[16f] required in paragraph .115L shall distinguish between derivative financial instruments held or issued for:

a. *Trading purposes,* including dealing[16g] and other trading activities measured at fair value[16h] with gains and losses recognized in earnings
b. *Purposes other than trading.* [FAS119, ¶9]

Disclosure about Derivative Financial Instruments Held or Issued for Trading Purposes

.115N Entities that hold or issue derivative financial instruments for *trading purposes* shall disclose, either in the body of the financial statements or in the accompanying notes, the following:

a. The average fair value of those derivative financial instruments during the reporting period,[16i] presented together with the related end-of-period fair value, distinguishing between assets and liabilities

---

[16f]If current disclosures [in] Management's Discussion and Analysis (MD&A) satisfy the requirements of this section, those disclosures could be included in the basic financial statements through incorporation by reference to MD&A. [FAS119, ¶99]

[16g]*Dealing* is the activity of standing ready to trade—either buying or selling—for the dealer's own account, thereby providing liquidity to the market. To facilitate this activity, dealers commonly hold contracts with customers for derivative financial instruments for indefinite periods and enter into other contracts to manage the risks arising from their trading account assets and liabilities. All of those activities are considered dealing. [FAS119, ¶47]

[16h]Some derivative financial instruments may be measured at fair value but not considered held or issued for *trading purposes.* For example, some hedging activities may entail the use of foreign exchange contracts that fail to meet the criteria for deferral accounting under Section F60. Those derivative financial instruments, although measured at fair value, may be categorized as held or issued for *purposes other than trading.* [FAS119, ¶48]

[16i]The calculation of average fair value based on daily balances is preferable to a calculation based on less frequent intervals. It is, however, sufficient to disclose average fair value based on the most frequent interval that a trader's systems generate for management, regulatory, or other reasons. [FAS119, ¶10, fn3]

b. The net gains or losses (often referred to as net trading revenues) arising from trading activities during the reporting period disaggregated by class, business activity, risk, or other category that is consistent with the management of those activities and where those net trading gains or losses are reported in the income statement. If the disaggregation is other than by class, the entity also shall describe for each category the classes of derivative financial instruments, other financial instruments, and nonfinancial assets and liabilities from which the net trading gains or losses arose.

Entities that trade other types of financial instruments or nonfinancial assets are encouraged, but not required, to present a more complete picture of their trading activities by also disclosing average fair value for those assets and liabilities. [FAS119, ¶10]

Disclosure about Derivative Financial Instruments Held or Issued for Purposes Other Than Trading

.115O Entities that hold or issue derivative financial instruments for *purposes other than trading* shall disclose the following:

a. A description of the entity's objectives for holding or issuing the derivative financial instruments, the context needed to understand those objectives, and its strategies for achieving those objectives, including the classes of derivative financial instruments used[16j]

b. A description of how each class of derivative financial instrument is reported in the financial statements including the policies for recognizing (or reasons for not recognizing) and measuring the derivative financial instruments held or issued, and when recognized, where those instruments and related gains and losses are reported in the statements of financial position and income

c. For derivative financial instruments that are held or issued and accounted for as hedges of anticipated transactions (both firm commitments and forecasted transactions for which there is no firm commitment), (1) a description of the anticipated transactions whose risks are hedged, including the period of time until the anticipated transactions are expected to occur, (2) a description of the classes of derivative financial instruments used to hedge the anticipated transactions, (3) the amount of hedging gains and losses explicitly deferred,[16k] and (4) a description of the transactions or other events

---

[16j]For example, if an entity's objective for a derivative position is to keep a risk arising from the entity's nonderivative assets below a specified level, the context would be a description of those assets and their risks, and a strategy might be purchasing put options in a specified proportion to the assets at risk. [FAS119, ¶11, fn4]

[16k]For purposes of the disclosure of hedging gains and losses, the term *explicitly deferred* refers to deferrals in separate accounts in the manner required by Section F80, "Futures Contracts," for hedges of anticipated transactions and by Section F60 for hedges of firm commitments. Those deferrals are in contrast to implicit deferrals that are (a) embedded in related carrying amounts for hedges of recognized assets and liabilities or (b) not recorded because changes in the value of the hedging instrument are not recognized. [FAS119, ¶11, fn5]

that result in the recognition in earnings of gains or losses deferred by hedge accounting. [FAS119, ¶11]

Encouraged Disclosure about All Derivative Financial Instruments Held or Issued

.115P Entities are encouraged, but not required, to disclose quantitative information about interest rate, foreign exchange, commodity price, or other market risks of derivative financial instruments that is consistent with the way the entity manages or adjusts those risks and that is useful for comparing the results of applying the entity's strategies to its objectives for holding or issuing the derivative financial instruments. Quantitative disclosures about the risks of derivative financial instruments are likely to be even more useful, and less likely to be perceived to be out of context or otherwise misunderstood, if similar information is disclosed about the risks of other financial instruments or nonfinancial assets and liabilities to which the derivative financial instruments are related by a risk management or other strategy.[16l] [FAS119, ¶12]

.115Q Appropriate ways of reporting the quantitative information encouraged in paragraph .115P will differ for different entities[16m] and will likely evolve over time as management approaches and measurement techniques evolve. Possibilities include disclosing:

a. More details about current positions and perhaps activity during the period [FAS119, ¶13]
   - An example for an entity with a small number of swaps might include disclosure of the fixed rates, the floating index, and the term of each swap. Entities, however, that use a large number of derivative financial instruments for managing or adjusting risk may find disclosure about each derivative impractical. [FAS119, ¶69]
b. The hypothetical effects on equity, or on annual income, of several possible changes in market prices [FAS119, ¶13]
   - An example of the effects of several possible changes in market prices might be disclosure of the effects of ±100 and ±200 basis point shifts in all interest rates; flattening of the yield curve by an increase in short rates or a decrease in long rates, or conversely, steepening of the curve; ±10 percent shifts in all exchange rates against the reporting currency; or ±20 percent shifts in prices of commodities that the entity purchases regularly. The indicated amounts of change ± are only illustrative. Entities choosing this disclosure would show some of the changes in market prices that they actually use in managing or adjusting risk. [FAS119, ¶69]

[16l]The quantitative disclosures encouraged in this paragraph, depending on the approach chosen, could measure either an entity's current risk position or its success in achieving prior objectives. Disclosure of both kinds of information may be useful. [FAS119, ¶73]

[16m]Some entities use one approach to manage risk in one part of their business and a different approach to manage risk in other parts of their business. Those entities are encouraged to provide separate disclosure for each part of their business. [FAS119, ¶74]

c. A gap analysis of interest rate repricing or maturity dates [FAS119, ¶13]
   - Gap analysis is an approach to the measurement of interest rate risk. The carrying amounts of rate-sensitive assets and liabilities, and the notional principal amounts of swaps and other unrecognized derivatives, are grouped by expected repricing or maturity date. The results are summed to show a cumulative interest sensitivity "gap" between assets and liabilities. [FAS119, ¶69]
d. The duration of the financial instruments [FAS119, ¶13]
   - Duration is the result of a calculation based on the timing of future cash flows and can be thought of as the life, in years, of a notional zero-coupon bond whose fair value would change by the same amount as the real bond or portfolio in response to a change in market interest rates. The usefulness of information about the duration of a bond or portfolio might be enhanced by also disclosing the convexity, which is the extent to which duration itself changes as prices change. [FAS119, ¶69]
e. The entity's value at risk from derivative financial instruments and from other positions at the end of the reporting period and the average value at risk during the year [FAS119, ¶13]
   - Value at risk is the expected loss from an adverse market movement with a specified probability over a period of time. For example, based on a simulation of a large number of possible scenarios, an entity can determine with 97.5 percent probability (corresponding to calculations using about 2 standard deviations) that any adverse change in the portfolio value over 1 day will not exceed a calculated amount, the value at risk. [FAS119, ¶69]

This list is not exhaustive, and entities are encouraged to develop other ways of reporting the quantitative information. [FAS119, ¶13]

Disclosures Related to Other Financial Instruments

.116 Generally accepted accounting principles and regulatory accounting requirements [have been and will be developed for certain specific financial instruments. Specific disclosure and accounting requirements for those instruments are found in other sections,] for example, Section F80, "Futures Contracts," paragraph .112 [presents disclosure for] only one type of financial instruments—futures contracts [FAS105, ¶4] [, whereas Section C32, paragraph .105 presents disclosure requirements for all long-term debt].

Illustrations Applying the Definition of a Financial Instrument

.117 [The following paragraphs] provide examples of instruments that are included in and excluded from the definition [of a financial instrument]. [FAS105, ¶23]

	Paragraph Numbers
Example 1—Cash	.118–.119
Example 2—Evidence of an Ownership Interest in an Entity	.120
Example 3—Contractual Right or Obligation to Receive or Deliver Cash	.121–.123
Example 4—Contractual Right or Obligation to Receive or Deliver Goods or Services	.124–.125
Example 5—Contractual Right or Obligation to Receive or Deliver Another Financial Instrument	.126
Example 6—Contractual Right or Obligation to Exchange Other Financial Instruments	.127–.130
Example 7—Contingent Rights or Obligations	.131–.132

[FAS105, Appendix A]

Example 1—Cash

.118 Currency[17] is a financial instrument even though generally the only contractual obligation placed on the issuing government is that it accept the currency as legal tender for payments due to it. [FAS105, ¶25]

.119 Demand deposits in banks are financial instruments of both the depositors and the banks. The depositors have a contractual right to receive currency on demand, and the banks have a contractual obligation to deliver currency on demand. The term *cash* as used in the definition includes both U.S. dollars and the currencies of other nations. [FAS105, ¶26]

Example 2—Evidence of an Ownership Interest in an Entity

.120 Common stock is a financial instrument that is evidence of an ownership interest in an entity, but others include preferred stock, partnership agreements, certificates of interest or participation, or warrants or options to subscribe to or purchase stock from the issuing entity. [FAS105, ¶27]

---

[17]The definition of a financial instrument could be written to exclude currency but include other forms of cash (for example, cash deposits) since currency does not generally represent a promise to pay. The definition includes currency in cash primarily as a matter of convenience. [FAS105, ¶25, fn14]

Example 3—Contractual Right or Obligation to Receive or Deliver Cash

.121 A contractual right to receive cash in the future is a financial instrument. Trade accounts, notes, loans, and bonds receivable all have that characteristic. An entity can have a contractual right to receive cash only if another entity has a contractual obligation to pay cash. [FAS105, ¶28]

.122 A contractual obligation to deliver cash in the future is also a financial instrument. Trade accounts, notes, loans, and bonds payable all have that characteristic. An entity can have a contractual obligation to pay cash only if another entity has the contractual right to receive cash. [FAS105, ¶29]

.123 Physical assets such as inventory, property, plant, and equipment, and leased assets including their unguaranteed residuals, as well as intangibles such as patents, trademarks, and goodwill, do not meet the definition of a financial instrument. Each of those assets could eventually lead to the receipt of cash; however, because no other entity has a present obligation to deliver cash, the entity has no present right to receive cash. [FAS105, ¶30]

Example 4—Contractual Right or Obligation to Receive or Deliver Goods or Services

.124 The definition of a financial instrument excludes many assets that contain contractual rights, such as prepaid expenses and advances to suppliers, because their probable future economic benefit is receipt of goods or services instead of a right to receive cash or an ownership interest in another entity. It also excludes many liabilities that contain contractual obligations, such as deferred revenue, advances from suppliers, and most warranty obligations, because their probable economic sacrifice is delivery of goods or services instead of an obligation to deliver cash or an ownership interest in another entity. [FAS105, ¶31]

.125 The definition excludes contracts that either require or permit settlement by the delivery of commodities. Those contracts are excluded because the future economic benefit is receipt of goods or services instead of a right to receive cash or an ownership interest in an entity and the economic sacrifice is delivery of goods or services instead of an obligation to deliver cash or an ownership interest in an entity. For example, bonds to be settled in ounces of gold or barrels of oil rather than in cash are not financial instruments under the definition. Similarly, contracts that entitle the holder to receive from the issuer *either* a financial instrument (such as the face value of a bond) *or* a physical asset (such as a specified amount of gold or oil) do not meet the definition of a financial instrument (regardless of the probability of settlement in cash rather than in goods or services). [FAS105, ¶32]

Example 5—Contractual Right or Obligation to Receive or Deliver Another Financial Instrument

.126 Another financial instrument is one whose future economic benefit or sacrifice is receipt or delivery of a financial instrument other than cash. For example, a note that is payable in U.S. Treasury bonds gives the holder the contractual right to receive and the issuer the contractual obligation to deliver bonds, not cash. But the bonds are financial instruments because they represent obligations of the U.S. Treasury to pay cash. Therefore, the note is also a financial instrument of the note holder and the note issuer. [FAS105, ¶33]

Example 6—Contractual Right or Obligation to Exchange Other Financial Instruments

.127 Another financial instrument is one that gives an entity the contractual right or obligation to exchange other financial instruments on potentially favorable or unfavorable terms. An example is a call option to purchase a U.S. Treasury note for $100,000 in 6 months. The holder of the option has a contractual right to exchange the financial instruments on potentially favorable terms; if the market value of the note exceeds $100,000 six months later, the terms will be favorable to the holder who will exercise the option. The writer of the call option has a contractual obligation because the writer has an obligation to exchange financial instruments on potentially unfavorable terms if the holder exercises the option. The writer is normally compensated by the holder for undertaking that obligation. A put option to sell a Treasury note has similar but opposite effects. A bank's commitment to lend $100,000 to a customer at a fixed rate of 10 percent any time during the next 6 months at the customer's option is also a financial instrument. [FAS105, ¶34]

.128 A more complex example is a forward contract in which the purchasing entity promises to exchange $100,000 cash for a U.S. Treasury note and the selling entity promises to exchange a U.S. Treasury note for $100,000 cash 6 months later. During the six-month period, both the purchaser and the seller have a contractual right and obligation to exchange financial instruments. The market price for the Treasury note might rise above $100,000, which would make the terms favorable to the purchaser and unfavorable to the seller, or fall below $100,000, which would have the opposite effect. Therefore, the purchaser has both a contractual right (a financial instrument) similar to a call option held and a contractual obligation (a financial instrument) similar to a put option written; the seller has a contractual right (a financial instrument) similar to a put option held and a contractual obligation (a financial instrument) similar to a call option written. [FAS105, ¶35]

.129 An interest rate swap can be viewed as a series of forward contracts to exchange, for example, fixed cash payments for variable cash receipts computed by multiplying a specified floating-rate market index by a notional amount. Those terms are potentially favorable or unfavorable depending on subsequent movements in the index, and an interest rate swap is both a contractual right and a contractual obligation to both parties. [FAS105, ¶36]

.130 Options and contracts that contain the right or obligation to exchange a financial instrument for a physical asset are not financial instruments. For example, 2 entities may enter into sale-purchase contracts in which the purchaser agrees to take delivery of gold or wheat 6 months later and pay the seller $100,000 on delivery. Because the sale-purchase contracts require the delivery of gold or wheat, which are not financial instruments, the sale-purchase contracts are not financial instruments. [FAS105, ¶37]

Example 7—Contingent Rights or Obligations

.131 Contingent items can be financial instruments under the definition. For example, in a typical financial guarantee, a borrower who borrows money from a lender simultaneously pays a fee to a guarantor; in return the guarantor agrees to pay the lender if the borrower defaults on the loan. The guarantee is a financial instrument of the guarantor (the contractual obligation to pay the lender if the borrower defaults) and a financial instrument of the lender (the contractual right to receive cash from the guarantor if the borrower defaults—normally reported together with the guaranteed loan). [FAS105, ¶38]

.132 Other contingent items that ultimately may require the payment of cash but do not as yet arise from contracts, such as contingent liabilities for tort judgments payable, are not financial instruments. However, if those obligations become enforceable by government or courts of law and are thereby contractually reduced to fixed payment schedules, the items would be financial instruments under the definition. [FAS105, ¶39]

Illustration Applying the Definition of a Financial Instrument with Off-Balance-Sheet Risk

.133 A financial instrument has off-balance-sheet risk of accounting loss if the risk of accounting loss to the entity may exceed the amount recognized as an asset, if any, or if the ultimate obligation may exceed the amount that is recognized as a liability in the statement of financial position. [FAS105, ¶40]

.134 Exhibit 134A presents some financial instruments that have and that do not have off-balance-sheet risk of accounting loss; it does not illustrate *all* financial instruments that are included in the scope of paragraphs .112 through .115. Off-balance-sheet risk of accounting loss for similar financial instruments may differ among entities using different methods of accounting. [FAS105, ¶42]

(This page intentionally left blank.)

Exhibit 134A

Financial Instrument	Off-Balance-Sheet (OBS) Risk of Accounting Loss					
	Holder[a]			Issuer[b]		
	OBS Risk[d]	Type of OBS Risk[c]		OBS Risk[d]	Type of OBS Risk[c]	
		CR	MR		CR	MR
Traditional items:						
Cash	No					
Foreign currency	No					
Time deposits (non-interest bearing, fixed rate, or variable rate)	No			No		
Bonds carried at amortized cost (fixed or variable rate bonds, with or without a cap)	No			No		
Bonds carried at market (in trading accounts, fixed or variable rate bonds, with or without a cap)	No			No		
Convertible bonds (convertible into stock of the issuer at a specified price at option of the holder; callable at a premium to face at option of the issuer)	No			No		
Accounts and notes receivable/payable (non-interest bearing, fixed rate, or variable rate)	No			No		
Loans (fixed or variable rate, with or without a cap)	No			No		
Refundable (margin) deposits	No			No		
Accrued expenses receivable/payable (wages, etc.)	No			No		
Common stock (equity investments—cost method or equity method)[e]	No			No		
Preferred stock (convertible or participating)	No			No		

Preferred stock (nonconvertible or nonparticipating)	No	No	
Cash dividends declared	No	No	
Obligations arising from financial instruments sold short	No	Yes	X

Note: Credit risk and market risk are present for many of the instruments included in this illustration. However, only those instruments with off-balance-sheet credit or market risk are denoted with an "X" (refer to footnote c).

[a]Holder includes buyer and investor.

[b]Issuer includes seller, borrower, and writer.

[c]An "X" in any of the columns (CR or MR) denotes the presence of the respective *off-balance-sheet* risk of accounting loss. The types of risk included are:
1. *Credit risk* (CR)—the possibility that a loss may occur from the failure of another party to perform according to the terms of a contract.
2. *Market risk* (MR)—the possibility that future changes in market prices may make a financial instrument less valuable or more onerous.

[d]A "Yes" in this column denotes the presence of off-balance-sheet risk of accounting loss; a "No" denotes no off-balance-sheet risk of accounting loss.

[e]Many joint ventures or other equity method investments are accompanied by guarantees of the debt of the investee. Debt guarantees of this nature present off-balance-sheet risk of accounting loss due to credit risk and should be evaluated with other financial guarantees.

Exhibit 134A (continued)

Financial Instrument	Off-Balance-Sheet (OBS) Risk of Accounting Loss					
	Holder			Issuer		
	OBS Risk	Type of OBS Risk		OBS Risk	Type of OBS Risk	
		CR	MR		CR	MR
Innovative items:						
Increasing rate debt	No			No		
Variable coupon redeemable notes	No			No		
Collateralized mortgage obligations (CMOs):						
CMO accounted for as a borrowing by issuer	No			No		
CMO accounted for as a sale by issuer	No			No[f]		
Transfer of receivables:						
Investor has recourse to the issuer at or below the receivable carrying amount—accounted for as a borrowing by issuer	No			No		
Investor has recourse to the issuer—accounted for as a sale by issuer	No			Yes	X	
Investor has recourse to the issuer and the agreement includes a floating interest rate provision—accounted for as a sale by issuer	No			Yes	X	X
Investor has no recourse to the issuer—accounted for as a sale by issuer	No			No		
Securitized receivables	Same as transfer of receivables					
(Reverse) Repurchase agreements:						
Accounted for as a borrowing by issuer	No			No		
Accounted for as a sale by issuer	No			Yes	X	X

Put option on stock (premium paid up front):				
Covered option	No	Yes		X
Naked option	No	Yes		X
Put option on interest rate contracts[g] (premium paid up front):				
Covered option	No	Yes	X	X
Naked option	No	Yes	X	X
Call option on stock, foreign currency, or interest rate contracts (premium paid up front):				
Covered option	No	Yes		X
Naked option	No	Yes		X
Loan commitment:				
Fixed rate	No	Yes	X	X
Variable rate	No	Yes	X	
Interest rate caps	No	Yes		X
Interest rate floors	No	Yes		X
Financial guarantees	No	Yes	X	
Note issuance facilities at floating rates	No	Yes	X	
Letters of credit (also standby letters of credit) at floating rates	No	Yes	X	

---

[f] Issuer refers to both the trust and the sponsor.

[g] Put options on interest rate contracts have credit risk if the underlying instrument that might be put (a particular bond, for example) is subject to credit risk.

Exhibit 134A (continued)

| Financial Instrument | Off-Balance-Sheet (OBS) Risk of Accounting Loss Both Counterparties[h] | Type of OBS Risk | |
	OBS Risk	CR	MR
Interest rate swaps—accrual basis:			
In a gain position	Yes		X
In a loss position	Yes		X
Gain or loss position netted: right of setoff exists[1]	Yes		X
Interest rate swaps—marked to market:			
In a gain position	Yes		X
In a loss position	Yes		X
Gain or loss position netted: right of setoff exists[1]	Yes		X
Currency swaps	Same as interest rate swaps		
Financial futures contracts—hedges (marked to market and gain or loss deferred—Section F60 or F80 accounting):			
In a gain position	Yes		X
In a loss position	Yes		X
Multiple contracts settled net	Yes		X
Financial futures contracts—nonhedges (marked to market—Section F60 or F80 accounting):			
In a gain position	Yes		X
In a loss position	Yes		X
Multiple contracts settled net	Yes		X

Forward contracts—hedges (marked to market and gain or loss deferred):		
In a gain position	Yes	X
In a loss position	Yes	X
Gain or loss position netted: right of setoff exists[i]	Yes	X
Forward contracts—nonhedges (marked to market and gain or loss recognized):		
In a gain position	Yes	X
In a loss position	Yes	X
Gain or loss position netted: right of setoff exists[i]	Yes	X
Forward contracts—not marked to market	Yes	X

[h]Swaps, forwards, and futures are two-sided transactions; therefore, the holder and issuer categories are not applicable. Risks are assessed in terms of the position held by the entity.

[i]Netting of receivable and payable amounts if right of setoff does not exist is in contravention of Section B10, "Balance Sheet Display: Offsetting." [Refer to paragraphs .101A, .101B, and .104 through .106 of Section B10.]

[FAS105, ¶42]

Illustrations Applying the Disclosure Requirements about Financial Instruments with Off-Balance-Sheet Risk and Concentrations of Credit Risk

.135 The examples that follow are guides to implementation of the disclosure requirements of paragraphs .112 through .115. Entities are not required to display the information contained herein in the specific manner or in the degree of detail illustrated. Alternative ways of disclosing the information are permissible as long as they satisfy the disclosure requirements of paragraphs .112 through .115. [FAS105, ¶43]

Example 1—Nonfinancial Entity

.136 This example illustrates the information that might be disclosed by Corporation A, a nonfinancial entity that has entered into interest rate swap agreements and foreign exchange contracts.[18] Corporation A has no significant concentrations of credit risk with any individual counterparty or groups of counterparties. [FAS105, ¶44]

.137 Corporation A might disclose the following:

Note U: Summary of Accounting Policies

[The accounting policies note to the financial statements might include the following.]

Interest Rate Swap Agreements

The differential to be paid or received is accrued as interest rates change and is recognized over the life of the agreements.

Foreign Exchange Contracts

The Corporation enters into foreign exchange contracts as a hedge against foreign accounts payable. Market value gains and losses are recognized, and the resulting credit or debit offsets foreign exchange gains or losses on those payables.

Note V: Interest Rate Swap Agreements[19]

The Corporation has entered into interest rate swap agreements to reduce the impact of changes in interest rates on its floating rate long-term debt. At December 31, 19X0, the

---

[18]This example might apply also to a financial entity that has a limited number of financial instruments with off-balance-sheet risk. [FAS105, ¶44, fn15]

[19]Placement within financial statements of the information that describes the extent of involvement an entity has in financial instruments with off-balance-sheet risk and the related nature, terms, and credit risk of those instruments is at the discretion of management. The example illustrates information that would be provided in a note "Interest Rate Swap Agreements." As an alternative, this same information could be included in the entity's note about long-term financing arrangements. [FAS105, ¶45, fn16]

Corporation had outstanding 2 interest rate swap agreements with commercial banks, having a total notional principal amount of $85 million. Those agreements effectively change the Corporation's interest rate exposure on its $35 million floating rate notes due 19X3 to a fixed 12 percent and its $50 million floating rate notes due 19X8 to a fixed 12.5 percent. The interest rate swap agreements mature at the time the related notes mature. The Corporation is exposed to credit loss in the event of nonperformance by the other parties to the interest rate swap agreements. However, the Corporation does not anticipate nonperformance by the counterparties.

Note W: Foreign Exchange Contracts

At December 31, 19X0, the Corporation had contracts maturing June 30, 19X1 to purchase $12.9 million in foreign currency (18 million deutsche marks and 5 million Swiss francs at the spot rate on that date). [FAS105, ¶45]

Example 2—Financial Entity

.138 This example illustrates the information that might be disclosed by Bank B, which has entered into the following financial instruments with off-balance-sheet risk: commitments to extend credit, standby letters of credit and financial guarantees written, interest rate swap agreements, forward and futures contracts, and options and interest rate caps and floors written. Bank B has (a) significant concentrations of credit risk in the semiconductor industry in its home state and (b) loans to companies with unusually high debt to equity ratios as a result of buyout transactions. [FAS105, ¶46]

.139 Bank B might disclose the following:

Note X: Summary of Accounting Policies

[The accounting policies note to the financial statements might include the following.]

Interest Rate Futures, Options, Caps and Floors, and Forward Contracts

The Corporation is party to a variety of interest rate futures, options, caps and floors, and forward contracts in its trading activities and in the management of its interest rate exposure.

Interest rate futures, options, caps and floors, and forward contracts used in trading activities are carried at market value. Realized and unrealized gains and losses are included in trading account profits.

Realized and unrealized gains and losses on interest rate futures, options, caps and floors, and forward contracts designated and effective as hedges of interest rate exposure are deferred and recognized as interest income or interest expense over the lives of the hedged assets or liabilities.

Interest Rate Swap Agreements

The Corporation is an intermediary in the interest rate swap market. It also enters into interest rate swap agreements both as trading instruments and as a means of managing its interest rate exposure.

As an intermediary, the Corporation maintains a portfolio of generally matched offsetting swap agreements. These swaps are carried at market value, with changes in value reflected in noninterest income. At inception of the swap agreements, the portion of the compensation related to credit risk and ongoing servicing is deferred and taken into income over the term of the swap agreements.

Interest rate swap agreements used in trading activities are valued at market. Realized and unrealized gains and losses are included in trading account profits. Unrealized gains are reported as assets and unrealized losses are reported as liabilities.

The differential to be paid or received on interest rate swap agreements entered into to reduce the impact of changes in interest rates is recognized over the life of the agreements.

Note Y: Financial Instruments with Off-Balance-Sheet Risk[20]

The Corporation is a party to financial instruments with off-balance-sheet risk in the normal course of business to meet the financing needs of its customers and to reduce its own exposure to fluctuations in interest rates. These financial instruments include commitments to extend credit, options written, standby letters of credit and financial guarantees, interest rate caps and floors written, interest rate swaps, and forward and futures contracts. Those instruments involve, to varying degrees, elements of credit and interest rate risk in excess of the amount recognized in the statement of financial position. The contract or notional amounts of those instruments reflect the extent of involvement the Corporation has in particular classes of financial instruments.

---

[20]Placement within financial statements of the information that describes the extent of involvement an entity has in financial instruments with off-balance-sheet risk and the related nature, terms, and credit risk of those instruments is at the discretion of management. The example illustrates information that would be provided in a note "Financial Instruments with Off-Balance-Sheet Risk." An entity may decide, however, to disclose this information in several separate notes. [FAS105, ¶47, fn17]

The Corporation's exposure to credit loss in the event of nonperformance by the other party to the financial instrument for commitments to extend credit and standby letters of credit and financial guarantees written is represented by the contractual notional amount of those instruments. The Corporation uses the same credit policies in making commitments and conditional obligations as it does for on-balance-sheet instruments. For interest rate caps, floors, and swap transactions, forward and futures contracts, and options written, the contract or notional amounts do not represent exposure to credit loss. The Corporation controls the credit risk of its interest rate swap agreements and forward and futures contracts through credit approvals, limits, and monitoring procedures.

Unless noted otherwise, the Corporation does not require collateral or other security to support financial instruments with credit risk.

	Contract or Notional Amount (in millions)
Financial instruments whose contract amounts represent credit risk:	
Commitments to extend credit	$ 2,780
Standby letters of credit and financial guarantees written	862
Financial instruments whose notional or contract amounts exceed the amount of credit risk:	
Forward and futures contracts	815
Interest rate swap agreements	10,520
Options written and interest rate caps and floors written	950

Commitments to extend credit are agreements to lend to a customer as long as there is no violation of any condition established in the contract. Commitments generally have fixed expiration dates or other termination clauses and may require payment of a fee. Since many of the commitments are expected to expire without being drawn upon, the total commitment amounts do not necessarily represent future cash requirements. The Corporation evaluates each customer's creditworthiness on a case-by-case basis. The amount of collateral obtained if deemed necessary by the Corporation upon extension of credit is based on management's credit evaluation of the counterparty. Collateral held varies but may include accounts receivable, inventory, property, plant, and equipment, and income-producing commercial properties.

Standby letters of credit and financial guarantees written are conditional commitments issued by the Corporation to guarantee the performance of a customer to a third party. Those guarantees are primarily issued to support public and private borrowing arrangements, including commercial paper, bond financing, and similar transactions. Except for short-term guarantees of $158 million, most guarantees extend for more than 5 years and expire in decreasing amounts through 20X0. The credit risk involved in issuing letters of credit is essentially the same as that involved in extending loan facilities to customers. The Corporation holds marketable securities as collateral supporting those commitments for which collateral is deemed necessary. The extent of collateral held for those commitments at December 31, 19X0 varies from 2 percent to 45 percent; the average amount collateralized is 24 percent.

Forward and futures contracts are contracts for delayed delivery of securities or money market instruments in which the seller agrees to make delivery at a specified future date of a specified instrument, at a specified price or yield. Risks arise from the possible inability of counterparties to meet the terms of their contracts and from movements in securities values and interest rates.

The Corporation enters into a variety of interest rate contracts—including interest rate caps and floors written, interest rate options written, and interest rate swap agreements—in its trading activities and in managing its interest rate exposure. Interest rate caps and floors written by the Corporation enable customers to transfer, modify, or reduce their interest rate risk. Interest rate options are contracts that allow the holder of the option to purchase or sell a financial instrument at a specified price and within a specified period of time from the seller or "writer" of the option. As a writer of options, the Corporation receives a premium at the outset and then bears the risk of an unfavorable change in the price of the financial instrument underlying the option.

Interest rate swap transactions generally involve the exchange of fixed and floating rate interest payment obligations without the exchange of the underlying principal amounts. Though swaps are also used as part of asset and liability management, most of the interest rate swap activity arises if the Corporation acts as an intermediary in arranging interest rate swap transactions for customers. The Corporation typically becomes a principal in the exchange of interest payments between the parties and, therefore, is exposed to loss should one of the parties default. The Corporation minimizes this risk by performing normal credit reviews on its swap customers and minimizes its exposure to the interest rate risk inherent in intermediated swaps by entering into offsetting swap positions that essentially counterbalance each other.

Entering into interest rate swap agreements involves not only the risk of dealing with counterparties and their ability to meet the terms of the contracts but also the interest rate risk associated with unmatched positions. Notional principal amounts often are used to express the volume of these transactions, but the amounts potentially subject to credit risk are much smaller.

Note Z: Significant Group Concentrations of Credit Risk

Most of the Corporation's business activity is with customers located within the state. As of December 31, 19X0, the Corporation's receivables from and guarantees of obligations of companies in the semiconductor industry were $XX million.

As of December 31, 19X0, the Corporation was also creditor for $XX of domestic loans and other receivables from companies with high debt to equity ratios as a result of buyout transactions. The portfolio is well diversified, consisting of XX industries. Generally, the loans are secured by assets or stock. The loans are expected to be repaid from cash flow or proceeds from the sale of selected assets of the borrowers. Credit losses arising from lending transactions with highly leveraged entities compare favorably with the Corporation's credit loss experience on its loan portfolio as a whole. The Corporation's policy for requiring collateral is [**state policy, along with information about the entity's access to that collateral or other security and a description of collateral**]. [FAS105, ¶47]

Example 3—Concentration of Credit Risk for Certain Entities

.140 For certain entities, industry or regional concentrations of credit risk may be disclosed adequately by a description of the business. For example:

a. *A Retailer*—Corporation C is a retailer of family clothing with three stores, all of which are located in Littletown. The Corporation grants credit to customers, substantially all of whom are local residents.
b. *A Bank*—Bank D grants agribusiness, commercial, and residential loans to customers throughout the state. Although the Bank has a diversified loan portfolio, a substantial portion of its debtors' ability to honor their contracts is dependent upon the agribusiness economic sector. [FAS105, ¶48]

Examples of Procedures for Estimating Fair Value

.141 Paragraphs .142 through .152 provide examples of procedures for estimating the fair value of financial instruments. The examples are illustrative and are not meant to portray all possible ways of estimating the fair value of a financial instrument in order to comply with the provisions of paragraphs .115C through .115F and .115I through .115K. [FAS107, ¶18]

.142 Fair value information is frequently based on information obtained from market sources. In broad terms, there are four kinds of markets in which financial instruments can be bought, sold, or originated; available information about prices differs by kind of market:

a. *Exchange market.* An exchange or "auction" market provides high visibility and order to the trading of financial instruments. Typically, closing prices and volume levels are readily available in an exchange market.

b. *Dealer market.* In a dealer market, dealers stand ready to trade—either buy or sell—for their own account, thereby providing liquidity to the market. Typically, current bid and asked prices are more readily available than information about closing prices and volume levels. "Over-the-counter" markets are dealer markets.

c. *Brokered market.* In a brokered market, brokers attempt to match buyers with sellers but do not stand ready to trade for their own account. The broker knows the prices bid and asked by the respective parties, but each party is typically unaware of another party's price requirements; prices of completed transactions are sometimes available.

d. *Principal-to-principal market.* Principal-to-principal transactions, both originations and resales, are negotiated independently, with no intermediary, and little, if any, information is typically released publicly. [FAS107, ¶19]

Financial Instruments with Quoted Prices

.143 As indicated in paragraph .115D, quoted market prices, if available, are the best evidence of fair value of financial instruments. Prices for financial instruments may be quoted in several markets; generally, the price in the most active market will be the best indicator of fair value. [FAS107, ¶20]

.144 In some cases, an entity's management may decide to provide further information about the fair value of a financial instrument. For example, an entity may want to explain that although the fair value of its long-term debt is less than the carrying amount, settlement at the reported fair value may not be possible or may not be a prudent management decision for other reasons; or the entity may want to state that potential taxes and other expenses that would be incurred in an actual sale or settlement are not taken into consideration. [FAS107, ¶21]

Financial Instruments with No Quoted Prices

.145 For financial instruments that do not trade regularly, or that trade only in principal-to-principal markets, an entity shall provide its best estimate of fair value. Judgments about the methods and assumptions to be used in various circumstances must be made by those who prepare and attest to an entity's financial statements. The following discussion provides some examples of how fair value might be estimated. [FAS107, ¶22]

.146 For some short-term financial instruments, the carrying amount in the financial statements may approximate fair value because of the relatively short period of time between the origination of the instruments and their expected realization. Likewise, for loans that reprice frequently at market rates, the carrying amount may normally be close enough to fair value to satisfy these disclosure requirements, provided there is no significant change in the credit risk of those loans. [FAS107, ¶23]

.147 Some financial instruments (for example, interest rate swaps and foreign currency contracts) may be "custom-tailored" and, thus, may not have a quoted market price. In those cases, an estimate of fair value might be based on the quoted market price of a similar financial instrument, adjusted as appropriate for the effects of the tailoring. Alternatively, the estimate might be based on the estimated current replacement cost of that instrument. [FAS107, ¶24]

.148 Other financial instruments that are commonly "custom-tailored" include various types of options (for example, put and call options on stock, foreign currency, or interest rate contracts). A variety of option pricing models that have been developed in recent years (such as the Black-Scholes model and binomial models) are regularly used to value options. The use of those pricing models to estimate fair value is appropriate under the requirements of this section. [FAS107, ¶25]

.149 For some predominantly financial entities, loans receivable may be the most significant category of financial instruments. Market prices may be more readily available for some categories of loans (such as residential mortgage loans) than for others. If no quoted market price exists for a category of loans, an estimate of fair value may be based on (a) the market prices of similar traded loans with similar credit ratings, interest rates, and maturity dates, (b) current prices (interest rates) offered for similar loans in the entity's own lending activities, or (c) valuations obtained from loan pricing services offered by various specialist firms or from other sources. [FAS107, ¶26]

.150 An estimate of the fair value of a loan or group of loans may be based on the discounted value of the future cash flows expected to be received from the loan or group of loans. The selection of an appropriate current discount rate reflecting the relative risks involved requires judgment, and several alternative rates and approaches are available to an entity. A single discount rate could be used to estimate the fair value of a homogeneous category of loans; for example, an entity might apply a single rate to each aggregated category of loans reported for regulatory purposes. An entity could use a discount rate commensurate with the credit, interest rate, and prepayment risks involved, which could be the rate at which the same loans would be made under current conditions. An entity also could select a discount rate that reflects the effects of interest rate changes and then make adjustments to reflect the effects of changes in credit risk. Those adjustments could include (a) revising cash flow estimates for cash flows not expected to be collected, (b) revising the discount rate to reflect any additional credit risk associated with that group of loans, or some combination of (a) and (b). [FAS107, ¶27]

.151 A fair value for financial liabilities for which quoted market prices are not available can generally be estimated using the same techniques used for estimating the value of financial assets. For example, a loan payable to a bank could be valued at the discounted amount of future cash flows using an entity's current incremental rate of borrowing for a similar liability; alternatively, the discount rate could be the rate that an entity would have to pay to a creditworthy third party to assume its obligation, with the creditor's legal consent (sometimes referred to as the "settlement rate"), or the rate that an entity would have to pay to acquire essentially risk-free assets to extinguish the obligation in accordance with the requirements of Section D14. [FAS107, ¶28]

.152 For deposit liabilities with defined maturities, such as certificates of deposit, an estimate of fair value might also be based on the discounted value of the future cash flows expected to be paid on the deposits. The discount rate could be the current rate offered for similar deposits with the same remaining maturities. For deposit liabilities with no defined maturities, paragraph .115E requires that the fair value to be disclosed be the amount payable on demand at the reporting date. [FAS107, ¶29]

Illustrations Applying the Disclosure Requirements about Fair Value of Financial Instruments

.153 The examples that follow are guides to implementation of the disclosure requirements of paragraphs .115C through .115F and .115I through .115K. Entities are not required to display the information contained herein in the specific manner illustrated. Alternative ways of disclosing the information are permissible as long as they satisfy the disclosure requirements of paragraphs .115C through .115F and .115I through .115K. Paragraphs .115E and .144 describe possible additional voluntary disclosures that may be appropriate in certain circumstances. [FAS107, ¶30]

Example 1—Financial Entity

.154 Bank A might disclose the following:

Note V: Disclosures about Fair Value of Financial Instruments

The following methods and assumptions were used to estimate the fair value of each class of financial instruments for which it is practicable to estimate that value:

Cash and short-term investments
For those short-term instruments, the carrying amount is a reasonable estimate of fair value.

Investment securities and trading account assets
For securities and derivative instruments held for trading purposes (which include bonds, interest rate futures, options, interest rate swaps, securities sold not owned, caps and floors, foreign currency contracts, and forward contracts) and marketable equity securities held for investment purposes, fair values are based on quoted market prices or dealer quotes. For other securities held as investments, fair value equals quoted market price, if available. If a quoted market price is not available, fair value is estimated using quoted market prices for similar securities.

Loan receivables
For certain homogeneous categories of loans, such as some residential mortgages, credit card receivables, and other consumer loans, fair value is estimated using the quoted market prices for securities backed by similar loans, adjusted for differences in loan characteristics. The fair value of other types of loans is estimated by discounting the future cash flows using the current rates at which similar loans would be made to borrowers with similar credit ratings and for the same remaining maturities.

Deposit liabilities
The fair value of demand deposits, savings accounts, and certain money market deposits is the amount payable on demand at the reporting date. The fair value of fixed-maturity certificates of deposit is estimated using the rates currently offered for deposits of similar remaining maturities.

Long-term debt
Rates currently available to the Bank for debt with similar terms and remaining maturities are used to estimate fair value of existing debt.

Interest rate swap agreements

The fair value of interest rate swaps (used for hedging purposes) is the estimated amount that the Bank would receive or pay to terminate the swap agreements at the reporting date, taking into account current interest rates and the current creditworthiness of the swap counterparties.

Commitments to extend credit, standby letters of credit, and financial guarantees written

The fair value of commitments is estimated using the fees currently charged to enter into similar agreements, taking into account the remaining terms of the agreements and the present creditworthiness of the counterparties. For fixed-rate loan commitments, fair value also considers the difference between current levels of interest rates and the committed rates. The fair value of guarantees and letters of credit is based on fees currently charged for similar agreements or on the estimated cost to terminate them or otherwise settle the obligations with the counterparties at the reporting date.

The estimated fair values of the Bank's financial instruments are as follows:

	19X9		19X8	
	Carrying Amount	Fair Value	Carrying Amount	Fair Value
Financial assets:				
Cash and short-term investments	$ XXX	$ XXX	$ XXX	$ XXX
Trading account assets	XXX	XXX	XXX	XXX
Investment securities	XXX	XXX	XXX	XXX
Loans	XXX		XXX	
Less: allowance for loan losses	(XXX)		(XXX)	
Loans, net of allowance	XXX	XXX	XXX	XXX
Financial liabilities:				
Deposits	XXX	XXX	XXX	XXX
Securities sold not owned	XXX	XXX	XXX	XXX
Long-term debt	XXX	XXX	XXX	XXX
Unrecognized financial instruments:*				
Interest rate swaps				
In a net receivable position	XXX	XXX	XXX	XXX
In a net payable position	(XXX)	(XXX)	(XXX)	(XXX)
Commitments to extend credit	(XXX)	(XXX)	(XXX)	(XXX)
Standby letters of credit	(XXX)	(XXX)	(XXX)	(XXX)
Financial guarantees written	(XXX)	(XXX)	(XXX)	(XXX)

*The amounts shown under "carrying amount" represent accruals or deferred income (fees) arising from those unrecognized financial instruments. Interest rate swaps and other derivative instruments entered into as trading activities are included in "trading account assets" or "securities sold not owned." [FAS107, ¶31]

Example 2—Nonfinancial Entity

[In this example, it is assumed that the carrying amounts of the short-term trade receivables and payables approximate their fair values.]

.155 Corporation B might disclose the following:

Note X: Disclosures about Fair Value of Financial Instruments

The following methods and assumptions were used to estimate the fair value of each class of financial instruments for which it is practicable to estimate that value:

Cash and short-term investments
The carrying amount approximates fair value because of the short maturity of those instruments.

Long-term investments
The fair values of some investments are estimated based on quoted market prices for those or similar investments. For other investments for which there are no quoted market prices, a reasonable estimate of fair value could not be made without incurring excessive costs. Additional information pertinent to the value of an unquoted investment is provided below.

Long-term debt
The fair value of the Corporation's long-term debt is estimated based on the quoted market prices for the same or similar issues or on the current rates offered to the Corporation for debt of the same remaining maturities.

Foreign currency contracts
The fair value of foreign currency contracts (used for hedging purposes) is estimated by obtaining quotes from brokers.

The estimated fair values of the Corporation's financial instruments are as follows:

	19X9		19X8	
	Carrying Amount	Fair Value	Carrying Amount	Fair Value
Cash and short-term investments	$ XXX	$ XXX	$ XXX	$ XXX
Long-term investments for which it is:				
Practicable to estimate fair value	XXX	XXX	XXX	XXX
Not practicable	XXX	—	XXX	—
Long-term debt	(XXX)	(XXX)	(XXX)	(XXX)
Foreign currency contracts	XXX	XXX	(XXX)	(XXX)

It was not practicable to estimate the fair value of an investment representing 12 percent of the issued common stock of an untraded company; that investment is carried at its original cost of $XXX (19X8, $XXX) in the statement of financial position. At year-end, the total assets reported by the untraded company were $XXX (19X8, $XXX) and the common stockholders' equity was $XXX (19X8, $XXX), revenues were $XXX (19X8, $XXX), and net income was $XXX (19X8, $XXX). [FAS107, ¶32]

Example 3—Small Nonfinancial Entity

.156 Corporation C, whose only financial instruments are cash, short-term trade receivables and payables for which their carrying amounts approximate fair values, and long-term debt, might disclose the following:

Note Z: Long-Term Debt

Based on the borrowing rates currently available to the Corporation for bank loans with similar terms and average maturities, the fair value of long-term debt is $XXX (19X8, $XXX). [FAS107, ¶33]

[**Note:** Additional guidance with respect to implementing Section F25 is presented in the FASB publication: *Illustrations of Financial Instrument Disclosures*. The publication presents four examples that illustrate the disclosure requirements of Section F25 and was written by FASB staff member Clark M. Anstis. This publication is available from the Order Department, Financial Accounting Standards Board, 401 Merritt 7, P.O. Box 5116, Norwalk, CT 06856-5116, telephone (203) 847-0700, extension 555.]

Glossary

.401 **Credit risk.** The possibility that a loss may occur from the failure of another party to perform according to the terms of a contract. [FAS105, ¶7]

.401A [Deleted 10/94 and renumbered as paragraph .401C.]

.401B **Derivative financial instrument.** Futures, forward, swap, or option contract, or other financial instrument with similar characteristics. [FAS119, ¶5] [Refer to paragraphs .105E and .105F for examples.]

.401C **Fair value.** [Refer to paragraph .115A.]

.402 **Financial instrument.** [Refer to paragraph .106.]

.403 **Market risk.** The possibility that future changes in market prices may make a financial instrument less valuable or more onerous. [FAS105, ¶7]

.404 **Risk of accounting loss.** Includes (a) the possibility that a loss may occur from the failure of another party to perform according to the terms of a contract (credit risk), (b) the possibility that future changes in market prices may make a financial instrument less valuable or more onerous (market risk), and (c) the risk of theft or physical loss. [FAS105, ¶7] Accounting loss refers to the loss that may have to be recognized [in the financial statements] due to credit and market risk as a direct result of the rights and obligations of a financial instrument. [FAS105, ¶7, fn4]

(The next page is 18351.)

Source: ARB 43, Chapter 2A

Summary

The presentation of comparative financial statements enhances the usefulness of annual and other reports. Ordinarily, it is desirable that financial statements of two or more periods be presented.

.101 The presentation of comparative financial statements in annual and other reports enhances the usefulness of such reports and brings out more clearly the nature and trends of current changes affecting the enterprise. Such presentation emphasizes the fact that statements for a series of periods are far more significant than those for a single period and that the accounts for one period are but an installment of what is essentially a continuous history. [ARB43, ch2A, ¶1]

.102 In any one year it is ordinarily desirable that the balance sheet, the income statement, [the statement of cash flows,] and the statement of [retained earnings] be given for one or more preceding years as well as for the current year.[1] Footnotes [and] explanations that appeared on the statements for the preceding years should be repeated, or at least referred to, in the comparative statements to the extent that they continue to be of significance. [ARB43, ch2A, ¶2]

.103 It is necessary that prior-year figures shown for comparative purposes be in fact comparable with those shown for the most recent period, or that any exceptions to comparability be clearly brought out. [ARB43, ch2A, ¶3]

(The next page is 19251.)

---

[1] Refer to Section A06, "Accounting Changes," concerning disclosure of changes made in the manner of or basis for presenting corresponding items for two or more periods. [ARB43, ch2A, ¶2]

Sources: FASB Statement 52; FASB Statement 95; FASB Statement 104;
FASB Statement 109; FASB Interpretation 37

Summary

The requirements in this section reflect these general conclusions:

a. The economic effects of an exchange rate change on an operation that is relatively self-contained and integrated within a foreign country relate to the net investment in that operation. Translation adjustments that arise from consolidating that foreign operation do not impact cash flows and are not included in net income.
b. The economic effects of an exchange rate change on a foreign operation that is an extension of the parent's domestic operations relate to individual assets and liabilities and impact the parent's cash flows directly. Accordingly, the exchange gains and losses in such an operation are included in net income.
c. Contracts, transactions, or balances that are, in fact, effective hedges of foreign exchange risk will be accounted for as hedges without regard to their form.

More specifically, this section presents standards for foreign currency translation that are designed to (a) provide information that is generally compatible with the expected economic effects of a rate change on an enterprise's cash flows and equity and (b) reflect in consolidated statements the financial results and relationships as measured in the primary currency in which each entity conducts its business (referred to as its *functional currency*).

An entity's functional currency is the currency of the primary economic environment in which that entity operates. The functional currency can be the dollar or a foreign currency depending on the facts. Normally, it will be the currency of the economic environment in which cash is generated and expended by the entity. An entity can be any form of operation, including a subsidiary, division, branch, or joint venture. This section provides guidance for this key determination in which management's judgment is essential in assessing the facts.

A currency in a highly inflationary environment (3-year inflation rate of approximately 100 percent or more) is not considered stable enough to serve as a functional currency and the more stable currency of the reporting parent is to be used instead.

The functional currency translation approach adopted in this section encompasses:

a. Identifying the functional currency of the entity's economic environment
b. Measuring all elements of the financial statements in the functional currency
c. Using the current exchange rate for translation from the functional currency to the reporting currency, if they are different
d. Distinguishing the economic impact of changes in exchange rates on a net investment from the impact of such changes on individual assets and liabilities that are receivable or payable in currencies other than the functional currency

Translation adjustments are an inherent result of the process of translating a foreign entity's financial statements from the functional currency to U.S. dollars. Translation adjustments are *not* included in determining net income for the period but are disclosed and accumulated in a separate component of consolidated equity until a sale in whole or in part or a complete or substantially complete liquidation of the net investment in the foreign entity takes place.

Transaction gains and losses are a result of the effect of exchange rate changes on transactions denominated in currencies other than the functional currency (for example, a U.S. enterprise may borrow Swiss francs or a French subsidiary may have a receivable denominated in kroner from a Danish customer). Gains and losses on those foreign currency transactions are generally included in determining net income for the period in which exchange rates change unless the transaction hedges a foreign currency commitment or a net investment in a foreign entity. Intercompany transactions of a long-term investment nature are considered part of a parent's net investment and hence do not give rise to gains or losses.

Introduction and Scope

.101 This section [contains] standards of financial accounting and reporting for **foreign currency transactions** in financial statements of a **reporting enterprise** (hereinafter, **enterprise**). It also [contains] the standards for translating foreign currency financial statements (hereinafter, **foreign currency statements**) that are incorporated in the financial statements of an enterprise by consolidation, combination, or the equity method of accounting. **Translation** of financial statements from one currency to another for purposes other than consolidation, combination, or the equity method is beyond the scope of this section. For example, this section does not cover translation of the financial statements of an enterprise from its **reporting currency** into another currency for the convenience of readers accustomed to that other currency. [FAS52, ¶2]

.102 The **functional currency** approach [described herein] applies equally to translation of financial statements of foreign investees whether accounted for by the equity method or consolidated. It also applies to translation after a business combination. Therefore, the foreign statements and the foreign currency transactions of an investee that are accounted for by the equity method should be translated in conformity with the requirements of this section in applying the equity method. Likewise, after a business combination accounted for by the purchase method, the amount allocated at the date of acquisition to the assets acquired and the liabilities assumed (including *goodwill* or *an excess of acquired net assets over cost*, as those terms are used in Section B50, "Business Combinations") should be translated in conformity with the requirements of this section. Accumulated **translation adjustments** attributable to minority interests should be allocated to and reported as part of the minority interest in the consolidated enterprise. [FAS52, ¶101]

Objectives of Translation

.103 Financial statements are intended to present information in financial terms about the performance, financial position, and cash flows of an enterprise. For this purpose, the financial statements of separate **entities** within an enterprise, which may exist and operate in different economic and currency environments, are consolidated and presented as though they were the financial statements of a single enterprise. Because it is not possible to combine, add, or subtract measurements expressed in different currencies, it is necessary to translate into a single reporting currency[1] those assets, liabilities, revenues, expenses, gains, and losses that are measured or denominated in a **foreign currency**.[2] However, the unity presented by such translation does

---

[1]For convenience, this section assumes that the enterprise uses the U.S. dollar (dollar) as its reporting currency. However, a currency other than the dollar may be the reporting currency in financial statements that are prepared in conformity with U.S. generally accepted accounting principles. For example, a foreign enterprise may report in its **local currency** in conformity with U.S. generally accepted accounting principles. If so, the requirements of this section apply. [FAS52, ¶4, fn2]

[2]To measure in foreign currency is to quantify an **attribute** of an item in a unit of currency other than the reporting currency. Assets and liabilities are denominated in a foreign currency if their amounts are fixed in terms of that foreign currency regardless of exchange rate changes. An asset or liability may be both measured and denominated in one currency, or it may be measured in one currency and denominated in another. To illustrate: Two foreign branches of a U.S. enterprise, one Swiss and one German, purchase identical assets on credit from a Swiss vendor at identical prices stated in Swiss francs. The German branch measures the cost (an attribute) of that asset in German marks. Although the corresponding liability is also measured in marks, it remains denominated in Swiss francs since the liability must be settled in a specified number of Swiss francs. The Swiss branch measures the asset and liability in Swiss francs. Its liability is both measured and denominated in Swiss francs. Although assets and liabilities can be measured in various currencies, rights to receive or obligations to pay fixed amounts of a currency are, by definition, denominated in that currency. [FAS52, ¶4, fn3]

not alter the underlying significance of the results and relationships of the constituent parts of the enterprise. It is only through the effective operation of its constituent parts that the enterprise as a whole is able to achieve its purpose. Accordingly, the translation of the financial statements of each component entity of an enterprise should accomplish the following objectives:

a. Provide information that is generally compatible with the expected economic effects of a rate change on an enterprise's cash flows and equity
b. Reflect in consolidated statements the financial results and relationships of the individual consolidated entities as measured in their functional currencies in conformity with U.S. generally accepted accounting principles [FAS52, ¶4]

The Functional Currency

.104 The assets, liabilities, and operations of a **foreign entity** shall be measured using the functional currency of that entity. An entity's functional currency is the currency of the primary economic environment in which the entity operates; normally, that is the currency of the environment in which an entity primarily generates and expends cash. Paragraphs .106 through .112 provide guidance for determination of the functional currency. [FAS52, ¶5]

.105 It is neither possible nor desirable to provide unequivocal criteria to identify the functional currency of foreign entities under all possible facts and circumstances and still fulfill the objectives of **foreign currency translation.** Arbitrary rules that might dictate the identification of the functional currency in each case would accomplish a degree of superficial uniformity but, in the process, might diminish the relevance and reliability of the resulting information. [FAS52, ¶40]

.106 Multinational enterprises may consist of entities operating in a number of economic environments and dealing in a number of foreign currencies. All foreign operations are not alike. In order to fulfill the objective in paragraph .102, it is necessary to recognize at least two broad classes of foreign operations. [FAS52, ¶79]

.107 In the first class are foreign operations that are relatively self-contained and integrated within a particular country or economic environment. The day-to-day operations are not dependent upon the economic environment of the parent's functional currency; the foreign operation primarily generates and expends foreign currency. The foreign currency net cash flows that it generates may be reinvested or converted and distributed to the parent. For this class, the foreign currency is the functional currency. [FAS52, ¶80]

.108 In the second class are foreign operations that are primarily a direct and integral component or extension of the parent company's operations. Significant assets may be acquired from the parent company or otherwise by expending dollars and, similarly, the sale of assets may generate dollars that are available to the parent. Financing is primarily by the parent or otherwise from dollar sources. In other words, the day-to-day operations are dependent on the economic environment of the parent's currency, and the changes in the foreign entity's individual assets and liabilities impact directly on the cash flows of the parent company in the parent's currency. For this case, the dollar is the functional currency. [FAS52, ¶81]

.109 The functional currency of an entity is, in principle, a matter of fact. In some cases, the facts will clearly identify the functional currency; in other cases they will not. [FAS52, ¶39] For example, if a foreign entity conducts significant amounts of business in two or more currencies, the functional currency might not be clearly identified. [FAS52, ¶8] In those instances in which the indicators are mixed and the functional currency is not obvious, management's judgment will be required in order to determine the functional currency that most faithfully portrays the economic results of the entity's operations and thereby best achieves the objectives of foreign currency translation set forth in paragraph .102. Management is in the best position to obtain the pertinent facts and weigh their relative importance in determining the functional currency for each operation. It is important to recognize that management's judgment is essential and paramount in this determination, provided only that it is not contradicted by the facts. [FAS52, ¶41]

.110 The salient economic factors set forth below, and possibly others, should be considered both individually and collectively when determining the functional currency.

a. Cash flow indicators
    (1) Foreign Currency—Cash flows related to the foreign entity's individual assets and liabilities are primarily in the foreign currency and do not directly impact the parent company's cash flows.
    (2) Parent's Currency—Cash flows related to the foreign entity's individual assets and liabilities directly impact the parent's cash flows on a current basis and are readily available for remittance to the parent company.
b. Sales price indicators
    (1) Foreign Currency—Sales prices for the foreign entity's products are not primarily responsive on a short-term basis to changes in exchange rates but are determined more by local competition or local government regulation.
    (2) Parent's Currency—Sales prices for the foreign entity's products are primarily responsive on a short-term basis to changes in exchange rates; for example, sales prices are determined more by worldwide competition or by international prices.
c. Sales market indicators
    (1) Foreign Currency—There is an active local sales market for the foreign entity's products, although there also might be significant amounts of exports.
    (2) Parent's Currency—The sales market is mostly in the parent's country or sales contracts are denominated in the parent's currency.

d.　Expense indicators
　　(1)　Foreign Currency—Labor, materials, and other costs for the foreign entity's products or services are primarily local costs, even though there also might be imports from other countries.
　　(2)　Parent's Currency—Labor, materials, and other costs for the foreign entity's products or services, on a continuing basis, are primarily costs for components obtained from the country in which the parent company is located.
e.　Financing indicators
　　(1)　Foreign Currency—Financing is primarily denominated in foreign currency, and funds generated by the foreign entity's operations are sufficient to service existing and normally expected debt obligations.
　　(2)　Parent's Currency—Financing is primarily from the parent or other dollar-denominated obligations, or funds generated by the foreign entity's operations are not sufficient to service existing and normally expected debt obligations without the infusion of additional funds from the parent company. Infusion of additional funds from the parent company for expansion is not a factor, provided funds generated by the foreign entity's expanded operations are expected to be sufficient to service that additional financing.
f.　Intercompany transactions and arrangements indicators
　　(1)　Foreign Currency—There is a low volume of intercompany transactions and there is not an extensive interrelationship between the operations of the foreign entity and the parent company. However, the foreign entity's operations may rely on the parent's or affiliates' competitive advantages, such as patents and trademarks.
　　(2)　Parent's Currency—There is a high volume of intercompany transactions and there is an extensive interrelationship between the operations of the foreign entity and the parent company. Additionally, the parent's currency generally would be the functional currency if the foreign entity is a device or shell corporation for holding investments, obligations, intangible assets, etc., that could readily be carried on the parent's or an affiliate's books. [FAS52, ¶42]

.111　An entity might have more than one distinct and separable operation, such as a division or branch, in which case each operation may be considered a separate entity. If those operations are conducted in different economic environments, they might have different functional currencies. [FAS52, ¶7] Similarly, a single subsidiary of a financial institution might have relatively self-contained and integrated operations in each of several different countries. In circumstances such as those described above, each operation may be considered to be an entity as that term is used in this section; and, based on the facts and circumstances, each operation might have a different functional currency. [FAS52, ¶43]

.112　Foreign investments that are consolidated or accounted for by the equity method are controlled by or subject to significant influence by the parent company. Likewise, the parent's currency is often used for measurements, assessments, evaluations, projections, etc., pertaining to foreign investments as part of the management decision-making process. Such management control, decisions, and resultant actions may reflect, indicate, or create economic facts and circumstances. However, the exercise of significant management control and the use of the parent's currency for decision-making purposes do not determine, per se, that the parent's currency is the functional currency for foreign operations. [FAS52, ¶44]

.113 Once the functional currency for a foreign entity is determined, that determination shall be used consistently unless significant changes in economic facts and circumstances indicate clearly that the functional currency has changed. Previously issued financial statements shall not be restated for any change in the functional currency. [FAS52, ¶9] (Section A06, "Accounting Changes," paragraph .106, states that "adoption or modification of an accounting principle necessitated by transactions or events that are clearly different in substance from those previously occurring" is not a change in accounting principles.) [FAS52, ¶45]

.114 If the functional currency changes from a foreign currency to the reporting currency, translation adjustments for prior periods should not be removed from equity and the translated amounts for nonmonetary assets at the end of the prior period become the accounting basis for those assets in the period of the change and subsequent periods. If the functional currency changes from the reporting currency to a foreign currency, the adjustment attributable to current-rate translation of nonmonetary assets as of the date of the change should be reported in the cumulative translation adjustments component of equity. [FAS52, ¶46]

.115 If an entity's books of record are not maintained in its functional currency, remeasurement into the functional currency is required. That remeasurement is required before translation into the reporting currency. If a foreign entity's functional currency is the reporting currency, remeasurement into the reporting currency obviates translation. The remeasurement process is intended to produce the same result as if the entity's books of record had been maintained in the functional currency. The remeasurement of and subsequent accounting for transactions denominated in a currency other than the functional currency shall be in accordance with the requirements of this section (refer to paragraphs .122 and .123). Paragraphs .146 through .152 provide guidance for remeasurement into the functional currency. [FAS52, ¶10]

Translation of Operations in Highly Inflationary Economies

.116 The financial statements of a foreign entity in a highly inflationary economy shall be remeasured as if the functional currency were the reporting currency. Accordingly, the financial statements of those entities shall be remeasured into the reporting currency according to the requirements of paragraph .115. For the purposes of this requirement, a highly inflationary economy is one that has cumulative inflation of approximately 100 percent or more over a 3-year period. [FAS52, ¶11]

.117 The definition of a highly inflationary economy as one that has cumulative inflation of *approximately* 100 percent or more over a 3-year period is necessarily an arbitrary decision. In some instances, the trend of inflation might be as important as the absolute rate. The definition of a highly inflationary economy [shall] be applied with judgment. [FAS52, ¶109]

Translation of Foreign Currency Statements

.118 All elements of financial statements shall be translated by using a **current exchange rate.** For assets and liabilities, the exchange rate at the balance sheet date shall be used. For revenues, expenses, gains, and losses, the exchange rate at the dates on which those elements are recognized shall be used. Because translation at the exchange rates at the dates the numerous revenues, expenses, gains, and losses are recognized is generally impractical, an appropriately weighted average exchange rate for the period may be used to translate those elements. [FAS52, ¶12] This also applies to accounting allocations (for example, depreciation, cost of sales, and amortization of deferred revenues and expenses) and requires translation at the current exchange rates applicable to the dates those allocations are included in revenues and expenses (that is, not the rates on the dates the related items originated). [FAS52, ¶99]

.118A A statement of cash flows of an enterprise with foreign currency transactions or foreign operations shall report the reporting currency equivalent of foreign currency cash flows using the exchange rates in effect at the time of the cash flows. An appropriately weighted average exchange rate for the period may be used for translation if the result is substantially the same as if the rates at the dates of the cash flows were used.[2aa] The statement shall report the effect of exchange rate changes on cash balances held in foreign currencies as a separate part of the reconciliation of the change in cash and cash equivalents during the period. [FAS95, ¶25] [Paragraphs .142 through .152 of Section C25, "Cash Flows Statement," present an example of a consolidating statement of cash flows for a U.S. parent company with two foreign subsidiaries.]

.119 If an entity's functional currency is a foreign currency, translation adjustments result from the process of translating that entity's financial statements into the reporting currency. Translation adjustments shall not be included in determining net income but shall be reported separately and accumulated in a separate component of equity. [FAS52, ¶13]

.120 Upon sale or upon complete or substantially complete liquidation of an investment in a foreign entity, the amount attributable to that entity and accumulated in the translation adjustment component of equity shall be removed from the separate component of equity and shall be reported as part of the gain or loss on sale or liquidation

---

[2aa]Paragraph .118 recognizes the general impracticality of translating revenues, expenses, gains, and losses at the exchange rates on dates they are recognized and permits an appropriately weighted average exchange rate for the period to be used to translate those elements. Section C25, "Cash Flows Statement," applies that provision to cash receipts and cash payments. [FAS95, ¶25, fn9]

of the investment for the period during which the sale or liquidation occurs.[2a] [FAS52, ¶14] If an enterprise sells part of its ownership interest in a foreign entity, a pro rata portion of the accumulated translation adjustment component of equity attributable to that investment shall be recognized in measuring the gain or loss on the sale.[2b] [FIN37, ¶2]

.121 [Deleted 11/87 because of FASB Statement 95, *Statement of Cash Flows*.]

Foreign Currency Transactions

.122 Foreign currency transactions are transactions denominated in a currency other than the entity's functional currency. Foreign currency transactions may produce receivables or payables that are fixed in terms of the amount of foreign currency that will be received or paid. [FAS52, ¶15] Examples [of foreign currency transactions] include a sale denominated in Swiss francs, a Swiss franc loan, and the holding of Swiss francs by an entity whose functional currency is the dollar. Likewise, a Swiss franc denominated transaction by a German entity or other entity whose functional currency is not the Swiss franc is a foreign currency transaction. For any entity whose functional currency is *not* the dollar, a dollar-denominated transaction is also a foreign currency transaction. [FAS52, ¶120] A change in exchange rates between the functional currency and the currency in which a transaction is denominated increases or decreases the expected amount of functional currency cash flows upon settlement of the transaction. [FAS52, ¶15] That is equally the case for transactions of the foreign entity denominated in the reporting currency. [FAS52, ¶96] That increase or decrease in expected functional currency cash flows is a foreign currency **transaction gain or loss** that generally shall be included in determining net income for the period in which the exchange rate changes. Likewise, a transaction gain or loss (measured from the **transaction date** or the most recent intervening balance sheet date, whichever is later) realized upon settlement of a foreign currency transaction generally shall be included in determining net income for the period in which the transaction is settled. The exceptions to this requirement for inclusion in net income of transaction gains and losses are set forth in paragraphs .127 and .130 and pertain to certain intercompany transactions and to transactions that are designated as, and effective as, economic hedges of net investments and foreign currency commitments. [FAS52, ¶15]

[2a][Some consider] a partial liquidation by a subsidiary may be considered to be similar to a sale of part of an ownership interest if the liquidation proceeds are distributed to the parent. However, extending pro rata recognition to such partial liquidations would require that their substance be distinguished from ordinary dividends. [It is felt] that such a distinction is [neither] possible nor desirable. This paragraph is restricted to clarifying that a sale includes an investor's partial, as well as complete, disposal of its ownership interest. [FIN37, ¶8]

[2b]Under Section I13, "Income Statement Presentation: Discontinued Operations," a gain or loss on disposal of part or all of a net investment may be recognized in a period other than that in which actual sale or liquidation occurs. This paragraph does not alter the period in which a gain or loss on sale or liquidation is recognized under existing generally accepted accounting principles. [FIN37, ¶2, fn1]

.123 For other than **forward exchange contracts** (refer to paragraphs .124 through .126), the following shall apply to all foreign currency transactions of an enterprise and its investees:

a. At the date the transaction is recognized, each asset, liability, revenue, expense, gain, or loss arising from the transaction shall be measured and recorded in the functional currency of the recording entity by use of the exchange rate in effect at that date (refer to paragraphs .136 through .138).

b. At each balance sheet date, recorded balances that are denominated in a currency other than the functional currency of the recording entity shall be adjusted to reflect the current exchange rate. [FAS52, ¶16]

Forward Exchange Contracts

.124 A forward exchange contract (forward contract) is an agreement to exchange different currencies at a specified future date and at a specified rate (the **forward rate**). A forward contract is a foreign currency transaction. A gain or loss on a forward contract that does not meet the conditions described in paragraph .127 or .130 shall be included in determining net income in accordance with the requirements for other foreign currency transactions (refer to paragraph .123). Agreements that are, in substance, essentially the same as forward contracts, for example, **currency swaps**, shall be accounted for in a manner similar to the accounting for forward contracts. [FAS52, ¶17]

.125 A gain or loss (whether or not deferred) on a forward contract, except a forward contract of the type discussed in paragraph .126, shall be computed by multiplying the foreign currency amount of the forward contract by the difference between the **spot rate** at the balance sheet date and the spot rate at the date of inception of the forward contract (or the spot rate last used to measure a gain or loss on that contract for an earlier period). The **discount or premium on a forward contract** (that is, the foreign currency amount of the contract multiplied by the difference between the contracted forward rate and the spot rate at the date of inception of the contract) shall be accounted for separately from the gain or loss on the contract and shall be included in determining net income over the life of the forward contract. However, if a gain or loss is deferred under paragraph .130, the forward contract's discount or premium that relates to the commitment period may be included in the measurement of the basis of the related foreign currency transaction when recorded. If a gain or loss is accounted for as a hedge of a net investment under paragraph .127, the forward contract's discount or premium may be included with translation adjustments in the separate component of equity. [FAS52, ¶18]

.126 A gain or loss on a speculative forward contract (that is, a contract that does not hedge an exposure) shall be computed by multiplying the foreign currency amount of the forward contract by the difference between the forward rate available for the remaining maturity of the contract and the contracted forward rate (or the forward rate last used to measure a gain or loss on that contract for an earlier period). No separate accounting recognition is given to the discount or premium on a speculative forward contract. [FAS52, ¶19]

.126A [In a statement of cash flows,] generally each cash receipt or payment is to be classified according to its nature without regard to whether it stems from an item intended as a hedge of another item. For example, the proceeds of a borrowing are a financing cash inflow even though the debt is intended as a hedge of an investment, and the purchase or sale of a futures contract is an investing activity even though the contract is intended as a hedge of a firm commitment to purchase inventory. However, cash flows from futures contracts, forward contracts, [(including foreign currency forward contracts,)] option contracts, or swap contracts that are accounted for as hedges of identifiable transactions or events (for example, a cash payment from a futures contract that hedges a purchase or sale of inventory), including anticipatory hedges, may be classified in the same category as the cash flows from the items being hedged provided that accounting policy is disclosed. If for any reason hedge accounting for an instrument that hedges an identifiable transaction or event is discontinued, then any cash flows subsequent to the date of discontinuance shall be classified consistent with the nature of the instrument. [FAS104, ¶7(b)]

Transaction Gains and Losses to Be Excluded from Determination of Net Income

.127 Gains and losses on the following foreign currency transactions shall not be included in determining net income but shall be reported in the same manner as translation adjustments (refer to paragraph .119):

a. Foreign currency transactions that are designated as, and are effective as, economic hedges of a net investment in a foreign entity, commencing as of the designation date
b. Intercompany foreign currency transactions that are of a long-term investment nature (that is, settlement is not planned or anticipated in the foreseeable future), when the entities to the transaction are consolidated, combined, or accounted for by the equity method in the reporting enterprise's financial statements. [FAS52, ¶20] [Intercompany] transactions and balances for which settlement is not planned or anticipated in the foreseeable future are considered to be part of the net investment. This might include balances that take the form of an advance or a demand note payable provided that payment is not planned or anticipated in the foreseeable future. [FAS52, ¶131]

.128 An example of the situation contemplated in paragraph .127(a) would be a U.S. parent company with a net investment in a subsidiary that is located in Switzerland and for which the Swiss franc is the functional currency. The U.S. parent might also borrow Swiss francs and designate the Swiss franc loan as a hedge of the net investment in the Swiss subsidiary. The loan is denominated in Swiss francs which are not the functional currency of the U.S. parent and, therefore, the loan is a foreign currency transaction. The loan is a liability, and the net investment in the Swiss subsidiary is an asset. Subsequent to a change in exchange rates, the adjustment resulting from translation of the Swiss subsidiary's balance sheet would go in the opposite direction from the adjustment resulting from translation of the U.S. parent company's Swiss franc debt. To the extent that the adjustment from translation of the Swiss franc loan (after tax effects, if any) is less than or equal to the adjustment from translation of the Swiss subsidiary's balance sheet, both adjustments should be included in the analysis of changes in the cumulative translation adjustment and reflected in the separate component of equity. However, any portion of the adjustment from translation of the U.S. parent company's Swiss franc debt (after tax effects, if any) that exceeds the adjustment from translation of the Swiss subsidiary's balance sheet is a transaction gain or loss that should be included in the determination of net income. [FAS52, ¶129]

.129 Ordinarily, a transaction that hedges a net investment should be denominated in the same currency as the functional currency of the net investment hedged. In some instances, it may not be practical or feasible to hedge in the same currency and, therefore, a hedging transaction also may be denominated in a currency for which the exchange rate generally moves in tandem with the exchange rate for the functional currency of the net investment hedged. [FAS52, ¶130]

.130 A gain or loss on a forward contract or other foreign currency transaction that is intended to hedge an identifiable foreign currency commitment (for example, an agreement to purchase or sell equipment) shall be deferred and included in the measurement of the related foreign currency transaction (for example, the purchase or the sale of the equipment). Losses shall not be deferred, however, if it is estimated that deferral would lead to recognizing losses in later periods. A foreign currency transaction shall be considered a hedge of an identifiable foreign currency commitment provided both of the following conditions are met:

a. The foreign currency transaction is designated as, and is effective as, a hedge of a foreign currency commitment.
b. The foreign currency commitment is firm.

The required accounting shall commence as of the designation date. The portion of a hedging transaction that shall be accounted for pursuant to this paragraph is limited to the amount of the related commitment. If a hedging transaction that meets conditions (a) and (b) above exceeds the amount of the related commitment, the gain or loss pertaining to the portion of the hedging transaction in excess of the commitment shall be deferred to the extent that the transaction is intended to provide a hedge on an after-tax basis. A gain or loss so deferred shall be included as an offset to the related tax effects in the period in which such tax effects are recognized; consequently, it shall not be included in the aggregate transaction gain or loss disclosure required by paragraph .140. A gain or loss pertaining to the portion of a hedging transaction in excess of the amount that provides a hedge on an after-tax basis shall not be deferred. Likewise, a gain or loss pertaining to a period after the transaction date of the related commitment shall not be deferred. If a foreign currency transaction previously considered a hedge of a foreign currency commitment is terminated before the transaction date of the related commitment, any deferred gain or loss shall continue to be deferred and accounted for in accordance with the requirements of this paragraph. [FAS52, ¶21]

.131 In some instances, it may not be practical or feasible to hedge in the same currency and, therefore, a hedging transaction also may be denominated in a currency for which the exchange rate generally moves in tandem with the exchange rate for the currency in which the hedged commitment is denominated. [FAS52, ¶133]

Income Tax Consequences of Rate Changes

.132 Interperiod tax allocation is required in accordance with [FAS52, ¶22] Section I27, "Income Taxes," [FAS109, ¶287] if taxable exchange gains or tax-deductible exchange losses resulting from an entity's foreign currency transactions are included in net income in a different period for financial statement purposes from that for tax purposes. [FAS52, ¶22]

.133 Translation adjustments are accumulated and reported in a separate component of equity. Reported as such, translation adjustments do not affect pretax accounting income and most such adjustments also do not affect taxable income. Adjustments that do not affect either accounting income or taxable income do not create [temporary differences] as defined by [Section I27]. However, reporting those adjustments as a component of equity does have the effect of increasing or decreasing equity, that is, increasing or decreasing an enterprise's net assets. Potential future tax effects related to those adjustments would partially offset the increase or decrease in net assets. Therefore, [temporary differences] relating to translation adjustments shall be accounted for in the same way as [temporary differences] relating to accounting income. The need for and the amount of deferred taxes shall be determined according to the requirements of [Section I27]. [FAS52, ¶135] [Section I27] provides that deferred taxes shall not be provided for unremitted earnings of a subsidiary in certain instances; in those instances, deferred taxes shall not be provided on translation adjustments. [FAS52, ¶23] [Similarly, Section I27] provides guidance as to how to compute the amount of deferred taxes; deferred taxes on translation adjustments should be computed in the same manner. [FAS52, ¶135]

.134 Section I27 [FAS109, ¶287] requires income tax expense to be allocated among income before extraordinary items, extraordinary items, adjustments of prior periods (or of the opening balance of retained earnings), and direct entries to other equity accounts. Some transaction gains and losses and all translation adjustments are reported in a separate component of equity. Any income taxes related to those transaction gains and losses and translation adjustments shall be allocated to that separate component of equity. [FAS52, ¶24]

Elimination of Intercompany Profits

.135 The elimination of intercompany profits that are attributable to sales or other transfers between entities that are consolidated, combined, or accounted for by the equity method in the enterprise's financial statements shall be based on the exchange rates at the dates of the sales or transfers. The use of reasonable approximations or averages is permitted. [FAS52, ¶25]

Exchange Rates

.136 The exchange rate is the ratio between a unit of one currency and the amount of another currency for which that unit can be exchanged at a particular time. If exchangeability between two currencies is temporarily lacking at the transaction date or balance sheet date, the first subsequent rate at which exchanges could be made shall be used for purposes of this section. If the lack of exchangeability is other than temporary, the propriety of consolidating, combining, or accounting for the foreign operation by the equity method in the financial statements of the enterprise shall be carefully considered. [FAS52, ¶26]

.137 The exchange rates to be used for translation of foreign currency transactions and foreign currency statements are as follows:

a. *Foreign Currency Transactions*—The applicable rate at which a particular transaction could be settled at the transaction date shall be used to translate and record the transaction. At a subsequent balance sheet date, the current rate is that rate at which the related receivable or payable could be settled at that date.
b. *Foreign Currency Statements*—In the absence of unusual circumstances, the rate applicable to **conversion** of a currency for purposes of dividend remittances shall be used to translate foreign currency statements.[3] [FAS52, ¶27]

.138 If a foreign entity whose balance sheet date differs from that of the enterprise is consolidated or combined with or accounted for by the equity method in the financial statements of the enterprise, the current rate is the rate in effect at the foreign entity's balance sheet date for purposes of applying the requirements of this section to that foreign entity. [FAS52, ¶28]

Use of Averages or Other Methods of Approximation

.139 Literal application of the standards in this section might require a degree of detail in record keeping and computations that could be burdensome as well as unnecessary to produce reasonable approximations of the results. Accordingly, it is acceptable to use averages or other methods of approximation. For example, the propriety of using average rates to translate revenue and expense amounts is noted in paragraph .118. Likewise, the use of other time- and effort-saving methods to approximate the results of detailed calculations is permitted. [FAS52, ¶29] Average rates used should be appropriately weighted by the volume of functional currency transactions occurring during the accounting period. For example, to translate revenue and expense accounts for an annual period, individual revenue and expense accounts for each quarter or month may be translated at that quarter's or that month's average rate. The translated amounts for each quarter or month should then be combined for the annual totals. [FAS52, ¶140]

---

[3]If unsettled intercompany transactions are subject to and translated using preference or penalty rates, translation of foreign currency statements at the rate applicable to dividend remittances may cause a difference between intercompany receivables and payables. Until that difference is eliminated by settlement of the intercompany transaction, the difference shall be treated as a receivable or payable in the enterprise's financial statements. [FAS52, ¶27, fn4]

Disclosure

.140 The aggregate transaction gain or loss included in determining net income for the period shall be disclosed in the financial statements or notes thereto. For that disclosure, gains and losses on forward contracts determined in conformity with the requirements of paragraphs .125 and .126 shall be considered transaction gains or losses. [Also refer to paragraph .130.] Certain enterprises, primarily banks, are dealers in foreign exchange. Although certain gains or losses from dealer transactions may fit the definition of transaction gains or losses in this section, they may be disclosed as dealer gains or losses rather than as transaction gains or losses. [Refer to Section F25, "Financial Instruments: Disclosure," for guidance on possible additional disclosure requirements.] [FAS52, ¶30]

.141 An analysis of the changes during the period in the separate component of equity for cumulative translation adjustments shall be provided in a separate financial statement, in notes to the financial statements, or as part of a statement of changes in equity. [FAS52, ¶31] This separate component of equity might be titled "Equity Adjustment from Foreign Currency Translation" or given a similar title. [FAS52, ¶142] At a minimum, the analysis shall disclose:

a. Beginning and ending amount of cumulative translation adjustments
b. The aggregate adjustment for the period resulting from translation adjustments (refer to paragraph .119) and gains and losses from certain hedges and intercompany balances (refer to paragraph .127)
c. The amount of income taxes for the period allocated to translation adjustments (refer to paragraph .134)
d. The amounts transferred from cumulative translation adjustments and included in determining net income for the period as a result of the sale or complete or substantially complete liquidation of an investment in a foreign entity (refer to paragraph .120). [FAS52, ¶31]

.142 An enterprise's financial statements shall not be adjusted for a rate change that occurs after the date of the enterprise's financial statements or after the date of the foreign currency statements of a foreign entity if they are consolidated, combined, or accounted for by the equity method in the financial statements of the enterprise. However, disclosure of the rate change and its effects on unsettled balances pertaining to foreign currency transactions, if significant, may be necessary. [FAS52, ¶32] If disclosed, the disclosure should include consideration of changes in unsettled transactions from the date of the financial statements to the date the rate changed. In some cases it may not be practicable to determine these changes; if so, that fact should be stated. [FAS52, ¶143]

.143 Management [is encouraged] to supplement the disclosures required by this section with an analysis and discussion of the effects of rate changes on the reported results of operations. This type of disclosure might include the mathematical effects of translating revenue and expenses at rates that are different from those used in a preceding period as well as the economic effects of rate changes, such as the effects on selling prices, sales volume, and cost structures. The purpose is to assist financial report users in understanding the broader economic implications of rate changes and to compare recent results with those of prior periods. [FAS52, ¶144]

.144 [Editorial deletion; this paragraph is contained in Section F65, "Foreign Operations," paragraph .102.]

.145 [Editorial deletion; this paragraph is contained in Section F65, "Foreign Operations," paragraph .103.]

Remeasurement of the Books of Record into the Functional Currency[4]

.146 If an entity's books of record are not maintained in its functional currency, this section (refer to paragraph .115) requires remeasurement into the functional currency prior to the translation process. If a foreign entity's functional currency is the reporting currency, remeasurement into the reporting currency obviates translation. The remeasurement process should produce the same result as if the entity's books of record had been initially recorded in the functional currency. To accomplish that result, it is necessary to use historical exchange rates between the functional currency and another currency in the remeasurement process for certain accounts (the current rate will be used for all others), and paragraph .147 identifies those accounts. To accomplish that result, it is also necessary to recognize currently in income all exchange gains and losses from remeasurement of monetary assets and liabilities that are not denominated in the functional currency (for example, assets and liabilities that are not denominated in dollars if the dollar is the functional currency). [FAS52, ¶47]

.147 The table below lists common nonmonetary balance sheet items and related revenue, expense, gain, and loss accounts that should be remeasured using historical rates in order to produce the same result in terms of the functional currency that would have occurred if those items had been initially recorded in the functional currency.

Accounts to Be Remeasured Using Historical Exchange Rates

Marketable securities carried at cost
 - Equity securities
 - Debt securities not intended to be held until maturity

Inventories carried at cost

Prepaid expenses such as insurance, advertising, and rent

---

[4]The guidance in paragraphs .146 through .153 applies only to those instances in which the books of record are not maintained in the functional currency. [FAS52, ¶47, fn*]

Property, plant, and equipment

Accumulated depreciation on property, plant, and equipment

Patents, trademarks, licenses, and formulas

Goodwill

Other intangible assets

Deferred charges and credits, except policy acquisition
   costs for life insurance enterprises

Deferred income

Common stock

Preferred stock carried at issuance price

Examples of revenues and expenses related to nonmonetary items:
   Cost of goods sold
   Depreciation of property, plant, and equipment
   Amortization of intangible items such as goodwill, patents, licenses, etc.
   Amortization of deferred charges or credits except
     policy acquisition costs for life insurance enterprises [FAS52, ¶48]

Inventories—Applying the Rule of Cost or Market, Whichever Is Lower, to Remeasure Inventory Not Recorded in the Functional Currency

.148 The rule of cost or market, whichever is lower (described in Section I78, "Inventory," [as *lower of cost or market*]), requires special application when the books of record are not kept in the functional currency. Inventories carried at cost in the books of record in another currency should be first remeasured to cost in the functional currency using historical exchange rates. Then, historical cost in the functional currency is compared with market as stated in the functional currency. Application of the rule in functional currency may require write-downs to market in the functional currency statements even though no write-down has been made in the books of record maintained in another currency. Likewise, a write-down in the books of record may need to be reversed if market exceeds historical cost as stated in the functional currency. If inventory[5] has been written down to market in the functional currency statements, that functional currency amount shall continue to be the carrying amount in the functional currency financial statements until the inventory is sold or a further write-down is necessary. [FAS52, ¶49]

---

[5]An asset other than inventory may sometimes be written down from historical cost. Although that write-down is not under the rule of cost or market, whichever is lower, the approach described in this paragraph might be appropriate. That is, a write-down may be required in the functional currency statements even though not required in the books of record, and a write-down in the books of record may need to be reversed before remeasurement to prevent the remeasured amount from exceeding functional currency historical cost. [FAS52, ¶49, fn5]

.149 Literal application of the rule of cost or market, whichever is lower, may require an inventory write-down[6] in functional currency financial statements for locally acquired inventory[7] if the value of the currency in which the books of record are maintained has declined in relation to the functional currency between the date the inventory was acquired and the date of the balance sheet. Such a write-down may not be necessary, however, if the replacement costs or selling prices expressed in the currency in which the books of record are maintained have increased sufficiently so that market exceeds historical cost as measured in functional currency. Paragraphs .150 through .152 illustrate this situation. [FAS52, ¶50]

.150 Assume the following:

a. When the rate is BR1 = FC2.40, a foreign subsidiary of a U.S. enterprise purchases a unit of inventory at a cost of BR500 (measured in functional currency, FC1,200).[8]
b. At the foreign subsidiary's balance sheet date, the current rate is BR1 = FC2.00 and the current replacement cost of the unit of inventory is BR560 (measured in functional currency, FC1,120).
c. Net realizable value is BR630 (measured in functional currency, FC1,260).
d. Net realizable value reduced by an allowance for an approximately normal profit margin is BR550 (measured in functional currency, FC1,100).

Because current replacement cost as measured in the functional currency (FC1,120) is less than historical cost as measured in the functional currency (FC1,200), an inventory write-down of FC80 is required in the functional currency financial statements. [FAS52, ¶51]

.151 Continue to assume the same information in the preceding example but substitute a current replacement cost at the foreign subsidiary's balance sheet date of BR620. Because market as measured in the functional currency (BR620 × FC2.00 = FC1,240) exceeds historical cost as measured in the functional currency (BR500 × FC2.40 = FC1,200), an inventory write-down is not required in the financial statements. [FAS52, ¶52]

---

[6]This paragraph is not intended to preclude recognition of gains in a later interim period to the extent of inventory losses recognized from market declines in earlier interim periods if losses on the same inventory are recovered in the same year, as provided by Section 173, "Interim Financial Reporting," paragraph .107(c), which states: "Inventory losses from market declines should not be deferred beyond the interim period in which the decline occurs. Recoveries of such losses on the same inventory in later interim periods of the same fiscal year through market price recoveries should be recognized as gains in the later interim period. Such gains should not exceed previously recognized losses. Some market declines at interim dates, however, can reasonably be expected to be restored in the fiscal year. Such *temporary* market declines need not be recognized at the interim date since no loss is expected to be incurred in the fiscal year." [FAS52, ¶50, fn6]

[7]An inventory write-down also may be required for imported inventory. [FAS52, ¶50, fn7]

[8][The following abbreviations are used:]
  BR = currency in which the books of record are maintained
  FC = functional currency [FAS52, ¶51, fn*]

.152 As another example, assume the information in paragraph .150, except that selling prices in terms of the currency in which the books of record are maintained have increased so that net realizable value is BR720 and net realizable value reduced by an allowance for an approximately normal profit margin is BR640. In that case, because replacement cost measured in functional currency (BR560 × FC2.00 = FC1,120) is less than net realizable value reduced by an allowance for an approximately normal profit margin measured in functional currency (BR640 × FC2.00 = FC1,280), market is FC1,280. Because market as measured in the functional currency (FC1,280) exceeds historical cost as measured in the functional currency (BR500 × FC2.40 = FC1,200), an inventory write-down is not required in the functional currency financial statements. [FAS52, ¶53]

.153 [Deleted 12/82 because of FASB Statement 70, *Financial Reporting and Changing Prices: Foreign Currency Translation*.]

Glossary

.401 Attribute. The quantifiable characteristic of an item that is measured for accounting purposes. For example, historical cost and current cost are attributes of an asset. [FAS52, ¶162]

.402 Conversion. The exchange of one currency for another. [FAS52, ¶162]

.403 Currency swaps. An exchange between two enterprises of the currencies of two different countries pursuant to an agreement to reexchange the two currencies at the same rate of exchange at a specified future date. [FAS52, ¶162]

.404 Current exchange rate. The current exchange rate is the rate at which one unit of a currency can be exchanged for (converted into) another currency. For purposes of translation of financial statements referred to in this section, the current exchange rate is the rate as of the end of the period covered by the financial statements or as of the dates of recognition in those statements in the case of revenues, expenses, gains, and losses. The requirements for applying the current exchange rate for translating financial statements are set forth in paragraph .113. Further information regarding exchange rates is provided in paragraphs .127 through .129. [FAS52, ¶162]

.405 Discount or premium on a forward contract. The foreign currency amount of the contract multiplied by the difference between the contracted forward rate and the spot rate at the date of inception of the contract. [FAS52, ¶162]

.406 Enterprise. Refer to **reporting enterprise.** [FAS52, ¶162]

.407 Entity. Refer to **foreign entity.** [FAS52, ¶162]

.408 Foreign currency. A currency other than the functional currency of the entity being referred to (for example, the dollar could be a foreign currency for a foreign entity). Composites of currencies, such as the Special Drawing Rights on the International Monetary Fund (SDRs), used to set prices or denominate amounts of loans, etc., have the characteristics of foreign currency for purposes of applying this section. [FAS52, ¶162]

.409 Foreign currency statements. Financial statements that employ as the unit of measure a functional currency that is not the reporting currency of the enterprise. [FAS52, ¶162]

.410 Foreign currency transactions. Transactions whose terms are denominated in a currency other than the entity's functional currency. Foreign currency transactions arise when an enterprise (a) buys or sells on credit goods or services whose prices are denominated in foreign currency, (b) borrows or lends funds and the amounts payable or receivable are denominated in foreign currency, (c) is a party to an unperformed forward exchange contract, or (d) for other reasons, acquires or disposes of assets, or incurs or settles liabilities denominated in foreign currency. [FAS52, ¶162]

.411 Foreign currency translation. The process of expressing in the reporting currency of the enterprise those amounts that are denominated or measured in a different currency. [FAS52, ¶162]

.412 Foreign entity. An operation (for example, subsidiary, division, branch, joint venture, etc.) whose financial statements (a) are prepared in a currency other than the reporting currency of the reporting enterprise and (b) are combined or consolidated with or accounted for on the equity basis in the financial statements of the reporting enterprise. [FAS52, ¶162]

.413 Forward exchange contract. An agreement to exchange at a specified future date currencies of different countries at a specified rate (forward rate). [FAS52, ¶162]

.414 Forward rate. Refer to **forward exchange contract.** [FAS52, ¶162]

.415 Functional currency. An entity's functional currency is the currency of the primary economic environment in which the entity operates; normally, that is the currency of the environment in which an entity primarily generates and expends cash (refer to paragraphs .104 through .115). [FAS52, ¶162]

.416 Local currency. The currency of a particular country being referred to. [FAS52, ¶162]

.417 Reporting currency. The currency in which an enterprise prepares its financial statements. [FAS52, ¶162]

.418 Reporting enterprise. An entity or group whose financial statements are being referred to. In this section, those financial statements reflect (a) the financial statements of one or more foreign operations by combination, consolidation, or equity accounting; (b) foreign currency transactions; or (c) both of the foregoing. [FAS52, ¶162]

.419 Spot rate. The exchange rate for immediate delivery of currencies exchanged. [FAS52, ¶162]

.420 Transaction date. The date at which a transaction (for example, a sale or purchase of merchandise or services) is recorded in accounting records in conformity with generally accepted accounting principles. A long-term commitment may have more than one transaction date (for example, the due date of each progress payment under a construction contract is an anticipated transaction date). [FAS52, ¶162]

.421 Transaction gain or loss. Transaction gains or losses result from a change in exchange rates between the functional currency and the currency in which a foreign currency transaction is denominated. They represent an increase or decrease in (a) the actual functional currency cash flows realized upon settlement of foreign currency transactions and (b) the expected functional currency cash flows on unsettled foreign currency transactions. [FAS52, ¶162]

.422 **Translation.** Refer to **foreign currency translation.** [FAS52, ¶162]

.423 **Translation adjustments.** Translation adjustments result from the process of translating financial statements from the entity's functional currency into the reporting currency. [FAS52, ¶162]

(The next page is 19501.)

Source: ARB 43, Chapter 12

Summary

Any foreign earnings reported beyond the amounts received in the United States shall be carefully considered in the light of all the facts.

.100A The recommendations made in this section apply to U.S. enterprises which have branches or subsidiaries operating in foreign countries. [ARB43, ch12, ¶1]

.100B Since World War I foreign operations have been influenced to a marked degree by wars, departures from the gold standard, devaluations of currencies, currency restrictions, government regulations, etc. [ARB43, ch12, ¶2]

.100C Although comparatively few countries in recent years have had unrestricted currencies and exchanges, it is nevertheless true that many companies have been doing business in foreign countries having varying degrees of restrictions; in some cases they have been carrying on all operations regarded as normal, including the transmission of funds. In view of the difficulties mentioned above, however, the accounting treatment of assets, liabilities, losses, and gains involved in the conduct of foreign business and to be included or reflected in the financial statements of the U.S. companies requires careful consideration. [ARB43, ch12, ¶3]

.101 A sound procedure for U.S. enterprises to follow is to show earnings from foreign operations in their own accounts only to the extent that funds have been received in the United States or unrestricted funds are available for transmission thereto. Appropriate provision shall be made for known losses. [ARB43, ch12, ¶4]

.102 Any foreign earnings reported beyond the amounts received in the United States shall be carefully considered in the light of all the facts. The amounts shall be disclosed if they are significant. [ARB43, ch12, ¶5]

.103 The accounting [for] assets held abroad shall take into consideration the fact that most foreign assets stand in some degree of jeopardy, so far as ultimate realization by U.S. owners is concerned. Under those conditions, it is important that especial care be taken in each case to make full disclosure in the financial statements of U.S. enterprises of the extent to which they include significant foreign items. [ARB43, ch12, ¶6]

(The next page is 19801.)

Sources: FASB Statement 80; FASB Statement 95; FASB Statement 104;
          FASB Statement 115

Summary

This section presents standards of accounting for exchange-traded futures contracts (other than contracts for foreign currencies).

A change in the market value of an open futures contract is required to be recognized as a gain or loss in the period of the change unless the contract qualifies as a hedge of certain exposures to price or interest rate risk. Immediate gain or loss recognition is also required if the futures contract is intended to hedge an item that is reported at fair value (which frequently will be the case for futures contracts used as hedges by investment companies, pension plans, and broker-dealers).

If the hedge criteria specified in this section are met, a change in the market value of the futures contract is either reported as an adjustment of the carrying amount of the hedged item or included in the measurement of a qualifying subsequent transaction. Enterprises are required to cease accounting for a contract as a hedge if high correlation of changes in the market value of the futures contract and the effects of price or interest rate changes on the hedged item has not occurred.

Introduction

.101 This section [presents] standards of financial accounting and reporting for **futures contracts,** except for futures contracts for foreign currencies.[1] This section

---

[1]The provisions of Section F60, "Foreign Currency Translation," apply to accounting for foreign currency futures. [FAS80, ¶1, fn2]

does not apply to forward placement or delayed delivery contracts and therefore does not prescribe or proscribe particular methods of accounting for such contracts.[2] [FAS80, ¶1]

.102 The basic issue addressed in this section is how to account for a change in the market value of a futures contract.[3] The general principle set forth in this section is that such a change is recognized in income when it occurs. However, for certain contracts, this section requires that the timing of recognition in income be related to the accounting for associated assets, liabilities, **firm commitments,** or transactions. Paragraphs .114 through .123 present examples that illustrate the applicability of [the requirements of] this section. [FAS80, ¶2]

Recognition of Changes in Market Value

.103 A change in the market value of a futures contract[4] shall be recognized as a gain or loss in the period of the change unless the contract meets the criteria specified in this section to qualify as a hedge[5] of an exposure to price or interest rate **risk.** If the hedge criteria are met, the accounting for the futures contract shall be related to the accounting for the hedged item so that changes in the market value of the futures contract are recognized in income when the effects of related changes in the price or interest rate of the hedged item are recognized. [FAS80, ¶3]

[2Accounting for options is not examined in this section.] Options and futures are different. Option holders acquire the right either to buy or to sell a commodity or **financial instrument** but have no obligation to do so; option writers have an obligation to sell or to buy the commodity or financial instrument if the buyer exercises the option. In contrast, futures contracts are "two-sided" in that buyers and sellers of futures both acquire a right and incur an obligation. Thus, the risk and return characteristics of options and futures are different, as is the system of margins in each market. [FAS80, ¶32] Exclusion of forward contracts from the section should not be construed as either acceptance or rejection of current practice for such contracts, nor should the exclusion be interpreted as an indication that the general principles of this section might not be appropriate in some circumstances for certain forward contracts. [FAS80, ¶34]

[3]Enterprises [are not required] to recognize an asset and a liability for the total amount of the commodity or financial instrument that underlies a futures contract. [FAS80, ¶35]

[4]For purposes of this section, the change in the market value of a futures contract equals the change in the contract's quoted market price multiplied by the contract size. For example, the change in the market value of a $100,000 U.S. Treasury bond futures contract whose price moves from 80-00 to 78-00 is $2,000. [FAS80, ¶3, fn3]

[5]The word *hedge* is used in a variety of ways by futures traders, accountants, and regulators, and there appears to be no generally accepted definition that is useful in making practical decisions. However, most, but not all, definitions are based on the notion of reducing exposure to price or interest rate risk. Risk reduction—that is, reducing the sensitivity of an enterprise's income to changes in prices or interest rates— should be the basis for delaying income recognition of the results of futures contracts. [FAS80, ¶42]

Hedge Criteria

.104 In applying this section, both of the following conditions shall be met for a futures contract to qualify as a hedge:

a.   *The item to be hedged exposes the enterprise to price (or interest rate) risk.* To meet this condition, the item or group of items intended to be hedged must contribute to the price or interest rate risk of the enterprise.[6] In determining if this condition is met, the enterprise shall consider whether other assets, liabilities,

---

[6]An interest-bearing financial instrument that an enterprise will retain to maturity does not, in and of itself, create interest rate risk if the instrument's interest rate is fixed. The amount of cash inflows or outflows is certain (assuming no default) and is not affected by changes in market interest rates. Notwithstanding that the cash flows associated with the instrument are fixed, the enterprise may be exposed to interest rate risk if it has funded its assets with instruments having earlier maturities or repricing dates. Futures contracts may qualify as a hedge of a fixed-rate financial instrument the enterprise intends to hold to maturity if the maturity or repricing characteristics of the instrument contribute to the enterprise's overall asset-liability mismatch. [FAS80, ¶4, fn4]

Hedge accounting [is] not permitted for so-called macro hedges where the futures contracts are not linked with identifiable assets, obligations, commitments, or anticipated transactions. Without such linkage, there is no objective method of either gauging the effectiveness of the futures contracts or ultimately recognizing the futures results in income. Futures contracts [cannot] be considered hedges of the interest spread between specifically identified assets and liabilities. The association of an asset with a specific funding source [is] an arbitrary process. Moreover, interest spreads per se cannot be hedged directly; there are no futures contracts for interest spreads. Clearly, the intent of the institution may be to reduce uncertainty about future interest spreads, but that is accomplished with futures by changing the revenue or expense component of the spread through hedges of existing or anticipated asset or liability positions. [FAS80, ¶62]

The determination and measurement of the interest rate risk of a financial institution may be complex and may involve significant estimates and judgements. [It was concluded that provision of] more specific guidance concerning when the risk condition of paragraph .104(a) is met by financial institutions was not feasible at present. The analysis and determination of an institution's interest rate sensitivity (and compilation of the necessary information) is an evolving process, and the approach followed may vary from institution to institution. There is [no] consensus among bankers and others about whether "gap" analysis, duration analysis, or some other method is the most appropriate way of assessing risk. [It was] concluded that it [was inappropriate] at this time to specify a single measure of interest rate sensitivity for use in applying the provisions of this section. [FAS80, ¶63]

firm commitments, and anticipated transactions already offset or reduce the exposure.[7] An enterprise that cannot assess risk by considering other relevant positions and transactions for the enterprise as a whole because it conducts its risk management activities on a decentralized basis can meet this condition if the item intended to be hedged exposes the particular business unit that enters into the contract.

b. *The futures contract reduces that exposure and is designated*[8] *as a hedge.* At the inception of the hedge and throughout the hedge period, high correlation of changes in (1) the market value of the futures contract(s) and (2) the fair value of, or interest income or expense associated with, the hedged item(s) shall be probable[9] so that the results of the futures contract(s) will substantially offset the effects of price or interest rate changes on the exposed item(s). In addition to assessing information about the correlation during relevant past periods, the enterprise also shall consider the characteristics of the specific hedge, such as the degree of correlation that can be expected at various levels of higher or lower market prices or interest rates. A futures contract for a commodity or a financial instrument different from the item intended to be hedged may qualify as a hedge provided there is a clear economic relationship between the prices of the two commodities or financial instruments, and provided high correlation is probable. [FAS80, ¶4]

---

[7]For example, assets held for resale may subject the enterprise to price risk, but that risk already may be wholly or partially offset by firm fixed-price sales commitments. Floating-rate debt may result in interest rate risk for one enterprise but not for another because of differences in the maturity or repricing characteristics of the assets owned by each enterprise. As a further example, unpriced anticipated raw material requirements may be a risk in some industries because finished product and raw material prices do not move together. For other industries, such as commodity trading, an exposure to risk may exist only when the commodity is held or when there are firm fixed-price commitments. [FAS80, ¶4, fn5] Determining whether an exposure already is hedged effectively by another item sometimes may not be clear and may require judgment. Such judgment is essential and must be exercised by those who have a thorough understanding of the enterprise's business and the specific circumstances. [FAS80, ¶44]

[8]One or more futures contracts may be designated as a hedge of either an individual item or an identifiable group of essentially similar items (for example, government securities that have similar maturities and coupon rates). [FAS80, ¶4, fn6]

[9]*Probable* is used here and in other parts of this section consistent with its use in Section C59, "Contingencies," [paragraph .104,] to mean that a transaction or event is likely to occur. [FAS80, ¶4, fn7]

Hedges of Items Reported at Fair Value

.105 If an enterprise includes unrealized changes in the fair value of a hedged item in income, a change in the market value of the related futures contract shall be recognized in income when the change occurs. The same accounting shall be applied to a futures contract that hedges an anticipated transaction if the asset to be acquired or liability to be incurred will be reported at fair value subsequent to acquisition or incurrence. Some enterprises report assets at fair value but include unrealized changes in that value in a separate component of stockholders' (or policyholders') equity pending sale or other disposition of the assets. A change in the market value of a futures contract that qualifies as a hedge of those assets also shall be included in that separate component of equity [FAS80, ¶5] until it is amortized or [FAS115, ¶129] until sale or disposition of the assets unless paragraph .111 requires earlier recognition of a gain or loss in income because high correlation has not occurred. [FAS80, ¶5]

Hedges of Existing Assets, Liabilities, and Firm Commitments

.106 A change in the market value of a futures contract that qualifies as a hedge of an existing asset or liability shall be recognized as an adjustment of the carrying amount of the hedged item. A change in the market value of a futures contract that is a hedge of a firm commitment shall be included in the measurement of the transaction that satisfies the commitment. An enterprise may recognize the premium or discount on a hedge contract in income over the life of the contract if the commodity or financial instrument being hedged is deliverable under the terms of the futures contract, and if it is probable that both the hedged item and the futures contract will be retained to the delivery date specified in the contract.[10] The premium or discount is computed at the inception of the hedge by reference to the contracted futures price and the fair value of the hedged item. [FAS80, ¶6]

.107 Recognition in income of the adjustment of the carrying amount of an asset or liability required by paragraph .106 shall be the same as other components of the carrying amount of that asset or liability.[11] An adjustment of the carrying amount of a hedged interest-bearing financial instrument that is otherwise reported at amortized cost shall be amortized as an adjustment of interest income or interest expense over the expected remaining life of the instrument. That amortization shall commence no later than the date that a particular contract is closed out, whether that contract is replaced by a similar contract for later delivery or not. [FAS80, ¶7]

---

[10]Relatively few hedges are likely to meet those conditions because most futures contracts are not held open up to the specified delivery date and because "cross hedges" will not qualify. [FAS80, ¶50]

[11]For example, an adjustment of the carrying amount of a hedged asset held for sale usually would be recognized in income when the asset is sold. However, earlier recognition may be necessary if other accounting standards, for example, Section I78, "Inventory," require that the adjusted carrying amount of the asset be written down to a lower amount. [FAS80, ¶7, fn8]

.108 Some enterprises (for example, commodity dealers) may use futures contracts to hedge a net exposure comprising inventory held for sale and firm commitments to purchase and sell essentially similar assets. If associating individual futures contracts with the assets on hand or specific commitments is impractical because of the volume and frequency of transactions, reasonable allocations of the results of futures contracts between assets or commitments on hand at the end of a reporting period and assets sold during the period may be used. The method of allocation shall be consistent from period to period. [FAS80, ¶8]

Hedges of Anticipated Transactions

.109 A futures contract may relate to transactions (other than transactions involving *existing* assets or liabilities, or transactions necessitated by *existing* firm commitments) an enterprise expects, but is not obligated, to carry out in the normal course of business. A change in the market value of a futures contract that hedges the price or interest rate of such an anticipated transaction shall be included in the measurement of the subsequent transaction if the two conditions in paragraph .104[12] *and* both of the following conditions are met:

a. *The significant characteristics and expected terms of the anticipated transaction are identified.* The significant characteristics and expected terms include the expected date of the transaction, the commodity or type of financial instrument involved, and the expected quantity to be purchased or sold.[13] For transactions involving interest-bearing financial instruments, the expected maturity of the instrument is also a significant term.

---

[12]Gross margins of certain enterprises that have not established a price for anticipated purchases (for example, probable raw material requirements for the next six months) may be as exposed to price risk as the gross margins of enterprises in other industries that have not covered their firm fixed-price sales commitments. However, not all unpriced anticipated transactions involve risk for an enterprise, and, therefore, not all futures contracts that some may consider to be "anticipatory hedges" will meet the hedge criteria in paragraph .104. As noted in footnote 7 to paragraph .104(a), because of differences in the pricing structure of various industries, some enterprises become exposed to risk only through owning a commodity or when the price of a transaction becomes fixed; others in effect are exposed when they have not established the price for an anticipated transaction. It follows that some futures contracts related to anticipated transactions actually increase an enterprise's exposure and should not be accounted for as hedges. [FAS80, ¶54]

[13]The purpose of requiring identification of the significant terms is threefold. First, without some idea of the timing and amount of the anticipated transaction, it is impossible to assess whether there is price or interest rate risk (paragraph .104(a)). Second, the information is also necessary to assess the likelihood that the transaction will occur ([see] paragraph (b)). Third, unless the expected terms of the transaction can be reasonably identified, it is unlikely that the correlation condition (paragraph .104(b)) can be met. Because the circumstances of each enterprise are different, the information needed to satisfy those three purposes may vary. [FAS80, ¶57]

b. *It is probable that the anticipated transaction will occur.*[14] Considerations in assessing the likelihood that a transaction will occur include the frequency of similar transactions in the past; the financial and operational ability of the enterprise to carry out the transaction; substantial commitments of resources to a particular activity (for example, a manufacturing facility that can be used in the short run only to process a particular type of commodity); the length of time to the anticipated transaction date; the extent of loss or disruption of operations that could result if the transaction does not occur; and the likelihood that transactions with substantially different characteristics might be used to achieve the same business purpose (for example, an enterprise that intends to raise cash may have several ways of doing so, ranging from short-term bank loans to common stock offerings). Enterprises sometimes may determine that two or more approximately similar alternative transactions are equally likely to occur. For example, a financial institution that plans to issue short-term obligations at a particular future date may have the choice of issuing various types of such obligations in domestic or foreign markets. In such cases, futures contracts are not precluded from qualifying as a hedge if all hedge criteria are met regardless of which transaction will be undertaken. [FAS80, ¶9]

.110 The accounting for a futures contract that hedges an anticipated acquisition of assets or an anticipated issuance of liabilities shall be consistent with the enterprise's method of accounting for those types of assets or liabilities. For example, a loss shall be recognized for a futures contract that relates to an anticipated inventory purchase to the extent there is evidence that the amount will not be recovered through sales. If a futures contract that has been accounted for as a hedge is closed before the date of the anticipated transaction, the accumulated change in value of the contract shall continue to be carried forward (subject to the other considerations in this paragraph and paragraph .111) and included in the measurement of the related transaction. A pro rata portion of the futures results that would otherwise be included in the measurement of a subsequent transaction shall be recognized as a gain or loss when it becomes probable that the quantity of the anticipated transaction will be less than that originally hedged. [FAS80, ¶10]

---

[14]A high level of assurance that a transaction will occur is necessary for [a] related futures contract to qualify as a hedge. Determination of the likelihood of a transaction's taking place should not be based solely on management's stated intent because that is not verifiable. Probability should be supported by observable facts and the attendant circumstances. [FAS80, ¶56]

Ongoing Assessment of Correlation

.111 An enterprise regularly shall assess the results of a futures contract designated as a hedge to determine if the high correlation required by paragraph .104(b) is being achieved. If that assessment indicates high correlation has not occurred, the enterprise shall cease to account for the futures contract as a hedge and shall recognize a gain or loss to the extent the futures results have not been offset by the effects of price or interest rate changes on the hedged item since inception of the hedge. If the effects of price or interest rate changes on the hedged item are not readily determinable by reference to quoted market prices or rates, reasonable estimates may be used. [FAS80, ¶11]

Disclosure

.112 An enterprise that has entered into futures contracts that have been accounted for as hedges shall disclose (a) the nature of the assets, liabilities, firm commitments, or anticipated transactions that are hedged with futures contracts and (b) the method of accounting for the futures contracts. The disclosure of the method shall include a description of the events or transactions that result in recognition in income of changes in value of the futures contracts.[15] [Refer to Section F25, "Financial Instruments: Disclosure," for guidance on possible additional disclosure requirements.] [FAS80, ¶12]

[15Technical] Bulletin [81-1] is rescinded by this section, but the provisions of Section A10, "Accounting Policies," continue to require the disclosures called for by the Bulletin for forward and standby contracts. [FAS80, ¶27]

Reporting Hedges in Cash Flows Statement

.112A A statement of cash flows shall classify cash receipts and cash payments as resulting from investing, financing, or operating activities. [FAS95, ¶14] Generally, each cash receipt or payment is to be classified according to its nature without regard to whether it stems from an item intended as a hedge of another item. For example, the proceeds of a borrowing are a financing cash inflow even though the debt is intended as a hedge of an investment, and the purchase or sale of a futures contract is an investing activity even though the contract is intended as a hedge of a firm commitment to purchase inventory. However, cash flows from futures contracts, forward contracts, option contracts, or swap contracts that are accounted for as hedges of identifiable transactions or events (for example, a cash payment from a futures contract that hedges a purchase or sale of inventory), including anticipatory hedges, may be classified in the same category as the cash flows from the items being hedged provided that accounting policy is disclosed. If for any reason hedge accounting for an instrument that hedges an identifiable transaction or event is discontinued, then any cash flows subsequent to the date of discontinuance shall be classified consistent with the nature of the instrument. [FAS104, ¶7b] [(Refer to Section C25, "Cash Flows Statement," for additional guidance on the statement of cash flows.)]

Examples

.113 Paragraphs .114 through .123 present examples that illustrate the application of [the requirements of] this section. The examples do not address all possible uses of futures contracts. The facts assumed are illustrative only and are not intended to modify or limit in any way the provisions of this section. For simplicity, commissions and other transaction costs, initial margin (except in Example 1), and income taxes are ignored. [FAS80, ¶16]

Example 1: Nonhedge Contract

.114 On September 15, 19X4, B Company purchases 10 March 19X5 U.S. Treasury bill (T-bill) futures contracts at 87.50 as an investment. (Each contract is for a three-month $1,000,000 face amount T-bill.) On that date, B Company makes an initial cash margin deposit of $30,000 with its broker. B Company holds the contracts through November 15, 19X4, when it closes out all contracts. The quoted market price of March 19X5 T-bill contracts increases during September (to 88.00) and October (to 88.20) and declines in November (to 87.80 by November 15). B Company withdraws some funds from its margin account at various times in September and October, deposits additional funds in November to meet margin calls, and withdraws the entire balance in its account when the futures position is closed out. Changes in the company's margin account are summarized on the following page.

	September	October	November
Beginning balance	$ 0	$32,500	$31,500
Deposit initial margin	30,000		
Change in the market value of the futures contracts[a]	12,500	5,000	(10,000)
Payments to (withdrawals from) account	(10,000)	(6,000)	8,500
Withdrawal of initial margin			(30,000)
Ending balance	$32,500	$31,500	$ 0

---

[a]Each basis point change in the price of a T-bill futures contract is equal to a $25 change in value. The gain for September is computed as follows:

September 30 price		88.00
September 15 price		87.50
	50 basis points	
	×	$ 25
		$ 1,250
Number of contracts	×	10
		$12,500

[FAS80, ¶17]

.115 B Company's financial statements for the months ended September 30 and October 31 would show $32,500 and $31,500, respectively, due from its broker. (If B Company satisfied the initial margin requirements by depositing government securities, such as T-bills, rather than cash, the securities would not be classified as part of the balance due from the broker.) Gains of $12,500 for September and $5,000 for October and a loss of $10,000 for November would be recognized. The income statement display of the gains and loss would be consistent with how the company reports other investment gains and losses. [FAS80, ¶18]

Example 2: Hedge of an Anticipated Purchase

.116 On November 1, 19X3, C Company, an enterprise that produces a grain-based industrial product, determines that it will require 100,000 bushels of the necessary grain in the last week of February 19X4. The finished product is not sold forward under fixed-price contracts but is sold at the going market price at the date of sale. Market conditions indicate that finished product selling prices are not likely to be affected significantly during the next few months by changes in the price of the grain during that period. On November 1, the enterprise purchases 20 March 19X4 futures contracts (each contract is for 5,000 bushels of the grain) at $3.00 per bushel. On December 31, 19X3, the enterprise's fiscal year-end, the closing price of the March 19X4 contract is $2.80 per bushel. On February 24, 19X4, the enterprise purchases 100,000 bushels of the grain through its normal commercial channels and closes out the futures contracts at $3.10 per bushel. [FAS80, ¶19]

.117 The changes in the value of the contracts during 19X3 and 19X4 are as follows:

	November 1– December 31, 19X3	January 1– February 24, 19X4
Futures price at beginning of period	$ 3.00	$ 2.80
Futures price at end of period	$ 2.80	$ 3.10
Change in price, per bushel	(0.20)	0.30
Bushels under contract (20 contracts @ 5,000 bushels each)	× 100,000	× 100,000
	$(20,000)	$ 30,000

Unless this transaction qualifies as a hedge, C Company would report a $20,000 loss for the period ending December 31, 19X3 and a $30,000 gain in 19X4. [FAS80, ¶20]

.118 If, however, the hedge conditions in paragraphs .104 and .109 are met and evidence at December 31 indicates the $20,000 will be recovered on sale of the finished product, the enterprise would not recognize a loss in its 19X3 financial statements. On February 24, 19X4, the cumulative change in the market value of the contracts is a $10,000 increase ($20,000 decline to December 31, 19X3 plus $30,000 appreciation in 19X4). That amount would be shown as a reduction of the cost of the grain acquired. [FAS80, ¶21]

Example 3: Hedge of Financial Instruments Held for Sale

.119 M Company, a mortgage banking enterprise, holds $10 million of mortgage loans that will be packaged and sold as mortgage-backed securities. M Company is exposed to the risk that interest rates will rise (and, thus, the value of the mortgages will fall) before the securities are sold. On April 1, 19X4, the enterprise sells June 19X4 futures contracts for mortgage-backed securities. Interest rates decline in April and increase in May, resulting in a $520,000 unfavorable change in the market value of the futures in April and a $940,000 favorable change in May. [FAS80, ¶22]

.120 The futures contracts qualify as a hedge of the mortgage loans if both conditions in paragraph .104 are met. If those hedge conditions are met, and as long as the correlation required in paragraph .104(b) is being achieved, the mortgage banker would adjust the carrying amount of the mortgages for changes in the market value of the futures contracts. The carrying amount of the mortgages in M Company's financial statements would be as follows:

	April	May
Mortgages, beginning of period	$10,000,000	$10,520,000
Adjustment for futures results	520,000	(940,000)
Mortgages, end of period[a]	$10,520,000	$ 9,580,000

[a]Paragraph .105 of Section Mo4, "Mortgage Banking Activities," requires mortgage banking enterprises to report mortgage loans held for sale at the lower of cost or market. Therefore, if the market value of the mortgages is less than the carrying amounts shown, a valuation allowance would be necessary.

[FAS80, ¶23]

.121 If M Company decides to transfer the mortgage loans to a long-term investment classification on May 31 rather than sell the assets, the mortgages would be transferred at the lower of their new cost basis ($9,580,000) or market value, in accordance with Section Mo4, "Mortgage Banking Activities." The difference between that amount and the outstanding principal balance would be amortized to income over the estimated remaining life of the mortgages. [FAS80, ¶24]

Example 4: Hedge of the Interest Expense Related to Short-Term Deposits

.122 The interest rate paid by a financial institution on its money market deposit accounts is revised every month and is a function of the current yield for three-month T-bills. On September 1, 19X4, the institution sells 30 futures contracts for three-month T-bills for the purpose of offsetting changes in the rate paid on the accounts for the 6 months commencing October 1. At each date the money market accounts are repriced, the enterprise closes out five of the contracts originally sold on September 1. [FAS80, ¶25]

.123 Changes in the market value of the futures contracts would be reported in income as those changes occur unless the hedge criteria of this section are met. In this situation, the futures contracts would have to qualify as anticipatory hedges because they relate to subsequent transactions—the payment of interest on the deposit accounts—that are not certain to occur. Therefore, in addition to meeting the hedge conditions in paragraph .104, the institution would also have to satisfy the conditions in paragraph .109 by demonstrating that it is probable that the deposits will be retained for the six-month period. Assuming the conditions in paragraphs .104 and .109 are met, changes in the value of the futures contracts would be reported as adjustments of interest expense. In this example, that would be accomplished by associating the change in value of the contracts closed with interest expense for the subsequent period. For example, changes in the market value of the contracts closed on October 1 would be amortized over the month of October as increases or decreases in interest expense on the deposits. [FAS80, ¶26]

[**Note:** Additional guidance with respect to implementing Section F80 is presented in FASB *Highlights,* "Futures Contracts: Guidance on Applying Statement 80," June 1985. The article addresses 33 questions and was written by FASB staff member Keith Wishon. This publication is available from the Order Department, Financial Accounting Standards Board, 401 Merritt 7, P.O. Box 5116, Norwalk, CT 06856-5116, telephone (203) 847-0700.]

Glossary

.401 **Financial Instrument.** The term is used broadly in this section to include instruments usually considered to be securities (such as notes, bonds, debentures, and equities) as well as other evidences of indebtedness (such as money market instruments, certificates of deposit, mortgages, and commercial paper) that often are not referred to as securities. [FAS80, ¶15]

.402 **Firm Commitment.** An agreement, usually legally enforceable, under which performance is probable because of sufficiently large disincentives for nonperformance. [FAS80, ¶15]

.403 **Futures Contract.** A legal agreement between a buyer or seller and the clearinghouse of a futures exchange. The futures contracts covered by this section include those traded on regulated futures exchanges in the United States and contracts having similar characteristics that are traded on exchanges in other countries. Futures contracts covered by this section have the following characteristics: (a) They obligate the purchaser (seller) to accept (make) delivery of a standardized quantity of a commodity or financial instrument at a specified date or during a specified period, or they provide for cash settlement rather than delivery,[401] (b) they effectively can be canceled before the delivery date by entering into an offsetting contract for the same commodity or financial instrument, and (c) all changes in value of open contracts are settled on a regular basis, usually daily. [FAS80, ¶15]

.404 **Risk.** [T]he sensitivity of an enterprise's income for one or more future periods to changes in market prices or yields of existing assets, liabilities, firm commitments, or anticipated transactions. [FAS80, ¶4]

(The next page is 23701.)

---

[401]Futures contracts for indexes of prices are considered to meet this condition even though there is no underlying commodity or financial instrument. [FAS80, ¶15, fn9]

Sources: FASB Statement 114; FASB Statement 115; FASB Statement 118; FASB Statement 121

Summary

This section presents standards for accounting for the impairment of (1) certain loans, (2) certain investments in debt and equity securities, (3) long-lived assets that will be held and used, including certain identifiable intangibles, and goodwill related to those assets, and (4) long-lived assets and certain identifiable intangibles to be disposed of. It also includes references to other sections in which impairment considerations are discussed.

For impaired loans this section is applicable to all creditors and, with limited exceptions, to all loans, uncollateralized as well as collateralized, that have been identified for impairment evaluation. It also applies to all loans that are restructured in a troubled debt restructuring involving a modification of terms.

Impaired loans that are within the scope of this section shall be measured based on the present value of expected future cash flows discounted at the loan's effective interest rate or, as a practical expedient, at the loan's observable market price or the fair value of the collateral if the loan is collateral dependent. Changes in these values are reflected in income and as adjustments to the allowance for credit losses.

This section requires that long-lived assets and certain identifiable intangibles to be held and used by an entity be reviewed for impairment whenever events or changes in circumstances indicate that the carrying amount of an asset may not be recoverable. In performing the review for recoverability, the entity should estimate the future cash flows expected to result from the use of the asset and its eventual disposition. If the sum of the expected future cash flows (undiscounted and without interest charges) is less than the carrying amount of the asset, an impairment loss is recognized. Otherwise, an impairment loss is not recognized. Measurement of an impairment loss for long-lived assets and identifiable intangibles that an entity expects to hold and use should be based on the fair value of the asset.

Long-lived assets and certain identifiable intangibles to be disposed of should be reported at the lower of carrying amount or fair value less cost to sell, except for assets that are covered by Section I13, "Income Statement Presentation: Discontinued Operations." Assets that are covered by Section I13 will continue to be reported at the lower of carrying amount or net realizable value.

This section also presents standards for recognizing other-than-temporary impairment of certain investments in debt and equity securities.

.101 [This section addresses the impairment of (a) loans in paragraphs .102 through .119, (b) certain investments in debt and equity securities in paragraph .120, and (c) long-lived assets to be held and used, including certain identifiable intangibles and goodwill related to those assets, and long-lived assets and certain identifiable intangibles to be disposed of in paragraphs .122 through .138. The accounting for impairment as it relates to other specific topics is included in other sections, [such as the following:

Asset or Topic	Section/Paragraph
Capitalized costs of the broadcasting industry	Br5.108
Capitalized costs of the motion picture industry	Mo6.115-.116
Capitalized computer software costs	Co2.109
Deferred policy acquisition costs of the insurance industry	In6.137D, .138-.143
Deferred tax assets	I27.119-.125
Disallowed costs of recently completed plants of regulated enterprises	Re6.127E
Disposal of a segment of a business	I13.101
Equity method of investments in common stock	I82.109(h)
Estimated residual value for sales-type, direct financing, and leveraged leases of lessors	L10.113
Identifiable intangibles specifically excluded in paragraph .122 of Section I08 and the goodwill identified with those intangibles	I60.112
Intangible assets of motor carriers	I60.125-.129
Long-term investments in mortgage loans by mortgage bankers	Mo4.108
Record masters of the record and music industry	Re4.106
Unproved properties of oil and gas producing companies	Oi5.104, .118-.120, .122(b), .124, .131, .138(g), and .138(h)

This section does not change the provisions of those sections.]

Impairment of a Loan

Scope

.102 For purposes of this section, a loan is a contractual right to receive money on demand or on fixed or determinable dates that is recognized as an asset in the creditor's statement of financial position. Examples include but are not limited to accounts receivable (with terms exceeding one year) and notes receivable. [FAS114, ¶4]

.103 This section applies to all creditors. It addresses the accounting by creditors for impairment of a loan by specifying how allowances for credit losses related to certain loans should be determined. This section also addresses the accounting by creditors for all loans that are restructured in a troubled debt restructuring involving a modification of terms of a receivable (except restructurings of loans excluded from the scope of this section in paragraph .104(b) through (d)) including [restructurings] involving a receipt of assets in partial satisfaction of a receivable. The term *troubled debt restructuring* is used in this section consistent with its use in Section D22, "Debt: Restructurings." [FAS114, ¶5] [A creditor in a troubled debt restructuring involving a modification of terms before the initial application of this section where the restructured loan is impaired based on the terms of the restructuring agreement shall apply this section and the relevant paragraphs of Section D22. A creditor in a troubled debt restructuring involving a modification of terms before the initial application of this section where the restructured loan is *not* impaired based on the terms of the restructuring agreement, may apply the relevant paragraphs of Section D22 unless the restructured loan meets the definition of a *security* in paragraph .406 of Section I80, "Investments: Debt and Equity Securities," in which case the provisions of Section I80 would apply.]

.104 This section applies to all loans that are identified for evaluation, uncollateralized as well as collateralized, except:

a. Large groups of smaller-balance homogeneous loans that are collectively evaluated for impairment. Those loans may include but are not limited to credit card, residential mortgage, and consumer installment loans.
b. Loans that are measured at fair value or at the lower of cost or fair value, for example, in accordance with Section Mo4, "Mortgage Banking Activities," or other specialized industry practice.
c. Leases as defined in Section L10, "Leases."
d. Debt securities as defined in Section I80.

[FAS114, ¶6]

.105 This section does not specify how a creditor should identify loans that are to be evaluated for collectibility.[1] A creditor should apply its normal loan review procedures in making that judgment. This section does not address when a creditor should record a direct write-down of an impaired loan, nor does it address how a creditor should assess the overall adequacy of the allowance for credit losses. In addition to the allowance calculated in accordance with this section, a creditor should continue to recognize an allowance for credit losses necessary to comply with Section C59, "Contingencies." [FAS114, ¶7]

Recognition of Impairment

.106 A loan is impaired when, based on current information and events, it is probable that a creditor will be unable to collect all amounts due according to the contractual terms of the loan agreement. As used in this section and in Section C59, *all amounts due according to the contractual terms* means that both the contractual interest payments and the contractual principal payments of a loan will be collected as scheduled in the loan agreement. [FAS114, ¶8] For a loan that has been restructured in a troubled debt restructuring, *the contractual terms of the loan agreement* refers to the contractual terms specified by the original loan agreement, not the contractual terms specified by the restructuring agreement. [FAS118, ¶6(a)] This section does not specify how a creditor should determine that it is probable that it will be unable to collect all amounts due according to the contractual terms of a loan. A creditor should apply its normal loan review procedures in making that judgment. An insignificant delay or insignificant shortfall in amount of payments does not require application of this section. A loan is not impaired during a period of delay in payment if the creditor expects to collect all amounts due including interest accrued at the contractual interest rate for the period of delay. Thus, a demand loan or other loan with no stated maturity is not impaired if the creditor expects to collect all amounts due including interest accrued at the contractual interest rate during the period the loan is outstanding. [FAS114, ¶8]

.107 Usually, a loan whose terms are modified in a troubled debt restructuring already will have been identified as impaired because the condition specified in paragraph .106

---

[1] Sources of information useful in identifying loans for evaluation that are listed in the AICPA's Auditing Procedure Study, *Auditing the Allowance for Credit Losses of Banks,* include a specific materiality criterion; regulatory reports of examination; internally generated listings such as "watch lists," past due reports, overdraft listings, and listings of loans to insiders; management reports of total loan amounts by borrower; historical loss experience by type of loan; loan files lacking current financial data related to borrowers and guarantors; borrowers experiencing problems such as operating losses, marginal working capital, inadequate cash flow, or business interruptions; loans secured by collateral that is not readily marketable or that is susceptible to deterioration in realizable value; loans to borrowers in industries or countries experiencing economic instability; and loan documentation and compliance exception reports. [FAS114, ¶7, fn1]

will have existed before a formal restructuring. However, if a loan is excluded from the scope of this section under paragraph .104(a), a creditor may not have accounted for that loan in accordance with this section before the loan was restructured. The creditor shall apply the provisions of this section to that loan when it is restructured. [FAS114, ¶9]

.108 The term *probable* is used in this section consistent with its use in paragraph .104 of Section C59. The conditions for accrual in paragraph .105 of Section C59 are not inconsistent with the accounting concept of conservatism. *Those conditions are not intended to be so rigid that they require virtual certainty before a loss is accrued.* They require only that it be *probable* that an asset has been impaired or a liability has been incurred and that the amount of loss be *reasonably* estimable. [FAS114, ¶10]

Measurement of Impairment

.109 Measuring [FAS114, ¶11] impairment of a loan [FAS118, ¶6(b)] requires judgment and estimates, and the eventual outcomes may differ from those estimates. Creditors should have latitude to develop measurement methods that are practical in their circumstances. Paragraphs .110 through .114 address those measurement methods. [FAS114, ¶11]

.110 Some impaired loans have risk characteristics that are unique to an individual borrower, and the creditor will apply the measurement methods described in paragraphs .111 through .114 on a loan-by-loan basis. However, some impaired loans may have risk characteristics in common with other impaired loans. A creditor may aggregate those loans and may use historical statistics, such as average recovery period and average amount recovered, along with a composite effective interest rate as a means of measuring [FAS114, ¶12] impairment of those loans. [FAS118, ¶6(c)]

.111 When a loan is impaired as defined in paragraph .106, a creditor shall measure impairment based on the present value of expected future cash flows discounted at the loan's effective interest rate, except that as a practical expedient, a creditor may measure impairment based on a loan's observable market price, or the fair value of the collateral if the loan is collateral dependent. Regardless of the measurement method, a creditor shall measure impairment based on the fair value of the collateral when the creditor determines that foreclosure is probable.[2] A loan is collateral dependent if the repayment

---

[2]When a creditor determines that foreclosure is probable, a creditor should remeasure the loan at the fair value of the collateral so that loss recognition is not delayed until actual foreclosure. The requirement in this section to discount expected future cash flows may not preclude the need to recognize additional loss when foreclosure is probable because estimates of expected future cash flows are not remeasured using a market rate and because estimates of expected future cash flows may change when a creditor determines that foreclosure is probable. [FAS114, ¶69] [Because of] the practical problems of accounting for the operations of an asset [(the collateral) that] the creditor does not possess, a loan for which foreclosure is probable should continue to be accounted for as a loan. [FAS114, ¶71]

of the loan is expected to be provided solely by the underlying collateral. The creditor may choose a measurement method on a loan-by-loan basis.[3] A creditor shall consider estimated costs to sell, on a discounted basis, in the measure of impairment if those costs are expected to reduce the cash flows available to repay or otherwise satisfy the loan.[4] If the [FAS114, ¶13] present value of expected future cash flows (or, alternatively, the observable market price of the loan or the fair value of the collateral) [FAS118, ¶6(d)] is less than the recorded investment in the loan[5] (including accrued interest, net deferred loan fees or costs, and unamortized premium or discount), a creditor shall recognize an impairment by creating a valuation allowance with a corresponding charge to bad-debt expense or by adjusting an existing valuation allowance for the impaired loan with a corresponding charge or credit to bad-debt expense. [FAS114, ¶13]

.112 If a creditor [FAS114, ¶14] bases its measure of loan impairment on [FAS118, ¶6(e)] a present value amount, the creditor shall calculate that present value amount based on an estimate of the expected future cash flows of the impaired loan, discounted at the loan's effective interest rate. The effective interest rate of a loan is the rate of return implicit in the loan (that is, the contractual interest rate adjusted for any net deferred loan fees or costs, premium, or discount existing at the origination or acquisition of the loan).[6] The effective interest rate for a loan restructured in a troubled debt restructuring is based on the original contractual rate, not the rate specified in the restructuring agreement. If the loan's contractual interest rate varies based on subsequent changes in an independent factor, such as an index or rate (for example, the prime rate, the London interbank offered rate, or the U.S. Treasury bill weekly average), that loan's effective interest rate may be calculated based on the factor as it changes over the life of the loan or may be fixed at the rate in effect at the date the loan meets the impairment criterion in paragraph .106. The creditor's choice shall be applied consistently for all loans whose

[3]The measurement method for an individual impaired loan shall be applied consistently to that loan and a change in method shall be justified by a change in circumstance. [FAS114, ¶53]

[4]For example, if repayment of a loan is dependent on the sale of the collateral, a creditor that uses a discounted cash flow method to measure impairment shall reduce its estimate of expected future cash flows by its estimates of costs to sell. Likewise, if a creditor uses the fair value of the collateral to measure impairment of a collateral-dependent loan and repayment or satisfaction of a loan is dependent on the sale of the collateral, the fair value of the collateral shall be adjusted to consider estimated costs to sell. However, if repayment or satisfaction of the loan is dependent only on the operation, rather than the sale, of the collateral, the measure of impairment would not incorporate estimated costs to sell the collateral. [FAS114, ¶46]

[5]The term *recorded investment in the loan* is distinguished from *net carrying amount of the loan* because the latter term is net of a valuation allowance, while the former term is not. The recorded investment in the loan does, however, reflect any direct write-down of the investment. [FAS114, ¶13, fn2]

[6]A loan may be acquired at a discount because of a change in credit quality or rate or both. When a loan is acquired at a discount that relates, at least in part, to the loan's credit quality, the effective interest rate is the discount rate that equates the present value of the investor's estimate of the loan's future cash flows with the purchase price of the loan. [FAS114, ¶14, fn3]

contractual interest rate varies based on subsequent changes in an independent factor. Projections of changes in the factor should not be made for purposes of determining the effective interest rate or estimating expected future cash flows. [FAS114, ¶14]

.113 If a creditor [FAS114, ¶15] bases its measure of loan impairment on [FAS118, ¶6(f)] a present value calculation, the estimates of expected future cash flows shall be the creditor's best estimate based on reasonable and supportable assumptions and projections. All available evidence, including estimated costs to sell if those costs are expected to reduce the cash flows available to repay or otherwise satisfy the loan, should be considered in developing the estimate of expected future cash flows. The weight given to the evidence should be commensurate with the extent to which the evidence can be verified objectively. If a creditor estimates a range for either the amount or timing of possible cash flows, the likelihood of the possible outcomes shall be considered in determining the best estimate of expected future cash flows. [FAS114, ¶15]

.114 Subsequent to the initial measurement of impairment, if there is a significant change (increase or decrease) in the amount or timing of an impaired loan's expected future cash flows, or if actual cash flows are significantly different from the cash flows previously projected, a creditor shall recalculate the impairment by applying the procedures specified in paragraphs .110 through .113 and by adjusting the valuation allowance. Similarly, a creditor that measures impairment based on the observable market price of an impaired loan or the fair value of the collateral of an impaired collateral-dependent loan shall adjust the valuation allowance if there is a significant change (increase or decrease) in either of those bases. However, the net carrying amount of the loan shall at no time exceed the recorded investment in the loan. [FAS114, ¶16]

Income Recognition

.115 This section does not address how a creditor should recognize, measure, or display interest income on an impaired loan.[6a] Some accounting methods for recognizing income may result in a recorded investment in an impaired loan that is less than the present value of expected future cash flows (or, alternatively, the observable market price of the loan or the fair value of the collateral). In that case, while the loan would meet the definition of an impaired loan in paragraph .106, no additional impairment would be recognized. Those accounting methods include recognition of interest income using a cost-recovery method, a cash-basis method, or some combination of those methods. The recorded investment in an impaired loan also may be less than the present value of expected fu-

---

[6a]This section does not preclude a creditor [from accruing] interest on the net carrying amount of the impaired loan and [reporting] other changes in the net carrying amount of the loan as an adjustment to bad-debt expense. This section [also] does not preclude a creditor [from recognizing] all changes in the net carrying amount of the loan as an adjustment to bad-debt expense. [FAS118, ¶4]

ture cash flows (or, alternatively, the observable market price of the loan or the fair value of the collateral) because the creditor has charged off part of the loan. [FAS118, ¶6(g)]

.116-.117 [Deleted 10/94 because of FASB Statement 118, *Accounting by Creditors for Impairment of a Loan—Income Recognition and Disclosures.*]

Disclosures

.118 A creditor shall disclose, either in the body of the financial statements or in the accompanying notes,[7] the following information about loans that meet the definition of an impaired loan in paragraph .106 of this section:

a. As of the date of each statement of financial position presented, the total recorded investment in the impaired loans at the end of each period and (1) the amount of that recorded investment for which there is a related allowance for credit losses determined in accordance with this section and the amount of that allowance and (2) the amount of that recorded investment for which there is no related allowance for credit losses determined in accordance with this section [Refer to Exhibit 121A for a summary of these disclosure requirements.]
b. The creditor's policy for recognizing interest income on impaired loans, including how cash receipts are recorded
c. For each period for which results of operations are presented, the average recorded investment[7a] in the impaired loans during each period, the related amount of interest income recognized during the time within that period that the loans were impaired, and, unless not practicable, the amount of interest income recognized using a cash-basis method of accounting during the time within that period that the loans were impaired.

Information about an impaired loan that has been restructured in a troubled debt restructuring involving a modification of terms need not be included in the disclosures required by (a) and (c) [above] in years after the restructuring if (i) the restructuring agreement specifies an interest rate equal to or greater than the rate that the creditor was willing to accept at the time of the restructuring for a new loan with comparable risk and (ii) the

---

[7]This section does not preclude a creditor from disclosing in the notes to the financial statements the effect of initially applying this section if the creditor believes it is practical to do so. [FAS114, ¶74]

[7a]This section does not specify how a creditor should calculate the average recorded investment in the impaired loans during the reporting period. A creditor should develop an appropriate method and averages based on month-end balances may be considered an appropriate method [by some creditors]. [FAS118, ¶17]

loan is not impaired based on the terms specified by the restructuring agreement. That exception shall be applied consistently for (a) and (c) [above] to all loans restructured in a troubled debt restructuring that meet the criteria in (i) and (ii) [above]. [FAS118, ¶6(i)]

.118A For each period for which results of operations are presented, a creditor also shall disclose the activity in the total allowance for credit losses related to loans, including the balance in the allowance at the beginning and end of each period, additions charged to operations, direct write-downs charged against the allowance, and recoveries of amounts previously charged off. The total allowance for credit losses related to loans includes those amounts that have been determined in accordance with Section C59 and with this section. [FAS118, ¶6(i)]

.119 [Deleted 10/94 because of FASB Statement 118.]

Impairment of Investments in Debt and Equity Securities

.120 For individual securities [as addressed in Section I80] classified as either available-for-sale or held-to-maturity, an enterprise shall determine whether a decline in fair value below the amortized cost basis is other than temporary. For example, if it is probable that the investor will be unable to collect all amounts due according to the contractual terms of a debt security not impaired at acquisition, an other-than-temporary impairment shall be considered to have occurred.[8] If the decline in fair value is judged to be other than temporary, the cost basis of the individual security shall be written down to fair value as a new cost basis and the amount of the write-down shall be included in earnings (that is, accounted for as a realized loss). The new cost basis shall not be changed for subsequent recoveries in fair value. Subsequent increases in the fair value of available-for-sale securities shall be included in the separate component of equity pursuant to paragraph .110 of Section I80; subsequent decreases in fair value, if not an other-than-temporary impairment, also shall be included in the separate component of equity. [FAS115, ¶16]

Illustration of Disclosure Requirements for Impaired Loans

.121 [Exhibit 121A presents a summary of the disclosure requirements in paragraph .118(a) for loans that are impaired under the definition in paragraph .106.]

---

[8] A decline in the value of a security that is other than temporary is also discussed in AICPA Auditing Interpretation, *Evidential Matter for the Carrying Amount of Marketable Securities*, which was issued in 1975 and incorporated in Statement on Auditing Standards No. 1, *Codification of Auditing Standards and Procedures*, as Interpretation 20, and in SEC Staff Accounting Bulletin No. 59, *Accounting for Noncurrent Marketable Equity Securities*. [FAS115, ¶16, fn4]

Exhibit 121A

Summary of Disclosure Requirements in Paragraph .118(a)

Description of Loans	Required Disclosures about the Recorded Investment in Loans That Meet the Definition of an Impaired Loan in Paragraph .106		
	(A) The Total Recorded Investment in the Impaired Loans	(B) The Amount of the Recorded Investment in (A) for Which There Is a Related Allowance for Credit Losses	(C) The Amount of the Recorded Investment in (A) for Which There Is No Related Allowance for Credit Losses
1. Loans that meet the definition of an impaired loan in paragraph .106 and that have *not* been charged off fully	Included. The amount disclosed in (A) must equal the sum of (B) and (C).	Included if there is a related allowance for credit losses.	Included if there is no related allowance for credit losses.
2. Loans that meet the definition of an impaired loan in paragraph .106 and that have been charged off fully	Excluded. The recorded investment and allowance for credit losses are equal to zero.		
3. Loans restructured in a troubled debt restructuring [before the date of adoption of the provisions in paragraphs .102–.119 and Section D22 (paragraphs .139–.146)] that are not impaired based on the terms specified by the restructuring agreement	Excluded. Disclosures should be provided in accordance with paragraphs .136 and .137 of Section D22.		

4. Loans restructured in a troubled debt restructuring [before the date of adoption of the provisions in paragraphs .102-.119 and Section D22 (paragraphs .139-.146)] that are impaired based on the terms specified by the restructuring agreement

Refer to items 1 and 2 above.

5. Loans restructured in a troubled debt restructuring [after the date of adoption of the provisions in paragraphs .102-.119 and Section D22 (paragraphs .139-.146)]

May be excluded in years after the restructuring if (a) the restructuring agreement specifies an interest rate equal to or greater than the rate that the creditor was willing to accept at the time of the restructuring for a new receivable with comparable risk and (b) the loan is not impaired based on the terms specified by the restructuring agreement. Otherwise, refer to items 1 and 2 above.

6. Large groups of smaller-balance homogeneous loans that are collectively evaluated for impairment and other loans that are excluded from the scope of this section as defined in paragraph .104

Excluded unless restructured in a troubled debt restructuring (refer to items 3-5 above and paragraph .107 for requirements for a restructured loan).

[FAS118, ¶24]

Impairment of Long-Lived Assets and Long-Lived Assets to Be Disposed Of

Scope

.122 Paragraphs .122 through .138 apply to long-lived assets, certain identifiable intangibles, and goodwill related to those assets to be held and used and to long-lived assets and certain identifiable intangibles to be disposed of. Those paragraphs apply to all entities. [However,] those paragraphs do not apply to financial instruments, long-term customer relationships of a financial institution (for example, core deposit intangibles and credit cardholder intangibles), mortgage and other servicing rights, deferred policy acquisition costs, or deferred tax assets. They also do not apply to assets whose accounting is prescribed by:

a. Section Re4, "Record and Music Industry"
b. Section Mo6, "Motion Picture Industry"
c. Section Br5, "Broadcasting Industry"
d. Section Co2, "Computer Software to Be Sold, Leased, or Otherwise Marketed"
e. Section Re6, "Regulated Operations," (for accounting for abandonments and disallowances of plant costs, paragraphs .127A through .127E).

All references to an asset in paragraphs .122 through .138 also refer to groups of assets representing the lowest level of identifiable cash flows as described in paragraph .127. [FAS121, ¶3]

Assets to Be Held and Used

Recognition and Measurement of Impairment

.123 An entity shall review long-lived assets and certain identifiable intangibles to be held and used for impairment whenever events or changes in circumstances indicate that the carrying amount of an asset may not be recoverable. [FAS121, ¶4]

.124 The following are examples of events or changes in circumstances that indicate that the recoverability of the carrying amount of an asset should be assessed:

a. A significant decrease in the market value of an asset
b. A significant change in the extent or manner in which an asset is used or a significant physical change in an asset
c. A significant adverse change in legal factors or in the business climate that could affect the value of an asset or an adverse action or assessment by a regulator

d. An accumulation of costs significantly in excess of the amount originally expected to acquire or construct an asset

e. A current period operating or cash flow loss combined with a history of operating or cash flow losses or a projection or forecast that demonstrates continuing losses associated with an asset used for the purpose of producing revenue.

[FAS121, ¶5]

.125 If the examples of events or changes in circumstances set forth in paragraph .124 are present or if other events or changes in circumstances indicate that the carrying amount of an asset that an entity expects to hold and use may not be recoverable, the entity shall estimate the future cash flows expected to result from the use of the asset and its eventual disposition. Future cash flows are the future cash inflows expected to be generated by an asset less the future cash outflows expected to be necessary to obtain those inflows. If the sum of the expected future cash flows (undiscounted and without interest charges) is less than the carrying amount of the asset, the entity shall recognize an impairment loss.[9] Otherwise, an impairment loss shall not be recognized; however, a review of depreciation policies may be appropriate.[10] [FAS121, ¶6]

.126 An impairment loss recognized in accordance with paragraph .125 shall be measured as the amount by which the carrying amount of the asset exceeds the fair value of the asset. The fair value of an asset is the amount at which the asset could be bought or sold in a current transaction between willing parties, that is, other than in a forced or liquidation sale. Quoted market prices in active markets are the best evidence of fair value and shall be used as the basis for the measurement, if available. If quoted market prices are not available, the estimate of fair value shall be based on the best information available in the circumstances. The estimate of fair value shall consider prices for similar assets and the results of valuation techniques to the extent available in the circum-

---

[9This] approach is consistent with the definition of an impairment as the inability to fully recover the carrying amount of an asset and with a basic presumption underlying a statement of financial position that the reported carrying amounts of assets should, at a minimum, be recoverable. [FAS121, ¶65]

[10]Paragraph .109 of Section A06, "Accounting Changes," addresses the accounting for changes in depreciation estimates, and paragraph .131 addresses the accounting for changes in the method of depreciation. Whenever there is reason to assess the recoverability of the carrying amount of an asset under paragraphs .123 and .124 of this section, there may be reason to review the depreciation estimates and method under paragraphs .109 and .131 of Section A06. However, an impairment loss that results from applying paragraphs .122 through .138 of this section should be recognized prior to performing that review. The provisions of Section A06 apply to the reporting of changes in the depreciation estimates and method regardless of whether an impairment loss is recognized under paragraph .125 of this section. [FAS121, ¶6, fn1]

stances. Examples of valuation techniques[11] include the present value of estimated expected future cash flows using a discount rate commensurate with the risks involved,[12] option-pricing models, matrix pricing, option-adjusted spread models, and fundamental analysis. [FAS121, ¶7]

.127 In estimating expected future cash flows for determining whether an asset is impaired (paragraph .125), and if expected future cash flows are used in measuring assets that are impaired (paragraph .126), assets shall be grouped[13] at the lowest level for which there are identifiable cash flows that are largely independent of the cash flows of other groups of assets. [FAS121, ¶8]

.128 Estimates of expected future cash flows shall be the best estimate based on reasonable and supportable assumptions and projections. All available evidence should be considered in developing estimates of expected future cash flows. The weight given to the evidence should be commensurate with the extent to which the evidence can be verified objectively. If a range is estimated for either the amount or timing of possible cash flows, the likelihood of possible outcomes shall be considered in determining the best estimate of future cash flows. [FAS121, ¶9]

---

[11]Valuation techniques for measuring an asset covered by this section should be consistent with the objective of measuring fair value and should incorporate assumptions that market participants would use in their estimate of the asset's fair value. [FAS121, ¶74]

[12]The discount rate commensurate with the risks involved is a rate that would be required for a similar investment with like risks. That rate is the asset-specific rate of return expected from the market—the return the entity would expect if it were to choose an equally risky investment as an alternative to operating the impaired asset. For some entities that have a well-developed capital budgeting process, the hurdle rate used to make investment decisions might be useful in estimating that rate. [FAS121, ¶93] This section does not require disclosure of the discount rate. [FAS121, ¶94]

[13]Assets should be grouped when they are used together; that is, when they are part of the same group of assets and are used together to generate joint cash flows. [FAS121, ¶95] Deciding the appropriate grouping of assets for impairment consideration requires considerable judgment. Varying facts and circumstances inevitably justify different groups. [FAS121, ¶96] [Consider the case where] an entity operates a bus company that provides service under contract with a municipality that requires minimum service on each of five separate routes. Assets devoted to serving each route and the cash flows from each route are discrete. One of the routes operates at a significant deficit that results in the inability to recover the carrying amounts of the dedicated assets. An appropriate level at which to group assets to test for and measure impairment would be the five bus routes because the entity does not have the option to curtail any one bus route. [FAS121, ¶97]

.129 In limited circumstances, the test specified in paragraph .125 will be applicable at only the entity[14] level because the asset being tested for recoverability does not have identifiable cash flows that are largely independent of other asset groupings. In those instances, if the asset is not expected to provide any service potential to the entity, the asset shall be accounted for as if abandoned or held for disposal in accordance with the provisions of paragraph .134. If the asset is expected to provide service potential, an impairment loss shall be recognized if the sum of the expected future cash flows (undiscounted and without interest charges) for the entity is less than the carrying amounts of the entity's assets covered by this section. [FAS121, ¶10]

.130 After an impairment is recognized, the reduced carrying amount of the asset shall be accounted for as its new cost. For a depreciable asset, the new cost shall be depreciated over the asset's remaining useful life. Restoration of previously recognized impairment losses is prohibited. [FAS121, ¶11]

Goodwill

.131 If an asset being tested for recoverability was acquired in a business combination accounted for using the purchase method, the goodwill that arose in that transaction shall be included as part of the asset grouping (paragraph .127) in determining recoverability. If some but not all of the assets acquired in that transaction are being tested, goodwill shall be allocated to the assets being tested for recoverability on a pro rata basis using the relative fair values of the long-lived assets and identifiable intangibles acquired at the acquisition date unless there is evidence to suggest that some other method of associating the goodwill with those assets is more appropriate. In instances where goodwill is identified with assets that are subject to an impairment loss, the carrying amount of the identified goodwill shall be eliminated before making any reduction of the carrying amounts of impaired long-lived assets and identifiable intangibles. [FAS121, ¶12]

---

[14]Not-for-profit organizations that rely in part on contributions to maintain their assets may need to consider those contributions in determining the appropriate cash flows to compare with the carrying amount of an asset. If future unrestricted contributions to the organization as a whole are not considered, the sum of the expected future cash flows may be negative, or positive but less than the carrying amount of the asset. For example, the costs of administering a museum may exceed the admission fees charged, but the organization may fund the cash flow deficit with unrestricted contributions. [FAS121, ¶99] Similar [situations might apply to] business enterprises. For example, the cost of operating assets such as corporate headquarters or centralized research facilities may be funded by revenue-producing activities at lower levels of the enterprise. Accordingly, the lowest level of identifiable cash flows that are largely independent of other asset groups may be the entity level. [FAS121, ¶100]

Reporting and Disclosure

.132 An impairment loss for assets to be held and used shall be reported as a component of income from continuing operations before income taxes for entities presenting an income statement and in the statement of activities of a not-for-profit organization. Although there is no requirement to report a subtotal such as "income from operations," entities that present such a subtotal must include the impairment loss in that subtotal. [FAS121, ¶13]

.133 An entity that recognizes an impairment loss shall disclose all of the following in financial statements that include the period of the impairment write-down:

a. A description of the impaired assets and the facts and circumstances leading to the impairment
b. The amount of the impairment loss and how fair value was determined
c. The caption in the income statement or the statement of activities in which the impairment loss is aggregated if that loss has not been presented as a separate caption or reported parenthetically on the face of the statement
d. If applicable, the business segment(s) affected.

[FAS121, ¶14]

Assets to Be Disposed Of

Recognition and Measurement

.134 Section I13, "Income Statement Presentation: Discontinued Operations," requires that certain assets to be disposed of be measured at the lower of carrying amount or net realizable value.[15] All long-lived assets and certain identifiable intangibles to be disposed of that are not covered by that section and for which management, having the authority to approve the action, has committed to a plan to dispose of the assets, whether by sale or abandonment, shall be reported at the lower of carrying amount or fair value

---

[15]Paragraphs .101 and .102 of Section I13 prescribe the accounting for the disposal of a segment of a business. Paragraph .404 defines a segment of a business as "a component of an entity whose activities represent a separate major line of business or class of customer." Paragraph .101 of that section prescribes the determination of a gain or loss on the disposal of a segment of a business and states:

> In the usual circumstance, it would be expected that the plan of disposal would be carried out within a period of one year from the measurement date and that such projections of operating income or loss would not cover a period exceeding approximately one year.

[FAS121, ¶15, fn2]

less cost to sell. The fair value of the assets to be disposed of shall be measured in accordance with paragraph .126 of this section. [FAS121, ¶15]

.135 Cost to sell an asset to be disposed of generally includes the incremental direct costs to transact the sale of the asset such as broker commissions, legal and title transfer fees, and closing costs that must be incurred before legal title can be transferred. Costs generally excluded from cost to sell an asset to be disposed of include insurance, security services, utility expenses, and other costs of protecting or maintaining an asset. However, if a contractual agreement for the sale of an asset obligates an entity to incur costs in the future to effect the ultimate sale, those costs shall be included as adjustments to the cost to sell an asset to be disposed of. If the fair value of an asset is measured by the current market value or by using the current selling price for a similar asset, that fair value shall be considered to be a current amount and that fair value and cost to sell shall not be discounted. If the fair value of an asset is measured by discounting expected future cash flows and if the sale is expected to occur beyond one year, the cost to sell also shall be discounted. Assets to be disposed of covered by paragraphs .134 through .136 shall not be depreciated (amortized) while they are held for disposal. [FAS121, ¶16] Goodwill related to assets to be disposed of by an entity should be accounted for under the provisions of paragraph .113 of Section I60, "Intangible Assets." [FAS121, ¶123]

.136 Subsequent revisions in estimates of fair value less cost to sell shall be reported as adjustments to the carrying amount of an asset to be disposed of, provided that the carrying amount of the asset does not exceed the carrying amount (acquisition cost or other basis less accumulated depreciation or amortization) of the asset before an adjustment was made to reflect the decision to dispose of the asset. [FAS121, ¶17]

Reporting and Disclosure

.137 An entity that holds assets to be disposed of that are accounted for in accordance with paragraphs .134 through .136 shall report gains or losses resulting from the application of those paragraphs as a component of income from continuing operations before income taxes for entities presenting an income statement and in the statement of activities of a not-for-profit organization. Although entities are not required to report a subtotal such as "income from operations," entities that present such a subtotal must include the gains or losses resulting from the application of paragraphs .134 through .136 in that subtotal. [FAS121, ¶18]

.138 An entity that accounts for assets to be disposed of in accordance with paragraphs .134 through .136 shall disclose all of the following in financial statements that include a period during which those assets are held:

a. A description of assets to be disposed of, the facts and circumstances leading to the expected disposal, the expected disposal date, and the carrying amount of those assets
b. If applicable, the business segment(s) in which assets to be disposed of are held
c. The loss, if any, resulting from the application of paragraph .134 of this section
d. The gain or loss, if any, resulting from changes in the carrying amounts of assets to be disposed of that arises from application of paragraph .136 of this section
e. The caption in the income statement or statement of activities in which the gains or losses in (c) and (d) are aggregated if those gains or losses have not been presented as a separate caption or reported parenthetically on the face of the statement
f. The results of operations for assets to be disposed of to the extent that those results are included in the entity's results of operations for the period and can be identified.

[FAS121, ¶19]

(The next page is 24275.)

Sources: APB Opinion 30; AICPA Interpretation of APB Opinion 30;
FASB Statement 16

Summary

This section specifies that the results of discontinued operations and the gain or loss on disposal shall be reported in the income statement separately from continuing operations but not as an extraordinary item. If a loss is expected from the discontinuance of a business segment, the estimated loss shall be provided for as of the measurement date. If a gain is expected, it shall be recognized when realized.

Determination of Gain or Loss on Disposal of a Segment of a Business

.101 If a loss is expected from the proposed sale or abandonment of a segment, the estimated loss shall be provided for at the **measurement date.**[1] If a gain is expected, it shall be recognized when realized, which ordinarily is the **disposal date.** The determination of whether a gain or a loss results from the disposal of a **segment of a business**[2] shall be made at the measurement date based on estimates at that date of the net realizable value of the segment after giving consideration to any estimated costs and expenses directly associated with the disposal and, if a plan of disposal is to be carried out over a period of time and contemplates continuing operations during that period, to any estimated income or losses from operations. If it is expected that net losses from operations will be incurred between the measurement date and the expected disposal date, the com-

---

[1] If financial statements for a date prior to the measurement date have not been issued, and the expected loss provides evidence of conditions that existed at the date of such statements and affects estimates inherent in the process of preparing them, the financial statements shall be adjusted for any change in estimates resulting from the use of such evidence. (Refer to Statement on Auditing Standards No. 1, *Codification of Auditing Standards and Procedures,* Section 560.03.) [APB30, ¶15, fn5]

[2] The disposal of a segment of a business shall be distinguished from other disposals of assets incident to the evolution of the enterprise's business, such as the disposal of part of a line of business, the shifting of production or marketing activities for a particular line of business from one location to another, the phasing out of a product line or class of service, and other changes occasioned by technological improvements. The disposal of two or more unrelated assets that individually do not constitute a segment of a business shall not be combined and accounted for as a disposal of a segment of a business. [APB30, ¶13] [Refer to paragraph .110 for guidance on accounting for long-lived assets to be disposed of that are unrelated to the disposal of a segment of a business.]

putation of the gain or loss on disposal shall also include an estimate of such amounts. If it is expected that income will be generated from operations during that period, the computation of the gain or loss shall include the estimated income, limited however to the amount of any loss otherwise recognizable from the disposal; any remainder shall be accounted for as income when realized. The estimated amounts of income or loss from operations of a segment between measurement date and disposal date included in the determination of loss on disposal shall be limited to those amounts that can be projected with reasonable accuracy. In the usual circumstance, it would be expected that the plan of disposal would be carried out within a period of one year from the measurement date and that such projections of operating income or loss would not cover a period exceeding approximately one year. [APB30, ¶15] When disposal is estimated to be completed within one year and subsequently is revised to a longer period of time, any revision of the net realizable value of the segment shall be treated as a change in estimate (refer to paragraph .104). [APB30, ¶15, fn6]

.102 Gain or loss from the disposal of a segment of a business shall not include adjustments, costs, and expenses associated with normal business activities that should have been recognized on a going-concern basis up to the measurement date, such as adjustments of accruals on long-term contracts or write-down or write-off of receivables, inventories, property, plant, and equipment used in the business, equipment leased to others, or intangible assets. However, such adjustments, costs, and expenses that (a) are clearly a *direct* result of the decision to dispose of the segment and (b) are clearly not the adjustments of carrying amounts or costs, or expenses that should have been recognized on a going-concern basis prior to the measurement date, shall be included in determining the gain or loss on disposal. Results of operations before the measurement date shall not be included in the gain or loss on disposal. [APB30, ¶16]

.103 Costs and expenses *directly* associated with the decision to dispose include items such as severance pay, additional pension costs, employee relocation expenses, and future rentals on long-term leases to the extent they are not offset by sublease rentals. [APB30, ¶17]

Adjustment of Amounts Reported in Prior Periods

.104 Circumstances attendant to disposals of a segment of a business frequently require estimates, for example, of associated costs and occasionally of associated revenue, based on judgment and evaluation of the facts known at the time of first accounting for the event. [APB30, ¶25] Each adjustment in the current period of a loss on disposal of a business segment that was reported in a prior period shall be separately disclosed as to year of origin, nature, and amount and classified separately in the current period [as a gain or loss on disposal of a segment]. [FAS16, ¶16(c)] If the adjustment is the correction of an error, the provisions of Section A35, "Adjustments of Financial Statements for Prior Periods," paragraphs .103(a) and .105, shall be applied. [APB30, ¶25]

Income Statement Presentation and Disclosure

.105 The results of continuing operations shall be reported separately from **discontinued operations** and any gain or loss from disposal of a segment of a business (determined in accordance with paragraphs .101 and .102) shall be reported in conjunction with the related results of discontinued operations, not as an extraordinary item. Accordingly, operations of a segment that has been or will be discontinued shall be reported separately as a component of income before extraordinary items and the cumulative effect of accounting changes (if applicable) in the following manner:

Income from continuing operations before income taxes*	$XXXX	
Provision for income taxes	XXX	
Income from continuing operations†		$XXXX
Discontinued operations (Note X):		
Income (loss) from operations of discontinued Division A (less applicable income taxes of $XXX)	$XXXX	
Loss on disposal of Division A, including provision of $XXX for operating losses during phase-out period (less applicable income taxes of $XXX)	XXXX	XXXX
Net Income		$XXXX

---

*This caption shall be modified appropriately when an enterprise reports an extraordinary item [(refer to Section I17, "Income Statement Presentation: Extraordinary Items")] or the cumulative effect of a change in accounting principle in accordance with Section A06, "Accounting Changes." The presentation of per share data shall be similarly modified. [APB30, ¶8, fn2]

†[Refer to footnote 3.]

Amounts of income taxes applicable to the results of discontinued operations and the gain or loss from disposal of the segment shall be disclosed on the face of the income statement or in related notes. Revenues applicable to the discontinued operations shall be separately disclosed in the related notes. [APB30, ¶8]

.106 Financial statements of *current and prior* periods that include results of operations prior to the measurement date shall disclose the results of operations of the disposed segment, less applicable income taxes, as a separate component of income before extraordinary items (refer to paragraph .105). [APB30, ¶13]

.107 Earnings per share data for income from continuing operations and net income, computed in accordance with Section E09, "Earnings per Share," shall be presented on the face of the income statement. If presented, per share data for the results of discontinued operations and gain or loss from disposal of the business segment may be included in the face of the income statement or in a related note. [APB30, ¶9]

.108 In addition to the amounts to be disclosed in the financial statements (refer to paragraph .105), the notes to financial statements for the period encompassing the measurement date shall disclose:

a. The identity of the segment of business that has been or will be discontinued
b. The expected disposal date, if known
c. The expected manner of disposal
d. A description of the remaining assets and liabilities of the segment at the balance sheet date[3]
e. The income or loss from operations and any proceeds from disposal of the segment during the period from the measurement date to the date of the balance sheet.

For periods subsequent to the measurement date and including the period of disposal, notes to the financial statements shall disclose the information listed in (a), (b), (c), and (d) above and also the information listed in (e) above compared with the prior estimates. [APB30, ¶18]

.109 If the loss on disposal cannot be estimated within reasonable limits, this fact shall be disclosed. [APB30, ¶18, fn7]

Determination of Gain or Loss on Long-Lived Assets to Be Disposed Of Unrelated to Disposal of a Segment of a Business

.110 [All long-lived assets and certain identifiable intangibles to be disposed of that are unrelated to the disposal of a segment of a business shall be accounted for in accordance with the provisions of paragraphs .134 through .138 of Section I08, "Impairment."]

---

[3]Consideration shall be given to disclosing this information by segregation in the balance sheet of the net assets and liabilities (current and noncurrent) of the discontinued segment. Only liabilities that will be assumed by others shall be designated as liabilities of the discontinued segment. [APB30, ¶18, fn7]

Glossary

.401 Discontinued operations. The operations of a segment of a business that has been sold, abandoned, spun off, or otherwise disposed of or, although still operating, is the subject of a formal plan for disposal. [APB30, ¶8]

.402 Disposal date. The date of closing the sale, if the disposal is by sale, or the date that operations cease, if the disposal is by abandonment. [APB30, ¶14]

.403 Measurement date of a disposal. The date on which the management having authority to approve the action commits itself to a formal plan to dispose of a segment of the business, whether by sale or abandonment. The plan of disposal shall include, as a minimum, identification of the major assets to be disposed of, the expected method of disposal, the period expected to be required for completion of the disposal, an active program to find a buyer if disposal is to be by sale, the estimated results of operations of the segment from the measurement date to the disposal date, and the estimated proceeds or salvage to be realized by disposal. [APB30, ¶14]

.404 Segment of a business. A component of an enterprise whose activities represent a separate major line of business or class of customer. A segment may be in the form of a subsidiary, a division, or a department, and in some cases a joint venture or other non-subsidiary investee, provided that its assets, results of operations, and activities can be clearly distinguished, physically and operationally and for financial reporting purposes, from the other assets, results of operations, and activities of the entity. The fact that the results of operations of the segment being sold or abandoned cannot be separately identified strongly suggests that the transaction should not be classified as the disposal of a segment of the business. [APB30, ¶13]

Supplemental Guidance

Illustrative Disposals of a Segment of a Business

.501 *Question*—What factors should be considered in determining whether the effects of a particular event or transaction are extraordinary items or should otherwise be set forth in the income statement, and how are these factors applied in practice? [AIN-APB30]

.502 *Interpretation*—The first question that generally should be considered in determining the appropriate classification of profit or loss items that appear to be unusual, infrequently occurring, or extraordinary is: Does the event or transaction involve the sale, abandonment, or other manner of disposal of a segment of a business? [AIN-APB30]

.503 The following are illustrative of disposals that should be classified as disposals of a segment of a business:

a. A sale by a diversified enterprise of a major division that represents the enterprise's only activities in the electronics industry. The assets and results of operations of the division are clearly segregated for internal financial reporting purposes from the other assets and results of operations of the enterprise.
b. A sale by a meat packing enterprise of a 25-percent interest in a professional football team that has been accounted for under the equity method. All other activities of the enterprise are in the meat packing business.
c. A sale by a communications enterprise of all its radio stations that represent 30 percent of gross revenues. The enterprise's remaining activities are three television stations and a publishing enterprise. The assets and results of operations of the radio stations are clearly distinguishable physically, operationally, and for financial reporting purposes.
d. A food distributor disposes of one of its two divisions. One division sells food wholesale primarily to supermarket chains and the other division sells food through its chain of fast food restaurants, some of which are franchised and some of which are owned by the enterprise. Both divisions are in the business of distributing food. However, the nature of selling food through fast food outlets is vastly different from that of wholesaling food to supermarket chains. Thus, by having two major classes of customers, the enterprise has two segments of its business.

[AIN-APB30]

.504 Certain disposals would not constitute disposals of a segment of a business because they do not meet the definition in paragraph .404. For example, the following disposals should not be classified as disposals of a segment of a business:

a. The sale of a major foreign subsidiary engaged in silver mining by a mining enterprise that represents all of the enterprise's activities in that particular country. Even though the subsidiary being sold may account for a significant percentage of gross revenue of the consolidated group and all of its revenues in the particular country, the fact that the enterprise continues to engage in silver mining activities in other countries would indicate that there was a sale of a part of a line of business.
b. The sale by a petrochemical enterprise of a 25-percent interest in a petrochemical plant that is accounted for as an investment in a corporate joint venture under the equity method. Since the remaining activities of the enterprise are in the same line of business as the 25-percent interest that has been sold, there has not been a sale of a major line of business but rather a sale of part of a line of business.
c. A manufacturer of children's wear discontinues all of its operations in Italy that were composed of designing and selling children's wear for the Italian market. In the context of determining a segment of a business by class of customer, the nationality of customers or slight variations in product lines in order to appeal to particular groups are not determining factors.
d. A diversified enterprise sells a subsidiary that manufactures furniture. The enterprise has retained its other furniture manufacturing subsidiary. The disposal of the subsidiary, therefore, is not a disposal of a segment of the business but rather a disposal of part of a line of business. Such disposals are incident to the evolution of the entity's business.
e. The sale of all the assets (including the plant) related to the manufacture of men's woolen suits by an apparel manufacturer in order to concentrate activities in the manufacture of men's suits from synthetic products. This would represent a disposal of a product line as distinguished from the disposal of a major line of business.

[AIN-APB30]

.505 The foregoing examples are illustrative. It should be recognized that all attendant circumstances, which can vary from those above, need to be considered in making the judgments required by this section. [AIN-APB30]

(The next page is 24467.)

INCOME STATEMENT PRESENTATION: EXTRAORDINARY ITEMS

Sources: APB Opinion 9; APB Opinion 16; APB Opinion 30;
AICPA Interpretations of APB Opinion 9;
AICPA Interpretation of APB Opinion 30;
FASB Statement 4; FASB Statement 44; FASB Statement 64;
FASB Statement 101; FASB Statement 109; FASB Statement 121;
FASB Technical Bulletin 85-6

Summary

This section specifies that an enterprise shall show extraordinary items separately as an item of net income for the period on the face of its income statement. Extraordinary items are events or transactions that are unusual and unrelated to the enterprise's ordinary activities and would occur infrequently.

Applicability

.101 This section applies to general purpose financial statements that purport to present results of operations in conformity with generally accepted accounting principles. Investment enterprises, insurance enterprises, and certain nonprofit enterprises have developed income statements with formats different from those of the typical commercial enterprise, designed to highlight the peculiar nature and sources of their income or operating results. The requirement of this section that net income be presented as one amount does not apply to such enterprises. [APB9, ¶6]

Income Statement Presentation and Disclosure

.102 In the absence of discontinued operations (refer to Section I13, "Income Statement Presentation: Discontinued Operations") and changes in accounting principles (refer to Section A06, "Accounting Changes"), the following main captions shall appear in an income statement if **extraordinary items** are reported:

Income before extraordinary items[1]	$XXX
Extraordinary items (less applicable income taxes of $XXX) (Note A)	XXX
Net income	$XXX

---

[1]This caption shall be modified appropriately when an enterprise reports the cumulative effect of an accounting change (refer to Section A06). [APB30, ¶11, fn4]

The caption "extraordinary items" shall be used to identify separately the effects of events and transactions, other than the disposal of a segment of a business, that meet the criteria for classification as extraordinary as discussed in paragraphs .106 through .111. Descriptive captions and the amounts for *individual* extraordinary events or transactions shall be presented, preferably on the face of the income statement, if practicable; otherwise, disclosure in related notes is acceptable. The nature of an extraordinary event or transaction and the principal items entering into the determination of an extraordinary gain or loss shall be described. The income taxes applicable to extraordinary items shall be disclosed on the face of the income statement; alternatively, disclosure in the related notes is acceptable. The caption *net income* shall replace the three captions shown above if the income statement includes no extraordinary items. [APB30, ¶11]

.103 Earnings per share data for income before extraordinary items and net income shall be presented on the face of the income statement, as prescribed by Section E09, "Earnings per Share." [APB30, ¶12]

.104 Gains or losses from extinguishment of debt that are classified as extraordinary items should be described sufficiently to enable users of financial statements to evaluate their significance. Accordingly, the following information, to the extent not shown separately on the face of the income statement, shall be disclosed in a single note to the financial statements or adequately cross-referenced if in more than one note:

a. A description of the extinguishment transactions, including the sources of any funds used to extinguish debt if it is practicable to identify the sources
b. The income tax effect in the period of extinguishment
c. The per share amount of the aggregate gain or loss net of related income tax effect.

[FAS4, ¶9]

.105 It has become customary for business enterprises to present historical, statistical-type summaries of financial data for a number of periods—commonly 5 or 10 years. The format for reporting extraordinary items described in paragraph .102 [is recommended] in such summaries. [APB9, ¶27]

Criteria for Extraordinary Items

.106 Judgment is required to segregate in the income statement the effects of events or transactions that are extraordinary items (as required by paragraph .102). An event or transaction shall be presumed to be an ordinary and usual activity of the reporting entity, the effects of which shall be included in income from operations, unless the evidence clearly supports its classification as an extraordinary item as defined in this section. [APB30, ¶19]

.107 Extraordinary items are events and transactions that are distinguished by their unusual nature *and* by the infrequency of their occurrence. Thus, *both* of the following criteria shall be met to classify an event or transaction as an extraordinary item:

a. *Unusual nature*—the underlying event or transaction possesses a high degree of abnormality and is of a type clearly unrelated to, or only incidentally related to, the ordinary and typical activities of the enterprise, taking into account the environment in which the enterprise operates (refer to paragraph .108).

b. *Infrequency of occurrence*—the underlying event or transaction is of a type that would not reasonably be expected to recur in the foreseeable future, taking into account the environment in which the enterprise operates (refer to paragraph .109).

[APB30, ¶20]

Unusual Nature

.108 The specific characteristics of the enterprise, such as type and scope of operations, lines of business, and operating policies, shall be considered in determining the enterprise's ordinary and typical activities. The environment in which an enterprise operates is a primary consideration in determining whether an underlying event or transaction is abnormal and significantly different from the ordinary and typical activities of the enterprise. The environment of an enterprise includes such factors as the characteristics of the industry or industries in which it operates, the geographical location of its operations, and the nature and extent of governmental regulation. Thus, an event or transaction may be unusual in nature for one enterprise but not for another because of differences in their respective environments. Unusual nature is not established by the fact that an event or transaction is beyond the control of management. [APB30, ¶21]

Infrequency of Occurrence

.109 For purposes of this section, an event or transaction of a type not reasonably expected to recur in the foreseeable future is considered to occur infrequently. Determining the probability of recurrence of a particular event or transaction in the foreseeable future shall take into account the environment in which an enterprise operates. Accordingly, a specific transaction of one enterprise might meet that criterion and a similar transaction of another enterprise might not because of different probabilities of recurrence. The past occurrence of an event or transaction for a particular enterprise provides evidence to assess the probability of recurrence of that type of event or transaction in the foreseeable future. By definition, extraordinary items occur infrequently. However, mere infrequency of occurrence of a particular event or transaction does not alone imply that its effects should be classified as extraordinary. An event or transaction of a type that

occurs frequently in the environment in which the enterprise operates cannot, by definition, be considered as extraordinary, regardless of its financial effect. [APB30, ¶22]

.110 Certain gains and losses shall not be reported as extraordinary items because they
are usual in nature or may be expected to recur as a consequence of customary and continuing business activities. Examples include:

a. Write-down or write-off of receivables,[2] inventories, equipment leased to others, or
   intangible assets
b. Gains or losses from exchange or translation of foreign currencies, including those
   relating to major devaluations and revaluations (refer to Section F60, "Foreign Currency Translation")
c. Gains or losses on disposal of a segment of a business (refer to Section I13)
d. Other gains or losses from sale or abandonment of property, plant, or equipment used
   in the business
e. Effects of a strike, including those against competitors and major suppliers
f. Adjustment of accruals on long-term contracts.

[APB30, ¶23]

.110A [Refer to paragraphs .503 through .510 for a discussion of additional examples
that should or should not be reported as extraordinary items.]

.111 In rare situations, an event or transaction may occur that clearly meets both criteria
specified in paragraph .107 and thus gives rise to an extraordinary gain or loss that includes one or more of the gains or losses enumerated above. In these circumstances,
gains or losses such as those described in subparagraphs .110(a) and .110(d) shall be
included in the extraordinary item if they are a direct result of a major casualty (such as
an earthquake), an expropriation, or a prohibition under a newly enacted law or regulation that clearly meets both criteria specified in paragraph .107. However, any portion of
such losses that would have resulted from a valuation of assets on a going concern basis
shall not be included in the extraordinary items. Disposals of a segment of a business
shall be accounted for and presented in the income statement pursuant to Section I13
even though the circumstances of the disposal meet the criteria specified in paragraph .107.[3] [APB30, ¶23]

---

[2]Refer to paragraphs .501 and .502 as to accounting for railroads' losses arising from charging off receivables from bankrupt railroads.]

[3]Refer to paragraphs .501 through .508 for further guidance in applying the criteria in paragraph .107.]

Exceptions to the Criteria for Extraordinary Items

.112 [Paragraphs .113 through .117A identify specific items that shall be reported as extraordinary items even though they do not meet the criteria set forth in paragraph .107.]

Extinguishment of Debt

.113 Gains and losses from extinguishment of debt that are included in the determination of net income shall be aggregated and, if material,[4] classified as an extraordinary item, net of related income tax effect. That conclusion shall apply whether an extinguishment is early or at scheduled maturity date or later. [FAS4, ¶8] The conclusion does not apply, however, to gains or losses from extinguishments of debt made to satisfy sinking-fund requirements that an enterprise must meet within one year of the date of the extinguishment.[5] [FAS64, ¶4] Those gains and losses shall be aggregated and the amount shall be identified as a separate item. [FAS4, ¶8]

Write-off of Operating Rights of Motor Carriers

.114 Unamortized costs of interstate operating rights subject to the provisions of the Motor Carrier Act of 1980 shall be charged to income and, if material, reported as an extraordinary item in accordance with paragraph .102. Subsequently, the cost of any other identifiable intangible asset or goodwill that is charged to income for reasons attributable to the Act shall not be reported as an extraordinary item. Tax benefits, if any, relating to the costs of interstate operating rights charged to income shall be reported in accordance with the provisions of [FAS44, ¶6] Section I27, "Income Taxes," [FAS109, ¶287] and paragraph .119 of this section. [FAS44, ¶6] In most cases, those sections would require tax benefits related to the charge to income of operating rights to be considered an adjustment of the extraordinary item. Therefore, in most cases any material recognized tax benefits should be included in motor carriers' financial statements as an extraordinary item whenever reported. [FAS44, ¶24]

.115 Other identifiable intangible assets and goodwill relating to motor carrier operations shall be accounted for in accordance with Section I60, "Intangible Assets." How-

---

[4]Refer to the first sentence of paragraph .118. [FAS4, ¶8, fn1]

[5]Some obligations to acquire debt have the essential characteristics of sinking-fund requirements, and resulting gains or losses are not required to be classified as extraordinary items if the obligations must be met within one year of the date of the extinguishment. [FAS64, ¶4] For example, if an enterprise is required each year to purchase a certain percentage of its outstanding bonds before their scheduled maturity, the gain or loss from such purchase is not required to be classified as an extraordinary item. Debt maturing serially, however, does not have the characteristics of sinking-fund requirements, and gain or loss from extinguishment of serial debt shall be classified as an extraordinary item. [FAS4, ¶8, fn2]

ever, the cost of intrastate operating rights shall be accounted for in accordance with the provisions of this section if a state deregulates motor carriers with effects similar to those of the Act. [FAS44, ¶7]

.116 [Deleted 2/92 because of FASB Statement 109, *Accounting for Income Taxes.*]

Significant Asset Disposition after a Pooling

.117 A combined enterprise shall disclose separately a profit or loss resulting from the disposal of a significant part of the assets or a separable segment of the previously separate enterprises, provided (a) the profit or loss is material in relation to the net income of the combined enterprise, (b) the disposition is within two years after the combination is consummated, [and (c) the combination was accounted for as a pooling of interests]. The disclosed profit or loss, less applicable income tax effect, shall be classified as an extraordinary item. [APB16, ¶60]

Discontinuation of Accounting for the Effects of Certain Types of Regulation

.117A When an enterprise discontinues application of [the specialized accounting for the effects of certain types of regulation as described in] Section Re6, "Regulated Operations," to all or part of its operations, that enterprise shall eliminate from its statement of financial position prepared for general-purpose external financial reporting the effects of any actions of regulators that had been recognized as assets and liabilities pursuant to Section Re6 but would not have been recognized as assets and liabilities by enterprises in general. However, the carrying amounts of plant, equipment, and inventory measured and reported pursuant to Section Re6 shall not be adjusted unless those assets are impaired, in which case the carrying amounts of those assets shall be reduced to reflect that impairment. Whether those assets have been impaired shall be judged in the same manner as for enterprises in general [FAS101, ¶6] and paragraphs .122 through .138 of Section I08, "Impairment," shall apply, except for the provisions for income statement reporting in paragraph .132 of that section. [FAS121, ¶33] The net effect of the adjustments required by this paragraph shall be included in income of the period in which the discontinuation occurs and shall be classified as an extraordinary item. [FAS101, ¶6] [For further guidance, refer to Section Re6, paragraphs .204 through .216.]

Materiality

.118 The effect of an extraordinary event or transaction shall be classified separately in the income statement in the manner described in paragraph .102 if it is material in relation to income before extraordinary items or to the trend of annual earnings before extraordinary items, or is material by other appropriate criteria. Items shall be considered individually and not in the aggregate in determining whether an extraordinary event or transaction is material. However, the effects of a series of related transactions arising from a single specific and identifiable event or plan of action that otherwise meets the two criteria in paragraph .107 shall be aggregated to determine materiality. [APB30, ¶24]

Adjustment of Amounts Reported in Prior Periods

.119 Circumstances attendant to extraordinary items frequently require estimates, for example, of associated costs and occasionally of associated revenue, based on judgment and evaluation of the facts known at the time of first accounting for the event. [APB30, ¶25] Each adjustment in the current period of an element of an extraordinary item that was reported in a prior period shall be separately disclosed as to year of origin, nature, and amount and classified separately in the current period [as an extraordinary item]. [FAS16, ¶16(c)] If the adjustment is the correction of an error, the provisions of Section A35, "Adjustments of Financial Statements for Prior Periods," paragraphs .103(a) and .105, shall be applied. [APB30, ¶25]

Glossary

.401 **Extraordinary items.** Events and transactions that are distinguished by their unusual nature *and* by the infrequency of their occurrence. Thus, *both* of the following criteria shall be met to classify an event or transaction as an extraordinary item:

a. *Unusual nature*—the underlying event or transaction possesses a high degree of abnormality and is of a type clearly unrelated to, or only incidentally related to, the ordinary and typical activities of the enterprise, taking into account the environment in which the enterprise operates.

b. *Infrequency of occurrence*—the underlying event or transaction is of a type that would not reasonably be expected to recur in the foreseeable future, taking into account the environment in which the enterprise operates.

[APB30, ¶20]

Supplemental Guidance

Losses Caused by Bankruptcies

.501 *Question*—Recent [1970] railroad bankruptcies raise the question of whether enterprises holding receivables from those railroads should account for losses arising from charging off such assets as ordinary losses or as extraordinary losses in determining net income. The Interstate Commerce Commission has ruled that railroads must write off certain past due payments from other railroads (for example, interline receivables) as extraordinary losses. Is this accounting treatment appropriate in the annual reports to railroads' shareholders and in the annual reports to shareholders of other (nonrailroad) enterprises? [AIN-APB9, #1]

.502 *Interpretation*—No, paragraph .110(a) specifies that, regardless of size, losses from receivables do *not* constitute extraordinary losses. The fact that the loss arises from a receivable from an enterprise in bankruptcy proceedings does not alter this answer in any way. Regulatory authorities often rule on the accounting treatment to be applied by enterprises under their jurisdiction. The above question is covered by [Section Re6, paragraph .114.] [AIN-APB9, #1]

Criteria for Extraordinary Items

.503 *Question*—As stated in paragraph .106, judgment is required to segregate in the income statement the effects of events or transactions that are extraordinary items. What factors must be considered in determining whether the effects of a particular event or transaction are extraordinary items or should otherwise be set forth in the income statement, and how are these factors applied in practice? [AIN-APB30, #1]

.504 *Interpretation*—The first question that generally should be considered in determining the appropriate classification of profit or loss items that appear to be unusual, infrequently occurring or extraordinary is: Does the event or transaction involve the sale, abandonment, or other manner of disposal of a segment of a business as defined in Section I13? If it has been determined that the particular event or transaction is not a disposal of a segment of a business, then the criteria for extraordinary items classification should be considered, that is, does the event or transaction meet both criteria of *unusual nature* and *infrequency of occurrence*. [AIN-APB30, #1]

.505 Events or transactions that would meet both criteria in the circumstances described are:

a. A large portion of a tobacco manufacturer's crops are destroyed by a hail storm. Severe damage from hail storms in the locality where the manufacturer grows tobacco is rare.

b. A steel fabricating enterprise sells the only land it owns. The land was acquired 10 years ago for future expansion, but shortly thereafter the enterprise abandoned all plans for expansion and held the land for appreciation.

c. An enterprise sells a block of common stock of a publicly traded enterprise. The block of shares, that represents less than 10 percent of the publicly held enterprise, is the only security investment the enterprise has ever owned.

d. An earthquake destroys one of the oil refineries owned by a large multinational oil enterprise.

[AIN-APB30, #1]

.506 The following illustrate events or transactions that do not meet both criteria in the circumstances described and thus should not be reported as extraordinary items:

a. A citrus grower's Florida crop is damaged by frost. Frost damage is normally experienced every three or four years. The criterion of infrequency of occurrence taking into account the environment in which the enterprise operates would not be met since the history of losses caused by frost damage provides evidence that such damage may reasonably be expected to recur in the foreseeable future.

b. An enterprise that operates a chain of warehouses sells the excess land surrounding one of its warehouses. When the enterprise buys property to establish a new warehouse, it usually buys more land than it expects to use for the warehouse with the expectation that the land will appreciate in value. In the past five years, there have been two instances in which the enterprise sold such excess land. The criterion of infrequency of occurrence has not been met since past experience indicates that such sales may reasonably be expected to recur in the foreseeable future.

c. A large diversified enterprise sells a block of shares from its portfolio of securities that it has acquired for investment purposes. This is the first sale from its portfolio of securities. Since the enterprise owns several securities for investment purposes, it should be concluded that sales of such securities are related to its ordinary and typical activities in the environment in which it operates and thus the criterion of unusual nature would not be met.

d. A textile manufacturer with only one plant moves to another location. It has not relocated a plant in 20 years and has no plans to do so in the foreseeable future. Notwithstanding the infrequency of occurrence of the event as it relates to this particular enterprise, moving from one location to another is an occurrence that is a consequence of customary and continuing business activities, some of which are finding more favorable labor markets, more modern facilities, and proximity to customers or suppliers. Therefore, the criterion of unusual nature has not been met and the moving expenses (and related gains and losses) should not be reported as an extraordinary item. Another example of an event that is a consequence of customary and typical business activities (namely financing) is an unsuccessful public registration, the cost of which should not be reported as an extraordinary item. (For additional examples refer to paragraph .110.)

[AIN-APB30, #1]

.507 Disposals of part of a line of business, such as the examples discussed in Section I13, paragraph .504, should not be classified as extraordinary items. As discussed in Section I13, footnote 2 to paragraph .101, such disposals are incident to the evolution of the enterprise's business and therefore the criterion of unusual nature would not be met. [AIN-APB30, #1]

.508 The foregoing examples are illustrative. It should be recognized that all attendant circumstances, which can vary from those above, need to be considered in making the judgments required by this section. [AIN-APB30, #1]

Costs Incurred in Defending against a Takeover Attempt

.509 *Question*—Should the costs incurred by an enterprise to defend itself from a takeover attempt or the cost attributed to a "standstill" agreement be classified as extraordinary items? [FTB85-6, ¶6]

.510 *Response*—No. Neither the costs incurred by an enterprise to defend itself from a takeover attempt nor the costs incurred as part of a "standstill" agreement meet the criteria for extraordinary classification as discussed in paragraph .107. The *event* that gave rise to those costs—a takeover attempt—cannot be considered to be both *unusual* and *infrequent* as those terms are used in this section. [FTB85-6, ¶7]

(The next page is 24667.)

Source: APB Opinion 30

Summary

An event or transaction that is either unusual in nature or occurs infrequently, but not both, shall be classified and reported as a separate component of income from continuing operations.

.101 A material event or transaction that is unusual in nature or occurs infrequently, but not both, and therefore does not meet both criteria for classification as an extraordinary item (refer to Section I17, "Income Statement Presentation: Extraordinary Items") shall be reported as a separate component of income from continuing operations. The nature and financial effects of each event or transaction shall be disclosed on the face of the income statement or, alternatively, in notes to the financial statements. Gains or losses of a similar nature that are not individually material shall be aggregated. Such items shall not be reported on the face of the income statement net of income taxes or in any manner inconsistent with the provisions of Section I13, "Income Statement Presentation: Discontinued Operations," or Section I17, or in any other manner that may imply that they are extraordinary items. Similarly, the earnings per share effects of those items shall not be disclosed on the face of the income statement.[1] [APB30, ¶26]

---

[1][Deleted as of 12/87 because of FASB Statement 97, *Accounting and Reporting by Insurance Enterprises for Certain Long-Duration Contracts and for Realized Gains and Losses from the Sale of Investments.*]

Supplemental Guidance

.501-.502 [Deleted 3/95 because of FASB Statement 121, *Accounting for the Impairment of Long-Lived Assets and for Long-Lived Assets to Be Disposed Of.*]

(The next page is 25331.)

Sources: APB Opinion 2; APB Opinion 4; APB Opinion 10;
         APB Opinion 23; AICPA Interpretations of APB Opinion 4;
         FASB Statement 37; FASB Statement 60; FASB Statement 95;
         FASB Statement 109; FASB Statement 115; FASB Technical Bulletin 82-1

Summary

This section presents financial accounting and reporting standards for the effects of income taxes that result from an enterprise's activities during the current and preceding years. An asset and liability approach is used in accounting for income taxes.

The objectives of accounting for income taxes are to recognize (a) the amount of taxes payable or refundable for the current year and (b) deferred tax liabilities and assets for the future tax consequences of events that have been recognized in an enterprise's financial statements or tax returns.

The following basic principles are applied in accounting for income taxes at the date of the financial statements:

a. A current tax liability or asset is recognized for the estimated taxes payable or refundable on tax returns for the current year.
b. A deferred tax liability or asset is recognized for the estimated future tax effects attributable to temporary differences and carryforwards.
c. The measurement of current and deferred tax liabilities and assets is based on provisions of the enacted tax law; the effects of future changes in tax laws or rates are not anticipated.
d. The measurement of deferred tax assets is reduced, if necessary, by the amount of any tax benefits that, based on available evidence, are not expected to be realized.

The tax consequences of most events recognized in the financial statements for a year are included in determining income taxes currently payable. However, tax laws often differ from the recognition and measurement requirements of financial accounting standards, and differences can arise between (a) the amount of taxable income and pretax financial income for a year and (b) the tax bases of assets or liabilities and their reported amounts in financial statements. All such differences collectively are referred to as *temporary differences* in this section.

Temporary differences ordinarily become taxable or deductible when the related asset is recovered or the related liability is settled. A deferred tax liability or asset represents the increase or decrease in taxes payable or refundable in future years as a result of temporary differences and carryforwards at the end of the current year.

A deferred tax liability is recognized for temporary differences that will result in taxable amounts in future years. For example, a temporary difference is created between the reported amount and the tax basis of an installment sale receivable if, for tax purposes, some or all of the gain on the installment sale will be included in the determination of taxable income in future years. Because amounts received upon recovery of that receivable will be taxable, a deferred tax liability is recognized in the current year for the related taxes payable in future years.

A deferred tax asset is recognized for temporary differences that will result in deductible amounts in future years and for carryforwards. For example, a temporary difference is created between the reported amount and the tax basis of a liability for estimated expenses if, for tax purposes, those estimated expenses are not deductible until a future year. Settlement of that liability will result in tax deductions in future years, and a deferred tax asset is recognized in the current year for the reduction in taxes payable in future years. A valuation allowance is recognized if, based on the weight of available evidence, it is *more likely than not* that some portion or all of the deferred tax asset will not be realized.

This section presents procedures to (a) measure deferred tax liabilities and assets using a tax rate convention and (b) assess whether a valuation allowance should be established for deferred tax assets. Enacted tax laws and rates are considered in determining the applicable tax rate and in assessing the need for a valuation allowance.

All available evidence, both positive and negative, is considered to determine whether, based on the weight of that evidence, a valuation allowance is needed for some portion or all of a deferred tax asset. Judgment must be used in considering the relative impact of negative and positive evidence. The weight given to the potential effect of negative and positive evidence should be commensurate with the extent to which it can be objectively verified. The more negative evidence that exists (a) the more positive evidence is necessary and (b) the more difficult it is to support a conclusion that a valuation allowance is not needed.

Deferred tax liabilities and assets are adjusted in the period of enactment for the effect of an enacted change in tax laws or rates. The effect is included in income from continuing operations.

This section also addresses the appropriate tax accounting treatment for the following areas:

a. Undistributed earnings of subsidiaries
b. Investments in corporate joint ventures

    c. Bad-debt reserves of savings and loan associations
    d. Policyholders' surplus of stock life insurance enterprises
    e. Investment tax credits
    f. Offsetting securities against taxes payable.

[**Note:** The reader should be aware that any references to income tax rules and regulations in this section are as they appear in the original pronouncement. No effect has been given to subsequent legislation, if any.]

Introduction

.101 This section addresses financial accounting and reporting for the effects of **income taxes** that result from an enterprise's activities during the current and preceding years. [FAS109, ¶1]

Scope

.102 This section [presents] standards of financial accounting and reporting for income taxes that are currently payable and for the tax consequences of:

a. Revenues, expenses, gains, or losses that are included in **taxable income** of an earlier or later year than the year in which they are recognized in financial income
b. Other **events** that create differences between the tax bases of assets and liabilities and their amounts for financial reporting
c. Operating loss or tax credit **carrybacks** for refunds of taxes paid in prior years and **carryforwards** to reduce taxes payable in future years. [FAS109, ¶3]

.103 The principles and requirements of this section are applicable to:

a. Domestic federal (national) income taxes (U.S. federal income taxes for U.S. enterprises) and foreign, state, and local (including franchise) taxes based on income
b. An enterprise's[1] domestic and foreign operations that are consolidated, combined, or accounted for by the equity method
c. Foreign enterprises in preparing financial statements in accordance with U.S. generally accepted accounting principles. [FAS109, ¶4]

---

[1]The term *enterprise* is used throughout this section because accounting for income taxes is primarily an issue for business enterprises. However, the requirements of this section apply to the activities of a not-for-profit organization that are subject to income taxes. [FAS109, ¶4, fn2]

.104 This section does not address accounting for income taxes in interim periods (other than the criteria for recognition of tax benefits and the effect of enacted changes in tax laws or rates and changes in valuation allowances). (Section I73, "Interim Financial Reporting," addresses that subject.) [FAS109, ¶5]

Objectives and Basic Principles

.105 One objective of accounting for income taxes is to recognize the amount of taxes payable or refundable for the current year. A second objective is to recognize **deferred tax liabilities and assets** for the future **tax consequences** of events[2] that have been recognized in an enterprise's financial statements or tax returns. [FAS109, ¶6]

.106 Ideally, the second objective might be stated more specifically to recognize the *expected* future tax consequences of events that have been recognized in the financial statements or tax returns. However, that objective is realistically constrained because (a) the tax payment or refund that results from a particular tax return is a joint result of all the items included in that return, (b) taxes that will be paid or refunded in future years are the joint result of events of the current or prior years and events of future years, and (c) information available about the future is limited. As a result, attribution of taxes to individual items and events is arbitrary and, except in the simplest situations, requires estimates and approximations. [FAS109, ¶7]

.107 To implement the objectives in light of those constraints, the following basic principles (the only exceptions are identified in paragraph .108) are applied in accounting for income taxes at the date of the financial statements:

a. A current tax liability or asset is recognized for the estimated taxes payable or refundable on tax returns for the current year.
b. A deferred tax liability or asset is recognized for the estimated future tax effects attributable to **temporary differences** and carryforwards.
c. The measurement of current and deferred tax liabilities and assets is based on provisions of the enacted tax law; the effects of future changes in tax laws or rates are not anticipated.
d. The measurement of deferred tax assets is reduced, if necessary, by the amount of any tax benefits that, based on available evidence, are not expected to be realized. [FAS109, ¶8]

.108 The only exceptions in applying those basic principles are:

a. The requirements for recognition of deferred taxes for the areas addressed in paragraphs .212 through .224

---

[2]Some events do not have tax consequences. Certain revenues are exempt from taxation and certain expenses are not deductible. In the United States, for example, interest earned on certain municipal obligations is not taxable and fines are not deductible. [FAS109, ¶6, fn3]

b. Special transitional procedures for temporary differences related to deposits in statutory reserve funds by U.S. steamship enterprises (refer to paragraph .131)
c. [The] accounting for leveraged leases, [including leveraged leases acquired in a purchase business combination], as required by Section L10, "Leases," (refer to paragraphs .183 through .185)
d. [The prohibition from recognizing] a deferred tax liability or asset related to goodwill (or the portion thereof) for which amortization is not deductible for tax purposes (refer to paragraph .129)
e. [The accounting] for income taxes paid on intercompany profits on assets remaining within the group, [as required by Section C51, "Consolidation,"] and [the prohibition from recognizing] a deferred tax asset for the difference between the tax basis of the assets in the buyer's tax jurisdiction and their cost as reported in the consolidated financial statements
f. [The prohibition from recognizing] a deferred tax liability or asset for differences related to assets and liabilities that, under [the provisions of] Section F60, "Foreign Currency Translation," are remeasured from the local currency into the functional currency using historical exchange rates and that result from (1) changes in exchange rates or (2) indexing for tax purposes. [FAS109, ¶9]

Temporary Differences

.109 **Income taxes currently payable**[3] for a particular year usually include the tax consequences of most events that are recognized in the financial statements for that year. However, because tax laws and financial accounting standards differ in their recognition and measurement of assets, liabilities, equity, revenues, expenses, gains, and losses, differences arise between:

a. The amount of taxable income and pretax financial income for a year
b. The tax bases of assets or liabilities and their reported amounts in financial statements. [FAS109, ¶10]

.110 An assumption inherent in an enterprise's statement of financial position prepared in accordance with generally accepted accounting principles is that the reported amounts of assets and liabilities will be recovered and settled, respectively. Based on that assumption, a difference between the tax basis of an asset or a liability and its reported amount in the statement of financial position will result in taxable or deductible amounts in some future year(s) when the reported amounts of assets are recovered and the reported amounts of liabilities are settled. Examples follow:

a. *Revenues or gains that are taxable after they are recognized in financial income.* An asset (for example, a receivable from an installment sale) may be recognized for revenues or gains that will result in future taxable amounts when the asset is recovered.

---

[3]References in this section to income taxes currently payable and (total) **income tax expense** are intended to include also **income taxes currently refundable** and (total) **income tax benefit,** respectively. [FAS109, ¶10, fn4]

b. *Expenses or losses that are deductible after they are recognized in financial income.* A liability (for example, a product warranty liability) may be recognized for expenses or losses that will result in future tax deductible amounts when the liability is settled.

c. *Revenues or gains that are taxable before they are recognized in financial income.* A liability (for example, subscriptions received in advance) may be recognized for an advance payment for goods or services to be provided in future years. For tax purposes, the advance payment is included in taxable income upon the receipt of cash. Future sacrifices to provide goods or services (or future refunds to those who cancel their orders) will result in future tax deductible amounts when the liability is settled.

d. *Expenses or losses that are deductible before they are recognized in financial income.* The cost of an asset (for example, depreciable personal property) may have been deducted for tax purposes faster than it was depreciated for financial reporting. Amounts received upon future recovery of the amount of the asset for financial reporting will exceed the remaining tax basis of the asset, and the excess will be taxable when the asset is recovered.

e. *A reduction in the tax basis of depreciable assets because of tax credits.*[4] Amounts received upon future recovery of the amount of the asset for financial reporting will exceed the remaining tax basis of the asset, and the excess will be taxable when the asset is recovered.

f. *Investment tax credit (ITC) accounted for by the deferral method.* In paragraph .228, ITC is viewed and accounted for as a reduction of the cost of the related asset (even though, for financial statement presentation, deferred ITC may be reported as deferred income). Amounts received upon future recovery of the reduced cost of the asset for financial reporting will be less than the tax basis of the asset, and the difference will be tax deductible when the asset is recovered.

g. *An increase in the tax basis of assets because of indexing whenever the local currency is the functional currency.* The tax law for a particular tax jurisdiction might require adjustment of the tax basis of a depreciable (or other) asset for the effects of inflation. The inflation-adjusted tax basis of the asset would be used to compute future tax deductions for depreciation or to compute gain or loss on sale of the asset. Amounts received upon future recovery of the local currency historical cost of the asset will be less than the remaining tax basis of the asset, and the difference will be tax deductible when the asset is recovered.

h. *Business combinations accounted for by the purchase method.* There may be differences between the assigned values and the tax bases of the assets and liabilities recognized in a business combination accounted for as a purchase under Section B50, "Business Combinations." Those differences will result in taxable or deductible amounts when the reported amounts of the assets and liabilities are recovered and settled, respectively. [FAS109, ¶11]

---

[4]The Tax Equity and Fiscal Responsibility Act of 1982 provided taxpayers with the choice of either (a) taking the full amount of Accelerated Cost Recovery System (ACRS) deductions and a reduced tax credit (that is, investment tax credit and certain other tax credits) or (b) taking the full tax credit and a reduced amount of ACRS deductions. [FAS109, ¶11, fn5]

.111 Examples (a) through (d) in paragraph .110 illustrate revenues, expenses, gains, or losses that are included in taxable income of an earlier or later year than the year in which they are recognized in pretax financial income. Those differences between taxable income and pretax financial income also create differences (sometimes accumulating over more than one year) between the tax basis of an asset or liability and its reported amount in the financial statements. Examples (e) through (h) in paragraph .110 illustrate other events that create differences between the tax basis of an asset or liability and its reported amount in the financial statements. For all eight examples, the differences result in taxable or deductible amounts when the reported amount of an asset or liability in the financial statements is recovered or settled, respectively. [FAS109, ¶12]

.112 This section refers collectively to the types of differences illustrated by those eight examples and to the ones described in paragraph .114 as *temporary differences.* Temporary differences that will result in taxable amounts in future years when the related asset or liability is recovered or settled are often referred to in this section as **taxable temporary differences** (examples (a), (d), and (e) in paragraph .110 are taxable temporary differences). Likewise, temporary differences that will result in deductible amounts in future years are often referred to as **deductible temporary differences** (examples (b), (c), (f), and (g) in paragraph .110 are deductible temporary differences). Business combinations accounted for by the purchase method (example (h)) may give rise to both taxable and deductible temporary differences. [FAS109, ¶13]

.113 Certain basis differences may not result in taxable or deductible amounts in future years when the related asset or liability for financial reporting is recovered or settled and, therefore, may not be temporary differences for which a deferred tax liability or asset is recognized. One example under current U.S. tax law is the excess of cash surrender value of life insurance over premiums paid. That excess is a temporary difference if the cash surrender value is expected to be recovered by surrendering the policy, but is not a temporary difference if the asset is expected to be recovered without tax consequence upon the death of the insured (there will be no taxable amount if the insurance policy is held until the death of the insured). [FAS109, ¶14]

.114 Some temporary differences are deferred taxable income or tax deductions and have balances only on the income tax balance sheet and therefore cannot be identified with a particular asset or liability for financial reporting. That occurs, for example, if a long-term contract is accounted for by the percentage-of-completion method for financial reporting and by the completed-contract method for tax purposes. The temporary difference (income on the contract) is deferred income for tax purposes that becomes taxable when the contract is completed. Another example is organizational costs that are recognized as expenses when incurred for financial reporting and are deferred and deducted in a later year for tax purposes. In both instances, there is no related, identifiable asset or liability for financial reporting, but there is a temporary difference that results from an event that has been recognized in the financial statements and, based on provisions in the tax law, the temporary difference will result in taxable or deductible amounts in future years. [FAS109, ¶15]

Recognition and Measurement

.115 An enterprise shall recognize a deferred tax liability or asset for all temporary differences[5] and operating loss and tax credit carryforwards in accordance with the provisions of paragraph .116. [FAS109, ¶16] [The deferred tax liability or asset] shall not be accounted for on a discounted basis. [APB10, ¶6] **Deferred tax expense or benefit** is the change during the year in an enterprise's deferred tax liabilities and assets.[6] For deferred tax liabilities and assets acquired in a purchase business combination during the year, it is the change since the combination date. Total income tax expense or benefit for the year is the sum of deferred tax expense or benefit and income taxes currently payable or refundable. [FAS109, ¶16]

Annual Computation of Deferred Tax Liabilities and Assets

.116 Deferred taxes shall be determined separately for each tax-paying component (an individual entity or group of entities that is consolidated for tax purposes) in each tax jurisdiction. That determination includes the following procedures:

a. Identify (1) the types and amounts of existing temporary differences and (2) the nature and amount of each type of operating loss and tax credit carryforward and the remaining length of the carryforward period
b. Measure the total deferred tax liability for taxable temporary differences using the applicable tax rate (refer to paragraph .117)
c. Measure the total deferred tax asset for deductible temporary differences and operating loss carryforwards using the applicable tax rate
d. Measure deferred tax assets for each type of tax credit carryforward
e. Reduce deferred tax assets by a **valuation allowance** if, based on the weight of available evidence, it is *more likely than not* (a likelihood of more than 50 percent) that some portion or all of the deferred tax assets will not be realized. The valuation allowance shall be sufficient to reduce the deferred tax asset to the amount that is more likely than not to be realized. [FAS109, ¶17]

.117 The objective is to measure a deferred tax liability or asset using the enacted tax rate(s) expected to apply to taxable income in the periods in which the deferred tax liability or asset is expected to be settled or realized. Under current U.S. federal tax law, if taxable income exceeds a specified amount, all taxable income is taxed, in substance, at

---

[5] Refer to paragraph .108. A deferred tax liability shall be recognized for the temporary differences addressed by paragraphs .212 through .224 in accordance with the requirements of paragraphs .130 through .133. [FAS109, ¶16, fn6]

[6] Paragraph .156 addresses the manner of reporting the transaction gain or loss that is included in the net change in a deferred foreign tax liability or asset if the reporting currency is the functional currency. [FAS109, ¶16, fn7]

a single flat tax rate. That tax rate shall be used for measurement of a deferred tax liability or asset by enterprises for which graduated tax rates are not a significant factor. Enterprises for which graduated tax rates are a significant factor shall measure a deferred tax liability or asset using the average graduated tax rate applicable to the amount of estimated annual taxable income in the periods in which the deferred tax liability or asset is estimated to be settled or realized (refer to paragraph .163). Other provisions of enacted tax laws should be considered when determining the tax rate to apply to certain types of temporary differences and carryforwards (for example, the tax law may provide for different tax rates on ordinary income and capital gains). If there is a phased-in change in tax rates, determination of the applicable tax rate requires knowledge about when deferred tax liabilities and assets will be settled and realized. [FAS109, ¶18]

.118 In the U.S. federal tax jurisdiction, the applicable tax rate is the regular tax rate, and a deferred tax asset is recognized for alternative minimum tax credit carryforwards in accordance with the provisions of paragraph .116(d) and (e) of this section. If alternative tax systems exist in jurisdictions other than the U.S. federal jurisdiction, the applicable tax rate is determined in a manner consistent with the tax law after giving consideration to any interaction (that is, a mechanism similar to the U.S. alternative minimum tax credit) between the two systems. [FAS109, ¶19]

.119 All available evidence, both positive and negative, shall be considered to determine whether, based on the weight of that evidence, a valuation allowance is needed. Information about an enterprise's current financial position and its results of operations for the current and preceding years ordinarily is readily available. That historical information is supplemented by all currently available information about future years. Sometimes, however, historical information may not be available (for example, start-up operations) or it may not be as relevant (for example, if there has been a significant, recent change in circumstances) and special attention is required. [FAS109, ¶20]

.120 Future realization of the tax benefit of an existing deductible temporary difference or carryforward ultimately depends on the existence of sufficient taxable income of the appropriate character (for example, ordinary income or capital gain) within the carryback, carryforward period available under the tax law. The following four possible sources of taxable income may be available under the tax law to realize a tax benefit for deductible temporary differences and carryforwards:

a. Future reversals of existing taxable temporary differences
b. Future taxable income exclusive of reversing temporary differences and carryforwards
c. Taxable income in prior carryback year(s) if carryback is permitted under the tax law
d. **Tax-planning strategies** (refer to paragraph .121) that would, if necessary, be implemented to, for example:
    (1) Accelerate taxable amounts to utilize expiring carryforwards
    (2) Change the character of taxable or deductible amounts from ordinary income or loss to capital gain or loss
    (3) Switch from tax-exempt to taxable investments.

Evidence available about each of those possible sources of taxable income will vary for different tax jurisdictions and, possibly, from year to year. To the extent evidence about one or more sources of taxable income is sufficient to support a conclusion that a valuation allowance is not necessary, other sources need not be considered. Consideration of each source is required, however, to determine the amount of the valuation allowance that is recognized for deferred tax assets. [FAS109, ¶21]

.121 In some circumstances, there are actions (including elections for tax purposes) that (a) are prudent and feasible, (b) an enterprise ordinarily might not take, but would take to prevent an operating loss or tax credit carryforward from expiring unused, and (c) would result in realization of deferred tax assets. This section refers to those actions as *tax-planning strategies*.[7] An enterprise shall consider tax-planning strategies[8] in determining the amount of valuation allowance required. Significant expenses to implement a tax-planning strategy or any significant losses that would be recognized if that strategy were implemented (net of any recognizable tax benefits associated with those expenses or losses) shall be included in the valuation allowance. Refer to paragraphs .173 through .178 for additional guidance. [FAS109, ¶22]

.122 Forming a conclusion that a valuation allowance is not needed is difficult if there is negative evidence such as cumulative losses in recent years. Other examples of negative evidence include (but are not limited to) the following:

a. A history of operating loss or tax credit carryforwards expiring unused
b. Losses expected in early future years (by a presently profitable entity)
c. Unsettled circumstances that, if unfavorably resolved, would adversely affect future operations and profit levels on a continuing basis in future years
d. A carryback, carryforward period that is so brief that it would limit realization of tax benefits if (1) a significant deductible temporary difference is expected to reverse in a single year or (2) the enterprise operates in a traditionally cyclical business. [FAS109, ¶23]

.123 Examples (not prerequisites) of positive evidence that might support a conclusion that a valuation allowance is not needed if there is negative evidence include (but are not limited to) the following:

a. Existing contracts or firm sales backlog that will produce more than enough taxable income to realize the deferred tax asset based on existing sales prices and cost structures

---

[7]Implementation of the tax-planning strategies must be primarily within the control of management but need not be within the unilateral control of management. [FAS109, ¶107]

[8]Under this section, the requirements for consideration of tax-planning strategies pertain only to the determination of a valuation allowance for a deferred tax asset. A deferred tax liability ordinarily is recognized for all taxable temporary differences. [FAS109, ¶251]

b. An excess of appreciated asset value over the tax basis of the entity's net assets in an amount sufficient to realize the deferred tax asset

c. A strong earnings history exclusive of the loss that created the future deductible amount (tax loss carryforward or deductible temporary difference) coupled with evidence indicating that the loss (for example, an unusual, infrequent, or extraordinary item) is an aberration rather than a continuing condition. [FAS109, ¶24]

.124 An enterprise must use judgment in considering the relative impact of negative and positive evidence. The weight given to the potential effect of negative and positive evidence shall be commensurate with the extent to which it can be objectively verified. The more negative evidence that exists (a) the more positive evidence is necessary and (b) the more difficult it is to support a conclusion that a valuation allowance is not needed for some portion or all of the deferred tax asset.[9] [FAS109, ¶25]

A Change in the Valuation Allowance

.125 The effect of a change in the beginning-of-the-year balance of a valuation allowance that results from a change in circumstances that causes a change in judgment about the realizability of the related deferred tax asset in future years ordinarily shall be included in income from continuing operations. The only exceptions are the initial recognition (that is, by elimination of the valuation allowance) of certain tax benefits that are allocated as required by paragraph .129 and paragraph .135 (items (c) and (e) through (g)). The effect of other changes in the balance of a valuation allowance are allocated among continuing operations and items other than continuing operations as required by paragraph .134. [FAS109, ¶26]

An Enacted Change in Tax Laws or Rates

.126 Deferred tax liabilities and assets shall be adjusted for the effect of a change in tax laws or rates. The effect shall be included in income from continuing operations for the period that includes the enactment date. [FAS109, ¶27]

A Change in the Tax Status of an Enterprise

.127 An enterprise's tax status may change from nontaxable to taxable or from taxable to nontaxable. An example is a change from a partnership to a corporation and vice versa. A deferred tax liability or asset[10] shall be recognized for temporary differences in accordance with the requirements of this section at the date that a nontaxable

---

[9]Future realization of a tax benefit sometimes will be expected for a portion but not all of a deferred tax asset, and the dividing line between the two portions may be unclear. In those circumstances, application of judgment based on a careful assessment of all available evidence is required to determine the portion of a deferred tax asset for which it is more likely than not a tax benefit will not be realized. [FAS109, ¶98]

[10There are] tax jurisdictions that have [various types of] tax holidays. [FAS109, ¶183] Recognition of a deferred tax asset for *any* tax holiday [is prohibited.] [FAS109, ¶184]

enterprise becomes a taxable enterprise. A deferred tax liability or asset shall be eliminated at the date an enterprise ceases to be a taxable enterprise. In either case, the effect of (a) an election for a voluntary change in tax status is recognized on the approval
date or on the filing date if approval is not necessary and (b) a change in tax status that
results from a change in tax law is recognized on the enactment date. The effect of
recognizing or eliminating the deferred tax liability or asset shall be included in income
from continuing operations. [FAS109, ¶28]

Regulated Enterprises

.128 Regulated enterprises that meet the criteria for application of Section Re6,
"Regulated Operations," are not exempt from the requirements of this section. Specifically, this section:

a. Prohibits net-of-tax accounting and reporting
b. Requires recognition of a deferred tax liability (1) for tax benefits that are flowed
   through to customers when temporary differences originate and (2) for the equity
   component of the allowance for funds used during construction
c. Requires adjustment of a deferred tax liability or asset for an enacted change in tax
   laws or rates.

If, as a result of an action by a regulator, it is probable that the future increase or decrease in taxes payable for items (b) and (c) above will be recovered from or returned to
customers through future rates, an asset or liability is recognized for that probable future revenue or reduction in future revenue pursuant to paragraphs .119 through .121 of
Section Re6. That asset or liability also is a temporary difference for which a deferred
tax liability or asset shall be recognized. [FAS109, ¶29]

Business Combinations

.129 A deferred tax liability or asset shall be recognized[11] in accordance with the requirements of this section for differences between the assigned values and the tax bases of the assets and liabilities (except the portion of goodwill for which amortization
is not deductible for tax purposes, unallocated "negative goodwill," leveraged leases,

---

[11]Discounting deferred tax assets or liabilities shall be prohibited for temporary differences (except for
leveraged leases) related to business combinations as it is for other temporary differences. [FAS109, ¶130]
An acquired enterprise's deductible temporary differences and carryforwards are not included in measuring a purchase transaction if the criteria for recognition of tax benefits are not met. Retroactive restatement of the purchase transaction and results of operations for intervening years [is not permitted] if the
criteria for recognition of tax benefits are met in subsequent periods. [FAS109, ¶136]

and acquired differences under paragraphs .212 through .224[12]) recognized in a purchase business combination (refer to paragraphs .186 through .199 for additional guidance). If a valuation allowance is recognized for the deferred tax asset for an acquired entity's deductible temporary differences or operating loss or tax credit carryforwards at the acquisition date, the tax benefits for those items that are first recognized (that is, by elimination of that valuation allowance) in financial statements after the acquisition date shall be applied (a) first to reduce to zero any goodwill related to the acquisition, (b) second to reduce to zero other noncurrent intangible assets related to the acquisition, and (c) third to reduce income tax expense. [FAS109, ¶30]

Temporary Differences under Paragraphs .212 through .224 and U.S. Steamship Enterprise Temporary Differences

.130 A deferred tax liability is not recognized for the following types of temporary differences unless it becomes apparent that those temporary differences will reverse in the foreseeable future:

a. An excess of the amount for financial reporting over the tax basis of an investment in a foreign subsidiary or a foreign corporate joint venture as defined in Section I82, "Investments: Equity Method," that is essentially permanent in duration
b. Undistributed earnings of a domestic subsidiary or a domestic corporate joint venture that is essentially permanent in duration that arose in fiscal years beginning on or before December 15, 1992[13]
c. "Bad debt reserves" for tax purposes of U.S. savings and loan associations (and other "qualified" thrift lenders) that arose in tax years beginning before December 31, 1987 (that is, the base-year amount)
d. "Policyholders' surplus" of stock life insurance companies that arose in fiscal years beginning on or before December 15, 1992.

The indefinite reversal criterion in paragraph .215 shall not be applied to analogous types of temporary differences. [FAS109, ¶31]

.131 A deferred tax liability shall be recognized for the following types of taxable temporary differences:

a. An excess of the amount for financial reporting over the tax basis of an investment in a domestic subsidiary that arises in fiscal years beginning after December 15, 1992

---

[12]Acquired differences under paragraphs .212 through .224 are accounted for in accordance with the requirements of paragraphs .130 through .133. [FAS109, ¶30, fn8]

[13]A last-in, first-out (LIFO) pattern determines whether reversals pertain to differences that arose in fiscal years beginning on or before December 15, 1992. [FAS109, ¶31, fn9]

b. An excess of the amount for financial reporting over the tax basis of an investment in a 50-percent-or-less-owned investee except as provided in paragraph .130(a) and (b) for a corporate joint venture that is essentially permanent in duration

c. "Bad debt reserves" for tax purposes of U.S. savings and loan associations (and other "qualified" thrift lenders) that arise in tax years beginning after December 31, 1987 (that is, amounts in excess of the base-year amount).

The tax effects of temporary differences related to deposits in statutory reserve funds by U.S. steamship enterprises that arose in fiscal years beginning on or before December 15, 1992 and that were not previously recognized shall be recognized when those temporary differences reverse or in their entirety at the beginning of the fiscal year for which this section is first applied. [FAS109, ¶32]

.132 Whether an excess of the amount for financial reporting over the tax basis of an investment in a more-than-50-percent-owned domestic subsidiary is a taxable temporary difference must be assessed. It is not a taxable temporary difference if the tax law provides a means by which the reported amount of that investment can be recovered tax-free and the enterprise expects that it will ultimately use that means. For example, under current U.S. federal tax law:

a. An enterprise may elect to determine taxable gain or loss on the liquidation of an 80-percent-or-more-owned subsidiary by reference to the tax basis of the subsidiary's net assets rather than by reference to the parent company's tax basis for the stock of that subsidiary.

b. An enterprise may execute a statutory merger whereby a subsidiary is merged into the parent company, the minority shareholders receive stock of the parent, the subsidiary's stock is cancelled, and no taxable gain or loss results if the continuity of ownership, continuity of business enterprise, and certain other requirements of the tax law are met.

Some elections for tax purposes are available only if the parent company owns a specified percentage of the subsidiary's stock. The parent company sometimes may own less than that specified percentage, and the price per share to acquire a minority interest may significantly exceed the per share equivalent of the amount reported as minority interest in the consolidated financial statements. In those circumstances, the excess of the amount for financial reporting over the tax basis of the parent's investment in the subsidiary is not a taxable temporary difference if settlement of the minority interest is expected to occur at the point in time when settlement would not result in a significant cost. That could occur, for example, toward the end of the life of the subsidiary, after it has recovered and settled most of its assets and liabilities, respectively. The fair value of the minority interest ordinarily will approximately equal its percentage of the subsidiary's net assets if those net assets consist primarily of cash. [FAS109, ¶33]

.133 A deferred tax asset shall be recognized for an excess of the tax basis over the amount for financial reporting of an investment in a subsidiary or corporate joint venture that is essentially permanent in duration only if it is apparent that the temporary difference will reverse in the foreseeable future. The need for a valuation allowance for that deferred tax asset and other deferred tax assets related to temporary differences under paragraphs .212 through .224 (for example, a deferred tax asset for foreign tax credit carryforwards or for a savings and loan association's bad-debt reserve for financial reporting) shall be assessed. Paragraph .120 identifies four sources of taxable income to be considered in determining the need for and amount of a valuation allowance for those and other deferred tax assets. One source is future reversals of temporary differences. Future reversals of taxable differences for which a deferred tax liability has not been recognized based on the exceptions cited in paragraph .130, however, shall not be considered. Another source is future taxable income exclusive of reversing temporary differences and carryforwards. Future distributions of future earnings of a subsidiary or corporate joint venture, however, shall not be considered except to the extent that a deferred tax liability has been recognized for existing undistributed earnings or earnings have been remitted in the past. [FAS109, ¶34]

Intraperiod Tax Allocation

.134 Income tax expense or benefit for the year shall be allocated among continuing operations, discontinued operations, extraordinary items, and items charged or credited directly to shareholders' equity (refer to paragraph .135). The amount allocated to continuing operations is the tax effect of the pretax income or loss from continuing operations that occurred during the year, plus or minus income tax effects of (a) changes in circumstances that cause a change in judgment about the realization of deferred tax assets in future years (refer to paragraph .125), (b) changes in tax laws or rates (refer to paragraph .126), (c) changes in tax status (refer to paragraph .127), and (d) tax-deductible dividends paid to shareholders (except as set forth in paragraph .135 for dividends paid on unallocated shares held by an employee stock ownership plan [ESOP] or any other stock compensation arrangement). The remainder is allocated to items other than continuing operations in accordance with the provisions of paragraph .137. [FAS109, ¶35]

.135 The tax effects of the following items occurring during the year are charged or credited directly to related components of shareholders' equity:

a. Adjustments of the opening balance of retained earnings for certain changes in accounting principles or a correction of an error
b. **Gains and losses included in comprehensive income but excluded from net income** (for example, translation adjustments under Section F60 and [FAS109, ¶36] changes in the unrealized holding gains and losses of securities classified as available-for-sale under Section I80, "Investments: Debt and Equity Securities") [FAS115, ¶133]
c. An increase or decrease in contributed capital (for example, deductible expenditures reported as a reduction of the proceeds from issuing capital stock)
d. An increase in the tax basis of assets acquired in a taxable business combination

accounted for as a pooling of interests and for which a tax benefit is recognized at the date of the business combination
e. Expenses for employee stock options recognized differently for financial reporting and tax purposes (refer to paragraph .117 of Section C47, "Compensation to Employees: Stock Purchase and Option Plans")
f. Dividends that are paid on unallocated shares held by an ESOP and that are charged to retained earnings
g. Deductible temporary differences and carryforwards that existed at the date of a quasi reorganization (except as set forth in paragraph .138). [FAS109, ¶36]

.136 The tax benefit of an operating loss carryforward or carryback (other than those carryforwards referred to at the end of this paragraph) shall be reported in the same manner as the source of the income or loss in the current year and not in the same manner as (a) the source of the operating loss carryforward or taxes paid in a prior year or (b) the source of expected future income that will result in realization of a deferred tax asset for an operating loss carryforward from the current year. The only exceptions are as follows:

a. Tax effects of deductible temporary differences and carryforwards that existed at the date of a purchase business combination and for which a tax benefit is initially recognized in subsequent years in accordance with the provisions of paragraph .129
b. Tax effects of deductible temporary differences and carryforwards that are allocated to shareholders' equity in accordance with the provisions of paragraph .135 (items (c) and (e) through (g)). [FAS109, ¶37]

.137 If there is only one item other than continuing operations, the portion of income tax expense or benefit for the year that remains after the allocation to continuing operations is allocated to that item. If there are two or more items other than continuing operations, the amount that remains after the allocation to continuing operations shall be allocated among those other items in proportion to their individual effects on income tax expense or benefit for the year. If there are two or more items other than continuing operations, the sum of the separately calculated, individual effects of each item sometimes may not equal the amount of income tax expense or benefit for the year that remains after the allocation to continuing operations. In those circumstances, the procedures to allocate the remaining amount to items other than continuing operations are as follows:

a. Determine the effect on income tax expense or benefit for the year of the total net loss for all net loss items
b. Apportion the tax benefit determined in (a) ratably to each net loss item
c. Determine the amount that remains, that is, the difference between (1) the amount to be allocated to all items other than continuing operations and (2) the amount allocated to all net loss items
d. Apportion the tax expense determined in (c) ratably to each net gain item.

Refer to paragraphs .200 through .203 for additional guidance. [FAS109, ¶38]

Certain Quasi Reorganizations

.138 The tax benefits of deductible temporary differences and carryforwards as of the date of a quasi reorganization as defined and contemplated in Section Q15, "Quasi Reorganizations," ordinarily are reported as a direct addition to contributed capital if the tax benefits are recognized in subsequent years. The only exception is for enterprises that have previously both adopted [the provisions of] FASB Statement 96, *Accounting for Income Taxes,* and effected a quasi reorganization that involves only the elimination of a deficit in retained earnings by a concurrent reduction in contributed capital prior to adopting [the provisions of] this section. For those enterprises, subsequent recognition of the tax benefit of prior deductible temporary differences and carryforwards is included in income and reported as required by paragraph .136 (without regard to the referenced exceptions) and then reclassified from retained earnings to contributed capital. Those enterprises shall disclose (a) the date of the quasi reorganization, (b) the manner of reporting the tax benefits and that it differs from present accounting requirements for other enterprises, and (c) the effect of those tax benefits on income from continuing operations, income before extraordinary items, and on net income (and on related per share amounts). [FAS109, ¶39]

Separate Financial Statements of a Subsidiary

.139 The consolidated amount of current and deferred tax expense for a group that files a consolidated tax return shall be allocated among the members of the group if those members issue separate financial statements. This section does not require a single allocation method. The method adopted, however, shall be systematic, rational, and consistent with the broad principles established by this section. A method that allocates current and deferred taxes to members of the group by applying this section to each member as if it were a separate taxpayer[14] meets those criteria. Examples of methods that are not consistent with the broad principles established by this section include:

a. A method that allocates only current taxes payable to a member of the group that has taxable temporary differences
b. A method that allocates deferred taxes to a member of the group using a method fundamentally different from the asset and liability method described in this section
c. A method that allocates no current or deferred tax expense to a member of the group that has taxable income because the consolidated group has no current or deferred tax expense.

Certain disclosures are also required (refer to paragraph .147). [FAS109, ¶40]

---

[14]In that situation, the sum of the amounts allocated to individual members of the group may not equal the consolidated amount. That may also be the result if there are intercompany transactions between members of the group. The criteria are satisfied, nevertheless, after giving effect to the type of adjustments (including eliminations) normally present in preparing consolidated financial statements. [FAS109, ¶40, fn10]

Financial Statement Presentation

.140 In a classified statement of financial position, an enterprise shall separate deferred tax liabilities and assets into a current amount and a noncurrent amount. Deferred tax liabilities and assets shall be classified as current or noncurrent based on the classification of the related[15] asset or liability for financial reporting. A deferred tax liability or asset that is not related to an asset or liability for financial reporting (refer to paragraph .114), including deferred tax assets related to carryforwards, shall be classified according to the expected reversal date of the [FAS109, ¶41] specific temporary difference. Such classification disregards any additional temporary differences that may arise and is based on the criteria used for classifying other assets and liabilities. [FAS109, ¶288p] [Refer to paragraphs .204 through .211 for illustrations of balance sheet classification.] The valuation allowance for a particular tax jurisdiction shall be allocated between current and noncurrent deferred tax assets for that tax jurisdiction on a pro rata basis. [FAS109, ¶41]

.141 For a particular tax-paying component of an enterprise and within a particular tax jurisdiction, (a) all current deferred tax liabilities and assets shall be offset and presented as a single amount and (b) all noncurrent deferred tax liabilities and assets shall be offset and presented as a single amount. However, an enterprise shall not offset deferred tax liabilities and assets attributable to different tax-paying components of the enterprise or to different tax jurisdictions. [FAS109, ¶42]

Financial Statement Disclosure

.142 The components of the net deferred tax liability or asset recognized in an enterprise's statement of financial position shall be disclosed as follows:

a. The total of all deferred tax liabilities measured in procedure (b) of paragraph .116
b. The total of all deferred tax assets measured in procedures (c) and (d) of paragraph .116
c. The total valuation allowance recognized for deferred tax assets determined in procedure (e) of paragraph .116.

The net change during the year in the total valuation allowance also shall be disclosed. A **public enterprise** shall disclose the approximate tax effect of each type of temporary difference and carryforward that gives rise to a significant portion of deferred tax liabilities and deferred tax assets (before allocation of valuation allowances). A **nonpublic enterprise** shall disclose the types of significant temporary differences and carryforwards but may omit disclosure of the tax effects of each type. A public enterprise that

---

[15]A temporary difference is related to an asset or liability if reduction of the asset or liability causes the temporary difference to reverse. As used here, the term *reduction* includes amortization, sale, or other realization of an asset and amortization, payment, or other satisfaction of a liability. [FAS109, ¶288p]

is not subject to income taxes because its income is taxed directly to its owners shall disclose that fact and the net difference between the tax bases and the reported amounts of the enterprise's assets and liabilities. [FAS109, ¶43]

.143 The following information shall be disclosed whenever a deferred tax liability is not recognized because of the exceptions to comprehensive recognition of deferred taxes for any of the areas addressed by paragraphs .212 through .224 or for deposits in statutory reserve funds by U.S. steamship enterprises:

a. A description of the types of temporary differences for which a deferred tax liability has not been recognized and the types of events that would cause those temporary differences to become taxable
b. The cumulative amount of each type of temporary difference
c. The amount of the unrecognized deferred tax liability for temporary differences related to investments in foreign subsidiaries and foreign corporate joint ventures that are essentially permanent in duration if determination of that liability is practicable or a statement that determination is not practicable
d. The amount of the deferred tax liability for temporary differences other than those in (c) above (that is, undistributed domestic earnings, the bad-debt reserve for tax purposes of a U.S. savings and loan association or other qualified thrift lender, the policyholders' surplus of a life insurance enterprise, and the statutory reserve funds of a U.S. steamship enterprise) that is not recognized in accordance with the provisions of paragraphs .130 and .131. [FAS109, ¶44]

.144 The significant components of income tax expense attributable to continuing operations for each year presented shall be disclosed in the financial statements or notes thereto. Those components would include, for example:

a. **Current tax expense or benefit**
b. Deferred tax expense or benefit (exclusive of the effects of other components listed below)
c. Investment tax credits
d. Government grants (to the extent recognized as a reduction of income tax expense)
e. The benefits of operating loss carryforwards
f. Tax expense that results from allocating certain tax benefits either directly to contributed capital or to reduce goodwill or other noncurrent intangible assets of an acquired entity
g. Adjustments of a deferred tax liability or asset for enacted changes in tax laws or rates or a change in the tax status of the enterprise
h. Adjustments of the beginning-of-the-year balance of a valuation allowance because of a change in circumstances that causes a change in judgment about the realizability of the related deferred tax asset in future years. [FAS109, ¶45]

.145 The amount of income tax expense or benefit allocated to continuing operations and the amounts separately allocated to other items (in accordance with the provisions of paragraphs .134 through .138) shall be disclosed for each year for which those items are presented. [FAS109, ¶46]

.146 A public enterprise shall disclose a reconciliation using percentages or dollar amounts of (a) the reported amount of income tax expense attributable to continuing operations for the year to (b) the amount of income tax expense that would result from applying domestic federal statutory tax rates to pretax income from continuing operations. The "statutory" tax rates shall be the regular tax rates if there are alternative tax systems. The estimated amount and the nature of each significant reconciling item shall be disclosed. A nonpublic enterprise shall disclose the nature of significant reconciling items but may omit a numerical reconciliation. If not otherwise evident from the disclosures required by this paragraph and paragraphs .142 through .145, all enterprises shall disclose the nature and effect of any other significant matters affecting comparability of information for all periods presented. [FAS109, ¶47]

.147 An enterprise shall disclose (a) the amounts and expiration dates of operating loss and tax credit carryforwards for tax purposes and (b) any portion of the valuation allowance for deferred tax assets for which subsequently recognized tax benefits will be allocated to reduce goodwill or other noncurrent intangible assets of an acquired entity or directly to contributed capital (refer to paragraphs .129 and .135). [FAS109, ¶48]

.148 An entity that is a member of a group that files a consolidated tax return shall disclose in its separately issued financial statements:

a. The aggregate amount of current and deferred tax expense for each statement of earnings presented and the amount of any tax-related balances due to or from affiliates as of the date of each statement of financial position presented
b. The principal provisions of the method by which the consolidated amount of current and deferred tax expense is allocated to members of the group and the nature and effect of any changes in that method (and in determining related balances to or from affiliates) during the years for which the disclosures in (a) above are presented. [FAS109, ¶49]

Application of the Standards in Paragraphs .101 through .148 to Specific Aspects of Accounting for Income Taxes

.149 Paragraphs .150 through .211 provide additional discussion and examples[16] that illustrate application of the standards [in paragraphs .101 through .148] to specific aspects of accounting for income taxes. [FAS109, ¶223]

CONTENTS

	Paragraph Numbers
Recognition of Deferred Tax Assets and Deferred Tax Liabilities	.150–.158
Offset of Taxable and Deductible Amounts	.153
Pattern of Taxable or Deductible Amounts	.154–.155
Change in Deferred Foreign Tax Assets and Liabilities	.156
Special Deductions	.157–.158
[Incremental Effect of Future Losses	.159]
Measurement of Deferred Tax Liabilities and Assets	.160–.166
Alternative Minimum Tax	.165–.166
Operating Loss and Tax Credit Carryforwards and Carrybacks	.167–.172
Recognition of a Tax Benefit for Carrybacks	.167
Recognition of a Tax Benefit for Carryforwards	.168–.171
Reporting the Tax Benefit of Operating Loss Carryforwards or Carrybacks	.172
Tax-Planning Strategies	.173–.178
Regulated Enterprises	.179–.182
Leveraged Leases	.183–.185
Business Combinations	.186–.199
Nontaxable Business Combinations	.187
Taxable Business Combinations	.188–.190
Carryforwards—Purchase Method	.191–.194
Subsequent Recognition of Carryforward Benefits— Purchase Method	.195–.196
Carryforwards—Pooling-of-Interests Method	.197–.199
Intraperiod Tax Allocation	.200–.203
[Balance Sheet Classification of Deferred Income Taxes	.204–.211]

---

[16]The discussion and examples in paragraphs .150 through .203 assume that the tax law requires offsetting net deductions in a particular year against net taxable amounts in the 3 preceding years and then in the 15 succeeding years. [These] assumptions about the tax law are for illustrative purposes only. The enacted tax law for a particular tax jurisdiction shall be used for recognition and measurement of deferred tax liabilities and assets. [FAS109, ¶223, fn14]

Recognition of Deferred Tax Assets and Deferred Tax Liabilities

.150   A deferred tax liability is recognized for all taxable temporary differences,[17] and a deferred tax asset is recognized for all deductible temporary differences and operating loss and tax credit carryforwards. A valuation allowance is recognized if it is more likely than not that some portion or all of the deferred tax asset will not be realized. [FAS109, ¶224]

.151   Exhibit 151A illustrates recognition of deferred tax assets and liabilities.

Exhibit 151A

Recognition of Deferred Tax Assets and Liabilities

At the end of year 3 (the current year), an enterprise has $2,400 of deductible temporary differences and $1,500 of taxable temporary differences.

A deferred tax liability is recognized at the end of year 3 for the $1,500 of taxable temporary differences, and a deferred tax asset is recognized for the $2,400 of deductible temporary differences. All available evidence, both positive and negative, is considered to determine whether, based on the weight of that evidence, a valuation allowance is needed for some portion or all of the deferred tax asset. If evidence about one or more sources of taxable income (refer to paragraph .120) is sufficient to support a conclusion that a valuation allowance is not needed, other sources of taxable income need not be considered. For example, if the weight of available evidence indicates that taxable income will exceed $2,400 in each future year, a conclusion that no valuation allowance is needed can be reached without considering the pattern and timing of the reversal of the temporary differences, the existence of qualifying tax-planning strategies, and so forth.

Similarly, if the deductible temporary differences will reverse within the next 3 years and taxable income in the current year exceeds $2,400, nothing needs to be known about future taxable income exclusive of reversing temporary differences because the deferred tax asset could be realized by carryback to the current year. A valuation allowance is needed, however, if the weight of available evidence indicates that some portion or all of the $2,400 of tax deductions from future reversals of the deductible temporary differences will not be realized by offsetting:

a.   The $1,500 of taxable temporary differences and $900 of future taxable income exclusive of reversing temporary differences
b. $2,400 of future taxable income exclusive of reversing temporary differences
c. $2,400 of taxable income in the current or prior years by loss carryback to those years
d. $2,400 of taxable income in one or more of the circumstances described above and as a result of a qualifying tax-planning strategy (refer to paragraphs .173 through .178).

---

[17]Refer to paragraph .108. [FAS109, ¶224, fn15]

Exhibit 151A (continued)

To the extent that evidence about one or more sources of taxable income is sufficient to eliminate any need for a valuation allowance, other sources need not be considered. Detailed forecasts, projections, or other types of analyses[18] are unnecessary if expected future taxable income is more than sufficient to realize a tax benefit. Detailed analyses are not necessary, for example, if the enterprise earned $500 of taxable income in each of years 1 through 3 and there is no evidence to suggest it will not continue to earn that level of taxable income in future years. That level of future taxable income is more than sufficient to realize the tax benefit of $2,400 of tax deductions over a period of at least 19 years (the year(s) of the deductions, 3 carryback years, and 15 carryforward years) in the U.S. federal tax jurisdiction. [FAS109, ¶225]

.152 Exhibit 152A illustrates recognition of a valuation allowance for a portion of a deferred tax asset in one year and a subsequent change in circumstances that requires adjustment of the valuation allowance at the end of the following year.

Exhibit 152A

Change in a Valuation Allowance

The assumptions are as follows:

a. At the end of the current year (year 3), an enterprise's only temporary differences are deductible temporary differences in the amount of $900.
b. Pretax financial income, taxable income, and taxes paid for each of years 1 through 3 are all positive, but relatively negligible, amounts.
c. The enacted tax rate is 40 percent for all years.

A deferred tax asset in the amount of $360 ($900 at 40 percent) is recognized at the end of year 3. If management concludes, based on an assessment of all available evidence (refer to guidance in paragraphs .119 through .124), that it is more likely than not that future taxable income will not be sufficient to realize a tax benefit for $400 of the $900 of deductible temporary differences at the end of the current year, a $160 valuation allowance ($400 at 40 percent) is recognized at the end of year 3.

---

[18] The terms *forecast* and *projection* refer to any process by which available evidence is accumulated and evaluated for purposes of estimating whether future taxable income will be sufficient to realize a deferred tax asset. Judgment is necessary to determine how detailed or formalized that evaluation process should be. Furthermore, information about expected future taxable income is necessary only to the extent positive evidence available from other sources (refer to paragraph .120) is not sufficient to support a conclusion that a valuation allowance is not needed. This section does not require either a *financial forecast* or a *financial projection* within the meaning of those terms in the Statements on Standards for Accountants' Services on Prospective Financial Information issued by the Auditing Standards Board of the American Institute of Certified Public Accountants. [FAS109, ¶225, fn16]

Exhibit 152A (continued)

Assume that pretax financial income and taxable income for year 4 turn out to be as follows:

Pretax financial loss	$ (50)
Reversing deductible temporary differences	(300)
Loss carryforward for tax purposes	$(350)

The $50 pretax loss in year 4 is additional negative evidence that must be weighed against available positive evidence to determine the amount of valuation allowance necessary at the end of year 4. Deductible temporary differences and carryforwards at the end of year 4 are as follows:

Loss carryforward from year 4 for tax purposes (refer to the above)	$350
Unreversed deductible temporary differences ($900 − $300)	600
	$950

The $360 deferred tax asset recognized at the end of year 3 is increased to $380 ($950 at 40 percent) at the end of year 4. Based on an assessment of all evidence available at the end of year 4, management concludes that it is more likely than not that $240 of the deferred tax asset will not be realized and, therefore, that a $240 valuation allowance is necessary. The $160 valuation allowance recognized at the end of year 3 is increased to $240 at the end of year 4. The $60 net effect of those 2 adjustments (the $80 increase in the valuation allowance less the $20 increase in the deferred tax asset) results in $60 of deferred tax expense that is recognized in year 4. [FAS109, ¶226]

_____

Offset of Taxable and Deductible Amounts

.153 The tax law determines whether future reversals of temporary differences will result in taxable and deductible amounts that offset each other in future years. The tax law also determines the extent to which deductible temporary differences and carry-forwards will offset the tax consequences of income that is expected to be earned in future years. For example, the tax law may provide that capital losses are deductible only to the extent of capital gains. In that case, a tax benefit is not recognized for temporary differences that will result in future deductions in the form of capital losses unless those deductions will offset either (a) other existing temporary differences that will result in future capital gains, (b) capital gains that are expected to occur in future years, or (c) capital gains of the current year or prior years if carryback (of those capital loss deductions from the future reversal years) is expected. [FAS109, ¶227]

Pattern of Taxable or Deductible Amounts

.154 The particular years in which temporary differences result in taxable or deductible amounts generally are determined by the timing of the recovery of the related asset or settlement of the related liability. However, there are exceptions to that general rule. For example, a temporary difference between the tax basis and the reported amount of inventory for which cost is determined on a LIFO basis does not reverse when present inventory is sold in future years if it is replaced by purchases or production of inventory in those same future years. A LIFO inventory temporary difference becomes taxable or deductible in the future year that inventory is liquidated and not replaced. [FAS109, ¶228]

.155 For some assets or liabilities, temporary differences may accumulate over several years and then reverse over several years. That pattern is common for depreciable assets. Future originating differences for existing depreciable assets and their subsequent reversals are a factor to be considered when assessing the likelihood of future taxable income (refer to paragraph .120(b)) for realization of a tax benefit for existing deductible temporary differences and carryforwards. [FAS109, ¶229]

Change in Deferred Foreign Tax Assets and Liabilities

.156 When the reporting currency (not the foreign currency) is the functional currency, remeasurement of an enterprise's deferred foreign tax liability or asset after a change in the exchange rate will result in a transaction gain or loss that is recognized currently in determining net income. Section F60 requires disclosure of the aggregate transaction gain or loss included in determining net income but does not specify how to display that transaction gain or loss or its components for financial reporting. Accordingly, a transaction gain or loss that results from remeasuring a deferred foreign tax liability or asset may be included in the reported amount of deferred tax benefit or expense if that presentation is considered to be more useful. If reported in that manner, that transaction gain or loss is still included in the aggregate transaction gain or loss for the period to be disclosed as required by Section F60. [FAS109, ¶230]

Special Deductions

.157 The tax benefit of statutory depletion[, as described in paragraph .141 of Section Oi5, "Oil and Gas Producing Activities,"] and other types of special deductions such as those for Blue Cross-Blue Shield and small life insurance companies in future years shall not be anticipated for purposes of offsetting a deferred tax liability for taxable temporary differences at the end of the current year. [FAS109, ¶231]

.158 As required above, the tax benefit of special deductions ordinarily is recognized no earlier than the year in which those special deductions are deductible on the tax return. However, some portion of the future tax effects of special deductions are implicitly recognized in determining (a) the average graduated tax rate to be used for measuring deferred taxes when graduated tax rates are a significant factor and (b) the need for a valuation allowance for deferred tax assets. In those circumstances, implicit recognition is unavoidable because (1) those special deductions are one of the determinants of future taxable income and (2) future taxable income determines the average graduated tax rate and sometimes determines the need for a valuation allowance. [FAS109, ¶232]

The Incremental Effect of Future Losses

.159 The tax consequences of tax losses expected in future years [shall not] be anticipated for purposes of:

a. Nonrecognition of a deferred tax liability for taxable temporary differences if there will be no future sacrifice because of future tax losses that otherwise would expire unused
b. Recognition of a deferred tax asset for the carryback refund of taxes paid for the current or a prior year because of future tax losses that otherwise would expire unused. [FAS109, ¶185]

Measurement of Deferred Tax Liabilities and Assets

.160 The tax rate that is used to measure deferred tax liabilities and deferred tax assets is the enacted tax rate(s) expected to apply to taxable income in the years that the liability is expected to be settled or the asset recovered. Measurements are based on elections (for example, an election for loss carryforward instead of carryback) that are expected to be made for tax purposes in future years. Presently enacted changes in tax laws and rates that become effective for a particular future year or years must be considered when determining the tax rate to apply to temporary differences reversing in that year or years. Tax laws and rates for the current year are used if no changes have been enacted for future years. An asset for deductible temporary differences that are expected to be realized in future years through carryback of a future loss to the current or a prior year (or a liability for taxable temporary differences that are expected to reduce the refund claimed for the carryback of a future loss to the current or a prior year) is measured using tax laws and rates for the current or a prior year, that is, the year for which a refund is expected to be realized based on loss carryback provisions of the tax law. [FAS109, ¶233]

.161 Exhibit 161A illustrates determination of the tax rate for measurement of a deferred tax liability for taxable temporary differences when there is a phased-in change in tax rates.

Exhibit 161A

Determination of the Tax Rate for Measurement of a Deferred Tax Liability with a Phased-in Change in Tax Rates

At the end of year 3 (the current year), an enterprise has $2,400 of taxable temporary differences, which are expected to result in taxable amounts of approximately $800 on the future tax returns for each of years 4 through 6. Enacted tax rates are 35 percent for years 1 through 3, 40 percent for years 4 through 6, and 45 percent for year 7 and thereafter.

The tax rate that is used to measure the deferred tax liability for the $2,400 of taxable temporary differences differs depending on whether the tax effect of future reversals of those temporary differences is on taxes payable for years 1 through 3, years 4 through 6, or year 7 and thereafter. The tax rate for measurement of the deferred tax liability is 40 percent whenever taxable income is expected in years 4 through 6. If tax losses are expected in years 4 through 6, however, the tax rate is:

a. 35 percent if realization of a tax benefit for those tax losses in years 4 through 6 will be by loss carryback to years 1 through 3
b. 45 percent if realization of a tax benefit for those tax losses in years 4 through 6 will be by loss carryforward to year 7 and thereafter. [FAS109, ¶234]

.162 Exhibit 162A illustrates determination of the tax rate for measurement of a deferred tax asset for deductible temporary differences when there is a change in tax rates.

Exhibit 162A

Determination of the Tax Rate for Measurement of a Deferred Tax Asset When There Is a Change in Tax Rates

The assumptions are as follows:

a. Enacted tax rates are 30 percent for years 1 through 3 and 40 percent for year 4 and thereafter.
b. At the end of year 3 (the current year), an enterprise has $900 of deductible temporary differences, which are expected to result in tax deductions of approximately $300 on the future tax returns for each of years 4 through 6.

The tax rate is 40 percent if the enterprise expects to realize a tax benefit for the deductible temporary differences by offsetting taxable income earned in future years. Alternatively, the tax rate is 30 percent if the enterprise expects to realize a tax benefit for the deductible temporary differences by loss carryback refund.

Exhibit 162A (continued)

Assume that (a) the enterprise recognizes a $360 ($900 at 40 percent) deferred tax asset to be realized by offsetting taxable income in future years and (b) taxable income and taxes payable in each of years 1 through 3 were $300 and $90, respectively. Realization of a tax benefit of at least $270 ($900 at 30 percent) is assured because carryback refunds totalling $270 may be realized even if no taxable income is earned in future years. Recognition of a valuation allowance for the other $90 ($360 − $270) of the deferred tax asset depends on management's assessment of whether, based on the weight of available evidence, a portion or all of the tax benefit of the $900 of deductible temporary differences will not be realized at 40 percent tax rates in future years.

Alternatively, if enacted tax rates are 40 percent for years 1 through 3 and 30 percent for year 4 and thereafter, measurement of the deferred tax asset at a 40 percent tax rate could only occur if tax losses are expected in future years 4 through 6. [FAS109, ¶235]

.163 Exhibit 163A illustrates determination of the average graduated tax rate for measurement of deferred tax liabilities and assets by an enterprise for which graduated tax rates ordinarily are a significant factor.

Exhibit 163A

Determination of the Average Graduated Tax Rate
for Measurement of Deferred Tax Liabilities and Assets

At the end of year 3 (the current year), an enterprise has $1,500 of taxable temporary differences and $900 of deductible temporary differences, which are expected to result in net taxable amounts of approximately $200 on the future tax returns for each of years 4 through 6. Enacted tax rates are 15 percent for the first $500 of taxable income, 25 percent for the next $500, and 40 percent for taxable income over $1,000. This example assumes that there is no income (for example, capital gains) subject to special tax rates.

The deferred tax liability and asset for those reversing taxable and deductible temporary differences in years 4 through 6 are measured using the average graduated tax rate for the estimated amount of annual taxable income in future years. Thus, the average graduated tax rate will differ depending on the expected level of annual taxable income (including reversing temporary differences) in years 4 through 6. The average tax rate will be:

a. 15 percent if the estimated annual level of taxable income in years 4 through 6 is $500 or less

Exhibit 163A (continued)

b. 20 percent if the estimated annual level of taxable income in years 4 through 6 is
$1,000

c. 30 percent if the estimated annual level of taxable income in years 4 through 6 is
$2,000.

Temporary differences usually do not reverse in equal annual amounts as in the example above, and a different average graduated tax rate might apply to reversals in different future years. However, a detailed analysis to determine the net reversals of temporary differences in each future year usually is not warranted. It is not warranted because the other variable (that is, taxable income or losses exclusive of reversing temporary differences in each of those future years) for determination of the average graduated tax rate in each future year is no more than an estimate. For that reason, an aggregate calculation using a single estimated average graduated tax rate based on estimated average annual taxable income in future years is sufficient. Judgment is permitted, however, to deal with unusual situations, for example, an abnormally large temporary difference that will reverse in a single future year, or an abnormal level of taxable income that is expected for a single future year. The lowest graduated tax rate shall be used whenever the estimated average graduated tax rate otherwise would be zero. [FAS109, ¶236]

.164 Deferred tax liabilities and assets are measured using enacted tax rates applicable to capital gains, ordinary income, and so forth, based on the expected type of taxable or deductible amounts in future years. For example, evidence based on all facts and circumstances should determine whether an investor's liability for the tax consequences of temporary differences related to its equity in the earnings of an investee should be measured using enacted tax rates applicable to a capital gain or a dividend. Computation of a deferred tax liability for undistributed earnings based on dividends shall also reflect any related dividends received deductions or foreign tax credits, and taxes that would be withheld from the dividend. [FAS109, ¶237]

Alternative Minimum Tax

.165 Temporary differences such as depreciation differences are one reason why [tentative minimum tax] (TMT) may exceed regular tax. Temporary differences, however, ultimately reverse and, absent a significant amount of preference items, total taxes paid over the entire life of the enterprise will be based on the regular tax system. Preference items are another reason why TMT may exceed regular tax. If preference items are large enough, an enterprise could be subject, over its lifetime, to the AMT system; and the cumulative amount of AMT credit carryforwards would expire unused. No one can know beforehand which scenario will prevail because that determination can only be made after the fact. In the meantime, this section requires procedures that provide a practical solution to that problem. [FAS109, ¶238]

.166 Under the requirements of this section, an enterprise shall:

a. Measure the total deferred tax liability and asset for regular tax temporary differences and carryforwards using the regular tax rate
b. Measure the total deferred tax asset for all AMT credit carryforward
c. Reduce the deferred tax asset for AMT credit carryforward by a valuation allowance if, based on the weight of available evidence, it is more likely than not that some portion or all of that deferred tax asset will not be realized.

Paragraph .120 identifies four sources of taxable income that shall be considered in determining the need for and amount of a valuation allowance. No valuation allowance is necessary if the deferred tax asset for AMT credit carryforward can be realized:

1. Under paragraph .120(a), by reducing a deferred tax liability from the amount of regular tax on regular tax temporary differences to not less than the amount of TMT on AMT temporary differences
2. Under paragraph .120(b), by reducing taxes on future income from the amount of regular tax on regular taxable income to not less than the amount of TMT on AMT income
3. Under paragraph .120(c), by loss carryback
4. Under paragraph .120(d), by a tax-planning strategy such as switching from tax-exempt to taxable interest income. [FAS109, ¶239]

Operating Loss and Tax Credit Carryforwards and Carrybacks

Recognition of a Tax Benefit for Carrybacks

.167 An operating loss, certain deductible items that are subject to limitations, and some tax credits arising but not utilized in the current year may be carried back for refund of taxes paid in prior years or carried forward to reduce taxes payable in future years. A receivable is recognized for the amount of taxes paid in prior years that is refundable by carryback of an operating loss or unused tax credits of the current year. [FAS109, ¶240]

Recognition of a Tax Benefit for Carryforwards

.168 A deferred tax asset is recognized for an operating loss or tax credit carryforward.[19] In assessing the need for a valuation allowance, provisions in the tax law that limit utilization of an operating loss or tax credit carryforward are applied in determining whether it is more likely than not that some portion or all of the deferred tax asset will not be realized by reduction of taxes payable on taxable income during the carryforward period. [FAS109, ¶241]

---

[19]This requirement pertains to all ITC carryforwards regardless of whether the flow-through or deferral method is used to account for ITC. [FAS109, ¶241, fn17]

.169 Exhibit 169A illustrates recognition of the tax benefit of an operating loss in the loss year and in subsequent carryforward years when a valuation allowance is necessary in the loss year.

Exhibit 169A

Recognition of the Tax Benefit of an Operating Loss When a Valuation Allowance Is Necessary in the Loss Year

The assumptions are as follows:

a. The enacted tax rate is 40 percent for all years.
b. An operating loss occurs in year 5.
c. The only difference between financial and taxable income results from use of accelerated depreciation for tax purposes. Differences that arise between the reported amount and the tax basis of depreciable assets in years 1 through 7 will result in taxable amounts before the end of the loss carryforward period from year 5.
d. Financial income, taxable income, and taxes currently payable or refundable are as follows:

	Year 1	Years 2-4	Year 5	Year 6	Year 7
Pretax financial income (loss)	$2,000	$5,000	$(8,000)	$ 2,200	$7,000
Depreciation differences	(800)	(2,200)	(800)	(700)	(600)
Loss carryback	—	—	2,800	—	—
Loss carryforward	—	—	—	(6,000)	(4,500)
Taxable income (loss)	$1,200	$2,800	$(6,000)	$(4,500)	$1,900
Taxes payable (refundable)	$ 480	$1,120	$(1,120)	$ —	$ 760

e. At the end of year 5, profits are not expected in years 6 and 7 and later years, and it is concluded that a valuation allowance is necessary to the extent realization of the deferred tax asset for the operating loss carryforward depends on taxable income (exclusive of reversing temporary differences) in future years.

The deferred tax liability for the taxable temporary differences is calculated at the end of each year as follows:

	Year 1	Years 2-4	Year 5	Year 6	Year 7
Unreversed differences:					
Beginning amount	$ —	$ 800	$3,000	$3,800	$4,500
Additional amount	800	2,200	800	700	600
Total	$800	$3,000	$3,800	$4,500	$5,100
Deferred tax liability (40 percent)	$320	$1,200	$1,520	$1,800	$2,040

Exhibit 169A (continued)

The deferred tax asset and related valuation allowance for the loss carryforward are calculated at the end of each year as follows:

	Year 1	Years 2-4	Year 5	Year 6	Year 7
Loss carryforward for tax purposes	$—	$—	$6,000	$4,500	$—
Deferred tax asset (40 percent)	$—	$—	$2,400	$1,800	$—
Valuation allowance equal to the amount by which the deferred tax asset exceeds the deferred tax liability	—	—	(880)	—	—
Net deferred tax asset	$—	$—	$1,520	$1,800	$—

Total tax expense for each period is as follows:

	Year 1	Years 2-4	Year 5	Year 6	Year 7
Deferred tax expense (benefit):					
Increase in deferred tax liability	$320	$ 880	$ 320	$280	$ 240
(Increase) decrease in net deferred tax asset	—	—	(1,520)	(280)	1,800
	320	880	(1,200)	—	2,040
Currently payable (refundable)	480	1,120	(1,120)	—	760
Total tax expense (benefit)	$800	$2,000	$(2,320)	$ —	$2,800

In year 5, $2,800 of the loss is carried back to reduce taxable income in years 2 through 4, and $1,120 of taxes paid for those years is refunded. In addition, a $1,520 deferred tax liability is recognized for $3,800 of taxable temporary differences, and a $2,400 deferred tax asset is recognized for the $6,000 loss carryforward. However, based on the conclusion described in assumption (e), a valuation allowance is recognized for the amount by which that deferred tax asset exceeds the deferred tax liability.

In year 6, a portion of the deferred tax asset for the loss carryforward is realized because taxable income is earned in that year. The remaining balance of the deferred tax asset for the loss carryforward at the end of year 6 equals the deferred tax liability for the taxable temporary differences. A valuation allowance is not needed.

In year 7, the remaining balance of the loss carryforward is realized, and $760 of taxes are payable on net taxable income of $1,900. A $2,040 deferred tax liability is recognized for the $5,100 of taxable temporary differences. [FAS109, ¶242]

.170 An operating loss or tax credit carryforward from a prior year (for which the deferred tax asset was offset by a valuation allowance) may sometimes reduce taxable income and taxes payable that are attributable to certain revenues or gains that the tax law requires be included in taxable income for the year that cash is received. For financial reporting, however, there may have been no revenue or gain and a liability is recognized for the cash received. Future sacrifices to settle the liability will result in deductible amounts in future years. Under those circumstances, the reduction in taxable income and taxes payable from utilization of the operating loss or tax credit carryforward gives no cause for recognition of a tax benefit because, in effect, the operating loss or tax credit carryforward has been replaced by temporary differences that will result in deductible amounts when a nontax liability is settled in future years. The requirements for recognition of a tax benefit for deductible temporary differences and for operating loss carryforwards are the same, and the manner of reporting the eventual tax benefit recognized (that is, in income or as required by paragraph .136) is not affected by the intervening transaction reported for tax purposes. [FAS109, ¶243]

.171 Exhibit 171A illustrates the interaction of loss carryforwards and temporary differences that will result in net deductible amounts in future years.

Exhibit 171A

**Interaction of Loss Carryforwards and Temporary Differences
That Will Result in Net Deductible Amounts in Future Years**

The assumptions are as follows:

a. The financial loss and the loss reported on the tax return for an enterprise's first year of operations are the same.
b. In year 2, a gain of $2,500 from a transaction that is a sale for tax purposes but a sale and leaseback for financial reporting is the only difference between pretax financial income and taxable income.

	Financial Income	Taxable Income
Year 1: Income (loss) from operations	$(4,000)	$(4,000)
Year 2: Income (loss) from operations	$ —	$ —
Taxable gain on sale		2,500
Taxable income before loss carryforward		2,500
Loss carryforward from year 1		(4,000)
Taxable income		$ —

The $4,000 operating loss carryforward at the end of year 1 is reduced to $1,500 at the end of year 2 because $2,500 of it is used to reduce taxable income. The $2,500 reduc-

Exhibit 171A (continued)

tion in the loss carryforward becomes $2,500 of deductible temporary differences that will reverse and result in future tax deductions when lease payments are made. The enterprise has no deferred tax liability to be offset by those future tax deductions, the future tax deductions cannot be realized by loss carryback because no taxes have been paid, and the enterprise has had pretax losses for financial reporting since inception. Unless positive evidence exists that is sufficient to overcome the negative evidence associated with those losses, a valuation allowance is recognized at the end of year 2 for the full amount of the deferred tax asset related to the $2,500 of deductible temporary differences and the remaining $1,500 of operating loss carryforward. [FAS109, ¶244]

Reporting the Tax Benefit of Operating Loss Carryforwards or Carrybacks

.172 Except as noted in paragraph .136, the manner of reporting the tax benefit of an operating loss carryforward or carryback is determined by the source of the income or loss in the current year and not by (a) the source of the operating loss carryforward or taxes paid in a prior year or (b) the source of expected future income that will result in realization of a deferred tax asset for an operating loss carryforward from the current year. Deferred tax expense or benefit that results because a change in circumstances causes a change in judgment about the future realization of the tax benefit of an operating loss carryforward is allocated to continuing operations (refer to paragraph .125). Thus, for example:

a. The tax benefit of an operating loss carryforward that resulted from an extraordinary loss in a prior year and that is first recognized in the financial statements for the current year:
   (1) Is allocated to continuing operations if it offsets the current or deferred tax consequences of income from continuing operations
   (2) Is allocated to an extraordinary gain if it offsets the current or deferred tax consequences of that extraordinary gain
   (3) Is allocated to continuing operations if it results from a change in circumstances that causes a change in judgment about future realization of a tax benefit
b. The current or deferred tax benefit of a loss from continuing operations in the current year is allocated to continuing operations regardless of whether that loss offsets the current or deferred tax consequences of an extraordinary gain that:
   (1) Occurred in the current year
   (2) Occurred in a prior year (that is, if realization of the tax benefit will be by carryback refund)
   (3) Is expected to occur in a future year. [FAS109, ¶245]

Tax-Planning Strategies

.173 Expectations about future taxable income incorporate numerous assumptions about actions, elections, and strategies to minimize income taxes in future years. For example, an enterprise may have a practice of deferring taxable income whenever possible by structuring sales to qualify as installment sales for tax purposes. Actions such as that are not *tax-planning strategies,* as that term is used in this section, because they are actions that management takes in the normal course of business. For purposes of applying the requirements of this section, a *tax-planning strategy* is an action that management ordinarily might not take but would take, if necessary, to realize a tax benefit for a carryforward before it expires. For example, a strategy to sell property and lease it back for the expressed purpose of generating taxable income to utilize a carryforward before it expires is not an action that management takes in the normal course of business. A qualifying tax-planning strategy is an action that:

a. *Is prudent and feasible.* Management must have the ability to implement the strategy and expect to do so unless the need is eliminated in future years. For example, management would not have to apply the strategy if income earned in a later year uses the entire amount of carryforward from the current year.
b. *An enterprise ordinarily might not take, but would take to prevent an operating loss or tax credit carryforward from expiring unused.* All of the various strategies that are expected to be employed for business or tax purposes other than utilization of carryforwards that would otherwise expire unused are, for purposes of this section, implicit in management's estimate of future taxable income and, therefore, are not tax-planning strategies as that term is used in this section.
c. *Would result in realization of deferred tax assets.* The effect of qualifying tax-planning strategies must be recognized in the determination of the amount of a valuation allowance. Tax-planning strategies need not be considered, however, if positive evidence available from other sources (refer to paragraph .120) is sufficient to support a conclusion that a valuation allowance is *not* necessary. [FAS109, ¶246]

.174 Tax-planning strategies may shift estimated future taxable income between future years. For example, assume that an enterprise has a $1,500 operating loss carryforward that expires at the end of next year and that its estimate of taxable income exclusive of the future reversal of existing temporary differences and carryforwards is approximately $1,000 per year for each of the next several years. That estimate is based, in part, on the enterprise's present practice of making sales on the installment basis and on provisions in the tax law that result in temporary deferral of gains on installment sales. A tax-planning strategy to increase taxable income next year and realize the full tax benefit of that operating loss carryforward might be to structure next year's sales in a manner that does not meet the tax rules to qualify as installment sales. Another strategy might be to change next year's depreciation procedures for tax purposes. [FAS109, ¶247]

.175 Tax-planning strategies also may shift the estimated pattern and timing of future reversals of temporary differences. For example, if an operating loss carryforward otherwise would expire unused at the end of next year, a tax-planning strategy to sell the enterprise's installment sale receivables next year would accelerate the future reversal of *taxable* temporary differences for the gains on those installment sales. In other circumstances, a tax-planning strategy to accelerate the future reversal of *deductible* temporary differences in time to offset taxable income that is expected in an early future year might be the only means to realize a tax benefit for those deductible temporary differences if they otherwise would reverse and provide no tax benefit in some later future year(s). Examples of actions that would accelerate the future reversal of deductible temporary differences include:

a. An annual payment that is larger than an enterprise's usual annual payment to reduce a long-term pension obligation (recognized as a liability in the financial statements) might accelerate a tax deduction for pension expense to an earlier year than would otherwise have occurred.
b. Disposal of obsolete inventory that is reported at net realizable value in the financial statements would accelerate a tax deduction for the amount by which the tax basis exceeds the net realizable value of the inventory.
c. Sale of loans at their reported amount (that is, net of an allowance for bad debts) would accelerate a tax deduction for the allowance for bad debts. [FAS109, ¶248]

.176 A significant expense might need to be incurred to implement a particular tax-planning strategy, or a significant loss might need to be recognized as a result of implementing a particular tax-planning strategy. In either case, that expense or loss (net of any future tax benefit that would result from that expense or loss) reduces the amount of tax benefit that is recognized for the expected effect of a qualifying tax-planning strategy. For that purpose, the future effect of a differential in interest rates (for example, between the rate that would be earned on installment sale receivables and the rate that could be earned on an alternative investment if the tax-planning strategy is to sell those receivables to accelerate the future reversal of related taxable temporary differences) is not considered. [FAS109, ¶249]

.177 Exhibit 177A illustrates recognition of a deferred tax asset based on the expected effect of a qualifying tax-planning strategy when a significant expense would be incurred to implement the strategy.

Exhibit 177A

Qualifying Tax-Planning Strategy with
Significant Expense to Implement the Strategy

The assumptions are as follows:

a. A $900 operating loss carryforward expires at the end of next year.
b. Based on historical results and the weight of other available evidence, the estimated level of taxable income exclusive of the future reversal of existing temporary differences and the operating loss carryforward next year is $100.
c. Taxable temporary differences in the amount of $1,200 ordinarily would result in taxable amounts of approximately $400 in each of the next 3 years.
d. There is a qualifying tax-planning strategy to accelerate the future reversal of all $1,200 of taxable temporary differences to next year.
e. Estimated legal and other expenses to implement that tax-planning strategy are $150.
f. The enacted tax rate is 40 percent for all years.

Without the tax-planning strategy, only $500 of the $900 operating loss carryforward could be realized next year by offsetting (a) $100 of taxable income exclusive of reversing temporary differences and (b) $400 of reversing taxable temporary differences. The other $400 of operating loss carryforward would expire unused at the end of next year. Therefore, the $360 deferred tax asset ($900 at 40 percent) would be offset by a $160 valuation allowance ($400 at 40 percent), and a $200 net deferred tax asset would be recognized for the operating loss carryforward.

With the tax-planning strategy, the $900 operating loss carryforward could be applied against $1,300 of taxable income next year ($100 of taxable income exclusive of reversing temporary differences and $1,200 of reversing taxable temporary differences). The $360 deferred tax asset is reduced by a $90 valuation allowance recognized for the net-of-tax expenses necessary to implement the tax-planning strategy. The amount of that valuation allowance is determined as follows:

Legal and other expenses to implement the tax-planning strategy	$150
Future tax benefit of those legal and other expenses—$150 at 40 percent	60
	$ 90

In summary, a $480 deferred tax liability is recognized for the $1,200 of taxable temporary differences, a $360 deferred tax asset is recognized for the $900 operating loss carryforward, and a $90 valuation allowance is recognized for the net-of-tax expenses of implementing the tax-planning strategy. [FAS109, ¶250]

.178 Under this section, the requirements for consideration of tax-planning strate-gies pertain only to the determination of a valuation allowance for a deferred tax asset. A deferred tax liability ordinarily is recognized for all taxable temporary dif-ferences. The only exceptions are identified in paragraph .108. Certain seemingly taxable temporary differences, however, may or may not result in taxable amounts when those differences reverse in future years. One example is an excess of cash sur-render value of life insurance over premiums paid (paragraph .113). Another exam-ple is an excess of the book over the tax basis of an investment in a domestic subsidi-ary (paragraph .132). The determination of whether those differences are taxable temporary differences does not involve a tax-planning strategy as that term is used in this section. [FAS109, ¶251]

Regulated Enterprises

.179 [The provisions of] paragraph .119 of Section Re6 require a regulated enterprise that applies Section Re6 to capitalize an incurred cost that would otherwise be charged to expense if the following criteria are met:

a. It is probable that future revenue in an amount at least equal to the capitalized cost will result from inclusion of that cost in allowable costs for rate-making purposes.
b. Based on available evidence, the future revenue will be provided to permit recovery of the previously incurred cost rather than to provide for expected levels of similar future costs.

If the income taxes that result from recording a deferred tax liability in accordance with this section meet those criteria, an asset is recognized for those income taxes when the deferred tax liability is recognized. That asset and the deferred tax liability are not offset for general-purpose financial reporting; rather, each is displayed separately. [FAS109, ¶252]

.180 Exhibit 180A illustrates recognition of an asset for the probable future revenue to recover future income taxes related to the deferred tax liability for the equity com-ponent of the allowance for funds used during construction (AFUDC).

Exhibit 180A

Regulated Enterprises—Equity Component of AFUDC

The assumptions are as follows:

a. During year 1, the first year of operations, total construction costs for financial re-porting and tax purposes are $400,000 (exclusive of AFUDC).
b. The enacted tax rate is 34 percent for all future years.

Exhibit 180A (continued)

c. AFUDC (consisting entirely of the equity component) is $26,000. The asset for probable future revenue to recover the related income taxes is calculated as follows:

34 percent of ($26,000 + A) = A (where A equals the asset for probable future revenue)

A = $13,394

At the end of year 1, the related accounts[20] are as follows:

Construction in progress	$426,000
Probable future revenue	$ 13,394
Deferred tax liability [34 percent of ($26,000 + $13,394)]	$ 13,394

[FAS109, ¶253]

.181 Exhibit 181A illustrates adjustment of a deferred tax liability for an enacted change in tax rates.

Exhibit 181A

Regulated Enterprises—Enacted Change in Tax Rates

The assumptions are the same as for the example in Exhibit 180A except that a change in the tax rate from 34 percent to 30 percent is enacted on the first day of year 2. As of the first day of year 2, the related accounts are adjusted so that the balances are as follows:

Construction in progress	$426,000
Probable future revenue	$ 11,143
Deferred tax liability [30 percent of ($26,000 + $11,143)]	$ 11,143

[FAS109, ¶254]

---

[20]In this example, if AFUDC had consisted entirely of a net-of-tax debt component in the amount of $26,000, the related accounts and their balances at the end of year 1 would be construction in progress in the amount of $439,394 and a deferred tax liability in the amount of $13,394. [FAS109, ¶253, fn18]

.182 Exhibit 182A illustrates adjustment of a deferred tax liability for an enacted change in tax rates when that deferred tax liability represents amounts already collected from customers for the future payment of income taxes. In that case, there would be no asset for "probable future revenue."

Exhibit 182A

Regulated Enterprises—Enacted Change in Tax Rates with Refund to Customers of Previously Collected Income Taxes

The assumptions are as follows:

a. Amounts at the end of year 1, the current year, are as follows:

Construction in progress for financial reporting	$400,000
Tax basis of construction in progress	$300,000
Deferred tax liability (34 percent of $100,000)	$ 34,000

b. A change in the tax rate from 34 percent to 30 percent is enacted on the first day of year 2. As a result of the reduction in tax rates, it is probable that $4,000 of the $34,000 (previously collected from customers for the future payment of income taxes) will be refunded to customers, together with the tax benefit of that refund, through a future rate reduction. The liability for the future rate reduction to refund a portion of the deferred taxes previously collected from customers is calculated as follows:

$4,000 + (30 percent of R) = R (where R equals the probable future reduction in revenue)

R = $5,714

As of the first day of year 2, the related accounts are adjusted so that the balances are as follows:

Construction in progress	$400,000
Probable reduction in future revenue	$ 5,714
Deferred tax liability [30 percent of ($100,000 − $5,714)]	$ 28,286

[FAS109, ¶255]

Leveraged Leases

.183 This section does not change (a) the pattern of recognition of after-tax income for leveraged leases as required by paragraph .141 in Section L10 or (b) the allocation of the purchase price in a purchase business combination to acquired leveraged leases as required by that Section. Integration[21] of the results of income tax accounting for leveraged leases with the other results of accounting for income taxes under this section is required when deferred tax credits related to leveraged leases are the only source (refer to paragraph .120) for recognition of a tax benefit for deductible temporary differences and carryforwards not related to leveraged leases. A valuation allowance is not necessary if deductible temporary differences and carryforwards will offset taxable amounts from future recovery of the net investment in the leveraged lease. However, to the extent that the amount of deferred tax credits for a leveraged lease as determined under Section L10 differs from the amount of the deferred tax liability related to the leveraged lease that would otherwise result from applying the requirements of this section, that difference is preserved and is not a source of taxable income for recognition of the tax benefit of deductible temporary differences and operating loss or tax credit carryforwards. [FAS109, ¶256]

.184 Paragraph .141 of Section L10 requires that the tax effect of any difference between the assigned value and the tax basis of a leveraged lease at the date of a business combination not be accounted for as a deferred tax credit. This section does not change that requirement. Any tax effects included in unearned and deferred income as required by Section L10 are not offset by the deferred tax consequences of other temporary differences or by the tax benefit of operating loss or tax credit carryforwards. However, deferred tax credits that arise after the date of a business combination are accounted for in the same manner as described above for leveraged leases that were not acquired in a purchase business combination. [FAS109, ¶257]

---

[21]Integration is an issue when all of the following exist:

(1) The accounting for a leveraged lease requires recognition of deferred tax credits.
(2) The requirements of this section limit the recognition of a tax benefit for deductible temporary differences and carryforwards not related to the leveraged lease.
(3) Unrecognized tax benefits could offset taxable amounts that result from future recovery of the net investment in the leveraged lease.

In those circumstances, integration should be required. However, integration should not override any results that are unique to income tax accounting for leveraged leases, for example, the manner of recognizing the tax effect of an enacted change in tax rates. [FAS109, ¶126]

.185 Exhibit 185A illustrates integration of the results of income tax accounting for leveraged leases with the other results of accounting for income taxes as required by this section.

Exhibit 185A

Integration of the Results of Income Tax Accounting for Leveraged Leases with Other Results of Accounting for Income Taxes

a. At the end of year 1, the current year, an enterprise has two temporary differences. One temporary difference is for a leveraged lease that was entered into in a prior year. During year 1, the enacted tax rate for year 2 and thereafter changed from 40 percent to 35 percent. After adjusting for the change in estimated total net income from the lease as a result of the change in tax rates as required by Section L10, the components of the investment in the leveraged lease at the end of year 1 are as follows:

Net rentals receivable plus residual value less unearned pretax income		$150,000
Reduced by:		
Deferred ITC	$ 9,000	
Deferred tax credits	39,000	48,000
Net investment in leveraged lease for financial reporting		$102,000

b. The other temporary difference is for a $120,000 estimated liability for warranty expense that will result in a tax deduction in year 5 when the liability is expected to be paid. Absent consideration of the deferred tax credits attributable to the leveraged lease, the weight of available evidence indicates that a valuation allowance is needed for the entire amount of the deferred tax asset related to that $120,000 deductible temporary difference.

c. The tax basis of the investment in the leveraged lease at the end of year 1 is $41,000. The amount of the deferred tax liability for that leveraged lease that would otherwise result from the requirements of this section is determined as follows:

Net rentals receivable plus residual value less unearned pretax income	$150,000
Temporary difference for deferred ITC	9,000
	141,000
Tax basis of leveraged lease	41,000
Temporary difference	$100,000
Deferred tax liability (35 percent)	$ 35,000

d. Loss carryback (to year 2) and loss carryforward (to year 20) of the $120,000 tax deduction for warranty expense in year 5 would offset the $100,000 of taxable amounts resulting from future recovery of the net investment in the leveraged lease over the remainder of the lease term.

Exhibit 185A (continued)

e. At the end of year 1, the enterprise recognizes a $42,000 ($120,000 at 35 percent) deferred tax asset and a related $7,000 valuation allowance. The effect is to recognize a $35,000 net deferred tax benefit for the reduction in deferred tax credits attributable to the leveraged lease. Deferred tax credits attributable to the leveraged lease determined under the requirements of Section L10 are $39,000. However, the deferred tax liability determined under the requirements of this section is only $35,000. The $4,000 difference is not available for offsetting. [FAS109, ¶258]

Business Combinations

.186 This section requires recognition of deferred tax liabilities and deferred tax assets (and related valuation allowances, if necessary) for the deferred tax consequences of differences between the assigned values and the tax bases of the assets and liabilities recognized in a business combination accounted for as a purchase under Section B50. A deferred tax liability or asset is not recognized for a difference between the reported amount and the tax basis of goodwill or the portion thereof for which amortization is not deductible for tax purposes (refer to paragraphs .189 and .190), unallocated "negative" goodwill, and leveraged leases (refer to paragraphs .183 through .185). Acquired differences under paragraphs .212 through .224 are accounted for in accordance with the requirements of paragraphs .130 through .133. [FAS109, ¶259]

Nontaxable Business Combinations

.187 Exhibit 187A illustrates recognition and measurement of a deferred tax liability and asset in a nontaxable business combination.

Exhibit 187A

Deferred Tax Liability and Asset in a Nontaxable Business Combination

The assumptions are as follows:

a. The enacted tax rate is 40 percent for all future years, and amortization of goodwill is not deductible for tax purposes.
b. An enterprise is acquired for $20,000, and the enterprise has no leveraged leases.
c. The tax basis of the net assets acquired is $5,000, and the assigned value (other than goodwill) is $12,000. Future recovery of the assets and settlement of the liabilities at their assigned values will result in $20,000 of taxable amounts and $13,000 of deductible amounts that can be offset against each other. Therefore, no valuation allowance is necessary.

Exhibit 187A (continued)

The amounts recorded to account for the purchase transaction are as follows:

Assigned value of the net assets (other than goodwill) acquired	$12,000
Deferred tax liability for $20,000 of taxable temporary differences	(8,000)
Deferred tax asset for $13,000 of deductible temporary differences	5,200
Goodwill	10,800
Purchase price of the acquired enterprise	$20,000

[FAS109, ¶260]

Taxable Business Combinations

.188 In a taxable business combination, the purchase price is assigned to the assets and liabilities recognized for tax purposes as well as for financial reporting. However, the amounts assigned to particular assets and liabilities may differ for financial reporting and tax purposes. A deferred tax liability and asset are recognized for the deferred tax consequences of those temporary differences in accordance with the recognition and measurement requirements of this section. For example, a portion of the amount of goodwill for financial reporting may be allocated to some other asset for tax purposes, and amortization of that other asset may be deductible for tax purposes. If a valuation allowance is recognized for that deferred tax asset at the acquisition date, recognized benefits for those tax deductions after the acquisition date shall be applied (a) first to reduce to zero any goodwill related to that acquisition, (b) second to reduce to zero other noncurrent intangible assets related to that acquisition, and (c) third to reduce income tax expense. [FAS109, ¶261]

.189 Amortization of goodwill is deductible for tax purposes in some tax jurisdictions. In those tax jurisdictions, the reported amount of goodwill and the tax basis of goodwill are each separated into two components as of the combination date for purposes of deferred tax calculations. The first component of each equals the lesser of (a) goodwill for financial reporting or (b) tax-deductible goodwill. The second component of each equals the remainder of each, that is, (1) the remainder, if any, of goodwill for financial reporting or (2) the remainder, if any, of tax-deductible goodwill. Any difference that arises between the book and tax basis of that first component of goodwill in future years is a temporary difference for which a deferred tax liability or asset is recognized based on the requirements of this section. No deferred taxes are recognized for the second component of goodwill. If that second component is an excess of tax-deductible goodwill over the reported amount of goodwill, the tax benefit for that excess is recognized when realized on the tax return, and that tax benefit is applied first to reduce to zero the goodwill related to that acquisition, second to reduce to zero other noncurrent intangible assets related to that acquisition, and third to reduce income tax expense. [FAS109, ¶262]

.190 Exhibit 190A illustrates accounting for the tax consequences of goodwill when amortization of goodwill is deductible for tax purposes.

Exhibit 190A

Accounting for Tax Consequences of Tax-Deductible Goodwill

The assumptions are as follows:

a. At the combination date, the reported amount and tax basis of goodwill are $600 and $800, respectively.
b. For tax purposes, amortization of goodwill will result in tax deductions of $400 in each of years 1 and 2. Those deductions result in a current tax benefit in years 1 and 2.
c. For financial reporting, amortization of goodwill is straight-line over years 1 through 4.
d. For purposes of simplification, the consequences of other temporary differences are ignored for years 1 through 4.
e. Income before amortization of goodwill and income taxes in each of years 1 through 4 is $1,000.
f. The tax rate is 40 percent for all years.

Income taxes payable for years 1 through 4 are:

	Year			
	1	2	3	4
Income before amortization of goodwill	$1,000	$1,000	$1,000	$1,000
Amortization of goodwill	400	400	—	—
Taxable income	$ 600	$ 600	$1,000	$1,000
Income taxes payable (40 percent)	$ 240	$ 240	$ 400	$ 400

At the combination date, goodwill is separated into two components as follows:

	Reported Amount	Tax Basis
First component	$600	$600
Second component	—	200
Total goodwill	$600	$800

A deferred tax liability is recognized at the end of years 1 through 3 for the excess of the reported amount over the tax basis of the first component of goodwill. A deferred tax asset is not recognized for the second component of goodwill; the tax benefit is allocated to reduce goodwill when realized on the tax returns for years 1 and 2.

Exhibit 190A (continued)

The second component of goodwill is deductible $100 per year in years 1 and 2. Those tax deductions provide $40 ($100 at 40 percent) of tax benefits that are realized in years 1 and 2. Allocation of those realized tax benefits to reduce the first component of goodwill produces a deferred tax benefit by reducing the taxable temporary difference related to that component of goodwill. Thus, the total tax benefit allocated to reduce the first component of goodwill in each of years 1 and 2 is the sum of (a) the $40 realized tax benefit allocated to reduce goodwill and (b) the deferred tax benefit from reducing the deferred tax liability related to goodwill. That total tax benefit (TTB) is determined as follows:

TTB = realized tax benefit plus (tax rate times TTB)
TTB = $40 + (.40 × TTB)
TTB = $67

Goodwill for financial reporting for years 1 through 4 is:

	Year			
	1	2	3	4
Balance at beginning of year	$600	$383	$188	$94
Amortization:				
$600 ÷ 4 years	150			
$383 ÷ 3 years		128		
$188 ÷ 2 years			94	94
Total tax benefit allocated to reduce goodwill	67	67	—	—
Balance at end of year	$383	$188	$ 94	$—

The deferred tax liability for the first component of goodwill and the related amount of deferred tax expense (benefit) for years 1 through 4 are:

	Year			
	1	2	3	4
Reported amount of goodwill at end of year	$383	$188	$ 94	$ —
Tax basis of goodwill (first component)	300	—	—	—
Taxable temporary difference	$ 83	$188	$ 94	$ —
Deferred tax liability:				
At end of year (40 percent)	$ 33	$ 75	$ 38	$ —
At beginning of year	—	33	75	38
Deferred tax expense (benefit) for the year	$ 33	$ 42	$(37)	$(38)

Exhibit 190A (continued)

Income for financial reporting for years 1 through 4 is:

	Year			
	1	**2**	**3**	**4**
Income before amortization of goodwill and income taxes	$1,000	$1,000	$1,000	$1,000
Amortization of goodwill	150	128	94	94
Pretax income	850	872	906	906
Income tax expense (benefit):				
Current	240	240	400	400
Deferred	33	42	(37)	(38)
Benefit applied to reduce goodwill	67	67	—	—
Income tax expense	340	349	363	362
Net income	$ 510	$ 523	$ 543	$ 544

[FAS109, ¶263]

Carryforwards—Purchase Method

.191 Accounting for a business combination shall reflect any provisions in the tax law that restrict the future use of either of the combining enterprises' deductible temporary differences or carryforwards to reduce taxable income or taxes payable attributable to the other enterprise subsequent to the business combination. For example, the tax law may limit the use of the acquired enterprise's deductible temporary differences and carryforwards to subsequent taxable income of the acquired enterprise in a consolidated tax return for the combined enterprise. In that circumstance, or if the acquired enterprise will file a separate tax return, the need for a valuation allowance for some portion or all of the acquired enterprise's deferred tax assets for deductible temporary differences and carryforwards is assessed based on the acquired enterprise's *separate* past and expected future results of operations. [FAS109, ¶264]

.192 Exhibit 192A illustrates (a) recognition of a deferred tax asset and the related valuation allowance for acquired deductible temporary differences at the date of a nontaxable business combination and in subsequent periods when (b) the tax law limits the use of an acquired enterprise's deductible temporary differences and carryforwards to subsequent taxable income of the acquired enterprise in a consolidated tax return.

Exhibit 192A

Recognition of a Deferred Tax Asset and the Related Valuation Allowance in a Nontaxable Business Combination When the Tax Law Limits the Use of Acquired Tax Benefits

The assumptions are as follows:

a. The enacted tax rate is 40 percent for all future years.
b. The purchase price is $20,000, and the assigned value of the net assets acquired is also $20,000.
c. The tax basis of the net assets acquired is $60,000. The $40,000 ($60,000 − $20,000) of deductible temporary differences at the combination date is primarily attributable to an allowance for loan losses. Provisions in the tax law limit the use of those future tax deductions to subsequent taxable income of the acquired enterprise.
d. The acquired enterprise's actual pretax results for the two preceding years and the expected results for the year of the business combination are as follows:

Year 1	$(15,000)
Year 2	(10,000)
Year 3 to the combination date	(5,000)
Expected results for the remainder of year 3	(5,000)

e. Based on assessments of all evidence available at the date of the business combination in year 3 and at the end of year 3, management concludes that a valuation allowance is needed at both dates for the entire amount of the deferred tax asset related to the acquired deductible temporary differences.

The acquired enterprise's pretax financial income and taxable income for year 3 (after the business combination) and year 4 are as follows:

	Year 3	Year 4
Pretax financial income	$15,000	$10,000
Reversals of acquired deductible temporary differences	(15,000)	(10,000)
Taxable income	$ —	$ —

At the end of year 4, the remaining balance of acquired deductible temporary differences is $15,000 ($40,000 − $25,000). The deferred tax asset is $6,000 ($15,000 at 40 percent). Based on an assessment of all available evidence at the end of year 4, management concludes that no valuation allowance is needed for that $6,000 deferred tax asset. Elimination of the $6,000 valuation allowance results in a $6,000 deferred tax benefit that is reported as a reduction of deferred income tax expense because there is no goodwill or other noncurrent intangible assets related to the acquisition. For the same reason, tax benefits realized in years 3 and 4 attributable to reversals of acquired deductible temporary differences are reported as a zero current income tax expense.

Exhibit 192A (continued)

The consolidated statement of earnings would include the following amounts attributable to the acquired enterprise for year 3 (after the business combination) and year 4:

	Year 3	Year 4
Pretax financial income	$15,000	$10,000
Income tax expense (benefit):		
Current	—	—
Deferred	—	(6,000)
Net income	$15,000	$16,000

[FAS109, ¶265]

.193 The tax law in some tax jurisdictions may permit the future use of either of the combining enterprises' deductible temporary differences or carryforwards to reduce taxable income or taxes payable attributable to the other enterprise subsequent to the business combination. If the combined enterprise expects to file a consolidated tax return, a deferred tax asset (net of a valuation allowance, if necessary) is recognized for deductible temporary differences or carryforwards of either combining enterprise based on an assessment of the *combined* enterprise's past and expected future results of operations as of the acquisition date. This either reduces goodwill or noncurrent assets (except long-term investments in marketable securities) of the acquired enterprise or creates or increases negative goodwill. [FAS109, ¶266]

.194 Exhibit 194A illustrates (a) elimination of the need for a valuation allowance for the deferred tax asset for an acquired loss carryforward based on offset against taxable temporary differences of the acquiring enterprise in a nontaxable business combination when (b) the tax law permits use of an acquired enterprise's deductible temporary differences and carryforwards to reduce taxable income or taxes payable attributable to the acquiring enterprise in a consolidated tax return.

Exhibit 194A

Recognition of an Acquired Loss Carryforward When the Tax Law Permits Acquired Tax Benefits to Be Utilized by the Acquiring Corporation

The assumptions are as follows:

a. The enacted tax rate is 40 percent for all future years.
b. The purchase price is $20,000. The tax basis of the identified net assets acquired is $5,000, and the assigned value is $12,000, that is, there are $7,000 of taxable temporary differences. The acquired enterprise also has a $16,000 operating loss carryforward, which, under the tax law, may be used by the acquiring enterprise in the consolidated tax return.

Exhibit 194A (continued)

c. The acquiring enterprise has temporary differences that will result in $30,000 of net taxable amounts in future years.
d. All temporary differences of the acquired and acquiring enterprises will result in taxable amounts before the end of the acquired enterprise's loss carryforward period.

In assessing the need for a valuation allowance, future taxable income exclusive of reversing temporary differences and carryforwards (paragraph .120(b)) need not be considered because the $16,000 operating loss carryforward will offset (a) the *acquired* enterprise's $7,000 of taxable temporary differences and (b) another $9,000 of the *acquiring* enterprise's taxable temporary differences. The amounts recorded to account for the purchase transaction are as follows:

Assigned value of the identified net assets acquired	$12,000
Deferred tax liability recognized for the acquired company's taxable temporary differences ($7,000 at 40 percent)	(2,800)
Deferred tax asset recognized for the acquired loss carryforward based on offset against the acquired company's taxable temporary differences ($7,000 at 40 percent)	2,800
Deferred tax asset recognized for the acquired loss carryforward based on offset against the acquiring company's taxable temporary differences ($9,000 at 40 percent)	3,600
Goodwill	4,400
Purchase price of the acquired enterprise	$20,000

[FAS109, ¶267]

Subsequent Recognition of Carryforward Benefits—Purchase Method

.195 If a valuation allowance is recognized for some portion or all of an acquired enterprise's deferred tax asset for deductible temporary differences and operating loss or tax credit carryforwards at the acquisition date, tax benefits for those items recognized in financial statements for a subsequent year(s) are:

a. First applied to reduce to zero any goodwill related to the acquisition
b. Second applied to reduce to zero other noncurrent intangible assets related to the acquisition
c. Third applied to reduce income tax expense.

Additional amounts of deductible temporary differences and operating loss or tax credit carryforwards may arise after the acquisition date and before recognition of the tax benefit of amounts existing at the acquisition date. Tax benefits are recognized in later years as follows:

a. The tax benefit of amounts existing at the acquisition date is first applied to reduce goodwill and other noncurrent intangible assets to zero. Any additional tax benefit reduces income tax expense.
b. The tax benefit of amounts arising after the acquisition date is recognized as a reduction of income tax expense.

Whether a tax benefit recognized in later years is attributable to an amount (for example, an operating loss carryforward) existing at or arising after the acquisition date is determined for financial reporting by provisions in the tax law that identify the sequence in which those amounts are utilized for tax purposes. If not determinable by provisions in the tax law, a tax benefit recognized for financial reporting is prorated between a reduction of (a) goodwill and other noncurrent intangible assets and (b) income tax expense. [FAS109, ¶268]

.196 Exhibit 196A illustrates recognition of tax benefits subsequent to a business combination.

Exhibit 196A

Recognition of Tax Benefits Subsequent to a Business Combination

The assumptions are as follows:

a. A nontaxable business combination occurs on the first day of year 1. Before considering any acquired deferred tax assets, the purchase transaction is summarized as follows:

	Assigned Value	Tax Basis
Net assets acquired	$5,000	$6,000
Excess of purchase price over the fair value of the net assets acquired*	1,500	
Purchase price	$6,500	

---
*There are no other noncurrent intangible assets.

Exhibit 196A (continued)

b. The only difference between pretax financial income and taxable income (amortization of goodwill is disregarded for this example) for years 1 through 3 is a $1,000 loss for tax purposes in year 1 from disposal of the acquired identified net assets at amounts equal to their $5,000 assigned value on the acquisition date.

	Year 1	Year 2	Year 3
Pretax financial income (loss)	$(3,000)	$2,500	$1,500
Disposal of acquired identified net assets	(1,000)	—	—
Taxable income (loss) before loss carryforward	(4,000)	2,500	1,500
Loss carryforward (loss carryback not permitted)	4,000	(2,500)	(1,500)
Taxable income after loss carryforward	$ —	$ —	$ —

c. The tax rate is 40 percent for all years.
d. Based on an assessment of all available evidence, management reaches the following conclusions at the acquisition date and at the end of years 1 and 2:
   (1) At the acquisition date, the portion of the $1,000 of deductible temporary differences ($6,000 – $5,000) for which it is more likely than not that a tax benefit will not be realized is $500.
   (2) At the end of year 1, the portion of the $4,000 loss carryforward for which it is more likely than not that a tax benefit will not be realized is $1,750.
   (3) At the end of year 2, it is more likely than not that a tax benefit will be realized for all of the remaining $1,500 of loss carryforward.

At the acquisition date, a $400 ($1,000 at 40 percent) deferred tax asset and a $200 ($500 at 40 percent) valuation allowance are recognized. The $200 net tax benefit reduces the excess of purchase price over the fair value of the net assets acquired from $1,500 to $1,300. Thus, the amount of goodwill recognized at the acquisition date is $1,300.

During year 1, the $1,000 of net deductible temporary differences at the acquisition date reverse and are part of the $4,000 loss carryforward for tax purposes at the end of year 1. An analysis of the components of that $4,000 loss carryforward follows:

	Acquired Deductions	Loss in Year 1	Total
Tax loss carryforward	$1,000	$3,000	$4,000
Portion for which a tax benefit was recognized at the acquisition date	500	—	500
Remainder available for recognition of a tax benefit at the end of year 1	$ 500	$3,000	$3,500

Exhibit 196A (continued)

Provisions in the tax law do not distinguish between those two components of the $3,500, and the component that is used first for tax purposes is indeterminable. However, the $500 of acquired deductions for which a tax benefit has not been recognized is one-seventh of the $3,500 total, and the $3,000 loss in year 1 is six-sevenths of the $3,500 total. The tax benefit of that $3,500 is prorated one-seventh to reduce goodwill and six-sevenths to reduce income tax expense when recognized in years 1 and 2.

At the end of year 1, a $1,600 ($4,000 at 40 percent) deferred tax asset and a $700 ($1,750 at 40 percent) valuation allowance are recognized. The tax benefit for the $700 increase in the net deferred tax asset (from $200 at the acquisition date to $900 at the end of year 1) is prorated as follows:

a. One-seventh or $100 to reduce goodwill
b. Six-sevenths or $600 to reduce tax expense.

During year 2, $1,000 ($2,500 at 40 percent) of the deferred tax asset recognized at the end of year 1 is realized. In addition, a tax benefit is recognized for the remaining $1,750 of future tax deductions by eliminating the $700 valuation allowance. That tax benefit is prorated $100 to reduce goodwill and $600 to reduce tax expense. The combined effect of the changes in the deferred tax asset and the related valuation allowance during year 2 is illustrated below:

| | Deferred Tax Asset | | Tax Expense |
	Year 1	Year 2	or (Benefit)
Deferred tax asset	$1,600	$600	$1,000
Valuation allowance	(700)	—	(700)
	$ 900	$600	300
Portion of $700 tax benefit allocated to reduce goodwill			100
Deferred tax expense for year 2			$ 400

The $600 deferred tax asset at the end of year 2 is realized in year 3, resulting in $600 of deferred tax expense for year 3. The consolidated statement of earnings would include the following amounts attributable to the acquired enterprise:

	Year 1	Year 2	Year 3
Pretax financial income (loss)	$(3,000)	$2,500	$1,500
Net deferred tax expense (benefit)	(600)	400	600
Net income (loss)	$(2,400)	$2,100	$ 900

[FAS109, ¶269]

Carryforwards—Pooling-of-Interests Method

.197 The separate financial statements of combining enterprises for prior periods are restated on a combined basis when a business combination is accounted for by the pooling-of-interests method. For restatement of periods prior to the combination date, a combining enterprise's operating loss carryforward does not offset the other enterprise's taxable income because consolidated tax returns cannot be filed for those periods. However, provisions in the tax law may permit an operating loss carryforward of either of the combining enterprises to offset combined taxable income subsequent to the combination date. [FAS109, ¶270]

.198 If the combined enterprise expects to file consolidated tax returns, a deferred tax asset is recognized for either combining enterprise's operating loss carryforward in a prior period. A valuation allowance is necessary to the extent it is more likely than not that a tax benefit will not be realized for that loss carryforward through offset of either (a) the other enterprise's deferred tax liability for taxable temporary differences that will reverse subsequent to the combination date or (b) combined taxable income subsequent to the combination date. Determined in that manner, the valuation allowance may be less than the sum of the valuation allowances in the separate financial statements of the combining enterprises prior to the combination date. That tax benefit is recognized as part of the adjustment to restate financial statements on a combined basis for prior periods. The same requirements apply to deductible temporary differences and tax credit carryforwards. [FAS109, ¶271]

.199 A taxable business combination may sometimes be accounted for by the pooling-of-interests method. The increase in the tax basis of the net assets acquired results in temporary differences. The deferred tax consequences of those temporary differences are recognized and measured the same as for other temporary differences. As of the combination date, recognizable tax benefits attributable to the increase in tax basis are allocated to contributed capital. Tax benefits attributable to the increase in tax basis that become recognizable after the combination date (that is, by elimination of a valuation allowance) are reported as a reduction of income tax expense. [FAS109, ¶272]

Intraperiod Tax Allocation

.200 If there is only one item other than continuing operations, the portion of income tax expense or benefit for the year that remains after the allocation to continuing operations is allocated to that item. If there are two or more items other than continuing operations, the amount that remains after the allocation to continuing operations is allocated among those other items in proportion to their individual effects on income tax expense or benefit for the year. [FAS109, ¶273]

.201 Exhibit 201A illustrates allocation of income tax expense if there is only one item other than income from continuing operations.

Exhibit 201A

Allocation of Income Tax Expense—One Item Other Than Income from Continuing Operations

The assumptions are as follows:

a. The enterprise's pretax financial income and taxable income are the same.
b. The enterprise's ordinary loss from continuing operations is $500.
c. The enterprise also has an extraordinary gain of $900 that is a capital gain for tax purposes.
d. The tax rate is 40 percent on ordinary income and 30 percent on capital gains. Income taxes currently payable are $120 ($400 at 30 percent).

Income tax expense is allocated between the pretax loss from operations and the extraordinary gain as follows:

Total income tax expense	$120
Tax benefit allocated to the loss from operations	(150)
Incremental tax expense allocated to the extraordinary gain	$270

The effect of the $500 loss from continuing operations was to offset an equal amount of capital gains that otherwise would be taxed at a 30 percent tax rate. Thus, $150 ($500 at 30 percent) of tax benefit is allocated to continuing operations. The $270 incremental effect of the extraordinary gain is the difference between $120 of total tax expense and the $150 tax benefit from continuing operations. [FAS109, ¶274]

.202 Exhibit 202A illustrates allocation of the tax benefit of a tax credit carryforward that is recognized as a deferred tax asset in the current year.

Exhibit 202A

Allocation of the Tax Benefit of an Originating Tax Credit Carryforward

The assumptions are as follows:

a. The enterprise's pretax financial income and taxable income are the same.
b. Pretax financial income for the year comprises $300 from continuing operations and $400 from an extraordinary gain.
c. The tax rate is 40 percent. Taxes payable for the year are zero because $330 of tax credits that arose in the current year more than offset the $280 of tax otherwise payable on $700 of taxable income.

Exhibit 202A (continued)

d. A $50 deferred tax asset is recognized for the $50 ($330 − $280) tax credit carryforward. Based on the weight of available evidence, management concludes that no valuation allowance is necessary.

Income tax expense or benefit is allocated between pretax income from continuing operations and the extraordinary gain as follows:

Total income tax benefit		$ (50)
Tax expense (benefit) allocated to income from continuing operations:		
Tax (before tax credits) on $300 of taxable income at 40 percent	$120	
Tax credits	(330)	(210)
Tax expense allocated to the extraordinary gain		$160

Absent the extraordinary gain and assuming it was not the deciding factor in reaching a conclusion that a valuation allowance is not needed, the entire tax benefit of the $330 of tax credits would be allocated to continuing operations. The presence of the extraordinary gain does not change that allocation. [FAS109, ¶275]

.203 Income taxes are sometimes allocated directly to shareholders' equity. Exhibit 203A illustrates the allocation of income taxes for translation adjustments under Section F60 directly to shareholders' equity.

Exhibit 203A

Allocation of Income Taxes Directly to Shareholders' Equity

a. A foreign subsidiary has earnings of FC600 for year 2. Its net assets (and unremitted earnings) are FC1,000 and FC1,600 at the end of years 1 and 2, respectively.
b. The foreign currency is the functional currency. For year 2, translated amounts are as follows:

	Foreign Currency	Exchange Rate	Dollars
Unremitted earnings, beginning of year	1,000	FC1 = $1.20	1,200
Earnings for the year	600	FC1 = $1.10	660
Unremitted earnings, end of year	1,600	FC1 = $1.00	1,600

c. A $260 translation adjustment ($1,200 + $660 − $1,600) is charged to the cumulative translation adjustment account in shareholders' equity for year 2.

Exhibit 203A (continued)

d. The U.S. parent expects that all of the foreign subsidiary's unremitted earnings will be remitted in the foreseeable future, and under paragraph .209, a deferred U.S. tax liability is recognized for those unremitted earnings.

e. The U.S. parent accrues the deferred tax liability at a 20 percent tax rate (that is, net of foreign tax credits, foreign tax credit carryforwards, and so forth). An analysis of the net investment in the foreign subsidiary and the related deferred tax liability for year 2 is as follows:

	Net Investment	Deferred Tax Liability
Balances, beginning of year	$1,200	$240
Earnings and related taxes	660	132
Translation adjustment and related taxes	(260)	(52)
Balances, end of year	$1,600	$320

f. For year 2, $132 of deferred taxes are charged against earnings, and $52 of deferred taxes are credited directly to the cumulative translation adjustment account in shareholders' equity. [FAS109, ¶276]

Balance Sheet Classification of Deferred Income Taxes

.204 Paragraphs .205 through .211 illustrate the balance sheet classification of certain types of deferred income taxes but do not encompass all possible circumstances. Accordingly, each situation should be resolved based on an evaluation of the facts, using these examples as guides to the extent that they are applicable. [FAS37, ¶16]

Accounting Change for Tax Purposes

.205 The deferred tax liability or asset [FAS109, ¶288p] associated with an accounting change for tax purposes would be classified like the associated asset or liability if reduction of that associated asset or liability will cause the [FAS37, ¶19] temporary difference [FAS109, ¶287] to reverse. If there is no associated asset or liability or if the [FAS37, ¶19] temporary difference [FAS109, ¶287] will reverse only over a period of time, the [FAS37, ¶19] deferred tax liability or asset [FAS109, ¶288p] would be classified based on the expected reversal date of the specific [FAS37, ¶19] temporary difference. [FAS109, ¶287]

.206 An enterprise changes its method of handling bad debts for tax purposes from the cash method to the reserve method. Ten percent of the effect of the change at the beginning of calendar year 19X1 will be included as a deduction from taxable income each year for 10 years. The enterprise uses a one-year time period as the basis for classifying current assets and current liabilities on its balance sheet. At December 31, 19X1, the amount of the effect of the change that is yet to be included as a deduction from taxable income and the balance of the related deferred income taxes are as follows:

Amount of the effect of the change that is yet to be included as a
  deduction from taxable income (⁹/₁₀ of total effect of the change)   <u>$5,125,000</u>

[FAS37, ¶20]

Deferred Tax Asset (40 percent is the enacted tax rate—no valuation
  allowance deemed necessary)   <u>$2,050,000</u>

[FAS109, ¶288p]

.207 The deferred tax asset does [FAS109, ¶288p] not relate to trade receivables or provisions for doubtful accounts because collection or write-off of the receivables will not cause the [FAS37, ¶21] temporary differences [FAS109, ¶287] to reverse; the [FAS37, ¶21] temporary differences [FAS109, ¶287] will reverse over time. Accordingly, the enterprise would classify the [FAS37, ¶21] deferred tax asset [FAS109, ¶288p] based on the scheduled reversal of the related [FAS37, ¶21] temporary differences. [FAS109, ¶287] One-ninth of the remaining [FAS37, ¶21] temporary differences [FAS109, ¶287] are scheduled to reverse in 19X2, so one-ninth of the related [FAS37, ¶21] deferred tax asset [FAS109, ¶288p] would be classified as current at December 31, 19X1 [FAS37, ¶21] ($227,778). [FAS109, ¶288p]

Method of Reporting Construction Contracts

.208 An enterprise reports profits on construction contracts on the completed contract method for tax purposes and the percentage-of-completion method for financial reporting purposes. The [FAS37, ¶22] temporary differences [FAS109, ¶288p] do not relate to an asset or liability that appears on the enterprise's balance sheet; the [FAS37, ¶22] temporary differences [FAS109, ¶287] will only reverse when the contracts are completed. Receivables that result from progress billings can be collected with no effect on the [FAS37, ¶22] temporary differences; [FAS109, ¶287] likewise, contract retentions can be collected with no effect on [FAS37, ¶22] temporary differences, [FAS109, ¶287] and the [FAS37, ¶22] temporary differences [FAS109, ¶287] will reverse when the contracts are deemed to be complete even if there is a waiting period before retentions will be received. Accordingly, the enterprise would classify the [FAS37, ¶22] deferred tax liability [FAS109, ¶288p] based on the estimated reversal of the related [FAS37, ¶22] temporary differences. [FAS109, ¶287] Deferred tax liabilities [FAS109, ¶288p] related to [FAS37, ¶22] temporary differences [FAS109, ¶287] that will reverse within the same time period used in classifying other contract-related assets and liabilities as current (for example, an operating cycle) would be classified as current. [FAS37, ¶22]

Unremitted Foreign Earnings of Subsidiaries

.209 An enterprise provides U.S. income taxes on the portion of its unremitted foreign earnings that are not considered to be permanently reinvested in its consolidated foreign subsidiary. The foreign earnings are included in U.S. taxable income in the year in which dividends are paid. The enterprise uses a one-year time period as the basis for classifying current assets and current liabilities on its balance sheet. At December 31, 19X1, the accumulated amount of unremitted earnings on which taxes have been provided and the balance of the related deferred income taxes are as follows:

Accumulated unremitted earnings on which taxes have been provided:

Expected to be remitted within one year	$ 9,800,000
Not expected to be remitted within one year	2,700,000
Total	$12,500,000

Accumulated [FAS37, ¶23] Deferred Tax Liability [FAS109, ¶288p]	
Related to Unremitted Earnings	$ 1,250,000

[FAS37, ¶23]

.210 The [FAS37, ¶24] deferred tax liability does [FAS109, ¶288p] not relate to an asset or liability on the consolidated balance sheet; the [FAS37, ¶24] temporary difference [FAS109, ¶287] will only reverse when the unremitted earnings are received from the foreign subsidiary by the parent. A payment between consolidated affiliates does not change the consolidated balance sheet, so no item on the consolidated balance sheet would be liquidated. Unremitted earnings expected to be remitted within the next year represent 78 percent of the total unremitted earnings for which tax has been provided ($9,800,000 ÷ $12,500,000). Therefore, 78 percent of the related [FAS37, ¶24] deferred tax liability [FAS109, ¶288p] would be classified as current on the consolidated balance sheet ($975,000). [FAS37, ¶24]

.211 If the subsidiary were accounted for on the equity method rather than consolidated (for example, a subsidiary reported on the equity method in separate parent company financial statements), the deferred income taxes would relate to the recorded investment in the subsidiary. The payment of dividends that causes the reversal of the [FAS37, ¶25] temporary difference [FAS109, ¶287] would be accompanied by a reduction of the recorded investment in the subsidiary. Therefore, the [FAS37, ¶25] deferred tax liability [FAS109, ¶288p] would be classified the same as the related investment in the subsidiary. [FAS37, ¶25]

Undistributed Earnings of Subsidiaries

.212 The inclusion of undistributed earnings of a subsidiary[22] in the pretax accounting income of a parent company, either through consolidation or accounting for the investment by the equity method [APB23, ¶9] results in a temporary difference. [FAS109, ¶288f]

Temporary Difference

.213 It should be presumed that all undistributed earnings of a subsidiary will be transferred to the parent company. Accordingly, the undistributed earnings of a subsidiary included in consolidated income shall be accounted for as a temporary difference unless the tax law provides a means by which the investment in a domestic subsidiary can be recovered tax free. However, a deferred tax liability is not recognized for (a) an excess of the amount for financial reporting over the tax basis of an investment in a foreign subsidiary that meets the criteria in paragraph .215 and (b) undistributed earnings of a domestic subsidiary that arose in fiscal years beginning on or before December 15, 1992 and that meet the criteria in paragraph .215. The criteria in paragraph .215 do not apply to undistributed earnings of domestic subsidiaries that arise in fiscal years beginning after December 15, 1992, and a deferred tax liability shall be recognized if the undistributed earnings are a taxable temporary difference. [FAS109, ¶288f]

.214 A deferred tax asset shall be recognized for an excess of the tax basis over the amount for financial reporting of an investment in a subsidiary in accordance with the requirements of paragraph .133. [FAS109, ¶288f]

Indefinite Reversal Criterion

.215 The presumption that all undistributed earnings will be transferred to the parent company may be overcome, and no income taxes shall be accrued by the parent company, if sufficient evidence shows that the subsidiary has invested or will invest the undistributed earnings indefinitely or that the earnings will be remitted in a tax-free liquidation. A parent company shall have evidence of specific plans for reinvestment of undistributed earnings of a subsidiary that demonstrate that remittance of the earnings will be postponed indefinitely. Experience of the enterprises and definite future programs of operations and remittances are examples of the types of evidence required to substantiate the parent company's representation of indefinite postponement of remittances from a subsidiary. If circumstances change and it becomes apparent that some or all of the undistributed earnings of a subsidiary will be remitted in the foreseeable future but income taxes have not been recognized by the parent company, it shall

---

[22]The conclusions of this section on undistributed earnings of a subsidiary also apply to the portion of the earnings of a Domestic International Sales Corporation (DISC) that is eligible for tax deferral. [APB23, ¶9, fn2]

accrue as an expense of the current period income taxes attributable to that remittance; income tax expense for such undistributed earnings shall not be accounted for as an extraordinary item. If it becomes apparent that some or all of the undistributed earnings of a subsidiary on which income taxes have been accrued will not be remitted in the foreseeable future, the parent company shall adjust income tax expense of the current period; such adjustment of income tax expense shall not be accounted for as an extraordinary item. [APB23, ¶12]

Change in Investment

.216 An investment in common stock of a subsidiary may change so that it is no longer a subsidiary because the parent company sells a portion of the investment, the subsidiary sells additional stock, or other transactions affect the investment. If the remaining investment in common stock should be accounted for by the equity method, the investor shall recognize income taxes on its share of current earnings of the investee enterprise in accordance with [APB23, ¶13] this section. [FAS109, ¶287] If a parent company did not recognize income taxes on its equity in undistributed earnings of a subsidiary for the reasons cited in paragraph .215 (and the enterprise in which the investment is held ceases to be a subsidiary), it shall accrue as a current period expense income taxes on undistributed earnings in the period that it becomes apparent[23] that any of those undistributed earnings (prior to the change in status) will be remitted; the accrual of those income taxes shall not be accounted for as an extraordinary item. [APB23, ¶13] If a parent company recognizes a deferred tax liability for the temporary difference arising from its equity in undistributed earnings of a subsidiary and subsequently reduces its investment in the subsidiary through a taxable sale or other transaction, the amount of the temporary difference and the related deferred tax liability will change. An investment in common stock of an investee (other than a subsidiary or corporate joint venture) may change so that the investee becomes a subsidiary because the investor acquires additional common stock, the investee acquires or retires common stock, or other transactions affect the investment. A temporary difference for the investor's share of the undistributed earnings of the investee prior to the date it becomes a subsidiary shall continue to be treated as a temporary difference for which a deferred tax liability shall continue to be recognized to the extent that dividends from the subsidiary do not exceed the parent company's share of the subsidiary's earnings subsequent to the date it became a subsidiary. [FAS109, ¶288f]

Disclosure

.217 Paragraphs .142 through .148 specify the requirements for financial statement disclosures [about income taxes]. [FAS109, ¶288f]

---

[23]The change in the status of an investment would not by itself mean that remittance of these undistributed earnings should be considered apparent. [APB23, ¶13, fn5]

Investments in Corporate Joint Ventures

.218 The principles applicable to undistributed earnings of subsidiaries (refer to paragraphs .212 through .216) also apply to tax effects of differences between taxable income and pretax accounting income attributable to earnings of corporate joint ventures that are essentially permanent in duration and are accounted for by the equity method.[24] [APB23, ¶17]

Disclosure

.219 The disclosure requirements set forth in paragraphs .142 through .148 also apply to earnings of corporate joint ventures. [APB23, ¶18]

Bad-Debt Reserves of Savings and Loan Associations

.220 Regulatory authorities require both stock and mutual savings and loan associations to appropriate a portion of earnings to general reserves[25] and to retain the reserves as a protection for depositors. Provisions of the U.S. Internal Revenue Code permit a savings and loan association to deduct an annual addition to a reserve for bad debts[26] in determining taxable income, subject to certain limitations. This annual addition permitted by the Code generally differs significantly from the bad-debt experience upon which determination of pretax accounting income is based. Thus, taxable income and pretax accounting income of an association usually differ. [APB23, ¶19]

.221 Although a general reserve determined according to requirements of the regulatory authorities is not directly related to a reserve for bad debts computed according to provisions of the U.S. Internal Revenue Code, the purposes and restrictions of each reserve are similar. Amounts of bad-debt deductions for income tax purposes are includable in taxable income of later years only if the bad-debt reserves are used subsequently for purposes other than to absorb bad-debt losses. [APB23, ¶20]

.222 The term *pretax accounting income,* as used in paragraphs .220 through .222, represents income or loss for a period, exclusive of related income tax expense, determined in conformity with generally accepted accounting principles. The term *taxable income,* as used in paragraphs .220 through .222, represents pretax accounting income

---

[24]Certain corporate joint ventures have a life limited by the nature of the venture, project, or other business activity. Therefore, a reasonable assumption is that a part or all of the undistributed earnings of the venture will be transferred to the investor in a taxable distribution. Deferred taxes shall be recorded, in accordance with [APB23, ¶17, fn7] this section [FAS109, ¶287], at the time the earnings (or losses) are included in the investor's income. [APB23, ¶17, fn7]

[25]The term *general reserves* is used in the context of the special meaning this term has in regulatory pronouncements and in the U.S. Internal Revenue Code. [APB23, ¶19, fn8]

[26]The term *reserve for bad debts* is used in the context of the special meaning this term has in regulatory pronouncements and in the U.S. Internal Revenue Code. [APB23, ¶19, fn8]

(a) adjusted for reversal of provisions for estimated losses on loans and property acquired in settlement of loans, gains or losses on the sales of such property, and adjusted for [APB23, ¶21] events that do not have tax consequences [FAS109, ¶288f] and (b) after giving effect to the bad-debt deduction allowable by the U.S. Internal Revenue Code assuming the applicable tax return were to be prepared based on such adjusted pretax accounting income. [APB23, ¶21]

.223 As described in paragraph .130, a savings and loan association[27] shall not provide deferred taxes on taxable temporary differences related to bad-debt reserves for tax purposes that arose in tax years beginning before December 31, 1987 (the base-year amount). [FAS109, ¶288f] However, if circumstances indicate that the association is likely to pay income taxes, either currently or in later years, because of known or expected reductions in the bad-debt reserve, income taxes attributable to that reduction shall be accrued as tax expense of the current period; the accrual of those income taxes shall not be accounted for as an extraordinary item. [APB23, ¶23]

Disclosure

.224 Paragraphs .142 through .148 specify the requirements for financial statement disclosures. [FAS109, ¶288f] [Those] disclosure requirements also apply to a parent company of a savings and loan association accounting for that investment either through consolidation or by the equity method. [APB23, ¶25]

Income Taxes of Stock Life Insurance Enterprises

Deferred Income Taxes

.225 Except as noted in paragraph .226, a deferred tax liability or asset shall be recognized for the deferred tax consequences of temporary differences in accordance with this section. [FAS109, ¶288t]

Policyholders' Surplus

.226 As described in paragraph .130, a life insurance enterprise shall not provide deferred taxes on taxable temporary differences related to policyholders' surplus that arose in fiscal years beginning on or before December 15, 1992. [FAS109, ¶288t] However, if circumstances indicate that the insurance enterprise is likely to pay income taxes, either currently or in later years, because of a known or expected reduction in policyholders' surplus, income taxes attributable to that reduction shall be accrued as a tax expense of the current period; the accrual of those income taxes shall not be accounted for as an extraordinary item. [FAS60, ¶59] Paragraphs .142 through .148 specify the requirements for financial statement disclosures about income taxes. [FAS109, ¶288t]

---

[27]The conclusions in this section apply to stock and mutual savings and loan associations and mutual savings banks. [APB23, ¶23, fn9]

Accounting for Investment Tax Credits

.227 [Tax law and regulations may] provide for an *investment [tax] credit* that, in general, is equal to a specified percentage of the cost of certain depreciable assets acquired and placed in service [during specified periods]. [APB2, ¶1]

.228 [It] shall be considered preferable [APB4, ¶10] [for] the allowable investment credit [to] be reflected in net income over the productive life of acquired property [(the deferral method)]. [APB2, ¶13] [However,] treating the credit as a reduction of federal income taxes of the year in which the credit arises [(the flow-through method)] is also acceptable. [APB4, ¶10]

.229 Disclosure [shall] be made of the method followed and amounts involved, when material. [APB4, ¶11]

.230 An investment credit shall be reflected in the financial statements to the extent it has been used as an offset against income taxes otherwise currently payable or to the extent its benefit is recognizable under the provisions of this section. Refer to paragraph .147 for required disclosures related to (a) tax credit carryforwards for tax purposes and (b) tax credit carryforwards for which a tax benefit has not been recognized for financial reporting. [FAS109, ¶288b]

Deferral Method

.231 While reflection of the allowable credit [on the balance sheet] as a reduction in the net amount at which the acquired property is stated (either directly or by inclusion in an offsetting account) may be preferable in many cases, [it is] recognized as equally appropriate [to display] the credit as deferred income, provided it is amortized over the productive life of the acquired property. [APB2, ¶14] [(Refer to paragraph .509 for supplemental guidance on applying the deferral method.)]

.232 It [is] preferable that the statement of income in the year in which the allowable investment credit arises shall be affected only by the results that flow from the accounting for the credit [under the deferral method] set forth in paragraph .228. Nevertheless, reflection of income tax provisions, in the income statement, in the amount payable (that is, after deduction of the allowable investment credit) is appropriate provided that a corresponding charge is made to an appropriate cost or expense (for example, to the provision for depreciation). [APB2, ¶15]

Offsetting Securities against Taxes Payable

.233 It is a general principle of accounting that the offsetting of assets and liabilities in the balance sheet is improper except when a right of setoff exists. [Refer to Section B10, "Balance Sheet Display: Offsetting," paragraphs .101A, .101B, and .107, for guidance on determining whether a right of setoff exists.] Accordingly, the offset of cash or other assets against the tax liability or other amounts owing to governmental bodies is not acceptable except in the circumstances described in paragraph .235. [APB10, ¶7(1)]

.234 Most securities now issued by governments are not by their terms designed specifically for the payment of taxes and, accordingly, shall not be deducted from taxes payable on the balance sheet. [APB10, ¶7(2)]

.235 The only exception to the general principle [in paragraph .233] occurs when it is clear that a purchase of securities (acceptable for the payment of taxes) is in substance an advance payment of taxes that will be payable in the relatively near future, so that in the special circumstances the purchase is tantamount to the prepayment of taxes. This occurs at times, for example, as an accommodation to a local government and in some instances when governments issue securities that are specifically designated as being acceptable for the payment of taxes of those governments. [APB10, ¶7(3)]

[**Note:** Additional guidance with respect to implementing Section I27 is presented in *A Guide to Implementation of Statement 109 on Accounting for Income Taxes: Questions and Answers.* The publication addresses 28 questions and was written by FASB staff members, Raymond E. Perry and E. Raymond Simpson. This publication is available from the Order Department, Financial Accounting Standards Board, 401 Merritt 7, P.O. Box 5116, Norwalk, CT 06856-5116, telephone (203) 847-0700.]

Glossary

.401 Carrybacks. Deductions or credits that cannot be utilized on the tax return during a year that may be carried back to reduce taxable income or taxes payable in a prior year. An operating loss carryback is an excess of tax deductions over gross income in a year; a tax credit carryback is the amount by which tax credits available for utilization exceed statutory limitations. Different tax jurisdictions have different rules about whether excess deductions or credits may be carried back and the length of the carryback period. [FAS109, ¶289]

.402 Carryforwards. Deductions or credits that cannot be utilized on the tax return during a year that may be carried forward to reduce taxable income or taxes payable in a future year. An operating loss carryforward is an excess of tax deductions over gross income in a year; a tax credit carryforward is the amount by which tax credits available for utilization exceed statutory limitations. Different tax jurisdictions have different rules about whether excess deductions or credits may be carried forward and the length of the carryforward period. The terms *carryforward, operating loss carryforward,* and *tax credit carryforward* refer to the amounts of those items, if any, reported in the tax return for the current year. [FAS109, ¶289]

.403 Current tax expense or benefit. The amount of income taxes paid or payable (or refundable) for a year as determined by applying the provisions of the enacted tax law to the taxable income or excess of deductions over revenues for that year. [FAS109, ¶289]

.404 Deductible temporary difference. Temporary differences that result in deductible amounts in future years when the related asset or liability is recovered or settled, respectively. Also refer to **Temporary difference.** [FAS109, ¶289]

.405 Deferred tax asset. The deferred tax consequences attributable to deductible temporary differences and carryforwards. A deferred tax asset is measured using the applicable enacted tax rate and provisions of the enacted tax law. A deferred tax asset is reduced by a valuation allowance if, based on the weight of evidence available, it is more likely than not that some portion or all of a deferred tax asset will not be realized. [FAS109, ¶289]

.406 Deferred tax expense or benefit. The change during the year in an enterprise's deferred tax liabilities and assets. For deferred tax liabilities and assets acquired in a purchase business combination during the year, it is the change since the combination date. Income tax expense or benefit for the year is allocated among continuing operations, discontinued operations, extraordinary items, and items charged or credited directly to shareholders' equity. [FAS109, ¶289]

.407 **Deferred tax liability.** The deferred tax consequences attributable to taxable temporary differences. A deferred tax liability is measured using the applicable enacted tax rate and provisions of the enacted tax law. [FAS109, ¶289]

.408 **Event.** A happening of consequence to an enterprise. The term encompasses both transactions and other events affecting an enterprise. [FAS109, ¶289]

.409 **Gains and losses included in comprehensive income but excluded from net income.** Under present practice, gains and losses included in comprehensive income but excluded from net income include certain changes in market values of investments in marketable equity securities classified as noncurrent assets, certain changes in market values of investments in industries having specialized accounting practices for marketable securities, adjustments from recognizing certain additional pension liabilities, and foreign currency translation adjustments. Future changes to generally accepted accounting principles may change what is included in this category. [FAS109, ¶289]

.410 **Income taxes.** Domestic and foreign federal (national), state, and local (including franchise) taxes based on income. [FAS109, ¶289]

.411 **Income taxes currently payable (refundable).** Refer to **Current tax expense or benefit.** [FAS109, ¶289]

.412 **Income tax expense (benefit).** The sum of current tax expense (benefit) and deferred tax expense (benefit). [FAS109, ¶289]

.413 **Nonpublic enterprise.** An enterprise other than one (a) whose debt or equity securities are traded in a public market, including those traded on a stock exchange or in the over-the-counter market (including securities quoted only locally or regionally), or (b) whose financial statements are filed with a regulatory agency in preparation for the sale of any class of securities. [FAS109, ¶289]

.414 **Public enterprise.** An enterprise (a) whose debt or equity securities are traded in a public market, including those traded on a stock exchange or in the over-the-counter market (including securities quoted only locally or regionally), or (b) whose financial statements are filed with a regulatory agency in preparation for the sale of any class of securities. [FAS109, ¶289]

.415 **Taxable income.** The excess of taxable revenues over tax deductible expenses and exemptions for the year as defined by the governmental taxing authority. [FAS109, ¶289]

.416 **Taxable temporary difference.** Temporary differences that result in taxable amounts in future years when the related asset or liability is recovered or settled, respectively. Also refer to **Temporary difference.** [FAS109, ¶289]

.417 **Tax consequences.** The effects on income taxes—current or deferred—of an event. [FAS109, ¶289]

.418 **Tax-planning strategy.** An action (including elections for tax purposes) that meets certain criteria (paragraph .121) and that would be implemented to realize a tax benefit for an operating loss or tax credit carryforward before it expires. Tax-planning strategies are considered when assessing the need for and amount of a valuation allowance for deferred tax assets. [FAS109, ¶289]

.419 **Temporary difference.** A difference between the tax basis of an asset or liability and its reported amount in the financial statements that will result in taxable or deductible amounts in future years when the reported amount of the asset or liability is recovered or settled, respectively. Paragraph .110 cites 8 examples of temporary differences. Some temporary differences cannot be identified with a particular asset or liability for financial reporting (refer to paragraph .114), but those temporary differences (a) result from events that have been recognized in the financial statements and (b) will result in taxable or deductible amounts in future years based on provisions of the tax law. Some events recognized in financial statements do not have tax consequences. Certain revenues are exempt from taxation and certain expenses are not deductible. Events that do not have tax consequences do not give rise to temporary differences. [FAS109, ¶289]

.420 **Valuation allowance.** The portion of a deferred tax asset for which it is more likely than not that a tax benefit will not be realized. [FAS109, ¶289]

Supplemental Guidance

Disclosure of the Sale or Purchase of Tax Benefits through Tax Leases

.501 **Question**—What disclosures are required for the sale or purchase of tax benefits through tax leases? [FTB82-1, ¶1] (This section does not address the accounting for the sale or purchase of tax benefits through tax leases.) [FTB82-1, ¶8]

.502 **Background**—The term *tax leases,* as used in this section, refers to leases that are entered into to transfer certain tax benefits as allowed by the leasing provisions of the Economic Recovery Tax Act of 1981. The tax benefits that can be transferred are deductions under the Accelerated Cost Recovery System and credits such as the investment tax credit and energy credit. Temporary Treasury regulations were issued on October 20, 1981, November 10, 1981, and December 28, 1981 that prescribe the conditions that must be met for a transaction to be characterized as a "safe harbor" lease for federal income tax purposes, thus enabling the parties to the transaction to transfer certain tax benefits between them. [FTB82-1, ¶2]

.503 **Response**—Section A10, "Accounting Policies," requires disclosure of all significant accounting policies for which alternative accounting principles or practices exist, including the methods of applying those accounting principles that materially affect the determination of financial position, [FTB82-1, ¶4] cash flows, [FAS95, ¶152] and results of operations. Because alternative accounting practices exist, the accounting policies or practices followed for those transactions should be disclosed in accordance with Section A10. The disclosure should include the method of recognizing revenue and allocating the income tax benefits and asset costs to current and future periods. [FTB82-1, ¶4]

.504 Paragraph .145 requires that (a) the reported amount of income tax expense attributable to continuing operations for the year be reconciled to the amount of income tax expense that would result from applying domestic federal statutory tax rates to pretax income from continuing operations and (b) the estimated amount and the nature of each significant reconciling item be disclosed. Transactions involving the sale or purchase of tax benefits through tax leases may give rise to a significant reconciling item that should be disclosed pursuant to the requirements of this section. [FAS109, ¶288cc]

.505 Section I22, "Income Statement Presentation: Unusual or Infrequent Items," paragraph .101, requires disclosure of material events or transactions that are unusual in nature or occur infrequently as a separate component of income from continuing operations. If material and unusual or infrequent to the enterprise, the nature and financial effects of transactions involving the sale or purchase of tax benefits through tax leases should be disclosed on the face of the income statement or, alternatively, in notes to the financial statements. [FTB82-1, ¶6]

.506 Disclosures in addition to those required by Sections A10, I22, and [FTB82-1, ¶7] this section [FAS109, ¶287] as discussed above may also be appropriate depending on the circumstances involved. For example, if significant contingencies exist with respect to the sale or purchase of tax benefits, disclosures in accordance with Section C59, "Contingencies," may be warranted. Also, as referred to in Section F43, "Financial Statements: Comparative Financial Statements," paragraph .102, if comparative financial statements are presented, disclosure should be made of any change in practice that significantly affects comparability. [FTB82-1, ¶7]

Investment Credit from Leased Property

.507 A financing institution may include the investment credit as part of the proceeds from leased property accounted for by the financing method and include it in determining the yield from the "loan," which is reflected in income over the term of the lease. However, the financing institution may account for the investment credit on property purchased for its own use by either the flow-through or the deferral method. [AIN-APB4, #3]

.508 The investment credit may be passed through to a lessee for leased property. The lessee should account for the credit by whichever method is used for purchased property. If the deferral method is used and the leased property is not capitalized, the term of the lease, generally including renewal options that are reasonably expected to be exercised, is the period over which the credit should be amortized. [AIN-APB4, #3]

Applying the Deferral Method of Accounting for Investment Credit

.509 Under the deferral method, the credit is reflected as a reduction of tax expense ratably over the period during which the asset is depreciated and follows the depreciation method used for financial reporting purposes. The amortization period may be the specific life of each asset or the composite life of all depreciable assets. However, amortization over the period [that] the asset must be held to avoid recapture of the credit rather than [over] the life of the asset is not acceptable because it is not based on depreciable life. [AIN-APB4, #3]

(The next page is 26155.)

Sources: FASB Statement 5; FASB Statement 113; FASB Technical Bulletin 85-4

Summary

Payments to insurance enterprises that do not involve transfer of risk shall be accounted for as a deposit by the insured or by the ceding enterprise in the case of reinsurance.

The amount that could be realized under a life insurance contract as of the date of the statement of financial position should be reported as an asset. The change in cash surrender or contract value during the period is an adjustment of premiums paid in determining the expense or income to be recognized under the contract for the period.

Payments to Insurance Enterprises That May Not Involve Transfer of Risk

.101 To the extent that an insurance contract or reinsurance contract does not, despite its form, provide for indemnification of the insured or the ceding enterprise by the insurer or reinsurer against loss or liability, the premium paid less the amount of the premium to be retained by the insurer or reinsurer shall be accounted for as a deposit by the insured or the ceding enterprise. Those contracts may be structured in various ways, but if, regardless of form, their substance is that all or part of the premium paid by the insured or the ceding enterprise is a deposit, it shall be accounted for as such.[1] [FAS5, ¶44]

.102 Operations in certain industries may be subject to such high risks that insurance is unavailable or is available only at what is considered to be a prohibitively high cost. Some enterprises in those industries have "pooled" their risks by forming a mutual insurance enterprise in which they retain an equity interest and to which they pay insurance premiums. For example, some electric utility enterprises have formed such a mutual insurance enterprise to insure risks related to nuclear power plants, and some oil enterprises have formed an enterprise to insure against risks associated with petroleum exploration and production. Whether the premium paid represents a payment for the transfer of risk or whether it represents merely a deposit will depend on the circumstances surrounding each enterprise's interest in and insurance arrangement with the mutual insurance enterprise. An analysis of the contract is required to determine whether risk has been transferred and to what extent. [FAS5, ¶45]

---

[1]Paragraphs .171 through .177 of Section In6, "Insurance Industry," identify conditions that are required for a reinsurance contract to indemnify the ceding enterprise against loss or liability and to be accounted for as reinsurance. Any transaction between enterprises to which Section In6 applies must meet those conditions to be accounted for as reinsurance. [FAS113, ¶30]

Supplemental Guidance

.501-.503 [Deleted 11/85 because of FASB Technical Bulletin No. 85-4, *Accounting for Purchases of Life Insurance.*]

Accounting for Purchases of Life Insurance

.504 *Question*—How should an enterprise[501] account for an investment in life insurance? [FTB85-4, ¶1]

.505 *Background*—A premium paid by a purchaser of life insurance serves a variety of purposes. A portion of the premium pays the insurer for assumption of mortality risk and provides for recovery of the insurer's contract acquisition, initiation, and maintenance costs. Another portion of the premium contributes to the accumulation of contract values. The relative amounts of premium payment credited to various contract attributes change over time as the age of the insured party increases and as earnings are credited to previously established contract values. [FTB85-4, ¶5]

.506 An insurance contract is significantly different from most investment agreements. The various attributes of the policy could be obtained separately through term insurance and purchase of investments. The combination of benefits and contract values could not, however, typically be acquired absent the insurance contract. Continued protection from mortality risk and realization of scheduled increases in contract accumulation usually requires payment of future premiums. [FTB85-4, ¶6]

.507 The payment of insurance premiums may take a number of different forms. The insurance contract may be purchased through payment of a single premium, as opposed to the typical series of future premiums. Alternatively, the premium payments may be made through loans from the insurance company that are secured by policy cash surrender values. The pattern of premium payments is a decision that does not alter the underlying nature of the insurance contract. [FTB85-4, ¶7]

.508 *Response*—The amount that could be realized under the insurance contract as of the date of the statement of financial position should be reported as an asset. The change in cash surrender or contract value during the period is an adjustment of premiums paid in determining the expense or income to be recognized under the contract for the period. [FTB85-4, ¶2]

---

[501]The provisions of paragraphs .504 through .509 apply to all enterprises that purchase life insurance in which the enterprise is either the owner or beneficiary of the contract, without regard to the funding objective of the purchase. Such purchases would typically include those intended to meet loan covenants or to fund deferred compensation agreements, buy-sell agreements, or postemployment death benefits. Purchases of life insurance by retirement plans that are subject to Section Pe5, "Pension Funds: Accounting and Reporting," are not covered by paragraphs .504 through .509. [FTB85-4, ¶1, fn1]

.509 [A] business exchange rider allows an enterprise to use values in an existing policy to insure a different employee when the originally insured employee leaves the enterprise. [FTB85-4, ¶14] The business exchange rider is a significant development in the design of business insurance products and reduces additional policy costs if a covered employee leaves the enterprise. Such a provision does not affect the realization of future benefits under the insurance contract, nor does it change the traditional underwriting decisions involved in insuring a new life. Instead, the provision only reduces the cost of obtaining those benefits by allowing a new employee to be insured without the costs that are typically associated with obtaining a new policy. [FTB85-4, ¶15]

(The next page is 26635.)

INTANGIBLE ASSETS

Sources: ARB 43, Chapter 5; APB Opinion 6; APB Opinion 17;
AICPA Interpretations of APB Opinion 17; FASB Statement 44;
FASB Statement 72; FASB Statement 109; FASB Statement 121;
FASB Interpretation 9; FASB Technical Bulletin 85-6

Summary

Accounting for an intangible asset involves determining an initial carrying amount, accounting for that amount after acquisition under normal business conditions, and accounting for that amount if the value declines substantially and permanently. The cost of intangible assets acquired prior to November 1, 1970 shall be either (a) accounted for as an asset and not amortized if the asset has no evident limited life or (b) amortized by systematic charges in the income statement over the period benefited if the asset does have a limited life.

The cost of intangible assets acquired after October 31, 1970 from other enterprises or individuals shall be recorded as an asset and shall be amortized over the period of its estimated useful life, but the period of amortization shall not exceed 40 years. Costs of developing, maintaining, or restoring intangible assets that are not specifically identifiable shall be recorded as expenses when incurred.

Introduction

.101 An enterprise may acquire intangible assets from others or may develop them itself. Many kinds of intangible assets may be identified and given reasonably descriptive names, for example, patents, franchises, trademarks, and the like. Other types of intangible assets lack specific identifiability. Both identifiable and unidentifiable assets may be developed internally. Identifiable intangible assets may be acquired singly, as a part of a group of assets, or as part of an entire enterprise, but unidentifiable assets cannot be acquired singly. The excess of the cost of an acquired enterprise over the sum of identifiable net assets, usually called **goodwill,** is the most common unidentifiable intangible asset. [APB17, ¶1]

.102 [Alternative accounting principles for intangible assets are required or permitted by this section depending on when the asset was acquired:]

a. [*Acquired after October 31, 1970*]—The provisions of paragraphs .103 through .113 shall be applied to account for intangible assets acquired after October 31, 1970. [APB17, ¶33]

b. [*Acquired before November 1, 1970*]—Application of paragraphs .108 through .112 [is encouraged] on a prospective basis to all intangible assets held on October 31, 1970. [APB17, ¶35] [However,] the provisions of paragraphs .108 through .112 shall not be applied retroactively to intangible assets acquired before November 1, 1970, whether in business combinations or otherwise. [APB17, ¶34] Unless the provisions of paragraphs .108 through .112 are applied prospectively, the accounting for intangible assets held on October 31, 1970 shall be in accordance with paragraphs .114 through .123. [APB17, ¶35]

c. [*Acquired in transaction in process on October 31, 1970*]—Intangible assets recognized in business combinations initiated before November 1, 1970 and consummated on or after that date under the terms prevailing on October 31, 1970[1] may be accounted for in accordance with paragraphs .103 through .113 or paragraphs .114 through .123. [APB17, ¶33]

Intangible Assets Acquired after October 31, 1970

.103 Paragraphs .105 through .113 cover the accounting for both identifiable and unidentifiable intangible assets that an enterprise acquires, including those acquired in business combinations. The conclusions of those paragraphs apply to intangible assets recorded, if any, on the acquisition of some or all of the stock held by minority stockholders of a subsidiary. Paragraphs .105 through .113 also cover accounting for costs of developing goodwill and other unidentifiable intangible assets with indeterminate lives. [APB17, ¶5]

.104 The provisions of paragraphs .105 through .113 apply to costs of developing identifiable intangible assets that an enterprise defers and records as assets. Some enterprises defer costs incurred to develop identifiable intangible assets [for example, preoperating costs,] while others record the costs as expenses as incurred. [Accounting for research and development costs represents a different problem and is described in Section R50, "Research and Development."] [APB17, ¶6]

---

[1] Section B50, "Business Combinations," paragraphs .105(a) and .106(a), defines date initiated and describes the effect of changes in terms of a plan of combination. [APB17, ¶33, fn2]

Acquisition of Intangible Assets

.105 An enterprise shall record as assets the costs of intangible assets acquired from other enterprises or individuals.[1a] Costs of developing, maintaining, or restoring intangible assets that are not specifically identifiable, have indeterminate lives, or are inherent in a continuing business and related to an enterprise as a whole—such as goodwill—shall be deducted from income when incurred. [APB17, ¶24]

.106 Intangible assets acquired singly shall be recorded at cost at date of acquisition. Cost is measured by the amount of cash disbursed, the fair value of other assets distributed, the present value of amounts to be paid for liabilities incurred, or the fair value of consideration received for stock issued as described in Section B50, paragraph .125. [APB17, ¶25]

.107 Intangible assets acquired as part of a group of assets or as part of an acquired enterprise also shall be recorded at cost at date of acquisition. Cost is measured differently for specifically identifiable intangible assets and those lacking specific identification. The cost of identifiable intangible assets is an assigned part of the total cost of the group of assets or enterprise acquired, normally based on the fair values of the individual assets. The cost of unidentifiable intangible assets is measured by the difference between the cost of the group of assets or enterprise acquired and the sum of the assigned costs of individual tangible and identifiable intangible assets acquired less liabilities assumed. Cost shall be assigned to all specifically identifiable intangible assets; cost of identifiable assets shall not be included in goodwill. Principles and procedures of determining cost of assets acquired, including intangible assets, are discussed in detail in Section B50, paragraphs .125 through .147.[2] [APB17, ¶26]

Amortization of Intangible Assets

.108 The recorded costs of intangible assets shall be amortized by systematic charges to income over the periods estimated to be benefited. Factors that shall be considered in estimating the useful lives of intangible assets include:

a. Legal, regulatory, or contractual provisions may limit the maximum useful life.
b. Provisions for renewal or extension may alter a specified limit on useful life.
c. Effects of obsolescence, demand, competition, and other economic factors may reduce a useful life.

[1a]Refer to paragraphs .507 and .508 for guidance on accounting for amounts paid to a shareholder or former shareholder attributable to an agreement precluding the shareholder or former shareholder from purchasing additional shares.]

[2]Refer to paragraphs .124 through .129 as to the applicability of paragraphs .105 through .113 to motor carriers.]

I60.108   *General Standards*

d. A useful life may parallel the service life expectancies of individuals or groups of employees.
e. Expected actions of competitors and others may restrict present competitive advantages.
f. An apparently unlimited useful life may in fact be indefinite and benefits cannot be reasonably projected.
g. An intangible asset may be a composite of many individual factors with varying effective lives.

The period of amortization of intangible assets shall be determined from the pertinent factors. [APB17, ¶27]

.109 The cost of each type of intangible asset shall be amortized on the basis of the estimated life of that specific asset and shall not be written off in the period of acquisition. Analysis of all factors should result in a reasonable estimate of the useful life of most intangible assets. A reasonable estimate of the useful life may often be based on upper and lower limits even though a fixed existence is not determinable. [APB17, ¶28]

.110 The period of amortization shall not, however, exceed 40 years. Analysis at the time of acquisition may indicate that the indeterminate lives of some intangible assets are likely to exceed 40 years and the cost of those assets shall be amortized over the maximum period of 40 years, not an arbitrary shorter period.[3] [APB17, ¶29]

.111 The straight-line method of amortization—equal annual amounts—shall be applied unless an enterprise demonstrates that another systematic method [refer to paragraph .132] is more appropriate.[4] The financial statements shall disclose the method and period of amortization. [APB17, ¶30]

.112 Identifiable intangible assets not covered by paragraphs .122 through .138 of Section I08, "Impairment," and goodwill not identified with assets that are subject to an impairment loss shall be evaluated as follows. [FAS121, ¶21] An enterprise shall evaluate the periods of amortization continually to determine whether later events and circumstances warrant revised estimates of useful lives. If estimates are changed, the unamortized cost shall be allocated to the increased or reduced number of remaining periods in the revised useful life but not to exceed 40 years after acquisition.[5] Estimation of value and future benefits of an intangible asset may indicate that the unamortized cost should

---

[3]Paragraphs .132 and .133 specify an exception to the provisions of this section with respect to the amortization of goodwill recognized in certain acquistions of banking or thrift institutions. [FAS72, ¶12]

[4Refer to footnote 3.]

[5Refer to footnote 3.]

be reduced significantly. However, a single loss year or even a few loss years together do not necessarily justify a [reduction of] all or a large part of the unamortized cost of intangible assets. The reason for [a significant reduction] shall be disclosed. [APB17, ¶31]

Disposal of Goodwill

.113 Ordinarily goodwill and similar intangible assets cannot be disposed of apart from the enterprise as a whole. However, [if] a large segment or separable group of assets of an acquired enterprise or the entire acquired enterprise [is] sold or otherwise liquidated, all or a portion of the unamortized cost of the goodwill recognized in the acquisition shall be included in the cost of the assets sold. [APB17, ¶32]

Intangible Assets Acquired Prior to November 1, 1970

.114 Intangible [assets], specifically, those acquired by the issuance of securities or purchased for cash or other consideration, may be purchased or acquired separately for a specified consideration, or may be purchased or acquired, together with other assets, for a lump-sum consideration without specification by either the seller or the purchaser, at the time of purchase, of the portions of the total price that are applicable to the respective assets thus acquired. Accounting for intangible [assets] developed in the regular course of business by research [and development activities is described in Section R50]. [ARB43, ch5, ¶1]

.115 The intangible [assets acquired prior to November 1, 1970] herein considered may be broadly classified as follows:

a. Those having a term of existence limited by law, regulation, or agreement, or by their nature (such as patents, copyrights, leases, licenses, franchises for a fixed term, and goodwill as to which there is evidence of limited duration)
b. Those having no such limited term of existence and as to which there is, at the time of acquisition, no indication of limited life (such as goodwill generally, going value, trade names, secret processes, subscription lists, perpetual franchises, and organization costs) [ARB43, ch5, ¶2]

.116 The intangible [assets acquired prior to November 1, 1970] described above are referred to [in paragraphs .116 through .123] as type (a) and type (b) intangible [assets], respectively. The portion of a lump-sum consideration deemed to have been paid for intangible elements when a mixed aggregate of tangible and intangible property is acquired, or the excess of a parent's investment in the stock of a subsidiary over its equity in the net assets of the subsidiary as shown by the latter's books at the date of acquisition, insofar as that excess would be treated as an intangible [asset] in consolidated financial statements of the parent and the subsidiary, may represent intangible [assets] of either type (a) or type (b) or a combination of both. [ARB43, ch5, ¶3]

Acquisition of Intangible Assets

.117 The initial amount assigned to all types of intangible [assets] shall be cost, in accordance with the generally accepted accounting principle that assets shall be stated at cost when they are acquired. In the case of noncash acquisitions, as, for example, if intangibles are acquired in exchange for securities, cost may be considered as being either the fair value of the consideration given or the fair value of the property or right acquired, whichever is the more clearly evident. [ARB43, ch5, ¶4]

Amortization of Intangible Assets

.118 The cost of type (a) intangible [assets] shall be amortized by systematic charges in the income statement over the period benefited, as in the case of other assets having a limited period of usefulness. If it becomes evident that the period benefited will be longer or shorter than originally estimated, recognition thereof may take the form of an appropriate decrease or increase in the rate of amortization or a partial write-down may be made by a charge to [ARB43, ch5, ¶5] [income].[6] [APB9, ¶17]

.119 If it becomes reasonably evident that the term of existence of a type (b) intangible [asset] has become limited and that it has therefore become a type (a) intangible [asset], its cost shall be amortized by systematic charges in the income statement over the estimated remaining period of usefulness. If, however, the period of amortization is relatively short so that misleading inferences might be drawn as a result of inclusion of substantial charges in the income statement, a partial write-down may be made by a charge to [ARB43, ch5, ¶6] income. [APB9, ¶17] The rest of the cost shall be amortized over the remaining period of usefulness. [ARB43, ch5, ¶6]

.120 If an enterprise decides that a type (b) intangible [asset] may not continue to have value during the entire life of the enterprise, it may amortize the cost of such intangible [asset] by systematic charges against income despite the fact that there are no present indications of limited existence or loss of value that would indicate that it has become type (a) and despite the fact that expenditures are being made to maintain its value. Such amortization is within the discretion of the enterprise and is not to be regarded as obligatory. The plan of amortization shall be reasonable; it shall be based on all the surrounding circumstances, including the basic nature of the intangible [asset] and the expendi-

---

[6]Such write-downs shall not be reported as extraordinary items as described in Section I17, "Income Statement Presentation: Extraordinary Items."]

tures currently being made for development, experimentation, and sales promotion. If the intangible [asset] is an important income-producing factor and is currently being maintained by advertising or otherwise, the period of amortization shall be reasonably long. [ARB43, ch5, ¶7]

Write-Off of Intangible Assets

.121 The cost of type (b) intangible [assets] shall be written off when it becomes reasonably evident that they have become worthless. Under such circumstances, the amount at which they are carried on the books shall be charged [ARB43, ch5, ¶8] to income. [APB9, ¶17] In determining whether an investment in type (b) intangible [assets] has become or is likely to become worthless, consideration shall be given to the fact that in some cases intangible [assets] acquired by purchase may merge with, or be replaced by, intangible [assets] acquired or developed with respect to other products or lines of business and that in such circumstances the discontinuance of a product or line of business may not in fact indicate loss of value. [ARB43, ch5, ¶8] [However, for motor carriers,] costs assigned to identifiable intangible assets, including **operating rights,** shall not be merged with or be replaced by amounts relating to other identifiable intangible assets or goodwill. Costs assigned to intangible assets shall not reflect costs of developing, maintaining, or restoring those intangibles after they were acquired ([refer to paragraphs .124 through .129]). [FAS44, ¶4]

.122 Lump-sum write-offs of intangible [assets] shall not be made to retained earnings immediately after acquisition, nor shall intangible [assets] be charged against paid-in capital. If not amortized systematically, intangible [assets] shall be carried at cost until an event has taken place that indicates a loss or a limitation on the useful life of the [assets]. [ARB43, ch5, ¶9]

Purchase of Subsidiary's Stock or Basket Purchase of Assets

.123 A problem arises if a group of intangibles or a mixed aggregate of tangible and intangible property is acquired for a lump-sum consideration, or if the consideration given for a stock investment in a subsidiary is greater than the net assets of such subsidiary applicable thereto, as carried on its books at the date of acquisition. In this latter type of situation there is a presumption that the parent, in effect, placed a valuation greater than their carrying amount on some of the assets of the subsidiary in arriving at the price it was willing to pay for its investment therein. The parent may have (a) paid amounts in excess of carrying amounts for specific assets of the subsidiary or (b) paid for the general goodwill of the subsidiary. In these cases, if practicable, there shall be an allocation, as between tangible and intangible property, of the cost of the mixed aggregate of property or of the excess of a parent's investment over its share of the amount at which the subsidiary carried its net assets on its books at the date of acquisition. Any amount allocated to intangibles shall be further allocated to determine, if practicable, a separate cost for each type (a) intangible and for at least the aggregate of all type (b) intangibles.[7] The amounts so allocated to intangibles shall thereafter be dealt with in accordance with the procedures outlined in paragraphs .114 through .123. [ARB43, ch5, ¶10]

Intangible Assets of Motor Carriers

.124 Paragraphs .125 through .129 clarify the accounting for certain intangible assets of motor carriers because enactment of the Motor Carrier Act of 1980[8] (Act) on July 1, 1980 raises questions regarding whether those intangibles shall continue to be reported as assets or charged to income. [FAS44, ¶1]

.125 When acquired, intangible assets of motor carriers may have included costs[9] related to expected benefits from established routes or customers, marketing or operating efficiencies, knowledge of the business, and other elements of goodwill as well as from specifically identifiable intangible assets, such as customer lists, favorable leases, or operating rights. The costs of intangible assets acquired may have been identified previously as operating rights or as goodwill. If not separately allocated in the past, the costs of intangible assets shall now be assigned to (a) interstate operating rights, (b) other identifiable intangible assets (including intrastate operating rights),[10] and (c) goodwill; the cost of identifiable intangible assets (including operating rights) shall not be included in goodwill. [FAS44, ¶3]

.126 For purposes of identifying and assigning costs to interstate operating rights, other identifiable intangible assets, and goodwill, a motor carrier shall apply the criteria in Section B50, paragraph .146, and paragraphs .105 through .107 of this section, based on the circumstances existing when the assets were acquired. Costs assigned to intangible assets shall not reflect costs of developing, maintaining, or restoring those intangibles after they were acquired. Costs assigned to identifiable intangibles, including operating rights, shall not be merged with or be replaced by amounts relating to other identifiable intangibles or goodwill. [FAS44, ¶4]

.127 If a motor carrier cannot separately identify its interstate operating rights, other identifiable intangible assets, and goodwill and cannot assign costs to them as specified

---

[7For motor carriers, the allocation of costs of intangible assets acquired is described in paragraph .125.]

[8]Public Law 96-296, 96th Congress, July 1, 1980. [FAS44, ¶1, fn1]

[9]*Cost,* as used in paragraphs .125 through .129, refers to the original cost or the unamortized cost of intangible assets as appropriate in the situation. [FAS44, ¶3, fn2]

[10]Refer to paragraph .129. [FAS44, ¶3, fn4]

by paragraphs .125 and .126 or finds that it is impracticable to do so, that motor carrier shall presume that all of those costs relate to interstate operating rights. [FAS44, ¶5]

.128 Unamortized costs of interstate operating rights subject to the provisions of the Act shall be charged to income and, if material, reported as an extraordinary item in accordance with Section I17, paragraph .102. Subsequently, the cost of any other identifiable intangible asset or goodwill that is charged to income for reasons attributable to the Act shall not be reported as an extraordinary item. Tax benefits, if any, relating to the cost of interstate operating rights charged to income shall be reported in accordance with the provisions of Section I17, paragraph .119, and [FAS44, ¶6] Section I27, "Income Taxes." [FAS109, ¶287]

.129 Other identifiable intangible assets and goodwill relating to motor carrier operations shall be accounted for in accordance with paragraphs .103 through .113 or paragraphs .114 through .123, as appropriate. However, the cost of intrastate operating rights shall be accounted for in accordance with the provisions of paragraphs .125 through .128 if a state deregulates motor carriers with effects similar to those of the Act. [FAS44, ¶7]

Acquisition of a Banking or Thrift Institution

.130 [Paragraphs .131 through .135 apply to the acquisition of a banking or thrift institution.[11]] Paragraphs .133 and .134 apply to only those acquisitions in which the fair value of liabilities assumed by the acquiring enterprise exceeds the fair value of tangible and identifiable intangible assets acquired, and those provisions specify an amortization method for the portion of any unidentifiable intangible asset up to the amount of that excess. Paragraphs .108 through .112 of this section also provide guidance as to the amortization of any additional unidentifiable intangible asset recognized in the acquisition. [FAS72, ¶2]

Identified Intangible Assets

.131 The purchase price paid for a [banking or thrift institution] may include an amount for one or more factors, such as the following:

a. Capacity of existing savings accounts and loan accounts to generate future income
b. Capacity of existing savings accounts and loan accounts to generate additional business or new business
c. Nature of territory served. [FIN9, ¶8]

In a business combination accounted for by the purchase method involving the acquisition of a banking or thrift institution, intangible assets acquired that can be separately

---

[11]Paragraphs .131 through .135 apply not only in the case of the acquisition of a savings and loan association but also in the case of the acquisition of a savings and loan association holding company, [FIN9, ¶1, fn1] a commercial bank, a mutual savings bank, a credit union, [or] other depository institutions having assets and liabilities of the same types as those institutions, and branches of such enterprises. [FAS72, ¶2]

identified shall be assigned a portion of the total cost of the acquired enterprise if the fair values of those assets can be reliably[12] determined. [FAS72, ¶4] The amount paid for [a] separately identified intangible shall be recorded as the cost of the intangible and amortized over [its] estimated life as specified by [paragraphs .108 through .112 of this section]. Any portion of the purchase price that cannot be assigned to specifically identifiable tangible and intangible assets acquired (refer to Section B50, "Business Combinations," paragraph .146(e) and footnote 13) less liabilities assumed shall be assigned to goodwill. [FIN9, ¶8] The fair values of [identified intangible] assets that relate to depositor or borrower relationships (refer to (a) and (b) [above]) shall be based on the estimated benefits attributable to the relationships that *exist* at the date of acquisition without regard to new depositors or borrowers that may replace them. Those identified intangible assets shall be amortized over the estimated lives of those existing relationships. [FAS72, ¶4]

Unidentifiable Intangible Asset

.132 An accelerated method would be appropriate and may be used to amortize goodwill [arising from a business combination treated as a purchase of a banking or thrift institution] when an enterprise demonstrates that (a) the amount assigned to goodwill represents an amount paid for factors such as those listed in paragraph .131 above, but there is not a satisfactory basis for determining appraised values for the individual factors, and (b) the benefits expected to be received from the factors decline over the expected life of those factors. Unless both (a) and (b) are demonstrated, straight-line amortization shall be used. [FIN9, ¶9] Paragraphs .133 and .134 of this section specify an exception to the provisions of this paragraph with respect to the amortization of goodwill recognized in certain acquisitions of banking or thrift institutions. [FAS72, ¶12]

.133 If, in a combination [involving a banking or thrift institution], the fair value of liabilities assumed exceeds the fair value of tangible and identified intangible assets acquired, that excess constitutes an unidentifiable intangible asset. That asset shall be amortized to expense over a period no greater than the estimated remaining life of the long-term interest-bearing assets[13] acquired. Amortization shall be at a constant rate when applied to the carrying amount[14] of those interest-bearing assets that, based on their terms, are expected to be outstanding at the beginning of each subsequent period. The prepayment assumptions, if any, used to determine the fair value of the long-term interest-

---

[12]Reliability embodies the characteristics of representational faithfulness and verifiability, as discussed in FASB Concepts Statement 2, *Qualitative Characteristics of Accounting Information.* [FAS72, ¶4, fn1]

[13]For purposes of paragraph .133, long-term interest-bearing assets are interest-bearing assets with a remaining term to maturity of more than one year. [FAS72, ¶5, fn3]

[14]Carrying amount is the face amount of the interest-bearing asset plus (or minus) the unamortized premium (or discount). [FAS72, ¶5, fn4]

bearing assets acquired also shall be used in determining the amount of those assets expected to be outstanding. However, if the assets acquired in such a combination do not include a significant amount of long-term interest-bearing assets, the unidentifiable intangible asset shall be amortized over a period not exceeding the estimated average remaining life of the existing customer (deposit) base acquired. The periodic amounts of amortization shall be determined as of the acquisition date and shall not be subsequently adjusted except as provided by paragraphs .134 and .135. Notwithstanding the other provisions of this paragraph, the period of amortization shall not exceed 40 years. [FAS72, ¶5]

.134 Paragraph .112 [of this section] specifies, among other things, that an enterprise should evaluate the periods of amortization of intangible assets continually to determine whether later events and circumstances warrant revised estimates of useful lives. In no event, however, shall the useful life of the unidentifiable intangible asset described in paragraph .133 be revised upward. [FAS72, ¶6]

.135 For purposes of applying paragraph .113 [of this section], if a large segment or separable group of the operating assets of an acquired banking or thrift institution, such as branches, is sold or liquidated, the portion of the unidentifiable intangible asset attributable to that segment or separable group shall be included in the cost of the assets sold. If a large segment or separable group of the interest-bearing assets of an acquired institution is sold or liquidated and if the benefits attributable to the unidentifiable intangible asset have been significantly reduced,[15] that reduction shall be recognized as a charge to income. [FAS72, ¶7]

[15]For example, if a sale of a large group of interest-bearing assets is accompanied by the loss of a significant and valuable customer base, a reduction in goodwill likely would be appropriate. On the other hand, if the proceeds of sale are reinvested in other forms of interest-bearing or other assets, no such reduction may be necessary. [FAS72, ¶7, fn6]

Glossary

.401 **Goodwill.** [Goodwill is] the excess of the cost of an acquired enterprise over the sum of identifiable net assets. [APB17, ¶1]

.402 **Operating right.** A franchise or permit issued by the Interstate Commerce Commission (ICC) or a similar state agency to a motor carrier to transport specified commodities over specified routes with limited competition. Those rights were either granted directly by the ICC or state agency, purchased from other motor carriers, or acquired through business combinations. [FAS44, ¶3, fn3]

Supplemental Guidance

Internally Developed Intangible Assets

.501 *Question*—Paragraphs .103 through .113 require that intangible assets acquired after October 31, 1970 be amortized over a period not exceeding 40 years. Do these paragraphs encourage the capitalization of identifiable internally developed intangible assets that have been generally charged to expense in the past? [AIN-APB17, #1]

.502 *Interpretation*—Paragraphs .103 through .113 do not change [earlier] accounting practice for intangible assets in any way except to require that intangible assets acquired after October 31, 1970 be amortized. Paragraph .104 notes that the costs of some identifiable intangible assets are now capitalized as deferred assets by some enterprises while other enterprises record the costs as expenses when incurred. Paragraph .104 also specifies that the question of whether the costs of identifiable internally developed intangible assets are to be capitalized or charged to expense is not covered by paragraphs .103 through .113. Therefore, these paragraphs do not encourage capitalizing the costs of a large initial advertising campaign for a new product or capitalizing the costs of training new employees. [AIN-APB17, #1]

Goodwill in a Step Acquisition

.503 *Question*—Goodwill and other intangible assets acquired before November 1, 1970 are not required to be amortized until their term of existence becomes limited (refer to paragraphs .114 through .123). Paragraphs .103 through .113 require all intangible assets acquired after October 31, 1970 to be amortized. If an enterprise purchases two or more blocks of voting common stock of another enterprise at various dates before and after November 1, 1970 and eventually obtains control or the ability to exercise significant influence over operating and financial policies of the other enterprise, how should the investor subsequently account for any goodwill related to the investment? [AIN-APB17, #2]

.504 *Interpretation*—If an enterprise in a series of purchases on a step-by-step basis acquires either a subsidiary that is consolidated or an investment that is accounted for under the equity method, the enterprise shall identify the cost of each investment, the fair value of the underlying assets acquired, and the goodwill for each step purchase. This process would then identify the goodwill associated with each step purchase made before November 1, 1970 or after October 31, 1970 for each investment.[501] [AIN-APB17, #2]

.505 Goodwill associated with each step purchase acquired prior to November 1, 1970 shall be accounted for in accordance with paragraphs .114 through .123. Although amortization is not required in the absence of evidence that the goodwill has a limited term of existence, paragraph .102(b) encourages prospective amortization of such goodwill. Retroactive amortization is prohibited by paragraph .102(b). [AIN-APB17, #2]

.506 Goodwill associated with each step purchase acquired after October 31, 1970 should be amortized in accordance with paragraphs .103 through .113. The period of amortization may not exceed 40 years as specified by paragraph .110. [AIN-APB17, #2]

Amounts Paid by an Enterprise to a Shareholder or Former Shareholder Attributed to an Agreement Precluding the Shareholder or Former Shareholder from Purchasing Additional Shares

.507 *Question*—Should amounts paid by an enterprise to a shareholder or former shareholder attributed to an agreement precluding the shareholder or former shareholder from purchasing additional shares be capitalized as assets and amortized over the period of the agreement? [FTB85-6, ¶4]

.508 *Response*—No. Payments by an enterprise to a shareholder or former shareholder attributed, for example, to a "standstill" agreement, or any agreement in which a shareholder or former shareholder agrees not to purchase additional shares, should be expensed as incurred. Such payments do not give rise to assets of the enterprise as defined in Concepts Statement 6. [FTB85-6, ¶5]

(The next page is 26971.)

---

[501]The accounting for a step acquisition of a subsidiary that is consolidated is described by Section C51, "Consolidation," paragraph .111 [(also refer to Section B50, paragraphs .145, .162, and .163)]. As specified by Section I82, "Investments: Equity Method," paragraphs .109(b) and .109(n), similar procedures apply for a step acquisition of an investment carried under the equity method. [AIN-APB17, #2, fn1]

INTEREST: CAPITALIZATION OF INTEREST COSTS

Sources: FASB Statement 34; FASB Statement 42; FASB Statement 58; FASB Statement 62; FASB Statement 87; FASB Statement 121; FASB Interpretation 33

Summary

Interest cost shall be capitalized as part of the historical cost of acquiring certain assets. To qualify for interest capitalization, assets must require a period of time to get them ready for their intended use. Examples are assets that an enterprise constructs for its own use (such as facilities) and assets intended for sale or lease that are constructed as discrete projects (such as ships or real estate projects). Interest capitalization is required for those assets if its effect, compared with the effect of expensing interest, is material. If the net effect is not material, interest capitalization is not required. However, interest cannot be capitalized for inventories that are routinely manufactured or otherwise produced in large quantities on a repetitive basis, or on qualifying assets acquired using gifts or grants that are restricted by the donor or grantor to acquisition of those assets to the extent that funds are available from such gifts or grants.

In situations involving qualifying assets financed with the proceeds of restricted tax-exempt borrowings, the amount of interest cost to be capitalized shall be all interest cost of those borrowings less any interest earned on temporary investment of the proceeds of those borrowings from the date of borrowing until the specified qualifying assets acquired with those borrowings are ready for their intended use.

In all other situations, the interest cost eligible for capitalization shall be the interest cost recognized on borrowings and other obligations. The amount capitalized is to be an allocation of the interest cost incurred during the period required to complete the asset. The interest rate for capitalization purposes is to be based on the rates of the enterprise's outstanding borrowings. If the enterprise associates a specific new borrowing with the asset, it may apply the rate on that borrowing to the appropriate portion of the expenditures for the asset. A weighted average of the rates on other borrowings is to be applied to expenditures not covered by specific new borrowings. Judgment is required in identifying the borrowings on which the average rate is based.

.101 This section [presents] standards of financial accounting and reporting for capitalizing interest cost as a part of the historical cost of acquiring certain assets. For the purposes of this section, *interest cost* includes interest recognized on obligations having explicit interest rates,[1] interest imputed on certain types of payables in accordance with Section I69, "Interest: Imputation of an Interest Cost," and interest related to a capital lease determined in accordance with Section L10, "Leases." [FAS34, ¶1] The interest cost component of net periodic pension cost [(Section P16, "Pension Costs")] shall not be considered to be interest for purposes of this section. [FAS87, ¶16, fn4]

.102 The historical cost of acquiring an asset includes the costs necessarily incurred to bring it to the condition and location necessary for its intended use.[2] If an asset requires a period of time in which to carry out the activities[3] necessary to bring it to that condition and location, the interest cost incurred during that period as a result of expenditures for the asset is a part of the historical cost of acquiring the asset. [FAS34, ¶6]

.103 The objectives of capitalizing interest are (a) to obtain a measure of acquisition cost that more closely reflects the enterprise's total investment in the asset and (b) to charge a cost that relates to the acquisition of a resource that will benefit future periods against the revenues of the periods benefited. [FAS34, ¶7]

.104 In concept, interest cost is capitalizable for all assets that require a period of time to get them ready for their intended use (an *acquisition period*). However, in many cases, the benefit in terms of information about enterprise resources and earnings may not justify the additional accounting and administrative cost involved in providing the information. [FAS34, ¶8] Accordingly, interest shall not be capitalized in the situations described in paragraph .106. [FAS42, ¶4]

Assets Qualifying for Interest Capitalization

.105 Interest shall be capitalized for the following types of assets ([referred to as] *qualifying assets*): [FAS42, ¶4]

a. Assets that are constructed or otherwise produced for an enterprise's own use (including assets constructed or produced for the enterprise by others for which deposits or progress payments have been made)

---

[1]Interest cost on these obligations includes amounts resulting from periodic amortization of discount or premium and issue costs on debt. [FAS34, ¶1, fn1]

[2]The term *intended use* embraces both readiness for use and readiness for sale, depending on the purpose of acquisition. [FAS34, ¶6, fn3]

[3]Refer to paragraph .114 for a definition of those activities for purposes of this section. [FAS34, ¶6, fn4]

b. Assets intended for sale or lease that are constructed or otherwise produced as discrete projects (for example, ships or real estate developments) [FAS34, ¶9]

c. Investments (equity, loans, and advances) accounted for by the equity method while the investee has activities in progress necessary to commence its planned principal operations provided that the investee's activities include the use of funds to acquire qualifying assets for its operations. [FAS58, ¶5]

.106 However, interest cost shall not be capitalized for inventories that are routinely manufactured or otherwise produced in large quantities on a repetitive basis because the informational benefit does not justify the cost of so doing. In addition, interest shall not be capitalized for the following types of assets:

a. Assets that are in use or ready for their intended use in the earning activities of the enterprise

b. Assets that are not being used in the earning activities of the enterprise and that are not undergoing the activities necessary to get them ready for use [FAS34, ¶10]

c. Assets that are not included in the consolidated balance sheet of the parent company and consolidated subsidiaries

d. Investments accounted for by the equity method after the planned principal operations of the investee begin

e. Investments in regulated investees that are capitalizing both the cost of debt and equity capital [FAS58, ¶6]

f. Assets acquired with gifts and grants that are restricted by the donor or grantor to acquisition of those assets to the extent that funds are available from such gifts and grants. Interest earned from temporary investment of those funds that is similarly restricted shall be considered an addition to the gift or grant for this purpose. [FAS62, ¶5]

.107 Land that is not undergoing activities necessary to get it ready for its intended use is not a qualifying asset. If activities are undertaken for the purpose of developing land for a particular use, the expenditures to acquire the land qualify for interest capitalization while those activities are in progress. The interest cost capitalized on those expenditures is a cost of acquiring the asset that results from those activities. If the resulting asset is a structure, such as a plant or a shopping center, interest capitalized on the land expenditures is part of the acquisition cost of the structure. If the resulting asset is developed land, such as land that is to be sold as developed lots, interest capitalized on the land expenditures is part of the acquisition cost of the developed land. [FAS34, ¶11]

.108 For oil and gas producing operations accounted for by the full cost method, assets whose costs are being currently depreciated, depleted, or amortized are assets in use in the earning activities of the enterprise and are not assets qualifying for capitalization of interest cost. Unusually significant investments in unproved properties and major development projects[4] that are not being currently depreciated, depleted, or amortized and on which exploration or development activities are in progress are assets qualifying for capitalization of interest cost. Similarly, in a cost center with no production, significant properties and projects on which exploration or development activities are in progress are assets qualifying for capitalization of interest cost. [FIN33, ¶2]

The Amount of Interest Cost to Be Capitalized

.109 The amount of interest cost to be capitalized for qualifying assets is intended to be that portion of the interest cost incurred during the assets' acquisition periods that theoretically could have been avoided (for example, by avoiding additional borrowings or by using the funds expended for the assets to repay existing borrowings) if expenditures for the assets had not been made. [FAS34, ¶12]

.110 The amount capitalized in an accounting period shall be determined by applying an interest rate(s) ([referred to as] the *capitalization rate*) to the average amount of accumulated expenditures for the asset during the period.[5] The capitalization rates used in an accounting period shall be based on the rates applicable to borrowings outstanding during the period. If an enterprise's financing plans associate a specific new borrowing with a qualifying asset, the enterprise may use the rate on that borrowing as the capitalization rate to be applied to that portion of the average accumulated expenditures for the asset that does not exceed that amount of that borrowing. If average accumulated expenditures for the asset exceed the amounts of specific new borrowings associated with the asset, the capitalization rate to be applied to such excess shall be a weighted average of the rates applicable to other borrowings of the enterprise. [FAS34, ¶13]

.111 In identifying the borrowings to be included in the weighted average rate, the objective is a reasonable measure of the cost of financing acquisition of the asset in terms of the interest cost incurred that otherwise could have been avoided. Accordingly, judgment will be required to make a selection of borrowings that best accomplishes that objective in the circumstances. For example, in some circumstances, it will be appropriate to include all borrowings of the parent company and its consolidated subsidiaries; for some multinational enterprises, it may be appropriate for each foreign subsidiary to use an average of the rates applicable to its own borrowings. However, the use of judgment

---

[4]Judgments as to what constitute *unusually significant* investments and *major* projects should be determined by an enterprise and its auditors based upon the enterprise's facts and circumstances. [FIN33, ¶12]

[5]If qualifying assets are financed with the proceeds of tax-exempt borrowings and those funds are externally restricted to the acquisition of specified qualifying assets or to service the related debt, the amount of interest cost capitalized shall be determined in accordance with paragraphs .116A and .116B of this section. [FAS62, ¶6]

in determining capitalization rates shall not circumvent the requirement that a capitalization rate be applied to all capitalized expenditures for a qualifying asset to the extent that interest cost has been incurred during an accounting period. [FAS34, ¶14]

.112 The total amount of interest cost capitalized in an accounting period shall not exceed the total amount of interest cost incurred by the enterprise in that period. In consolidated financial statements, that limitation shall be applied by reference to the total amount of interest cost incurred by the parent company and consolidated subsidiaries on a consolidated basis. In any separately issued financial statements of a parent company or a consolidated subsidiary and in the financial statements (whether separately issued or not) of unconsolidated subsidiaries and other investees accounted for by the equity method, the limitation shall be applied by reference to the total amount of interest cost (including interest on intercompany borrowings) incurred by the separate entity. [FAS34, ¶15]

.113 For purposes of this section, *expenditures* to which capitalization rates are to be applied are capitalized expenditures (net of progress payment collections) for the qualifying asset that have required the payment of cash, the transfer of other assets, or the incurring of a liability on which interest is recognized (in contrast to liabilities, such as trade payables, accruals, and retainages on which interest is not recognized). However, reasonable approximations of net capitalized expenditures may be used. For example, capitalized costs for an asset may be used as a reasonable approximation of capitalized expenditures unless the difference is material. [FAS34, ¶16]

The Capitalization Period

.114 In situations involving qualifying assets financed with the proceeds of tax-exempt borrowings that are externally restricted as specified in paragraph .116A, the capitalization period begins at the date of the borrowing. [FAS62, ¶7] [In other situations,] the capitalization period shall begin when [the following] three conditions are present:

a. Expenditures (as defined in paragraph .113) for the asset have been made.
b. Activities that are necessary to get the asset ready for its intended use are in progress.
c. Interest cost is being incurred.

Interest capitalization shall continue as long as those three conditions are present. The term *activities* is to be construed broadly. It encompasses more than physical construction; it includes all the steps required to prepare the asset for its intended use. For example, it includes administrative and technical activities during the preconstruction stage, such as the development of plans or the process of obtaining permits from governmental authorities; it includes activities undertaken after construction has begun in order to overcome unforeseen obstacles, such as technical problems, labor disputes, or litigation. If the enterprise suspends substantially all activities related to acquisition of the asset, interest capitalization shall cease until activities are resumed. However, brief interruptions in activities, interruptions that are externally imposed, and delays that are inherent in the asset acquisition process shall not require cessation of interest capitalization. [FAS34, ¶17]

.115 The capitalization period shall end when the asset is substantially complete[6] and ready for its intended use. Some assets are completed in parts, and each part is capable of being used independently while work is continuing on other parts. An example is a condominium. For such assets, interest capitalization shall stop on each part when it is substantially complete and ready for use. Some assets must be completed in their entirety before any part of the asset can be used. An example is a facility designed to manufacture products by sequential processes. For such assets, interest capitalization shall continue until the entire asset is substantially complete and ready for use. Some assets cannot be used effectively until a separate facility has been completed. Examples are the oil wells drilled in Alaska before completion of the pipeline. For such assets, interest capitalization shall continue until the separate facility is substantially complete and ready for use. [FAS34, ¶18]

.116 Interest capitalization shall not cease when present accounting principles require recognition of a lower value for the asset than acquisition cost; the provision required to reduce acquisition cost to such lower value shall be increased appropriately. [FAS34, ¶19] The provisions of paragraphs .122 through .132 of Section I08, "Impairment," apply in recognizing impairment of assets held for use. [FAS121, ¶26]

Capitalization of Interest Cost in Situations Involving Certain Tax-Exempt Borrowings and Certain Gifts and Grants

.116A Interest earned shall not be offset against interest cost in determining either capitalization rates or limitations on the amount of interest cost to be capitalized except in situations involving acquisition of qualifying assets financed with the proceeds of tax-exempt borrowings if those funds are externally restricted to finance acquisition of specified qualifying assets or to service the related debt. [FAS62, ¶3]

---

[6]The term *substantially complete* is used to prohibit continuation of interest capitalization in situations in which completion of the asset is intentionally delayed. For example, it is customary for a condominium developer to defer installation of certain fixtures and fittings until units are sold, so that buyers may choose the types and colors they want. An intentional delay of that kind is related more to marketing of the asset than to the exigencies of the asset acquisition process. Similarly, interest is not to be capitalized during periods when the enterprise intentionally defers or suspends activities related to the asset. Interest cost incurred during such periods is a holding cost, not an acquisition cost. [FAS34, ¶58]

.116B The amount of interest cost capitalized on qualifying assets acquired with proceeds of tax-exempt borrowings that are externally restricted as specified in paragraph .116A shall be all interest cost of the borrowing less any interest earned on related interest-bearing investments acquired with proceeds of the related tax-exempt borrowings[7] from the date of the borrowing until the assets are ready for their intended use. Interest cost of a tax-exempt borrowing shall be eligible for capitalization on other qualifying assets of the entity when the specified qualifying assets are no longer eligible for interest capitalization. [FAS62, ¶4]

Example

.116C The following example illustrates the application of [paragraphs .116A and .116B] in the situation described below:

a. The entity is committed to construct Project A at a cost of $10 million. Project A is to be financed from three sources:
   (1) $4 million government grant restricted to use for the specified construction project, payable $1 million per year
   (2) $4 million tax-exempt borrowing at an interest rate of 8 percent ($320,000 per year)
   (3) $2 million from operations
b. The entity has $10 million in other borrowings that are outstanding throughout the construction of Project A. The interest rate on those borrowings is 6 percent. Other qualifying assets of the entity never exceed $5 million during the construction of Project A.
c. The proceeds from the borrowing and the initial phase of the grant are received 1 year in advance of starting construction on Project A and are temporarily invested in interest-bearing investments yielding 12 percent. Interest income earned from temporary investments is not reinvested.
d. Project A will take 4 years after start of construction to complete.
e. The table on the following page sets forth the amount of interest to be capitalized as part of the entity's investment in Project A.
f. Over the course of construction the net cost of financing is $678,000, the sum of the interest capitalized for the 5 years. Accordingly, the entity's total net investment in Project A will be $10,678,000.

---

[7]The interest cost and interest earned on any portion of the proceeds of the tax-exempt borrowings that are not designated for the acquisition of specified qualifying assets and servicing the related debt are excluded. The entire interest cost on that portion of the proceeds that is available for other uses (such as refunding of an existing debt issue other than a construction loan related to those assets) is eligible for capitalization on other qualifying assets. [FAS62, ¶4, fn1]

	Year				
	19X1	**19X2**	**19X3**	**19X4**	**19X5**
	(amounts in thousands)				
(1) Assumed average qualifying assets	$ 0	$2,000	$5,000	$8,000	$9,000
(2) Average funding received					
borrowing	4,000	4,000	4,000	4,000	4,000
grant	1,000	2,000	3,000	4,000	4,000
(3) Average temporary investments ((2) − (1), not less than zero)*					
borrowing	4,000	3,000	1,000	0	0
grant	1,000	1,000	1,000	0	0
(4) Interest earned ((3) × 12 percent)					
(a) borrowing	480	360	120	0	0
(b) grant	120	120	120	0	0
(5) Average qualifying assets in excess of borrowing, grant, and interest earned on grant†	0	0	0	0	640
(6) Interest cost capitalized—other borrowings ((5) × 6 percent)	0	0	0	0	38
(7) Interest cost—tax-exempt borrowings	320	320	320	320	320
(8) Interest capitalized ((6) + (7) − (4)(a))‡	(160)	(40)	200	320	358

---

*Balances of unexpended borrowings and unexpended grants can vary depending on the source from which the entity elects to disburse funds.

†That is, (1) average qualifying assets minus the sum of ((2) average funding received plus (4)(b) cumulative interest earned on grant), not less than zero.

‡Note that amounts in parentheses are reductions in the cost of the asset.

[FAS62, ¶10]

Disposition of the Amount Capitalized

.117 Because interest cost is an integral part of the total cost of acquiring a qualifying asset, its disposition shall be the same as that of other components of asset cost. [FAS34, ¶20] Interest capitalized on an investment accounted for by the equity method shall be accounted for in accordance with Section I82, "Investments: Equity Method," paragraph .109(b), which states: "A difference between the cost of an investment and the amount of underlying equity in net assets of an investee should be accounted for as if the investee were a consolidated subsidiary." [FAS58, ¶7]

Disclosures

.118 The following information with respect to interest cost shall be disclosed in the financial statements or related notes:

a. For an accounting period in which no interest cost is capitalized, the amount of interest cost incurred and charged to expense during the period
b. For an accounting period in which some interest cost is capitalized, the total amount of interest cost incurred during the period and the amount thereof that has been capitalized. [FAS34, ¶21]

Supplemental Guidance

.501-.503 [Deleted 6/82 because of FASB Statement 62, *Capitalization of Interest Cost in Situations Involving Certain Tax-Exempt Borrowings and Certain Gifts and Grants.*]

(The next page is 27087.)

INTEREST: IMPUTATION OF AN INTEREST COST SECTION I69

Sources: APB Opinion 12; APB Opinion 21; AICPA Interpretation of APB Opinion 21; FASB Statement 34; FASB Statement 109

Summary

Receivables and payables (notes) that are contractual rights to receive or pay money at a fixed or determinable date are recorded at the present value of the consideration given or received in the exchange.

This section does not apply to:

a. Receivables and payables from the normal course of business maturing in less than one year
b. Amounts that will be applied to the purchase price of property, goods, or services
c. Security deposits and retainages
d. Financial institutions' customary lending activities
e. Transactions when interest rates are affected by tax attributes or legal restrictions prescribed by a governmental agency
f. Parent-subsidiary transactions.

When a note is exchanged for cash only, the present value of the note is measured by the cash proceeds given or received. If rights or privileges are exchanged in addition to cash, the difference between the present value of the note and the cash exchanged is considered applicable to those rights and privileges.

When a note is exchanged for property, goods, or services in an arm's-length transaction, there is a general presumption that the note's stipulated rate of interest is fair and adequate unless (a) no interest rate is stated, (b) the stated rate is unreasonable, or (c) the face amount of the note differs materially from the current cash sales price of the property, goods, or services exchanged for the note or the market value of the note. In these circumstances, the exchange is valued at the fair value of the property, goods, or services or at an amount that reasonably approximates the market value of the note, whichever is more clearly determinable. In the absence of established exchange prices for the property, goods, or services or evidence of the market price of the note, the present value of the note is determined by discounting all future payments using an imputed rate of interest. The imputed interest rate used is one that approximates the rate that an independent borrower and lender would have negotiated in a similar transaction.

Any difference between the face amount of the note and its present value is accounted for as a discount or premium and amortized over the life of the note by the interest method or any other method that produces approximately the same results.

Applicability

.101 This section is applicable to receivables and payables that represent contractual rights to receive money or contractual obligations to pay money on fixed or determinable dates, whether or not there is any stated provision for interest, except as stated in paragraphs .102 and .103. Such receivables and payables are collectively referred to in this section as *notes*. Examples are secured and unsecured notes, debentures, bonds, mortgage notes, equipment obligations, and some accounts receivable and payable. [APB21, ¶2]

.102 Except that paragraph .109 covering statement presentation of discount and premium is applicable in all circumstances, this section is not intended to apply to:

a. Receivables and payables arising from transactions with customers or suppliers in the normal course of business that are due in customary trade terms not exceeding approximately one year
b. Amounts that do not require repayment in the future, but rather will be applied to the purchase price of the property, goods, or services involved (for example, deposits or progress payments on construction contracts, advance payments for acquisition of resources and raw materials, advances to encourage exploration in the extractive industries)
c. Amounts intended to provide security for one party to an agreement (for example, security deposits, retainages on contracts)
d. The customary cash lending activities and demand or savings deposit activities of financial institutions whose primary business is lending money
e. Transactions when interest rates are affected by the tax attributes or legal restrictions prescribed by a governmental agency (for example, industrial revenue bonds, tax-exempt obligations, government-guaranteed obligations, income tax settlements)
f. Transactions between parent company and subsidiaries and between subsidiaries of a common parent.

[APB21, ¶3]

.103 This section is also not intended to apply to the application of the *present value*[1] measurement (valuation) technique to estimates of contractual or other obligations assumed in connection with sales of property, goods, or services—for example, a warranty for product performance. [APB21, ¶4]

Notes Exchanged for Cash or for Cash and Rights or Privileges

.104 When a note[2] is received or issued solely for cash and no other right or privilege is exchanged, it is presumed to have a present value at issuance measured by the cash proceeds exchanged. If cash and some other rights or privileges are exchanged for a note, the value of the rights or privileges shall be given accounting recognition [APB21, ¶11] by establishing a note discount or premium account. In such instances, the effective interest rate differs from the stated rate. For example, an enterprise may lend a supplier cash which is to be repaid five years hence with no stated interest. Such a noninterest-bearing loan may be partial consideration under a purchase contract for supplier products at lower than the prevailing market prices. In this circumstance, the difference between the present value of the receivable and the cash loaned to the supplier is appropriately regarded as an addition to the cost of products purchased during the contract term. The note discount is amortized as interest income over the five-year life of the note. [APB21, ¶7]

Notes Exchanged for Property, Goods, or Services

.105 When a note is exchanged for property, goods, or services in a bargained transaction entered into at arm's length, there shall be a general presumption that the rate of interest stipulated by the parties to the transaction represents fair and adequate compensation to the supplier for the use of the related funds. That presumption, however, must not permit the form of the transaction to prevail over its economic substance and thus would not apply if (a) interest is not stated or (b) the stated interest rate is unreasonable (refer to paragraphs .106 and .107) or (c) the stated face amount of the note is materially different from the current cash sales price for the same or similar items or from the market value of the note at the date of the transaction. In these circumstances, the note, the sales price, and the cost of the property, goods, or services exchanged for the note shall be recorded at the fair value of the property, goods, or services or at an amount that reasonably approximates the market value of the note, whichever is the more clearly determinable. That amount may or may not be the same as its face amount, and any resulting discount or premium shall be accounted for as an element of interest over the life of the note (refer to paragraph .108). In the absence of established exchange prices for the

---

[1]*Present value* is the sum of the future payments discounted to the present date at an appropriate rate of interest (refer to paragraphs .111 and .112 for examples). [APB21, ¶1, fn1]

[2]Paragraphs .101 through .103 describe the applicability of this section. [APB21, ¶11, fn6]

related property, goods, or services or evidence of the market value of the note, the present value of a note that stipulates either no interest or a rate of interest that is clearly unreasonable shall be determined by discounting all future payments on the notes using an imputed rate of interest as described in paragraphs .106 and .107. This determination shall be made at the time the note is issued, assumed, or acquired; any subsequent changes in prevailing interest rates shall be ignored. [APB21, ¶12]

Determining an Appropriate Interest Rate

.106 The variety of transactions encountered precludes any specific interest rate from being applicable in all circumstances. However, some general guides may be stated. The choice of a rate may be affected by the credit standing of the issuer, restrictive covenants, the collateral payment and other terms pertaining to the debt, and, if appropriate, the tax consequences to the buyer and seller. The prevailing rates for similar instruments of issuers with similar credit ratings will normally help determine the appropriate interest rate for determining the present value of a specific note at its date of issuance. In any event, the rate used for valuation purposes will normally be at least equal to the rate at which the debtor can obtain financing of a similar nature from other sources at the date of the transaction. The objective is to approximate the rate that would have resulted if an independent borrower and an independent lender had negotiated a similar transaction under comparable terms and conditions with the option to pay the cash price upon purchase or to give a note for the amount of the purchase which bears the prevailing rate of interest to maturity. [APB21, ¶13]

.107 The selection of a rate may be affected by many considerations. For instance, where applicable, the choice of a rate may be influenced by (a) an approximation of the prevailing market rates for the source of credit that would provide a market for sale or assignment of the note; (b) the prime or higher rate for notes that are discounted with banks, giving due weight to the credit standing of the maker; (c) published market rates for similar quality bonds; (d) current rates for debentures with substantially identical terms and risks that are traded in open markets; and (e) the current rate charged by investors for first or second mortgage loans on similar property. [APB21, ¶14]

Amortization of Discount and Premium

.108 With respect to a note that by the provisions of this section requires the imputation of interest, the difference between the present value and the face amount shall be treated as discount or premium[3] and amortized as interest expense or income over the life of the note in such a way as to result in a constant rate of interest when applied to the amount outstanding at the beginning of any given period. This is the *interest* method.[4] Other methods of amortization may be used if the results obtained are not materially different from those that would result from the *interest* method. [APB21, ¶15]

Statement Presentation of Discount and Premium

.109 The discount or premium resulting from the determination of present value in cash or noncash transactions is not an asset or liability separable from the note that gives rise to it. Therefore, the discount or premium shall be reported in the balance sheet as a direct deduction from or addition to the face amount of the note. It shall not be classified as a deferred charge or deferred credit. The description of the note shall include the effective interest rate; the face amount shall also be disclosed in the financial statements or in the notes to the statements.[1] Amortization of discount or premium shall be reported as interest expense. Issue costs shall be reported in the balance sheet as deferred charges. [APB21, ¶16]

Eligibility for Interest Capitalization

.110 Paragraphs .108 and .109 provide that the discount or premium that results from imputing interest for certain types of payables shall be amortized as interest expense over the life of the payable and reported as such in the statement of income. The amount chargeable to interest expense under the provisions of those paragraphs is eligible for inclusion in the amount of interest cost [that is] capitalizable [as a part of the historical cost of acquiring certain assets] in accordance with Section I67, "Interest: Capitalization of Interest Costs." [FAS34, ¶2]

---

[3]Differences between the recognition for financial accounting purposes and income tax purposes of discount or premium resulting from determination of the present value of a note should be treated as [APB21, ¶15, fn8] temporary differences [in accordance with] Section I27, "Income Taxes." [FAS109, ¶287]

[4]The *interest* method of amortization is an acceptable method [APB12, ¶17] [for determining] the periodic amortization of discount and expense or premium on debt (that is, the difference between the net proceeds, after expense, received upon issuance of debt and the amount repayable at its maturity) over its term. The objective of the interest method is to arrive at a periodic interest cost (including amortization) which will represent a level effective rate on the sum of the face amount of the debt and (plus or minus) the unamortized premium or discount and expense at the beginning of each period. The difference between the periodic interest cost so calculated and the nominal interest on the outstanding amount of the debt is the amount of periodic amortization. [APB12, ¶16]

[5]Refer to paragraph .113 for illustrations of balance sheet presentation. [APB21, ¶16, fn9]

Examples of Determining Present Value

Example 1

.111 Consider the issuance of a $1,000, 20-year bond which bears interest at 10 percent annually. If we assume that 10 percent is an appropriate market rate of interest for such a bond, the proceeds at issuance will be $1,000. The bond payable would be recorded at $1,000 which represents the amount repayable at maturity and also the present value at issuance which is equal to the proceeds. However, under similar circumstances, if the prevailing market rate were more (less) than 10 percent, a 20-year, 10-percent bond with a face amount of $1,000 would usually have a value at issuance and provide cash proceeds of less (more) than $1,000. The significant point is that, upon issuance, a bond is valued at (a) the present value of the future coupon interest payments plus (b) the present value of the future principal payments (face amount). These two sets of future cash payments are discounted at the prevailing market rate of interest (for an equivalent security) at the date of issuance of the debt. As the 8-percent and 12-percent columns show, premium or discount arises when the prevailing market rate of interest differs from the coupon rate:

	Assume prevailing market rate of		
	10%	8%	12%
1. Present value of annual interest payments of $100 (the coupon rate of 10% of $1,000) for 20 years	$ 851	$ 982	$747
2. Present value of payment of the face amount of $1,000 at the end of year 20	149	215	104
Present value and proceeds at date of issuance	$1,000	$1,197	$851

[APB21, ¶18]

Example 2

.112 In the case of a $1,000, non-interest-bearing 20-year note, when the prevailing market rate for comparable credit risks is 10 percent, the following valuation shall be made:

1. Present value of no annual interest payments $ 0
2. Present value of payment of the face amount of $1,000 at the end of year 20   149
    Present value and proceeds at date of issuance $149

Comparison of the results of the illustrations in paragraph .111 with the illustration above shows the significant impact of interest. [APB21, ¶19]

Illustrations of Balance Sheet Presentation of Notes That Are Discounted

Example 1

.113 [Balance sheet presentation of] discount presented in the caption [is as follows:]

	December 31,	
	19Y0	**19X9**
Note Receivable from Sale of Property:		
$1,000,000 face amount, noninterest bearing, due December 31, 19Y5 (less unamortized discount based on imputed interest rate of 8%—19Y0, $320,000; 19X9, $370,000)	$680,000	$630,000

[APB21, ¶20]

Example 2

.114 [Balance sheet presentation of] discount presented separately [is as follows:]

	December 31,	
	19Y0	**19X9**
Note Receivable from Sale of Property:		
Non-interest-bearing note due December 31, 19Y5	$1,000,000	$1,000,000
Less unamortized discount based on imputed interest rate of 8%	320,000	370,000
Note receivable less unamortized discount	$ 680,000	$ 630,000

[APB21, ¶20]

Example 3

.115 [Balance sheet presentation of] several notes involved [is as follows:]

	December 31,	
	19Y0	**19X9**
Long-Term Debt (Note A):		
Principal amount	$24,000,000	$24,000,000
Less unamortized discount	2,070,000	2,192,000
Long-term debt less unamortized discount	$21,930,000	$21,808,000

Note A—Long-Term Debt: Long-term debt at December 31, 19Y0 consisted of the following:

	Principal	Unamortized Discount
6% subordinated debentures, due 19Z4 (discount is based on imputed interest rate of 7%)	$20,000,000	$1,750,000
6½% of bank loan, due 19Y3	3,000,000	
Non-interest-bearing note issued in connection with acquisition of property, due 19Y5 (discount is based on imputed interest rate of 8%)	1,000,000	320,000
Total	$24,000,000	$2,070,000

[APB21, ¶20]

Supplemental Guidance

Advance Not Requiring Imputation

.501 *Question*—This section requires interest to be imputed for some rights to receive or obligations to pay money on fixed or determinable dates. In certain transactions, pipeline enterprises make advances to encourage exploration. These advances are satisfied by delivery of future production, but there is also a definite obligation to repay if the future production is insufficient to discharge the obligation by a definite date. Does this section apply to such advances? [AIN-APB21]

.502 *Interpretation*—No, paragraph .102 states that this section is not intended to apply to "amounts that do not require repayment in the future, but rather will be applied to the purchase price of the property, goods, or services involved (for example, deposits or progress payments on construction contracts, advance payments for acquisition of resources and raw materials, advances to encourage exploration in the extractive industries)." The advance described in the paragraph above is covered by the exclusion in paragraph .102 even though there may be an obligation to repay should the future production prove insufficient to discharge the obligation. [AIN-APB21]

(The next page is 27279.)

Sources: APB Opinion 28; FASB Statement 3; FASB Statement 16;
FASB Statement 69; FASB Statement 95; FASB Statement 109;
FASB Interpretation 18; FASB Technical Bulletin 79-9

Summary

Each interim period shall be viewed primarily as an integral part of an annual period. The results for each interim period shall be based on the accounting principles and practices used by an enterprise in the preparation of its latest annual financial statements unless a change in an accounting practice or policy has been adopted in the current year. However, certain accounting principles and practices followed for annual reporting purposes may require modification at interim reporting dates so that the reported results for the interim period may better relate to the results of operations for the annual period.

This section provides guidance concerning modifications that are necessary or desirable at interim dates in accounting principles or practices followed for annual periods. It also requires that an enterprise make at the end of each interim period its best estimate of the effective tax rate expected to be applicable for the full fiscal year. The rate so determined shall be used in providing for income taxes on a current year-to-date basis.

Introduction

.101 This section indicates the applicability of generally accepted accounting principles [APB28, ¶3] to interim reporting and sets forth minimum disclosure requirements for interim financial reports of publicly traded enterprises.[1] This section does not deal with unresolved matters of accounting related to annual reporting. [APB28, ¶6]

.102 [Generally accepted] accounting principles and reporting practices shall apply to interim financial information in the manner set forth in this section. The guides expressed in this section are applicable whenever an enterprise issues interim financial information. [APB28, ¶7]

---

[1] A publicly traded enterprise for purposes of this section includes any enterprise whose securities trade in a public market on either (a) a stock exchange (domestic or foreign) or (b) in the over-the-counter market (including securities quoted only locally or regionally). When an enterprise makes a filing with a regulatory agency in preparation for sale of its securities in a public market, it is considered a publicly traded enterprise for this purpose. [APB28, ¶6, fn1]

Determining Interim Financial Information

.103 Each interim period shall be viewed primarily as an integral part of an annual period. [APB28, ¶9] The results for each interim period shall be based on the accounting principles and practices used by an enterprise in the preparation of its latest annual financial statements unless a change in an accounting practice or policy has been adopted in the current year (refer to paragraphs .131 through .145). However, certain accounting principles and practices followed for annual reporting purposes shall require modification at interim reporting dates so that the reported results for the interim period may better relate to the results of operations for the annual period. Paragraphs .105 through .123 set forth the modifications that are necessary or desirable at interim dates in accounting principles or practices followed for annual periods. [APB28, ¶10]

Revenue

.104 Revenue from products sold or services rendered shall be recognized as earned during an interim period on the same basis as followed for the full year.[2] [APB28, ¶11]

Costs and Expenses

.105 Costs and expenses for interim reporting purposes shall be classified as:

a. Costs associated with revenue—those costs that are associated directly with or allocated to the products sold or to the services rendered and are charged against income in those interim periods in which the related revenue is recognized.
b. All other costs and expenses—those costs and expenses that are not allocated to the products sold or to the services rendered and are charged against income in interim fiscal periods as incurred, or are allocated among interim periods based on an estimate of time expired, benefit received, or other activity associated with the periods. [APB28, ¶12]

Costs Associated with Revenue

.106 Those costs and expenses that are associated directly with or allocated to the products sold or to the services rendered for annual reporting purposes (including, for example, material costs, wages and salaries and related fringe benefits, manufacturing overhead, and warranties) shall be similarly treated for interim reporting purposes. [APB28, ¶13]

---

[2]For example, revenues from long-term construction-type contracts accounted for under the percentage-of-completion method shall be recognized in interim periods on the same basis followed for the full year. Losses projected on such contracts shall be recognized in full during the interim period in which the existence of such losses becomes evident. [APB28, ¶11]

.107 [An enterprise shall] generally use the same inventory pricing methods and make provisions for write-downs to market at interim dates on the same basis as used at annual inventory dates with the following exceptions, as appropriate, at interim reporting dates:

a. Some enterprises use estimated gross profit rates to determine the costs of goods sold during interim periods or use other methods different from those used at annual inventory dates. Those enterprises shall disclose the method used at the interim date and any significant adjustments that result from reconciliations with the annual physical inventory.

b. An enterprise that uses the LIFO method may encounter a liquidation of base period inventories at an interim date that is expected to be replaced by the end of the annual period. In such a case the inventory at the interim reporting date shall not give effect to the LIFO liquidation, and costs of sales for the interim reporting period shall include the expected cost of replacement of the liquidated LIFO base.

c. Inventory losses from market declines shall not be deferred beyond the interim period in which the decline occurs. Recoveries of such losses on the same inventory in later interim periods of the same fiscal year through market price recoveries shall be recognized as gains in the later interim period. Such gains shall not exceed previously recognized losses. Some market declines at interim dates, however, can reasonably be expected to be restored in the fiscal year. Such *temporary* market declines need not be recognized at the interim date since no loss is expected to be incurred in the fiscal year.

d. An enterprise that uses standard cost accounting systems for determining inventory and product costs shall generally follow the same procedures in reporting purchase price, wage rate, usage or efficiency variances from standard cost at the end of an interim period as followed at the end of a fiscal year. Purchase price variances or volume or capacity cost variances that are planned and expected to be absorbed by the end of the annual period shall be deferred at interim reporting dates. The effect of unplanned or unanticipated purchase price or volume variances, however, shall be reported at the end of an interim period following the same procedures used at the end of a fiscal year. [APB28, ¶14]

All Other Costs and Expenses

.108 The following standards shall apply in accounting for costs and expenses other than product costs in interim periods:

a. Costs and expenses other than product costs shall be charged to income in interim periods as incurred, or be allocated among interim periods based on an estimate of time expired, benefit received or activity associated with the periods. Procedures adopted for assigning specific cost and expense items to an interim period shall be consistent with the bases followed by the enterprise in reporting results of operations at annual reporting dates. However, if a specific cost or expense item charged to expense for annual reporting purposes benefits more than one interim period, the cost or expense item shall be allocated to those interim periods (refer to paragraph .150).

b. Costs and expenses incurred in an interim period that cannot be readily identified with the activities or benefits of other interim periods shall be charged to the interim period in which incurred. Disclosure shall be made as to the nature and amount of such costs unless items of a comparable nature are included in both the current interim period and in the corresponding interim period of the preceding year.

c. Arbitrary assignment of the amount of such costs to an interim period shall not be made.

d. Gains and losses that arise in any interim period similar to those that would not be deferred at year-end shall not be deferred to later interim periods within the same fiscal year. [APB28, ¶15]

[Refer to paragraph .150 for examples of accounting for costs and expenses other than product costs.]

.109 The amounts of certain costs and expenses are frequently subjected to year-end adjustments even though they can reasonably be approximated at interim dates. To the extent possible, such adjustments shall be estimated and the estimated costs and expenses assigned to interim periods so that the interim periods bear a reasonable portion of the anticipated annual amount. Examples of such items include inventory shrinkage, allowances for uncollectible accounts, allowances for quantity discounts, and discretionary year-end bonuses. [APB28, ¶17]

Seasonal Revenue, Costs, or Expenses

.110 Revenues of certain enterprises are subject to material seasonal variations. To avoid the possibility that interim results with material seasonal variations may be taken as fairly indicative of the estimated results for a full fiscal year, such businesses shall disclose the seasonal nature of their activities, and consider supplementing their interim reports with information for 12-month periods ended at the interim date for the current and preceding years. [APB28, ¶18]

Income Tax Provisions

Estimated Annual Effective Tax Rate[3]

.111 At the end of each interim period the enterprise shall make its best estimate of the effective tax rate expected to be applicable for the full fiscal year. The rate so determined shall be used in providing for income taxes on a current year-to-date basis. The effective tax rate shall reflect anticipated investment tax credits, foreign tax rates, per-

---

[3]Refer also to paragraph .113 when the enterprise has operations taxable in multiple jurisdictions. [FIN18, ¶8, fn3]

centage depletion, capital gains rates, and other available tax planning alternatives.[4] [APB28, ¶19] It also includes the effect of any valuation allowance expected to be necessary at the end of the year for deferred tax assets related to originating deductible temporary differences and carryforwards during the year. [FAS109, ¶288y] However, in arriving at this effective tax rate no effect shall be included for the tax related to significant, unusual, or extraordinary items that will be separately reported or reported net of their related tax effect in reports for the interim period or for the fiscal year. [APB28, ¶19]

.112 The rate is revised, if necessary, as of the end of each successive interim period during the fiscal year to the enterprise's best *current* estimate of its annual effective tax rate. In some cases, the rate will be the statutory rate modified as may be appropriate in particular circumstances. In other cases, the rate will be the enterprise's estimate of the **tax (or benefit)** that will be provided for the fiscal year, stated as a percentage of its estimated **ordinary income (or loss)** for the fiscal year (refer to paragraphs .121 through .123 if an ordinary loss is anticipated for the fiscal year).[5] [FIN18, ¶8] The tax (or benefit) related to ordinary income (or loss) shall be computed at an estimated annual effective tax rate[6] and the tax (or benefit) related to all other items shall be individually computed and recognized when the items occur. [FIN18, ¶6] Disclosure shall be made of the reasons for significant variations in the customary relationship between income tax expense and pretax accounting income, if they are not otherwise ap-

[4]Certain investment tax credits may be excluded from the estimated annual effective tax rate. If an enterprise includes allowable investment tax credits as part of its provision for income taxes over the productive life of acquired property and not entirely in the year the property is placed in service, amortization of deferred investment tax credits need not be taken into account in estimating the annual effective tax rate; however, if the investment tax credits are taken into account in the estimated annual effective tax rate, the amount taken into account shall be the amount of amortization that is anticipated to be included in income in the current year (refer to Section 127, "Income Taxes," paragraphs .228 and .232). Further, Section L10, "Leases," paragraphs .145 and .146, specifies that the investment tax credits related to leases that are accounted for as leveraged leases shall be deferred and accounted for as return on the net investment in the leveraged leases in the years in which the net investment is positive. Section L10, footnote 39, explains that the use of the term *years* is not intended to preclude application of the accounting described to shorter periods. If an enterprise accounts for investment tax credits related to leveraged leases in accordance with Section L10, paragraphs .145 and .146, for interim periods, those investment tax credits shall not be taken into account in estimating the annual effective tax rate. [FIN18, ¶8, fn6]

[5]Estimates of the annual effective tax rate at the end of interim periods are, of necessity, based on evaluations of possible future events and transactions and may be subject to subsequent refinement or revision. If a reliable estimate cannot be made, the actual effective tax rate for the year to date may be the best estimate of the annual effective tax rate. If an enterprise is unable to estimate a part of its ordinary income (or loss) or the related tax (or benefit) but is otherwise able to make a reliable estimate, the tax (or benefit) applicable to the item that cannot be estimated shall be reported in the interim period in which the item is reported. [FIN18, ¶8, fn7]

[6][Deleted 11/92 because of FASB Statement 111, *Rescission of FASB Statement No. 32 and Technical Corrections.*]

parent from the financial statements or from the nature of the enterprise's business [APB28, ¶19, fn2] (refer to Section I27, paragraph .147). [FAS109, ¶288h]

Operations Taxable in Multiple Jurisdictions

.113 If an enterprise that is subject to tax in multiple jurisdictions pays taxes based on identified income in one or more individual jurisdictions, interim period tax (or benefit) related to consolidated ordinary income (or loss) for the year to date shall be computed in accordance with paragraphs .116 through .123 using one overall estimated annual effective tax rate except that:

a. If in a separate jurisdiction an enterprise anticipates an ordinary loss for the fiscal year or has an ordinary loss for the year to date for which, in accordance with paragraphs .121 through .123, no tax benefit can be recognized, the enterprise shall exclude ordinary income (or loss) in that jurisdiction and the related tax (or benefit) from the overall computations of the estimated annual effective tax rate and interim period tax (or benefit). A separate estimated annual effective tax rate shall be computed for that jurisdiction and applied to ordinary income (or loss) in that jurisdiction in accordance with paragraphs .116 through .123.

b. If an enterprise is unable to estimate an annual effective tax rate in a foreign jurisdiction in dollars or is otherwise unable to make a reliable estimate of its ordinary income (or loss) or of the related tax (or benefit) for the fiscal year in a jurisdiction, the enterprise shall exclude ordinary income (or loss) in that jurisdiction and the related tax (or benefit) from the overall computations of the estimated annual effective tax rate and interim period tax (or benefit). The tax (or benefit) related to ordinary income (or loss) in that jurisdiction[7] shall be recognized in the interim period in which the ordinary income (or loss) is reported. [FIN18, ¶22]

(1) The effect of translating foreign currency financial statements may make it difficult to estimate an annual effective foreign currency tax rate in dollars. For example, depreciation is translated at historical exchange rates, whereas many transactions included in income are translated at current period average exchange rates. If depreciation is large in relation to earnings, a change in the estimated ordinary income that does not change the effective foreign currency tax rate can change the effective tax rate in the dollar financial statements. This result can occur with no change in exchange rates during the current year if there have been exchange rate changes in past years. If the enterprise is unable to estimate its annual effective tax rate in dollars or is otherwise unable to make a reliable estimate of its ordinary income (or loss) or of the related tax (or benefit) for the fiscal year in a jurisdiction, the tax (or benefit) applicable to ordinary income (or loss) in that jurisdiction shall be recognized in the interim period in which the ordinary income (or loss) is reported. [FIN18, ¶85]

---

[7]The tax (or benefit) related to ordinary income (or loss) in a jurisdiction may not be limited to tax (or benefit) in that jurisdiction. It might also include tax (or benefit) in another jurisdiction that results from providing taxes on unremitted earnings, foreign tax credits, etc. [FIN18, ¶22, fn24]

Effect of New Tax Legislation

.114 Paragraph .122 sets forth the requirements for recognition of the tax effects of a change in tax law or rates. That paragraph refers to effective dates prescribed in the statutes. Paragraph .115 describes the determination of when new legislation becomes effective. [FAS109, ¶288y]

Effective Date

.115 Legislation generally becomes effective on the date prescribed in the statutes. However, tax legislation may prescribe changes that become effective during an enterprise's fiscal year that are administratively implemented by applying a portion of the change to the full fiscal year. For example, if the statutory tax rate applicable to calendar-year corporations were increased from 48 percent to 52 percent, effective January 1, the increased statutory rate might be administratively applied to a corporation with a fiscal year ending at June 30 in the year of the change by applying a 50 percent rate to its taxable income for the fiscal year, rather than 48 percent for the first 6 months and 52 percent for the last 6 months. In that case the legislation becomes effective for that enterprise at the beginning of the enterprise's fiscal year. [FIN18, ¶24] (Refer to paragraphs .501 through .503 for supplemental guidance.)

Computation of Interim Period Tax (or Benefit)

.116 The estimated annual effective tax rate, described in paragraph .111 above, shall be applied to the year-to-date ordinary income (or loss) at the end of each interim period to compute the year-to-date tax (or benefit) related to ordinary income (or loss).[8] The interim period tax (or benefit) related to ordinary income (or loss) shall be the difference between the amount so computed and the amounts reported for previous interim periods of the fiscal year. [FIN18, ¶9]

Ordinary Income Anticipated for Fiscal Year

Year-to-Date Ordinary Income

.117 If an enterprise has ordinary income for the year to date at the end of an interim period and anticipates ordinary income for the fiscal year, the interim period tax shall be computed as described in paragraph .116. [FIN18, ¶10]

[[7a]Deleted 2/92 because of FASB Statement 109, *Accounting for Income Taxes.*]

[8]One result of the year-to-date computation is that, if the tax benefit of an ordinary loss that occurs in the early portions of the fiscal year is not recognized because realization of the tax benefits is not assured, tax is not provided for subsequent ordinary income until the unrecognized tax benefit of the earlier ordinary loss is offset (refer to paragraph .122). [FIN18, ¶9, fn8]

Year-to-Date Ordinary Loss

.118 If an enterprise has an ordinary loss for the year to date at the end of an interim period and anticipates ordinary income for the fiscal year, the interim period tax benefit shall be computed as described in paragraph .116 except that the year-to-date tax benefit recognized shall be limited to the amount determined in accordance with paragraphs .121 and .123. [FIN18, ¶11]

Ordinary Loss Anticipated for Fiscal Year

Year-to-Date Ordinary Income

.119 If an enterprise has ordinary income for the year to date at the end of an interim period and anticipates an ordinary loss for the fiscal year, the interim period tax shall be computed as described in paragraph .116. The estimated tax benefit for the fiscal year, used to determine the estimated annual effective tax rate described in paragraph .112, shall not exceed the tax benefit determined in accordance with paragraphs .121 through .123. [FIN18, ¶12]

Year-to-Date Ordinary Loss

.120 If an enterprise has an ordinary loss for the year to date at the end of an interim period and anticipates an ordinary loss for the fiscal year, the interim period tax benefit shall be computed as described in paragraph .116. The estimated tax benefit for the fiscal year, used to determine the estimated annual effective tax rate described in paragraph .112, shall not exceed the tax benefit determined in accordance with paragraphs .121 through .123. In addition to that limitation in the effective rate computation, if the year-to-date ordinary loss exceeds the anticipated ordinary loss for the fiscal year, the tax benefit recognized for the year to date shall not exceed the tax benefit determined, based on the year-to-date ordinary loss, in accordance with paragraphs .121 through .123. [FIN18, ¶13]

Limitations Applicable to Losses

Recognition of the Tax Benefit of a Loss

.121 Paragraph .122 provides that a tax benefit is recognized for a loss that arises early in a fiscal year if the tax benefits are expected to be (a) realized during the year or (b) recognizable as a deferred tax asset at the end of the year in accordance with the provisions of Section I27. Paragraph .116(e) of Section I27 requires that a valuation allowance be recognized if it is more likely than not that the tax benefit of some portion or all of a deferred tax asset will not be realized. Those limitations shall be applied in determining the estimated tax benefit of an ordinary loss for the fiscal year, used to determine the estimated annual effective tax rate described in paragraph .112, and the year-to-date tax benefit of a loss. [FAS109, ¶288y]

.122 The tax effects of losses that arise in the early portion of a fiscal year shall be recognized only when [APB28, ¶20] the tax benefits are expected to be (a) realized during the year or (b) recognizable as a deferred tax asset at the end of the year in accordance with the provisions of Section I27. [FAS109, ¶288h] An established seasonal pattern of loss in early interim periods offset by income in later interim periods shall constitute evidence that realization is [APB28, ¶20] more likely than not [FAS109, ¶288h], unless other evidence indicates the established seasonal pattern will not prevail. The tax effects of losses incurred in early interim periods shall be recognized in a later interim period of a fiscal year if their realization, although initially uncertain, later becomes [APB28, ¶20] more likely than not. [FAS109, ¶288h] If the tax effects of losses that arise in the early portions of a fiscal year are not recognized in that interim period, no tax provision shall be made for income that arises in later interim periods until the tax effects of the previous interim losses are utilized.[9] [APB28, ¶20] The tax effect of a valuation allowance expected to be necessary for a deferred tax asset at the end of the year for originating deductible temporary differences and carryforwards during the year should be included in the effective tax rate. The effect of a change in the beginning-of-the-year balance of a valuation allowance as a result of a change in judgment about the realizability of the related deferred tax asset in future years shall not be apportioned among interim periods through an adjustment of the effective tax rate but shall be recognized in the interim period in which the change occurs. The effects of new tax legislation shall not be recognized prior to enactment. The tax effect of a change in tax laws or rates on taxes currently payable or refundable for the current year shall be reflected after the effective dates prescribed in the statutes in the computation of the annual effective tax rate beginning no earlier than the first interim period that includes the enactment date of the new legislation. The effect of a change in tax laws or rates on a deferred tax liability or asset shall not be apportioned among interim periods through an adjustment of the annual effective tax rate. The tax effect of a change in tax laws or rates on taxes payable or refundable for a prior year shall be recognized as of the enactment date of the change as tax expense (benefit) for the current year. [FAS109, ¶288h]

Reversal of Taxable Temporary Differences

.123 A deferred tax liability related to existing taxable temporary differences is a source of evidence for recognition of a tax benefit when (a) an enterprise anticipates an ordinary loss for the fiscal year or has a year-to-date ordinary loss in excess of the anticipated ordinary loss for the fiscal year, (b) the tax benefit of that loss is not expected to be realized during the year, and (c) recognition of a deferred tax asset for that loss at the end of the fiscal year is expected to depend on taxable income from the reversal of existing taxable temporary differences (that is, a higher valuation allowance (refer to paragraph .116(e) of Section I27) would be necessary absent the existing taxable temporary differences). If the tax benefit relates to an estimated ordinary loss for

---

[8a]Deleted 2/92 because of FASB Statement 109.]

[9]The tax benefits of interim losses accounted for in this manner would not be reported as extraordinary items in the results of operations of the interim period. [APB28, ¶20, fn3]

the fiscal year, it shall be considered in determining the estimated annual effective tax rate described in paragraph .112. If the tax benefit relates to a year-to-date ordinary loss, it shall be considered in computing the maximum tax benefit that shall be recognized for the year-to-date. [FAS109, ¶288y]

Disposal of a Segment of a Business and Extraordinary, Unusual, Infrequently Occurring, and Contingent Items

.124 Extraordinary items shall be disclosed separately and included in the determination of net income for the interim period in which they occur. In determining materiality, extraordinary items shall be related to the estimated income for the full fiscal year. Effects of disposals of a segment of a business and unusual and infrequently occurring transactions and events that are material with respect to the operating results of the interim period but that are not designated as extraordinary items in the interim statements shall be reported separately. In addition, matters such as unusual seasonal results, business combinations treated for accounting purposes as poolings of interests, and acquisition of a significant business in a purchase shall be disclosed to provide information needed for a proper understanding of interim financial reports. Extraordinary items, gains or losses from disposal of a segment of a business, and unusual or infrequently occurring items shall not be prorated over the balance of the fiscal year. [APB28, ¶21]

Contingent Items

.125 Contingencies and other uncertainties that affect the fairness of presentation of financial data at an interim date shall be disclosed in interim reports in the same manner required for annual reports.[12] Such disclosures shall be repeated in interim and annual reports until the contingencies have been removed, resolved, or have become immaterial. [APB28, ¶22]

---

[10][Deleted 2/92 because of FASB Statement 109.]

[11][Deleted 2/92 because of FASB Statement 109.]

[12]The significance of a contingency or uncertainty shall be judged in relation to annual financial statements. Disclosures of such items shall include, but not be limited to, those matters that form the basis of a qualification of an independent auditor's report. [APB28, ¶22, fn4]

Tax (or Benefit) Applicable to Significant Unusual or Infrequently Occurring Items, Discontinued Operations, or Extraordinary Items

Basis of Tax Provision

.126 Paragraph .111 excludes taxes related to "significant unusual or extraordinary items that will be separately reported or reported net of their related tax effect"[13] from the estimated annual effective tax rate calculation. [FIN18, ¶16] Paragraph .122 excludes the effects of changes in judgment about beginning-of-year valuation allowances and effects of changes in tax laws or rates from the estimated effective tax rate calculation. [FAS109, ¶288y] Paragraph .124 requires that those items be recognized in the interim period in which they occur. [FIN18, ¶16] Section I27, paragraphs .134 through .137, [FAS109, ¶288y] describes the method of applying tax allocation within a period. This computation shall be made using the estimated fiscal-year ordinary income and the items described in footnote 13 for the year to date. [FIN18, ¶16]

Financial Statement Presentation

.127 Extraordinary items and discontinued operations that will be presented net of related tax effects in the financial statements for the fiscal year shall be presented net of related tax effects in interim financial statements. Unusual or infrequently occurring items that will be separately disclosed in the financial statements for the fiscal year shall be separately disclosed as a component of pretax income from continuing operations, and the tax (or benefit) related to such items shall be included in the tax (or benefit) related to continuing operations. Paragraphs .128 and .129 describe the application of the above to specific situations. [FIN18, ¶17]

Recognition of the Tax Benefit of a Loss

.128 If an enterprise has a significant unusual, infrequently occurring, or extraordinary loss or a loss from discontinued operations, the tax benefit of that loss [FIN18, ¶18] shall be recognized when the tax benefit of the loss is expected to be (a) realized during the year or (b) recognizable as a deferred tax asset at the end of the year in accordance with the provisions of Section I27. Realization would appear to be more likely than not if future taxable income from (ordinary) income during the current year is expected based on an established seasonal pattern of loss in early interim periods offset by income in later interim periods.[14] If recognition of a deferred tax asset at the end of the fiscal year for all or a portion of the tax benefit of the loss depends on taxable income from the reversal of existing taxable temporary differences, refer to paragraph .123

---

[13] In the context of paragraph .124, which is consistent with Sections I17, "Income Statement Presentation: Extraordinary Items," and I22, "Income Statement Presentation: Unusual or Infrequent Items," this description includes unusual items, infrequently occurring items, discontinued operations, and extraordinary items. [FIN18, ¶16, fn16]

[14] Refer to paragraph .122. [FIN18, ¶18, fn19]

above. [FAS109, ¶288y] If all or a part of the tax benefit is not realized and future realization is not [FIN18, ¶18] more likely than not [FAS109, ¶288y] in the interim period of
occurrence but becomes [FIN18, ¶18] more likely than not [FAS109, ¶288y] in a subsequent interim period of the same fiscal year, the previously unrecognized tax benefit
shall be reported in that subsequent interim period in the same manner that it would
have been reported if realization had been [FIN18, ¶18] more likely than not [FAS109,
¶288y] in the interim period of occurrence, that is, as a tax benefit relating to continuing
operations, discontinued operations, or an extraordinary item. [FIN18, ¶18]

Discontinued Operations

.129 The computations described in paragraphs .126 through .128 shall be the basis
for the tax (or benefit) related to both (a) the income (or loss) from operations of the
discontinued segment[15] prior to the measurement date and (b) the gain (or loss) on
disposal of discontinued operations (including any provision for operating loss subsequent to the measurement date). Income (or loss) from operations of the discontinued
segment prior to the interim period in which the measurement date occurs will have
been included in ordinary income (or loss) of prior periods and thus will have been
included in the estimated annual effective tax rate and tax (or benefit) calculations.
The *total* tax (or benefit) provided in the prior interim periods shall not be recomputed
but shall be divided into two components, applicable to the remaining ordinary income (or loss) and to the income (or loss) from operations of the discontinued segment as follows. A revised estimated annual effective tax rate and resulting tax (or
benefit) shall be computed, in accordance with paragraphs .111 through .123, for the
remaining ordinary income (or loss), based on the estimates applicable to such operations used in the original calculations for each prior interim period. The tax (or benefit) related to the operations of the discontinued segment shall be the total of (a) the
difference between the tax (or benefit) originally computed for ordinary income (or
loss) and the recomputed amount for the remaining ordinary income (or loss) and
(b) the tax computed in accordance with paragraphs .126 through .128 for any unusual or infrequently occurring items of the discontinued segment. [FIN18, ¶19]

Using a Prior-Year Operating Loss Carryforward

.130 Paragraph .136 of Section I27 requires that the manner of reporting the tax
benefit of an operating loss carryforward recognized in a subsequent year generally is
determined by the source of the income in that year, and not by (a) the source of the
operating loss carryforward or (b) the source of expected future income that will result
in realization of a deferred tax asset for the operating loss carryforward. The tax benefit is allocated first to reduce tax expense from continuing operations to zero with any
excess allocated to the other source(s) of income that provides the means of realization, for example, extraordinary items, discontinued operations, and so forth. That

---

[15]The term *discontinued segment* refers to a discontinued segment of the business as described in Section I13,
paragraph .404. [FIN18, ¶19, fn20]

requirement also pertains to reporting the tax benefit of an operating loss carryforward in interim periods. The tax benefit of an operating loss carryforward from prior years shall be included in the effective tax rate computation if the tax benefit is expected to be realized as a result of ordinary income in the current year. Otherwise, the tax benefit shall be recognized in the manner described above in each interim period to the extent that income in the period and for the year to date is available to offset the operating loss carryforward or, in the case of a change in judgment about realizability of the related deferred tax asset in future years, the effect shall be recognized in the interim period in which the change occurs. [FAS109, ¶288y]

Accounting Changes in Interim Periods

.131 Each report of interim financial information shall indicate any change in accounting principles or practices from those applied in (a) the comparable interim period of the prior annual period, (b) the preceding interim periods in the current annual period, and (c) the prior annual report. [APB28, ¶23]

.132 Changes in an interim or annual accounting practice or policy made in an interim period shall be reported in the period in which the change is made in accordance with the provisions of Section A06, "Accounting Changes." [APB28, ¶24]

.133 The effect of a change in an accounting estimate, including a change in the estimated effective annual tax rate, shall be accounted for in the period in which the change in estimate is made. No restatement of previously reported interim information shall be made for changes in estimates, but the effect on earnings of a change in estimate made in a current interim period shall be reported in the current and subsequent interim periods, if material in relation to any period presented and shall continue to be reported in the interim financial information of the subsequent year for as many periods as necessary to avoid misleading comparisons. Such disclosure shall conform with Section A06, paragraph .132. [APB28, ¶26]

.134 If possible, [it is recommended that] enterprises adopt any accounting changes during the first interim period of a fiscal year. Changes in accounting principles and practices adopted after the first interim period in a fiscal year tend to obscure operating results and complicate disclosure of interim financial information. [APB28, ¶28]

Cumulative Effect-Type Accounting Changes Other Than Changes to LIFO

.135 If a cumulative effect-type accounting change is made during the *first* interim period of an enterprise's fiscal year, the cumulative effect of the change on retained earnings at the *beginning of that fiscal year* shall be included in net income of the first interim period (and in last-12-months-to-date financial reports that include that first interim period). [FAS3, ¶9]

.136 If a cumulative effect-type accounting change is made in *other than the first* interim period of an enterprise's fiscal year, *no* cumulative effect of the change shall be included in net income of the period of change. Instead, financial information for the prechange interim periods of the fiscal year in which the change is made shall be restated by applying the newly adopted accounting principle to those prechange interim periods. The cumulative effect of the change on retained earnings at the *beginning of that fiscal year* shall be included in restated net income of the first interim period of the fiscal year in which the change is made (and in any year-to-date or last-12-months-to-date financial reports that include the first interim period). If financial information that includes those prechange interim periods is presented, it shall be presented on the restated basis. [FAS3, ¶10]

.137 The following disclosures about a cumulative effect-type accounting change shall be made in interim financial reports:

a. In financial reports for the interim period in which the new accounting principle is adopted, disclosure shall be made of the nature of and justification for the change.
b. In financial reports for the interim period in which the new accounting principle is adopted, disclosure shall be made of the effect of the change on income from continuing operations, net income, and related per share amounts for the interim period in which the change is made. In addition, if the change is made in other than the first interim period of a fiscal year, financial reports for the period of change shall also disclose (1) the effect of the change on income from continuing operations, net income, and related per share amounts for each prechange interim period of that fiscal year and (2) income from continuing operations, net income, and related per share amounts for each prechange interim period restated in accordance with paragraph .136.
c. In financial reports for the interim period in which the new accounting principle is adopted, disclosure shall be made of income from continuing operations, net income, and related per share amounts computed on a pro forma basis for (1) the interim period in which the change is made and (2) any interim periods of prior fiscal years for which financial information is being presented. If no financial information for interim periods of prior fiscal years is being presented, disclosure shall be made, in the period of change, of the actual and pro forma amounts of income from continuing operations, net income, and related per share amounts for the interim period of the immediately preceding fiscal year that corresponds to the interim period in which the changes are made. In all cases, the pro forma amounts shall be computed and presented in conformity with Section A06, paragraphs .115, .117, .118, and .121.
d. In year-to-date and last-12-months-to-date financial reports that include the interim period in which the new accounting principle is adopted, the disclosures specified in the first sentence of subparagraph (b) above and in subparagraph (c) above shall be made.
e. In financial reports for a subsequent (postchange) interim period of the fiscal year in which the new accounting principle is adopted, disclosure shall be made of the

effect of the change on income from continuing operations, net income, and related per share amounts for that postchange interim period. [FAS3, ¶11]

.138 In determining materiality for the purpose of reporting the cumulative effect of an accounting change or correction of an error, amounts shall be related to the estimated income for the full fiscal year and also to the effect on the trend of earnings. Changes that are material with respect to an interim period but not material with respect to the estimated income for the full fiscal year or to the trend of earnings shall be separately disclosed in the interim period. [APB28, ¶29]

.139 Section A06 specifies that the related income tax effect of a cumulative effect-type accounting change shall be computed as though the new accounting principle had been applied retroactively for all prior periods that would have been affected. [FIN18, ¶21]

Changes to the LIFO Method of Inventory Pricing and Similar Situations

.140 Section A06, paragraph .122, indicates that in rare situations—principally a change to the LIFO method of inventory pricing[16]—neither the cumulative effect of the change on retained earnings at the beginning of the fiscal year in which the change is made nor the pro forma amounts can be computed. In those situations, the paragraph requires an explanation of the reasons for omitting (a) accounting for a cumulative effect and (b) disclosure of pro forma amounts for prior years. If a change of that type is made in the *first* interim period of an enterprise's fiscal year, the disclosures specified in paragraph .137 shall be made (except the pro forma amounts for interim periods of prior fiscal years called for by paragraph .137(c) will not be disclosed). [FAS3, ¶12]

.141 If the change is made in *other than the first* interim period of an enterprise's fiscal year, the disclosure specified in paragraph .137 shall be made (except the pro forma amounts for interim periods of prior fiscal years called for by paragraph .137(c) will not be disclosed) and in addition, financial information for the prechange interim periods of that fiscal year shall be restated by applying the newly adopted accounting principle to those prechange interim periods. If financial information that includes those prechange interim periods is presented, it shall be presented on the restated basis. [FAS3, ¶13]

.142 Certain changes in accounting principle, such as those described in Section A06, paragraphs .103 and .123, require retroactive restatement of previously issued financial statements. Section A35, "Adjustments of Financial Statements for Prior Periods," paragraph .107, requires similar treatment for prior period adjustments. Previously issued financial statements also must be restated for a change in the reporting entity (refer to Section A35, paragraphs .112 and .113) and for correction of an error (refer to Section A35, paragraphs .103 and .105). Previously issued interim financial

---

[16]In making disclosures about changes to the LIFO method, enterprises should be aware of the limitations the Internal Revenue Service has placed on such disclosures. [FAS3, ¶12, fn1]

information shall be similarly restated. Sections A06 and A35 specify the required disclosures. [APB28, ¶25]

Adjustments Related to Prior Interim Periods of the Current Fiscal Year

.143 For purposes of this section, an "adjustment related to prior *interim* periods of the current fiscal year" is an adjustment or settlement of litigation or similar claims, of income taxes [FAS16, ¶13] (except for the effects of retroactive tax legislation) [FAS109, ¶288n], of renegotiation proceedings, or of utility revenue under rate-making processes provided that the adjustment or settlement meets each of the following criteria:

a. The effect of the adjustment or settlement is material in relation to income from continuing operations of the current fiscal year or in relation to the trend of income from continuing operations or is material by other appropriate criteria.
b. All or part of the adjustment or settlement can be specifically identified with and is directly related to business activities of specific prior interim periods of the current fiscal year.
c. The amount of the adjustment or settlement could not be reasonably estimated prior to the current interim period but becomes reasonably estimable in the current interim period.

Criterion (b) is not met solely because of incidental effects such as interest on a settlement. Criterion (c) would be met by the occurrence of an event with currently measurable effects such as a final decision on a rate order. Treatment as adjustments related to prior interim periods of the current fiscal year shall not be applied to the normal recurring corrections and adjustments that are the result of the use of estimates inherent in the accounting process. Changes in provisions for doubtful accounts shall not be considered to be adjustments related to prior interim periods of the current fiscal year even though the changes result from litigation or similar claims. [FAS16, ¶13]

.144 If an item of profit or loss occurs in *other than the first* interim period of the enterprise's fiscal year and all or a part of the item of profit or loss is an adjustment related to prior interim periods of the current fiscal year, as defined in paragraph .143, the item shall be reported as follows:

a. The portion of the item that is directly related to business activities of the enterprise during the current interim period, if any, shall be included in the determination of net income for that period.
b. Prior interim periods of the current fiscal year shall be restated to include the portion of the item that is directly related to business activities of the enterprise during each prior interim period in the determination of net income for that period.

[16aDeleted 2/92 because of FASB Statement 109.]

c. The portion of the item that is directly related to business activities of the enterprise during prior fiscal years, if any, shall be included in the determination of net income of the first interim period of the current fiscal year. [FAS16, ¶14]

.145 The following disclosures shall be made in interim financial reports about an adjustment related to prior interim periods of the current fiscal year. In financial reports for the interim period in which the adjustment occurs, disclosure shall be made of (a) the effect on income from continuing operations, net income, and related per share amounts for each prior interim period of the current fiscal year and (b) income from continuing operations, net income, and related per share amounts for each prior interim period restated in accordance with paragraph .144. [FAS16, ¶15]

Disclosure of Summarized Interim Financial Data by Publicly Traded Companies

.146 If publicly traded companies[17] report summarized financial information to their security holders at interim dates (including reports on fourth quarters), the following data shall be reported, as a minimum:[18]

a. Sales or gross revenues, provision for income taxes, extraordinary items (including related income tax effects), cumulative effect of a change in accounting principles or practices, and net income
b. Primary and fully diluted earnings per share data for each period presented, determined in accordance with the provisions of Section E09, "Earnings per Share"
c. Seasonal revenue, costs, or expenses (refer to paragraph .110)
d. Significant changes in estimates or provisions for income taxes (refer to paragraphs .111 and .112)
e. Disposal of a segment of a business and extraordinary, unusual or infrequently occurring items (refer to paragraph .124)
f. Contingent items (refer to paragraph .125)
g. Changes in accounting principles or estimates (refer to paragraphs .131 through .145)
h. Significant changes in financial position (refer to paragraph .149)

If summarized financial data are regularly reported on a quarterly basis, the foregoing information with respect to the current quarter and the current year to date or the last 12 months to date shall be furnished together with comparable data for the preceding year. [APB28, ¶30]

.147 If interim financial data and disclosures are not separately reported for the fourth quarter, security holders often make inferences about that quarter by subtract-

---

[17]Refer to footnote 1. [APB28, ¶30, fn6]

[18]The minimum disclosures of summarized interim financial data required of publicly traded companies by this section do not constitute a fair presentation of financial position and results of operations in conformity with generally accepted accounting principles. [APB28, ¶30, fn7]

ing data based on the third quarter interim report from the annual results. In the absence of a separate fourth quarter report or disclosure of the results (as outlined in paragraph .146) for that quarter in the annual report, [accounting changes made during the fourth quarter], disposals of segments of a business, and extraordinary, unusual, or infrequently occurring items recognized in the fourth quarter, as well as the aggregate effect of year-end adjustments that are material to the results of that quarter (refer to paragraph .109), shall be disclosed in the annual report in a note to the annual financial statements. [APB28, ¶31] Disclosures about the effect of an accounting change on interim periods that are required by paragraphs .131 through .137 and .140 and .141 shall be included, as appropriate. [FAS3, ¶14]

.148 Disclosure of the impact on the financial results for interim periods of the matters discussed in paragraphs .124 through .141 is desirable for as many subsequent periods as necessary to keep the reader fully informed. There is a presumption that users of summarized interim financial data will have read the latest published annual report, including the financial disclosures required by generally accepted accounting principles and management's commentary concerning the annual financial results, and that the summarized interim data will be viewed in that context. In this connection, the management is encouraged to provide commentary relating to the effects of significant events upon the interim financial results. [APB28, ¶32]

.149 Publicly traded enterprises are encouraged to publish balance sheet and [APB28, ¶33] cash flow data [FAS95, ¶151] at interim dates since these data often assist security holders in their understanding and interpretation of the income data reported. If condensed interim balance sheet information or [APB28, ¶33] cash flow data [FAS95, ¶151] are not presented at interim reporting dates, significant changes since the last reporting period with respect to liquid assets, net working capital, long-term liabilities, or stockholders' equity shall be disclosed. [APB28, ¶33]

Disclosures Required by Publicly Traded[19] Enterprises with Oil and Gas Producing Activities

.149A The disclosures set forth in Section Oi5, "Oil and Gas Producing Activities," paragraphs .156 through .186, are not required in interim financial reports. However, interim financial reports [of publicly traded enterprises with significant oil and gas producing activities] shall include information about a major discovery or other favorable or adverse event that causes a significant change from the information presented in the most recent annual financial report concerning oil and gas reserve quantities [refer to Section Oi5, paragraphs .160 through .167]. [FAS69, ¶9]

[19Refer to Section Oi5, "Oil and Gas Producing Activities," paragraph .157.]

Examples of Accounting for Costs and Expenses Other Than Product Costs

.150 A complete listing of examples of application of the standards set forth in paragraph .108 is not practical; however, the following examples of applications may be helpful:

a. If a cost that is expensed for annual reporting purposes clearly benefits two or more interim periods (for example, annual major repairs), each interim period shall be charged for an appropriate portion of the annual cost by the use of accruals or deferrals.

b. If quantity discounts are allowed customers based upon annual sales volume, the amount of such discounts charged to each interim period shall be based on the sales to customers during the interim period in relation to estimated annual sales.

c. Property taxes (and similar costs such as interest and rent) may be accrued or deferred at the annual reporting date, to achieve a full year's charge of taxes to costs and expenses. Similar procedures shall be adopted at each interim reporting date to provide an appropriate cost in each period.

d. Advertising costs may be deferred within a fiscal year if the benefits of an expenditure made clearly extend beyond the interim period in which the expenditure is made. Advertising costs may be accrued and assigned to interim periods in relation to sales prior to the time the service is received if the advertising program is clearly implicit in the sales arrangement. [APB28, ¶16]

Examples of Reporting a Cumulative Effect-Type Accounting Change (Other Than a Change to LIFO)

.151 The following are examples of application of this section, and the requirements of Section A06 as they are incorporated by reference in this section. The examples do not encompass all possible circumstances and are not intended to indicate a preference for a particular format. [FAS3, Appendix A]

Assumptions

.152 In the year 19X5, ABC Company decides to adopt the straight-line method of depreciation for plant equipment. The straight-line method will be used for new acquisitions as well as for previously acquired plant equipment for which depreciation had been provided on an accelerated method. [FAS3, Appendix A]

.153 These examples assume that the effects of the change are limited to the effect on depreciation, incentive compensation, and related income tax provisions and that the effect on inventories is not material. The pro forma amounts have been adjusted for an assumed 10 percent pretax effect of the change on the provisions for incentive compensation and an assumed 50 percent income tax rate. The per share amounts are computed assuming that throughout the 2 years 19X4 and 19X5, 1,000,000 shares of common stock were issued and outstanding with no potential dilution. Other data assumed for these examples are:

Period	Net Income on the Basis of Old Accounting Principle (Accelerated Depreciation)	Gross Effect of Change to Straight-Line Depreciation	Gross Effect Less Income Taxes	Net Effect after Incentive Compensation and Related Income Taxes
Prior to first quarter 19X4		$ 20,000	$ 10,000	$ 9,000
First quarter 19X4	$1,000,000	30,000	15,000	13,500
Second quarter 19X4	1,200,000	70,000	35,000	31,500
Third quarter 19X4	1,100,000	50,000	25,000	22,500
Fourth quarter 19X4	1,100,000	80,000	40,000	36,000
Total at beginning of 19X5	$4,400,000	$250,000	$125,000	$112,500
First quarter 19X5	$1,059,500	$ 90,000	$ 45,000	$ 40,500
Second quarter 19X5	1,255,000	100,000	50,000	45,000
Third quarter 19X5	1,150,500	110,000	55,000	49,500
Fourth quarter 19X5	1,146,000	120,000	60,000	54,000
[Total at end of 19X5]	$4,611,000	$420,000	$210,000	$189,000

[FAS3, Appendix A]

Example 1

.154 The change in depreciation method is made in the first quarter of 19X5. The manner of reporting the change in the first quarter of 19X5, with comparative information for the first quarter of 19X4, is as follows:

| | 3 Months Ended March 31, | |
	19X5	19X4
Income before cumulative effect of a change in accounting principle	$1,100,000	$1,000,000
Cumulative effect on prior years (to December 31, 19X4) of changing to a different depreciation method (Note A)	125,000	
Net income	$1,225,000	$1,000,000
Amounts per common share:		
Income before cumulative effect of a change in accounting principle	$1.10	$1.00
Cumulative effect on prior years (to December 31, 19X4) of changing to a different depreciation method (Note A)	.13	
Net income	$1.23	$1.00
Pro forma amounts assuming the new depreciation method is applied retroactively (Note A):		
Net income	$1,100,000	$1,013,500
Net income per common share	$1.10	$1.01

Note A—Change in Depreciation Method for Plant Equipment

In the first quarter of 19X5, the method of computing depreciation of plant equipment was changed from the . . . (state previous method) . . . used in prior years, to the straight-line method . . . (state justification for the change in method) . . . and the new method has been applied to equipment acquisitions of prior years. The $125,000 cumulative effect of the change on prior years (after reduction for income taxes of $125,000) is included in income of the first quarter of 19X5. The effect of the change on the first quarter of 19X5 was to increase income before cumulative effect of a change in accounting principle $40,500 ($.04 per share) and net income $165,500 ($.17 per share). The pro forma amounts reflect the effect of retroactive application on depreciation, the change in provisions for incentive compensation that would have been made in 19X4 had the new method been in effect, and related income taxes. [FAS3, Appendix A]

Example 2

.155 Assume the same facts as in Example 1, except that the change is made in the third quarter of 19X5. [FAS3, Appendix A]

.156 The manner of reporting the change in the third quarter of 19X5, with year-to-date information and comparative information for similar periods of 19X4, is as follows:

	3 Months Ended September 30,		9 Months Ended September 30,	
	19X5	**19X4**	**19X5**	**19X4**
Income before cumulative effect of a change in accounting principle	$1,200,000	$1,100,000	$3,600,000	$3,300,000
Cumulative effect on prior years (to December 31,19X4) of changing to a different depreciation method (Note A)			125,000	
Net income	$1,200,000	$1,100,000	$3,725,000	$3,300,000
Amounts per common share: Income before cumulative effect of a change in accounting principle	$1.20	$1.10	$3.60	$3.30
Cumulative effect on prior years (to December 31, 19X4) of changing to a different depreciation method (Note A)			.13	
Net income	$1.20	$1.10	$3.73	$3.30
Pro forma amounts assuming the new depreciation method is applied retroactively (Note A): Net income	$1,200,000	$1,122,500	$3,600,000	$3,367,500
Net income per common share	$1.20	$1.12	$3.60	$3.37

Note A—Change in Depreciation Method for Plant Equipment

In the third quarter of 19X5, the method of computing depreciation of plant equipment was changed from the . . . (state previous method) . . . used in prior years, to the straight-line method . . . (state justification for the change in method) . . . and the new method has been applied to equipment acquisitions of prior years. The $125,000 cumulative effect of the change on prior years (after reduction for income taxes of $125,000) is included in income of the 9 months ended September 30, 19X5.

The effect of the change on the 3 months ended September 30, 19X5 was to increase net income $49,500 ($.05 per share); the effect of the change on the 9 months ended September 30, 19X5 was to increase income before cumulative effect of a change in accounting principle $135,000 ($.14 per share) and net income $260,000 ($.26 per share). The pro forma amounts reflect the effect of retroactive application on depreciation, the change in provisions for incentive compensation that would have been made in 19X4 had the new method been in effect, and related income taxes. The effect of the change on the first quarter of 19X5 was to increase income before cumulative effect of a change in accounting principle $40,500 ($.04 per share) to $1,100,000 ($1.10 per share) and net income $165,500 ($.17 per share) to $1,225,000 ($1.23 per share); the effect of the change on the second quarter was to increase net income $45,000 ($.04 per share) to $1,300,000 ($1.30 per share). [FAS3, Appendix A]

.157 Alternatively, the last sentence of Note A could be replaced with the following tabular disclosure:

The effect of the change on the first and second quarters of 19X5 is as follows:

	3 Months Ended	
	March 31, 19X5	**June 30, 19X5**
Net income as originally reported*	$1,059,500	$1,255,000
Effect of change in depreciation method	40,500	45,000
Income before cumulative effect of a change in accounting principle	1,100,000	1,300,000
Cumulative effect on prior years (to December 31, 19X4) of changing to a different depreciation method	125,000	
Net income as restated	$1,225,000	$1,300,000
Per share amounts:		
Net income as originally reported*	$1.06	$1.26
Effect of change in depreciation method	.04	.04
Income before cumulative effect of a change in accounting principle	1.10	1.30
Cumulative effect on prior years (to December 31, 19X4) of changing to a different depreciation method	.13	
Net income as restated	$1.23	$1.30

---

*Disclosure of net income as originally reported is not required.

[FAS3, Appendix A]

Reporting a Change to the LIFO Method of Inventory Pricing

.158 The following are examples of application of this section, and the requirements of Section A06 as they are incorporated by reference in this section. The examples do not encompass all possible circumstances and are not intended to indicate a preference for a particular format. [FAS3, Appendix B]

Assumptions

.159 In the year 19X5, XYZ Company decides to change to the LIFO method of inventory pricing. These examples assume that the effects of the change are limited to the effect on inventory, incentive compensation, and related income tax provisions. A 10 percent pretax effect of the change on incentive compensation and a 50 percent income tax rate are assumed. The per share amounts are computed assuming that throughout 19X4 and 19X5, 1,000,000 shares of common stock were issued and outstanding with no potential dilution. Other data assumed for these examples are:

Period	Net Income on the Basis of Old Accounting Principle	Gross Effect of Change to LIFO	Net Effect after Incentive Compensation and Income Taxes
First quarter 19X5	$1,095,500	$ (90,000)	$ (40,500)
Second quarter 19X5	1,295,000	(100,000)	(45,000)
Third quarter 19X5	1,194,500	(110,000)	(49,500)
Fourth quarter 19X5	1,194,000	(120,000)	(54,000)
[Total]	$4,779,000	$(420,000)	$(189,000)

[FAS3, Appendix B]

Example 3

.160 The change to LIFO is made in the first quarter of 19X5. The manner of reporting the change in the first quarter of 19X5, with comparative information for the first quarter of 19X4, is as follows:

	3 Months Ended March 31,	
	19X5	**19X4**
Net income (Note A)	$1,055,000	$1,000,000
Net income per common share (Note A)	$1.06	$1.00

Note A—Change to LIFO Method of Inventory Pricing

In the first quarter of 19X5, the enterprise changed its method of inventory pricing from . . . (state previous method) . . . used previously to the LIFO method because . . . (state justification for change and reasons for not disclosing a cumulative effect on, and pro forma amounts for, prior periods). The effect of the change on the first quarter of 19X5 was to decrease net income $40,500 ($.04 per share). [FAS3, Appendix B]

Example 4

.161 Assume the same facts as in Example 3, except that the change is made in the third quarter of 19X5. [FAS3, Appendix B]

.162 The manner of reporting the change in the third quarter of 19X5, with year-to-date information and comparative information for similar periods of 19X4, is as follows:

	3 Months Ended September 30,		9 Months Ended September 30,	
	19X5	**19X4**	**19X5**	**19X4**
Net income (Note A)	$1,145,000	$1,200,000	$3,450,000	$3,400,000
Net income per common share (Note A)	$1.15	$1.20	$3.45	$3.40

Note A—Change to LIFO Method of Inventory Pricing

In the third quarter of 19X5, the enterprise changed its method of inventory pricing from . . . (state previous method) . . . used previously to the LIFO method because . . . (state justification for change and reasons for not disclosing a cumulative effect on, and pro forma amounts for, prior periods). The effect of the change on the 3 months and 9 months ended September 30, 19X5 was to decrease net income $49,500 ($.05 per share) and $135,000 ($.14 per share), respectively. The effect of the change on the first and second quarters of 19X5 was to decrease net income $40,500 ($.04 per share) to $1,055,000 ($1.06 per share) and $45,000 ($.05 per share) to $1,250,000 ($1.25 per share), respectively. [FAS3, Appendix B]

.163 Alternatively, the last sentence of Note A could be replaced with the following tabular disclosure:

The effect of the change on the first and second quarters of 19X5 is as follows:

	3 Months Ended	
	March 31, 19X5	**June 30, 19X5**
Net income as originally reported*	$1,095,500	$1,295,000
Effect of change to LIFO method of inventory pricing	(40,500)	(45,000)
Net income as restated	$1,055,000	$1,250,000
Per share amounts:		
Net income as originally reported*	$1.10	$1.30
Effect of change to LIFO method of inventory pricing	(.04)	(.05)
Net income as restated	$1.06	$1.25

*Disclosure of net income as originally reported is not required.

[FAS3, Appendix B]

.164 This paragraph provides a cross-reference from the paragraphs of this section to other paragraphs that illustrate the application of those paragraphs.

Text Paragraph Numbers		Example at Paragraph Numbers
.112	Estimated annual effective tax rate	.167, .174, .178, .179
	Changes in estimates	.172, .173
.113	Operations taxable in multiple jurisdictions	.198
.113(a)	Ordinary loss, realization not assured	.200
.113(b)	Unable to estimate in a jurisdiction	.201
	Effect of new tax legislation:	
.114	Effective in future interim period	.204, .205
.116	Computation of interim period tax (or benefit) applicable to ordinary income (or loss):	
	Ordinary income anticipated for fiscal year:	
.117	Year-to-date ordinary income	.168, .169

Text Paragraph Numbers		Example at Paragraph Numbers
.118	Year-to-date ordinary loss	.170, .171
	Ordinary loss anticipated for fiscal year:	
.119	Year-to-date ordinary income	.176, .179
.120	Year-to-date ordinary loss	.175, .177, .178
.121	Recognition of the tax benefit of a loss	.175, .177, .178, .179
	Year-to-date loss—special computation	.170, .171, .176
.123	Reversal of net deferred tax credits	.180, .181
.126	Tax (or benefit) applicable to significant unusual, infrequently occurring, or extraordinary items	.183, 184
.127	Financial statement presentation	.208
.128	Recognition of the tax benefit of a loss	.183, .184
.129	Tax (or benefit) applicable to discontinued operations	.188, .189, .190, .191, .192, .193, .194, .195
.139	Cumulative effects of changes in accounting principles	.196, .197

[FIN18, ¶40]

Examples of Computations of Interim Period Income Taxes

.165 Paragraphs .167 through .208 provide examples of application of this section for some specific situations. In general, the examples illustrate matters unique to accounting for income taxes at interim dates. The examples do not include consideration of the nature of tax credits and [FIN18, ¶41] events that do not have tax consequences [FAS109, ¶288y] or illustrate all possible combinations of circumstances. [FIN18, ¶41]

.166 Specific situations illustrated are:

	Paragraph Numbers
Accounting for income taxes applicable to ordinary income (or loss) at an interim date if ordinary income is anticipated for the fiscal year:	
Facts, paragraphs .168 through .171	.167
Ordinary income on all interim periods	.168
Ordinary income and losses in interim periods:	
Year-to-date ordinary income	.169
Year-to-date ordinary losses, realization assured	.170
Year-to-date ordinary losses, realization not assured	.171
Changes in estimates	.172, .173
Accounting for income taxes applicable to ordinary income (or loss) at an interim date if an ordinary loss is anticipated for the fiscal year:	
Facts, paragraphs .175 through .179	.174
Realization of the tax benefit of the loss is assured:	
Ordinary losses in all interim periods	.175
Ordinary income and losses in interim periods	.176
Realization of the tax benefit of the loss is not assured	.177
Partial realization of the tax benefit of the loss is assured:	
Ordinary losses in all interim periods	.178
Ordinary income and losses in interim periods	.179
[Reduction of deferred tax liability]	.180, .181
Accounting for income taxes applicable to unusual, infrequently occurring, or extraordinary items:	
Ordinary income expected for the fiscal year:	
Explanation of paragraphs .183 and .184	.182
Unusual, infrequently occurring, or extraordinary loss with:	
Realization of the tax benefit assured at date of occurrence	.183
Realization of the tax benefit not assured at date of occurrence	.184
Accounting for income taxes applicable to income (or loss) from discounted operations at an interim date	.188-.195
Accounting for income taxes applicable to the cumulative effect of a change in accounting principle:	
Cumulative effect of the change on retained earnings at the beginning of the fiscal year	.196
Effect of the change on prechange interim periods of the current fiscal year	.197

	Paragraph Numbers
Accounting for income taxes applicable to ordinary income if an enterprise is subject to tax in multiple jurisdictions:	
Ordinary income in all jurisdictions	.198, .199
Ordinary loss in a jurisdiction; realization of the tax benefit not assured	.200
Ordinary income tax cannot be estimated in one jurisdiction	.201, .202
Effect of new tax legislation:	
Facts, paragraphs .204 through [.205]	.203
Legislation effective in a future interim period	.204, .205

[FIN18, ¶42]

Accounting for Income Taxes Applicable to Ordinary Income (or Loss) at an Interim Date If Ordinary Income Is Anticipated for the Fiscal Year

.167 The following assumed facts are applicable to the examples of application of this section in paragraphs .168 through .171:

> For the full fiscal year, an enterprise anticipates ordinary income of $100,000. All income is taxable in 1 jurisdiction at a 50-percent rate. Anticipated tax credits for the fiscal year total $10,000. No [FIN18, ¶43] events that do not have tax consequences [FAS109, ¶288y] are anticipated. No changes in estimated ordinary income, tax rates, or tax credits occur during the year.
>
> Computation of the estimated annual effective tax rate applicable to ordinary income is as follows:

Tax at statutory rate ($100,000 at 50%)	$50,000
Less anticipated tax credits	(10,000)
Net tax to be provided	$40,000
Estimated annual effective tax rate ($40,000 ÷ $100,000)	40%

Tax credits are generally subject to limitations, usually based on the amount of tax payable before the credits. In computing the estimated annual effective tax rate, anticipated tax credits are limited to the amounts that are expected to be realized or are expected to be [FIN18, ¶43] recognizable at the end of the current year in accordance with the provisions of Section I27. [FAS109, ¶288y] If an enterprise is unable to estimate the amount of its tax credits for the year, refer to paragraph .112, footnote 5. [FIN18, ¶43]

.168 Assume the facts stated in paragraph .167. The enterprise has ordinary income in all interim periods. Quarterly tax computations are:

Reporting Period	Ordinary Income Reporting Period	Year-to-Date	Estimated Annual Effective Tax Rate	Tax Year-to-Date	Less Previously Provided	Reporting Period
First quarter	$ 20,000	$ 20,000	40%	$ 8,000	$ —	$ 8,000
Second quarter	20,000	40,000	40%	16,000	8,000	8,000
Third quarter	20,000	60,000	40%	24,000	16,000	8,000
Fourth quarter	40,000	100,000	40%	40,000	24,000	16,000
Fiscal year	$100,000					$40,000

[FIN18, ¶44]

.169 Assume the facts stated in paragraph .167. The enterprise has ordinary income and losses in interim periods; there is not an ordinary loss for the fiscal year to date at the end of any interim period. Quarterly tax computations are:

Reporting Period	Ordinary Income (Loss) Reporting Period	Year-to-Date	Estimated Annual Effective Tax Rate	Tax (or Benefit) Year-to-Date	Less Previously Provided	Reporting Period
First quarter	$ 40,000	$ 40,000	40%	$16,000	$ —	$16,000
Second quarter	40,000	80,000	40%	32,000	16,000	16,000
Third quarter	(20,000)	60,000	40%	24,000	32,000	(8,000)
Fourth quarter	40,000	100,000	40%	40,000	24,000	16,000
Fiscal year	$100,000					$40,000

[FIN18, ¶45]

.170 Assume the facts stated in paragraph .167. The enterprise has ordinary income and losses in interim periods, and there is an ordinary loss for the year to date at the end of an interim period. [FIN18, ¶46] Established seasonal patterns provide evidence that realization in the current year of the tax benefit of the year-to-date loss and of anticipated tax credits is more likely than not. [FAS109, ¶288y] Quarterly tax computations are:

Reporting Period	Ordinary Income (Loss) Reporting Period	Year-to-Date	Estimated Annual Effective Tax Rate	Tax (or Benefit) Year-to-Date	Less Previously Provided	Reporting Period
First quarter	$(20,000)	$(20,000)	40%	$(8,000)	$ —	$ (8,000)
Second quarter	10,000	(10,000)	40%	(4,000)	(8,000)	4,000
Third quarter	15,000	5,000	40%	2,000	(4,000)	6,000
Fourth quarter	95,000	100,000	40%	40,000	2,000	38,000
Fiscal year	$100,000					$40,000

[FIN18, ¶46]

.171 Assume the facts stated in paragraph .167. The enterprise has ordinary income and losses in interim periods, and there is a year-to-date ordinary loss during the year. [FIN18, ¶47] There is no established seasonal pattern and it is more likely than not that the tax benefit of the year-to-date loss and the anticipated tax credits will not be realized in the current or future years. [FAS109, ¶288y] Quarterly tax computations are:

Reporting Period	Ordinary Income (Loss) Reporting Period	Year-to-Date	Estimated Annual Effective Tax Rate	Tax Year-to-Date	Less Previously Provided	Reporting Period
First quarter	$(20,000)	$(20,000)	—*	$ —	$ —	$ —
Second quarter	10,000	(10,000)	—*	—	—	—
Third quarter	15,000	5,000	40%	2,000	—	$ 2,000
Fourth quarter	95,000	100,000	40%	40,000	2,000	38,000
Fiscal year	$100,000					$40,000

*No benefit recognized because the tax benefit of the year-to-date loss is not [FIN18, ¶47] expected to be (a) realized during the current year or (b) recognizable as a deferred tax asset at the end of the current year in accordance with the provisions of Section I27. [FAS109, ¶288y]

.172 During the fiscal year, all of an enterprise's operations are taxable in one jurisdiction at a 50 percent rate. No [FIN18, ¶48] events that do not have tax consequences [FAS109, ¶288y] are anticipated. Estimates of ordinary income for the year and of anticipated credits at the end of each interim period are as shown below. Changes in the estimated annual effective tax rate result from changes in the ratio of anticipated tax credits to tax computed at the statutory rate. Changes consist of an unanticipated strike that reduced income in the second quarter, an increase in the capital budget resulting in an increase in anticipated investment tax credit in the third quarter, and better than anticipated sales and income in all interim periods. Computations of the estimated annual effective tax rate based on the estimate made at the end of each quarter are:

	Estimated, End of			Actual Fiscal Year
	First Quarter	Second Quarter	Third Quarter	
Estimated ordinary income for the fiscal year	$100,000	$80,000	$80,000	$100,000
Tax at 50% statutory rate	50,000	$40,000	$40,000	$ 50,000
Less anticipated credits	(5,000)	(5,000)	(10,000)	(10,000)
Net tax to be provided	$ 45,000	$35,000	$30,000	$ 40,000
Estimated annual effective tax rate	45%	43.75%	37.5%	40%

[FIN18, ¶48]

.173 Quarterly tax computations are:

	Ordinary Income		Estimated Annual Effective Tax Rate	Tax		
Reporting Period	Reporting Period	Year-to-Date		Year-to-Date	Less Previously Provided	Reporting Period
First quarter	$ 25,000	$ 25,000	45%	$11,250	$ —	$11,250
Second quarter	5,000	30,000	43.75%	13,125	11,250	1,875
Third quarter	25,000	55,000	37.5%	20,625	13,125	7,500
Fourth quarter	45,000	100,000	40%	40,000	20,625	19,375
Fiscal year	$100,000					$40,000

[FIN18, ¶48]

Accounting for Income Taxes Applicable to Ordinary Income (or Loss) at an Interim Date If an Ordinary Loss Is Anticipated for the Fiscal Year

.174 The following assumed facts are applicable to the examples of application of this section in paragraphs .175 through .179:

> For the full fiscal year, an enterprise anticipates an ordinary loss of $100,000. The enterprise operates entirely in one jurisdiction where the tax rate is 50 percent. Anticipated tax credits for the fiscal year total $10,000. No [FIN18, ¶49] events that do not have tax consequences [FAS109, ¶288y] are anticipated. [FIN18, ¶49]
>
> If there is a recognizable tax benefit for [both] the loss and the tax credits pursuant to the requirements of Section I27 [FAS109, ¶288y], computation of the estimated annual effective tax rate applicable to the ordinary loss would be as follows:

Tax benefit at statutory rate ($100,000 at 50%)	$(50,000)
Tax credits	(10,000)
Net tax benefit	$(60,000)
Estimated annual effective tax rate ($60,000 ÷ $100,000)	60%

The examples in paragraphs .175 through .179 state varying assumptions with respect to assurance of realization of the components of the net tax benefit. When realization of a component of the benefit is not [FIN18, ¶49] expected to be (a) realized during the current year or (b) recognizable as a deferred tax asset at the end of the current year in accordance with the provisions of Section I27, [FAS109, ¶288y] that component is not included in the computation of the estimated annual effective tax rate. [FIN18, ¶49]

.175 Assume the facts stated in paragraph .174. The enterprise has ordinary losses in all interim periods. [FIN18, ¶50] The full tax benefit of the anticipated ordinary loss and the anticipated tax credits will be realized by carryback. [FAS109, ¶288y] Quarterly tax computations are:

	Ordinary Loss		Estimated Annual Effective Tax Rate	Tax Benefit		
Reporting Period	Reporting Period	Year-to-Date		Year-to-Date	Less Previously Provided	Reporting Period
First quarter	$ (20,000)	$ (20,000)	60%	$(12,000)	$ —	$(12,000)
Second quarter	(20,000)	(40,000)	60%	(24,000)	(12,000)	(12,000)
Third quarter	(20,000)	(60,000)	60%	(36,000)	(24,000)	(12,000)
Fourth quarter	(40,000)	(100,000)	60%	(60,000)	(36,000)	(24,000)
Fiscal Year	$(100,000)					$(60,000)

[FIN18, ¶50]

.176 Assume the facts stated in paragraph .174. The enterprise has ordinary income and losses in interim periods and for the year to date. [FIN18, ¶51] The full tax benefit of the anticipated ordinary loss and the anticipated tax credits will be realized by carryback. The full tax benefit of the maximum year-to-date ordinary loss can also be realized by carryback. [FAS109, ¶288y] Quarterly tax computations are:

| Reporting Period | Ordinary Income (Loss) | | Estimated Annual Effective Tax Rate | Tax (or Benefit) | | | |
| | Reporting Period | Year-to-Date | | Year-to-Date | | Less Previously Provided | Reporting Period |
				Computed	Limited to		
First quarter	$ 20,000	$ 20,000	60%	$ 12,000		$ —	$ 12,000
Second quarter	(80,000)	(60,000)	60%	(36,000)		12,000	(48,000)
Third quarter	(80,000)	(140,000)	60%	(84,000)	$(80,000)*	(36,000)	(44,000)
Fourth quarter	40,000	(100,000)	60%	(60,000)		(80,000)	20,000
Fiscal year	$(100,000)						$(60,000)

---

*Because the year-to-date ordinary loss exceeds the anticipated ordinary loss for the fiscal year, the tax benefit recognized for the year to date is limited to the amount that would be recognized if the year-to-date ordinary loss were the anticipated ordinary loss for the fiscal year. The limitation is computed as follows:

Year-to-date ordinary loss times the statutory rate ($140,000 at 50%)	$(70,000)
Estimated tax credits for the year	(10,000)
Year-to-date benefit limited to	$(80,000)

[FIN18, ¶51]

.177 In the examples in paragraphs .175 and .176, if neither the tax benefit of the anticipated loss for the fiscal year [FIN18, ¶52] nor [FAS109, ¶288y] anticipated tax credits were [FIN18, ¶52] recognizable pursuant to Section I27 [FAS109, ¶288y], the estimated annual effective tax rate for the year would be zero and no tax (or benefit) would be recognized in any quarter. That conclusion is not affected by changes in the mix of income and loss in interim periods during a fiscal year. However, refer to paragraph .112, footnote 5. [FIN18, ¶52]

Partial Realization of the Tax Benefit of the Loss Is Assured

.178 Assume the facts stated in paragraph .174. The enterprise has an ordinary loss in all interim periods. [FIN18, ¶53] It is more likely than not that [FAS109, ¶288y] the tax benefit of the loss [FIN18, ¶53] in excess [FAS109, ¶288y] of $40,000 of prior income available to be offset by carryback ($20,000 of tax at the 50 percent statutory rate) [FIN18, ¶53] will not be realized. [FAS109, ¶288y] Therefore, the estimated annual effective tax rate is 20 percent ($20,000 benefit assured divided by $100,000 estimated fiscal-year ordinary loss). Quarterly tax computations are:

Reporting Period	Ordinary Loss Reporting Period	Year-to-Date	Estimated Annual Effective Tax Rate	Tax Benefit Year-to-Date	Less Previously Provided	Reporting Period
First quarter	$ (20,000)	$ (20,000)	20%	$ (4,000)	$ —	$ (4,000)
Second quarter	(20,000)	(40,000)	20%	(8,000)	(4,000)	(4,000)
Third quarter	(20,000)	(60,000)	20%	(12,000)	(8,000)	(4,000)
Fourth quarter	(40,000)	(100,000)	20%	(20,000)	(12,000)	(8,000)
Fiscal year	$(100,000)					$(20,000)

[FIN18, ¶53]

.179 Assume the facts stated in paragraph .174. The enterprise has ordinary income and losses in interim periods and for the year to date. [FIN18, ¶54] It is more likely than not that [FAS109, ¶288y] the tax benefit of the anticipated ordinary loss [FIN18, ¶54] in excess [FAS109, ¶288y] of $40,000 of prior income available to be offset by carryback ($20,000 of tax at the 50 percent statutory rate) [FIN18, ¶54] will not be realized. [FAS109, ¶288y] Therefore, the estimated annual effective tax rate is 20 percent ($20,000 benefit assured divided by $100,000 estimated fiscal-year ordinary loss), and the benefit that can be recognized for the year to date is limited to $20,000 (the benefit that is assured of realization). Quarterly tax computations are:

Reporting Period	Ordinary Income (Loss) Reporting Period	Year-to-Date	Estimated Annual Effective Tax Rate	Tax (or Benefit) Year-to-Date Computed	Limited to	Less Previously Provided	Reporting Period
First quarter	$ 20,000	$ 20,000	20%	$ 4,000		$ —	$ 4,000
Second quarter	(80,000)	(60,000)	20%	(12,000)		4,000	(16,000)
Third quarter	(80,000)	(140,000)	20%	(28,000)	$(20,000)	(12,000)	(8,000)
Fourth quarter	40,000	(100,000)	20%	(20,000)		(20,000)	—
Fiscal year	$(100,000)						$(20,000)

[FIN18, ¶54]

.180 The enterprise anticipates a fiscal year ordinary loss. The loss cannot be carried back, and future profits [FIN18, ¶55] exclusive of reversing temporary differences are unlikely. [FAS109, ¶288y] Net deferred tax [FIN18, ¶55] liabilities [FAS109, ¶288y] arising from [FIN18, ¶55] existing net taxable temporary differences [FAS109, ¶288y] are present. A portion of the [FIN18, ¶55] existing net taxable temporary differences [FAS109, ¶288y] relating to those [FIN18, ¶55] liabilities [FAS109, ¶288y] will reverse within the loss carryforward period. Computation of the estimated annual tax rate to be used [FIN18, ¶55] (refer to paragraph .123) [FAS109, ¶288y] is as follows:

Estimated fiscal year ordinary loss	$(100,000)

The tax benefit to be recognized is the lesser of:

Tax effect of the loss carryforward ($100,000 at 50% statutory rate)	$50,000
Amount of the net deferred tax [FIN18, ¶55] liabilities [FAS109, ¶288y] that would otherwise have been [FIN18, ¶55] settled [FAS109, ¶288y] during the carryforward period	$24,000
Estimated annual effective tax rate ($24,000 ÷ $100,000)	24%

[FIN18, ¶55]

.181 Quarterly tax computations are:

Reporting Period	Ordinary Loss Reporting Period	Ordinary Loss Year-to-Date	Estimated Annual Effective Tax Rate	Tax Benefit Year-to-Date	Tax Benefit Less Previously Provided	Tax Benefit Reporting Period
First quarter	$ (20,000)	$ (20,000)	24%	$ (4,800)	$ —	$ (4,800)
Second quarter	(20,000)	(40,000)	24%	(9,600)	(4,800)	(4,800)
Third quarter	(20,000)	(60,000)	24%	(14,400)	(9,600)	(4,800)
Fourth quarter	(40,000)	(100,000)	24%	(24,000)	(14,400)	(9,600)
Fiscal year	$(100,000)					$(24,000)

Note: Changes in the timing of the loss by quarter would not change the above computation. [FIN18, ¶55]

Accounting for Income Taxes Applicable to Unusual, Infrequently Occurring, or Extraordinary Items

.182 The examples of computations in paragraphs .183 and .184 illustrate the computation of the tax (or benefit) applicable to unusual, infrequently occurring, or extraordinary items when ordinary income is anticipated for the fiscal year. These examples are based on the facts and computations given in paragraphs .167 through .171 plus additional information supplied in paragraphs .183 and .184. The computation of the tax (or benefit) applicable to the ordinary income is not affected by the occurrence of an unusual, infrequently occurring, or extraordinary item; therefore, each example refers to one or more of the examples of that computation in paragraphs .168 through .171 and does not reproduce the computation and the facts assumed. The income statement display for tax (or benefit applicable to unusual, infrequently occurring, or extraordinary items) is illustrated in paragraph .208. [FIN18, ¶56]

.183 As explained in paragraph .182, this example is based on the computations of tax applicable to ordinary income that are illustrated in paragraph .168. In addition, the enterprise experiences a tax-deductible unusual, infrequently occurring, or extraordinary loss of $50,000 (tax benefit $25,000) in the second quarter. Because the loss can be carried back, the benefit of the loss is assured beyond any reasonable doubt at the time of occurrence. Quarterly tax provisions are:

Reporting Period	Ordinary Income	Unusual, Infrequently Occurring, or Extraordinary Loss	Tax (or Benefit) Applicable to Ordinary Income	Unusual, Infrequently Occurring, or Extraordinary Loss
First quarter	$ 20,000		$ 8,000	
Second quarter	20,000	$(50,000)	8,000	$(25,000)
Third quarter	20,000		8,000	
Fourth quarter	40,000		16,000	
Fiscal year	$100,000	$(50,000)	$40,000	$(25,000)

Note: Changes in assumptions would not change the timing of the recognition of the tax benefit applicable to the unusual, infrequently occurring, or extraordinary item as long as realization is assured beyond any reasonable doubt. [FIN18, ¶57]

.184 As explained in paragraph .182, this example is based on the computations of tax applicable to ordinary income that are illustrated in paragraphs .168 and .169. In addition, the enterprise experiences a tax-deductible unusual, infrequently occurring, or extraordinary loss of $50,000 (potential benefit $25,000) in the second quarter. [FIN18, ¶58] The loss cannot be carried back, and available evidence indicates that a valuation allowance is needed for all of the deferred tax asset. [FAS109, ¶288y] As a result, the tax benefit of the unusual, infrequently occurring, or extraordinary loss is [FIN18, ¶58] recognized only [FAS109, ¶288y] to the extent of offsetting ordinary income for the year to date. Quarterly tax provisions under two different assumptions for the occurrence of ordinary income are:

Assumptions and Reporting Period	Ordinary Income (Loss)	Unusual, Infrequently Occurring, or Extraordinary Loss	Tax (or Benefit) Applicable to				
			Ordinary Income (Loss)		Unusual, Infrequently Occurring, or Extraordinary Loss		
			Reporting Period	Year-to-Date	Year-to-Date	Less Previously Provided	Reporting Period
Income in all quarters:							
First quarter	$ 20,000		$ 8,000	$ 8,000			
Second quarter	20,000	$(50,000)	8,000	16,000	$(16,000)	$ —	$(16,000)
Third quarter	20,000		8,000	24,000	(24,000)	(16,000)	(8,000)
Fourth quarter	40,000		16,000	40,000	(25,000)	(24,000)	(1,000)
Fiscal year	$100,000	$(50,000)	$40,000				$(25,000)
Income and loss quarters:							
First quarter	$ 40,000		$16,000	$16,000			
Second quarter	40,000	$(50,000)	16,000	32,000	$(25,000)	$ —	$(25,000)
Third quarter	(20,000)		(8,000)	24,000	(24,000)	(25,000)	1,000
Fourth quarter	40,000		16,000	40,000	(25,000)	(24,000)	(1,000)
Fiscal year	$100,000	$(50,000)	$40,000				$(25,000)

[FIN18, ¶58]

.185-.187 [Deleted 2/92 because of FASB Statement 109.]

Accounting for Income Taxes Applicable to Income (or Loss) from Discontinued Operations at an Interim Date

.188 An enterprise anticipates ordinary income for the year of $100,000 and tax credits of $10,000. The enterprise has ordinary income in all interim periods. The estimated annual effective tax rate is 40 percent, computed as follows:

Estimated pretax income	$100,000
Tax at 50% statutory rate	$ 50,000
Less anticipated credits	$ (10,000)
Net tax to be provided	$ 40,000
Estimated annual effective tax rate	40%

[FIN18, ¶62]

.189 Quarterly tax computations for the first two quarters are:

| | Ordinary Income | | Estimated Annual | Tax Benefit | | |
| | Reporting | Year-to- | Effective | Year-to- | Less Previously | Reporting |
Reporting Period	Period	Date	Tax Rate	Date	Provided	Period
First quarter	$20,000	$20,000	40%	$ 8,000	$ —	$ 8,000
Second quarter	25,000	45,000	40%	18,000	8,000	10,000

[FIN18, ¶62]

.190 In the third quarter a decision is made to discontinue the operations of Division X, a segment of the business that has recently operated at a loss (before income taxes). The pretax income (and losses) of the continuing operations of the enterprise and of Division X through the third quarter and the estimated fourth quarter results are as follows:

| | | Division X | |
Reporting Period	Revised Ordinary Income from Continuing Operations	Loss from Operations	Provision for Loss on Disposal
First quarter	$ 25,000	$ (5,000)	
Second quarter	35,000	(10,000)	
Third quarter	50,000	(10,000)	$(55,000)
Fourth quarter	50,000*	—	—
Fiscal year	$160,000	$(25,000)	$(55,000)

---

*Estimated.

[FIN18, ¶62]

.191 No changes have occurred in continuing operations that would affect the estimated annual effective tax rate. Anticipated annual tax credits of $10,000 included $2,000 of credits related to the operations of Division X. The revised estimated annual effective tax rate applicable to ordinary income from continuing operations is 45 percent, computed as follows:

Estimated ordinary income from continuing operations	$160,000
Tax at 50% statutory rate	$ 80,000
Less anticipated tax credits applicable to continuing operations	(8,000)
Net tax to be provided	$ 72,000
Estimated annual effective tax rate	45%

[FIN18, ¶62]

.192 Quarterly computations of tax applicable to ordinary income from continuing operations are as follows:

Reporting Period	Ordinary Income Reporting Period	Ordinary Income Year-to-Date	Estimated Annual Effective Tax Rate	Tax Year-to-Date	Tax Less Previously Provided	Tax Reporting Period
First quarter	$ 25,000	$ 25,000	45%	$11,250	$ —	$11,250
Second quarter	35,000	60,000	45%	27,000	11,250	15,750
Third quarter	50,000	110,000	45%	49,500	27,000	22,500
Fourth quarter	50,000	160,000	45%	72,000	49,500	22,500
Fiscal year	$160,000					$72,000

[FIN18, ¶62]

.193 Tax benefit applicable to Division X for the first two quarters is computed as follows:

Reporting Period	Tax Applicable to Ordinary Income Previously Reported (A)	Tax Applicable to Ordinary Income Recomputed (above) (B)	Tax Benefit Applicable to Division X (A – B)
First quarter	$ 8,000	$11,250	$(3,250)
Second quarter	10,000	15,750	(5,750)
			$(9,000)

[FIN18, ¶62]

.194 The third quarter tax benefits applicable to both the loss from operations and the provision for loss on disposal of Division X are computed based on estimated annual income with and without the effects of the Division X losses. Current year tax credits related to the operations of Division X have not been recognized. It is assumed that the tax benefit of those credits will not be realized because of the discontinuance of Division X operations. Any reduction in tax benefits resulting from recapture of previously recognized tax credits resulting from discontinuance or current year tax credits applicable to the discontinued operations would be reflected in the tax benefit recognized for the loss on disposal or loss from operations as appropriate. If, because of capital gains and losses, etc., the individually computed tax effects of the items do not equal the aggregate tax effects of the items, the aggregate tax effects are allocated to the individual items in the same manner that they will be allocated in the annual financial statements. The computations are as follows:

	Loss from Operations of Division X	Provision for Loss on Disposal
Estimated annual income from continuing operations	$160,000	$160,000
Loss from Division X operations	(25,000)	
Provision for loss on disposal of Division X		(55,000)
Total	$135,000	$105,000
Tax at 50% statutory rate	$ 67,500	$ 52,500
Anticipated credits from continuing operations	(8,000)	(8,000)
Tax credits of Division X and recapture of previously recognized tax credits resulting from discontinuance	—	—
Taxes on income after effect of Division X losses	59,500	44,500
Taxes on income before effect of Division X losses—refer to computation above	72,000	72,000
Tax benefit applicable to the losses of Division X	(12,500)	(27,500)
Amounts previously recognized—refer to computation above	(9,000)	—
Tax benefit recognized in third quarter	$ (3,500)	$(27,500)

[FIN18, ¶62]

.195 The resulting revised quarterly tax provisions are summarized as follows:

	Pretax Income (Loss)			Tax (or Benefit) Applicable to		
Reporting Period	Continuing Operations	Operations of Division X	Provision for Loss on Disposal	Continuing Operations	Operations of Division X	Provision for Loss on Disposal
First quarter	$ 25,000	$ (5,000)		$11,250	$ (3,250)	
Second quarter	35,000	(10,000)		15,750	(5,750)	
Third quarter	50,000	(10,000)	$(55,000)	22,500	(3,500)	$(27,500)
Fourth quarter	50,000			22,500		
Fiscal year	$160,000	$(25,000)	$(55,000)	$72,000	$(12,500)	$(27,500)

[FIN18, ¶62]

Accounting for Income Taxes Applicable to the Cumulative Effect of a Change in Accounting Principle

.196 The tax (or benefit) applicable to the cumulative effect of the change on retained earnings at the beginning of the fiscal year shall be computed the same as for the annual financial statements. [FIN18, ¶63]

.197 When an enterprise makes a cumulative effect-type accounting change in other than the first interim period of the enterprise's fiscal year, paragraph .136 requires that financial information for the prechange interim periods of the fiscal year shall be restated by applying the newly adopted accounting principle to those prechange interim periods. The tax (or benefit) applicable to those prechange interim periods shall be recomputed. The restated tax (or benefit) shall reflect the year-to-date amounts and annual estimates originally used for the prechange interim periods, modified only for the effect of the change in accounting principle on those year-to-date and estimated annual amounts. [FIN18, ¶64]

Accounting for Income Taxes Applicable to Ordinary Income If an Enterprise Is Subject to Tax in Multiple Jurisdictions

.198 An enterprise operates through separate corporate entities in two countries. Applicable tax rates are 50 percent in the United States and 20 percent in Country A. The enterprise has no unusual or extraordinary items during the fiscal year and anticipates no tax credits or [FIN18, ¶65] events that do not have tax consequences. [FAS109, ¶288y] (The effect of foreign tax credits and the necessity of providing tax on undistributed earnings are ignored because of the wide range of tax-planning alternatives available.) For the full fiscal year the enterprise anticipates ordinary income of $60,000 in the United States and $40,000 in Country A. The enterprise is able to make a reliable estimate of its Country A ordinary income and tax for the fiscal year in dollars. Computation of the overall estimated annual effective tax rate is as follows:

Anticipated ordinary income for the fiscal year:	
In the United States	$ 60,000
In Country A	40,000
Total	$100,000
Anticipated tax for the fiscal year:	
In the United States ($60,000 at 50% statutory rate)	$ 30,000
In Country A ($40,000 at 20% statutory rate)	8,000
Total	$ 38,000
Overall estimated annual effective tax rate ($38,000 ÷ $100,000)	38%

[FIN18, ¶65]

.199 Quarterly tax computations are as follows:

Reporting Period	Ordinary Income U.S.	Ordinary Income Country A	Ordinary Income Total	Year-to-Date	Overall Estimated Annual Effective Tax Rate	Tax Year-to-Date	Tax Less Previously Reported	Reporting Period
First quarter	$ 5,000	$15,000	$ 20,000	$ 20,000	38%	$ 7,600	$ —	$ 7,600
Second quarter	10,000	10,000	20,000	40,000	38%	15,200	7,600	7,600
Third quarter	10,000	10,000	20,000	60,000	38%	22,800	15,200	7,600
Fourth quarter	35,000	5,000	40,000	100,000	38%	38,000	22,800	15,200
Fiscal year	$60,000	$40,000	$100,000					$38,000

[FIN18, ¶65]

.200 Assume the facts stated in paragraphs .198 and .199. In addition, the enterprise operates through a separate corporate entity in Country B. Applicable tax rates in Country B are 40 percent. Operations in Country B have resulted in losses in recent years and an ordinary loss is anticipated for the current fiscal year in Country B. [FIN18, ¶66] It is expected that [FAS109, ¶288y] the tax benefit of those losses [FIN18, ¶66] will not be recognizable as a deferred tax asset at the end of the current year pursuant to Section I27 [FAS109, ¶288y]; accordingly, no tax benefit is recognized for losses in Country B, and interim period tax (or benefit) is separately computed for the ordinary loss in Country B and for the overall ordinary income in the United States and Country A. The tax applicable to the overall ordinary income in the United States and Country A is computed as in paragraphs .198 and .199. Quarterly tax provisions are as follows:

Reporting Period	Ordinary Income (or Loss) U.S.	Ordinary Income (or Loss) Country A	Ordinary Income (or Loss) Combined Excluding Country B	Ordinary Income (or Loss) Country B	Ordinary Income (or Loss) Total	Tax (or Benefit) Overall Excluding Country B	Tax (or Benefit) Country B	Tax (or Benefit) Total
First quarter	$ 5,000	$15,000	$ 20,000	$ (5,000)	$15,000	$ 7,600	$—	$ 7,600
Second quarter	10,000	10,000	20,000	(25,000)	(5,000)	7,600	—	7,600
Third quarter	10,000	10,000	20,000	(5,000)	15,000	7,600	—	7,600
Fourth quarter	35,000	5,000	40,000	(5,000)	35,000	15,200	—	15,200
Fiscal year	$60,000	$40,000	$100,000	$(40,000)	$60,000	$38,000	$—	$38,000

[FIN18, ¶66]

.201 Assume the facts stated in paragraphs .198 and .199. In addition, the enterprise operates through a separate corporate entity in Country C. Applicable tax rates in Country C are 40 percent in foreign currency. Depreciation in that country is large and exchange rates have changed in prior years. The enterprise is unable to make a reasonable estimate of its ordinary income for the year in Country C and thus is unable to reasonably estimate its annual effective tax rate in Country C in dollars. Accordingly, tax (or benefit) in Country C is separately computed as ordinary income (or loss) occurs in Country C. The tax applicable to the overall ordinary income in the United States and Country A is computed as in paragraphs .198 and .199. Quarterly computations of tax applicable to Country C are as follows:

	Foreign Currency Amounts		Translated Amounts in Dollars	
Reporting Period	**Ordinary Income in Reporting Period**	**Tax (at 40% Rate)**	**Ordinary Income in Reporting Period**	**Tax**
First quarter	FC10,000	FC 4,000	$12,500	$ 3,000
Second quarter	5,000	2,000	8,750	1,500
Third quarter	30,000	12,000	27,500	9,000
Fourth quarter	15,000	6,000	16,250	4,500
Fiscal year	FC60,000	FC24,000	$65,000	$18,000

[FIN18, ¶67]

.202 Quarterly tax provisions are as follows:

	Ordinary Income					Tax		
Reporting Period	**U.S.**	**Country A**	**Combined Excluding Country C**	**Country C**	**Total**	**Overall Excluding Country C**	**Country C**	**Total**
First quarter	$ 5,000	$15,000	$ 20,000	$12,500	$ 32,500	$ 7,600	$ 3,000	$10,600
Second quarter	10,000	10,000	20,000	8,750	28,750	7,600	1,500	9,100
Third quarter	10,000	10,000	20,000	27,500	47,500	7,600	9,000	16,600
Fourth quarter	35,000	5,000	40,000	16,250	56,250	15,200	4,500	19,700
Fiscal year	$60,000	$40,000	$100,000	$65,000	$165,000	$38,000	$18,000	$56,000

[FIN18, ¶67]

Effect of New Tax Legislation

.203 The following assumed facts are applicable to the examples of application in paragraphs .204 and .205:

> For the full fiscal year, an enterprise anticipates ordinary income of $100,000. All income is taxable in 1 jurisdiction at a 50 percent rate. Anticipated tax credits for the fiscal year total $10,000. No [FIN18, ¶68] events that do not have tax consequences [FAS109, ¶288y] are anticipated.

Computation of the estimated annual effective tax rate applicable to ordinary income is as follows:

Tax at statutory rate ($100,000 at 50%)	$50,000
Less anticipated tax credits	(10,000)
Net tax to be provided	$40,000
Estimated annual effective tax rate ($40,000 ÷ $100,000)	40%

[FIN18, ¶68]

.204 Assume the facts stated in paragraph .203. In addition, assume that new legislation creating additional tax credits is enacted during the second quarter of the enterprise's fiscal year. The new legislation is effective on the first day of the third quarter. As a result of the estimated effect of the new legislation, the enterprise revises its estimate of its annual effective tax rate to the following:

Tax at statutory rate ($100,000 at 50%)	$50,000
Less anticipated tax credits	(12,000)
Net tax to be provided	$38,000
Estimated annual effective tax rate ($38,000 ÷ $100,000)	38%

[FIN18, ¶69]

.205 The effect of the new legislation shall not be reflected until it is effective or administratively effective. Accordingly, quarterly tax computations are:

Reporting Period	Ordinary Income Reporting Period	Year-to-Date	Estimated Annual Effective Tax Rate	Year-to-Date	Tax Less Previously Provided	Reporting Period
First quarter	$ 20,000	$ 20,000	40%	$ 8,000	$ —	$ 8,000
Second quarter	20,000	40,000	40%	16,000	8,000	8,000
Third quarter	20,000	60,000	38%	22,800	16,000	6,800
Fourth quarter	40,000	100,000	38%	38,000	22,800	15,200
Fiscal year	$100,000					$38,000

[FIN18, ¶69]

.206-.207 [Deleted 2/92 because of FASB Statement 109.]

[19aDeleted 2/92 because of FASB Statement 109.]

Illustration of Income Taxes in Income Statement Display

.208 Exhibit 208A illustrates the location in an income statement display of the various tax amounts computed under this section. [FIN18, ¶71]

Exhibit 208A

Illustrative Income Statement

*Net sales		$XXXX
*Other income		XXX
		XXXX
Costs and expenses:		
*Cost of sales	$XXXX	
*Selling, general, and administrative expenses	XXXX	
*Interest expense	XXX	
*Other deductions	XX	
Unusual items	XXX	
Infrequently occurring items	XXX	XXXX
Income (loss) from continuing operations before income taxes and other items listed below		XXXX
†Provision for income taxes (benefit)		XXXX
Income (loss) from continuing operations before other items listed below		XXXX
Discontinued operations:		
Income (loss) from operations of discontinued Division X (less applicable income taxes of $XXXX)	XXXX	
Income (loss) on disposal of Division X, including provision of $XXXX for operating losses during phase-out period (less applicable income taxes of $XXXX)	XXXX	XXXX
Income (loss) before extraordinary items and cumulative effect of a change in accounting principle		XXXX
Extraordinary items (less applicable income taxes of $XXXX)		XXXX
‡Cumulative effect on prior years of a change in accounting principle (less applicable income taxes of $XXXX)		XXXX
Net income (loss)		$XXXX

*Components of ordinary income (loss).

†Consists of the total income taxes (or benefits) applicable to (a) ordinary income, (b) unusual items, and (c) infrequently occurring items.

‡This amount is net of applicable income taxes. The amount of the applicable income taxes is usually separately disclosed but that is not required.

[FIN18, ¶71]

Glossary

.401 **Annual effective tax rate.** Best estimate of [an enterprise's] effective tax rate expected to be applicable for the full fiscal year [(refer to paragraph .111)]. [APB28, ¶19]

.402 **Ordinary income or loss.** "Income (or loss) from continuing operations before income taxes (or benefits)" excluding significant "unusual or infrequently occurring items." Extraordinary items, discontinued operations, and cumulative effects of changes in accounting principles are also excluded from this term.[401] The term is *not* used in the income tax context of ordinary income versus capital gain. [FIN18, ¶5]

.403 **Tax (or benefit).** The total income tax expense (or benefit) including the provision (or benefit) for income taxes both currently payable and deferred. [FIN18, ¶5]

---

[401]The terms used in this definition are described in Sections A06, I13, and I17. Refer to Section I13, paragraphs .105 and .401, for *income (or loss) from continuing operations before income taxes (or benefits)* and *discontinued operations.* Refer to Section I17, paragraph .107, for *unusual items* and *infrequently occurring items.* Refer to Section A06, paragraph .116, for *cumulative effects of changes in accounting principles.* [FIN18, ¶5, fn1]

Supplemental Guidance

Reduction in Tax Rate Effective for Part of Fiscal Year

.501 *Question*—How should an enterprise with a fiscal year other than a calendar year account during interim periods for the reduction in the corporate tax rate resulting from the Revenue Act of 1978? [FTB79-9, ¶1]

.502 *Background*—The Revenue Act of 1978, among other things, reduced the corporate income tax rate from 48 percent to 46 percent. [FTB79-9, ¶2]

.503 *Response*—Paragraph .115 requires that the effect of a change in tax rates be reflected in a revised annual effective tax rate calculation in the same way that the change will be applied to the enterprise's taxable income for the year. The revised annual effective tax rate would then be applied to pretax income for the year to date at the end of the current interim period. [FTB79-9, ¶3]

.504-.507 [Deleted 2/92 because of FASB Statement 109.]

(The next page is 27519.)

Sources: ARB 43, Chapter 3A; ARB 43, Chapter 4

Summary

Inventory shall be stated at the lower of cost or market except in certain exceptional cases when it may be stated above cost. *Cost* is defined as the sum of the applicable expenditures and charges directly or indirectly incurred in bringing inventories to their existing condition and location. Cost for inventory purposes may be determined under any one of several assumptions as to the flow of cost factors (such as first-in, first-out; average; and last-in, first-out).

Introduction

.101 Whenever the operation of a business includes the ownership of a stock of goods, it is necessary for adequate financial accounting purposes that **inventories** be properly compiled periodically and recorded in the accounts.[1] [ARB43, ch4, ¶1] This section sets forth the general principles applicable to the pricing of inventories of mercantile and manufacturing enterprises. Its conclusions are not directed to or necessarily applicable to noncommercial businesses or to regulated utilities. [ARB43, ch4, ¶2]

Definition of Inventory

.102 [In this section,] the term *inventory* is used to designate the aggregate of those items of tangible personal property that (a) are held for sale in the ordinary course of business [(finished goods)], (b) are in process of production for such sale [(work in process)], or (c) are to be currently consumed either directly or indirectly in the production of goods or services to be available for sale [(raw materials and supplies)]. [ARB43, ch4, ¶3]

.103 This definition of inventories excludes long-term assets subject to depreciation accounting or goods that, when put into use, will be so classified. [In addition,] a depreciable asset [that] is retired from regular use and held for sale [shall] not be classified as part of the inventory. Raw materials and supplies purchased for production may be used or consumed for the construction of long-term assets or other purposes not related to production, but the fact that inventory items representing a small portion of the total [inventory] may not be absorbed ultimately in the production process shall not require

---

[1] Prudent reliance upon perpetual inventory records is not precluded. [ARB43, ch4, ¶1, fn1]

separate classification. By trade practice, operating materials and supplies of certain types of enterprises, such as oil producers, are usually treated as inventory. [ARB43, ch4, ¶3]

Accounting Objective

.104 [Revenues from the sale of inventory, or from the sale of the goods or services in whose production it is used, normally arise] in a continuous repetitive process or cycle of operations by which goods are acquired and sold, and further goods are acquired for additional sales. The major objective [in accounting for the goods in the inventory] is the matching of appropriate **costs** against revenues in order that there may be a proper determination of the realized income. Thus, the inventory at any given date is the balance of costs applicable to goods on hand remaining after the matching of absorbed costs with concurrent revenues. This balance [shall be] carried to future periods provided it does not exceed an amount properly chargeable against the revenues expected to be obtained from ultimate disposition of the goods carried forward.[2] In practice, this balance is determined by the process of pricing the articles in the inventory.[3] [ARB43, ch4, ¶4]

Accounting for Inventories

Cost Basis

.105 In keeping with the principle that accounting is primarily based on cost, there is a presumption that inventories shall be stated at cost.[3] [ARB43, ch4, ¶5]

.106 Although principles for the determination of inventory costs may be easily stated, their application, particularly to such inventory items as work in process and finished goods, is difficult because of the variety of problems encountered in the allocation of costs and charges. For example, under some circumstances, items such as idle facility expense, excessive spoilage, double freight, and rehandling costs may be so abnormal as to require treatment as current period charges rather than as a portion of the inventory cost. Also, general and administrative expenses shall be included as period charges, except for the portion of such expenses that [are] clearly related to production and thus constitute a part of inventory costs (product charges). Selling expenses [are not] part of inventory costs. Exclusion of all overheads from inventory costs does not constitute an accepted accounting procedure. [ARB43, ch4, ¶5]

.107 Cost for inventory purposes shall be determined under any one of several assumptions as to the flow of cost factors (such as first-in, first-out; average; and last-in, first-out); the major objective in selecting a method shall be to choose the one that most clearly

[2 Refer to paragraph .109 for guidance if the utility of inventory is not as great as its cost.]

[3 Refer to paragraphs .109 and .119 for exceptions to this rule.]

reflects periodic income. [ARB43, ch4, ¶6] [Refer to Section I73, "Interim Financial Reporting," paragraph .107, for a discussion of the application of those methods at an interim reporting date.]

.108 The cost to be matched against revenue from a sale may not be the identified cost of the specific item that is sold, especially in cases in which similar goods are purchased at different times and at different prices. While in some lines of business specific lots are clearly identified from the time of purchase through the time of sale and are costed on this basis, ordinarily the identity of goods is lost between the time of acquisition and the time of sale. If the materials purchased in various lots are identical and interchangeable, the use of identified cost of the various lots may not produce the most useful financial statements. This fact has resulted in the development of general acceptance of several assumptions with respect to the flow of cost factors (such as first-in, first-out; average; and last-in, first-out) to provide practical bases for the measurement of periodic income.[4] In some situations, a reversed mark-up procedure of inventory pricing, such as the retail inventory method, may be both practical and appropriate. The business operations in some cases may be such as to make it desirable to apply one of the acceptable methods of determining cost to one portion of the inventory or components thereof and another of the acceptable methods to other portions of the inventory. [ARB43, ch4, ¶6]

Lower of Cost or Market Basis

.109 A departure from the cost basis of pricing the inventory is required when the utility of the goods is no longer as great as its cost. [If the utility of goods is impaired by damage,] deterioration, obsolescence, changes in price levels, or other causes, [a loss shall be reflected as a charge against the revenues of the period in which it occurs.] The measurement of such losses shall be accomplished by applying the rule of pricing inventories at **cost or market, whichever is lower.** This provides a practical means of measuring utility and thereby determining the amount of the loss to be recognized and accounted for in the current period. [ARB43, ch4, ¶8]

---

[4]Standard costs are acceptable if adjusted at reasonable intervals to reflect current conditions so that at the balance sheet date standard costs reasonably approximate costs computed under one of the recognized bases. In such cases, descriptive language shall be used that will express this relationship, as, for instance, "approximate costs determined on the first-in, first-out basis," or, if it is desired to mention standard costs, "at standard costs, approximating average costs." [ARB43, ch4, ¶6, fn3]

.110 As used in the phrase *lower of cost or market* the term **market** means current replacement cost (by purchase or by reproduction, as the case may be) except that:

a. Market shall not exceed the net realizable value (i.e., estimated selling price in the ordinary course of business less reasonably predictable costs of completion and disposal); and

b. Market shall not be less than net realizable value reduced by an allowance for an approximately normal profit margin. [ARB43, ch4, ¶9]

.111 The rule of *cost or market, whichever is lower* [shall] provide a means of measuring the residual usefulness of an inventory expenditure. The term *market* shall therefore be interpreted as indicating utility on the inventory date and should be thought of in terms of the equivalent expenditure that would have to be made in the ordinary course [of business] at that date to procure corresponding utility. As a general guide, utility is indicated primarily by the current cost of replacement of the goods as they would be obtained by purchase or reproduction. In applying the rule, however, judgment should always be exercised and no loss shall be recognized unless the evidence indicates clearly that a loss has been sustained. There are exceptions to such a standard. Replacement or reproduction prices [are] not appropriate as a measure of utility [if] the estimated sales value, reduced by the costs of completion and disposal, is lower, in which case the realizable value so determined more appropriately measures utility. Furthermore, [if] the evidence indicates that cost will be recovered with an approximately normal profit upon sale in the ordinary course of business, no loss shall be recognized even though replacement or reproduction costs are lower. This might be true, for example, in the case of production under firm sales contracts at fixed prices, or [if] a reasonable volume of future orders is assured at stable selling prices. [ARB43, ch4, ¶9]

.112 Because of the many variations of circumstances encountered in inventory pricing, paragraphs .110 and .111 are intended as a guide rather than a literal rule. They should be applied realistically in the light of the objectives expressed in this section and with due regard to the form, content, and composition of the inventory. For example, the retail inventory method, if adequate markdowns are currently taken, accomplishes the objectives described herein. If a business is expected to lose money for a sustained period, the inventory shall not be written down to offset a loss inherent in the subsequent operations. [ARB43, ch4, ¶10]

.113 Depending on the character and composition of the inventory, the rule of *cost or market, whichever is lower* may be properly applied either directly to each item or to the total of the inventory (or, in some cases, to the total of the components of each major category). The method shall be that which most clearly reflects periodic income. [ARB43, ch4, ¶11]

.114 The purpose of reducing inventory to *market* is to reflect fairly the income of the period. The most common practice is to apply the *lower of cost or market* rule separately to each item of the inventory. However, if there is only one end-product category the cost utility of the total stock—the inventory in its entirety—may have the greatest significance for accounting purposes. Accordingly, the reduction of individual items to *market* may not always lead to the most useful result if the utility of the total inventory to the business is not below its cost. This might be the case if selling prices are not affected by temporary or small fluctuations in current costs of purchase or manufacture. Similarly, [if] more than one major product or operational category exists, the application of the *cost or market, whichever is lower* rule to the total of the items included in such major categories may result in the most useful determination of income. [ARB43, ch4, ¶11]

.115 [If] no loss of income is expected to take place as a result of a reduction of cost prices of certain goods because others forming components of the same general categories of finished products have a market equally in excess of cost, such components need not be adjusted to market to the extent that they are in balanced quantities. Thus, in such cases, the rule of *cost or market, whichever is lower* shall be applied directly to the totals of the entire inventory, rather than to the individual inventory items, if they enter into the same category of finished product and if they are in balanced quantities, provided the procedure is applied consistently from year to year. [ARB43, ch4, ¶12]

.116 To the extent, however, that the stocks of particular materials or components are excessive in relation to others, the more widely recognized procedure of applying the *lower of cost or market* to the individual items constituting the excess shall be followed. This would also apply in cases in which the items enter into the production of unrelated products or products having a material variation in the rate of turnover. Unless an effective method of classifying categories is practicable, the rule shall be applied to each item in the inventory. [ARB43, ch4, ¶13]

.117 [If] substantial and unusual losses result from the application of this rule, the amount of the loss [shall be disclosed] in the income statement as a charge separately identified from the consumed inventory costs described as *cost of goods sold*. [ARB43, ch4, ¶14]

.118 [The application of the lower of cost or market rule to inventories in translated financial statements is discussed in Section F60, "Foreign Currency Translation," paragraphs .148 through .152.]

Stating Inventories above Cost

.119 Only in exceptional cases may inventories be stated above cost. For example, precious metals having a fixed monetary value with no substantial cost of marketing may be stated at such monetary value; any other exceptions must be justifiable by inability to determine appropriate approximate costs, immediate marketability at quoted market price, and the characteristic of unit interchangeability. [Stating inventories above cost] is not uncommon for inventories representing agricultural, mineral, and other products, units of which are interchangeable and have an immediate marketability at quoted prices and for which appropriate costs may be difficult to obtain. [If] such inventories are stated at sales prices, they [shall be] reduced by expenditures to be incurred in disposal. [If goods are stated above cost, this fact] shall be fully disclosed. [ARB43, ch4, ¶16]

Disclosure

.120 The amounts at which [inventories] are stated [shall] be supplemented by information which reveals for the various classifications of inventory items, the basis upon which their amounts are stated and, where practicable, [an] indication of the method of determining the cost—e.g., *average cost, first-in first-out, last-in first-out,* etc. [ARB43, ch3A, ¶9] The basis of stating inventories shall be consistently applied and shall be disclosed in the financial statements;[5] whenever a significant change is made therein, there shall be disclosure of the nature of the change and, if material, the effect on income, [as discussed in Section A06, "Accounting Changes," paragraphs .107 and .108 and .113 through .124]. [ARB43, ch4, ¶15]

Net Losses on Firm Purchase Commitments

.121 Accrued net losses on firm purchase commitments for goods for inventory, measured in the same way as are inventory losses, shall, if material, be recognized in the accounts and the amounts thereof separately disclosed in the income statement. [ARB43, ch4, ¶17]

.122 The recognition in a current period of losses arising from the decline in the utility of cost expenditures is equally applicable to similar losses that are expected to arise from firm, uncancelable, and unhedged commitments for the future purchase of inventory items. The net loss on such commitments shall be measured in the same way as are inventory losses and, if material, shall be recognized in the [financial statements] and separately disclosed in the income statement. The utility of such commitments is not impaired, and hence there is no loss, [if] the amounts to be realized from the disposition of the future inventory items are adequately protected by firm sales contracts or if there are other circumstances that reasonably assure continuing sales without price decline. [ARB43, ch4, ¶17]

[5Refer to Section A10, "Accounting Policies," for guidance regarding disclosure.]

Glossary

.401 Cost.[401] The price paid or consideration given to acquire an asset; [it includes] the applicable expenditures and charges directly or indirectly incurred in bringing [the asset] to its existing condition and location. [ARB43, ch4, ¶5]

.402 Inventory. The aggregate of those items of tangible personal property that (a) are held for sale in the ordinary course of business (finished goods), (b) are in process of production for such sale (work in process), or (c) are to be currently consumed either directly or indirectly in the production of goods or services to be available for sale (raw materials and supplies). [ARB43, ch4, ¶3]

.403 Lower of Cost or Market [Rule] . The rule of **cost or market, whichever is lower** [shall] provide a means of measuring the residual usefulness of an inventory expenditure. In applying the rule, however, judgment should always be exercised and no loss shall be recognized unless the evidence indicates clearly that a loss has been sustained. There are exceptions to such a standard. Replacement or reproduction prices [are] not appropriate as a measure of utility [if] the estimated sales value, reduced by the costs of completion and disposal, is lower, in which case the realizable value so determined more appropriately measures utility. Furthermore, [if] the evidence indicates that cost will be recovered with an approximately normal profit upon sale in the ordinary course of business, no loss shall be recognized even though replacement or reproduction costs are lower. This might be true, for example, in the case of production under firm sales contracts at fixed prices, or [if] a reasonable volume of future orders is assured at stable selling prices. [ARB43, ch4, ¶9]

.404 Market. The term **market** means current replacement cost (by purchase or by reproduction, as the case may be) except that:

a. Market shall not exceed the net realizable value (i.e., estimated selling price in the ordinary course of business less reasonably predictable costs of completion and disposal); and

b. Market shall not be less than net realizable value reduced by an allowance for an approximately normal profit margin.

The term *market* shall be interpreted as indicating utility on the inventory date and should be thought of in terms of the equivalent expenditure that would have to be made in the ordinary course [of business] at that date to procure corresponding utility. As a general guide, utility is indicated primarily by the current cost of replacement of the goods as they would be obtained by purchase or reproduction. [ARB43, ch4, ¶9]

(The next page is 27631.)

---

[401] In the case of goods that have been written down below cost at the close of a fiscal period (refer to paragraph .109), such reduced amounts shall be considered the cost for subsequent accounting purposes. [ARB43, ch4, ¶5, fn2]

Sources: ARB 43; FASB Statement 91; FASB Statement 115;
          FASB Technical Bulletin 79-19; FASB Technical Bulletin 94-1

Summary

This section addresses the accounting and reporting for investments in equity securities that have readily determinable fair values and for all investments in debt securities. Those investments are to be classified in three categories and accounted for as follows:

- Debt securities that the enterprise has the positive intent and ability to hold to maturity are classified as *held-to-maturity securities* and reported at amortized cost.
- Debt and equity securities that are bought and held principally for the purpose of selling them in the near term are classified as *trading securities* and reported at fair value, with unrealized gains and losses included in earnings.
- Debt and equity securities not classified as either held-to-maturity securities or trading securities are classified as *available-for-sale securities* and reported at fair value, with unrealized gains and losses excluded from earnings and reported in a separate component of shareholders' equity.

This section does not apply to unsecuritized loans. However, after mortgage loans are converted to mortgage-backed securities, they are subject to its provisions.

Scope

.101 This section addresses the accounting and reporting for certain investments in **debt securities** and **equity securities**. [FAS115, ¶1] Except as indicated in paragraph .102, this section establishes standards of financial accounting and reporting for investments in equity securities that have readily determinable **fair values** and for all investments in debt securities.

a. The fair value of an equity security is readily determinable if sales prices or bid-and-asked quotations are currently available on a **securities** exchange registered with the Securities and Exchange Commission (SEC) or in the over-the-counter market, provided that those prices or quotations for the over-the-counter market are publicly reported by the National Association of Securities Dealers Automated

Quotations systems or by the National Quotation Bureau. Restricted stock[1] does not meet that definition.
b. The fair value of an equity security traded only in a foreign market is readily determinable if that foreign market is of a breadth and scope comparable to one of the U.S. markets referred to above.
c. The fair value of an investment in a mutual fund is readily determinable if the fair value per share (unit) is determined and published and is the basis for current transactions. [FAS115, ¶3]

.102 This section does not apply to investments in equity securities accounted for under the equity method nor to investments in consolidated subsidiaries. [Refer to Section 182, "Investments: Equity Method."] This section does not apply to enterprises whose specialized accounting practices include accounting for substantially all investments in debt and equity securities at market value or fair value, with changes in value recognized in earnings (income) or in the change in net assets. Examples of those enterprises are brokers and dealers in securities, defined benefit pension plans, and investment companies. This section also does not apply to not-for-profit organizations[2]; however, it does apply to cooperatives and mutual enterprises, including credit unions and mutual insurance companies. [FAS115, ¶4] This section does not address the accounting for other financial instruments used to hedge investments in securities. However, the accounting for those instruments may be affected if they are hedges of securities whose accounting is [addressed] by this section. [Refer to paragraph .113.] [FAS115, ¶115] The accounting for discounts, premiums, and commitment fees associated with the purchase of loans and other debt securities such as corporate bonds, Treasury notes and bonds, groups of loans, and loan-backed securities (such as pass-through certificates, collateralized mortgage obligations, and other so-called "securitized" loans) is addressed in Section L20, "Lending Activities." [FAS91, ¶3] [Refer to paragraphs .503 and .504 for further guidance on the applicability of this section to loans restructured in a troubled debt restructuring.]

Accounting for Certain Investments in Debt and Equity Securities

.103 At acquisition, an enterprise shall classify debt and equity securities into one of three categories: held-to-maturity, available-for-sale, or trading. At each reporting date, the appropriateness of the classification shall be reassessed. [FAS115, ¶6]

---

[1]*Restricted stock,* for the purpose of this section, means equity securities for which sale is restricted by governmental or contractual requirement (other than in connection with being pledged as collateral) except if that requirement terminates within one year or if the holder has the power by contract or otherwise to cause the requirement to be met within one year. Any portion of the security that can be reasonably expected to qualify for sale within one year, such as may be the case under Rule 144 or similar rules of the SEC, is not considered restricted. [FAS115, ¶3, fn2]

[2]Not-for-profit organizations include] religious, charitable, scientific, educational, and similar nonprofit institutions, municipalities, professional firms, and the like. [ARB43, Intro., ¶5]

Held-to-Maturity Securities

.104 Investments in debt securities shall be classified as *held-to-maturity* and measured at amortized cost in the statement of financial position only if the reporting enterprise has the positive intent[3] and ability to hold those securities to maturity. [FAS115, ¶7]

.105 The following changes in circumstances, however, may cause the enterprise to change its intent to hold a certain security to maturity without calling into question its intent to hold other debt securities to maturity in the future. Thus, the sale or transfer of a held-to-maturity security due to one of the following changes in circumstances shall not be considered to be inconsistent with its original classification:

a. Evidence of a significant deterioration[4] in the issuer's creditworthiness
b. A change in tax law that eliminates or reduces the tax-exempt status of interest on the debt security (but not a change in tax law that revises the marginal tax rates applicable to interest income[5])
c. A major business combination or major disposition (such as sale of a segment) that necessitates the sale or transfer of held-to-maturity securities to maintain the enterprise's existing interest rate risk position or credit risk policy[6]
d. A change in statutory or regulatory requirements significantly modifying either what constitutes a permissible investment or the maximum level of investments in certain kinds of securities, thereby causing an enterprise to dispose of a held-to-maturity security
e. A significant increase by the regulator in the industry's capital requirements that causes the enterprise to downsize by selling held-to-maturity securities[7]
f. A significant increase in the risk weights of debt securities used for regulatory risk-based capital purposes.

---

[3]In establishing intent, an enterprise shall consider pertinent historical experience, such as sales and transfers of debt securities classified as held-to-maturity. A pattern of sales or transfers of those securities is inconsistent with an expressed current intent to hold similar debt securities to maturity. [FAS115, ¶59]

[4]The sale of a held-to-maturity security must be in response to an actual deterioration, not mere speculation. That deterioration shall be supported by evidence about the issuer's creditworthiness; however, the enterprise need not await an actual downgrading in the issuer's published credit rating or inclusion on a "credit watch" list. [FAS115, ¶72]

[5Similarly, selling] held-to-maturity securities to generate taxable gains to offset existing taxable losses, or vice versa, [or selling] those securities in response to changes in the enterprise's anticipated future profitability [is not permitted]. Securities that may need to be sold to implement tax-planning strategies should be classified as available-for-sale, not held-to-maturity. [FAS115, ¶71]

[6]Those necessary transfers or sales should occur concurrent with or shortly after the business combination or disposition. [FAS115, ¶74]

[7However,] an enterprise's ability and intent to hold securities to maturity would be called into question by the sale of held-to-maturity securities to realize gains to replenish regulatory capital that had been reduced by a provision for loan losses. [FAS115, ¶76]

In addition to the foregoing changes in circumstances, other events that are isolated, nonrecurring, and unusual for the reporting enterprise that could not have been reasonably anticipated may cause the enterprise to sell or transfer a held-to-maturity security without necessarily calling into question its intent to hold other debt securities to maturity. All sales and transfers of held-to-maturity securities shall be disclosed pursuant to paragraph .121. [FAS115, ¶8]

.106 An enterprise shall not classify a debt security as held-to-maturity if the enterprise has the intent to hold the security for only an indefinite period. Consequently, a debt security should not, for example, be classified as held-to-maturity if the enterprise anticipates that the security would be available to be sold in response to:

a. Changes in market interest rates and related changes in the security's prepayment risk
b. Needs for liquidity (for example, due to the withdrawal of deposits, increased demand for loans, surrender of insurance policies, or payment of insurance claims)
c. Changes in the availability of and the yield on alternative investments
d. Changes in funding sources and terms
e. Changes in foreign currency risk. [FAS115, ¶9]

.107 Although its asset-liability management may encompass consideration of the maturity and repricing characteristics of all investments in debt securities, an enterprise may decide that it can accomplish the necessary adjustments under its asset-liability management without having all of its debt securities available for disposition. In that case, the enterprise may choose to designate certain debt securities as unavailable to be sold to accomplish those ongoing adjustments deemed necessary under its asset-liability management, thereby enabling those debt securities to be accounted for at amortized cost on the basis of a positive intent and ability to hold them to maturity. [FAS115, ¶10]

.108 Sales of debt securities that meet either of the following two conditions may be considered as maturities for purposes of the classification of securities under paragraphs .104 and .109 and the disclosure requirements under paragraph .121:

a. The sale of a security occurs near enough to its maturity date (or call date if exercise of the call is probable) that interest rate risk is substantially eliminated as a pricing factor. That is, the date of sale is so near the maturity or call date (for example, within three months) that changes in market interest rates would not have a significant effect on the security's fair value.
b. The sale of a security occurs after the enterprise has already collected a substantial portion (at least 85 percent) of the principal outstanding at acquisition [FAS115, ¶11] (not the principal outstanding at issuance for securities purchased in the secondary market) [FAS115, ¶66] due either to prepayments on the debt security or to scheduled payments on a debt security payable in equal installments (both princi-

pal and interest) over its term. For variable-rate securities, the scheduled payments need not be equal. [FAS115, ¶11]

Trading Securities and Available-for-Sale Securities

.109 Investments in debt securities that are not classified as held-to-maturity and equity securities that have readily determinable fair values shall be classified in one of the following categories and measured at fair value in the statement of financial position:

a. *Trading securities.* Securities that are bought and held principally for the purpose of selling them in the near term (thus held for only a short period of time) shall be classified as *trading securities.* Trading generally reflects active and frequent buying and selling, and trading securities are generally used with the objective of generating profits on short-term differences in price. Mortgage-backed securities that are held for sale in conjunction with mortgage banking activities, as described in Section Mo4, "Mortgage Banking Activities," shall be classified as trading securities. (Other mortgage-backed securities not held for sale in conjunction with mortgage banking activities shall be classified based on the criteria in this paragraph and paragraph .104.)

b. *Available-for-sale securities.* Investments not classified as trading securities (nor as held-to-maturity securities) shall be classified as *available-for-sale securities.* [FAS115, ¶12]

Reporting Changes in Fair Value

.110 Unrealized **holding gains and losses** for trading securities shall be included in earnings. Unrealized holding gains and losses for available-for-sale securities (including those classified as current assets) shall be excluded from earnings and reported as a net amount in a separate component of shareholders' equity until realized. Paragraph .135 of Section I27, "Income Taxes," provides guidance on reporting the tax effects of unrealized holding gains and losses reported in a separate component of shareholders' equity. [FAS115, ¶13]

.111 Dividend and interest income, including amortization of the premium and discount arising at acquisition, for all three categories of investments in securities shall continue to be included in earnings. This section does not affect the methods used for recognizing and measuring the amount of dividend and interest income. Realized gains and losses for securities classified as either available-for-sale or held-to-maturity also shall continue to be reported in earnings. [FAS115, ¶14]

Determining Fair Value

.112 Quoted market prices, if available, provide the most reliable measure of fair value. [FAS115, ¶110] Although quoted market prices are not available for all debt securities, a reasonable estimate of fair value can be made or obtained for the remaining debt securities required to be valued at fair value by this section. For debt securities that do not trade regularly or that trade only in principal-to-principal markets, a reasonable estimate of fair value can be made using a variety of pricing techniques, including, but not limited to, discounted cash flow analysis, matrix pricing, option-adjusted spread models, and fundamental analysis. [FAS115, ¶111]

Financial Instruments Used to Hedge Investments at Fair Value

.113 Gains and losses on instruments that hedge securities classified as trading should be reported in earnings, consistent with the reporting of unrealized gains and losses on the trading securities. Gains and losses on instruments that hedge available-for-sale securities are initially reported in a separate component of equity, consistent with the reporting for those securities, but then should be amortized as a yield adjustment. The reporting of available-for-sale securities at fair value does not change the recognition and measurement of interest income. [FAS115, ¶115]

Transfers between Categories of Investments

.114 The transfer of a security between categories of investments shall be accounted for at fair value.[8] At the date of the transfer, the security's unrealized holding gain or loss shall be accounted for as follows:

a. For a security transferred from the trading category, the unrealized holding gain or loss at the date of the transfer will have already been recognized in earnings and shall not be reversed.
b. For a security transferred into the trading category, the unrealized holding gain or loss at the date of the transfer shall be recognized in earnings immediately.
c. For a debt security transferred into the available-for-sale category from the held-to-maturity category, the unrealized holding gain or loss at the date of the transfer shall be recognized in a separate component of shareholders' equity.
d. For a debt security transferred into the held-to-maturity category from the available-for-sale category, the unrealized holding gain or loss at the date of the transfer shall continue to be reported in a separate component of shareholders' equity but shall be amortized over the remaining life of the security as an adjustment of yield in a manner consistent with the amortization of any premium or discount. The amortization of an unrealized holding gain or loss reported in equity will offset or mitigate the effect on interest income of the amortization of the premium or discount (discussed in footnote 8) for that held-to-maturity security.

---

[8]For a debt security transferred into the held-to-maturity category, the use of fair value may create a premium or discount that, under amortized cost accounting, shall be amortized thereafter as an adjustment of yield pursuant to Section L20. [FAS115, ¶15, fn3]

Consistent with paragraphs .104 through .106, transfers from the held-to-maturity category should be rare, except for transfers due to the changes in circumstances identified in subparagraphs .105(a) through .105(f). Given the nature of a trading security, transfers into or from the trading category also should be rare. [FAS115, ¶15]

Impairment of Securities

.115 For individual securities classified as either available-for-sale or held-to-maturity, an enterprise shall determine whether a decline in fair value below the amortized cost basis is other than temporary. For example, if it is probable that the investor will be unable to collect all amounts due according to the contractual terms of a debt security not impaired at acquisition, an other-than-temporary impairment shall be considered to have occurred.[9] If the decline in fair value is judged to be other than temporary, the cost basis of the individual security shall be written down to fair value as a new cost basis and the amount of the write-down shall be included in earnings (that is, accounted for as a realized loss)[10]. The new cost basis shall not be changed for subsequent recoveries in fair value. Subsequent increases in the fair value of available-for-sale securities shall be included in the separate component of equity pursuant to paragraph .110; subsequent decreases in fair value, if not an other-than-temporary impairment, also shall be included in the separate component of equity. [FAS115, ¶16]

Financial Statement Presentation

.116 An enterprise that presents a classified statement of financial position shall report all trading securities as current assets and shall report individual held-to-maturity securities and individual available-for-sale securities as either current or noncurrent, as appropriate, under the provisions of Section B05, "Balance Sheet Classification: Current Assets and Current Liabilities."[11] [FAS115, ¶17] Presentation of individual

---

[9]A decline in the value of a security that is other than temporary is also discussed in AICPA Auditing Interpretation, *Evidential Matter for the Carrying Amount of Marketable Securities,* which was issued in 1975 and incorporated in Statement on Auditing Standards No. 1, *Codification of Auditing Standards and Procedures,* as Interpretation 20, and in SEC Staff Accounting Bulletin No. 59, *Accounting for Noncurrent Marketable Equity Securities.* [FAS115, ¶16, fn4]

[10]The impairment provisions of this section differ from those in Section I08, "Impairment," [paragraphs .102 through .119, in that] this section requires that the measure of impairment be based on the fair value of the security, whereas Section I08 permits measurement of an unsecuritized loan's impairment based on either fair value (of the loan or the collateral) or the present value of the expected cash flows discounted at the loan's effective interest rate. [FAS115, ¶113]

[11]Section B05, paragraph .105 indicates that "the term *current assets* is used to designate cash and other assets or resources commonly identified as those which are reasonably expected to be realized in cash or sold or consumed during the normal operating cycle of the business." That paragraph further indicates that the term also comprehends "marketable securities representing the investment of cash available for current operations." Paragraph .106 indicates that "a one-year time period is to be used as a basis for the segregation of current assets in cases where there are several operating cycles occurring within a year." [FAS115, ¶17, fn5]

amounts for the three categories of investments on the face of the statement of financial position [is not required], provided the information is presented in the notes. [FAS115, ¶117]

.117 Cash flows from purchases, sales, and maturities of available-for-sale securities and held-to-maturity securities shall be classified as cash flows from investing activities and reported gross for each security classification in the statement of cash flows. Cash flows from purchases, sales, and maturities of trading securities shall be classified as cash flows from operating activities. [FAS115, ¶18]

Disclosures

.118 For securities classified as available-for-sale and separately for securities classified as held-to-maturity, all reporting enterprises shall disclose the aggregate fair value, gross unrealized holding gains, gross unrealized holding losses, and amortized cost basis by major security type as of each date for which a statement of financial position is presented. In complying with this requirement, financial institutions[12] shall include in their disclosure the following major security types, though additional types also may be included as appropriate:

a. Equity securities
b. Debt securities issued by the U.S. Treasury and other U.S. government corporations and agencies
c. Debt securities issued by states of the United States and political subdivisions of the states
d. Debt securities issued by foreign governments
e. Corporate debt securities
f. Mortgage-backed securities
g. Other debt securities. [FAS115, ¶19]

.119 For investments in debt securities classified as available-for-sale and separately for securities classified as held-to-maturity, all reporting enterprises shall disclose information about the contractual maturities of those securities as of the date of the most recent statement of financial position presented. Maturity information may be combined in appropriate groupings. In complying with this requirement, financial institutions shall disclose the fair value and the amortized cost of debt securities based on at least 4 maturity groupings: (a) within 1 year, (b) after 1 year through 5 years, (c) after 5 years through 10 years, and (d) after 10 years. Securities not due at a single maturity date, such as mortgage-backed securities, may be disclosed separately rather than allocated over several maturity groupings; if allocated, the basis for allocation also shall be disclosed. [FAS115, ¶20]

---

[12]For purposes of the disclosure requirements of paragraphs .118 and .119, the term *financial institutions* includes banks, savings and loan associations, savings banks, credit unions, finance companies, and insurance companies, consistent with the usage of that term in AICPA Statement of Position 90-11, *Disclosure of Certain Information by Financial Institutions About Debt Securities Held as Assets.* [FAS115, ¶19, fn6]

.120 For each period for which the results of operations are presented, an enterprise shall disclose:

a. The proceeds from sales of available-for-sale securities and the gross realized gains and gross realized losses on those sales
b. The basis on which cost was determined in computing realized gain or loss (that is, specific identification, average cost, or other method used)
c. The gross gains and gross losses included in earnings from transfers of securities from the available-for-sale category into the trading category
d. The change in net unrealized holding gain or loss on available-for-sale securities that has been included in the separate component of shareholders' equity during the period
e. The change in net unrealized holding gain or loss on trading securities [held at period-end] that has been included in earnings during the period. [FAS115, ¶21]

.121 For any sales of or transfers from securities classified as held-to-maturity, the amortized cost amount of the sold or transferred security, the related realized or unrealized gain or loss, and the circumstances leading to the decision to sell or transfer the security shall be disclosed in the notes to the financial statements for each period for which the results of operations are presented. Such sales or transfers should be rare except for sales and transfers due to the changes in circumstances identified in subparagraphs .105(a) through .105(f). [FAS115, ¶22]

Glossary

.401 Debt security. Any security representing a creditor relationship with an enterprise. It also includes (a) preferred stock that by its terms either must be redeemed by the issuing enterprise or is redeemable at the option of the investor and (b) a collateralized mortgage obligation (CMO) (or other instrument) that is issued in equity form but is required to be accounted for as a nonequity instrument regardless of how that instrument is classified (that is, whether equity or debt) in the issuer's statement of financial position. However, it excludes option contracts, financial futures contracts, forward contracts, and lease contracts.

- Thus, the term *debt security* includes, among other items, U.S. Treasury securities, U.S. government agency securities, municipal securities, corporate bonds, convertible debt, commercial paper, all securitized debt instruments, such as CMOs and real estate mortgage investment conduits (REMICs), and interest-only and principal-only strips.
- Trade accounts receivable arising from sales on credit by industrial or commercial enterprises and loans receivable arising from consumer, commercial, and real estate lending activities of financial institutions are examples of receivables that do not meet the definition of *security;* thus, those receivables are not debt securities (unless they have been securitized, in which case they would meet the definition). [FAS115, ¶137]

.402 Equity security. Any security representing an ownership interest in an enterprise (for example, common, preferred, or other capital stock) or the right to acquire (for example, warrants, rights, and call options) or dispose of (for example, put options) an ownership interest in an enterprise at fixed or determinable prices. However, the term does not include convertible debt or preferred stock that by its terms either must be redeemed by the issuing enterprise or is redeemable at the option of the investor. [FAS115, ¶137]

.403 Fair value. The amount at which a financial instrument could be exchanged in a current transaction between willing parties, other than in a forced or liquidation sale. If a quoted market price is available for an instrument, the fair value to be used in applying this section is the product of the number of trading units of the instrument times its market price. [FAS115, ¶137]

.404 Holding gain or loss. The net change in fair value of a security exclusive of dividend or interest income recognized but not yet received and exclusive of any write-downs for other-than-temporary impairment. [FAS115, ¶137]

.405 Restricted stock. Equity securities for which sale is restricted by governmental or contractual requirement (other than in connection with being pledged as collateral) except if that requirement terminates within one year or if the holder has the power by contract or otherwise to cause the requirement to be met within one year. Any portion of the security that can be reasonably expected to qualify for sale within one year, such as may be the case under Rule 144 or similar rules of the SEC, is not considered restricted. [FAS115, ¶3, fn2]

.406 **Security.** A share, participation, or other interest in property or in an enterprise of the issuer or an obligation of the issuer that (a) either is represented by an instrument issued in bearer or registered form or, if not represented by an instrument, is registered in books maintained to record transfers by or on behalf of the issuer, (b) is of a type commonly dealt in on securities exchanges or markets or, when represented by an instrument, is commonly recognized in any area in which it is issued or dealt in as a medium for investment, and (c) either is one of a class or series or by its terms is divisible into a class or series of shares, participations, interests, or obligations. [FAS115, ¶137]

Supplemental Guidance

Unrealized Losses on Marketable Securities Owned by an Equity Method Investee

.501 *Question*—How should a parent or investor account for its share of the [FTB79-19, ¶1] unrealized holding gains or losses on investments in debt and equity securities [FAS115, ¶135(a)] included in stockholders' equity of an investee accounted for under the equity method? [FTB79-19, ¶1]

.502 *Response*—If a subsidiary or other investee that is accounted for by the equity method is required to include unrealized holding gains and losses on investments in debt and equity securities in the stockholders' equity section of the balance sheet pursuant to the provisions of this section, the parent or investor shall adjust its investment in that investee by its proportionate share of the unrealized gains and losses and a like amount shall be included in the stockholders' equity section of its balance sheet. [FAS115, ¶135(b)]

Application of This Section to Debt Securities Restructured in a Troubled Debt Restructuring

.503 *Question*—For a loan that was restructured in a troubled debt restructuring involving a modification of terms, does this section apply to the accounting by the creditor (that is, investor) [as described in paragraph .101A of Section D22, "Debt: Restructurings,"] if the restructured loan meets the definition of a *security* in paragraph .406? [FTB94-1, ¶1]

.504 *Response*—This section applies to all loans that meet the definition of a *security* in paragraph .406. Thus, any loan that was restructured in a troubled debt restructuring involving a modification of terms, [as described in paragraph .126 of Section D22] including those restructured [in fiscal years beginning before December 16, 1994] would be subject to the provisions of this section if the debt instrument meets the definition of a *security*. [FTB94-1, ¶3]

(The next page is 27715.)

Sources: APB Opinion 18; AICPA Interpretations of APB Opinion 18;
FASB Statement 58; FASB Statement 94; FASB Statement 109;
FASB Statement 115; FASB Interpretation 35; FASB Technical Bulletin 79-19

Summary

The equity method is a method of accounting for investments. An investor using the equity method initially records an investment at cost. Subsequently, the carrying amount of the investment is increased to reflect the investor's share of income of the investee and is reduced to reflect the investor's share of losses of the investee or dividends received from the investee. The investor's share of the income or losses of the investee is included in the investor's net income as the investee reports them. Adjustments similar to those made in preparing consolidated financial statements, such as elimination of intercompany gains and losses and amortization of the difference between cost and underlying equity in net assets, also are applicable to the equity method. Under the equity method, an investment in common stock is generally shown in the balance sheet of an investor as a single amount. Likewise, an investor's share of earnings or losses from its investment is ordinarily shown in its income statement as a single amount.

This section requires that an investor use the equity method to account for investments in corporate joint ventures. This section also requires use of the equity method to account for other investments in common stock if the investor has the ability to exercise significant influence over operating and financial policies of the investee enterprise. That ability is presumed to exist for investments of 20 percent or more and is presumed not to exist for investments of less than 20 percent; both presumptions may be overcome by predominant evidence to the contrary.

Scope

.101 This section does not apply to investments in common stock held by (a) investment enterprises registered under the Investment Company Act of 1940 or investment enterprises that would be included under the Act (including small business investment enterprises) except that the number of stockholders is limited and the securities are not offered publicly or (b) nonbusiness entities, such as estates, trusts, and individuals. The section also does not apply to investments in common stock other than those described in this section. [APB18, ¶2] This section [does not address] parent-company financial statements prepared for purposes other than issuance as the general-purpose financial statements of the primary reporting entity. [FAS94, ¶15, fn3]

Criteria for Applying the Equity Method

.102 Section C51, "Consolidation," paragraphs .102 and .103, requires consolidation of all majority-owned **subsidiaries** except the few that meet conditions described in paragraph .102 of that section. The **equity method** is not a valid substitute for consolidation. Moreover, since Section C51 requires the general-purpose financial statements of companies having one or more majority-owned subsidiaries to be consolidated statements, parent-company statements are not a valid substitute for consolidated financial statements.[1] [FAS94, ¶15(c)]

.103 Investors shall account for investments in common stock of **corporate joint ventures** by the equity method in consolidated financial statements.[2] [FAS94, ¶15(e)]

.104 The equity method of accounting for an investment in common stock also shall be followed by an **investor** whose investment in voting stock gives it the ability to exercise significant influence over operating and financial policies of an **investee** even though the investor holds 50 percent or less of the voting stock. Ability to exercise that influence may be indicated in several ways, such as representation on the board of directors, participation in policymaking processes, material intercompany transactions, interchange of managerial personnel, or technological dependency. Another important consideration is the extent of ownership by an investor in relation to the concentration of other shareholdings, but substantial or majority ownership of the voting stock of an investee by another investor does not necessarily preclude the ability to exercise significant influence by the investor. Determining the ability of an investor to exercise such influence is not always clear and applying judgment is necessary to assess the status of each investment. In order to achieve a reasonable degree of uniformity in application, an investment (direct or indirect) of 20 percent or more of the voting stock of an investee shall

---

[1]Paragraphs .102 and .103 of Section C51 describe the conditions under which a majority-owned subsidiary shall not be consolidated. The limitations in paragraphs .102 and .103 of Section C51 shall also be applied as limitations to the use of the equity method. [FAS94, ¶15(d)]

[2]The equity method shall not be applied to the investments described in this paragraph insofar as the limitations on the use of the equity method outlined in footnote 1 would be applicable to investments other than those in subsidiaries. [APB18, ¶16, fn6] [Supplemental guidance regarding applicability to investments in partnerships and unincorporated joint ventures is provided in paragraphs .508 through .512.]

lead to a presumption that in the absence of evidence to the contrary an investor has the ability to exercise significant influence over an investee. Conversely, an investment of less than 20 percent of the voting stock of an investee shall lead to a presumption that an investor does not have the ability to exercise significant influence unless such ability can be demonstrated.[3] [APB18, ¶17]

.105 An investor's *voting stock interest* in an investee shall be based on those currently outstanding securities whose holders have present voting privileges. Potential voting privileges that may become available to holders of securities of an investee shall be disregarded. An investor's *share of the earnings or losses* of an investee shall be based on the shares of *common* stock held by an investor without recognition of securities of the investee that are designated as *common stock equivalents* under Section E09, "Earnings per Share."[4] [APB18, ¶18]

.106 Paragraph .104 requires that the equity method of accounting be followed by an investor whose investment in voting stock gives it the ability to exercise significant influence over operating and financial policies of an investee. The presumptions in paragraph .104 are intended to provide a reasonable degree of uniformity in applying the equity method. The presumptions can be overcome by predominant evidence to the contrary. [FIN35, ¶2]

.107 Evidence that an investor owning 20 percent or more of the voting stock of an investee may be unable to exercise significant influence over the investee's operating and financial policies requires an evaluation of all the facts and circumstances relating to the investment. The presumption that the investor has the ability to exercise significant influence over the investee's operating and financial policies stands until overcome by predominant evidence to the contrary.[5] [FIN35, ¶3]

---

[3]The equity method shall not be applied to the investments described in this paragraph insofar as the limitations on the use of the equity method outlined in footnote 1 would be applicable to investments other than those in subsidiaries. [APB18, ¶17, fn7]

[4]Section E09, paragraph .132, states: "The designation of securities as common stock equivalents in this section is solely for the purpose of determining primary earnings per share. No changes from present practices are recommended in the accounting for such securities, in their presentation within the financial statements or in the manner of determining net assets per common share. Information is available in the financial statements and elsewhere for readers to make judgments as to the present and potential status of the various securities outstanding." Paragraphs .156 through .160 in Section E09 discuss the treatment of common stock equivalents of subsidiaries in computing earnings per share of a parent company. The provisions of those paragraphs also apply to investments in common stock of corporate joint ventures and investee enterprises accounted for under the equity method. [APB18, ¶18, fn8]

[5]Subject to the limitations on the use of the equity method identified in footnote 1. [FIN35, ¶3, fn1]

.108 Examples of indications that an investor may be unable to exercise significant influence over the operating and financial policies of an investee include:

a. Opposition by the investee, such as litigation or complaints to governmental regulatory authorities, challenges the investor's ability to exercise significant influence.
b. The investor and investee sign an agreement under which the investor surrenders significant rights as a shareholder.[6]
c. Majority ownership of the investee is concentrated among a small group of shareholders who operate the investee without regard to the views of the investor.
d. The investor needs or wants more financial information to apply the equity method than is available to the investee's other shareholders (for example, the investor wants quarterly financial information from an investee that publicly reports only annually), tries to obtain that information, and fails.[7]
e. The investor tries and fails to obtain representation on the investee's board of directors.

This list is illustrative and is not all-inclusive. None of the individual circumstances is necessarily conclusive that the investor is unable to exercise significant influence over the investee's operating and financial policies. However, if any of these or similar circumstances exists, an investor with ownership of 20 percent or more shall evaluate all facts and circumstances relating to the investment to reach a judgment about whether the presumption that the investor has the ability to exercise significant influence over the investee's operating and financial policies is overcome. It may be necessary to evaluate the facts and circumstances for a period of time before reaching a judgment. [FIN35, ¶4]

---

[6][Sometimes,] an investor and an investee have signed an agreement under which the investor agrees to limit its shareholding in the investee. (Because the investor usually agrees not to increase its current holdings, such agreements often are called *stand-still agreements*.) Those agreements commonly are used to compromise disputes when an investee is fighting against a takeover attempt or an increase in an investor's percentage ownership. Depending on their provisions, the agreements may modify an investor's rights or may increase certain rights and restrict others compared with the situation of an investor without such an agreement. If the investor surrenders significant rights as a shareholder under the provisions of such an agreement, the investor shall assess all the facts and circumstances of the investment to determine whether they are sufficient to overcome the presumption. [FIN35, ¶9]

[7]The subject of inability to obtain financial information also is addressed in the American Institute of Certified Public Accountants' *Codification of Statements on Auditing Standards,* AU Section 332, "Evidential Matter for Long-Term Investments," paragraph 9. [FIN35, ¶4, fn3]

Applying the Equity Method

.109 The procedures set forth below shall be followed by an investor in applying the equity method of accounting to investments in common stock of corporate joint ventures and other investees that qualify for the equity method:

a. Intercompany profits and losses shall be eliminated until realized by the investor or investee as if a corporate joint venture or investee enterprise were consolidated.[8]

b. A difference between the cost of an investment and the amount of underlying equity in **net assets of an investee** shall be accounted for as if the investee were a consolidated subsidiary.[9]

c. The investment(s) in common stock shall be shown in the balance sheet of an investor as a single amount, and the investor's share of earnings or losses of an investee(s) shall ordinarily be shown in the income statement as a single amount except for the extraordinary items as specified in (d) below.

d. The investor's share of extraordinary items and its share of prior period adjustments reported in the financial statements of the investee in accordance with Section I17, "Income Statement Presentation: Extraordinary Items," and Section A06, "Accounting Changes," shall be classified in a similar manner unless they are immaterial in the income statement of the investor.

e. A transaction of an investee of a capital nature that affects the investor's share of stockholders' equity of the investee shall be accounted for as if the investee were a consolidated subsidiary. [For purchases by an investee of its own stock, refer to Section B50, "Business Combinations," paragraphs .101 and .102.]

f. Sales of stock of an investee by an investor shall be accounted for as gains or losses equal to the difference at the time of sale between selling price and carrying amount of the stock sold.

g. If financial statements of an investee are not sufficiently timely for an investor to apply the equity method currently, the investor ordinarily shall record its share of the earnings or losses of an investee from the most recent available financial statements. A lag in reporting shall be consistent from period to period.

h. A loss in value of an investment that is other than a temporary decline shall be recognized. Evidence of a loss in value might include, but would not necessarily be limited to, absence of an ability to recover the carrying amount of the investment or inability of the investee to sustain an earnings capacity that would justify the carrying amount of the investment. A current fair value of an investment that is less than its carrying

---

[8Supplemental guidance on eliminating intercompany profits is provided in paragraphs .501 through .507.]

[9For investments made prior to November 1, 1970, investors are not required to amortize any goodwill in the absence of evidence that the goodwill has a limited term of existence; prospective amortization of such goodwill is encouraged. [APB18, ¶19, fn9]

amount may indicate a loss in value of the investment. However, a decline in the quoted market price below the carrying amount or the existence of operating losses is not necessarily indicative of a loss in value that is other than temporary. All are factors to be evaluated.[10]

i. An investor's share of losses of an investee may equal or exceed the carrying amount of an investment accounted for by the equity method plus advances made by the investor. The investor ordinarily shall discontinue applying the equity method when the investment (and net advances) is reduced to zero and shall not provide for additional losses unless the investor has guaranteed obligations of the investee or is otherwise committed to provide further financial support for the investee.[11] If the investee subsequently reports net income, the investor shall resume applying the equity method only after its share of that net income equals the share of net losses not recognized during the period the equity method was suspended.

j. [Accounting for income taxes on undistributed earnings of investees accounted for by the equity method is discussed in Section I27, "Income Taxes," paragraphs .212 through .217.]

k. If an investee has outstanding cumulative preferred stock, an investor shall compute its share of earnings (losses) after deducting the investee's preferred **dividends,** whether or not such dividends are declared.

l. An investment in voting stock of an investee enterprise may fall below the level of ownership described in paragraph .104 from sale of a portion of an investment by the investor, sale of additional stock by an investee, or other transactions and the investor may thereby lose the ability to influence policy, as described in that paragraph. An investor shall discontinue accruing its share of the earnings or losses of the investee for an investment that no longer qualifies for the equity method. The earnings or losses that relate to the stock retained by the investor and that were previously accrued shall remain as a part of the carrying amount of the investment. The investment account shall not be adjusted retroactively under the conditions described in this subparagraph. However, dividends received by the investor in subsequent periods that exceed [the investor's] share of earnings for such periods shall be applied in reduction of the carrying amount of the investment (refer to paragraph .402). [APB18, ¶19] Section I80, "Investments: Debt and Equity Securities," addresses the accounting for investments in equity securities with readily determinable fair values that are not consolidated or accounted for under the equity method. [FAS115, ¶126]

---

[10]Supplemental guidance on reporting unrealized losses on marketable securities owned by an equity method investee is provided in paragraphs .513 and .514.]

[11]An investor shall, however, provide for additional losses when the imminent return to profitable operations by an investee appears to be assured. For example, a material, nonrecurring loss of an isolated nature may reduce an investment below zero even though the underlying profitable operating pattern of an investee is unimpaired. [APB18, ¶19, fn10]

m. An investment in common stock of an investee that was previously accounted for on other than the equity method [(that is, by the **cost method**)] may become qualified for use of the equity method by an increase in the level of ownership described in paragraph .104 (that is, acquisition of additional voting stock by the investor, acquisition or retirement of voting stock by the investee, or other transactions). When an investment qualifies for use of the equity method, the investor shall adopt the equity method of accounting. The investment, results of operations (current and prior periods presented), and retained earnings of the investor shall be adjusted retroactively in a manner consistent with the accounting for a step-by-step acquisition of a subsidiary.[12] [(Refer to Section C51, paragraph .111, for a description of the step-by-step acquisition method.)]

n. The carrying amount of an investment in common stock of an investee that qualifies for the equity method of accounting as described in subparagraph (m) may differ from the underlying equity in net assets of the investee. The difference shall affect the determination of the amount of the investor's share of earnings or losses of an investee as if the investee were a consolidated subsidiary. However, if the investor is unable to relate the difference to specific accounts of the investee, the difference shall be considered to be goodwill and amortized over a period not to exceed 40 years, in accordance with Section I60, "Intangible Assets."[13]

[APB18, ¶19]

Disclosures

.110 The significance of an investment to the investor's financial position and results of operations shall be considered in evaluating the extent of disclosures of the financial position and results of operations of an investee. If the investor has more than one investment in common stock, disclosures wholly or partly on a combined basis may be appropriate. The following disclosures are generally applicable to the equity method of accounting for investments in common stock:

a. Financial statements of an investor shall disclose parenthetically, in notes to financial statements, or in separate statements or schedules (1) the name of each investee and percentage of ownership of common stock, (2) the accounting policies of the investor

---

[12]The amount of interest cost capitalized through application of Section I67, "Interest: Capitalization of Interest Cost," shall not be changed when restating financial statements of prior periods [to reflect the use of the equity method for an investee that was previously accounted for on other than the equity method]. [FAS58, ¶8]

[13]For investments made prior to November 1, 1970, investors are not required to amortize any goodwill in the absence of evidence that the goodwill has a limited term of existence; prospective amortization of such goodwill is encouraged. [APB18, ¶19, fn12]

with respect to investments in common stock,[14] and (3) the difference, if any, between the amount at which an investment is carried and the amount of underlying equity in net assets and the accounting treatment of the difference.

b. For those investments in common stock for which a quoted market price is available, the aggregate value of each identified investment based on the quoted market price usually shall be disclosed. This disclosure is not required for investments in common stock of subsidiaries.

c. [Deleted 11/87 because of FASB Statement 94, *Consolidation of All Majority-Owned Subsidiaries.*]

d. If investments in common stock of corporate joint ventures or other investments accounted for under the equity method are, in the aggregate, material in relation to the financial position or results of operations of an investor, it may be necessary for summarized information as to assets, liabilities, and results of operations of the investees to be presented in the notes or in separate statements, either individually or in groups, as appropriate.

e. Conversion of outstanding convertible securities, exercise of outstanding options and warrants, and other contingent issuances of an investee may have a significant effect on an investor's share of reported earnings or losses. Accordingly, material effects of possible conversions, exercises, or contingent issuances shall be disclosed in notes to the financial statements of an investor.[15]

[APB18, ¶20]

---

[14]Disclosure shall include the names of any significant investee corporations in which the investor holds 20 percent or more of the voting stock, but the common stock is not accounted for on the equity method, together with the reasons why the equity method is not considered appropriate, and the names of any significant investee corporations in which the investor holds less than 20 percent of the voting stock and the common stock is accounted for on the equity method, together with the reasons why the equity method is considered appropriate. [APB18, ¶19, fn13]

[15]Refer to footnote 4. [APB18, ¶19, fn14]

Glossary

.401 Corporate joint venture. An enterprise owned and operated by a small group of businesses (the *joint venturers*) as a separate and specific business or project for the mutual benefit of the members of the group. A government also may be a member of the group. The purpose of a corporate joint venture frequently is to share risks and rewards in developing a new market, product, or technology; to combine complementary technological knowledge; or to pool resources in developing production or other facilities. A corporate joint venture also usually provides an arrangement under which each joint venturer may participate, directly or indirectly, in the overall management of the joint venture. Joint venturers thus have an interest or relationship other than as passive investors. An enterprise that is a subsidiary of one of the joint venturers is not a corporate joint venture. The ownership of a corporate joint venture seldom changes, and its stock is usually not traded publicly. A minority public ownership, however, does not preclude an enterprise from being a corporate joint venture. [APB18, ¶3]

.402 Cost method. [A method of accounting for an investment under which] an investor records an investment in the stock of an investee at cost, and recognizes as income dividends received that are distributed from net accumulated earnings of the investee since the date of acquisition by the investor. The net accumulated earnings of an investee subsequent to the date of investment are recognized by the investor only to the extent distributed by the investee as dividends. Dividends received in excess of earnings subsequent to the date of investment are considered a return of investment and are recorded as reductions of cost of the investment. [APB18, ¶6(a)]

.403 Dividends. Dividends paid or payable in cash, other assets, or another class of stock and does not include, for purposes of this section, stock dividends or stock splits. [APB18, ¶3] [Section C20, "Capital Stock: Stock Dividends and Stock Splits," discusses accounting for stock dividends and stock splits.]

.404 Earnings or losses of an investee and financial position of an investee. Net income (or net loss) and financial position of an investee determined in accordance with accounting principles generally accepted in the United States. [APB18, ¶3]

.405 Equity method. [A method of accounting for an investment under which] an investor initially records an investment in the stock of an investee at cost, and adjusts the carrying amount of the investment to recognize the investor's share of the earnings or losses of the investee after the date of acquisition. The amount of the adjustment is included in the determination of net income by the investor and such amount reflects adjustments similar to those made in preparing consolidated statements including adjustments to eliminate intercompany gains and losses, and to amortize, if appropriate, any difference between investor cost and underlying equity in net assets of the investee at the date of investment. The investment of an investor also is adjusted to reflect the investor's share of changes in the investee's capital. Dividends received from an investee reduce the carrying amount of the investment. [APB18, ¶6(b)] Under the equity method, an investment in common stock is generally shown in the balance sheet of an investor as a single amount. Likewise, an investor's share of earnings or losses from its investment is ordinarily shown in its income statement as a single amount. [APB18, ¶11]

.406 **Investee.** An enterprise that issued voting stock held by an investor. [APB18, ¶3]

.407 **Investor.** A business enterprise that holds an investment in voting stock of another enterprise. [APB18, ¶3]

.408 **Subsidiary.** An enterprise that is controlled, directly or indirectly, by another enterprise. The usual condition for control is ownership of a majority (over 50 percent) of the outstanding voting stock. The power to control also may exist with a lesser percentage of ownership, for example, by contract, lease, agreement with other stockholders, or by court decree. [APB18, ¶3]

Supplemental Guidance

Intercompany Profit Elimination

.501 *Question*—In applying the equity method of accounting, intercompany profits or losses on assets still remaining with an investor or investee should be eliminated, giving effect to any income taxes on the intercompany transactions (refer to paragraph .109(a) and Section C51, paragraphs .109 and .110). Should all of the intercompany profit or loss be eliminated or only that portion related to the investor's common stock interest in the investee? [AIN-APB18, #1]

.502 *Interpretation*—Paragraph .109 normally requires an investor's net income and stock-holders' equity to be the same from application of the equity method as would result from consolidation. Because the equity method is a *one-line* consolidation, however, the details reported in the investor's financial statements under the equity method will not be the same as would be reported in consolidated financial statements (refer to paragraph .109(c)). All intercompany transactions are eliminated in consolidation, but under the equity method intercompany profits or losses are normally eliminated only on assets still remaining on the books of an investor or an investee. [AIN-APB18, #1]

.503 Section C51, paragraph .115, provides for complete elimination of intercompany profits or losses in consolidation. It also states that the elimination of intercompany profit or loss may be allocated proportionately between the majority and minority interests. Whether all or a proportionate part of the intercompany profit or loss shall be eliminated under the equity method depends largely upon the relationship between the investor and the investee. [AIN-APB18, #1]

.504 If an investor controls an investee through majority voting interest and enters into a transaction with an investee which is not on an *arm's-length* basis, none of the inter-company profit or loss from the transaction shall be recognized in income by the inves-tor until it has been realized through transactions with third parties. The same treatment also applies for an investee established with the cooperation of an investor (including an investee established for the financing and operation or leasing of property sold to the investee by the investor) if control is exercised through guarantees of indebtedness, ex-tension of credit and other special arrangements by the investor for the benefit of the investee, or because of ownership by the investor of warrants, convertible securities, etc., issued by the investee. [AIN-APB18, #1]

.505 In other cases, it would be appropriate for the investor to eliminate intercompany profit in relation to the investor's common stock interest in the investee. In these cases, the percentage of intercompany profit to be eliminated would be the same regardless of whether the transaction is *downstream* (that is, a sale by the investor to the investee) or *upstream* (that is, sale by the investee to the investor). The following examples illustrate how these eliminations might be made. The examples assume an investor owns 30 percent of the common stock of an investee, the investment is accounted for under the equity method, and the income tax rate to both the investor and the investee is 40 percent. [AIN-APB18, #1]

.506 Assume an investor sells inventory items to the investee (*downstream* [transaction]). At the investee's balance sheet date, the investee holds inventory for which the investor has recorded a gross profit of $100,000. The investor's net income would be reduced $18,000 to reflect a $30,000 reduction in gross profit and a $12,000 reduction in income tax expense. The elimination of intercompany profit might be reflected in the investor's balance sheet in various ways. The income statement and balance sheet presentations will depend upon what is the most meaningful in the circumstances. [AIN-APB18, #1]

.507 Assume an investee sells inventory items to the investor (*upstream* [transaction]). At the investor's balance sheet date, the investor holds inventory for which the investee has recorded a gross profit of $100,000. In computing the investor's equity "pickup," $60,000 ($100,000 less 40 percent of income tax) would be deducted from the investee's net income and $18,000 (the investor's share of the intercompany gross profit after income tax) would thereby be eliminated from the investor's equity income. Usually, the investor's investment account would also reflect the $18,000 intercompany profit elimination, but the elimination also might be reflected in various other ways; for example, the investor's inventory might be reduced $18,000. [AIN-APB18, #1]

Investments in Partnerships and Unincorporated Ventures

.508 *Question*—Do the provisions of this section apply to investments in partnerships and unincorporated joint ventures? [AIN-APB18, #2]

.509 *Interpretation*—This section applies only to investments in common stock of enterprises and does not cover investments in partnerships and unincorporated joint ventures (also called undivided interests in ventures). Many of the provisions of the section would be appropriate in accounting for investments in these unincorporated entities, however, as discussed below. [AIN-APB18, #2]

.510 Partnership profits and losses accrued by investor-partners are generally reflected in their financial statements as described in paragraphs .109(c) and .109(d). Likewise, most of the other provisions of paragraph .109 would be appropriate in accounting for a partnership interest, such as the elimination of intercompany profits and losses (refer to paragraph .109(a)). [AIN-APB18, #2]

.511 However, income taxes shall be provided on the profits accrued by investor-partners regardless of the tax basis employed in the partnership return. The tax liabilities applicable to partnership interests relate directly to the partners, and the accounting for income taxes generally contemplated by [AIN-APB18, #2] Section I27 [FAS109, ¶287] is appropriate. [AIN-APB18, #2]

.512 Generally, the above discussion of partnerships also would apply to unincorporated joint ventures, particularly the elimination of intercompany profits and the accounting for income taxes. However, because the investor-venturer owns an undivided interest in each asset and is proportionately liable for its share of each liability, the provisions of paragraph .109(c) may not apply in some industries. For example, if it is the established industry practice (such as in some oil and gas venture accounting), the investor-venturer may account in its financial statements for its pro rata share of the assets, liabilities, revenues, and expenses of the venture. [AIN-APB18, #2]

Unrealized Losses on Marketable Securities Owned by an Equity Method Investee

.513 *Question*—How should a parent or investor account for its share of the [FTB79-19, ¶1] unrealized holding gains or losses on investments in debt and equity securities [FAS115, ¶135(a)] included in stockholders' equity of an investee accounted for under the equity method? [FTB79-19, ¶1]

.514 *Response*—If a subsidiary or other investee that is accounted for by the equity method is required to include unrealized holding gains and losses on investments in debt and equity securities in the stockholders' equity section of the balance sheet pursuant to the provisions of Section I80, the parent or investor shall adjust its investment in that investee by its proportionate share of the unrealized gains and losses and a like amount shall be included in the stockholders' equity section of its balance sheet. [FAS115, ¶135(b)]

(The next page is 29141.)

Sources: FASB Statement 13; FASB Statement 22; FASB Statement 23;
FASB Statement 27; FASB Statement 28; FASB Statement 29;
FASB Statement 76; FASB Statement 77; FASB Statement 91;
FASB Statement 94; FASB Statement 98; FASB Statement 109;
FASB Interpretation 19; FASB Interpretation 21;
FASB Interpretation 23; FASB Interpretation 24;
FASB Interpretation 26; FASB Interpretation 27;
FASB Technical Bulletin 79-10; FASB Technical Bulletin 79-12;
FASB Technical Bulletin 79-13; FASB Technical Bulletin 79-14;
FASB Technical Bulletin 79-15; FASB Technical Bulletin 79-16(R);
FASB Technical Bulletin 85-3; FASB Technical Bulletin 86-2;
FASB Technical Bulletin 88-1

Summary

The accounting for leases, as provided in this section, is derived from the view that a lease that transfers substantially all of the benefits and risks of ownership should be accounted for as the acquisition of an asset and the incurrence of an obligation by the lessee (a capital lease) and as a sale or financing by the lessor (a sales-type, direct financing, or leveraged lease). Other leases should be accounted for as operating leases, that is, the rental of property.

A lessee classifies a lease as either a capital lease or an operating lease. If a particular lease meets any one of the following classification criteria, it is a capital lease:

a. The lease transfers ownership of the property to the lessee by the end of the lease term.
b. The lease contains an option to purchase the leased property at a bargain price.
c. The lease term is equal to or greater than 75 percent of the estimated economic life of the leased property.
d. The present value of rental and other minimum lease payments equals or exceeds 90 percent of the fair value of the leased property less any investment tax credit retained by the lessor.

The last 2 criteria are not applicable when the beginning of the lease term falls within the last 25 percent of the total estimated economic life of the leased property.

The amount to be recorded by the lessee as an asset and an obligation under a capital lease is the lesser of the present value of the rental and other minimum lease payments or the fair value of the leased property. Leased property under a capital lease is amortized in a manner consistent with the lessee's normal depreciation policy for owned assets; the amortization period is restricted to the lease term, rather than the life of the asset, unless the lease provides for transfer of title or includes a bargain purchase option. The periodic rental payments are treated as payments of the lease obligation and interest is recorded on the remaining balance of the obligation.

If none of the criteria is met, the lease is classified as an operating lease by a lessee. Neither an asset nor an obligation is recorded for operating leases. Rental payments are recorded as rental expense in the income statement in a systematic manner, which is usually straight-line.

From the lessor's perspective, a lease is classified as a sales-type, direct financing, leveraged, or operating lease. For a lease involving real estate whose fair value is different from its carrying amount, the lease is classified as a sales-type lease if the lease transfers ownership of the property to the lessee by the end of the lease term; otherwise, such lease is classified as an operating lease. For a lease involving real estate whose fair value is the same as its carrying amount and for all leases not involving real estate, to be classified as a sales-type, direct financing, or leveraged lease, a lease must meet one of the four classification criteria specified above and *both* of the following two further criteria:

a. Collectibility of the minimum lease payments is reasonably predictable.
b. No important uncertainties surround the amount of unreimbursable costs yet to be incurred by the lessor under the lease.

A lease not involving real estate that meets those criteria is classified as a sales-type lease if the fair value of the leased property is different from its carrying amount. Otherwise, unless the lease meets certain additional criteria for leveraged leases, a lease not involving real estate that meets one of the first four criteria and both of the last two is classified as a direct financing lease. Similarly, a lease involving real estate whose fair value is the same as its carrying amount is classified as a direct financing lease if it meets one of the first four criteria and both of the last two, unless the lease meets certain additional criteria for leveraged leases. Leases that fail to meet the foregoing criteria are classified as operating leases.

For sales-type leases of real estate, the method of profit recognition is determined under Section R10, "Real Estate." For other sales-type leases, the present value of the minimum lease payments receivable from the lessee is reported as sales and the carrying amount of the leased property plus any initial direct costs, less the present value of any unguaranteed residual value, is charged as cost of sales. The lessor reports as an asset on the balance sheet the net investment in a sales-type lease calculated by recording the gross investment (the sum of the minimum lease payments and the unguaranteed residual value) at its present value, using the interest rate implicit in the lease as the discount factor. The difference between the gross investment and the net investment is unearned income, which is amortized over the lease term so as to produce a constant periodic rate of return on the net investment.

For a lease classified as a direct financing lease, the lessor reports as an asset on the balance sheet the net investment in a lease consisting of gross investment less unearned income and the unamortized initial direct costs. The gross investment is calculated by adding the minimum lease payments and the unguaranteed residual value. Unearned income is determined by subtracting the sum of the cost or carrying amount of the leased property from the gross investment. Unearned income and the initial direct costs are amortized over the lease term so as to produce a constant periodic rate of return on the net investment. The practice of recognizing a portion of the unearned income at inception of the lease to offset initial direct costs or other costs of direct financing leases is not acceptable.

A leveraged lease is a direct financing lease that additionally has all of the following characteristics:

a. It involves at least three parties: a lessee, a long-term creditor, and a lessor.
b. The financing provided by the long-term creditor is substantial to the transaction and is nonrecourse to the lessor.
c. The lessor's net investment declines during the early years and increases during the later years of the lease term.
d. Any investment tax credit retained by the lessor is accounted for as one of the cash flow components of the lease.

The lessor records the investment in a leveraged lease net of the nonrecourse debt. Income is recognized only in periods in which the net investment net of related deferred taxes is positive. The total net income over the lease term is calculated by deducting the original investment from total cash receipts. By using projected cash receipts and disbursements, the rate of return on the net investment in the years in which the investment is positive is determined and applied to the net investment to determine the periodic income to be recognized. The assumption that underlies this accounting is that the lessor will earn other income during the years in which the investment is negative (net funds are provided by the lease) and will not expect the lease to provide income during those years.

A lessor accounts for leases not meeting the criteria for classification as sales-type, direct financing, or leveraged leases as operating leases. Leased property under operating leases is recorded in the same way as other property, plant, and equipment; rent is reported as income over the lease term in a systematic manner, which is usually straight-line; and the leased property is depreciated like other productive assets.

Leases involving real estate are also addressed. Briefly, if the leased property is land only, the lease is classified as an operating lease unless it provides for transfer of title or includes a bargain purchase option. If the leased property is land and buildings, this section specifies whether and how the elements are to be separated and which criteria are to be applied. Leases that cover only part of a building are addressed and guidance is provided in determining whether the fair value of that part of a building can be determined objectively.

A sale-leaseback transaction involving real estate, including real estate with equipment, is accounted for as a sale only if the transaction qualifies as a sale under the provisions of Section R10 and the seller-lessee will actively use the property during the lease term. If the transaction does not qualify as a sale, it should be accounted for by the deposit method or as a financing.

Required disclosures of lessees and lessors are specified and special guidance is provided for various matters, including leveraged leases, leases involving real estate, leases involving related parties, subleases, the effect of business combinations on the classification of leases, and sale-leaseback transactions.

.101 This section [presents] standards of financial accounting and reporting for leases by lessees and lessors.[1] A **lease** is defined as an agreement conveying the right to use property, plant, or equipment (land or depreciable assets or both) usually for a stated period of time. It includes agreements that, although not nominally identified as leases, meet the above definition, such as a *heat supply contract* for nuclear fuel.[2] This

---

[1]Paragraphs .512 and .513 discuss the applicability of this section to current value financial statements.]

[2]Under present generally accepted accounting principles, a nuclear fuel installation constitutes a depreciable asset. Thus, a nuclear fuel lease conveys the right to use a depreciable asset, whereas contracts to supply coal or oil do not. [FAS13, ¶64] Heat supply (also called *burn-up*) contracts usually provide for payments by the user-lessee based upon nuclear fuel utilization in the period plus a charge for the unrecovered cost base. The residual value usually accrues to the lessee, and the lessor furnishes no service other than the financing. [FAS13, ¶1, fn1]

definition does not include agreements that are contracts for services that do not transfer the right to use property, plant, or equipment from one contracting party to the other. On the other hand, agreements that do transfer the right to use property, plant, or equipment meet the definition of a lease even though substantial services by the contractor (lessor) may be called for in connection with the operation or maintenance of such assets. This section does not apply to lease agreements concerning the rights to explore for or to exploit natural resources such as oil, gas, minerals, and timber. Nor does it apply to licensing agreements for items such as motion picture films, plays, manuscripts, patents, and copyrights. [FAS13, ¶1]

Classification of Leases

.102 For purposes of applying the accounting and reporting standards [herein], leases are classified as follows:

a. Classifications from the standpoint of the lessee:
  (1) *Capital leases.* Leases that meet one or more of the criteria in paragraph .103.
  (2) *Operating leases.* All other leases.
b. Classifications from the standpoint of the lessor: [FAS13, ¶6]
  (1) *Sales-type leases.* Leases that give rise to manufacturer's or dealer's profit (or loss) to the lessor (that is, the **fair value of the leased property** at the **inception of the lease** is greater or less than its cost or carrying amount, if different) and that meet one or more of the criteria in paragraph .103 and both of the criteria in paragraph .104, except as indicated in the following sentence. A lease involving real estate shall be classified as a sales-type lease only if it meets the criterion in paragraph .103(a), in which case the criteria in paragraph .104 do not apply. [FAS98, ¶22c] Normally, sales-type leases will arise when manufacturers or dealers use leasing as a means of marketing their products. Leases involving lessors that are primarily engaged in financing operations normally will not be sales-type leases if they qualify under paragraphs .103 and .104, but will most often be **direct financing leases,** described in paragraph .102(b)(2) below. However, a lessor need not be a dealer to realize dealer's profit (or loss) on a transaction, for example, if a lessor, not a dealer, leases an asset that at the inception of the lease has a fair value that is greater or less than its cost or carrying amount, if different, such a transaction is a sales-type lease, assuming the criteria referred to are met. [FAS13, ¶6] Leases of a manufacturing company's equipment sold to a leasing subsidiary that are accounted for as direct financing leases on the subsidiary's financial statements normally would be sales-type capital leases in the consolidated financial statements. [FAS94, ¶52] A **renewal or extension** of an existing sales-type or direct financing lease that otherwise qualifies as a sales-type lease shall be classified as a direct financing lease unless the renewal or extension occurs at or near the end of the original term[3] specified in the existing lease, in which case it shall be classified as a

[3]A renewal or extension that occurs in the last few months of an existing lease is considered to have occurred at or near the end of the existing **lease term.** [FAS27, ¶6]

sales-type lease (refer to paragraph .113(f)). [FAS27, ¶6]

(2) *Direct financing leases.* Leases other than **leveraged leases** that do not give rise to manufacturer's or dealer's profit (or loss) to the lessor but that meet one or more of the criteria in paragraph .103 and both of the criteria in paragraph .104. In such leases, the cost or carrying amount, if different, and fair value of the leased property are the same at the inception of the lease. [FAS13, ¶6] An exception arises when an existing sales-type or direct financing lease is renewed or extended[4] during the term of the existing lease. [FAS27, ¶7] In such cases, the fact that the carrying amount of the property at the end of the original lease term is different from its fair value at that date shall not preclude the classification of the renewal or extension as a direct financing lease (refer to paragraph .113(f)).

(3) *Leveraged leases.* Leases that meet the criteria of paragraph .144. [FAS13, ¶6]

(4) *Operating leases.* All other leases, including leases that involve real estate and give rise to manufacturer's or dealer's profit (or loss) to the lessor but do not meet the criterion in paragraph .103(a). [FAS98, ¶22d]

Criteria for Classifying Leases (Other Than Leveraged Leases)

.103 The criteria for classifying leases set forth in this paragraph and in paragraph .104 derive from the concept [FAS13, ¶7] that a lease that transfers substantially all of the benefits and risks incident to the ownership of property should be accounted for as the acquisition of an asset and the incurrence of an obligation by the lessee and as a sale or financing by the lessor. All other leases should be accounted for as operating leases. In a lease that transfers substantially all of the benefits and risks of ownership, the economic effect on the parties is similar, in many respects, to that of an installment purchase. [FAS13, ¶60] If at its inception a lease meets one or more of the following four criteria, the lease shall be classified as a capital lease by the lessee. Otherwise, it shall be classified as an operating lease. (Refer to paragraph .150 and Exhibit 150C for an illustration of the application of these criteria.)

a. The lease transfers ownership of the property to the lessee by the end of the lease term.[4a]

b. The lease contains a **bargain purchase option.**

c. The lease term is equal to 75 percent or more of the estimated economic life of the leased property. However, if the beginning of the lease term falls within the last 25 percent of the total **estimated economic life of the leased property,** including earlier years of use, this criterion shall not be used for purposes of classifying the lease.

---

[4] Refer to paragraph .419. [FAS13, ¶6, fn10]

[4a]This criterion is met in situations in which the lease agreement provides for the transfer of title at or shortly after the end of the lease term in exchange for the payment of a nominal fee, for example, the minimum required by statutory regulation to transfer title. [FAS98, ¶22e]

d. The present value[5] at the beginning of the lease term of the **minimum lease payments,** excluding that portion of the payments representing **executory costs,** to be paid by the lessor, including any profit thereon, equals or exceeds 90 percent of the excess of the fair value of the leased property to the lessor at the inception of the lease over any related investment tax credit retained by the lessor and expected to be realized by [the lessor].[6] However, if the beginning of the lease term falls within the last 25 percent of the total estimated economic life of the leased property, including earlier years of use, this criterion shall not be used for purposes of classifying the lease. A lessor shall compute the present value of the minimum lease payments using the interest rate implicit in the lease. A lessee shall compute the present value of the minimum lease payments using its incremental borrowing rate, unless (1) it is practicable for [the lessee] to learn the implicit rate computed by the lessor and (2) the implicit rate computed by the lessor is less than the lessee's incremental borrowing rate. If both of those conditions are met, the lessee shall use the implicit rate. [FAS13, ¶7]

.104 From the standpoint of the lessor, a lease involving real estate shall be classified as a sales-type lease only if it meets the criterion in paragraph .103(a) as appropriate under paragraph .102(b)(1). Otherwise, if the lease at inception meets any one of the four criteria in paragraph .103 and in addition meets both of the following criteria, it shall be classified as a sales-type lease, a direct financing lease, a leveraged lease, or an operating lease as appropriate under paragraph .102(b). If the lease does not meet any of the criteria of paragraph .103 or both of the following criteria, the lease shall be classified as an operating lease.

a. Collectibility of the minimum lease payments is reasonably predictable. A lessor shall not be precluded from classifying a lease as a sales-type lease, a direct financing lease, or a leveraged lease simply because the receivable is subject to an estimate of uncollectibility based on experience with groups of similar receivables. [FAS98, ¶22f]
b. No important uncertainties surround the amount of unreimbursable costs yet to be incurred by the lessor under the lease.[7] Important uncertainties might include commitments by the lessor to guarantee performance of the leased property in a manner more extensive than the typical product warranty or to effectively protect the lessee from obsolescence of the leased property. However, the necessity of estimating executory costs to be paid by the lessor (refer to paragraphs .113(a) and .114(a)) shall not by itself constitute an important uncertainty as referred to herein. [FAS13, ¶8]

---

[5]Refer to paragraphs .509 through .511 for supplemental guidance on the interest rate to be used in calculating the present value of minimum lease payments.]

[6]The 90-percent test is stated as a lower limit rather than as a guideline. [FIN19, ¶4]

[7]If the property covered by the lease is yet to be constructed or has not been acquired by the lessor at the inception of the lease, the classification criterion of paragraph .104(b) shall be applied at the date that construction of the property is completed or the property is acquired by the lessor. [FAS23, ¶7]

.105 If at any time the lessee and lessor agree to change the provisions of the lease, other than by renewing the lease or extending its term, in a manner that would have resulted in a different classification of the lease under the criteria in paragraphs .103 and .104 had the changed terms been in effect at the inception of the lease, the revised agreement shall be considered as a new agreement over its term, and the criteria in paragraphs .103 and .104 shall be applied for purposes of classifying the new lease. Likewise, except when a guarantee or **penalty** is rendered inoperative as described in paragraphs .108 and .113(e), any action that extends the lease beyond the expiration of the existing lease term, such as the exercise of a lease renewal option other than those already included in the lease term, shall be considered as a new agreement, which shall be classified according to the provisions of paragraphs .102 through .104. Changes in estimates (for example, changes in estimates of the economic life or of the residual value of the leased property) or changes in circumstances (for example, default by the lessee), however, shall not give rise to a new classification of a lease for accounting purposes. [FAS13, ¶9]

Accounting and Reporting by Lessees

Capital Leases

.106 The lessee shall record a capital lease as an asset and an obligation at an amount equal to the present value at the beginning of the lease term of minimum lease payments during the lease term, excluding that portion of the payments representing executory costs to be paid by the lessor, together with any profit thereon. However, if the amount so determined exceeds the fair value of the leased property at the inception of the lease, the amount recorded as the asset and obligation shall be the fair value.[8] If the portion of the minimum lease payments representing executory costs, including profit thereon, is not determinable from the provisions of the lease, an estimate of the amount shall be made. The discount rate to be used in determining present value of the minimum lease payments shall be that prescribed for the lessee in paragraph .103(d). (Refer to paragraph .150 and Exhibit 150C for an illustration.) [FAS13, ¶10]

.107 Except as provided in paragraphs .121 and .122 with respect to leases involving land, the asset recorded under a capital lease shall be amortized as follows:

a.   If the lease meets the criterion of either paragraph .103(a) or .103(b), the asset shall be amortized in a manner consistent with the lessee's normal depreciation policy for owned assets.

---

[8]If the lease agreement or commitment, if earlier, includes a provision to escalate minimum lease payments for increases in construction or acquisition cost of the leased property or for increases in some other measure of cost or value, such as general price levels, during the construction or preacquisition period, the effect of any increases that have occurred shall be considered in the determination of "fair value of the leased property at the inception of the lease" for purposes of this paragraph. [FAS23, ¶8]

b. If the lease does not meet either criterion .103(a) or .103(b), the asset shall be amortized in a manner consistent with the lessee's normal depreciation policy except that the period of amortization shall be the lease term. The asset shall be amortized to its expected value, if any, to the lessee at the end of the lease term. As an example, if the lessee guarantees a residual value at the end of the lease term and has no interest in any excess which might be realized, the expected value of the leased property to [the lessee] is the amount that can be realized from it up to the amount of the guarantee. [FAS13, ¶11]

.108 During the lease term, each minimum lease payment shall be allocated between a reduction of the obligation and interest expense so as to produce a constant periodic rate of interest on the remaining balance of the obligation.[9] (Refer to paragraph .150 for illustrations.) In leases containing a residual guarantee by the lessee or a penalty for failure to renew the lease at the end of the lease term,[10] following the above method of amortization will result in a balance of the obligation at the end of the lease term that will equal the amount of the guarantee or penalty at that date. In the event that a renewal or extension of the lease term renders the guarantee or penalty inoperative, the asset and the obligation under the lease shall be adjusted by an amount equal to the difference between the present value of the future minimum lease payments under the revised agreement and the present balance of the obligation. The present value of the future minimum lease payments under the revised agreement shall be computed using the rate of interest used to record the lease initially. In accordance with paragraph .105, other renewals and extensions of the lease term shall be considered new agreements, which shall be accounted for in accordance with the provisions of paragraph .109. [FAS13, ¶12] **Contingent rentals** shall be included in the determination of income as accruable. [FAS29, ¶13] [(Refer to paragraph .165 for an illustration involving contingent rentals.)]

.109 Except for a change in the provisions of a lease that results from a refunding by the lessor of tax-exempt debt, including an advance refunding in which the perceived economic advantages of the refunding are passed through to the lessee by a change in the provisions of the lease agreement and the revised agreement is classified as a capital lease (refer to paragraph .110), a change in the provisions of a lease, a renewal or extension of an existing lease, and a termination of a lease prior to the expiration of the lease term shall be accounted for as follows: [FAS22, ¶14]

a. If the provisions of the lease are changed in a way that changes the amount of the remaining minimum lease payments and the change either (1) does not give rise to a new agreement under the provisions of paragraph .105 or (2)

---

[9]This is the *interest* method described in Section I69, "Interest: Imputation of an Interest Cost," paragraph .108 and footnote 4. [FAS13, ¶12, fn11]

[10]Residual guarantees and termination penalties that serve to extend the lease term are excluded from minimum lease payments and are thus distinguished from those guarantees and penalties referred to in this paragraph. [FAS13, ¶12, fn12]

does give rise to a new agreement but such agreement is also classified as a capital lease, the present balances of the asset and the obligation shall be adjusted by an amount equal to the difference between the present value of the future minimum lease payments under the revised or new agreement and the present balance of the obligation. The present value of the future minimum lease payments under the revised or new agreement shall be computed using the rate of interest used to record the lease initially. If the change in the lease provisions gives rise to a new agreement classified as an operating lease, the asset and obligation under the lease shall be removed, gain or loss shall be recognized for the difference, and the new lease agreement shall thereafter be accounted for as any other operating lease.

b. Except when a guarantee or penalty is rendered inoperative as described in paragraph .108, a renewal or an extension of an existing lease shall be accounted for as follows:

    (1) If the renewal or extension is classified as a capital lease, it shall be accounted for as described in subparagraph (a) above.

    (2) If the renewal or extension is classified as an operating lease, the existing lease shall continue to be accounted for as a capital lease to the end of its original term, and the renewal or extension shall be accounted for as any other operating lease.

c. A termination of a capital lease shall be accounted for by removing the asset and obligation, with gain or loss recognized for the difference.[11] [FAS13, ¶14]

.110 If prior to the expiration of the lease term a change in the provisions of the lease results from a refunding by the lessor of tax-exempt debt, including an advance refunding,[12] in which the perceived economic advantages of the refunding are passed through to the lessee and the revised agreement is classified as a capital lease by the lessee, the change shall be accounted for [by the lessee] as follows:

a. If a change in the provisions of a lease results from a refunding by the lessor of tax-exempt debt, including an advance refunding that is accounted for as an early extinguishment of debt, the lessee shall adjust the lease obligation to the present value of the future minimum lease payments under the revised lease using the effective interest rate applicable to the revised agreement and

---

[11] The termination of the capital lease that results from the purchase of a leased asset by the lessee is not the type of transaction contemplated by this paragraph but rather is an integral part of the purchase of the leased asset. The purchase by the lessee of property under a capital lease shall be accounted for like a renewal or extension of a capital lease that, in turn, is classified as a capital lease, that is, any difference between the purchase price and the carrying amount of the lease obligation shall be recorded as an adjustment of the carrying amount of the asset. [FIN26, ¶5]

[12] An advance refunding involves the issuance of new debt to replace existing debt with the proceeds from the new debt placed in trust or otherwise restricted to retire the existing debt at a determinable future date or dates. [FAS22, ¶1, fn1] Section D14, "Debt: Extinguishments," provides criteria for determining whether the advance refunding should be recognized as an extinguishment of the existing debt at the date of the advance refunding. [FAS76, ¶10]

shall recognize any resulting gain or loss currently as a gain or loss on early extinguishment of debt. Any gain or loss so determined shall be classified in accordance with Section D14, "Debt: Extinguishments." [Paragraphs .162 and .163 illustrate the accounting prescribed by this subparagraph.]

b. If the provisions of a lease are changed in connection with an advance refunding by the lessor of tax-exempt debt that is not accounted for as an early extinguishment of debt at the date of the advance refunding and the lessee is obligated to reimburse the lessor for any costs related to the debt to be refunded that have been or will be incurred, such as unamortized discount or issue costs or a call premium, the lessee shall accrue those costs by the *interest* method[13] over the period from the date of the advance refunding to the call date of the debt to be refunded. [FAS22, ¶12]

Operating Leases

.111 Normally, rental on an operating lease shall be charged to expense over the lease term as it becomes payable. If rental payments are not made on a straight-line basis,[13a] rental expense nevertheless shall be recognized on a straight-line basis unless another systematic and rational basis is more representative of the time pattern in which use benefit is derived from the leased property, in which case that basis shall be used. [FAS13, ¶15]

Disclosures

.112 The following information with respect to leases shall be disclosed in the lessee's financial statements or the footnotes thereto. (Refer to paragraphs .151 and .152 for illustrations.)

a. For capital leases:
    (1) The gross amount of assets recorded under capital leases as of the date of each balance sheet presented by major classes according to nature or function. This information may be combined with the comparable information for owned assets.
    (2) Future *minimum lease payments* as of the date of the latest balance sheet presented, in the aggregate and for each of the five succeeding fiscal years, with separate deductions from the total for the amount representing *executory costs,* including any profit thereon, included in the *minimum lease payments* and for the amount of the imputed interest necessary to reduce the net *minimum lease payments* to present value.
    (3) The total of minimum sublease rentals to be received in the future under noncancelable subleases as of the date of the latest balance sheet presented.

---

[13]Refer to paragraph .108 and footnote 9 thereto. [FAS22, ¶12, fn3]

[[13a]Refer to paragraphs .525 through .527F for supplemental guidance on accounting for operating leases with scheduled rent increases and lease incentives.]

(4) Total *contingent rentals* actually incurred for each period for which an income statement is presented. [FAS13, ¶16]

(5) Assets recorded under capital leases and the accumulated amortization thereon shall be separately identified in the lessee's balance sheet or in footnotes thereto. Likewise, the related obligations shall be separately identified in the balance sheet as obligations under capital leases and shall be subject to the same considerations as other obligations in classifying them with current and noncurrent liabilities in classified balance sheets. Unless the charge to income resulting from amortization of assets recorded under capital leases is included with depreciation expense and the fact that it is so included is disclosed, the amortization charge shall be separately disclosed in the financial statements or footnotes thereto. [FAS13, ¶13]

b. For operating leases having initial or remaining noncancelable *lease terms* in excess of one year:

(1) Future minimum rental payments required as of the date of the latest balance sheet presented, in the aggregate and for each of the five succeeding fiscal years.

(2) The total of minimum rentals to be received in the future under noncancelable subleases as of the date of the latest balance sheet presented.

c. For all operating leases, rental expense for each period for which an income statement is presented, with separate amounts for minimum rentals, contingent rentals, and sublease rentals. Rental payments under leases with *terms* of a month or less that were not renewed need not be included.

d. A general description of the lessee's leasing arrangements including, but not limited to, the following:

(1) The basis on which contingent rental payments are determined.

(2) The existence and terms of renewal or purchase options and escalation clauses.

(3) Restrictions imposed by lease agreements, such as those concerning dividends, additional debt, and further leasing. [FAS13, ¶16]

Accounting and Reporting by Lessors

Sales-Type Leases

.113 Sales-type leases shall be accounted for by the lessor as follows:

a. The minimum lease payments (net of amounts, if any, included therein with respect to executory costs to be paid by the lessor, together with any profit thereon) plus the **unguaranteed residual value** accruing to the benefit of the lessor shall be recorded as the gross investment in the lease.[13b] [FAS13, ¶17] The estimated residual value used to compute the unguaranteed residual value accruing to the benefit of the lessor shall not exceed the amount estimated at the inception of the

---

[13b]Paragraphs .536 and .537 further discuss residual value retained by a lessor that sells rental payments.]

lease.[14] [FAS23, ¶9] However, if the sales-type lease involves real estate, the lessor shall account for the transaction under the provisions of Section R10, "Real Estate," in the same manner as a *seller* of the same property. [FAS98, ¶22g]

b. The difference between the gross investment in the lease in (a) above and the sum of the present values of the two components of the gross investment shall be recorded as unearned income. The discount rate to be used in determining the present values shall be the interest rate implicit in the lease. The net investment in the lease shall consist of the gross investment less the unearned income. The unearned income shall be amortized to income over the lease term so as to produce a constant periodic rate of return on the net investment in the lease.[15] However, other methods of income recognition may be used if the results obtained are not materially different from those which would result from the prescribed method. The net investment in the lease shall be subject to the same considerations as other assets in classification as current or noncurrent assets in a classified balance sheet. [FAS13, ¶17] Contingent rentals shall be included in the determination of income as accruable. [FAS29, ¶13] [(Refer to paragraph .165 for an illustration involving contingent rentals.)]

c. The present value of the minimum lease payments (net of executory costs, including any profit thereon), computed at the interest rate implicit in the lease, shall be recorded as the sales price. The cost or carrying amount, if different, of the leased property, plus any **initial direct costs,** less the present value of the unguaranteed residual value accruing to the benefit of the lessor, computed at the interest rate implicit in the lease, shall be charged against income in the same period.

d. The estimated residual value shall be reviewed at least annually.[16] If the review results in a lower estimate than had been previously established, a determination must be made as to whether the decline in estimated residual value is other than temporary. If the decline in estimated residual value is judged to be other than temporary, the accounting for the transaction shall be revised using the changed estimate. The resulting reduction in the net investment shall be recognized as a loss in the period in which the estimate is changed. An upward adjustment of the estimated residual value shall not be made.

---

[14]If the lease agreement or commitment, if earlier, includes a provision to escalate minimum lease payments for increases in construction or acquisition cost of the leased property or for increases in some other measure of cost or value, such as general price levels, during the construction or preacquisition period, the effect of any increases that have occurred shall be considered in the determination of "the **estimated residual value of the leased property** at the inception of the lease" for purposes of this paragraph. [FAS23, ¶9]

[15]This is the interest method described in Section 169, paragraph .108 and footnote 4. [FAS13, ¶12, fn11]

[16]Paragraphs .514 through .517 discuss upward adjustment of guaranteed residual values.]

e. In leases containing a residual guarantee or a penalty for failure to renew the lease at the end of the lease term,[17] following the method of amortization described in (b) above will result in a balance of minimum lease payments receivable at the end of the lease term that will equal the amount of the guarantee or penalty at that date. In the event that a renewal or other extension of the lease term renders the guarantee or penalty inoperative, the existing balances of the minimum lease payments receivable and the estimated residual value shall be adjusted for the changes resulting from the revised agreement (subject to the limitation on the residual value imposed by subparagraph (d) above) and the net adjustment shall be charged or credited to unearned income. [FAS13, ¶17]

f. Except for a change in the provisions of a lease that results from a refunding by the lessor of tax-exempt debt, including an advance refunding, in which the perceived economic advantages of the refunding are passed through to the lessee by a change in the provisions of the lease agreement and the revised agreement is classified as a direct financing lease (refer to paragraph .110), a change in the provisions of a lease, a renewal or extension of an existing lease, and a termination of a lease prior to the expiration of the lease term shall be accounted for as follows: [FAS22, ¶15]

    (1) If the provisions of a lease are changed in a way that changes the amount of the remaining minimum lease payments and the change either (a) does not give rise to a new agreement under the provisions of paragraph .105 or (b) does give rise to a new agreement but such agreement is classified as a direct financing lease, the balance of the minimum lease payments receivable and the estimated residual value, if affected, shall be adjusted to reflect the change (subject to the limitation on the residual value imposed by subparagraph (d) above), and the net adjustment shall be charged or credited to unearned income. If the change in the lease provisions gives rise to a new agreement classified as an operating lease, the remaining net investment shall be removed from the accounts, the leased asset shall be recorded as an asset at the lower of its original cost, present fair value, or present carrying amount, and the net adjustment shall be charged to income of the period. The new lease shall thereafter be accounted for as any other operating lease.

    (2) Except when a guarantee or penalty is rendered inoperative as described in subparagraph (e) above, a renewal or an extension of an existing lease shall be accounted for as follows:

        (a) If the renewal or extension is classified as a direct financing lease, it shall be accounted for as described in subparagraph (f)(1) above.

        (b) If the renewal or extension is classified as an operating lease, the existing lease shall continue to be accounted for as a sales-type lease to the end of its original term, and the renewal or extension shall be

[17]Residual guarantees and termination penalties that serve to extend the lease term are excluded from minimum lease payments and are thus distinguished from those guarantees and penalties referred to in this paragraph. [FAS13, ¶17, fn17]

accounted for as any other operating lease. [FAS13, ¶17]

(c) If a renewal or extension that occurs at or near the end of the term[18] of the existing lease is classified as a sales-type lease, the renewal or extension shall be accounted for as a sales-type lease. [FAS27, ¶8]

(3) A termination of the lease shall be accounted for by removing the net investment from the accounts, recording the leased asset at the lower of its original cost, present fair value, or present carrying amount, and the net adjustment shall be charged to income of the period. [FAS13, ¶17]

g. If prior to the expiration of the lease term a change in the provisions of a lease results from a refunding by the lessor of tax-exempt debt, including an advance refunding,[19] in which the perceived economic advantages of the refunding are passed through to the lessee and the revised agreement is classified as a direct financing lease by the lessor, the change shall be accounted for as follows:[20]

(1) If a change in the provisions of a lease results from a refunding of tax-exempt debt, including an advance refunding that is accounted for as an early extinguishment of debt, the lessor shall adjust the balance of the minimum lease payments receivable and the estimated residual value, if affected (that is, the gross investment in the lease), in accordance with the requirements of paragraphs .114(c) and .113(f)(1). The adjustment of unearned income shall be the amount required to adjust the net investment in the lease to the sum of the present values of the two components of the gross investment based on the interest rate applicable to the revised lease agreement. The combined adjustment resulting from applying the two preceding sentences shall be recognized as a gain or loss in the current period. [Paragraphs .162 and .163 illustrate the accounting prescribed by this paragraph.]

(2) If a change in the provisions of the lease results from an advance refunding that is not accounted for as an early extinguishment of debt at the date of the advance refunding, the lessor shall systematically recognize, as revenue, any reimbursements to be received from the lessee for costs related to the debt to be refunded, such as unamortized discount or issue costs or a call premium, over the period from the date of the advance refunding to the call date of debt to be refunded. [FAS22, ¶12]

---

[18]A renewal or extension that occurs in the last few months of an existing lease is considered to have occurred at or near the end of the existing lease term. [FAS27, ¶8]

[19]An advance refunding involves the issuance of new debt to replace existing debt with the proceeds from the new debt placed in trust or otherwise restricted to retire the existing debt at a determinable future date or dates. [FAS22, ¶1, fn1] Section D14, "Debt: Extinguishments," provides criteria for determining whether the advance refunding should be recognized as an extinguishment of the existing debt at the date of the advance refunding. [FAS76, ¶10]

[20]This paragraph prescribes the accounting for a direct financing lease by governmental units that classify and account for leases of that kind. [FAS22, ¶12, fn4]

Direct Financing Leases

.114 Direct financing leases shall be accounted for by the lessor as follows (refer to paragraph .150 for illustrations): [FAS13, ¶18]

a. The sum of (1) the minimum lease payments (net of amounts, if any, included therein with respect to executory costs, such as maintenance, taxes, and insurance, to be paid by the lessor, together with any profit thereon) and (2) the unguaranteed residual value accruing to the benefit of the lessor shall be recorded as the gross investment in the lease.[20a] The estimated residual value used to compute the unguaranteed residual value accruing to the benefit of the lessor shall not exceed the amount estimated at the inception of the lease.[21] [FAS98, ¶22h]

b. The difference between the gross investment in the lease in (a) above and the cost or carrying amount, if different, of the leased property shall be recorded as unearned income. The net investment in the lease shall consist of the gross investment plus any unamortized initial direct costs less the unearned income. The unearned income and initial direct costs shall be amortized to income over the lease term[21a] so as to produce a constant periodic rate of return on the net investment in the lease.[22] However, other methods of income recognition may be used if the results obtained are not materially different from those that would result from the prescribed method in the preceding sentence. The net investment in the lease shall be subject to the same considerations as other assets in classification as current or noncurrent assets in a classified balance sheet. Contingent rentals shall be included in the determination of income as accruable. [FAS98, ¶22i]

c. In leases containing a residual guarantee or penalty for failure to renew the lease at the end of the lease term,[23] the lessor shall follow the accounting procedure described in paragraph .113(e). The accounting provisions of paragraphs .113(f) and .113(g) with respect to renewals and extensions not dealt with in paragraph .113(e), terminations, and other changes in lease provisions shall also be followed with respect to direct financing leases.

[20a]Paragraphs .536 and .537 further discuss residual value retained by a lessor that sells rental payments.]

[21]If the lease agreement or commitment, if earlier, includes a provision to escalate minimum lease payments for increases in construction or acquisition cost of the leased property or for increases in some other measure of cost or value, such as general price levels, during the construction or preacquisition period, the effect of any increases that have occurred shall be considered in the determination of "the estimated residual value of the leased property at the inception of the lease" for purposes of this paragraph. [FAS23, ¶9]

[21a]The practice of accelerating the recognition of lease finance revenues to offset initial direct costs or other costs of direct financing leases [is not] acceptable. [FAS91, ¶44]

[22]This is the interest method described in Section I69, paragraph .108 and footnote 4, [FAS13, ¶12, fn11] [and in Section L20, "Lending Activities," paragraph .117].

[23]Residual guarantees and termination penalties that serve to extend the lease term are excluded from minimum lease payments and are thus distinguished from those guarantees and penalties referred to in this paragraph. [FAS13, ¶12, fn12]

d. The estimated residual value shall be reviewed at least annually[24] and, if neces-
    sary, adjusted in the manner prescribed in paragraph .113(d). [FAS13, ¶18]

Operating Leases

.115 Operating leases shall be accounted for by the lessor as follows:

a. The leased property shall be included with or near property, plant, and equipment
    in the balance sheet. The property shall be depreciated following the lessor's nor-
    mal depreciation policy, and in the balance sheet the accumulated depreciation
    shall be deducted from the investment in the leased property.
b. Rent shall be reported as income over the lease term as it becomes receivable
    according to the provisions of the lease. However, if the rentals vary from a
    straight-line basis,[24a] the income shall be recognized on a straight-line basis
    unless another systematic and rational basis is more representative of the time
    pattern in which use benefit from the leased property is diminished, in which case
    that basis shall be used.
c. Initial direct costs shall be deferred and allocated over the lease term in propor-
    tion to the recognition of rental income. However, initial direct costs may be
    charged to expense as incurred if the effect is not materially different from that
    which would have resulted from the use of the method prescribed in the preceding
    sentence. [FAS13, ¶19]
d. If, at the inception of the lease, the fair value of the property in an operating lease
    involving real estate that would have been classified as a sales-type lease except
    that it did not meet the criterion in paragraph .103(a) is less than its cost or carry-
    ing amount, if different, then a loss equal to that difference shall be recognized at
    the inception of the lease. [FAS98, ¶22j]

Participation by Third Parties

.116 The sale or assignment of a lease or of property subject to a lease that was
accounted for as a sales-type lease or direct financing lease shall not negate the
original accounting treatment accorded the lease. [FAS13, ¶20] Any profit or loss on
the sale or assignment shall be recognized at the time of the transaction except that (a)
if the sale or assignment is between **related parties,** the provisions of paragraphs .125
and .126 shall be applied or (b) if the sale or assignment is with recourse, it shall be
accounted for in accordance with Section R20, "Receivables Sold with Recourse."
[FAS77, ¶10]

.117 The sale of property subject to an operating lease, or of property that is leased
by or intended to be leased by the third-party purchaser to another party, shall not be

---

[24]Paragraphs .514 through .517 discuss upward adjustment of guaranteed residual values.]

[24a]Refer to paragraphs .525 through .527F for supplemental guidance on accounting for operating
leases with scheduled rent increases and lease incentives.]

treated as a sale if the seller or any party related to the seller retains substantial risks of ownership in the leased property. A seller may by various arrangements assure recovery of the investment by the third-party purchaser in some operating lease transactions and thus retain substantial risks in connection with the property. For example, in the case of default by the lessee or termination of the lease, the arrangements may involve a formal or informal commitment by the seller to (a) acquire the lease or the property, (b) substitute an existing lease, or (c) secure a replacement lessee or a buyer for the property under a remarketing agreement. However, a remarketing agreement by itself shall not disqualify accounting for the transaction as a sale if the seller (1) will receive a reasonable fee commensurate with the effort involved at the time of securing a replacement lessee or buyer for the property and (2) is not required to give priority to the re-leasing or disposition of the property owned by the third-party purchaser over similar property owned or produced by the seller. (For example, a first-in, first-out remarketing arrangement is considered to be a priority.) [FAS13, ¶21]

.118 If a sale to a third party of property subject to an operating lease or of property that is leased by or intended to be leased by the third-party purchaser to another party is not to be recorded as a sale because of the provisions of paragraph .117, the transaction shall be accounted for as a borrowing. (Transactions of these types are in effect collateralized borrowings.) The proceeds from the *sale* shall be recorded as an obligation on the books of the *seller*. Until that obligation has been amortized under the procedure described herein, rental payments made by the lessee(s) under the operating lease or leases shall be recorded as revenue by the *seller,* even if such rentals are paid directly to the third-party purchaser. A portion of each rental shall be recorded by the *seller* as interest expense, with the remainder to be recorded as a reduction of the obligation. The interest expense shall be calculated by application of a rate determined in accordance with the provisions of Section I69, paragraphs .106 and .107. The leased property shall be accounted for as prescribed in paragraph .115(a) for an operating lease, except that the term over which the asset is depreciated shall be limited to the estimated amortization period of the obligation. The sale or assignment by the lessor of lease payments due under an operating lease shall be accounted for as a borrowing as described above. [FAS13, ¶22]

Disclosures

.119 When leasing, exclusive of leveraged leasing, is a significant part of the lessor's business activities in terms of revenue, net income, or assets, the following information with respect to leases shall be disclosed in the financial statements or footnotes thereto (refer to paragraphs .151 and .153 for illustrations):

a. For sales-type and direct financing leases: [FAS13, ¶23]
   (1) The components of the net investment in sales-type and direct financing leases as of the date of each balance sheet presented:
      (a) Future minimum lease payments to be received, with separate deductions

for (i) amounts representing executory costs, including any profit thereon, included in the minimum lease payments and (ii) the accumulated allowance for uncollectible minimum lease payments receivable.

(b) The unguaranteed residual values accruing to the benefit of the lessor.

(c) For direct financing leases only, initial direct costs (see paragraph .411).

(d) Unearned income (refer to paragraphs .113(b) and .114(b)). [FAS91, ¶25d]

(2) Future minimum lease payments to be received for each of the five succeeding fiscal years as of the date of the latest balance sheet presented.

(3) [Deleted 12/86 because of the issuance of FASB Statement 91, *Accounting for Nonrefundable Fees and Costs Associated with Originating or Acquiring Loans and Initial Direct Costs of Leases.*]

(4) Total contingent rentals included in income for each period for which an income statement is presented.

b. For operating leases:

(1) The cost and carrying amount, if different, of property on lease or held for leasing by major classes of property according to nature or function, and the amount of accumulated depreciation in total as of the date of the latest balance sheet presented.

(2) Minimum future rentals on noncancelable leases as of the date of the latest balance sheet presented, in the aggregate and for each of the five succeeding fiscal years.

(3) Total contingent rentals included in income for each period for which an income statement is presented.

c. A general description of the lessor's leasing arrangements. [FAS13, ¶23]

Leases Involving Real Estate

.120 For purposes of this section, leases involving real estate can be divided into four categories: (a) leases involving land only, (b) leases involving land and building(s), (c) leases involving equipment as well as real estate, and (d) leases involving only part of a building. [FAS13, ¶24]

Leases Involving Land Only

.121 If land is the sole item of property leased and the criterion in either paragraph .103(a) or .103(b) is met, the lessee shall account for the lease as a capital lease otherwise, as an operating lease. If the lease gives rise to manufacturer's or dealer's profit (or loss) and the criterion of paragraph .103(a) is met, the lessor shall classify the lease as a sales-type lease as appropriate under paragraph .102(b)(1) and account for the transaction under the provisions of Section R10 in the same manner as a *seller* of the same property. If the lease does not give rise to manufacturer's or dealer's profit (or loss) and the criterion of paragraph .103(a) and both criteria of paragraph .104 are met, the lessor shall account for the lease as a direct financing lease or a leveraged lease as appropriate under paragraph .102(b). If the criterion of paragraph .103(b) and both criteria of paragraph .104 are met, the lessor shall account for the lease as a direct financing lease, a leveraged lease, or an operating lease as appropriate under paragraph .102(b). If the lease does not meet the criteria of paragraph .104, the lessor shall account for the lease as an operating lease. [FAS98, ¶22k] Criteria .103(c) and .103(d) are not applicable to land leases. Because ownership of the land is expected to pass to the lessee if either criterion .103(a) or .103(b) is met, the asset recorded under the capital lease would not normally be amortized. [FAS13, ¶25]

Leases Involving Land and Buildings

.122 Leases involving both land and building(s) shall be accounted for as follows:

a. Lease meets either criterion .103(a) or .103(b):
   (1) Lessee's accounting: If either criterion (a) or (b) of paragraph .103 is met, the land and building shall be separately capitalized by the lessee. For this purpose, the present value of the minimum lease payments after deducting executory costs, including any profit thereon, shall be allocated between the two elements in proportion to their fair values at the inception of the lease.[25] The building shall be amortized in accordance with the provisions of paragraph .107(a). As stated in paragraph .121, land capitalized under a lease that meets criterion (a) or (b) of paragraph .103 would not normally be amortized. [FAS13, ¶26]
   (2) Lessor's accounting if the lease meets criterion .103(a): If the lease gives rise to manufacturer's or dealer's profit (or loss), the lessor shall classify the lease as a sales-type lease as appropriate under paragraph .102(b)(1) and account for the lease as a single unit under the provisions of Section R10 in the same manner as a *seller* of the same property. If the lease does not give rise to manufacturer's or dealer's profit (or loss) and meets both criteria of paragraph .104, the lessor shall account for the lease as a direct financing lease or a leveraged lease as appropriate under paragraph .102(b)(2) or .102(b)(3). If the lease does not give rise to manufacturer's or dealer's profit (or loss) and does not meet both criteria of paragraph .104, the lessor shall account for the lease as an operating lease.
   (3) Lessor's accounting if the lease meets criterion .103(b): If the lease gives rise to manufacturer's or dealer's profit (or loss), the lessor shall classify the lease as an operating lease as appropriate under paragraph .102(b)(4). If the lease does not give rise to manufacturer's or dealer's profit (or loss) and meets both criteria of paragraph .104, the lessor shall account for the lease as a direct financing lease or a leveraged lease as appropriate under paragraph .102(b)(2) or .102(b)(3). If the lease does not give rise to manufacturer's or dealer's profit (or loss) and does not meet both criteria of paragraph .104, the lessor shall account for the lease as an operating lease. [FAS98, ¶22l]

---

[25]If the lease agreement or commitment, if earlier, includes a provision to escalate *minimum lease payments* for increases in construction or acquisition cost of the leased property or for increases in some other measure of cost or value, such as general price levels, during the construction or preacquisition period, the effect of any increases that have occurred shall be considered in the determination of "fair value of the leased property at the inception of the lease" for purposes of this paragraph. [FAS23, ¶8]

b. Lease meets neither criterion .103(a) nor .103(b):
  (1) If the fair value of the land is less than 25 percent of the total fair value of the leased property at the inception of the lease: Both the lessee and the lessor shall consider the land and the building as a single unit for purposes of applying the criteria of paragraphs .103(c) and .103(d). For purposes of applying the criterion of paragraph .103(c), the estimated economic life of the building shall be considered as the estimated economic life of the unit.
    (a) Lessee's accounting: If either criterion (c) or (d) of paragraph .103 is met, the lessee shall capitalize the land and building as a single unit and amortize it in accordance with the provisions of paragraph .107(b); otherwise, the lease shall be accounted for as an operating lease. [FAS13, ¶26]
    (b) Lessor's accounting: If either criterion (c) or (d) of paragraph .103 and both criteria of paragraph .104 are met, the lessor shall account for the lease as a single unit as a direct financing lease, a leveraged lease, or an operating lease as appropriate under paragraph .102(b). If the lease meets neither criterion (c) nor (d) of paragraph .103 or does not meet both criteria of paragraph .104, the lease shall be accounted for as an operating lease. [FAS98, ¶22m]
  (2) If the fair value of the land is 25 percent or more of the total fair value of the leased property at the inception of the lease: Both the lessee and lessor shall consider the land and the building separately for purposes of applying the criteria of paragraphs .103(c) and .103(d). The minimum lease payments after deducting executory costs, including any profit thereon, applicable to the land and the building shall be separated both by the lessee and the lessor by determining the fair value of the land and applying the lessee's incremental borrowing rate to it to determine the annual minimum lease payments applicable to the land element; the remaining minimum lease payments shall be attributed to the building element.
    (a) Lessee's accounting: If the building element of the lease meets criterion (c) or (d) of paragraph .103, the building element shall be accounted for as a capital lease and amortized in accordance with the provisions of paragraph .107(b). The land element of the lease shall be accounted for separately as an operating lease. If the building element of the lease meets neither criterion (c) nor (d) of paragraph .103, both the building element and the land element shall be accounted for as a single operating lease. [FAS13, ¶26]
    (b) Lessor's accounting: If the building element of the lease meets either criterion (c) or (d) of paragraph .103 and both criteria of paragraph .104, the building element shall be accounted for as a direct financing lease, a leveraged lease, or an operating lease as appropriate under paragraph .102(b). [FAS98, 22n] The land element of the lease shall be accounted for separately as an operating lease. If the building element of the lease meets neither criterion (c) nor (d) of paragraph .103 or does not meet the criteria of paragraph .104, both the building element and the land element shall be accounted for as a single operating lease. [FAS13, ¶26]

Leases Involving Equipment as Well as Real Estate

.123 If a lease involving real estate also includes equipment, the portion of the minimum lease payments applicable to the equipment element of the lease shall be estimated by whatever means are appropriate in the circumstances. The equipment shall be considered separately for purposes of applying the criteria in paragraphs .103 and .104 and shall be accounted for separately according to its classification by both lessees and lessors. [FAS13, ¶27]

Leases Involving Only Part of a Building

.124 When the leased property is part of a larger whole, its cost (or carrying amount) and fair value[26] may not be objectively determinable, as for example, when an office or floor of a building is leased. If the cost and fair value of the leased property are objectively determinable, both the lessee and the lessor shall classify and account for the lease according to the provisions of paragraph .122. Unless both the cost and the fair value are objectively determinable, the lease shall be classified and accounted for as follows:

a. Lessee:
   (1) If the fair value of the leased property is objectively determinable, the lessee shall classify and account for the lease according to the provisions of paragraph .122.
   (2) If the fair value of the leased property is not objectively determinable, the lessee shall classify the lease according to the criterion of paragraph .103(c) only, using the estimated economic life of the building in which the leased premises are located. If that criterion is met, the leased property shall be capitalized as a unit and amortized in accordance with the provisions of paragraph .107(b).
b. Lessor:
   If either the cost or the fair value of the property is not objectively determinable, the lessor shall account for the lease as an operating lease.

---

[26]If there are no sales of property similar to the leased property, other evidence may provide a basis for an objective determination of fair value. For example, reasonable estimates of the leased property's fair value might be objectively determined by referring to an independent appraisal of the leased property or to estimated replacement cost information. [FIN24, ¶6] [However,] this section does not intend to impose a requirement to obtain an appraisal or similar valuation as a general matter but does [indicate] that kind of information be obtained whenever possible if (a) classification as a capital lease seems likely and (b) the effects of capital lease classification would be significant to the financial statements of a lessee. [Although] the applicability of this paragraph [is not] limited to lessees of a significant portion of a facility, [it is] recognized that a lessee's ability to make a reasonable estimate of the leased property's fair value will vary depending on the size of the leased property in relation to the entire facility. For example, obtaining a meaningful appraisal of an office or a floor of a multi-story building may not be possible, whereas similar information may be readily obtainable if the leased property is a major part of that facility. [FIN24, ¶4]

Because of special provisions normally present in leases involving terminal space and other airport facilities owned by a governmental unit or authority, the economic life of such facilities for purposes of classifying the lease is essentially indeterminate. Likewise, the concept of fair value is not applicable to such leases. Since such leases also do not provide for a transfer of ownership or a bargain purchase option, they shall be classified as operating leases.[27] Leases of other facilities owned by a governmental unit or authority wherein the rights of the parties are essentially the same as in a lease of airport facilities described above shall also be classified as operating leases. Examples of such leases may be those involving facilities at ports and bus terminals. [FAS13, ¶28]

Leases between Related Parties

.125 Except as noted below, leases between related parties shall be classified in accordance with the criteria in paragraphs .103 and .104. Insofar as the separate financial statements of the related parties are concerned, the classification and accounting shall be the same as for similar leases between **unrelated parties,** except in cases in which it is clear that the terms of the transaction have been significantly affected by the fact that the lessee and lessor are related. In such cases, the classification or accounting or both shall be modified as necessary to recognize economic substance rather than legal form. The nature and extent of leasing transactions with related parties shall be disclosed. [FAS13, ¶29]

.126 In consolidated financial statements or in financial statements for which an interest in an investee is accounted for on the equity basis, any profit or loss on a leasing transaction with the related party shall be accounted for in accordance with the principles set forth in Section C51, "Consolidation," or Section I82, "Investments: Equity Method," whichever is applicable. [FAS13, ¶30]

---

[27][This automatic classification as an operating lease applies] only if all of the following conditions are met:

a. The leased property is owned by a governmental unit or authority.

b. The leased property is part of a larger facility, such as an airport, operated by or on behalf of the lessor.

c. The leased property is a permanent structure or a part of a permanent structure, such as a building, that normally could not be moved to a new location.

d. The lessor, or in some cases a higher governmental authority, has the explicit right under the lease agreement or existing statutes or regulations applicable to the leased property to terminate the lease at any time during the lease term, such as by closing the facility containing the leased property or by taking possession of the facility. [FIN23, ¶8] ([However, it is not intended] that leases of government-owned property would be classified as operating leases merely because sovereign rights, such as the right of eminent domain, exist.) [FIN23, ¶6]

e. The lease neither transfers ownership of the leased property to the lessee nor allows the lessee to purchase or otherwise acquire ownership of the leased property.

f. The leased property or equivalent property in the same service area [FIN23, ¶8] (property that would allow continuation of essentially the same service or activity as afforded by the leased property without any appreciable difference in economic results to the lessee) [FIN23, ¶8, fn1] cannot be purchased nor can such property be leased from a nongovernmental unit or authority. [FIN23, ¶8]

Leases of property not meeting all of these conditions are subject to the same criteria for classifying leases that are applicable to leases not involving government-owned property. [FIN23, ¶9]

.127 The accounts of subsidiaries (regardless of when organized or acquired) whose principal business activity is leasing property of facilities to the parent of other affiliated enterprises shall be consolidated. The equity method is not adequate for fair presentation of those subsidiaries because their assets and liabilities are significant to the consolidated financial position of the enterprise. [FAS13, ¶31]

Sale-Leaseback Transactions

.128 Sale-leaseback transactions involve the sale of property by the owner and a lease of the property back to the seller. A sale of property that is accompanied by a leaseback of all or any part of the property for all or part of its remaining economic life shall be accounted for by the seller-lessee in accordance with the provisions of paragraph .129 [except that a sale-leaseback involving real estate, property improvements, or integral equipment[27a] shall be accounted for in accordance with the provisions of paragraphs .130A through .130M]. A sale of property that is accompanied by a leaseback of all or any part of the property for all or part of its remaining economic life shall be accounted for by the [buyer-lessor] in accordance with the provisions of paragraph .130. [FAS28, ¶2] [See paragraphs .544 through .545 for supplemental guidance in accounting for sale-leaseback transactions when nonrecourse debt is obtained using the lease rentals or lease rentals and the leased asset as collateral and the nonrecourse debt is sold with the asset to a third party investor (a wrap lease transaction).]

.129 If the lease meets one of the criteria for treatment as a capital lease (refer to paragraph .103), the seller-lessee shall account for the lease as a capital lease; otherwise, as an operating lease. Any profit or loss on the sale[28] shall be deferred and amortized in proportion to the amortization of the leased asset,[29] if a capital lease, or in proportion to the related gross rental charged to expense over the lease term, if an operating lease, unless:

a. The seller-lessee relinquishes the right to substantially all of the remaining use of the property sold (retaining only a minor portion of such use),[30] in which case the sale and the leaseback shall be accounted for as separate transactions based on their respective terms. However, if the amount of rentals called for by the lease is unreasonable under market conditions at the inception of the lease, an appropri-

---

[27a]The terms *property improvements* and *integral equipment* are discussed in paragraph .130A and footnote 32a.]

[28]*Profit or loss on the sale* is used in this paragraph to refer to the profit or loss that would be recognized on the sale if there were no leaseback. For example, on a sale of real estate subject to Section R10, the profit on the sale to be deferred and amortized in proportion to the leaseback would be the profit that could otherwise be recognized in accordance with that section. [FAS28, ¶3]

[29]If the leased asset is land only, the amortization shall be on a straight-line basis over the lease term. [FAS13, ¶33, fn23]

[30]*Substantially all* and *minor* are used here in the context of the concepts underlying the classification criteria of this section. In that context, a test based on the 90-percent recovery criterion of paragraph .103(d) could be used as a guideline; that is, if the present value of a reasonable amount of rental for the leaseback represents 10 percent or less of the *fair value* of the asset sold, the seller-lessee could be presumed to have transferred to the [buyer-lessor] the right to substantially all of the remaining use of the property sold, and the seller-lessee could be presumed to have retained only a minor portion of such use. [FAS28, ¶3a]

ate amount shall be deferred or accrued, by adjusting the profit or loss on the sale, and amortized as specified in the introduction of this paragraph to adjust those rentals to a reasonable amount.

b. The seller-lessee retains more than a minor part but less than substantially all[31] of the use of the property through the leaseback and realizes a profit on the sale[32] in excess of (1) the present value of the minimum lease payments over the lease term, if the leaseback is classified as an operating lease, or (2) the recorded amount of the leased asset, if the leaseback is classified as a capital lease. In that case, the profit on the sale in excess of either the present value of the minimum lease payments or the recorded amount of the leased asset, whichever is appropriate, shall be recognized at the date of the sale. For purposes of applying this provision, the present value of the minimum lease payments for an operating lease shall be computed using the interest rate that would be used to apply the 90 percent recovery criterion of paragraph .103(d).

c. The fair value of the property at the time of the transaction is less than its undepreciated cost, in which case a loss shall be recognized immediately up to the amount of the difference between undepreciated cost and fair value. [FAS28, ¶3]

.130 If the lease meets the criteria in paragraphs .103 and .104, the [buyer-lessor] shall record the transaction as a purchase and a direct financing lease; otherwise, the [buyer-lessor] shall record the transaction as a purchase and an operating lease. [FAS13, ¶34]

Sale-Leaseback Transactions Involving Real Estate

.130A Paragraphs .130A through .130M [present] standards of financial accounting and reporting by a seller-lessee for sale-leaseback transactions involving real estate, including real estate with equipment, such as manufacturing facilities, power plants, and office buildings with furniture and fixtures. A sale-leaseback transaction involving real estate with equipment includes any sale-leaseback transaction in which the equipment and the real estate are sold and leased back as a package, irrespective of the relative value of the equipment and the real estate. Those paragraphs also address sale-leaseback transactions in which the seller-lessee sells property improvements or integral equipment[32a] to a buyer-lessor and leases them back while retaining the un-

---

[31] *Substantially all* is used here in the context of the concepts underlying the classification criteria of this section. In that context, if a leaseback of *the entire property sold* meets the criteria of this section for classification as a capital lease, the seller-lessee would be presumed to have retained substantially all of the remaining use of the property sold. [FAS28, ¶3b]

[32] *Profit or loss on the sale* is used in this paragraph to refer to the profit or loss that would be recognized on the sale if there were no leaseback. For example, on a sale of real estate subject to Section R10, the profit on the sale to be deferred and amortized in proportion to the leaseback would be the profit that could otherwise be recognized in accordance with that section. [FAS28, ¶3]

[32a] The terms *property improvements* or *integral equipment* as used in paragraphs .130A through .130M of this section refer to any physical structure or equipment attached to the real estate, or other parts thereof, that cannot be removed and used separately without incurring significant cost. Examples include an office building, a manufacturing facility, a power plant, and a refinery. [FAS98, ¶6, fn2]

derlying land.[32b] [FAS98, ¶6]

Sale-Leaseback Accounting

.130B Sale-leaseback accounting is a method of accounting for a sale-leaseback transaction in which the seller-lessee records the sale, removes all property and related liabilities from its balance sheet, recognizes gain or loss from the sale in accordance with [paragraphs .129 and .130A through .130M] and Section R10, and classifies the leaseback in accordance with this section. [FAS98, ¶70]

Criteria for Sale-Leaseback Accounting

.130C Sale-leaseback accounting shall be used by a seller-lessee only if a sale-leaseback transaction includes all of the following:

a. A normal leaseback as described in paragraph .130D
b. Payment terms and provisions that adequately demonstrate the buyer-lessor's initial and continuing investment in the property (refer to paragraphs .111 through .119 of Section R10)
c. Payment terms and provisions that transfer *all* of the other risks and rewards of ownership as demonstrated by the absence of *any* other continuing involvement by the seller-lessee described in paragraphs .130G through .130I of this section and paragraphs .128 through .142 and .144 through .146 of Section R10. [FAS98, ¶7]

.130D A *normal leaseback* is a lessee-lessor relationship that involves the active use of the property by the seller-lessee in consideration for payment of rent, including contingent rentals that are based on the future operations of the seller-lessee,[32c] and excludes other continuing involvement provisions or conditions described in paragraphs .130G through .130I of this section. The phrase *active use of the property by the seller-lessee* refers to the use of the property during the lease term in the seller-lessee's trade or business, provided that subleasing of the leased back property is minor.[32d] If

---

[32b]Paragraphs .141 and .142 of Section R10 address transactions in which the seller sells property improvements to a buyer and leases the underlying land to the buyer of the improvements. Under certain circumstances, paragraph .141 of Section R10 precludes **sales recognition** for such transactions and requires that they be accounted for as leases of both the land and improvements. Paragraphs .130A through .130M of this section are not intended to modify paragraph .141 of Section R10; thus, they do not address a sale-leaseback transaction that does not qualify for sales recognition under the provisions of paragraph .141 of Section R10. However, those paragraphs do address a sale-leaseback transaction that qualifies for sales recognition under the provisions of paragraph .142 of Section R10. [FAS98, ¶6, fn3]

[32c]Paragraphs .130A through .130M distinguish between contingent rentals that are based on the future operations of the seller-lessee and those that are based on some predetermined or determinable level of future operations of the buyer-lessor. The latter type of contingent rental is addressed in paragraph .130H(e) of this section. [FAS98, ¶8, fn4]

[32d][The term] *minor* is used here in the context of the definition in footnote 30 to paragraph .129. [FAS98, ¶8, fn6]

the present value of a reasonable amount of rental for that portion of the leaseback that is subleased is not more than 10 percent of the fair value of the asset sold, the leased back property under sublease is considered minor. Active use of the property may involve the providing of services where the occupancy of the property is generally transient or short-term and is integral to the ancillary services being provided. Those ancillary services include, but are not limited to, housekeeping, inventory control, entertainment, bookkeeping, and food services. Thus, the use of property by a seller-lessee engaged in the hotel or bonded warehouse business or the operation of a golf course or a parking lot, for example, is considered active use. [FAS98, ¶8]

Terms of the Sale-Leaseback Transaction

.130E Terms of the sale-leaseback transaction that are substantially different from terms that an independent third-party lessor or lessee would accept represent an exchange of some stated or unstated rights or privileges. Those rights or privileges shall be considered in evaluating the continuing involvement provisions in paragraphs .130G through .130I of this section. Those terms or conditions include, but are not limited to, the sales price, the interest rate, and other terms of any loan from the seller-lessee to the buyer-lessor. The fair value of the property used in making that evaluation shall be based on objective evidence, for example, an independent third-party appraisal or recent sales of comparable property. [FAS98, ¶9]

Continuing Involvement

.130F A sale-leaseback transaction that does not qualify for sale-leaseback accounting because of any form of continuing involvement by the seller-lessee other than a normal leaseback shall be accounted for by the deposit method or as a financing, whichever is appropriate under Section R10. The provisions or conditions described in paragraphs .130G through .130I of this section are examples of continuing involvement for the purpose of applying paragraphs .130A through .130M. [FAS98, ¶10]

.130G Paragraphs .128 through .142 and .144 through .146 of Section R10 describe forms of continuing involvement by the seller-lessee with the leased property that result in the seller-lessee not transferring the risks or rewards of ownership to the buyer-lessor. Two examples of continuing involvement specified in those paragraphs that are frequently found in sale-leaseback transactions are provisions or conditions in which:

a. The seller-lessee has an obligation or an option[32e] to repurchase the property or the buyer-lessor can compel the seller-lessee to repurchase the property.
b. The seller-lessee guarantees the buyer-lessor's investment or a return on that investment for a limited or extended period of time. [FAS98, ¶11]

[32e]A right of first refusal based on a bona fide offer by a third party ordinarily is not an obligation or an option to repurchase. An agreement that allows the seller-lessee to repurchase the asset in the event no third-party offer is made is an option to repurchase. [FAS98, ¶11, fn7]

.130H Other provisions or conditions that are guarantees and that do not transfer all of the risks of ownership shall constitute continuing involvement for the purpose of applying paragraphs .130A through .130M to sale-leaseback transactions and include, but are not limited to, the following:

a. The seller-lessee is required to pay the buyer-lessor at the end of the lease term for a decline in the fair value of the property below the estimated residual value on some basis other than excess wear and tear of the property levied on inspection of the property at the termination of the lease.

b. The seller-lessee provides **nonrecourse financing** to the buyer-lessor for any portion of the sales proceeds or provides recourse financing in which the only recourse is to the leased asset.

c. The seller-lessee is not relieved of the obligation under any existing debt related to the property.

d. The seller-lessee provides collateral on behalf of the buyer-lessor other than the property directly involved in the sale-leaseback transaction, the seller-lessee or a related party to the seller-lessee guarantees the buyer-lessor's debt, or a related party to the seller-lessee guarantees a return of or on the buyer-lessor's investment.

e. The seller-lessee's rental payment is contingent on some predetermined or determinable level of future operations of the buyer-lessor.[32f] [FAS98, ¶12]

.130I The following provisions or conditions also shall be considered examples of continuing involvement for the purpose of applying paragraphs .130A through .130M to sale-leaseback transactions:

a. The seller-lessee enters into a sale-leaseback transaction involving property improvements or integral equipment[32g] without leasing the underlying land to the buyer-lessor.[32h]

b. The buyer-lessor is obligated to share with the seller-lessee any portion of the appreciation of the property.

[32f]Paragraphs .130A through .130M distinguish between contingent rentals that are based on the future operations of the seller-lessee and those that are based on some predetermined or determinable level of future operations of the buyer-lessor. [FAS98, ¶8, fn4]

[32g]The terms *property improvements* or *integral equipment* as used in paragraphs .130A through .130M refer to any physical structure or equipment attached to the real estate, or other parts thereof, that cannot be removed and used separately without incurring significant cost. Examples include an office building, a manufacturing facility, a power plant, and a refinery. [FAS98, ¶6, fn2]

[32h]Paragraphs .141 and .142 of Section R10 address transactions in which the seller sells property improvements to a buyer and leases the underlying land to the buyer of the improvements. Under certain circumstances, paragraph .141 of Section R10 precludes sales recognition for such transactions and requires that they be accounted for as leases of both the land and improvements. Paragraph .130A through .130M of this section are not intended to modify paragraph .141 of Section R10; thus, they do not address a sale-leaseback transaction that does not qualify for sales recognition under the provisions of paragraph .141 of Section R10. However, those paragraphs do address a sale-leaseback transaction that qualifies for sales recognition under the provisions of paragraph .142 of Section R10. [FAS98, ¶6, fn3]

c. Any other provision or circumstance that allows the seller-lessee to participate in any future profits of the buyer-lessor or the appreciation of the leased property, for example, a situation in which the seller-lessee owns or has an option to acquire any interest in the buyer-lessor. [FAS98, ¶13]

Sale-Leaseback Transactions by Regulated Enterprises

.130J The provisions of paragraphs .130A through .130M apply to sale-leaseback transactions of a regulated enterprise subject to Section Re6, "Regulated Operations." That accounting may result in a difference between the timing of income and expense recognition required by those paragraphs and the timing of income and expense recognition for rate-making purposes. That difference shall be accounted for as follows:

a. If the difference in timing of income and expense recognition constitutes all or a part of a phase-in plan, as defined in paragraph .125A of Section Re6, it shall be accounted for in accordance with paragraphs .125A through .125F of Section Re6.
b. Otherwise, the timing of income and expense recognition related to the sale-leaseback transaction shall be modified as necessary to conform to Section Re6. That modification required for a transaction that is accounted for by the deposit method or as a financing is further described in paragraphs .125I and .125J of Section Re6. [FAS98, ¶14]

Financial Statement Presentation and Disclosure

.130K In addition to the [other] disclosure requirements of this section and Section R10, the financial statements of a seller-lessee shall include a description of the terms of the sale-leaseback transaction, including future commitments, obligations, provisions, or circumstances that require or result in the seller-lessee's continuing involvement. [FAS98, ¶17]

.130L The financial statements of a seller-lessee that has accounted for a sale-leaseback transaction by the deposit method or as a financing according to the provisions of this section and Section R10 also shall disclose:

a. The obligation for future minimum lease payments as of the date of the latest balance sheet presented in the aggregate and for each of the five succeeding fiscal years
b. The total of minimum sublease rentals, if any, to be received in the future under noncancelable subleases in the aggregate and for each of the five succeeding fiscal years. [FAS98, ¶18]

Other

.130M Paragraphs .160A through .160M provide additional discussion and illustrations of how the provisions of paragraphs .130A through .130M shall be applied to specific aspects of accounting for sale-leaseback transactions [involving real estate, property improvements, and equipment integral to real estate]. Paragraphs .160A through .160M constitute an integral part of the requirements of paragraphs .130A through .130M. [FAS98, ¶19]

Accounting and Reporting for Subleases and Similar Transactions

.131 Paragraphs .132 through .136 deal with the following types of leasing transactions:

a. The leased property is re-leased by the original lessee[33] to a third party, and the lease agreement between the two original parties remains in effect (a sublease).
b. A new lessee is substituted under the original lease agreement. The new lessee becomes the primary obligor under the agreement, and the original lessee may or may not be secondarily liable.
c. A new lessee is substituted through a new agreement, with cancellation of the original lease agreement. [FAS13, ¶35]

Accounting by the Original Lessor

.132 If the original lessee enters into a sublease or the original lease agreement is sold or transferred by the original lessee to a third party, the original lessor shall continue to account for the lease as before. [FAS13, ¶36]

.133 If the original lease agreement is replaced by a new agreement with a new lessee, the lessor shall account for the termination of the original lease as provided in paragraph .113(f) and shall classify and account for the new lease as a separate transaction. [FAS13, ¶37]

Accounting by the Original Lessee

.134 If the nature of the transaction is such that the original lessee is relieved of the primary obligation under the original lease, as would be the case in transactions of the type described in paragraphs .131(b) and .131(c), the termination of the original lease agreement shall be accounted for as follows:

a. If the original lease was a capital lease, the asset and obligation representing the original lease shall be removed from the accounts, gain or loss shall be recognized for the difference, and, if the original lessee is secondarily liable, the loss contingency shall be treated as provided by Section C59, "Contingencies." Any consideration paid or received upon termination shall be included in the determination of gain or loss to be recognized.

---

[33] An *original lessee* includes any lessee who acts as sublessor on a sublease. [FIN27, ¶1, fn1]

b. If the original lease was an operating lease and the original lessee is secondarily liable, the loss contingency shall be treated as provided by Section C59. [FAS13, ¶38]

.135 If the nature of the transaction[34] is such that the original lessee is not relieved of the primary obligation under the original lease, as would be the case in transactions of the type described in paragraph .131(a), the original lessee, as sublessor, shall account for the transaction as follows:

a. If the original lease met either criterion (a) or (b) of paragraph .103, the original lessee shall classify the new lease in accordance with the criteria of paragraphs .103 and .104. If the new lease meets one of the criteria of paragraph .103 and both of the criteria of paragraph .104, it shall be accounted for as a sales-type or direct financing lease, as appropriate, and the unamortized balance of the asset under the original lease shall be treated as the cost of the leased property. If the new lease does not qualify as a sales-type or direct financing lease, it shall be accounted for as an operating lease. In either case, the original lessee shall continue to account for the obligation related to the original lease as before.

b. If the original lease met either criterion (c) or (d) but not criterion (a) or (b) of paragraph .103, the original lessee shall, with one exception, classify the new lease in accordance with the criteria of paragraphs .103(c) and .104 only. If it meets those criteria, it shall be accounted for as a direct financing lease, with the unamortized balance of the asset under the original lease treated as the cost of the leased property; otherwise, as an operating lease. In either case, the original lessee shall continue to account for the obligation related to the original lease as before. The one exception arises when the timing and other circumstances surrounding the sublease are such as to suggest that the sublease was intended as an integral part of an overall transaction in which the original lessee serves only as an intermediary. In that case, the sublease shall be classified according to the criteria of paragraphs .103(c) and .103(d), as well as the criteria of paragraph .104. In applying the criterion of paragraph .103(d), the fair value of the leased property shall be the fair value to the original lessor at the inception of the original lease.

c. If the original lease is an operating lease, the original lessee shall account for both it and the new lease as operating leases. [FAS13, ¶39]

This paragraph does not prohibit the recognition of a loss by an original lessee who disposes of leased property or mitigates the cost of an existing lease commitment by subleasing the property.[34a] [FIN27, ¶2] If a sublease is entered into as part of a dis-

---

[34]Paragraphs .518 through .520 discuss the accounting for loss on a sublease not involving the disposal of a segment.]

[34a]See paragraphs .527C through .527F for guidance on the lessee's recognition of a loss on a lease that is assumed by a new lessor as an incentive to enter into a new lease with that lessor.]

posal of a segment of a business[35] as defined in Section I13, "Income Statement Presentation: Discontinued Operations," paragraph .404, the anticipated future cash flows that will result from the original lease and the sublease, as well as the carrying amount of any related recorded assets or obligations, shall be taken into account in determining the overall gain or loss on the disposal. [FIN27, ¶3]

Accounting by the New Lessee

.136 The new lessee shall classify the lease in accordance with the criteria of paragraph .103 and account for it accordingly. [FAS13, ¶40]

Accounting for Leases in a Business Combination

Summary

.137 The classification of a lease in accordance with the criteria of this section shall not be changed as a result of a business combination unless the provisions of the lease are modified (refer to paragraph .138). [FIN21, ¶12]

Changes in the Provisions of the Lease

.138 If in connection with a business combination, whether accounted for by the purchase method or by the pooling-of-interests method, the provisions of a lease are modified in a way that would require the revised agreement to be considered a new agreement under paragraph .105, the new lease shall be classified by the combined enterprise according to the criteria set forth in this section, based on conditions as of the date of the modification of the lease. [FIN21, ¶13]

Pooling of Interests

.139 In a business combination that is accounted for by the pooling-of-interests method, each lease shall retain its previous classification under this section unless the provisions of the lease are modified as indicated in paragraph .138 and shall be accounted for by the combined enterprise in the same manner that it would have been classified and accounted for by the combining enterprise. [FIN21, ¶14]

---

[35]Section I22, "Income Statement Presentation: Unusual or Infrequent Items," paragraph .502, states that "the gain or loss on sale of a portion of a line of business which is not a segment of a business . . . should be calculated using the same measurement principles as if it were a segment of a business (refer to Section I13, paragraphs .102 through .104)." [FIN27, ¶3, fn3]

Purchase Combination

.140 In a business combination that is accounted for by the purchase method, the acquiring enterprise shall retain the previous classification in accordance with this section for the leases of an acquired enterprise unless the provisions of the lease are modified as indicated in paragraph .138. The amounts assigned to individual assets acquired and liabilities assumed at the date of the combination shall be determined in accordance with the general guides for that type of asset or liability in Section B50, "Business Combinations," paragraph .146. Subsequent to the recording of the amounts called for by that section, the leases shall thereafter be accounted for in accordance with this section.[36] Paragraphs .141 and .142 explain application of this paragraph to a leveraged lease by an enterprise that acquires a lessor. [FIN21, ¶15]

.141 In a business combination that is accounted for by the purchase method, the acquiring enterprise shall apply the following procedures to the acquired enterprise's investment as a lessor in a leveraged lease. The acquiring enterprise shall retain the classification of a leveraged lease at the date of the combination. The acquiring enterprise shall assign an amount to the acquired net investment in the leveraged lease in accordance with the general guides in Section B50, paragraph .146, based on the remaining future cash flows and giving appropriate recognition to the estimated future tax effects of those cash flows. Once determined, that net investment shall be broken down into its components, namely, net rentals receivable, estimated residual value, and unearned income including discount to adjust other components to present value. The acquiring enterprise thereafter shall account for that investment in a leveraged lease in accordance with the provisions of this section. [FIN21, ¶16]

.142 Paragraph .161 illustrates the application of paragraph .141. [FIN21, ¶16]

Accounting and Reporting for Leveraged Leases

.143 From the standpoint of the lessee, leveraged leases shall be classified and accounted for in the same manner as nonleveraged leases. The balance of this section deals with leveraged leases from the standpoint of the lessor. [FAS13, ¶41]

.144 For the purposes of this section, a leveraged lease is defined as one having all of the following characteristics:

a. Except for the exclusion of leveraged leases from the definition of a direct financing lease as set forth in paragraph .102(b)(2), it otherwise meets that

---

[36]The subsequent accounting for amounts recorded for favorable or unfavorable operating leases [is not addressed here]. Accordingly, present practice is not changed with respect to the amortization of those amounts. [FIN21, ¶15, fn3]

definition. Leases that meet the definition of sales-type leases set forth in paragraph .102(b)(1) shall not be accounted for as leveraged leases but shall be accounted for as prescribed in paragraph .113.

b.   It involves at least three parties: a lessee, a long-term creditor, and a lessor (commonly called the equity participant).

c.   The financing provided by the long-term creditor is nonrecourse as to the general credit of the lessor (although the creditor may have recourse to the specific property leased and the unremitted rentals relating to it). The amount of the financing is sufficient to provide the lessor with substantial *leverage* in the transaction.

d.   The lessor's net investment, as defined in paragraph .145, declines during the early years once the investment has been completed and rises during the later years of the lease before its final elimination. Such decreases and increases in the net investment balance may occur more than once.

A lease meeting the preceding definition shall be accounted for by the lessor using the method described in paragraphs .145 through .149.[36a] An exception arises if the investment tax credit is accounted for other than as stated in paragraphs .145 and .146,[37] in which case the lease shall be classified as a direct financing lease and accounted for in accordance with paragraph .114. A lease not meeting the definition of a leveraged lease shall be accounted for in accordance with its classification under paragraph .102(b). [FAS13, ¶42]

.145   The lessor shall record its investment in a leveraged lease net of the nonrecourse debt.[37a] The net of the balances of the following accounts shall represent the initial and continuing investment in leveraged leases:

a.   Rentals receivable, net of that portion of the rental applicable to principal and interest on the nonrecourse debt.

b.   A receivable for the amount of the investment tax credit to be realized on the transaction.

c.   The estimated residual value of the leased asset. [FAS13, ¶43] The estimated residual value shall not exceed the amount estimated at the inception of the lease except as provided in footnote 38.[38] [FAS23, ¶10]

d.   Unearned and deferred income consisting of (1) the estimated pretax lease income (or loss), after deducting initial direct costs, remaining to be allocated

---

[36a]Paragraphs .536 and .537 further discuss residual value retained by a lessor that sells rental payments.]

[37]It is recognized that the investment tax credit may be accounted for other than as prescribed here, as provided by Congress in the Revenue Act of 1971. [FAS13, ¶42, fn24]

[37a]Footnote 502 further discusses nonrecourse debt collateralized by a lease receivable.]

[38]If the lease agreement or commitment, if earlier, includes a provision to escalate minimum lease payments for increases in construction or acquisition cost of the leased property or for increases in some other measure of cost or value, such as general price levels, during the construction or preacquisition period, the effect of any increases that have occurred shall be considered in the determination of "the estimated residual value of the leased property at the inception of the lease" for purposes of this paragraph. [FAS23, ¶10]

to income over the lease term and (2) the investment tax credit remaining to be allocated to income over the lease term.

The investment in leveraged leases less deferred taxes arising from differences between pretax accounting income and taxable income shall represent the lessor's net investment in leveraged leases for purposes of computing periodic net income from the lease, as described in paragraph .146. [FAS13, ¶43]

.146 Given the original investment and using the projected cash receipts and disbursements over the term of the lease, the rate of return on the net investment in the years[39] in which it is positive shall be computed. The rate is that rate which when applied to the net investment in the years in which the net investment is positive will distribute the net income to those years (refer to Exhibit 154C) and is distinct from the *interest rate implicit in the lease*. In each year whether positive or not, the difference between the net cash flow and the amount of income recognized, if any, shall serve to increase or reduce the net investment balance. The net income recognized shall be composed of three elements: two, pretax lease income (or loss) and investment tax credit, shall be allocated in proportionate amounts from the unearned and deferred income included in net investment, as described in paragraph .145; the third element is the tax effect of the pretax lease income (or loss) recognized, which shall be reflected in tax expense for the year. The tax effect of the difference between pretax accounting income (or loss) and taxable income (or loss) for the year shall be charged or credited to deferred taxes. The accounting prescribed in paragraph .145 and in this paragraph is illustrated in paragraph .154. [FAS13, ¶44]

.147 If the projected net cash receipts[40] over the term of the lease are less than the lessor's initial investment, the deficiency shall be recognized as a loss at the inception of the lease. Likewise, if at any time during the lease term the application of the method prescribed in paragraphs .145 and .146 would result in a loss being allocated to future years, that loss shall be recognized immediately. This situation might arise in cases in which one of the important assumptions affecting net income is revised (refer to paragraph .148). [FAS13, ¶45]

.148 Any estimated residual value and all other important assumptions affecting estimated total net income from the lease shall be reviewed at least annually.[41] If during the lease term the estimate of the residual value is determined to be excessive and the decline in the residual value is judged to be other than temporary or if the revision of

---

[39]The use of the term *years* is not intended to preclude application of the accounting prescribed in this paragraph to shorter accounting periods. [FAS13, ¶44, fn25]

[40]For purposes of this paragraph, net cash receipts shall be gross cash receipts less gross cash disbursements exclusive of the lessor's initial investment. [FAS13, ¶45, fn26]

[[41]Refer to paragraphs .521 through .524 for supplemental guidance on the effect of a change in income tax rate on the accounting for leveraged leases.]

another important assumption changes the estimated total net income from the lease, the rate of return and the allocation of income to positive investment years shall be recalculated from the inception of the lease following the method described in paragraph .146 and using the revised assumption. The accounts constituting the net investment balance shall be adjusted to conform to the recalculated balances, and the change in the net investment shall be recognized as a gain or loss in the year in which the assumption is changed. An upward adjustment of the estimated residual value shall not be made.[41a] The accounting prescribed in this paragraph is illustrated in paragraph .154. [FAS13, ¶46]

Accounting for Income Taxes

.148A Section 127, "Income Taxes," does not change (a) the pattern of recognition of after-tax income for leveraged leases as required by this section or (b) the allocation of the purchase price in a purchase business combination to acquired leveraged leases as required by paragraphs .140 through .142. Integration[41b] of the results of income tax accounting for leveraged leases with the other results of accounting for income taxes under Section 127 is required when deferred tax credits related to leveraged leases are the only source (refer to paragraph .120 of Section 127) for recognition of a tax benefit for deductible temporary differences and carryforwards not related to leveraged leases. A valuation allowance is not necessary if deductible temporary differences and carryforwards will offset taxable amounts from future recovery of the net investment in the leveraged lease. However, to the extent that the amount of deferred tax credits for a leveraged lease as determined under this section differs from the amount of the deferred tax liability related to the leveraged lease that would otherwise result from applying the requirements of Section 127, that difference is preserved and is not a source of taxable income for recognition of the tax benefit of deductible temporary differences and operating loss or tax credit carryforwards. [FAS109, ¶256]

.148B Paragraph .141 requires that the tax effect of any difference between the assigned value and the tax basis of a leveraged lease at the date of a business combination not be accounted for as a deferred tax credit. Section 127 does not change that requirement. Any tax effects included in unearned and deferred income as required by this section are not offset by the deferred tax consequences of other temporary differences or by the tax benefit of operating loss or tax credit carryforwards. However, de-

---

[41a]Paragraphs .536 and .537 further discuss residual value retained by a lessor that sells rental payments.]

[41b]Integration is an issue when all of the following exist:

a. The accounting for a leveraged lease requires recognition of deferred tax credits.
b. The requirements of Section 127 limit the recognition of a tax benefit for deductible temporary differences and carryforwards not related to the leveraged lease.
c. Unrecognized tax benefits could offset taxable amounts that result from future recovery of the net investment in the leveraged lease.

In those circumstances, integration shall be required. However, integration should not override any results that are unique to income tax accounting for leveraged leases, for example, the manner of recognizing the tax effect of an enacted change in tax rates. [FAS109, ¶126]

ferred tax credits that arise after the date of a business combination are accounted for in the same manner as described above for leveraged leases that were not acquired in a purchase business combination. [FAS109, ¶257] [Exhibit 185A in Section I27 presents an example that integrates the] accounting for leveraged leases [as required by this section] and the accounting for income taxes required by Section I27. [FAS109, ¶258]

Disclosures

.149 For purposes of presenting the investment in a leveraged lease in the lessor's balance sheet, the amount of related deferred taxes shall be presented separately (from the remainder of the net investment). In the income statement or the notes thereto, separate presentation (from each other) shall be made of pretax income from the leveraged lease, the tax effect of pretax income, and the amount of investment tax credit recognized as income during the period. When leveraged leasing is a significant part of the lessor's business activities in terms of revenue, net income, or assets, the components of the net investment balance in leveraged leases as set forth in paragraph .145 shall be disclosed in the footnotes to the financial statements. Paragraph .154 contains an illustration of the balance sheet, income statement, and footnote presentation for a leveraged lease. [FAS13, ¶47]

Illustrations of Accounting by Lessees and Lessors

.150 This paragraph contains the following exhibits illustrating the accounting requirements of this section as applied to a particular example (an automobile lease):

a. Lease example—terms and assumptions, Exhibit 150A
b. Computation of minimum lease payments (lessee and lessor) and lessor's computation of rate of interest implicit in the lease, Exhibit 150B
c. Classification of the lease, Exhibit 150C
d. Journal entries for the first month of the lease, as well as for the disposition of the leased property at the end of the lease term, Exhibit 150D [FAS13, ¶121]

Exhibit 150A

Lease Example
Terms and Assumptions

Lessor's cost of the leased property (automobile)	$5,000
Fair value of the leased property at inception of the lease (1/1/X7)	$5,000
Estimated economic life of the leased property	5 years

Lease terms and assumptions: The lease has a fixed noncancelable term of 30 months, with a rental of $135 payable at the beginning of each month. The lessee

Exhibit 150A (continued)

guarantees the residual value at the end of the 30-month lease term in the amount of $2,000. The lessee is to receive any excess of sales price of property over the guaranteed amount at the end of the lease term. The lessee pays executory costs. The lease is renewable periodically based on a schedule of rentals and guarantees of the residual values decreasing over time. The rentals specified are deemed to be fair rentals (as distinct from bargain rentals), and the guarantees of the residual are expected to approximate realizable values. No investment tax credit is available. [FAS13, ¶121]

The residual value at the end of the lease term is estimated to be $2,000. The lessee depreciates its owned automobiles on a straight-line basis. The **lessee's incremental borrowing rate** is $10^1/_2$ percent per year. There were no initial direct costs of negotiating and closing the transaction. At the end of the lease term the asset is sold for $2,100. [FAS13, ¶121]

Exhibit 150B

Computation of Minimum Lease Payments for Lessee and Lessor

In accordance with paragraph .416, minimum lease payments for both the lessee and lessor are computed as follows:

Minimum rental payments over the lease term ($135 × 30 months)	$4,050
Lessee guarantee of the residual value at the end of the lease term	2,000
Total minimum lease payments	$6,050

Lessor's Computation of Rate of Interest Implicit in the Lease

In accordance with paragraph .412, the **interest rate implicit in the lease** is that rate implicit in the recovery of the fair value of the property at the inception of the lease ($5,000) through the minimum lease payments (30 monthly payments of $135 and the lessee's guarantee of the residual value in the amount of $2,000 at the end of the lease term). That rate is 12.036 percent (1.003 percent per month). [FAS13, ¶121]

Exhibit 150C

Classification of the Lease

**Criteria set forth
in paragraph**

.103(a) *Not met.* The lease does not transfer ownership of the property to the lessee by the end of the lease term.

.103(b) *Not met.* The lease does not contain a bargain purchase option.

.103(c) *Not met.* The lease term is not equal to 75 percent or more of the estimated economic life of the property. (In this case, it represents only 50 percent of the estimated economic life of the property.)

.103(d) *Met.* In the lessee's case, the present value ($5,120) of the minimum lease payments using the incremental borrowing rate (10 1/2 percent) exceeds 90 percent of the fair value of the property at the inception of the lease. (Refer to [the following] computation.) Even if the lessee knows the implicit rate, the lessee uses its incremental rate because it is lower. The lessee classifies the lease as a capital lease. In the lessor's case, the present value ($5,000) of the minimum lease payments using the implicit rate also exceeds 90 percent of the fair value of the property. (Refer to [the following] computation.) Having met this criterion and assuming that the criteria of paragraph .104 are also met, the lessor will classify the lease as a direct financing lease (as opposed to a sales-type lease) because the cost and fair value of the asset are the same at the inception of the lease (refer to paragraph .102(b)(2)).

| | **Present Values** | |
	Lessee's computation using the incremental borrowing rate of 10 1/2% (.875% per month)*	**Lessor's computation using the implicit interest rate of 12.036% (1.003% per month)**
Minimum lease payments:		
Rental payments	$3,580	$3,517
Residual guarantee by lessee	1,540	1,483
Total	$5,120	$5,000
Fair value of the property at inception of the leases	$5,000	$5,000
Minimum lease payments as a percentage of fair value	102%	100%

*In this case, the lessee's incremental borrowing rate is used because it is lower than the implicit rate (refer to paragraph .103(d)).

[FAS13, ¶121]

Exhibit 150D

Journal Entries for the First
Month of the Lease as Well as for the
Disposition of the Leased Property at the End of the Lease Term

First Month of the Lease

LESSEE

		Debit	Credit
1/1/X7	Leased property under capital leases	5,000	
	Obligations under capital leases		5,000
	To record capital lease at the fair value of the property. (Since the present value of the minimum lease payments using the lessee's incremental borrowing rate as the discount rate [refer to paragraph .103(d) for selection of rate to be used] is greater than the fair value of the property, the lessee capitalizes only the fair value of the property [refer to paragraph .106].)		
1/1/X7	Obligations under capital leases	135	
	Cash		135
	To record first month's rental payment		
1/31/X7	Interest expense	49	
	Accrued interest on obligations under capital leases		49*
	To recognize interest expense for the first month of the lease. Obligation balance outstanding during month $4,865 ($5,000−$135) × 1.003% (rate implicit in the liquidation of the $5,000 obligation through (a) 30 monthly payments of $135 made at the beginning of each month and (b) a $2,000 guarantee of the residual value at the end of 30 months) = $49 (refer to paragraph .108).		

---

*In accordance with paragraph .108, the February 1, 19X7 rental payment of $135 will be allocated as follows: $86 (principal reduction) against obligations under capital leases and $49 against accrued interest on obligations under capital leases.

Exhibit 150D (continued)

	Debit	Credit

LESSEE

1/31/X7	Depreciation expense	100	
	Leased property under capital leases		100

        To record first month's depreciation on a straight-line basis over 30 months to a salvage value of $2,000, which is the estimated residual value to the lessee (refer to paragraph .107(b)).

LESSOR

1/1/X7	Minimum lease payments receivable	6,050	
	Automobile		5,000
	Unearned income		1,050

        To record lessor's investment in the direct financing lease (refer to paragraphs .114(a) and .114(b)).

1/1/X7	Cash	135	
	Minimum lease payments receivable		135

        To record receipt of first month's rental payment under the lease.

1/31/X7	Unearned income	49	
	Earned income		49

        To recognize the portion of unearned income that is earned during the first month of the lease. Net investment outstanding for month $4,865 (gross investment $5,915 [$6,050−$135] less unearned income $1,050) × 1.003% (monthly implicit rate in the lease) = $49 (refer to paragraph .114(b)).

29181

Exhibit 150D (continued)

Disposition of Asset for $2,100 (refer to following Note)

LESSEE

		Debit	Credit
7/1/X9	Cash	100	
	Obligations under capital leases	1,980	
	Accrued interest on obligations under capital leases	20	
	Leased property under capital leases		2,000
	Gain on disposition of leased property		100
	To record the liquidation of the obligations under capital leases and receipt of cash in excess of the residual guarantee through the sale of the leased property.		

LESSOR

		Debit	Credit
7/1/X9	Cash	2,000	
	Minimum lease payments receivable		2,000
	To record the receipt of the amount of the lessee's guarantee.		

Note to Disposition of Asset

Had the lessee elected at July 1, 19X9 to renew the lease, it would render inoperative the guarantee as of that date. For that reason, the renewal would not be treated as a new agreement, as would otherwise be the case under paragraph .105, but would instead be accounted for as provided in paragraph .108. The lessee would accordingly adjust the remaining balances of the asset and obligation from the original lease, which at June 30, 19X9 were equal, by an amount equal to the difference between the present value of the future minimum lease payments under the revised agreement and the remaining balance of the obligation. The present value of the future minimum lease payments would be computed using the rate of interest used to record the lease initially.

From the lessor's standpoint, the revised agreement would be accounted for in accordance with paragraph .113(e). Accordingly, the remaining balance of minimum lease payments receivable would be adjusted to the amount of the payments called for by the revised agreement, and the adjustment would be credited to unearned income. [FAS13, ¶121]

Illustrations of Disclosure by Lessees and Lessors

.151 Paragraphs .152 and .153 illustrate one way of meeting the disclosure requirements of this section, except for those relating to leveraged leases which are illustrated in paragraph .154. The illustrations do not encompass all types of leasing arrangements for which disclosures are required. For convenience, the illustrations have been constructed as if the section had been in effect in prior years. [FAS13, ¶122]

.152 Lessee's disclosure [is illustrated in Exhibits 152A and 152B]. [FAS13, ¶122]

Exhibit 152A

[Lessee] Company X
Balance Sheet

ASSETS				LIABILITIES	
	December 31,				December 31,
	19X6	19X5			19X6	19X5
Leased property under capital leases, less accumulated amortization (Note 2)	XXX	XXX	Current: Obligations under capital leases (Note 2)	XXX	XXX
			Noncurrent: Obligations under capital leases (Note 2)	XXX	XXX

Footnotes appear in Exhibit 152B.

Exhibit 152B

Footnotes for Exhibit 152A

Note 1—Description of Leasing Arrangements

The Company conducts a major part of its operations from leased facilities which include a manufacturing plant, 4 warehouses, and 26 stores. The plant lease, which is for 40 years expiring in 19Z9, is classified as a capital lease. The warehouses are under operating leases that expire over the next seven years. Most of the leases of store facilities are classified as capital leases. All of the leases of store facilities expire over the next 15 years.

Most of the operating leases for warehouses and store facilities contain one of the following options: (a) the Company can, after the initial lease term, purchase the property at the then fair value of the property or (b) the Company can, at the end of the initial lease term, renew its lease at the then fair rental value for periods of 5 to 10 years. These options enable the Company to retain use of facilities in desirable operating areas. The rental payments under a store facility lease are based on a minimum rental plus a percentage of the store's sales in excess of stipulated amounts. Portions of store space and warehouse space are sublet under leases expiring during the next three years.

In addition, the Company leases transportation equipment (principally trucks) and data processing equipment under operating leases expiring during the next 3 years.

In most cases, management expects that in the normal course of business, leases will be renewed or replaced by other leases.

The plant lease prohibits the Company from entering into future lease agreements if, as a result of new lease agreements, aggregate annual rentals under all leases will exceed $XXX.

Note 2—Capital Leases

The following is an analysis of the leased property under capital leases by major classes:

Classes of Property	Asset Balances at December 31,	
	19X6	19X5
Manufacturing plant	$XXX	$XXX
Store facilities	XXX	XXX
Other	XXX	XXX
Less: Accumulated amortization	(XXX)	(XXX)
	$XXX	$XXX

Exhibit 152B (continued)

The following is a schedule by years of future minimum lease payments under capital leases together with the present value of the net minimum lease payments as of December 31, 19X6:

Year ending December 31:

19X7	$XXX
19X8	XXX
19X9	XXX
19Y0	XXX
19Y1	XXX
Later years	XXX
Total minimum lease payments[1]	XXX
Less: Amount representing estimated executory costs (such as taxes, maintenance, and insurance), including profit thereon, included in total minimum lease payments	(XXX)
Net minimum lease payments	XXX
Less: Amount representing interest[2]	(XXX)
Present value of net minimum lease payments[3]	$XXX

[1]Minimum payments have not been reduced by minimum sublease rentals of $XXX due in the future under noncancelable subleases. They also do not include contingent rentals which may be paid under certain store leases on the basis of a percentage of sales in excess of stipulated amounts. Contingent rentals amounted to $XXX in 19X6 and $XXX in 19X5.

[2]Amount necessary to reduce net minimum lease payments to present value calculated at the Company's incremental borrowing rate at the inception of the leases.

[3]Reflected in the balance sheet as current and noncurrent obligations under capital leases of $XXX and $XXX, respectively.

Note 3—Operating Leases

The following is a schedule by years of future minimum rental payments required under operating leases that have initial or remaining noncancelable lease terms in excess of one year as of December 31, 19X6:

Exhibit 152B (continued)

Year ending December 31:

19X7	$ XXX
19X8	XXX
19X9	XXX
19Y0	XXX
19Y1	XXX
Later years	XXX
Total minimum payments required*	$ XXX

The following schedule shows the composition of total rental expense for all operating leases except those with terms of a month or less that were not renewed:

	Year ending December 31,	
	19X6	**19X5**
Minimum rentals	$ XXX	$ XXX
Contingent rentals	XXX	XXX
Less: Sublease rentals	(XXX)	(XXX)
	$ XXX	$ XXX

---

*Minimum payments have not been reduced by minimum sublease rentals of $XXX due in the future under noncancelable subleases.

[FAS13, ¶122]

.153 Lessor's disclosure (other than for leveraged leases) [is illustrated in Exhibits 153A and 153B]. [FAS13, ¶122]

Exhibit 153A

[Lessor] Company X
Balance Sheet

	December 31,	
ASSETS	**19X6**	**19X5**
Current assets:		
Net investment in direct financing and sales-type leases (Note 2)	XXX	XXX
Noncurrent assets:		
Net investment in direct financing and sales-type leases (Note 2)	XXX	XXX
Property on operating leases and property held for leases (net of accumulated depreciation of $XXX and $XXX for 19X6 and 19X5, respectively) (Note 3)	XXX	XXX

Footnotes appear in Exhibit 153B.

Exhibit 153B

Footnotes to Exhibit 153A

Note 1—Description of Leasing Arrangements

The Company's leasing operations consist principally of the leasing of various types of heavy construction and mining equipment, data processing equipment, and transportation equipment. With the exception of the leases of transportation equipment, the bulk of the Company's leases are classified as direct financing leases. The construction equipment and mining equipment leases expire over the next 10 years and the data processing equipment leases expire over the next 8 years. Transportation equipment (principally trucks) is leased under operating leases that expire during the next 3 years.

Note 2—Net Investment in Direct Financing and Sales-Type Leases

The following lists the components of the net investment in direct financing and sales-type leases as of December 31:

	19X6	19X5
Total minimum lease payments to be received*	$ XXX	$ XXX
Less: Amounts representing estimated executory costs (such as taxes, maintenance, and insurance), including profit thereon, included in total minimum lease payments	(XXX)	(XXX)
Minimum lease payments receivable	XXX	XXX
Less: Allowance for uncollectibles	(XXX)	(XXX)
Net minimum lease payments receivable	XXX	XXX
Estimated residual values of leased property (unguaranteed)	XXX	XXX
Less: Unearned income	(XXX)	(XXX)
Net investment in direct financing and sales-type leases	$ XXX	$ XXX

---

*Minimum lease payments do not include contingent rentals which may be received under certain leases of data processing equipment on the basis of hours of use in excess of stipulated minimums. Contingent rentals amounted to $XXX in 19X6 and $XXX in 19X5. At December 31, 19X6, minimum lease payments for each of the five succeeding fiscal years are as follows: $XXX in 19X7, $XXX in 19X8, $XXX in 19X9, $XXX in 19Y0, and $XXX in 19Y1.

Exhibit 153B (continued)

Note 3—Property on Operating Leases and Property Held for Lease

The following schedule provides an analysis of the Company's investment in property on operating leases and property held for lease by major classes as of December 31, 19X6:

Construction equipment	$ XXX
Mining equipment	XXX
Data processing equipment	XXX
Transportation equipment	XXX
Other	XXX
	XXX
Less: Accumulated depreciation	(XXX)
	$ XXX

Note 4—Rentals under Operating Leases

The following is a schedule by years of minimum future rentals on noncancelable operating leases as of December 31, 19X6:

Year ending December 31:

19X7	$XXX
19X8	XXX
19X9	XXX
19Y0	XXX
19Y1	XXX
Later years	XXX
Total minimum future rentals*	$XXX

---

*This amount does not include contingent rentals which may be received under certain leases of data processing equipment on the basis of hours of use in excess of stipulated minimums. Contingent rentals amounted to $XXX in 19X6 and $XXX in 19X5.

[FAS13, ¶122]

Illustrations of Accounting and Financial Statement Presentation for Leveraged Leases

.154 This paragraph illustrates the accounting requirements of this section and one way of meeting its disclosure requirements as applied to a leveraged lease. The illustrations do not encompass all circumstances that may arise in connection with leveraged leases; rather, the illustrations are based on a single example of a leveraged lease, the terms and assumptions of which are stated in Exhibit 154A. The elements of accounting and reporting illustrated for this example of a leveraged lease are as follows:

a. Leveraged lease example—terms and assumptions, Exhibit 154A
b. Cash flow analysis by years, Exhibit 154B
c. Allocation of annual cash flow to investment and income, Exhibit 154C
d. Journal entries for lessor's initial investment and first year of operation, Exhibit 154D
e. Financial statements including footnotes at end of second year, Exhibit 154E
f. Accounting for a revision in the estimated residual value of the leased asset assumed to occur in the eleventh year of the lease (from $200,000 to $120,000):
    (1) Revised allocation of annual cash flow to investment and income, Exhibit 154F
    (2) Balances in investment accounts at beginning of the eleventh year before revised estimate, Exhibit 154G
    (3) Journal entries, Exhibit 154H
    (4) Adjustment of investment accounts, Exhibit 154I

[FAS13, ¶123]

Exhibit 154A

Leveraged Lease Example Terms and Assumptions

Cost of leased asset (equipment)	$1,000,000.
Lease term	15 years, dating from January 1, 19X5.
Lease rental payments	$90,000 per year (payable last day of each year).
Residual value	$200,000 estimated to be realized one year after lease termination. In the eleventh year of the lease the estimate is reduced to $120,000.
Financing: Equity investment by lessor	$400,000.
Long-term nonrecourse debt	$600,000, bearing interest at 9% and repayable in annual installments (on last day of each year) of $74,435.30.
Depreciation allowable to lessor for income tax purposes	7-year ADR life using double-declining-balance method for the first 2 years (with the half-year convention election applied in the first year) and sum-of-years'-digits method for remaining life, depreciated to $100,000 salvage value.
Lessor's income tax rate (federal and state)	50.4% (assumed to continue in existence throughout the term of the lease).
Investment tax credit	10% of equipment cost or $100,000 (realized by the lessor on last day of first year of lease).
Initial direct costs	For simplicity, initial direct costs have not been included in the illustration.

[FAS13, ¶123]

(This page intentionally left blank.)

General Standards

Exhibit 154B

Cash Flow Analysis by Years

Year	1 Gross lease rentals and residual value	2 Depreciation (for income tax purposes)	3 Loan interest payments	4 Taxable income (loss) (col. 1 − 2 − 3)
Initial investment	—	—	—	—
1	$ 90,000	$ 142,857	$ 54,000	$(106,857)
2	90,000	244,898	52,161	(207,059)
3	90,000	187,075	50,156	(147,231)
4	90,000	153,061	47,971	(111,032)
5	90,000	119,048	45,589	(74,637)
6	90,000	53,061	42,993	(6,054)
7	90,000	—	40,163	49,837
8	90,000	—	37,079	52,921
9	90,000	—	33,717	56,283
10	90,000	—	30,052	59,948
11	90,000	—	26,058	63,942
12	90,000	—	21,704	68,296
13	90,000	—	16,957	73,043
14	90,000	—	11,785	78,215
15	90,000	—	6,145	83,855
16	200,000	100,000	—	100,000
Totals	$1,550,000	$1,000,000	$516,530	$ 33,470

[FAS13, ¶123]

5 Income tax credits (charges) (col. 4 × 50.4%)	6 Loan principal payments	7 Investment tax credit realized	8 Annual cash flow (col. 1 − 3 + 5 − 6 + 7)	9 Cumulative cash flow
—	—	—	$(400,000)	$(400,000)
$ 53,856	$ 20,435	$100,000	169,421	(230,579)
104,358	22,274	—	119,923	(110,656)
74,204	24,279	—	89,769	(20,887)
55,960	26,464	—	71,525	50,638
37,617	28,846	—	53,182	103,820
3,051	31,442	—	18,616	122,436
(25,118)	34,272	—	(9,553)	112,883
(26,672)	37,357	—	(11,108)	101,775
(28,367)	40,719	—	(12,803)	88,972
(30,214)	44,383	—	(14,649)	74,323
(32,227)	48,378	—	(16,663)	57,660
(34,421)	52,732	—	(18,857)	38,803
(36,813)	57,478	—	(21,248)	17,555
(39,420)	62,651	—	(23,856)	(6,301)
(42,263)	68,290	—	(26,698)	(32,999)
(50,400)	—	—	149,600	116,601
$(16,869)	$600,000	$100,000	$116,601	

Exhibit 154C

Allocation of Annual Cash Flow to Investment and Income

	1	2	3	4
			Annual Cash Flow	
Year	Lessor's net investment at beginning of year	Total (from Exhibit 154B, col. 8)	Allocated to investment	Allocated to income[1]
1	$400,000	$169,421	$134,833	$34,588
2	265,167	119,923	96,994	22,929
3	168,173	89,769	75,227	14,542
4	92,946	71,525	63,488	8,037
5	29,458	53,182	50,635	2,547
6	(21,177)	18,616	18,616	—
7	(39,793)	(9,553)	(9,553)	—
8	(30,240)	(11,108)	(11,108)	—
9	(19,132)	(12,803)	(12,803)	—
10	(6,329)	(14,649)	(14,649)	—
11	8,320	(16,663)	(17,382)	719
12	25,702	(18,857)	(21,079)	2,222
13	46,781	(21,248)	(25,293)	4,045
14	72,074	(23,856)	(30,088)	6,232
15	102,162	(26,698)	(35,532)	8,834
16	137,694	149,600	137,694	11,906
Totals		$516,601	$400,000	$116,601

[1]Lease income is recognized as 8.647 percent of the unrecovered investment at the beginning of each year in which the net investment is positive. The rate is that rate which when applied to the net investment in the years in which the net investment is positive will distribute the net income (net cash flow) to those years. The rate for allocation used in this exhibit is calculated by a trial and error process. The allocation is calculated based upon an initial estimate of the rate as a starting point. If the total thus allocated to income (column 4) differs under the estimated rate from the net cash flow (Exhibit 154B, column 8) the estimated rate is increased or decreased, as appropriate, to derive a revised allocation. This process is repeated until a rate is selected which develops a total amount allocated to income that is precisely equal to the net cash flow. As a practical matter, a computer program is used to calculate Exhibit 154C under successive iterations until the correct rate is determined.

[FAS13, ¶123]

	5	6	7
		Components of Income[2]	
Year	**Pretax income**	**Tax effect of pretax income**	**Investment tax credit**
1	$9,929	$(5,004)	$29,663
2	6,582	(3,317)	19,664
3	4,174	(2,104)	12,472
4	2,307	(1,163)	6,893
5	731	(368)	2,184
6	—	—	—
7	—	—	—
8	—	—	—
9	—	—	—
10	—	—	—
11	206	(104)	617
12	637	(321)	1,906
13	1,161	(585)	3,469
14	1,789	(902)	5,345
15	2,536	(1,278)	7,576
16	3,418	(1,723)	10,211
Totals	$33,470	$(16,869)	$100,000

[2]Each component is allocated among the years of positive net investment in proportion to the allocation of net income in column 4.

Exhibit 154D

Illustrative Journal Entries for Year Ending December 31, 19X5

	Debit	Credit
Lessor's Initial Investment		
Rentals receivable (Exhibit 154B, total of column 1 less residual value, less totals of columns 3 and 6)	233,470	
Investment tax credit receivable (Exhibit 154B, column 7)	100,000	
Estimated residual value (Exhibit 154A)	200,000	
Unearned and deferred income (Exhibit 154C, totals of columns 5 and 7)		133,470
Cash		400,000
To record lessor's initial investment.		

First Year of Operation

Journal Entry 1

	Debit	Credit
Cash	15,565	
Rentals receivable (Exhibit 154B, column 1 less columns 3 and 6)		15,565
Collection of first year's net rental		

Journal Entry 2

	Debit	Credit
Cash*	100,000	
Investment tax credit receivable (Exhibit 154B, column 7)		100,000
Receipt of investment tax credit		

---

*Receipts of the investment tax credit and other tax benefits are shown as cash receipts for simplicity only. Those receipts probably would not be in the form of immediate cash inflow. Instead, they likely would be in the form of reduced payments of taxes on other income of the lessor or on the combined income of the lessor and other entities whose operations are joined with the lessor's operations in a consolidated tax return.

Exhibit 154D (continued)

	Debit	Credit

Journal Entry 3

Unearned and deferred income   9,929

  Income from leveraged leases (Exhibit 154C,
    column 5)   9,929

    Recognition of first year's portion of pretax income
    allocated in the same proportion as the allocation
    of total income, [computed as follows:]

$$\frac{34,588}{116,601} \times 33,470 = 9,929$$

Journal Entry 4

Unearned and deferred income   29,663

  Investment tax credit recognized (Exhibit 154C,
    column 7)   29,663

    Recognition of first year's portion of investment tax
    credit allocated in the same proportion as the
    allocation of total income, [computed as follows:]

$$\frac{34,588}{116,601} \times 100,000 = 29,663$$

Journal Entry 5

Cash (Exhibit 154B, column 5)   53,856

Income tax expense (Exhibit 154C, column 6)   5,004

  Deferred taxes   58,860
    To record receipt of first year's tax credit from
    lease operation, to charge income tax expense for
    tax effect of pretax accounting income, and to
    recognize as deferred taxes the tax effect of the
    difference between pretax accounting income and
    the tax loss for the year, calculated as follows:

Exhibit 154D (continued)

	Debit	Credit

Tax loss (Exhibit 154B, column 4) $(106,857)
Pretax accounting income   9,929

Difference $(116,786)

Deferred taxes ($116,786 x 50.4%) $ 58,860

[FAS13, ¶123]

Exhibit 154E

**Illustrative Partial Financial Statements
Including Footnotes**

Balance Sheet

	ASSETS December 31,			LIABILITIES December 31,	
	19X6	**19X5**		**19X6**	**19X5**
Investment in leveraged leases	$334,708	$324,027	Deferred taxes arising from leveraged leases	$166,535	$58,860

Income Statement
(Ignoring all income and expense items other than
those relating to leveraged leasing)

	19X6	19X5
Income from leveraged leases	$ 6,582	$ 9,929
Income before taxes and investment tax credit	6,582	9,929
Less: Income tax expense*	(3,317)	(5,004)
	3,265	4,925
Investment tax credit recognized*	19,664	29,663
Net income	$22,929	$34,588

Footnotes appear on the following pages.

---

*These two items may be netted for purposes of presentation in the income statement, provided that the separate amounts are disclosed in a note to the financial statements.

Exhibit 154E (continued)

Footnotes

Investment in Leveraged Leases

The Company is the lessor in a leveraged lease agreement entered into in 19X5 under which mining equipment having an estimated economic life of 18 years was leased for a term of 15 years. The Company's equity investment represented 40 percent of the purchase price; the remaining 60 percent was furnished by third-party financing in the form of long-term debt that provides for no recourse against the Company and is secured by a first lien on the property. At the end of the lease term, the equipment is turned back to the Company. The residual value at that time is estimated to be 20 percent of cost. For federal income tax purposes, the Company receives the investment tax credit and has the benefit of tax deductions for depreciation on the entire leased asset and for interest on the long-term debt. Since during the early years of the lease those deductions exceed the lease rental income, substantial excess deductions are available to be applied against the Company's other income. In the later years of the lease, rental income will exceed the deductions and taxes will be payable. Deferred taxes are provided to reflect this reversal.

The Company's net investment in leveraged leases is composed of the following elements:

| | December 31, | |
	19X6	19X5
Rentals receivable (net of principal and interest on the nonrecourse debt)	$202,340	$217,905
Estimated residual value of leased assets	200,000	200,000
Less: Unearned and deferred income	(67,632)	(93,878)
Investment in leveraged leases	334,708	324,027
Less: Deferred taxes arising from leveraged leases	(166,535)	(58,860)
Net investment in leveraged leases	$168,173	$265,167

[FAS13, ¶123]

(This page intentionally left blank.)

Exhibit 154F

Allocation of Annual Cash Flow to Investment and Income
Revised to Include New Residual Value Estimate

	1	2	3	4
			Annual Cash Flow	
Year	Lessor's net investment at beginning of year	Total	Allocated to investment	Allocated to income[1]
1	$400,000	$169,421	$142,458	$26,963
2	257,542	119,923	102,563	17,360
3	154,979	89,769	79,323	10,446
4	75,656	71,525	66,425	5,100
5	9,231	53,182	52,560	622
6	(43,329)	18,616	18,616	—
7	(61,945)	(9,553)	(9,553)	—
8	(52,392)	(11,108)	(11,108)	—
9	(41,284)	(12,803)	(12,803)	—
10	(28,481)	(14,649)	(14,649)	—
11	(13,832)	(16,663)	(16,663)	—
12	2,831	(18,857)	(19,048)	191
13	21,879	(21,248)	(22,723)	1,475
14	44,602	(23,856)	(26,862)	3,006
15	71,464	(26,698)	(31,515)	4,817
16	102,979	109,920	102,979	6,941
Totals		$476,921	$400,000	$76,921

[1] The revised allocation rate is 6.741%.

[FAS13, ¶123]

	5	6	7
		Components of Income	
Year	**Pretax loss**	**Tax effect of pretax loss**	**Investment tax credit**
1	$(16,309)	$ 8,220	$ 35,052
2	(10,501)	5,293	22,568
3	(6,319)	3,184	13,581
4	(3,085)	1,555	6,630
5	(377)	190	809
6	—	—	—
7	—	—	—
8	—	—	—
9	—	—	—
10	—	—	—
11	—	—	—
12	(115)	58	248
13	(892)	450	1,917
14	(1,819)	916	3,909
15	(2,914)	1,469	6,262
16	(4,199)	2,116	9,024
Totals	$(46,530)	$23,451	$100,000

Exhibit 154G

Balances in Investment Accounts before
Revised Estimate of Residual Value

	1 Rentals receivable[1]	2 Estimated residual value	3 Investment tax credit receivable
Initial investment	$233,470	$200,000	$100,000
Changes in year of operation			
1	(15,565)	—	(100,000)
2	(15,565)	—	—
3	(15,565)	—	—
4	(15,565)	—	—
5	(15,565)	—	—
6	(15,565)	—	—
7	(15,565)	—	—
8	(15,564)	—	—
9	(15,564)	—	—
10	(15,565)	—	—
Balances, beginning of eleventh year	$ 77,822	$200,000	$ —

[FAS13, ¶123]

---

[1]Exhibit 154B, column 1, excluding residual value, less columns 3 and 6.
[2]Exhibit 154C, column 5.
[3]Exhibit 154C, column 7.
[4]50.4% of difference between taxable income (loss), Exhibit 154B, column 4, and pretax accounting income (loss), Exhibit 154C, column 5.

4	5	6	7
			Net investment (col. 1+2+3) less (col. 4+5+6)
Unearned and Deferred Income			
Pretax income (loss)[2]	Investment tax credit[3]	Deferred taxes[4]	
$33,470	$100,000	$ —	$400,000
(9,929)	(29,663)	58,860	(134,833)
(6,582)	(19,664)	107,675	(96,994)
(4,174)	(12,472)	76,308	(75,227)
(2,307)	(6,893)	57,123	(63,488)
(731)	(2,184)	37,985	(50,635)
—	—	3,051	(18,616)
—	—	(25,118)	9,553
—	—	(26,672)	11,108
—	—	(28,367)	12,803
—	—	(30,214)	14,649
$ 9,747	$ 29,124	$230,631	$ 8,320

Exhibit 154H

Illustrative Journal Entries
Reduction in Residual Value In Eleventh Year

	Debit	Credit
Journal Entry 1		
Pretax income (or loss)	$60,314	
Unearned and deferred income	27,450	
Pretax income (loss):		
Balance at end of 10th year	$ 9,747[a]	
Revised balance	(9,939)[b]	
Adjustment	(19,686)	
Deferred investment tax credit:		
Balance at end of 10th year	29,124[c]	
Revised balance	21,360[d]	
Adjustment	(7,764)	
Investment tax credit recognized		$ 7,764
Estimated residual value		80,000

To record:

a. The cumulative effect on pretax income
   and the effect on future income resulting
   from the decrease in estimated residual
   value:

Reduction in estimated residual value	$80,000
Less portion attributable to future years (unearned and deferred income)	(19,686)
Cumulative effect (charged against current income)	$60,314

b. The cumulative and future effect of the
   change in allocation of the investment
   tax credit resulting from the reduction in
   estimated residual value

---

[a]Exhibit 154G, column 4.
[b]Exhibit 154F, total of column 5 less amounts applicable to the first 10 years.
[c]Exhibit 154G, column 5.
[d]Exhibit 154F, total of column 7 less amounts applicable to the first 10 years.

Exhibit 154H (continued)

	Debit	Credit

Journal Entry 2

	Debit	Credit
Deferred taxes	30,398	
Income tax expense		30,398

To recognize deferred taxes for the difference
between pretax accounting income (or loss)
and taxable income (or loss) for the effect
of the reduction in estimated residual value:

Pretax accounting loss per journal entry 1	$(60,314)
Tax income (or loss)	—
Difference	$(60,314)
Deferred taxes ($60,314 × 50.4%)	$(30,398)

[FAS13, ¶123]

Exhibit 154I

Adjustment of Investment Accounts for Revised Estimate of Residual Value in Eleventh Year

	1 Rentals receivable	2 Estimated residual value
Balances, beginning of eleventh year (Exhibit 154G)	$77,822	$200,000
Adjustment of estimated residual value and unearned and deferred income (Exhibit 154H – journal entry 1)	—	(80,000)
Adjustment of deferred taxes for the cumulative effect on pretax accounting income (Exhibit 154H – journal entry 2)	—	—
Adjusted balances, beginning of eleventh year	$77,822	$120,000

[FAS13, ¶123]

3	4	5	6
Unearned and Deferred Income			**Net investment**
Pretax income (loss)	**Investment tax credit**	**Deferred taxes**	**(col. 1 + 2) less (col. 3 + 4 + 5)**
$ 9,747	$29,124	$230,631	$ 8,320
(19,686)	(7,764)	—	(52,550)
—	—	(30,398)	30,398
$ (9,939)	$21,360	$200,233	$(13,832)[1]

---

[1] Exhibit 154F, column 1.

Illustrations of Accounting for Sale-Leaseback Transactions

.155 Paragraphs .156 through .160M illustrate the accounting for certain sales with leasebacks but do not encompass all possible circumstances. Accordingly, each situation should be resolved based on an evaluation of the facts, using the examples in these paragraphs as guidance to the extent that they are applicable to the facts of the individual sale and leaseback. [FAS28, ¶22] Examples [in paragraphs .160A through .160M] assume that the initial transaction occurs on the first day of the year and that subsequent transactions and payments are made on the last day of each year. [FAS98, ¶26]

Sales Qualifying for Full and Immediate Profit Recognition

Minor Leaseback

.156 An enterprise constructs a regional shopping center and sells it to a real estate management firm. The sale meets [the criteria of paragraph .130C for sale-leaseback accounting and] the criteria of Section R10 for full and immediate profit recognition. At the same time, the seller leases back for 40 years a part of the facility, estimated to be approximately 8 percent of the total rental value of the center. Pertinent data are:

Sales price	$11,200,000
Cost of shopping center	$10,000,000

The rental called for by the lease appears to be reasonable in view of current market conditions. The seller-lessee would record the sale and recognize $1,200,000 profit. The seller-lessee would account for the leaseback as though it were unrelated to the sale because the leaseback is minor as indicated in paragraph .129(a). [FAS28, ¶23]

.157 An enterprise sells real estate, consisting of land and a factory. The factory has an estimated remaining life of approximately 40 years. The sale meets [the criteria of paragraph .130C for sale-leaseback accounting and] the criteria of Section R10 for full and immediate profit recognition. The seller negotiates a leaseback of the factory for one year because its new facilities are under construction and approximately one year will be required to complete the new facilities and relocate. Pertinent data are:

Sales price	$20,000,000
Carrying value of real estate	$ 6,000,000
Annual rental under leaseback	$ 900,000
Estimated annual market rental	$ 1,800,000

The leaseback is minor as indicated in paragraph .129(a) because the present value of the leaseback ($1,800,000) is less than 10 percent of the fair value of the asset sold (approximately $20,900,000, based on the sales price and the prepaid rental that apparently has reduced the sales price). Accordingly, the seller-lessee would record the sale and would recognize profit. An amount of $900,000 would be deferred and amortized as additional rent expense over the term of the leaseback to adjust the leaseback rentals to a reasonable amount.[42] Accordingly, the seller-lessee would recognize $14,900,000 as profit on the sale ($14,000,000 of profit based on the terms of the sale increased by $900,000 to adjust the leaseback rentals to a reasonable amount). [FAS28, ¶24]

Leasebacks That Are Not Minor but Do Not Cover Substantially All of the Use of the Property Sold

.158 An enterprise sells an existing shopping center to a real estate management firm. The sale meets [the criteria of paragraph .130C for sale-leaseback accounting and] the criteria of Section R10 for full and immediate profit recognition. At the same time, the seller leases back the anchor store (with corresponding use of the related land), estimated to be approximately 30 percent of the total rental value of the shopping center, for 20 years, which is substantially all of the remaining economic life of the building. Pertinent data are:

Sales price of shopping center	$3,500,000
Estimated to consist of:	
Land	$1,000,000
Buildings and improvements	2,500,000
	$3,500,000
Carrying value of shopping center	$1,000,000
Monthly rentals called for by leaseback	$ 12,600
Seller-lessee's incremental borrowing rate*	10%

*Believed to be approximately the same as the implicit rate calculated by the lessor.

The seller-lessee estimates the ratio of land to building for the leaseback to be the same as for the property as a whole. The seller-lessee would apply paragraph .122(b)(2)(a) because the land value exceeds 25 percent of the total fair value of the leased property and would account for the leaseback of the land as a separate operating lease. The seller-lessee would account for $2,500 as monthly land rental (10 percent annual rate applied to the $300,000 value of the land leased back—30 percent of the land value of the shopping center). The balance of the monthly rental (10,000) would be allocated to the building and improvements and would be accounted for as a capital lease pursuant to the 75 percent of economic life criterion. The leased building and improvements would be recorded at the present value of the $10,100 monthly rentals for 20 years at the seller-lessee's 10 percent incremental borrowing rate, or $1,046,608. The seller-lessee would compute the profit to be recognized on the sale as follows:

---

[42]If the term of a prepayment of rent were significant, the amount deferred would be the amount required to adjust the rental to the market rental for an equivalent property if that rental were also prepaid. [FAS28, ¶24, fn††]

Profit on the sale		$2,500,000
Recorded amount of leased asset (capital lease)	$1,046,608	
Present value of operating lease rentals at 10% rate	259,061	
Profit to be deferred and amortized		1,305,669
Profit to be recognized		$1,194,331

The deferred profit would be amortized in relation to the separate segments of the lease. The amount attributable to the capital lease ($1,046,608) would be amortized in proportion to the amortization of the leased asset over the term of the lease. The amount attributable to the operating lease ($259,061) would be amortized on a straight-line basis over the term of the lease. [FAS28, ¶25]

.159 An enterprise sells an airplane with an estimated remaining economic life of 10 years. At the same time, the seller leases back the airplane for three years. Pertinent data are:

Sales price	$600,000
Carrying value of airplane	$100,000
Monthly rental under leaseback	$ 6,330
Interest rate implicit in the lease as computed by the lessor*	12%

*Used because it is lower than the lessee's incremental borrowing rate.

The leaseback does not meet any of the criteria for classification as a capital lease; hence, it would be classified as an operating lease. The seller-lessee would compute the profit to be recognized on the sale as follows:

Profit on the sale	$500,000
Present value of operating lease rentals ($6,330 for 36 months at 12%)	190,581
Profit to be recognized	$309,419

The $190,581 deferred profit would be amortized in equal monthly amounts over the lease term because the leaseback is classified as an operating lease. [FAS28, ¶26]

Leaseback That Covers Substantially All of the Use of the Property Sold

.160 An enterprise sells equipment with an estimated remaining economic life of 15 years. At the same time, the seller leases back the equipment for 12 years. All profit on the sale would be deferred and amortized in relation to the amortization of the leased asset because the leaseback of *all* of the property sold covers a period in excess of 75 percent of the remaining economic life of the property and, thus, meets one of the criteria for classification as a capital lease. [FAS28, ¶27]

Sales Not Qualifying for Full and Immediate Profit Recognition

Sales Recognition

.160A A sale-leaseback transaction [that involves real estate, property improvements, or equipment integral to real estate and] that qualifies for sales recognition under the provisions of paragraphs .130A through .130M of this section is accounted for using sale-leaseback accounting by the seller-lessee whether the leaseback is classified as a capital lease or an operating lease in accordance with paragraph .102(a). The proper approach is first to determine the gain that would be recognized under Section R10 as if the transaction were a sale without a leaseback and then to allocate that gain as provided by this section over the remaining lease term. Under the provisions of footnote 28 to paragraph .129 of this section, the gain to be deferred and amortized in proportion to the leaseback is the gain that would otherwise be recognized in that year under the provisions of Section R10, except for the amount that can be recognized currently under paragraph .129 of this section. The total gain is recognized immediately if the leaseback is considered minor under the context of paragraph .129(a). The gain to be recognized currently under paragraph .129(b) is the amount of gain in excess of (a) the present value of the minimum lease payments if the leaseback is classified as an operating lease or (b) the recorded amount of the leased asset if the leaseback is classified as a capital lease. [FAS98, ¶27]

Example 1—Sale-Leaseback Transaction Accounted for as a Sale with Gain Recognized under the Installment Method and the Leaseback Classified as an Operating Lease

.160B Company A (a seller-lessee) sells the building at its principal manufacturing facility with an estimated remaining life of 15 years and a cost less accumulated depreciation of $800,000 to a buyer-lessor for $950,000 (the fair value of the property as determined by an independent third-party appraisal) and enters into an agreement to lease back the building. In exchange for the building, the seller-lessee receives $50,000 and a 10-year $900,000 recourse note with a 10 percent annual interest rate with annual payments of $146,471. Under the terms of the agreement, the seller-lessee is required to lease the building back for $100,000 a year for an initial period of 5 years. In addition, the seller-lessee has the option to renew the lease for an additional 5 years at $110,000 (estimated to be the then fair-market rental). [FAS98, ¶28]

.160C The sale-leaseback transaction does not include any form of continuing involvement that would preclude the seller-lessee from using sale-leaseback accounting. The initial down payment is inadequate for the seller-lessee to account for the transaction under the full accrual method described in Section R10. Under the provisions of Section R10, the seller-lessee elects to use the installment method to recognize the gain on the transaction. The property and any related debt would be removed from the seller-lessee's balance sheet and the note receivable net of unamortized deferred profit would be reported on the balance sheet. The renewal of the lease is included in the lease term for purposes of classifying the lease and amortizing income because the loss of the property at the end of the initial lease term is considered to be a penalty. The leaseback is classified as an operating lease because none of the criteria of paragraph .103 of this section is met. [FAS98, ¶29] [Exhibit 160A presents the calculation of the total gain and the portion to be recognized in each period.]

Exhibit 160A

Recognition of the Gain on the Transaction in Example 1

Calculation of the Gain

Sales price	$950,000
Cost less accumulated depreciation	800,000
Total gain to be recognized	$150,000

Gain Recognition under Section R10
(Installment Method Absent the Leaseback)

Day 1	$ 7,895
End of Year 1	8,916
Year 2	9,808
Year 3	123,381
Total	$150,000

Exhibit 160A (continued)

Gain Recognition for the Sale-Leaseback under This Section

Allocation of Annual Gain under the Installment Method with the Leaseback

Period Recognized	Day 1 Gain	End of Year 1 Gain	Year 2 Gain	Year 3 Gain	Total Gain Recognized
Year 1	$ 789				$ 789
Year 2	789	$ 990			1,779
Year 3	789	990	$1,226		3,005
Year 4	789	990	1,226	$ 17,625	20,630
Year 5	789	991	1,226	17,626	20,632
Year 6	790	991	1,226	17,626	20,633
Year 7	790	991	1,226	17,626	20,633
Year 8	790	991	1,226	17,626	20,633
Year 9	790	991	1,226	17,626	20,633
Year 10	790	991	1,226	17,626	20,633
Total	$7,895	$8,916	$9,808	$123,381	$150,000

Note: The installment method as described in paragraph .150 of Section R10 requires profit to be allocated to the down payment and subsequent collections on the buyer-lessor's note (principal portion only) by the percentage of profit inherent in the transaction (in this example, 15.79 percent). In addition, paragraph .155 of Section R10 allows a seller to switch from the installment method to the full accrual method of recognizing profit when the transaction meets the requirements for the full accrual method on a cumulative basis. In this example, it is assumed that for the seller-lessee to recognize profit in year 3 under the full accrual method, the buyer-lessor must have an investment in the property of 20 percent of the sales price to meet the minimum investment requirement and that the seller-lessee elects to switch to the full accrual method in the first full year after the minimum initial and continuing investment criteria are met.

[FAS98, ¶29, Illustration 1]

Deposit Method

.160D Paragraphs .123 through .125, .131, and .135 of Section R10 describe certain circumstances in which it is appropriate to account for a transaction using the deposit method (as described in paragraphs .159 through .161 of Section R10). If a sale-leaseback transaction is accounted for by the deposit method, lease payments decrease and collections on the buyer-lessor's note, if any, increase the seller-lessee's deposit account. The property and any related debt continue to be included in the seller-lessee's balance sheet, and the seller-lessee continues to depreciate the property. Under the provisions of paragraph .124 of Section R10, a seller-lessee that is accounting for any transaction by the deposit method according to the provisions of this section shall recognize a loss if at any time the net carrying amount of the property exceeds the sum of the balance in the deposit account, the fair value of the unrecorded note receivable, and any debt assumed by the buyer. [FAS98, ¶30]

.160E If a sale-leaseback transaction accounted for by the deposit method subsequently qualifies for sales recognition under this section and Section R10, the transaction is accounted for using sale-leaseback accounting, and the gain or loss is recognized in accordance with the provisions of paragraph .160A of this section. In addition, the leaseback is classified and accounted for in accordance with this section as if the sale had been recognized at the inception of the lease. If the leaseback meets one of the criteria for classification as a capital lease, the asset and liability accounts related to the leaseback, including accumulated amortization, are recorded as of the date that the sale is recognized to reflect amortization that would have been charged to expense had the lease been recorded as a capital lease at its inception. The change in the related lease accounts that would have been recorded from the inception of the lease had the transaction initially qualified for sale-leaseback accounting is included in computing the gain or loss recognized in accordance with paragraph .160A of this section. [FAS98, ¶31]

Example 2—Sale-Leaseback Transaction Accounted for by the Deposit Method with Subsequent Sales Recognition and the Leaseback Classified as a Capital Lease

.160F Company B (a seller-lessee) sells the building at one of its manufacturing facilities to a buyer-lessor for $950,000 (the fair value of the property as determined by an independent third-party appraisal) and enters into an agreement to lease the building back for 10 years at $150,000 per year. The property has a historical cost of $1,300,000 and accumulated depreciation at the date of the transaction of $400,000. Depreciation expense is $80,000 per year. In exchange for the building, the seller-lessee receives $50,000 and a 10-year $900,000 recourse note with a 10 percent annual interest rate with annual payments of $146,471. [FAS98, ¶32]

.160G The sale-leaseback transaction does not include any continuing involvement provisions, but the buyer-lessor has a questionable credit rating. Based on the poor credit standing of the buyer-lessor and the inadequate initial investment, the seller-lessee elects to account for the transaction by the deposit method. The initial and continuing investment must equal 20 percent of the sales price before it is appropriate to recognize profit by the full accrual method. Based on the amortization schedule of the buyer-lessor's note and assuming an improved credit rating of the buyer-lessor, income recognition under the full accrual method will be appropriate for the transaction at the end of year 3. The leaseback meets the criteria for classification as a capital lease in accordance with the provisions of paragraphs .103(c) and .103(d) of this section. [FAS98, ¶33] [Exhibit 160B presents the calculation of the total gain and the portion to be recognized in each period. Exhibit 160C presents the related journal entries. Exhibit 160D presents balance sheet information.]

Exhibit 160B

Recognition of the Gain on the Transaction in Example 2

Calculation of the Gain

Sales price (at inception)	$950,000
Cost less accumulated depreciation (end of year 3)	660,000
	290,000
Adjustments required by the deposit method or provisions of this section:	
Amortization of capital asset not recognized	(285,000)
Interest income credited to the deposit account in years 1-3 (credited to the deposit account as part of note payments received)	252,495
Interest expense charged to the deposit account in years 1-3 (charged to the deposit account as part of lease payments)	(247,363)
Total gain to be recognized	$ 10,132

Under the provisions of Section R10 and absent the leaseback, a gain of $10,132 would be recognized at the end of year 3 under the full accrual method.

Allocation of Gain Recognition
under This Section

Period Recognized	Year 3 Gain
Year 4	$ 1,447
Year 5	1,447
Year 6	1,447
Year 7	1,447
Year 8	1,448
Year 9	1,448
Year 10	1,448
Total	$10,132

[FAS98, ¶33, Illustration 2]

Exhibit 160C

Journal Entries for Example 2

	Debit	Credit
At inception:		
Cash	50,000	
Deposit		50,000

To record the receipt of the down payment on the property

Recurring journal entries in years 1-3:

Cash	146,471	
Deposit		146,471

To record the receipt of collections on the buyer-lessor's note (the annual payment required for a 10-year $900,000 note)

Deposit	150,000	
Cash		150,000

To record the lease payments

Depreciation expense	80,000	
Accumulated depreciation		80,000

To record the depreciation expense

When the sale is recognized at end of year 3:

Deposit	39,413	
Capital asset	950,000	
Note receivable	713,082	
Accumulated depreciation	640,000	
Property, plant, and equipment		1,300,000
Capital lease obligation		747,363
Accumulated amortization of the capital asset		285,000
Deferred gain		10,132

To recognize the sale and to record the capitalization of the leased asset

[FAS98, ¶33, Illustration 3]

(This page intentionally left blank.)

Exhibit 160D

Annual Balances in the Related Balance Sheet Accounts for Example 2

(1)	(2)	(3)	(4)	(5)	(6)	(7)	(8)	(9)	(10)	(11)	(12)	(13)
								Memo entries only in years 1-3				
Period	Deposit Account	Property, Plant, and Equipment	Accum. Depr.	Deferred Gain	Deferred Interest Income	Gross Note Receiv.	Net Note Receiv.	Deferred Interest Expense	Gross Lease Oblig.	Net Lease Oblig.	Capital Lease Asset	Capital Lease Accum. Amort.
At inception	$50,000	$1,300,000	$400,000	$ 0	$564,710	$1,464,710	$900,000	$550,000	$1,500,000	$950,000	$950,000	$ 0
Year 1	46,471	1,300,000	480,000	0	474,710	1,318,239	843,529	461,635	1,350,000	888,365	950,000	95,000
Year 2	42,942	1,300,000	560,000	0	390,357	1,171,768	781,411	379,003	1,200,000	820,997	950,000	190,000
Year 3	39,413	1,300,000	640,000	0	312,215	1,025,297	713,082	302,637	1,050,000	747,363	950,000	285,000
After sale is recognized	0	0	0	10,132	312,215	1,025,297	713,082	302,637	1,050,000	747,363	950,000	285,000
Year 4	0	0	0	8,685	240,907	878,826	637,919	233,120	900,000	666,880	950,000	380,000
Year 5	0	0	0	7,238	177,115	732,355	555,240	171,090	750,000	578,910	950,000	475,000
Year 6	0	0	0	5,791	121,591	585,884	464,293	117,242	600,000	482,758	950,000	570,000
Year 7	0	0	0	4,344	75,162	439,413	364,251	72,337	450,000	377,663	950,000	665,000
Year 8	0	0	0	2,896	38,736	292,942	254,206	37,209	300,000	262,791	950,000	760,000
Year 9	0	0	0	1,448	13,316	146,471	133,155	12,765	150,000	137,235	950,000	855,000
Year 10	0	0	0	0	0	0	0	0	0	0	950,000	950,000

Computations:

Column (2)   Original deposit plus collections on the buyer-lessor's note net of payments on the lease.

Column (3)   Plant balance at inception of lease.

Column (4)   Accumulated depreciation at inception of lease plus annual depreciation expense.

Column (5)   Deferred gain account less amount recognized annually per Exhibit 160B.

Column (6)   Column 7 less column 8.

Column (7)   Balance of remaining payments on the buyer-lessor's note.

Column (8)   The present value of the remaining note payments discounted at 10 percent.

Column (9)   Column 10 less column 11.

Column (10)   Accumulated balance of the remaining payments on the seller-lessee's lease obligation.

Column (11)   The present value of the remaining lease payments discounted at 9.301595 percent (assumed to be the seller-lessee's incremental borrowing rate).

Column (12)   Balance of the capital lease asset.

Column (13)   Accumulated balance of annual amortization of $95,000.

[FAS98, ¶33, Illustration 4]

Financing Method

.160H This section and paragraphs .128 through .142 and .144 through .146 of Section R10 describe some common forms of continuing involvement with the property by the seller that preclude a sale-leaseback transaction from sale-leaseback accounting. Depending on the nature and duration of the continuing involvement with the property, those provisions may require a sale-leaseback transaction to be accounted for as a financing. If a sale-leaseback transaction is reported as a financing, lease payments, exclusive of an interest portion, decrease and collections on the buyer-lessor's note increase the seller-lessee's liability account with a portion of the lease payments being recognized under the interest method. The seller-lessee reports the sales proceeds as a liability, continues to report the real estate or the real estate and equipment as an asset, and continues to depreciate the property. [FAS98, ¶34]

.160I If a sale-leaseback transaction accounted for as a financing subsequently qualifies for sales recognition under this section and Section R10, the transaction is then recorded using sale-leaseback accounting, and the cumulative change in the related balance sheet accounts is included in the computation of the gain recognized in accordance with the provisions of paragraph .160A of this section. In addition, the leaseback is classified and accounted for in accordance with paragraph .103 of this section as if the sale had been recognized at the inception of the lease. If the leaseback meets one of the criteria for classification as a capital lease, the related lease accounts, including accumulated amortization, are established as of the date the sale is recognized to reflect accumulated amortization and interest that would have been charged to expense had the lease been recorded at its inception. The change in the related lease accounts from the inception of the lease to the date the sale is recognized is included in the gain recognized in accordance with paragraph .160A of this section. [FAS98, ¶35]

Example 3—Sale-Leaseback Transaction (with Seller-Lessee Providing Financing) Accounted for as a Financing with Subsequent Sales Recognition and the Leaseback Classified as an Operating Lease

.160J Company C (a seller-lessee) sells one of its older special-purpose buildings at its principal manufacturing facility to a buyer-lessor for $950,000 (the fair value of the property as determined by an independent third-party appraisal) and enters into an agreement to lease the building back for 5 years at $100,000 per year. In addition, the agreement includes an option that allows the seller-lessee to renew the lease for an additional 5 years at $100,000 per year (estimated to be the then fair-market rental). The lease agreement also includes a fair value repurchase option during the initial lease term, and the seller-lessee guarantees that the residual value of the property will be no less than $920,000 at the end of the initial lease period. The special-purpose building has a historical cost of $3,510,000 and accumulated depreciation at the date of the transaction of $2,660,000. Depreciation expense is $70,000 per year. In exchange for the building, the seller-lessee receives $50,000 and a 10-year $900,000 recourse note with a 10 percent annual interest rate. [FAS98, ¶36]

.160K The seller-lessee accounts for this transaction as a financing because of the continuing involvement associated with the guarantee and the repurchase option. At the end of year 5, the seller-lessee exercises the renewal option, and the continuing involvement with the property is no longer at issue because the repurchase option and the guarantee no longer exist. The seller-lessee recognizes the transaction as a sale and classifies the leaseback as an operating lease because none of the criteria of paragraph .103 of this section is met. [FAS98, ¶37] [Exhibit 160E presents the calculation of the total gain and the portion to be recognized in each period. Exhibit 160F presents the related journal entries. Exhibit 160G presents balance sheet information.]

Exhibit 160E

Recognition of the Gain on the Transaction in Example 3

Calculation of the Gain

Sales price (at inception)	$950,000
Cost less accumulated depreciation (end of year 5)	500,000
	450,000
Adjustments required by the provisions of this section:	
Rent charged to the finance obligation account in years 1-5	(500,000)
Interest expense charged to income during years 1-5	82,405
Interest income credited to the finance obligation account in years 1-5	387,595
Total gain to be recognized	$420,000

Under the provisions of Section R10 and absent the leaseback, a gain of $420,000 would be recognized at the end of year 5 under the full accrual method.

Exhibit 160E (continued)

Allocation of Gain Recognition
under This Section

Period Recognized	Year 5 Gain
Year 5	$ 34,060*
Year 6	77,188
Year 7	77,188
Year 8	77,188
Year 9	77,188
Year 10	77,188
Total	$420,000

---

*Represents the amount by which the total gain to be recognized exceeds the present value of the future minimum lease payments discounted at the seller-lessee's incremental borrowing rate, assumed to be 9.301595 percent ($420,000 − $385,940 = $34,060).

[FAS98, ¶37, Illustration 5]

Exhibit 160F

Journal Entries for Example 3

	Debit	Credit
At inception:		
Cash	50,000	
Finance obligation		50,000
To record the receipt of the down payment on the property		
Recurring journal entries in years 1-5:		
Cash	146,471	
Finance obligation		146,471

To record the receipt of collections on the buyer-lessor's note (the annual payment required for a 10-year $900,000 note)

	Debit	Credit
Depreciation expense	70,000	
Accumulated depreciation		70,000
To record the depreciation expense		

Exhibit 160F (continued)

	Debit	Credit

Nonrecurring journal entries:

Year 1

	Debit	Credit
Finance obligation	94,972	
Interest expense	5,028	
Cash		100,000

To record the lease payments (Interest expense is calculated under the interest method using an effective yield of 10.0562 percent and the guaranteed residual value as the last payment.)

Year 2

	Debit	Credit
Finance obligation	89,793	
Interest expense	10,207	
Cash		100,000

To record the lease payments

Year 3

	Debit	Credit
Finance obligation	84,093	
Interest expense	15,907	
Cash		100,000

To record the lease payments

Year 4

	Debit	Credit
Finance obligation	77,820	
Interest expense	22,180	
Cash		100,000

To record the lease payments

Year 5

	Debit	Credit
Finance obligation	70,917	
Interest expense	29,083	
Cash		100,000

To record the lease payments

When the sale is recognized:

	Debit	Credit
Finance obligation	364,760	
Note receivable	555,240	
Accumulated depreciation	3,010,000	
Property, plant, and equipment		3,510,000
Deferred gain		385,940
Gain on sale		34,060

To record the transaction as a sale

[FAS98, ¶37, Illustration 6]

Exhibit 160G

Annual Balances in the Related Balance Sheet Accounts for Example 3

(1)	(2)	(3)	(4)	(5)	(6)	(7)	(8)
						Memo entries only in years 1-5	
		Property,			Deferred	Gross	Net
	Finance	Plant, and	Accumulated	Deferred	Interest	Note	Note
Period	Obligation	Equipment	Depreciation	Gain	Income	Receivable	Receivable
At inception	$ 50,000	$3,510,000	$2,660,000	$ 0	$564,710	$1,464,710	$900,000
Year 1	101,499	3,510,000	2,730,000	0	474,710	1,318,239	843,529
Year 2	158,177	3,510,000	2,800,000	0	390,357	1,171,768	781,411
Year 3	220,555	3,510,000	2,870,000	0	312,215	1,025,297	713,082
Year 4	289,206	3,510,000	2,940,000	0	240,907	878,826	637,919
Year 5	364,760	3,510,000	3,010,000	0	177,115	732,355	555,240
After sale is							
recognized	0	0	0	385,940	177,115	732,355	555,240
Year 6	0	0	0	308,752	121,591	585,884	464,293
Year 7	0	0	0	231,564	75,162	439,413	364,251
Year 8	0	0	0	154,376	38,736	292,942	254,206
Year 9	0	0	0	77,188	13,316	146,471	133,155
Year 10	0	0	0	0	0	0	0

Computations:

Column (2) Collections on the buyer-lessor's note net of payments on the lease applied to the finance obligation account.

Column (3) Plant balance at inception of lease.

Column (4) Accumulated depreciation at inception of lease plus annual depreciation expense.

Column (5) Deferred gain less amounts recognized annually per Exhibit 160E.

Column (6) Column 7 less column 8.

Column (7) Balance of remaining payments on the buyer-lessor's note.

Column (8) The present value of the remaining note payments discounted at 10 percent.

[FAS98, ¶37, Illustration 7]

Example 4—Sale-Leaseback Transaction (All Cash) Accounted for as a Financing with Subsequent Sales Recognition

.160L Company D (a seller-lessee) sells the building at one of its manufacturing facilities to a buyer-lessor for $950,000 (the fair value of the property as determined by an independent third-party appraisal) and enters into an agreement to lease the building back for 5 years at $100,000 per year. In addition, the seller-lessee has an option to renew the lease for an additional 5 years at $110,000 (estimated to be the then fair-market rental). The lease agreement also includes a fair value repurchase option, and the seller-lessee guarantees that the residual value of the property will be no less than $950,000 at the end of the initial lease period. The property has a historical cost of $1,200,000 and accumulated depreciation at the date of the transaction of $400,000. Depreciation expense is $80,000 per year. [FAS98, ¶38]

.160M Because of the continuing involvement associated with the guarantee and the repurchase option, the seller-lessee accounts for this transaction as a financing in accordance with the provisions of this section. At the inception of the lease, it is known that the seller-lessee is developing a new manufacturing process that will require a different manufacturing facility. The new technology becomes available at the end of the initial lease term, and the seller-lessee vacates the property. The fair value of the property (as determined by an independent third-party appraisal) at that time is $915,000. The seller-lessee honors the $950,000 guarantee of the property by paying the buyer-lessor $35,000 and recognizes the sale of the property. [FAS98, ¶39] [Exhibits 160H, 160I, and 160J present the calculation of the gain before the effect of the guarantee, the related journal entries, and balance sheet information, respectively.]

Exhibit 160H

Recognition of the Gain on the Transaction in Example 4

Calculation of the Gain before the Effect of the Guarantee

Sales price (at inception)	$950,000
Cost less accumulated depreciation (end of year 5)	400,000
Total gain to be recognized	$550,000

[FAS98, ¶39, Illustration 8]

Exhibit 160I

Journal Entries for Example 4

	Debit	Credit
At inception:		
Cash	950,000	
Finance obligation		950,000

To record the receipt of the proceeds from the sale of the property

Recurring journal entries in years 1-5:

	Debit	Credit
Depreciation expense	80,000	
Accumulated depreciation		80,000

To record the depreciation expense

	Debit	Credit
Interest expense	100,000	
Cash		100,000

To record the lease payments (Interest expense is calculated under the interest method using an effective yield of 10.5263 percent and the guaranteed residual as the last payment.)

When the sale is recognized:

	Debit	Credit
Accumulated depreciation	800,000	
Finance lease obligation	950,000	
Property, plant, and equipment		1,200,000
Cash		35,000
Gain on sale of property		515,000

To record the transaction as a sale

Under the provisions of this section, gain deferral is not required because the seller-lessee no longer occupies or otherwise benefits from the property and no longer has any guarantee or other continuing involvement.

[FAS98, ¶39, Illustration 9]

Exhibit 160J

Annual Balances in the Related Balance Sheet Accounts for Example 4

(1) Period	(2) Finance Obligation	(3) Property, Plant, and Equipment	(4) Accumulated Depreciation
At inception	$950,000	$1,200,000	$400,000
Year 1	950,000	1,200,000	480,000
Year 2	950,000	1,200,000	560,000
Year 3	950,000	1,200,000	640,000
Year 4	950,000	1,200,000	720,000
Year 5	950,000	1,200,000	800,000
When property is vacated	0	0	0

[FAS98, ¶39, Illustration 10]

Illustration of the Accounting for a Leveraged Lease in a Purchase Combination

.161 This paragraph illustrates one way that a lessor's investment in a leveraged lease might be valued by the acquiring enterprise in a business combination accounted for by the purchase method and the subsequent accounting for investment. The elements of accounting and reporting illustrated for this example are as follows:

a. Leveraged lease example—terms and assumptions, Exhibit 161A
b. Acquiring enterprise's cash flow analysis by years, Exhibit 161B
c. Acquiring enterprise's valuation of investment in the leveraged lease, Exhibit 161C
d. Acquiring enterprise's allocation of annual cash flow to investment and income, Exhibit 161D
e. Journal entry for recording allocation of purchase price to net investment in the leveraged lease, Exhibit 161E
f. Journal entries for the year ending December 31, 19Y4 (year 10 of the lease), Exhibit 161F [FIN21, ¶19]

Exhibit 161A

Leveraged Lease Example
Term and Assumptions

Cost of leased asset (equipment) $1,000,000.

Lease term 15 years, dating from January 1, 19X5.

Lease rental payments $90,000 per year (payable last day of each year).

Residual value $200,000 estimated to be realized 1 year after lease termination.

Financing:
  Equity investment by lessor $400,000.
  Long-term nonrecourse debt $600,000 bearing interest at 9% and repayable in annual installments (on last day of each year) of $74,435.30.

Depreciation allowable to lessor
  for income tax purposes 7-year ADR life using double-declining-balance method for the first 2 years (with the half-year convention election applied in the first year) and sum-of-years-digits' method for remaining life, depreciated to $100,000 salvage value.

Lessor's income tax rate
  (federal and state) 50.4% (assumed to continue in existence throughout the term of the lease).

Investment tax credit 10% of equipment cost or $100,000 (realized by the lessor on last day of first year of lease).

Initial direct costs For simplicity, initial direct costs have not been included in the illustration.

Date of business combination January 1, 19X2.

Tax status of business combination Nontaxable transaction.

Appropriate interest rate for
  valuing net-of-tax return
  on investment 4 1/2%
[FIN21, ¶19]

Exhibit 161B

Acquiring Enterprise's Cash Flow Analysis by Years

	1 Gross lease rentals and residual	2 Depreciation (for income tax	3 Loan interest	4 Taxable income	5 Income tax (charges) (col. 4 x	6 Loan principal	7 Annual cash flow (col. 1-3
Year	value	purposes)	payments	(col. 1-2-3)	50.4%)	payments	+5-6)
8	$ 90,000	-	$ 37,079	$ 52,921	$ (26,672)	$ 37,357	$ (11,108)
9	90,000	-	33,717	56,283	(28,367)	40,719	(12,803)
10	90,000	-	30,052	59,948	(30,214)	44,383	(14,649)
11	90,000	-	26,058	63,942	(32,227)	48,378	(16,663)
12	90,000	-	21,704	68,296	(34,421)	52,732	(18,857)
13	90,000	-	16,957	73,043	(36,813)	57,478	(21,248)
14	90,000	-	11,785	78,215	(39,420)	62,651	(23,856)
15	90,000	-	6,145	83,855	(42,263)	68,290	(26,698)
16	200,000	$100,000	-	100,000	(50,400)	-	149,600
Totals	$920,000	$100,000	$183,497	$636,503	$(320,797)	$411,988	$ 3,718

[FIN21, ¶19]

Exhibit 161C

Acquiring Enterprise's
Valuation of Investment in the Leveraged Lease

Cash Flow	Present Value at 4 1/2% Net-of-Tax Rate
1. Rentals receivable (net of principal and interest on the nonrecourse debt) ($15,564.70 at the end of each year for 8 years)	$102,663
2. Estimated residual value ($200,000 realizable at the end of 9 years)	134,581
3. Future tax payments (various amounts payable over 9 years—refer to Exhibit 161B)	(253,489)
Net present value	$ (16,245)

[FIN21, ¶19]

Exhibit 161D

Acquiring Enterprise's
Allocation of Annual Cash Flow to Investment and Income

	1	2	3	4	5	6
		Annual Cash Flow			Components of Income[b]	
Year	Net investment at beginning of year	Total from Exhibit 161B col. 7	Allocated to investment	Allocated to income[a]	Pretax income	Tax effect of pretax income
8	$(16,245)	$(11,108)	$(11,108)	–	–	–
9	(5,137)	(12,803)	(12,803)	–	–	–
10	7,666	(14,649)	(14,973)	$ 324	$ 5,530	$ (5,206)
11	22,639	(16,663)	(17,621)	958	16,353	(15,395)
12	40,260	(18,857)	(20,561)	1,704	29,087	(27,383)
13	60,821	(21,248)	(23,822)	2,574	43,937	(41,363)
14	84,643	(23,856)	(27,439)	3,583	61,160	(57,577)
15	112,082	(26,698)	(31,443)	4,745	80,995	(76,250)
16	143,525	149,600	143,525	6,075	103,698	(97,623)
Totals		$ 3,718	$(16,245)	$19,963	$340,760	$(320,797)

[a]Lease income is recognized as 4.233 percent of the unrecovered investment at the beginning of each year in which the net investment is positive. The rate is that rate which when applied to the net investment in the years in which the net investment is positive will distribute the net income (net cash flow) to those years. The rate for allocation used in this exhibit is calculated by a trial and error process. The allocation is calculated based upon an initial estimate of the rate as a starting point. If the total thus allocated to income (column 4) differs under the estimated rate from the net cash flow (column 2 less column 3), the estimated rate is increased or decreased, as appropriate, to derive a revised allocation. This process is repeated until a rate is selected which develops a total amount allocated to income that is precisely equal to the net cash flow. As a practical matter, a computer program is used to calculate Exhibit 161D under successive iterations until the correct rate is determined.

[b]Each component is allocated among the years of positive net investment in proportion to the allocation of net income in column 4. Journal entry 2 in Exhibit 161F of this paragraph includes an example of this computation.

[FIN21, ¶19]

Exhibit 161E

Illustrative Journal Entry for Recording
Allocation of Purchase Price to Net Investment in the Leveraged Lease

	Debit	Credit
Rentals receivable (Exhibit 161B, total of column 1 less residual value, less totals of columns 3 and 6)	$124,515	
Estimated residual value (Exhibit 161A)	200,000	
Purchase price allocation clearing account (Exhibit 161C, present value)	16,245	
Unearned and deferred income (Exhibit 161C, present value, less total of rentals receivable and estimated residual value)		$340,760

[FIN21, ¶19]

Exhibit 161F

Illustrative Journal Entries for the Year Ending December 31, 19Y4

Third Year of Operation after the Business
Combination (Year 10 of the Lease)

Journal Entry 1

	Debit	Credit
Cash	$15,565	
Rentals receivable (Exhibit 161B, column 1, less columns 3 and 6)		$15,565
Collection of year's net rental		

Journal Entry 2

	Debit	Credit
Unearned and Deferred Income	$ 5,530	
Income from leveraged leases (Exhibit 161D, column 5)		$5,530

Recognition of pretax income for the year
allocated in the same proportion as the
allocation of total income, [computed as follows:]

$$\frac{\$\ 324}{\$19,963} \times \$340,760 = \$5,530$$

Journal Entry 3

	Debit	Credit
Deferred taxes (Exhibit 161B, column 5, less Exhibit 161D, column 6)	$25,008	
Income tax expense (Exhibit 161D, column 6)	$ 5,206	
Cash (Exhibit 161B, column 5)		$30,214

To record payment of tax for the year.

[FIN21, ¶19]

_____

Illustration of Lessor and Lessee Accounting Required by Paragraphs .110 and .113(g) regarding Refunding of Tax-Exempt Debt

.162 Exhibits 163B and 163C illustrate the application of the requirements of paragraphs .110(a) and .113(g)(1) when a refunding of tax-exempt debt results in a change in the provisions of a lease agreement and the revised lease is classified as a direct financing lease by the lessor and as a capital lease by the lessee. [FAS22, ¶17]

Computation Information

.163 Exhibit 163A summarizes the total debt service requirements of the serial obligation to be refunded and of the refunding obligation. It is presumed that the perceived economic advantages of the refunding results from the lower interest rate applicable to the refunding obligation. The resulting reduction in total debt service requirements will be passed through to the lessee by changing the terms of the lease to conform with the debt service requirements of the refunding obligation. All costs that have been or that will be incurred by the lessor in connection with the refunding transaction will be passed through to the lessee. [FAS22, ¶17]

Exhibit 163A

Fifteen-Year Serial Debt Service Requirements ($000 omitted)

Obligation to Be Refunded			Refunding Obligation*			
Face Amount	Interest 7%	Total	Face Amount	Interest 5%	Total	Difference
$50,000	$32,300	$82,300	$52,000	$23,150	$75,150	$7,150

*The face amount of the refunding obligation ($52,000,000) is equal to the face amount of the obligation to be refunded ($50,000,000) plus the redemption premium applicable to the obligation to be refunded ($1,500,000) and the costs of issuance ($500,000).

[FAS22, ¶17]

Exhibit 163B

Lessor Accounting

**Computation of Required Adjustments to Reflect Changes in the Terms
of a Lease Resulting from a Refunding of Tax-Exempt Debt**

Adjustment to Balance of Minimum Lease Payments Receivable:
Present balance of minimum lease payments receivable
(equal to debt service requirements of obligation
to be refunded) .... $ 82,300,000
Minimum lease payments receivable under revised agreement
(equal to debt service requirements of refunding obligation) 75,150,000

Adjustment to reflect reduction in minimum lease payments
receivable .... $ 7,150,000

Adjustment to Unearned Income:
Change in the sum of the present value of the two components
of the gross investment using the interest rate applicable to
each agreement .... $ 2,000,000
Change in sum of the present value of the two components
of the gross investment using the interest rate applicable to
each agreement 7,150,000

Adjustment to reflect reduction in balance of unearned
income .... $ 9,150,000

Summary of Adjustments ($000 omitted):

	Minimum Lease Payments Receivable	Unearned Income	Net Investment
Balance before refunding	$82,300	$32,300	$50,000
Adjustment	(7,150)	(9,150)	2,000
Balance after refunding	$75,150	$23,150	$52,000

Exhibit 163B (continued)

Journal Entries to Record the Refunding and Changes in the Terms of the Lease Resulting from Refunding of Tax-Exempt Debt

	Debit	Credit
Recoverable deferred issue costs	500,000	
Loss resulting from refunding of tax-exempt debt	1,500,000	
7% outstanding obligation	50,000,000	
5% refunding obligation		52,000,000

To record loss from refunding $50,000,000—7% obligation with $52,000,000—5% refunding obligation in accordance with the provisions of Section D18.

	Debit	Credit
Unearned income	9,150,000	
Minimum lease payments receivable		7,150,000
Gain resulting from adjustment of lease terms		1,500,000
Recoverable deferred issue costs		500,000

To adjust unearned income by the amount required to adjust the net investment in the lease to the sum of the present values of the two components of the gross investment based on the interest rate applicable to the revised lease agreement in accordance with this section.

[FAS22, ¶17]

Exhibit 163C

Lessee Accounting

Computation of Required Adjustment to Lease Obligation to Reflect Changes in the Terms of the Lease Resulting from Refunding of Tax-Exempt Debt

Adjustment to Balance of Lease Obligation:
Present balance of lease obligation under
original agreement .... $ 50,000,000

Present value of future minimum lease payments
under revised agreement 51,500,000

Adjustment to Lease Obligation .... $ 1,500,000

Journal Entry to Record Adjustment to Lease Obligation Resulting from Refunding of Tax-Exempt Debt

	Debit	Credit
Loss resulting from revision to lease agreement	1,500,000	
Obligation under capital lease		1,500,000

> To record the loss resulting from changes in the lease terms resulting from a refunding of tax-exempt debt. For purposes of calculating the present value of the future minimum lease payments, deferred issue costs were considered as additional interest in determining the effective interest rate applicable to the revised agreement. (The loss shall be classified in accordance with Section D14.)

[FAS22, ¶17]

Illustrations of Determining Contingent Rentals

.164 Paragraphs .165 and .166 illustrate the application of the provisions of this section in determining contingent rentals. The examples do not comprehend all possible combinations of circumstances. [FAS29, ¶15]

.165 Paragraph .404 indicates that lease payments that depend on an existing index or rate, such as the prime interest rate, shall be included in the minimum lease payments based on the index or rate existing at the inception of the lease. As an example, an equipment lease could stipulate a monthly base rental of $2,000 and a monthly supplemental rental of $15 for each percentage point in the prime interest rate in effect at the beginning of each month. If the prime interest rate at the inception of the lease is 10 percent, minimum lease payments would be based on a monthly rental of $2,150 [$2,000 + ($15 × 10) = $2,150]. If the lease term is 48 months and no executory costs are included in the rentals, minimum lease payments would be $103,200 [$2,150 × 48]. If the lease is classified as a capital lease and the prime interest rate subsequently increases to 11 percent, the $15 increase in the monthly rentals would be a contingent rental included in the determination of income as it accrues. If the prime interest rate subsequently decreases to 9 percent, the $15 reduction in the monthly rentals would affect income as accruable. In the case of either the increase or decrease, minimum lease payments would continue to be $103,200. [FAS29, ¶16]

.166 Paragraph .404 also indicates that lease payments that depend on a factor directly related to the future use of the leased property, such as machine hours of use or sales volume during the lease term, are contingent rentals and accordingly, are excluded from minimum lease payments in their entirety. For example, a lease agreement for retail store space could stipulate a monthly base rental of $200 and a monthly supplemental rental of 1/4 of one percent of monthly sales volume during the lease term. Even if the lease agreement is a renewal for store space that had averaged monthly sales of $25,000 for the past 2 years, minimum lease payments would include only the $200 monthly base rental; the supplemental rental is a contingent rental that is excluded from minimum lease payments. The future sales for the lease term do not exist at the inception of the lease, and future rentals would be limited to $200 per month if the store were subsequently closed and no sales were made thereafter. [FAS29, ¶17]

Glossary

.401 Bargain purchase option. A provision allowing the lessee, at [the lessee's] option, to purchase the leased property for a price that is sufficiently lower than the expected fair value of the property at the date the option becomes exercisable that exercise of the option appears, at the inception of the lease, to be reasonably assured. [FAS13, ¶5d]

.402 Bargain renewal option. A provision allowing the lessee, at [the lessee's] option, to renew the lease for a rental sufficiently lower than the fair rental[401] of the property at the date the option becomes exercisable that exercise of the option appears, at the inception of the lease, to be reasonably assured. [FAS13, ¶5e]

.403 Capital lease. [Refer to paragraph .102(a)(1).]

.404 Contingent rentals. The increases or decreases in lease payments that result from changes occurring subsequent to the inception of the lease in the factors (other than the passage of time) on which lease payments are based, except as provided in the following sentence. Any escalation of minimum lease payments relating to increases in construction or acquisition cost of the leased property or for increases in some measure of cost or value during the construction or preconstruction period, as discussed in footnote 13, shall be excluded from contingent rentals. Lease payments that depend on a factor directly related to the future use of the leased property, such as machine hours of use or sales volume during the lease term, are contingent rentals and, accordingly, are excluded from minimum lease payments in their entirety. However, lease payments that depend on an existing index or rate, such as the consumer price index or the prime interest rate, shall be included in minimum lease payments based on the index or rate existing at the inception of the lease; any increases or decreases in lease payments that result from subsequent changes in the index or rate are contingent rentals and thus affect the determination of income as accruable. [FAS29, ¶11]

.405 Direct financing leases. [Refer to paragraph .102(b)(2).]

.406 Estimated economic life of leased property. The estimated remaining period during which the property is expected to be economically usable by one or more users, with normal repairs and maintenance, for the purpose for which it was intended at the inception of the lease, without limitation by the lease term. [FAS13, ¶5g]

.407 Estimated residual value of leased property. The estimated fair value of the leased property at the end of the lease term. [FAS13, ¶5h]

---

[401] *Fair rental* in this context shall mean the expected rental for equivalent property under similar terms and conditions. [FAS13, ¶5, fn2]

.408 Executory costs. [Those costs] such as insurance, maintenance, and taxes [incurred for leased property, whether paid by the lessor or lessee. Amounts paid by a lessee in consideration for a guarantee from an unrelated third party of the residual value are also executory costs. If executory costs are paid by a lessor, any lessor's profit on those costs is considered the same as executory costs.] [FAS13, ¶7&10]

.409 Fair value of the leased property. The price for which the property could be sold in an arm's-length transaction between unrelated parties. The following are examples of the determination of fair value:

a. When the lessor is a manufacturer or dealer, the fair value of the property at the inception of the lease will ordinarily be its normal selling price, reflecting any volume or trade discounts that may be applicable. However, the determination of fair value shall be made in light of market conditions prevailing at the time, which may indicate that the fair value of the property is less than the normal selling price and, in some instances, less than the cost of the property.

b. When the lessor is not a manufacturer or dealer, the fair value of the property at the inception of the lease will ordinarily be its cost, reflecting any volume or trade discounts that may be applicable. However, when there has been a significant lapse of time between the acquisition of the property by the lessor and the inception of the lease, the determination of fair value shall be made in light of market conditions prevailing at the inception of the lease, which may indicate that the fair value of the property is greater or less than its cost or carrying amount, if different (refer to paragraph .102). [FAS13, ¶5c]

.410 Inception of the lease. The date of the lease agreement or commitment, if earlier.[402] For purposes of this definition, a commitment shall be in writing, signed by the parties in interest to the transaction, and shall specifically set forth the principal provisions of the transaction. If any of the principal provisions [is] yet to be negotiated, such a preliminary agreement or commitment does not qualify for purposes of this definition. [FAS23, ¶6]

.411 Initial direct costs.[402a] Only those costs incurred by the lessor that are (a) costs to

---

[402]If a master lease agreement specifies that the lessee must take a minimum number of units or dollar value of equipment and if all other principal provisions are stated, the inception of the lease is the date of the master lease agreement with respect to the specified minimum. The inception of the lease for equipment *take-downs* in excess of the specified minimum is the date that the lessee orders the equipment because the lessee does not agree to lease the equipment until that date. To the extent that lease payments for required take-downs are based on value at the date of the take-down, the lease, in effect, has a preacquisition period escalator provision based on value. Footnotes 18, 24, 31, and 35 address that situation. If a master lease agreement does not require the lessee to take down any minimum quantity or dollar value of equipment, the agreement is merely an offer by the lessor to rent equipment at an agreed price and the inception of the lease is the date that the lessee orders the equipment. [FAS23, ¶14]

[402a]Initial direct cost shall be offset by nonrefundable fees that are yield adjustments as prescribed in Section L20. [FAS91, ¶24, fn*] The provisions of paragraphs .104 through .108 of Section L20 apply to lessors in determining the net amount of *initial direct costs*. [FAS91, ¶23]

originate a lease incurred in transactions with independent third parties that (i) result directly from and are essential to acquire that lease and (ii) would not have been incurred had that leasing transaction not occurred and (b) certain costs directly related to specified activities performed by the lessor for that lease. Those activities are: evaluating the prospective lessee's financial condition; evaluating and recording guarantees, collateral, and other security arrangements; negotiating lease terms; preparing and processing lease documents; and closing the transaction. The costs directly related to those activities shall include only that portion of the employees' total compensation and payroll-related fringe benefits directly related to time spent performing those activities for that lease and other costs related to those activities that would not have been incurred but for that lease. Initial direct costs shall not include costs related to activities performed by the lessor for advertising, soliciting potential lessees, servicing existing leases, and other ancillary activities related to establishing and monitoring credit policies, supervision, and administration. Initial direct costs shall not include administrative costs, rent, depreciation, any other occupancy and equipment costs and employees' compensation and fringe benefits related to activities described in the previous sentence, unsuccessful origination efforts, and idle time. [FAS91, ¶24]

.412 **Interest rate implicit in the lease.** The discount rate that, when applied to (a) the minimum lease payments, excluding that portion of the payments representing executory costs to be paid by the lessor, together with any profit thereon, and (b) the unguaranteed residual value accruing to the benefit of the lessor[403] causes the aggregate present value at the beginning of the lease term to be equal to the fair value of the leased property to the lessor at the inception of the lease, minus any investment tax credit retained by the lessor and expected to be realized by him. (This definition does not necessarily purport to include all factors that a lessor might recognize in determining his rate of return, for example, refer to paragraph .146.) [FAS13, ¶5k]

.413 **Lease.** An agreement conveying the right to use property, plant, or equipment (land or depreciable assets or both) usually for a stated period of time. [FAS13, ¶1]

.414 **Lease term.** The fixed noncancelable term of the lease plus (a) all periods, if any, covered by bargain renewal options (as defined in paragraph .402), (b) all periods, if any, for which failure to renew the lease imposes a penalty (as defined in paragraph .418A) on the lessee in such amount that a renewal appears, at the inception of the lease, to be reasonably assured, (c) all periods, if any, covered by ordinary renewal options[405] during which a guarantee by the lessee of the lessor's debt directly or indi-

---

[403]If the lessor is not entitled to any excess of the amount realized on disposition of the property over a guaranteed amount, no unguaranteed residual value would accrue to the lessor's benefit. [FAS13, ¶5k, fn8]

[404Deleted 5/88 because of FASB Statement 98, *Accounting for Leases: Sale-Leaseback Transactions Involving Real Estate, Sales-Type Leases of Real Estate, Definition of the Lease Term, and Initial Direct Costs of Direct Financing Leases.*]

[405Paragraphs .501 through .505 address fiscal funding clauses in lease agreements.]

rectly related to the leased property[405a] is expected to be in effect or a loan from the lessee to the lessor directly or indirectly related to the leased property is expected to be outstanding, (d) all periods, if any, covered by ordinary renewal options preceding the date as of which a bargain purchase option (as defined in paragraph .401) is exercisable, and (e) all periods, if any, representing renewals or extensions of the lease at the lessor's option; however, in no case shall the lease term be assumed to extend beyond the date a bargain purchase option becomes exercisable. A lease that is cancelable (1) only upon the occurrence of some remote contingency, (2) only with the permission of the lessor, (3) only if the lessee enters into a new lease with the same lessor, or (4) only if the lessee incurs a penalty in such amount that continuation of the lease appears, at inception, reasonably assured shall be considered "noncancelable" for purposes of this definition. [FAS98, ¶22a]

.415 **Lessee's incremental borrowing rate.** The rate that, at the inception of the lease, the lessee would have incurred to borrow over a similar term the funds necessary to purchase the leased asset.[406] [FAS13, ¶5l]

.416 **Leveraged lease.** [Refer to paragraphs .102(b)(3) and .144.]

.417 **Minimum lease payments.**

a. *From the standpoint of the lessee:* The payments that the lessee is obligated to make or can be required to make in connection with the leased property. [FAS13, ¶5j] (Contingent rentals, as defined in paragraph .404, shall be excluded from minimum lease payments.) [FAS29, ¶10] However, a guarantee by the lessee of the lessor's debt and the lessee's obligation to pay (apart from the rental payments) executory costs in connection with the leased property shall be excluded. If the lease contains a bargain purchase option, only the minimum rental payments over the lease term (as defined in paragraph .413) and the payment called for by the bargain purchase option shall be included in the minimum lease payments. Otherwise, minimum lease payments include the following:
   (1) The minimum rental payments called for by the lease over the lease term.
   (2) Any guarantee by the lessee or any party related to the lessee of the residual value at the expiration of the lease term, whether or not payment of

---

[405a]The phrase *indirectly related to the leased property* is used in this paragraph to describe provisions or conditions that in substance are guarantees of the lessor's debt or loans to the lessor by the lessee that are related to the leased property but are structured in such a manner that they do not represent a direct guarantee or loan. Examples include a party related to the lessee guaranteeing the lessor's debt on behalf of the lessee, or the lessee financing the lessor's purchase of the leased asset using collateral other than the leased property. [FAS98, ¶22a]

[406Paragraphs .509 through .511 further discuss the interest rate used in calculating the present value of the minimum lease payments.]

the guarantee constitutes a purchase of the leased property.[407] When the lessor has the right to require the lessee to purchase the property at termination of the lease for a certain or determinable amount, that amount shall be considered a lessee guarantee. When the lessee agrees to make up any deficiency[408] below a stated amount in the lessor's realization of the residual value, the guarantee to be included in the minimum lease payments shall be the stated amount,[409] rather than an estimate of the deficiency to be made up.

(3) Any payment that the lessee must make or can be required to make upon failure to renew or extend the lease at the expiration of the lease term, whether or not the payment would constitute a purchase of the lease property. In this connection, it should be noted that the definition of lease term (refer to paragraph .413) includes "all periods, if any, for which failure to renew the lease imposes a penalty on the lessee in an amount such that renewal appears, at the inception of the lease, to be reasonably assured." If the lease term has been extended because of that provision, the related penalty shall not be included in minimum lease payments.

b. *From the standpoint of the lessor:* The payments described above plus any guarantee of the residual value or of rental payments beyond the lease term by a third party unrelated to either the lessee or the lessor,[410] provided the third party is financially capable of discharging the obligations that may arise from the guarantee. [FAS13, ¶5j]

.417A [Deleted 1/89 and renumbered .417C.]

---

[407] A guarantee of the residual value obtained by the lessee from an unrelated third party for the benefit of the lessor shall not be used to reduce the amount of the lessee's minimum lease payments except to the extent that the lessor explicitly releases the lessee from obligation, including secondary obligation if the guarantor defaults, to make up a residual value deficiency. Amounts paid in consideration for a guarantee by an unrelated third party are executory costs and are not included in the lessee's minimum lease payments. [FIN19, ¶5]

[408] A lease provision requiring the lessee to make up a residual value deficiency that is attributable to damage, extraordinary wear and tear, or excessive usage is similar to contingent rentals in that the amount is not determinable at the inception of the lease. Such a provision does not constitute a lessee guarantee of the residual value. [FIN19, ¶3]

[409] If a lease limits the amount of the lessee's obligation to make up a residual value deficiency to an amount less than the stipulated residual value of the leased property at the end of the lease term, the amount of the lessee's guarantee to be included in minimum lease payments shall be limited to the specified maximum deficiency the lessee can be required to make up. The *stated amount* is the specified maximum deficiency that the lessee is obligated to make up. If that maximum deficiency clearly exceeds any reasonable estimate of a deficiency that might be expected to arise in normal circumstances, the lessor's risk associated with the portion of the residual in excess of the maximum may appear to be negligible. However, the fact remains that the lessor must look to the resale market or elsewhere rather than to the lessee to recover the unguaranteed portion of the stipulated residual value of the leased property. The lessee has not guaranteed full recovery of the residual value, and the parties should not base their accounting on the assumption that the lessee has guaranteed it. [FIN19, ¶4]

[410] If the guarantor is related to the lessor, the residual value shall be considered as unguaranteed. [FAS13, ¶5j, fn8]

.417B **Money-over-money lease transaction.** [Refer to paragraph .542.]

.417C **Nonrecourse financing.** Lending or borrowing activities in which the creditor does not have general recourse to the debtor but rather has recourse only to the property used for collateral in the transaction or other specific property. [FAS98, ¶70]

.418 **Operating lease.** [Refer to paragraphs .102(a)(2) and .102(b)(4).]

.418A **Penalty.** Any requirement that is imposed or can be imposed on the lessee by the lease agreement or by factors outside the lease agreement to disburse cash, incur or assume a liability, perform services, surrender or transfer an asset or rights to an asset or otherwise forego an economic benefit, or suffer an economic detriment. Factors to consider when determining if an economic detriment may be incurred include, but are not limited to, the uniqueness of purpose or location of the property, the availability of a comparable replacement property, the relative importance or significance of the property to the continuation of the lessee's line of business or service to its customers, the existence of leasehold improvements or other assets whose value would be impaired by the lessee vacating or discontinuing use of the leased property, adverse tax consequences, and the ability or willingness of the lessee to bear the cost associated with relocation or replacement of the leased property at market rental rates or to tolerate other parties using the leased property. [FAS98, ¶22b]

.419 **Related parties.** A parent company and its subsidiaries, an owner enterprise and its joint ventures (corporate or otherwise) and partnerships, and an investor (including a natural person) and its investees, provided that the parent company, owner enterprise, or investor has the ability to exercise significant influence over operating and financial policies of the related party, as significant influence is defined in Section 182, paragraph .104. In addition to the examples of significant influence set forth in that paragraph, significant influence may be exercised through guarantees of indebtedness, extensions of credit, or through ownership of warrants, debt obligations, or other securities. If two or more enterprises are subject to the significant influence of a parent company, owner enterprise, investor (including a natural person), or common officers or directors, those enterprises shall be considered related parties with respect to each other. [FAS13, ¶5a]

.420 **Renewal or extension of a lease.** [The continuation of a lease agreement beyond the original lease term including] a new lease under which the lessee continues to use the same property. [FAS13, ¶6, fn9]

.420A **Sale-leaseback accounting.** For purposes of this section, a method of accounting for a sale-leaseback transaction in which the seller-lessee records the sale, removes all property and related liabilities from its balance sheet, recognizes gain or loss from the sale, and classifies the leaseback in accordance with this section. [FAS98, ¶70]

.420B Sales recognition. Any method that is described in Section R10 as a method to record a transaction involving real estate, other than the deposit method, or the methods to record transactions accounted for as financing, leasing, or profit-sharing arrangements. Profit recognition methods described in Section R10 commonly used to record transactions involving real estate include, but are not limited to, the full accrual method, the installment method, the cost recovery method, and the reduced profit method. [FAS98, ¶70]

.421 Sales-type lease. [Refer to paragraph .102(b)(1).]

.422 Unguaranteed residual value. The estimated residual value of the leased property exclusive of any portion guaranteed by the lessee or by any party related to the lessee or by a third party unrelated to the lessor.[411] [FAS13, ¶5i]

.423 Unrelated parties. [All parties that are not related parties as defined above.]

.424 Wrap lease transaction. [Refer to paragraph .544.]

---

[411]If the guarantor is related to the lessor, the residual value shall be considered as unguaranteed. [FAS13, ¶5i, fn4]

Supplemental Guidance

Fiscal Funding Clauses in Lease Agreements

.501 *Question*—What effect, if any, should the existence of a fiscal funding clause in a lease agreement have on the classification of the lease under this section? [FTB79-10, ¶1]

.502 *Background*—A fiscal funding clause is commonly found in a lease agreement in which the lessee is a governmental unit. A fiscal funding clause generally provides that the lease is cancelable if the legislature or other funding authority does not appropriate the funds necessary for the governmental unit to fulfill its obligations under the lease agreement. [FTB79-10, ¶2]

.503 *Response*—[Under] paragraph .413, a cancelable lease, such as a lease containing a fiscal funding clause, [must] be evaluated to determine whether the uncertainty of possible lease cancellation is a remote contingency. That paragraph states that "a lease which is cancelable (1) only upon occurrence of some *remote* contingency . . . shall be considered for purposes of this definition" of lease term. (Emphasis added.) [FTB79-10, ¶3]

.504 In discussing the likelihood of the occurrence of a future event or events to confirm a loss contingency, Section C59, paragraph .104, defines *remote* as relating to conditions when "the chance of the future event or events occurring is slight." The evaluation of the uncertainty of possible lease cancellation should be consistent with that definition. [FTB79-10, ¶4]

.505 The existence of a fiscal funding clause in a lease agreement would necessitate an assessment of the likelihood of lease cancellation through exercise of the fiscal funding clause. If the likelihood of exercise of the fiscal funding clause is assessed as being remote, a lease agreement containing such a clause would be considered a noncancelable lease; otherwise, the lease would be considered cancelable and thus classified as an operating lease. [FTB79-10, ¶5]

.506-.508 [Deleted 5/88 because of FASB Statement 98, *Accounting for Leases: Sale-Leaseback Transactions Involving Real Estate, Sales-Type Leases of Real Estate, Definition of the Lease Term, and Initial Direct Costs of Direct Financing Leases.*]

Interest Rate Used in Calculating the Present Value of Minimum Lease Payments

.509 *Question*—May a lessee use its secured borrowing rate in calculating the present value of minimum lease payments in applying the provisions of this section? [FTB79-12, ¶1]

.510 *Background*—Paragraph .103(d) requires the lessee to use its incremental borrowing rate (or the lessor's implicit interest rate in certain circumstances) to calculate the present value of minimum lease payments. The incremental borrowing rate is defined in paragraph .414 as "the rate that . . . the lessee would have incurred to borrow over a similar term the funds necessary to purchase the leased asset." [FTB79-12, ¶2]

.511 *Response*—Paragraph .414 does not proscribe the lessee's use of a secured borrowing rate as its incremental borrowing rate if that rate is determinable, reasonable, and consistent with the financing that would have been used in the particular circumstances. [FTB79-12, ¶3]

Applicability of This Section to Current Value Financial Statements

.512 *Question*—Are financial statements prepared on a current value basis exempt from the provisions of this section? [FTB79-13, ¶1]

.513 *Response*—This section would not be inapplicable merely because financial statements are prepared on a current value basis. For example, if at its inception a lease involving property meets one or more of the four criteria of paragraph .103 and both of the criteria of paragraph .104, the lessor would classify the lease as a sales-type or direct financing lease, whichever is appropriate. Subsequently, the carrying amount of the recorded investment in the lease payments receivable would be adjusted in accordance with the valuation techniques employed in preparing the financial statements on a current value basis. [FTB79-13, ¶2]

Upward Adjustment of Guaranteed Residual Values

.514 *Question*—Does the prohibition against upward adjustments of estimated residual values in this section also apply to upward adjustments that result from renegotiations of the guaranteed portions of residual values? [FTB79-14, ¶1]

.515 *Background*—Paragraphs .113(d), .114(d), and .148 require the lessor to review annually the estimated residual value of sales-type leases, direct financing leases, and leveraged leases, respectively. Those paragraphs also contain a provision that prohibits any upward adjustment of the estimated residual value. [FTB79-14, ¶2]

.516 *Response*—The prohibitions of paragraphs .113(d), .114(d), and .148 against upward adjustments to the leased property's estimated residual value are equally applicable to the guaranteed portion. If a lease initially transferred substantially all of the benefits and risks incident to the ownership of the leased property, it would not seem appropriate that the lessor could subsequently increase the benefits that were accounted for as having been retained initially. [FTB79-14, ¶3]

.517 Recording upward adjustments to the leased property's residual value would, in essence, result in recognizing a sale of the residual value interest. In this respect, the prohibition of an upward adjustment in the leased property's residual value is similar to the prohibition in Section C59, paragraph .118, of recognizing gain contingencies because to do so might be recognizing revenue before realization. Realization of the residual value interest might also be contingent on factors, such as the physical condition of the leased property or the requirements and related costs, if any, relating to remarketing agreements at the end of the lease term. [FTB79-14, ¶4]

Accounting for Loss on a Sublease Not Involving the Disposal of a Segment

.518 *Question*—Should a loss on a sublease not involving the disposal of a segment be recognized and how is it determined? [FTB79-15, ¶1]

.519 *Response*—The general principle of recognizing losses on transactions and the applicability of that general principle to contracts that are expected to result in a loss are well established. Accordingly, if costs expected to be incurred under an operating sublease (that is, executory costs and either amortization of the leased asset or rental payments on an operating lease, whichever is applicable) exceed anticipated revenue on the operating sublease, a loss should be recognized by the sublessor. Similarly, a loss should be recognized on a direct financing sublease if the carrying amount of the investment in the sublease exceeds the total of rentals expected to be received and estimated residual values unless the sublessor's tax benefits from the transaction are sufficient to justify that result. [FTB79-15, ¶2]

.520 The absence of explicit reference to accounting for these transactions in this section does not affect the necessity to follow general principles of loss recognition. [FTB79-15, ¶3]

Effect of a Change in Income Tax Rate on the Accounting for Leveraged Leases

.521 *Question*—What effect, if any, does a change in the income tax rate have on the accounting for leveraged leases under this section? [FTB79-16(R), ¶1]

.522 *Background*—Paragraph .148 provides that, when an important assumption changes, the rate of return and the allocation of income shall be recalculated from the inception of the lease, and the change in the recalculated balances of net investment shall be recognized as a gain or loss in the year in which the assumption is changed. [FTB79-16(R), ¶2]

.523 *Response*—The lessor's income tax rate is an important assumption in accounting for a leveraged lease. Accordingly, the income effect of a change in the income tax rate should be recognized in the first accounting period ending on or after the date on which the legislation effecting a rate change becomes law. [FTB79-16(R), ¶3]

.524 If accounting for the effect on leveraged leases of the change in tax rates results in a significant variation from the customary relationship between income tax expense and pretax accounting income and the reason for that variation is not otherwise apparent, [FTB79-16(R), ¶4] Section I27, paragraph .146, [FAS109, ¶288bb] requires that the reason for that variation should be disclosed. [FTB79-16(R), ¶4]

Accounting for Operating Leases

Accounting for Operating Leases with Scheduled Rent Increases

.525 *Question*—Certain operating lease agreements specify scheduled rent increases over the lease term. Such scheduled rent increases may, for example, be designed to provide an inducement or "rent holiday" for the lessee, to reflect the anticipated effects of inflation, to ease the lessee's near-term cash flow requirements, or to acknowledge the time value of money. For operating leases that include scheduled rent increases, is it ever appropriate for lessees or lessors to recognize rent expense or rental income on a basis other than the straight-line basis required by this section? [FTB85-3, ¶1]

.526 *Response*—The effects of those scheduled rent increases, which are included in minimum lease payments [refer to paragraph .417], should be recognized by lessors and lessees on a straight-line basis over the lease term unless another systematic and rational allocation basis is more representative of the time pattern in which the leased property is physically employed. [See paragraph .527B.] Using factors such as the time value of money, anticipated inflation, or expected future revenues to allocate scheduled rent increases is inappropriate because these factors do not relate to the *time pattern* of the physical usage of the leased property. However, such factors may affect the periodic reported rental income or expense if the lease agreement involves contingent rentals [refer to paragraph .404], which are excluded from minimum lease payments and accounted for separately [refer to paragraphs .108, .113, and .114]. [FTB85-3, ¶2]

.527 There is an important substantive difference between lease rentals that are contingent upon some specified future event and scheduled rent increases that are unaffected by future events. [FTB85-3, ¶13] This section differentiates between (a) scheduled rent increases that are not dependent on future events and (b) increases or decreases in rentals that are dependent on future events such as future sales volume, future inflation, future property taxes, and so forth. The former are minimum lease payments to be accounted for under paragraphs .111 and .115(b). The latter are contingent rentals that affect the measure of expense or income as accruable, as specified in paragraphs .108, .113, and .114. [FTB85-3, ¶12] If the lessor and lessee eliminate the risk of variable payments inherent in contingent rentals by agreeing to scheduled rent increases, the accounting should reflect those different circumstances. [FTB85-3, ¶13]

Time Pattern of the Physical Use of the Property in an Operating Lease

.527A *Question*—A lease agreement may include scheduled rent increases designed to accommodate the lessee's projected physical use of the property. For example, rents may escalate in contemplation of the lessee's physical use of the property even though the lessee takes possession of or controls the physical use of the property at the inception of the lease, or rents may escalate under a master lease agreement as the lessee adds additional equipment to the leased property or requires additional space or capacity (hereinafter referred to as additional leased property). For operating leases that include those provisions, how should the rental payment obligation be recognized by the lessee and lessor in accordance with paragraphs .111, [.115,] and .525 through .527? [FTB88-1, ¶1]

.527B *Response*—Both the lessee and the lessor should recognize the lease payments under paragraphs .111, [.115,] and .525 through .527 as follows:

a. If rents escalate in contemplation of the lessee's physical use of the leased property, including equipment, but the lessee takes possession of or controls the physical use[501a] of the property at the beginning of the lease term, all rental payments, including the escalated rents, should be recognized as rental expense or rental revenue on a straight-line basis in accordance with paragraphs .111, [.115,] and .525 through .527 starting with the beginning of the lease term.
b. If rents escalate under a master lease agreement because the lessee gains access to and control over additional leased property at the time of the escalation, the escalated rents should be considered rental expense or rental revenue attributable to the leased property and recognized in proportion to the additional leased property in the years that the lessee has control over the use of the additional leased property. The amount of rental expense or rental revenue attributed to the additional leased property should be proportionate to the relative fair value of the additional property, as determined at the inception of the lease, in the applicable time periods during which the lessee controls its use. [FTB88-1, ¶2]

Lease Incentives in an Operating Lease

.527C *Question*—An operating lease agreement with a new lessor may include incentives for the lessee to sign the lease, such as an up-front cash payment to the lessee,

---

[501] Deleted 1/89 and renumbered as footnote 501b.]

[501a] The right to control the use of the leased property [is considered] the equivalent of physical use. When the lessee controls the use of the leased property, recognition of rental expense or rental revenue should not be affected by the extent to which the lessee utilizes that property. [FTB88-1, ¶4]

payment of costs for the lessee (such as moving expenses), or the assumption by the lessor of the lessee's preexisting lease with a third party. For operating leases that include such incentives, should lessees or lessors ever recognize those incentives as rental expense or rental revenue other than on a straight-line basis in accordance with paragraphs .111, [.115,] and .525 through .527? [FTB88-1, ¶6]

.527D *Response*—Payments made to or on behalf of the lessee represent incentives that should be considered reductions of rental expense by the lessee and reductions of rental revenue by the lessor over the term of the new lease. Similarly, losses incurred by the lessor as a result of assuming a lessee's preexisting lease with a third party should be considered an incentive by both the lessor and the lessee. Incentives should be recognized on a straight-line basis over the term of the new lease in accordance with paragraphs .111, [.115,] and .525 through .527B. [FTB88-1, ¶7]

.527E The lessee's immediate recognition of expenses or losses, such as moving expenses, losses on subleases, or the write-off of abandoned leasehold improvements, is not changed by paragraph .527D. Rather, paragraph .527D addresses the question of when to recognize the incentive related to the new lessor's assumption of that expense or loss. The new lessor and the lessee should independently estimate any loss attributable to the assumption of a preexisting lease with a third party. For example, the lessee's estimate of the incentive could be based on a comparison of the new lease with the market rental rate available for similar lease property or the market rental rate from the same lessor without the lease assumption, and the lessor should estimate any loss based on the total remaining costs reduced by the expected benefits from the sublease or use of the assumed leased property. [FTB88-1, ¶8]

.527F For example, in conjunction with an operating lease of property for eight years, the lessor assumes the lessee's preexisting lease with a third party that has four years remaining. Assume that the old lease payment is $800 per year and the new lease payment is $1,200 per year. Also assume that the lessor estimates the loss on the assumed lease of $1,000 over its remaining term based on the ability to sublease the property for $550 per year. The lessee estimates the incentive as $960 based on a comparison of the preexisting lease rate to current rates for similar property. Exhibit 527A [presents the journal entries for] accounting for that incentive. [FTB88-1, ¶9]

Exhibit 527A

Journal Entries for Lease Incentives

	Debit	Credit
Lessor Accounting		
At inception:		
Incentive to lessee	1,000	
Liability on sublease assumed		1,000
To record deferred cost and liability related to loss on assumption of remaining lease		
Recurring journal entries in years 1 through 4:		
Liability on sublease assumed (1,000/ 4 years)	250	
Sublease expense	550	
Cash		800
To record cash payment on sublease assumed and amortization of the liability on the sublease assumed		
Cash	550	
Sublease revenue		550
To record cash received from sublease of the property		
Recurring journal entries in years 1 through 8:		
Cash	1,200	
Rental revenue		1,075
Incentive to lessee (1,000/ 8 years)		125
To record cash received on new lease and amortization of incentive over new lease term		
Lessee Accounting		
At inception:		
Loss on sublease assumed by lessor	960	
Incentive from lessor		960
To record loss on sublease assumed in conjunction with new lease agreement		
Recurring journal entries in years 1 through 8:		
Lease expense	1,080	
Incentive from lessor (960/ 8 years)	120	
Cash		1,200
To record cash payment on new lease and amortization of incentive over the new lease term		

[FTB88-1, ¶9]

Accounting for the Acquisition of an Interest in Residual Value

.528 *Question*—How should an enterprise account for the acquisition from a lessor of the unconditional right to own and possess, at the end of the lease term, an asset subject to a lease? Also, how should an enterprise account for the acquisition of the right to receive all, or a portion, of the proceeds from the sale of a leased asset at the end of the lease term? [FTB86-2, ¶1]

.529 *Response*—At the date the rights are acquired, both transactions involve a right to receive, at the end of the lease term, all, or a portion, of any future benefit to be derived from the leased asset and should be accounted for as the acquisition of an asset. (Hereinafter, both transactions are referred to as the acquisition of an interest in the residual value of a leased asset.) [FTB86-2, ¶2]

Measuring Cost of Acquired Residual Value

.530 *Question*—How should an enterprise acquiring an interest in the residual value of a leased asset measure the cost of the acquisition? [FTB86-2, ¶3]

.531 *Response*—An interest in the residual value of a leased asset should be recorded as an asset at the amount of cash disbursed, the fair value of other consideration given, and the present value of liabilities assumed at the date the right is acquired. The fair value of the interest in the residual value of the leased asset at the date of the agreement should be used to measure its cost if that fair value is more clearly evident than the fair value of assets surrendered, services rendered, or liabilities assumed. [FTB86-2, ¶4]

Accounting for an Interest in the Residual Value of a Leased Asset during Lease Term

.532 *Question*—A lessor recognizes increases in the residual value of a leased asset accounted for as a sales-type or direct financing lease to its estimated value at the end of the lease term. How should an enterprise acquiring an interest in the residual value of a leased asset account for that asset during the lease term? [FTB86-2, ¶5]

.533 *Response*—An enterprise acquiring an interest in the residual value of any leased asset, irrespective of the classification of the related lease by the lessor, should not recognize increases to the asset's estimated value over the remaining term of the related lease, and the asset should be reported at no more than its acquisition cost until sale or disposition. If it is subsequently determined that the fair value of the residual value of a leased asset has declined below the carrying amount of the acquired interest and that decline is other than temporary, the asset should be written down to fair value, and the amount of the write-down should be recognized as a loss. That fair value becomes the asset's new carrying amount, and the asset should not be increased for any subsequent increase in its fair value prior to its sale or disposition. [FTB86-2, ¶6]

Applicability to Lease Brokers

.534 *Question*—Do paragraphs .529, .531, and .533 apply to lease brokers? [FTB86-2, ¶7]

.535 *Response*—Yes. An interest in the residual value of a leased asset acquired by a lease broker for cash, liabilities assumed, and the fair value of other consideration given, including services rendered, should be accounted for under those paragraphs.[501b] [FTB86-2, ¶8]

Residual Value Retained by Lessor That Sells Rental Payments

.536 *Question*—If a lessor sells substantially all of the minimum rental payments associated with a sales-type, direct financing, or leveraged lease and retains an interest in the residual value of the leased asset, how should the lessor account for that asset over the remaining lease term? [FTB86-2, ¶9]

.537 *Response*—A lessor retaining an interest in the residual value of the leased asset should not recognize increases in the value of the lease residual to its estimated value over the remaining lease term. The lessor should report any remaining interest thereafter at its carrying amount at the date of the sale of the lease payments.[502] If it is subsequently determined that the fair value of the residual value of the leased asset has declined below the carrying amount of the interest retained and that decline is other than temporary, the asset should be written down to fair value, and the amount of the write-down should be recognized as a loss. That fair value becomes the asset's new carrying amount, and the asset should not be increased for any subsequent increase in its fair value prior to its sale or disposition. [FTB86-2, ¶10]

[501b]This section prohibits a lease broker from recognizing increases in the asset's estimated value over the remaining term of the lease. In that respect, it differs from the AICPA Issues Paper, "Accounting by Lease Brokers." It does not address other areas of fee recognition by lease brokers, or any other provisions of that Issues Paper. [FTB86-2, ¶16]

[502This] paragraph only addresses those transactions structured as a sale of the related lease receivable and is not intended to consider any circumstance in which nonrecourse debt is collateralized by a lease receivable. In that circumstance, recognizing increases in the carrying amount of an interest in the residual value of a leased asset is appropriate under this section. However, Section I27, paragraph .233 states:

> It is a general principle of accounting that the offsetting of assets and liabilities in the balance sheet is improper except where a right of setoff exists.

Therefore, offsetting the lease receivable with nonrecourse debt is appropriate only in those circumstances in which a legal right of offset exists or when, at the inception of the lease, the lease meets all of the characteristics of paragraph .144 and is appropriately classified as a leveraged lease. Otherwise, the guidance provided in paragraph .233 of Section I27 should be applied. [FTB86-2, ¶21]

Guaranteed Residual Value of a Leased Asset

.538 *Question*—If an interest in the residual value of a leased asset is guaranteed, does the guarantee change the nature of the asset or the accounting [described in paragraphs .529, .531, .533, .535, and .537]? [FTB86-2, ¶11]

.539 *Response*—No. A guarantee does not change the nature of an interest in the residual value of a leased asset or its historical acquisition cost. [FTB86-2, ¶12]

Applicability of Leveraged Lease Accounting to Existing Assets of the Lessor

.540 *Question*—Paragraph .102(b)(2) requires that the cost or carrying amount, if different, and the fair value of the asset be the same at the inception of the lease for it to be classified as a direct financing lease. Paragraph .144(a) requires that a lease qualify as a direct financing lease for the lessor to classify that lease as a leveraged lease. How does a lessor apply those requirements to leasing an asset the lessor has owned and had previously placed in service? [FTB88-1, ¶11]

.541 *Response*—Paragraphs .102(b)(2) and .144(a) should be applied literally. Although the carrying amount (cost less accumulated depreciation) of an asset previously placed in service may not be significantly different from its fair value, the two amounts will not likely be the same. Therefore, leveraged lease accounting will not be appropriate, generally, other than when an asset to be leased is acquired by the lessor. If the carrying amount of an existing asset of the lessor before any related write-down is equal to fair value as established in transactions by unrelated third parties, that asset could qualify for leveraged lease accounting. However, any write-down to the existing asset's fair value in contemplation of leasing the asset precludes the transaction from leveraged lease accounting. [FTB88-1, ¶12]

Money-over-Money Lease Transactions

.542 *Question*—An enterprise manufactures or purchases an asset, leases the asset to a lessee, and obtains nonrecourse financing in excess of the asset's cost using the leased asset and the future lease rentals as collateral (commonly referred to as a **money-over-money lease transaction**). Should the enterprise ever recognize any of the amount by which the cash received plus the present value of any estimated residual retained exceeds the carrying amount of the leased asset as profit on that transaction at the beginning of the lease term? If not, how should the enterprise account for the transaction? [FTB88-1, ¶16]

.543 *Response*—Other than the recognition of manufacturer's or dealer's profit in a sales-type lease, an enterprise should never recognize as income the proceeds from the borrowing in a money-over-money lease transaction at the beginning of the lease term. The enterprise should account for that transaction as (a) the manufacture or purchase of an asset, (b) the leasing of the asset under an operating, direct financing, or sales-type lease as required by paragraphs .102 through .104, and (c) the borrowing of funds. The asset (if an operating lease) or the lease receivable (if a direct financing or sales-type lease) and the liability for the nonrecourse financing should not be offset in the statement of financial position unless a right of setoff exists. [FTB88-1, ¶17] [See Section B10, "Balance Sheet Display: Offsetting," paragraphs .101A, .101B, and .107, for guidance on determining whether a right of setoff exists.]

Wrap Lease Transactions

.544 *Question*—An enterprise purchases an asset, leases the asset to a lessee, obtains nonrecourse financing using the lease rentals or the lease rentals and the asset as collateral, sells the asset subject to the lease and the nonrecourse debt to a third-party investor, and leases the asset back while remaining the substantive principal lessor under the original lease (commonly referred to as a **wrap lease transaction**). Other than as required by this section, should an enterprise ever recognize any profit on the wrap lease transaction at its inception? If not, how should the enterprise account for the transaction? [FTB88-1, ¶21]

.545 *Response*—If the property involved is real estate, paragraphs .130A through .130M and .160A through .160M of this section and paragraphs .125H through .125J of Section Re6 apply to the sale-leaseback transaction. If the property involved is not real estate, the enterprise should account for the transaction as a sale-leaseback transaction in accordance with paragraphs .128 through .130 and the lease to the end user should be accounted for as a sublease in accordance with paragraph .132. Under this section the asset should be removed from the books of the original enterprise, the leaseback should be classified in accordance with paragraph .102, and any gain on the transaction should be recognized or deferred and amortized in accordance with paragraph .129. The enterprise would also reflect the retained residual interest, gross sublease receivable, nonrecourse third-party debt, the leaseback obligation, and the note receivable from the investor in the statement of financial position. As in accounting for a money-over-money lease transaction (refer to paragraph .543), the sublease asset and the related nonrecourse debt should not be offset in the statement of financial position unless a right of setoff exists. [FTB88-1, ¶22] [See Section B10, paragraphs .101A, .101B, and .107, for guidance on determining whether a right of setoff exists.]

(The next page is 30101.)

Sources: FASB Statement 91; FASB Statement 115

Summary

This section presents the accounting for nonrefundable fees and costs associated with lending, committing to lend, or purchasing a loan or group of loans.

This section applies to all types of loans (including debt securities) as well as to all types of lenders (including banks, thrift institutions, insurance companies, mortgage bankers, and other financial and nonfinancial institutions).

The section specifies that:

- Loan origination fees shall be recognized over the life of the related loan as an adjustment of yield.
- Certain direct loan origination costs shall be recognized over the life of the related loan as a reduction of the loan's yield.
- All loan commitment fees shall be deferred except for certain retrospectively determined fees; commitment fees meeting specified criteria shall be recognized over the loan commitment period; all other commitment fees shall be recognized as an adjustment of yield over the related loan's life or, if the commitment expires unexercised, recognized in income upon expiration of the commitment.
- Loan fees, certain direct loan origination costs, and purchase premiums and discounts on loans shall be recognized as an adjustment of yield generally by the interest method based on the contractual terms of the loan. However, prepayments may be anticipated in certain specified circumstances.

Scope

.101 This section [presents] standards of financial accounting and reporting for nonrefundable fees and costs associated with lending activities and loan purchases. Lending, committing to lend, refinancing or restructuring loans, arranging standby letters of credit, syndicating loans, and leasing activities are "lending activities" for purposes of this section. The lender's activities that precede the disbursement of funds can generally be distinguished between (a) efforts to identify and attract potential borrowers and (b) efforts necessary to originate a loan or loan commitment after a potential borrower requests a loan or loan commitment. Non-refundable fees have many different names in practice, such as **origination fees**, points, placement fees, **commitment fees**, application fees, management fees, restructuring fees, and syndication fees, but, for purposes of this section, they are referred to as loan origination fees, commitment fees, or syndication fees. [FAS91, ¶2]

.102 This section addresses the recognition and the balance sheet classification of nonrefundable fees and costs associated with lending activities. The accounting for discounts, premiums, and commitment fees associated with the purchase of loans and other debt securities such as corporate bonds, Treasury notes and bonds, groups of loans, and loan-backed securities (such as pass-through certificates, collateralized mortgage obligations, and other so-called "securitized" loans) is also addressed by this section. This section does not [address] loan origination or commitment fees that are refundable; however, the provisions of this section do apply when such fees subsequently become nonrefundable. It also does not [address] costs that are incurred by the lender in transactions with independent third parties if the lender bills those costs directly to the borrower. The provisions of this section do not apply to nonrefundable fees and costs associated with originating or acquiring loans that are carried at market value [FAS91, ¶3] if the changes in market value are included in earnings. [FAS115, ¶130(a)]

General

.103 An enterprise may acquire a loan by lending (originating the loan) or by purchasing (acquiring a loan from a party other than the borrower). This section applies to both a lender and a purchaser. This section shall be applied to individual loan contracts. Aggregation of similar loans for purposes of recognizing net fees or costs and purchase premiums or discounts is permitted if the provisions of paragraph .118 are met or if the resulting recognition does not differ materially from the amount that would have been recognized on an individual loan-by-loan basis. [FAS91, ¶4]

Loan Origination Fees and Costs

.104 Loan origination fees[1] shall be deferred and recognized over the life of the

---

[1]Origination fees consist of:

a. Fees that are being charged to the borrower as "prepaid" interest or to reduce the loan's nominal interest rate, such as interest "buy-downs" (explicit yield adjustments)
b. Fees to reimburse the lender for origination activities
c. Other fees charged to the borrower that relate directly to making the loan (for example, fees that are paid to the lender as compensation for granting a complex loan or agreeing to lend quickly)
d. Fees that are not conditional on a loan being granted by the lender that receives the fee but are, in substance, implicit yield adjustments because a loan is granted at rates or terms that would not have otherwise been considered absent the fee (for example, certain syndication fees addressed in paragraph .110).

Designation of a fee or cost as an origination fee or cost for a loan that is purchased is inappropriate because a purchased loan has already been originated by another party. [FAS91, ¶36]

loan as an adjustment of yield[2] (interest income). Likewise, direct loan origination costs defined in paragraph .105 shall be deferred and recognized as a reduction in the yield of the loan except as set forth in paragraph .113 (for a troubled debt restructuring). Loan origination fees and related direct loan origination costs for a given loan shall be offset and only the net amount shall be deferred and amortized. The practice of recognizing a portion of loan origination fees as revenue in a period to offset all or part of the costs of origination shall no longer be acceptable. [FAS91, ¶5]

.105 Direct loan origination costs of a completed loan shall include only (a) **incremental direct costs** of loan origination incurred in transactions with independent third parties for that loan and (b) certain costs directly related to specified activities performed by the lender for that loan. Those activities are: evaluating the prospective borrower's financial condition; evaluating and recording guarantees, collateral, and other security arrangements; negotiating loan terms; preparing and processing loan documents; and closing the transaction. The costs directly related to those activities shall include only that portion of the employees' total compensation and payroll-related fringe benefits directly related to time spent performing those activities for that loan and other costs related to those activities that would not have been incurred but for that loan. [FAS91, ¶6]

.106 All other lending-related costs, including costs related to activities performed by the lender for advertising, soliciting potential borrowers, servicing existing loans, and other ancillary activities related to establishing and monitoring credit policies, supervision, and administration, shall be charged to expense as incurred. Employees' compensation and fringe benefits related to those activities, unsuccessful loan origination efforts, and idle time shall be charged to expense as incurred. Administrative costs, rent, depreciation, and all other occupancy and equipment costs are considered indirect costs and shall be charged to expense as incurred. [FAS91, ¶7]

Commitment Fees and Costs

.107 Except as set forth in subparagraphs (a) and (b) below, fees received for a commitment to originate or purchase a loan or group of loans shall be deferred and, if the commitment is exercised, recognized over the life of the loan as an adjustment of yield or, if the commitment expires unexercised, recognized in income upon expiration of the commitment.

---

[2]Methods for recognition of deferred fees and direct loan origination costs over the life of the loan as an adjustment of yield are set forth in paragraphs .117 through .119. [FAS91, ¶5, fn2]

a. If the enterprise's experience with similar arrangements indicates that the likelihood that the commitment will be exercised is remote,[3] the commitment fee shall be recognized over the commitment period on a straight-line basis as service fee income. If the commitment is subsequently exercised during the commitment period, the remaining unamortized commitment fee at the time of exercise shall be recognized over the life of the loan as an adjustment of yield.
b. If the amount of the commitment fee is determined retrospectively as a percentage of the line of credit available but unused in a previous period, if that percentage is nominal in relation to the stated interest rate on any related borrowing, and if that borrowing will bear a market interest rate at the date the loan is made, the commitment fee shall be recognized as service fee income as of the determination date. [FAS91, ¶8]

.108 Direct loan origination costs (described in paragraph .105) incurred to make a commitment to originate a loan shall be offset against any related commitment fee and the net amount recognized as set forth in paragraph .107. [FAS91, ¶9]

.109 Available lines of credit under credit card and similar charge card arrangements are loan commitments, and fees collected in connection with such cards (**credit card fees**) are viewed in part as being loan commitment fees. However, those fees generally cover many services to cardholders. Accordingly, fees that are periodically charged to cardholders shall be deferred and recognized on a straight-line basis over the period the fee entitles the cardholder to use the card. This accounting shall also apply to other similar card arrangements that involve an extension of credit by the card issuer. [FAS91, ¶10]

Syndication Fees

.110 The enterprise managing a loan syndication (the syndicator) shall recognize loan syndication fees when the syndication is complete unless a portion of the syndication loan is retained. If the yield on the portion of the loan retained by the syndicator is less than the average yield to the other syndication participants after considering the fees passed through by the syndicator, the syndicator shall defer a portion of the syndication fee to produce a yield on the portion of the loan retained that is not less than the average yield on the loans held by the other syndication participants. [FAS91, ¶11]

Fees and Costs in Refinancings or Restructurings

.111 If the terms of the new loan resulting from a loan refinancing or restructuring other than a troubled debt restructuring are at least as favorable to the

---

[3]The term *remote* is used here, consistent with its use in Section C59, "Contingencies," to mean that the likelihood is slight that a loan commitment will be exercised prior to its expiration. [FAS91, ¶8, fn3]

lender as the terms for comparable loans to other customers with similar collection risks who are not refinancing or restructuring a loan with the lender, the refinanced loan shall be accounted for as a new loan. This condition would be met if the new loan's effective yield is at least equal to the effective yield for such loans.[4] Any unamortized net fees or costs and any prepayment penalties from the original loan shall be recognized in interest income when the new loan is granted. [FAS91, ¶12]

.112 If the refinancing or restructuring does not meet the condition set forth in paragraph .111 or if only minor modifications are made to the original loan contract, the unamortized net fees or costs from the original loan and any prepayment penalties shall be carried forward as a part of the net investment in the new loan. In this case, the investment in the new loan shall consist of the remaining net investment in the original loan,[5] any additional amounts loaned, any fees received, and direct loan origination costs set forth in paragraph .105 associated with the refinancing or restructuring. [FAS91, ¶13]

.113 Fees received in connection with a modification of terms of a troubled debt restructuring as defined in Section D22, "Debt: Restructurings," shall be applied as a reduction of the recorded investment in the loan. All related costs, including direct loan origination costs, shall be charged to expense as incurred. [FAS91, ¶14]

Purchase of a Loan or Group of Loans

.114 The initial investment in a purchased loan or group of loans shall include the amount paid to the seller plus any fees paid or less any fees received. The initial investment frequently differs from the related loan's principal amount at the date of purchase. This difference shall be recognized as an adjustment of yield over the life of the loan. All other costs incurred in connection with acquiring purchased loans or committing to purchase loans shall be charged to expense as incurred. [FAS91, ¶15]

.115 In applying the provisions of this section to loans purchased as a group, the purchaser may allocate the initial investment to the individual loans or may account for the initial investment in the aggregate. The cash flows provided by the underlying loan contracts shall be used to apply the interest method, except as set

---

[4]The effective yield comparison considers the level of nominal interest rate, commitment and origination fees, and direct loan origination costs and would also consider comparison of other factors where appropriate, such as compensating balance arrangements. [FAS91, ¶12, fn4]

[5]The net investment in the original loan includes the unpaid loan principal, any remaining unamortized net fees or costs, any remaining unamortized purchase premium or discount, and any accrued interest receivable. [FAS91, ¶13, fn5]

forth in paragraph .118. If prepayments are not anticipated pursuant to paragraph .118 and prepayments occur or a portion of the purchased loans is sold, a proportionate amount of the related deferred fees and purchase premium or discount shall be recognized in income so that the effective interest rate on the remaining portion of loans continues unchanged. [FAS91, ¶16]

Other

.116 Deferred net fees or costs shall not be amortized during periods in which interest income on a loan is not being recognized because of concerns about the realization of loan principal or interest. [FAS91, ¶17]

Application of the Interest Method and Other Amortization Matters

.117 Net fees or costs that are required to be recognized as yield adjustments over the life of the related loan(s) shall be recognized by the interest method except as set forth in paragraph .119. The objective of the interest method is to arrive at periodic interest income (including recognition of fees and costs) at a constant effective yield on the net investment in the receivable (that is, the principal amount of the receivable adjusted by unamortized fees or costs and purchase premium or discount). The difference between the periodic interest income so determined and the stated interest on the outstanding principal amount of the receivable is the amount of periodic amortization.[6] Under the provisions of this section, the interest method shall be applied as follows when the stated interest rate is not constant throughout the term of the loan:

a. If the loan's stated interest rate increases during the term of the loan (so that interest accrued under the interest method in early periods would exceed interest at the stated rate), interest income shall not be recognized to the extent that the net investment in the loan would increase to an amount greater than the amount at which the borrower could settle the obligation.[7] Prepayment penalties shall be considered in determining the amount at which the borrower could settle the obligation only to the extent that such penalties are imposed throughout the loan term. (Refer to paragraphs .133 through .135.)

---

[6]The "interest" method is also described in footnote 4 of Section I69, "Interest: Imputation of an Interest Cost" and in the first sentence of paragraph .108 of that section. [FAS91, ¶18, fn6]

[7]This paragraph imposes a limit on the amount of periodic amortization that can be recognized. However, that limitation does not apply to the capitalization of costs incurred (such as direct loan origination costs and purchase premiums) that cause the investment in the loan to be in excess of the amount at which the borrower could settle the obligation. [It was] concluded that the capitalization of costs incurred is different from increasing the net investment in a loan through accrual of interest income that is only contingently receivable. [FAS91, ¶54]

b. If the loan's stated interest rate decreases during the term of the loan, the stated periodic interest received early in the term of the loan would exceed the periodic interest income that is calculated under the interest method. In that circumstance, the excess shall be deferred and recognized in those future periods when the constant effective yield under the interest method exceeds the stated interest rate. (Refer to paragraph .136.)

c. If the loan's stated interest rate varies based on future changes in an independent factor, such as an index or rate (for example, the prime rate, the London Interbank Offered Rate (LIBOR), or the U.S. Treasury bill weekly average rate), the calculation of the constant effective yield necessary to recognize fees and costs shall be based either on the factor (the index or rate) that is in effect at the inception of the loan or on the factor as it changes over the life of the loan.[8] (Refer to paragraphs .137 and .138.) [FAS91, ¶18]

.118 Except as stated in the following sentence, the calculation of the constant effective yield necessary to apply the interest method shall use the payment terms required by the loan contract, and prepayments of principal shall not be anticipated to shorten the loan term. If the enterprise holds a large number of similar loans[9] for which prepayments are probable and the timing and amount of prepayments can be reasonably estimated, the enterprise may consider estimates of future principal prepayments in the calculation of the constant effective yield necessary to apply the interest method. If the enterprise anticipates prepayments in applying the interest method and a difference arises between the prepayments anticipated and actual prepayments received, the enterprise shall recalculate the effective yield to reflect actual payments to date and anticipated future payments. The net investment in the loans shall be adjusted to the amount that would have existed had the new effective yield been applied since the acquisition of the loans. The investment in the loans shall be adjusted to the new balance with a corresponding charge or credit to interest income. Enterprises that anticipate prepayments shall disclose that policy and the significant assumptions underlying the prepayment estimates. The practice of recognizing net fees over the estimated average life of a group of loans shall no longer be acceptable. (Refer to paragraphs .128 through .132.) [FAS91, ¶19]

.119 Certain loan agreements provide no scheduled payment terms (demand loans); others provide the borrower with the option to make multiple borrowings

---

[8]A variable rate loan whose initial rate differs from the rate its base factor would produce is also subject to the provisions of paragraphs .117(a) and (b). [FAS91, ¶18, fn7]

[9]The loans [that are] grouped together should have sufficiently similar characteristics that prepayment experience of the loans can be expected to be similar in a variety of interest rate environments [and] should have sufficiently similar levels of net fees or costs so that, in the event that an individual loan is sold, recalculation of that loan's carrying amount will be practicable. [FAS91, ¶58]

up to a specified maximum amount, to repay portions of previous borrowings, and then reborrow under the same contract (revolving lines of credit).

a. For a loan that is payable at the lender's demand, any net fees or costs may be recognized as an adjustment of yield on a straight-line basis over a period that is consistent with (1) the understanding between the borrower and lender or (2) if no understanding exists, the lender's estimate of the period of time over which the loan will remain outstanding; any unamortized amount shall be recognized when the loan is paid in full.

b. For revolving lines of credit (or similar loan arrangements), the net fees or costs shall be recognized in income on a straight-line basis over the period the revolving line of credit is active, assuming that borrowings are outstanding for the maximum term provided in the loan contract. If the borrower pays all borrowings and cannot reborrow under the contract, any unamortized net fees or costs shall be recognized in income upon payment. The interest method shall be applied to recognize net unamortized fees or costs when the loan agreement provides a schedule for payment and no additional borrowings are provided for under the agreement.[10] [FAS91, ¶20]

Balance Sheet Classification

.120 The unamortized balance of loan origination, commitment, and other fees and costs and purchase premiums and discounts that is being recognized as an adjustment of yield pursuant to this section shall be reported on the enterprise's balance sheet as part of the loan balance to which it relates. [FAS91, ¶21]

Income Statement Classification

.121 Amounts of loan origination, commitment, and other fees and costs recognized as an adjustment of yield shall be reported as part of interest income. Amortization of other fees, such as commitment fees that are being amortized on a straight-line basis over the commitment period or included in income when the commitment expires, shall be reported as service fee income. [FAS91, ¶22]

Application to Leasing Activities

.122 [As discussed in Section L10, "Leases,"] the provisions of paragraphs .104 through .108 of this section apply to lessors in determining the net amount of *ini-*

---

[10]For example, if the loan agreement provides the borrower with the option to convert a one-year revolving line of credit to a five-year term loan, during the term of the revolving line of credit the lender would recognize the net fees or costs as income on a straight-line basis using the combined life of the revolving line of credit and term loan. If the borrower elects to convert the line of credit to a term loan, the lender would recognize the unamortized net fees or costs as an adjustment of yield using the interest method. If the revolving line of credit expires and borrowings are extinguished, the unamortized net fees or costs would be recognized in income upon payment. [FAS91, ¶20, fn8]

tial direct costs as that term is used in Section L10. Lessors shall account for initial direct costs as part of the investment in a direct financing lease. The practice of recognizing a portion of the unearned income at inception of the lease to offset initial direct costs [is not] acceptable. [FAS91, ¶23]

Examples of Application of This Section

.123 The examples and estimates used are illustrative only and are not intended to modify or limit in any way the provisions of this section. All examples assume that principal and interest payments are made on the last day of the year. [FAS91, ¶64]

Case 1—Amortization Based on Contractual Payment Terms

.124 On January 1, 19X7, Company A originates a 10-year $100,000 loan with a 10 percent stated interest rate. The contract specifies equal annual payments of $16,275 through December 31, 19Y6. The contract also specifies that no penalty will be charged for prepayments of the loan. Company A charges a 3 percent ($3,000) nonrefundable fee to the borrower and incurs $1,000 in direct loan origination costs (attorney fees, appraisal, title insurance, wages and payroll-related fringe benefits of employees performing origination activities, outside broker's fee). The carrying amount of the loan is computed as follows:

Loan principal	$100,000
Origination fees	(3,000)
Direct loan origination costs	1,000
Carrying amount of loan	$ 98,000

[FAS91, ¶65]

.125 Company A accounts for this loan using contractual payments to apply the interest method of amortization. In calculating the effective rate to apply the interest method, the discount rate necessary to equate 10 annual payments of $16,275 to the initial carrying amount of $98,000 is approximately 10.4736 percent. The amortization if no prepayment occurs is shown in Exhibit 125A. [FAS91, ¶66]

Exhibit 125A   Amortization Based on Contractual Payment Terms

Year	(1) Cash (Out) Inflow	(2) Stated Interest	(3) Amortization	(4) Interest Income	(5) Remaining Principal	(6) Unamortized Net Fees	(7) Carrying Amount
	$ (98,000)				$100,000		$ 98,000
1	16,275	$ 10,000	$ 264	$ 10,264	93,725	$ 1,736	91,989
2	16,275	9,373	262	9,635	86,823	1,474	85,349
3	16,275	8,682	257	8,939	79,230	1,217	78,013
4	16,275	7,923	248	8,171	70,878	969	69,909
5	16,275	7,088	234	7,322	61,691	735	60,956
6	16,275	6,169	215	6,384	51,585	520	51,065
7	16,275	5,159	189	5,348	40,469	331	40,138
8	16,275	4,047	157	4,204	28,241	174	28,067
9	16,275	2,824	116	2,940	14,790	58	14,732
10	16,275	1,485[a]	58	1,543	0	0	0

Total amortization $ 2,000

Computations:

Column (1)—Contractual payments

Column (2)—Column (5) for prior year × the loan's stated interest rate (10%)

Column (3)—Column (4) – Column (2)

Column (4)—Column (7) for prior year × the effective interest rate (10.4736%)[b]

Column (5)—Column (5) for prior year – (Column (1) – Column (2))

Column (6)—Initial net fees – amortization to date

Column (7)—Column (5) – Column (6)

[a]$6 rounding adjustment.

[b]The effective interest rate is the discount rate that equates the present value of the future cash inflows to the initial net cash outflow of $98,000.

[FAS91, ¶66]

Case 2—Amortization Based on Contractual Payment Terms with Full Prepayment in Year 3

.126 On January 1, 19X7, Company B originates a 10-year $100,000 loan with a 10 percent stated interest rate. The contract specifies equal annual payments of $16,275 through December 31, 19Y6. The contract also specifies that no penalty will be charged for prepayments of the loan. Company B charges a 3 percent ($3,000) nonrefundable fee to the borrower and incurs $1,000 in direct loan origination costs. [FAS91, ¶67]

.127 Company B accounts for this loan using contractual payments to apply the interest method of amortization. The amortization if the borrower prepays the remaining principal at the end of year 3 is shown in Exhibit 127A. [FAS91, ¶68]

Exhibit 127A

Amortization Based on Contractual Payment Terms with Full Prepayment in Year 3

Year	(1) Cash (Out) Inflow	(2) Stated Interest	(3) Amortization	(4) Interest Income	(5) Remaining Principal	(6) Unamortized Net Fees	(7) Carrying Amount
	$ (98,000)				$ 100,000		$ 98,000
1	16,275	$ 10,000	$ 264	$ 10,264	93,725	$ 1,736	91,989
2	16,275	9,373	262	9,635	86,823	1,474	85,349
3	95,505	8,682	1,474	10,156	0	0	0
Total amortization			$ 2,000				

Computations:

Column (1)—Contractual payments + prepayments

Column (2)—Column (5) for prior year × the loan's stated interest rate (10%)

Column (3)—Column (4) – Column (2)

Column (4)—Column (7) for prior year × the effective interest rate (10.4736%) plus in year 3 an adjustment of $1,217 representing the unamortized net fees recognized when the loan is paid in full

Column (5)—Column (5) for prior year – (Column (1) – Column (2))

Column (6)—Initial net fees – amortization to date

Column (7)—Column (5) – Column (6)

[FAS91, ¶68]

Case 3—Amortization Based on Estimated Prepayment Patterns

.128 On January 1, 19X7, Company C originates 1,000 10-year $10,000 loans with 10 percent stated interest rates. Each contract specifies equal annual payments through December 31, 19Y6. The contracts also specify that no penalty will be charged for prepayments. Company C charges each borrower a 3 percent ($300) fee and incurs $100 in direct origination costs for each loan. The carrying amount of the loans is computed as follows:

Loan principal amounts	$ 10,000,000
Origination fees	(300,000)
Direct loan origination costs	100,000
Carrying amount of loans	$ 9,800,000

[FAS91, ¶69]

.129 Company C chooses to account for this large number of loans using anticipated prepayment patterns to apply the interest method of amortization. Company C estimates a constant prepayment rate of 6 percent per year, which is consistent with Company C's prior experience with similar loans and Company C's expectation of ongoing experience. The amortization when prepayments occur as anticipated is shown in Exhibit 129A. [FAS91, ¶70]

Exhibit 129A

Amortization Based on Estimated Prepayment Patterns

Year	(1) Cash (Out) Inflow	(2) Stated Interest	(3) Amortization	(4) Interest Income	(5) Remaining Principal	(6) Unamortized Net Fees	(7) Carrying Amount
	$ (9,800,000)				$ 10,000,000		$ 9,800,000
1	2,227,454	$ 1,000,000	$ 35,141	$ 1,035,141	8,772,546	$ 164,859	8,607,687
2	2,049,623	877,255	31,946	909,201	7,600,178	132,913	7,467,265
3	1,880,619	760,018	28,724	788,742	6,479,577	104,189	6,375,388
4	1,719,716	647,958	25,453	673,411	5,407,819	78,736	5,329,083
5	1,566,144	540,782	22,111	562,893	4,382,457	56,625	4,325,832
6	1,419,028	438,246	18,677	456,923	3,401,675	37,948	3,363,727
7	1,277,230	340,168	15,131	355,299	2,464,613	22,817	2,441,796
8	1,138,934	246,461	11,458	257,919	1,572,140	11,359	1,560,781
9	1,000,180	157,214	7,646	164,860	729,174	3,713	725,461
10	802,091	72,917	3,713	76,630	0	0	0

Total amortization $ 200,000

Computations:

Column (1)—Contractual payments + 6% of Column (5) for the prior year (except in year 10)

Column (2)—Column (5) for prior year × the loan's stated interest rate (10%)

Column (3)—Column (4) – Column (2)

Column (4)—Column (7) for the prior year × the effective interest rate (10.5627%)

Column (5)—Column (5) for prior year – (Column (1) – Column (2))

Column (6)—Initial net fees – amortization to date

Column (7)—Column (5) – Column (6)

[FAS91, ¶70]

Case 4—Amortization Based on Estimated Prepayment Patterns Adjusted for Change in Estimate

.130 On January 1, 19X7, Company D originates 1,000 10-year $10,000 loans with 10 percent stated interest rates. Each contract specifies equal annual payments through December 31, 19Y6. The contracts also specify that no penalty will be charged for prepayments. Company D charges each borrower a 3 percent ($300) fee and incurs $100 in direct origination costs for each loan. [FAS91, ¶71]

.131 Company D chooses to account for this portfolio of loans using anticipated prepayment patterns to apply the interest method of amortization. Company D estimates a constant prepayment rate of 6 percent per year, which is consistent with Company D's prior experience with similar loans and Company D's expectation of ongoing experience. [FAS91, ¶72]

.132 Exhibit 132A illustrates the adjustment required by paragraph .118 of this section when an enterprise's actual prepayment experience differs from the amounts anticipated. The loans have actually prepaid at a rate of 6 percent in years 1 and 2 and 20 percent in year 3, and based on the new information at the end of year 3, Company D revises its estimate of prepayment experience to anticipate that 10 percent of the loans will prepay in year 4 and 6 percent of the loans will prepay in remaining years. The carrying amount of the loans at the end of year 3 is adjusted to the amount that would have existed had the new effective yield been applied since January 1, 19X7. Included in amortization in year 3 is an adjustment for the difference in the prior effective yield and the new effective yield applied to amounts outstanding in years 1 and 2. Amortization in years 4-10 assumes the new estimates of prepayment experience occur as anticipated. [FAS91, ¶73]

Exhibit 132A   Amortization Based on Estimated Prepayment Patterns Adjusted for a Change in Estimate

Year	(1) Cash (Out) Inflow	(2) Stated Interest	(3) Amortization	(4) Interest Income	(5) Remaining Principal	(6) Unamortized Net Fees	(7) Carrying Amount
	$ (9,800,000)				$ 10,000,000		$ 9,800,000
1	2,227,454	$ 1,000,000	$ 35,141	$ 1,035,141	8,772,546	$ 164,859	8,607,687
2	2,049,623	877,255	31,946	909,201	7,600,178	132,913	7,467,265
3	2,944,644	760,018	41,951	801,969	5,415,552	90,962	5,324,590
4	1,653,939	541,555	23,294	564,849	4,303,168	67,668	4,235,500
5	1,246,229	430,317	18,998	449,315	3,487,256	48,670	3,438,586
6	1,129,164	348,726	16,050	364,776	2,706,818	32,620	2,674,198
7	1,016,331	270,682	13,005	283,687	1,961,169	19,615	1,941,554
8	906,285	196,117	9,849	205,966	1,251,001	9,766	1,241,235
9	795,875	125,100	6,574	131,674	580,226	3,192	577,034
10	638,249	58,023	3,192	61,215	0	0	0
Total amortization			$ 200,000				

Computations:

Column (1)—Contractual payments + prepayments

Column (2)—Column (5) for prior year × the loan's stated interest rate (10%)

Column (3)—Column (4) – Column (2)

Column (4)—Column (7) for the prior year × the effective rate (10.5627% for years 1 and 2, and 10.6083% for years 3–10, + an adjustment of $8,876 in year 3 representing the cumulative effect[c] applicable to years 1 and 2 of changing the estimated effective rate)

Column (5)—Column (5) for prior year – (Column (1) – Column (2))

Column (6)—Initial net fees – amortization to date

Column (7)—Column (5) – Column (6)

[c]An adjustment would also be required if the level of prepayments realized was less than anticipated.

[FAS91, ¶73]

Case 5—Application of Paragraph .117(a)—When the Loan's Prepayment Penalty Is Effective throughout the Entire Term

.133 Company E grants a 10-year $100,000 loan with an 8 percent stated interest rate in year 1 and 10 percent in years 2-10. Company E receives net fees of $1,000 related to this loan. The contract specifies that the borrower must pay a penalty equal to 1 percent of any principal prepaid. Application of the effective yield to recognize an amount in excess of net fees is appropriate for a loan with an increasing stated interest rate only to the extent that the loan agreement provides for a prepayment penalty that is effective throughout the loan term. [Exhibit 133A illustrates the application of paragraph .117(a) when the prepayment penalty is effective throughout the entire term of the loan.] [FAS91, ¶74]

Exhibit 133A

Application of Paragraph .117(a)—When the Loan's Prepayment Penalty is Effective throughout the Entire Term

Year	(1) Cash (Out) Inflow	(2) Stated Interest	(3) Amortization	(4) Interest Income	(5) Remaining Principal	(6) Unamortized Net Fees^d	(7) Carrying Amount	(8) Settlement Amount
	$ (99,000)				$ 100,000		$ 99,000	
1	14,903	$ 8,000	$ 1,710	$ 9,710	93,097	$ (710)	93,807	$ 94,028
2	16,165	9,310	(108)	9,202	86,242	(602)	86,844	87,104
3	16,165	8,624	(106)	8,518	78,701	(496)	79,197	79,488
4	16,165	7,870	(102)	7,768	70,406	(394)	70,800	71,110
5	16,165	7,041	(97)	6,944	61,282	(297)	61,579	61,895
6	16,165	6,128	(88)	6,040	51,245	(209)	51,454	51,757
7	16,165	5,124	(78)	5,046	40,204	(131)	40,335	40,606
8	16,165	4,021	(65)	3,956	28,060	(66)	28,126	28,340
9	16,165	2,806	(47)	2,759	14,701	(19)	14,720	14,848
10	16,165	1,464^e	(19)^e	1,445	0	0	0	0

Total amortization $ 1,000

Computations:
Column (1)—Contractual payments
Column (2)—Column (5) for prior year × the loan's stated interest rate (8% in year 1, 10% in years 2-10)
Column (3)—Column (4) − Column (2)
Column (4)—Column (5) for the prior year × the effective interest rate (9.8085%)
Column (5)—Column (5) for prior year − (Column (1) − Column (2))
Column (6)—Initial net fees − amortization to date
Column (7)—Column (5) − Column (6)
Column (8)—Column (5) × 1.01 (to calculate the settlement amount including prepayment penalty)

^d Unamortized net fee and accrued interest.
^e $6 rounding adjustment.

[FAS91, ¶74]

Case 6—Application of Paragraph .117(a)—With No Prepayment Penalty

.134 Company F grants a 10-year $100,000 loan. The contract provides for 8 percent interest in year 1 and 10 percent interest in years 2-10. Company F receives net fees of $1,000 related to this loan. The contract specifies that no penalty will be charged for prepayment of principal. [FAS91, ¶75]

.135 The discount factor that equates the present value of the cash inflows in Column 1 with the initial cash outflow of $99,000 is 9.8085 percent. In year 1, recognition of interest income on the investment of $99,000 at a rate of 9.8085 percent would cause the investment to be $93,807, or $710 greater than the amount at which the borrower could settle the obligation. Because the condition set forth in paragraph .117(a) is not met, recognition of an amount greater than the net fee is not permitted, [as illustrated in Exhibit 135A.] [FAS91, ¶76]

Exhibit 135A

Application of Paragraph .117(a)—With No Prepayment Penalty

Year	(1) Cash (Out) Inflow	(2) Stated Interest	(3) Amortization	(4) Interest Income	(5) Remaining Principal	(6) Unamortized Net Fees	(7) Carrying Amount
	$ (99,000)				$ 100,000		$ 99,000
1	14,903	$ 8,000	$ 1,000	$ 9,000	93,097	$0	93,097
2	16,165	9,310	0	9,310	86,242	0	86,242
3	16,165	8,624	0	8,624	78,701	0	78,701
4	16,165	7,870	0	7,870	70,406	0	70,406
5	16,165	7,041	0	7,041	61,282	0	61,282
6	16,165	6,128	0	6,128	51,245	0	51,245
7	16,165	5,124	0	5,124	40,204	0	40,204
8	16,165	4,021	0	4,021	28,060	0	28,060
9	16,165	2,806	0	2,806	14,701	0	14,701
10	16,165	1,464f	0	1,464	0	0	0

Total amortization　　$ 1,000

Computations:
Column (1)—Contractual payments
Column (2)—Column (5) for prior year × the loan's stated interest rate (8% in year 1, 10% in years 2-10)
Column (3)—Column (4) − Column (2)
Column (4)—Column (7) for the prior year × the effective interest rate (9.8085%) as limited by paragraph .117(a) of this section
Column (5)—Column (5) for prior year − (Column (1) − Column (2))
Column (6)—Initial net fees − amortization to date
Column (7)—Column (5) − Column (6)

f$6 rounding adjustment.

[FAS91, ¶76]

Case 7—Application of Paragraph .117(b)

.136 Company G grants a 10-year $100,000 mortgage. Company G receives net fees of $1,000 related to this loan. The contract provides for an interest rate of 12 percent in year 1, 11 percent in year 2, and 10 percent thereafter. [Exhibit 136A illustrates the application of paragraph .117(b).] [FAS91, ¶77]

Exhibit 136A

Application of Paragraph .117(b)

Year	(1) Cash (Out) Inflow	(2) Stated Interest	(3) Amortization	(4) Interest Income	(5) Remaining Principal	(6) Unamortized Net Fees[g]	(7) Carrying Amount
	$ (99,000)				$ 100,000		$ 99,000
1	17,698	$ 12,000	$(1,259)	$ 10,741	94,302	$2,259	92,043
2	17,031	10,373	(388)	9,985	87,644	2,647	84,997
3	16,428	8,764	458	9,222	79,980	2,189	77,791
4	16,428	7,998	441	8,439	71,550	1,748	69,802
5	16,428	7,155	418	7,573	62,277	1,330	60,947
6	16,428	6,228	385	6,613	52,077	945	51,132
7	16,428	5,208	339	5,547	40,857	606	40,251
8	16,428	4,086	281	4,367	28,515	325	28,190
9	16,428	2,852	206	3,058	14,939	119	14,820
10	16,428	1,489[h]	119	1,608	0	0	0

Total amortization $ 1,000

Computations:
Column (1)—Contractual payments
Column (2)—Column (5) for prior year × the loan's stated interest rate (12% in year 1, 11% for year 2, and 10% in years 3-10)
Column (3)—Column (4) – Column (2)
Column (4)—Column (7) for the prior year × effective interest rate (10.8491%)
Column (5)—Column (5) for prior year – (Column (1) – Column (2))
Column (6)—Initial net fees – amortization to date
Column (7)—Column (5) – Column (6)

[g]Unamortized net fee and deferred interest.
[h]$5 rounding adjustment.
[FAS91, ¶77]

Case 8—Application of Paragraph .117(c)—Amortization Based on Factor at Inception

.137 Company H grants a 10-year variable rate mortgage. The loan's interest rate and payment are adjusted annually based on the weekly Treasury bill index plus 1 percent. At the date the loan is granted, this index is 7 percent and does not change until the end of year 3. The first year loan interest rate is 8 percent (equal to the Treasury bill index plus 1 percent). Company H receives net fees of $3,000. At the end of year 3 the index changes to 9 percent and does not change again. Therefore, the loan's stated interest rate is 8 percent for years 1-3 and 10 percent for years 4-10. Company H chooses to determine the amortization based on the index at the date the loan is granted and to ignore subsequent changes in the factor, [as illustrated in Exhibit 137A.] [FAS91, ¶78]

Exhibit 137A Application of Paragraph .117(c)—Amortization Based on Factor at Inception

Year	(1) Cash (Out) Inflow	(2) Stated Interest	(3) Amortization	(4) Interest Income	(5) Remaining Principal	(6) Unamortized Net Fees	(7) Carrying Amount
	$ (97,000)				$ 100,000		$ 97,000
1	14,903	$ 8,000	$ 420	$ 8,420	93,097	$ 2,580	90,517
2	14,903	7,448	410	7,858	85,642	2,170	83,472
3	14,903	6,851	395	7,246	77,590	1,775	75,815
4	15,937	7,759	375	8,134	69,412	1,400	68,012
5	15,937	6,941	347	7,288	60,416	1,053	59,363
6	15,937	6,042	314	6,356	50,521	739	49,782
7	15,937	5,052	272	5,324	39,636	467	39,169
8	15,937	3,964	221	4,185	27,663	246	27,417
9	15,937	2,766	160	2,926	14,492	86	14,406
10	15,937	1,445[i]	86	1,531	0	0	0
Total amortization			$ 3,000				

Computations:
Column (1)—Contractual payments
Column (2)—Column (5) for prior year × the loan's stated interest rate (8% in years 1-3, and 10% in years 4-10)
Column (3)—Calculated as if the index did not change—that is, the amount that would have been recognized for an 8%, 10-year $100,000 mortgage with no prepayments and a $3,000 net fee
Column (4)—Column (2) + Column (3)
Column (5)—Column (5) for prior year – (Column (1) – Column (2))
Column (6)—Initial net fees – amortization to date
Column (7)—Column (5) – Column (6)

[i]$4 rounding adjustment.

[FAS91, ¶78]

Case 9—Application of Paragraph .117(c)—Amortization Recalculated for Subsequent Changes in Factor

.138 Company I grants a 10-year variable rate mortgage. The loan's interest rate and payment are adjusted annually based on the weekly Treasury bill index plus 1 percent. At the date the loan is granted, this index is 7 percent and does not change until the end of year 3. The first year loan interest rate is 8 percent (equal to the Treasury bill index plus 1 percent). Company I receives net fees of $3,000. At the end of year 3 the index changes to 9 percent and does not change again. Therefore, the loan's stated interest rate is 8 percent for years 1-3 and 10 percent for years 4-10. Company I chooses to recalculate a new amortization schedule each time the loan's index changes, [as illustrated in Exhibit 138A.] [FAS91, ¶79]

Exhibit 138A

Application of Paragraph .117(c)—Amortization Recalculated for Subsequent Changes in Factor

Year	(1) Cash (Out) Inflow	(2) Stated Interest	(3) Amortization	(4) Interest Income	(5) Remaining Principal	(6) Unamortized Net Fees	(7) Carrying Amount
	$(97,000)				$100,000		$97,000
1	14,903	$8,000	$ 420	$8,420	93,097	$2,580	90,517
2	14,903	7,448	410	7,858	85,642	2,170	83,472
3	14,903	6,851	395	7,246	77,590	1,775	75,815
4	15,937	7,759	358	8,117	69,412	1,417	67,995
5	15,937	6,941	340	7,281	60,416	1,077	59,339
6	15,937	6,042	311	6,353	50,521	766	49,755
7	15,937	5,052	275	5,327	39,636	491	39,145
8	15,937	3,964	227	4,191	27,663	264	27,399
9	15,937	2,766	168	2,934	14,492	96	14,396
10	15,937	1,445^j	96	1,541	0	0	0
Total amortization			$3,000				

Computations:

Column (1)—Contractual payments

Column (2)—Column (5) for prior year × the loan's stated interest rate (8% in years 1-3, and 10% in years 4-10)

Column (3)—Column (4) – Column (2)

Column (4)—Column (7) for the prior year × the effective interest rate (8.6809%) for years 1-3 and Column (7) for the prior year × the effective interest rate (10.7068%) for years 4-10

Column (5)—Column (5) for prior year – (Column (1) – Column (2))

Column (6)—Initial net fees – amortization to date

Column (7)—Column (5) – Column (6)

---

^j $4 rounding adjustment.

[FAS91, ¶79]

Glossary

.401 **Commitment fees.** Fees charged for entering into an agreement that obligates the enterprise to make or acquire a loan or to satisfy an obligation of the other party under a specified condition. For purposes of this section, the term *commitment fees* includes fees for letters of credit and obligations to purchase a loan or group of loans and pass-through certificates. [FAS91, ¶80]

.402 **Credit card fees.** The periodic uniform fees that entitle cardholders to use credit cards. The amount of such fees generally is not dependent upon the level of credit available or frequency of usage. Typically the use of credit cards facilitates the cardholder's payment for the purchase of goods and services on a periodic, as-billed basis (usually monthly), involves the extension of credit, and, if payment is not made when billed, involves imposition of interest or finance charges. For purposes of this section, the term *credit card fees* includes fees received in similar arrangements, such as charge card and cash card fees. [FAS91, ¶80]

.403 **Incremental direct costs.** Costs to originate a loan that (a) result directly from and are essential to the lending transaction and (b) would not have been incurred by the lender had that lending transaction not occurred. [FAS91, ¶80]

.404 **Origination fees.** Fees charged to the borrower in connection with the process of originating, refinancing, or restructuring a loan. This term includes, but is not limited to, points, management, arrangement, placement, application, underwriting, and other fees pursuant to a lending or leasing transaction and also includes syndication and participation fees to the extent they are associated with the portion of the loan retained by the lender. [FAS91, ¶80]

[Note: Additional guidance with respect to implementing Section L20 is presented in *A Guide to Implementation of Statement 91 on Accounting for Nonrefundable Fees and Costs Associated with Originating or Acquiring Loans and Initial Direct Costs of Leases: Questions and Answers.* The publication, which addresses 65 questions and was edited by Christopher S. Lynch, FASB staff, is available from the Order Department, Financial Accounting Standards Board, 401 Merritt 7, P.O. Box 5116, Norwalk, CT 06856-5116, telephone (203) 847-0700.]

(The next page is 31981.)

Sources: APB Opinion 29; FASB Statement 109; FASB Interpretation 30

Summary

In general, accounting for nonmonetary transactions shall be based on the fair values of the assets (or services) involved. This is the same basis as that used for monetary transactions. If a nonmonetary asset is involuntarily converted to a monetary asset (such as cash), a gain or loss shall be recognized even though an enterprise reinvests or is obligated to reinvest the monetary assets in replacement nonmonetary assets.

Applicability

.101 This section does not apply to the following transactions:

a. A business combination accounted for by an enterprise according to the provisions of Section B50, "Business Combinations"
b. A transfer of **nonmonetary assets** solely between enterprises or persons under common control, such as between a parent company and its subsidiaries or between two subsidiary enterprises of the same parent, or between a corporate joint venture and its owners
c. Acquisition of nonmonetary assets or services on issuance of the capital stock of an enterprise
d. Stock issued or received in stock dividends and stock splits which are accounted for in accordance with Section C20, "Capital Stock: Stock Dividends and Stock Splits"

Some exchanges of nonmonetary assets involve a small monetary consideration, referred to as *boot,* even though the exchange is essentially nonmonetary. This section also applies to those transactions. For purposes of applying this section, events and transactions in which nonmonetary assets are involuntarily converted [1] (for example, as a result of total or partial destruction, theft, seizure, or condemnation) to **monetary assets** that are then reinvested in other nonmonetary assets are monetary transactions. [APB29, ¶4]

---

[1]Paragraphs .114 through .119 discuss the appropriate accounting for *involuntary* conversions of nonmonetary assets to monetary assets.]

Examples of Nonmonetary Transactions

Nonreciprocal Transfers with Owners

.102 Some **nonmonetary transactions** are **nonreciprocal transfers** between an enterprise and its owners. Examples include (a) distribution of nonmonetary assets, such as marketable equity securities, to stockholders as dividends [(refer to Section C11, "Capital Stock: Dividends-in-Kind")]; (b) distribution of nonmonetary assets, such as marketable equity securities, to stockholders to redeem or acquire outstanding capital stock of the enterprise; (c) distribution of nonmonetary assets, such as capital stock of subsidiaries, to stockholders in corporate liquidations or plans of reorganization that involve disposing of all or a significant segment of the business (the plans are variously referred to as spin-offs, split-ups, and split-offs); and (d) distribution of nonmonetary assets to groups of stockholders, pursuant to plans of rescission or other settlements relating to a prior business combination, to redeem or acquire shares of capital stock previously issued in a business combination. [APB29, ¶5]

Nonreciprocal Transfers with Other Than Owners

.103 Other nonmonetary transactions are nonreciprocal transfers between an enterprise and entities other than its owners. Examples are the contribution of nonmonetary assets by an enterprise to a charitable organization and the contribution of land by a governmental unit for construction of productive facilities by an enterprise. [APB29, ¶6]

Exchanges

.104 Many nonmonetary transactions are **exchanges** of nonmonetary assets or services with another entity. Examples include (a) exchange of product held for sale in the ordinary course of business (inventory) for dissimilar property as a means of selling the product to a customer; (b) exchange of product held for sale in the ordinary course of business (inventory) for similar product as an accommodation—that is, at least one party to the exchange reduces transportation costs, meets immediate inventory needs, or otherwise reduces costs or facilitates ultimate sale of the product—and not as a means of selling the product to a customer; and (c) exchange of **productive assets**—assets employed in production rather than held for sale in the ordinary course of business—for similar productive assets or for an equivalent interest in **similar productive assets.** Examples of exchanges in category (c) include the trade of player contracts by professional sports organizations, exchange of leases on mineral properties, exchange of one form of interest in an oil-producing property for another form of interest, [and] exchange of real estate for real estate. [APB29, ¶7]

Basic Principle

.105 Accounting for nonmonetary transactions shall be based on the fair values[2] of the assets (or services) involved, which is the same basis as that used in monetary transactions. Thus, the cost of a nonmonetary asset acquired in exchange for another nonmonetary asset is the fair value of the asset surrendered to obtain it, and a gain or loss shall be recognized on the exchange. The fair value of the asset received shall be used to measure the cost if it is more clearly evident than the fair value of the asset surrendered. Similarly, a nonmonetary asset received in a nonreciprocal transfer shall be recorded at the fair value of the asset received. A transfer of a nonmonetary asset to a stockholder or to another entity in a nonreciprocal transfer shall be recorded at the fair value of the asset transferred, and a gain or loss should be recognized on the disposition of the asset. The fair value of an enterprise's own stock reacquired may be a more clearly evident measure of the fair value of the asset distributed in a nonreciprocal transfer if the transaction involves distribution of a nonmonetary asset to eliminate a disproportionate part of owners' interests (that is, to acquire stock for the treasury or for retirement). [APB29, ¶18]

.106 Certain modifications of the basic principle are required to accommodate problems of measurement and questions about the conditions for recognizing revenue. These modifications are specified in paragraphs .107 through .110. [APB29, ¶19]

Modifications of the Basic Principle

Fair Value Not Determinable

.107 Accounting for a nonmonetary transaction shall not be based on the fair values of the assets transferred unless those fair values are determinable within reasonable limits (refer to paragraph .111). [APB29, ¶20]

Exchanges

.108 If the exchange is not essentially the culmination of an earning process, accounting for an exchange of a nonmonetary asset between an enterprise and another entity shall be based on the recorded amount (after reduction, if appropriate, for an indicated impairment of value) of the nonmonetary asset relinquished. The following two types of nonmonetary exchange transactions do not culminate an earning process:

a. An exchange of a product or property held for sale in the ordinary course of business for a product or property to be sold in the same line of business to

---

[2]Refer to paragraph .111 for determination of fair value. [APB29, ¶18, fn5]

facilitate sales to customers other than the parties to the exchange

b. An exchange of a productive asset not held for sale in the ordinary course of business for a similar productive asset or an equivalent interest in the same or similar productive asset (examples are given in paragraph .104)[3] [APB29, ¶21]

.109 The exchanges of nonmonetary assets that would otherwise be based on recorded amounts (refer to paragraph .108) may include an amount of monetary consideration. The recipient of the monetary consideration has realized gain on the exchange to the extent that the amount of the monetary receipt exceeds a proportionate share of the recorded amount of the asset surrendered. The portion of the cost applicable to the realized amount shall be based on the ratio of the monetary consideration to the total consideration received (monetary consideration plus the estimated fair value of the nonmonetary asset received) or, if more clearly evident, the fair value of the nonmonetary asset transferred. The enterprise paying the monetary consideration shall not recognize any gain on a transaction covered in paragraph .108 but shall record the asset received at the amount of the monetary consideration paid plus the recorded amount of the nonmonetary asset surrendered. If a loss is indicated by the terms of a transaction described in this paragraph or in paragraph .108, the entire indicated loss on the exchange shall be recognized. [APB29, ¶22]

Nonreciprocal Transfers to Owners

.110 Accounting for the distribution of nonmonetary assets to owners of an enterprise in a spin-off or other form of reorganization or liquidation or in a plan that is in substance the rescission of a prior business combination shall be based on the recorded amount (after reduction, if appropriate, for an indicated impairment of value) of the nonmonetary assets distributed. A pro rata distribution to owners of an enterprise of shares of a subsidiary or other enterprise that has been or is being consolidated or that has been or is being accounted for under the equity method is to be considered to be equivalent to a spin-off. Other nonreciprocal transfers of nonmonetary assets to owners shall be accounted for at fair value if the fair value of the nonmonetary asset distributed is objectively measurable and would be clearly realizable to the distributing entity in an outright sale at or near the time of the distribution. [APB29, ¶23]

Applying the Basic Principle

.111 Fair value of a nonmonetary asset transferred to or from an enterprise in a nonmonetary transaction shall be determined by referring to estimated realizable values in cash transactions of the same or similar assets, quoted market prices, in-

---

[3]The fact that an exchange of productive assets is not a taxable transaction for tax purposes may be evidence that the assets exchanged are similar for purposes of applying this section. [APB29, ¶21, fn6]

dependent appraisals, estimated fair values of assets or services received in exchange, and other available evidence. If one of the parties in a nonmonetary transaction could have elected to receive cash instead of the nonmonetary asset, the amount of cash that could have been received may be evidence of the fair value of the nonmonetary assets exchanged. [APB29, ¶25]

.112 Fair value shall be regarded as not determinable within reasonable limits if major uncertainties exist about the realizability of the value that would be assigned to an asset received in a nonmonetary transaction accounted for at fair value. An exchange involving parties with essentially opposing interests is not considered a prerequisite to determining a fair value of a nonmonetary asset transferred; nor does an exchange insure that a fair value for accounting purposes can be ascertained within reasonable limits. If neither the fair value of a nonmonetary asset transferred nor the fair value of a nonmonetary asset received in exchange is determinable within reasonable limits, the recorded amount of the nonmonetary asset transferred from the enterprise may be the only available measure of the transaction. [APB29, ¶26]

.113 A difference between the amount of gain or loss recognized for tax purposes and that recognized for accounting purposes may constitute a [APB29, ¶27] temporary difference [FAS109, ¶287] to be accounted for according to [APB29, ¶27] Section I27, "Income Taxes." [FAS109, ¶287]

Accounting for Involuntary Conversions of Nonmonetary Assets to Monetary Assets

.114 Involuntary conversions of nonmonetary assets to monetary assets are monetary transactions for which gain or loss shall be recognized even though an enterprise reinvests or is obligated to reinvest the monetary assets in replacement nonmonetary assets. [FIN30, ¶2] The gain or loss on the involuntary conversion is the difference between the cost[4] of the nonmonetary asset and the amount of monetary assets received. [FIN30, ¶1]

.115 The requirement to recognize gain in paragraph .114 does not apply to certain involuntary conversions of LIFO inventories[5] [FIN30, ¶2] for which replacement is intended but not made by year-end and the taxpayer does not recognize gain for income tax reporting purposes. [FIN30, ¶11]

---

[4]As used in this section, the term *cost* refers to the cost of a nonmonetary asset or to its carrying amount, if different. [FIN30, ¶1, fn2]

[5]Section I73, "Interim Financial Reporting," paragraph .107(b), provides an exception for the liquidation of a LIFO inventory at an interim date if replacement is expected by year-end. Accordingly, that exception applies to an involuntary conversion of a LIFO inventory if replacement is expected by year-end. [FIN30, ¶2, fn3]

.116 An involuntary conversion of a nonmonetary asset to monetary assets and the subsequent reinvestment of the monetary assets is [not] equivalent to an exchange transaction between an enterprise and another entity. The conversion of a nonmonetary asset to monetary assets is a monetary transaction, whether the conversion is voluntary or involuntary, and such a conversion differs from exchange transactions that involve only nonmonetary assets. To the extent the cost of a nonmonetary asset differs from the amount of monetary assets received, the transaction results in the realization of a gain or loss that shall be recognized. The cost of subsequently acquired nonmonetary assets shall be measured by the consideration paid and not be affected by a previous transaction. [FIN30, ¶10]

.117 In some cases, a nonmonetary asset may be destroyed or damaged in one accounting period, and the amount of monetary assets to be received is not determinable until a subsequent accounting period. In those cases, gain or loss shall be recognized in accordance with Section C59, "Contingencies." [FIN30, ¶3]

.118 Gain or loss resulting from an involuntary conversion of a nonmonetary asset to monetary assets shall be classified in accordance with the provisions of Section I17, "Income Statement Presentation: Extraordinary Items," and Section I22, "Income Statement Presentation: Unusual or Infrequent Items." [FIN30, ¶4]

.119 Gain or loss resulting from an involuntary conversion of a nonmonetary asset to monetary assets that is not recognized for income tax reporting purposes in the same period in which the gain or loss is recognized for financial reporting purposes is a [FIN30, ¶5] temporary difference [FAS109, ¶287] for which comprehensive [recognition of deferred taxes], as described in [FIN30, ¶5] Section I27, [FAS109, ¶287] is required. [FIN30, ¶5]

Disclosure

.120 An enterprise that engages in one or more nonmonetary transactions during a period shall disclose in financial statements for the period the nature of the transactions, the basis of accounting for the assets transferred, and gains or losses recognized on transfers.[6] [APB29, ¶28]

---

[6]Section C51, "Consolidation," paragraph .113, includes additional disclosures that are preferred if a parent company disposes of a subsidiary during the year. [APB29, ¶28, fn7]

Glossary

.401 Exchange (or exchange transaction). A reciprocal transfer between an enterprise and another entity that results in the enterprise's acquiring assets or services or satisfying liabilities by surrendering other assets or services or incurring other obligations.[401] [APB29, ¶3]

.402 Monetary assets (and liabilities). Assets and liabilities whose amounts are fixed in terms of units of currency by contract or otherwise. Examples are cash, short- or long-term accounts and notes receivable in cash, and short- or long-term accounts and notes payable in cash.[402] [APB29, ¶3]

.403 Nonmonetary assets (and liabilities). Assets and liabilities other than monetary ones. Examples are inventories; investments in common stocks; property, plant, and equipment; and liabilities for rent collected in advance.[403] [APB29, ¶3]

.404 Nonmonetary transactions. Exchanges and nonreciprocal transfers that involve little or no monetary assets or liabilities. [APB29, ¶1] [Some nonmonetary transactions are described in paragraphs .102 through .104.]

.405 Nonreciprocal transfer.[404] A transfer of assets or services in one direction, either from an enterprise to its owners (whether or not in exchange for their ownership interests) or another entity or from owners or another entity to the enterprise. An enterprise's reacquisition of its outstanding stock is an example of a nonreciprocal transfer. [APB29, ¶3]

.406 Productive assets. Assets held for or used in the production of goods or services by the enterprise. Productive assets include an investment in another entity if the investment is accounted for by the equity method but exclude an investment not accounted for by that method. [APB29, ¶3]

.407 Similar productive assets. Productive assets that are of the same general type, that perform the same function or that are employed in the same line of business. [APB29, ¶3]

(The next page is 34201.)

---

[401] APB Statement No. 4, *Basic Concepts and Accounting Principles Underlying Financial Statements of Business Enterprises,* paragraphs 180 through 183, contains a more complete explanation of exchanges and nonreciprocal transfers. [APB29, ¶3, fn3]

[402] Refer to APB Statement No. 3, *Financial Statements Restated for General Price-Level Changes,* paragraphs 17 through 19 and Appendix B, [and Section C28, "Changing Prices: Reporting Their Effects in Financial Reports," for a] more complete explanation of monetary and nonmonetary items. [APB29, ¶3, fn2]

[403] [Refer to footnote 402.] [APB29, ¶3, fn2]

[404] [Refer to footnote 401.] [APB29, ¶3, fn3]

Sources: FASB Statement 87; FASB Statement 88; FASB Statement 106;
FASB Statement 109

Summary

The conclusions in this section derive from the basic idea that a defined benefit pension is an exchange between the employer and the employee. In exchange for services provided by the employee, the employer promises to provide, in addition to current wages and other benefits, an amount of retirement income. It follows from that basic view that pension benefits are not gratuities but instead are part of an employee's compensation, and since payment is deferred, the pension is a type of deferred compensation. It also follows that the employer's obligation for that compensation is incurred when the services are rendered.

This section addresses three fundamental aspects of pension accounting: *delaying recognition* of certain events, reporting *net cost*, and *offsetting* liabilities and assets.

The delayed recognition feature means that changes in the pension obligation (including those resulting from plan amendments) and changes in the value of assets set aside to meet those obligations are not recognized as they occur but are recognized systematically and gradually over subsequent periods.

The net cost feature means that the recognized consequences of events and transactions affecting a pension plan are reported as a single net amount in the employer's financial statements. That approach aggregates at least three items that might be reported separately for any other part of an employer's operations: the compensation cost of benefits promised, interest cost resulting from deferred payment of those benefits, and the results of investing what are often significant amounts of assets.

The offsetting feature means that recognized values of assets contributed to a plan and liabilities for pensions recognized as net pension cost of past periods are shown net in the employer's statement of financial position, even though the liability has not been settled, the assets may still be largely controlled, and substantial risks and rewards associated with both of those amounts are clearly borne by the employer.

Within those three features that are retained from prior standards, more useful financial reporting is achieved through the following changes:

1. A standardized method is required for measuring net periodic pension cost that is intended to improve comparability and understandability by recognizing the compensation cost of an employee's pension (including prior service cost) over the employee's approximate service period and by relating cost more directly to the terms of the plan
2. Immediate recognition of a liability (the minimum liability) is required in certain circumstances when the accumulated benefit obligation exceeds the fair value of plan assets, although recognition of the offsetting amount as an increase in net periodic pension cost continues to be delayed
3. Expanded disclosures are required that are intended to provide more complete and more current information than that incorporated in the financial statements.

This section defines the limits of delayed recognition of certain previously unrecognized amounts. It also identifies certain events or transactions that trigger the immediate recognition of gains or losses and unrecognized prior service costs. Those events or transactions include settlements of pension obligations and curtailment of defined benefits. This section also addresses the accounting for termination benefits.

Prior to issuance of this section, an employer that entered into an asset reversion transaction involving the termination of one plan and the establishment of a successor defined benefit plan was precluded from immediately recognizing any resulting gain in earnings. This section specifies how that employer should determine the gain to be recognized in earnings at the time of initial application of this section.

.101 This section [presents] standards of financial accounting and reporting for an employer that offers **pension benefits** to its employees. Ordinarily, such benefits are periodic pension payments to retired employees or their survivors, but they may also include benefits payable as a single lump sum and, except as noted in the following paragraph, other types of **benefits** such as death benefits [(also referred to as life insurance)] provided through a pension plan. An employer's arrangement to provide pension benefits may take a variety of forms and may be financed in different ways. This section applies to any arrangement that is similar in substance to a pension plan regardless of the form or means of financing. This section applies to a written plan and to a plan whose existence may be implied from a well-defined, although perhaps unwritten, practice of paying postretirement benefits. [FAS87, ¶7] This section [also] applies to an employer that sponsors a **defined benefit pension plan** if all or part of the plan's pension benefit obligation is settled or the plan is curtailed. [In addition,] it applies to an employer that offers benefits to employees in connection with their termination of employment. [FAS88, ¶2]

.102 This section does not apply to life insurance benefits provided outside a pension plan or to other postretirement health and welfare benefits. The accounting for those benefits is set forth in Section P40, "Postretirement Benefits Other Than Pensions." [FAS106, ¶14] This section does not change or supersede any of the requirements set forth in Section Pe5, "Pension Funds: Accounting and Reporting by Defined Benefit Pension Plans," for the financial statements of a pension plan. [FAS87, ¶8]

.103 This section is intended to specify accounting objectives and results rather than specific computational means of obtaining those results. If estimates, averages, or computational shortcuts can reduce the cost of applying this section, their use is appropriate, provided the results are reasonably expected not to be materially different from the results of a detailed application. [FAS87, ¶10]

Single-Employer Defined Benefit Pension Plans

.104 For purposes of this section, a defined benefit pension plan is one that defines an amount of pension benefit to be provided, usually as a function of one or more factors such as age, years of **service,** or compensation. [FAS87, ¶11]

.105 A pension benefit is part of the compensation paid to an employee for services. In a defined benefit pension plan, the employer promises to provide, in addition to current wages, retirement income payments in future years after the employee retires or terminates service. Generally, the amount of benefit to be paid depends on a number of future events that are incorporated in the **plan's benefit formula,** often including how long the employee and any survivors live, how many years of service the employee renders, and the employee's compensation in the years immediately before retirement or termination. In most cases, services are rendered over a number of years before an employee retires and begins collecting the pension. Even though the services rendered by an employee are complete and the employee has retired, the total amount of benefit that the employer has promised and the cost to the employer of the services rendered are not precisely determinable but can only be estimated using the **benefit formula** and estimates of the relevant future events, many of which the employer cannot control. [FAS87, ¶12]

---

[1][Deleted 12/90 because of FASB Statement 106, *Employers' Accounting for Postretirement Benefits Other Than Pensions.*]

Basic Elements of Pension Accounting

.106 Conceptually, compensation cost should be recognized in the period in which the employee renders services. Although the complexity and uncertainty of the pension arrangement may preclude complete achievement of that goal, a fundamental objective of this section is to approximate more closely the recognition of the compensation cost of an employee's pension benefits over that employee's service period. [FAS87, ¶95]

.107 Any method of pension accounting that recognizes cost before the payment of benefits to retirees must deal with two problems stemming from the nature of the defined benefit pension contract. First, estimates or **assumptions** must be made concerning the future events that will determine the amount and timing of the benefit payments. Second, some approach to attributing the cost of pension benefits to individual years of service must be selected. [FAS87, ¶13]

.108 This section requires use of assumptions, each of which individually represents the best estimate of a particular future event. [FAS87, ¶14] That method of selecting assumptions is referred to as an **explicit approach.** [FAS87, ¶191]

.109 The assumptions and the **attribution** of cost to periods of employee service are fundamental to the measurements of **net periodic pension cost** and pension obligations required by this section. The basic elements of pension accounting are described in paragraphs .110 through .113; they are the foundation of the accounting and reporting requirements set forth in this section. [FAS87, ¶15]

.110 Net periodic pension cost is made up of several *components* that reflect different aspects of the employer's financial arrangements as well as the cost of benefits earned by employees. The cost of a benefit can be determined without regard to how the employer decides to finance the plan. The **service cost component** of net periodic pension cost is the **actuarial present value** of benefits attributed by the plan's benefit formula to services rendered by employees during the period. The service cost component is conceptually the same for an unfunded plan, a plan with minimal funding, and a well-funded plan. The other components of net periodic pension cost are interest cost[2] (interest on the **projected benefit obligation,** which is a discounted amount), **actual return on plan assets, amortization** of **unrecognized prior service cost,** and **gain or loss.** Both the **return on plan assets** and interest cost components are in substance financial items rather than employee compensation costs. [FAS87, ¶16]

.111 The projected benefit obligation as of a date is the actuarial present value of all benefits attributed by the plan's benefit formula to employee service rendered prior to that date. The projected benefit obligation is measured using an assumption as to future compensation levels if the **pension benefit formula** is based on those future com-

---

[2]The **interest cost component** of net periodic pension cost shall not be considered to be interest for purposes of applying Section I67, "Interest: Capitalization of Interest Costs." [FAS87, ¶16, fn4]

pensation levels. Plans for which the pension benefit formula is based on future compensation are sometimes called pay-related, **final-pay**, final-average-pay, or **career-average-pay plans.** Plans for which the pension benefit formula is not based on future compensation levels are called non-pay-related or **flat-benefit plans.** The projected benefit obligation is a measure of benefits attributed to service to date assuming that the plan continues in effect and that estimated future events (including compensation increases, **turnover,** and **mortality**) occur. [FAS87, ¶17]

.112 The **accumulated benefit obligation** as of a date is the actuarial present value of benefits attributed by the pension benefit formula to employee service rendered prior to that date and based on current and past compensation levels. The accumulated benefit obligation differs from the projected benefit obligation in that it includes no assumption about future compensation levels. For plans with flat-benefit or non-pay-related pension benefit formulas, the accumulated benefit obligation and the projected benefit obligation are the same. The accumulated benefit obligation and the **vested benefit obligation** provide information about the obligation the employer would have if the plan were discontinued. [FAS87, ¶18]

.113 **Plan assets** are assets—usually stocks, bonds, and other investments—that have been segregated and restricted (usually in a trust) to provide for pension benefits. The amount of plan assets includes amounts contributed by the employer (and by employees for a **contributory plan**) and amounts earned from investing the contributions, less benefits paid. Plan assets ordinarily cannot be withdrawn by the employer except under certain circumstances when a plan has assets in excess of obligations and the employer has taken certain steps to satisfy existing obligations. Assets not segregated in a trust or otherwise effectively restricted so that they cannot be used by the employer for other purposes are not plan assets for purposes of this section even though it may be intended that such assets be used to provide pensions. Amounts accrued by the employer but not yet paid to the plan are not plan assets for purposes of this section. Securities of the employer held by the plan are includable in plan assets provided they are transferable. [FAS87, ¶19]

Recognition of Net Periodic Pension Cost

.114 The following components shall be included in the net pension cost recognized for a period by an employer sponsoring a defined benefit pension plan:

a. Service cost
b. Interest cost
c. Actual return on plan assets, if any
d. Amortization of unrecognized prior service cost, if any
e. Gain or loss (including the effects of changes in assumptions) to the extent recognized (paragraph .128)

f. Amortization of the unrecognized net obligation (and loss or cost) or unrecognized net asset (and gain) existing at the date of initial application of this section.[3] [FAS87, ¶20]

Service Cost

.115 The service cost component recognized in a period shall be determined as the actuarial present value of benefits attributed by the pension benefit formula to employee service during that period. The measurement of the service cost component requires use of an attribution method and assumptions. That measurement is discussed in paragraphs .133 through .138 and paragraphs .141 through .144 of this section. [FAS87, ¶21]

Interest Cost

.116 The interest cost component recognized in a period shall be determined as the increase in the projected benefit obligation due to the passage of time. Measuring the projected benefit obligation as a present value requires accrual of an interest cost at rates equal to the assumed **discount rates.** [FAS87, ¶22]

Actual Return on Plan Assets

.117 For a funded plan, the actual return on plan assets shall be determined based on the fair value of plan assets at the beginning and the end of the period, adjusted for contributions and benefit payments. [FAS87, ¶23]

Prior Service Cost

.118 **Plan amendments** (including initiation of a plan) often include provisions that grant increased benefits based on services rendered in prior periods. Because plan amendments are granted with the expectation that the employer will realize economic benefits in future periods, this section does not require the cost of providing such **retroactive benefits** (that is, **prior service cost**) to be included in net periodic pension cost entirely in the year of the amendment but provides for recognition during the future service periods of those employees active at the date of the amendment who are expected to receive benefits under the plan. [FAS87, ¶24]

---

[3]For a defined benefit plan, an employer shall determine as of the **measurement date** (paragraph .148) for the beginning of the fiscal year in which this section is first applied, the amounts of (a) the projected benefit obligation and (b) the **fair value** of plan assets plus previously recognized **unfunded accrued pension cost** or less previously recognized **prepaid pension cost.** The difference between those two amounts, whether it represents an unrecognized net obligation (and loss or cost) or an unrecognized net asset (and gain), shall be amortized on a straight-line basis over the average remaining service period of employees expected to receive benefits under the plan, except that, (a) if the average remaining service period is less than 15 years, the employer may elect to use a 15-year period, and (b) if all or almost all of a plan's **participants** are inactive, the employer shall use the inactive participants' average remaining life expectancy period. That same amortization shall also be used to recognize any unrecognized net obligation related to a **defined contribution plan.** [FAS87, ¶77]

.119 The cost of retroactive benefits (including benefits that are granted to retirees) is the increase in the projected benefit obligation at the date of the amendment. Except as specified in paragraphs .120 and .121, that prior service cost shall be amortized by assigning an equal amount to each future period of service of each employee active at the date of the amendment who is expected to receive benefits under the plan. If all or almost all of a plan's participants are inactive, the cost of retroactive plan amendments affecting benefits of inactive participants shall be amortized based on the remaining life expectancy of those participants instead of based on the remaining service period. [FAS87, ¶25]

.120 To reduce the complexity and detail of the computations required, consistent use of an alternative amortization approach that more rapidly reduces the unrecognized cost of retroactive amendments is acceptable. For example, a straight-line amortization of the cost over the average remaining service period of employees expected to receive benefits under the plan is acceptable. The alternative method used shall be disclosed. [FAS87, ¶26] Use of [a] more precise method [that] recognize[s] the cost of each individual's added benefits over that individual's remaining service period is, of course, appropriate. [FAS87, ¶163]

.121 In some situations a history of regular plan amendments and other evidence may indicate that the period during which the employer expects to realize economic benefits from an amendment granting retroactive benefits is shorter than the entire remaining service period of the active employees. Identification of such situations requires an assessment of the individual circumstances and the substance of the particular plan situation. In those circumstances [FAS87, ¶27] [and when] the benefits of a plan amendment have been impaired, [FAS87, ¶167] the amortization of prior service cost shall be accelerated to reflect the more rapid expiration of the employer's economic benefits and to recognize the cost in the periods benefited. [FAS87, ¶27]

.122 A plan amendment can reduce, rather than increase, the projected benefit obligation. Such a reduction shall be used to reduce any existing unrecognized prior service cost, and the excess, if any, shall be amortized on the same basis as the cost of benefit increases. [FAS87, ¶28]

Gains and Losses

.123 **Gains and losses** are changes in the amount of either the projected benefit obligation or plan assets resulting from experience different from that assumed and from changes in assumptions. This section does not distinguish between those sources of gains and losses. Gains and losses include amounts that have been realized, for example by sale of a security, as well as amounts that are unrealized. Because gains and losses may reflect refinements in estimates as well as real changes in economic values and because some gains in one period may be offset by losses in another or vice versa, this section does not require recognition of gains and losses as components of net pension cost of the period in which they arise.[4] [FAS87, ¶29]

.124 The **expected return on plan assets** shall be determined based on the **expected long-term rate of return on plan assets** and the **market-related value of plan assets.** The market-related value of plan assets shall be either fair value or a calculated value that recognizes changes in fair value in a systematic and rational manner over not more than five years. Different ways of calculating market-related value may be used for different classes of assets (for example, an employer might use fair value for bonds and a five-year-moving-average value for equities), but the manner of determining market-related value shall be applied consistently from year to year for each asset class. [FAS87, ¶30]

.125 Asset gains and losses are differences between the actual return on assets during a period and the expected return on assets for that period. Asset gains and losses include both (a) changes reflected in the market-related value of assets and (b) changes not yet reflected in the market-related value (that is, the difference between the fair value of assets and the market-related value). Asset gains and losses not yet reflected in market-related value are not required to be amortized under paragraphs .126 and .127. [FAS87, ¶31]

.126 As a minimum, amortization of an **unrecognized net gain or loss** (excluding asset gains and losses not yet reflected in market-related value) shall be included as a component of net pension cost for a year if, as of the beginning of the year, that unrecognized net gain or loss exceeds 10 percent of the greater of the projected benefit obligation or the market-related value of plan assets. If amortization is required, the minimum amortization[5] shall be that excess divided by the average remaining service period of active employees expected to receive benefits under the plan. If all or almost all of a plan's participants are inactive, the average remaining life expectancy of the inactive participants shall be used instead of average remaining service. [FAS87, ¶32]

.127 Any systematic method of amortization of unrecognized gains or losses may be used in lieu of the minimum specified in the previous paragraph provided that (a) the minimum is used in any period in which the minimum amortization is greater (reduces the net balance by more), (b) the method is applied consistently, (c) the method is applied similarly to both gains and losses, and (d) the method used is disclosed. [FAS87, ¶33]

.128 The gain or loss component of net periodic pension cost shall consist of (a) the difference between the actual return on plan assets and the expected return on plan assets and (b) amortization of the unrecognized net gain or loss from previous periods. [FAS87, ¶34]

---

[4]Accounting for **plan terminations** and **curtailments** and other circumstances in which recognition of gains and losses might not be delayed is addressed in paragraphs .171 through .188. [FAS87, ¶29, fn5]

[5]The amortization must always reduce the beginning-of-the-year balance. Amortization of a net unrecognized gain results in a decrease in net periodic pension cost; amortization of a net unrecognized loss results in an increase in net periodic pension cost. [FAS87, ¶32, fn6]

Recognition of Liabilities and Assets

.129 A liability (unfunded accrued pension cost) is recognized if net periodic pension cost recognized pursuant to this section exceeds amounts the employer has contributed to the plan. An asset (prepaid pension cost) is recognized if net periodic pension cost is less than amounts the employer has contributed to the plan. [FAS87, ¶35]

.130 If the accumulated benefit obligation exceeds the fair value of plan assets, the employer shall recognize in the statement of financial position a liability (including unfunded accrued pension cost) that is at least equal to the **unfunded accumulated benefit obligation.** Recognition of an additional minimum liability is required if an unfunded accumulated benefit obligation exists and (a) an asset has been recognized as prepaid pension cost, (b) the liability already recognized as unfunded accrued pension cost is less than the unfunded accumulated benefit obligation, or (c) no accrued or prepaid pension cost has been recognized. [FAS87, ¶36]

.131 If an additional minimum liability is recognized pursuant to paragraph .130, an equal amount shall be recognized as an intangible asset, provided that the asset recognized shall not exceed the amount of unrecognized prior service cost.[6] If an additional liability required to be recognized exceeds unrecognized prior service cost, the excess (which would represent a net loss not yet recognized as net periodic pension cost) shall be reported as a separate component (that is, a reduction) of equity, net of any tax benefits that result from considering such losses as [FAS87, ¶37] temporary differences [FAS109, ¶287] for purposes of applying the provisions of [FAS87, ¶37] Section I27, "Income Taxes." [FAS109, ¶287]

.132 When a new determination of the amount of additional liability is made to prepare a statement of financial position, the related intangible asset and separate component of equity shall be eliminated or adjusted as necessary. [FAS87, ¶38]

Measurement of Cost and Obligations

.133 The service component of net periodic pension cost, the projected benefit obligation, and the accumulated benefit obligation are based on an attribution of pension benefits to periods of employee service and on the use of actuarial assumptions to calculate the actuarial present value of those benefits. Actuarial assumptions reflect the time value of money (discount rate) and the probability of payment (assumptions as to mortality, turnover, early retirement, and so forth). [FAS87, ¶39]

Attribution

.134 For purposes of this section, pension benefits ordinarily shall be attributed to periods of employee service based on the plan's benefit formula to the extent that the for-

---

[6]For purposes of this paragraph, an unrecognized net obligation existing at the date of initial application of this section [(see footnote 3)] shall be treated as unrecognized prior service cost. [FAS87, ¶37, fn7]

mula states or implies an attribution. For example, if a plan's formula provides for a pension benefit of $10 per month for life for each year of service, the benefit attributed to each year of an employee's service is $10 times the number of months of life expectancy after retirement, and the cost attributable to each year is the actuarial present value of that benefit. For plan benefit formulas that define benefits similarly for all years of service, that attribution is a **"benefit/years-of-service" approach** because it attributes the same amount of the pension benefit to each year of service.[7] For final-pay and career-average-pay plans, that attribution is also the same as the "projected unit credit" or "unit credit with service prorate" actuarial cost method. For a flat-benefit plan, it is the same as the "unit credit" actuarial cost method. [FAS87, ¶40] [The] use of a standardized [attribution approach will] improve comparability, even though some differences that are not necessarily reflective of real differences will remain because of the exercise of judgement in the selection of assumptions. [FAS87, ¶127]

.135 In some situations a history of regular increases in non-pay-related benefits or benefits under a career-average-pay plan and other evidence may indicate that an employer has a present commitment to make future amendments and that the substance of the plan is to provide benefits attributable to prior service that are greater than the benefits defined by the written terms of the plan. In those situations, the substantive commitment shall be the basis for the accounting, and the existence and nature of the commitment to make future amendments shall be disclosed. [FAS87, ¶41] [In the absence of such a commitment,] plan amendments should [not] be anticipated or estimated before they are made. [A] present obligation ordinarily [does not exist] for benefits to be promised in future amendments. [FAS87, ¶168]

.136 Some plans may have benefit formulas that attribute all or a disproportionate share of the total benefits provided to later years of service, thereby achieving in substance a delayed vesting of benefits. For example, a plan that provides no benefits for the first 19 years of service and a vested benefit of $10,000 for the 20th year is substantively the same as a plan that provides $500 per year for each of 20 years and requires 20 years of service before benefits vest. For such plans the total projected benefit shall be considered to accumulate in proportion to the ratio of the number of completed years of service to the number that will have been completed when the benefit is first fully vested. If a plan's benefit formula does not specify how a particular benefit relates to services rendered, the benefit shall be considered to accumulate as follows:

---

[7]Some plans define different benefits for different years of service. For example, a step-rate plan might provide a benefit of 1 percent of final pay for each year of service up to 20 years and 1 1/2 percent of final pay for years of service in excess of 20. Another plan might provide 1 percent of final pay for each year of service but limit the total benefit to no more than 20 percent of final pay. For such plans the attribution called for by this section will not assign the same amount of pension benefit to each year of service. [FAS87, ¶40, fn8]

a. For benefits of a type includable in **vested benefits**,[8] in proportion to the ratio of the number of completed years of service to the number that will have been completed when the benefit is first fully vested
b. For benefits of a type not includable in vested benefits,[9] in proportion to the ratio of completed years of service to total projected years of service. [FAS87, ¶42]

Assumptions

.137 Each significant assumption used shall reflect the best estimate solely with respect to that individual assumption. All assumptions shall presume that the plan will continue in effect in the absence of evidence that it will not continue. [FAS87, ¶43]

.138 Assumed discount rates shall reflect the rates at which the pension benefits could be effectively settled.[9a] It is appropriate in estimating those rates to look to available information about rates implicit in current prices of **annuity contracts** that could be used to effect settlement of the obligation (including information about [FAS87, ¶44] [certain] [FAS87, ¶196] available annuity rates currently published by the Pension Benefit Guaranty Corporation). In making those estimates, employers may also look to rates of return on high-quality fixed-income investments currently available and expected to be available during the period to maturity of the pension benefits.[9b] Assumed discount rates are used in measurements of the projected, accumulated, and vested benefit obligations and the service and interest cost components of net periodic pension cost. [FAS87, ¶44] [M]aterial changes in long-term rates should [not] be ignored solely to avoid adjusting assumed interest discount rates. [FAS87, ¶201]

.139 **Interest rates** vary depending on the duration of investments; for example, U.S. Treasury bills, 7-year bonds, and 30-year bonds have different interest rates. Thus, the

---

[8]For example, a supplemental early retirement benefit that is a vested benefit after a stated number of years. [FAS87, ¶42, fn9]

[9]For example, a death or disability benefit that is payable only if death or disability occurs during active service. [FAS87, ¶42, fn10]

[9a]As opposed to "settling" the obligation, which incorporates the insurer's risk factor, "effectively settling" the obligation focuses only on the time value of money and ignores the insurer's cost for assuming the risk of experience losses. [FAS106, ¶188]

[9b]The objective of selecting assumed discount rates is to measure the single amount that, if invested at the measurement date in a portfolio of high-quality debt instruments, would provide the necessary future cash flows to pay the benefit [obligation] when due. Notionally, that single amount, the [projected,] accumulated [,or vested] benefit obligation, would equal the current market value of a portfolio of high-quality zero coupon bonds whose maturity dates and amounts would be the same as the timing and amount of the [respective] future benefit payments. Because cash inflows would equal cash outflows in timing and amount, there would be no reinvestment risk in the yields to maturity of the portfolio. However, in other than a zero coupon portfolio, such as a portfolio of long-term debt instruments that pay semiannual interest payments or whose maturities do not extend far enough into the future to meet expected benefit payments, the assumed discount rates (the yield to maturity) need to incorporate expected reinvestment rates available in the future. Those rates should be extrapolated from the existing yield curve at the measurement date. Assumed discount rates should be reevaluated at each measurement date. If the general level of interest rates rises or declines, the assumed discount rates should change in a similar manner. [FAS106, ¶186]

weighted-average discount rate (interest rate) inherent in the prices of annuities (or a dedicated bond portfolio) will vary depending on the length of time remaining until individual benefit payment dates. A plan covering only retired employees would be expected to have significantly different discount rates from one covering a work force of 30-year-olds. The disclosures required by this section regarding components of the pension benefit obligation will be more representationally faithful if individual discount rates applicable to various benefit deferral periods are selected. A properly weighted average rate can be used for aggregate computations such as the interest cost component of net pension cost for the period. [FAS87, ¶199]

.140 An insurance company deciding on the price of an annuity contract will consider the rates of return available to it for investing the premium received and the rates of return expected to be available to it for reinvestment of future cash flows from the initial investment during the period until benefits are payable. That consideration is indicative of a relationship between rates inherent in the prices of annuity contracts and rates available in investment markets. [It is] appropriate for employers to consider that relationship and information about investment rates in estimating the discount rates required for application of this section. [FAS87, ¶200] A current settlement rate best meets that objective and also is consistent with measurement of plan assets at fair value for purposes of disclosing the plan's funded status. [FAS87, ¶198] The volatility of the unfunded or overfunded obligation may be less than some expect if the explicit assumptions used in the valuation of the obligation are changed to reflect fully the changes in interest rate structures that affect the fair values of plan assets, because changes in the assets may tend to offset changes in the obligation. [FAS87, ¶174]

.141 The expected long-term rate of return on plan assets shall reflect the average rate of earnings expected on the funds invested or to be invested to provide for the benefits included in the projected benefit obligation. In estimating that rate, appropriate consideration should be given to the returns being earned by the plan assets in the **fund** and the rates of return expected to be available for reinvestment.[10] The expected long-term rate of return on plan assets is used (with the market-related value of assets) to compute the expected return on assets. [FAS87, ¶45]

.142 The service cost component of net periodic pension cost and the projected benefit obligation shall reflect future compensation levels to the extent that the pension benefit formula defines pension benefits wholly or partially as a function of future compensation levels (that is, for a final-pay plan or a career-average-pay plan). Future increases for which a present commitment exists as described in paragraph .135 shall be similarly considered. Assumed compensation levels shall reflect an estimate of the actual future compensation levels of the individual employees involved, including future changes attributed to general price levels, productivity, seniority, promotion, and other factors. All assumptions shall be consistent to the extent that each reflects expec-

---

[10]An expected long-term-return-on-assets rate significantly below the rate at which the obligation could be settled implies that settlement would be economically advantageous. [FAS87, ¶179]

tations of the same future economic conditions, such as future rates of inflation. Measuring service cost and the projected benefit obligation based on estimated future compensation levels entails considering indirect effects, such as changes under existing law in social security benefits or benefit limitations[11] that would affect benefits provided by the plan. [FAS87, ¶46]

.143 The accumulated benefit obligation shall be measured based on employees' *history* of service and *compensation* without an estimate of future compensation levels. Excluding estimated future compensation levels also means excluding indirect effects of future changes such as increases in the social security wage base. In measuring the accumulated benefit obligation, projected years of service shall be a factor only in determining employees' expected eligibility for particular benefits, such as:

a. Increased benefits that are granted provided a specified number of years of service are rendered (for example, a pension benefit that is increased from $9 per month to $10 per month for each year of service if 20 or more years of service are rendered)
b. Early retirement benefits
c. Death benefits
d. Disability benefits. [FAS87, ¶47]

.144 Automatic benefit increases specified by the plan (for example, automatic cost-of-living increases) that are expected to occur shall be included in measurements of the projected, accumulated, and vested benefit obligations, and the service cost component required by this section. Also, retroactive plan amendments shall be included in the computation of the projected and accumulated benefit obligations once they have been contractually agreed to, even if some provisions take effect only in future periods. For example, if a plan amendment grants a higher benefit level for employees retiring after a future date, the higher benefit level shall be included in current-period measurements for employees expected to retire after that date. [FAS87, ¶48]

Measurement of Plan Assets

.145 For purposes of measuring the minimum liability required by the provisions of paragraph .130 and for purposes of the disclosures required by paragraph .150, plan investments, whether equity or debt securities, real estate, or other, shall be measured at their fair value as of the measurement date. The fair value of an investment is the amount that the plan could reasonably expect to receive for it in a current sale between a willing buyer and a willing seller, that is, other than in a forced or liquidation sale. Fair value shall be measured by the market price if an active market exists for the investment. If no active market exists for an investment but such a market exists for similar investments, selling prices in that market may be helpful in estimating fair value. If a market price is not available, a forecast of expected cash flows may aid in

---

[11]For example, those currently imposed by Section 415 of the Internal Revenue Code. [FAS87, ¶46, fn11]

estimating fair value, provided the expected cash flows are discounted at a current rate commensurate with the risk involved.[12] [FAS87, ¶49]

.146 For purposes of determining the expected return on plan assets and accounting for asset gains and losses pursuant to paragraphs .123 through .128, a market-related asset value, defined in paragraph .124, is used. [FAS87, ¶50]

.147 Plan assets used in plan operations (for example, buildings, equipment, furniture and fixtures, and leasehold improvements) shall be measured at cost less accumulated depreciation or amortization for all purposes. [FAS87, ¶51]

Measurement Dates

.148 The measurements of plan assets and obligations required by this section shall be as of the date of the financial statements or, if used consistently from year to year, as of a date not more than three months prior to that date. Requiring that the pension measurements be as of a particular date is not intended to require that all procedures be performed after that date. As with other financial statement items requiring estimates, much of the information can be prepared as of an earlier date and projected forward to account for subsequent events (for example, employee service). The additional minimum liability reported in interim financial statements shall be the same additional minimum liability (paragraph .130) recognized in the previous year-end statement of financial position, adjusted for subsequent accruals and contributions, unless measures of both the obligation and plan assets are available as of a more current date or a significant event occurs, such as a plan amendment, that would ordinarily call for such measurements. [FAS87, ¶52]

.149 Measurements of net periodic pension cost for both interim and annual financial statements shall be based on the assumptions used for the previous year-end measurements unless more recent measurements of both plan assets and obligations are available or a significant event occurs, such as a plan amendment, that would ordinarily call for such measurements. [FAS87, ¶53]

Disclosures

.150 An employer sponsoring a defined benefit pension plan shall disclose the following:

a. A description of the plan including employee groups covered, type of benefit formula, **funding policy,** types of assets held and significant nonbenefit liabilities, if

---

[12]For an indication of factors to be considered in determining the discount rate, refer to Section I69, "Interest: Imputation of an Interest Cost," paragraphs .106 and .107. If significant, the fair value of an investment shall reflect the brokerage commissions and other costs normally incurred in a sale. [FAS87, ¶49, fn12]

any, and the nature and effect of significant matters affecting comparability of information for all periods presented

b. The amount of net periodic pension cost for the period showing separately the service cost component, the interest cost component, the actual return on assets for the period, and the net total of other components[13]

c. A schedule reconciling the funded status of the plan with amounts reported in the employer's statement of financial position, showing separately:

(1) The fair value of plan assets

(2) The projected benefit obligation identifying the accumulated benefit obligation and the vested benefit obligation

(3) The amount of unrecognized prior service cost

(4) The amount of unrecognized net gain or loss (including asset gains and losses not yet reflected in market-related value)

(5) The amount of any remaining unrecognized net obligation or net asset existing at the date of initial application of this section

(6) The amount of any additional liability recognized pursuant to paragraph .130

(7) The amount of net pension asset or liability recognized in the statement of financial position pursuant to paragraphs .129 and .130 (which is the net result of combining the preceding six items)

d. The weighted-average assumed discount rate and rate of compensation increase (if applicable) used to measure the projected benefit obligation and the weighted-average expected long-term rate of return on plan assets

e. If applicable, the amounts and types of securities of the employer and related parties included in plan assets, and the approximate amount of annual benefits of employees and retirees covered by annuity contracts issued by the employer and related parties. Also, if applicable, the alternative amortization method used pursuant to paragraphs .120 and .127, and the existence and nature of the commitment discussed in paragraph .135. [FAS87, ¶54]

.151 It [is] appropriate for employers to consider disclosing [the following items] if they decide to disclose more information about pension plans than the minimum required by this section, for example, because their plans are large relative to their overall operations[:] [FAS87, ¶224]

a. The ratio of net periodic pension cost to covered payroll

b. The separate amounts of amortization of unrecognized prior service and amortization of unrecognized net gain or loss

---

[13]The net total of other components is the net effect during the period of certain delayed recognition provisions of this section. That net total includes:

a. The net asset gain or loss during the period deferred for later recognition (in effect, an offset or a supplement to the actual return on assets)

b. Amortization of the net gain or loss from earlier periods

c. Amortization of unrecognized prior service cost

d. Amortization of the unrecognized net obligation or net asset existing at the date of initial application of this section. [FAS87, ¶54, fn13]

c. Information about the cash flows of the plan separately showing employer contributions, other contributions, and benefits paid during the period
d. The amounts of plan assets classified by major asset category
e. The amounts of the vested benefit obligation owed to retirees and to others
f. The change in the projected benefit obligation that would result from a one-percentage-point change in (1) the assumed discount rate and (2) the assumed rate of compensation increase
g. The change in the service cost and interest cost components of net periodic pension cost that would result from a one-percentage-point change in (1) the assumed discount rate and (2) the assumed rate of compensation increase. [FAS87, ¶223]

Employers with Two or More Plans

.152 An employer that sponsors two or more separate defined benefit pension plans shall determine net periodic pension cost, liabilities, and assets by separately applying the provisions of this section to each plan. In particular, unless an employer clearly has a right to use the assets of one plan to pay benefits of another, a liability required to be recognized pursuant to paragraph .129 or .130 for one plan shall not be reduced or eliminated because another plan has assets in excess of its accumulated benefit obligation or because the employer has prepaid pension cost related to another plan. [FAS87, ¶55]

.153 Except as noted below, disclosures required by this section may be aggregated for all of an employer's single-employer defined benefit plans, or plans may be disaggregated in groups so as to provide the most useful information. For purposes of the disclosures required by paragraph .150(c), plans with assets in excess of the accumulated benefit obligation shall not be aggregated with plans that have accumulated benefit obligations that exceed plan assets. Disclosures for plans outside the U.S. shall not be combined with those for U.S. plans unless those plans use similar economic assumptions. [FAS87, ¶56]

Annuity Contracts

.154 An annuity contract is a contract in which an insurance company[14] unconditionally undertakes a legal obligation to provide specified benefits to specific individuals in return for a fixed consideration or premium. An annuity contract is irrevocable and involves the transfer of significant risk from the employer to the insurance company. Some annuity contracts (**participating annuity contracts**) provide that the purchaser (either the plan or the employer) may participate in the experience of the insurance

---

[14]If the insurance company does business primarily with the employer and related parties (a **captive insurer**), or if there is any reasonable doubt that the insurance company will meet its obligations under the contract, the contract is not an annuity contract for purposes of paragraphs .101 through .170 of this section. Some contracts provide for a refund of premiums if an employee for whom an annuity is purchased does not render sufficient service for the benefit to vest under the terms of the plan. Such a provision shall not by itself preclude a contract from being treated as an annuity contract for purposes of this section. [FAS87, ¶57, fn14]

company. Under those contracts, the insurance company ordinarily pays dividends to the purchaser. If the substance of a participating contract is such that the employer remains subject to all or most of the risks and rewards associated with the benefit obligation covered and the assets transferred to the insurance company, that contract is not an annuity contract for purposes of this section. [FAS87, ¶57] [Refer also to paragraph .158.]

.155 To the extent that benefits currently earned are covered by annuity contracts, the cost of those benefits shall be the cost of purchasing the contracts, except as provided in paragraph .158. That is, if all the benefits attributed by the plan's benefit formula to service in the current period are covered by **nonparticipating annuity contracts**, the cost of the contracts determines the service cost component of net pension cost for that period. [FAS87, ¶58]

.156 Benefits provided by the pension benefit formula beyond benefits provided by annuity contracts (for example, benefits related to future compensation levels) shall be accounted for according to the provisions of this section applicable to plans not involving insurance contracts. [FAS87, ¶59]

.157 Benefits covered by annuity contracts shall be excluded from the projected benefit obligation and the accumulated benefit obligation. Except as provided in paragraph .158, annuity contracts shall be excluded from plan assets. [FAS87, ¶60]

.158 Some annuity contracts provide that the purchaser (either the plan or the employer) may participate in the experience of the insurance company. Under those contracts, the insurance company ordinarily pays dividends to the purchaser, the effect of which is to reduce the cost of the plan. The purchase price of a participating annuity contract ordinarily is higher than the price of an equivalent contract without **participation rights.** The difference is the cost of the participation right. The cost of the participation right shall be recognized at the date of purchase as an asset. In subsequent periods, the participation right shall be measured at its fair value if the contract is such that fair value is reasonably estimable. Otherwise, the participation right shall be measured at its amortized cost (not in excess of its net realizable value), and the cost shall be amortized systematically over the expected dividend period under the contract. [FAS87, ¶61]

Other Contracts with Insurance Companies

.159 Insurance contracts that are in substance equivalent to the purchase of annuities shall be accounted for as such. Other contracts with insurance companies shall be accounted for as investments and measured at fair value. For some contracts, the best available evidence of fair value may be contract value. If a contract has a determinable cash surrender value or conversion value, that is presumed to be its fair value. [FAS87, ¶62]

Defined Contribution Plans

.160 For purposes of this section, a defined contribution pension plan is a plan that provides pension benefits in return for services rendered, provides an individual account for each participant, and has terms that specify how contributions to the individual's account are to be determined rather than the amount of pension benefits the individual is to receive. Under a defined contribution plan, the pension benefits a participant will receive depend only on the amount contributed to the participant's account, the returns earned on investments of those contributions, and forfeitures of other participants' benefits that may be allocated to the participant's account. [FAS87, ¶63]

.161 To the extent that a plan's defined contributions to an individual's account are to be made for periods in which that individual renders services, the net pension cost for a period shall be the contribution called for in that period. If a plan calls for contributions for periods after an individual retires or terminates, the estimated cost shall be accrued during the employee's service period. [FAS87, ¶64]

.162 An employer that sponsors one or more defined contribution plans shall disclose the following separately from its defined benefit plan disclosures:

a. A description of the plan(s) including employee groups covered, the basis for determining contributions, and the nature and effect of significant matters affecting comparability of information for all periods presented
b. The amount of cost recognized during the period. [FAS87, ¶65]

.163 A pension plan having characteristics of both a defined benefit plan and a defined contribution plan requires careful analysis. If the *substance* of the plan is to provide a defined benefit, as may be the case with some "target benefit" plans, the accounting and disclosure requirements shall be determined in accordance with the provisions of this section applicable to a defined benefit plan. [FAS87, ¶66]

Multiemployer Plans

.164 For purposes of this section, a **multiemployer plan** is a pension plan to which two or more unrelated employers contribute, usually pursuant to one or more collective-bargaining agreements. A characteristic of multiemployer plans is that assets contributed by one participating employer may be used to provide benefits to employees of other participating employers since assets contributed by an employer are not segregated in a separate account or restricted to provide benefits only to employees of that employer. A multiemployer plan usually is administered by a board of trustees composed of management and labor representatives and may also be referred to as a "joint trust" or "union" plan. Generally, many employers participate in a multiemployer plan, and an employer may participate in more than one plan. The employers participating in multiemployer plans usually have a common industry bond, but for some plans the employers are in different industries, and the labor union may be their only common bond. Some multiemployer plans do not involve a union. For example, local chapters of a not-for-profit organization may participate in a plan established by the related national organization. [FAS87, ¶67]

.165 An employer participating in a multiemployer plan shall recognize as net pension cost the required contribution for the period and shall recognize as a liability any contributions due and unpaid. [FAS87, ¶68]

.166 An employer that participates in one or more multiemployer plans shall disclose the following separately from disclosures for a **single-employer plan:**

a. A description of the multiemployer plan(s) including the employee groups covered, the type of benefits provided (defined benefit or defined contribution), and the nature and effect of significant matters affecting comparability of information for all periods presented
b. The amount of cost recognized during the period. [FAS87, ¶69]

.167 In some situations, withdrawal from a multiemployer plan may result in an employer's having an obligation to the plan for a portion of its unfunded benefit obligations. If withdrawal under circumstances that would give rise to an obligation is either probable or reasonably possible, the provisions of Section C59, "Contingencies," shall apply. [FAS87, ¶70]

Multiple-Employer Plans

.168 Some pension plans to which two or more unrelated employers contribute are not multiemployer plans[, but are **multiple-employer plans**]. Rather, they are in substance aggregations of single-employer plans combined to allow participating employers to pool their assets for investment purposes and to reduce the costs of plan administration. Those plans ordinarily do not involve collective-bargaining agreements. They may also have features that allow participating employers to have different benefit formulas, with the employer's contributions to the plan based on the benefit formula selected by the employer. Such plans shall be considered single-employer plans rather than multiemployer plans for purposes of this section, and each employer's accounting shall be based on its respective interest in the plan. [FAS87, ¶71]

Non-U.S. Pension Plans

.169 This section includes no special provisions applicable to pension arrangements outside the United States. To the extent that those arrangements are in substance similar to pension plans in the United States, they are subject to the provisions of this section for purposes of preparing financial statements in accordance with accounting principles generally accepted in the United States. The substance of an arrangement is determined by the nature of the obligation and by the terms or conditions that define the amount of benefits to be paid, not by whether (or how) a plan is funded, whether benefits are payable at intervals or as a single amount, or whether the benefits are required by law or custom or are provided under a plan the employer has elected to sponsor. [FAS87, ¶72]

.170 It is customary or required in some countries to provide benefits in the event of a voluntary or involuntary severance of employment (also called termination indemnities). If such an arrangement is in substance a pension plan (for example, if the benefits are paid for virtually all terminations), it is subject to the provisions of this section. [FAS87, ¶73] [Refer to paragraph .185.]

Settlements and Curtailments of Pension Plans and Termination Benefits

.171 Paragraphs .172 through .188 address an employer's accounting for a **settlement** or a curtailment of its defined benefit pension plan and for termination benefits. [FAS88, ¶1] [No] other events [have been identified that do] not [involve] settlement of obligation[s] or curtailment[s] of plan[s that should result] in recognition of prior service cost [(paragraphs .118 through .122)] and unrecognized net gain or loss [(paragraphs .123 through .128)]. [FAS88, ¶45]

.172 Examples of transactions that constitute a settlement include (a) making lump-sum cash payments to plan participants in exchange for their rights to receive specified pension benefits and (b) purchasing nonparticipating annuity contracts to cover vested benefits. [FAS88, ¶3] A transaction that does not meet all of the criteria of [a settlement as defined in] paragraph .457 does not constitute a settlement for purposes of this section. For example, investing in a portfolio of high-quality fixed-income securities with principal and interest payment dates similar to the estimated payment dates of benefits may avoid or minimize certain risks. However, that does not constitute a settlement because the investment decision can be reversed and such a strategy does not relieve the employer (or the plan) of primary responsibility for a pension obligation nor does it eliminate significant risks related to the obligation. [FAS88, ¶4]

.173 Curtailments include:

a. Termination of employees' services earlier than expected, which may or may not involve closing a facility or discontinuing a segment of a business
b. Termination or **suspension** of a plan so that employees do not earn additional defined benefits for future services. In the latter situation, future service may be counted toward vesting of benefits accumulated based on past service. [FAS88, ¶6]

.174 A [plan] settlement and a curtailment may occur separately or together. If benefits to be accumulated in future periods are reduced (for example, because half of a work force is dismissed or a plant is closed) but the plan remains in existence and continues to pay benefits, to invest assets, and to receive contributions, a curtailment has occurred but not a settlement. If an employer purchases nonparticipating annuity contracts for vested benefits and continues to provide defined benefits for future service, either in the same plan or in a successor plan, a settlement has occurred but not a curtailment. If a plan is terminated (that is, the obligation is settled and the plan ceases to exist) and not replaced by a successor defined benefit plan, both a settlement and a curtailment have occurred (whether or not the employees continue to work for the employer). [FAS88, ¶7]

.175 Paragraphs .177, .179, and .181 through .185 of this section describe the accounting for a settlement, a plan curtailment, and for termination benefits that are not directly related to a disposal of a segment of a business. Paragraph .186 addresses the accounting if those events are directly related to a disposal of a segment of a business. [FAS88, ¶8]

.176 [A determination] as to the proper sequence of events to follow in measuring the effects of a settlement and a curtailment that are to be recognized at the same time is arbitrary. [A]n employer should consistently apply the same sequence of events in determining the effects of all settlements and curtailments that are to be recognized at the same time. [FAS88, ¶47]

Accounting for Settlement of the Pension Obligation

.177 For purposes of paragraphs .171 through .188, the maximum gain or loss subject to recognition in earnings when a pension obligation is settled is the unrecognized net gain or loss defined in paragraph .123 of this section plus any remaining unrecognized net asset existing at the date of initial application of this section.[15] That maximum amount includes any gain or loss first measured at the time of settlement. The maximum amount shall be recognized in earnings if the entire projected benefit obligation is settled. If only part of the projected benefit obligation is settled, the employer shall recognize in earnings a pro rata portion of the maximum amount equal to the percentage reduction in the projected benefit obligation. [FAS88, ¶9]

.178 An *annuity contract* is a contract in which an insurance company[16] unconditionally undertakes a legal obligation to provide specified benefits to specific individuals in return for a fixed consideration or premium. An annuity contract is irrevocable and involves the transfer of significant risk from the employer to the insurance company. Some annuity contracts (participating annuity contracts) provide that the purchaser (either the plan or the employer) may participate in the experience of the insurance

---

[15]At the time of initial application of this section an employer may have an unrecognized net asset [refer to footnote 3. T]he portion of such an unrecognized net asset remaining unamortized at the date of a subsequent settlement or curtailment shall be treated as an unrecognized net gain and shall be combined with the unrecognized net gain or loss arising subsequent to transition to this section before applying the provisions of this paragraph and paragraph .183. [FAS88, ¶21]

[16]If the insurance company is controlled by the employer, or if there is any reasonable doubt that the insurance company will meet its obligations under the contract, the purchase of the contract does not constitute a settlement for purposes of paragraphs .171 through .188. [FAS88, ¶5, fn1]

company. Under those contracts, the insurance company ordinarily pays dividends to the purchaser. If the substance of a participating annuity contract is such that the employer remains subject to all or most of the risks and rewards associated with the benefit obligation covered or the assets transferred to the insurance company, the purchase of the contract does not constitute a settlement. [FAS88, ¶5]

.179 If the purchase of a participating annuity contract constitutes a settlement, the maximum gain (but not the maximum loss) shall be reduced by the cost of the participation right before determining the amount to be recognized in earnings. [FAS88, ¶10]

.180 It is difficult to determine the extent to which a participating contract exposes the purchaser to the risk of unfavorable experience, which would be reflected in lower than expected future dividends. Under some annuity contracts described as participating the purchaser might remain subject to all or most of the same risks and rewards related to future experience that would have existed had the contract not been purchased. Some participating contracts may require or permit payment of additional premiums if experience is unfavorable. If a participating contract requires or permits payment of additional premiums because of experience losses, or if the substance of the contract is such that the purchaser retains all or most of the related risks and rewards, the purchase of that contract does not constitute a settlement. [FAS88, ¶34]

.181 If the cost of all settlements[17] in a year is less than or equal to the sum of the service cost and interest cost components of net periodic pension cost for the plan for the year, gain or loss recognition is permitted but not required for those settlements. However, the accounting policy adopted shall be applied consistently from year to year. [FAS88, ¶11]

Accounting for a Plan Curtailment

.182 The unrecognized prior service cost associated with years of service no longer expected to be rendered as the result of a curtailment is a loss. For example, if a curtailment eliminates half of the estimated remaining future years of service of those who were employed at the date of a prior plan amendment and were expected to receive benefits under the plan, then the loss associated with the curtailment is half of the remaining unrecognized prior service cost related to that plan amendment. For purposes of applying the provisions of this paragraph, unrecognized prior service cost includes the cost of retroactive plan amendments (refer to paragraphs .118 and .119)

---

[17]For the following types of settlements, the cost of the settlement is:

a. For a cash settlement, the amount of cash paid to employees

b. For a settlement using nonparticipating annuity contracts, the cost of the contracts

c. For a settlement using participating annuity contracts, the cost of the contracts less the amount attributed to participation rights. (Refer to paragraph .158 of this section.) [FAS88, ¶11, fn3]

and any remaining unrecognized net obligation existing at the date of initial application of this section.[18] [FAS88, ¶12]

.183 The projected benefit obligation may be decreased (a gain) or increased (a loss) by a curtailment.[19]

a. To the extent that such a gain exceeds any unrecognized net loss (or the entire gain, if an unrecognized net gain exists), it is a *curtailment gain.*
b. To the extent that such a loss exceeds any unrecognized net gain (or the entire loss, if an unrecognized net loss exists), it is a *curtailment loss.*

For purposes of applying the provisions of this paragraph, any remaining unrecognized net asset existing at the date of initial application of this section shall be treated as an unrecognized net gain and shall be combined with the unrecognized net gain or loss arising subsequent to transition to this section. [FAS88, ¶13]

.184 If the sum of the effects identified in paragraphs .182 and .183 is a net loss, it shall be recognized in earnings when it is probable that a curtailment will occur and the effects described are reasonably estimable. If the sum of those effects is a net gain, it shall be recognized in earnings when the related employees terminate or the plan suspension or amendment is adopted. [FAS88, ¶14]

Termination Benefits

.185 An employer may provide benefits to employees in connection with their termination of employment. They may be either *special termination benefits* offered only for a short period of time or *contractual termination benefits* required by the terms of a plan only if a specified event, such as a plant closing, occurs. An employer that offers special termination benefits to employees shall recognize a liability and a loss when the employees accept the offer and the amount can be reasonably estimated. An employer that provides contractual termination benefits shall recognize a liability and a loss when it is probable that employees will be entitled to benefits and the amount can be reasonably estimated. Termination benefits may take various forms including lump-sum payments, periodic future payments, or both. They may be paid directly from an employer's assets, an existing pension plan, a new employee benefit plan, or a combination of those means. The cost of termination benefits recognized as a liability and a loss shall include the amount of any lump-sum payments and the present value of any expected future payments. A situation involving termination benefits may also

---

[18] At the time of initial application of this section, an employer may have an unrecognized net obligation [refer to footnote 3. T]he portion of such an unrecognized net obligation remaining unamortized at the date of a subsequent curtailment shall be treated as unrecognized prior service cost before applying the provisions of [this] paragraph. [FAS88, ¶21]

[19]Increases in the projected benefit obligation that reflect termination benefits are excluded from the scope of this paragraph. (Refer to paragraph .187 of this section.) [FAS88, ¶13, fn4]

involve a curtailment to be accounted for under paragraphs .182 through .184. [FAS88, ¶15]

Disposal of a Segment

.186 If the gain or loss measured in accordance with paragraphs .177, .179, .182, .183, and .185 is directly related to a disposal of a segment of a business, it shall be included in determining the gain or loss associated with that event and recognized pursuant to the requirements of Section I13, "Income Statement Presentation: Discontinued Operations." [FAS88, ¶16]

Disclosure and Presentation

.187 An employer that recognizes a gain or loss under the provisions of paragraphs .171 through .188, whether directly related to the disposal of a segment of a business or otherwise, shall disclose the following:

a. A description of the nature of the event(s)
b. The amount of gain or loss recognized. [FAS88, ¶17]

When the criteria of Section I17, "Income Statement Presentation: Extraordinary Items," are met, gains or losses recognized under paragraphs .177, .179, .182, .183, and .185 of this section should be accounted for as extraordinary items. For many enterprises those gains or losses generally do not result from the type of unusual and infrequently occurring event or transaction required by Section I17 to be reported as an extraordinary item. [FAS88, ¶48]

Asset Reversions

.188 Certain employers have settled significant portions of their pension obligations as part of transactions in which plan assets in excess of obligations reverted to the employer (asset reversion transactions). Consistent with prior standards, an employer that previously entered into an asset reversion transaction and continued to provide defined benefits recognized a credit on its statement of financial position for the amount withdrawn instead of recognizing a gain at the time of the withdrawal. Net periodic pension costs of subsequent periods were then reduced by amortization of the deferred gain (that is, the amount withdrawn). An employer that entered into such a transaction before the effective date of this section shall recognize a gain as the cumulative effect of a change in accounting principle at the time of initial application of this section. The amount of gain recognized shall be the lesser of:

a. The unamortized amount related to the asset reversion
b. Any unrecognized net asset for the plan (or the successor plan) existing at the time of transition [see footnote 3]. [FAS88, ¶20]

Illustrations

.189 Pages 34225 through 34262 contain illustrations of the following requirements
of this section:

	Page Numbers
1. Delayed recognition and reconciliation of funded status	34225-34229
2. Transition	34230-34231
3. Amortization of unrecognized prior service cost	34232-34235
4. Accounting for gain or loss and timing of measurements	34236-34248
5. Recognition of pension liabilities, including minimum liability . . .	34249-34257
6. Disclosure	34258-34261
7. Accounting for a business combination	34262

Illustration 1—Delayed Recognition and Reconciliation of Funded Status

This section provides for delayed recognition of the effects of a number of types of
events that change the measures of the projected benefit obligation and the fair value
of plan assets. Those events include retroactive plan amendments and gains and
losses. Gains and losses as defined in this section include the effects of changes in
assumptions.

This section also requires disclosure of a reconciliation of the funded status of a
plan to the net pension liability or asset recognized in the employer's financial statements. This illustration shows how that reconciliation provides information about
items that have not been recognized due to delayed recognition. The illustration starts
with an assumed funded status at the date of initial application of this section and
shows how a series of events that change the obligation or the plan assets are reflected
in the reconciliation. (Throughout this illustration the fair value of plan assets exceeds
the accumulated benefit obligation and, therefore, no recognition of an additional
minimum liability is required.)

Case 1—Company T at Transition

The reconciliation as of the date of initial application of this section is as follows:

Projected benefit obligation	$(10,000)
Plan assets at fair value	6,500
Funded status	(3,500)
Unrecognized net (gain) or loss	0
Unrecognized prior service cost	0
Unrecognized net obligation or (net asset) at date of initial application	3,500
(Accrued)/prepaid pension cost	$ 0

The unrecognized net gain or loss and the unrecognized prior service cost are both initially zero by definition. The unrecognized net obligation or asset at transition is defined in paragraph .114 as the difference between the funded status and the accrued or prepaid pension cost already recognized. If, as in this case, the past contributions were equal to amounts recognized as net pension cost in past periods, there is no recognized accrued or prepaid pension cost in the statement of financial position and, therefore, the unrecognized net obligation or asset at transition is equal to the funded status.

Case 2—Past Contributions Lower by $400

If Company T had not made a contribution of $400 for the last year before the date of initial application but had recognized the same net periodic pension cost as in Case 1, the situation would be as follows:

Projected benefit obligation	$(10,000)
Plan assets at fair value	6,100
Funded status	(3,900)
Unrecognized net (gain) or loss	0
Unrecognized prior service cost	0
Unrecognized net obligation or (net asset) at date of initial application	3,500
(Accrued)/prepaid pension cost	$ (400)

The unrecognized net obligation at transition is unchanged. It is the amount of the projected benefit obligation not yet recognized in net periodic pension cost and is not directly affected by funding decisions.

Case 3—Past Contributions Greater by $800

If, instead, the employer had made a contribution in excess of net periodic pension cost of $800, but the company had recognized the same net periodic pension cost as in Case 1, the reconciliation would be as follows:

Projected benefit obligation	$ (10,000)
Plan assets at fair value	7,300
Funded status	(2,700)
Unrecognized net (gain) or loss	0
Unrecognized prior service cost	0
Unrecognized net obligation or (net asset) at date of initial application	3,500
(Accrued)/prepaid pension cost	$ 800

After Initial Application

At any date after initial application, any change in the projected benefit obligation or the plan assets (other than contributions and benefit payments) either is unrecognized or has been included in net pension cost for some period. Contributions decrease the accrued pension cost or increase the prepaid pension cost, and benefit payments reduce the obligation and the plan assets equally. Thus, all changes in either the obligation or the assets are reflected in the reconciliation. Using Case 1 above as the starting point, the following reconciliations illustrate the effect of various events that change either the projected benefit obligation or the plan assets.

Case 4—Fair Value of Assets Increases by $400

	Before	After
Projected benefit obligation	$ (10,000)	$ (10,000)
Plan assets at fair value	6,500	6,900
Funded status	(3,500)	(3,100)
Unrecognized net (gain) or loss	0	(400)
Unrecognized prior service cost	0	0
Unrecognized net obligation or (net asset) at date of initial application	3,500	3,500
(Accrued)/prepaid pension cost	$ 0	$ 0

Case 5—Increase in Discount Rate Reduces Obligation by $900

	Before	After
Projected benefit obligation	$ (10,000)	$ (9,100)
Plan assets at fair value	6,500	6,500
Funded status	(3,500)	(2,600)
Unrecognized net (gain) or loss	0	(900)
Unrecognized prior service cost	0	0
Unrecognized net obligation or (net asset) at date of initial application	3,500	3,500
(Accrued)/prepaid pension cost	$ 0	$ 0

Case 6—Plan Amendment Increases the Obligation by $1,500

	Before	After
Projected benefit obligation	$ (10,000)	$ (11,500)
Plan assets at fair value	6,500	6,500
Funded status	(3,500)	(5,000)
Unrecognized net (gain) or loss	0	0
Unrecognized prior service cost	0	1,500
Unrecognized net obligation or (net asset) at date of initial application	3,500	3,500
(Accrued)/prepaid pension cost	$ 0	$ 0

Case 7—Employer Accrues Net Pension Cost

Net pension cost includes:

Service cost	$ 600
Interest cost	1,000
Amortization of initial unrecognized net obligation	233
Return on assets	(650)
	$ 1,183

No contribution is made.

	Before	After
Projected benefit obligation	$ (10,000)	$ (11,600)
Plan assets at fair value	6,500	7,150
Funded status	(3,500)	(4,450)
Unrecognized net (gain) or loss	0	0
Unrecognized prior service cost	0	0
Unrecognized net obligation or (net asset) at date of initial application	3,500	3,267
(Accrued)/prepaid pension cost	$ 0	$ (1,183)

Illustration 2—Transition

Case 1

As of December 31, 1985, the projected benefit obligation and plan assets of a non-contributory defined benefit plan sponsored by Company A were:

Projected benefit obligation	$ (1,500,000)
Plan assets at fair value	1,200,000
Initial unfunded obligation	$ (300,000)

Company A elected to apply the provisions of this section for its financial statements for the year ending December 31, 1986. At December 31, 1985, no prepaid or accrued pension cost had been recognized in Company A's statement of financial position (that is, all amounts accrued as net periodic pension cost had been contributed to the plan). The average remaining service period of active plan participants expected to receive benefits was estimated to be 16 years at the date of transition. In this situation the initial unrecognized net obligation (and loss or cost) of $300,000 is to be amortized (recognized as a component of net periodic pension cost) on a straight-line basis over the average remaining service period of 16 years [refer to footnote 3] as follows:

Year	Beginning-of-Year Balance	Amortization[a]	End-of-Year Balance
1986	300,000	18,750	281,250
1987	281,250	18,750	262,500
1988	262,500	18,750	243,750
1989	243,750	18,750	225,000
1990	225,000	18,750	206,250
1991	206,250	18,750	187,500
1992	187,500	18,750	168,750
1993	168,750	18,750	150,000
1994	150,000	18,750	131,250
1995	131,250	18,750	112,500
1996	112,500	18,750	93,750
1997	93,750	18,750	75,000
1998	75,000	18,750	56,250
1999	56,250	18,750	37,500
2000	37,500	18,750	18,750
2001	18,750	18,750	0

---

[a]300,000/16 = 18,750.

Case 2

As of December 31, 1985, the projected benefit obligation and plan assets of a non-contributory defined benefit plan sponsored by Company B were:

Projected benefit obligation	$ (1,400,000)
Plan assets at fair value	1,600,000
Initial overfunded obligation	$ 200,000

Company B elected to apply the provisions of this section for its financial statements for the year ending December 31, 1986. In previous periods, Company B's plan was deemed to be fully funded for tax purposes, and the company decided not to make contributions that would not have been currently tax deductible. As a result, contributions were less than net pension cost for those periods, and the company had recognized unfunded accrued pension cost (a liability) of $150,000 at December 31, 1985.

The unrecognized net asset at transition defined in [footnote 3] consists of amounts previously charged to net pension cost in excess of the projected benefit obligation. Amounts charged to net pension cost in past periods include amounts contributed (plan assets) and amounts unfunded. In this case, at December 31, 1985 those amounts were:

Plan assets in excess of obligation	$ 200,000
Unfunded accrued pension cost	150,000
Unrecognized net asset	$ 350,000

The average remaining service period of active plan participants expected to receive benefits was estimated to be 10 years at the date of transition. In this situation, the initial unrecognized net asset of $350,000 may be amortized on a straight-line basis over either 10 years or 15 years [refer to footnote 3]. That amortization will result in an annual credit to net periodic pension cost of either $35,000 or $23,333.

Illustration 3—Amortization of Unrecognized Prior Service Cost

Case 1—Assigning Equal Amounts to Future Years of Service

Determination of Expected Future Years of Service

The amortization of unrecognized prior service cost defined in paragraph .119 is based on the expected future years of service of participants active at the date of the amendment who are expected to receive benefits under the plan. Calculation of the expected future years of service considers population decrements based on the actuarial assumptions and is not weighted for benefits or compensation. Each expected future service year is assigned an equal share of the initially determined prior service cost. The portion of prior service cost to be recognized in each of the future years is determined by the service years rendered in that year.

The following chart illustrates the calculation of the expected future years of service for the defined benefit plan of Company E. At the date of the amendment (January 1, 19X2), the company has 100 employees who are expected to receive benefits under the plan. Five percent of that group (5 employees) are expected to leave (either retire or quit) in each of the next 20 years. Employees hired after that date do not affect the amortization. Initial estimates of expected future years of service related to each amendment are subsequently adjusted only for a curtailment.

Determination of Expected Years of Service

Service Years Rendered in Each Year

Individuals	Future Service Years	1	2	3	4	5	6	7	8	9	10	11	12	13	14	15	16	17	18	19	20
A1-A5	5	5																			
B1-B5	10	5	5																		
C1-C5	15	5	5	5																	
D1-D5	20	5	5	5	5																
E1-E5	25	5	5	5	5	5															
F1-F5	30	5	5	5	5	5	5														
G1-G5	35	5	5	5	5	5	5	5													
H1-H5	40	5	5	5	5	5	5	5	5												
I1-I5	45	5	5	5	5	5	5	5	5	5											
J1-J5	50	5	5	5	5	5	5	5	5	5	5										
K1-K5	55	5	5	5	5	5	5	5	5	5	5	5									
L1-L5	60	5	5	5	5	5	5	5	5	5	5	5	5								
M1-M5	65	5	5	5	5	5	5	5	5	5	5	5	5	5							
N1-N5	70	5	5	5	5	5	5	5	5	5	5	5	5	5	5						
O1-O5	75	5	5	5	5	5	5	5	5	5	5	5	5	5	5	5					
P1-P5	80	5	5	5	5	5	5	5	5	5	5	5	5	5	5	5	5				
Q1-Q5	85	5	5	5	5	5	5	5	5	5	5	5	5	5	5	5	5	5			
R1-R5	90	5	5	5	5	5	5	5	5	5	5	5	5	5	5	5	5	5	5		
S1-S5	95	5	5	5	5	5	5	5	5	5	5	5	5	5	5	5	5	5	5	5	
T1-T5	100	5	5	5	5	5	5	5	5	5	5	5	5	5	5	5	5	5	5	5	5
	1,050																				
Service Years Rendered		100	95	90	85	80	75	70	65	60	55	50	45	40	35	30	25	20	15	10	5
Amortization Fraction		$\frac{100}{1,050}$	$\frac{95}{1,050}$	$\frac{90}{1,050}$	$\frac{85}{1,050}$	$\frac{80}{1,050}$	$\frac{75}{1,050}$	$\frac{70}{1,050}$	$\frac{65}{1,050}$	$\frac{60}{1,050}$	$\frac{55}{1,050}$	$\frac{50}{1,050}$	$\frac{45}{1,050}$	$\frac{40}{1,050}$	$\frac{35}{1,050}$	$\frac{30}{1,050}$	$\frac{25}{1,050}$	$\frac{20}{1,050}$	$\frac{15}{1,050}$	$\frac{10}{1,050}$	$\frac{5}{1,050}$

Amortization of Unrecognized Prior Service Cost

On January 1, 19X2, Company E granted retroactive credit for prior service pursuant to a plan amendment. This amendment generated unrecognized prior service cost of $750,000. The amortization of the unrecognized prior service cost resulting from the plan amendment is based on the expected future years of service of active participants as discussed in the previous paragraph.

Amortization of Unrecognized Prior Service Cost

Year	Beginning-of-Year Balance	Amortization Rate	Amortization	End-of-Year Balance
19X2	750,000	100/1050	71,429	678,571
19X3	678,571	95/1050	67,857	610,714
19X4	610,714	90/1050	64,286	546,428
19X5	546,428	85/1050	60,714	485,714
19X6	485,714	80/1050	57,143	428,571
19X7	428,571	75/1050	53,571	375,000
19X8	375,000	70/1050	50,000	325,000
19X9	325,000	65/1050	46,429	278,571
19Y0	278,571	60/1050	42,857	235,714
19Y1	235,714	55/1050	39,286	196,428
19Y2	196,428	50/1050	35,714	160,714
19Y3	160,714	45/1050	32,143	128,571
19Y4	128,571	40/1050	28,571	100,000
19Y5	100,000	35/1050	25,000	75,000
19Y6	75,000	30/1050	21,429	53,571
19Y7	53,571	25/1050	17,857	35,714
19Y8	35,714	20/1050	14,286	21,428
19Y9	21,428	15/1050	10,714	10,714
19Z0	10,714	10/1050	7,143	3,571
19Z1	3,571	5/1050	3,571	0

Case 2—Using Straight-Line Amortization over Average Remaining Service Period

Determination of Expected Future Years of Service

To reduce the complexity and detail of the computations shown in Illustration 3, Case 1, alternative amortization approaches that recognize the cost of retroactive amendments more quickly may be consistently used (paragraph .120). For example, a straight-line amortization of the cost over the average remaining service period of employees expected to receive benefits under the plan is acceptable.

If Company E (Case 1) had elected to use straight-line amortization over the average remaining service period of employees expected to receive benefits (1,050 future service years/100 employees = 10.5 years), the amortization would have been as follows:

Amortization of Unrecognized Prior Service Cost

Year	Beginning-of-Year Balance	Amortization[a]	End-of-Year Balance
19X2	750,000	71,429	678,571
19X3	678,571	71,429	607,142
19X4	607,142	71,429	535,713
19X5	535,713	71,429	464,284
19X6	464,284	71,429	392,855
19X7	392,855	71,429	321,426
19X8	321,426	71,429	249,997
19X9	249,997	71,429	178,568
19Y0	178,568	71,429	107,139
19Y1	107,139	71,429	35,710
19Y2	35,710	35,710	0

---

[a]750,000/10.5 = 71,429.

Illustration 4—Accounting for Gains and Losses and Timing of Measurements

The following shows the funded status of Company I's pension plan at December 31, 1986 and its assumptions and expected components of net periodic pension cost for the following year (all amounts are in thousands):

DECEMBER 1986—INITIAL SITUATION

Assumptions:

Discount rate	10.00%
Expected long-term rate of return on plan assets	10.00%
Average remaining service	10 years

	Actual 12/31/86	For 1987	Projected 12/31/87
Projected benefit obligation	$ (1,000)		$ (1,060)
Plan assets at fair value	800		880
Funded status	(200)		(180)
Unrecognized net obligation existing at January 1, 1987	200		180
Unrecognized prior service cost	0		0
Unrecognized net (gain) or loss	0		0
(Accrued)/prepaid	$ 0		$ 0
Service cost component		$ 60ª	
Interest cost component		100	
Expected return on assets		(80)	

Amortization of:

Unrecognized net obligation existing at	
January 1, 1987	20
Unrecognized prior service cost	0
Unrecognized net (gain) or loss	0
Net cost	$ 100
Contribution	$ 100
Benefits paid	$ 100

Company I elected to apply the provisions of this section as of January 1, 1987 rather than as of an earlier date. Also, the company elected to measure pension-related amounts as of year-end. Alternatively, the company could have chosen to make the measurements as of another date not earlier than September 30. (Throughout this illustration it is assumed that the fair value of plan assets exceeds the accumulated benefit obligation and, therefore, no recognition of an additional minimum liability is required. For simplicity, all contributions and benefit payments are assumed to occur on the last day of the year.)

---

[a]Throughout this illustration the service cost component is assumed as an input rather than calculated as part of the illustration.

1987—LIABILITY LOSS

When Company I's plan assets and obligations were measured at December 31, 1987, the amount of the projected benefit obligation was not equal to the expected amount. Because the discount rate had declined to 9 percent and for various other reasons not specifically identified, the projected benefit obligation was higher than had been projected (a loss had occurred). The results, were as follows:

Assumptions:

Discount rate	10.00%	9.00%
Expected long-term rate of return on plan assets	10.00%	10.00%
Average remaining service	10 years	10 years

	Actual 12/31/86	For 1987	Projected 12/31/87	Actual 12/31/87	For 1988	Projected 12/31/88
Projected benefit obligation	$ (1,000)		$ (1,060)	$ (1,200)		$ (1,266)[b]
Plan assets at fair value	800		880	880		968[c]
Funded status	(200)		(180)	(320)		(298)
Unrecognized net obligation existing at January 1, 1987	200		180	180		160
Unrecognized prior service cost	0		0	0		0
Unrecognized net (gain) or loss	0		0	140		138
(Accrued)/prepaid	$ 0		$ 0	$ 0		$ 0
Service cost component		$ 60			$ 72	
Interest cost component		100			108	
Expected return on assets		(80)			(88)	

Market-related value of assets	$ 800	$ 880
Actual return on assets—		
(increase)/decrease		(80)
Amortization of:		
Unrecognized net obligation existing at		
January 1, 1987	20	20
Unrecognized prior service cost	0	0
Unrecognized net (gain) or loss	0[d]	2[d]
Net cost	$ 100	$ 114
Contribution	$ 100	$ 114
Benefits paid	$ 100	$ 114

The 1987 financial statements will include the following disclosures:

Cost Components

Service cost	$ 60
Interest cost	100
Actual return on assets	(80)
Net amortization and deferral	20[e]
Net cost	$ 100

Reconciliation of Funded Status

Projected benefit obligation	$ (1,200)
Plan assets at fair value	880
Funded status	(320)
Unrecognized net obligation existing at	
January 1, 1987	180
Unrecognized prior service cost	0
Unrecognized net (gain) or loss	140
(Accrued)/prepaid	$ 0[f]

b(Actual projected benefit obligation at 12/31/87) + (service component) + (interest component) – (benefits paid).

c(Actual plan assets at 12/31/87) + (expected return on assets) + (contributions) – (benefits paid).

dParagraph .126 provides that net periodic pension cost may be based on unrecognized net gain or loss as of the beginning of the period. In the year of transition (1987) the beginning balance of unrecognized net gain or loss is zero by definition. The minimum amortization of unrecognized net gain or loss is calculated as follows:

	1987	1988
Unrecognized net (gain) or loss at 1/1	$ 0	$ 140
Plus asset gain or less asset loss not yet in market-related value of assets at 1/1— (fair value of plan assets) – (market-related value of plan assets)	0	0
Unrecognized net (gain) or loss subject to amortization	0	140
Corridor = 10% of the greater of projected benefit obligation or market-related value of assets at 1/1	100	120
Unrecognized net (gain) or loss outside corridor	0	20
× 1/average remaining service	0.10	0.10
Amortization	$ 0	$ 2

eThe "net amortization and deferral" consists of:

Amortization of unrecognized net obligation existing at January 1, 1987	$ 20
Amortization of unrecognized prior service cost	0
Amortization of unrecognized net (gain) or loss	0
Asset gain/(loss) deferred	0
	$ 20

fThe (accrued)/prepaid is the amount included in the company's statement of financial position. If the accumulated benefit obligation had been greater than the plan assets, an additional minimum liability would have been required and would have been shown as an additional item in this reconciliation.

(This page intentionally left blank.)

1988—ASSET GAIN

When Company I's plan assets and obligations were measured at December 31, 1988, the amount of plan assets was not equal to the expected amount because of market performance better than the expected or assumed 10 percent. The results were as follows:

Assumptions:

Discount rate	9.00%	9.00%
Expected long-term rate of return on plan assets	10.00%	10.00%
Average remaining service	10 years	10 years

	Actual 12/31/87	For 1988	Projected 12/31/88	Actual 12/31/88	For 1989	Projected 12/31/89
Projected benefit obligation	$ (1,200)		$ (1,266)	$ (1,266)		$ (1,345)
Plan assets at fair value	880		968	1,068		1,167
Funded status	(320)		(298)	(198)		(178)
Unrecognized net obligation existing at January 1, 1987	180		160	160		140
Unrecognized prior service cost	0		0	0		0
Unrecognized net (gain) or loss	140		138	38		38
(Accrued)/prepaid	$ 0		$ 0	$ 0		$ 0
Service cost component		$ 72			$ 76	
Interest cost component		108			114	
Expected return on assets		(88)			(99)g	

Market-related value of assets	$ 880	$ 988[h]
Actual return on assets—(increase)/decrease	(80)	(188)
Amortization of:		
Unrecognized net obligation existing at January 1, 1987	20	20
Unrecognized prior service cost	0	0
Unrecognized net (gain) or loss	2[i]	0[i]
Net cost	$ 114	$ 111
Contribution	$ 114	$ 111
Benefits paid	$ 114	$ 111

The 1988 financial statements will include the following disclosures:

Cost Components

Service cost	$ 72
Interest cost	108
Actual return on assets	(188)
Net amortization and deferral	122[j]
Net cost	$ 114

Reconciliation of Funded Status

Projected benefit obligation	$ (1,266)
Plan assets at fair value	1,068
Funded status	(198)
Unrecognized net obligation existing at January 1, 1987	160
Unrecognized prior service cost	0
Unrecognized net (gain) or loss	38
(Accrued)/prepaid	$ 0

gExpected return on plan assets = (expected long-term rate of return on plan assets) × (market-related value of plan assets). If contributions occurred other than at the end of the year, market-related value would consider those amounts.

hMarket-related asset values may be calculated in a variety of ways. This example uses an approach that adds in 20% of each of the last five years' gains and losses. The only objective of the market-related calculation is to reduce the volatility of net pension cost.

Market-related value of assets at 1/1	$ 880
Expected return on assets	88
Contributions	114
Benefits paid	(114)
20% of last five years' asset gains and (losses)	20
Market-related value of assets at 12/31	$ 988

iAmortization of unrecognized net gain or loss is calculated as follows:

	1988	1989
Unrecognized net (gain) or loss at 1/1	$ 140	$ 38
Plus asset gain or less asset loss not yet in market-related value of assets at 1/1— (fair value of plan assets) − (market-related value of plan assets)	0	80
Unrecognized net (gain) or loss subject to amortization	140	118
Corridor = 10% of the greater of projected benefit obligation or market-related value of assets at 1/1	120	127
Unrecognized net (gain) or loss outside corridor	20	0
× 1/average remaining service	0.10	0.10
Amortization	$ 2	$ 0

jThe "net amortization and deferral" consists of:

Amortization of unrecognized net obligation existing at January 1, 1987	$ 20
Amortization of unrecognized prior service cost	0
Amortization of unrecognized net (gain) or loss	2
Asset gain/(loss) deferred	100
	$ 122

(This page intentionally left blank.)

1989—ASSET LOSS AND LIABILITY GAIN

When Company I's plan assets and obligations were measured at December 31, 1989, both an asset loss and a liability gain were discovered.

Assumptions:

Discount rate	9.00%	9.25%
Expected long-term rate of return on plan assets	10.00%	10.00%
Average remaining service	10 years	10 years

	Actual 12/31/88	For 1989	Projected 12/31/89	Actual 12/31/89	For 1990	Projected 12/31/90
Projected benefit obligation	$ (1,266)		$ (1,345)	$ (1,320)		$ (1,409)
Plan assets at fair value	1,068		1,167	1,097		1,206
Funded status	(198)		(178)	(223)		(203)
Unrecognized net obligation existing at January 1, 1987	160		140	140		120
Unrecognized prior service cost	0		0	0		0
Unrecognized net (gain) or loss	38		38	83		83
(Accrued)/prepaid	$ 0		$ 0	$ 0		$ 0
Service cost component		$ 76			$ 79	
Interest cost component		114			122	
Expected return on assets		(99)			(109)	

Market-related value of assets	$ 988	$ 1,093[k]
Actual return on assets—(increase)/decrease	(188)	(29)
Amortization of:		
Unrecognized net obligation existing at January 1, 1987	20	20
Unrecognized prior service cost	0	0
Unrecognized net (gain) or loss	0[l]	0[l]
Net cost	$ 111	$ 112
Contribution	$ 111	$ 112
Benefits paid	$ 111	$ 112

The 1989 financial statements will include the following disclosures:

Cost Components

Service cost	$ 76
Interest cost	114
Actual return on assets	(29)
Net amortization and deferral	(50)[m]
Net cost	$ 111

Reconciliation of Funded Status

Projected benefit obligation	$ (1,320)
Plan assets at fair value	1,097
Funded status	(223)
Unrecognized net obligation existing at January 1, 1987	140
Unrecognized prior service cost	0
Unrecognized net (gain) or loss	83
(Accrued)/prepaid	$ 0

^{k}Market-related asset values may be calculated in a variety of ways. This example uses an approach that adds in 20% of each of the last five years' gains and losses. The only objective of the market-related calculation is to reduce the volatility of net pension cost.

Market-related value of assets at 1/1	$ 988
Expected return on assets	99
Contributions	111
Benefits paid	(111)
20% of last five years' asset gains and (losses) = .20 (100 − 70) =	6
Market-related value of assets at 12/31	$ 1,093

^{l}Amortization of unrecognized net gain or loss is calculated as follows:

	1989	1990
Unrecognized net (gain) or loss at 1/1	$ 38	$ 83
Plus asset gain or less asset loss not yet in market-related value of assets at 1/1— (fair value of plan assets) − (market-related value of plan assets)	80	4
Unrecognized net (gain) or loss subject to amortization	118	87
Corridor = 10% of the greater of projected benefit obligation or market-related value of assets at 1/1	127	132
Unrecognized net (gain) or loss outside corridor	0	0
× 1/average remaining service	0.10	0.10
Amortization	$ 0	$ 0

^{m}The "net amortization and deferral" consists of:

Amortization of unrecognized net obligation existing at January 1, 1987	$ 20
Amortization of unrecognized prior service cost	0
Amortization of unrecognized net (gain) or loss	0
Asset gain/(loss) deferred	(70)
	$ (50)

Illustration 5—Recognition of Pension Liability, Including Minimum Liability

Case 1—Minimum Liability Less Than Unrecognized Prior Service Cost

Company K elected to apply the provisions of this section, including those requiring recognition of minimum liability, for its 1986 financial statements. The funded status of its plan for the years 1988 through 1991 is shown below.

	As of December 31,			
	1988	**1989**	**1990**	**1991**
		(in thousands)		
FUNDED STATUS—COMPANY K				
Assets and obligations:				
Accumulated benefit obligation	$ (1,254)	$ (1,628)	$ (1,616)	$ (1,554)
Plan assets at fair value	1,165	1,505	1,622	1,517
Unfunded accumulated benefits	$ (89)	$ (123)		$ (37)
Overfunded accumulated benefits			$ 6	
Projected benefit obligation	$ (1,879)	$ (2,442)	$ (2,424)	$ (2,331)
Plan assets at fair value	1,165	1,505	1,622	1,517
Items not yet recognized in earnings:				
Unrecognized net obligation (net asset) at January 1, 1986	280	260	240	220
Unrecognized prior service cost	715	1,314	1,172	1,039
Unrecognized net gain	(251)	(557)	(460)	(476)
(Accrued)/prepaid pension cost	$ 30	$ 80	$ 150	$ (31)

DETERMINATION OF AMOUNTS TO BE RECOGNIZED

(Accrued)/prepaid pension cost at beginning of year	$ 0	$ 30	$ 80	$ 150
Net periodic pension cost	(304)	(335)	(397)	(361)
Contribution	334	385	467	180
(Accrued)/prepaid pension cost at end of year	$ 30	$ 80	$ 150	$ (31)
Required minimum liability (unfunded accumulated benefits)	$ (89)	$ (123)	$ 0	$ (37)
Adjustment required to reflect minimum liability:				
Additional liability[a]	$ (119)	$ (84)	$ 203	$ (6)
Intangible asset (not to exceed unrecognized prior service cost)	$ 119	$ 84	$ (203)	$ 6
Balance of additional liability	$ (119)	$ (203)	$ 0	$ (6)
Balance of intangible asset	$ 119	$ 203	$ 0	$ 6

---

[a]This amount is equal to unfunded accumulated benefits, plus prepaid (or minus accrued) pension cost, minus the previous balance. For financial statement presentation, the additional liability is combined with the (accrued)/prepaid pension cost.

Journal Entries

The journal entries required to reflect the accounting for the company's pension plan for the years 1988 through 1991 are as follows (in thousands):

Year 1988

Journal Entry 1

Net periodic pension cost	304	
Accrued/prepaid pension cost		304
To record net pension cost for the period (paragraph .129)		

Journal Entry 2

Accrued/prepaid pension cost	334	
Cash		334
To record contribution (paragraph .129)		

Journal Entry 3

Intangible asset	119	
Additional liability		119

    To record an additional liability to reflect the required minimum liability (For financial statement presentation, the additional liability account balance is combined with the accrued/prepaid pension cost account balance. Since prepaid pension cost of $30 has been recognized, an additional liability of $119 is needed to reflect the required minimum liability of $89 [equal to unfunded accumulated benefits]. Because the additional liability is less than unrecognized prior service cost, an intangible asset also is recognized.) (paragraphs .130 and .131)

Year 1989

Journal Entry 1

Net periodic pension cost	335	
Accrued/prepaid pension cost		335
To record net pension cost for the period (paragraph .129)		

Journal Entry 2

Accrued/prepaid pension cost	385	
Cash		385
To record contribution (paragraph .129)		

Journal Entry 3

Intangible asset	84	
Additional liability		84

    To adjust the additional liability to reflect the required minimum liability (For financial statement presentation, the additional liability account balance is combined with the accrued/prepaid pension cost account balance. The required minimum liability is determined independently of any prior years' amounts. Since unfunded accumulated benefits are $123 and a prepaid pension cost of $80 has been recognized, the amount of the additional liability is $203 or an increase of $84 from the previous period. Because the balance of the additional liability is less than unrecognized prior service cost, an intangible asset also is recognized.) (paragraphs .130 and .131)

Year 1990

Journal Entry 1

Net periodic pension cost	397	
Accrued/prepaid pension cost		397
To record net pension cost for the period (paragraph .129)		

Journal Entry 2

Accrued/prepaid pension cost	467	
Cash		467
To record contribution (paragraph .129)		

Journal Entry 3

Additional liability	203	
Intangible asset		203

    To reverse additional liability no longer required (Since plan assets exceed accumulated benefits, no additional liability is necessary.) (paragraph .132)

Year 1991

Journal Entry 1

Net periodic pension cost	361	
Accrued/prepaid pension cost		361

To record net pension cost for the period (paragraph .129)

Journal Entry 2

Accrued/prepaid pension cost	180	
Cash		180

To record contribution (paragraph .129)

Journal Entry 3

Intangible asset	6	
Additional liability		6

To record an additional liability to reflect the required minimum liability amount (For financial statement presentation, the additional liability account balance is combined with the accrued/prepaid pension cost account balance. Since unfunded accumulated benefits of $37 exceed unfunded accrued pension cost of $31, recognition of an additional liability of $6 is necessary. Because the balance of additional liability is less than unrecognized prior service cost, an intangible asset also is recognized.) (paragraphs .130 and .131)

Case 2—Minimum Liability in Excess of Unrecognized Prior Service Cost

Company L elected to apply the provisions of this section, including those requiring recognition of minimum liability, for its 1986 financial statements. The funded status of its plan for the years 1988 and 1989 is shown below.

	As of December 31,	
	1988	1989
	(in thousands)	
FUNDED STATUS—COMPANY L		
Assets and obligations:		
Accumulated benefit obligation	$ (1,270)	$ (1,290)
Plan assets at fair value	1,200	1,304
Unfunded accumulated benefits	$ (70)	
Overfunded accumulated benefits		$ 14
Projected benefit obligation	$ (1,720)	$ (1,807)
Plan assets at fair value	1,200	1,304
Items not yet recognized in earnings:		
Unrecognized prior service cost	92	86
Unrecognized net loss	486	497
(Accrued)/prepaid pension cost	$ 58	$ 80

DETERMINATION OF AMOUNTS TO BE RECOGNIZED

(Accrued)/prepaid pension cost at beginning of year	$ 0	$ 58
Net periodic pension cost	(141)	(144)
Contribution	199	166
(Accrued)/prepaid pension cost at end of year	$ 58	$ 80
Required minimum liability (unfunded accumulated benefits)	$ 70	$ 0
Adjustment required to reflect minimum liability:		
Additional liability[a]	$ (128)	$ 128
Intangible asset (not to exceed unrecognized prior service cost)	$ 92	$ (92)
Charge to equity (excess of additional pension liability over unrecognized prior service cost)	$ 36	$ (36)
Balance of additional liability	$ (128)	$ 0
Balance of intangible asset	$ 92	$ 0
Balance of equity account	$ 36	$ 0

---

[a]This amount is equal to unfunded accumulated benefits, plus prepaid (or minus accrued) pension cost, minus the previous balance. For financial statement presentation, the additional liability is combined with the (accrued)/prepaid pension cost.

Journal Entries

The journal entries required to reflect the accounting for the company's pension plan for the years 1988 and 1989 are as follows (in thousands):

Year 1988

Journal Entry 1

Net periodic pension cost	141	
Accrued/prepaid pension cost		141
To record net pension cost for the period (paragraph .129)		

Journal Entry 2

Accrued/prepaid pension cost	199	
Cash		199
To record contribution (paragraph .129)		

Journal Entry 3

Excess of additional pension liability over unrecognized prior service cost	36	
Intangible asset	92	
Additional liability		128

To record an additional liability to reflect the required minimum liability (For financial statement presentation, the additional liability account balance is combined with the accrued/prepaid pension cost account balance. Since prepaid pension cost of $58 has been recognized, an additional liability of $128 is needed to reflect the required minimum liability of $70 [equal to unfunded accumulated benefits]. Because the additional liability is greater than unrecognized prior service cost, an intangible asset is recognized for the amount of additional liability up to the amount of unrecognized prior service cost, and equity is charged for the excess of the additional liability over unrecognized prior service cost.) (paragraphs .130 and .131)

Year 1989

Journal Entry 1

Net periodic pension cost	144	
Accrued/prepaid pension cost		144
To record net pension cost for the period (paragraph .129)		

Journal Entry 2

Accrued/prepaid pension cost	166	
Cash		166
To record contribution (paragraph .129)		

Journal Entry 3

Additional liability	128	
Excess of additional pension liability over		
unrecognized prior service cost		36
Intangible asset		92
To reverse additional liability no longer required (Since plan		
assets exceed accumulated benefits, no additional liability is		
necessary.) (paragraph .132)		

Illustration 6—Disclosure Requirements

Case 1—Simple Case

The following illustrates the disclosure for a sponsor with a single-employer defined benefit pension plan presenting only one year's financial statements.

Note P: The company has a defined benefit pension plan covering substantially all of its employees. The benefits are based on years of service and the employee's compensation during the last five years of employment. The company's funding policy is to contribute annually the maximum amount that can be deducted for federal income tax purposes. Contributions are intended to provide not only for benefits attributed to service to date but also for those expected to be earned in the future.

The following table sets forth the plan's funded status and amounts recognized in the company's statement of financial position at December 31, 1988 (in thousands):

Actuarial present value of benefit obligations:	
Accumulated benefit obligation, including vested benefits of $287	$ (335)
Projected benefit obligation for service rendered to date	$ (500)
Plan assets at fair value, primarily listed stocks and U.S. bonds	475
Projected benefit obligation in excess of plan assets	(25)
Unrecognized net gain from past experience different from that assumed and effects of changes in assumptions	(53)
Prior service cost not yet recognized in net periodic pension cost	19
Unrecognized net obligation at January 1, 1986 being recognized over 15 years	77
Prepaid pension cost included in other assets	$ 18

Net pension cost for 1988 included the following components (in thousands):

Service cost—benefits earned during the period	$ 26
Interest cost on projected benefit obligation	39
Actual return on plan assets	(45)
Net amortization and deferral[a]	10
Net periodic pension cost	$ 30

The weighted-average discount rate and rate of increase in future compensation levels used in determining the actuarial present value of the projected benefit obligation were 9 percent and 6 percent, respectively. The expected long-term rate of return on assets was 10 percent.

---

[a]The net effects of delayed recognition of certain events (for example, unanticipated investment performance) arising during the current period and amortization (recognition) of the net unrecognized effects of past similar events at a rate based on employees' average remaining service life.

Case 2—Disclosures for Multiple Plans

Note S: The company and its subsidiaries have a number of noncontributory pension plans covering substantially all U.S. employees. Plans covering salaried and management employees provide pension benefits that are based on the employee's compensation during the three years before retirement. The company's funding policy for those plans is to contribute annually at a rate that is intended to remain a level percentage of compensation for the covered employees (presently 12.9 percent). Plans covering hourly employees and union members generally provide benefits of stated amounts for each year of service and provide for significant supplemental benefits for employees who retire with 30 years of service before age 65. The company's funding policy for those plans is to make the minimum annual contributions required by applicable regulations.

Net periodic pension cost for 19X3 and 19X2 included the following components (in thousands):

	19X3	19X2
Service cost—benefits earned during the period	$ 66	$ 66
Interest cost on projected benefit obligation	100	96
Actual return on assets	(79)	(63)
Net amortization and deferral	88	78
Net periodic pension cost	$ 175	$ 177

Assumptions used in the accounting were:

	As of December 31,	
	19X3	19X2
Discount rates	9.0%	8.75%
Rates of increase in compensation levels	6.0%	6.0%
Expected long-term rate of return on assets	9.5%	9.5%

The following table sets forth the plan's funded status and amounts recognized in the company's statement of financial position at December 31, 19X3 and 19X2, for its U.S. pension plans (in thousands):

| | December 31, 19X3 | | December 31, 19X2 | |
	Assets Exceed Accumulated Benefits	Accumulated Benefits Exceed Assets	Assets Exceed Accumulated Benefits	Accumulated Benefits Exceed Assets
Actuarial present value of benefit obligations:				
Vested benefit obligation	$(298)	$(385)	$(268)	$(363)
Accumulated benefit obligation	$(339)	$(442)	$(311)	$(427)
Projected benefit obligation[a]	$(502)	$(620)	$(470)	$(640)
Plan assets at fair value[b]	604	228	548	205
Projected benefit obligation (in excess of) or less than plan assets	102	(392)	78	(435)
Unrecognized net (gain) or loss	(114)	30	(117)	41
Prior service cost not yet recognized in net periodic pension cost	120	292	132	321
Unrecognized net obligation at January 1, 19X1	180	225	200	250
Adjustment required to recognize minimum liability	0	(369)	0	(399)
Prepaid pension cost (pension liability) recognized in the statement of financial position	$ 288	$(214)	$ 293	$(222)

---

[a]The projected benefit obligation and plan assets at December 31, 19X3 and 19X2 do not include amounts related to an annuity contract purchased from an affiliated company covering annual benefits of approximately $42.

[b]Plan assets include common stock of the company of $50 and $45 at December 31, 19X3 and 19X2, respectively. About half of the plan assets are invested in listed stocks and bonds. The balance is invested in income-producing real estate.

Case 3—Disclosure for a Defined Contribution Plan

Note T: The company sponsors a defined contribution pension plan covering substantially all of its employees in both its engine parts and tire subsidiaries. Contributions and cost are determined as 1.5 percent of each covered employee's salary and totaled $231,000 in 19X2 and $215,000 in 19X1.

Case 4—Disclosure for a Multiemployer Plan

Note W: One of the company's subsidiaries participates in a multiemployer plan. The plan provides defined benefits to substantially all unionized workers in the company's trucking subsidiary. Amounts charged to pension cost and contributed to the plan in 19X2 and 19X1 totaled $598,000 and $553,000, respectively.

Illustration 7—Accounting for a Business Combination

The following example illustrates how the liability (or asset) recognized by the acquiring firm at the date of a business combination accounted for as a purchase would be reduced in years subsequent to the date of the business combination.

Company R purchased Company S on January 1, 19X2. Company S sponsors a single-employer defined benefit pension plan. The reconciliation of funded status of the Company S plan before and after the combination was as follows (in thousands):

	Precombination	Postcombination
Pension benefit obligation	$ (1,000)	$ (1,000)
Plan assets at fair value	500	500
Unrecognized loss	200	0
Unrecognized prior service cost	300	0
Liability recognized in the statement of financial position—unfunded accrued pension cost	$ 0	$ (500)

In subsequent periods, net periodic pension cost would not include any amortization of either the unrecognized prior service cost or the unrecognized loss existing at the date of the combination. However, the funding of the plan is not directly affected by a business combination. Whatever the basis of funding, it will, over time, reflect the past amendments and losses that underlie those amounts. As they are reflected in the funding process, contributions will, in some periods, exceed the net pension cost, and that will reduce the liability (unfunded accrued pension cost) recognized at the date of acquisition. [FAS87, ¶261]

.190 Pages 34263 through 34283 contain separate illustrations of the following requirements of this section:

	Page Numbers
1. Accounting for a plan termination without a replacement defined benefit plan	34263-34265
2. Accounting for a settlement of a pension obligation	34266-34271
3. Accounting for a plan curtailment	34272-34275
4. Calculation of unrecognized prior service cost associated with services of terminated employees	34276-34278
5. Accounting for a plan curtailment when termination benefits are offered to employees	34279-34281
6. Transition for an employer that completed an asset reversion prior to the initial application of this section	34282-34283

Illustration 1—Accounting for a Plan Termination without a Replacement Defined Benefit Plan

Company A sponsored a final-pay noncontributory defined benefit plan. On November 16, 19X3, the employer terminated the plan, settled the accumulated benefit obligation of $1,500,000 (nonvested benefits became vested upon termination of the plan) by purchasing nonparticipating annuity contracts, and withdrew excess assets. Defined benefits were not provided under any successor plan. The plan ceased to exist as an entity.

As a result, Company A recognized a gain of $900,000, determined as follows:

	Before Termination	Company A (in thousands) Effect of Termination	After Termination
Assets and obligations:			
Accumulated benefit obligation	$ (1,500)	$ 1,500[a]	$ 0
Effects of projected future compensation levels	(400)	400[b]	0
Projected benefit obligation	(1,900)	1,900	0
Plan assets at fair value	2,100	(1,500)[a] / (600)[c]	0
Items not yet recognized in earnings:			
Unrecognized net asset at transition[d,e]	(200)	200	0
Unrecognized net gain subsequent to transition[e]	(300)	300	0
(Accrued)/prepaid pension cost on the statement of financial position	$ (300)	$ 300	$ 0

[a]The accumulated benefits of $1,500 were settled by using an equivalent amount of plan assets to purchase nonparticipating annuity contracts.

[b]The effects of projected future compensation levels ceased to be an obligation of the plan or the employer due to the termination of all plan participants. Under paragraph .183 of this section, the gain (that is, the decrease in the projected benefit obligation) resulting from the curtailment is first offset against any existing unrecognized net loss. Because the previously unrecognized amount in this case was a gain ($200 unrecognized net asset at transition plus $300 unrecognized net gain subsequent to transition), the $400 gain from the curtailment was recognized.

[c]Plan assets, in excess of the amount used to settle the pension benefits, were withdrawn from the plan.

[d]An unrecognized net asset at transition is treated as an unrecognized net gain for purposes of this section [refer to footnote 15].

[e]A pro rata amount of the maximum gain (paragraph .177), which includes the unrecognized net gain subsequent to transition ($300) and the unamortized net asset from transition ($200), is recognized due to settlement. The projected benefit obligation was reduced from $1,500 to $0 (the curtailment initially reduced the projected benefit obligation from $1,900 to $1,500 as described in footnote b), a reduction of 100 percent. Accordingly, the entire unrecognized net gain of $500 ($300 + $200) was recognized.

The journal entry required to reflect the accounting for the plan termination was:

Cash	600	
Accrued/prepaid pension cost	300	
Gain from plan termination		900

The gain from the plan termination without a replacement defined benefit plan was composed of the following:

Gain from curtailment	$ 400
Gain from settlement	500
Total gain	$ 900

Illustration 2—Accounting for a Settlement of a Pension Obligation

The following examples illustrate the accounting for a settlement of a pension obligation in three specific situations. The first example (Company B) had an unrecognized net obligation at the date of transition to this section, and the second and third examples (Company C and Company D) each had unrecognized net assets at the date of transition. Each company settled a portion of the obligation subsequent to transition to this section. Company B had a retroactive plan amendment after transition; Company C and Company D did not.

Example 2A—Projected Benefit Obligation Exceeds Plan Assets

Company B sponsors a final-pay noncontributory defined benefit plan. On December 31, 19X3, the plan settled the vested benefit portion ($1,300,000) of the projected benefit obligation through the purchase of nonparticipating annuity contracts.

As a result, Company B recognized a gain of $195,000, determined as follows:

	Company B (in thousands)		
	Before Settlement	**Effect of Settlement**	**After Settlement**
Assets and obligations:			
Vested benefit obligation	$ (1,300)	$ 1,300[a]	$ 0
Nonvested benefits	(200)		(200)
Accumulated benefit obligation	(1,500)	1,300	(200)
Effects of projected future compensation levels	(500)		(500)
Projected benefit obligation	(2,000)	1,300	(700)
Plan assets at fair value	1,400	(1,300)[a]	100
Items not yet recognized in earnings:			
Unrecognized net obligation at transition[b]	650		650
Unrecognized prior service cost from amendment subsequent to transition	150		150
Unrecognized net gain subsequent to transition[c]	(300)	195	(105)
(Accrued)/prepaid pension cost on the statement of financial position	$ (100)	$ 195	$ 95

---

[a]The vested benefits of $1,300 were settled by using plan assets to purchase nonparticipating annuity contracts.

[b]An unrecognized net obligation at transition is treated as unrecognized prior service cost and therefore is not affected by settlement of the obligation [refer to footnote 15].

[c]A pro rata portion of the maximum gain (paragraph .177), the unrecognized net gain subsequent to transition, is recognized due to settlement. The projected benefit obligation was reduced from $2,000 to $700, a reduction of 65 percent. Accordingly, 65 percent of the maximum gain of $300, a gain of $195, was recognized. The journal entry required to reflect the accounting for the plan settlement was:

Accrued/prepaid pension cost	195	
Gain from settlement		195

Example 2B—Plan Assets Exceed the Projected Benefit Obligation

Company C sponsors a final-pay noncontributory defined benefit plan. On December 31, 19X3, the plan settled the vested benefit portion ($1,300,000) of the projected benefit obligation through the purchase of nonparticipating annuity contracts.

As a result, Company C recognized a gain of $325,000, determined as follows:

	Before Settlement	Effect of Settlement	After Settlement
Company C (in thousands)			
Assets and obligations:			
Vested benefit obligation	$ (1,300)	$ 1,300[a]	$ 0
Nonvested benefits	(200)		(200)
Accumulated benefit obligation	(1,500)	1,300	(200)
Effects of projected future compensation levels	(500)		(500)
Projected benefit obligation	(2,000)	1,300	(700)
Plan assets at fair value	2,100	(1,300)[a]	800
Items not yet recognized in earnings:			
Unrecognized net asset at transition[b,c]	(200)	130	(70)
Unrecognized net gain subsequent to transition[c]	(300)	195	(105)
(Accrued)/prepaid pension cost on the statement of financial position	$ (400)	$ 325	$ (75)

---

[a]The vested benefits of $1,300 were settled by using plan assets to purchase nonparticipating annuity contracts.

[b]An unrecognized net asset at transition is treated as an unrecognized net gain for purposes of this section [refer to footnote 15].

[c]A pro rata amount of the maximum gain (paragraph .177), which includes the unrecognized net gain subsequent to transition ($300) and the unamortized net asset from transition ($200), is recognized due to settlement. The projected benefit obligation was reduced from $2,000 to $700, a reduction of 65 percent. Accordingly, 65 percent of the maximum gain of $500 ($300 + $200), a gain of $325, was recognized. The journal entry required to reflect the accounting for the plan settlement was:

Accrued/prepaid pension cost	325	
Gain from settlement		325

Example 2C—Plan Assets Exceed the Projected Benefit Obligation and a Participating Annuity Contract Is Purchased to Settle Benefits

Company D sponsors a final-pay noncontributory defined benefit plan. On December 31, 19X3, the plan settled the vested benefit portion ($1,300,000) of the projected benefit obligation through the purchase of a participating annuity contract at a cost of $1,430,000. The plan could have purchased a nonparticipating contract covering the same benefits for $1,300,000. The participation features of the contract warranted a conclusion that its purchase constituted a settlement.

As a result, Company D recognized a gain of $240,000 (rounded), determined as follows:

	Company D (in thousands)		
	Before Settlement	Effect of Settlement	After Settlement
Assets and obligations:			
Vested benefit obligation	$ (1,300)	$ 1,300[a]	$ 0
Nonvested benefits	(200)		(200)
Accumulated benefit obligation	(1,500)	1,300	(200)
Effects of projected future compensation levels	(500)		(500)
Projected benefit obligation	(2,000)	1,300	(700)
Plan assets at fair value:			
Participation right		130[a]	130
Other plan assets	2,100	(1,430)[a]	670
Items not yet recognized in earnings:			
Unrecognized net asset at transition[b,c]	(200)	130[d]	(70)
Unrecognized net gain subsequent to transition[c]	(300)	110[d]	(190)
(Accrued)/prepaid pension cost on the statement of financial position	$ (400)	$ 240	$ (160)

34270

[a]The vested benefits of $1,300 were settled by using $1,430 of plan assets to purchase a participating annuity contract. However, a nonparticipating contract covering the same benefits could have been purchased for $1,300. The plan paid the additional $130 to obtain the participation right.

[b]An unrecognized net asset at transition is treated as an unrecognized net gain for purposes of this section [refer to footnote 15].

[c]A pro rata amount of the maximum gain (paragraph .177), which includes the unrecognized net gain subsequent to transition ($300) and the unamortized net asset from transition ($200), was recognized due to settlement. However, any gain on a settlement that uses a participating annuity contract shall be computed by first reducing the maximum gain by the cost of the participation right [$200 + ($300 − $130) = $370]. The projected benefit obligation was reduced from $2,000 to $700, a reduction of 65 percent. Accordingly, a gain of $240 (rounded) was recognized (.65 × $370). The journal entry required to reflect the accounting for the plan settlement was:

Accrued/prepaid pension cost	240	
Gain from settlement		240

[d]The amount of gain from settlement was allocated as follows (rounded):

Unrecognized net asset at transition (.65 × $200)	$ 130
Unrecognized net gain subsequent to transition [.65 × ($300 − $130)]	110
	$ 240

34271

Illustration 3—Accounting for a Plan Curtailment

The following examples illustrate the accounting for a curtailment in two specific situations. The first example (Company E) had an unrecognized net obligation at the date of transition to this section and a retroactive plan amendment after transition. The second example (Company F) had an unrecognized net asset at the date of transition. Both companies curtailed their plans subsequent to transition to this section.

Example 3A—Disposal of a Segment—Projected Benefit Obligation Exceeds Plan Assets

Company E sponsors a final-pay noncontributory defined benefit plan. On January 1, 1988 (one year after transition) the company had a retroactive plan amendment resulting in $800,000 of prior service cost. On December 31, 1989, the management of Company E committed itself to a formal plan to dispose of a segment of its business. In connection with the disposal, the number of employees accumulating benefits under the plan would be reduced significantly. The portion of the projected benefit obligation based on the expected future compensation levels of the terminated employees was $90,000, and nonvested benefits of the terminated employees amounted to $20,000. The plan also had an unrecognized net obligation at the date of transition to this section that is treated as unrecognized prior service cost for purposes of applying this section. The remaining expected future years of service associated with those employees present at the date of transition was reduced by 30 percent due to the termination of employees. Accordingly, 30 percent of the unrecognized net obligation remaining unamortized at December 31, 1989 was a loss which amounted to $120,000.

The unrecognized prior service cost (which relates to the plan amendment of January 1, 1988) associated with the previously expected years of service of the terminated employees that will not be rendered was a loss which amounted to $160,000.

The sum of the effects resulting from the plan curtailment was a loss of $170,000, determined as follows:

	Before Curtailment	**Effect of Curtailment**	**After Curtailment**
		Company E **(in thousands)**	
Assets and obligations:			
Vested benefit obligation	$ (1,300)		$ (1,300)
Nonvested benefits	(200)	$ 20	(180)
Accumulated benefit obligation	(1,500)	20	(1,480)
Effects of projected future compensation levels	(500)	90	(410)
Projected benefit obligation	(2,000)	110[a]	(1,890)
Plan assets at fair value	1,400		1,400
Items not yet recognized in earnings:			
Unrecognized net obligation at transition[b]	400	(120)[b]	280
Unrecognized prior service cost resulting from plan amendment[c]	651	(160)[c]	491
Unrecognized net gain subsequent to transition	(151)		(151)
(Accrued)/prepaid pension cost on the statement of financial position	$ 300	$ (170)[d]	$ 130

[a]Under paragraph .183 of this section, the gain (that is, the decrease in the projected benefit obligation) resulting from the curtailment is first offset against any existing unrecognized net loss. Because the previously unrecognized amount in this case was a gain ($151 unrecognized net gain subsequent to transition), the $110 gain from the curtailment was recognized.

[b]Because the plan had an unrecognized net obligation at the date of transition to this section [refer to footnote 3], the unrecognized amount is treated as prior service cost for purposes of applying this section. The remaining expected future years of service associated with those employees present at the date of transition was reduced by 30 percent due to the termination of employees. Accordingly, 30 percent of the unrecognized net obligation remaining unamortized at the date of the curtailment was recognized which amounted to $120.

[c]The unrecognized prior service cost (which related to the plan amendment of January 1, 1988) associated with the previously expected years of service of the terminated employees that will not be rendered was $160.

[d]Under paragraph .186 of this section, the loss, which amounted to $170, should be recognized with other gains and losses resulting from the disposal of the segment.

Example 3B—Plan Assets Exceed the Projected Benefit Obligation

Company F sponsors a final-pay noncontributory defined benefit plan. On July 27, 1990, the management of Company F decided to reduce significantly the operations of a line of business products. Although the decision did not result in closing down any facilities, it required the termination of a significant number of employees. The termination of employees [will take] place on November 1, 1990.

The portion of the projected benefit obligation based on expected future compensation levels of the terminated employees was $90,000, and the portion of nonvested benefits related to the terminated employees was $20,000.

As a result, Company F recognized a gain of $110,000 on November 1, 1990,* determined as follows:

---

*Under paragraph .184 of this section, if the sum of the effects resulting from the curtailment is a net loss, it is to be recognized when it is probable that the curtailment will occur and the effects are reasonably estimable. If the sum of those effects is a net gain, it [shall] be recognized when the related employees terminate. Company F estimated at July 27, 1990 that a net curtailment gain would result. Accordingly, the gain was recognized on the date employees terminated (November 1, 1990) and *was based on plan assets and obligations measured as of that date.*

Company F
(in thousands)

As of November 1, 1990

	Before Realization of Curtailment Gain	Effect of Curtailment	After Realization of Curtailment Gain
Assets and obligations:			
Vested benefit obligation	$ (1,300)		$ (1,300)
Nonvested benefits	(300)	$ 20	(280)
Accumulated benefit obligation	(1,600)	20	(1,580)
Effects of projected future compensation levels	(400)	90	(310)
Projected benefit obligation	(2,000)	110[a]	(1,890)
Plan assets at fair value	2,100		2,100
Items not yet recognized in earnings:			
Unrecognized net asset at transition[a]	(200)	0[a]	(200)
Unrecognized net loss subsequent to transition	100	0[a]	100
(Accrued)/prepaid pension cost on the statement of financial position	$ 0	$ 110	$ 110

---

[a]Under paragraph .183 of this section, the curtailment gain (that is, the decrease in the projected benefit obligation) is first offset against any existing unrecognized net loss. The unrecognized net asset from transition is treated as an unrecognized net gain [refer to footnote 15]. Thus the net amount of previously unrecognized gain or loss was a gain of $100 (unrecognized net loss of $100 plus the remaining unrecognized net asset from transition of $200). Because the previously unrecognized net amount was a gain, the $110 gain from curtailment was recognized.

If the previously existing unrecognized net amount had been a loss including the unrecognized net asset at transition and that loss exceeded the curtailment gain, the curtailment gain would have been offset, and no gain would have been recognized.

The journal entry required to reflect the accounting for the plan curtailment was:

Accrued/prepaid pension cost   110
  Gain from curtailment   110

Illustration 4—Calculation of Unrecognized Prior Service Cost Associated with Services of Terminated Employees

Company S sponsors a final-pay noncontributory defined benefit plan. On January 1, 19X3, the company had a retroactive plan amendment resulting in prior service cost of $800,000.

The unrecognized prior service cost that results from the plan amendment is amortized based on the expected future years of service of participants active as of January 1, 19X3 who are expected to receive benefits under the plan.

As of January 1, 19X3, the company had 100 employees who were expected to receive benefits under the plan. Based on the assumption that 5 percent of that group (5 employees) leaves (either quits or retires) in each of the next 20 years, the expected future years of service amounted to 1,050.

The amount of prior service cost associated with each expected future year of service is $762 ($800,000 ÷ 1,050). Exhibit A illustrates the originally expected expiration of the anticipated service years.

On December 31, 19X5, Company S terminated 25 employees active at the date of the plan amendment. Immediately prior to the curtailment, 765 expected future years of service remained (1,050 less 285 years of service rendered in the previous 3 years). The curtailment reduced the total expected future years of service at December 31, 19X5 from 765 to 555 (210) as illustrated in Exhibit B. Therefore, Company S will recognize $160,020 ($762 × 210) of prior service cost in conjunction with the curtailment.

Exhibit A   Determination of Expected Years of Service Rendered in Each Year Before Curtailment

Individuals	Future Service Years	X3	X4	X5	X6	X7	X8	X9	Y0	Y1	Y2	Y3	Y4	Y5	Y6	Y7	Y8	Y9	Z0	Z1	Z2
A1-A5	5	5																			
B1-B5	10	5	5																		
C1-C5	15	5	5	5																	
D1-D5	20	5	5	5	5																
E1-E5	25	5	5	5	5	5															
F1-F5	30	5	5	5	5	5	5														
G1-G5	35	5	5	5	5	5	5	5													
H1-H5	40	5	5	5	5	5	5	5	5												
I1-I5	45	5	5	5	5	5	5	5	5	5											
J1-J5	50	5	5	5	5	5	5	5	5	5	5										
K1-K5	55	5	5	5	5	5	5	5	5	5	5	5									
L1-L5	60	5	5	5	5	5	5	5	5	5	5	5	5								
M1-M5	65	5	5	5	5	5	5	5	5	5	5	5	5	5							
N1-N5	70	5	5	5	5	5	5	5	5	5	5	5	5	5	5						
O1-O5	75	5	5	5	5	5	5	5	5	5	5	5	5	5	5	5					
P1-P5	80	5	5	5	5	5	5	5	5	5	5	5	5	5	5	5	5				
Q1-Q5	85	5	5	5	5	5	5	5	5	5	5	5	5	5	5	5	5	5			
R1-R5	90	5	5	5	5	5	5	5	5	5	5	5	5	5	5	5	5	5	5		
S1-S5	95	5	5	5	5	5	5	5	5	5	5	5	5	5	5	5	5	5	5	5	
T1-T5	100	5	5	5	5	5	5	5	5	5	5	5	5	5	5	5	5	5	5	5	5
	1,050																				
Service Years Rendered		100	95	90	85	80	75	70	65	60	55	50	45	40	35	30	25	20	15	10	5
Amortization Fraction		100	95	90	85	80	75	70	65	60	55	50	45	40	35	30	25	20	15	10	5
		1,050	1,050	1,050	1,050	1,050	1,050	1,050	1,050	1,050	1,050	1,050	1,050	1,050	1,050	1,050	1,050	1,050	1,050	1,050	1,050
Expected Future Years of Service Remaining at Year-End		950	855	765	680	600	525	455	390	330	275	225	180	140	105	75	50	30	15	5	0

Prior Service Cost $ 800,000

Total Expected Future Years of Service   1,050

Amortization Amount per Each Year of Service $ 762

Exhibit B   Determination of Expected Years of Service Rendered in Each Year After Curtailment

Individuals	Year																			
	X3	X4	X5	X6	X7	X8	X9	Y0	Y1	Y2	Y3	Y4	Y5	Y6	Y7	Y8	Y9	Z0	Z1	Z2
A1-A5	5																			
B1-B5	5	5																		
C1-C5	5	5	5																	
D1-D5*	5	5	5																	
E1-E5	5	5	5	5	5															
F1-F5	5	5	5	5	5	5														
G1-G5	5	5	5	5	5	5	5													
H1-H5*	5	5	5																	
I1-I5	5	5	5	5	5	5	5	5	5											
J1-J5	5	5	5	5	5	5	5	5	5	5										
K1-K5	5	5	5	5	5	5	5	5	5	5	5									
L1-L5*	5	5	5																	
M1-M5	5	5	5	5	5	5	5	5	5	5	5	5	5							
N1-N5	5	5	5	5	5	5	5	5	5	5	5	5	5	5						
O1-O5*	5	5	5																	
P1-P5	5	5	5	5	5	5	5	5	5	5	5	5	5	5	5	5				
Q1-Q5	5	5	5	5	5	5	5	5	5	5	5	5	5	5	5	5	5			
R1-R5*	5	5	5																	
S1-S5	5	5	5	5	5	5	5	5	5	5	5	5	5	5	5	5	5	5	5	
T1-T5	5	5	5	5	5	5	5	5	5	5	5	5	5	5	5	5	5	5	5	5
Service Years Rendered	100	95	90	60	60	55	50	45	45	40	35	30	30	25	20	20	15	10	10	5
Adjustment for Termination			210																	
Total	100	95	300	60	60	55	50	45	45	40	35	30	30	25	20	20	15	10	10	5
Amortization Fraction	1,050	1,050	1,050	1,050	1,050	1,050	1,050	1,050	1,050	1,050	1,050	1,050	1,050	1,050	1,050	1,050	1,050	1,050	1,050	1,050
Expected Future Years of Service Remaining at Year-End	950	855	555	495	435	380	330	285	240	200	165	135	105	80	60	40	25	15	5	0

*Terminated group of employees.

Illustration 5—Accounting for a Plan Curtailment When Termination Benefits Are Offered to Employees

Company G sponsors a final-pay noncontributory defined benefit plan. The company had an unrecognized net obligation at the date of transition to this section and did not have a retroactive plan amendment after that date. On May 11, 19X5, the company offered for a short period of time (until June 30, 19X5) special benefits to its employees in connection with their voluntary termination of employment (special termination benefits). The special termination benefit was a lump-sum payment to be made upon termination, payable in addition to the employee's regular plan benefits. The special termination benefit was paid directly from the employer's assets rather than from the plan assets.

On June 30, 15 percent of the employees accepted the offer. The amount of the special termination benefit payment was $125,000.

The portion of the projected benefit obligation based on the expected future compensation levels of the terminated employees amounted to $100,000, and all the employees terminated were fully vested in their accumulated benefits. The portion of the unrecognized net obligation at transition associated with the years of service no longer expected from the terminated employees was $150,000.

As a result, Company G recognized a loss of $175,000 that includes the cost of the special termination benefits and the loss* from the curtailment determined as follows:

---

*Under paragraph .184 of this section, if the sum of the effects resulting from the curtailment is a net loss, it is to be recognized when it is probable that the curtailment will occur and the effects are reasonably estimable. In this example, the effects resulting from the curtailment were not reasonably estimable until June 30, 19X5, the acceptance date for the offer of special termination benefits.

	Company G (in thousands)		
	Before Curtailment	Effect of Curtailment	After Curtailment
Assets and obligations:			
Vested benefit obligation	$ (1,300)		$ (1,300)
Nonvested benefits	(200)		(200)
Accumulated benefit obligation	(1,500)		(1,500)
Effects of projected future compensation levels	(500)	$ 100	(400)
Projected benefit obligation	(2,000)	100[a]	(1,900)
Plan assets at fair value	1,400		1,400
Items not yet recognized in earnings:			
Unrecognized net obligation at transition[b]	800	(150)	650
Unrecognized net gain subsequent to transition	(300)		(300)
(Accrued)/prepaid pension cost on the statement of financial position	$ (100)	$ (50)	$ (150)
Loss on curtailment		$ 50	
Cost of special termination benefits (lump-sum payments to terminated employees)		125	
Total loss		$ 175[c]	

^aUnder paragraph .183 of this section, the curtailment gain (that is, the decrease in the projected benefit obligation) is first offset against any existing unrecognized net loss. Since the previously unrecognized amount was a gain ($300 unrecognized net gain subsequent to transition), the $100 gain from the curtailment was recognized.

^bAn unrecognized net obligation at the date of transition to this section is treated as unrecognized prior service cost for purposes of applying this section. The portion of unrecognized prior service cost associated with the years of service no longer expected from the terminated employees ($150) was recognized.

^cThe loss Company G recognized was $175, which includes the cost of the special termination benefits of $125, the gain related to salary progression of $100 and the recognition of prior service cost of $150. The journal entry required to reflect the accounting for this event was:

Loss on employee terminations	175	
Accrued/prepaid pension cost		50
Liability for termination benefits		125

If the company had paid the termination benefits from the pension plan (by amending the plan and using plan assets), the same loss would have been recognized, but $175 would have been credited to the accrued pension cost liability.

Illustration 6—Transition for an Employer That Completed an Asset Reversion Prior to the Initial Application of this Section

Company H sponsors a final-pay noncontributory defined benefit pension plan. On September 9, 1981, the company settled a portion of its pension obligation through the purchase of annuity contracts and withdrew excess assets. The company continued to provide defined benefits to its employees. No gain was recognized on the transaction, and Company H recognized a credit in its statement of financial position equal to the amount of cash withdrawn. For financial reporting purposes, that amount was grouped with accrued or prepaid pension cost. In subsequent periods the amount of the reversion (a deferred gain) was amortized as a reduction of net periodic pension cost. The company had no other past differences between net periodic pension cost and amounts contributed and, therefore, had recognized no other accrued or prepaid pension cost.

As of January 1, 1985, the time of initial application of this section, the unamortized amount of the reversion gain was $287,000. Company H's transition to this section would be accomplished as follows:

	Company H Computation of Unrecognized Net Asset (in thousands)	
Projected benefit obligation		$ (800)
Plan assets at fair value	$ 950	
Accrued pension cost on the statement of financial position	287	1,237
Unrecognized net asset		$ 437

Company H
(in thousands)

	Before Recognition of Reversion Gain	Effect of Recognition of Reversion Gain	After Recognition of Reversion Gain
Assets and obligations:			
Projected benefit obligation	$ (800)		$ (800)
Plan assets at fair value	950		950
Item not yet recognized in earnings:			
Unrecognized net asset at transition	(437)	$ 287[a]	(150)
(Accrued)/prepaid pension cost on the statement of financial position	$ (287)	$ 287[a]	$ 0

[FAS88, ¶57]

---

[a]Under paragraph .188 of this section, an employer that completed an asset reversion prior to the effective date of this section should recognize a gain as the cumulative effect of a change in accounting principle at the time of initial application of this section.

The gain recognized by Company H amounts to $287, which is the lesser of the unamortized amount of the reversion gain ($287) and the unrecognized net asset from transition ($437). The journal entry required to reflect the accounting as of January 1, 1985 was:

Accrued/prepaid pension cost	287	
Cumulative effect of a change in accounting principle		287

[**Note:** Additional guidance with respect to implementing Section P16 is presented in two FASB publications: *A Guide to Implementation of Statement 87 on Employers' Accounting for Pensions: Questions and Answers,* which addresses 107 questions, and *A Guide to Implementation of Statement 88 on Employers' Accounting for Settlements and Curtailments of Defined Benefit Pension Plans and for Termination Benefits: Questions and Answers,* which addresses 70 other questions. Both publications were written by FASB staff members, Joan Lordi Amble and Jules M. Cassel, and are available from the Order Department, Financial Accounting Standards Board, 401 Merritt 7, P.O. Box 5116, Norwalk, CT 06856-5116, telephone (203) 847-0700.]

Glossary

.401 Accumulated benefit obligation. The actuarial present value of benefits (whether vested or nonvested) attributed by the pension benefit formula to employee service rendered before a specified date and based on employee service and compensation (if applicable) prior to that date. The accumulated benefit obligation differs from the projected benefit obligation in that it includes no assumption about future compensation levels. For plans with flat-benefit or non-pay-related pension benefit formulas, the accumulated benefit obligation and the projected benefit obligation are the same. [FAS87, ¶264]

.402 Actual return on plan assets component (of net periodic pension cost). The difference between fair value of plan assets at the end of the period and the fair value at the beginning of the period, adjusted for contributions and payments of benefits during the period. [FAS87, ¶264]

.403 Actuarial present value. The value, as of a specified date, of an amount or series of amounts payable or receivable thereafter, with each amount adjusted to reflect (a) the time value of money (through discounts for interest) and (b) the probability of payment (by means of decrements for events such as death, disability, withdrawal, or retirement) between the specified date and the expected date of payment. [FAS87, ¶264]

.404 Allocated contract. A contract with an insurance company under which payments to the insurance company are currently used to purchase immediate or deferred annuities for individual participants. See also **Annuity contract.** [FAS87, ¶264]

.405 Amortization. Usually refers to the process of reducing a recognized liability systematically by recognizing revenues or reducing a recognized asset systematically by recognizing expenses or costs. In pension accounting, amortization is also used to refer to the systematic recognition in net pension cost over several periods of previously *unrecognized* amounts, including unrecognized prior service cost and unrecognized net gain or loss. [FAS87, ¶264]

.406 Annuity contract. A contract in which an insurance company unconditionally undertakes a legal obligation to provide specified pension benefits to specific individuals in return for a fixed consideration or premium. An annuity contract is irrevocable and involves the transfer of significant risk from the employer to the insurance company. Annuity contracts are also called allocated contracts. [FAS87, ¶264] [I]f there is any reasonable doubt that the insurance company will meet its obligation under the contract, the contract is not an annuity [contract] for purposes of this section. [In addition,] if the insurance company does business primarily with the employer and related parties (a captive insurer), the contract is not an annuity contract for purposes of paragraphs .154 through .158. [FAS87, ¶57, fn14] If the insurance company is controlled by the employer, the purchase of the contract does not constitute a settlement for purposes of [applying paragraphs .178 through .181]. [FAS88, ¶5, fn1] Some annuity contracts (participating annuity contracts) provide that the purchaser (either the plan or the employer) may participate in the experience of the insurance company. Under those contracts, the insurance company ordinarily pays dividends to the purchaser. If the substance of a participating annuity contract is such that the employer remains subject to all or most of the risks and rewards associated with the benefit obligation covered or the assets transferred to the insurance company, that contract is not an annuity contract for purposes of this section [FAS87, ¶57] [and] the purchase of the contract does not constitute a settlement. [FAS88, ¶5]

.407 Assumptions. Estimates of the occurrence of future events affecting pension costs, such as mortality, withdrawal, disablement and retirement, changes in compensation and national pension benefits, and discount rates to reflect the time value of money. [FAS87, ¶264]

.408 Attribution. The process of assigning pension benefits or cost to periods of employee service. [FAS87, ¶264]

.409 Benefit formula. See **Pension benefit formula.** [FAS87, ¶264]

.410 Benefits. Payments to which participants may be entitled under a pension plan, including pension benefits, death benefits, and benefits due on termination of employment. [FAS87, ¶264]

.411 Benefit/years-of-service approach. Under this approach, an equal portion of the total estimated benefit is attributed to each year of service. The actuarial present value of the benefits is derived after the benefits are attributed to the periods. [FAS87, ¶264]

.412 Captive [insurer]. An insurance company that does business primarily with related entities. [FAS87, ¶264]

.413 Career-average-pay formula (Career-average-pay plan). A benefit formula that bases benefits on the employee's compensation over the entire period of service with the employer. A career-average-pay plan is a plan with such a formula. [FAS87, ¶264]

.414 Contributory plan. A pension plan under which employees contribute part of the cost. In some contributory plans, employees wishing to be covered must contribute; in other contributory plans, employee contributions result in increased benefits. [FAS87, ¶264]

.415 Curtailment. See **Plan curtailment.** [FAS87, ¶264]

.416 Defined benefit pension plan. A pension plan that defines an amount of pension benefit to be provided, usually as a function of one or more factors such as age, years of service, or compensation. Any pension plan that is not a defined contribution pension plan is, for purposes of this section, a defined benefit pension plan. [FAS87, ¶264]

.417 Defined contribution pension plan. A plan that provides pension benefits in return for services rendered, provides an individual account for each participant, and specifies how contributions to the individual's account are to be determined instead of specifying the amount of benefits the individual is to receive. Under a defined contribution pension plan, the benefits a participant will receive depend solely on the amount contributed to the participant's account, the returns earned on investments of those contributions, and forfeitures of other participants' benefits that may be allocated to such participant's account. [FAS87, ¶264]

.418 Discount rate. The interest rate used to adjust for the time value of money. See also **Actuarial present value.** [FAS87, ¶264]

.419 Expected long-term rate of return on plan assets. An assumption as to the rate of return on plan assets reflecting the average rate of earnings expected on the funds invested or to be invested to provide for the benefits included in the projected benefit obligation. [FAS87, ¶264]

.420 Expected return on plan assets. An amount calculated as a basis for determining the extent of delayed recognition of the effects of changes in the fair value of assets. The expected return on plan assets is determined based on the expected long-term rate of return on plan assets and the market-related value of plan assets. [FAS87, ¶264]

.421 Explicit approach to assumptions. An approach under which each significant assumption used reflects the best estimate of the plan's future experience solely with respect to that assumption. [FAS87, ¶264]

.422 Fair value. The amount that a pension plan could reasonably expect to receive for an investment in a current sale between a willing buyer and a willing seller, that is, other than in a forced or liquidation sale. [FAS87, ¶264]

.423 Final-pay formula (Final-pay plan). A benefit formula that bases benefits on the employee's compensation over a specified number of years near the end of the employee's service period or on the employee's highest compensation periods. For example, a plan might provide annual pension benefits equal to 1 percent of the employee's average salary for the last five years (or the highest consecutive five years) for each year of service. A final-pay plan is a plan with such a formula. [FAS87, ¶264]

.424 Flat-benefit formula (Flat-benefit plan). A benefit formula that bases benefits on a fixed amount per year of service, such as $20 of monthly retirement income for each year of credited service. A flat-benefit plan is a plan with such a formula. [FAS87, ¶264]

.425 Fund. Used as a verb, to pay over to a funding agency (as to fund future pension benefits or to fund pension cost). Used as a noun, assets accumulated in the hands of a funding agency for the purpose of meeting pension benefits when they become due. [FAS87, ¶264]

.426 Funding policy. The program regarding the amounts and timing of contributions by the employer(s), participants, and any other sources (for example, state subsidies or federal grants) to provide the benefits a pension plan specifies. [FAS87, ¶264]

.427 Gain or loss. A change in the value of either the projected benefit obligation or the plan assets resulting from experience different from that assumed or from a change in an actuarial assumption. See also **Unrecognized net gain or loss.** [FAS87, ¶264]

.428 Gain or loss (component of net periodic pension cost). The sum of (a) the difference between the actual return on plan assets and the expected return on plan assets and (b) the amortization of the unrecognized net gain or loss from previous periods. The gain or loss component is the net effect of delayed recognition of gains and losses (the net change in the unrecognized net gain or loss) except that it does not include changes in the projected benefit obligation occurring during the period and deferred for later recognition. [FAS87, ¶264]

.429 Interest cost component (of net periodic pension cost). The increase in the projected benefit obligation due to passage of time. [FAS87, ¶264]

.430 Interest rate. See **Discount rate.** [FAS87, ¶264]

.431 Loss. See **Gain or loss.** [FAS87, ¶264]

.432 Market-related value of plan assets. A balance used to calculate the expected return on plan assets. Market-related value can be either fair market value or a calculated value that recognizes changes in fair value in a systematic and rational manner over not more than five years. Different ways of calculating market-related value may be used for different classes of assets, but the manner of determining market-related value shall be applied consistently from year to year for each asset class. [FAS87, ¶264]

.433 Measurement date. The date as of which plan assets and obligations are measured. [FAS87, ¶264]

.434 Mortality rate. The proportion of the number of deaths in a specified group to the number living at the beginning of the period in which the deaths occur. Actuaries use mortality tables, which show death rates for each age, in estimating the amount of pension benefits that will become payable. [FAS87, ¶264]

.435 Multiemployer plan. A pension plan to which two or more unrelated employers contribute, usually pursuant to one or more collective-bargaining agreements. A characteristic of multiemployer plans is that assets contributed by one participating employer may be used to provide benefits to employees of other participating employers since assets contributed by an employer are not segregated in a separate account or restricted to provide benefits only to employees of that employer. A multiemployer plan is usually administered by a board of trustees composed of management and labor representatives and may also be referred to as a "joint trust" or "union" plan. Generally, many employers participate in a multiemployer plan, and an employer may participate in more than one plan. The employers participating in multiemployer plans usually have a common industry bond, but for some plans the employers are in different industries and the labor union may be their only common bond. [FAS87, ¶264]

.436 Multiple-employer plan. A pension plan maintained by more than one employer but not treated as a multiemployer plan. Multiple-employer plans are not as prevalent as single-employer and multiemployer plans, but some of the ones that do exist are large and involve many employers. Multiple-employer plans are generally not collectively bargained and are intended to allow participating employers, commonly in the same industry, to pool their assets for investment purposes and reduce the costs of plan administration. A multiple-employer plan maintains separate accounts for each employer so that contributions provide benefits only for employees of the contributing employer. Some multiple-employer plans have features that allow participating employers to have different benefit formulas, with the employer's contributions to the plan based on the benefit formula selected by the employer. [FAS87, ¶264]

.437 Net periodic pension cost. The amount recognized in an employer's financial statements as the cost of a pension plan for a period. Components of net periodic pension cost are service cost, interest cost, actual return on plan assets, gain or loss, amortization of unrecognized prior service cost, and amortization of the unrecognized net obligation or asset existing at the date of initial application of this section. This section uses the term *net periodic pension cost* instead of *net pension expense* because part of the cost recognized in a period may be capitalized along with other costs as part of an asset such as inventory. [FAS87, ¶264]

.438 Nonparticipating annuity contract. An annuity contract that does not provide for the purchaser to participate in the investment performance or in other experience of the insurance company. See also **Annuity contract.** [FAS87, ¶264]

.439 Participant. Any employee or former employee, or any member or former member of a trade or other employee association, or the beneficiaries of those individuals, for whom there are pension plan benefits. [FAS87, ¶264]

.440 Participating annuity contract. An annuity contract that provides for the purchaser to participate in the investment performance and possibly other experience (for example, mortality experience) of the insurance company. [FAS87, ¶264]

.441 **Participation right.** A purchaser's right under a participating contract to receive future dividends or retroactive rate credits from the insurance company. [FAS87, ¶264]

.442 **Pension benefit formula (plan's benefit formula or benefit formula).** The basis for determining payments to which participants may be entitled under a pension plan. Pension benefit formulas usually refer to the employee's service or compensation or both. [FAS87, ¶264]

.443 **Pension benefits.** Periodic (usually monthly) payments made pursuant to the terms of the pension plan to a person who has retired from employment or to that person's beneficiary. [FAS87, ¶264]

.444 **Plan amendment.** A change in the terms of an existing plan or the initiation of a new plan. A plan amendment may increase benefits, including those attributed to years of service already rendered. See also **Retroactive benefits.** [FAS87, ¶264]

.445 **Plan assets.** Assets—usually stocks, bonds, and other investments—that have been segregated and restricted (usually in a trust) to provide benefits. Plan assets include amounts contributed by the employer (and by employees for a contributory plan) and amounts earned from investing the contributions, less benefits paid. Plan assets cannot ordinarily be withdrawn by the employer except in certain circumstances when a plan has assets in excess of obligations and the employer has taken certain steps to satisfy existing obligations. For purposes of this section, assets not segregated in a trust or otherwise effectively restricted so that they cannot be used by the employer for other purposes are not plan assets even though it may be intended that such assets be used to provide pensions. Amounts accrued by the employer as net periodic pension cost but not yet paid to the plan are not plan assets for purposes of this section. Securities of the employer held by the plan are includable in plan assets provided they are transferable. If a plan has liabilities other than for benefits, those nonbenefit obligations may be considered as reductions of plan assets for purposes of this section. [FAS87, ¶264]

.446 **Plan assets available for benefits.** See **Plan assets.** [FAS87, ¶264]

.447 **Plan curtailment.** An event that significantly reduces the expected years of future service of present employees or eliminates for a significant number of employees the accrual of defined benefits for some or all of their future services. [FAS87, ¶264] Curtailments include:

a. Termination of employees' services earlier than expected, which may or may not involve closing a facility or discounting a segment of a business

b. Termination or suspension of a plan so that employees do not earn additional defined benefits for future services. In the latter situation, future service may be counted toward vesting of benefits accumulated based on past service. [FAS88, ¶6]

.448 Plan's benefit formula. See **Pension benefit formula.** [FAS87, ¶264]

.449 Plan termination. An event in which the pension plan ceases to exist and all benefits are settled by purchase of annuities or other means. The plan may or may not be replaced by another plan. A plan termination with a replacement plan may or may not be in substance a plan termination for accounting purposes. [FAS87, ¶264]

.450 Prepaid pension cost. Cumulative employer contributions in excess of accrued net pension cost. [FAS87, ¶264]

.451 Prior service cost. The cost of retroactive benefits granted in a plan amendment. See also **Unrecognized prior service cost.** [FAS87, ¶264]

.452 Projected benefit obligation. The actuarial present value as of a date of all benefits attributed by the pension benefit formula to employee service rendered prior to that date. The projected benefit obligation is measured using assumptions as to future compensation levels if the pension benefit formula is based on those future compensation levels (pay-related, final-pay, final-average-pay, or career-average-pay plans). [FAS87, ¶264]

.453 Retroactive benefits. Benefits granted in a plan amendment (or initiation) that are attributed by the pension benefit formula to employee services rendered in periods prior to the amendment. The cost of the retroactive benefits is referred to as prior service cost. [FAS87, ¶264]

.454 Return on plan assets. See **Actual return on plan assets component** and **Expected return on plan assets.** [FAS87, ¶264]

.455 Service. Employment taken into consideration under a pension plan. Years of employment before the inception of a plan constitute an employee's past service; years thereafter are classified in relation to the particular actuarial valuation being made or discussed. Years of employment (including past service) prior to the date of a particular valuation constitute prior service; years of employment following the date of the valuation constitute future service; a year of employment adjacent to the date of valuation, or in which such date falls, constitutes current service. [FAS87, ¶264]

.456 Service cost component (of net periodic pension cost). The actuarial present value of benefits attributed by the pension benefit formula to employee services rendered by employees during that period. The service cost component is a portion of the projected benefit obligation and is unaffected by the funded status of the plan. [FAS87, ¶264]

.457 Settlement. A transaction that (a) is an irrevocable action, (b) relieves the employer (or the plan) of primary responsibility for a pension benefit obligation, and (c) eliminates significant risks related to the obligation and the assets used to effect the settlement. Examples of transactions that constitute a settlement include (a) making lump-sum cash payments to plan participants in exchange for their rights to receive specified pension benefits and (b) purchasing nonparticipating annuity contracts to cover vested benefits. [FAS88, ¶3]

.458 Single-employer plan. A pension plan that is maintained by one employer. The term also may be used to describe a plan that is maintained by related parties such as a parent and its subsidiaries. [FAS87, ¶264]

.459 Suspension. An event in which the pension plan is frozen and no further benefits accrue. Future service may continue to be the basis for vesting of nonvested benefits existing at the date of suspension. The plan may still hold assets, pay benefits already accrued, and receive additional employer contributions for any unfunded benefits. Employees may or may not continue working for the employer. [FAS87, ¶264]

.460 Turnover. Termination of employment for a reason other than death or retirement. [FAS87, ¶264]

.461 Unfunded accrued pension cost. Cumulative net pension cost accrued in excess of the employer's contributions. [FAS87, ¶264]

.462 Unfunded accumulated benefit obligation. The excess of the accumulated benefit obligation over plan assets. [FAS87, ¶264]

.463 Unrecognized net gain or loss. The cumulative net gain or loss that has not been recognized as a part of net periodic pension cost. See **Gain or loss.** [FAS87, ¶264]

.464 Unrecognized prior service cost. That portion of prior service cost that has not been recognized as a part of net periodic pension cost. [FAS87, ¶264]

.465 Vested benefit obligation. The actuarial present value of vested benefits. [FAS87, ¶264]

.466 Vested benefits. Benefits for which the employee's right to receive a present or future pension benefit is no longer contingent on remaining in the service of the employer. (Other conditions, such as inadequacy of the pension fund, may prevent the employee from receiving the vested benefit.) Under graded vesting, the initial vested right may be to receive in the future a stated percentage of a pension based on the number of years of accumulated credited service; thereafter, the percentage may increase with the number of years of service or of age until the right to receive the entire benefit has vested. [FAS87, ¶264]

(The next page is 34851.)

Source: FASB Statement 112

Summary

This section presents standards for employers' accounting for postemployment benefits provided to former or inactive employees, including their beneficiaries and covered dependents, after employment but before retirement. Postemployment benefits may be paid as the result of a disability, layoff, death, or other event and may be provided in cash or in kind. If an obligation is not accrued only because the amount cannot be reasonably estimated, the financial statements shall disclose that fact.

Scope

.101 This section applies to all types of **postemployment benefits** provided to former or **inactive employees**, their beneficiaries, and covered dependents after employment but before retirement, except as noted in paragraph .102. Benefits may be provided in cash or in kind and may be paid as a result of a disability, layoff, death, or other event. Benefits may be paid immediately upon cessation of active employment or over a specified period of time. Employees' rights to benefits may accumulate or vest as they render service. [FAS112, ¶4]

.102 This section does not apply to:

a. Postemployment benefits provided through a pension or postretirement benefit plan (Sections P16, "Pensions," and P40, "Postretirement Benefits Other Than Pensions," specify the accounting for those costs.)
b. Individual deferred compensation arrangements that are addressed by Section C38, "Compensation to Employees: Deferred Compensation Agreements"
c. Special or contractual termination benefits covered by Sections P16 and P40
d. Stock compensation plans that are addressed by Section C47, "Compensation to Employees: Stock Purchase and Option Plans." [FAS112, ¶5]

Accounting for Postemployment Benefits

.103 Postemployment benefits that are within the scope of this section and that meet the conditions in paragraph .104 of Section C44, "Compensation to Employees: Paid Absences," shall be accounted for in accordance with [the provisions of] that section. Postemployment benefits that do not meet the conditions of paragraph .104 of Section C44, shall be accounted for in accordance with [the provisions of] paragraph .105

of Section C59, "Contingencies," [FAS112, ¶6] which requires recognition of a loss contingency when it is probable that an asset has been impaired or a liability has been incurred and the amount of loss can be reasonably estimated.[1] [FAS112, ¶21]

.104 [This section does not] provide guidance on how to measure an employer's postemployment benefit obligation. Sections P16 and P40 discuss measurement issues extensively. To the extent that similar issues apply to postemployment benefit plans, employers may refer to those sections for guidance in measuring their obligations in compliance with the requirements of this section. [In addition, this section does not] provide explicit guidance on discounting. As a result, the use of discounting in measuring postemployment benefit obligations [is] permitted but not required. [FAS111, ¶23]

Disclosures

.105 If an obligation for postemployment benefits is not accrued in accordance with Sections C44 or C59 only because the amount cannot be reasonably estimated, the financial statements shall disclose that fact. [FAS112, ¶7]

---

[1]For example, an employer may provide any former employee on permanent disability with continued medical insurance coverage until that employee meets the requirements for participation in the employer's postretirement medical plan. If the level of benefits provided is the same for any disabled employee regardless of years of service, the cost of those benefits should be recognized when the event causing a permanent disability occurs and a reasonable estimate can be made as specified by Section C59. [FAS112, ¶22]

Glossary

.401 **Inactive employees.** Employees who are not currently rendering service to the employer and who have not been terminated. They include those who have been laid off and those on disability leave, regardless of whether they are expected to return to active status. [FAS112, ¶1]

.402 **Postemployment benefits.** Benefits provided to former and inactive employees after employment but before retirement. Postemployment benefits include, but are not limited to, salary continuation, supplemental unemployment benefits, severance benefits, disability-related benefits (including workers' compensation), job training and counseling, and continuation of benefits such as health care benefits and life insurance coverage. [FAS112, ¶1]

(The next page is 35011.)

Sources: FASB Statement 88; FASB Statement 106; FASB Statement 112

Summary

This section presents standards for employers' accounting for postretirement benefits other than pensions (hereinafter referred to as postretirement benefits). Although it applies to all forms of post-retirement benefits, this section focuses principally on postretirement health care benefits. This section requires accrual, during the years that the employee renders the necessary service, of the expected cost of providing those benefits to an employee and the employee's beneficiaries and covered dependents.

An employer's practice of providing postretirement benefits to selected employees under individual contracts, with specific terms determined on an individual-by-individual basis, does not constitute a postretirement benefit plan under this section. The accounting for those contracts is presented in Section C38, "Compensation to Employees: Deferred Compensation Agreements."

The accounting in this section is similar, in many respects, to the accounting for pensions as presented in Section P16, "Pension Costs." In applying accrual accounting to postretirement benefits, three fundamental aspects of pension accounting are adopted: delayed recognition of certain events, reporting net cost, and offsetting liabilities and related assets.

Delayed recognition means that certain changes in the obligation for postretirement benefits, including those changes arising as a result of a plan initiation or amendment, and certain changes in the value of plan assets set aside to meet that obligation are not recognized as they occur. Rather, those changes are recognized systematically over future periods. All changes in the obligation and plan assets ultimately are recognized unless they are first reduced by other changes. The changes that have been identified and quantified but not yet recognized in the employer's financial statements as components of net periodic postretirement benefit cost and as a liability or asset are disclosed.

Net cost means that the recognized consequences of the transactions affecting a postretirement benefit plan are a single amount in the employer's financial statement. or amount includes at least three types of events the might otherwise be reported separately transactions—exchanging a promise of defer form of postretirement benefits for emplo

arising from the passage of time until those benefits are paid, and the returns from the investment of plan assets—are disclosed separately as components of net periodic postretirement benefit cost.

Offsetting means that plan assets restricted for the payment of postretirement benefits offset the accumulated postretirement benefit obligation in determining amounts recognized in the employer's statement of financial position and that the return on those plan assets offsets postretirement benefit cost in the employer's statement of income. That offsetting is reflected even though the obligation has not been settled, the investment of the plan assets may be largely controlled by the employer, and substantial risks and rewards associated with both the obligation and the plan assets are borne by the employer.

This section requires that the accounting for postretirement benefits reflect the terms of the exchange transaction that takes place between an employer that provides postretirement benefits and the employees who render services in exchange for those benefits. Generally the extant written plan provides the best evidence of that exchange transaction. However, in some situations, an employer's cost-sharing policy or a past practice of regular increases in certain monetary benefits may indicate that the substantive plan—the plan as understood by the parties to the exchange transaction—differs from the extant written plan. The substantive plan is the basis for the accounting.

This section requires that an employer's obligation for postretirement benefits expected to be provided to or for an employee be fully accrued by the date that employee attains full eligibility for all of the benefits expected to be received by that employee, any beneficiaries, and covered dependents (the full eligibility date), even if the employee is expected to render additional service beyond that date. That accounting reflects the fact that at the full eligibility date the employee has provided all of the service necessary to earn the right to receive all of the benefits that employee is expected to receive under the plan.

The beginning of the attribution (accrual) period is the employee's date of hire unless the plan only grants credit for service from a later date, in which case benefits are generally attributed from the beginning of that credited service period. An equal amount of the expected postretirement benefit obligation is attributed to each year of service in the attribution period unless the plan attributes a disproportionate share of the expected benefits to employees' early service.

.101 This section establishes standards of financial accounting and reporting for an employer that offers **postretirement benefits other than pensions** (hereinafter referred to as **postretirement benefits**) to its employees.[1] [FAS106, ¶1]

Scope

.102 This section applies to *all* postretirement benefits expected to be provided by an employer[2] to current and former employees (including **retirees**, disabled employees,[3] and other former employees who are expected to receive postretirement benefits), their beneficiaries, and covered dependents, pursuant to the terms of an employer's undertaking to provide those **benefits**. Postretirement benefits include, but are not limited to, postretirement health care;[4] life insurance provided outside a pension plan to retirees; and other welfare benefits such as tuition assistance, day care, legal services, and housing subsidies provided after retirement. Often those benefits are in the form of a reimbursement to plan participants or direct payment to providers for the cost of specified services as the need for those services arises, but they may also include benefits payable as a lump sum, such as death benefits. This section also applies to **settlement** of all or a part of an employer's **accumulated postretirement benefit obligation** or **curtailment** of a postretirement benefit plan and to an employer that provides postretirement benefits as part of a special **termination benefits** offer. [FAS106, ¶6]

---

[1] The accounting for benefits paid after employment but before retirement (for example, layoff benefits) is [FAS106, ¶1, fn2] [covered in Section P32, "Postemployment Benefits."] That section applies to all types of postemployment benefits provided to former or inactive employees, their beneficiaries, and covered dependents after employment but before retirement. [FAS112, ¶4]

[2] For some rate-regulated enterprises, [the provisions of] Section Re6, "Regulated Operations," may require that the difference between **net periodic postretirement benefit cost** as defined in this section and amounts of postretirement benefit cost considered for rate-making purposes be recognized as an asset or a liability created by the actions of the regulator. Those actions of the regulator change the timing of recognition of net periodic postretirement benefit cost as an expense; they do not otherwise affect the requirements of this section. [FAS106, ¶364]

[3] Health and other welfare benefits expected to be provided to employees deemed to be on a disability retirement are within the scope of this section. [FAS106, ¶136] The determination of disability benefits to be accrued pursuant to this section is based on the terms of the **postretirement benefit plan** defining when a disabled employee is entitled to postretirement benefits. [FAS106, ¶6, fn4] For example, the provisions of the postretirement health care plan may provide postretirement health care coverage after a disabled employee attains a specified number of years of credited service (which may include credit for periods after the employee is disabled), with a separate disability plan that provides health benefits prior to that date. Or, the postretirement health care plan may have special provisions for disabled employees that entitle them to benefit coverage under the postretirement benefit plan at a date earlier than that coverage would commence for other employees who are not disabled. [FAS106, ¶137] [Refer to the illustrations in paragraphs .218 through .220]

[4] Postretirement health care benefits are likely to be the most significant in terms of cost and prevalence, and certain of the issues that arise in measuring those benefits are unique. Therefore, much of the language of this section focuses on postretirement health care plans. Nevertheless, this section applies equally to all postretirement benefits. [FAS106, ¶6, fn5]

.103 For the purposes of this section, a postretirement benefit plan is an arrangement that is mutually understood by an employer and its employees, whereby an employer undertakes to provide its current and former employees with benefits after they retire in exchange for the employees' services over a specified period of time, upon attaining a specified age while in service, or both. Benefits may commence immediately upon termination of service or may be deferred until retired employees attain a specified age. [FAS106, ¶7]

.104 An employer's practice of providing postretirement benefits may take a variety of forms and the obligation may or may not be funded. This section applies to any arrangement that is in substance a postretirement benefit plan, regardless of its form or the means or timing of its funding. This section applies both to written plans and to unwritten plans whose existence is discernible either from a practice of paying postretirement benefits or from oral representations made to current or former employees. Absent evidence to the contrary, it shall be presumed that an employer that has provided postretirement benefits in the past or is currently promising those benefits to employees will continue to provide those future benefits. [FAS106, ¶8]

.105 This section applies to deferred compensation contracts with individual employees if those contracts, taken together, are equivalent to a **plan** that provides postretirement benefits. It does not apply to an employer's practice of providing postretirement benefits to selected employees under individual contracts with specific terms determined on an individual-by-individual basis. Those contracts shall be accounted for individually, following the terms of the contract. To the extent the contract does not attribute the benefits to individual years of service, the expected future benefits shall be accrued over the period of service required to be rendered in exchange for the benefits. (Refer to Section C38, "Compensation to Employees: Deferred Compensation Agreements," paragraph .101A.) [FAS106, ¶9]

.106 A postretirement benefit plan may be part of a larger plan or arrangement that provides benefits currently to active employees as well as to retirees. In those circumstances, the promise to provide benefits to present and future retirees under the plan shall be segregated from the promise to provide benefits currently to active employees and shall be accounted for in accordance with the provisions of this section. [FAS106, ¶10]

.107 This section does not apply to pension or life insurance benefits provided through a pension plan. The accounting for those benefits is set forth in Section P16, "Pension Costs."[5] [FAS106, ¶11]

---

[5]Two Special Reports prepared by the FASB staff, *A Guide to Implementation of Statement 87 on Employers' Accounting for Pensions*, and *A Guide to Implementation of Statement 88 on Employers' Accounting for Settlements and Curtailments of Defined Benefit Pension Plans and for Termination Benefits*, provide accounting guidance on implementation questions raised in connection with Statements 87 and 88. Many of the provisions in this section are the same as or are similar to the provisions of Statements 87 and 88. Consequently, the guidance provided in those Special Reports should be useful in understanding and implementing many of the provisions of this section. [FAS106, ¶11, fn6]

Use of Reasonable Approximations

.108 This section is intended to specify accounting objectives and results rather than computational means of obtaining those results. If estimates, averages, or computational shortcuts can reduce the cost of applying this section, their use is appropriate, provided the results are reasonably expected not to be materially different from the results of a detailed application. [FAS106, ¶15]

Single-Employer Defined Benefit Postretirement Plans

.109 This section primarily focuses on an employer's accounting for a **single-employer plan** that defines the postretirement benefits to be provided to retirees. For purposes of this section, a **defined benefit postretirement plan** is one that defines the postretirement benefits in terms of (a) monetary amounts (for example, $100,000 of life insurance) or (b) benefit coverage to be provided (for example, up to $200 per day for hospitalization, 80 percent of the cost of specified surgical procedures, and so forth). (Specified monetary amounts and benefit coverage are hereinafter collectively referred to as *benefits*.) [FAS106, ¶16]

.110 In some cases, an employer may limit its obligation through an individual or an aggregate "cap" on the employer's cost or benefit obligation. For example, an employer may elect to limit its annual postretirement benefit obligation for each retired plan participant to a maximum of $5,000. Or, an employer may elect to limit its share of the aggregate cost of covered postretirement health care benefits for a period to an amount determined based on an average per capita cost per retired plan participant. Plans of that nature are considered to be defined benefit postretirement plans. Paragraphs .269 through .275 illustrate measurement considerations for defined-dollar capped plans. [FAS106, ¶17]

.111 A postretirement benefit is part of the compensation paid to an employee for services rendered. In a defined benefit plan, the employer promises to provide, in addition to current wages and benefits, future benefits during retirement. Generally, the amount of those benefits depends on the **benefit formula** (that may include factors such as the number of years of service rendered or the employee's compensation before retirement or termination), the longevity of the retiree and any beneficiaries and covered dependents, and the incidence of events requiring benefit payments (for example, illnesses affecting the amount of health care required). In most cases, services are rendered over a number of years before an employee retires and begins to receive benefits or is entitled to receive benefits as a need arises. Even though the services rendered by the employee are complete and the employee has retired, the total amount of benefits the employer has promised and the cost to the employer of the services rendered are not precisely determinable but can be estimated using the plan's benefit formula and estimates of the effects of relevant future events. [FAS106, ¶18]

Basic Elements of Accounting for Postretirement Benefits

.112 Any method of accounting that recognizes the cost of postretirement benefits over employee service periods (before the payment of benefits to retirees) must deal with two factors that stem from the nature of the arrangement. First, estimates or **assumptions** must be made about the future events that will determine the amount and timing of the benefit payments. Second, an **attribution** approach that assigns benefits and the cost of those benefits to individual years of service must be selected. [FAS106, ¶19]

.113 The **expected postretirement benefit obligation** for an employee is the **actuarial present value** as of a particular date of the postretirement benefits expected to be paid by the employer's plan to or for the employee, the employee's beneficiaries, and any covered dependents pursuant to the terms of the plan. Measurement of the expected postretirement benefit obligation is based on the expected amount and timing of future benefits, taking into consideration the expected future cost of providing the benefits and the extent to which those costs are shared by the employer, the employee (including consideration of contributions required during the employee's active service period and following retirement, deductibles, coinsurance provisions, and so forth), or others (such as through governmental programs). [FAS106, ¶20]

.114 The accumulated postretirement benefit obligation[6] as of a particular date is the actuarial present value of all future benefits attributed to an employee's service rendered to that date pursuant to paragraphs .138 and .139 and .147 through .150, assuming the plan continues in effect and that all assumptions about future events are fulfilled. Prior to the date on which an employee attains **full eligibility** for the benefits that employee is expected to earn under the terms of the postretirement benefit plan (the **full eligibility date**), the accumulated postretirement benefit obligation for an employee is a portion of the expected postretirement benefit obligation. On and after the full eligibility date, the accumulated postretirement benefit obligation and the expected postretirement benefit obligation for an employee are the same. Determination of the full eligibility date is affected by plan terms that provide incremental benefits expected to be received by or on behalf of an employee for additional years of service, unless those incremental benefits are trivial. Determination of the full eligibility date is not affected by plan terms that define when benefit payments commence or by an employee's current **dependency status.** (Paragraphs .209 through .220 illustrate determination of the full eligibility date.) [FAS106, ¶21]

---

[6]The accumulated postretirement benefit obligation generally reflects a ratable allocation of expected future benefits to employee service already rendered in the attribution period; the accumulated benefit obligation under Section P16 generally reflects the future benefits allocated to employee service in accordance with the benefit formula. In addition, unlike Section P16, this section implicitly considers salary progression in the measurement of the accumulated postretirement benefit obligation of a pay-related plan. [FAS106, ¶21, fn7] Thus, the accumulated postretirement benefit obligation disclosed pursuant to this section is defined in terms notionally more comparable to the projected benefit obligation under Section P16. [FAS106, ¶168]

.115 Net periodic postretirement benefit cost[7] comprises several components that reflect different aspects of the employer's financial arrangements. The **service cost** component of net periodic postretirement benefit cost is the actuarial present value of benefits attributed to services rendered by employees during the period (the portion of the expected postretirement benefit obligation attributed to service in the period). The service cost component is the same for an unfunded plan, a plan with minimal funding, and a well-funded plan. The other components of net periodic postretirement benefit cost are **interest cost**[8] (interest on the accumulated postretirement benefit obligation, which is a discounted amount), **actual return on plan assets**, **amortization** of **unrecognized prior service cost**, amortization of the **transition obligation** or **transition asset**, and the **gain or loss component.** [FAS106, ¶22]

Measurement of Cost and Obligations

Accounting for the Substantive Plan

.116 An objective of this section is that the accounting reflect the terms of the exchange transaction that takes place between an employer that provides postretirement benefits and the employees who render services in exchange for those benefits, as those terms are understood by both parties to the transaction. Generally, the extant written plan provides the best evidence of the terms of that exchange transaction. However, in some situations, an employer's **cost-sharing** policy, as evidenced by past practice or by communication of intended changes to a plan's cost-sharing provisions (refer to paragraphs .117 and .118), or a past practice of regular increases in certain monetary benefits (refer to paragraph .119) may indicate that the **substantive plan**—the plan as understood by the parties to the exchange transaction—differs from the extant written plan. The substantive plan shall be the basis for the accounting. [FAS106, ¶23]

.117 Except as provided in paragraph .118, an employer's cost-sharing policy, as evidenced by the following past practice or communication, shall constitute the cost-sharing provisions of the substantive plan if either of the following conditions exist. Otherwise, the extant written plan shall be considered to be the substantive plan.

a. The employer has a past practice[9] of (1) maintaining a consistent level of cost sharing between the employer and its retirees through changes in deductibles, coinsurance provisions, retiree contributions, or some combination of those changes

---

[7]This section uses the term *net periodic postretirement cost* rather than *net postretirement benefit expense* because part of the cost recognized in a period may be capitalized along with other costs as part of an asset such as inventory. [FAS106, ¶5, fn3]

[8]The interest cost component of postretirement benefit cost shall not be considered interest for purposes of applying Section I67, " Interest: Capitalization of Interest Costs." [FAS106, ¶22, fn8]

[9]A past practice would be indicated when the nature of the change and duration of the past practice are sufficient to warrant a presumption that it is understood by the plan participants. [FAS106, ¶176]

or (2) consistently increasing or reducing the employer's share of the cost of the covered benefits through changes in retired or **active plan participants'** contributions toward their retiree health care benefits, deductibles, coinsurance provisions, out-of-pocket limitations, and so forth, in accordance with the employer's established cost-sharing policy

b. The employer has the ability, and has communicated to affected **plan participants** its intent, to institute different cost-sharing provisions at a specified time or when certain conditions exist (for example, when health care cost increases exceed a certain level). [FAS106, ¶24]

.118 An employer's past practice of maintaining a consistent level of cost sharing with its retirees or consistently increasing or reducing its share of the cost of providing the covered benefits shall not constitute provisions of the substantive plan if accompanied by identifiable offsetting changes in other benefits or compensation[10] or if the employer incurred significant costs, such as work stoppages, to effect that cost-sharing policy.[11] Similarly, an employer's communication of its intent to institute cost-sharing provisions that differ from the extant written plan or the past cost-sharing practice shall not constitute provisions of the substantive plan (a) if the plan participants would be unwilling to accept the change without adverse consequences to the employer's operations or (b) if other modifications of the plan, such as the level of benefit coverage, or providing offsetting changes in other benefits, such as pension benefits, would be required to gain plan participants' acceptance of the change to the cost-sharing arrangement. [FAS106, ¶25]

.119 A past practice of regular increases in postretirement benefits defined in terms of monetary amounts may indicate that the employer has a present commitment to make future *improvements* to the plan and that the plan will provide monetary benefits attributable to prior service that are greater than the monetary benefits defined by the extant written plan. In those situations, the substantive commitment to increase those benefits shall be the basis for the accounting. Changes in the benefits, other than benefits defined in terms of monetary amounts, covered by a postretirement health care plan or by other postretirement benefit plans shall not be anticipated. [FAS106, ¶26]

---

[10]For example, a past practice of increasing retiree contributions annually based on a specified index or formula may appear to indicate that the substantive plan includes a determinable indexing of the retirees' annual contributions to the plan. However, if that past practice of increasing retiree contributions is accompanied by identifiable offsetting changes in other benefits or compensation, those offsetting changes would indicate that the substantive plan incorporates only the *current* cost-sharing provisions. Therefore, future increases or reductions of those cost-sharing provisions shall not be incorporated in measuring the expected postretirement benefit obligation. [FAS106, ¶25, fn9]

[11]By definition, an employer does not have the unilateral right to change a collectively bargained plan. Therefore, if the postretirement benefits are the subject of collective bargaining, the extant written plan shall be the substantive plan unless the employer can demonstrate its ability to maintain (a) a consistent level of cost sharing or (b) a consistent practice of increasing or reducing its share of the cost of the covered benefits in past negotiations without making offsetting changes in other benefits or compensation of the affected plan participants or by incurring other significant costs to maintain that cost-sharing arrangement. [FAS106, ¶25, fn10]

.120 Contributions expected to be received from active employees toward the cost of their postretirement benefits and from retired plan participants are treated similarly for purposes of measuring an employer's expected postretirement benefit obligation. That obligation is measured as the actuarial present value of the benefits expected to be provided under the plan, reduced by the actuarial present value of contributions expected to be received from the plan participants during their remaining active service and postretirement periods. In determining the amount of the contributions expected to be received from those participants toward the cost of their postretirement benefits, consideration is given to any related substantive plan provisions, such as an employer's past practice of consistently increasing or reducing the contribution rates as described in paragraphs .117 and .118. An obligation to return contributions received from employees who do not attain eligibility for postretirement benefits and, if applicable, any interest accrued on those contributions shall be recognized as a component of an employer's postretirement benefit obligation. [FAS106, ¶27]

.121 Automatic benefit changes[12] specified by the plan that are expected to occur shall be included in measurements of the expected and accumulated postretirement benefit obligations and the service cost component of net periodic postretirement benefit cost. Also, **plan amendments** shall be included in the computation of the expected and accumulated postretirement benefit obligations once they have been contractually agreed to, even if some provisions take effect only in future periods. For example, if a plan amendment grants a different benefit level for employees retiring after a future date, that increased or reduced benefit level shall be included in current-period measurements for employees expected to retire after that date. [FAS106, ¶28]

Assumptions

.122 This section requires the use of **explicit assumptions**, each of which individually represents the best estimate of a particular future event, to measure the expected postretirement benefit obligation.[13] A portion of that expected postretirement benefit obligation is attributed to each period of an employee's service associated with earning the postretirement benefits, and that amount is accrued as service cost for that period. [FAS106, ¶29]

---

[12]For purposes of this section, a plan that promises to provide retirees a benefit in kind, such as health care benefits, rather than a defined dollar amount of benefit, is considered to be a plan that specifies automatic benefit changes. (The assumed rate of change in the future cost of providing health care benefits, the assumed health care cost trend rate, is discussed in paragraph .134.) Because automatic benefit changes are not conditional on employees rendering additional years of service, the full eligibility date is not affected by those changes. A benefit in kind includes the direct rendering of services, the payment directly to others who provide the services, or the reimbursement of the retiree's payment for those services. [FAS106, ¶28, fn11]

[13]Measurement of an employer's postretirement benefit obligation is based on the current plan participants (a "closed group" approach). [FAS106, ¶183]

.123 The service cost component of postretirement benefit cost, any **prior service cost,** and the accumulated postretirement benefit obligation are measured using actuarial assumptions and present value techniques to calculate the actuarial present value of the expected future benefits attributed to periods of employee service. Each assumption used shall reflect the best estimate solely with respect to that individual assumption. All assumptions shall presume that the plan will continue in effect in the absence of evidence that it will not continue. Principal actuarial assumptions include the time value of money (**discount rates**); participation rates (for **contributory plans**); retirement age; factors affecting the amount and timing of future benefit payments, which for **postretirement health care benefits** consider past and present **per capita claims cost by age, health care cost trend rates, Medicare reimbursement rates,** and so forth; salary progression (for **pay-related plans**); and the probability of payment (turnover, dependency status, mortality, and so forth). [FAS106, ¶30]

.124 Many of the other assumptions used in postretirement benefit measurements also are similar to assumptions used in pension measurements, but the sensitivity of the measures to changes in the assumptions may be more significant. For example, the turnover assumption may have a more significant effect for postretirement benefits than for pension benefits because, in many cases, eligibility for postretirement benefits is an all-or-nothing proposition, while most pension plans provide reduced benefits for relatively short periods of service. The dependency status assumption also may have a more significant effect on postretirement benefit measurements than on pension measurements. Plan provisions that entitle an employee's spouse and other dependents to health care and other welfare benefits may substantially increase an employer's cost and obligation for postretirement benefits. [FAS106, ¶194]

.125 Postretirement benefit measurements are more sensitive to assumptions about retirement ages and the probability of retiring at each age than are pension measurements. For example, employer-provided postretirement health care benefits are significantly more expensive before Medicare coverage begins than after. Many pension arrangements provide for an actuarially reduced pension benefit for employees retiring before the normal retirement age; however, for an employee retiring early, there typically is no reduction in the postretirement benefit levels, and those benefits will be paid over a longer period of time and at a higher annual cost to the employer than if the employee retired at the normal retirement age. Similarly, postretirement benefit measurements are more sensitive than pension measurements to the life expectancy assumption. In particular, health care benefits are sensitive to that assumption because health care costs generally increase with age. [FAS106, ¶195]

.126 Assumed discount rates shall reflect the time value of money as of the **measurement date** in determining the present value of future cash outflows currently expected to be required to satisfy the postretirement benefit obligation. In making that assumption, employers shall look to rates of return on high-quality fixed-income investments currently available whose cash flows match the timing and amount of expected benefit payments.[14] If settlement of the obligation with third-party insurers is possible (for example, the purchase of nonparticipating life insurance contracts to provide death benefits), the interest rates inherent in the amount at which the postretirement benefit obligation could be settled are relevant in determining the assumed discount rates. Assumed discount rates are used in measurements of the expected and accumulated postretirement benefit obligations and the service cost and interest cost components of net periodic postretirement benefit cost. [FAS106, ¶31]

.127 The **expected long-term rate of return on plan assets** shall reflect the average rate of earnings expected on the existing assets that qualify as **plan assets** and contributions to the plan expected to be made during the period. In estimating that rate, appropriate consideration shall be given to the returns being earned on the plan assets currently invested and the rates of return expected to be available for reinvestment. If the return on plan assets is taxable to the trust or other fund under the plan, the expected long-term rate of return shall be reduced to reflect the related income taxes expected to be paid under existing law. The expected long-term rate of return on plan assets is used with the **market-related value of plan assets** to compute the **expected return on plan assets**. (Refer to paragraph .152.) There is no assumption of an expected long-term rate of return on plan assets for plans that are unfunded or that have no assets that qualify as plan assets pursuant to this section. [FAS106, ¶32]

.128 The service cost component of net periodic postretirement benefit cost and the expected and accumulated postretirement benefit obligations shall reflect future compensation levels to the extent the postretirement benefit formula defines the benefits wholly or partially as a function of future compensation levels.[15] For pay-related plans, assumed compensation levels shall reflect the best estimate of the actual future compensation levels of the individual employees involved, including future changes attributed to general price levels, productivity, seniority, promotion, and other factors. All assumptions shall be consistent to the extent that each reflects expectations about the same fu-

---

[14]The objective of selecting assumed discount rates is to measure the single amount that, if invested at the measurement date in a portfolio of high-quality debt instruments, would provide the necessary future cash flows to pay the accumulated benefits when due. Notionally, that single amount, the accumulated postretirement benefit obligation, would equal the current market value of a portfolio of high-quality zero coupon bonds whose maturity dates and amounts would be the same as the timing and amount of the expected future benefit payments. Because cash inflows would equal cash outflows in timing and amount, there would be no reinvestment risk in the yields to maturity of the portfolio. However, in other than a zero coupon portfolio, such as a portfolio of long-term debt instruments that pay semiannual interest payments or whose maturities do not extend far enough into the future to meet expected benefit payments, the assumed discount rates (the yield to maturity) need to incorporate expected reinvestment rates available in the future. Those rates should be extrapolated from the existing yield curve at the measurement date. Assumed discount rates should be reevaluated at each measurement date. If the general level of interest rates rises or declines, the assumed discount rates should change in a similar manner. [FAS106, ¶186]

[15]For pay-related plans, salary progression is included in measuring the expected postretirement benefit obligation. For example, a postretirement health care plan may define the deductible amount or copayment, or a postretirement life insurance plan may define the amount of death benefit, based on the employee's average or final level of annual compensation. [FAS106, ¶33, fn12]

ture economic conditions, such as future rates of inflation. Measuring service cost and the expected and accumulated postretirement benefit obligations based on estimated future compensation levels entails considering any indirect effects, such as benefit limitations, that would affect benefits provided by the plan.[16] [FAS106, ¶33]

Assumptions Unique to Postretirement Health Care Benefits

.129 Measurement of an employer's postretirement health care obligation requires the use of several assumptions unique to health care benefits. Most significantly, it includes several assumptions about factors that will affect the amount and timing of future benefit payments for postretirement health care. Those factors include consideration of historical per capita claims cost by age, health care cost trend rates (for plans that provide a benefit in kind), and medical coverage to be paid by governmental authorities and other providers of health care benefits. [FAS106, ¶34]

.130 In principle, an employer's share of the expected future postretirement health care cost for a plan participant is developed by reducing the **assumed per capita claims cost** at each age at which the plan participant is expected to receive benefits under the plan by (a) the effects of coverage by Medicare and other providers of health care benefits, and (b) the effects of the cost-sharing provisions of the plan (deductibles, copayment provisions, out-of-pocket limitations, caps on the limits of the employer-provided payments, and retiree contributions).[17] The resulting amount represents the assumed **net incurred claims cost** at each age at which the plan participant is expected to receive benefits under the plan. If contributions are required to be paid by active plan participants toward their postretirement health care benefits, the actuarial present value of the plan participants' future contributions reduces the actuarial present value of the aggregate assumed net incurred claims costs. [FAS106, ¶35]

.131 The assumed per capita claims cost by age is the annual per capita cost, for periods after the measurement date, of providing the postretirement health care benefits covered by the plan from the earliest age at which an individual could begin to receive benefits under the plan through the remainder of the individual's life or the covered

---

[16]For example, a plan may define the maximum benefit to be provided under the plan (a fixed cap). In measuring the expected postretirement benefit obligation under that plan, the projected benefit payments would be limited to that cap. For a plan that automatically adjusts the maximum benefit to be provided under the plan for the effects of inflation (an adjustable cap), the expected postretirement benefit obligation would be measured based on adjustments to that cap consistent with the assumed inflation rate reflected in other inflation-related assumptions. [FAS106, ¶33, fn13]

[17]In some cases, retiree contributions are established based on the average per capita cost of benefit coverage under an employer's health care plan that provides coverage to both active employees and retirees. However, the medical cost of the retirees may cause the average per capita cost of benefit coverage under the plan to be higher than it would be if only active employees were covered by the plan. In that case, the employer has a postretirement benefit obligation for the portion of the expected future cost of the retiree health care benefits that are not recovered through retiree contributions, Medicare, or other providers of health care benefits. [FAS106, ¶35, fn14]

period, if shorter. The assumed per capita claims cost shall be the best estimate of the expected future cost of the benefits covered by the plan.[18] It may be appropriate to consider other factors in addition to age, such as sex and geographical location, in developing the assumed per capita claims cost. [FAS106, ¶36]

.132 Past and present claims data for the plan, such as a historical pattern of gross claims by age (claims curve), shall be used in developing the current per capita claims cost to the extent that those data are considered to be indicative of the current cost of providing the benefits covered by the plan. Those current claims data shall be adjusted by the assumed health care cost trend rate. The resulting assumed per capita claims cost by age, together with the **plan demographics**, determines the amount and timing of expected future **gross eligible charges**. [FAS106, ¶37]

.133 In the absence of sufficiently reliable plan data about the current cost of the benefits covered by the plan, the current per capita claims cost shall be based, entirely or in part, on the claims information of other employers to the extent those costs are indicative of the current cost of providing the benefits covered by the plan. For example, the current per capita claims cost may be based on the claims experience of other employers [FAS106, ¶38] in the same industry or geographical location [FAS106, ¶197] derived from information in data files developed by insurance companies, actuarial firms, or employee benefits consulting firms. [FAS106, ¶38] National or regional statistics about claims cost patterns also may provide information that may be used for developing the per capita claims cost by age. [FAS106, ¶197] The current per capita claims cost developed on those bases shall be adjusted to best reflect the terms of the employer's plan and the plan demographics. For example, the information shall be adjusted, as necessary, for differing demographics, such as the age and sex of plan participants, health care utilization patterns by men and women at various ages, and the expected geographical location of retirees and their dependents, and for significant differences between the nature and types of benefits covered by the employer's plan and those encompassed by the underlying data. [FAS106, ¶38]

.134 The assumption about health care cost trend rates represents the expected annual rates of change in the cost of health care benefits currently provided by the postretirement benefit plan, due to factors other than changes in the demographics of the plan participants, for each year from the measurement date until the end of the period in which benefits are expected to be paid. Past and current health care cost trends shall be used in developing an employer's assumed health care cost trend rates, which implicitly consider estimates of health care inflation, changes in health care utilization or delivery patterns, technological advances, and changes in the health status of plan

---

[18]If significant, the internal and external costs directly associated with administering the postretirement benefit plan also shall be accrued as a component of assumed per capita claims cost. [FAS106, ¶36, fn15]

participants.[19] Differing services, such as hospital care and dental care, may require the use of different health care cost trend rates. It is appropriate for that assumption to reflect changes in health care cost trend rates over time. For example, the health care cost trend rates may be assumed to continue at the present level for the near term, or increase for a period of time, and then grade down over time to an estimated health care cost trend rate ultimately expected to prevail. [FAS106, ¶39]

.135 Certain medical claims may be covered by governmental programs under existing law or by other providers of health care benefits.[20] Benefit coverage by those governmental programs shall be assumed to continue as provided by the present law and by other providers pursuant to their present plans. Presently enacted changes in the law or amendments of the plans of other health care providers that take effect in future periods and that will affect the future level of their benefit coverage shall be considered in current-period measurements for benefits expected to be provided in those future periods. Future changes in laws concerning medical costs covered by governmental programs and future changes in the plans of other providers shall not be anticipated. [FAS106, ¶40]

.136 In some cases, determining the assumed per capita claims cost by age as described in paragraphs .131 through .133 may not be practical because credible historical information about the gross per capita cost of covered benefits may not be available or determinable to satisfy the stated measurement approach. However, credible historical information about **incurred claims costs** may be available. In those cases, an alternative method of developing the assumed per capita claims cost may be used provided the method results in a measure that is the best estimate of the expected future cost of the benefits covered by the plan. For example, the assumed health care cost trend rates may be determined by adjusting the expected change in the employer's share of per capita incurred claims cost by age by a factor that reflects the effects of the plan's cost-sharing provisions. However, an approach that projects net incurred claims costs using unadjusted assumed health care cost trend rates would implicitly assume changes in the plan's cost-sharing provisions at those assumed rates and, therefore, is not acceptable unless the plan's cost-sharing provisions are indexed in that manner or the substantive plan (refer to paragraphs .117 through .119) operates in that manner. [FAS106, ¶41]

---

[19]An assumption about changes in the health status of plan participants considers, for example, the probability that certain claims costs will be incurred based on expectations of future events, such as the likelihood that some retirees will incur claims requiring technology currently being developed or that historical claims experience for certain medical needs may be reduced as a result of participation in a wellness program. [FAS106, ¶39, fn16]

[20]For example, a retiree's spouse also may be covered by the spouse's present (or former) employer's health care plan. In that case, the spouse's employer (or former employer) may provide either primary or secondary postretirement health care benefits to the retiree's spouse or dependents. [FAS106, ¶40, fn17]

.137 Assumed discount rates include an inflationary element that reflects the expected general rate of inflation. Assumed compensation levels include consideration of future changes attributable to general price levels. Similarly, assumed health care cost trend rates include an element that reflects expected general rates of inflation for the economy overall and an element that reflects price changes of health care costs in particular. To the extent that those assumptions consider similar inflationary effects, the assumptions about those effects shall be consistent. [FAS106, ¶42]

Attribution[21]

.138 An equal amount of the expected postretirement benefit obligation for an employee generally shall be attributed to each year of service in the **attribution period** (a benefit/years-of-service approach). However, some plans may have benefit formulas that attribute a disproportionate share of the expected postretirement benefit obligation to employees' early years of service. For that type of plan, the expected postretirement benefit obligation shall be attributed in accordance with the plan's benefit formula. [FAS106, ¶43] [Refer to illustrations in paragraphs .223 and .224.]

.139 The beginning of the attribution period generally shall be the date of hire. However, if the plan's benefit formula grants credit only for service from a later date and that **credited service period** is not nominal in relation to employees' total years of service prior to their full eligibility dates, the expected postretirement benefit obligation shall be attributed from the beginning of that credited service period. In all cases, the end of the attribution period[22] shall be the full eligibility date.[23] (Paragraphs .221 through .224 illustrate the attribution provisions of this section.) [FAS106, ¶44]

Recognition of Net Periodic Postretirement Benefit Cost

.140 As with other forms of deferred compensation, the cost of providing postretirement benefits shall be attributed to the periods of employee service rendered in exchange for those future benefits pursuant to the terms of the plan. That cost notionally represents the change in the **unfunded accumulated postretirement benefit obligation** for the period, ignoring employer contributions to the plan, plan settlements, and payments made by the employer directly to retirees. However, changes in that unfunded obligation that arise from experience gains and losses and the effects of

---

[21]Attribution is the process of assigning the expected cost of benefits to periods of employee service. The general objective is to assign to each year of service the cost of benefits earned or assumed to have been earned in that year. [FAS106, ¶200]

[22]Accrual of an obligation over the period of employee service rendered in exchange for that benefit is applicable to all forms of compensation. [FAS106, ¶135]

[23]For postretirement benefit plans that are pay-related or that otherwise index benefits during employees' service periods to their retirement date, the full eligibility date and retirement date generally will be the same. The attribution period for those benefits will differ from the attribution period for a similarly defined pension benefit with a capped credited service period. [FAS106, ¶227]

changes in assumptions may be recognized as a component of net periodic postretirement benefit cost on a delayed basis. In addition, the effects of a plan initiation or amendment generally are recognized on a delayed basis. [FAS106, ¶45]

.141 The following components shall be included in the net postretirement benefit cost recognized for a period by an employer sponsoring a defined benefit postretirement plan:

a. Service cost (refer to paragraph .142)
b. Interest cost (refer to paragraph .143)
c. Actual return on plan assets, if any (refer to paragraph .144)
d. Amortization of unrecognized prior service cost, if any (refer to paragraphs .145 through .150)
e. **Gain or loss** (including the effects of changes in assumptions) to the extent recognized (refer to paragraphs .151 through .157)
f. Amortization of the unrecognized obligation or asset existing at the date of initial application of this section,[24] hereinafter referred to as the **unrecognized transition obligation**[25] or **unrecognized transition asset**. [FAS106, ¶46] [There is a constraint on delayed recognition of a transition obligation. (Refer to paragraphs .200 and .201.)]

Service Cost

.142 The service cost component recognized in a period shall be determined as the portion of the expected postretirement benefit obligation attributed to employee service during that period. The measurement of the service cost component requires identification of the substantive plan and the use of assumptions and an attribution method, which are discussed in paragraphs .116 through .139. [FAS106, ¶47]

Interest Cost

.143 The interest cost component recognized in a period shall be determined as the increase in the accumulated postretirement benefit obligation to recognize the effects

---

[24]For a defined benefit plan, an employer shall determine as of the measurement date (paragraph .167) for the beginning of the fiscal year in which this section is first applied (the transition date), the amounts of (a) the accumulated postretirement benefit obligation and (b) the fair value of plan assets plus any recognized accrued postretirement benefit cost or less any recognized prepaid postretirement benefit cost. The difference between those two amounts, whether it represents a transition obligation or a transition asset, may be recognized either immediately in net income of the period of the change as the effect of a change in accounting principle, or on a delayed basis as a component of net periodic postretirement benefit cost. [FAS106, ¶110] [(Refer to Appendix C, "Effective Dates of Pronouncements," for illustrations of the determination of the transition amount and the timing of the recognition of the transition obligation.)]

[25]Amortization of the unrecognized transition obligation or asset will be adjusted prospectively to recognize the effects of (a) a negative plan amendment pursuant to paragraph .150, (b) a constraint on immediate recognition of a net gain or loss pursuant to paragraph .155, (c) settlement accounting pursuant to paragraphs .184 and .185, (d) plan curtailment accounting pursuant to paragraphs .189 through .191, and (e) a constraint on delayed recognition of the unrecognized transition obligation pursuant to paragraph .200. [FAS106, ¶46, fn18]

of the passage of time. Measuring the accumulated postretirement benefit obligation as a present value requires accrual of an interest cost at rates equal to the assumed discount rates. [FAS106, ¶48]

Actual Return on Plan Assets

.144 For a funded plan, the actual return on plan assets shall be determined based on the **fair value** of plan assets (refer to paragraphs .160 and .161) at the beginning and end of the period, adjusted for contributions and benefit payments. If the fund holding the plan assets is a taxable enterprise,[26] the actual return on plan assets shall reflect the tax expense or benefit for the period determined in accordance with generally accepted accounting principles. Otherwise, no provision for taxes shall be included in the actual return on plan assets. [FAS106, ¶49]

Prior Service Cost

.145 Plan amendments (including initiation of a plan) may include provisions that attribute the increase or reduction in benefits to employee service rendered in prior periods or only to employee service to be rendered in future periods. For purposes of measuring the accumulated postretirement benefit obligation, the effect of a plan amendment on a plan participant's expected postretirement benefit obligation shall be attributed to each year of service in that plan participant's attribution period, including years of service already rendered by that plan participant, in accordance with the attribution of the expected postretirement benefit obligation to years of service as discussed in paragraphs .138 and .139. [FAS106, ¶50] If an employer amends the benefits to be provided by the plan, the effect of the amendment is recognized immediately in measuring the employer's expected and accumulated postretirement benefit obligations, even if the effective date of the change in benefits is delayed until a specified date in the future. [FAS106, ¶174] If a plan is initiated that grants benefits solely in exchange for employee service after the date of the plan initiation or a future date, no portion of the expected postretirement benefit obligation is attributed to prior service periods because, in that case, the credited service period for the current employees who are expected to receive benefits under the plan begins at the date of the plan initiation or the future date. [FAS106, ¶50]

---

[26]Unlike most pension plans, the return on postretirement benefit plan assets may be subject to income tax because of the lack of tax-exempt vehicles for funding those benefits. At present, even if postretirement benefit plan assets are restricted and segregated within a trust, the income generated by those assets generally is taxable. If the plan has taxable income, the assessed tax will reduce the returns available for payment of benefits or reinvestment. When the trust or other entity holding the plan assets is taxed as a separate entity on the return on *plan assets* (as defined herein), the expected long-term rate of return should be·determined by giving consideration to anticipated income taxes under enacted tax law. However, if the tax on income generated by plan assets is not a liability of the plan, but of the employer, the expected long-term rate of return should not anticipate a tax on those earnings, because that tax will be reflected in the employer's accounting for income taxes. [FAS106, ¶295]

.146 Plan amendments that improve benefits are granted with the expectation that the employer will realize economic benefits in future periods. Consequently, except as discussed in paragraph .149, this section does not permit the cost of benefit improvements (that is, prior service cost) to be included in net periodic postretirement benefit cost entirely in the year of the amendment. Rather, paragraph .147 provides for recognition of prior service cost arising from benefit improvements during the remaining years of service to the full eligibility dates of those plan participants active at the date of the plan amendment. (Refer to paragraph .150 for plan amendments that reduce benefits.) [FAS106, ¶51]

.147 The cost of benefit improvements (including improved benefits that are granted to **fully eligible plan participants**) is the increase in the accumulated postretirement benefit obligation as a result of the plan amendment, measured at the date of the amendment. Except as specified in the next sentence and in paragraphs .148 and .149, that prior service cost shall be amortized by assigning an equal amount to each remaining year of service to the full eligibility date of each plan participant active at the date of the amendment who was not yet fully eligible for benefits at that date. If all or almost all of a plan's participants are fully eligible for benefits, the prior service cost shall be amortized based on the remaining life expectancy of those plan participants rather than on the remaining years of service to the full eligibility dates of the active plan participants. [FAS106, ¶52]

.148 To reduce the complexity and detail of the computations required, consistent use of an alternative amortization approach that more rapidly reduces unrecognized prior service cost is permitted. For example, a straight-line amortization of the cost over the average remaining years of service to full eligibility for benefits of the active plan participants is acceptable. [FAS106, ¶53]

.149 In some situations, a history of regular plan amendments and other evidence may indicate that the period during which the employer expects to realize economic benefits from an amendment that grants increased benefits is shorter than the remaining years of service to full eligibility for benefits of the active plan participants. Identification of those situations requires an assessment of the individual circumstances of the particular plan. In those circumstances, the amortization of prior service cost shall be accelerated to reflect the more rapid expiration of the employer's economic benefits and to recognize the cost in the periods benefited. [FAS106, ¶54]

.150 A plan amendment can reduce, rather than increase, the accumulated postretirement benefit obligation. A reduction in that obligation shall be used first to reduce any existing unrecognized prior service cost, then to reduce any remaining unrecognized transition obligation. The excess, if any, shall be amortized on the same basis as specified in paragraph .147 for prior service cost. Immediate recognition of the excess is not permitted. [FAS106, ¶55]

Gains and Losses

.151 Gains and losses are changes in the amount of either the accumulated postretirement benefit obligation or plan assets resulting from experience different from that assumed or from changes in assumptions. This section generally does not distinguish between those sources of gains and losses. Gains and losses include amounts that have been realized, for example, by the sale of a security, as well as amounts that are unrealized. Because gains and losses may reflect refinements in estimates as well as real changes in economic values and because some gains in one period may be offset by losses in another or vice versa, this section does not require recognition of gains and losses as components of net postretirement benefit cost in the period in which they arise, except as described in paragraph .156. (Gain and loss recognition in accounting for settlements and curtailments is addressed in paragraphs .182 through .191.) [FAS106, ¶56]

.152 The expected return on plan assets shall be determined based on the expected long-term rate of return on plan assets (refer to paragraph .127) and the market-related value of plan assets. The market-related value of plan assets shall be either fair value or a calculated value that recognizes changes in fair value in a systematic and rational manner over not more than five years. Different methods of calculating market-related value may be used for different classes of assets (for example, an employer might use fair value for bonds and a five-year-moving-average value for equities), but the manner of determining market-related value shall be applied consistently from year to year for each class of plan assets. [FAS106, ¶57]

.153 Plan asset gains and losses are differences between the actual return on plan assets during a period and the expected return on plan assets for that period. Plan asset gains and losses include both (a) changes reflected in the market-related value of plan assets and (b) changes not yet reflected in the market-related value of plan assets (that is, the difference between the fair value and the market-related value of plan assets). Plan asset gains and losses not yet reflected in market-related value are not required to be amortized under paragraphs .154 and .155. [FAS106, ¶58]

.154 As a minimum, amortization of an **unrecognized net gain or loss** (excluding plan asset gains and losses not yet reflected in market-related value) shall be included as a component of net postretirement benefit cost for a year if, as of the beginning of the year, that unrecognized net gain or loss exceeds 10 percent of the greater of the accumulated postretirement benefit obligation or the market-related value of plan assets. If amortization is required, the minimum amortization[27] shall be that excess divided by the average remaining service period of active plan participants. If all or almost all of a plan's participants are inactive, the average remaining life expectancy of the inactive participants shall be used instead of the average remaining service period. [FAS106, ¶59]

---

[27] The amortization must always reduce the beginning-of-the-year balance. Amortization of an unrecognized net gain results in a decrease in net periodic postretirement benefit cost; amortization of an unrecognized net loss results in an increase in net periodic postretirement benefit cost. [FAS106, ¶59, fn19]

.155 Any systematic method of amortization of unrecognized gains and losses may be used in place of the minimum amortization specified in paragraph .154 provided that (a) the minimum amortization is recognized in any period in which it is greater (reduces the unrecognized amount by more) than the amount that would be recognized under the method used, (b) the method is applied consistently, (c) the method is applied similarly to both gains and losses, and (d) the method used is disclosed. If an enterprise uses a method of consistently recognizing gains and losses immediately, any gain that does not offset a loss previously recognized in income pursuant to this paragraph shall first offset any unrecognized transition obligation; any loss that does not offset a gain previously recognized in income pursuant to this paragraph shall first offset any unrecognized transition asset. [FAS106, ¶60]

.156 In some situations, an employer may forgive a retrospective adjustment of the current or past years' cost-sharing provisions of the plan as they relate to benefit costs *already incurred* by retirees[28] or may otherwise deviate from the provisions of the substantive plan to increase or decrease the employer's share of the benefit costs *incurred in the current or past periods*. The effect of a decision to temporarily deviate from the substantive plan shall be immediately recognized as a loss or gain. [FAS106, ¶61]

.157 The gain or loss component of net periodic postretirement benefit cost shall consist of (a) the difference between the actual return on plan assets and the expected return on plan assets, (b) any gain or loss immediately recognized or the amortization of the unrecognized net gain or loss from previous periods, and (c) any amount immediately recognized as a gain or loss pursuant to paragraph .156. [FAS106, ¶62]

Measurement of Plan Assets

.158 Plan assets are assets—usually stocks, bonds, and other investments (except certain **insurance contracts** as noted in paragraph .162)—that have been segregated and restricted (usually in a trust) to be used for postretirement benefits. [FAS106, ¶63] Whether certain funding vehicles can be restricted solely for the provision of postretirement benefits, as opposed to funding both active employees' and retirees' benefits (and therefore, qualify as plan assets) is subject to legal, not accounting, interpretation. [FAS106, ¶308] The amount of plan assets includes amounts contributed by the employer, and by plan participants for a contributory plan, and amounts earned from investing the contributions, less benefits, income taxes, and other expenses incurred. Plan assets ordinarily cannot be withdrawn by the employer except under certain cir-

---

[28]For example, the terms of a substantive postretirement health care plan may provide that any shortfall resulting from current year benefit payments in excess of the employer's stated share of incurred claims cost and retiree contributions for that year is to be recovered from increased retiree contributions in the subsequent year. The employer may subsequently determine that increasing retiree contributions for the shortfall in the prior year would be onerous and make a decision to bear the cost of the shortfall for that year. The employer's decision to bear the shortfall represents a change in intent and the resulting loss shall be recognized immediately. Future decisions by the employer to continue to bear the shortfall suggest an amendment of the substantive plan that shall be accounted for as described in paragraphs .145 through .150. [FAS106, ¶61, fn20]

cumstances when a plan has assets in excess of obligations and the employer has taken certain steps to satisfy existing obligations. Securities of the employer held by the plan are includable in plan assets provided they are transferable. [FAS106, ¶63]

.159 Assets not segregated in a trust, or otherwise effectively restricted, so that they cannot be used by the employer for other purposes are not plan assets for purposes of this section, even though the employer may intend that those assets be used to provide postretirement benefits. Those assets shall be accounted for in the same manner as other employer assets of a similar nature and with similar restrictions. Amounts accrued by the employer but not yet paid to the plan are not plan assets for purposes of this section. [FAS106, ¶64]

.160 For purposes of the disclosures required by paragraph .169, plan investments, whether equity or debt securities, real estate, or other, shall be measured at their fair value as of the measurement date. The fair value of an investment is the amount that the plan could reasonably expect to receive for it in a current sale between a willing buyer and a willing seller, that is, other than in a forced or liquidation sale. Fair value shall be measured by the market price if an active market exists for the investment. If no active market exists for an investment but an active market exists for similar investments, selling prices in that market may be helpful in estimating fair value. If a market price is not available, a forecast of expected cash flows may aid in estimating fair value, provided the expected cash flows are discounted at a current rate commensurate with the risk involved.[29] (Refer to paragraph .166.) [FAS106, ¶65]

.161 Plan assets used in plan operations (for example, buildings, equipment, furniture and fixtures, and leasehold improvements) shall be measured at cost less accumulated depreciation or amortization for all purposes. [FAS106, ¶66]

Insurance Contracts

.162 For purposes of this section, an insurance contract is defined as a contract in which an insurance company unconditionally undertakes a legal obligation to provide specified benefits to specific individuals in return for a fixed consideration or premium; an insurance contract is irrevocable and involves the transfer of significant risk from the employer (or the plan) to the insurance company.[30] Benefits covered by in-

---

[29]For an indication of factors to be considered in determining the discount rate, refer to Section I69, "Interest: Imputation of an Interest Cost," paragraphs .106 and .107. If significant, the fair value of an investment shall reflect the brokerage commissions and other costs normally incurred in a sale. [FAS106, ¶65, fn21]

[30]If the insurance company providing the contract does business primarily with the employer and related parties (a **captive insurer**) or if there is any reasonable doubt that the insurance company will meet its obligations under the contract, the contract is not an insurance contract for purposes of this section. [FAS106, ¶67, fn22]

surance contracts shall be excluded from the accumulated postretirement benefit obligation. Insurance contracts shall be excluded from plan assets, except as provided in paragraph .164 for the cost of **participation rights**. [FAS106, ¶67]

.163 Some insurance contracts (**participating insurance contracts**) provide that the purchaser (either the plan or the employer) may participate in the [FAS106, ¶68] investment performance or [FAS106, ¶367] experience of the insurance company. Under those contracts, [FAS106, ¶68] if the insurance company has favorable experience, [FAS106, ¶367] the insurance company ordinarily pays dividends to the purchaser, the effect of which is to reduce the cost of the plan. [FAS106, ¶68] For example, if the insurance company's investment return is better than anticipated, or perhaps if actual experience related to mortality or other assumptions is favorable, the purchaser will receive dividends that reduce the cost of the contract. [FAS106, ¶367] If the participating insurance contract causes the employer to remain subject to all or most of the risks and rewards associated with the benefit obligation covered or the assets transferred to the insurance company, that contract is not an insurance contract for purposes of this section, and the purchase of that contract does not constitute a settlement pursuant to paragraphs .182 through .187. [FAS106, ¶68]

.164 The purchase price of a participating insurance contract ordinarily is higher than the price of an equivalent contract without a participation right. The difference is the cost of the participation right. The cost of the participation right shall be recognized at the date of purchase as an asset. In subsequent periods, the participation right shall be measured at its fair value if the contract is such that fair value is reasonably estimable. Otherwise the participation right shall be measured at its amortized cost (not in excess of its net realizable value), and the cost shall be amortized systematically over the expected dividend period under the contract. [FAS106, ¶69]

.165 To the extent that insurance contracts are purchased during the period to cover postretirement benefits attributed to service in the current period (such as life insurance benefits), the cost of those benefits shall be the cost of purchasing the coverage under the contracts, except as provided in paragraph .164 for the cost of a participation right. If all the postretirement benefits attributed to service in the current period are covered by **nonparticipating insurance contracts** purchased during that period, the cost of the contracts determines the service cost component of net postretirement benefit cost for that period. Benefits attributed to current service in excess of benefits provided by nonparticipating insurance contracts purchased during the current period shall be accounted for according to the provisions of this section applicable to plans not involving insurance contracts. [FAS106, ¶70]

.166 Other contracts with insurance companies may not meet the definition of an insurance contract because the insurance company does not unconditionally undertake a legal obligation to provide specified benefits to specified individuals. Those contracts shall be accounted for as investments and measured at fair value. If a contract has a determinable cash surrender value or conversion value, that is presumed to be its fair value. For some contracts, the best available estimate of fair value may be contract value. [FAS106, ¶71]

Measurement Date

.167 The measurements of *plan assets and obligations* required by this section shall be as of the date of the financial statements or, if used consistently from year to year, as of a date not more than three months prior to that date. Even though the postretirement benefit measurements are required as of a particular date, all procedures are not required to be performed after that date. As with other financial statement items requiring estimates, much of the information can be prepared as of an earlier date and projected forward to account for subsequent events (for example, employee service). [FAS106, ¶72]

.168 Measurements of *net periodic postretirement benefit cost* for both interim and annual financial statements generally shall be based on the assumptions at the beginning of the year (assumptions used for the previous year-end measurements of plan assets and obligations) unless more recent measurements of both plan assets and the accumulated postretirement benefit obligation are available. For example, if a significant event occurs, such as a plan amendment, settlement, or curtailment, that ordinarily would call for remeasurement, the assumptions used for those later measurements shall be used to remeasure net periodic postretirement benefit cost from the date of the event to the year-end measurement date. [FAS106, ¶73]

Disclosures

.169 This section requires disclosures about an employer's obligation to provide postretirement benefits and the cost of providing those benefits that are intended to enhance the usefulness of the financial statements to investors, creditors, and other users of financial information. An employer sponsoring one or more defined benefit postretirement plans (refer to paragraphs .172 and .173) shall disclose, if applicable, the following information about those plans:

a. A description of the substantive plan(s) that is the basis for the accounting (refer to paragraphs .116 through .121), including the nature of the plan, any modifications of the existing cost-sharing provisions that are encompassed by the substantive plan(s) (refer to paragraphs .117 and .118), and the existence and nature of any commitment to increase monetary benefits provided by the postretirement benefit plan (refer to paragraph .119), employee groups covered, types of benefits provided, **funding policy**, types of assets held and significant nonbenefit liabilities, and the nature and effect of significant matters affecting the comparability of information for all periods presented, such as the effect of a business combination or divestiture

b. The amount of net periodic postretirement benefit cost showing separately the service cost component, the interest cost component, the actual return on plan assets for the period, amortization of the unrecognized transition obligation or transition asset, and the net total of other components[31]

c. A schedule reconciling the funded status of the plan(s) with amounts reported in the employer's statement of financial position, showing separately:

   (1) The fair value of plan assets

   (2) The accumulated postretirement benefit obligation, identifying separately the portion attributable to retirees, other fully eligible plan participants, and other active plan participants

   (3) The amount of unrecognized prior service cost

   (4) The amount of unrecognized net gain or loss (including plan asset gains and losses not yet reflected in market-related value)

   (5) The amount of any remaining unrecognized transition obligation or transition asset

   (6) The amount of net postretirement benefit asset or liability recognized in the statement of financial position, which is the net result of combining the preceding five items

d. The assumed health care cost trend rate(s) used to measure the expected cost of benefits covered by the plan (gross eligible charges) for the next year and a general description of the direction and pattern of change in the assumed trend rates thereafter, together with the ultimate trend rate(s) and when that rate is expected to be achieved

e. The weighted-average of the assumed discount rate(s) and rate(s) of compensation increase (for pay-related plans) used to measure the accumulated postretirement benefit obligation and the weighted-average of the expected long-term rate(s) of return on plan assets and, for plans whose income is segregated from the employer's investment income for tax purposes, the estimated income tax rate(s) included in that rate of return

---

[31] The net total of other components is generally the net effect during the period of certain delayed recognition provisions of this section. That net total includes:

a. The net asset gain or loss during the period deferred for later recognition (in effect, an offset or a supplement to the actual return on plan assets)

b. Amortization of unrecognized prior service cost

c. Amortization of the net gain or loss from earlier periods

d. Any gain or loss recognized due to a temporary deviation from the substantive plan (paragraph .156).

[FAS106, ¶74, fn23]

f. The effect of a one-percentage-point increase in the assumed health care cost trend rates for each future year on (1) the aggregate of the service and interest cost components of net periodic postretirement health care benefit cost and (2) the accumulated postretirement benefit obligation for health care benefits[32] (For purposes of this disclosure, all other assumptions shall be held constant and the effects shall be measured based on the substantive plan that is the basis for the accounting.)

g. The amounts and types of securities of the employer and related parties included in plan assets, and the approximate amount of future annual benefits of plan participants covered by insurance contracts issued by the employer and related parties

h. Any alternative amortization method used pursuant to paragraphs .148 or .155

i. The amount of gain or loss recognized during the period for a settlement or curtailment and a description of the nature of the event(s) (Refer to paragraphs .182 through .191.)

j. The cost of providing special or contractual termination benefits recognized during the period and a description of the nature of the event(s). (Refer to paragraphs .193 and .194.) [FAS106, ¶74]

Employers with Two or More Plans

.170 Postretirement benefits offered by an employer may vary in nature and may be provided to different groups of employees. As discussed in paragraph .171, in some cases an employer may aggregate data from unfunded plans for measurement purposes in lieu of performing separate measurements for each unfunded plan (including plans whose designated assets are not appropriately segregated and restricted and thus have no plan assets as that term is used in this section). Net periodic postretirement benefit cost, the accumulated postretirement benefit obligation, and plan assets shall be determined for each separately measured plan or aggregation of plans by applying the provisions of this section to each such plan or aggregation of plans. [FAS106, ¶75]

.171 The data from all unfunded postretirement health care plans may be aggregated for measurement purposes if those plans provide different benefits to the same group of employees. [FAS106, ¶76] For example, an employer may have separate medical care, dental care, and eye care plans that provide benefit coverage to all retirees of the company. Similarly, an employer may combine two or more unfunded plans [if those plans] provide the same benefits to different groups of plan participants. For example, an employer may have identical postretirement medical care plans at each of its operating locations. This section permits combining plans in those situations because the differences in the plans are not substantive. Combining information in those cases results in combined measurements for accounting and disclosure purposes. [FAS106, ¶357] Data from other unfunded postretirement welfare benefit plans may be aggre-

---

[32]Measuring the sensitivity of the accumulated postretirement benefit obligation and the combined service and interest cost components to a change in the assumed health care cost trend rates requires remeasuring the accumulated postretirement benefit obligation as of the beginning and end of the year. [FAS106, ¶354]

gated for measurement purposes in similar circumstances, such as when an employer has a variety of welfare benefit plans that provide benefits to the same group of employees. However, a plan that has plan assets (as defined herein) shall not be aggregated with other plans but shall be measured separately. [FAS106, ¶76]

.172 Disclosures for plans with plan assets in excess of the accumulated postretirement benefit obligation generally may be aggregated with disclosures for plans that have accumulated postretirement benefit obligations that exceed plan assets. However, for purposes of the disclosures required by paragraph .169(c), the aggregate plan assets and the aggregate accumulated postretirement benefit obligation of the underfunded plans shall be separately disclosed. Otherwise, except as described in paragraph .173, the disclosures required by this section may be aggregated for all of an employer's single-employer defined benefit plans, or plans may be disaggregated in groups to provide more useful information. [FAS106, ¶77]

.173 The disclosures required by this section shall be presented separately for the following:

a. Plans that provide primarily postretirement health care benefits and plans that provide primarily other postretirement welfare benefits if the accumulated postretirement benefit obligation of the latter plans is significant relative to the aggregate accumulated postretirement benefit obligation for all of the plans
b. Plans inside the United States and plans outside the United States if the accumulated postretirement benefit obligation of the latter plans is significant relative to the aggregate accumulated postretirement benefit obligation for all of the plans. [FAS106, ¶78]

Multiemployer Plans

.174 For purposes of this section, a **multiemployer plan** is a postretirement benefit plan to which two or more unrelated employers contribute, usually pursuant to one or more collective-bargaining agreements. A characteristic of multiemployer plans is that assets contributed by one participating employer may be used to provide benefits to employees of other participating employers since assets contributed by an employer are not segregated in a separate account or restricted to provide benefits only to employees of that employer. [FAS106, ¶79]

.175 A multiemployer plan usually is administered by a board of trustees composed of management and labor representatives and may also be referred to as a "joint trust" or "union plan." Generally, many employers participate in a multiemployer plan, and an employer may participate in more than one plan. The employers participating in multiemployer plans usually have a common industry bond, but for some plans the employers are in different industries, and the labor union may be their only common bond. Some multiemployer plans do not involve a union. For example, local chapters of a not-for-profit organization may participate in a plan established by the related national organization. [FAS106, ¶80]

.176 In a multiemployer setting, eligibility for benefits is defined by the plan; retired employees continue to receive benefits whether or not their former employers continue to contribute to the plan. On the other hand, plan participants not yet eligible for benefits may lose accumulated postretirement benefits if their current or former employer withdraws from a plan unless they take or have a job with other employers who participate in the plan. While the plan may have the option of cancelling the accrued service credits that apply toward the required service, within the bargaining unit, of plan participants who were employed by a withdrawing employer and who become or are employed by another participating employer, that rarely occurs because of the difficulty of matching employees to specific employers. For example, in certain industries, an employee may work for more than one employer in a single day and different employers on different days, making it difficult to associate any portion of that employee's past service with a specific employer. [FAS106, ¶377]

.177 An employer participating in a multiemployer plan shall recognize as net postretirement benefit cost the required contribution for the period, which shall include both cash and the fair market value of noncash contributions, and shall recognize as a liability any unpaid contributions required for the period. [FAS106, ¶81]

.178 An employer that participates in one or more multiemployer plans shall disclose the following separately from disclosures for a single-employer plan:

a. A description of the multiemployer plan(s) including the employee groups covered, the type of benefits provided (defined benefits or defined contribution), and the nature and effect of significant matters affecting comparability of information for all periods presented
b. The amount of postretirement benefit cost recognized during the period, if available. Otherwise, the amount of the aggregate required contribution for the period to the general health and welfare benefit plan that provides health and welfare benefits to both active employees and retirees shall be disclosed. [FAS106, ¶82]

.179 In some situations, withdrawal from a multiemployer plan may result in an employer's having an obligation to the plan for a portion of the plan's unfunded accumulated postretirement benefit obligation. If it is either probable or reasonably possible that (a) an employer would withdraw from the plan under circumstances that would give rise to an obligation or (b) an employer's contribution to the fund would be increased during the remainder of the contract period to make up a shortfall in the funds necessary to maintain the negotiated level of benefit coverage (a "maintenance of benefits" clause), the employer shall apply the provisions of Section C59, "Contingencies." [FAS106, ¶83]

Multiple-Employer Plans

.180 Some postretirement benefit plans to which two or more unrelated employers contribute are not multiemployer plans. Rather, those **multiple-employer plans** are in substance aggregations of single-employer plans, combined to allow participating employers to pool plan assets for investment purposes or to reduce the costs of plan administration. Those plans ordinarily do not involve collective-bargaining agreements. They may also have features that allow participating employers to have different benefit formulas, with the employer's contributions to the plan based on the benefit formula selected by the employer. Those plans shall be considered single-employer plans rather than multiemployer plans for purposes of this section, and each employer's accounting shall be based on its respective interest in the plan. [FAS106, ¶84]

Postretirement Benefit Plans outside the United States

.181 Except for [the date this section must be applied, (refer to Appendix C, "Effective Dates of Pronouncements")] this section includes no special provisions applicable to postretirement benefit arrangements outside the United States. Those arrangements are subject to the provisions of this section for purposes of preparing financial statements in accordance with accounting principles generally accepted in the United States. The applicability of this section to those arrangements is determined by the nature of the obligation and by the terms or conditions that define the amount of benefits to be paid, not by whether or how a plan is funded, whether benefits are payable at intervals or as a single amount, or whether the benefits are required by law or custom or are provided under a plan the employer has elected to sponsor. [FAS106, ¶85]

Accounting for Settlement of a Postretirement Benefit Obligation

.182 For purposes of this section, a settlement is defined as a transaction that (a) is an irrevocable action, (b) relieves the employer (or the plan) of primary responsibility for a postretirement benefit obligation, and (c) eliminates significant risks related to the obligation and the assets used to effect the settlement.[33] Examples of transactions that constitute a settlement include making lump-sum cash payments to plan participants in exchange for their rights to receive specified postretirement benefits and purchasing long-term nonparticipating insurance contracts for the accumulated postretirement benefit obligation for some or all of the plan participants. [FAS106, ¶90]

.183 A transaction that does not meet the three criteria of paragraph .182 does not constitute a settlement for purposes of this section. For example, investing in a portfolio of high-quality fixed-income securities with principal and interest payment dates similar to the estimated payment dates of benefits may avoid or minimize certain risks. However, that investment decision does not constitute a settlement because that

---

[33] If an insurance contract is purchased from an insurance company controlled by the employer, the purchase of the contract does not constitute a settlement. [FAS106, ¶90, fn24]

decision can be reversed, and investing in that portfolio does not relieve the employer (or the plan) of primary responsibility for a postretirement benefit obligation nor does it eliminate significant risks related to that obligation. [FAS106, ¶91]

.184 For purposes of this section, the maximum gain or loss subject to recognition in income when a postretirement benefit obligation is settled is the unrecognized net gain or loss defined in paragraphs .151 through .155 plus any remaining unrecognized transition asset. That maximum gain or loss includes any gain or loss resulting from remeasurements of plan assets and the accumulated postretirement benefit obligation at the time of settlement. [FAS106, ¶92]

.185 If the entire accumulated postretirement benefit obligation is settled and the maximum amount subject to recognition is a gain, the settlement gain shall first reduce any remaining unrecognized transition obligation;[34] any excess gain shall be recognized in income.[35] If the entire accumulated postretirement benefit obligation is settled and the maximum amount subject to recognition is a loss, the maximum settlement loss shall be recognized in income. If only part of the accumulated postretirement benefit obligation is settled, the employer shall recognize in income the excess of the pro rata portion (equal to the percentage reduction in the accumulated postretirement benefit obligation) of the maximum settlement gain over any remaining unrecognized transition obligation or a pro rata portion of the maximum settlement loss. [FAS106, ¶93]

.186 If the purchase of a participating insurance contract constitutes a settlement (refer to paragraphs .162 and .182), the maximum gain (but not the maximum loss) shall be reduced by the cost of the participation right before determining the amount to be recognized in income. [FAS106, ¶94]

.187 If the cost of all settlements[36] in a year is less than or equal to the sum of the service cost and interest cost components of net postretirement benefit cost for the plan for the year, gain or loss recognition is permitted but not required for those settlements. However, the accounting policy adopted shall be applied consistently from year to year. [FAS106, ¶95]

---

[34] As discussed in paragraph .200, in measuring the gain or loss subject to recognition in income when a postretirement benefit obligation is settled, it shall first be determined whether recognition of an additional amount of any unrecognized transition obligation is required. [FAS106, ¶93, fn25]

[35] Because the plan is the unit of accounting, the determination of the effects of a settlement considers only the unrecognized net gain or loss and unrecognized transition obligation or asset related to the plan for which all or a portion of the accumulated postretirement benefit obligation is being settled. [FAS106, ¶93, fn26]

[36] For the following types of settlements, the cost of the settlement is:

a. For a cash settlement, the amount of cash paid to plan participants
b. For a settlement using nonparticipating insurance contracts, the cost of the contracts
c. For a settlement using participating insurance contracts, the cost of the contracts less the amount attributed to participation rights. (Refer to paragraphs .163 and .164.) [FAS106, ¶95, fn27]

Accounting for a Plan Curtailment

.188 For purposes of this section, a curtailment is an event that significantly reduces the expected years of future service of active plan participants or eliminates the accrual of defined benefits for some or all of the future services of a significant number of active plan participants. Curtailments include:

a. Termination of employees' services earlier than expected, which may or may not involve closing a facility or discontinuing a segment of a business
b. Termination or suspension of a plan so that employees do not earn additional benefits for future service. In the latter situation, future service may be counted toward eligibility for benefits accumulated based on past service. [FAS106, ¶96]

.189 The unrecognized prior service cost associated with the portion of the future years of service that had been expected to be rendered, but as a result of a curtailment are no longer expected to be rendered, is a loss. For purposes of measuring the effect of a curtailment, unrecognized prior service cost includes the cost of plan amendments and any remaining unrecognized transition obligation. For example, a curtailment may result from the termination of a significant number of employees who were plan participants at the date of a prior plan amendment.[37] The loss associated with that curtailment is measured as (a) the portion of the remaining unrecognized prior service cost related to that (and any prior) plan amendment attributable to the previously expected remaining future years of service of the employees who were terminated and (b) the portion of the remaining unrecognized transition obligation attributable to the previously expected remaining future years of service of the terminated employees who were plan participants at the date of transition. [FAS106, ¶97]

.190 The accumulated postretirement benefit obligation may be decreased (a gain) or increased (a loss) by a curtailment.[38] That (gain) loss shall reduce any unrecognized net loss (gain).

a. To the extent that such a gain exceeds any unrecognized net loss (or the entire gain, if an unrecognized net gain exists), it is a curtailment gain.
b. To the extent that such a loss exceeds any unrecognized net gain (or the entire loss, if an unrecognized net loss exists), it is a curtailment loss.

---

[37]A curtailment also may result from terminating the accrual of additional benefits for the future services of a significant number of employees. The loss in that situation is (a) a proportionate amount of the remaining unrecognized prior service cost based on the portion of the remaining expected years of service in the amortization period that originally was attributable to those employees who were plan participants at the date of the plan amendment and whose future accrual of benefits has been terminated and (b) a proportionate amount of the remaining unrecognized transition obligation based on the portion of the remaining years of service of all participants active at the date of transition that originally was attributable to the remaining expected future years of service of the employees whose future accrual of benefits has been terminated. [FAS106, ¶97, fn28]

[38]Increases in the accumulated postretirement benefit obligation that reflect termination benefits are excluded from the scope of this paragraph. (Refer to paragraphs .193 and .194.) [FAS106, ¶98, fn29]

For purposes of applying the provisions of this paragraph, any remaining unrecognized transition asset shall be treated as an unrecognized net gain and shall be combined with the unrecognized net gain or loss arising subsequent to transition to this section. [FAS106, ¶98]

.191 If the sum of the effects identified in paragraphs .189 and .190 is a net loss, it shall be recognized in income when it is probable that a curtailment will occur and the net effect is reasonably estimable. If the sum of those effects is a net gain, it shall be recognized in income when the related employees terminate or the plan suspension or amendment is adopted. [FAS106, ¶99]

Relationship of Settlements and Curtailments to Other Events

.192 A settlement and a curtailment may occur separately or together. If benefits expected to be paid in future periods are eliminated for some plan participants (for example, because a significant portion of the work force is dismissed or a plant is closed) but the plan remains in existence and continues to pay benefits, to invest assets, and to receive contributions, a curtailment has occurred but not a settlement. If an employer purchases nonparticipating insurance contracts for the accumulated postretirement benefit obligation and continues to provide defined benefits for future service, either in the same plan or in a successor plan, a settlement has occurred but not a curtailment. If a **plan termination** occurs (that is, the obligation is settled and the plan ceases to exist) and the plan is not replaced by a successor defined benefit plan, both a settlement and a curtailment have occurred (whether or not the employees continue to work for the employer). [FAS106, ¶100]

Measurement of the Effects of Termination Benefits

.193 Postretirement benefits offered as special or contractual termination benefits shall be recognized in accordance with paragraph .185 of Section P16.[39] That is, an employer that offers special termination benefits to employees shall recognize a liability and a loss when the employees accept the offer and the amount can be reasonably estimated. An employer that provides contractual termination benefits shall recognize a liability and a loss when it is probable that employees will be entitled to benefits and the amount can be reasonably estimated. A situation involving special or contractual

---

[39]An employer may provide benefits to employees in connection with their termination of employment. They may be either *special termination benefits* offered only for a short period of time or *contractual termination benefits* required by the terms of a plan only if a specified event, such as a plant closing occurs. An employer that offers special termination benefits to employees shall recognize a liability and a loss when the employees accept the offer and the amount can be reasonably estimated. An employer that provides contractual termination benefits shall recognize a liability and a loss when it is probable that employees will be entitled to benefits and the amount can be reasonably estimated. [FAS88, ¶15] Section P16 therefore applies to other benefits in addition to pensions. [This section reiterates] the applicability of Section P16, since practice may have been to exclude postretirement health care costs from the measurement of termination benefits. [FAS106, ¶333]

termination benefits may also result in a curtailment to be accounted for under paragraphs .188 through .191 of this section. [FAS106, ¶101]

.194 The liability and loss recognized for employees who accept an offer of special termination benefits to be provided by a postretirement benefit plan shall be the difference between (a) the accumulated postretirement benefit obligation for those employees, assuming that those employees (active plan participants) not yet fully eligible for benefits would terminate at their full eligibility date and that fully eligible plan participants would retire immediately, without considering any special termination benefits and (b) the accumulated postretirement benefit obligation as measured in (a) adjusted to reflect the special termination benefits. [FAS106, ¶102]

Disposal of a Segment

.195 If the gain or loss measured in accordance with paragraphs .184 through .186, .189 through .191, or .193 and .194 is directly related to disposal of a segment of a business or a portion of a line of business, it shall be included in determining the gain or loss associated with that event. The net gain or loss attributable to the disposal shall be recognized pursuant to the requirements of Section I13, "Income Statement Presentation: Discontinued Operations." [FAS106, ¶103]

Defined Contribution Plans

.196 For purposes of this section, a **defined contribution postretirement plan** is a plan that provides postretirement benefits in return for services rendered, provides *an individual account* for each participant, and has terms that specify how contributions to the individual's account are to be determined rather than the amount of postretirement benefits the individual is to receive.[40] Under a defined contribution plan, the postretirement benefits a plan participant will receive are limited to the amount contributed to the plan participant's account, the returns earned on investments of those contributions, and forfeitures of other plan participants' benefits that may be allocated to the plan participant's account. [FAS106, ¶104] The employer's present obligation under the terms of [a defined contribution] plan is fully satisfied when the contribution for the period is made, provided that costs (defined contributions) are not being deferred and recognized in periods after the related service period of the individual to whose account the contributions are to be made. [FAS106, ¶382]

---

[40]For example, an employer may establish individual postretirement health care accounts for each employee, each year contributing a specified amount to each active employee's account. The balance in each employee's account may be used by that employee after the employee's retirement to purchase health care insurance or for other health care benefits. Rather than providing for defined health care benefits, the employer is providing a defined amount of money that may be used by retirees toward the payment of their health care costs. [FAS106, ¶104, fn30]

.197 To the extent a plan's defined contributions to an individual's account are to be made for periods in which that individual renders services, the net postretirement benefit cost for a period shall be the contribution called for in that period. If a plan calls for contributions for periods after an individual retires or terminates, the estimated cost shall be accrued during the employee's service period. [FAS106, ¶105]

.198 An employer that sponsors one or more defined contribution plans shall disclose the following separately from its defined benefit plan disclosures:

a. A description of the plan(s) including employee groups covered, the basis for determining contributions, and the nature and effect of significant matters affecting comparability of information for all periods presented
b. The amount of cost recognized during the period. [FAS106, ¶106]

.199 A postretirement benefit plan having characteristics of both a defined benefit plan and a defined contribution plan requires careful analysis. If the *substance* of the plan is to provide a defined benefit, as may be the case with some "target benefit" plans, the accounting and disclosure requirements shall be determined in accordance with the provisions of this section applicable to a defined benefit plan. [FAS106, ¶107]

Amortization of Transition Obligation

.200 Amortization of the transition obligation shall be accelerated if the cumulative benefit payments subsequent to the transition date to all plan participants exceed the cumulative postretirement benefit cost accrued subsequent to the transition date. In that situation, an additional amount of the unrecognized transition obligation shall be recognized equal to the excess cumulative benefit payments. For purposes of applying this provision, cumulative benefit payments shall be reduced by any plan assets or any recognized accrued postretirement benefit obligation at the transition date. Payments made pursuant to a settlement, as discussed in paragraphs .182 through .186, shall be included in the determination of cumulative benefit payments made subsequent to the transition date. [FAS106, ¶112]

.201 If at the measurement date for the beginning of an employer's fiscal year it is expected that additional recognition of any remaining unrecognized transition obligation will be required pursuant to paragraph .200, amortization of the transition obligation for interim reporting purposes shall be based on the amount expected to be amortized for the year, except for the effects of applying paragraph .200 for any settlement required to be accounted for pursuant to paragraphs .182 through .186. Those effects shall be recognized when the related settlement is recognized. The effects of changes during the year in the initial assessment of whether additional recognition of the unrecognized transition obligation will be required for the year shall be recognized over the remainder of the year. The amount of the unrecognized transition obligation to be recognized for a year shall be finally determined at the measurement date for the end of the year based on the constraints on delayed recognition discussed in paragraph .200; any difference between the amortization of the transition obligation recognized during interim periods and the amount required to be recognized for the year shall be recognized immediately. [FAS106, ¶113]

Application of Standards in Paragraphs .101 through .201 to Specific Aspects of Accounting for Postretirement Benefits Other Than Pensions

.202 Paragraphs .205 through .308 provide additional discussion and examples that illustrate the application of certain requirements of this section to specific aspects of employers' accounting for postretirement benefits other than pensions. [FAS106, ¶391]

CONTENTS

	Paragraph Numbers
Introduction	.203–.204
Illustration 1—Illustration of Terms	.205–.224
Case 1A—Expected Postretirement Benefit Obligation and Accumulated Postretirement Benefit Obligation	.205–.208
Case 1B—Full Eligibility Date	.209–.220
Case 1C—Attribution	.221–.224
Illustration 2—Delayed Recognition and Reconciliation of Funded Status	.225–.237
Case 2A—Unrecognized Obligation at Date of Transition	.226–.228
Case 2B—Employer Accrual of Net Periodic Postretirement Benefit Cost	.229–.230
Case 2C—Plan Amendment That Increases Benefits	.231–.233
Case 2D—Negative Plan Amendment	.234–.236
Case 2E—Change in Assumption	.237
Illustration 3—Constraint on Delayed Recognition of Transition Obligation	.238–.245
Illustration 4—Plan Amendments and Prior Service Cost	.246–.251
Case 4A—Equal Amount Assigned to Each Future Year of Service to Full Eligibility Date	.248–.250
Case 4B—Straight-Line Amortization over Average Remaining Years of Service to Full Eligibility Date	.251
Illustration 5—Accounting for Gains and Losses and Timing of Measurements	.252–.268
Case 5A—Loss on Obligation	.254–.258
Case 5B—Gain on Assets	.259–.261
Case 5C—Loss on Assets and Gain on Obligation	.262–.264
Supporting Schedules	.265–.268

	Paragraph Numbers
Illustration 6—Defined-Dollar Capped Plans	.269–.275
Case 6A—Dollar Cap Defined on Individual Coverage	.270–.272
Case 6B—Dollar Cap Defined in the Aggregate for the Retiree Group	.273–.275
Illustration 7—Disclosure Requirements	.276–.280
Case 7A—Single-Employer Defined Benefit Postretirement Plan	.277
Case 7B—Defined Contribution Plan	.278
Case 7C—Multiemployer Plan	.279–.280
Illustration 8—Accounting for Settlements	.281–.292
Case 8A—Settlement When an Unrecognized Transition Obligation Exists	.282–.283
Case 8B—Settlement When an Unrecognized Transition Asset Exists	.284–.285
Case 8C—Effect of Mid-Year Settlement on Transition Constraint	.286–.292
Illustration 9—Accounting for Curtailments	.293–.298
Case 9A—Curtailment When an Unrecognized Gain and an Unrecognized Transition Obligation Exist	.295–.296
Case 9B—Curtailment Related to a Disposal of a Portion of the Business and an Unrecognized Loss and Unrecognized Transition Obligation Exist	.297–.298
Illustration 10—Accounting for a Partial Settlement and a Full Curtailment That Occur as a Direct Result of a Sale of a Line of Business	.299–.303
Illustration 11—Accounting for the Effects of an Offer of Special Termination Benefits	.304–.308

Introduction

.203 The illustrations are referenced to the applicable paragraph(s) of this section where appropriate. Certain illustrations have been included to facilitate the understanding and application of certain provisions of this section that apply in specific circumstances that may not be encountered frequently by employers. The fact patterns shown may not be representative of actual situations but are presented only to illustrate those requirements. [FAS106, ¶391]

.204 Throughout these illustrations the accumulated postretirement benefit obligation and service cost are assumed as inputs rather than calculated based on some underlying population. For simplicity, benefit payments are assumed to be made at the end of the year, service cost is assumed to include interest on the portion of the expected postretirement benefit obligation attributed to the current year, and interest cost is based on the accumulated postretirement benefit obligation as of the beginning of the year. For unfunded plans, benefits are assumed to be paid directly by the employer and are reflected as a reduction in the accrued postretirement benefit cost. The required disclosure of the reconciliation of the funded status of the plan is illustrated in many of the cases; however, for simplicity, the components of the accumulated postretirement benefit obligation are not included in those reconciliations as required by paragraph .169(c)(2). In many of the cases, application of the underlying concepts has been simplified by focusing on a single employee for purposes of illustration. In practice, the determination of the full eligibility date and the measurement of postretirement benefit cost and obligation are based on employee groups and consider various possible retirement dates and the probabilities associated with retirement at each of those dates. [FAS106, ¶392]

Illustration 1—Illustration of Terms

Case 1A—Expected Postretirement Benefit Obligation and Accumulated Postretirement Benefit Obligation

.205 This section uses two terms to describe certain measures of the obligation to provide postretirement benefits: *expected postretirement benefit obligation* and *accumulated postretirement benefit obligation.* The expected postretirement benefit obligation for an employee is the actuarial present value as of a measurement date of the postretirement benefits expected to be paid to or for the employee, the employee's beneficiaries, and any covered dependents. Prior to the date on which an employee attains full eligibility for the benefits that employee is expected to earn under the terms of the postretirement benefit plan (the full eligibility date), the accumulated postretirement benefit obligation for an employee is a portion of the expected postretirement benefit obligation. On and after the full eligibility date, the accumulated postretirement benefit obligation and the expected postretirement benefit obligation for an employee are the same. (Refer to paragraphs .113 and .114.) The following example illustrates the notion of the expected postretirement benefit obligation and the relationship between that obligation and the accumulated postretirement benefit obligation at various dates. [FAS106, ¶393]

.206 Company A's plan provides postretirement health care benefits to all employees who render at least 10 years of service and attain age 55 while in service. A 50-year-old employee, hired January 1, 19V3 at age 30 and eligible for benefits upon attaining age 55, is expected to terminate employment at age 62 and is expected to live to age 77. A discount rate of 8 percent is assumed.

At December 31, 19X2, Company A estimates the expected amount and timing of benefit payments for that employee as follows:

| | Expected | Present Value at Age | | |
Age	Future Claims	50	53	55
63	$ 2,796	$1,028	$1,295	$1,511
64	3,093	1,052	1,326	1,547
65	856	270	339	396
66	947	276	348	406
67	1,051	284	357	417
68	1,161	291	366	427
69	1,282	297	374	436
70	1,425	306	385	449
71	1,577	313	394	460
72	1,744	321	404	471
73	1,934	329	415	484
74	2,137	337	424	495
75	2,367	346	435	508
76	2,620	354	446	520
77	3,899	488	615	717
	$28,889	$6,292	$7,923	$9,244

[FAS106, ¶394]

.207 The expected and accumulated postretirement benefit obligations at December 31, 19X2 (age 50) are $6,292 and $5,034 (20/25 of $6,292), respectively. An equal amount of the expected postretirement benefit obligation is attributed to each year of service from the employee's date of hire to the employee's full eligibility date (age 55) (paragraphs .138 and .139). Therefore, when the employee is age 50, the accumulated postretirement benefit obligation is measured as 20/25 of the expected postretirement benefit obligation, as the employee has rendered 20 years of the 25-year credited service period. Refer to Case 1B (paragraphs .209 through .220) for additional illustrations on the full eligibility date and Case 1C (paragraphs .221 through .224) for additional illustrations on attribution. [FAS106, ¶395]

.208 Assuming no changes in health care costs or other circumstances, the accumulated postretirement benefit obligation at December 31, 19X5 (age 53) is $7,289 (23/25 of $7,923). At the end of the employee's 25th year of service and thereafter, the expected postretirement benefit obligation and the accumulated postretirement benefit obligation are equal. In this example, at December 31, 19X7, when the employee is 55 and fully eligible for benefits, the accumulated and expected postretirement benefit obligations are $9,244. At the end of the 26th year of service (December 31, 19X8) when the employee is 56, those obligations are $9,984 ($9,244 plus interest at 8 percent for 1 year). [FAS106, ¶396]

Case 1B—Full Eligibility Date

.209 The *full eligibility date* (paragraph .114) is the date at which an employee has rendered all of the service necessary to have earned the right to receive all of the benefits expected to be received by that employee under the terms of the postretirement benefit plan. Therefore, the present value of all of the benefits expected to be received by or on behalf of an employee is attributed to the employee's credited service period, which ends at the full eligibility date. Determination of an employee's full eligibility date is affected by plan terms that provide incremental benefits expected to be received by the employee for additional years of service, unless those incremental benefits are trivial. Determination of the full eligibility date is *not* affected by an employee's current dependency status or by plan terms that define when benefit payments commence. The following examples (paragraphs .210 through .220) are presented to assist in understanding the full eligibility date. [FAS106, ¶397]

Plans That Provide Incremental Benefits for Additional Years of Service

Graded benefit formula

.210 Some plans have benefit formulas that define different benefits for different years of service. To illustrate, assume a plan in which the percentage of postretirement health care coverage to be provided by an employer is defined by groups of years of service. The plan provides 20 percent postretirement health care coverage for 10 years of service after age 35, 50 percent for 20 years of service after age 35, 70 percent for 25 years of service after age 35, and 100 percent for 30 years of service after age 35. The full eligibility date for an employee who was hired at age 35 and is expected to retire at age 62 is at age 60. At that date the employee has rendered 25 years of service after age 35 and is eligible to receive a benefit of 70 percent health care coverage after retirement. The employee receives no additional benefits for the last two years of service. [FAS106, ¶398]

Pay-related plans

.211 Some plans may base the amount of benefits or level of benefit coverage on employees' compensation, for example, as a percentage of their final pay. To the extent the plan's postretirement benefit formula defines benefits wholly or partially as a function of future compensation (that is, the plan provides incremental benefits for additional years of service when it is assumed that final pay will increase), determination of the full eligibility date for an employee is affected by those additional years of service the employee is expected to render (paragraph .114). In addition, measurements of the postretirement benefit obligation and service cost reflect the best estimate of employees' future compensation levels (paragraph .128). [FAS106, ¶399]

.212 For example, assume a plan provides life insurance benefits to employees who render 20 years of service and attain age 55 while in service; the benefit is equal to 20 percent of final pay. A 55-year-old employee, who currently earns a salary of $90,000, has worked 22 years for the company. The employee is expected to retire at age 60 and is expected to be earning $120,000 at that time. The employee is eligible for life insurance coverage under the plan at age 55, when the employee has met the age and service requirements. However, because the employee's salary continues to increase each year, the employee is not *fully eligible* for benefits until age 60 when the employee retires because the employee earns an incremental benefit for each additional year of service beyond age 55. That is, the employee earns an additional benefit equal to 20 percent of the increase in salary each year from age 55 to retirement at age 60 for service during each of those years. [FAS106, ¶400]

Spousal coverage

.213 Some postretirement benefit plans provide spousal or dependent coverage or both if the employee works a specified number of years beyond the date at which the employee attains eligibility for single coverage. For example, a postretirement health care plan provides single coverage to employees who work 10 years and attain age 50 while in service; the plan provides coverage for dependents if the employee works 20 years and attains age 60 while in service. Because the additional 10 years of service may provide an incremental benefit to employees, for employees expected to satisfy the age and service requirements and to have covered dependents during the period following the employee's retirement, their full eligibility date is the date at which they have both rendered 20 years of service and attained age 60 while in service. For employees not expected to have covered dependents after their retirement or who are not expected to render at least 20 years of service or attain age 60 while in service, or both, their full eligibility date is the date at which they have both rendered 10 years of service and attained age 50 while in service. [FAS106, ¶401]

Single Plan Provides Health Care and Life Insurance Benefits

.214 Some postretirement benefit plans may have different eligibility requirements for different types of benefits. For example, assume a plan provides a postretirement death benefit of $100,000 to employees who render 20 or more years of service. Fifty percent health care coverage is provided to eligible employees who render 10 years of service, 70 percent coverage to those who render 20 years of service, and 100 percent coverage to those who render 30 years of service. Employees are eligible for the health care and death benefits if they attain age 55 while in service. [FAS106, ¶402]

.215 The full eligibility date for an individual hired at age 30 and expected to terminate employment at age 62 is the date on which that employee has rendered 30 years of service and attained age 55 while in service (age 60 in this example). At that date the employee is eligible for all of the benefits expected to be paid to or on behalf of that employee under the postretirement benefit plan ($100,000 death benefits and 100 percent health care coverage). The full eligibility date for an employee hired at age 37 and expected to retire at age 62 is the date on which that employee has rendered 20 years of service and attained age 55 while in service (age 57 in this example). At that date the employee is eligible for all of the benefits expected to be paid to or on behalf of that employee under the postretirement benefit plan ($100,000 death benefits and 70 percent health care coverage). [FAS106, ¶403]

Plans That Provide Benefits Based on Status at Date of Termination

.216 Some postretirement benefit plans provide coverage for the spouse to whom an employee is married when the employee terminates service; that is, the marital status of an employee upon termination of employment determines whether single or spousal coverage is to be provided. In measuring the expected postretirement benefit obligation, consideration is given to factors such as when benefit coverage will commence, who will receive benefits (employee and any covered dependents), and the expected need for and utilization of benefit coverage. However, determination of an employee's full eligibility date is not affected by plan terms that define when payments commence or by an employee's current marital (or dependent) status (paragraph .114). [FAS106, ¶404]

.217 For example, assume a plan provides postretirement health care coverage to employees who render at least 10 years of service and attain age 55 while in service; health care coverage also is provided to employees' spouses at the date of the employees' retirement. A 55-year-old employee is single, has worked for the company for 30 years, and is expected to marry at age 59 and to retire at age 62. Although the employee is entitled to spousal coverage only if married at retirement, at age 55 the employee has earned the right to spousal coverage. The probability that the employee will be married when the employee retires is included in the actuarial assumptions developed to measure the expected postretirement benefit obligation for that plan participant. The full eligibility date (age 55 in this example) is not affected by that measurement assumption. [FAS106, ¶405]

Postretirement Benefits to Be Received by Disabled Plan Participants

.218 Some plans provide postretirement benefits to disabled employees. For example, Company B provides disability income and health care benefits to employees who become disabled while in service and have rendered 10 or more years of service. Retiree health care benefits are provided to employees who render 20 or more years of service and attain age 55 while in service. Employees receiving disability benefits continue to accrue "credit" toward their eligibility for retiree health care benefits. Under this plan, an employee hired at age 25, who becomes permanently disabled at age 40, is entitled to receive retiree health care benefits commencing at age 55 (in addition to any disability income benefits commencing at age 40) because that employee worked for Company B for more than 10 years before becoming disabled. Under the terms of the plan the employee is given credit for working to age 55 even though no actual service is rendered by the employee after the disabling event occurs. [FAS106, ¶406]

.219 Because the employee is permanently disabled, the full eligibility date is accelerated to recognize the shorter period of service required to be rendered in exchange for the retiree health care benefits—in this case the full eligibility date is age 40, the date of the disabling event. For a similar employee who is temporarily disabled at age 40 but returns to work and attains age 55 while in service, the full eligibility date is age 55. Company B's expected postretirement benefit health care obligation for the permanently disabled employee is based on the employee's expected health care costs commencing at age 55 and is attributed ratably to that employee's active service to age 40. [FAS106, ¶407]

.220 Only some employees become and remain disabled. Therefore, in measuring the expected postretirement benefit obligation and in determining the attribution period for plan participants expected to become disabled, the probability and timing of a disabling event is considered in determining whether employees are likely to become disabled and whether they will be entitled to receive postretirement benefits. [FAS106, ¶408]

Case 1C—Attribution

Attribution Period

.221 Paragraph .139 states that the beginning of the *attribution period* shall be the date of hire unless the plan's benefit formula grants credit only for service from a later date, in which case benefits generally shall be attributed from the beginning of that credited service period. For example, for a plan that provides benefit coverage to employees who render 30 or more years of service or who render at least 10 years of service and attain age 55 while in service, without specifying when the credited service period begins, the expected postretirement benefit obligation is attributed to service from the date of hire to the earlier of the date at which a plan participant has rendered 30 years of service or has rendered 10 years of service and attained age 55 while in service. However, for a plan that provides benefit coverage to employees who render at least 20 years of service after age 35, the expected postretirement benefit obligation is attributed to a plan participant's first 20 years of service after attaining age 35 or after the date of hire, if later than age 35. [FAS106, ¶409]

.222 For a plan with a benefit formula that attributes benefits to a credited service period that is nominal in relation to employees' total years of service prior to their full eligibility dates, an equal amount of the expected postretirement benefit obligation for an employee is attributed to each year of that employee's service from date of hire to date of full eligibility for benefits. For example, a plan with a benefit formula that defines 100 percent benefit coverage for service for the year in which employees attain age 60 has a 1-year credited service period. If plan participants are expected to have rendered an average of 20 years of service at age 60, the credited service period is nominal in relation to their total years of service prior to their full eligibility dates. In that case, the service cost is recognized from date of hire to age 60. [FAS106, ¶410]

Attribution Pattern

.223 For all plans, except those that "frontload" benefits, the expected postretirement benefit obligation is attributed ratably to each year of service in the attribution period (paragraph .138). That is, an equal amount of the expected postretirement benefit obligation is attributed to each year of service from the employee's date of hire or beginning of the credited service period, if later, to the employee's full eligibility date unless (a) the credited service period is nominal relative to the total years of service prior to the full eligibility date (paragraph .222) or (b) the benefit formula frontloads benefits (paragraph .224). [FAS106, ¶411]

Frontloaded plans

.224 Some plans may have a benefit formula that defines benefits in terms of specific periods of service to be rendered in exchange for those benefits but attributes all or a disproportionate share of the expected postretirement benefit obligation to employees' early years of service in the credited service period. An example would be a life insurance plan that provides postretirement death benefits of $250,000 for 10 years of service after age 45 and $5,000 of additional death benefits for each year of service thereafter up to age 65 (maximum benefit of $300,000). For plans that frontload the benefit, the expected postretirement benefit obligation is attributed to employee service in accordance with the plan's benefit formula (paragraph .138). In this example, the actuarial present value of a $25,000 death benefit is attributed to each of the first 10 years of service after age 45, and the actuarial present value of an additional $5,000 death benefit is attributed to each year of service thereafter up to age 65. [FAS106, ¶412]

Illustration 2—Delayed Recognition and Reconciliation of Funded Status

.225 Pursuant to the provisions of this section, the recognition of certain changes affecting measurement of the accumulated postretirement benefit obligation or the fair value of plan assets may be delayed. Those changes include plan amendments (paragraph .146) and gains and losses due to experience different from that assumed or from changes in assumptions (paragraph .151). Information about the effect of the changes that have been afforded delayed recognition is provided through disclosure of the reconciliation of the funded status of a plan to the accrued or prepaid postretirement benefit cost recognized in the employer's statement of financial position (paragraph .169(c)). The following cases (2A through 2E, paragraphs .226 through .237) show how events that change the accumulated postretirement benefit obligation are reflected in that reconciliation. [FAS106, ¶417]

Case 2A—Unrecognized Obligation at Date of Transition

.226 For an unfunded plan with an accumulated postretirement benefit obligation of $600,000 at the date of transition (January 1, 19X3), the reconciliation of the funded status of the plan with the amount shown in the statement of financial position as of that date is as follows:

Accumulated postretirement benefit obligation	$(600,000)[a]
Plan assets at fair value	0
Funded status	(600,000)
Transition obligation at January 1, 19X3	600,000
(Accrued)/prepaid postretirement benefit cost	$ 0

[a]The actuarial present value of the obligation for fully eligible plan participants' expected postretirement benefits and the portion of the expected postretirement benefit obligation for other active plan partici- pants attributed to service to December 31, 19X2. For example, assume a plan provides benefits to em- ployees who render at least 20 years of service after age 35. For employees age 45 with 10 years of service at December 31, 19X2, the accumulated postretirement benefit obligation is 50% of the expected postre- tirement benefit obligation for those employees. For employees age 55 or older who have rendered 20 or more years of service at December 31, 19X2 and retirees (collectively referred to as fully eligible plan par- ticipants), the accumulated postretirement benefit obligation is the full amount of the expected postretire- ment benefit obligation for those employees.

[FAS106, ¶418]

.227 The transition obligation or asset is the difference between (a) the accumulated postretirement benefit obligation and (b) the fair value of plan assets plus any recog- nized accrued postretirement benefit cost or less any recognized prepaid postretire- ment benefit cost at the date of transition (paragraph .141, footnote 24). If, as in this case, advance contributions were not made and postretirement benefit cost was not accrued in prior periods, there is no accrued or prepaid postretirement benefit cost recognized in the statement of financial position, and, therefore, the transition obliga- tion is equal to the unfunded status ($600,000). [FAS106, ¶419]

Unrecognized Amounts after Date of Transition

.228 After the date of transition, any change in the accumulated postretirement bene- fit obligation or the plan assets (other than contributions and benefit payments) either is unrecognized, due to the delayed recognition provisions of this section, or is in- cluded in net periodic postretirement benefit cost. Contributions by the employer in- crease plan assets and decrease the accrued postretirement benefit cost or increase the prepaid postretirement benefit cost, subject to the provision of paragraph .200 requir- ing recognition of an additional amount of the unrecognized transition obligation in certain situations. All changes in the accumulated postretirement benefit obligation and plan assets are reflected in the reconciliation. Using Case 2A as the starting point, the following reconciliations (Cases 2B through 2E [paragraphs .229 through .237]) illustrate the effect of changes in assumptions or changes in the plan on measurement of the accumulated postretirement benefit obligation. [FAS106, ¶420]

Case 2B—Employer Accrual of Net Periodic Postretirement Benefit Cost

.229 Benefit payments of $42,000 are made at the end of 19X3. Changes in accrued postretirement benefit cost, accumulated postretirement benefit obligation, and unrecognized transition obligation in 19X3 are summarized as follows:

	Accrued Postretirement Benefit Cost	Accumulated Postretirement Benefit Obligation	Unrecognized Transition Obligation
Beginning of year	$ 0	$(600,000)	$600,000
Recognition of components of net periodic postretirement benefit cost:			
Service cost	(32,000)	(32,000)	
Interest cost[a]	(48,000)	(48,000)	
Amortization of transition obligation[b]	(30,000)		(30,000)
	(110,000)	(80,000)	(30,000)
Benefit payments	42,000	42,000	
Net change	(68,000)	(38,000)	(30,000)
End of year	$ (68,000)	$(638,000)	$570,000

[a]Assumed discount rate of 8% applied to the accumulated postretirement benefit obligation at the beginning of the year.

[b]The transition obligation of $600,000 is amortized on a straight-line basis over 20 years. Illustration 3 (paragraphs .239 through .245) illustrates the constraint on delayed recognition of the transition obligation pursuant to paragraph .200.

[FAS106, ¶421]

.230 The funded status of the plan at January 1, 19X3 and December 31, 19X3 is reconciled with the amount shown in the statement of financial position at those dates as follows:

	1/1/X3	Net Change	12/31/X3
Accumulated postretirement benefit obligation	$(600,000)	$(38,000)	$(638,000)
Plan assets at fair value	0		0
Funded status	(600,000)	(38,000)	(638,000)
Unrecognized transition obligation	600,000	(30,000)	570,000
Accrued postretirement benefit cost	$ 0	$(68,000)	$ (68,000)

[FAS106, ¶422]

Case 2C—Plan Amendment That Increases Benefits

.231 The plan is amended on January 2, 19X4, resulting in a $90,000 increase in the accumulated postretirement benefit obligation. The effects of plan amendments are reflected immediately in measurement of the accumulated postretirement benefit obligation; however, the effects of the amendment are not recognized immediately in the financial statements, but rather are recognized on a delayed basis (paragraph .147). [FAS106, ¶423]

.232 Benefit payments of $39,000 are made at the end of 19X4. Changes in accrued postretirement benefit cost, accumulated postretirement benefit obligation, unrecognized transition obligation, and unrecognized prior service cost in 19X4 are summarized as follows:

	Accrued Postretirement Benefit Cost	Accumulated Postretirement Benefit Obligation	Unrecognized Transition Obligation	Unrecognized Prior Service Cost
Beginning of year	$ (68,000)	$(638,000)	$570,000	$ 0
Plan amendment		(90,000)		90,000
Recognition of components of net periodic postretirement benefit cost:				
Service cost	(30,000)	(30,000)		
Interest cost[a]	(58,240)	(58,240)		
Amortization of transition obligation	(30,000)		(30,000)	
Amortization of prior service cost[b]	(9,000)			(9,000)
	(127,240)	(178,240)	(30,000)	81,000
Benefit payments	39,000	39,000		
Net change	(88,240)	(139,240)	(30,000)	81,000
End of year	$(156,240)	$(777,240)	$540,000	$81,000

[a]Assumed discount rate of 8% applied to the accumulated postretirement benefit obligation at the beginning of the year and to the increase in that obligation for the unrecognized prior service cost at the date of the plan amendment [($638,000 × 8%) + ($90,000 × 8%)].

[b]As permitted by paragraph .148, prior service cost of $90,000 is amortized on a straight-line basis over the average remaining years of service to *full eligibility* for benefits of the active plan participants (10 years in this example).

[FAS106, ¶424]

.233 The funded status of the plan at December 31, 19X3 and 19X4 is reconciled with amount shown in the statement of financial position at those dates as follows:

	12/31/X3	Net Change	12/31/X4
Accumulated postretirement benefit obligation	$(638,000)	$(139,240)	$(777,240)
Plan assets at fair value	0		0
Funded status	(638,000)	(139,240)	(777,240)
Unrecognized prior service cost	0	81,000	81,000
Unrecognized transition obligation	570,000	(30,000)	540,000
Accrued postretirement benefit cost	$ (68,000)	$ (88,240)	$(156,240)

[FAS106, ¶425]

Case 2D—Negative Plan Amendment

.234 The plan is amended on January 4, 19X5, resulting in a $99,000 reduction in the accumulated postretirement benefit obligation. As with a plan amendment that increases benefits, the effect of a negative plan amendment (an amendment that decreases benefits) is reflected immediately in the measurement of the accumulated postretirement benefit obligation. The effects of the negative plan amendment are recognized by first reducing any existing unrecognized prior service cost and then any existing unrecognized transition obligation; the remainder is recognized in the financial statements on a delayed basis. [FAS106, ¶426]

.235 Benefit payments in 19X5 are $40,000. Changes in accrued postretirement benefit cost, accumulated postretirement benefit obligation, unrecognized transition obligation, and unrecognized prior service cost in 19X5 are summarized as follows:

	Accrued Postretirement Benefit Cost	Accumulated Postretirement Benefit Obligation	Unrecognized Transition Obligation	Unrecognized Prior Service Cost
Beginning of year	$(156,240)	$(777,240)	$540,000	$ 81,000
Plan amendment[a]		99,000	(18,000)	(81,000)
Recognition of components of net periodic postretirement benefit cost:				
Service cost	(30,000)	(30,000)		
Interest cost[b]	(54,259)	(54,259)		
Amortization of transition obligation[c]	(29,000)		(29,000)	
Amortization of prior service cost	0			0
	(113,259)	14,741	(47,000)	(81,000)
Benefit payments	40,000	40,000		
Net change	(73,259)	54,741	(47,000)	(81,000)
End of year	$(229,499)	$(722,499)	$493,000	$ 0

[a]Paragraph .150 requires that the effects of a plan amendment that reduces the accumulated postretirement benefit obligation be used first to reduce any existing unrecognized prior service cost, then any unrecognized transition obligation. Any remaining effects are recognized on a delayed basis over the remaining years of service to full eligibility for those plan participants who were active at the date of the amendment. If all or almost all of the plan participants were fully eligible at that date, the remaining effects should be recognized over the remaining life expectancy of those plan participants.

[b]Assumed discount rate of 8% applied to the accumulated postretirement benefit obligation at the beginning of the year and to the decrease in that obligation at the date of the plan amendment [($777,240 × 8%) − ($99,000 × 8%)].

[c]Unrecognized transition obligation of $522,000 ($540,000 − $18,000) is amortized on a straight-line basis over the 18 years remaining in the transition period.

[FAS106, ¶427]

.236 The funded status of the plan at December 31, 19X4 and 19X5 is reconciled with the amount shown in the statement of financial position at those dates as follows:

	12/31/X4	Net Change	12/31/X5
Accumulated postretirement benefit obligation	$(777,240)	$ 54,741	$(722,499)
Plan assets at fair value	0		0
Funded status	(777,240)	54,741	(722,499)
Unrecognized prior service cost	81,000	(81,000)	0
Unrecognized transition obligation	540,000	(47,000)	493,000
Accrued postretirement benefit cost	$(156,240)	$(73,259)	$(229,499)

[FAS106, ¶428]

Case 2E—Change in Assumption

.237 The assumed health care cost trend rates are changed at December 31, 19X5, resulting in a $55,000 increase in the accumulated postretirement benefit obligation. The net loss that results from a change in the health care cost trend rates assumption is reflected immediately in the measurement of the accumulated postretirement benefit obligation. However, as with most other gains and losses, the effect of a change in assumption may be recognized in the financial statements either immediately or on a delayed basis, as long as the recognition method is applied consistently.

	Before Change	Net Loss	After Change
Accumulated postretirement benefit obligation	$(722,499)	$(55,000)	$(777,499)
Plan assets at fair value	0		0
Funded status	(722,499)	(55,000)	(777,499)
Unrecognized net loss[a]	0	55,000	55,000
Unrecognized transition obligation	493,000		493,000
Accrued postretirement benefit cost	$(229,499)	$ 0	$(229,499)

---

[a]This section generally does not require recognition of gains and losses in the period in which they arise (paragraphs .151 through .156). However, at a minimum, amortization of an unrecognized net gain or loss is required to be recognized as a component of net periodic postretirement benefit cost for a year if, as of the beginning of the year, the unrecognized net gain or loss exceeds 10% of the greater of the accumulated postretirement benefit obligation or the market-related value of plan assets. Applications of those provisions are included in Illustration 5 (paragraphs .252 through .268).

[FAS106, ¶429]

Illustration 3—Constraint on Delayed Recognition of Transition Obligation

.238 [As indicated in paragraph .200] phasing in recognition of a transition obligation should not result in less rapid recognition than would have resulted under pay-as-you-go accounting. That is, after the transition date, the cumulative postretirement benefit cost accrued should not be less than cumulative benefit payments. Paragraphs .239 through .245 illustrate a situation in which recognition of the transition obligation is accelerated as a result of that constraint. [FAS106, ¶430]

.239 At December 31, 19X2, the accumulated (and unrecognized) postretirement benefit obligation and plan assets of a defined benefit postretirement plan sponsored by Company D [were] as follows:

Accumulated postretirement benefit obligation	$(255,000)
Plan assets at fair value	0
Transition obligation	$(255,000)

[FAS106, ¶435]

.240 Company D adopts [the provisions of] this section for the year beginning January 1, 19X3. At December 31, 19X2, Company D [had] no prepaid or accrued postretirement benefit cost. Company D [elected] to amortize the transition obligation over the average remaining service period of active plan participants at the date of transition—17 years. [FAS106, ¶436]

.241 Benefit payments in 19X3 are $45,000. Changes in accrued postretirement benefit cost, accumulated postretirement benefit obligation, and unrecognized transition obligation in 19X3 are summarized as follows:

	Accrued Postretirement Benefit Cost	Accumulated Postretirement Benefit Obligation	Unrecognized Transition Obligation
Beginning of year	$ 0	$(255,000)	$255,000
Recognition of components of net periodic postretirement benefit cost:			
Service cost	(30,000)	(30,000)	
Interest cost[a]	(20,400)	(20,400)	
Amortization of transition obligation[b]	(15,000)		(15,000)
	(65,400)	(50,400)	(15,000)
Benefit payments	45,000	45,000	
Net change	(20,400)	(5,400)	(15,000)
End of year	$(20,400)	$(260,400)	$240,000

[a]An 8% discount rate is assumed.

[b]$255,000 ÷ 17 years = $15,000 per year.

[FAS106, ¶437]

.242 In 19X4, benefit payments increase to $95,000 and service cost increases to $35,000. Changes in accrued postretirement benefit cost, accumulated postretirement benefit obligation, and unrecognized transition obligation in 19X4 are summarized as follows:

	Accrued Postretirement Benefit Cost	Accumulated Postretirement Benefit Obligation	Unrecognized Transition Obligation
Beginning of year	$(20,400)	$(260,400)	$240,000
Recognition of components of net periodic postretirement benefit cost:			
Service cost	(35,000)	(35,000)	
Interest cost	(20,832)	(20,832)	
Amortization of transition obligation[c]	(18,768)		(18,768)
	(74,600)	(55,832)	(18,768)
Benefit payments	95,000	95,000	
Net change	20,400	39,168	(18,768)
End of year	$ 0	$(221,232)	$221,232

[c]Amortization of the transition obligation in 19X4 includes straight-line amortization of $15,000 plus additional recognition of $3,768. The additional recognition is required because in 19X4 cumulative benefit payments subsequent to the January 1, 19X3 transition date exceed cumulative postretirement benefit cost accrued subsequent to that date (paragraph .200). The additional transition obligation required to be recognized ($3,768) is determined as follows:

	19X3	19X4
Benefit payments:		
1/1/X3 to beginning of current year		$ 45,000
Current year	$45,000	95,000
Cumulative 1/1/X3 to end of current year	$45,000	$140,000
Postretirement benefit cost recognized:		
1/1/X3 to beginning of current year		$ 65,400
Current year prior to recognition of any additional amount pursuant to paragraph .200	$65,400	70,832
Cumulative 1/1/X3 to end of current year before applying paragraph .200 constraint	65,400	136,232
Additional amount required to be recognized pursuant to paragraph .200	0	3,768
Cumulative 1/1/X3 to end of current year	$65,400	$140,000

[FAS106, ¶439]

.243 The objective of the constraint on delayed recognition of the transition obligation (paragraph .200) is to preclude slower recognition of postretirement benefit cost (as a result of applying the delayed recognition provisions of this section) than would have resulted under pay-as-you-go accounting for costs. An indication that the constraint may apply is the existence of a prepaid postretirement benefit cost after the date of transition for an enterprise that prior to the application of this section was on a pay-as-you-go basis of accounting for other postretirement benefits. For example, in paragraph .242, if the employer had not recognized the additional $3,768 of transition obligation, the employer would have had a prepaid postretirement benefit cost equal to that amount. [FAS106, ¶440]

.244 The funded status of the plan at December 31, 19X3 and 19X4 is reconciled with the amount shown in the statement of financial position at those dates as follows:

	12/31/X3	**Net Change**	**12/31/X4**
Accumulated postretirement benefit obligation	$(260,400)	$ 39,168	$(221,232)
Plan assets at fair value	0		0
Funded status	(260,400)	39,168	(221,232)
Unrecognized transition obligation	240,000	(18,768)	221,232[d]
Accrued postretirement benefit cost	$ (20,400)	$ 20,400	$ 0

---

[d] In 19X5, the straight-line amortization of the unrecognized transition obligation will be $14,749 ($221,232 ÷ 15 years remaining in the transition period).

[FAS106, ¶441]

.245 Paragraph .201 states that if at the measurement date for the beginning of an employer's fiscal year it is expected that additional recognition of any remaining unrecognized transition obligation will be required pursuant to paragraph .200, amortization of the transition obligation for interim reporting purposes shall be based on the amount expected to be amortized for the year, except for the effects of applying the constraint in paragraph .200 for any settlement required to be accounted for pursuant to paragraphs .182 through .186. Those effects shall be recognized when the related settlement is recognized. The effects of changes during the year in the initial assessment of whether additional recognition of the unrecognized transition obligation will be required for the year shall be recognized over the remainder of the year. The amount of the unrecognized transition obligation to be recognized for a year shall be finally determined at the end of the year (or the measurement date, if earlier) based on the constraints on delayed recognition discussed in paragraph .200; any difference between the amortization of the transition obligation recognized during interim periods and the amount required to be recognized for the year shall be recognized immediately. [FAS106, ¶442]

Illustration 4—Plan Amendments and Prior Service Cost

. .246 This section requires that, at a minimum, prior service cost arising from a plan initiation or plan amendment be recognized by assigning an equal amount of the prior service cost to each remaining year of service to the full eligibility date of each plan participant active at the date of the plan initiation or amendment (paragraph .147). Consistent use of an alternative amortization method that more rapidly reduces the unrecognized prior service cost is permitted (paragraph .148). [FAS106, ¶449]

.247 Company H has a postretirement benefit plan that provides benefits to employees who render at least 20 years of service after age 35. On January 2, 19X4, Company H amends its postretirement benefit plan to increase the lifetime cap on benefits provided, resulting in unrecognized prior service cost of $750,000 (the increase in the accumulated postretirement benefit obligation as a result of the plan amendment). Amortization of that unrecognized prior service cost is illustrated in Cases 4A and 4B (paragraphs .248 through .251). [FAS106, ¶450]

Case 4A—Equal Amount Assigned to Each Future Year of Service to Full Eligibility Date

.248 The determination of the amortization of prior service cost is based on remaining years of service prior to the full eligibility date of each plan participant active at the date of the amendment but not yet fully eligible for benefits. (Refer to paragraph .453 for the definition of plan participant.) Future years of service of active employees who are not plan participants are excluded. Each remaining year of service prior to the full eligibility date of each active plan participant not yet fully eligible for benefits is assigned an equal share of the prior service cost (paragraph .147). Thus, the portion of prior service cost to be recognized in each of those future years is weighted based on the number of those plan participants expected to render service in each of those future years. [FAS106, ¶451]

.249 At the date of the amendment (January 2, 19X4), the Company H has 165 employees of whom 15 are fully eligible for benefits, 10 are under age 35, and 40 are expected to terminate before becoming eligible for any benefits. Because the 10 employees under age 35 have not met the age requirements to participate in the plan (only service after age 35 is credited) and 40 employees are not expected to receive benefits under the plan, those 50 employees are not considered to be plan participants and, therefore, are excluded from the calculation. The 15 fully eligible plan participants also are excluded from the calculation because they do not have to render any additional service to earn the added benefits. The remaining 100 employees have not yet earned the full amount of the benefits they are expected to earn under the plan. Those employees are expected to become fully eligible for those benefits over the next 20 years. Their remaining years of service to full eligibility for benefits is the basis for amortization of the prior service cost. [FAS106, ¶452]

.250 The following schedules illustrate the calculation of the expected remaining years of service prior to full eligibility (Schedule 1) and the amortization schedule for recognizing the prior service cost (Schedule 2). Employees hired after the date of the plan amendment or who attain age 35 after the date of the plan amendment do not affect the amortization nor do revised estimates of remaining years of service, except those due to a curtailment.

Schedule 1—Determination of Expected Remaining Years of Service Prior to Full Eligibility as of January 2, 19X4

Indiv.	Remaining Years of Service Prior to Full Elig.	19X4	19X5	19X6	19X7	19X8	19X9	19Y0	19Y1	19Y2	19Y3	19Y4	19Y5	19Y6	19Y7	19Y8	19Y9	19Z0	19Z1	19Z2	19Z3	Total Remaining Years of Service Prior to Full Elig.
A1-A4	1	4																				4
B1-B6	2	6	6																			12
C1-C5	3	5	5	5																		15
D1-D5	4	5	5	5	5																	20
E1-E7	5	7	7	7	7	7																35
F1-F5	6	5	5	5	5	5	5															30
G1-G9	7	9	9	9	9	9	9	9														63
H1-H7	8	7	7	7	7	7	7	7	7													56
I1-I5	9	5	5	5	5	5	5	5	5	5												45
J1-J5	10	5	5	5	5	5	5	5	5	5	5											50
K1-K4	11	4	4	4	4	4	4	4	4	4	4	4										44
L1-L8	12	8	8	8	8	8	8	8	8	8	8	8	8									96
M1-M8	13	8	8	8	8	8	8	8	8	8	8	8	8	8								104
N1-N5	14	5	5	5	5	5	5	5	5	5	5	5	5	5	5							70
O1-O4	15	4	4	4	4	4	4	4	4	4	4	4	4	4	4	4						60
P1-P3	16	3	3	3	3	3	3	3	3	3	3	3	3	3	3	3	3					48
Q1-Q4	17	4	4	4	4	4	4	4	4	4	4	4	4	4	4	4	4	4				68
R1-R3	18	3	3	3	3	3	3	3	3	3	3	3	3	3	3	3	3	3	3			54
S1-S2	19	2	2	2	2	2	2	2	2	2	2	2	2	2	2	2	2	2	2	2		38
T1	20	1	1	1	1	1	1	1	1	1	1	1	1	1	1	1	1	1	1	1	1	20
Service Years Rendered		100	96	90	85	80	73	68	59	52	47	42	38	30	22	17	13	10	6	3	1	932
Amortization Fraction		$\frac{100}{932}$	$\frac{96}{932}$	$\frac{90}{932}$	$\frac{85}{932}$	$\frac{80}{932}$	$\frac{73}{932}$	$\frac{68}{932}$	$\frac{59}{932}$	$\frac{52}{932}$	$\frac{47}{932}$	$\frac{42}{932}$	$\frac{38}{932}$	$\frac{30}{932}$	$\frac{22}{932}$	$\frac{17}{932}$	$\frac{13}{932}$	$\frac{10}{932}$	$\frac{6}{932}$	$\frac{3}{932}$	$\frac{1}{932}$	$\frac{932}{932}$

Note: To determine total remaining service years prior to full eligibility, consideration is given to the remaining number of years of service to the full eligibility date of each plan participant or group of plan participants active at the date of the plan amendment who is not yet fully eligible for benefits. For example, in 19X4, individuals A1-A4 meet the company's age and service requirements for full eligibility for the benefits they are expected to receive under the plan. Although it may be expected that those employees will work beyond 19X4, benefits are not attributed to years of service beyond their full eligibility date (paragraph .114). Refer to Case 4B, paragraph .251, for less complex amortization approaches.

Schedule 2—Amortization of Unrecognized Prior Service Cost

Year	Beginning-of-Year Balance	Amortization Rate	Amortization	End-of-Year Balance
19X4	$750,000	100/932	$80,472	$669,528
19X5	669,528	96/932	77,253	592,275
19X6	592,275	90/932	72,425	519,850
19X7	519,850	85/932	68,401	451,449
19X8	451,449	80/932	64,378	387,071
19X9	387,071	73/932	58,745	328,326
19Y0	328,326	68/932	54,721	273,605
19Y1	273,605	59/932	47,479	226,126
19Y2	226,126	52/932	41,845	184,281
19Y3	184,281	47/932	37,822	146,459
19Y4	146,459	42/932	33,798	112,661
19Y5	112,661	38/932	30,579	82,082
19Y6	82,082	30/932	24,142	57,940
19Y7	57,940	22/932	17,704	40,236
19Y8	40,236	17/932	13,680	26,556
19Y9	26,556	13/932	10,461	16,095
19Z0	16,095	10/932	8,047	8,048
19Z1	8,048	6/932	4,828	3,220
19Z2	3,220	3/932	2,414	806
19Z3	806	1/932	806	0

[FAS106, ¶453]

Case 4B—Straight-Line Amortization over Average Remaining Years of Service to Full Eligibility Date

.251 To reduce the complexity and detail of the computations shown in Case 4A (paragraph .250, Schedules 1 and 2), alternative amortization approaches that recognize prior service cost related to plan amendments more rapidly may be applied if used consistently (paragraph .148). For example, if Company H (Case 4A) elects to use straight-line amortization of prior service cost over the average remaining years of service prior to full eligibility for benefits of the active plan participants (932 future service years ÷ 100 employees = 9.32 years), the amortization would be as follows:

Year	Beginning-of-Year Balance	Amortization	End-of-Year Balance
19X4	$750,000	$80,472[a]	$669,528
19X5	669,528	80,472	589,056
19X6	589,056	80,472	508,584
19X7	508,584	80,472	428,112
19X8	428,112	80,472	347,640
19X9	347,640	80,472	267,168
19Y0	267,168	80,472	186,696
19Y1	186,696	80,472	106,224
19Y2	106,224	80,472	25,752
19Y3	25,752	25,752	0

[a]$750,000 ÷ 9.32 years = $80,472.

Note: Under this approach, the first year's amortization is the same as the first year's amortization under the weighted remaining years of service method illustrated in Case 4A (paragraph .250, Schedule 2). Thereafter, the amortization pattern will differ.

[FAS106, ¶454]

Illustration 5—Accounting for Gains and Losses and Timing of Measurements

.252 Gains and losses are changes in the amount of the accumulated postretirement benefit obligation or plan assets resulting from experience different from that assumed or changes in assumptions (paragraph .151). This illustration demonstrates the effects of gains and losses in accounting for postretirement benefits for Company I from 19X3 to 19X5. Case 5A (paragraphs .254 through .258) illustrates the accounting for a loss resulting from changes in assumptions in measuring the accumulated postretirement benefit obligation. Case 5B (paragraphs .259 through .261) illustrates the effect of a gain when the return on plan assets exceeds projections. Case 5C (paragraphs .262 through .264) illustrates the accounting in a year when both gains and losses are experienced. [FAS106, ¶455]

.253 Company I adopts [the provisions of] this section for the fiscal year beginning January 1, 19X3 and elects a December 31 measurement date (date at which the accumulated postretirement benefit obligation and plan assets are measured). Alternatively, as discussed in paragraph .167, the company could choose a measurement date not earlier than September 30. The company's accumulated postretirement benefit obligation on December 31, 19X2 is $6,000,000, and the plan is unfunded. Beginning in 19X3, and unless otherwise noted, the company funds at the end of each year an amount equal to the benefits paid that year plus the service cost and interest cost for that year. For illustrative purposes, the following assumptions are used to project changes in the accumulated postretirement benefit obligation and plan assets during the period 19X3 through 19X5:

	19X3	**19X4**	**19X5**
Discount rate	9.5%	9.0%	9.0%
Expected long-term rate of return on plan assets		10.0%	10.0%
Average remaining years of service of active plan participants	12	12	12

[FAS106, ¶456]

Case 5A—Loss on Obligation

.254 The reconciliation of the funded status of Company I's postretirement benefit plan with the amount shown in the statement of financial position at the date of transition (January 1, 19X3) follows:

	Actual 1/1/X3
Accumulated postretirement benefit obligation	$(6,000,000)
Plan assets at fair value	0
Funded status	(6,000,000)
Unrecognized transition obligation	6,000,000
(Accrued)/prepaid postretirement benefit cost	$ 0

[FAS106, ¶457]

.255 Company I elects to amortize the unrecognized transition obligation over a 20-year period rather than the average remaining service period of active plan participants at the date of transition (12 years). Projected changes in prepaid postretirement benefit cost, accumulated postretirement benefit obligation, unrecognized transition obligation, and plan assets in 19X3 are summarized as follows:

	Prepaid Postretirement Benefit Cost	Accumulated Postretirement Benefit Obligation	Unrecognized Transition Obligation	Plan Assets
Beginning of year	$ 0	$(6,000,000)	$6,000,000	$ 0
Recognition of components of net periodic postretirement benefit cost:				
Service cost	(300,000)	(300,000)		
Interest cost	(570,000)	(570,000)		
Amortization of transition obligation	(300,000)		(300,000)	
	(1,170,000)	(870,000)	(300,000)	
Assets contributed to plan	1,500,000			1,500,000
Benefit payments from plan		630,000		(630,000)
Net change	330,000	(240,000)	(300,000)	870,000
End of year—projected	$ 330,000	$(6,240,000)	$5,700,000	$ 870,000

[FAS106, ¶458]

.256 When Company I's plan assets and obligations are measured at December 31, 19X3, the accumulated postretirement benefit obligation is $760,000 greater than had been projected (a loss occurs) because the discount rate declined to 9 percent and for various other reasons not specifically identified. Company I elects to amortize amounts in excess of the "corridor" over the average remaining service period of active plan participants.[41] [FAS106, ¶459]

---

[41] Paragraph .154 states that, at a minimum, amortization of an unrecognized net gain or loss is included as a component of net periodic postretirement benefit cost if, as of the beginning of the year, that unrecognized net gain or loss exceeds 10 percent of the greater of the accumulated postretirement benefit obligation or market-related value of plan assets. As used herein, *amounts in excess of the corridor* refers to the portion of the unrecognized net gain or loss in excess of the greater of those defined amounts. [FAS106, ¶459, fna]

.257 The change in the funded status of the plan at December 31, 19X3 from amounts projected and the reconciliation of the funded status of the plan with the amount shown in the statement of financial position at that date follow:

	Projected 12/31/X3	Net Loss	Actual 12/31/X3
Accumulated postretirement benefit obligation	$(6,240,000)	$(760,000)	$(7,000,000)
Plan assets at fair value	870,000		870,000
Funded status	(5,370,000)	(760,000)	(6,130,000)
Unrecognized net loss		760,000	760,000
Unrecognized transition obligation	5,700,000		5,700,000
Prepaid postretirement benefit cost	$ 330,000	$ 0	$ 330,000

[FAS106, ¶460]

.258 In addition to the funded status reconciliation, the 19X3 financial statements include the following disclosure of the components of net periodic postretirement benefit cost (as required by paragraph .169(b)):

Service cost	$ 300,000
Interest cost	570,000
Amortization of transition obligation	300,000
Net periodic postretirement benefit cost	$1,170,000

[FAS106, ¶461]

Case 5B—Gain on Assets

.259 Changes in prepaid postretirement benefit cost, accumulated postretirement benefit obligation, unrecognized transition obligation, unrecognized net loss, and plan assets are projected at the beginning of the year. That projection serves as the basis for interim accounting until a subsequent event occurs requiring remeasurement. The projection at the beginning of 19X4 follows:

	Prepaid Postretirement Benefit Cost	Accumulated Postretirement Benefit Obligation	Unrecognized Transition Obligation	Unrecognized Net Loss	Plan Assets
Beginning of year	$ 330,000	$(7,000,000)	$5,700,000	$760,000	$ 870,000
Recognition of components of net periodic postretirement benefit cost:					
Service cost	(320,000)	(320,000)			
Interest cost	(630,000)	(630,000)			
Amortization of transition obligation	(300,000)		(300,000)		
Amortization of unrecognized net loss[a]	(5,000)			(5,000)	
Expected return on plan assets[b]	87,000				87,000
	(1,168,000)	(950,000)	(300,000)	(5,000)	87,000
Assets contributed to plan	1,650,000				1,650,000
Benefit payments from plan		700,000			(700,000)
Net change	482,000	(250,000)	(300,000)	(5,000)	1,037,000
End of year—projected	$ 812,000	$(7,250,000)	$5,400,000	$755,000	$1,907,000

[a]Refer to Schedule 2 (paragraph .266) for computation.
[b]Refer to Schedule 1 (paragraph .265) for computation.

[FAS106, ¶462]

.260 When Company I's plan assets and obligations are measured at December 31, 19X4, the fair value of the plan assets is $150,000 greater than expected (an experience gain) because market performance was better than the 10 percent return that was assumed. The change in the funded status of the plan at December 31, 19X4 from amounts projected and the reconciliation of the funded status of the plan with the amount shown in the statement of financial position at that date follow:

	Projected 12/31/X4	Net Gain	Actual 12/31/X4
Accumulated postretirement benefit obligation	$(7,250,000)		$(7,250,000)
Plan assets at fair value	1,907,000	$150,000[c]	2,057,000
Funded status	(5,343,000)	150,000	(5,193,000)
Unrecognized net (gain) or loss	755,000	(150,000)	605,000
Unrecognized transition obligation	5,400,000		5,400,000
Prepaid postretirement benefit cost	$ 812,000	$ 0	$ 812,000

[c]Refer to Schedule 1 (paragraph .265) for computation.

[FAS106, ¶463]

.261 The 19X4 financial statements include the following disclosure of the components of net periodic postretirement benefit cost:

Service cost	$ 320,000
Interest cost	630,000
Actual return on plan assets[d]	(237,000)
Amortization of transition obligation	300,000
Net amortization and deferral[e]	155,000
Net periodic postretirement benefit cost	$1,168,000

[d]Refer to Schedule 3 (paragraph .267) for computation.
[e]Refer to Schedule 4 (paragraph .268) for computation.

[FAS106, ¶464]

Case 5C—Loss on Assets and Gain on Obligation

.262 Projected changes in prepaid postretirement benefit cost, accumulated postretirement benefit obligation, unrecognized transition obligation, unrecognized net loss, and plan assets for 19X5 are summarized as follows:

	Prepaid Postretirement Benefit Cost	Accumulated Postretirement Benefit Obligation	Unrecognized Transition Obligation	Unrecognized Net Loss	Plan Assets
Beginning of year	$ 812,000	$(7,250,000)	$5,400,000	$605,000	$2,057,000
Recognition of components of net periodic postretirement benefit cost:					
Service cost	(360,000)	(360,000)			
Interest cost	(652,500)	(652,500)			
Amortization of transition obligation	(300,000)		(300,000)		
Amortization of unrecognized net loss[a]	0			0	
Expected return on plan assets[b]	193,700				193,700
	(1,118,800)	(1,012,500)	(300,000)	0	193,700
Assets contributed to plan	1,912,500				1,912,500
Benefit payments from plan		900,000			(900,000)
Net change	793,700	(112,500)	(300,000)	0	1,206,200
End of year—projected	$1,605,700	$(7,362,500)	$5,100,000	$605,000	$3,263,200

[a]Refer to Schedule 2 (paragraph .266) for computation.
[b]Refer to Schedule 1 (paragraph .265) for computation.

[FAS106, ¶465]

.263 When Company I's plan assets and obligations are measured at December 31, 19X5, both an asset loss of $220,360 and a liability gain of $237,260 are determined. The change in the funded status of the plan at December 31, 19X5 from amounts projected and the reconciliation of the funded status of the plan with the amount shown in the statement of financial position at that date follow:

	Projected 12/31/X5	Net Gain/Loss	Actual 12/31/X5
Accumulated postretirement benefit obligation	$(7,362,500)	$237,260	$(7,125,240)
Plan assets at fair value	3,263,200	(220,360)[c]	3,042,840
Funded status	(4,099,300)	16,900	(4,082,400)
Unrecognized net (gain) or loss	605,000	(16,900)	588,100
Unrecognized transition obligation	5,100,000		5,100,000
Prepaid postretirement benefit cost	$ 1,605,700	$ 0	$ 1,605,700

[c]Refer to Schedule 1 (paragraph .265) for computation.

[FAS106, ¶466]

.264 The 19X5 financial statements include the following disclosure of the components of net periodic postretirement benefit cost:

Service cost	$ 360,000
Interest cost	652,500
Actual loss on plan assets[d]	26,660
Amortization of transition obligation	300,000
Net amortization and deferral[e]	(220,360)
Net periodic postretirement benefit cost	$1,118,800

[d]Refer to Schedule 3 (paragraph .267) for computation.
[e]Refer to Schedule 4 (paragraph .268) for computation.

[FAS106, ¶467]

Supporting Schedules

Schedule 1—Plan Assets

.265 This section requires use of an assumption about the long-term rate of return on plan assets and a market-related value of plan assets to calculate the expected return on plan assets. If the fund holding plan assets is a taxable entity, the expected long-term rate of return on plan assets is net of estimated income taxes, and the nonbenefit liability for accrued income taxes reduces plan assets. This section defines market-related asset value as either fair value or a calculated value that recognizes changes in fair value in a systematic and rational manner over not more than five years (paragraph .152). This schedule reflects the calculation of market-related value, the fair value of plan assets, the actual return on plan assets, and the deferred asset gain or loss for the year (the difference between actual and expected return on plan assets included in the net amortization and deferral component of net periodic postretirement benefit cost).

	19X3	19X4	19X5
Expected long-term rate of return on plan assets		10.0%	10.0%
Beginning balance, market-related value[a]	$ 0	$ 870,000	$1,937,000
Contributions to plan (end of year)	1,500,000	1,650,000	1,912,500
Benefits paid by plan	(630,000)	(700,000)	(900,000)
Expected return on plan assets		87,000	193,700
	870,000	1,907,000	3,143,200
20% of each of last 5 years' asset gains (losses)		30,000	(14,072)
Ending balance, market-related value	$ 870,000	$1,937,000	$3,129,128
Beginning balance, fair value of plan assets	$ 0	$ 870,000	$2,057,000
Contributions to plan	1,500,000	1,650,000	1,912,500
Benefits paid	(630,000)	(700,000)	(900,000)
Actual return (loss) on plan assets[b]	0	237,000	(26,660)
Ending balance, fair value of plan assets	$ 870,000	$2,057,000	$3,042,840
Deferred asset gain (loss) for year[c]	$ 0	$ 150,000	$ (220,360)
Gain (loss) not included in ending balance market-related value[d]	$ 0	$ 120,000	$ (86,288)

---

[a]This example uses an approach that adds in 20% of each of the last 5 years' gains or losses.

[b]Refer to Schedule 3 (paragraph .267) for computation.

[c](Actual return on plan assets) − (expected return on plan assets).

[d](Ending balance, fair value of plan assets) − (ending balance, market-related value of plan assets).

[FAS106, ¶468]

Schedule 2—Test for Amortization of Unrecognized Net Gain or Loss

.266 This section generally does not require recognition of any of the gain or loss in the period in which it arises and permits a minimum amortization of an unrecognized net gain or loss whereby the net amount in excess of the "corridor" is amortized over the average remaining service period of active plan participants (paragraph .154 and paragraph .256, footnote 41). That allows a reasonable opportunity for gains and losses to offset each other without affecting net periodic postretirement benefit cost.

	19X3	19X4	19X5
10% of beginning balance of accumulated postretirement benefit obligation	$600,000	$700,000	$725,000
10% of beginning balance of market-related value of plan assets[e]	$ 0	$ 87,000	$193,700
Greater of the above	$600,000	$700,000	$725,000
Unrecognized net (gain) loss at beginning of year		$760,000	$605,000
Asset gain (loss) not included in beginning balance of market-related value[f]		0	120,000
Amount subject to amortization		$760,000	$725,000
Amount in excess of the corridor subject to amortization		$ 60,000	$ 0
Divided by average remaining service period (years)		12	
Required amortization		$ 5,000	

---

[e]Refer to Schedule 1 (paragraph .265) for calculation of market-related value of plan assets.

[f]Refer to Schedule 1 (paragraph .265) for calculation of gain or loss not included in prior year's ending balance market-related value.

[FAS106, ¶469]

Schedule 3—Determination of Actual Return or Loss on Plan Assets

.267 The determination of the actual return or loss on plan assets component of net periodic postretirement benefit cost is as follows:

	19X3	19X4	19X5
Plan assets at fair value, beginning of year	$ 0	$ 870,000	$2,057,000
Plus: assets contributed to plan	1,500,000	1,650,000	1,912,500
Less: benefit payments from plan	(630,000)	(700,000)	(900,000)
	870,000	1,820,000	3,069,500
Less: plan assets at fair value, end of year	(870,000)	(2,057,000)	(3,042,840)
Actual (return) loss on plan assets	$ 0	$ (237,000)	$ 26,660

[FAS106, ¶470]

Schedule 4—Determination of Net Amortization and Deferral

.268 The net amortization and deferral component of net periodic postretirement benefit cost required to be disclosed pursuant to paragraph .169(b) is determined as follows:

	19X4	19X5
Amortization of unrecognized net (gain) or loss[g]	$ 5,000	$ 0
Deferred asset gain (loss) for year[h]	150,000	(220,360)
Net amortization and deferral	$155,000	$(220,360)

---

[g]Refer to Schedule 2 (paragraph .266) for computation.
[h]Refer to Schedule 1 (paragraph .265) for computation.

[FAS106, ¶471]

Illustration 6—Defined-Dollar Capped Plans

.269 The following cases (6A and 6B, paragraphs .270 through .275) demonstrate the operation of defined-dollar capped plans and the possible effect of the "cap" on projecting costs for purposes of measuring the accumulated postretirement benefit obligation and net periodic postretirement benefit cost. The examples are simplified and illustrate only one aspect of the measurement process (paragraph .110 and paragraph .128, footnote 16). [FAS106, ¶472]

Case 6A—Dollar Cap Defined on Individual Coverage

.270 Company J sponsors a postretirement health care plan for its salaried employees. The plan has an annual limitation (a "cap") on the dollar amount of the employer's share of the cost of covered benefits incurred by a plan participant. The retiree is responsible, therefore, for the amount by which the cost of the benefit coverage under the plan incurred during a year exceeds that cap. The company adjusts the cap annually for the effects of inflation. For 19X3, the cap is $1,500; the inflation adjustment in 19X4 and 19X5 is assumed to be 4 percent. The employer's health care cost trend rate assumption is 13 percent for 19X4 and 12 percent for 19X5. [FAS106, ¶473]

.271 The employer's projected cost of providing benefit coverage in 19X3 through 19X5 for a 67-year-old retiree follows. Similar projections are made for each age at which a plan participant is expected to receive benefits under the plan. In this example, the incurred claims cost exceeds the cap on the employer's share of the cost in each year.

	Expected Cost for 67-Year-Old Retiree		
	19X3	19X4	19X5
Gross eligible charges	$3,065	$3,463	$3,879
Medicare[a]	(890)	(1,003)	(1,125)
Deductible/coinsurance	(325)	(340)	(355)
Incurred claims cost	$1,850	$2,120	$2,399
Annual cap on employer's cost	$1,500	$1,560	$1,622
Employer's share of incurred claims cost	$1,500	$1,560	$1,622
Retiree's share of gross eligible charges[b]	$ 675	$ 900	$1,132

[a]The change in Medicare reflects the portion of the gross eligible charges for which Medicare is responsible under enacted Medicare legislation.

[b]Deductible/coinsurance plus share of incurred claims: 19X3—[$325 + ($1,850 − $1,500)]; 19X4—[$340 + ($2,120 − $1,560)]; 19X5—[$355 + ($2,399 − $1,622)].

[FAS106, ¶474]

.272 If, based on the health care cost trend rate assumptions, the employer's share of costs for each plan participant is not expected to be less than the cap in the future, Company J could measure its expected postretirement benefit obligation by projecting the annual cap. However, if per capita claims data for some plan participants or estimates of the health care cost trend rate indicate that in the future the employer's share of the incurred claims cost will be less than the cap for at least some plan participants, the employer's obligation is to be measured as described in paragraphs .129 through .137. [FAS106, ¶475]

Case 6B—Dollar Cap Defined in the Aggregate for the Retiree Group

.273 Company K sponsors a contributory postretirement health care plan for its hourly employees. The plan has an annual limitation (a "cap") on the dollar amount of the employer's share of the cost of covered benefits incurred by the retiree group as a whole. The Company agrees to bear annual costs equal to a specified dollar amount ($1,500 in 19X3) multiplied by the number of retired plan participants (the employer contribution); participating retirees are required to contribute a stated amount each year ($1,000 in 19X3). The cap on the employer's share of annual costs and the retirees' contribution rates are increased 5 percent annually. The shortfall in a year (the amount by which incurred claims cost exceed the combined employer and retiree contributions) is initially borne by the employer but is passed back to retirees in the subsequent year through supplemental retiree contributions for that year (a retrospective adjustment). [FAS106, ¶476]

.274 The employer projects the aggregate cost of benefits expected to be paid to current plan participants (40 retirees) in each future period as follows:

	19X3	19X4	19X5
Gross eligible charges	$160,000	$215,000	$197,000
Medicare	(46,500)	(62,350)	(57,300)
Deductible/coinsurance	(20,750)	(27,440)	(24,700)
Incurred claims cost	$ 92,750	$125,210	$115,000
Retiree contributions[a]	$ 40,000	$ 42,000	$ 44,080
Maximum employer contribution[b]	60,000	63,000	66,160
	$100,000	$105,000	$110,240
Shortfall (to be recovered by additional retiree contributions in subsequent year)		$ 20,210	$ 4,760
Supplemental contribution from retirees due to shortfall in prior year			$ 20,210

[a]Per retiree: 19X3—$1,000; 19X4—$1,050; 19X5—$1,102.

[b]Per retiree: 19X3—$1,500; 19X4—$1,575; 19X5—$1,654.

[FAS106, ¶477]

.275 If, as in this example, retirees absorb the entire shortfall in annual contributions and if there is a projected shortfall for all future years, the employer could measure its expected postretirement benefit obligation by projecting its annual contribution (contribution rate × expected number of retirees = expected obligation for the year). [FAS106, ¶478]

Illustration 7—Disclosure Requirements

.276 This section requires an employer to disclose information in its financial statements about the obligation to provide postretirement benefits and the cost of providing those benefits. Paragraph .169 describes the disclosures required for defined benefit postretirement plans (paragraphs .172 and .173 describe how those disclosures may be aggregated by an employer with more than one postretirement benefit plan), paragraph .198 describes the disclosures required for defined contribution plans, and paragraph .178 describes the disclosures required for multiemployer plans. The following cases (7A through 7C, paragraphs .277 through .280) illustrate those disclosure requirements. For simplicity, comparative financial statements are not presented. [FAS106, ¶479]

Case 7A—Single-Employer Defined Benefit Postretirement Plan

.277 Paragraph .173(a) permits an employer to combine the disclosures for health and other welfare benefit plans unless the accumulated postretirement benefit obligation of the plans that provide primarily other postretirement welfare benefits is significant relative to the aggregate accumulated postretirement benefit obligation of all the employer's postretirement benefit plans. For an employer that provides more than one defined benefit postretirement plan, the disclosure for the year ended December 31, 19X3 would be as follows. Because the life insurance plan is not significant, it is combined with the health care plan for disclosure purposes as permitted by paragraph .173.

Note X: The company sponsors two defined benefit postretirement plans that cover both salaried and nonsalaried employees. One plan provides medical and dental benefits, and the other provides life insurance benefits. The postretirement health care plan is contributory, with retiree contributions adjusted annually; the life insurance plan is noncontributory. The accounting for the health care plan anticipates future cost-sharing changes to the written plan that are consistent with the company's expressed intent to increase retiree contributions each year by 50 percent of the excess of the expected general inflation rate over 6 percent. On July 24, 19X3, the company amended its postretirement health care plan to provide vision coverage. Beginning in 19X3, the company adopted a funding policy for its postretirement health care plan similar to its funding policy for its life insurance plan—an amount equal to a level percentage of the employees' salaries is contributed to the plan annually. For 19X3, that percentage was 4.25, and the aggregate contribution for both plans was $34,000.

The following table sets forth the plans' combined funded status reconciled with the amount shown in the company's statement of financial position at December 31, 19X3:

Accumulated postretirement benefit obligation:	
Retirees	$(187,000)
Fully eligible active plan participants	(100,000)
Other active plan participants	(297,400)
	(584,400)
Plan assets at fair value, primarily listed U.S. stocks and bonds	87,960
Accumulated postretirement benefit obligation in excess of plan assets	(496,440)
Unrecognized net gain from past experience different from that assumed and from changes in assumptions	(40,000)
Prior service cost not yet recognized in net periodic postretirement benefit cost	19,000
Unrecognized transition obligation	470,250
Accrued postretirement benefit cost	$ (47,190)

The company's postretirement health care plan is underfunded; the accumulated postretirement benefit obligation and plan assets for that plan are $552,400 and $36,800, respectively.

Net periodic postretirement benefit cost for 19X3 included the following components:

Service cost—benefits attributed to service during the period	$15,000
Interest cost on accumulated postretirement benefit obligation	44,400
Actual return on plan assets	(3,960)
Amortization of transition obligation over 20 years	24,750
Net amortization and deferral	1,000
Net periodic postretirement benefit cost	$81,190

For measurement purposes, a 16 percent annual rate of increase in the per capita cost of covered health care benefits was assumed for 19X4; the rate was assumed to decrease gradually to 6 percent for [19Z9] and remain at that level thereafter. The health care cost trend rate assumption has a significant effect on the amounts reported. To illustrate, increasing the assumed health care cost trend rates by 1 percentage point in each year would increase the accumulated postretirement benefit obligation as of December 31, 19X3 by $73,000 and the aggregate of the service and interest cost components of net periodic postretirement benefit cost for the year then ended by $13,000.

The weighted-average discount rate used in determining the accumulated postretirement benefit obligation was 8 percent. The trust holding the plan assets is subject to federal income taxes at a 34 percent tax rate. The expected long-term rate of return on plan assets after estimated taxes was 6.6 percent. [FAS106, ¶480]

Case 7B—Defined Contribution Plan

.278 An illustration of the disclosure for a defined contribution plan follows:

Note X: The company sponsors a defined contribution postretirement health care plan covering substantially all of its employees in both its chemicals and automotive subsidiaries. The company's contributions and cost are determined annually as 1.5 percent of each covered employee's salary and totaled $569,000 in 19X3. [FAS106, ¶481]

Case 7C—Multiemployer Plan

.279 An illustration of the disclosure for a multiemployer plan follows:

Note X: The company's trucking subsidiary participates in a multiemployer plan that provides defined postretirement health care benefits to substantially all unionized workers in that subsidiary. Amounts charged to postretirement benefit cost and contributed to the plan totaled $319,000 in 19X3. [FAS106, ¶482]

.280 If the information regarding the amount of postretirement benefit cost recognized during the period (disclosed in paragraph .279) is not available and the postretirement health and welfare benefits are provided through a general health and welfare plan, the amount of the aggregate required contribution to the general health and welfare benefit plan should be disclosed as follows (paragraph .178(b)):

Note X: The company's trucking subsidiary participates in a multiemployer plan that provides substantially all unionized workers in that subsidiary with health care and other welfare benefits during their working lives and after retirement. Amounts charged to benefit cost and contributed to the health and welfare plan for those benefits totaled $400,000 in 19X3. [FAS106, ¶483]

Illustration 8—Accounting for Settlements

.281 This section provides for delayed recognition of the effects of a plan initiation or a plan amendment, the transition obligation or transition asset, and gains or losses arising in the ordinary course of operations. In certain circumstances, however, recognition of some or all of those previously delayed amounts is appropriate. Settlements are events that may require income or expense recognition of certain previously unrecognized amounts and adjustments to liabilities or assets recognized in the employer's statement of financial position. The settlement of all or part of the accumulated postretirement benefit obligation is the event that requires recognition of all or part of a previously unrecognized net gain or loss and unrecognized transition asset. A settlement also may accelerate recognition of a transition obligation under the constraint in paragraph .200 (paragraphs .184 and .185). The following cases (8A through 8C, paragraphs .282 through .292) illustrate the accounting for settlements in various circumstances. [FAS106, ¶484]

Case 8A—Settlement When an Unrecognized Transition Obligation Exists

.282 Company L sponsors a postretirement life insurance plan. On January 1, 19X3, the company adopts [the provisions of] this section; prior to that date it accounted for postretirement benefits on a pay-as-you-go (cash) basis. On December 31, 19X4, Company L settles the accumulated postretirement benefit obligation for its current retirees ($70,000) through the purchase of nonparticipating life insurance contracts. [FAS106, ¶485]

.283 In accounting for the settlement, Company L must determine whether recognition of an additional amount of any unrecognized transition obligation is required pursuant to the constraint on delayed recognition of the transition obligation (paragraphs .200 and .201). At December 31, 19X4, the cumulative postretirement benefit cost accrued subsequent to the date of transition exceeds the cumulative benefit payments subsequent to that date (including payments made pursuant to the settlement) in this example; thus, the constraint on delayed recognition of the transition obligation is not operative. The results of the settlement are as follows:

	December 31, 19X4		
	Before Settlement	Settlement	After Settlement
Accumulated postretirement benefit obligation	$(257,000)	$70,000	$(187,000)
Plan assets at fair value	73,000	(70,000)[a]	3,000
Funded status	(184,000)	0	(184,000)
Unrecognized net gain	(44,575)	12,124[a]	(32,451)
Unrecognized prior service cost	33,000		33,000
Unrecognized transition obligation	195,000	(12,124)[a]	182,876
Accrued postretirement benefit cost	$ (575)	$ 0	$ (575)

[a] The maximum settlement gain subject to recognition is the unrecognized net gain subsequent to transition plus any unrecognized transition asset ($44,575 + $0 = $44,575) (paragraph .184). If, as in this case, only part of the accumulated postretirement benefit obligation is settled, a pro rata portion of the maximum gain based on the relationship of the accumulated postretirement benefit obligation settled to the total accumulated postretirement benefit obligation ($70,000 ÷ $257,000 or 27.2%) is subject to recognition. That amount ($44,575 × 27.2% = $12,124) must first reduce any unrecognized transition obligation; any excess is recognized in income in the current period (paragraph .185). In this case, the settlement gain is entirely offset against the unrecognized transition obligation.

[FAS106, ¶486]

Case 8B—Settlement When an Unrecognized Transition Asset Exists

.284 Company M sponsors a postretirement life insurance plan. On January 2, 19X5, Company M settles the accumulated postretirement benefit obligation for its current retirees ($200,000) through the purchase of nonparticipating life insurance contracts. [FAS106, ¶487]

.285 Pursuant to paragraphs .184 and .185, a settlement gain of $78,506 is recognized, determined as follows:

| | January 2, 19X5 | | |
	Before Settlement	Settlement	After Settlement
Accumulated postretirement benefit obligation	$(257,000)	$200,000	$(57,000)
Plan assets at fair value	350,900	(200,000)	150,900
Funded status	93,900	0	93,900
Unrecognized net gain	(44,575)	34,679[a]	(9,896)
Unrecognized prior service cost	33,000		33,000
Unrecognized transition asset	(56,333)	43,827[a]	(12,506)
Prepaid postretirement benefit cost	$ 25,992	$ 78,506	$104,498

---

[a]The maximum settlement gain is measured as the unrecognized net gain subsequent to transition plus the unrecognized transition asset ($44,575 + $56,333 = $100,908) (paragraph .184). Since only a portion of the accumulated postretirement benefit obligation is settled, a pro rata portion of the maximum gain based on the relationship of the accumulated postretirement benefit obligation settled to the total accumulated postretirement benefit obligation ($200,000 ÷ $257,000 or 77.8%) is subject to recognition. That amount ($100,908 × 77.8% = $78,506) must first reduce any unrecognized transition obligation ($0); any excess is recognized in income in the current period (paragraph .185). In this case, the entire settlement gain of $78,506 is recognized in income. The transition constraint of paragraph .200 that requires additional recognition of a *transition obligation* in certain circumstances is not applicable because there is an unrecognized *transition asset*.

[FAS106, ¶488]

Case 8C—Effect of Mid-Year Settlement on Transition Constraint

.286 A settlement is an event that requires remeasurement of the accumulated postretirement benefit obligation prior to the settlement. This case illustrates the accounting for a settlement of part of the accumulated postretirement benefit obligation that occurs mid-year and the interaction between that event and other provisions of the section, such as the constraint on delayed recognition of the transition obligation. [FAS106, ¶489]

.287 Company N adopts [the provisions of] this section for the fiscal year beginning January 1, 19X3 and elects a year-end (December 31) measurement date. At the date of transition, the company's accumulated postretirement benefit obligation for its postretirement life insurance plan is $6,000,000, and there are no plan assets. In 19X3, the company establishes a policy of funding at the end of each year an amount equal to the benefits paid during the year plus the service and interest cost for the year. Benefits are paid at the end of each year and in 19X3 are $630,000, which is less than the net periodic postretirement benefit cost accrued for the year ($1,170,000); thus, no additional transition obligation is recognized pursuant to paragraph .200. Company N elects to amortize net unrecognized gains and losses in excess of the "corridor" over the average remaining service period of plan participants (paragraph .154 and paragraph .256, footnote 41). [FAS106, ¶490]

.288 At the beginning of 19X4, Company N projects the life insurance benefits expected to be paid in 19X4 to retirees' beneficiaries to determine whether recognition of an additional amount of the unrecognized transition obligation will be required (paragraph .201). Although Company N is considering settling a portion of the accumulated postretirement benefit obligation, the effects of the settlement are not included in the projection because plan settlements are not anticipated for measurement or recognition prior to their occurrence. The projection indicates that no additional amount is required to be recognized. On June 30, 19X4, Company N contributes additional funds ($1,430,000) and settles a portion ($1,900,000) of the accumulated postretirement benefit obligation for its current retirees through the purchase of nonparticipating life insurance contracts. [FAS106, ¶491]

.289 The changes in the funded status of the plan during the first six months of the year and a reconciliation of the funded status of the plan with the amount shown in the statement of financial position immediately prior to the settlement are as follows:

	Actual 12/31/X3	Six Months Postretirement Benefit Cost	Assets Contributed to Plan	Effects of Remeasurement Immediately before Settlement	Before Settlement 6/30/X4
Accumulated post-retirement benefit obligation	$(6,600,000)	$(457,000)[a]		$420,000[b]	$(6,637,000)
Plan assets at fair value	870,000	43,500[c]	$1,430,000	0[b]	2,343,500
Funded status	(5,730,000)	(413,500)	1,430,000	420,000	(4,293,500)
Unrecognized net (gain) or loss	360,000	0		(420,000)[b]	(60,000)
Unrecognized transition obligation	5,700,000	(150,000)			5,550,000
Prepaid postretirement benefit cost	$ 330,000	$(563,500)	$1,430,000	$ 0	$ 1,196,500[d]

[a]Represents 6 months' service cost of $160,000 and interest cost of $297,000 on the accumulated postretirement benefit obligation for 19X4, assuming a 9% discount rate.

[b]A gain results from the remeasurement of the accumulated postretirement benefit obligation immediately prior to the settlement as a result of a change in the assumed discount rates based on the interest rates inherent in the price at which the accumulated postretirement benefit obligation for the retirees will be settled. No gain or loss results from remeasurement of plan assets.

[c]Represents 6 months' return on plan assets, assuming a 10% return.

[d]Because there is a settlement (treated as a benefit payment) and a prepaid asset exists as a result of providing the funds to effect that settlement, the constraint on delayed recognition of the transition obligation pursuant to paragraph .200 may be applicable. The test to determine whether additional recognition is necessary should be done based on amounts for the full year (paragraph .291).

[FAS106, ¶492]

.290 In accounting for a settlement, an employer must determine whether recognition of an additional amount of any unrecognized transition obligation is required pursuant to the constraint on delayed recognition (paragraph .200). Any additional transition obligation required to be recognized as a result of a settlement is recognized when the related settlement is recognized (paragraph .201) as illustrated in the following table. Detailed calculations are presented in paragraph .291.

| | **June 30, 19X4** | | | |
	Before Settlement	**Settlement**	**Recognition of Transition Obligation**	**After Settlement**
Accumulated postretirement benefit obligation	$(6,637,000)	$1,900,000		$(4,737,000)
Plan assets at fair value	2,343,500	(1,900,000)		443,500
Funded status	(4,293,500)	0		(4,293,500)
Unrecognized net (gain) or loss	(60,000)	17,160^e		(42,840)
Unrecognized transition obligation	5,550,000	(17,160)^e	$(718,822)	4,814,018
Prepaid postretirement benefit cost	$ 1,196,500	$ 0	$(718,822)	$ 477,678

^{e}The maximum settlement gain subject to recognition is the unrecognized net gain subsequent to transition plus any unrecognized transition asset ($60,000 + $0 = $60,000). If, as in this case, only part of the accumulated postretirement benefit obligation is settled, a pro rata portion of the maximum gain based on the relationship of the accumulated postretirement benefit obligation settled to the total accumulated postretirement benefit obligation ($1,900,000 ÷ $6,637,000 or 28.6%) is subject to recognition. That amount ($60,000 × 28.6% = $17,160) must first reduce any unrecognized transition obligation (paragraph .185); any excess is recognized. In this situation, the settlement gain is entirely offset against the unrecognized transition obligation.

[FAS106, ¶493]

.291 When a settlement occurs in the middle of the year, as in this example, the additional transition obligation to be recognized, if any, pursuant to the constraint in paragraph .200 is determined based on projected amounts for the full year. In this case, at June 30, 19X4, cumulative benefit payments from the date of transition (January 1, 19X3) to December 31, 19X4 are projected to exceed cumulative postretirement benefit cost accrued for that same period as illustrated in the following table. The additional transition obligation to be recognized is the amount by which cumulative benefit payments exceed cost accrued, or $718,822.

	Projected 12/31/X4
Benefit payments:	
1/1/X3 to beginning of 19X4	$ 630,000
19X4 excluding settlement	410,000
Settlement	1,900,000
Cumulative benefit payments	$2,940,000
Postretirement benefit cost recognized:	
1/1/X3 to beginning of 19X4	$1,170,000
19X4	1,051,178[f]
Cumulative cost recognized	$2,221,178
Benefit payments in excess of cost recognized	$ 718,822

[f]$563,500 for period 1/1/X4 through 6/30/X4 plus $487,678 for period 7/1/X4 through 12/31/X4. The net postretirement benefit cost of $487,678 recognized in the second half of 19X4 (paragraph .292) includes amortization ($130,108) of the unrecognized transition obligation that remains after recognizing an additional portion ($718,822) of the unrecognized transition obligation pursuant to paragraph .200. Because determination of the additional portion of the transition obligation to be recognized and the transition obligation amortized in the second half of 19X4 are interrelated, those amounts are determined in a single computation that is intended to result in unrecognized transition obligation at the end of the year that appropriately reflects the constraint of paragraph .200.

[FAS106, ¶494]

.292 After the settlement, net periodic postretirement benefit cost for the remainder of the year is remeasured. The projected funded status of the plan reconciled to the projected amounts to be shown in the statement of financial position follows:

	After Settlement 6/30/X4	Six Months Postretirement Benefit Cost	Benefit Payments	Assets Contributed to Plan	Projected 12/31/X4
Accumulated postretirement benefit obligation	$(4,737,000)	$(379,745)[g]	$410,000		$(4,706,745)
Plan assets at fair value	443,500	22,175[h]	(410,000)	$1,246,745	1,302,420
Funded status	(4,293,500)	(357,570)	0	1,246,745	(3,404,325)
Unrecognized net gain	(42,840)	0			(42,840)
Unrecognized transition obligation	4,814,018	(130,108)[i]			4,683,910
(Accrued)/prepaid postretirement cost	$ 477,678	$(487,678)	$ 0	$1,246,745	$ 1,236,745

[g]Represents 6 months' service cost of $150,000 and interest cost of $229,745 on the accumulated postretirement benefit obligation, assuming a 9.7% discount rate.

[h]Represents 6 months' return on plan assets, assuming a 10% return.

[i]Unrecognized transition obligation at 6/30/X4 of $4,814,018 ÷ 18.5 years remaining in amortization period = $260,217; half-year amortization = $130,108.

[FAS106, ¶495]

Illustration 9—Accounting for Curtailments

.293 This section provides for delayed recognition of the effects of a plan initiation or a plan amendment, the transition obligation or transition asset, and gains or losses arising in the ordinary course of operations. In certain circumstances, however, recognition of some or all of those previously delayed amounts is appropriate. Curtailments are events that may require income or expense recognition of certain previously unrecognized amounts and adjustments to liabilities or assets recognized in the employer's statement of financial position. [FAS106, ¶496]

.294 A curtailment is an event that significantly reduces the expected years of future service of active plan participants or eliminates the accrual of defined benefits for some or all of the future services of a significant number of active plan participants. Such a reduction or elimination raises doubt about the continued existence of the future economic benefits of prior plan amendments. Therefore, an appropriate portion of the remaining unrecognized prior service cost should be recognized when it is probable that a curtailment will occur, the effects are reasonably estimable, and the estimated effects of the curtailment are a net loss. When the estimated effects of a curtailment are a net gain, the gain should be recognized in income when the related employees terminate or the plan suspension or amendment is adopted (paragraphs .189 through .191). For purposes of measuring those effects, any remaining unrecognized transition obligation is treated as unrecognized prior service cost. The following cases (9A and 9B, paragraphs .295 through .298) illustrate the accounting for curtailments. [FAS106, ¶497]

Case 9A—Curtailment When an Unrecognized Gain and an Unrecognized Transition Obligation Exist

.295 Company P sponsors a postretirement benefit plan. On October 29, 19X4, Company P decides to reduce its operations by terminating a significant number of employees effective December 31, 19X4. On October 29, 19X4, it is expected that a curtailment gain will result from the termination. A consequence of the curtailment is a significant reduction in the number of employees accumulating benefits under the plan. The *remaining years of expected service* associated with those terminated employees who were plan participants at the date of transition is 22 percent of the remaining years of service of all plan participants at the date of transition. The *remaining years of service prior to full eligibility* associated with those terminated employees who were plan participants at the date of a prior plan amendment is 18 percent of the remaining years of service of all plan participants at the date of that plan amendment. [FAS106, ¶498]

.296 The sum of the effects of the plan curtailment is a gain of $5,160 that should be recognized in income when the related employees terminate (paragraph .191). That gain is determined as follows:

	December 31, 19X4		
	Before Curtailment	Curtailment	After Curtailment
Accumulated postretirement benefit obligation	$(257,000)	$54,000[a]	$(203,000)
Plan assets at fair value	73,000		73,000
Funded status	(184,000)	54,000	(130,000)
Unrecognized net gain	(44,575)		(44,575)
Unrecognized prior service cost	33,000	(5,940)[a]	27,060
Unrecognized transition obligation	195,000	(42,900)[a]	152,100
(Accrued)/prepaid postretirement benefit cost	$ (575)	$ 5,160	$ 4,585

[a]The effect of the curtailment consists of two components:

1. The unrecognized transition obligation and unrecognized prior service cost associated with remaining years of service no longer expected to be rendered—measured as 22% (reduction in the remaining years of expected service associated with those terminated employees who were plan participants at the date of transition) of the unrecognized transition obligation of $195,000 ($42,900) and 18% (reduction in the remaining years of service prior to full eligibility for benefits associated with those terminated employees who were plan participants at the date of a prior plan amendment) of the unrecognized prior service cost of $33,000 related to that amendment ($5,940) (paragraph .189)
2. The gain from the decrease in the accumulated postretirement benefit obligation of $54,000 (due to the termination of employees whose accumulated benefits were not vested under the plan) in excess of the unrecognized net loss of $0, or $54,000 (paragraph .190(a)).

[FAS106, ¶499]

Case 9B—Curtailment Related to a Disposal of a Portion of the Business and an Unrecognized Loss and Unrecognized Transition Obligation Exist

.297 Company R sponsors a postretirement benefit plan. On December 31, 19X4, Company R sells a portion of its business at a gain of $100,000 before considering the effect of the related curtailment of its postretirement benefit plan. In connection with the sale, the number of employees accumulating benefits under the plan is significantly reduced; thus, a curtailment occurs. The *remaining years of expected service* associated with the terminated employees who were plan participants at the date of transition is 22 percent of the remaining years of service of all plan participants at the date of transition. The *remaining years of service prior to full eligibility* associated with the terminated employees who were plan participants at the date of that prior plan amendment is 18 percent of the remaining years of service of all plan participants at the date of that plan amendment. [FAS106, ¶500]

.298 The sum of the effects of the plan curtailment is a loss of $36,265 that should be recognized with the gain of $100,000 associated with Company R's sale of a portion of its business. The loss is determined as follows:

	December 31, 19X4		
	Before Curtailment	Curtailment	After Curtailment
Accumulated postretirement benefit obligation	$(343,000)	$ 54,000[a]	$(289,000)
Plan assets at fair value	73,000		73,000
Funded status	(270,000)	54,000	(216,000)
Unrecognized net loss	41,425	(41,425)[a]	0
Unrecognized prior service cost	33,000	(5,940)[a]	27,060
Unrecognized transition obligation	195,000	(42,900)[a]	152,100
Accrued postretirement benefit cost	$ (575)	$(36,265)	$ (36,840)

---

[a]The effect of the curtailment consists of two components:

1. The unrecognized transition obligation and unrecognized prior service cost associated with remaining years of service no longer expected to be rendered—measured as 22% (reduction in the remaining years of expected service associated with those terminated employees who were plan participants at the date of transition) of the unrecognized transition obligation of $195,000 ($42,900) and 18% (reduction in the remaining years of service prior to full eligibility for benefits associated with those terminated employees who were plan participants at the date of a prior plan amendment) of the unrecognized prior service cost of $33,000 related to that amendment ($5,940) (paragraph .189)
2. The gain from the decrease in the accumulated postretirement benefit obligation of $54,000 (due to the termination of employees whose accumulated benefits were not vested under the plan) in excess of the unrecognized net loss of $41,425, or $12,575 (paragraph .190(a)).

[FAS106, ¶501]

Illustration 10—Accounting for a Partial Settlement and a Full Curtailment That Occur as a Direct Result of a Sale of a Line of Business

.299 Company S sells a line of business on December 31, 19X4; prior to that date, the company had no formal plan for disposal of those operations. Company S has a separate postretirement benefit plan that provides health care benefits to retirees of the division that is sold. In connection with that sale, (a) all of the employees of that division are terminated by Company S resulting in no further accumulation of benefits under the postretirement benefit plan (a full curtailment), (b) most of the terminated employees are hired by the acquiring company (some terminated employees fully eligible for benefits elect to retire immediately), (c) an accumulated postretirement benefit obligation of $80,000 for postretirement benefits related to the hired employees is assumed by the acquiring company (a partial settlement, since the obligation for current retirees is retained by Company S), and (d) plan assets of $100,000, representing $80,000 for the settlement of the accumulated postretirement benefit obligation and $20,000 as an excess contribution, are transferred from the plan to the acquiring company. A $300,000 gain from the sale is calculated before considering the related effects on the plan. [FAS106, ¶502]

.300 The employer's accounting policy is to determine the effects of a curtailment before determining the effects of a settlement when both events occur simultaneously. Pursuant to paragraph .189, the unrecognized prior service cost associated with the portion of the future years of service that had been expected to be rendered, but as a result of a curtailment are no longer expected to be rendered, is a loss. When a full curtailment occurs, the entire remaining unrecognized prior service cost and unrecognized transition obligation is a loss because there are no future years of service to be rendered. [FAS106, ¶503]

.301 The net loss from the curtailment is $228,000, which is recognized with the $300,000 gain resulting from the disposal of the division. The effect of the curtailment is determined as follows:

| | December 31, 19X4 | | |
	Before Curtailment	Curtailment-Related Effects Resulting from Sale	After Curtailment
Accumulated postretirement benefit obligation	$(257,000)	$ (10,000)[a]	$(267,000)
Plan assets at fair value	110,000		110,000
Funded status	(147,000)	(10,000)	(157,000)
Unrecognized net gain	(49,575)	10,000[a]	(39,575)
Unrecognized prior service cost	33,000	(33,000)[b]	0
Unrecognized transition obligation	195,000	(195,000)[c]	0
(Accrued)/prepaid postretirement benefit cost	$ 31,425	$(228,000)	$(196,575)

[a]The increase in the accumulated postretirement benefit obligation as a result of the fully eligible employees retiring earlier than expected is a loss of $10,000. That loss reduces the unrecognized net gain of $49,575; any excess (none in this case) would be recognized as the effect of a curtailment (paragraph .190).

[b]Measured as 100% (reduction in the remaining years of service prior to full eligibility for benefits associated with those terminated employees who were plan participants at the date of a prior plan amendment) of the unrecognized prior service cost of $33,000 related to that amendment (paragraph .189).

[c]Measured as 100% (reduction in the remaining years of expected service associated with those terminated employees who were plan participants at the date of transition) of the unrecognized transition obligation of $195,000 (paragraph .189).

[FAS106, ¶504]

.302 The $8,128 loss related to the settlement and transfer of plan assets that is recognized with the gain from the sale is determined as follows:

	After Curtailment	Settlement and Transfer of Plan Assets	After Settlement
		December 31, 19X4	
Accumulated postretirement benefit obligation	$(267,000)	$ 80,000[d]	$(187,000)
Plan assets at fair value	110,000	(100,000)[d]	10,000
Funded status	(157,000)	(20,000)	(177,000)
Unrecognized net gain	(39,575)	11,872[e]	(27,703)
Unrecognized prior service cost	0		0
Unrecognized transition obligation	0		0
Accrued postretirement benefit cost	$(196,575)	$ (8,128)	$(204,703)

[d]The accumulated postretirement benefit obligation for the employees hired by the purchaser is determined to be $80,000 and is settled when Company S transfers plan assets of an equal amount to the purchaser. In connection with the purchase agreement, Company S transfers an additional $20,000 of plan assets.

[e]Represents a pro rata amount of the maximum gain based on the relationship of the accumulated postretirement benefit obligation settled to the total accumulated postretirement benefit obligation ($80,000 ÷ $267,000 or 30%). The maximum gain is measured as the unrecognized net gain subsequent to transition plus any unrecognized transition asset ($39,575 + $0 = $39,575). The settlement gain is, therefore, 30% of $39,575, or $11,872; recognition of that gain is subject to first reducing any remaining unrecognized transition obligation. As there is no remaining unrecognized transition obligation (the remainder was recognized in connection with the curtailment), the gain of $11,872 is recognized together with the excess $20,000 transfer of plan assets as part of the net gain from the sale (paragraphs .184 and .185).

[FAS106, ¶505]

.303 The sum of the effects related to postretirement benefits resulting from the sale is a loss of $236,128, the components of which are as follows:

Curtailment loss (paragraph .301)	$228,000
Settlement gain and loss from transfer of plan assets (paragraph .302)	8,128
Effects of sale	$236,128

[FAS106, ¶506]

Illustration 11—Accounting for the Effects of an Offer of Special Termination Benefits

.304 The measurement of the effects of an offer of special termination benefits pursuant to paragraphs .193 and .194 and the accounting for the related curtailment are illustrated in the following paragraphs. [FAS106, ¶507]

.305 On January 16, 19X5, Company T offers for a short period of time (until January 30, 19X5) special benefits to its employees who elect voluntary termination of employment during that period (special termination benefits). As part of the offer, employees who voluntarily terminate will be credited with an additional five years of service and five years of age to determine eligibility for postretirement health care benefits. Employees are normally eligible for those benefits upon attaining age 55 and rendering at least 20 years of service. [FAS106, ¶508]

.306 On January 30, 19X5, employees representing 18 percent of the work force accept the offer of special termination benefits. For those employees, the accumulated postretirement benefit obligation attributed to prior service periods based on their previously expected retirement dates (without consideration of the special offer) is $280,000. If those employees were assumed to terminate (retire) immediately upon attaining full eligibility for benefits (age 55 with 20 years of service), the accumulated postretirement benefit obligation for those employees would be $450,000. The accumulated postretirement benefit obligation for those employees after they accept the offer of the special termination benefits (full eligibility date accelerated, benefit coverage begins immediately) is $630,000. [FAS106, ¶509]

.307 The *remaining years of expected service* associated with the terminated employees who were plan participants at the date of transition is 24 percent of the remaining years of service of all plan participants at the date of transition. In addition, the portion of the unrecognized prior service cost arising from a prior plan amendment associated with the *remaining years of service prior to full eligibility* that are no longer expected to be rendered by the terminated employees is $25,000. [FAS106, ¶510]

.308 Pursuant to paragraph .191, if the sum of the effects resulting from a curtailment is a net loss, it shall be recognized in income when it is probable that a curtailment will occur and the effects are reasonably estimable. In this illustration, the effects resulting from the curtailment are not reasonably estimable until January 30, 19X5, the acceptance date of the offer of special termination benefits. Consequently, at January 30, 19X5, the employer recognizes a loss of $453,400 that includes the cost of the special termination benefits ($180,000) and the net loss from the curtailment ($273,400) determined as follows:

	January 30, 19X5			
	Before Employee Terminations	Special Termination Benefits	Effect of Curtailment	After Employee Terminations
Accumulated postretirement benefit obligation:				
Employees accepting offer	$(280,000)	$(180,000)[a]	$(170,000)[b]	$ (630,000)
Other employees	(633,000)			(633,000)
	(913,000)	(180,000)	(170,000)	(1,263,000)
Plan assets at fair value	141,000			141,000
Funded status	(772,000)	(180,000)	(170,000)	(1,122,000)
Unrecognized net gain	(88,000)		88,000[b]	0
Unrecognized prior service cost	148,500		(25,000)[c]	123,500
Unrecognized transition obligation	693,333		(166,400)[c]	526,933
Accrued postretirement benefit cost	$ (18,167)	$(180,000)	$(273,400)	$ (471,567)

[a]The loss from acceptance of the special termination benefits is $180,000 ($450,000 − $630,000), representing the difference between (1) the accumulated postretirement benefit obligation measured assuming that active plan participants not yet fully eligible for benefits would terminate employment at their full eligibility date and that fully eligible plan participants would retire immediately and (2) the accumulated postretirement benefit obligation reflecting the special termination benefits (paragraph .194).

[b]The increase in the accumulated postretirement benefit obligation as a result of the employees (fully eligible plan participants and other active plan participants not yet fully eligible for benefits) retiring at a date earlier than expected is a loss of $170,000 ($280,000 − $450,000). That amount is reduced by the unrecognized net gain of $88,000 (paragraph .190(b)) as part of the accounting for the curtailment.

[c]Additional effects of the curtailment are (1) the reduction of $25,000 in the unrecognized prior service cost (arising from a prior plan amendment) associated with the remaining years of service prior to full eligibility that are no longer expected to be rendered by the terminated employees and (2) the reduction of $166,400 in the unrecognized transition obligation associated with remaining years of service no longer expected to be rendered—measured as 24% (reduction in the remaining years of expected service associated with those employees affected by the early retirement who were plan participants at the date of transition) of the unrecognized transition obligation of $693,333 (paragraph .189).

[FAS106, ¶511]

[**Note:** Additional guidance with respect to implementing Section P40 is presented in FASB publication: *A Guide to Implementation of Statement 106 on Employers' Accounting for Postretirement Benefits Other Than Pensions: Questions and Answers.* The publication addresses 64 questions and was written by FASB staff members Kenneth E. Dakdduk and Jules M. Cassel. This publication is available from the Order Department, Financial Accounting Standards Board, 401 Merritt 7, P.O. Box 5116, Norwalk, CT 06856-5116, telephone (203) 847-0700.]

GLOSSARY

.401 Accumulated postretirement benefit obligation. The actuarial present value of benefits attributed to employee service rendered to a particular date. Prior to an employee's full eligibility date, the accumulated postretirement benefit obligation as of a particular date for an employee is the portion of the expected postretirement benefit obligation attributed to that employee's service rendered to that date; on and after the full eligibility date, the accumulated and expected postretirement benefit obligations for an employee are the same. [FAS106, ¶518]

.402 Active plan participant. Any active employee who has rendered service during the credited service period and is expected to receive benefits, including benefits to or for any beneficiaries and covered dependents, under the postretirement benefit plan. Also refer to **Plan participant**. [FAS106, ¶518]

.403 Actual return on plan assets (component of net periodic postretirement benefit cost). The change in the fair value of the plan's assets for a period including the decrease due to expenses incurred during the period (such as income tax expense incurred by the fund, if applicable), adjusted for contributions and benefit payments during the period. [FAS106, ¶518]

.404 Actuarial present value. The value, as of a specified date, of an amount or series of amounts payable or receivable thereafter, with each amount adjusted to reflect (a) the time value of money (through discounts for interest) and (b) the probability of payment (for example, by means of decrements for events such as death, disability, or withdrawal) between the specified date and the expected date of payment. [FAS106, ¶518]

.405 Amortization. Usually refers to the process of reducing a recognized liability systematically by recognizing revenues or of reducing a recognized asset systematically by recognizing expenses or costs. In accounting for postretirement benefits, amortization is also used to refer to the systematic recognition in net periodic postretirement benefit cost over several periods of previously *unrecognized* amounts, including unrecognized prior service cost, unrecognized net gain or loss, and any unrecognized transition obligation or asset. [FAS106, ¶518]

.406 Assumed per capita claims cost (by age). The annual per capita cost, for periods after the measurement date, of providing the postretirement health care benefits covered by the plan from the earliest age at which an individual could begin to receive benefits under the plan through the remainder of the individual's life or the covered period, if shorter. To determine the assumed per capita claims cost, the per capita claims cost by age based on historical claims costs is adjusted for assumed health care cost trend rates. The resulting assumed per capita claims cost by age reflects expected future costs and is applied with the plan demographics to determine the amount and timing of future gross eligible charges. Also refer to **Gross eligible charges** and **Per capita claims cost by age**. [FAS106, ¶518]

.407 Assumptions. Estimates of the occurrence of future events affecting postretirement benefit costs, such as turnover, retirement age, mortality, dependency status, per capita claims costs by age, health care cost trend rates, levels of Medicare and other health care providers' reimbursements, and discount rates to reflect the time value of money. [FAS106, ¶518]

.408 Attribution. The process of assigning postretirement benefit cost to periods of employee service. [FAS106, ¶518]

.409 Attribution period. The period of an employee's service to which the expected postretirement benefit obligation for that employee is assigned. The beginning of the attribution period is the employee's date of hire unless the plan's benefit formula grants credit only for service from a later date, in which case the beginning of the attribution period is generally the beginning of that credited service period. The end of the attribution period is the full eligibility date. Within the attribution period, an equal amount of the expected postretirement benefit obligation is attributed to each year of service unless the plan's benefit formula attributes a disproportionate share of the expected postretirement benefit obligation to employees' early years of service. In that case, benefits are attributed in accordance with the plan's benefit formula. Also refer to **Credited service period**. [FAS106, ¶518]

.410 Benefit formula. The basis for determining benefits to which participants may be entitled under a postretirement benefit plan. A plan's benefit formula specifies the years of service to be rendered, age to be attained while in service, or a combination of both that must be met for an employee to be eligible to receive benefits under the plan. A plan's benefit formula may also define the beginning of the credited service period and the benefits earned for specific periods of service. [FAS106, ¶518]

.411 Benefits. The monetary or in-kind benefits or benefit coverage to which participants may be entitled under a postretirement benefit plan, including health care benefits, life insurance not provided through a pension plan, and legal, educational, and advisory services. [FAS106, ¶518]

.412 Captive insurer. An insurance company that does business primarily with related entities. [FAS106, ¶518]

.413 Contributory plan. A plan under which retirees or active employees contribute part of the cost. In some contributory plans, retirees or active employees wishing to be covered must contribute; in other contributory plans, participants' contributions result in increased benefits. [FAS106, ¶518]

.414 Cost-sharing (provisions of the plan). The provisions of the postretirement benefit plan that describe how the costs of the covered benefits are to be shared between the employer and the plan participants. Cost-sharing provisions describe retired and active plan participants' contributions toward their postretirement health care benefits, deductibles, coinsurance, out-of-pocket limitations on participant costs, caps on employer costs, and so forth. [FAS106, ¶518]

.415 Credited service period. Employee service period for which benefits are earned pursuant to the terms of the plan. The beginning of the credited service period may be the date of hire or a later date. For example, a plan may provide benefits only for service rendered after a specified age. Service beyond the end of the credited service period does not earn any additional benefits under the plan. Also refer to **Attribution period**. [FAS106, ¶518]

.416 Curtailment (of a postretirement benefit plan). An event that significantly reduces the expected years of future service of active plan participants or eliminates the accrual of defined benefits for some or all of the future services of a significant number of active plan participants. [FAS106, ¶518]

.417 Defined benefit postretirement plan. A plan that defines postretirement benefits in terms of monetary amounts (for example, $100,000 of life insurance) or benefit coverage to be provided (for example, up to $200 per day for hospitalization, 80 percent of the cost of specified surgical procedures, and so forth). Any postretirement benefit plan that is not a defined contribution postretirement plan is, for purposes of this section, a defined benefit postretirement plan. [FAS106, ¶518]

.418 Defined contribution postretirement plan. A plan that provides postretirement benefits in return for services rendered, provides an individual account for each plan participant, and specifies how contributions to the individual's account are to be determined rather than specifies the amount of benefits the individual is to receive. Under a defined contribution postretirement plan, the benefits a plan participant will receive depend solely on the amount contributed to the plan participant's account, the returns earned on investments of those contributions, and the forfeitures of other plan participants' benefits that may be allocated to that plan participant's account. [FAS106, ¶518]

.419 Dependency status. The status of a current or former employee having dependents (for example, a spouse or other relatives) who are expected to receive benefits under a postretirement benefit plan that provides dependent coverage. [FAS106, ¶518]

.420 Discount rates. The rates used to reflect the time value of money. Discount rates are used in determining the present value as of the measurement date of future cash flows currently expected to be required to satisfy the postretirement benefit obligation. Also refer to **Actuarial present value**. [FAS106, ¶518]

.421 Expected long-term rate of return on plan assets. An assumption about the rate of return on plan assets reflecting the average rate of earnings expected on existing plan assets and expected contributions to the plan during the period. [FAS106, ¶518]

.422 **Expected postretirement benefit obligation**. The actuarial present value as of a particular date of the benefits expected to be paid to or for an employee, the employee's beneficiaries, and any covered dependents pursuant to the terms of the postretirement benefit plan. [FAS106, ¶518]

.423 **Expected return on plan assets**. An amount calculated as a basis for determining the extent of delayed recognition of the effects of changes in the fair value of plan assets. The expected return on plan assets is determined based on the expected long-term rate of return on plan assets and the market-related value of plan assets. [FAS106, ¶518]

.424 **Explicit (approach to) assumptions**. An approach under which each significant assumption used reflects the best estimate of the plan's future experience solely with respect to that assumption. [FAS106, ¶518]

.425 **Fair value**. The amount that a plan could reasonably expect to receive for an investment in a current sale between a willing buyer and a willing seller, that is, other than a forced or liquidation sale. [FAS106, ¶518]

.426 **Full eligibility (for benefits)**. The status of an employee having reached the employee's full eligibility date. Full eligibility for benefits is achieved by meeting specified age, service, or age and service requirements of the postretirement benefit plan. Also refer to **Full eligibility date**. [FAS106, ¶518]

.427 **Full eligibility date**. The date at which an employee has rendered all of the service necessary to have earned the right to receive all of the benefits expected to be received by that employee (including any beneficiaries and dependents expected to receive benefits). Determination of the full eligibility date is affected by plan terms that provide incremental benefits expected to be received by or on behalf of an employee for additional years of service, unless those incremental benefits are trivial. Determination of the full eligibility date is *not* affected by plan terms that define when benefit payments commence or by an employee's current dependency status. [FAS106, ¶518]

.428 **Fully eligible plan participants**. Collectively, that group of former employees (including retirees) and active employees who have rendered service to or beyond their full eligibility date and who are expected to receive benefits under the plan, including benefits to their beneficiaries and covered dependents. [FAS106, ¶518]

.429 **Funding policy**. The program regarding the amounts and timing of contributions by the employer(s), plan participants, and any other sources to provide the benefits a postretirement benefit plan specifies. [FAS106, ¶518]

.430 **Gain or loss**. A change in the value of either the accumulated postretirement benefit obligation or the plan assets resulting from experience different from that assumed or from a change in an actuarial assumption, or the consequence of a decision to temporarily deviate from the substantive plan. Also refer to **Unrecognized net gain or loss**. [FAS106, ¶518]

.431 Gain or loss component (of net periodic postretirement benefit cost). The sum of (a) the difference between the actual return on plan assets and the expected return on plan assets, (b) any gain or loss immediately recognized or the amortization of the unrecognized net gain or loss from previous periods, and (c) any amount immediately recognized as a gain or loss pursuant to a decision to temporarily deviate from the substantive plan. The gain or loss component is generally the net effect of delayed recognition of gains and losses (the net change in the unrecognized net gain or loss) except that it does not include changes in the accumulated postretirement benefit obligation occurring during the period and deferred for later recognition. [FAS106, ¶518]

.432 Gross eligible charges. The cost of providing the postretirement health care benefits covered by the plan to a plan participant, before adjusting for expected reimbursements from Medicare and other providers of health care benefits and for the effects of the cost-sharing provisions of the plan. [FAS106, ¶518]

.433 Health care cost trend rates. An assumption about the annual rate(s) of change in the cost of health care benefits currently provided by the postretirement benefit plan, due to factors other than changes in the composition of the plan population by age and dependency status, for each year from the measurement date until the end of the period in which benefits are expected to be paid. The health care cost trend rates implicitly consider estimates of health care inflation, changes in health care utilization or delivery patterns, technological advances, and changes in the health status of the plan participants. Differing types of services, such as hospital care and dental care, may have different trend rates. [FAS106, ¶518]

.434 Incurred claims cost (by age). The cost of providing the postretirement health care benefits covered by the plan to a plan participant, after adjusting for reimbursements from Medicare and other providers of health care benefits and for deductibles, coinsurance provisions, and other specific claims costs borne by the retiree. Also refer to **Net incurred claims cost (by age)**. [FAS106, ¶518]

.435 Insurance contract. A contract in which an insurance company unconditionally undertakes a legal obligation to provide specified benefits to specific individuals in return for a fixed consideration or premium. An insurance contract is irrevocable and involves the transfer of significant risk from the employer (or the plan) to the insurance company. If the insurance company providing the contract is a captive insurer, or if there is any reasonable doubt that the insurance company will meet its obligations under the contract, the contract is not an insurance contract for purposes of this section. [FAS106, ¶518]

.436 Interest cost component (of net periodic postretirement benefit cost). The accrual of interest on the accumulated postretirement benefit obligation due to the passage of time. [FAS106, ¶518]

.437 Market-related value of plan assets. A balance used to calculate the expected return on plan assets. Market-related value can be either fair value or a calculated value that recognizes changes in fair value in a systematic and rational manner over not more than five years. Different methods of calculating market-related value may be used for different classes of plan assets, but the manner of determining market-related value shall be applied consistently from year to year for each class of plan asset. [FAS106, ¶518]

.438 Measurement date. The date of the financial statements or, if used consistently from year to year, a date not more than three months prior to that date, as of which plan assets and obligations are measured. [FAS106, ¶518]

.439 Medicare reimbursement rates. The health care cost reimbursements expected to be received by retirees through Medicare as mandated by currently enacted legislation. Medicare reimbursement rates vary by the type of benefits provided. [FAS106, ¶518]

.440 Multiemployer plan. A postretirement benefit plan to which two or more unrelated employers contribute, usually pursuant to one or more collective-bargaining agreements. A characteristic of multiemployer plans is that assets contributed by one participating employer may be used to provide benefits to employees of other participating employers since assets contributed by an employer are not segregated in a separate account or restricted to provide benefits only to employees of that employer. A multiemployer plan is usually administered by a board of trustees composed of management and labor representatives and may also be referred to as a "joint trust" or "union plan." Generally, many employers participate in a multiemployer plan, and an employer may participate in more than one plan. The employers participating in multiemployer plans usually have a common industry bond, but for some plans the employers are in different industries and the labor union may be their only common bond. [FAS106, ¶518]

.441 Multiple-employer plan. A postretirement benefit plan maintained by more than one employer but not treated as a multiemployer plan. Multiple-employer plans are generally not collectively bargained and are intended to allow participating employers, commonly in the same industry, to pool their plan assets for investment purposes and to reduce the cost of plan administration. A multiple-employer plan maintains separate accounts for each employer so that contributions provide benefits only for employees of the contributing employer. Multiple-employer plans may have features that allow participating employers to have different benefit formulas, with the employer's contributions to the plan based on the benefit formula selected by the employer. [FAS106, ¶518]

.442 **Net incurred claims cost (by age).** The employer's share of the cost of providing the postretirement health care benefits covered by the plan to a plan participant; incurred claims cost net of retiree contributions. Also refer to **Incurred claims cost (by age).** [FAS106, ¶518]

.443 **Net periodic postretirement benefit cost.** The amount recognized in an employer's financial statements as the cost of a postretirement benefit plan for a period. Components of net periodic postretirement benefit cost include service cost, interest cost, actual return on plan assets, gain or loss, amortization of unrecognized prior service cost, and amortization of the unrecognized transition obligation or asset. [FAS106, ¶518]

.444 **Nonparticipating insurance contract.** An insurance contract that does not provide for the purchaser to participate in the investment performance or in other experience of the insurance company. Also refer to **Insurance contract.** [FAS106, ¶518]

.445 **Participating insurance contract.** An insurance contract that provides for the purchaser to participate in the investment performance and possibly other experience (for example, morbidity experience) of the insurance company. Also refer to **Insurance contract.** [FAS106, ¶518]

.446 **Participation right.** A purchaser's right under a participating insurance contract to receive future dividends or retroactive rate credits from the insurance company. [FAS106, ¶518]

.447 **Pay-related plan.** A plan that has a benefit formula that bases benefits or benefit coverage on compensation, such as a final-pay or career-average-pay plan. [FAS106, ¶518]

.448 **Per capita claims cost by age.** The current cost of providing postretirement health care benefits for one year at each age from the youngest age to the oldest age at which plan participants are expected to receive benefits under the plan. Also refer to **Assumed per capita claims cost (by age).** [FAS106, ¶518]

.449 **Plan.** An arrangement that is mutually understood by an employer and its employees, whereby an employer undertakes to provide its employees with benefits after they retire in exchange for their services over a specified period of time, upon attaining a specified age while in service, or a combination of both. A plan may be written or it may be implied by a well-defined, although perhaps unwritten, practice of paying postretirement benefits or from oral representations made to current or former employees. Also refer to **Substantive plan.** [FAS106, ¶518]

.450 **Plan amendment.** A change in the existing terms of a plan. A plan amendment may increase or decrease benefits, including those attributed to years of service already rendered. [FAS106, ¶518]

.451 **Plan assets**. Assets—usually stocks, bonds, and other investments—that have been segregated and restricted (usually in a trust) to provide for postretirement benefits. The amount of plan assets includes amounts contributed by the employer (and by plan participants for a contributory plan) and amounts earned from investing the contributions, less benefits, income taxes, and other expenses incurred. Plan assets ordinarily cannot be withdrawn by the employer except under certain circumstances when a plan has assets in excess of obligations and the employer has taken certain steps to satisfy existing obligations. Assets not segregated in a trust, or otherwise effectively restricted, so that they cannot be used by the employer for other purposes are not plan assets, even though it may be intended that those assets be used to provide postretirement benefits. Amounts accrued by the employer as net periodic postretirement benefit cost but not yet paid to the plan are not plan assets. Securities of the employer held by the plan are includable in plan assets provided they are transferable. If a plan has liabilities other than for benefits, those nonbenefit obligations are considered as reductions of plan assets. [FAS106, ¶518]

.452 **Plan demographics**. The characteristics of the plan population including geographical distribution, age, sex, and marital status. [FAS106, ¶518]

.453 **Plan participant**. Any employee or former employee who has rendered service in the credited service period *and is expected to receive employer-provided benefits* under the postretirement benefit plan, including benefits to or for any beneficiaries and covered dependents. Also refer to **Active plan participant**. [FAS106, ¶518]

.454 **Plan termination**. An event in which the postretirement benefit plan ceases to exist and all benefits are settled by the purchase of insurance contracts or by other means. The plan may or may not be replaced by another plan. A plan termination with a replacement plan may or may not be in substance a plan termination for accounting purposes. [FAS106, ¶518]

.455 **Postretirement benefit plan**. Refer to **Plan**. [FAS106, ¶518]

.456 **Postretirement benefits**. All forms of benefits, other than retirement income, provided by an employer to retirees. Those benefits may be defined in terms of specified benefits, such as health care, tuition assistance, or legal services, that are provided to retirees as the need for those benefits arises, such as certain health care benefits, or they may be defined in terms of monetary amounts that become payable on the occurrence of a specified event, such as life insurance benefits. [FAS106, ¶518]

.457 **Postretirement benefits other than pensions**. Refer to **Postretirement benefits**. [FAS106, ¶518]

.458 **Postretirement health care benefits**. A form of postretirement benefit provided by an employer to retirees for defined health care services or coverage of defined health care costs, such as hospital and medical coverage, dental benefits, and eye care. [FAS106, ¶518]

.459 Prior service cost. The cost of benefit improvements attributable to plan participants' prior service pursuant to a plan amendment or a plan initiation that provides benefits in exchange for plan participants' prior service. Also refer to **Unrecognized prior service cost.** [FAS106, ¶518]

.460 Retirees. Collectively, that group of plan participants that includes retired employees, their beneficiaries, and covered dependents. [FAS106, ¶518]

.461 Service cost component (of net periodic postretirement benefit cost). The portion of the expected postretirement benefit obligation attributed to employee service during a period. [FAS106, ¶518]

.462 Settlement (of a postretirement benefit plan). An irrevocable action that relieves the employer (or the plan) of primary responsibility for a postretirement benefit obligation and eliminates significant risks related to the obligation and the assets used to effect the settlement. Examples of transactions that constitute a settlement include (a) making lump-sum cash payments to plan participants in exchange for their rights to receive specified postretirement benefits and (b) purchasing nonparticipating insurance contracts for the accumulated postretirement benefit obligation for some or all of the plan participants. [FAS106, ¶518]

.463 Single-employer plan. A postretirement benefit plan that is maintained by one employer. The term also may be used to describe a plan that is maintained by related parties such as a parent and its subsidiaries. [FAS106, ¶518]

.464 Substantive plan. The terms of the postretirement benefit plan as understood by an employer that provides postretirement benefits and the employees who render services in exchange for those benefits. The substantive plan is the basis for the accounting for that exchange transaction. In some situations an employer's cost-sharing policy, as evidenced by past practice or by communication of intended changes to a plan's cost-sharing provisions, or a past practice of regular increases in certain monetary benefits may indicate that the substantive plan differs from the extant written plan. [FAS106, ¶518]

.465 Termination benefits. Benefits provided by an employer to employees in connection with their termination of employment. They may be either special termination benefits offered only for a short period of time or contractual benefits required by the terms of a plan only if a specified event, such as a plant closing, occurs. [FAS106, ¶518]

.466 Transition asset. The unrecognized amount, as of the date this section is initially applied, of (a) the fair value of plan assets plus any recognized accrued postretirement benefit cost or less any recognized prepaid postretirement benefit cost in excess of (b) the accumulated postretirement benefit obligation. [FAS106, ¶518]

.467 **Transition obligation**. The unrecognized amount, as of the date this section is initially applied, of (a) the accumulated postretirement benefit obligation in excess of (b) the fair value of plan assets plus any recognized accrued postretirement benefit cost or less any recognized prepaid postretirement benefit cost. [FAS106, ¶518]

.468 **Unfunded accumulated postretirement benefit obligation**. The accumulated postretirement benefit obligation in excess of the fair value of plan assets. [FAS106, ¶518]

.469 **Unrecognized net gain or loss**. The cumulative net gain or loss that has not been recognized as a part of net periodic postretirement benefit cost or as a part of the accounting for the effects of a settlement or a curtailment. Also refer to **Gain or loss**. [FAS106, ¶518]

.470 **Unrecognized prior service cost**. The portion of prior service cost that has not been recognized as a part of net periodic postretirement benefit cost, as a reduction of the effects of a negative plan amendment, or as a part of the accounting for the effects of a curtailment. [FAS106, ¶518]

.471 **Unrecognized transition asset**. The portion of the transition asset that has not been recognized either immediately as the effect of a change in accounting or on a delayed basis as a part of net periodic postretirement benefit cost, as an offset to certain losses, or as a part of accounting for the effects of a settlement or a curtailment. [FAS106, ¶518]

.472 **Unrecognized transition obligation**. The portion of the transition obligation that has not been recognized either immediately as the effect of a change in accounting or on a delayed basis as a part of net periodic postretirement benefit cost, as an offset to certain gains, or as a part of accounting for the effects of a settlement or a curtailment. [FAS106, ¶518]

(The next page is 35157.)

The material in this section has been superseded by FASB Statement 106, *Employers' Accounting for Postretirement Benefits Other Than Pensions.* Due to the delayed effective date for FAS 106, this section has been moved to Appendix E for those users who have not yet adopted FAS 106. However, the supplemental guidance provided by FASB Technical Bulletin 87-1, *Accounting for a Change in Method of Accounting for Certain Postretirement Benefits,* has been deleted from Section P50. FTB 87-1 was rescinded immediately by FAS 106.

(The next page is 37647.)

Sources: ARB 43, Chapter 7A; ARB 46; FASB Statement 109

Summary

If an enterprise elects to restate the carrying values of the balance sheet amounts to fair value as part of a quasi reorganization or corporate readjustment, the offsetting adjustment shall be charged to retained earnings. If the adjustment exceeds the balance in the retained earnings account, any difference shall be charged to additional paid-in capital. A new retained earnings account shall be established at the effective date of such readjustment, and the effective date generally shall be disclosed for a period of 10 years.

.101 [As noted in] Section A31, "Additional Paid-In Capital," additional paid-in capital, however created, shall not be used to relieve the income account of the current or future years of charges that otherwise would be made against income. This rule might be subject to the exception that if, upon reorganization, a reorganized enterprise would be relieved of charges that would be made against income if the existing enterprise were continued, it might be regarded as permissible to accomplish the same result without reorganization provided the facts were as fully revealed to and the action as formally approved by the shareholders as in reorganization. [ARB43, ch7A, ¶1]

.102 Readjustments of the kind mentioned in the [above] exception to the rule fall in the category of what are called *quasi reorganizations.* This section does not deal with the general question of quasi reorganizations, but only with cases in which the exception permitted [in paragraph .101] is availed of by an enterprise. Hereinafter, such cases are referred to as *readjustments.* [ARB43, ch7A, ¶2]

.103 [This section provides guidance on the accounting during and after a readjustment. It does not address any] other types of readjustments, such as correcting erroneous credits made to additional paid-in capital in the past. [ARB43, ch7A, ¶12]

Accounting for a Readjustment

.104 An enterprise [that] elects to restate its assets, capital stock, additional paid-in capital, and retained earnings through a readjustment and thus avail itself of permission to relieve its future income account or retained earnings of charges that would otherwise

be made against it shall make a clear report to its shareholders of the restatements proposed to be made, and obtain their formal consent. It shall present a fair balance sheet as
at the date of the readjustment, in which the adjustment of carrying amounts is reasonably complete, in order that there may be no continuation of the circumstances that
justify charges to additional paid-in capital. [ARB43, ch7A, ¶3]

.105 Assets shall be carried forward as of the date of readjustment at fair and not unduly
conservative amounts, determined with due regard for the accounting to be employed by
the enterprise thereafter. If the fair value of any asset is not readily determinable a conservative estimate may be made, but in that case the amount shall be described as an
estimate and any material difference arising through realization or otherwise and not attributable to events occurring or circumstances arising after that date shall not be carried
to income or retained earnings. [ARB43, ch7A, ¶4]

.106 If potential losses or charges are known to have arisen prior to the date of readjustment but the amounts thereof are then indeterminate, provision may properly be made to
cover the maximum *probable* losses or charges. [Section C59, "Contingencies," contains more detailed guidance for accounting for contingent losses.] If the amounts provided are subsequently found to have been excessive or insufficient, the differences shall
not be carried to retained earnings nor used to offset losses or gains originating after the
readjustment, but shall be carried to additional paid-in capital. [ARB43, ch7A, ¶5]

.107 When the amounts to be written off in a readjustment have been determined, they
shall be charged first against retained earnings to the full extent of such retained earnings; any balance shall then be charged against additional paid-in capital. An enterprise
that has subsidiaries shall apply this rule in such a way that no consolidated retained
earnings survive a readjustment in which any part of losses has been charged to additional paid-in capital. [ARB43, ch7A, ¶6]

.108 If the retained earnings of any subsidiaries cannot be applied against the losses
before resort is had to additional paid-in capital, the parent company's interest in such
retained earnings shall be regarded as capitalized by the readjustment just as retained
earnings at the date of acquisition are capitalized, so far as the parent is concerned. [ARB43,
ch7A, ¶7] [The parent company's accounting for its investments in subsidiaries is discussed in Section C51, "Consolidation."]

.109 The effective date of the readjustment, from which the income of the enterprise is
thereafter determined, shall be as near as practicable to the date on which formal consent
of the stockholders is given, and shall ordinarily not be prior to the close of the last completed fiscal year. [ARB43, ch7A, ¶8]

Accounting after a Readjustment

.110 When the readjustment has been completed, the enterprise's accounting shall be substantially similar to that appropriate for a new enterprise. [ARB43, ch7A, ¶9]

.111 After such a readjustment retained earnings previously accumulated cannot properly be carried forward under that title. A new retained earnings account shall be established, dated to show that it runs from the effective date of the readjustment, and this dating shall be disclosed in financial statements until such time as the effective date is no longer deemed to possess any special significance. [ARB43, ch7A, ¶10] The dating of retained earnings following a quasi reorganization would rarely, if ever, be of significance after a period of 10 years and there may be exceptional circumstances in which the discontinuance of the dating of retained earnings could be justified at the conclusion of a period less than 10 years. [ARB46, ¶2]

.112 Additional paid-in capital originating in such a readjustment is restricted in the same manner as that of a new enterprise; charges against it shall be only those that may properly be made against the initial additional paid-in capital of a new enterprise. [ARB43, ch7A, ¶11]

Accounting for a Tax Benefit

.113 The tax benefits of deductible temporary differences and carryforwards as of the date of a quasi reorganization as defined and contemplated in this section ordinarily are reported as a direct addition to contributed capital if the tax benefits are recognized in subsequent years. The only exception is for enterprises that have previously both adopted [the provisions of] FASB Statement 96, *Accounting for Income Taxes*, and effected a quasi reorganization that involves only the elimination of a deficit in retained earnings by a concurrent reduction in contributed capital prior to adopting [the provisions of] Section I27, "Income Taxes." For those enterprises, subsequent recognition of the tax benefit of prior deductible temporary differences and carryforwards is included in income and reported as required by paragraph .136 of Section I27 (without regard to the referenced exceptions) and then reclassified from retained earnings to contributed capital. Those enterprises shall disclose (a) the date of the quasi reorganization, (b) the manner of reporting the tax benefits and that it differs from present accounting requirements for other enterprises and (c) the effect of those tax benefits on income from continuing operations, income before extraordinary items, and on net income (and on related per share amounts). [FAS109, ¶39]

(The next page is 38295.)

Sources: FASB Statement 66; FASB Statement 67; FASB Statement 98; FASB Statement 121

Summary

The accounting for certain real estate transactions is covered in Sections Re1, "Real Estate: Sales," and Re2, "Real Estate: Accounting for Costs and Initial Rental Operations of Real Estate Projects."

Sections Re1 and Re2 relate to enterprises in the real estate industry that are frequently involved in highly complex transactions. This section includes the contents of each of the above two sections that are pertinent to occasional real estate transactions of those enterprises in other than the real estate industry. This section describes which of the above two sections is pertinent to a particular situation.

.101 Section Re1, "Real Estate: Sales," [presents] standards for recognition of profit on all real estate sales transactions without regard to the nature of the seller's business. [FAS66, ¶1]

.102 Although Section Re1 applies to all sales of real estate, many of the extensive provisions were developed over several years to deal with complex transactions that are frequently encountered in enterprises that specialize in real estate transactions [and, therefore, the accounting requirements are contained within Section Re1]. The decision tree [in paragraph .178 highlights] the major provisions of this section and will help a user identify criteria that determine when and how profit is recognized. Those accounting for relatively simple real estate sales transactions will need to apply only limited portions of Section Re1. [Those requirements are reproduced in paragraphs .106 through .178 of this section.] The general requirements for recognizing all of the profit on a nonretail land sale at the date of sale are set forth in paragraphs .106 through .108, and are highlighted on the decision tree in paragraph .178. Paragraphs .109 through .177 elaborate on those general provisions. [FAS66, ¶2]

.103 Section Re2, "Real Estate: Accounting for Costs and Initial Rental Operations of Real Estate Projects," [presents] accounting and reporting standards for acquisition, development, construction, selling, and rental costs associated with real estate projects. It also provides guidance for the accounting for initial rental operations and criteria for determining when the status of a rental project changes from nonoperating to operating. [FAS67, ¶1]

.104 Section Re2 does not apply to:

a. Real estate developed by an enterprise for use in its own operations,[1] other than for sale or rental.
b. "Initial direct costs" of sales-type, operating, and other types of leases, which are defined in Section L10, "Leases," paragraph .411. The accounting for initial direct costs is prescribed in Section L10.
c. Costs directly related to manufacturing, merchandising, or service activities as distinguished from real estate activities.

Paragraphs .120 through .123 of Section Re2 do not apply to real estate rental activity in which the predominant rental period is less than one month. [FAS67, ¶2]

.105 [Deleted 11/92 because of FASB Statement 111, *Rescission of FASB Statement No. 32 and Technical Corrections.*]

Real Estate Sales Other Than Retail Land Sales

Recognition of Profit by the Full Accrual Method

.106 Profit shall be recognized in full when real estate is sold, provided (a) the profit is determinable, that is, the collectibility of the sales price is reasonably assured or the amount that will not be collectible can be estimated, and (b) the earnings process is virtually complete, that is, the seller is not obliged to perform significant activities after the sale to earn the profit. Unless both conditions exist, recognition of all or part of the profit shall be postponed. Recognition of all of the profit at the time of sale or at some later date when both conditions exist is referred to as the *full accrual method* in this section. [FAS66, ¶3]

.107 In accounting for sales of real estate, collectibility of the sales price is demonstrated by the buyer's commitment to pay, which in turn is supported by substantial initial and continuing investments that give the buyer a stake in the property sufficient that the risk of loss through default motivates the buyer to honor its obligation to the seller. Collectibility shall also be assessed by considering factors such as the credit standing of the buyer, age and location of the property, and adequacy of cash flow from the property. [FAS66, ¶4]

---

[1]In this context, "real estate developed by an enterprise for use in its own operations" includes real estate developed by a member of a consolidated group for use in the operations of another member of the group (for example, a manufacturing facility developed by a subsidiary for use in its parent's operations) when the property is reported in the group's consolidated financial statements. However, such property is not "real estate developed for use in the enterprise's operations" when reported in the separate financial statements of the entity that developed it. [FAS67, ¶2, fn1]

.108 Profit on real estate sales transactions[2] shall not be recognized by the full accrual method until all of the following criteria are met:

a. A sale is consummated (refer to paragraph .109).
b. The buyer's initial and continuing investments are adequate to demonstrate a commitment to pay for the property (refer to paragraphs .111 through .119).
c. The seller's receivable is not subject to future subordination (refer to paragraph .120).
d. The seller has transferred to the buyer the usual risks and rewards of ownership in a transaction that is in substance a sale and does not have a substantial continuing involvement with the property (refer to paragraph .121).

Paragraphs .122 through .146 describe appropriate accounting if the above criteria are not met. [FAS66, ¶5]

Consummation of a Sale

.109 A sale shall not be considered consummated until (a) the parties are bound by the terms of a contract, (b) all consideration has been exchanged, (c) any permanent financing for which the seller is responsible has been arranged, and (d) all conditions[3] precedent to closing have been performed. Usually, those four conditions are met at the time of closing or after closing, not when an agreement to sell is signed or at a preclosing. [FAS66, ¶6]

Buyer's Initial and Continuing Investment

.110 "Sales value" shall be determined by:

a. Adding to the stated sales price the proceeds from the issuance of a real estate option that is exercised and other payments that are in substance additional sales proceeds. These nominally may be management fees, points, or prepaid interest or fees that are required to be maintained in an advance status and applied against the amounts due to the seller at a later date.
b. Subtracting from the sale price a discount to reduce the receivable to its present value and by the net present value of services that the seller commits to perform without compensation or by the net present value of the services in excess of the compensa-

---

[2]Profit on a sale of a partial interest in real estate shall be subject to the same criteria for profit recognition as a sale of a whole interest. [FAS66, ¶5, fn1]

[3]Paragraph .123 provides an exception to this requirement if the seller is constructing office buildings, condominiums, shopping centers, or similar structures. [FAS66, ¶6, fn2]

tion that will be received. Paragraph .134 specifies appropriate accounting if services are to be provided by the seller without compensation or at less than prevailing rates. [FAS66, ¶7]

.111 Adequacy of a buyer's initial investment shall be measured by (a) its composition (refer to paragraphs .112 and .113) and (b) its size compared with the sales value of the property (refer to paragraph .114). [FAS66, ¶8]

.112 The buyer's initial investment shall include only: (a) cash paid as a down payment, (b) the buyer's notes supported by irrevocable letters of credit from an independent established lending institution,[4] (c) payments by the buyer to third parties to reduce existing indebtedness on the property, and (d) other amounts paid by the buyer that are part of the sales value. Other consideration received by the seller, including other notes of the buyer, shall be included as part of the buyer's initial investment only when that consideration is sold or otherwise converted to cash without recourse to the seller. [FAS66, ¶9]

.113 The initial investment shall not include:

a. Payments by the buyer to third parties for improvements to the property
b. A permanent loan commitment by an independent third party to replace a loan made by the seller
c. Any funds that have been or will be loaned, refunded, or directly or indirectly provided to the buyer by the seller or loans guaranteed or collateralized by the seller for the buyer[5]

[FAS66, ¶10]

.114 The buyer's initial investment shall be adequate to demonstrate the buyer's commitment to pay for the property and shall indicate a reasonable likelihood that the seller will collect the receivable. Lending practices of independent established lending institutions provide a reasonable basis for assessing the collectibility of receivables from buyers of real estate. Therefore, to qualify, the initial investment shall be equal to at least a major part of the difference between usual loan limits and the sales value of the property. Guidance on minimum initial investments is provided in paragraphs .147 and .148. [FAS66, ¶11]

---

[4] An "independent established lending institution" is an unrelated institution such as a commercial bank unaffiliated with the seller. [FAS66, ¶9, fn3]

[5] As an example, if unimproved land is sold for $100,000, with a down payment of $50,000 in cash, and the seller plans to loan the buyer $35,000 at some future date, the initial investment is $50,000 minus $35,000, or $15,000. [FAS66, ¶10, fn4]

.115 The buyer's continuing investment in a real estate transaction shall not qualify unless the buyer is contractually required to pay each year on its total debt for the purchase price of the property an amount at least equal to the level annual payment that would be needed to pay that debt and interest on the unpaid balance over no more than (a) 20 years for debt for land and (b) the customary amortization term of a first mortgage loan by an independent established lending institution for other real estate. For this purpose, contractually required payments by the buyer on its debt shall be in the forms specified in paragraph .112 as acceptable for an initial investment. Except as indicated in the following sentence, funds to be provided directly or indirectly by the seller (refer to paragraph .113(c)) shall be subtracted from the buyer's contractually required payments in determining whether the initial and continuing investments are adequate. If a future loan on normal terms from an established lending institution bears a fair market interest rate and the proceeds of the loan are conditional on use for specified development of or construction on the property, the loan need not be subtracted in determining the buyer's investment. [FAS66, ¶12]

Release Provisions

.116 An agreement to sell property (usually land) may provide that part or all of the property may be released from liens securing related debt by payment of a release price or that payments by the buyer may be assigned first to released property. If either of those conditions is present, a buyer's initial investment shall be sufficient both to pay release prices on property released at the date of sale and to constitute an adequate initial investment on property not released or not subject to release at that time in order to meet the criterion of an adequate initial investment for the property as a whole. [FAS66, ¶13]

.117 If the release conditions described in paragraph .116 are present, the buyer's investment shall be sufficient, after the released property is paid for, to constitute an adequate continuing investment on property not released in order to meet the criterion of an adequate continuing investment for the property as a whole (refer to paragraph .115). [FAS66, ¶14]

.118 If the amounts applied to unreleased portions do not meet the initial and continuing-investment criteria as applied to the sales value of those unreleased portions, profit shall be recognized on each released portion when it meets the criteria in paragraph .108 as if each release were a separate sale. [FAS66, ¶15]

.119 Tests of adequacy of a buyer's initial and continuing investments described in paragraphs .111 through .118 shall be applied cumulatively when the sale is consummated and annually afterward. If the initial investment exceeds the minimum prescribed, the excess shall be applied toward the required annual increases in the buyer's investment. [FAS66, ¶16]

Future Subordination

.120 The seller's receivable shall not be subject to future subordination. This restriction shall not apply if (a) a receivable is subordinate to a first mortgage on the property existing at the time of sale or (b) a future loan, including an existing permanent loan commitment, is provided for by the terms of the sale and the proceeds of the loan will be applied first to the payment of the seller's receivable. [FAS66, ¶17]

Continuing Involvement without Transfer of Risks and Rewards

.121 If a seller is involved with a property after it is sold in any way that results in retention of substantial risks or rewards of ownership, except as indicated in paragraph .146, the absence-of-continuing-involvement criterion has not been met. Forms of involvement that result in retention of substantial risks or rewards by the seller, and accounting therefor, are described in paragraphs .128 through .145. [FAS66, ¶18]

Recognition of Profit When the Full Accrual Method Is Not Appropriate

.122 If a real estate sales transaction does not satisfy the criteria in paragraphs .106 through .121 for recognition of profit by the full accrual method, the transaction shall be accounted for as specified in the following paragraphs. [FAS66, ¶19]

Sale Not Consummated

.123 The deposit method of accounting described in paragraphs .159 through .161 shall be used until a sale has been consummated (refer to paragraph .109). "Consummation" usually requires that all conditions precedent to closing have been performed, including that the building be certified for occupancy. However, because of the length of the construction period of office buildings, apartments, condominiums, shopping centers, and similar structures, such sales and the related income may be recognized during the process of construction, subject to the criteria in paragraphs .144 and .145, even though a certificate of occupancy, which is a condition precedent to closing, has not been obtained. [FAS66, ¶20]

.124 If the net carrying amount of the property exceeds the sum of the deposit received, the fair value of the unrecorded note receivable, and the debt assumed by the buyer, the seller shall recognize the loss at the date the agreement to sell is signed.[6] If a buyer defaults, or if circumstances after the transaction indicate that it is probable the buyer will

---

[6]Section Re2, "Real Estate: Accounting for Costs and Initial Rental Operations of Real Estate Projects," paragraph .124, specifies the accounting for property that has not yet been sold but is substantially complete and ready for its intended use. [FAS121, ¶30]

default and the property will revert to the seller, the seller shall evaluate whether the circumstances indicate a decline in the value of the property for which an allowance for loss should be provided. [FAS66, ¶21]

Initial or Continuing Investments Do Not Qualify

.125 If the buyer's initial investment does not meet the criteria specified in paragraphs .111 through .114 for recognition of profit by the full accrual method and if recovery of the cost of the property is reasonably assured if the buyer defaults, the installment method described in paragraphs .150 through .155 shall be used. If recovery of the cost of the property is not reasonably assured if the buyer defaults or if cost has already been recovered and collection of additional amounts is uncertain, the cost recovery method (described in paragraphs .156 through .158) or the deposit method (described in paragraphs .159 through .161) shall be used. The cost recovery method may be used to account for sales of real estate for which the installment method would be appropriate. [FAS66, ¶22]

.126 If the initial investment meets the criteria in paragraphs .111 through .114 but the continuing investment by the buyer does *not* meet the criteria in paragraphs .115 and .119, the seller shall recognize profit by the reduced profit method described in paragraphs .162 and .163 at the time of sale if payments by the buyer each year will at least cover both of the following:

a. The interest and principal amortization on the maximum first mortgage loan that could be obtained on the property
b. Interest, at an appropriate rate,[7] on the excess of the aggregate actual debt on the property over such a maximum first mortgage loan

If the criteria specified in this paragraph for use of the reduced profit method are not met, the seller may recognize profit by the installment method (refer to paragraphs .150 through .155) or the cost recovery method (refer to paragraphs .156 through .158). [FAS66, ¶23]

Receivable Subject to Future Subordination

.127 If the seller's receivable is subject to future subordination as described in paragraph .120, profit shall be recognized by the cost recovery method (refer to paragraphs .156 through .158). [FAS66, ¶24]

---

[7]Section 169, "Interest: Imputation of an Interest Cost," paragraphs .106 and .107, provide criteria for selecting an appropriate rate for present-value calculations. [FAS66, ¶23, fn6]

Continuing Involvement without Transfer of Risks and Rewards

.128 If the seller has some continuing involvement with the property and does not transfer substantially all of the risks and rewards of ownership, profit shall be recognized by a
method determined by the nature and extent of the seller's continuing involvement. Generally, profit shall be recognized at the time of sale if the amount of the seller's loss of
profit because of continued involvement with the property is limited by the terms of the
sales contract. The profit recognized shall be reduced by the maximum exposure to loss.
Paragraphs .129 through .146 describe some common forms of continuing involvement
and specify appropriate accounting if those forms of involvement are present. If the seller
has some other form of continuing involvement with the property, the transaction shall
be accounted for according to the nature of the involvement. [FAS66, ¶25]

.129 *The seller has an obligation to repurchase the property, or the terms of the transaction allow the buyer to compel the seller or give an option[8] to the seller to repurchase
the property.* The transaction shall be accounted for as a financing, leasing, or profit-
sharing arrangement rather than as a sale. [FAS66, ¶26]

.130 *The seller is a general partner in a limited partnership that acquires an interest in
the property sold (or has an extended, noncancelable management contract requiring
similar obligations) and holds a receivable from the buyer for a significant[9] part of the
sales price.* The transaction shall be accounted for as a financing, leasing, or profit-
sharing arrangement. [FAS66, ¶27]

.131 *The seller guarantees[10] the return of the buyer's investment or a return on that
investment for a limited or extended period.* For example, the seller guarantees cash flows,
subsidies, or net tax benefits. If the seller guarantees return of the buyer's investment or
if the seller guarantees a return on the investment for an extended period, the transaction
shall be accounted for as a financing, leasing, or profit-sharing arrangement. If the guar-

---

[8] A right of first refusal based on a bona fide offer by a third party ordinarily is not an obligation or an option
to repurchase. [FAS66, ¶26, fn7]

[9] For this purpose, a significant receivable is a receivable in excess of 15 percent of the maximum first-lien
financing that could be obtained from an independent established lending institution for the property. It
would include:

a. A construction loan made or to be made by the seller to the extent that it exceeds the minimum funding
   commitment for permanent financing from a third party that the seller will not be liable for
b. An all-inclusive or wraparound receivable held by the seller to the extent that it exceeds prior-lien financing for which the seller has no personal liability
c. Other funds provided or to be provided directly or indirectly by the seller to the buyer
d. The present value of a land lease when the seller is the lessor (refer to paragraph .142, footnote 16).

[FAS66, ¶27, fn8]

[10] Guarantees by the seller may be limited to a specified period of time. [FAS66, ¶28, fn9]

antee of a return on the investment is for a limited period, the deposit method shall be used until operations of the property cover all operating expenses, debt service, and contractual payments. At that time, profit shall be recognized on the basis of performance of the services required, as illustrated in paragraphs .171 through .175. [FAS66, ¶28]

.132 *The seller is required to initiate or support operations or continue to operate the property at its own risk, or may be presumed to have such a risk, for an extended period, for a specified limited period, or until a specified level of operations has been obtained, for example, until rentals of a property are sufficient to cover operating expenses and debt service.* If support is required or presumed to be required[11] for an *extended* period of time, the transaction shall be accounted for as a financing, leasing, or profit-sharing arrangement. If support is required or presumed to be required for a *limited* time, profit on the sale shall be recognized on the basis of performance of the services required. Performance of those services shall be measured by the costs incurred and to be incurred over the period during which the services are performed. Profit shall begin to be recognized when there is reasonable assurance that future rent receipts will cover operating expenses and debt service including payments due the seller under the terms of the transaction. Reasonable assurance that rentals will be adequate would be indicated by objective information regarding occupancy levels and rental rates in the immediate area. In assessing whether rentals will be adequate to justify recognition of profit, total estimated future rent receipts of the property shall be reduced by one-third as a reasonable safety factor unless the amount so computed is less than the rents to be received from signed leases. In this event, the rents from signed leases shall be substituted for the computed amount. Application of this method is illustrated in paragraphs .171 through .176. [FAS66, ¶29]

.133 If the sales contract does not stipulate the period during which the seller is obligated to support operations of the property, support shall be presumed for at least two years from the time of initial rental unless actual rental operations cover operating expenses, debt service, and other contractual commitments before that time. If the seller is contractually obligated for a longer time, profit recognition shall continue on the basis of performance until the obligation expires. Calculation of profits on the basis of performance of services is illustrated in paragraphs .171 through .176. [FAS66, ¶30]

---

[11]Support shall be presumed to be required if: (a) a seller obtains an interest as a general partner in a limited partnership that acquires an interest in the property sold; (b) a seller retains an equity interest in the property, such as an undivided interest or an equity interest in a joint venture that holds an interest in the property; (c) a seller holds a receivable from a buyer for a significant part of the sales price and collection of the receivable depends on the operation of the property; or (d) a seller agrees to manage the property for the buyer on terms not usual for the services to be rendered, and the agreement is not terminable by either the seller or the buyer. [FAS66, ¶29, fn10]

.134 If the sales contract requires the seller to provide management services relating to the property after the sale without compensation or at compensation less than prevailing rates for the service required (refer to paragraph .110) or on terms not usual for the services to be rendered (refer to paragraph .132, footnote 11(d)), compensation shall be imputed when the sale is recognized and shall be recognized in income as the services are performed over the term of the management contract. [FAS66, ¶31]

.135 *The transaction is merely an option to purchase the property.* For example, undeveloped land may be "sold" under terms that call for a very small initial investment by the buyer (substantially less than the percentages specified in paragraph .148) and postponement of additional payments until the buyer obtains zoning changes or building permits or other contingencies specified in the sales agreement are satisfactorily resolved. Proceeds from the issuance of the option by a property owner shall be accounted for as a deposit (refer to paragraphs .159 through .161). Profit shall not be recognized until the option either expires or is exercised. When an option to purchase real estate is sold by an option holder,[12] the seller of the option shall recognize income by the cost recovery method (refer to paragraphs .156 through .158) to the extent nonrefundable cash proceeds exceed the seller's cost of the option if the buyer's initial and continuing investments are not adequate for profit recognition by the full accrual method (refer to paragraphs .110 through .119). [FAS66, ¶32]

.136 *The seller has made a partial sale.* A sale is a partial sale if the seller retains an equity interest in the property or has an equity interest in the buyer. Profit (the difference between the sales value and the proportionate cost of the partial interest sold) shall be recognized at the date of sale if:

a. The buyer is independent of the seller.
b. Collection of the sales price is reasonably assured (refer to paragraph .107).
c. The seller will not be required to support the operations of the property or its related obligations to an extent greater than its proportionate interest.

[FAS66, ¶33]

.137 If the buyer is not independent of the seller, for example, if the seller holds or acquires an equity interest in the buyer, the seller shall recognize the part of the profit proportionate to the outside interests in the buyer at the date of sale. If the seller controls the

---

[12]When an option to purchase real estate is sold by an option holder, the sales value includes the exercise price of the option and the sales price of the option. For example, if the option is sold for $150,000 ($50,000 cash and a $100,000 note) and the exercise price is $500,000, the sales value is $650,000. [FAS66, ¶32, fn11]

buyer, no profit on the sale shall be recognized until it is realized from transactions with outside parties through sale or operations of the property. [FAS66, ¶34]

.138 If collection of the sales price is not reasonably assured, the cost recovery or installment method of recognizing profit shall be used. [FAS66, ¶35]

.139 If the seller is required to support the operations of the property after the sale, the accounting shall be based on the nature of the support obligation. For example, the seller may retain an interest in the property sold and the buyer may receive preferences as to profits, cash flows, return on investment, and so forth. If the transaction is in substance a sale, the seller shall recognize profit to the extent that proceeds from the sale, including receivables from the buyer, exceed all of the seller's costs related to the entire property. Other examples of support obligations are described in paragraphs .132 through .134. [FAS66, ¶36]

.140 If individual units in condominium projects[13] or time-sharing interests are being sold separately and all the following criteria are met, profit shall be recognized by the percentage-of-completion method on the sale of individual units or interests:

a. Construction is beyond a preliminary stage.[14]
b. The buyer is committed to the extent of being unable to require a refund except for nondelivery of the unit or interest.[15]
c. Sufficient units have already been sold to assure that the entire property will not revert to rental property. In determining whether this condition has been met, the seller shall consider the requirements of state laws, the condominium or time-sharing contract, and the terms of the financing agreements.
d. Sales prices are collectible (refer to paragraph .107).
e. Aggregate sales proceeds and costs can be reasonably estimated. Consideration shall be given to sales volume, trends of unit prices, demand for the units including

---

[13]A condominium project may be a building, a group of buildings, or a complete project. [FAS66, ¶37, fn12]

[14]Construction is not beyond a preliminary stage if engineering and design work, execution of construction contracts, site clearance and preparation, excavation, and completion of the building foundation are incomplete. [FAS66, ¶37, fn13]

[15]The buyer may be able to require a refund, for example, if a minimum status of completion of the project is required by state law and that status has not been attained; if state law requires that a "Declaration of Condominium" be filed and it has not been filed, except that in some states the filing of the declaration is a routine matter and the lack of such filing may not make the sales contract voidable; if the sales contract provides that permanent financing at an acceptable cost must be available to the buyer at the time of closing and it is not available; or if the condominium units must be registered with either the Office of Interstate Land Sales Registration of the Department of Housing and Urban Development or the Securities and Exchange Commission, and they are not so registered. [FAS66, ¶37, fn14]

seasonal factors, developer's experience, geographical location, and environmental factors.

If any of the above criteria is not met, proceeds shall be accounted for as deposits until the criteria are met. [FAS66, ¶37]

.141 *The seller sells property improvements and leases the underlying land to the buyer of the improvements.* In these circumstances, the transactions are interdependent and it is impracticable to distinguish between profits on the sale of the improvements and profits under the related lease. The transaction shall be accounted for as a lease of both the land and improvements if the term of the land lease to the buyer from the seller of the improvements either (a) does not cover substantially all of the economic life of the property improvements, thus strongly implying that the transaction is in substance a lease of both land and improvements, or (b) is not for a substantial period, for example, 20 years. [FAS66, ¶38]

.142 If the land lease described in paragraph .138 covers substantially all of the economic life of the improvements and extends for at least 20 years, the profit to be recognized on the sale of the improvements at the time of sale shall be (a) the present value of the rental payments[16] not in excess of the seller's cost of the land plus (b) the sales value of the improvements minus (c) the carrying value of the improvements and the land. Profit on (1) the buyer's rental payments on the land in excess of the seller's cost of the land and (2) the rent to be received on the land after the maturity of the primary indebtedness on the improvements or other customary amortization term shall be recognized when the land is sold or the rents in excess of the seller's cost of the land are accrued under the lease. Calculations of profit in those circumstances are illustrated in paragraphs .169 and .170. [FAS66, ¶39]

.143 *The sale of the property is accompanied by a leaseback to the seller of all or any part of the property for all or part of its remaining economic life.* Real estate sale-leaseback transactions shall be accounted for in accordance with Section L10, paragraphs .130A through .130M and .160A through .160M. [FAS98, ¶23]

.144 *The sales contract or an accompanying agreement requires the seller to develop the property in the future, to construct facilities on the land, or to provide off-site improvements or amenities.* The seller is involved with future development or construction work if the buyer is unable to pay amounts due for that work or has the right under

---

[16]The present value of the specified rental payments is the present value of the lease payments specified in the lease over the term of the primary indebtedness, if any, on the improvements, or over the customary amortization term of primary debt instruments on the type of improvements involved. The present value is computed at an interest rate appropriate for (a) primary debt if the lease is not subordinated or (b) secondary debt if the lease is subordinated to loans with prior liens. [FAS66, ¶39, fn15]

the terms of the arrangement to defer payment until the work is done. If future costs of development can be reasonably estimated at the time of sale, profit allocable to (a) performance before the sale of the land and (b) the sale of the land shall be recognized when the sale of the land meets the criteria in paragraph .108. Profit allocable to performance after the sale shall be recognized by the percentage-of-completion method as development and construction proceed, provided that cost and profit can be reasonably estimated from the seller's previous experience. [FAS66, ¶41]

.145 The profit shall be allocated to the sale of the land and the later development or construction work on the basis of estimated costs of each activity; the same rate of profit shall be attributed to each activity. No profit shall be recognized at the time of sale if future costs of development cannot be reasonably estimated at that time. [FAS66, ¶42]

.146 *The seller will participate in future profit from the property without risk of loss (such as participation in operating profits or residual values without further obligation).* If the transaction otherwise qualifies for recognition of profit by the full accrual method, the transfer of risks and rewards of ownership and absence of continuing involvement criterion shall be considered met. The contingent future profits shall be recognized when they are realized.[17] All the costs of the sale shall be recognized at the time of sale; none shall be deferred to periods when the contingent profits are recognized. [FAS66, ¶43]

Minimum Initial Investments

.147 Minimum initial investment requirements for sales, other than retail land sales, that are to be accounted for by the full accrual method are specified in paragraph .114. The table of minimum initial investments in paragraph .148 is based on usual loan limits for various types of properties. However, lenders' appraisals of specific properties may differ. Therefore, if a recently placed permanent loan or firm permanent loan commitment for maximum financing of the property exists with an independent established lending institution, the minimum initial investment should be whichever of the following is greater:

a. The minimum percentage of the sales value (refer to paragraph .110) of the property specified in paragraph .148
b. The lesser of:
   (1) The amount of the sales value of the property in excess of 115 percent of the amount of a newly placed permanent loan or firm permanent loan commitment from a primary lender that is an independent established lending institution
   (2) Twenty-five percent of the sales value

[FAS66, ¶53]

---

[17]Section C59, "Contingencies," paragraph .118, addresses accounting for gain contingencies. [FAS66, ¶43, fn16]

.148 This table does not cover every type of real estate property. To evaluate initial investments on other types of property, enterprises may make analogies to the types of properties specified, or the risks of a particular property can be related to the risks of the properties specified. Use of this table is illustrated in paragraphs .164 through .170.

	Minimum Initial Investment Expressed as a Percentage of Sales Value
Land	
Held for commercial, industrial, or residential development to commence within two years after sale	20
Held for commercial, industrial, or residential development to commence after two years	25
Commercial and Industrial Property	
Office and industrial buildings, shopping centers, and so forth:	
Properties subject to lease on a long-term lease basis to parties with satisfactory credit rating; cash flow currently sufficient to service all indebtedness	10
Single-tenancy properties sold to a buyer with a satisfactory credit rating	15
All other	20
Other income-producing properties (hotels, motels, marinas, mobile home parks, and so forth):	
Cash flow currently sufficient to service all indebtedness	15
Start-up situations or current deficiencies in cash flow	25
Multifamily Residential Property	
Primary residence:	
Cash flow currently sufficient to service all indebtedness	10
Start-up situations or current deficiencies in cash flow	15
Secondary or recreational residence:	
Cash flow currently sufficient to service all indebtedness	15
Start-up situations or current deficiencies in cash flow	25
Single-Family Residential Property (including condominium or cooperative housing)	
Primary residence of the buyer	5[a]
Secondary or recreational residence	10[a]

[FAS66, ¶54]

---

[a]If collectibility of the remaining portion of the sales price cannot be supported by reliable evidence of collection experience, the minimum initial investment shall be at least 60 percent of the difference between the sales value and the financing available from loans guaranteed by regulatory bodies such as the Federal Housing Authority (FHA) or the Veterans Administration (VA), or from independent, established lending institutions. This 60-percent test applies when independent first-mortgage financing is not utilized and the seller takes a receivable from the buyer for the difference between the sales value and the initial investment. If independent first-mortgage financing is utilized, the adequacy of the initial investment on sales of single-family residential property should be determined in accordance with paragraph .147. [FAS66, ¶54, fn(a)]

Description of Certain Methods of Accounting for Real Estate Sales Transactions

.149 Paragraphs .150 through .163 describe several of the methods of profit recognition that are provided for by this section. [FAS66, ¶55]

Installment Method

.150 The installment method apportions each cash receipt and principal payment by the buyer on debt assumed between cost recovered and profit. The apportionment is in the same ratio as total cost and total profit bear to the sales value. The calculation is illustrated in paragraph .177. [FAS66, ¶56]

.151 If the stated interest rate is equal to or less than an appropriate interest rate, it is acceptable not to reduce the receivable to its present value. This ordinarily results in reducing profit recognized in the earlier years. [FAS66, ¶57]

.152 Under the installment method, the receivable less profits not recognized does not exceed what the property value would have been if the property had not been sold. [FAS66, ¶58]

.153 The income statement, or related footnotes, for the period including the date of sale presents the sales value, the gross profit that has not yet been recognized, and the total cost of the sale. Revenue and cost of sales (or gross profit) are presented as separate items on the income statement or are disclosed in the footnotes when profit is recognized as earned. This presentation is illustrated [for a retail land sale transaction] in paragraph .194 [of Re1, "Real Estate: Sales."] [FAS66, ¶59]

.154 Paragraph [.173 of Section Re1, "Real Estate: Sales"[18]] describes accounting for obligations for future improvement costs under the percentage-of-completion method. That description applies as well to accounting for those obligations under the installment method. [FAS66, ¶60]

---

[18]If there is an obligation for future improvement costs that is recognized under the percentage-of-completion method:

a. Estimates are based on costs generally expected in the construction industry locally.
b. Unrecoverable costs of off-site improvements, utilities, and amenities are provided for. In determining the amount of unrecoverable costs, estimates of amounts to be recovered from future sale of the improvements, utilities, and amenities are discounted to present value as of the date the net unrecoverable costs are recognized.

[FAS66, ¶75]

.155 If after adoption of the installment method the transaction meets the requirements for the full accrual method (specified in paragraphs .106 through .121) of recognizing profit for real estate sales other than retail land sales, the seller may then change to the full accrual method. The remaining profit that was not recognized is recognized in income at that time. [FAS66, ¶61]

Cost Recovery Method

.156 Under the cost recovery method, no profit is recognized until cash payments by the buyer, including principal and interest on debt due to the seller and on existing debt assumed by the buyer, exceed the seller's cost of the property sold.[19] The receivable less profits not recognized, if any, does not exceed what the depreciated property value would have been if the property had not been sold. [FAS66, ¶62]

.157 The income statement for the period including the date of sale presents the sales value, the gross profit that has not yet been recognized, and the total cost of the sale. Gross profit not yet recognized is offset against the related receivable on the balance sheet. Principal collections reduce the related receivable, and interest collections on such receivables increase the unrecognized gross profit on the balance sheet. Gross profit is presented as a separate item of revenue on the income statement when it is recognized as earned. [FAS66, ¶63]

.158 If, after the adoption of the cost recovery method, the transaction meets the requirements for the full accrual method (specified in paragraphs .106 through .121), the seller may then change to the full accrual method. The remaining profit that was not recognized is recognized in income at that time. [FAS66, ¶64]

Deposit Method

.159 Under the deposit method, the seller does not recognize any profit, does not record notes receivable, continues to report in its financial statements the property and the related existing debt even if it has been assumed by the buyer, and discloses that those items are subject to a sales contract. The seller continues to charge depreciation to expense as a period cost for the property for which deposits have been received. Cash received from the buyer, including the initial investment and subsequent collections of principal and interest, is reported as a deposit on the contract except that, for sales that are not retail land sales, portions of cash received that are designated by the contract as interest and are not subject to refund offset carrying charges (property taxes and interest on

---

[19]For an all-inclusive or "wraparound" receivable held by the seller, interest collected is recognized as income to the extent of, and as an appropriate offset to, interest expense on prior-lien financing for which the seller remains responsible. [FAS66, ¶62, fn23]

existing debt) on the property. Interest collected that is subject to refund and is included in the deposit account before a sale is consummated is accounted for as part of the buyer's initial investment (refer to paragraph .110) at the time the sale is consummated. [FAS66, ¶65]

.160 When a contract is canceled without a refund, deposits forfeited are recognized as income. [FAS66, ¶66]

.161 The seller's balance sheet presents nonrecourse debt assumed by the buyer among the liabilities; the debt assumed is not offset against the related property. The seller reports the buyer's principal payments on mortgage debt assumed as additional deposits with corresponding reductions of the carrying amount of the mortgage debt. [FAS66, ¶67]

Reduced-Profit Method

.162 A reduced profit is determined by discounting the receivable from the buyer to the present value of the lowest level of annual payments required by the sales contract over the maximum period specified in paragraph .112 and excluding requirements to pay lump sums. The present value is calculated using an appropriate interest rate,[20] but not less than the rate stated in the sales contract. This method permits profit to be recognized from level payments on the buyer's debt over the maximum term established in paragraph .115 and postpones recognition of other profits until lump sum or other payments are made. [FAS66, ¶68]

.163 To illustrate, assume a sale of land that cost the seller $800,000 and is being sold for $1,000,000 with the following financing:

Buyer's initial investment	$ 250,000
First mortgage note payable to an independent lending institution (Terms—15 percent interest payable annually over 20 years: $79,881 per year including principal and interest)	500,000
Second mortgage note payable to seller (Terms—12 percent interest payable annually over 25 years: $31,875 per year including principal and interest)	250,000
Total selling price	$1,000,000

The amortization term of the second mortgage (25 years) exceeds the term permitted by paragraph .112 (20 years for sales of land). It is assumed that the payments by the buyer each year will meet the requirement in paragraph .123, that the reduced-profit method is to be applied, and that the market interest rate is 16 percent.

---

[20]Section I69, paragraphs .106 and .107, provide criteria for selecting an appropriate rate for present-value calculations. [FAS66, ¶68, fn24]

The present value of $31,875 per year for 20 years at a market rate of 16 percent is $31,875 × 5.92884 = $188,982.

The profit to be recognized at the time of sale is reduced by the difference between the face amount of the seller's receivable ($250,000) and the reduced amount ($188,982), or $61,018. The profit recognized at the time of sale is $1,000,000 (sales price) minus $800,000 (cost) minus $61,018, or $138,982. Additional profit of $61,018 is recognized as the second mortgage payments are received in years 21 through 25. [FAS66, ¶69]

Exhibit I

Illustration of Effect of Land Lease—New Multifamily Residential Property

.164 Land improvements may be sold and concurrently the land under the improvements may be leased to the buyer of the improvements. [FAS66, ¶77]

.165 This exhibit illustrates the effect of loans issued in connection with long-term land leases on evaluations of the adequacy of a buyer's initial investment if improvements on the land are sold separately. In addition, it demonstrates the limit that a lease places on profit recognition if the leased land is owned by the seller of the improvements, making the lease of land and sale of improvements interdependent transactions. [FAS66, ¶78]

.166 The calculations are illustrated for four different circumstances: two examples with a primary land lease and two with a subordinated land lease. [FAS66, ¶79]

.167 Primary Land Lease: Land Owned by Third Party Lessor—Nonqualifying

Assumptions:

Sales price of improvements	$875,000
Represented by proceeds of:	
Cash down payment	$125,000
Loan by insurance company: lien on leasehold improvements, 28-year term, 8½%, payable in equal monthly installments of principal and interest	657,000
Note received by seller from buyer: 12-year term, 9½%, payable in equal monthly installments of principal and interest	93,000
	$875,000

Land lease for 99 years @ $19,000/year, net, payable monthly in advance

Cost of constructing improvements—$750,000

No continuing involvement by seller

Computations:

Present value of 336 monthly payments on land lease of $1,583.33

  discounted at 8½% (interest rate on loan from insurance company):

$1,583.33 + ($1,583.33 × 127.9071)	$ 204,000
Loan from insurance company	657,000
Equivalent primary debt	861,000
Note receivable from buyer	93,000
Total debt or equivalent	954,000
Down payment	125,000
Sales value	$1,079,000

Because 15% of the sales value of the improvements is $161,850, the initial investment of $125,000 (about 12% of adjusted sales value) is inadequate to recognize profit on the sale of improvements. The second test is therefore irrelevant. [FAS66, ¶80]

.168 Primary Land Lease: Land Owned by Third-Party Lessor—Qualifying

Assumptions:

Sales price of improvements	$875,000
Represented by proceeds of:	
Cash down payment	$165,000
Loan by insurance company: lien on leasehold improvements, 28-year term, 8½%, payable in equal monthly installments of principal and interest	657,000
Note received by seller from buyer: 12-year term, 9½%, payable in equal monthly installments of principal and interest	53,000
	$875,000

Land lease for 99 years @ $17,880/year, net, payable monthly in advance

Cost of constructing improvements—$750,000

No continuing involvement by seller

Computations:

Present value of 336 monthly payments on land lease of $1,490
discounted at 8½% (interest rate on loan from insurance company):

$1,490 + ($1,490 × 127.9071)	$ 192,000
Loan from insurance company	657,000
Equivalent primary debt	849,000
Note receivable from buyer	53,000
Total debt or equivalent	902,000
Down payment	165,000
Sales value	$1,067,000

Because 15% of the sales value of the improvements is $160,050, the initial investment of $165,000 (15% of the sales value) is adequate to recognize profit on the sale of improvements. However, the second test must also be applied.

The initial investment required by the second test is:

Sales value	$1,067,000
115% of $849,000 (loan from primary lender)	976,350
	$ 90,650

The initial investment of $165,000 exceeds the amount required, so recognition of profit on sale of improvements is appropriate. The second test may alternatively be applied as the ratio of total debt or equivalent to the equivalent primary debt: $902,000/$849,000 = 106%. Because 106% is less than 115%, the initial investment exceeds the difference between the sales value of the property and 115% of the equivalent primary debt.

Profit recognition:

Sales price of improvements	$875,000
Less: Cost of improvements	750,000
Profit recognized at time of sale	$125,000

[FAS66, ¶81]

.169 Subordinated Land Lease: Land Owned by Seller—Qualifying

Assumptions:

Sales price of improvements	$ 914,000
Represented by proceeds of:	
Cash down payment	$ 154,000
Loan by insurance company: first lien on the fee or on subordinated leasehold, 28-year term, 8¼%, payable in equal monthly installments of principal and interest	760,000
	$ 914,000

Land lease for 99 years @ $11,580/year, net, payable monthly in advance,
and 5% of gross rents
Cost of land—$200,000
Cost of constructing improvements—$750,000
No continuing involvement by seller

Computations:

Present value of 336 monthly payments on land lease at $965 discounted at 12% (imputed interest for a second lien receivable):	
$965 + ($965 × 96.432696)	$ 94,000
Loan from insurance company (primary debt)	760,000
Total debt or equivalent	854,000
Down payment	154,000
Sales value	$1,008,000

The initial investment ($154,000) is more than 15% of the sales value. (15% × $1,008,000 = $151,200).

The initial investment is also larger than the excess of the sales value over 115% of the primary debt.

Sales value	$1,008,000
115% of $760,000	874,000
Excess of sales value over 115% of debt	$ 134,000

Therefore, the initial investment of $154,000 is adequate, and recognizing profit on the sale of the improvements is appropriate.

Profit recognition:

Sales value		$1,008,000
Less: Cost of improvements	$750,000	
Cost of land	200,000	950,000
Profit recognized at time of sale		$ 58,000

The effect of including the present value of the lease is to reduce profit recognized by $106,000: $94,000 (present value of the land lease) − $200,000 (cost of land). [FAS66, ¶82]

.170 Subordinated Land Lease: Land Owned by Seller—Nonqualifying

Assumptions:

Sales price of improvements	$ 875,000

Represented by proceeds of:

Cash down payment	$ 132,000
Loan by insurance company: first lien on the fee or on subordinated leasehold, 28-year term, 8¼%, payable in equal monthly installments of principal and interest	743,000
	$ 875,000

Land lease for 99 years @ $19,332/year, net, payable monthly
in advance
Cost of land—$200,000
Cost of improvements—$750,000
No continuing involvement by seller

Computations:

Present value of 336 monthly payments on land lease of $1,611 discounted at 12% (imputed interest for a second lien receivable):	
$1,611 + ($1,611 × 96.432696)	$ 157,000
Loan from insurance company (primary debt)	743,000
Total debt or equivalent	900,000
Down payment	132,000
Sales value	$1,032,000

The initial investment ($132,000) is less than 15% of the sales value (15% × $1,032,000 = $154,800), and therefore is inadequate to recognize profit on sale of improvements. Profit recognized at time of sale should not exceed that recognizable under the installment method as if the subordinated lease were an installment receivable.

Profit recognition on installment method:

Sales value		$1,032,000
Less: Cost of improvements	$750,000	
Cost of land	200,000	950,000
Anticipated profit on sale of improvements		$ 82,000

Cash received or to be received by the seller, other than the proceeds of the primary loan, is:

Down payment	$132,000
Present value of land lease payments	157,000
	$289,000

The percentage of profit in each collection is therefore:

$$\frac{\$ 82,000}{\$289,000} = 28.37\%$$

Profit recognizable in the period of sale is 28.37% of the down payment of $132,000, or $37,450. The remaining profit of $44,550 will be recognized at the rate of 28.37% of the portion of each lease payment that is equivalent to a reduction of principal on a loan of $157,000 for 28 years at 12%.

The effect of including the present value of the lease in the sales value of the improvements is to reduce the profit recognized on the improvements by $43,000: $157,000 (present value of the land lease) − $200,000 (cost of the land). [FAS66, ¶83]

Exhibit II

Illustration of Profit Recognition—Sale of Property with Construction and Support Obligations by Seller

.171 This exhibit illustrates the method of accounting required for a sale of property in which the seller is obligated to construct multifamily units and in which cash flow deficits are anticipated. The example applies to obligations of the seller specified in paragraphs .131 through .133. [FAS66, ¶84]

.172 Assumptions:

a. Company X develops and sells multifamily residential projects. The Company performs directly all developmental activities, including initial planning, site acquisition, obtaining of financing, and physical construction of the project.

b. During the year ended December 31, 19X1 the Company began a project of 100 units. The project was planned and substantial activity had been performed in 19X1 but physical construction had not started as of December 31, 19X1. However, all contracts had been let, and the Company had obtained construction financing.

c. On December 31, 19X1, the Company sold the project to a limited partnership syndication (fully formed) in which it is the sole general partner:

Sales value	**$1,100,000**

Represented by proceeds of:

Cash down payment	$ 165,000
Permanent financing assumed by the buyer, consisting of a 28-year 8½% fully amortizing first mortgage loan by a conventional lender, payable in equal monthly payments of principal and interest to maturity	825,000
Second mortgage note received by the Company payable in equal monthly installments including interest at 9½% over 12 years	110,000
	$1,100,000

d. The closing occurred on December 31, 19X1 and included delivery or performance of the following:

   (1) The Company delivered to the buyer a legal title to the land and all existing improvements.

   (2) The Company delivered to the buyer a firm commitment from an outside lender for permanent financing, and the buyer assumed permanent financing formerly in the name of the Company.

   (3) The Company received from the buyer $165,000 cash and a second mortgage note for $110,000.

   (4) The Company signed a contract to deliver the completed project for a single price of $1,100,000.

e. Costs incurred by the Company and total costs estimated to complete the project, as of December 31, 19X1, were:

	Costs to Date	Estimated Costs to Complete	Total Estimated Costs
Land	$117,000		$117,000
Feasibility, zoning, architectural	35,000		35,000
Finance and other	85,000	$ 10,000	95,000
Site improvements		20,000	20,000
Building construction		571,000	571,000
Total	$237,000	$601,000	$838,000

f. The Company has completed an extensive market research and feasibility study analyzing its cost estimates, the rent-up incubation period, and subsequent rent levels. The initial rent-up will commence in 19X2. Accordingly, a support period of two years is presumed for 19X3 and 19X4.

g. Based on its market analysis, the projected results are as follows:

	19X2	19X3	19X4
Rental expense	$ 37,000	$ 58,000	$ 58,000
Debt service	93,000	93,000	93,000
Total	130,000	151,000	151,000
Rental revenue	(75,000)	(150,000)	(180,000)*
Anticipated net deficit (surplus) in cash flow	55,000	1,000	(29,000)
Safety factor of ⅓ of rental revenue	25,000	50,000	60,000
Adjusted anticipated net deficit in cash flow	$ 80,000	$ 51,000	$ 31,000

*$180,000 equals 95% of gross scheduled rents.

h. Initial cost estimates by the Company on previous projects have never varied from final costs by more than one-half of one % of total costs. [FAS66, ¶85]

.173 Calculations of Profit to Be Recognized:

Schedules A and B (refer to paragraphs .174 and .175) illustrate calculations of profit to be recognized in the period of sale, in the period of construction, and in each period in which the seller will support operations (19X2-19X4). The following features should be noted:

a. The percentage of estimated total profit to be recognized each period is determined by the ratio of gross costs incurred to the end of the period to total estimated gross costs of the project, including gross costs during the period of support of operations. (Construction costs should be included even if construction is performed by parties other than the seller.)

b. The estimated total profit that is the basis of the calculation in each period (that is, the profit to which the percentage in (a) is applied) is determined by adding the sales value and two-thirds of the projected revenue during the period of support of operations and deducting the estimated total costs of the project, including costs of operating the property and debt service.

(1) Actual amounts of revenue and costs are substituted for estimated amounts in the calculation as the actual amounts are known. However, in this illustration, remain-

ing estimates of future revenue and expense are not changed because of actual results even though experience might indicate that projections of future amounts should be revised.

(2) Projected and actual revenues in the calculation should exclude amounts that accrue to the buyer, for example, revenue in excess of the sum of operating expenses and debt service.

(3) One-third of projected revenue should be excluded from the estimate of profit to provide a margin of safety (refer to paragraph .172(g)). Actual results incorporated in the calculation need not be reduced by a safety factor.

(4) The calculation illustrated should be applied only if objective information is available regarding occupancy levels and rental rates for similar property in the immediate area. This will provide reasonable assurance that rent revenue from the project will be sufficient to cover operating expenses and debt service, including payments due to the seller under the terms of the transaction. Unless that evidence is available, no profit should be recognized on the transaction until rent revenue actually reaches levels that assure coverage of those costs.

c. Schedule A shows calculation of profit to be recognized each period on the assumption that actual revenue and costs are the same as those projected in paragraph .172(g) *adjusted* for the safety margin of one-third of revenue.

d. Schedule B shows calculation of profit to be recognized each period on the assumption that actual revenue and costs are the same as those projected in paragraph .172(g) *before* adjustment for safety margin.

e. Schedule C illustrates the calculation of estimated future rent receipts by adjustment for a safety margin.

[FAS66, ¶86]

.174 Schedule A

Example of Profit Calculation
(assuming actual rental revenue equals *adjusted* projection)

Revenues

Sales value	$1,100,000
Adjusted—projected rental revenue*	
19X2	50,000
19X3	100,000
19X4	120,000
	1,370,000

---

*Two-thirds of projected revenue during periods of support of operations; this can also be calculated as projected rental expenses plus projected debt service less projected deficit cash flow. [FAS66, ¶87, fn29]

Costs

Total estimated costs of project (paragraph .172(e))	838,000
Estimated rental expenses and debt service	
19X2	130,000
19X3	151,000
19X4	151,000
	1,270,000
Total projected profit	$ 100,000

Profit to be recognized:

$$\frac{\text{Cost to date}}{\text{Total costs}} \times \text{projected profit}$$

Profit recognized in period of sale:

$$\frac{\$\ 237,000}{1,270,000} \times \$100,000 = \$18,661$$

Total profit to date	$	18,661
Less profit previously reported		0
Current profit recognition	$	18,661

Profit recognized in period of construction:

$$\frac{\$\ 838,000}{1,270,000} \times \$100,000 = \$65,984$$

Total profit to date	$	65,984
Less profit previously recognized		18,661
Current profit recognition	$	47,323

Profit recognized during support period (19X2):

$$\frac{\$\ 968,000}{1,270,000} \times \$100,000 = \$76,221$$

Total profit to date	$	76,221
Less profit previously recognized		65,984
Current profit recognition	$	10,237

Profit recognized during support period (19X3):

$$\frac{\$1,119,000}{1,270,000} \times \$100,000 = \$88,110$$

Total profit to date	$	88,110
Less profit previously recognized		76,221
Current profit recognition	$	11,889

Profit recognized during support period (19X4):

$$\frac{\$1,270,000}{1,270,000} \times \$100,000 = \$100,000$$

Total profit to date	$100,000
Less profit previously recognized	88,110
Current profit recognition	$ 11,890

[FAS66, ¶87]

.175 **Schedule B**

Example of Profit Calculation
(assuming actual rental revenue equals *unadjusted* projection)
(in thousands)

	Profit Recognized in Period of Sale	Profit Recognized in Period of Construction	Profit Recognized during Support Period		
			19X2	**19X3**	**19X4**
Revenues					
Sales value	$1,100	$1,100	$1,100	$1,100	$1,100
Adjusted—projected rental revenue*					
19X2	50	50	75[†]	75[†]	75[†]
19X3	100	100	100	150[†]	150[†]
19X4	120	120	120	150[‡]	151[§]
	1,370	1,370	1,395	1,475	1,476
Costs					
Same as Schedule A	1,270	1,270	1,270	1,270	1,270
Total projected profit	$ 100	$ 100	$ 125	$ 205	$ 206

---

[*]Two-thirds of projected revenue during periods of support of operation; this can also be calculated as projected rental expenses plus projected debt service less projected deficit cash flow.

[†]Actual rental revenue.

[‡]Actual rental revenue excluding amounts not needed to meet cash flow requirements of the property.

[§]Because the property has attained a level of occupancy in excess of the original adjusted projection, and there is no reason to believe that such occupancy level cannot be sustained, the projected 19X4 rental revenue should be adjusted to 19X3 actual rental revenue.

Profit to be recognized:

$$\frac{\text{Cost to date}}{\text{Total costs}} \times \text{projected profit}$$

Profit recognized in period of sale:

$$\frac{\$\ 237,000}{1,270,000} \times \$100,000 = \$18,661$$

Total profit to date	$ 18,661
Less profit previously reported	0
Current profit recognition	$ 18,661

Profit recognized in period of construction:

$$\frac{\$\ 838,000}{1,270,000} \times \$100,000 = \$65,984$$

Total profit to date	$ 65,984
Less profit previously reported	18,661
Current profit recognition	$ 47,323

Profit recognized during support period (19X2):

$$\frac{\$\ 968,000}{1,270,000} \times \$125,000 = \$95,276$$

Total profit to date	$ 95,276
Less profit previously reported	65,984
Current profit recognition	$ 29,292

Profit recognized during support period (19X3):

$$\frac{\$1,119,000}{1,270,000} \times \$205,000 = \$180,626$$

Total profit to date	$180,626
Less profit previously reported	95,276
Current profit recognition	$ 85,350

Profit recognized during support period (19X4):

$$\frac{\$1,270,000}{1,270,000} \times \$206,000 = \$206,000$$

Total profit to date	$206,000
Less profit previously reported	180,626
Current profit recognition	$ 25,374

[FAS66, ¶88]

.176 Schedule C

Calculation of Adjusted Projected Rental Revenue

Assume an office building under development is sold together with an agreement to support operations of the property for three years. The projected annual rent roll is $1,000,000 of which $350,000 is supported by signed lease agreements. The projected rental revenue for the first year of operation is $600,000; the second year $750,000; and the third year $1,000,000. At the time of sale, the amounts to be included in the calculation would be as follows:

Year	Projected Rental Revenue	Safety Factor (33⅓%)	Adjusted Projected Rental Revenue
1	$ 600,000	$200,000	$400,000
2	750,000	250,000	500,000
3	1,000,000	333,333	666,667

If at the time of sale there were signed lease agreements for $450,000, then the $450,000 would be used in year 1 because it is greater than the adjusted projected rental revenue. The adjusted projected rental revenue for years 2 and 3 would remain $500,000 and $666,667, respectively. [FAS66, ¶89]

Exhibit III

Illustration of Profit Recognition—Installment Method, with Debt Assumed by Buyer

.177 Assumptions:

Cash down payment	$ 150,000
Second mortgage payable by buyer to seller (10-year amortization of principal plus interest)	350,000
Total cash to be received by seller	500,000
First mortgage assumed by buyer (20-year amortization of principal plus interest)	500,000
Total sales price and sales value	1,000,000
Cost	600,000
Total profit	$ 400,000

The initial investment is assumed to be inadequate for full profit recognition, and the installment method of accounting is assumed to be appropriate. It is also assumed that, after the down payment, the buyer pays $25,000 of principal on the first mortgage and $35,000 of principal on the second mortgage.

Profit recognition: Under the installment method, profit recognition attributable to the down payment is $60,000, representing 40% ($400,000/$1,000,000) of $150,000.

Profit recognition attributable to the principal payments by the buyer on the first and second mortgages is $24,000, representing 40% of $60,000 ($25,000 + $35,000).

[FAS66, ¶90]

Decision Tree

.178 The following decision tree [is] intended to provide an overview of the major provisions in this section that relate to the accounting for sales of real estate. It should not be used without further reference to the section. The highlighted boxes describe the general requirements for recognizing all of the profit on a sale of real estate other than a retail land sale at the date of sale. [FAS66, ¶123]

**SALES OF REAL ESTATE
OTHER THAN RETAIL LAND SALES**

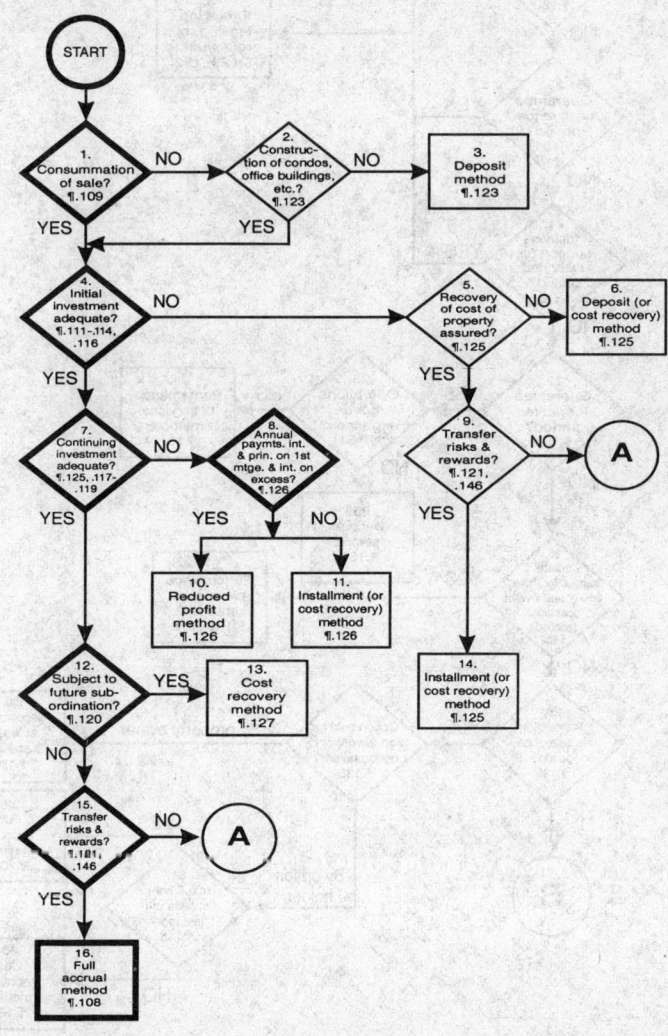

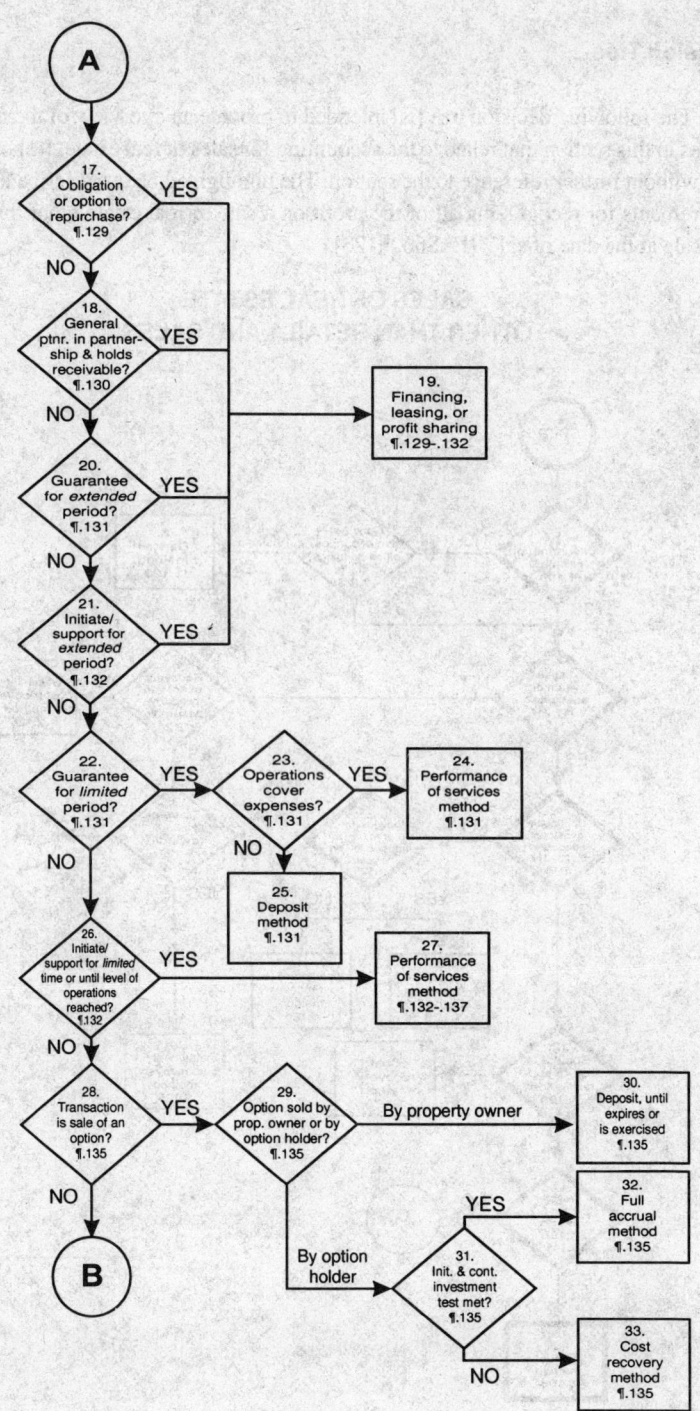

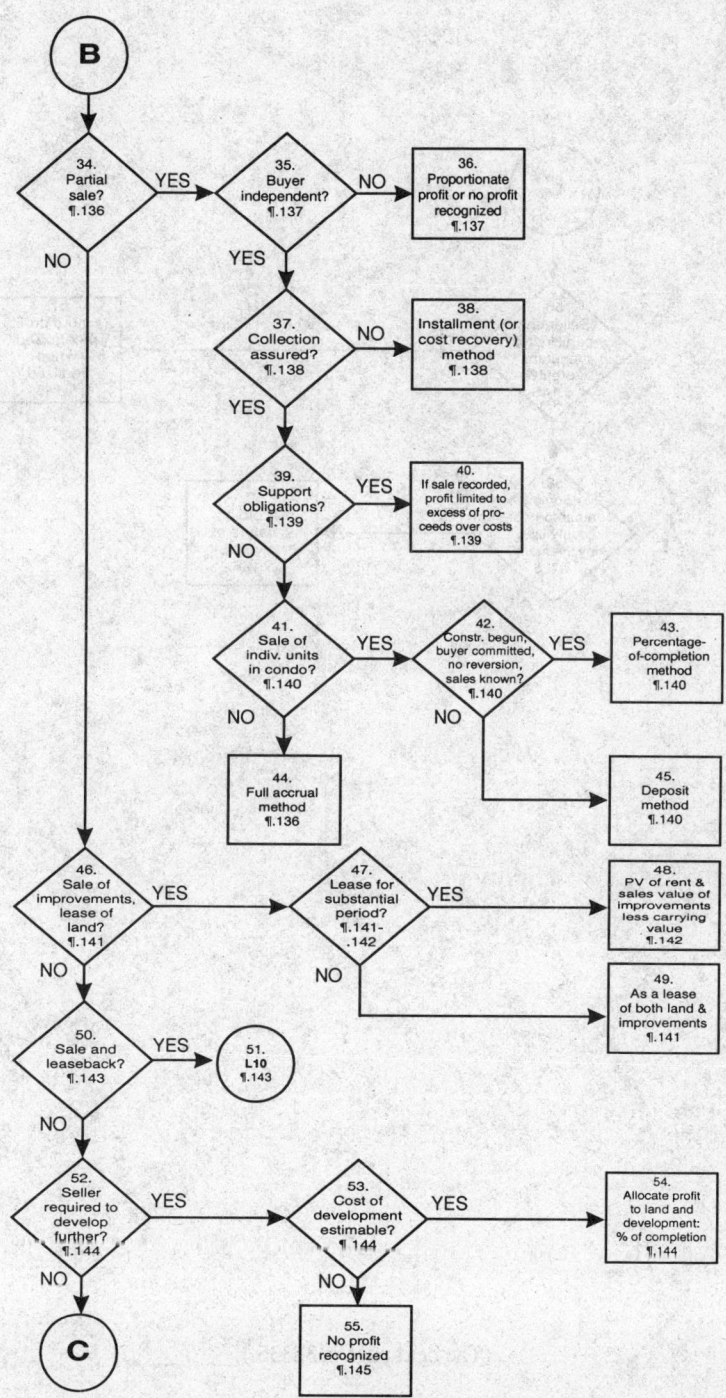

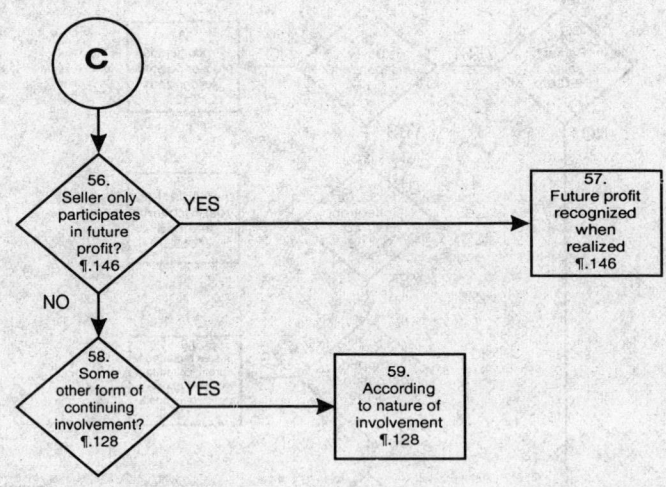

(The next page is 38335.)

Sources: FASB Statement 77; FASB Statement 105

Summary

This section specifies that a transferor ordinarily should report a sale of receivables with recourse transaction as a sale if (a) the transferor surrenders its control of the future economic benefits relating to the receivables, (b) the transferor can reasonably estimate its obligation under the recourse provisions, and (c) the transferee cannot return the receivables to the transferor except pursuant to the recourse provisions. If those conditions do not exist, the amount of proceeds from the transfer should be reported as a liability.

.101 An enterprise may borrow money and pledge receivables as collateral for a loan or may sell receivables with **recourse.** Whether the enterprise pledges or sells the receivables, either the borrower-seller or the lender-purchaser may thereafter bill and collect the receivables,[1] or they may share the servicing of the receivables. Sales of receivables with recourse may have many of the same characteristics as loans collateralized by receivables. This section clarifies the circumstances under which a transfer of receivables with recourse should be recognized by the transferor as a loan or, alternatively, as a sale. [FAS77, ¶1]

Scope

.102 This section [presents] standards of financial accounting and reporting by transferors for transfers of receivables with recourse that purport to be sales of receivables. It also applies to participation agreements (that is, transfers of specified interests in a particular receivable or pool of receivables) that provide for recourse, factoring agreements that provide for recourse, and sales or assignments with recourse of leases or property subject to leases that were accounted for as sales-type or direct financing leases.[2] [FAS77, ¶3]

---

[1]The transfer agreement normally stipulates which party is to perform the administration and routine collection functions (usually referred to as "servicing") for the receivables that are transferred. If the transferor retains the servicing function when receivables are sold, the agreement may require the transferee to pay a servicing fee. Even though the agreement does not specifically provide for compensation to the party performing the servicing, compensation for the future servicing will nevertheless be reflected in the transfer price of the receivables. [FAS77, ¶15]

[2]Refer to Section L10, "Leases," paragraphs .102(b) and .116. [FAS77, ¶3, fn2]

.103 This section does not address accounting and reporting by transferees, nor does it address accounting and reporting of loans collateralized by receivables, for which the receivables and the loan are reported on the borrower's balance sheet. It also does not address the accounting and reporting for exchanges of substantially identical receivables or exchanges of other assets. [FAS77, ¶4]

.104 This section does not modify any of the provisions of any other sections and does not apply to transactions for which the accounting or reporting is specified by those sections. In addition, the provisions of other sections apply to transfers of receivables with recourse as appropriate. For example, the requirements for elimination of intercompany gain or loss of Section C51, "Consolidation," and Section I82, "Investments: Equity Method," apply to a transfer of receivables to a finance subsidiary. [FAS77, ¶20]

Accounting and Reporting

Transfer Recognized as a Sale

.105 A transfer of receivables with recourse shall be recognized as a sale[3] if all of the following conditions are met:

a. *The transferor surrenders control of the future economic benefits embodied in the receivables.*[4] Control has not been surrendered if the transferor has an option[5] to repurchase the receivables at a later date.

---

[3]Risks retained by the seller shall be recognized either by accruing the costs to be incurred or, if those costs are not subject to reasonable estimation, by postponing recognition of the sale. In most transactions, the benefits of ownership can be transferred even though some of the risks of ownership are retained. [FAS77, ¶24] Some risk retention by itself is not sufficient to prohibit recognizing a sale. [FAS77, ¶22]

[4]In considering whether control has been relinquished, paragraph 115 of FASB Concepts Statement No. 3, *Elements of Financial Statements of Business Enterprises,* is pertinent. It states in part:

> Every asset is an asset of some entity; moreover, no asset can simultaneously be an asset of more than one entity. . . . To have an asset, a business enterprise must control future economic benefit to the extent that it can benefit from the asset and generally can deny or regulate access to that benefit by others. . . .

To apply that concept to a transfer of receivables with recourse, determining what constitutes control over a receivable is necessary. Although the legal document relating to a transfer of receivables may specify which party has legal title to the related future economic benefits, paragraph 119 of Concepts Statement 3 states that ". . . legal enforceability of a right is not an indispensible prerequisite for an enterprise to have an asset if the enterprise otherwise will probably obtain the future economic benefit involved." [FAS77, ¶26]

[5][If the transfer agreement included] an option [for the transfer] to reacquire the receivables at fair value, such a transfer shall not be recognized as a sale. [FAS77, ¶28] [However,] a right of first refusal based on a bona fide offer by an unrelated third party ordinarily is not an option to repurchase. [FAS77, ¶5, fn3] [See also footnote 6.]

b. *The transferor's obligation under the recourse provisions can be reasonably estimated.* Lack of experience with receivables with characteristics similar to those being transferred or other factors that affect a determination at the transfer date of the collectibility of the receivables may impair the ability to make a reasonable estimate of the probable bad debt losses and related costs of collections and repossessions. A transfer of receivables shall not be recognized as a sale if collectibility of the receivables and related costs of collection and repossession are not subject to reasonable estimation.

c. *The transferee cannot require the transferor to repurchase*[6] *the receivables except pursuant to the recourse provisions.*[7] [FAS77, ¶5]

.106 If a transfer qualifies to be recognized as a sale, all **probable adjustments** in connection with the recourse obligations to the transferor shall be accrued in accordance with Section C59, "Contingencies." The difference between (a) the sales price (adjusted for the accrual for probable adjustments) and (b) the **net receivables** shall be recognized as a gain or loss on the sale of receivables. If receivables are sold with servicing retained and the stated servicing fee rate differs materially from a **current (normal) servicing fee rate**[7a] or no servicing fee is specified, the sales price shall be adjusted to provide for a normal servicing fee in each subsequent servicing period, which shall not be less than the estimated servicing costs. [FAS77, ¶6]

.107 If a transfer qualifies to be recognized as a sale and the sales price is subject to change during the term of the receivables because of a floating interest rate provision, the sales price shall be estimated using an appropriate market interest rate[8] at the transfer date. Subsequent changes in interest rates from the rate used at the transfer date shall be considered changes in the estimate of the sales price and not as interest cost or interest income. The effect shall be reported in income in the period the interest rate changes in accordance with Section A06, "Accounting Changes," paragraph .130. [FAS77, ¶7]

[6Including] a put option (or a call option) in the transfer agreement with terms to ensure that the option would never be exercised [to avoid reporting a transfer as a sale] (for example, to avoid loss recognition) [would be contrary to] paragraph 160 of FASB Concepts Statement No. 2, *Qualitative Characteristics of Accounting Information,* [which] states that "the quality of reliability and, in particular, of representational faithfulness leaves no room for accounting representations that subordinate substance to form." [When options are] without economic substance, professional judgment can eliminate abuses. [FAS77, ¶34]

[7]Some transfer agreements require or permit the transferor to repurchase transferred receivables when the amount of outstanding receivables is minor to keep the cost of servicing those receivables from becoming unreasonable. If those reversionary interests are not significant to the transferor, their existence alone does not preclude a transfer from being recognized as a sale. [FAS77, ¶5, fn4]

[7aFor mortgage receivables, refer to Section Mo4, "Mortgage Banking Activities," paragraphs .504 through .507 for further guidance on determining a normal servicing fee rate.]

[8]Section I69, "Interest: Imputation of an Interest Cost," paragraph .107, discusses the considerations that may affect the selection of a rate. [FAS77, ¶7, fn5]

Transfer Recognized as a Liability

.108 If any of the conditions in paragraph .105 is not met, the amount of the proceeds from the transfer of receivables shall be reported as a liability. [FAS77, ¶8]

Disclosures

.109 For transfers of receivables with recourse reported as sales, the transferor's financial statements shall disclose (a) the proceeds to the transferor during each period for which an income statement is presented and [FAS77, ¶9] (b) information required by Section F25, "Financial Instruments: Disclosure," paragraphs .112, .113, and .115.[9] [FAS105, ¶21] [This section does not] include other disclosure requirements, such as the amount of any contingent liability, significant terms of the transfer agreement and recourse provisions, and so forth [because] most of those disclosures, if material, are already required by other sections. The following are examples:

a. Section C59, paragraph .113, requires disclosure of the nature and amount of certain contingencies even though the possibility of loss may be remote. Examples of such contingencies include guarantees to repurchase receivables under recourse provisions (or, in some cases, to repurchase the repossessed property underlying the receivables) and guarantees of a specified return or yield on the transferred receivables, including a floating interest rate provision. Section C59, paragraph .118, also requires disclosure of contingencies that might result in gains.

b. Section I22, "Income Statement Presentation: Unusual or Infrequent Items," paragraph .101, requires that the nature and financial effects of a material transaction that occurs infrequently be disclosed as a separate component of income from continuing operations on the face of the income statement or in the notes thereto. A material gain or loss on a sale of receivables with recourse might qualify.

c. Section A06, paragraph .132, requires disclosure of the effect on income before extraordinary items, net income, and related per share amounts of the current period for a change in estimate that affects several future periods, such as a change in interest rates if the sales price of a sale of receivables with recourse is subject to a floating interest rate provision.

d. Section R36, "Related Parties," paragraph .102, requires disclosure of material related party transactions, such as a sale of receivables with recourse by a parent company or an affiliate to an unconsolidated finance subsidiary. [FAS77, ¶39]

---

[9]Aggregation of similar transfers may be appropriate for these disclosures. [FAS77, ¶9, fn7]

Glossary

.401 Current (normal) servicing fee rate. A servicing fee rate that is representative of servicing fee rates most commonly used in comparable servicing agreements covering similar types of receivables. [FAS77, ¶12]

.402 Net receivables. The gross amount of the receivables, including finance and service charges and fees owed by the debtor included in the recorded receivables, less related unearned finance and service charges and fees. [FAS77, ¶12]

.403 Probable adjustments. Adjustments for (a) failure of the debtors to pay when due, for example, estimated bad debt losses and related costs of collections and repossessions accounted for in accordance with Section C59, (b) estimated effects of prepayments, and (c) defects in the eligibility of the transferred receivables, for example, defects in the legal title of the transferred receivables. [FAS77, ¶12]

.404 Recourse. The right of a transferee of receivables to receive payment from the transferor of those receivables for (a) failure of the debtors to pay when due, (b) the effects of prepayments, or (c) adjustments resulting from defects in the eligibility of the transferred receivables. [FAS77, ¶12] Recourse provisions vary. Examples of various forms of recourse provisions include the following:

a. Under some recourse provisions, the transferor must reimburse the transferee in full (by repurchasing the receivable or otherwise) in the event of default by the debtor regardless of whether property that is collateral for the receivable is recovered from the debtor.

b. Under other recourse provisions, the transferee is obligated to repossess property that is collateral for the receivable from the debtor and return it to the transferor before the transferor is compelled to perform under the recourse provisions. Sometimes a recourse provision is effective only if the property is reacquired within a stated period of time, such as 90 days. The recourse provision may require that the transferee sell the repossessed property, apply the proceeds against the balance of the receivable, and charge the transferor for any remaining receivable balance.

c. Under some recourse provisions, the right of the transferee to demand payment from the transferor is limited to a stipulated maximum dollar amount or percentage of transferred receivables. Depending on the type of receivables transferred and the value of collateral securing the receivables, transfers that appear to be with limited recourse actually might be with full recourse. For example, in the absence of unusual economic conditions or of a material unexpected loss, a recourse provision for an amount in excess of the anticipated loss might assure that the transferee will recover its investment and will suffer no loss from defaults on the receivables.

d. Sometimes the transferee may retain a portion of the transfer price of the receivables until the receivables are collected to ensure performance by the transferor under the recourse provisions. The retained amounts are generally referred to as dealers' reserves or holdbacks, and the terms governing them usually are specified in the transfer agreement. The amount of a dealer's reserve may be determined by the transferee based on previous experience in transactions with the transferor or others. Amounts retained in a dealer's reserve account are sometimes remitted to the transferor as the reserve account exceeds stipulated percentages of the uncollected receivables. Agreements may provide that the dealer's reserve be charged for credit losses if a debtor defaults. Some agreements may limit the transferee's recourse to the transferor to the amount set aside in the dealer's reserve. The holdback is the mechanism by which the recourse provisions in the agreement are effected; they are part of the transfer price and are a receivable of the transferor from the transferee if the transfer qualifies to be recognized as a sale. [FAS77, ¶13]

e. Sometimes the transferor guarantees the transferee a minimum specified return or profit on the transfer. For example, the transferor guarantees that the transferee will earn 10 percent after deducting all expenses and credit losses. Those arrangements may require the transferor to provide the required yield in addition to repurchasing a defaulted receivable. Prepayments by debtors also might reduce the transferee's yield and require the transferor to pay the difference. [FAS77, ¶14]

(The next page is 38345.)

RELATED PARTIES

Sources: ARB 43, Chapter 1A; FASB Statement 57; FASB Statement 109

Summary

Financial statements shall include disclosures of material related party transactions, other than compensation arrangements, expense allowances, and other similar items in the ordinary course of business. The nature of certain common control relationships shall be disclosed if the nature of those relationships could significantly affect the reporting enterprise. The reporting of certain related party transactions is specified in other sections.

Introduction

.101 Examples of transactions between **related parties** include transactions between (a) a parent company and its subsidiaries; (b) subsidiaries of a common parent; (c) an enterprise and trusts for the benefit of employees, such as pension and profit-sharing trusts that are managed by or under the trusteeship of the enterprise's **management;** (d) an enterprise and its **principal owners,** management, or members of their **immediate families;** and (e) **affiliates.** Transactions between related parties commonly occur in the normal course of business. Some examples of common types of transactions with related parties are: sales, purchases, and transfers of realty and personal property; services received or furnished, for example, accounting, management, engineering, and legal services; use of property and equipment by lease or otherwise; borrowings and lendings; guarantees; maintenance of bank balances as compensating balances for the benefit of another; intercompany billings based on allocations of common costs; and filings of consolidated tax returns. Transactions between related parties are considered to be related party transactions even though they may not be given accounting recognition. For example, an enterprise may receive services from a related party without charge and not record receipt of the services. [FAS57, ¶1]

Disclosures

.102 Financial statements shall include disclosures of material related party transactions, other than compensation arrangements, expense allowances, and other similar items in the ordinary course of business. However, disclosure of transactions that are eliminated in the preparation of consolidated or combined financial statements is not required in those statements.[1] The disclosures shall include:[2]

a. The nature of the relationship(s) involved
b. A description of the transactions, including transactions to which no amounts or nominal amounts were ascribed, for each of the periods for which income statements are presented, and such other information deemed necessary to an understanding of the effects of the transactions on the financial statements
c. The dollar amounts of transactions for each of the periods for which income statements are presented and the effects of any change in the method of establishing the terms from that used in the preceding period
d. Amounts due from or to related parties as of the date of each balance sheet presented and, if not otherwise apparent, the terms and manner of settlement [FAS57, ¶2]
e. The information required by paragraph .149 of Section I27, "Income Taxes." [FAS109, ¶288(s)]

.103 Transactions involving related parties cannot be presumed to be carried out on an arm's-length basis, as the requisite conditions of competitive, free-market dealings may not exist. Representations about transactions with related parties, if made, shall not imply that the related party transactions were consummated on terms equivalent to those that prevail in arm's-length transactions unless such representations can be substantiated. [FAS57, ¶3]

.104 If the reporting enterprise and one or more other enterprises are under common ownership or management **control** and the existence of that control could result in operating results or financial position of the reporting enterprise significantly different from those that would have been obtained if the enterprises were autonomous, the nature of the control relationship shall be disclosed even though there are no transactions between the enterprises. [FAS57, ¶4]

---

[1]The requirements of this section are applicable to separate financial statements of each or combined groups of each of the following: a parent company, a subsidiary, a corporate joint venture, or a 50-percent-or-less owned investee. However, it is not necessary to duplicate disclosures in a set of separate financial statements that is presented in the financial report of another enterprise (the primary reporting enterprise) if those separate financial statements also are consolidated or combined in a complete set of financial statements and both sets of financial statements are presented in the same financial report. [FAS57, ¶2, fn2]

[2]In some cases, aggregation of similar transactions by type of related party may be appropriate. Sometimes, the effect of the relationship between the parties may be so pervasive that disclosure of the relationship alone will be sufficient. If necessary to the understanding of the relationship, the name of the related party should be disclosed. [FAS57, ¶2, fn3]

.105 Notes or accounts receivable due from officers, employees, or affiliated enterprises shall be shown separately and not included under a general heading, such as notes receivable or accounts receivable. [ARB43, ch1A, ¶5]

Reporting of Certain Related Party Transactions

.106 [The reporting of certain related party transactions is specified in other sections. Inclusion of subsidiaries in consolidated financial statements is discussed in Section C51, "Consolidation," paragraphs .102 through .105, and Section I82, "Investments: Equity Method." The reporting of leases between related parties is discussed in Section L10, "Leases," paragraphs .125 through .127. Certain transfers and exchanges between enterprises under common control are discussed in Section N35, "Nonmonetary Transactions," paragraph .110. The reporting of substitution or addition of debtors in troubled debt restructurings involving related parties is specified in Section D22, "Debt: Restructurings," paragraph .138.]

Glossary

.401 **Affiliate.** A party that, directly or indirectly through one or more intermediaries, controls, is controlled by, or is under common control with an enterprise. [FAS57, ¶24(a)]

.402 **Control.** The possession, direct or indirect, of the power to direct or cause the direction of the management and policies of an enterprise through ownership, by contract, or otherwise. [FAS57, ¶24(b)]

.403 **Immediate family.** Family members whom a principal owner or a member of management might control or influence or by whom they might be controlled or influenced because of the family relationship. [FAS57, ¶24(c)]

.404 **Management.** Persons who are responsible for achieving the objectives of the enterprise and who have the authority to establish policies and make decisions by which those objectives are to be pursued. Management normally includes members of the board of directors, the chief executive officer, chief operating officer, vice presidents in charge of principal business functions (such as sales, administration, or finance), and other persons who perform similar policymaking functions. Persons without formal titles also may be members of management. [FAS57, ¶24(d)]

.405 **Principal owners.** Owners of record or known beneficial owners of more than 10 percent of the voting interests of the enterprise. [FAS57, ¶24(e)]

.406 **Related parties.** Affiliates of the enterprise; entities for which investments are accounted for by the equity method by the enterprise; trusts for the benefit of employees, such as pension and profit-sharing trusts that are managed by or under the trusteeship of management; principal owners of the enterprise; its management; members of the immediate families of principal owners of the enterprise and its management; and other parties with which the enterprise may deal if one party controls or can significantly influence the management or operating policies of the other to an extent that one of the transacting parties might be prevented from fully pursuing its own separate interests. Another party also is a related party if it can significantly influence the management or operating policies of the transacting parties or if it has an ownership interest in one of the transacting parties and can significantly influence the other to an extent that one or more of the transacting parties might be prevented from fully pursuing its own separate interests. [FAS57, ¶24(f)]

(The next page is 38847.)

RESEARCH AND DEVELOPMENT

Sources: FASB Statement 2; FASB Statement 86; FASB Interpretation 6

Summary

Research and development costs shall be charged to expense when incurred. Disclosure in the financial statements is required for the total research and development costs charged to expense in each period for which an income statement is presented.

Scope

.101 This section specifies:

a. Those activities that shall be identified as research and development for financial accounting and reporting purposes
b. The elements of costs that shall be identified with research and development activities
c. The accounting for research and development costs
d. The financial statement disclosures related to research and development costs [FAS2, ¶1]

.102 Accounting for the costs of research and development activities conducted for others under a contractual arrangement is a part of accounting for contracts in general [(refer to Sections Co4, "Contractor Accounting: Construction-Type Contracts," and Co5, "Contractor Accounting: Government Contracts")] and is beyond the scope of this section. Indirect costs that are specifically reimbursable under the terms of a contract are also excluded. [FAS2, ¶2] [Refer to Section Co2, "Computer Software to Be Sold, Leased, or Otherwise Marketed," for the accounting and reporting of research and development costs related thereto. The accounting and reporting for certain other software costs are addressed in paragraphs .113 through .119.]

.103 This section does not apply to activities that are unique to enterprises in the extractive industries, such as prospecting, acquisition of mineral rights, exploration, drilling, mining, and related mineral development. It does apply, however, to research and development activities of enterprises in the extractive industries that are comparable in nature to research and development activities of other enterprises, such as development or improvement of processes and techniques including those employed in exploration, drilling, and extraction. [FAS2, ¶3]

Activities Constituting Research and Development

.104 For purposes of this section, **research** and **development** are defined as follows:

a. *Research* is planned search or critical investigation aimed at discovery of new knowledge with the hope that such knowledge will be useful in developing a new product or service (hereinafter *product*) or a new process or technique (hereinafter *process*) or in bringing about a significant improvement to an existing product or process.

b. *Development* is the translation of research findings or other knowledge into a plan or design for a new product or process or for a significant improvement to an existing product or process whether intended for sale or use. It includes the conceptual formulation, design, and testing of product alternatives, construction of prototypes, and operation of pilot plants. It does not include routine or periodic alterations to existing products, production lines, manufacturing processes, and other ongoing operations, even though those alterations may represent improvements, and it does not include market research or market-testing activities. [FAS2, ¶8]

.105 A process [(refer to paragraph .104(a))] may be a system whose output is to be sold, leased, or otherwise marketed to others. A process also may be used internally as a part of a manufacturing activity or a service activity where the service itself is marketed. A process may be intended to achieve cost reductions as opposed to revenue generation. Paragraph .104(b), however, specifically excludes from research and development activities "market research or market-testing activities." [It is intended] that the acquisition, development, or improvement of a process by an enterprise for use in its selling or administrative activities be excluded from the definition of research and development activities. [FIN6, ¶4]

.106 [Examples of activities that typically would be included in research and development activities and those that typically would be excluded are presented in paragraphs .111 and .112, respectively. Application of this section to costs incurred to obtain or develop computer software is presented in paragraphs .113 through .119.]

Elements of Costs to Be Identified with Research and Development Activities

.107 Elements of costs shall be identified with research and development activities as follows:

a. *Materials, equipment, and facilities.* The costs of materials (whether from the enterprise's normal inventory or acquired specially for research and development activities) and equipment or facilities that are acquired or constructed for research and development activities and that have alternative future uses (in research and development projects or otherwise) shall be capitalized as tangible assets when acquired or constructed. The cost of such materials consumed in research and development activities and the depreciation of such equipment or facilities used in those activities are research and development costs. However, the costs of materials, equipment, or facilities that are acquired or constructed for a particular research and development project and that have no alternative future uses (in other research and development projects or otherwise) and therefore no separate economic values are research and development costs at the time the costs are incurred.

b. *Personnel.* Salaries, wages, and other related costs of personnel engaged in research and development activities shall be included in research and development costs.

c. *Intangibles purchased from others.* The costs of intangibles that are purchased from others for use in research and development activities and that have alternative future uses (in research and development projects or otherwise) shall be capitalized and amortized as intangible assets.[1] The amortization of those intangible assets used in research and development activities is a research and development cost. However, the costs of intangibles that are purchased from others for a particular research and development project and that have no alternative future uses (in other research and development projects or otherwise) and therefore no separate economic values are research and development costs at the time the costs are incurred.[2]

d. *Contract services.* The costs of services performed by others in connection with the research and development activities of an enterprise, including research and development conducted by others [on] behalf of the enterprise, shall be included in research and development costs.

e. *Indirect costs.* Research and development costs shall include a reasonable allocation of indirect costs. However, general and administrative costs that are not clearly related to research and development activities shall not.be included as research and development costs. [FAS2, ¶11]

Accounting for Research and Development Costs

.108 All research and development costs encompassed by this section shall be charged to expense when incurred. [FAS2, ¶12]

Disclosure

.109 Disclosure shall be made in the financial statements of the total research and development costs charged to expense in each period for which an income statement is presented. [FAS2, ¶13]

---

[1] Accounting for intangible assets is described in Section I60, "Intangible Assets."]

[2] Paragraph .107(c) is not intended to alter the conclusions in Section B50, "Business Combinations," regarding allocation of cost to assets acquired in a business combination accounted for by the purchase method. [FAS2, ¶34]

.110 [Deleted 12/82 because of FASB Statement 71, *Accounting for the Effects of Certain Types of Regulation.*]

Examples

.111 The following are examples of activities that typically would be included in research and development in accordance with paragraph .104 (unless conducted for others under a contractual arrangement—refer to paragraph .102):

a. Laboratory research aimed at discovery of new knowledge
b. Searching for applications of new research findings or other knowledge
c. Conceptual formulation and design of possible product or process alternatives
d. Testing in search for or evaluation of product or process alternatives
e. Modification of the formulation or design of a product or process
f. Design, construction, and testing of preproduction prototypes and models
g. Design of tools, jigs, molds, and dies involving new technology
h. Design, construction, and operation of a pilot plant that is not of a scale economically feasible to the enterprise for commercial production
i. Engineering activity required to advance the design of a product to the point that it meets specific functional and economic requirements and is ready for manufacture [FAS2, ¶9]

.112 The following are examples of activities that typically would be excluded from research and development in accordance with paragraph .104:

a. Engineering follow-through in an early phase of commercial production
b. Quality control during commercial production including routine testing of products
c. Trouble-shooting in connection with breakdowns during commercial production
d. Routine, ongoing efforts to refine, enrich, or otherwise improve upon the qualities of an existing product
e. Adaptation of an existing capability to a particular requirement or customer's need as part of a continuing commercial activity
f. Seasonal or other periodic design changes to existing products
g. Routine design of tools, jigs, molds, and dies
h. Activity, including design and construction engineering, related to the construction, relocation, rearrangement, or start-up of facilities or equipment other than (1) pilot plants (refer to paragraph .111(h)) and (2) facilities or equipment whose sole use is for a particular research and development project (refer to paragraph .107(a))
i. Legal work in connection with patent applications or litigation and the sale or licensing of patents [FAS2, ¶10]

Computer Software

.113 Computer software is developed for many and diverse uses. Accordingly, in each case the nature of the activity for which the software is being developed should be considered in relation to the guidelines in paragraphs .104, .111, and .112 to determine whether software costs should be included or excluded. [FAS2, ¶31]

Purchase or Lease of Software

.114 Costs incurred to purchase or lease computer software developed by others are not research and development costs unless the software is for use in research and development activities. [FIN6, ¶5] The phrase "for use in research and development activities" includes tools used to facilitate research and development or components of a product or process that are undergoing research and development activities. [FAS86, ¶50]

Internal Development of Software

.115 An enterprise may undertake development of computer software internally for its own use. The software may be intended, for example, to be used in the research and development activities of the enterprise or as a part of a newly developed or significantly improved product or process. [FIN6, ¶6]

.116 [Deleted 8/85 because of FASB Statement 86, *Accounting for the Costs of Computer Software to Be Sold, Leased, or Otherwise Marketed.*]

.117 Costs incurred by an enterprise in developing computer software internally for use in its research and development activities are research and development costs and, therefore, shall be charged to expense when incurred.[3] This includes costs incurred during all phases of software development because all of those costs are incurred in a research and development activity. [FIN6, ¶8]

.118 [Deleted 8/85 because of FASB Statement 86, *Accounting for the Costs of Computer Software to Be Sold, Leased, or Otherwise Marketed.*]

.119 To the extent that the acquisition, development, or improvement of a process by an enterprise for use in its selling or administrative activities includes costs for com-

---

[3]The alternative future-use test does not apply to the internal development of computer software; paragraph .107(c) applies only to intangibles *purchased from others.* [FIN6, ¶8, fn2]

puter software, those costs are not research and development costs.[4] Examples of the excluded costs of software are those incurred for development by an airline of a computerized reservation system or for development of a general management information system. [FIN6, ¶4]

---

[4]Accounting for the costs of [development of software for an enterprise's own use] is not currently [considered] a significant problem and, therefore, [has not been included in Section Co2, "Computer Software to Be Sold, Leased, or Otherwise Marketed."] The majority of companies expense all costs of developing software for internal use, and [it has not been concluded] that this predominant practice is improper. Also, Section Co2 clarifies activities that are research and development activities and establishes a high capitalization threshold that is likely to be applied to costs incurred in developing software for internal use as well as for sale or lease to others. [FAS86, ¶26]

Glossary

.401 **Development.** Translation of research findings or other knowledge into a plan or design for a new product or process or for a significant improvement to an existing product or process, whether intended for sale or use. It includes the conceptual formulation, design, and testing of product alternatives, construction of prototypes, and operation of pilot plants. It does not include routine or periodic alterations to existing products, production lines, manufacturing processes, and other ongoing operations even though those alterations may represent improvements and it does not include market research or market-testing activities. [FAS2, ¶8]

.402 **Research.** Planned search or critical investigation aimed at discovery of new knowledge with the hope that such knowledge will be useful in developing a new product or service (hereinafter *product*) or a new process or technique (hereinafter *process*) or in bringing about a significant improvement to an existing product or process. [FAS2, ¶8]

Supplemental Guidance

.501-.502 [Deleted 8/85 because of FASB Statement 86, *Accounting for the Costs of Computer Software to Be Sold, Leased, or Otherwise Marketed.*]

(The next page is 38887.)

Sources: FASB Statement 68; FASB Technical Bulletin 84-1

Summary

This section specifies how an enterprise should account for its obligation under an arrangement for the funding of its research and development by others. The enterprise must determine whether it is obligated only to perform contractual research and development for others, or is otherwise obligated. To the extent that the enterprise is obligated to repay the other parties, it records a liability and charges research and development costs to expense as incurred.

Scope

.101 This section [presents] standards of financial accounting and reporting for an enterprise that is a party to a research and development arrangement[1] through which it can obtain the results of research and development funded partially or entirely by others. It applies whether the research and development is performed by the enterprise, the funding parties, or a third party. Although the limited-partnership form of arrangement is used for illustrative purposes in this section, this section also applies for other forms. This section does not address reporting of government-sponsored research and development. [FAS68, ¶3]

Accounting and Reporting

.102 An enterprise shall determine the nature of the obligation it incurs when it enters into an arrangement with other parties who fund its research and development. The factors discussed in paragraphs .103 through .109 and other factors that may be present and relevant to a particular arrangement shall be considered when determining the nature of the enterprise's obligation. [FAS68, ¶4]

---

[1]The legal structure of a research and development arrangement may take a variety of forms and often is influenced by federal and state income tax and securities regulations. An enterprise might have an equity interest in the arrangement, or its legal involvement might be only contractual (for example, a contract to provide services and an option to acquire the results of the research and development). [FAS68, ¶2]

Obligation Is a Liability to Repay the Other Parties

.103 If the enterprise is obligated to repay any of the funds provided by the other parties regardless of the outcome of the research and development, the enterprise shall estimate and recognize that liability. This requirement applies whether the enterprise may settle the liability by paying cash, by issuing securities, or by some other means. [FAS68, ¶5]

.104 To conclude that a liability does not exist, the transfer of the financial risk involved with research and development from the enterprise to the other parties must be substantive and genuine. To the extent that the enterprise is committed to repay any of the funds provided by the other parties regardless of the outcome of the research and development, all or part of the risk has not been transferred. The following are some examples in which the enterprise is committed to repay:

a. The enterprise guarantees, or has a contractual commitment that assures, repayment of the funds provided by the other parties regardless of the outcome of the research and development.
b. The other parties can require the enterprise to purchase their interest in the research and development regardless of the outcome.
c. The other parties automatically will receive debt or equity securities of the enterprise upon termination or completion of the research and development regardless of the outcome.

[FAS68, ¶6]

.105 Even though the written agreements or contracts under the arrangement do not require the enterprise to repay any of the funds provided by the other parties, surrounding conditions might indicate that the enterprise is likely to bear the risk of failure of the research and development. If those conditions suggest that it is probable[2] that the enterprise will repay any of the funds regardless of the outcome of the research and development, there is a presumption that the enterprise has an obligation to repay the other parties. That presumption can be overcome only by substantial evidence to the contrary. [FAS68, ¶7]

.106 Examples of conditions leading to the presumption that the enterprise will repay the other parties include the following:

a. The enterprise has indicated an intent to repay all or a portion of the funds provided regardless of the outcome of the research and development.

---

[2]*Probable* is used here consistent with its use in Section C59, "Contingencies," to mean that repayment is likely. [FAS68, ¶7, fn1]

b. The enterprise would suffer a severe economic penalty if it failed to repay any of the funds provided to it regardless of the outcome of the research and development. An economic penalty is considered "severe" if in the normal course of business an enterprise would probably choose to pay the other parties rather than incur the penalty. For example, an enterprise might purchase the partnership's interest in the research and development if the enterprise had provided the partnership with proprietary basic technology necessary for the enterprise's ongoing operations without retaining a way to recover that technology, or prevent it from being transferred to another party, except by purchasing the partnership's interest.

c. A significant related party[3] relationship between the enterprise and the parties funding the research and development exists at the time the enterprise enters into the arrangement.

d. The enterprise has essentially completed the project before entering into the arrangement.

[FAS68, ¶8]

.107 An enterprise that incurs a liability to repay the other parties shall charge the research and development costs to expense as incurred. The amount of funds provided by the other parties might exceed the enterprise's liability. That might be the case, for example, if license agreements or partial buy-out provisions permit the enterprise to use the results of the research and development or to reacquire certain basic technology or other assets for an amount that is less than the funds provided. Those agreements or provisions might limit the extent to which the enterprise is economically compelled to buy out the other parties regardless of the outcome. In those situations, the liability to repay the other parties might be limited to a specified price for licensing the results or for purchasing a partial interest in the results. If the enterprise's liability is less than the funds provided, the enterprise shall charge its portion of the research and development costs to expense in the same manner as the liability is incurred. For example, the liability might arise as the initial funds are expended, or the liability might arise on a pro rata basis. [FAS68, ¶9]

---

[3]Related parties are defined in Section R36, "Related Parties." [FAS68, ¶8, fn2] Although transactions between related parties commonly occur in the normal course of business, the conditions of competitive free-market dealings between independent parties may not exist. Accordingly, the enterprise might be influenced by considerations other than those that would exist in arm's-length transactions with unrelated parties. This is particularly true if the related parties can directly or indirectly influence the enterprise's decision whether or not to acquire the results of the research and development. However, the enterprise's obligation should not be accounted for as a liability just because the enterprise is the general partner. [FAS68, ¶32]

Obligation Is to Perform Contractual Services

.108 To the extent that the financial risk associated with the research and development has been transferred because repayment of any of the funds provided by the other parties depends *solely* on the results of the research and development having future economic benefit, the enterprise shall account for its obligation as a contract to perform research and development for others. [FAS68, ¶10]

.109 If the enterprise's obligation is to perform research and development for others and the enterprise subsequently decides to exercise an option to purchase the other parties' interests in the research and development arrangement or to obtain the exclusive rights to the results of the research and development, the nature of those results and their future use shall determine the accounting for the purchase transaction.[4] [FAS68, ¶11]

Loan or Advance to the Other Parties

.110 If repayment to the enterprise of any loan or advance by the enterprise to the other parties depends solely on the results of the research and development having future economic benefit, the loan or advance shall be accounted for as costs incurred by the enterprise. The costs shall be charged to research and development expense unless the loan or advance to the other parties can be identified as relating to some other activity, for example, marketing or advertising, in which case the costs shall be accounted for according to their nature. [FAS68, ¶12]

Issuance of Warrants or Similar Instruments

.111 If warrants or similar instruments are issued in connection with the arrangement, the enterprise shall report a portion of the proceeds to be provided by the other parties as paid-in capital. The amount so reported shall be the fair value of the instruments at the date of the arrangement. [FAS68, ¶13]

---

[4]Section B50, "Business Combinations," paragraph .152 states: ". . . the accounting for the cost of an item to be used in research and development activities is the same under Section R50, 'Research and Development,' paragraphs .107 and .108, whether the item is purchased singly, or as part of a group of assets, or as part of an entire enterprise in a business combination accounted for by the purchase method." The accounting for other identifiable intangible assets acquired by the enterprise is specified in Section I60, "Intangible Assets." [FAS68, ¶11, fn3]

Disclosures

.112 An enterprise that under the provisions of this section accounts for its obligation under a research and development arrangement as a contract to perform research and development for others shall disclose[5] the following:[6]

a. The terms of significant agreements under the research and development arrange-ment (including royalty arrangements, purchase provisions, license agreements, and commitments to provide additional funding) as of the date of each balance sheet presented
b. The amount of compensation earned and costs incurred under such contracts for each period for which an income statement is presented.

[FAS68, ¶14]

---

[5]Section R36 specifies additional disclosure requirements for related party transactions and certain control relationships. [FAS68, ¶14, fn4]

[6]An enterprise that is a party to more than one research and development arrangement need not separately disclose each arrangement unless separate disclosure is necessary to understand the effects on the financial statements. Aggregation of similar arrangements by type may be appropriate. [FAS68, ¶14, fn5]

Supplemental Guidance

Accounting for Stock Issued to Acquire the Results of a Research and Development Arrangement

.501 *Question*—How should an enterprise account for stock issued to acquire the results of a research and development arrangement? [FTB84-1, ¶1]

.502 *Background*—[An] enterprise [that is a party to a research and development arrangement] usually has an option either to purchase the [other parties'] interest in or to obtain the exclusive rights to the entire results of the research and development in return for a lump sum payment or royalty payments to the [other parties]. Some arrangements contain a provision that permits the enterprise to acquire complete ownership of the results for a specified amount of the enterprise's stock or cash at some future time. In some of those purchase agreements, the [other parties have] the option to receive either the enterprise's stock or cash; in others, the enterprise makes the decision. Sometimes, warrants or similar instruments to purchase the enterprise's stock are issued in connection with the arrangement. [FTB84-1, ¶2]

.503 *Response*—When an enterprise that is or was a party to a research and development arrangement acquires the results of the research and development arrangement in exchange for cash, common stock of the enterprise, or other consideration, the transaction is a purchase of tangible or intangible assets resulting from the activities of the research and development arrangement. Although such a transaction is not a business combination, paragraph .125 of Section B50 describes the general principles that apply in recording the purchase of such an asset. [FTB84-1, ¶6]

.504 Accordingly, when an enterprise that is or was a party to a research and development arrangement exchanges stock for the results of the research and development arrangement, whether pursuant to the exercise of warrants or similar instruments issued in connection with the arrangement or otherwise, the enterprise should record the stock issued at its fair value, or at the fair value of consideration received, whichever is more clearly evident. The transaction should be accounted for in this manner whether the enterprise exchanges stock for the results of the research and development arrangement, for rights to use the results, or for ownership interests in the arrangement or a successor to the arrangement. The fair value should be determined as of the date the enterprise exercises its option to acquire the results of the research and development arrangement. [FTB84-1, ¶7]

(The next page is 39567.)

RETAINED EARNINGS

Sources: ARB 43, Chapter 1A; ARB 51; FASB Statement 5

Summary

Preacquisition retained earnings or deficit of a purchased subsidiary shall not be included in consolidated retained earnings. Dividends declared from the preacquisition retained earnings of a subsidiary shall not be credited to income of the parent company.

Appropriation of retained earnings shall be shown within stockholders' equity. Costs or losses shall not be charged to an appropriation of retained earnings and no part of an appropriation shall be transferred to income.

.101 The retained earnings or deficit of a purchased[1] subsidiary at the date of acquisition by the parent shall not be included in consolidated retained earnings. [ARB51, ¶9]

.102 [No dividend declared out of the retained earnings of a subsidiary created prior to acquisition shall] be credited to the income account of the parent company. [ARB43, ch1A, ¶3]

.103 [If] a portion of retained earnings [is] "appropriated" for loss contingencies, the appropriation of retained earnings [shall be] shown within the stockholders' equity section of the balance sheet and be clearly identified as an appropriation of retained earnings. Costs or losses shall not be charged to an appropriation of retained earnings, and no part of the appropriation shall be transferred to income. [FAS5, ¶15]

.104 [Section Q15, "Quasi Reorganizations," provides guidance on the treatment of retained earnings in quasi reorganizations.]

(The next page is 39747.)

---

[1]Refer to Section B50, "Business Combinations," for the difference in treatment between a purchase and a pooling of interests.]

Sources: ARB 43, Chapter 1A; APB Opinion 10; FASB Statement 48;
         FASB Statement 111; FASB Technical Bulletin 90-1

Summary

Profit ordinarily shall be recognized at the time a sale in the ordinary course of business is effected. Accordingly, revenues ordinarily shall be recognized at the time a transaction is completed, with appropriate provision for uncollectible accounts. The installment method of recognizing revenue is not acceptable unless collection of the sale price is not reasonably assured.

Revenue from sales transactions in which the buyer has a right to return the product shall be recognized at time of sale only if specified conditions are met. If those conditions are not met, revenue recognition is postponed; if they are met, sales revenue and cost of sales shall be reported in the income statement and shall be reduced to reflect estimated returns. Expected costs or losses relating to sales returns also shall be accrued.

Revenue from the sale of separately priced extended warranty and product maintenance contracts should be deferred and generally recognized in income on a straight-line basis. Costs that are directly related to the acquisition of those contracts are deferred and charged to expense in proportion to the revenue recognized. All other costs are charged to expense as incurred.

Profit and Revenue Recognition

.101 Profit is realized when a sale in the ordinary course of business is effected, unless the circumstances are such that the collection of the sale price is not reasonably assured. [ARB43, ch1A, ¶1] [Accordingly,] revenues shall ordinarily be [recognized] at the time a transaction is completed, with appropriate provision for uncollectible accounts. [APB10, ¶12] In the absence of the circumstances referred to above or other specific guidance, such as in Sections R10, "Real Estate," or Re1, "Real Estate: Sales," the installment method is not acceptable. [FAS111, ¶8(a)] An exception to the general [principle] may be made with respect to inventories in industries, such as [the] packing-house industry, in which, owing to the impossibility of determining costs, it is a trade custom to [account for] inventories at net selling prices, which may exceed cost. [ARB43, ch1A, ¶1]

.102 Unrealized profit shall not be credited to income of the enterprise either directly or indirectly, by charging against such unrealized profits amounts that ordinarily would be charged against income. [ARB43, ch1A, ¶1]

Installment Method of Accounting

.103 The installment method of recognizing revenue is not acceptable unless the circumstances[1] are such that the collection of the sale price is not reasonably assured. [APB10, ¶12]

Other Guidance on Revenue Recognition

.104 [Refer to Sections Co4, "Contractor Accounting: Construction-Type Contracts" and Co5, "Contractor Accounting: Government Contracts," for principles regarding accounting for profits on contracts. In addition, refer to Sections Fr3, "Franchising: Accounting by Franchisors," and L20, "Lending Activities," for accounting principles on recognition of franchisor and loan fee revenue.]

Revenue Recognition When Right of Return Exists

Applicability and Scope

.105 Paragraphs .107 through .109 specify criteria for recognizing revenue on a sale in which a product may be returned, whether as a matter of contract or as a matter of existing practice, either by the ultimate customer or by a party who resells the product to others. The product may be returned for a refund of the purchase price, for a credit applied to amounts owed or to be owed for other purchases, or in exchange for other products. The purchase price or credit may include amounts related to incidental services, such as installation. [FAS48, ¶3]

.106 Paragraphs .107 through .109 do not apply to [the following]:

a. Accounting for revenue in service industries if part or all of the service revenue may be returned under cancellation privileges granted to the buyer
b. Transactions involving real estate or leases
c. Sales transactions in which a customer may return defective goods, such as under warranty provisions. [FAS48, ¶4]

---

[1]There are exceptional cases in which receivables are collectible over an extended period and, because of the terms of the transactions or other conditions, there is no reasonable basis for estimating the degree of collectibility. When those circumstances exist, and as long as they exist, either the installment method or the cost-recovery method of accounting may be used. (Under the cost-recovery method, equal amounts of revenue and expense are recognized as collections are made until all costs have been recovered, postponing any recognition of profit until that time.) [APB10, ¶12, fn8]

Criteria for Recognizing Revenue When Right of Return Exists

.107 If an enterprise sells its product but gives the buyer the right to return the product, revenue from the sales transaction shall be recognized at time of sale only if *all* of the following conditions are met:

a. The seller's price to the buyer is substantially fixed or determinable at the date of sale.
b. The buyer has paid the seller, or the buyer is obligated to pay the seller and the obligation is not contingent on resale of the product.[2]
c. The buyer's obligation to the seller would not be changed in the event of theft or physical destruction or damage of the product.
d. The buyer acquiring the product for resale has economic substance apart from that provided by the seller.[3]
e. The seller does not have significant obligations for future performance to directly bring about resale of the product by the buyer.
f. The amount of future returns[4] can be reasonably estimated (refer to paragraph .109).[5]

Sales revenue and cost of sales that are not recognized at time of sale because the foregoing conditions are not met shall be recognized either when the return privilege has substantially expired or if those conditions subsequently are met, whichever occurs first. [FAS48, ¶6]

.108 If sales revenue is recognized because the conditions of paragraph .107 are met, any costs or losses that may be expected in connection with any returns shall be accrued in accordance with Section C59, "Contingencies." Sales revenue and cost of sales reported in the income statement shall be reduced to reflect estimated returns. [FAS48, ¶7]

---

[2]This condition is met if the buyer pays the seller at time of sale or if the buyer does not pay at time of sale but is obligated to pay at a specified date or dates. If, however, the buyer does not pay at time of sale and the buyer's obligation to pay is contractually or implicitly excused until the buyer resells the product, then the condition is not met. [FAS48, ¶22]

[3]This condition relates primarily to buyers that exist "on paper," that is, buyers that have little or no physical facilities or employees. It prevents enterprises from recognizing sales revenue on transactions with parties that the sellers have established primarily for the purpose of recognizing such sales revenue. [FAS48, ¶6, fn2]

[4]Exchanges by ultimate customers of one item for another of the same kind, quality, and price (for example, one color or size for another) are not considered returns for purposes of this section. [FAS48, ¶6, fn3]

[5Because] detailed record keeping for returns for each product line might be costly in some cases, reasonable aggregations and approximations of product returns [are permitted]. [FAS48, ¶20]

.109 The ability to make a reasonable estimate of the amount of future returns depends on many factors and circumstances that will vary from one case to the next. However, the following factors may impair the ability to make a reasonable estimate:

a. The susceptibility of the product to significant external factors, such as technological obsolescence or changes in demand
b. Relatively long periods in which a particular product may be returned
c. Absence of historical experience with similar types of sales of similar products, or inability to apply such experience because of changing circumstances, for example, changes in the selling enterprise's marketing policies or relationships with its customers
d. Absence of a large volume of relatively homogeneous transactions.

The existence of one or more of the above factors, in light of the significance of other factors, may not be sufficient to prevent making a reasonable estimate; likewise, other factors may preclude a reasonable estimate. [FAS48, ¶8]

Supplemental Guidance

Accounting for Separately Priced Extended Warranty and Product Maintenance Contracts

.501 *Question*—How should revenue and costs from a separately priced extended warranty[501] or product maintenance contract be recognized? [FTB90-1, ¶1]

.502 *Background*—An *extended warranty* is an agreement to provide warranty protection in addition to the scope of coverage of the manufacturer's original warranty, if any, or to extend the period of coverage provided by the manufacturer's original warranty. A *product maintenance contract* is an agreement to perform certain agreed-upon services to maintain a product for a specified period of time. The terms of the contract may take different forms, such as an agreement to periodically perform a particular service a specified number of times over a specified period of time, or an agreement to perform a particular service as the need arises over the term of the contract. Some contracts may provide both extended warranty coverage and product maintenance services. A contract is *separately priced* if the customer has the option to purchase the services provided under the contract for an expressly stated amount separate from the price of the product. [FTB90-1, ¶2]

.503 *Response*—Revenue from separately priced extended warranty and product maintenance contracts should be deferred and recognized in income on a straight-line basis over the contract period except in those circumstances in which sufficient historical evidence indicates that the costs of performing services under the contract are incurred on other than a straight-line basis. In those circumstances, revenue should be recognized over the contract period in proportion to the costs expected to be incurred in performing services under the contract.[502] [FTB90-1, ¶3]

.504 Costs that are directly related to the acquisition of a contract and that would have not been incurred but for the acquisition of that contract (incremental direct acquisition costs)[503] should be deferred and charged to expense in proportion to the

---

[501]Warranties are explicitly included within the scope of Section C59, [which] addresses warranty obligations that are incurred in connection with the sale of the product, that is, obligations that are not separately priced or sold but are included in the sale of the product. [FTB90-1, ¶8]

[502]The pattern of cost incurrence may vary depending on characteristics of the product or may be a function of the coverage provided under the contract. [For example,] when the coverage under the contract varies, such as those situations in which the period of the extended warranty partially overlaps the period of the product's original warranty, or the extended warranty contains a graduating deductible, costs of providing services under the contract may vary proportionate to that coverage. [FTB90-1, ¶9]

[503]Acquisition costs should be identified consistent with guidance in paragraph .105 of Section L20, which defines acquisition costs in terms of incremental direct costs. [FTB90-1, ¶12]

revenue recognized. All other costs, such as costs of services performed under the contract, general and administrative expenses, advertising expenses, and costs associated with the negotiation of a contract that is not consummated, should be charged to expense as incurred. [FTB90-1, ¶4]

.505 A loss should be recognized on extended warranty or product maintenance contracts if the sum of expected costs of providing services under the contracts and unamortized acquisition costs exceeds related unearned revenue. Extended warranty or product maintenance contracts should be grouped in a consistent manner to determine if a loss exists. A loss should be recognized first by charging any unamortized acquisition costs to expense. If the loss is greater than the unamortized acquisition costs, a liability should be recognized for the excess. [FTB90-1, ¶5]

(The next page is 41727.)

Sources: FASB Statement 14; FASB Statement 18; FASB Statement 21;
FASB Statement 24; FASB Statement 30; FASB Statement 69;
FASB Statement 95; FASB Statement 111;
FASB Technical Bulletin 79-4; FASB Technical Bulletin 79-5;
FASB Technical Bulletin 79-8

Summary

The financial statements of a business enterprise whose securities are publicly traded or that is required to file financial statements with the SEC shall include disaggregated information about the enterprise's operations in different industries, its foreign operations and export sales, and its major customers. For each reportable segment and for foreign operations an enterprise shall present information about:

a. Sales to unaffiliated customers and sales or transfers to other industry segments of the enterprise
b. Operating profit or loss
c. The aggregate carrying amount of identifiable assets
d. Other related disclosures

Applicability

.101 The provisions of this section [have been] suspended and need not be applied by a **nonpublic enterprise**[1] pending further action by the FASB. [FAS21, ¶15] [Enterprises are not required] to disclose the information specified by this section in a complete set of separately issued financial statements of a subsidiary, corporate joint venture, or other investee that is a nonpublic enterprise. [FAS21, ¶12]

.102 Any [segment] information that is presented in the financial statements [of nonpublic enterprises] shall be consistent with the requirements of this section. [FAS21, ¶14]

.103 [Deleted because the guidance on economic dependency under AICPA Statement on Auditing Standards No. 6 (SAS 6), *Related Party Standards,* is no longer applicable. Related party disclosures are now required by FASB Statement 57, *Related Party Disclosures,* which states that it "does not address the issues pertaining to economic dependency."]

[1 Refer to paragraphs .505 through .507 as to the applicability of this section to certain brokers and dealers in securities.]
2 [Deleted because the guidance from SAS 6 is no longer applicable.]

Inclusion in Financial Statements

.104 If an enterprise issues a **complete set of financial statements** that present financial position at the end of the enterprise's fiscal year and results of operations and [FAS14, ¶3] cash flows [FAS95, ¶152] for that fiscal year in conformity with generally accepted accounting principles, those financial statements shall include certain information relating to:

a. The enterprise's operations in different industries—paragraphs .112 through .136
b. Its foreign operations and export sales—paragraphs .137 through .144
c. Its major customers—paragraph .145

If such statements are presented for more than one fiscal year, the information required by this section shall be presented for each such year. [FAS14, ¶3]

.105 The information specified in paragraph .104 is not required in financial statements for interim periods. [FAS18, ¶7] Any segment information that is presented in interim period financial statements shall be consistent with the requirements of this section. [FAS18, ¶8]

Purpose of Segment Information

.106 The purpose of the information required to be reported by this section is to assist financial statement users in analyzing and understanding the enterprise's financial statements by permitting better assessment of the enterprise's past performance and future prospects. Information prepared in conformity with this section may be of limited usefulness for comparing a segment of one enterprise with a similar segment of another enterprise. [FAS14, ¶5]

Accounting Principles Used in Preparing Segment Information

.107 The information required to be reported by this section is a disaggregation of the **consolidated financial information** included in the enterprise's financial statements. The accounting principles underlying the disaggregated information should be the same accounting principles as those underlying the consolidated information, except that most intersegment transactions that are eliminated from consolidated financial information are included in segment information (refer to paragraph .111). For example, a segment for which information is required to be reported by this section may include a consolidated subsidiary that prepares separate financial statements. Amounts reported in the subsidiary's financial statements sometimes differ from amounts included in consolidation for reasons other than intersegment transactions, for instance, because the subsidiary was acquired in a business combination accounted for by the purchase method. In that event, the segment information required to be reported by this section with respect to the consolidated financial statements shall be based on the amounts included in consolidation, not on the amounts reported in the subsidiary's financial statements. [FAS14, ¶6]

.108 Enterprises are not required by this section to disaggregate financial information pertaining to unconsolidated subsidiaries or other unconsolidated investees. Unconsolidated subsidiaries and investments in corporate joint ventures and 50 percent or less owned enterprises are normally accounted for by the equity method, and financial information about equity method investees is required to be disclosed in the investor's financial statements in accordance with Section I82, "Investments: Equity Method," paragraph .110. In addition, Section F65, "Foreign Operations," requires the disclosure of certain financial information about foreign subsidiaries of an enterprise. However, in addition to those disclosures, identification shall be made of both the industries and the geographic areas in which the equity method investees operate. Also, paragraph .133(c) requires special disclosures with respect to an equity method investee whose operations are vertically integrated with those of a **reportable segment** of the enterprise. Disaggregation of financial information pertaining to unconsolidated subsidiaries and other unconsolidated equity method investees is encouraged when that is considered to be desirable for an understanding of the enterprise's operations. [FAS14, ¶7]

.109 If a complete set of financial statements is presented for a parent company, subsidiary, corporate joint venture, or 50 percent or less owned investee, each such entity or a combined group of such entities is considered to be an enterprise as that term is used in this section and thus is subject to its requirements if those financial statements are *issued separately.* However, disclosure of the information that would otherwise be required by this section need not be made in a complete set of financial statements that is presented in another enterprise's **financial report** (that is, the primary reporting enterprise):

a. If those financial statements are also consolidated or combined in a complete set of financial statements and both sets of financial statements are presented in the same financial report

b. If those financial statements are presented for a **foreign investee that is not a subsidiary of the primary reporting enterprise** unless that foreign investee's *separately issued* financial statements disclose the information required by this section, for example, because the investee prepares its *separately issued* financial statements in accordance with U.S. generally accepted accounting principles

c. If those financial statements are presented in the financial report of a [nonpublic] enterprise that is not subject to the requirements of this section [FAS24, ¶5]

.110 Unless exempted above, if a complete set of financial statements for an investee (that is, subsidiary, corporate joint venture, or 50 percent or less owned investee) accounted for by the cost or equity method is presented in another enterprise's financial report, the information required by this section shall be presented for the investee if that information is significant in relation to the financial statements of the primary reporting entity in that financial report (for example, the consolidated or combined financial statements). To determine the information required by this section to be disclosed for an investee in such situations, the percentage tests specified in paragraphs .119, .138, and .145 shall be applied as specified in those paragraphs in relation to the financial statements of the primary reporting entity without adjustment for the **revenues, operating profit or loss,** or **identifiable assets** of the investee. [FAS24, ¶5]

.111 Transactions between a parent and its subsidiaries or between two subsidiaries are eliminated in preparing consolidated financial statements (refer to Section C51, "Consolidation," paragraph .109). In preparing the information required to be reported by this section, however, transactions between the segments of an enterprise shall be included in the segment information. Thus, for example, revenue reported for a segment includes both sales to unaffiliated customers (that is, customers outside the enterprise) and intersegment sales or transfers. Similarly, expenses relating both to sales to unaffiliated customers and to intersegment sales or transfers are deducted in measuring a segment's profitability. Exceptions to the general rule that intersegment transactions are not eliminated from segment information are provided in paragraphs .405, .408, and .411 for certain intersegment advances and loans and related interest revenue and expense. Paragraphs .136 and .144 require reconciliation of segment information with amounts reported in consolidated financial statements. [FAS14, ¶8]

Information about an Enterprise's Operations in Different Industries

.112 The financial statements of an enterprise shall include certain information about the **industry segments** of the enterprise. Criteria for determining industry segments for which information shall be reported are in paragraphs .113 through .127. The type of information to be presented for each reportable industry segment is specified in paragraphs .128 through .133. Requirements for presenting that information in financial statements are in paragraphs .133 through .136. [FAS14, ¶9]

Determining Reportable Segments

.113 The reportable segments of an enterprise shall be determined by (a) identifying the individual products and services from which the enterprise derives its revenue, (b) grouping those products and services by industry lines into industry segments (refer to paragraphs .114 through .118), and (c) selecting those industry segments that are significant with respect to the enterprise as a whole (refer to paragraphs .119 through .127). [FAS14, ¶11]

Grouping Products and Services by Industry Lines

.114 No single set of characteristics is universally applicable in determining the industry segments of all enterprises, nor is any single characteristic determinative in all cases. [(Refer to paragraphs .149 through .156 for information on standard industrial classification.)] Consequently, determination of an enterprise's industry segments must depend to a considerable extent on the judgment of the management of the enterprise. [FAS14, ¶12]

.115 Among the factors that should be considered in determining whether products and services are related (and, therefore, should be grouped into a single industry segment) or unrelated (and, therefore, should be separated into two or more industry segments) are the following:

a. *The nature of the product.* Related products or services have similar purposes or end uses. Thus, they may be expected to have similar rates of profitability, similar degrees of risk, and similar opportunities for growth.
b. *The nature of the production process.* Sharing of common or interchangeable production or sales facilities, equipment, labor force, or service group or use of the same or similar basic raw materials may suggest that products or services are related. Likewise, similar degrees of labor intensiveness or similar degrees of capital intensiveness may indicate a relationship among products or services.
c. *Markets and marketing methods.* Similarity of geographic marketing areas, types of customers, or marketing methods may indicate a relationship among products or services. For instance, the use of a common or interchangeable sales force may suggest a relationship among products or services. The sensitivity of the market to price changes and to changes in general economic conditions may also indicate whether products or services are related or unrelated. [FAS14, ¶100]

.116 Broad categories such as *manufacturing, wholesaling, retailing,* and *consumer products* are not per se indicative of the industries in which an enterprise operates, and those terms should not be used without identification of a product or service to describe an enterprise's industry segments. [FAS14, ¶101]

.117 An enterprise's existing **profit centers**—the smallest units of activity for which revenue and expense information is accumulated for internal planning and control purposes—represent a logical starting point for determining the enterprise's industry segments. If an enterprise's existing profit centers cross industry lines, it will be necessary to disaggregate its existing profit centers into smaller groups of related products and services (except as provided in paragraph .118). If an enterprise operates in more than one industry but does not presently accumulate any information on a less-than-total-enterprise basis (that is, its only profit center is the enterprise as a whole), it shall disaggregate its operations along industry lines (except as provided in paragraph .118). [FAS14, ¶13]

.118 Industry segmentation on a worldwide basis is a desirable objective but it may be impracticable for some enterprises. To the extent that revenue and profitability information is accumulated along industry lines for an enterprise's foreign operations, as defined in paragraph .137, or that it would be practicable to do so, industry segments shall be determined on a worldwide basis. To the extent that it is impracticable to disaggregate part or all of its foreign operations along industry lines, the enterprise shall disaggregate along industry lines its domestic operations and its foreign operations for which disaggregation is practicable and shall treat the aggregate of its foreign operations for which disaggregation is not practicable as a single industry segment. When that segment qualifies as a reportable industry segment (refer to paragraphs .119 through .127), disclosure shall be made of the types of industry operations included in the foreign operations that have not been disaggregated. [FAS14, ¶14]

Selecting Reportable Segments

.119 Each industry segment that is significant to an enterprise as a whole shall be identified as a reportable segment. For purposes of this section, an industry segment shall be regarded as significant—and therefore identified as a reportable segment (refer to paragraph .122)—if it satisfies one or more of the following tests. The tests shall be applied separately for each fiscal year for which financial statements are presented.

a. Its revenue (including both sales to unaffiliated customers and intersegment sales or transfers) is 10 percent or more of the combined revenue (sales to unaffiliated customers and intersegment sales or transfers) of all of the enterprise's industry segments.

b. The absolute amount of its operating profit or operating loss is 10 percent or more of the greater, in absolute amount, of:

(1) The combined operating profit of all industry segments that did not incur an operating loss.

(2) The combined operating loss of all industry segments that did incur an operating loss. (Paragraphs .120 and .121 illustrate the application of paragraph .119(b).)

c. Its identifiable assets are 10 percent or more of the combined identifiable assets of all industry segments.

Revenue, operating profits or loss, and identifiable assets relating to those foreign operations that have not been disaggregated along industry lines on grounds of impracticability (refer to paragraph .118) shall be included in computing the combined revenue, combined operating profit or operating loss, and combined identifiable assets of the enterprise's industry segments. [FAS14, ¶15]

.120 To illustrate how paragraph .119(b) is applied, assume that an enterprise has seven industry segments some of which incurred operating losses, as follows:

Industry Segment	Operating Profit or (Operating Loss)	
A	$100	
B	500	$1,000
C	400	
D	(295)	
E	(600)	(1,100)
F	(100)	
G	(105)	
[Total]	$(100)	

[FAS14, ¶103]

.121 The combined operating profit of all industry segments that did not incur a loss (A, B, and C) is $1,000. The absolute amount of the combined operating loss of those segments that did incur a loss (D, E, F, and G) is $1,100. Under paragraph .119(b), therefore, industry segments B, C, D, and E are significant because the absolute amount of their individual operating profit or operating loss equals or exceeds $110 (10 percent of $1,100). Additional industry segments might, of course, also be deemed significant under the revenue and identifiable assets tests in paragraphs .119(a) and .119(b). [FAS14, ¶104]

.122 The results of applying the percentage tests in paragraph .119 shall be evaluated from the standpoint of interperiod comparability before final determination of an enterprise's reportable segments is made. For instance, interperiod comparability would most likely require that an industry segment that has been significant in the past and is expected to be significant in the future be regarded as a reportable segment even though it fails to satisfy the tests in paragraph .119 in the current year. Conversely, a relatively insignificant industry segment may happen to satisfy the tests in paragraph .119 in the current fiscal year because its revenue or operating profit or loss is abnormally high or the combined revenue or operating profit or loss of all industry segments is abnormally low. In that case, it may be inappropriate to regard it as a reportable segment. Appropriate explanation of such circumstances shall be included as a part of the enterprise's segment information. [FAS14, ¶16]

.123 The reportable segments of an enterprise shall represent a substantial portion of the enterprise's total operations. The following test shall be applied to determine whether a substantial portion of an enterprise's operations is explained by its segment information: The combined revenue from sales to unaffiliated customers of all reportable segments (that is, revenue not including intersegment sales or transfers) shall constitute at least 75 percent of the combined revenue from sales to unaffiliated customers of all industry segments. The test shall be applied separately for each fiscal year for which financial statements are presented. Revenue relating to those foreign operations that have not been disaggregated along industry lines on grounds of impracticability shall be included in the denominator of the computation required by this paragraph and will be included in the numerator if those operations have been identified (in accordance with paragraphs .118 and .119) as a reportable segment. [FAS14, ¶17]

.124 If the industry segments identified as reportable in accordance with paragraphs .119 and .122 do not satisfy the 75 percent test in paragraph .123, additional industry segments shall be identified as reportable segments (subject to the provisions of paragraph .125) until the 75 percent test is met. [FAS14, ¶18]

.125 [There is a] need for a practical limit to the number of industry segments for which an enterprise reports information; beyond that limit, segment information may become overly detailed. Without attempting to define that limit precisely, [it is suggested] that as the number of industry segments that would be identified as reportable segments in accordance with paragraphs .119 through .124 increases above 10, the question of whether a practical limit has been reached comes increasingly into consideration, and combining the most closely related industry segments into broader reportable segments may be appropriate. Combinations shall be made, however, only to the extent necessary to contain the number of reportable segments within practical limits while still meeting the 75 percent test. [FAS14, ¶19]

.126 An enterprise may operate exclusively in a single industry or a dominant portion of an enterprise's operations may be in a single industry segment with the remaining portion in one or more other industry segments. The disclosures required by paragraphs .128 through .136 need not be applied to a dominant industry segment, except that the financial statements of an enterprise that operates predominantly or exclusively in a single industry shall identify that industry. An industry segment may be regarded as dominant if its revenue, operating profit or loss, and identifiable assets (as defined in paragraphs .405, .408, and .411) each constitute more than 90 percent of related combined totals for all industry segments, and no other industry segment meets any of the 10 percent tests in paragraph .119. [FAS14, ¶20]

.127 Paragraphs .113 through .126 and the guidelines for grouping products and services into industry segments set forth in paragraphs .115 and .116 are not intended to prohibit a more detailed disaggregation if that is considered to be desirable for an understanding of the enterprise's operations. [FAS14, ¶21]

Information to Be Presented

.128 The following shall be presented for each of an enterprise's reportable segments determined in accordance with paragraphs .113 through .127 (including those foreign operations that have not been disaggregated along industry lines on grounds of impracticability—refer to paragraph .118) and in the aggregate for the remainder of the enterprise's industry segments not deemed reportable segments:

a. Revenue information as set forth in paragraph .129
b. Profitability information as set forth in paragraphs .130 and .131
c. Identifiable assets information as set forth in paragraph .132
d. Other related disclosures as set forth in paragraph .133

In addition, the types of products and services from which the revenue of each reportable segment is derived shall be identified, and the accounting policies relevant to the information reported for industry segments shall be described to the extent not adequately explained by the disclosures of the enterprise's accounting policies required by Section A10, "Accounting Policies." Presentation of additional information for some or all of an enterprise's reportable segments beyond that specified in paragraphs .129 through .133 may be considered to be desirable, and this section does not preclude those additional disclosures. [FAS14, ¶22]

Revenue

.129 Sales to unaffiliated customers and sales or transfers to other industry segments of the enterprise shall be separately disclosed in presenting revenue of a reportable segment. As indicated in paragraph .411, for purposes of this section, sales or transfers to other industry segments shall be accounted for on the basis used by the enterprise to price the intersegment sales or transfers. The basis of accounting for intersegment sales or transfers shall be disclosed. If the basis is changed, disclosure shall be made of the nature of the change and its effect on the reportable segments' operating profit or loss in the period of change. [FAS14, ¶23]

Profitability

.130 Operating profit or loss as defined in paragraph .408 shall be presented for each reportable segment. As part of its segment information, an enterprise shall explain the nature and amount of any unusual or infrequently occurring items (refer to Section I22, "Income Statement Presentation: Unusual or Infrequent Items," paragraph .101) reported in its consolidated income statement that have been added or deducted in computing the operating profit or loss of a reportable segment in accordance with paragraph .408. Methods used to allocate operating expenses among industry segments in computing operating profit or loss should be consistently applied from period to period (but, if changed, disclosure shall be made of the nature of the change and its effect on the reportable segments' operating profit or loss in the period of change). [FAS14, ¶24]

Other Profitability Information

.131 In addition to presenting operating profit or loss as required by paragraph .130, an enterprise may choose to present some other measure of profitability for some or all of its segments. If the enterprise elects to present a measure of contribution to operating profit or loss, the enterprise shall describe the differences between contribution and operating profit or loss. If the enterprise elects to present net income or a measure of profitability between operating profit or loss and net income, the nature and amount of each category of revenue or expense that was added or deducted and the methods of allocation, if any, shall be disclosed. Those methods should be consistently applied from period to period (but, if changed, disclosure shall be made of the nature and effect of the change in the period of change). [FAS14, ¶25]

Identifiable Assets

.132 The aggregate carrying amount of identifiable assets as defined in paragraph .405 shall be presented for each reportable segment. [FAS14, ¶26]

Other Related Disclosures

.133 Disclosures relating to the information for reportable segments shall be made as follows:

a. Disclosure shall be made of the aggregate amount of depreciation, depletion, and amortization expense for each reportable segment.
b. Disclosure shall be made of the amount of each reportable segment's capital

expenditures, that is, additions to its property, plant, and equipment.

c. For each reportable segment, disclosure shall be made of the enterprise's equity in the net income from and investment in the net assets of equity method investees whose operations are vertically integrated with the operations of that segment. Disclosure shall also be made of the geographic areas in which those vertically integrated equity method investees operate.

d. Section A06, "Accounting Changes," paragraph .113, requires that the effect on income of a change in accounting principle be disclosed in the financial statements of an enterprise in the period in which the change is made. Disclosure shall also be made of the effect of the change on the operating profit of reportable segments in the period in which the change is made.[3] [FAS14, ¶27]

Publicly Traded Enterprises[4] Having Significant Oil and Gas Producing Activities

.133A If oil and gas producing activities[5] constitute a business segment, [refer to] paragraph .406, and the business segment activities are located substantially in a single geographic area, the results of operations information required by Section Oi5, "Oil and Gas Producing Activities," paragraphs .174 through .179, may be included with segment information disclosed elsewhere in the financial report. [FAS69, ¶24, fn7]

Methods of Presentation

.134 Information about the reportable segments of a business enterprise shall be included in the enterprise's financial statements in any of the following ways:

a. Within the body of the financial statements, with appropriate explanatory disclosures in the footnotes to the financial statements
b. Entirely in the footnotes to the financial statements
c. In a separate schedule that is included as an integral part of the financial statements. If, in a report to security holders, that schedule is located on a page that is not clearly a part of the financial statements, the schedule shall be referenced in the financial statements as an integral part thereof. [FAS14, ¶28]

.135 Financial information such as revenue, operating profit or loss, and identifiable assets of reportable segments shall be presented as dollar amounts. Corresponding percentages may be shown in addition to dollar amounts. [FAS14, ¶29]

---

[3]The pro forma effects of retroactive application, which are required to be disclosed on a consolidated basis by Section A06, paragraph .117, need not be disclosed for individual reportable segments. Also, the pro forma supplemental information relating to a business combination accounted for by the purchase method required to be presented by Section B50, "Business Combinations," paragraph .165, need not be presented for individual reportable segments. [FAS14, ¶27, fn10]

[4]Refer to Section Oi5, "Oil and Gas Producing Activities," paragraph .157.]

[5]Refer to Section Oi5, paragraph .101.]

.136 The information required to be presented by paragraphs .128 through .133 for individual reportable segments and in the aggregate for industry segments not deemed reportable shall be reconciled to related amounts in the financial statements of the enterprise as a whole, as follows: Revenue shall be reconciled to revenue reported in the consolidated income statement, and operating profit or loss shall be reconciled to pretax income from continuing operations (before gain or loss on discontinued operations, extraordinary items, and cumulative effect of a change in accounting principle) in the consolidated income statement. Also, identifiable assets shall be reconciled to consolidated total assets, with assets maintained for general corporate purposes separately identified in the reconciliation. An illustration is presented in paragraphs .147 and .148. [FAS14, ¶30]

Information about Foreign Operations and Export Sales

.137 The financial statements of an enterprise shall include information about its foreign operations. The features that identify an operation as foreign vary among enterprises. Thus, the identification of foreign operations will depend on the facts and circumstances of the particular enterprise. For purposes of this section, an enterprise's foreign operations include those revenue-producing operations (except for unconsolidated subsidiaries and other unconsolidated investees (refer to paragraph .108)) that (a) are located outside of the enterprise's home country (the United States for U.S. enterprises)[6] and (b) are generating revenue either from sales to unaffiliated customers or from intraenterprise sales or transfers between geographic areas.[7] Similarly, an enterprise's domestic operations include those revenue-producing operations of the enterprise located in the enterprise's home country that generate revenue either from sales to unaffiliated customers or from intraenterprise sales or transfers between geographic areas. Operations, either domestic or foreign (and regardless of whether part

---

[6]An enterprise whose home country is other than the United States but that prepares financial statements in conformity with U.S. generally accepted accounting principles shall classify operations outside of its home country as foreign operations. [FAS14, ¶31, fn11] [Refer to paragraphs .501 and .502 as to the status of Puerto Rico and other areas under U.S. sovereignty or some type of American jurisdiction.]

[7]Difficulties may arise in classifying the activities of certain types of enterprises. The following examples may provide useful guidelines:

a. Determination of whether the employment of an enterprise's mobile assets, such as offshore drilling rigs or ocean-going vessels, constitutes foreign operations should depend on whether such assets are normally identified with operations located and generating revenue from outside the home country. If they are normally identified with the enterprise's foreign operations, revenue generated from abroad would be considered foreign revenue. If they are normally identified with the enterprise's domestic operations, revenue generated from abroad would be considered export sales.

b. Services rendered by the foreign offices of a service enterprise, such as a consulting firm, having offices or facilities located both in the home country and in foreign countries would be considered foreign operations, and the revenue should be considered foreign revenue. Revenue generated abroad from services provided by domestic offices should be considered export sales. [FAS14, ¶31, fn12]

of a branch or a division of the enterprise or part of a consolidated subsidiary), should have identified with them the revenues generated by those operations, the assets employed in or associated with generating those revenues, and the costs and expenses incurred in generating those revenues or employing those assets. [FAS14, ¶31]

.138 The information specified in paragraph .142 shall be presented for (1) an enterprise's foreign operations, either in the aggregate or, if appropriate under paragraph .139, by geographic area, and (2) its domestic operations,[8] if either of the following conditions is met:

a. Revenue generated by the enterprise's foreign operations from sales to unaffiliated customers is 10 percent or more of consolidated revenue as reported in the enterprise's income statement.
b. Identifiable assets of the enterprise's foreign operations are 10 percent or more of consolidated total assets as reported in the enterprise's balance sheet. [FAS14, ¶32]

.139 If an enterprise's foreign operations are conducted in two or more geographic areas as defined in paragraph .140, the information specified in paragraph .141 shall be presented separately for each significant foreign geographic area, and in the aggregate for all other foreign geographic areas not deemed significant. A geographic area shall be regarded as *significant,* for the purpose of applying this paragraph, if its revenue from sales to unaffiliated customers or its identifiable assets are 10 percent or more of related consolidated amounts. [FAS14, ¶33]

.140 For purposes of this section, foreign *geographic areas* are individual countries or groups of countries as may be determined to be appropriate in an enterprise's particular circumstances. No single method of grouping the countries in which an enterprise operates into the geographic areas can reflect all of the differences among international business environments. Each enterprise shall group its foreign operations on the basis of the differences that are most important in its particular circumstances. Factors to be considered include proximity, economic affinity, similarities in business environments, and the nature, scale, and degree of interrelationship of the enterprise's operations in the various countries. [FAS14, ¶34]

.141 The following information shall be presented for an enterprise's foreign operations and for its domestic operations as appropriate in accordance with paragraphs .138 through .140:

a. Revenue as defined in paragraph .411, with sales to unaffiliated customers and sales or transfers between geographic areas shown separately. For purposes of this

---

[8]Separate information about domestic operations need not be presented if domestic operations' revenue from sales to unaffiliated customers and domestic operations' identifiable assets are less than 10 percent of related consolidated amounts. [FAS14, ¶32, fn13]

section, intraenterprise sales or transfers between geographic areas shall be accounted for on the basis used by the enterprise to price the intraenterprise sales or transfers. The basis of accounting for intraenterprise sales or transfers shall be disclosed. If the basis is changed, disclosure shall be made of the nature of the change and its effect in the period of change.

b.   Operating profit or loss as defined in paragraph .408 *or* net income *or* some other measure of profitability between operating profit or loss and net income. A common level of profitability shall be reported for all geographic areas, although an enterprise may choose to report additional profitability information for some or all of its geographic areas of operations.

c.   Identifiable assets as defined in paragraph .405. [FAS14, ¶35]

.142 With respect to an enterprise's *domestic* operations, sales to unaffiliated customers include both (a) sales to customers within the enterprise's home country and (b) sales to customers in foreign countries, that is, export sales. If the amount of export sales from an enterprise's home country to unaffiliated customers in foreign countries is 10 percent or more of total revenue from sales to unaffiliated customers as reported in the enterprise's consolidated income statement, that amount shall be separately reported, in the aggregate and by such geographic areas as are considered appropriate in the circumstances. The disclosure required by this paragraph shall be made even if the enterprise is not required by this section to report information about its operations in different industries or foreign operations. [FAS14, ¶36]

.143 Information about the foreign operations and export sales of a business enterprise may be included in the enterprise's financial statements in any of the ways identified in paragraph .134. Financial information shall be presented as U.S. dollar amounts; corresponding percentages may be shown in addition to dollar amounts. The geographic areas into which an enterprise's foreign operations have been disaggregated shall be identified. [FAS14, ¶37]

.144 The information about revenue, profitability, and identifiable assets required to be presented for foreign operations shall be reconciled to related amounts in the financial statements of the enterprise as a whole, in a manner similar to that described in paragraph .136 [and illustrated in paragraphs .147 and .148]. [FAS14, ¶38]

Information about Major Customers

.145 An enterprise shall disclose information about the extent of the enterprise's reliance on its major customers.[9] If 10 percent or more of the revenue of an enterprise is derived from sales to any single customer, that fact and the amount of revenue from each such customer shall be disclosed. For this purpose, a group of entities under common control shall be regarded as a single customer, and the federal government, a

---

[9]Refer to paragraphs .503 and .504 as to the meaning of *customers* of health care facilities.]

state government, a local government (for example, a county or municipality), or a foreign government shall each be considered as a single customer.[10] The identity of the customer need not be disclosed, but the identity of the industry segment or segments making the sales shall be disclosed. The disclosures required by this paragraph shall be made by an enterprise subject to this section even if the enterprise operates only in one industry or has no foreign operations. [FAS30, ¶6]

Restatement of Previously Reported Segment Information

.146 If prior period information about an enterprise's reportable industry segments, its foreign operations and export sales, and its major customers is being presented with corresponding information for the current period, the prior period information shall be retroactively restated in the following circumstances, with appropriate disclosure of the nature and effect of the restatement:

a. When the financial statements of the enterprise as a whole have been retroactively restated, for example, for a change in accounting principle of the type described in Section A06, paragraphs .123 and .125, or for a business combination accounted for by the pooling-of-interests method

b. When there has been a change in the way the enterprise's products and services are grouped into industry segments or a change in the way the enterprise's foreign operations are grouped[11] into geographic areas and such changes affect the segment or geographic area information being reported [FAS14, ¶40]

Illustrations of Financial Statement Disclosures

.147 Paragraph .148 contains examples of disclosures of the type that this section requires to be included in the financial statements of an enterprise. The illustrations do not encompass all possible circumstances, nor do the formats used indicate [preferable practice]. [FAS14, ¶105]

.148 Exhibit 148A presents the consolidated income statement of a hypothetical enterprise for the year ended December 31, 19X1. Exhibit 148B illustrates how the enterprise might present information about its operations in different industries and its reliance on major customers. Exhibit 148C illustrates how the enterprise might present information about its foreign operations in different geographic areas and its export sales.

---

[10]If sales are concentrated in a particular department or agency of government, disclosure of that fact and the amount of revenue derived from each such source is encouraged. [FAS30, ¶6]

[11]Restatement is not required when an enterprise's reportable segments change as a result of a change in the nature of an enterprise's operations or as a result of applying the tests in paragraphs .119 through .126. [FAS14, ¶40, fn14]

Exhibit 148A

X Company
Consolidated Income Statement
Year Ended December 31, 19X1

Sales		$4,700
Cost of sales	$3,000	
Selling, general, and administrative expense	700	
Interest expense	200	3,900
[Total]		800
Equity in net income of Z Co. (25% owned)		100
Income from continuing operations before		
income taxes		900
Income taxes		400
Income from continuing operations		500
Discontinued operations:		
Loss from operations of discontinued		
West Coast division (net of income tax		
effect of $50)	70	
Loss on disposal of West Coast division		
(net of income tax effect of $100)	130	200
Income before extraordinary gain and		
before cumulative effect of change in		
accounting principle		300
Extraordinary gain (net of income tax effect		
of $80)		90
Cumulative effect on prior years of change		
from straight-line to accelerated depreciation		
(net of income tax effect of $60)		(60)
Net income		$ 330

[FAS14, ¶106]

Exhibit 148B

X Company

Information about the Company's Operations in Different Industries

Year Ended December 31, 19X1

	Industry A	Industry B	Industry C	Other Industries	Adjustments and Eliminations	Consolidated
Sales to unaffiliated customers	$1,000	$2,000	$1,500	$ 200		$ 4,700
Intersegment sales	200		500		$ (700)	
Total revenue	$1,200	$2,000	$2,000	$ 200	$ (700)	$ 4,700
Operating profit	$ 200	$ 290	$ 600	$ 50	$ (40)	$ 1,100
Equity in net income of Z Co.						100
General corporate expenses						(100)
Interest expense						(200)
Income from continuing operations before income taxes						$ 900
Identifiable assets at December 31, 19X1	$2,000	$4,050	$6,000	$1,000	$ (50)	$13,000
Investment in net assets of Z Co.						400
Corporate assets						1,600
Total assets at December 31, 19X1						$15,000

Refer to accompanying note.

Exhibit 148B (continued)

Note: The Company operates principally in three industries, A, B, and C. Operations in Industry A involve production and sale of (describe types of products and services). Operations in Industry B involve production and sale of (describe types of products and services). Operations in Industry C involve production and sale of (describe types of products and services). Total revenue by industry includes both sales to unaffiliated customers, as reported in the Company's consolidated income statement, and intersegment sales, which are accounted for by (describe the basis of accounting for intersegment sales).

Operating profit is total revenue less operating expenses. In computing operating profit, none of the following items has been added or deducted: general corporate expenses, interest expense, income taxes, equity in income from an unconsolidated investee, loss from discontinued operations of the West Coast division (which was a part of the Company's operations in Industry B), extraordinary gain (which relates to the Company's operations in Industry A), and the cumulative effect of the change from straight-line to accelerated depreciation (of which $30 relates to the Company's operations in Industry A, $10 to Industry B, and $20 to Industry C). Depreciation for Industries A, B, and C, respectively, was $80, $100, and $150. Capital expenditures for the 3 industries were $100, $200, and $400, respectively.

The effect of the change from straight-line to accelerated depreciation was to reduce the 19X1 operating profit of Industries A, B, and C, respectively, by $40, $30, and $20.

Identifiable assets by industry are those assets that are used in the Company's operations in each industry. Corporate assets are principally cash and marketable securities.

The Company has a 25-percent interest in Z Co., whose operations are in the United States and are vertically integrated with the Company's operations in Industry A. Equity in net income of Z Co. was $100; investment in net assets of Z Co. was $400.

To reconcile industry information with consolidated amounts, the following eliminations have been made: $700 of intersegment sales; $40 relating to the net change in intersegment operating profit in beginning and ending inventories; and $50 intersegment operating profit in inventory at December 31, 19X1.

Contracts with a U.S. government agency account for $1,100 of the sales to unaffiliated customers of Industry B. [FAS14, ¶106]

Exhibit 148C

X Company

Information about the Company's Operations in Different Geographic Areas

Year Ended December 31, 19X1

	United States	Geographic Area A	Geographic Area B	Adjustments and Eliminations	Consolidated
Sales to unaffiliated customers	$3,000	$1,000	$ 700		$ 4,700
Transfers between geographic areas	1,000			$(1,000)	
Total revenue	$4,000	$1,000	$ 700	$(1,000)	$ 4,700
Operating profit	$ 800	$ 400	$ 100	$ (200)	$ 1,100
Equity in net income of Z Co.					100
General corporate expenses					(100)
Interest expense					(200)
Income from continuing operations before income taxes					$ 900
Identifiable assets at December 31, 19X1	$7,300	$3,400	$2,450	$ (150)	$13,000
Investment in net assets of Z Co.					400
Corporate assets					1,600
Total assets at December 31, 19X1					$15,000

Refer to accompanying note.

Exhibit 148C (continued)

Note: Transfers between geographic areas are accounted for by (describe the basis of accounting for such transfers). Operating profit is total revenue less operating expenses. In computing operating profit, none of the following items has been added or deducted: general corporate expenses, interest expense, income taxes, equity in income from unconsolidated investee, loss from discontinued operations of West Coast division (which was part of the Company's U.S. operations), extraordinary gain (which relates to the Company's operations in Geographic Area B), and the cumulative effect of the change from straight-line to accelerated depreciation (which relates entirely to the Company's operations in the United States).

Identifiable assets are those assets of the Company that are identified with the operations in each geographic area. Corporate assets are principally cash and marketable securities.

Of the $3,000 U.S. sales to unaffiliated customers, $1,200 were export sales, principally to Geographic Area C. [FAS14, ¶106]

.149 [There are] several systems that have been developed for classifying business activities, such as the Standard Industrial Classification [(SIC)] and the Enterprise Standard Industrial Classification systems. None is, by itself, suitable to determine industry segments as that term is used in this section. Nonetheless, those systems may provide guidance for the exercise of the judgment required to group an enterprise's products and services by industry lines. [FAS14, ¶91]

.150 As set forth in the *Standard Industrial Classification Manual* prepared by the Statistical Policy Division of the U.S. Office of Management and Budget, SIC is a system for classifying business establishments (generally, individual plants, stores, banks, etc.) by the type of economic activity in which they are engaged. An establishment is not necessarily identical with a business enterprise, which may consist of one or more establishments. [FAS14, ¶92]

.151 The manual contains one-digit, two-digit, three-digit, and four-digit SIC industry codes, each of which is described in detail. At the one-digit level, the SIC classifies business activities into 11 divisions:

A Agriculture, forestry, and fishing
B Mining
C Construction
D Manufacturing
E Transportation, communications, electric, gas, and sanitary services
F Wholesale trade
G Retail trade

H   Finance, insurance, and real estate
I   Services
J   Public administration
K   Nonclassifiable establishments [FAS14, ¶93]

.152 Each of those divisions is subdivided into two-digit major groups. There are a total of 84 two-digit groups. For example, the 20 major groups in manufacturing are:

a.   Food and kindred products
b.   Tobacco manufacturers
c.   Textile mill products
d.   Apparel and other finished products made from fabrics and similar materials
e.   Lumber and wood products, except furniture
f.   Furniture and fixtures
g.   Paper and allied products
h.   Printing, publishing, and allied [industries]
i.   Chemicals and allied products
j.   Petroleum refining and related industries
k.   Rubber and miscellaneous plastics products
l.   Leather and leather products
m.   Stone, clay, glass, and concrete products
n.   Primary metal industries
o.   Fabricated metal products, except machinery and transportation equipment
p.   Machinery, except electrical
q.   Electrical and electronic machinery, equipment, and supplies
r.   Transportation equipment
s.   Measuring, analyzing, and controlling instruments; photographic, medical, and optical goods; watches and clocks
t.   Miscellaneous manufacturing industries [FAS14, ¶94]

.153 Each of the two-digit SIC major groups, in turn, is further subdivided into three-digit industry groups. There are [420] three-digit groups. For example, the "machinery, except electrical" group includes the following industry groups:

a.   Engines and turbines
b.   Farm and garden machinery and equipment
c.   Construction, mining, and materials handling machinery and equipment
d.   Metalworking machinery and equipment
e.   Special industry machinery, except metalworking machinery
f.   General industry machinery and equipment
g.   Office, computing, and accounting machines
h.   Refrigeration and service industry machinery
i.   Miscellaneous machinery, except electrical [FAS14, ¶95]

.154 The three-digit SIC industry groups are still further subdivided by product lines into over 1,000 narrower, four-digit industry groups. Metalworking machinery and equipment (a three-digit industry group), for example, is divided into metal cutting machine tools, metal forming machine tools, power driven hand tools, rolling mill machinery and equipment, and so on. [FAS14, ¶96]

.155 The *Standard Industrial Classification Manual* is revised periodically. It is available for sale by the Superintendent of Documents, U.S. Government Printing Office. [FAS14, ¶97]

.156 The *Enterprise Standard Industrial Classification Manual,* like the *SIC Manual,* is prepared by the Statistical Policy Division of the U.S. Office of Management and Budget. It classifies enterprises (companies, firms, partnerships, etc.) rather than establishments (plants, stores, banks, etc.). The structure of *ESIC* follows closely the structure of the SIC codes. It includes [11] classes of enterprises at the one-digit level, [75] at the two-digit level, [241] at the three-digit level, and [278] at the four-digit level. [FAS14, ¶98]

Glossary

.401 Complete set of financial statements. A set of financial statements (including necessary footnotes) that present financial position, results of operations, and [FAS24, ¶1, fn2] cash flows [FAS95, ¶152] in conformity with generally accepted accounting principles. [FAS24, ¶1, fn2]

.402 Consolidated financial information. Aggregate [financial] information relating to an enterprise as a whole whether or not the enterprise has consolidated subsidiaries. [FAS14, ¶6, fn1]

.403 Financial report. Includes any compilation of information that includes one or more complete sets of financial statements, such as in an annual report to stockholders or in a filing with the Securities and Exchange Commission. [FAS24, ¶1]

.404 Foreign investee that is not a subsidiary of the primary reporting enterprise. An [investee] enterprise incorporated or otherwise organized and domiciled in a foreign country if 50 percent or more of that enterprise's voting stock is owned by residents of a foreign country. [FAS24, ¶5]

.405 Identifiable assets. Those tangible and intangible enterprise assets that are used by the industry segment, including (a) assets that are used exclusively by that industry segment and (b) an allocated portion of assets used jointly by two or more industry segments. Assets used jointly by two or more industry segments shall be allocated among the industry segments on a reasonable basis. Because the assets of an industry segment that transfers products or services to another industry segment are not used in the operations of the receiving segment, no amount of those assets shall be allocated to the receiving segment. Assets that represent part of an enterprise's investment in an industry segment, such as goodwill, shall be included in the industry segment's identifiable assets.[401] Assets maintained for general corporate purposes (that is, those not used in the operations of any industry segment) shall not be allocated to industry segments. The identifiable assets of an industry segment shall not include advances or loans to or investments in another industry segment, except that advances or loans to other industry segments shall be included in the identifiable assets of a financial segment because the income therefrom is included in computing the financial segment's operating profit or loss (refer to footnote 408). Asset valuation allowances such as the following shall be taken into account in computing the amount of an industry segment's identifiable assets: allowance for doubtful accounts, accumulated depreciation, and marketable securities valuation allowance. [FAS14, ¶10]

---

[401]Any related depreciation or amortization expense is deducted in determining the operating profit of the industry segment. [FAS14, ¶10, fn9]

.406 **Industry segment.**[402] A component of an enterprise engaged in providing a product or service or a group of related products and services primarily to unaffiliated customers (that is, customers outside the enterprise) for a profit.[403] By defining an industry segment in terms of products and services that are sold primarily to unaffiliated customers, this section does not require the disaggregation of the vertically integrated operations of an enterprise. [FAS14, ¶10a]

.407 **Nonpublic enterprise.** An enterprise other than one (a) whose debt or equity securities trade in a public market on a foreign or domestic stock exchange or in the over-the-counter market (including securities quoted only locally or regionally) or (b) that is required to file financial statements with the Securities and Exchange Commission. An enterprise is no longer considered a nonpublic enterprise when its financial statements are issued in preparation for the sale of any class of securities in a public market. [FAS21, ¶13] [Nonpublic] enterprises include certain mutual associations, cooperatives, nonbusiness organizations, and partnerships that often make their financial statements available to a broad class, such as insurance policyholders, depositors, members, contributors, or partners. [FAS21, ¶8]

.408 **Operating profit or loss.** Revenue minus all operating expenses. As used herein, operating expenses include expenses that relate to both revenue from sales to unaffiliated customers and revenue from intersegment sales or transfers; those operating expenses incurred by an enterprise that are not directly traceable to an industry segment shall be allocated on a reasonable basis among those industry segments for whose benefit the expenses were incurred (refer to paragraph .130). For purposes of this section, intersegment purchases shall be accounted for on the same basis as intersegment sales or transfers (that is, on the basis used by the enterprise to price the intersegment sales or transfers—refer to the last sentence of paragraph .411). None of the following shall be added or deducted, as the case may be, in computing the operating profit or loss of an industry segment: revenue earned at the corporate level and not derived from the operations of any industry

---

[402]The meaning of the term *industry segment* as it is used in this section is different from the use of the term *segment* in pronouncements of the [former] Cost Accounting Standards Board. [FAS14, ¶10, fn2]

[403]In some industries, it is normal practice for an enterprise to purchase and sell substantially identical commodities to minimize transportation or other costs. In those situations, sales and purchases of substantially identical commodities should be netted for the purpose of determining whether a product or service or a group of related products and services is sold primarily to unaffiliated customers. Although those sales and purchases are netted for the purpose of identifying an industry segment, it is not intended that this rule change an enterprise's accounting practice with respect to determining the revenue of the enterprise or any of its industry segments. [FAS14, ¶10, fn3]

segment; general corporate expenses;[404] interest expense;[405] domestic and foreign income taxes; equity in income or loss from unconsolidated subsidiaries and other unconsolidated investees; gain or loss on discontinued operations (as defined in Section I13, "Income Statement Presentation: Discontinued Operations"); extraordinary items; minority interest; and the cumulative effect of a change in accounting principles (refer to Section A06). [FAS14, ¶10d]

.409 Profit center. Those components of an enterprise that sell primarily to out-side markets and for which information about revenue and profitability is accumulated. [They are] the smallest units of activity for which revenue and expense information is accumulated for internal planning and control purposes. [FAS14, ¶13]

.410 Reportable segment. An industry segment (or, in certain cases, a group of two or more closely related industry segments—refer to paragraph .125) for which information is required to be reported by this section. [FAS14, ¶10b]

.411 Revenue. The revenue of an industry segment includes revenue both from sales[406] to unaffiliated customers (that is, revenue from customers outside the enterprise as reported in the enterprise's income statement) and from intersegment sales or transfers, if any, of products and services similar to those sold to unaffiliated customers.[407] Interest from sources outside the enterprise and interest earned on intersegment trade receivables is included in revenue if the asset on which the interest is earned is included among the industry segment's identifiable assets (refer to paragraph .405), but interest earned on advances or loans to other industry segments is not included.[408] For purposes of this section, revenue from intersegment sales or transfers shall be accounted for on the basis used by the enterprise to price the intersegment sales or transfers. [FAS14, ¶10c]

---

[404]Some of the expenses incurred at an enterprise's central administrative office may not be general corporate expenses, but rather may be operating expenses of industry segments that should therefore be allocated to those industry segments. The nature of an expense rather than the location of its incurrence should determine whether it is an operating expense. Only those expenses identified by their nature as operating expenses should be allocated as operating expenses in computing an industry segment's operating profit or loss. [FAS14, ¶10, fn7]

[405]Interest expense is deducted in computing the operating profit or loss of an industry segment whose operations are principally of a financial nature (for example, banking, insurance, leasing, or financing). [FAS14, ¶10, fn8]

[406]For convenience, the term *sales* is used in this section to include the sale of a product, the rendering of a service, and other types of transactions by which revenue is earned. [FAS14, ¶10, fn4]

[407]Intersegment billings for the cost of shared facilities or other jointly incurred costs do not represent intersegment sales or transfers as that term is used in this section. [FAS14, ¶10, fn5]

[408]Interest earned on advances or loans to other industry segments is included in computing the operating profit or loss of an industry segment whose operations are principally of a financial nature (for example, banking, insurance, leasing, or financing). [FAS14, ¶10, fn6]

Supplemental Guidance

Segment Reporting of Puerto Rican Operations

.501 *Question*—Are Puerto Rican operations and operations related to other areas under U.S. sovereignty or some type of American jurisdiction, such as the Virgin Islands and American Samoa, to be considered *foreign* operations and thus subject to the disclosure requirements of paragraphs .137 through .144? [FTB79-4, ¶1]

.502 *Response*—The degree of interrelationship between the United States and Puerto Rico (as well as non-self-governing U.S. territories such as the Virgin Islands and American Samoa) is such that Puerto Rican operations of U.S. enterprises should be considered domestic operations. Factors such as proximity, economic affinity, and similarities in business environments also indicate this classification for the Puerto Rican operations of U.S. enterprises. This section does not prohibit additional disclosures about Puerto Rican operations that might be useful in analyzing and understanding an enterprise's financial statements. [FTB79-4, ¶3]

Customers of Health Care Facilities

.503 *Question*—Would an insuring entity (such as Blue Cross) be considered a *customer* of a health care facility as that term is defined in paragraph .145? [FTB79-5, ¶1]

.504 *Response*—An insuring entity should not be considered the *customer* of a health care facility as that term is used in this section. The fact that an insuring entity is a paying agent for the patient does not make the insuring entity the customer of the health care facility because the insuring entity does not decide which services to purchase and from which health care facility to purchase the services. The latter two factors are important in determining the customer. [FTB79-5, ¶3]

Applicability to Certain Brokers and Dealers in Securities

.505 *Question*—Should closely held brokers or dealers in securities that file financial statements with the Securities and Exchange Commission be considered nonpublic enterprises for purposes of applying this section? [FTB79-8, ¶1]

.506 *Background*—All security brokers and dealers registered with the SEC must file complete sets of financial statements with the SEC for use by the SEC's Division of Market Regulation for regulatory purposes, whether they are closely held or publicly held. Although the statement of financial condition filed by a broker-dealer must be available for public inspection, the income statement and statement of [FTB79-8, ¶5] cash flows [FAS111, ¶8(aa)] may be treated as *confidential* if so requested by the broker-dealer. A publicly held broker-dealer that is subject to Sections 12 and 13 of the Securities Exchange Act of 1934 must, in addition, file a complete set of financial statements and various forms with the SEC in the same manner as is required of other publicly held enterprises subject to those sections of the 1934 Act. [FTB79-8, ¶5]

.507 *Response*—The fact that financial statements are required to be filed for broker-dealer regulatory purposes with the SEC does not make an otherwise *nonpublic* enterprise public for purposes of this section. Thus, the suspension in paragraph .101 applies to closely held broker-dealers that are required to file financial statements with the SEC only for use by its Division of Market Regulation, principally because the broker-dealer can cause a significant portion of those financial statements (that is, the income statement and statement of [FTB79-8, ¶6] cash flows [FAS111, ¶8(aa)]) to be unavailable for public inspection by requesting confidential treatment. [FTB79-8, ¶6]

(The next page is 42687.)

TAXES: REAL AND PERSONAL PROPERTY TAXES

Source: ARB 43, Chapter 10A

Summary

Real and personal property taxes are generally accrued on the tax-payer's books during the fiscal period of the taxing authority for which the taxes are levied.

Background Information

.101 In practice, real and personal property taxes have been charged against the income of various periods, as indicated below:

a. Year in which paid (cash basis)
b. Year ending on assessment (or lien) date
c. Year beginning on assessment (or lien) date
d. Calendar or fiscal year of taxpayer prior to assessment (or lien) date
e. Calendar or fiscal year of taxpayer including assessment (or lien) date
f. Calendar or fiscal year of taxpayer prior to payment date
g. Fiscal year of governing body levying the tax
h. Year appearing on tax bill.

[ARB43, ch10A, ¶10]

.102 Some of these periods may coincide, as when the fiscal year of the taxing body and that of the taxpayer are the same. The charge to income is sometimes made in full at one time, sometimes ratably on a monthly basis, and sometimes on the basis of prior estimates adjusted during or after the period. [ARB43, ch10A, ¶11]

.103 The various periods mentioned represent varying degrees of conservatism in accrual accounting. Some justification may be found for each usage, but all the circumstances relating to a particular tax must be considered before a satisfactory conclusion is reached. [ARB43, ch10A, ¶12]

.104 Consistency of application from year to year is the important consideration and selection of any of the periods mentioned is a matter for individual judgment. [ARB43, ch10A, ¶13]

Basis Considered Most Acceptable

.105 Generally, the most acceptable basis of providing for property taxes is monthly accrual on the taxpayer's books during the fiscal period of the taxing authority for which the taxes are levied. The books will then show, at any closing date, the appropriate accrual or prepayment. [ARB43, ch10A, ¶14]

Treatment in Financial Statements

Balance Sheet

.106 An accrued liability for real and personal property taxes, whether estimated or definitely known, shall be included among the current liabilities. If estimates are subject to a substantial measure of uncertainty, the liability shall be described as estimated. [ARB43, ch10A, ¶16]

Income Statement

.107 While it is sometimes proper to capitalize in property accounts the amount of real estate taxes applicable to property that is being developed for use or sale, these taxes are generally regarded as an expense of doing business. They may be (a) charged to operating expenses; (b) shown as a separate deduction from income; or (c) distributed among the several accounts to which they are deemed to apply, such as factory overhead, rental income, and selling or general expenses. [ARB43, ch10A, ¶17]

.108 In condensed income statements appearing in published reports, the amounts of real and personal property taxes, however charged in the accounts, are rarely shown separately. They are frequently combined with other taxes but not with taxes on income. [ARB43, ch10A, ¶18]

(The next page is 44703.)

VALUATION: USE OF VALUATION ALLOWANCES

Source: APB Opinion 12

Summary

Valuation allowances are items that reduce or increase the carrying amount of an asset or a liability. For purposes of financial statement presentation, valuation allowances shall be deducted from or added to the assets or liabilities to which they relate.

.101 [A **valuation allowance** is described in paragraphs 34 and 43 of FASB Concepts Statement No. 6, *Elements of Financial Statements,* as a separate item that reduces or increases the carrying amount of an asset or a liability. For example, an estimate of uncollectible amounts reduces receivables to the amount expected to be collected, or a premium on a bond receivable increases the receivable to its cost or present value. Concepts Statement 6 concludes that valuation allowances are part of the related assets or liabilities and are neither assets nor liabilities in their own right.]

.102 [For purposes of financial statement presentation,] accumulated allowances for depreciation and depletion and asset valuation allowances for losses such as those on receivables and investments [APB12, ¶2] shall be deducted from the assets or groups of assets to which the allowances relate, with appropriate disclosure. [APB12, ¶3]

.103 [Specific requirements and guidance applicable to valuation allowances are included in this text in the sections that address the assets to which they relate. For example, the valuation allowance for receivables is discussed in Section C59, "Contingencies," paragraphs .128 and .129, and Section D22, "Debt: Restructurings," footnote 6, and the valuation allowance for mortgage loans is discussed in Section Mo4, "Mortgage Banking Activities," paragraph .105.]

Glossary

.401 **Valuation allowance.** A separate item that reduces or increases the carrying amount of an asset or a liability. Valuation allowances are part of the related assets or liabilities and are neither assets nor liabilities in their own right. [Concepts Statement 6, ¶34 & 43]

(The next page is T-1.)

**Refer to Volume II of the
Current Text for the appendixes.**

Topical Index

INTRODUCTION TO THE TOPICAL INDEX

The topical index includes references to documents contained in the *Original Pronouncements* volumes, all sections of the *Current Text* volumes, matters discussed by the FASB Emerging Issues Task Force (EITF), and supplemental guidance published by the FASB in the form of question-and-answer *Highlights* and Special Reports.

Original Pronouncements References

For *Original Pronouncements,* the topical index generally excludes references to introductory paragraphs and those paragraphs that provide background information or bases for conclusions. However, if those paragraphs facilitate an understanding of an accounting standard, they are referenced. Superseded paragraphs and pronouncements are not indexed except for those superseded pronouncements with significantly delayed effective dates. The related pronouncements are also retained in the text but shaded to alert the reader that the material has been superseded. The effective date and transition paragraphs are also not indexed, but the principal effective dates are listed in Appendix C, "Effective Dates of Pronouncements."

Current Text References

The topical index provides references to specific paragraphs of all sections of the *Current Text.* It also includes references to all sections that have been superseded by pronouncements with significantly delayed effective dates; those superseded sections are presented in Appendix E of the *Current Text.*

EITF Issue References

References to issues discussed by the FASB Emerging Issues Task Force are also included in the topical index. In this volume, Appendix D presents a listing of all issues discussed to date and their status (through the May 18-19, 1995 meeting). Those matters are summarized by issue number in a separate publication, *EITF Abstracts.*

Other References

Also included in the topical index are references to supplemental guidance published by the FASB in the following documents:

* FASB *Highlights,* "Futures Contracts: Guidance on Applying Statement 80," June 1985 (Q&A.80)

- FASB *Highlights,* "Computer Software: Guidance on Applying Statement 86," February 1986 (Q&A.86)
- FASB Special Report, *A Guide to Implementation of Statement 87 on Employers' Accounting for Pensions: Questions and Answers* (Q&A.87)
- FASB Special Report, *A Guide to Implementation of Statement 88 on Employers' Accounting for Settlements and Curtailments of Defined Benefit Pension Plans and for Termination Benefits: Questions and Answers* (Q&A.88)
- FASB Special Report, *A Guide to Implementation of Statement 91 on Accounting for Nonrefundable Fees and Costs Associated with Originating or Acquiring Loans and Initial Direct Costs of Leases: Questions and Answers* (Q&A.91)
- FASB Special Report, *A Guide to Implementation of Statement 106 on Employers' Accounting for Postretirement Benefits Other Than Pensions: Questions and Answers* (Q&A.106)
- FASB Special Report, *A Guide to Implementation of Statement 109 on Accounting For Income Taxes: Questions and Answers* (Q&A.109)
- FASB Viewpoints, "Accounting for Reinsurance: Questions and Answers about Statement 113," FASB *Status Report,* February 26, 1993 (Q&A.113). [**Note:** For the convenience of the user, this article is reproduced in Topic No. D-34 of *EITF Abstracts.*]
- FASB Special Report, *Illustrations of Financial Instrument Disclosures* (Q&A.FinDisc)
- FASB *Highlights,* "Time for a Change—Implementing FASB Statements 116 and 117," January 1995 (Q&A.116/117)

Organization of the Topical Index

References in the topical index are made to the source documents in the following manner:

- *Current Text*—to the CT section and paragraph number
- *Original Pronouncements*—to the document and paragraph number
- EITF Issues—to the issue number or to Appendix D in *EITF Abstracts*
- Supplemental guidance—to the *Highlights* or FASB Special Report by the applicable FAS number and question number.

An example follows:

	OP	CT	EITF/Other
FUTURES CONTRACTS			
Hedges			
. . Ongoing Assessment of Correlation ...	FAS80, ¶11	F80.111	EITF.85-6
			Q&A.80 #20-21

The reference FAS80, ¶11 indicates paragraph 11 of FASB Statement No. 80, *Accounting for Futures Contracts*. F80.111 indicates paragraph .111 of the *Current Text* Section F80, "Futures Contracts." The reference to EITF.85-6 indicates EITF Issue No. 85-6, "Futures Implementation Questions." Q&A.80 #20-21 refers to questions 20 and 21 of the FASB *Highlights*, "Futures Contracts: Guidance on Applying Statement 80."

Multiple references on an individual topic are listed in alphabetical and numerical order and there is not necessarily a direct relationship between references listed on the same line.

Order Information on Source Material

Copies of *EITF Abstracts*, EITF Issue Summary packages and related meeting minutes, and the FASB *Highlights*, Viewpoints, and Special Reports listed above can be obtained from the FASB Order Department. The *Original Pronouncements* loose-leaf service also may be obtained from the FASB. In addition, for non-AICPA members, the *Current Text* loose-leaf service may be obtained from the FASB. For information call 203-847-0700, ext. 555.

AICPA members may obtain copies of the annual bound volumes of the *Original Pronouncements* and *Current Text,* as well as the *Current Text* loose-leaf service, from the American Institute of Certified Public Accountants. Members who wish to order copies of these publications should write or phone the Order Department, American Institute of CPAs, Harborside Financial Center, 201 Plaza III, Jersey City, NJ 07311. Call 800-862-4272.

Non-AICPA members may obtain copies of the annual bound volumes of the *Original Pronouncements* and *Current Text* from John Wiley & Sons, Inc. Call 800-225-5945; outside the United States call 908-469-4400.

	Original Pronouncements	Current Text	EITF and Other

ABANDONED PROPERTY
See Oil and Gas Producing Activities
See Real Estate: Costs and Initial
  Operations of Real Estate Projects
See Regulated Operations
ABANDONMENTS
See Regulated Operations
ABNORMAL COSTS
See Extraordinary Items
Inventory .... ARB43, Ch.4, ¶5   I78.106
Unusual or Infrequent Items .... APB30, ¶26   I22.101
ACCELERATED COST RECOVERY SYSTEM (ACRS)
See Depreciation
ACCELERATED DEPRECIATION
See Depreciation
ACCOUNTING CHANGES
See Adjustments of Financial Statements
  for Prior Periods
See Disclosure
See Earnings per Share
See Interim Financial Reporting
AICPA Statements of Position (SOPs) .... FAS111, ¶10   A06.127
.... FIN20, ¶5
Accounting Policies .... APB22, ¶14   A10.107
Accounting Principles .... APB20, ¶7-8   A06.105-106
Amortization or Depreciation .... APB20, ¶23-24   A06.119-120
  . . Oil and Gas Producing Activities .... FAS19, ¶30   Oi5.121
Audit and Accounting Guides
 . . Specialized Accounting and
    Reporting .... FAS111, ¶7   A06.112
Business Combinations
 . . Combined Enterprise,
    Pooling-of-Interests Method .... APB16, ¶52   B50.111
 . . Disclosure .... APB16, ¶64   B50.123
Change for Tax Purposes .... FAS37, ¶19-21   I27.205-207
.... FAS109, ¶287-288
Change in Accounting Estimate .... APB20, ¶10   A06.109
.... APB20, ¶31-33   A06.130-132
 . . Core Deposit Intangibles EITF.85-33
Change in Accounting Principle
 . . Cumulative Effect .... APB20, ¶18-20   A06.114-116
 . . Effected by Change in Accounting
    Principle .... APB20, ¶11   A06.110
 . . Examples .... APB20, ¶9   A06.107-108
.... FIN1, ¶5
Change in Goodwill Amortization Method
 . . Business Combinations Initiated Prior
    to Effective Date of Statement 72 ....   EITF.89-19

FAS–FASB Statements   FIN–FASB Interpretations   FTB–FASB Technical Bulletins
APB–APB Opinions   AIN–AICPA Interpretations   ARB–Accounting Research Bulletins
CON–FASB Concepts   EITF–EITF Issues   Q&A–FASB Special Reports

	Original Pronouncements	Current Text	EITF and Other
ACCOUNTING CHANGES—continued			
Changes Based on Tentative FASB Decision to Change GAAP			EITF.86-4
Computer Software Costs			EITF.85-35
Cumulative Effect Not Determinable	APB20, ¶26	A06.122	
Exemption for Initial Public Distribution	APB20, ¶29-30	A06.125-126	
Functional Currency	FAS52, ¶9	F60.113	
Glossary	APB20, ¶6-7	A06.401-402	
Historical Summaries of Financial Information	APB20, ¶39	A06.134	
Illustrations of Disclosures by Types of Changes	APB20, ¶41-48	A06.135-142	
Implementation of an EITF Consensus			EITF.D-1
Inventory Valuation	ARB43, Ch.4, ¶15	I78.120	
. . Capitalizing Indirect Costs			EITF.86-46
. . Change in Composition of Cost Elements	FIN1, ¶5	A06.108	
. . LIFO Adopted Due to Repeal of *Insilco* Decision			EITF.84-10
Investments			
. . Equity Method	APB18, ¶19	I82.109	
Materiality	APB20, ¶38	A06.133	
Methods of Reporting	APB20, ¶18-22	A06.114-118	
Postemployment Benefits Other Than Pensions			
. . Change from Cash to Accrual Basis after Acquisition			EITF.86-20
. . Prospective or Cumulative Catch-up Adjustment			EITF.86-19
Prior-Period Adjustments			
. . Relation to	FAS16, ¶12	A35.101	
Pro Forma Amounts Not Determinable	APB20, ¶25	A06.121	
Pro Forma Effects of Retroactive Application	APB20, ¶21-22	A06.117-118	
Real Estate: Costs and Initial Operations of Real Estate Projects			
. . Installment to Percentage-of-Completion Method	FAS66, ¶49	Re1.149	
Regulated Operations	FAS71, ¶31-32	Re6.136-137	
Relation to Consistency	CON2, ¶122		
Retroactive Application of Change			
. . From LIFO Method of Inventory Pricing	APB20, ¶27	A06.123	
. . From/To Full Cost Method of Accounting in Extractive Industries	APB20, ¶27	A06.123	
. . Long-Term Construction-Type Contracts	APB20, ¶27	A06.123	

See "Terminology" for references to defined terms presented in various accounting pronouncements.
See the Introduction to the Topical Index for details on the use of this index.

	Original Pronouncements	Current Text	EITF and Other
ACCOUNTING CHANGES—continued			
Retroactive Application of Change in Accounting Principle			EITF.85-22
Retroactive Application of FASB Technical Bulletins			EITF.85-22
Scope of Accounting and Reporting Requirements	APB20, ¶2-4	A06.101-103	
	FAS111, ¶7		
Segment of Business Reporting	FAS14, ¶27	S20.133	
Specialized Accounting and Reporting	APB20, ¶15-16	A06.111-112	
	FAS111, ¶7	A06.127	
	FAS111, ¶10		
	FAS111, ¶17		
	FIN20, ¶5		
Types	APB20, ¶6	A06.104	
ACCOUNTING ESTIMATE CHANGES			
See Accounting Changes			
See Adjustments of Financial Statements for Prior Periods			
ACCOUNTING POLICIES			
See Disclosure			
Accounting Changes	APB22, ¶14	A10.107	
Defined Benefit Pension Plans	FAS35, ¶27	Pe5.126	
Definition	APB22, ¶6	A10.401	
Description	APB22, ¶6	A10.101	
Investments: Equity Method . . Disclosure	APB18, ¶20	I82.110	
Scope of Accounting and Reporting Requirements	APB22, ¶8-10	A10.102-104	
	FAS95, ¶152		
ACCOUNTING PRINCIPLE			
See Accounting Changes			
Definition	APB20, ¶7	A06.402	
ACCOUNTING PRINCIPLE CHANGES			
See Accounting Changes			
See Adjustments of Financial Statements for Prior Periods			
ACCOUNTING PRINCIPLES AND METHODS			
Choice of	CON2, ¶6-20		
ACCOUNTING TERMINOLOGY			
See Terminology			
ACCOUNTS PAYABLE (TRADE)			
See Balance Sheet Classification: Current Assets and Liabilities			
ACCOUNTS RECEIVABLE			
See Balance Sheet Classification: Current Assets and Liabilities			

FAS–FASB Statements   FIN–FASB Interpretations   FTB–FASB Technical Bulletins
APB–APB Opinions   AIN–AICPA Interpretations   ARB–Accounting Research Bulletins
CON–FASB Concepts   EITF–EITF Issues   Q&A–FASB Special Reports

	Original Pronouncements	Current Text	EITF and Other
ACCOUNTS RECEIVABLE—continued			
See Receivables			
From Officers, Employees, or Affiliates......	ARB43, Ch.1A, ¶5	R36.105	
ACCRUAL			
Balance Sheet Classification	ARB43, Ch.3A, ¶7	B05.108	
Definition	CON6, ¶141		
ACCRUAL BASIS OF ACCOUNTING			
Allocation and Amortization	CON6, ¶141-142		
Compared to Cash Basis	CON4, ¶50		
....	CON6, ¶139-140		
....	CON6, ¶144-145		
Deferral	CON6, ¶141-142		
Definition	CON6, ¶139-141		
Description	CON6, ¶134-142		
Elements of Financial Statements	CON6, ¶134-152		
Enterprise Performance	CON1, ¶44-48		
Not-for-Profit Organizations	CON4, ¶50		
Relation to Matching of Costs and Revenues	CON6, ¶145-151		
Transactions, Events, and Circumstances ...	CON6, ¶135-138		
ACQUIRING ENTERPRISE			
See Business Combinations Intangible Assets			
. . Regulated Operations	FAS71, ¶29-30	Re6.134-135	
ACQUISITIONS			
See Business Combinations			
ACQUISITIONS AND MERGERS			
See Business Combinations			
ACRS (ACCELERATED COST RECOVERY SYSTEM)			
See Depreciation			
ACTUARIAL ASSUMPTIONS			
See Defined Benefit Pension Plans			
See Pension Costs			
See Postretirement Benefits Other Than Pensions			
ADDITIONAL PAID-IN CAPITAL			
Accounting	ARB43, Ch.1A, ¶2	A31.101	
Charges Against			
. . Quasi Reorganizations	ARB43, Ch.7A, ¶2	Q15.102	
Disclosure	APB12, ¶10	C08.102	
Employee Stock Purchase and Stock Option Plans	APB25, ¶17	C47.117	
....	FTB82-2, ¶13	C47.516	
Transactions	APB14, ¶16	C08.103-104	
....	ARB43, Ch.1A, ¶6		
ADJUSTMENTS OF FINANCIAL STATEMENTS FOR PRIOR PERIODS			
See Disclosure			

See "Terminology" for references to defined terms presented in various accounting pronouncements.

See the Introduction to the Topical Index for details on the use of this index.

Topical Index

	Original Pronouncements	Current Text	EITF and Other
ADJUSTMENTS OF FINANCIAL STATEMENTS FOR PRIOR PERIODS—continued			
Accounting	FAS16, ¶13-14	A35.103	
	FAS109, ¶288	A35.109-110	
Accounting for Discontinued Operations			
Subsequently Retained			EITF.90-16
. . Disclosure by SEC Registrants			EITF.90-16
Change from Unacceptable to Acceptable			
Accounting Principle	APB20, ¶13	A35.104	
	FAS111, ¶9		
Change in Accounting Principle			
. . Adopting LIFO Inventory Pricing			EITF.84-10
. . First Public Offering	APB20, ¶27	A35.114	
	APB20, ¶29		
. . From LIFO Inventory Pricing	APB20, ¶27	A35.114	
	APB20, ¶29		
. . From Retirement-Replacement-Betterment Accounting to Depreciation Accounting	FAS73, ¶2	A35.114	
	FAS73, ¶5-7		
. . Full Cost Method in Extractive Industries	APB20, ¶27	A35.114	
	APB20, ¶29		
. . Illustrations	APB20, ¶45-48	A35.116-119	
. . Long-Term Construction-Type Contracts	APB20, ¶27	A35.114	
. . Reporting Entity/Business Combinations	APB20, ¶34-35	A35.112-113	
Change in Estimates	APB20, ¶13	A35.104	
Comparative Financial Statements	APB9, ¶18	A35.106	
	FAS16, ¶16		
Correction of Errors	APB20, ¶13	A35.103-105	
	APB20, ¶37		
	FAS109, ¶288		
Disposal of a Segment of a Business See Income Statement Presentation: Discontinued Operations			
Earnings per Share	APB15, ¶18	E09.109	
Exclusions from Net Income	FAS109, ¶288	A35.103	
Extraordinary Items	FAS16, ¶16	I17.119	
Historical Summaries of Financial Data	APB9, ¶27	A35.108	
Implementation of an EITF Consensus			EITF.D-1
Interim Periods, Adjustments within Year	FAS16, ¶13	A35.109	
	FAS109, ¶288		
. . Disclosure	FAS16, ¶14-15	A35.110-111	
. . Effect of Tax Reform Act of 1986			EITF.86-11
. . Restatement	FAS16, ¶14	A35.110	
Investments: Equity Method	APB18, ¶19	I82.109	
Relation to Accounting Changes	FAS16, ¶12	A35.101	

FAS–FASB Statements   FIN–FASB Interpretations   FTB–FASB Technical Bulletins
APB–APB Opinions   AIN–AICPA Interpretations   ARB–Accounting Research Bulletins
CON–FASB Concepts   EITF–EITF Issues   Q&A–FASB Special Reports

	Original Pronouncements	Current Text	EITF and Other
ADJUSTMENTS OF FINANCIAL STATEMENTS FOR PRIOR PERIODS—continued			
Relation to Current Period Net Income	FAS16, ¶10	A35.102	
Restatement Reflected as Adjustments to Opening Retained Earnings	APB9, ¶18	A35.106-107	
	APB9, ¶26		
	FAS16, ¶16		
Retroactive Application of FASB Technical Bulletins			EITF.85-22
ADVANCE REFUNDING			
See Debt: Extinguishments			
See Leases			
AFFILIATES			
See Business Combinations			
See Consolidation			
See Related Parties			
AFFORDABLE HOUSING PROJECTS TAX BENEFITS			
See Income Taxes			
AGRICULTURE			
Inventory	ARB43, Ch.4, ¶16	I78.119	
AICPA			
See AICPA Practice Bulletins			
See AICPA Statement on Auditing Standards (SAS)			
See AICPA Statements of Position (SOPs)			
AICPA AUDIT AND ACCOUNTING GUIDES			
See Accounting Changes			
AICPA PRACTICE BULLETINS			
Accounting Changes	FAS111, ¶10	A06.127	
	FIN20; ¶5		
AICPA STATEMENT ON AUDITING STANDARDS (SAS)			
SAS No. 69			
. . Required Changes in Accounting Principle	FAS111, ¶7	A06.112	
AICPA STATEMENTS OF POSITION (SOPS)			
Accounting Changes	FAS111, ¶10	A06.127	
	FIN20, ¶5		
ALLOCATION OF COSTS			
See Accrual Basis of Accounting			
See Interim Financial Reporting			
See Segment of Business Reporting			
Definition	CON6, ¶142		
Matching of Costs and Revenues	CON6, ¶149		
ALLOCATION OF INCOME TAXES			
See Income Taxes			

See "Terminology" for references to defined terms presented in various accounting pronouncements.

See the Introduction to the Topical Index for details on the use of this index.

	Original Pronouncements	Current Text	EITF and Other
ALLOWABLE COSTS			
See Regulated Operations			
Definition	FAS71, ¶1	Re6.111	
ALLOWANCE FOR DOUBTFUL ACCOUNTS			
See Valuation Allowances			
Sale of Bad-Debt Recovery Rights			EITF.86-8
ALLOWANCE FOR EARNINGS ON SHAREHOLDERS' INVESTMENT			
See Regulated Operations			
ALTERNATIVE MINIMUM TAX (AMT)			
See Income Taxes			
Accounting for AMT			EITF.87-8
Business Combinations			EITF.87-8
Leases			EITF.87-8
. . Leveraged Leases			EITF.86-43
Tax Credit Carryforwards			EITF.86-41
ALTERNATIVE TAX SYSTEMS			
See Income Taxes			
AMORTIZATION			
See Depreciation			
See Income Taxes			
See Intangible Assets			
See Lending Activities			
See Motion Picture Industry			
See Pension Costs			
See Postretirement Benefits Other Than Pensions			
Accounting Changes	APB20, ¶23-24	A06.119-120	
	FAS19, ¶30	Oi5.121	
Accounting for Individual Credit Card Acquisitions			EITF.93-1
Accounting Policy Disclosure	APB22, ¶13	A10.106	
Amortization Period for Net Deferred Credit Card Origination Costs			EITF.92-5
Cable Television Industry	FAS51, ¶10	Ca4.108	
Core Deposit Intangibles of Thrifts			EITF.85-8
Credit Cardholder Relationship			EITF.88-20
Definition	CON6, ¶142		
Goodwill			
. . Business Combinations Initiated Prior to Effective Date of Statement 72			EITF.89-19
Imputed Interest	APB21, ¶16	I69.108	
Investment in Certain CMOs and Mortgage-Backed Interest-Only Certificates			EITF.89-4
Matching of Costs and Revenues	CON6, ¶149		
Methods for Debt Discount	CON6, ¶235-239		
Mortgage Servicing Rights			EITF.86-38

FAS–FASB Statements   FIN–FASB Interpretations   FTB–FASB Technical Bulletins
APB–APB Opinions   AIN–AICPA Interpretations   ARB–Accounting Research Bulletins
CON–FASB Concepts   EITF–EITF Issues   Q&A–FASB Special Reports

	Original Pronouncements	Current Text	EITF and Other

AMORTIZATION—continued

Negative Amortization of Loan Principle

. . Applying Profit Recognition Criteria
   for Sale of Real Estate .... | | | EITF.84-17

. . Interest Income Recognition .... | | | EITF.85-38

. . Sale of Negative Amortizing Loans ...... | | | EITF.85-38

Recognition Guidance .... CON5, ¶86

Unidentifiable Intangible Assets of
   Thrifts .... | | | EITF.85-8

. . Business Combinations Initiated Prior
   to Effective Date of Statement 72 .... | | | EITF.89-19

ANNUITIES

See Contributions

See Insurance Industry

See Pension Costs

ANTICIPATORY HEDGES

See Cash Flows Statement

See Financial Instruments

See Futures Contracts

ANTI-DILUTION

See Earnings per Share

APPRAISALS

Not Allowed for Depreciable Assets .... APB6, ¶17 | D40.102

ARM'S-LENGTH TRANSACTIONS

See Related Parties

ART

See Works of Art

ARTICULATION

Definition .... CON6, ¶20-21

ASBESTOS TREATMENT COSTS

Capitalization

. . Acquisition of Property with Known
   Asbestos Problem .... | | | EITF.89-13

Charged to Expense .... | | | EITF.89-13

Deferral

. . Costs Incurred in Anticipation of Sale
   of Property .... | | | EITF.89-13

ASSESSMENT ENTERPRISES

See Insurance Industry

Definition .... FAS60, ¶66 | In6.403

ASSESSMENTS

See Contingencies

**ASSET REVERSIONS (OF DEFINED
BENEFIT PENSION PLANS)**

See Pension Costs

ASSETS

See Balance Sheet Classification: Current
Assets and Liabilities

See Impairment

See "Terminology" for references to defined terms presented in various accounting pronouncements.

See the Introduction to the Topical Index for details on the use of this index.

	Original Pronouncements	Current Text	EITF and Other
ASSETS—continued			
Characteristics	CON6, ¶26-31		
	CON6, ¶171-191		
Classifying Notes Received for Capital Stock			EITF.85-1
Control by Entity	CON6, ¶183-189		
Criteria for Recognition	CON5, ¶58-65		
	CON5, ¶67-69		
	CON5, ¶73-77		
Definition	CON6, ¶25-31		
Elements of Financial Statements	CON6, ¶25-34		
Future Economic Benefits	CON6, ¶28		
	CON6, ¶172-182		
Items Not Qualified as	CON6, ¶169		
Measurement of	CON5, ¶67-69		
Past Transactions	CON6, ¶190-191		
Qualification as	CON6, ¶168		
	CON6, ¶174		
Recognition of Changes in	CON5, ¶88-90		
Relation to Control	CON6, ¶183-189		
Relation to Costs	CON6, ¶178-182		
Relation to Future Economic Benefits	CON6, ¶190-191		
Revaluation of Depreciable Basis for Tax Purposes			EITF.84-43
Service Potential	CON6, ¶28		
Transactions and Events Affecting	CON6, ¶32-33		
Uncertainty of Recognition	CON6, ¶44-48		
Valuation of Assets and Liabilities by Liquidating Bank			EITF.88-25
ASSETS TO BE DISPOSED OF			
See Impairment: Long-Lived Assets			
See Income Statement Presentation: Discontinued Operations			
ASSOCIATED COMPANIES			
See Mortgage Banking Activities			
See Related Parties			
ATTRIBUTES			
See Measurement			
ATTRIBUTION			
See Postretirement Benefits Other Than Pensions			
AVERAGE COST			
Inventory	ARB43, Ch.4, ¶6	I78.107-108	
AWARDS			
See Compensation to Employees: Stock Purchase and Stock Option Plans			
See Contributions			

(The next page is T-21.)

FAS–FASB Statements	FIN–FASB Interpretations	FTB–FASB Technical Bulletins
APB–APB Opinions	AIN–AICPA Interpretations	ARB–Accounting Research Bulletins
CON–FASB Concepts	EITF–EITF Issues	Q&A–FASB Special Reports

	Original Pronouncements	Current Text	EITF and Other

BAD-DEBT ALLOWANCES
See Impairment: Loans
See Valuation Allowances
Accounting for Income Tax Benefits from Bad Debts of a Savings and Loan Association EITF.91-3
Sale of Bad-Debt Recovery Rights EITF.86-8
BAD-DEBT RESERVES
See Banking and Thrift Industries
BALANCE SHEET
See Balance Sheet Classification: Current Assets and Liabilities
See Not-for-Profit Organizations
See Offsetting
See Statement of Financial Position
BALANCE SHEET CLASSIFICATION: CURRENT ASSETS AND LIABILITIES
See Disclosure
See Offsetting
Accounts Receivable .... ARB43, Ch.3A, ¶4 ... B05.105
Callable Obligations .... FAS78, ¶5 ... B05.109A-109B ... EITF.86-30
.... FAS78, ¶13
. . Obligations with Scheduled Repayment Terms EITF.86-5
Classification of Amount Received from Investor for Future Revenue EITF.88-18
Classified Balance Sheet .... FAS6, ¶7 ... B05.102
Classifying Notes Received for Capital Stock EITF.85-1
Classifying Obligations .... FAS6, ¶32-33 ... B05.119-120
. . Acquisition of Noncurrent Assets .... FAS6, ¶48-49 ... B05.135-136
. . Covenant Violation Waived by Creditor EITF.86-30
. . Effect of Restriction on Transferring Funds, Foreign Subsidiary .... FAS6, ¶37-38 ... B05.124-125
. . Financing Agreement Used to Refinance Existing Obligation .... FAS6, ¶34-36 ... B05.121-123
. . Financing Agreement with Fluctuating Maximum Borrowings .... FAS6, ¶45-47 ... B05.132-134
. . Increasing-Rate Debt EITF.86-15
. . Refinancing Classified as Current .... FAS6, ¶50 ... B05.137
. . Refinancing Post Balance Sheet Date ... FAS6, ¶39-42 ... B05.126-129
. . Repaid Prior to Replacement by a Long-Term Security .... FIN8, ¶2 ... B05.138-139
.... FIN8, ¶4
. . Revolving Credit Agreement .... FAS6, ¶43-44 ... B05.130-131
. . Subjective Acceleration Clauses and Debt Classification EITF.D-23

FAS–FASB Statements   FIN–FASB Interpretations   FTB–FASB Technical Bulletins
APB–APB Opinions   AIN–AICPA Interpretations   ARB–Accounting Research Bulletins
CON–FASB Concepts   EITF–EITF Issues   Q&A–FASB Special Reports

	Original Pronouncements	Current Text	EITF and Other
BALANCE SHEET CLASSIFICATION: CURRENT ASSETS AND LIABILITIES—continued			
Classifying Obligations—continued			
. . Subsidiary's Loan Payable When Subsidiary's and Parent's Fiscal Years Differ			EITF.88-15
Creditors	ARB43, Ch.3A, ¶7	B05.108	
Current Assets	ARB43, Ch.3A, ¶4-6	B05.105-107A	
	FAS115, ¶125		
. . Description and Examples	ARB43, Ch.3A, ¶4	B05.105	
	FAS115, ¶125		
Current Liabilities	ARB43, Ch.3A, ¶7	B05.108	
. . Compensated Absences	FAS43, ¶6	C44.104	
. . Deferred Taxes and Income Taxes	FAS37, ¶16	I27.204	
. . Description and Examples	ARB43, Ch.3A, ¶7-8	B05.108-109	
. . Employee Stock Purchase and Stock Option Plans	APB25, ¶13-15	C47.113-115	
. . Long-Term Obligations, Criteria for Inclusion	FAS78, ¶1	B05.109A-109B	EITF.86-5
	FAS78, ¶5		EITF.86-30
	FAS78, ¶13		
. . Long-Term Obligations, Grace Period within Which to Cure a Violation	FAS78, ¶5	B05.109A	EITF.86-30
Deferred Taxes	FAS109, ¶41-42	I27.140-141	
	FAS109, ¶288		
Definition			
. . Callable Obligations	FAS78, ¶1	B05.400	
. . Current Assets	ARB43, Ch.3A, ¶4	B05.401	
. . Current Liabilities	ARB43, Ch.3A, ¶7	B05.402	
. . Long-Term Obligations	FAS6, ¶2	B05.403	
. . Operating Cycle	ARB43, Ch.3A, ¶5	B05.404	
. . Short-Term Obligations	FAS6, ¶2	B05.405	
. . Subjective Acceleration Clause	FAS78, ¶10	B05.405A	
. . Working Capital	ARB43, Ch.3A, ¶3	B05.406	
Demand Notes			EITF.86-30
. . Obligations with Scheduled Repayment Terms			EITF.86-5
Investment Tax Credits	APB2, ¶14	I27.231	
Investments	ARB43, Ch.3A, ¶6	B05.107	
Long-Term Obligations	FAS6, ¶2	B05.111	
Marketable Securities	ARB43, Ch.3A, ¶4	B05.105	
	ARB43, Ch.3A, ¶9	B05.107A	
	FAS115, ¶125		
Mortgage Banking Activities			
. . Mortgage-Backed Securities and Loans	FAS65, ¶28	Mo4.129	
Motion Picture Industry			
. . Balance Sheet Classification	FAS53, ¶19-21	Mo6.118-120	
Noncurrent Assets	ARB43, Ch.3A, ¶6	B05.107	

See "Terminology" for references to defined terms presented in various accounting pronouncements.
See the Introduction to the Topical Index for details on the use of this index.

	Original Pronouncements	Current Text	EITF and Other

BALANCE SHEET CLASSIFICATION:
CURRENT ASSETS AND
LIABILITIES—continued

Operating Cycle .... ARB43, Ch.3A, ¶2   B05.103
.... ARB43, Ch.3A, ¶4-5 B05.106
.... ARB43, Ch.3A, ¶7   B05.108
Prepaid Expenses .... ARB43, Ch.3A, ¶4   B05.105
Refinancing Agreements .... FAS6, ¶2   B05.111
Revolving Credit Agreement .... FAS6, ¶14   B05.116
Scope of Accounting and Reporting
  Requirements .... FAS6, ¶7   B05.102
Securities with a Put Option Held by an
  ESOP EITF.89-11
Short-Term Debt .... ARB43, Ch.3A, ¶7   B05.108
Short-Term Obligations Expected to Be
  Refinanced .... FAS6, ¶1-2   B05.110-117
.... FAS6, ¶8-14
.... FIN8, ¶3
Sinking Fund Accruals .... ARB43, Ch.3A, ¶6   B05.107
Subjective Acceleration Clauses in
  Long-Term Debt Agreements .... FAS78, ¶10   B05.405A
.... FTB79-3, ¶1-3   B05.501-503
Unclassified Balance Sheet .... FAS6, ¶7   B05.102
.... FAS78, ¶5   B05.118
Unearned Discount .... ARB43, Ch.3A, ¶9   B05.107A
Working Capital .... ARB43, Ch.3A, ¶3   B05.102
.... FAS6, ¶7   B05.104

BALANCE SHEET CLASSIFICATION:
DEBT VS. EQUITY

Classifying Obligations
. . Debt Repayable by a Capital Stock
    Transaction EITF.84-40

BANKER'S ACCEPTANCES
See Banking and Thrift Industries
See Financial Instruments
BANKING AND THRIFT
INDUSTRIES
See Collateralized Mortgage Obligations
See Disclosure
See Financial Instruments
See Impairment: Loans
See Lending Activities
See Mortgage Banking Activities
See Savings and Loan Associations

Accounting for Individual Credit Card
  Acquisitions EITF.93-1

FAS–FASB Statements   FIN–FASB Interpretations   FTB–FASB Technical Bulletins
APB–APB Opinions   AIN–AICPA Interpretations   ARB–Accounting Research Bulletins
CON–FASB Concepts   EITF–EITF Issues   Q&A–FASB Special Reports

	Original Pronouncements	Current Text	EITF and Other
BANKING AND THRIFT INDUSTRIES—continued			
Acquisition of a Banking or Thrift Institution	FAS72, ¶2-12	Bt7.102-115	
	FIN9, ¶1		
	FIN9, ¶4-5		
	FIN9, ¶7-9		
. . Adjustments of Allocation of Original Purchase Price			EITF.85-3
. . Amortization of Unidentifiable Intangible Assets			EITF.85-8
. . FSLIC-Assisted Acquisitions of Thrifts			EITF.88-19
. . Goodwill			EITF.85-42
. . Identifiable Intangible Assets	FAS72, ¶4	Bt7.106	EITF.85-42
	FIN9, ¶8		
. . Net-Spread Method	FIN9, ¶1	Bt7.103	
	FIN9, ¶4		
. . Regulatory-Assisted Acquisitions of Thrifts			EITF.88-19
. . Regulatory-Assisted Combinations	FAS72, ¶3	Bt7.111-115	
	FAS72, ¶8-11		
. . Sale of Assets of Acquired Banking or Thrift Institution	FAS72, ¶7	Bt7.110	
. . Separate-Valuation Method	FIN9, ¶1	Bt7.103	
	FIN9, ¶4		
. . Unidentifiable Intangible Assets	FAS72, ¶5-7	Bt7.107-110	EITF.85-8
	FAS72, ¶12		EITF.85-42
. . Valuation of Assets	FIN9, ¶5	Bt7.104	
. . Valuation of Liabilities	FIN9, ¶7	Bt7.105	
Acquisition of a Savings and Loan Association by a Bank			
. . Accounting for Exit and Entrance Fees Incurred in a Conversion from the Savings Association Insurance Fund to the Bank Insurance Fund			EITF.90-11
. . Tax Implications of Excess Bad-Debt Reserves			EITF.86-31
Acquisition, Development, and Construction Loans			EITF.84-4
			EITF.86-21
Amortization Period for Net Deferred Credit Card Origination Costs			EITF.92-5
Bad Debts			
. . Accounting for Income Tax Benefits from Bad Debts of a Savings and Loan Association			EITF.91-3
Banker's Acceptances			
. . Accounting for Risk Participations			EITF.85-34

See "Terminology" for references to defined terms presented in various accounting pronouncements.

See the Introduction to the Topical Index for details on the use of this index.

	Original Pronouncements	Current Text	EITF and Other
BANKING AND THRIFT INDUSTRIES—continued			
Cash Flows Statement	FAS104, ¶7	C25.111A Bt7.123	
Change in Accounting Estimate			
. . Core Deposit Intangibles			EITF.85-33
Collateralized Mortgage Obligations (CMOs)			
. . Purchased Investment			EITF.89-4 EITF.93-18
Commitment Fees and Costs			
. . Loan Guarantees			EITF.85-20
. . Long-Term Credit Commitment			EITF.87-30
Conversion of Savings and Loan Association to a Bank			
. . Accounting for Exit and Entrance Fees Incurred in a Conversion from the Savings Association Insurance Fund to the Bank Insurance Fund			EITF.90-11
. . Tax Imposed on Excess Bad-Debt Reserves			EITF.86-31
Credit Card Portfolio—Purchase			
. . Accounting for Difference between Initial Investment and Principal Amount of Loans			EITF.88-20
. . Accounting for Individual Credit Card Acquisitions			EITF.93-1
. . Amortization of Cardholder Relationships Acquired			EITF.88-20
Credit Card Portfolio Securitization			EITF.88-22 EITF.90-18
Deferred Interest Rate Setting Arrangements			EITF.84-14
Deferred Tax Debits in Regulatory Reports			EITF.85-31
Definition			
. . Carrying Amount	FAS72, ¶5	Bt7.401	
. . General Reserve	APB23, ¶19	Bt7.402	
. . Long-Term Interest-Bearing Assets	FAS72, ¶5	Bt7.403	
. . Net-Spread Method	FIN9, ¶2	Bt7.404	
. . Pretax Accounting Income	APB23, ¶21	Bt7.405	
. . Reserve for Bad Debts	APB23, ¶19	Bt7.406	
. . Separate-Valuation Method	FIN9, ¶3	Bt7.407	
. . Taxable Income	APB23, ¶21	Bt7.408	
Deposit Float of Banks			EITF.84-9
Deposit Insurance			
. . Accounting for Exit and Entrance Fees Incurred in a Conversion from the Savings Association Insurance Fund to the Bank Insurance Fund			EITF.90-11

FAS–FASB Statements   FIN–FASB Interpretations   FTB–FASB Technical Bulletins
APB–APB Opinions   AIN–AICPA Interpretations   ARB–Accounting Research Bulletins
CON–FASB Concepts   EITF–EITF Issues   Q&A–FASB Special Reports

	Original Pronouncements	Current Text	EITF and Other
BANKING AND THRIFT INDUSTRIES—continued			
Deposits of Savings and Loan Institutions			
. . Equity Certificates of Deposit			EITF.84-31
Earnings per Share			
. . Conversion from Mutual Ownership to Stock Ownership................................			EITF.84-22
Equity Certificates of Deposit			
. . Recognizing Contingent Interest Expense...			EITF.84-31
Equity Kickers			EITF.84-4
....			EITF.86-21
Exchange of Interest-Only and Principal-Only Securities for a Mortgage-Backed Security			EITF.90-2
Federal Home Loan Mortgage Corporation (FHLMC)			
. . Accounting for Distribution of FHLMC Participating Preferred Stock..	FAS115, ¶136		
....	FTB85-1, ¶1-4	Bt7.501-504	
. . Disclosure of Relationship of District Banks and Member Banks..................	FTB85-1, ¶14	Bt7.505	
. . Receipt of FHLMC Participating Preferred Stock	FTB85-1, ¶1-4	Bt7.501-504	EITF.85-7
. . Relationship of District Banks and Member Banks....................................	FTB85-1, ¶14	Bt7.505	
Federal Savings and Loan Insurance Corporation (FSLIC)			
. . FSLIC-Assisted Acquisitions of Thrifts......................................			EITF.88-19
. . Management Consignment Program			EITF.85-41
. . Net Worth Certificates			EITF.85-41
. . Write-off of Prepayments to the Secondary Reserve			EITF.87-22
Financial Institutions Reform, Recovery, and Enforcement Act of 1989 (FIRREA)			
. . Divestiture of Certain Investment Securities......................................			EITF.89-18
Flip Transactions...			EITF.85-38
Futures Contracts, Hedges...........................	FAS80, ¶63	F80.104	EITF.86-34
GNMA Dollar Rolls			EITF.84-20
Goodwill Amortization			
. . Business Combinations Initiated Prior to Effective Date of Statement 72.......			EITF.89-19
Hedging Reverse Repurchase Agreements ..			EITF.86-34
Hedging with Cash Securities			EITF.87-1
High-Risk Mortgage Security			EITF.D-39

See "Terminology" for references to defined terms presented in various accounting pronouncements.
See the Introduction to the Topical Index for details on the use of this index.

	Original Pronouncements	Current Text	EITF and Other

BANKING AND THRIFT INDUSTRIES—continued

Impairment

. . Mortgage Obligation Instrument or Mortgage-Backed Interest-Only Certificate .... | | | EITF.93-18

Implementation of Statement 107 .... | | | EITF.D-29

Intangible Assets

. . Adjustments of Allocation of Original Purchase Price...................................... | | | EITF.85-3

. . Amortization of Unidentifiable Intangible Assets............................... | | | EITF.85-8

. . Change in Amortization Method for Goodwill .... | | | EITF.89-19

. . Core Deposit Intangibles...................... | | | EITF.85-33

. . Identifiable Intangible Assets .... | | | EITF.85-42

. . Unidentifiable Intangible Assets .... | | | EITF.85-8

.... | | | EITF.85-42

Interest Rate Swap Transactions .... | | | EITF.84-36

.... | | | EITF.88-8

. . Termination or Sale .... | | | EITF.84-7

Investments

. . Classification of Interest-Only Securities as Held-to-Maturity .... | | | EITF.94-4

. . Divestiture of Certain Investment Securities under FIRREA .... | | | EITF.89-18

. . Mutual Funds That Invest in U.S. Government Securities .... | | | EITF.86-40

. . Purchase of Collateralized Mortgage Obligation Instruments .... | | | EITF.89-4

.... | | | EITF.93-18

. . Purchase of Mortgage-Backed Interest-Only Certificates................... | | | EITF.89-4

.... | | | EITF.93-18

Liquidation of a Banking Institution

. . Valuation of Assets and Liabilities by Liquidating Bank .... | | | EITF.88-25

Loan Acquisitions Involving Table Funding Arrangements............................ | | | EITF.92-10

Loan Guarantees

. . Revenue Recognition of Fees............... | | | EITF.85-20

Loan Loss Allowances

. . Differences between GAAP and RAP .. | | | EITF.85-44

. . Impairment of Loans .... FAS114, ¶13 — I08.111

.... FAS114, ¶16 — I08.114

.... FAS118, ¶6 — I08.118-118A

. . Loss Reserves in a Business Combination...................................... | | | EITF.84-35

FAS–FASB Statements	FIN–FASB Interpretations	FTB–FASB Technical Bulletins
APB–APB Opinions	AIN–AICPA Interpretations	ARB–Accounting Research Bulletins
CON–FASB Concepts	EITF–EITF Issues	Q&A–FASB Special Reports

	Original Pronouncements	Current Text	EITF and Other

BANKING AND THRIFT INDUSTRIES—continued

Loans

. . Accounting for Conversion of a Loan into a Debt Security in a Debt Restructuring...................................... — EITF.94-8

. . Brady Bonds... — EITF.D-39

. . Negative Amortization of Principal ...... — EITF.85-38

. . Payment Modifications Involving Forgiveness of Principal..................... — EITF.84-19

. . Sale of Bad-Debt Recovery Rights....... — EITF.86-8

. . Sale of Mortgage Loan by CMO Established through Third Party........ — EITF.86-24

. . Sale of Mortgage Loan with Servicing Rights Retained.................................. — EITF.86-39

. . Sale of Mortgage Servicing Rights....... — EITF.85-13

.... — EITF.89-5

.... — EITF.94-5

.... — EITF.95-5

. . Sale of Mortgage Servicing Rights with Subservicing Agreement .... — EITF.87-34

.... — EITF.90-21

. . Sale of Short-Term Loan under Long-Term Credit Commitment .... — EITF.87-30

. . Sale to Special-Purpose Entities............ — EITF.84-30

. . Sale with a Partial Participation Retained .... — EITF.84-21

Modification of Debt Terms When Debtor Is Experiencing Financial Difficulties ...... — EITF.89-15

Mortgage Derivative Product

. . Effect of Potential Designation as a High-Risk Security .... — EITF.D-39

Mortgage Servicing Rights

. . Recognition of Sale of Mortgage Servicing Rights................................. — EITF.89-5

.... — EITF.94-5

.... — EITF.95-5

. . Sale of Mortgage Loan with Servicing Rights Retained.................................. — EITF.86-39

. . Sale of Mortgage Servicing Rights....... — EITF.85-13

.... — EITF.89-5

.... — EITF.94-5

.... — EITF.95-5

. . Sale of Mortgage Servicing Rights with Subservicing Agreement .... — EITF.87-34

.... — EITF.90-21

Mortgage Swaps..................................... — EITF.88-8

Participation in Future Payment Stream

. . Unanticipated Mortgage Prepayments.. — EITF.86-38

Receipt of FHLMC Participating Preferred Stock... — EITF.85-7

See "Terminology" for references to defined terms presented in various accounting pronouncements.

See the Introduction to the Topical Index for details on the use of this index.

	Original Pronouncements	Current Text	EITF and Other
BANKING AND THRIFT INDUSTRIES—continued			
Regulatory-Assisted Acquisitions of Thrifts			EITF.88-19
. . Disclosure Requirements			EITF.88-19
Relationship between Statement 15 and Savings and Loan Audit Guide			
. . Loan Loss Allowances			EITF.87-5
Reorganization of a Banking or Thrift Institution			
. . Regulatory-Assisted Combinations			EITF.85-41
. . Valuation of Assets and Liabilities			EITF.85-41
Revenue Recognition			
. . Credit Card Portfolio Securitizations with a "Removal of Accounts" Provision			EITF.90-18
. . Fees Associated with Loan Syndications and Loan Participations			EITF.88-17
. . Sale of Convertible, Adjustable-Rate Mortgages with Contingent Repayment Agreement			EITF.87-25
. . Sale of Mortgage Loan with Servicing Rights Retained			EITF.86-39
. . Sale of Mortgage Servicing Rights			EITF.85-13
			EITF.89-5
			EITF.94-5
			EITF.95-5
. . Sale of Mortgage Servicing Rights with Subservicing Agreement			EITF.87-34
. . Sale of Short-Term Loan under Long-Term Credit Commitment			EITF.87-30
. . Sale with a Partial Participation Retained			EITF.84-21
. . Securitization of Credit Card Portfolio			EITF.88-22
Reverse Repurchase Agreements			EITF.84-20
Sale of Bad-Debt Recovery Rights			EITF.86-8
Sale of Loan with a Partial Participation Retained			EITF.84-21
Sale of Short-Term Loan under Long-Term Credit Commitment			EITF.87-30
Savings and Loan Associations			
. . Accounting for Income Tax Benefits from Bad Debts			EITF.91-3
. . Bad-Debt Reserves	APB23, ¶19-21	Bt7.116-121	
	APB23, ¶23		
	APB23, ¶25		
	FAS109, ¶288		
. . Conversion from Mutual Ownership to Stock Ownership			EITF.84-22

FAS–FASB Statements	FIN–FASB Interpretations	FTB–FASB Technical Bulletins
APB–APB Opinions	AIN–AICPA Interpretations	ARB–Accounting Research Bulletins
CON–FASB Concepts	EITF–EITF Issues	Q&A–FASB Special Reports

	Original Pronouncements	Current Text	EITF and Other

BANKING AND THRIFT INDUSTRIES—continued

Savings and Loan Associations—continued
. . Divestiture of Certain Investment
    Securities under FIRREA .... | | | EITF.89-18
. . Write-off of Prepayments to the
    Secondary Reserve of the FSLIC .... | | | EITF.87-22
Shared Appreciation Mortgages .... | | | EITF.86-21
Tax Benefits Relating to Asset
  Dispositions after Acquisition.................. | | | EITF.85-3
Tax Deduction Disallowed
. . Core Deposit Intangibles...................... | | | EITF.85-33
Troubled Debt Restructurings
. . Accounting for Conversion of a Loan
    into a Debt Security in a Debt
    Restructuring.................................... | | | EITF.94-8
. . Loan Loss Allowance under Savings
    and Loan Audit Guide........................ | | | EITF.87-5

BANKRUPTCY

See Debt: Restructurings
See Extraordinary Items
Assurance That a Right of Setoff Is
  Enforceable in a Bankruptcy under
  FASB Interpretation 39............................ | | | EITF.D-43
Consideration of the Impact of Bankruptcy
  in Determining Plan Assets under
  Statement 106..................................... | | | EITF.93-3

BANKS

See Banking and Thrift Industries
See Lending Activities
Activities Similar to Mortgage Banking
  Enterprise .... FAS65, ¶3 | Mo4.104 |
Dealers in Foreign Currency .... FAS52, ¶30 | F60.140 |
Futures Contracts
. . Hedges .... FAS80, ¶4 | F80.104 |
Mutual Savings
. . Exemption from Earnings per Share
    Reporting Requirements.................... FAS21, ¶12 | E09.102 |

BARTER TRANSACTIONS

See Broadcasting Industry
See Nonmonetary Transactions
See Television Barter Syndicators
Accounting for Barter Transactions
  Involving Barter Credits .... | | | EITF.93-11
Barter Credits.. | | | EITF.93-11
Definition .... FAS63, ¶14 | Br5.401 |
Guidance in Recognizing Revenues and
  Gains... CON5, ¶84 | |

See "Terminology" for references to defined terms presented in various accounting pronouncements.
See the Introduction to the Topical Index for details on the use of this index.

	Original Pronouncements	Current Text	EITF and Other
BENEFITS (PENSION, POSTEMPLOYMENT, AND RETIREMENT)			
See Defined Benefit Pension Plans			
See Pension Costs			
See Postemployment Benefits			
See Postretirement Benefits Other Than Pensions			
See Postretirement Health Care and Life Insurance Benefits			
BEQUEST			
See Not-for-Profit Organizations			
BIAS			
Definition	CON2, Glossary		
Relation to Representational Faithfulness	CON2, ¶77-78		
BOND DISCOUNT			
See Debt Discount			
BOND PREMIUM			
See Debt Premium			
BONDS			
See Debt			
See Financial Instruments			
See Long-Term Obligations			
BOOT			
Monetary Transactions			EITF.87-29
Nonmonetary Transactions	APB29, ¶4	N35.101	EITF.84-29
			EITF.86-29
			EITF.87-29
BRADY BONDS			
See Investments: Debt and Equity Securities			
BROADCASTING INDUSTRY			
See Disclosure			
See Television Barter Syndicators			
Barter Transactions	FAS63, ¶8	Br5.109	
. . Advertising Time for Programming			EITF.87-10
Glossary	FAS63, ¶14	Br5.401-405	
License Agreement for Program Material			
. . Amortization of Capitalized Costs	FAS63, ¶5-6	Br5.106-107	
. . Asset Valuation	FAS63, ¶7	Br5.108	
. . Capitalization of Costs	FAS63, ¶3-4	Br5.104-105	
Network Affiliation Agreements	FAS63, ¶9	Br5.110	
Nonmonetary Transactions	FAS63, ¶9	Br5.109	
Scope of Accounting and Reporting Requirements	FAS63, ¶1	Br5.102	
BROKERS AND DEALERS IN SECURITIES			
See Earnings per Share			
See Financial Instruments			

FAS–FASB Statements	FIN–FASB Interpretations	FTB–FASB Technical Bulletins
APB–APB Opinions	AIN–AICPA Interpretations	ARB–Accounting Research Bulletins
CON–FASB Concepts	EITF–EITF Issues	Q&A–FASB Special Reports

	Original Pronouncements	Current Text	EITF and Other
BROKERS AND DEALERS IN SECURITIES—continued			
See Mutual Fund Distributors			
See Segment of Business Reporting			
Investments in Debt and Equity Securities...	FAS115, ¶4	I80.102	
Stock Market Decline			
. . Subsequent Events Disclosure			EITF.D-11
Unclassified Balance Sheet	FAS6, ¶7	B05.102	
BUDGETS			
Not-for-Profit Organizations	CON4, ¶9		
....	CON4, ¶21-22		
BUILDING AND LOAN ASSOCIATIONS			
See Banking and Thrift Industries			
See Lending Activities			
See Savings and Loan Associations			
BUILDINGS			
See Depreciation			
See Interest: Capitalization of Interest Costs			
See Leases			
See Property, Plant, and Equipment			
See Real Estate			
BUSINESS COMBINATIONS			
See Disclosure			
See Earnings per Share			
See Income Taxes			
See Intangible Assets			
Accounting for a Business Combination Involving a Majority-Owned Investee of a Venture Capital Company			EITF.90-10
Accounting for Simultaneous Common Control Mergers			EITF.90-13
Accounting for the Present Value of Future Profits Resulting from the Acquisition of a Life Insurance Company........................			EITF.92-9
. . Disclosure by SEC Registrants			EITF.92-9
Accounting Methods			
. . Pooling-of-Interests	APB16, ¶42-44	B50.102-103	
. . Purchase..	APB16, ¶42-44	B50.102-103	
Acquisition Date	APB16, ¶93-94	B50.162-163	
....	ARB51, ¶9		
Acquisition of Minority Interest................	AIN-APB16, #26	B50.102	EITF.85-4
....	APB16, ¶42-43	B50.593-596D	
....	FTB85-5, ¶5-7		
....	FTB85-5, ¶12		
Banking or Thrift Institution, Acquisition			
. . Adjustments of Allocation of Original Purchase Price....................................			EITF.85-3

See "Terminology" for references to defined terms presented in various accounting pronouncements.
See the Introduction to the Topical Index for details on the use of this index.

	Original Pronouncements	Current Text	EITF and Other
BUSINESS COMBINATIONS—continued			
Banking or Thrift Institution, Acquisition—continued			
. . Amortization of Goodwill			EITF.85-42
. . Amortization of Goodwill for Business Combinations Initiated Prior to the Effective Date of Statement 72			EITF.89-19
. . Amortization of Unidentifiable Intangible Assets			EITF.85-8
. . FSLIC-Assisted Acquisitions of Thrifts			EITF.88-19
. . Identifiable Intangible Assets	FAS72, ¶4	B50.158	
	FIN9, ¶8		
. . Net-Spread Method	FIN9, ¶1	B50.155	
	FIN9, ¶4		
. . Regulatory-Assisted Acquisitions of Thrifts			EITF.88-19
. . Regulatory-Assisted Combinations	FAS72, ¶3	B50.158B-158F	
	FAS72, ¶8-11		
. . Separate-Valuation Method	FIN9, ¶4	B50.155	
	FIN9, ¶8	B50.158	
. . Unidentifiable Intangible Assets	FAS72, ¶5	B50.158A	
. . Valuation of Assets	APB16, ¶43	B50.102	
	FAS72, ¶3-5	B50.155-158E	
	FAS72, ¶8-10		
	FIN9, ¶1		
	FIN9, ¶4-5		
	FIN9, ¶7-8		
Basis of Accounting			
. . Allocating Basis to Individual Assets and Liabilities under Issue No. 88-16			EITF.90-12
. . New Basis of Accounting Resulting from Change in Ownership			EITF.85-21
. . Predecessor Cost Carried Over in Leveraged Buyout			EITF.86-16
			EITF.88-16
. . Push-down Accounting in Separate Statements of Acquired Entity			EITF.86-9
. . Push-down of Parent Company's Debt to Subsidiary			EITF.84-42
. . Valuation of Shareholder's Interest in a Leveraged Buyout			EITF.86-16
			EITF.88-16
Common Control in a Business Combination	AIN-APB16, #27	B50.597-605	EITF.86-16
			EITF.88-16
. . Accounting for Simultaneous Common Control Mergers			EITF.90-13

FAS–FASB Statements   FIN–FASB Interpretations   FTB–FASB Technical Bulletins
APB–APB Opinions   AIN–AICPA Interpretations   ARB–Accounting Research Bulletins
CON–FASB Concepts   EITF–EITF Issues   Q&A–FASB Special Reports

	Original Pronouncements	Current Text	EITF and Other
BUSINESS COMBINATIONS—continued			
Contingencies	APB16, ¶77	C59.119	
Contingent Assets/Liabilities	FAS38, ¶6	B50.148	
Contingent Consideration	FAS38, ¶4	C59.119	
Cost of Acquired Enterprise	APB16, ¶77-86	B50.135-144	
	FTB85-5, ¶1-2	B50.651-652	
Costs of Maintaining an Acquisitions Department	AIN-APB16, #31	B50.620	
	AIN-APB16, #33	B50.627-628	
Definition			
. . Allocation Period	FAS38, ¶4	B50.401	
. . Contingent Consideration	APB16, ¶78	B50.402	
. . Goodwill	APB16, ¶87	B50.403	
. . Negative Goodwill	APB16, ¶87	B50.404	
. . Nonpublic Enterprise	FAS79, ¶5	B50.404A	
	FAS79, ¶16		
. . Pooling-of-Interests Method	APB16, ¶45	B50.405	
. . Preacquisition Contingencies	FAS38, ¶4	B50.406	
. . Purchase Method	APB16, ¶44	B50.407	
Different Tax and Accounting Bases for Acquired Assets and Liabilities	FAS109, ¶30	I27.129	
Different Tax and Accounting Bases for Depreciation of Property			
. . Unrecognized Tax Benefits			EITF.85-3
Divestiture	APB16, ¶46	B50.105	
Downstream Mergers	AIN-APB16, #26	B50.593-596	EITF.85-4
	FTB85-5, ¶13-14	B50.596E-596F	
Effect of Change in Tax Rate			EITF.86-42
Excess of Acquired Net Assets over Cost	APB16, ¶91-92	B50.160-161	
Exchange of Assets for Noncontrolling Equity Interest in New Entity			EITF.89-7
Exchange of Interest in Subsidiary for Noncontrolling Equity Interest in New Entity			EITF.89-7
Exchanges of Ownership Interests between Entities under Common Control			EITF.90-5
Federal Savings and Loan Insurance Corporation (FSLIC)			
. . FSLIC-Assisted Acquisitions of Thrifts			EITF.88-19
. . Management Consignment Program			EITF.85-41
Foreign Operations	FAS52, ¶101	F60.102	
Franchisor Acquisition of Franchisee's Business	FAS45, ¶19	Fr3.115	
Goodwill			
. . Amortization	APB16, ¶90	B50.159	
Guaranteed Future Value of Stock Issued by Acquirer			EITF.87-31

See "Terminology" for references to defined terms presented in various accounting pronouncements.
See the Introduction to the Topical Index for details on the use of this index.

	Original Pronouncements	Current Text	EITF and Other

BUSINESS COMBINATIONS—continued

Initiation Date

.. Description... APB16, ¶46 — B50.105

.. Effect of Terminating a Plan of
    Combination...................................... AIN-APB16, #10 — B50.528-529

.. Notification to Stockholders................. AIN-APB16, #2 — B50.505-508

.. Option to Exchange Shares................... AIN-APB16, #29 — B50.609-612

.. Ratio of Exchange .... AIN-APB16, #1 — B50.501-504

Interim Financial Reporting .... APB28, ¶21 — I73.124

Leveraged Buyout

.. Allocating Basis to Individual Assets
    and Liabilities under Issue
    No. 88-16 .... — — EITF.90-12

.. Carryover of Predecessor Cost.............. — — EITF.86-16

.... — — EITF.88-16

.. Financed by Loan to ESOP.................... — — EITF.85-11

.. Purchase of Stock Options and SARs
    by Target Company............................. — — EITF.84-13

.. Valuation of Shareholder's Interest....... — — EITF.86-16

.... — — EITF.88-16

Loss Carryforwards

.. Purchased... — — EITF.85-15

.... — — EITF.86-1

.. Realization of Income Tax Benefit........ — — EITF.86-1

Master Limited Partnerships

.. Carryover of Predecessor Cost.............. — — EITF.87-21

.. Recording Assets Acquired and
    Liabilities Assumed .... — — EITF.87-21

Nonmonetary Transactions........................... APB29, ¶4 — N35.101 — EITF.85-43

.... — — EITF.86-29

.. Exchange of Assets for Noncontrolling
    Equity Interest in New Entity .... — — EITF.89-7

.. Exchange of Interest in Subsidiary for
    Noncontrolling Equity Interest in
    New Entity .... — — EITF.89-7

.. Nonmonetary Exchange of
    Cost-Method Investments.................... — — EITF.91-5

.. Transfer of Nonmonetary Assets to a
    New Corporation .... — — EITF.84-39

.. Transfers between Entities under
    Common Control .... — — EITF.84-39

Nonpublic Enterprises .... FAS79, ¶6 — B50.165

Normal Dividends .... APB16, ¶47 — B50.106

Operations Held for Sale after a Business
  Combination

.. Disclosure by SEC Registrants .... — — EITF.87-11

.... — — EITF.90-6

Part Purchase, Part Pooling .... AIN-APB16, #15 — B50.102

.... APB16, ¶42 — B50.545-548

FAS–FASB Statements   FIN–FASB Interpretations   FTB–FASB Technical Bulletins
APB–APB Opinions   AIN–AICPA Interpretations   ARB–Accounting Research Bulletins
CON–FASB Concepts   EITF–EITF Issues   Q&A–FASB Special Reports

	Original Pronouncements	Current Text	EITF and Other

BUSINESS
COMBINATIONS—continued

Personal Holding Enterprises
. . Pooling by Subsidiary of .... AIN-APB16, #28 — B50.606-608

Pooling-of-Interests Method
. . Abnormal Dividends .... APB16, ¶47 — B50.106
. . Absence of Controlling Class of
    Common Stock .... — — EITF.87-27
    .... — — EITF.88-26
. . Absence of Planned Transactions .... APB16, ¶45 — B50.104
    .... APB16, ¶48 — B50.107
. . Accounting for a Business
    Combination Involving a
    Majority-Owned Investee of a
    Venture Capital Company................... — — EITF.90-10
. . All Shares Must Be Exchanged,
    Ninety Percent Test............................. AIN-APB16, #25 — B50.106 — EITF.85-14
    .... APB16, ¶47 — B50.584-592 — EITF.86-10
    .... — — EITF.87-16
. . Altering Terms of Plan of
    Combination....................................... APB16, ¶47 — B50.106
. . Application of Method .... APB16, ¶50-65 — B50.109-124
. . Assets and Liabilities Combined........... APB16, ¶51-52 — B50.110-111
. . Attributes of Combining Enterprises .... APB16, ¶46 — B50.105
. . Autonomy .... APB16, ¶46 — B50.105
. . Bailouts .... AIN-APB16, #21 — B50.106
    .... AIN-APB16, #37 — B50.569-571
    .... APB16, ¶47 — B50.638-640
. . Change in Equity Interest..................... APB16, ¶47 — B50.106
. . Combined Enterprises Have Different
    Accounting.. APB16, ¶52 — B50.111
. . Conditions Required............................. APB16, ¶45-47 — B50.104-106
. . Consummation Date for a Business
    Combination....................................... AIN-APB16, #4 — B50.111
    .... APB16, ¶52 — B50.512-515
. . Contingency, Management
    Representations.................................. AIN-APB16, #30 — B50.106
    .... APB16, ¶47 — B50.613-619
    .... FAS111, ¶8
. . Contingent Shares Defeat Pooling .... AIN-APB16, #14 — B50.106
    .... APB16, ¶47 — B50.542-544
. . Convertible Securities Acquired for
    Cash.. — — EITF.85-14
. . Date of Recording Combination .... APB16, ¶61-62 — B50.120-121
. . Delay in Consummation, Government
    Approval .... APB16, ¶47 — B50.106

See "Terminology" for references to defined terms presented in various accounting pronouncements.
See the Introduction to the Topical Index for details on the use of this index.

	Original Pronouncements	Current Text	EITF and Other
BUSINESS			
COMBINATIONS—continued			
Pooling-of-Interests Method—continued			
. . Disposition of Assets after			
Combination..	AIN-APB16, #22	B50.107	
....	APB16, ¶48	B50.118-119	
....	APB16, ¶59-60	B50.572-574	
....		I17.117	
. . Dissenters' Rights.................................			EITF.87-16
. . Dissenting Shareholders........................	APB16, ¶47	B50.106	
. . Dissolution after Combination	APB16, ¶49	B50.108	
. . Earnings per Share for Prior Years			
after Conversion and Pooling			EITF.84-22
. . Effect of Acquisition of Employer			
Shares for/by an Employee Benefit			
Trust on Accounting for Business			
Combinations......................................			EITF.93-2
. . Effect of Unallocated Shares in an			
Employee Stock Ownership Plan.......			EITF.88-27
. . Employment Contingencies	AIN-APB16, #31	B50.620-623	
. . Equity and Debt Issued for Common			
Stock before Pooling	AIN-APB16, #19	B50.560-561	
. . Expenses Related to Combination	APB16, ¶58	B50.117	
. . Forced Sale of Stock..............................	AIN-APB16, #34	B50.630-631	
. . Fractional Shares	APB16, ¶47	B50.106	
. . Identical Common Shares	AIN-APB16, #13	B50.539-541B	EITF.84-38
....	FTB85-5, ¶16-19		
. . Identity of Issuer and Its Effect			EITF.87-16
. . Impact of Treasury Shares Acquired to			
Satisfy Conversions in a Leveraged			
Preferred Stock ESOP			EITF.D-19
. . Independence	APB16, ¶46	B50.105	
. . Intercompany Eliminations	APB16, ¶56	B50.115	
. . Intercorporate Investment Exceeding			
Ten Percent Limit.................................	APB16, ¶47	B50.106	
. . Issuance or Retirement of Securities.....	AIN-APB16, #3	B50.105-106	
....	APB16, ¶46-47	B50.509-510	
. . Leases	FIN21, ¶12-14	L10.137-139	
. . Loan Guarantees...................................	APB16, ¶48	B50.107	
. . Manner of Combining Interests	APB16, ¶45	B50.104	
. . Mutual and Cooperative Enterprises.....	FTB85-5, ¶21-24	B50.653-655	
. . Nature of Consideration	APB16, ¶47	B50.106	
. . New Enterprise	APB16, ¶46	B50.105	
. . Normal Dividends	APB16, ¶47	B50.106	
. . Notification to Stockholders..................	AIN-APB16, #2	B50.505-508	
. . Options Acquired for Cash....................			EITF.85-14
. . Plan of Combination..............................	APB16, ¶47	B50.106	
. . Planned Change in Common Stock	APB16, ¶48	B50.107	
. . Planned Sale of Securities.....................			EITF.D-40

	Original Pronouncements	Current Text	EITF and Other
BUSINESS			
COMBINATIONS—continued			
Pooling-of-Interests Method—continued			
. . Pooling Not Completed within One Year	AIN-APB16, #5	B50.516-518	
. . Pooling a Bank and a Savings and Loan Association			EITF.86-31
. . Pro Rata Distribution Prohibited	APB16, ¶47	B50.106	
. . Ratio of Exchange	AIN-APB16, #1	B50.501-504	
. . Registered Stock Exchanged for Restricted Stock	AIN-APB16, #6	B50.519-520	
. . Reporting Combined Operations	APB16, ¶56-57	B50.115-116	
. . Restricted Stock Used to Effect Business Combination	AIN-APB16, #11	B50.530-533	
. . Right of First Refusal	FTB85-5, ¶16-17	B50.541A-541B	EITF.84-38
. . Securities Acquired for Cash			EITF.85-14
. . Shares Must Be Exchanged	AIN-APB16, #25	B50.584-592	
. . Standstill Agreements			EITF.87-15
. . Stock Options in a Pooling	AIN-APB16, #32	B50.624-626	
. . Stockholders' Equity Combined	APB16, ¶53-55	B50.112-114	
. . Ten Percent Cash Payout Determined by Lottery			EITF.86-10
. . Transfer of Net Assets	APB16, ¶47	B50.106	
. . Treasury Stock Allowed with Pooling	AIN-APB16, #20	B50.106	
	APB16, ¶47	B50.562-568	
. . Voting Common Stock	APB16, ¶47	B50.106	
. . Voting Ratio Maintained	APB16, ¶47	B50.106	
. . Warrants Acquired for Cash			EITF.85-14
. . Warrants May Defeat Pooling	AIN-APB16, #12	B50.534-538	
. . Wholly Owned Subsidiary, Use of Pooling	AIN-APB16, #18	B50.556-559	
	AIN-APB16, #36	B50.635-637	
Preacquisition Contingencies	FAS38, ¶4-6	B50.148-150	EITF.93-7
	FAS38, ¶23	C59.119	
Preacquisition Dividends of Subsidiary	ARB43, Ch.1A, ¶3	R70.102	
Preacquisition Earnings of Purchased Subsidiary	ARB51, ¶9	R70.101	
Prior-Period Adjustments			
. . Change in Reporting Entity	APB20, ¶12	A35.112-113	
	APB20, ¶35		
Pro Forma Information	FAS79, ¶6	B50.165	
Purchase Method			
. . Accrual of Liabilities			EITF.84-35
			EITF.95-3
. . Acquiring Assets, Accounting after Acquisition	APB16, ¶69	B50.127	
. . Acquiring Assets, Allocating Cost	APB16, ¶68	B50.126	EITF.87-8
. . Acquiring Assets, Principles	APB16, ¶67	B50.125	
. . Acquiring Enterprise, Characteristics and Identification	APB16, ¶70-71	B50.128-129	

See "Terminology" for references to defined terms presented in various accounting pronouncements.

See the Introduction to the Topical Index for details on the use of this index.

	Original Pronouncements	Current Text	EITF and Other

BUSINESS COMBINATIONS—continued
Purchase Method—continued

	Original Pronouncements	Current Text	EITF and Other
. . Adjustments of Allocation of Original Purchase Price			EITF.85-3
			EITF.95-3
. . Adjustments to Purchase Price Allocation under IRC Section 338			EITF.86-3
. . Allocating Basis to Individual Assets and Liabilities under Issue No. 88-16			EITF.90-12
. . Allocating Cost to Assets to Be Sold			EITF.87-11
. . Allocating Cost to Assets to Be Sold When Sale Is Not Completed within Holding Period			EITF.90-6
. . Alternative Minimum Tax			EITF.87-8
. . Compensation in Contingent Agreements	APB16, ¶86	B50.144	
. . Contingent Consideration	APB16, ¶77-86	B50.135-144	
. . Contingent Consideration Based on Earnings	APB16, ¶80	B50.138	
. . Contingent Consideration Based on Security Prices	APB16, ¶81-83	B50.139-141	
. . Cost of an Acquired Enterprise			EITF.84-35
. . Costs of Acquisition	APB16, ¶76	B50.134	
. . Costs of Closing Duplicate Facilities of an Acquirer	FTB85-5, ¶1-4	B50.651-652	EITF.84-35
. . Costs to Exit an Activity of an Acquired Company			EITF.95-3
. . Costs to Involuntarily Terminate Employees of an Acquired Company			EITF.95-3
. . Costs to Relocate an Employee of an Acquired Company			EITF.95-3
. . Determining Cost of an Acquired Enterprise	APB16, ¶72-75	B50.130-133	
. . Duplicate Facilities Sold or Closed			EITF.84-35
. . Earnout	APB16, ¶80	B50.138	
. . Effect of Tax Rate Changes on Assets and Liabilities Acquired			EITF.86-42
. . Effect of Tax Regulations on Purchase Price Allocations			EITF.86-3
. . Fair Value of Consideration	APB16, ¶67	B50.125	
. . Indirect and General Costs of an Acquisition			EITF.95-3
. . Integration Costs			EITF.95-3
. . Interest or Dividends during Contingency Period	APB16, ¶84	B50.142	

	Original Pronouncements	Current Text	EITF and Other
BUSINESS			
COMBINATIONS—continued			
Purchase Method—continued			
. . Leases	FIN21, ¶12	L10.137	
	FIN21, ¶15-16	L10.140-142	
. . Leveraged Buyout			EITF.86-16
			EITF.88-16
. . Leveraged Leases	FIN21, ¶19	L10.161	
. . Loss Carryforwards Purchased			EITF.85-15
			EITF.86-1
. . Pension Obligations			EITF.84-35
. . Percentage of Total Stock to Be Acquired	AIN-APB16, #8	B50.521-527	
. . Postemployment Benefits Other Than Pensions			EITF.86-20
. . Preacquisition Contingencies	FAS38, ¶5-6	B50.148-150	
	FAS38, ¶23		
. . Pro Forma Information	APB16, ¶96	B50.165	
. . Recognition of Liabilities in Connection with a Purchase Business Combination			EITF.95-3
. . Recording Assets Acquired and Liabilities Assumed	APB16, ¶87-88	B50.145-146	EITF.86-16
	FAS87, ¶74		EITF.86-42
	FAS106, ¶86-88		EITF.87-11
	FAS109, ¶288		EITF.88-16
			EITF.90-6
			EITF.95-3
. . Registration Costs	AIN-APB16, #35	B50.632-634	
. . Research and Development Costs Acquired	FIN4, ¶4-5	B50.151-152	EITF.86-14
. . Settlement of Stock Options and Awards by Acquired Company			EITF.85-45
. . Step Acquisitions			EITF.86-16
			EITF.88-16
. . Stock Options and SARs Purchased by Acquired Company			EITF.84-13
. . Subsequent Realization of Unrecognized Tax Benefits	FAS109, ¶30	I27.129	EITF.85-3
. . Subsidiary's Stock, Intangible Assets	ARB43, Ch.5, ¶10	I60.123	
. . Tax Deduction Subsequently Disallowed; Core Deposit Intangibles			EITF.85-33
. . Tax Effect of Imputed Interest, Contingencies	APB16, ¶85	B50.143	
. . Transactions between Enterprises under Common Control			EITF.86-16
			EITF.88-16
. . Uncertainties Related to Income Taxes in a Purchase Business Combination			EITF.93-7

See "Terminology" for references to defined terms presented in various accounting pronouncements.
See the Introduction to the Topical Index for details on the use of this index.

	Original Pronouncements	Current Text	EITF and Other
BUSINESS COMBINATIONS—continued			
Purchase Method—continued			
. . Valuation of Assets and Liabilities Acquired	APB16, ¶88	B50.146	EITF.86-42
	FAS87, ¶74		
	FAS106, ¶86-88		
	FAS109, ¶288		
Push-down Accounting			EITF.85-21
			EITF.86-9
. . Parent Company's Debt to Subsidiary			EITF.84-42
Recognition and Measurement of the Tax Benefit of Excess Tax-Deductible Goodwill Resulting from a Retroactive Change in Tax Law			EITF.93-12
Recognition of Liabilities in Connection with a Purchase Business Combination			EITF.95-3
Scope of Accounting and Reporting Requirements	APB16, ¶5	B50.101	
Separate Financial Statements of Acquired Company			
. . Push-down Accounting			EITF.86-9
Several Enterprises in a Single Business Combination	AIN-APB16, #38	B50.641-644	
Stock Options Acquired by Acquired Company with Assistance from Acquiring Company			EITF.85-45
Stock Options and SARs Purchased by Acquired Company			EITF.84-13
Takeover Attempt			
. . Costs Incurred in a Takeover Defense			EITF.85-2
Transactions between Enterprises under Common Control	AIN-APB16, #39	B50.596A-596D	EITF.85-4
	FTB85-5, ¶5-7		
	FTB85-5, ¶12		
Transitional Matters			
. . Changes in Intercorporate Investments	AIN-APB16, #16	B50.549-551	
. . General Provisions	APB16, ¶99	B50.167-168	
. . Grandfather Clause for Subsidiaries	AIN-APB16, #24	B50.580-583	
. . Intercorporate Investment at October 31, 1970	AIN-APB16, #17	B50.552-555	
. . Part Purchase, Part Pooling	AIN-APB16, #15	B50.545-548	
BUSINESS ENTERPRISE			
Cash Flow Prospects	CON1, ¶39		
Compared to Not-for-Profit Organizations	CON4, ¶6-9		
	CON4, ¶14-22		
Earning Process	CON1, ¶42-48		
Performance Measurement	CON1, ¶42-55		
Return on Investment	CON1, ¶45		

FAS–FASB Statements FIN–FASB Interpretations FTB–FASB Technical Bulletins
APB–APB Opinions AIN–AICPA Interpretations ARB–Accounting Research Bulletins
CON–FASB Concepts EITF–EITF Issues Q&A–FASB Special Reports

	Original Pronouncements	Current Text	EITF and Other

BUSINESS ENTERPRISE OBJECTIVES

Compared to Not-for-Profit Organizations'
Objectives.. CON4, ¶67

BUSINESS INTERRUPTION

See Contingencies

BUSINESS SEGMENTS

See Segment of Business Reporting

(The next page is T-51.)

See "Terminology" for references to defined terms presented in various accounting pronouncements.
See the Introduction to the Topical Index for details on the use of this index.

	Original Pronouncements	Current Text	EITF and Other
CABLE TELEVISION INDUSTRY			
Amortization of Capitalized Costs	FAS51, ¶10	Ca4.108	
. . Franchise Costs	FAS51, ¶13	Ca4.111	
. . Hookup Revenue and Costs	FAS51, ¶11-12	Ca4.109-110	
. . Recoverability of Costs	FAS51, ¶14	Ca4.112	
Glossary	FAS51, ¶17	Ca4.401-404	
Prematurity Period			
. . Accounting during	FAS51, ¶6-9	Ca4.104-107	
. . Definition	FAS51, ¶17	Ca4.403	
. . Establishment by Management	FAS51, ¶4	Ca4.102	
. . Interest Capitalization	FAS51, ¶9	Ca4.107	
. . Portion of System in	FAS51, ¶5	Ca4.103	
Scope of Accounting and Reporting Requirements	FAS51, ¶1	Ca4.101	
CAPITAL			
Description	CON6, ¶212		
CAPITAL IN EXCESS OF PAR VALUE			
See Additional Paid-in Capital			
CAPITAL LEASES			
See Leases			
See Regulated Operations			
Definition	FAS13, ¶7	L10.102	
CAPITAL LOSSES			
See Quasi Reorganizations			
CAPITAL MAINTENANCE			
Concepts, Physical Capital and Financial Capital	CON5, ¶45-48		
	CON6, ¶71-72		
Disclosure in Cash Flows Statement	FAS95, ¶99	C25.115	
Maintenance of Net Assets			
. . Not-for-Profit Organizations	CON6, ¶103-106		
Relation to Price-Level Changes	CON6, ¶71		
Relation to Return on Investment (Business Enterprises)	CON6, ¶71		
CAPITAL STOCK			
See Earnings per Share			
CAPITAL STOCK: CAPITAL TRANSACTIONS			
See Business Combinations			
See Capital Stock: Dividends-in-Kind			
See Capital Stock: Preferred Stock			
See Capital Stock: Stock Dividends and Stock Splits			
See Capital Stock: Treasury Stock			
See Debt: Convertible Debt and Debt with Stock Purchase Warrants			
See Disclosure			
Accounting for Financial Instruments Indexed to, and Potentially Settled in, a Company's Own Stock			EITF.94-7

FAS–FASB Statements	FIN–FASB Interpretations	FTB–FASB Technical Bulletins
APB–APB Opinions	AIN–AICPA Interpretations	ARB–Accounting Research Bulletins
CON–FASB Concepts	EITF–EITF Issues	Q&A–FASB Special Reports

	Original Pronouncements	Current Text	EITF and Other
CAPITAL STOCK: CAPITAL TRANSACTIONS—continued			
Changes in Capital Accounts......................	APB12, ¶10	C08.102	
Contingent Stock Purchase Warrants..........			EITF.84-8
Costs Incurred in a Takeover Defense			EITF.85-2
Debt Exchanged for Common or Preferred Shares...	FAS111, ¶8	D14.501-504	
....	FTB80-1, ¶1-4		
Debt Repayable by a Capital Stock Transaction...			EITF.84-40
Detachable Stock Purchase Warrants Issued in Connection with Debt................	APB14, ¶16	C08.104	
. . Includes Put for Stock Purchased..........			EITF.86-35
Development Stage Enterprises	FAS7, ¶11	De4.107	
....	FAS95, ¶151		
Employee Purchases at a Discount			
. . Employee Can Put Stock to Issuer........			EITF.84-34
. . Issuer Has Right of First Refusal			EITF.84-34
Exchanges of Ownership Interests between Entities under Common Control...			EITF.90-5
Excluded from Income			
. . Retained Earnings Appropriations	APB9, ¶28	C08.101	
. . Treasury Stock Transactions	APB9, ¶28	C08.101	
Nonmonetary Transactions..........................	APB29, ¶4	N35.101	EITF.86-29
Notes Received for Capital Stock			EITF.85-1
Paid-in Capital	APB14, ¶16	C08.103-104	
....	ARB43, Ch.1A, ¶6		
Partnership Withdrawals..............................			EITF.85-46
Redeemable Stock	FAS47, ¶9-10	C32.104-105	
....	FAS47, ¶31-32	C32.113-114	
. . Purchase by Parent Company			EITF.86-32
. . Sale of Put Options on Issuer's Stock...			EITF.87-31
Sale of Capital Stock by Subsidiary............			EITF.84-27
Sale of Put Options on Issuer's Stock........			EITF.87-31
Shareholder Appreciation Rights Program (SHARP)..			EITF.87-31
Shareholder/Former Shareholder Payments			
. . Greenmail	FTB85-6, ¶3-5	C23.503-504	EITF.85-2
....	FTB85-6, ¶14-16	I60.507-508	
. . Payments for Precluding Further Share Purchases..	FTB85-6, ¶4-7	I60.507-508	EITF.85-2
Stock Issued for Property and Subsequently Contributed Back to Enterprise..	ARB43, Ch.1A, ¶6	C08.103	
Takeover Attempts.......................................	FTB85-6, ¶4-7	I17.509-510	
....		I60.507-508	
. . Costs Incurred in a Takeover Defense ..			EITF.85-2
Variable Stock Purchase Warrants...............			EITF.84-8
Warrants Issued in Conjunction with Sales Agreement...			EITF.84-8

See "Terminology" for references to defined terms presented in various accounting pronouncements.

See the Introduction to the Topical Index for details on the use of this index.

	Original Pronouncements	Current Text	EITF and Other
CAPITAL STOCK: DIVIDENDS-IN-KIND			
See Capital Stock: Capital Transactions			
See Capital Stock: Preferred Stock			
See Capital Stock: Stock Dividends and Stock Splits			
See Capital Stock: Treasury Stock			
See Disclosure			
Distributions of Loans Receivable to Shareholders			EITF.87-17
Scope of Accounting and Reporting Requirements	APB29, ¶4	C11.101	
	APB29, ¶18		
CAPITAL STOCK: PREFERRED STOCK			
See Capital Stock: Capital Transactions			
See Capital Stock: Dividends-in-Kind			
See Capital Stock: Stock Dividends and Stock Splits			
See Capital Stock: Treasury Stock			
See Disclosure			
Conversion to Common Stock	APB12, ¶10	C08.102	
Debt Repayable by a Capital Stock Transaction			EITF.84-40
Disclosure Requirements	APB10, ¶10-11	C16.101-102	
	APB15, ¶50		
Effect of a Redemption Agreement on Carrying Value of Investment			EITF.85-23
FHLMC Participating Preferred Stock			
. . Receipt of Stock			EITF.85-7
Foreign Currency Translation	FAS52, ¶48	F60.147	
Imputation of Dividends When Initial Dividend Rate Is Below Market			EITF.86-45
Redeemable Stock	FAS47, ¶9-10	C32.104-105	
	FAS47, ¶31-32	C32.113-114	
. . Purchase by Parent Company			EITF.86-32
Redemption or Induced Conversion			
. . Calculation of Earnings per Share			EITF.D-42
CAPITAL STOCK: STOCK DIVIDENDS AND STOCK SPLITS			
See Capital Stock: Capital Transactions			
See Capital Stock: Dividends-in-Kind			
See Capital Stock: Preferred Stock			
See Capital Stock: Treasury Stock			
Accounting by the Issuer			
. . Stock Dividends	ARB43, Ch.7B, ¶10-14	C20.103-107	
. . Stock Dividends of Subsidiaries	ARB51, ¶18	C20.110	
. . Stock Splits	ARB43, Ch.7B, ¶15-16	C20.108-109	

FAS–FASB Statements   FIN–FASB Interpretations   FTB–FASB Technical Bulletins
APB–APB Opinions   AIN–AICPA Interpretations   ARB–Accounting Research Bulletins
CON–FASB Concepts   EITF–EITF Issues   Q&A–FASB Special Reports

	Original Pronouncements	Current Text	EITF and Other
CAPITAL STOCK: STOCK DIVIDENDS AND STOCK SPLITS—continued			
Accounting by the Recipient	ARB43, Ch.7B, ¶9	C20.102	
. . Distribution of FHLMC Participating			
Preferred Stock	FAS115, ¶136	Bt7.501-504	EITF.85-7
	FTB85-1, ¶1-4		
Definition			
. . Stock Dividend	ARB43, Ch.7B, ¶1	C20.401	
. . Stock Split	ARB43, Ch.7B, ¶2	C20.402	
Federal Home Loan Mortgage Corporation (FHLMC)			
. . Accounting for Distribution of FHLMC Participating Preferred			
Stock	FAS115, ¶136	Bt7.501-504	
	FTB85-1, ¶1-4		
Legal Requirements	ARB43, Ch.7B, ¶14	C20.107	
Nonmonetary Transactions	APB29, ¶4	N35.101	
Scope of Accounting and Reporting Requirements	ARB43, Ch.7B, ¶3	C20.101	
Shareholder Appreciation Rights Program (SHARP)			EITF.87-31
Special, Large, and Nonrecurring Dividends			EITF.90-9
CAPITAL STOCK: TREASURY STOCK			
See Capital Stock: Capital Transactions			
See Capital Stock: Dividends-in-Kind			
See Capital Stock: Preferred Stock			
See Capital Stock: Stock Dividends and Stock Splits			
See Disclosure			
Accounting for Treasury Stock in Leveraged Preferred Stock ESOPs			EITF.D-19
Business Combinations	AIN-APB16, #20	B50.106	
	APB16, ¶47	B50.562-568	
Dividends	ARB43, Ch.1A, ¶4	C23.101	
Earnings per Share	AIN-APB15, Exh.4	E09.910	
Effect of Acquisition of Employer Shares for/by an Employee Benefit Trust on Accounting for Business Combinations			EITF.93-2
Effect of Unallocated Shares on Applying Pooling-of-Interests Method to a Business Combination			EITF.88-27
Employer's Stock Contributed to Defined Contribution Plan			
. . Excess Assets Not Allocated to Participants			EITF.86-27

See "Terminology" for references to defined terms presented in various accounting pronouncements.
See the Introduction to the Topical Index for details on the use of this index.

	Original Pronouncements	Current Text	EITF and Other
CAPITAL STOCK: TREASURY STOCK—continued			
Employer's Stock Contributed to Employee Stock Ownership Plan			
. . Excess Assets Not Allocated to Participants...........................			EITF.86-27
Held Not for Retirement.............................	APB6, ¶12	C23.103	EITF.85-2
....	ARB43, Ch.1A, ¶4	C23.501-503	
....	FTB85-6, ¶1-3		
Investment by Subsidiary in Treasury Stock of Parent..	ARB51, ¶13	C51.114	
Legal Requirements....................................	APB6, ¶13	C23.104	
Purchase of Treasury Shares			
. . Price Significantly in Excess of the Current Market Price of the Shares....	FTB85-6, ¶1-3	C23.501-504	EITF.85-2
....	FTB85-6, ¶14-16		
Retirement..	APB6, ¶12	C23.102	
Tainted Shares..	AIN-APB16, #20	B50.567	EITF.88-27
....			EITF.93-2
....			EITF.D-19
Transactions Excluded from Income	APB9, ¶28	C08.101	
CAPITAL SURPLUS			
See Additional Paid-in Capital			
See Quasi Reorganizations			
CAPITAL TRANSACTIONS			
See Capital Stock: Capital Transactions			
CAPITALIZATION			
See Earnings per Share			
See Leases			
See Regulated Operations			
CAPITALIZATION OF INTEREST			
See Interest: Capitalization of Interest Costs			
See Oil and Gas Producing Activities			
CAPITALIZED COSTS			
Asbestos Treatment			EITF.89-13
Costs to Clean Up Environmental Contamination..			EITF.90-8
Deferred Costs			
. . Development Stage Enterprises	FAS7, ¶10	De4.105	
. . Direct Loan Origination Costs	FAS91, ¶5-7	L20.104-106	
. . Loan Commitment Fees and Costs	FAS91, ¶8-10	L20.107-109	
Regulated Operations	FAS71, ¶4	Re6.114	
....	FAS71, ¶9-10	Re6.119-120	
....	FAS90, ¶3-5	Re6.127A-127C	
. . Allowance for Earnings on Shareholders' Investment	FAS92, ¶8-9	Re6.125G	
. . Discontinuation of Accounting for the Effects of Certain Types of Regulation..	FAS101, ¶5-7	Re6.204-206	

FAS–FASB Statements   FIN–FASB Interpretations   FTB–FASB Technical Bulletins
APB–APB Opinions   AIN–AICPA Interpretations   ARB–Accounting Research Bulletins
CON–FASB Concepts   EITF–EITF Issues   Q&A–FASB Special Reports

	Original Pronouncements	Current Text	EITF and Other
CAPITALIZED COSTS—continued			
Regulated Operations—continued			
. . Phase-in Plan	FAS92, ¶4-5	Re6.125B-125C	
CAPITALIZED INTEREST			
See Interest: Capitalization of Interest Costs			
See Interest: Imputation of an Interest Cost			
CARRYFORWARDS AND CARRYBACKS			
See Income Taxes			
CARRYING AMOUNT			
See Banking and Thrift Industries			
See Debt: Restructurings			
Definition	FAS72, ¶5	Bt7.401	
Extinguished Debt	APB26, ¶19	D14.102	
Of Payables			
. . Definition	FAS15, ¶13	D22.401	
CASH			
See Financial Instruments			
Balance Sheet Classification	ARB43, Ch.3A, ¶4	B05.105	
Medium of Exchange	CON1, ¶10		
	CON6, ¶29		
Restricted in Use	ARB43, Ch.3A, ¶6	B05.107	
CASH BASIS OF ACCOUNTING			
Compared to Accrual Basis of Accounting	CON4, ¶50		
	CON6, ¶139-140		
	CON6, ¶144-145		
CASH FLOWS			
See Cash Flows Statement			
See Recognition and Measurement in Financial Statements			
Cash Flow per Share	FAS95, ¶33	C25.135	
	FAS95, ¶125		
Information Useful in Assessing	CON1, ¶37-39		
Performance Measurement	CON1, ¶43-49		
Relation to Earnings	CON1, ¶43-49		
Statement of	CON5, ¶52-54		
Users' Needs for Information	CON1, ¶25		
	CON1, ¶30		
CASH FLOWS STATEMENT			
See Disclosure			
Anticipatory Hedges	FAS104, ¶7	C25.112	
Banks, Savings Institutions, and Credit Unions	FAS104, ¶7	C25.111A	
Cash and Cash Equivalents	FAS95, ¶7-10	C25.105-108	
Cash Flow per Share	FAS95, ¶33	C25.135	
	FAS95, ¶125		

See "Terminology" for references to defined terms presented in various accounting pronouncements.
See the Introduction to the Topical Index for details on the use of this index.

	Original Pronouncements	Current Text	EITF and Other

CASH FLOWS
STATEMENT—continued
Classification of Cash Receipts and
Payments .... FAS95, ¶14-24   C25.112-122B
.... FAS102, ¶8-9   I80.117
.... FAS104, ¶7
.... FAS115, ¶18
.... FAS115, ¶132
. . Financing Activities.............................. FAS95, ¶18-20   C25.116-118
.... FAS117, ¶30
. . Hedging Transactions .... FAS104, ¶7   C25.112
. . Investing Activities............................... FAS95, ¶15-17   C25.113-115
.... FAS95, ¶99   C25.122A-122B
.... FAS102, ¶8-9
.... FAS115, ¶132
. . Operating Activities.............................. FAS95, ¶21-24   C25.119-122B
.... FAS102, ¶8-9
.... FAS102, ¶26-27
Complementary Relationship to Other
Financial Statements .... CON5, ¶24
Content and Form of Statement .... FAS95, ¶26-31   C25.124-129
.... FAS117, ¶30
Description and Recognition
Considerations.. CON5, ¶52-54
Direct Method.. FAS95, ¶27   C25.125
.... FAS95, ¶29-30   C25.127-128
.... FAS95, ¶131   C25.137
.... FAS95, ¶133-149   C25.139-155
.... FAS102, ¶30-32
. . Direct Method Indirectly Determined... FAS95, ¶115-118   C25.130-133
.... FAS95, ¶135   C25.141
Exemptions from the Requirement to
Provide a Statement of Cash Flows.......... FAS102, ¶5-7   C25.135A-135C
.... FAS102, ¶15
.... FAS102, ¶20-22
Foreign Currency Cash Flows.................... FAS95, ¶25   C25.123
.... FAS95, ¶136-146   C25.142-152
Gross and Net Cash Flows .... FAS95, ¶11-13   C25.109-111A
.... FAS104, ¶7
. . Banks, Savings Institutions, and Credit
Unions.. FAS104, ¶7   C25.111A
Illustrative Examples.................................. FAS95, ¶130-149   C25.136-155
.... FAS102, ¶30-32
. . Direct Method.. FAS95, ¶131   C25.137
.... FAS95, ¶133-149   C25.139-155
.... FAS102, ¶30-32
. . Direct Method Indirectly Determined... FAS95, ¶135   C25.141
. . Foreign Operations............................... FAS95, ¶136-146   C25.142-152
. . Indirect Method .... FAS95, ¶132-134   C25.138-140
. . Not-for-Profit Organizations .... FAS117, ¶160   No5.135

FAS–FASB Statements　　FIN–FASB Interpretations　　FTB–FASB Technical Bulletins
APB–APB Opinions　　AIN–AICPA Interpretations　　ARB–Accounting Research Bulletins
CON–FASB Concepts　　EITF–EITF Issues　　Q&A–FASB Special Reports

	Original Pronouncements	Current Text	EITF and Other
CASH FLOWS			
STATEMENT—continued			
Indirect Method	FAS95, ¶28-30	C25.126-128	
	FAS95, ¶132-134	C25.138-140	
Investments in Debt and Equity			
Securities	FAS115, ¶18	I80.117	
Noncash Investing and Financing			
Activities	FAS95, ¶32	C25.134	
	FAS117, ¶30		
Operating Activities	FAS95, ¶27-30	C25.125-128	
. . Direct Method	FAS95, ¶27	C25.125	
	FAS95, ¶29-30	C25.127-128	
. . Indirect Method	FAS95, ¶28-30	C25.126-128	
Scope and Purpose of Accounting and			
Reporting	FAS95, ¶3-6	C25.101-104	
. . Employee Benefit Plans	FAS102, ¶10	C25.101	
. . Investment Enterprises	FAS102, ¶10	C25.101	
. . Not-for-Profit	FAS117, ¶30	C25.101	
CASH SURRENDER VALUE			
Life Insurance			
. . Provision for Deferred Taxes on			
Increases in CSV			EITF.87-28
. . Temporary Differences	FAS109, ¶14	I27.113	
CASUALTY LOSSES			
See Extraordinary Items			
See Insurance Industry			
Loss Contingencies	FAS5, ¶4	C59.122	
Unasserted Claims	FAS5, ¶38	C59.144	
CATCH-UP ADJUSTMENT			
See Cumulative Accounting Adjustments			
CHANGE IN ACCOUNTING			
PRINCIPLES/ESTIMATES/ENTITY			
See Accounting Changes			
CHANGE IN BASIS OF ASSETS AND			
LIABILITIES			
See Business Combinations			
Adjustments for Payments during Rent-up			
Period of Real Estate			EITF.85-27
Basis of Accounting under FSLIC			
Management Consignment Program			EITF.85-41
Exchanges of Ownership Interests			
between Entities under Common			
Control			EITF.90-5
Leveraged Buyout Transactions			EITF.86-16
			EITF.88-16
. . Allocating Basis to Individual Assets			
and Liabilities under Issue No. 88-16			EITF.90-12
Liquidation of a Banking Institution			
. . Valuation of Assets and Liabilities by			
Liquidating Bank			EITF.88-25

See "Terminology" for references to defined terms presented in various accounting pronouncements.
See the Introduction to the Topical Index for details on the use of this index.

	Original Pronouncements	Current Text	EITF and Other

CHANGE IN BASIS OF ASSETS AND LIABILITIES—continued

Master Limited Partnership Transactions ...			EITF.87-21
New Basis of Accounting Resulting from Change in Ownership.............................			EITF.85-21
Push-down Accounting in Separate Statements of Acquired Entity.................			EITF.86-9
Push-down of Parent Company's Debt to Subsidiary......................................			EITF.84-42
Transfer of Nonmonetary Assets to a New Corporation			EITF.84-39
Transfers between Entities under Common Control..			EITF.84-39
Valuation in Simultaneous Common Control Mergers			EITF.90-13

CHANGES IN FINANCIAL POSITION

See Accounting Changes

See Adjustments of Financial Statements for Prior Periods

See Capital Stock: Capital Transactions

See Cash Flows Statement

Definition	CON6, ¶20		

CHANGING PRICES: REPORTING THEIR EFFECTS IN FINANCIAL REPORTS

See Disclosure

Application of Statement 109 in Foreign Financial Statements Restated for General Price-Level Changes			EITF.93-9
Calculations of Current Cost/Constant Purchasing Power Information			
. . Illustrations	FAS89, ¶46-95	C28.141-190	
. . Measurement	FAS89, ¶16-43	C28.112-139	
Glossary	FAS89, ¶44	C28.401-419	
Illustrations of Disclosure............................	FAS89, ¶45	C28.140	
Income from Continuing Operations	FAS89, ¶12-13	C28.108-109	
....	FAS89, ¶32-33	C28.128-129	
Income-Producing Real Estate...................	FAS89, ¶25	C28.121	
Income Tax Expense...................................	FAS89, ¶33	C28.129	
Inventory			
. . Current Cost Amounts...........................	FAS89, ¶16-17	C28.112-113	
....	FAS89, ¶19-21	C28.115-117	
. . Increase or Decrease............................	FAS89, ¶34-35	C28.130-131	
....	FAS89, ¶67-68	C28.162-163	
Lower Recoverable Amount	FAS89, ¶29-31	C28.125-127	
Mineral Reserve Assets	FAS89, ¶14-15	C28.110-111	
....	FAS89, ¶23	C28.119	

FAS–FASB Statements	FIN–FASB Interpretations	FTB–FASB Technical Bulletins
APB–APB Opinions	AIN–AICPA Interpretations	ARB–Accounting Research Bulletins
CON–FASB Concepts	EITF–EITF Issues	Q&A–FASB Special Reports

T-59

	Original Pronouncements	Current Text	EITF and Other
CHANGING PRICES: REPORTING THEIR EFFECTS IN FINANCIAL REPORTS—continued			
Monetary and Nonmonetary Items			
. . Classification	FAS89, ¶41	C28.137	
	FAS89, ¶96-108	C28.191-203	
	FAS109, ¶288		
Motion Picture Films	FAS89, ¶25	C28.121	
Net Assets	FAS89, ¶27-28	C28.123-124	
Oil and Gas Reserves	FAS89, ¶24	C28.120	
Parity Adjustment	FAS89, ¶39	C28.135	
	FAS89, ¶95	C28.190	
Property, Plant, and Equipment			
. . Current Cost Amounts	FAS89, ¶16	C28.112	
	FAS89, ¶18-22	C28.114-118	
. . Increase or Decrease	FAS89, ¶34-35	C28.130-131	
	FAS89, ¶69-70	C28.164-165	
Purchasing Power Gain or Loss	FAS89, ¶40-43	C28.136-139	
	FAS89, ¶66	C28.161	
	FAS89, ¶83-84	C28.178-179	
	FAS89, ¶90-93	C28.185-188	
Rate Regulated Enterprise			
. . Recoverable Amount	FAS89, ¶31	C28.127	
Recoverable Amount	FAS89, ¶29-31	C28.125-127	
Restate-Translate Method	FAS89, ¶37	C28.133	
. . Purchasing Power Gain or Loss	FAS89, ¶43	C28.139	
	FAS89, ¶90-93	C28.185-188	
. . Translation Adjustment	FAS89, ¶39	C28.135	
	FAS89, ¶94-95	C28.189-190	
Restatement of Current Cost Information			
Using the CPI(U)	FAS89, ¶36-37	C28.132-133	
	FAS89, ¶82-83	C28.177-178	
	FAS89, ¶90-91	C28.185-186	
Scope	FAS89, ¶3	C28.101	
Specialized Assets	FAS89, ¶23-26	C28.119-122	
Timberlands and Growing Timber	FAS89, ¶25-26	C28.121-122	
Translate-Restate Method	FAS89, ¶37	C28.133	
. . Purchasing Power Gain or Loss	FAS89, ¶42	C28.138	
	FAS89, ¶83-84	C28.178-179	
. . Translation Adjustment	FAS89, ¶38	C28.135	
	FAS89, ¶85	C28.189-190	
CHARITABLE INSTITUTIONS			
See Not-for-Profit Organizations			
CIRCUMSTANCES			
Definition	CON6, ¶136		
CLAIM COST RECOGNITION			
Insurance Contracts	FAS60, ¶17-20	In6.117-120	
CLAIMS			
See Insurance Industry			

See "Terminology" for references to defined terms presented in various accounting pronouncements.
See the Introduction to the Topical Index for details on the use of this index.

	Original Pronouncements	Current Text	EITF and Other
CLAIMS—continued			
Accrual and Disclosure	FAS5, ¶33-39	C59.139-145	
. . Accounting by Insureds for Claims-Made Insurance Policies			EITF.86-12
Definition	FAS60, ¶66	In6.404	
Loss Contingencies	FAS5, ¶4	C59.122	
. . Accounting by Insureds for Claims-Made Insurance Policies			EITF.86-12
CLASSIFICATION OF ASSETS AND LIABILITIES			
See Balance Sheet Classification: Current Assets and Liabilities			
See Balance Sheet Classification: Debt vs. Equity			
CLOSELY HELD COMPANIES			
See Earnings per Share			
See Mortgage Banking Activities			
See Related Parties			
CLOSING DUPLICATE FACILITIES OF AN ACQUIRER			
See Business Combinations			
Facilities of an Acquirer Duplicated by a Business Combination	FTB85-5, ¶1-2	B50.651-652	EITF.84-35
CLUBS			
See Not-for-Profit Organizations			
CMOs			
See Collateralized Mortgage Obligations			
COAL INDUSTRY			
Accounting for Estimated Payments in Connection with the Coal Industry Retiree Health Benefit Act of 1992			EITF.92-13
CO-BRANDING			
See Lending Activities			
COLLATERAL			
See Financial Instruments			
For Loans			
. . Collateral-Dependent Loans	FAS114, ¶13	I08.111	
. . Loss Contingency	FAS5, ¶18	C59.120	
COLLATERALIZED MORTGAGE OBLIGATIONS (CMOs)			
See Financial Instruments			
Accounting by Issuer	FTB85-2, ¶2	C30.502	
Consolidation of Issuer with Sponsor	FTB85-2, ¶3	C30.503	EITF.85-28
Definition			
. . Collateralized Mortgage Obligations	FTB85-2, ¶1	C30.501	
. . Nominal	FTB85-2, ¶2	C30.502	
Establishment through Third Party			
. . Gain or Loss Recognition by Seller of Mortgages			EITF.86-24
Offsetting Collateral against Liability	FTB85-2, ¶4	C30.504	

FAS–FASB Statements   FIN–FASB Interpretations   FTB–FASB Technical Bulletins
APB–APB Opinions   AIN–AICPA Interpretations   ARB–Accounting Research Bulletins
CON–FASB Concepts   EITF–EITF Issues   Q&A–FASB Special Reports

	Original Pronouncements	Current Text	EITF and Other
COLLATERALIZED MORTGAGE OBLIGATIONS (CMOs)—continued			
Purchased Investment			EITF.89-4
. . Impairment Recognition			EITF.93-18
COLLECTIONS—WORKS OF ART, HISTORICAL TREASURES, AND SIMILAR ASSETS			
Definition	FAS116, ¶128	C67.111	
	FAS116, ¶209	C67.401	
Examples of Contributed Collections	FAS116, ¶185-189	C67.137-141	
Financial Statement Presentation and			
Disclosure	FAS116, ¶26-27	C67.123-124	
	FAS116, ¶141	No5.142	
Optional Recognition and Capitalization			
of Contributed Collections	FAS116, ¶11-13	C67.111-113	
	FAS116, ¶135		
COMBINATIONS OF BUSINESSES			
See Business Combinations			
COMBINED FINANCIAL STATEMENTS			
See Consolidation			
Related Parties	ARB51, ¶22-23	C51.121-122	
COMMERCIAL BANKS			
See Banking and Thrift Industries			
COMMERCIAL PAPER			
See Financial Instruments			
Balance Sheet Classification	FAS6, ¶1	B05.110	
COMMITMENT FEES			
See Lending Activities			
See Loan Origination and Commitment Fees			
See Mortgage Banking Activities			
COMMITMENTS			
See Financial Instruments			
See Futures Contracts			
Contractor Accounting: Construction-Type			
Contracts	ARB45, ¶16	Co4.113	
Contributions Payable (Promises to Give)	FAS116, ¶18-21	C67.114-117	
Purchase, Losses—Qualification as a			
Liability	CON6, ¶251-253		
Recognition of Executory Contracts	CON6, ¶251-253		
COMMITMENTS: LONG-TERM OBLIGATIONS			
See Disclosure			
See Financial Instruments			
See Futures Contracts			
Glossary	FAS47, ¶23	C32.401-404	
Inventory			
. . Losses	ARB43, Ch.4, ¶17	I78.121-122	

See "Terminology" for references to defined terms presented in various accounting pronouncements.
See the Introduction to the Topical Index for details on the use of this index.

	Original Pronouncements	Current Text	EITF and Other
COMMITMENTS: LONG-TERM OBLIGATIONS—continued			
Long-Term Debt			
. . Disclosure Requirements	FAS47, ¶10	C32.105	
Redeemable Stock	FAS47, ¶31-32	C32.113-114	
. . Accounting	FAS47, ¶9	C32.104	
. . Redemption Requirements	FAS47, ¶10	C32.105	
. . Sinking Fund Requirements for Long-Term Borrowings	FAS47, ¶10	C32.105	
. . Unconditional Purchase Obligations	FAS47, ¶10	C32.105	
Relation to Leases	FAS47, ¶6	C32.101	
Scope of Accounting and Reporting Requirements	FAS47, ¶1	C32.101	
	FAS47, ¶6		
Take-or-Pay Contract	FAS47, ¶29-32	C32.111-114	
Throughput Contract	FAS47, ¶24-28	C32.106-110	
Unconditional Purchase Obligations	FAS47, ¶1	C32.101	
	FAS47, ¶6		
Unrecorded Obligations	FAS47, ¶7-8	C32.102-103	
COMMODITY FUTURES CONTRACTS			
See Financial Instruments			
See Futures Contracts			
COMMODITY TRADERS			
Futures Contracts	FAS80, ¶8	F80.108	
COMMON CONTROL			
See Related Parties			
Accounting for Simultaneous Common Control Mergers			EITF.90-13
Acquisition of Minority Interests			EITF.85-4
			EITF.90-5
Business Combinations	AIN-APB16, #27	B50.596A-605	
	AIN-APB16, #39	B50.645-648	
	FTB85-5, ¶5-7		
	FTB85-5, ¶12		
. . Accounting for Simultaneous Common Control Mergers			EITF.90-13
. . Downstream Mergers	FTB85-5, ¶13-14	B50.596E-596F	EITF.85-4
. . Leveraged Buyout			EITF.86-16
			EITF.88-16
Exchanges of Ownership Interests between Entities under Common Control			EITF.90-5
Master Limited Partnerships			
. . Carryover of Predecessor Cost			EITF.87-21
Nonmonetary Transactions	APB29, ¶4	N35.101	EITF.84-39
Transfers between Entities under Common Control			EITF.84-39
COMMON STOCK			
See Capital Stock: Capital Transactions			

FAS–FASB Statements	FIN–FASB Interpretations	FTB–FASB Technical Bulletins
APB–APB Opinions	AIN–AICPA Interpretations	ARB–Accounting Research Bulletins
CON–FASB Concepts	EITF–EITF Issues	Q&A–FASB Special Reports

	Original Pronouncements	Current Text	EITF and Other
COMMON STOCK—continued			
See Capital Stock: Stock Dividends and Stock Splits			
See Capital Stock: Treasury Stock			
See Debt: Convertible Debt and Debt with Stock Purchase Warrants			
See Earnings per Share			
Definition	APB15, App.D	E09.403	
Issued to Extinguish Debt Early	FAS111, ¶8	D14.501-504	
	FTB80-1, ¶1-4		
COMMON STOCK EQUIVALENTS			
See Earnings per Share			
COMPARABILITY			
Accounting for Similar Circumstances	CON2, ¶16		
As a Quality	CON2, ¶111-119		
Between Enterprises			
. . Primary Qualitative Characteristic	CON2, ¶111		
Definition	CON2, Glossary		
Primary Qualitative Characteristic	CON2, ¶111-122		
COMPARATIVE FINANCIAL STATEMENTS			
See Adjustments of Financial Statements for Prior Periods			
See Disclosure			
See Financial Statements: Comparative Financial Statements			
See Segment of Business Reporting			
Development Stage Enterprises	FAS7, ¶13	De4.109	
Earnings per Share	AIN-APB15, #23	E09.587-589	
COMPENSATION TO EMPLOYEES			
Lump-Sum Payments under Union Contracts			EITF.88-23
Recognition by Sponsor of Leveraged Employee Stock Ownership Plan (ESOP)			EITF.89-8
COMPENSATION TO EMPLOYEES: DEFERRED			
See Compensation to Employees: Paid Absences			
See Compensation to Employees: Stock Purchase and Stock Option Plans			
Deferred Compensation Agreements	APB12, ¶6-7	C38.101-102	
	FAS106, ¶13		
. . Illustrations	FAS106, ¶413-416	C38.103-106	
Qualification as a Liability	CON6, ¶196		
COMPENSATION TO EMPLOYEES: PAID ABSENCES			
See Disclosure			

See "Terminology" for references to defined terms presented in various accounting pronouncements.

See the Introduction to the Topical Index for details on the use of this index.

	Original Pronouncements	Current Text	EITF and Other
COMPENSATION TO EMPLOYEES: PAID ABSENCES—continued			
Conditions for Accrual	FAS43, ¶6-7	C44.104-106	
	FAS43, ¶12	C44.109	
	FAS43, ¶18		
. . Disclosure If Criteria Met and Liability Not Accrued	FAS43, ¶6	C44.104	
. . Nonvesting Accumulating Rights to Receive Sick Pay Benefits	FAS43, ¶7	C44.108	
	FAS43, ¶15		
. . Nonvesting Rights	FAS43, ¶13	C44.107	
Definition	FAS43, ¶1	C44.401	
Regulated Operations	FAS71, ¶48-49	Re6.153-154	
Relation to Contingencies	FAS5, ¶7	C59.102	
Scope of Accounting and Reporting Requirements	FAS43, ¶1	C44.101-103	
	FAS43, ¶20		
	FAS112, ¶8-9		
COMPENSATION TO EMPLOYEES: STOCK PURCHASE AND STOCK OPTION PLANS			
See Compensation to Employees: Deferred			
See Disclosure			
Accounting for a Reload Stock Option			EITF.90-7
Accruing Compensation Cost	APB25, ¶13-15	C47.113-115	
Alternate Stock Plans	APB25, ¶34	C47.137	
Book Value Stock Option Plans			
. . Effect of Initial Public Offering on Compensation Expense			EITF.88-6
Book Value Stock Purchase Plans			
. . Accounting by a Privately Held Company			EITF.87-23
. . Accounting by a Publicly Held Company			EITF.88-6
. . Effect of an Initial Public Offering			EITF.88-6
Buyout of Compensatory Stock Options			EITF.94-6
Cancellation and Reissuance of Options			EITF.87-33
Changes to Fixed Employee Stock Option Plans as a Result of Equity Restructuring			EITF.90-9
Compensation Cost Measured at Date of Grant or Award	APB25, ¶23	C47.126	
. . Stock Bonus or Award Plans	APB25, ¶26	C47.129	
. . Stock Purchase and Stock Option Plans	APB25, ¶25	C47.128	
. . Typical Plans with Fixed and Determinable Terms	APB25, ¶24	C47.127	

	Original Pronouncements	Current Text	EITF and Other
COMPENSATION TO EMPLOYEES: STOCK PURCHASE AND STOCK OPTION PLANS—continued			
Compensation Cost Measured at Other Than Date of Grant or Award	APB25, ¶27	C47.130	
. . Accounting	APB25, ¶28	C47.131	
. . Book Value Stock Purchase Plans			EITF.87-23
. . Combination and Elective Plans	APB25, ¶33-34	C47.136-137	
. . Junior Stock Option, Purchase and Award Plans	FIN38, ¶2	C47.135A	
	FIN38, ¶4-6	C47.135C-135E	
. . Phantom Stock Plans	APB25, ¶32	C47.135	
. . Plans with Variable Terms	APB25, ¶29	C47.119	
	FIN28, ¶2	C47.132	
	FIN38, ¶3	C47.135B	
	FIN38, ¶22		
. . Settlement of Stock Options and Awards			EITF.85-45
. . Shadow Stock Plans	APB25, ¶32	C47.135	
. . Stock Bonus or Award Plans	APB25, ¶31-32	C47.134-135	
. . Stock Option and Stock Purchase Plans	APB25, ¶30	C47.133	
. . Stock Options Acquired in Business Combinations			EITF.85-45
. . Stock Options Acquired in Leveraged Buyouts			EITF.84-13
Compensatory Plans			
. . Accounting for Income Tax Benefits	APB25, ¶17-18	C47.117-118	
	FAS109, ¶287-288		
. . Accruing Compensation Cost	APB25, ¶12	C47.112	
. . Deferred Compensation Agreements	APB25, ¶12	C47.112	
. . Description	APB25, ¶8	C47.107-108	
	ARB43, Ch.13B, ¶3		
. . Employee Services as Consideration for Stock Issued	APB25, ¶9	C47.109	
	ARB43, Ch.13B, ¶14		
. . Income Tax Benefits	APB25, ¶16-17	C47.116-117	
	FAS109, ¶287-288		
. . Measuring Compensation for Services	APB25, ¶10-11	C47.110-111	
Definition			
. . Junior Stock	FIN38, ¶1	C47.400	
. . Measurement Date	APB25, ¶10	C47.401	
. . Plan	APB25, ¶4	C47.402	
. . Service Period	FIN28, ¶3	C47.402A	
. . Stock Appreciation Rights	FIN28, ¶9	C47.403	
. . Variable Stock Option, Purchase and Award Plans	APB25, ¶29	C47.405	

See "Terminology" for references to defined terms presented in various accounting pronouncements.
See the Introduction to the Topical Index for details on the use of this index.

	Original Pronouncements	Current Text	EITF and Other
COMPENSATION TO EMPLOYEES: STOCK PURCHASE AND STOCK OPTION PLANS—continued			
Incentive Stock Options under the Economic Recovery Tax Act of 1981	FTB82-2, ¶1-4	C47.507-516	
	FTB82-2, ¶8-13		
. . Combination of Circumstances	FTB82-2, ¶12	C47.515	
. . Description	FTB82-2, ¶1-4	C47.507-510	
. . Repricing	FTB82-2, ¶8-9	C47.511-512	
. . Tandem Plans	FTB82-2, ¶10-11	C47.513-514	
. . Taxes	FTB82-2, ¶13	C47.516	
Incentive Stock Options under the Tax Reform Act of 1986			
. . Disqualifications of ISOs			EITF.87-6
Measurement Date	APB25, ¶10-11	C47.110-111	EITF.87-6
	APB25, ¶13	C47.113	
	APB25, ¶22	C47.119	
	APB25, ¶27-28	C47.121	
	FIN28, ¶2	C47.125	
	FIN28, ¶4	C47.130-131	
. . Book Value Stock Purchase Plans			EITF.87-23
. . Changes to Fixed Employee Stock Option Plans as a Result of Equity Restructuring			EITF.90-9
. . Junior Stock Option, Purchase and Award Plans	FIN38, ¶2-3	C47.135A-135B	
	FIN38, ¶5-6	C47.135D-135E	
Measuring and Accounting for Compensation under Typical Plans	APB25, ¶21-22	C47.124-125	
Measuring Compensation for Services	APB25, ¶11	C47.111	
. . Junior Stock Option, Purchase and Award Plans	FIN38, ¶2	C47.135A	
	FIN38, ¶4-6	C47.135C-135E	
Noncompensatory Plans	APB25, ¶7	C47.104-106	
	ARB43, Ch.13B, ¶4-5		
Paid-in Capital	APB25, ¶17	C47.117	
	FTB82-2, ¶13	C47.516	
Performance Plans			EITF.87-23
			EITF.88-6
Permanent Discount Restricted Stock Purchase Plans			EITF.84-34
Phantom Stock Plans	APB25, ¶34	C47.137	
Phantom Stock-for-Stock Exercise of Stock Options			EITF.87-6
Plans with Tax Offset Cash Bonuses			EITF.87-6
Purchase of Stock Options and SARs in Leveraged Buyouts			EITF.84-13
Pyramid Stock Option Plans			EITF.84-18
Repricing of Options			EITF.87-33
			EITF.90-9

FAS–FASB Statements   FIN–FASB Interpretations   FTB–FASB Technical Bulletins
APB–APB Opinions   AIN–AICPA Interpretations   ARB–Accounting Research Bulletins
CON–FASB Concepts   EITF–EITF Issues   Q&A–FASB Special Reports

	Original Pronouncements	Current Text	EITF and Other
COMPENSATION TO EMPLOYEES: STOCK PURCHASE AND STOCK OPTION PLANS—continued			
Repurchase of Options			EITF.87-33
			EITF.94-6
Scope of Accounting and Reporting Requirements	APB25, ¶1-2	C47.101-103	
	APB25, ¶4		
Stapled Options			EITF.90-9
. . Nonstapled Options			EITF.90-9
Stock Appreciation Rights and Other Variable Stock Option or Award Plans	FIN28, ¶2-5	C47.119-122	EITF.87-23
	FIN28, ¶19-27	C47.138-146	EITF.88-6
			EITF.D-18
Stock Depreciation Rights			EITF.87-33
Stock Indemnification Rights			EITF.87-33
Stock Market Decline			EITF.87-33
Stock Options Acquired by Acquired Company with Assistance from Acquiring Company			EITF.85-45
Stock Plans Established by a Principal Stockholder	AIN-APB25, #1	C47.501-506	
Stock-for-Stock Exercise of Stock Options			
. . Accounting for a Reload Stock Option			EITF.90-7
. . Phantom Stock-for-Stock Exercises			EITF.87-6
. . Pyramiding			EITF.84-18
Tandem Stock Plans	APB25, ¶34	C47.137	
Use of Shares to Cover Tax Withholding			EITF.87-6
COMPLETED CONTRACT METHOD			
See Contractor Accounting: Construction-Type Contracts			
COMPLETENESS			
Definition	CON2, Glossary		
Relation to Representational Faithfulness	CON2, ¶79-80		
COMPLETE SET OF FINANCIAL STATEMENTS			
Not-for-Profit Organizations	FAS117, ¶1-3	No5.104-105	
	FAS117, ¶6-7		
	FAS117, ¶70		
Segment of Business Reporting	FAS14, ¶3	S20.104	
	FAS95, ¶152		
COMPREHENSIVE INCOME			
See Earnings			
See Losses			
See Revenues			
Change in Terms from Concepts Statement 1	CON5, ¶11		
Characteristics	CON6, ¶73-77		
	CON6, ¶215-218		

See "Terminology" for references to defined terms presented in various accounting pronouncements.

See the Introduction to the Topical Index for details on the use of this index.

	Original Pronouncements	Current Text	EITF and Other

COMPREHENSIVE INCOME—continued

Component of Full Set of Financial Statements .... CON5, ¶13

Components .... CON6, ¶73-77

Definition .... CON6, ¶70

Display Issues .... CON6, ¶220

Element of Financial Statements.................. CON6, ¶70-77

Equivalent Terms... CON5, ¶40

Financial Capital Concept .... CON6, ¶71-72

Information about Sources .... CON6, ¶219

Relation to Price-Level Changes.................. CON6, ¶73-75

Relation to Profit and Loss .... CON6, ¶16

Relationship between Earnings and Comprehensive Income .... CON5, ¶42-44

Statement of Comprehensive Income

. . Complementary Relationship to Other Financial Statements........................... CON5, ¶24

Statement of Earnings and Comprehensive Income .... CON5, ¶30-32

Total Nonowner Changes in Equity (or Equivalent Term) .... CON5, ¶40

COMPUTER SOFTWARE

See Disclosure

See Research and Development

Amortization of Capitalized Software Costs .... FAS86, ¶8 — Co2.107 — Q&A.86 #15-17

. . Estimated Useful Life of Product Enhancements .... — — Q&A.86 #24

Capitalization of Costs .... FAS86, ¶4-7 — Co2.103-106

Computer Software to Be Sold, Leased, or Otherwise Marketed

. . Balance Sheet Presentation .... — — Q&A.86 #21

. . Costs Incurred to Establish Technological Feasibility of Software Products... FAS86, ¶3-4 — Co2.102-103 — EITF.85-35

. . Created for Others under a Contractual Arrangement .... FAS2, ¶2 — Co2.101

.... FAS86, ¶2

. . Development of Software to Be Used as a Product or Process .... FAS86, ¶5 — Co2.104

.... FIN6, ¶8 — R50.117

. . Evaluation of Capitalized Costs .... FAS86, ¶10 — Co2.109 — Q&A.86 #22

. . Glossary .... FAS86, ¶10 — Co2.401-410

.... FAS86, ¶52

. . Indirect Production Costs .... — — Q&A.86 #11

. . Inventory Costs...................................... FAS86, ¶9 — Co2.108

. . Maintenance and Customer Support Costs... FAS86, ¶6 — Co2.105 — Q&A.86# 12

.... FAS86, ¶45

	Original Pronouncements	Current Text	EITF and Other
COMPUTER SOFTWARE—continued			
Computer Software to Be Sold, Leased, or Otherwise Marketed—continued			
. . Producing Product Masters	FAS86, ¶5	Co2.104	
. . Product Enhancement Costs			EITF.85-35
			Q&A.86 #23-25
. . Purchased Computer Software	FAS86, ¶7	Co2.106	Q&A.86 #14
	FAS86, ¶39		
. . Purchase of Computer Software to Be Used as Part of a Product or Process	FAS86, ¶5	Co2.104	Q&A.86 #13-14
. . Research and Development Costs of Computer Software	FAS86, ¶3-4	Co2.102-103	Q&A.86 #5
Criteria for Capitalization of Costs	FAS86, ¶4	Co2.103	Q&A.86 #6-10
. . For Product Enhancements			Q&A.86 #23
			Q&A.86 #25
. . Indirect Production Costs			Q&A.86 #11
Definitions			
. . Software Product	FAS86, ¶2	Co2.101	Q&A.86 #1
. . Software as Part of a Process	FAS86, ¶2	Co2.101	Q&A.86 #2
. . Technological Feasibility	FAS86, ¶3	Co2.102	Q&A.86 #9
. . Working Model	FAS86, ¶4	Co2.103	Q&A.86 #10
Development of Software to Be Used as a Product or Process	FIN6, ¶4	R50.119	
For Internal Use			
. . Created for Internal Use	FAS86, ¶26	Co2.101	
. . Development of Software to Be Used in Research and Development Activities	FAS86, ¶3	Co2.102	
	FIN6, ¶8	R50.117	
. . Internal Development of Software	FIN6, ¶6	R50.115	
. . Purchase or Lease of Software	FAS86, ¶50	R50.114	
	FIN6, ¶5		
. . Subsequently Offered for Sale			Q&A.86 #3
Scope of Accounting and Reporting Requirements	FAS86, ¶2	Co2.101	Q&A.86 #1-4
Timing of Capitalization of Costs	FAS86, ¶4	Co2.103	Q&A.86 #6-8
CONCEPTUAL FRAMEWORK			
As Basis for Standards	CON1, ¶3		
History of Need for	CON1, ¶57-60		
Not-for-Profit Organizations	CON4, ¶1-2		
Relation to Current Value	CON1, ¶2		
Relation to Financial Accounting Standards	CON1, ¶3		
CONDITIONAL CONTRACT			
Definition	FIN39, ¶3	B10.104	
CONDOMINIUMS			
See Real Estate: Sales Other Than Retail Land Sales			
CONGLOMERATES			
See Segment of Business Reporting			

See "Terminology" for references to defined terms presented in various accounting pronouncements.
See the Introduction to the Topical Index for details on the use of this index.

	Original Pronouncements	Current Text	EITF and Other

CONSERVATISM
Definition .... CON2, Glossary
Recognition Implication for Earnings .... CON5, ¶50
Relation to Reliability .... CON2, ¶91-97
CONSISTENCY
Accounting for Similar Circumstances .... CON2, ¶16
Definition .... CON2, Glossary
Relation to Comparability .... CON2, ¶120-122
Relation to Conservatism .... CON2, ¶91-97
CONSOLIDATED FINANCIAL STATEMENTS
Classification of Subsidiary's Loan Payable in Consolidated Balance Sheet When Subsidiary's and Parent's Fiscal Years Differ EITF.88-15
Fiscal Year of Parent and Subsidiary Differs
. . Classification of Subsidiary's Loan Payable in Consolidated Balance Sheet EITF.88-15
Specialized Accounting Principles of Subsidiaries
. . Small Business Investment Company ... EITF.85-12
. . Subsidiary Venture Capital Investment Company EITF.85-12
CONSOLIDATION
See Disclosure
See Earnings per Share
See Foreign Currency Translation
See Interim Financial Reporting
See Related Parties
See Segment of Business Reporting
Arbitrage Transactions of an Unconsolidated Subsidiary EITF.84-41
Classification of Subsidiary's Loan Payable in Consolidated Balance Sheet When Subsidiary's and Parent's Fiscal Years Differ EITF.88-15
Combined Statements
. . Commonly Controlled Enterprises .... ARB51, ¶22   C51.121
. . Intercompany Balances and Transactions .... ARB51, ¶23   C51.122
Consolidated Tax Return .... FAS109, ¶49   C51.108A
Controlling Financial Interest .... FAS94, ¶13   C51.102
Definition .... ARB51, ¶1   C51.401
Development Stage Enterprises .... FIN7, ¶4   De4.106
Different Fiscal Periods .... ARB51, ¶4   C51.107
Equity Method vs. Consolidated Statements .... FAS94, ¶15   I82.102

FAS–FASB Statements   FIN–FASB Interpretations   FTB–FASB Technical Bulletins
APB–APB Opinions   AIN–AICPA Interpretations   ARB–Accounting Research Bulletins
CON–FASB Concepts   EITF–EITF Issues   Q&A–FASB Special Reports

	Original Pronouncements	Current Text	EITF and Other
CONSOLIDATION—continued			
Fiscal Year of Parent and Subsidiary Differs			
. . Classification of Subsidiary's Loan Payable in Consolidated Balance Sheet			EITF.88-15
Foreign Subsidiaries			
. . Elimination of Write-ups	APB6, ¶17	D40.102	
Instantaneous In-Substance Defeasance by an Unconsolidated Subsidiary			EITF.84-41
Intercompany Balances and Transactions			
. . Combined Financial Statements	ARB51, ¶23	C51.122	
. . Income Taxes Paid on Intercompany Profits	ARB51, ¶17	C51.110	
. . Regulated Operations	FAS71, ¶16-17	Re6.126-127	
Limitations on Use of Equity Method	FAS94, ¶13	I82.102	
Minority Interests			
. . Allocation of Intercompany Profit Elimination	ARB51, ¶14	C51.115	
. . Losses in Minority Interest Exceed Equity Interest	ARB51, ¶15	C51.116	
Objectives	ARB51, ¶1	C51.101	
Oil and Gas Producing Activities	FAS69, ¶10	Oi5.160	
Parent and Subsidiary with Different Year-Ends			
. . Both Have Portfolios of Marketable Securities	ARB51, ¶4	C51.107	
Parent Company Statements	ARB51, ¶24	C51.123	
Policy for	ARB51, ¶5	C51.108	
Related Parties		R36.106	
Separate Statements of Subsidiaries			
. . Allocating Consolidated Tax Provision			EITF.86-9
. . Push-down Accounting			EITF.86-9
Separate vs. Consolidated Statements	FAS94, ¶13-14	C51.102-103	
. . Segment of Business Reporting	FAS14, ¶7	S20.108	
Shares of Parent Held by a Subsidiary	ARB51, ¶13	C51.114	
Special-Purpose Entities	FTB85-2, ¶3	C30.503	
. . Accounting for Lease Transactions			EITF.90-15
. . Collateralized Mortgage Obligation Issuer			EITF.85-28
. . Grantor Trusts			EITF.84-15

See "Terminology" for references to defined terms presented in various accounting pronouncements.
See the Introduction to the Topical Index for details on the use of this index.

	Original Pronouncements	Current Text	EITF and Other

CONSOLIDATION—continued

Special-Purpose Entities—continued

. . Grantor Trusts Owned by a Subsidiary .. | | | EITF.84-40

. . Sale of Loans to Special-Purpose Entities .... | | | EITF.84-30

Step Acquisition

. . Consolidation Procedure .... ARB51, ¶10-11 | C51.111-112 |

Subsidiary

. . Acquired in Year................................. ARB51, ¶10-11 | C51.111-112 |

. . Allocating Consolidated Tax Provision .... | | | EITF.86-9

. . Disposed of in Year............................. ARB51, ¶12 | C51.113 |

. . Investment in Parent Treasury Stock .... ARB51, ¶13 | C51.114 |

. . Stock Dividends.................................... ARB51, ¶18 | C51.117 |

. . Unconsolidated.................................... FAS14, ¶7 | S20.108 |

Subsidiary with No Equity Ownership .... | | | EITF.84-30

Temporary Control .... FAS94, ¶13 | C51.102 |

. . Sponsor Intends to Sell CMO Issuer..... | | | EITF.85-28

. . Subsidiary Acquired to Realize Parent's NOL Carryforward .... | | | EITF.84-33

Transactions Involving Special-Purpose Entities... | | | EITF.D-14

Unconsolidated Subsidiaries in Consolidated Statements

. . Disclosure about Formerly Unconsolidated Subsidiaries .... FAS94, ¶14 | C51.120A |

. . Limitations on Use of Equity Method .. FAS94, ¶13 | C51.102 |

Users' Needs for Information...................... FAS94, ¶14 | C51.120A |

CONSTRUCTION CONTRACTS

See Contractor Accounting: Construction-Type Contracts

See Contractor Accounting: Government Contracts

See Income Taxes

Accounting Policy Disclosure..................... APB22, ¶13 | A10.106 |

Profit Recognition

. . Construction of House on Builder's Lot... | | | EITF.86-7

CONSTRUCTION LOANS

Balance Sheet Classification .... FAS6, ¶1 | B05.110 |

CONSTRUCTIVE OBLIGATIONS

Definition .... CON6, ¶40

CONSUMER PRICE INDEX

See Changing Prices: Reporting Their Effects in Financial Reports

CONSUMPTION OF BENEFITS

Guidance in Applying Recognition Criteria to Expenses .... CON5, ¶86

FAS–FASB Statements   FIN–FASB Interpretations   FTB–FASB Technical Bulletins
APB–APB Opinions   AIN–AICPA Interpretations   ARB–Accounting Research Bulletins
CON–FASB Concepts   EITF–EITF Issues   Q&A–FASB Special Reports

	Original Pronouncements	Current Text	EITF and Other
CONTINGENCIES			
See Commitments: Long-Term Obligations			
See Disclosure			
See Financial Instruments			
See Impairment: Loans			
See Quasi Reorganizations			
See Receivables Sold with Recourse			
Accounting for Estimated Payments in Connection with the Coal Industry Retiree Health Benefit Act of 1992			EITF.92-13
Accounting for Multiple-Year Retrospectively Rated Contracts by Ceding and Assuming Enterprises............			EITF.93-6
....			EITF.D-35
See Insurance Industry			
Accounting for Multiple-Year Retrospectively Rated Insurance Contracts by Insurance Enterprises and Other Enterprises.......................................			EITF.93-14
Accounting for Restructuring Charges			EITF.94-3
Business Combinations	AIN-APB16, #30-31	B50.106	
....	APB16, ¶47	B50.135-144	
....	APB16, ¶77-86	B50.148-150	
....	FAS38, ¶5-6	B50.613-623	
....	FAS38, ¶23		
Contingent Stock Purchase Warrants			EITF.84-8
Debt: Restructurings....................................	FAS15, ¶22	D22.118	
....	FAS15, ¶36	D22.132	
Definition			
. . Contingencies	FAS5, ¶1	C59.401	
. . Indirect Guarantee of Indebtedness of Others..	FIN34, ¶2	C59.402	
. . Probable	FAS5, ¶3	C59.403	
. . Reasonably Possible.............................	FAS5, ¶3	C59.404	
. . Remote...	FAS5, ¶3	C59.405	
Description of Term....................................	FAS5, ¶1	C59.101	
Funded Catastrophe Covers			EITF.93-6
Gain Contingencies	FAS5, ¶17	C59.118	
General or Unspecified Business Risks	FAS5, ¶14	C59.116	
Interim Financial Reporting	APB28, ¶22	I73.125	
Lease Rentals..	FAS29, ¶15-17	L10.164-166	
Liability Recognition for Costs to Exit an Activity...			EITF.94-3
....			EITF.95-3
Loan Covenant Restrictions on Distribution	FAS5, ¶18-19	C59.120	
Loan Guarantees			
. . Recognition of Liability			EITF.85-20
. . Revenue Recognition of Fees...............			EITF.85-20

See "Terminology" for references to defined terms presented in various accounting pronouncements.
See the Introduction to the Topical Index for details on the use of this index.

	Original Pronouncements	Current Text	EITF and Other

CONTINGENCIES—continued

	Original Pronouncements	Current Text	EITF and Other
Loss Contingencies	FAS5, ¶2	C59.105-107	
	FAS5, ¶4	C59.121-151	
	FAS5, ¶8		
	FAS5, ¶21-45		
	FAS113, ¶30		
	FAS114, ¶21		
	FIN14, ¶4-7		
. . Accounting by Insureds for Claims-Made Insurance Policies			EITF.86-12
. . Accounting for Environmental Liabilities			EITF.93-5
. . Appropriations of Retained Earnings	FAS5, ¶15	C59.117	
. . Business Combinations, Contingent Consideration	APB16, ¶77	C59.119	
. . Business Combinations, Preacquisition Contingencies	APB16, ¶77	C59.119	
. . Business Interruption	FAS5, ¶29-30	C59.135-136	
. . Catastrophe Losses of Property and Casualty Insurance Enterprises	FAS5, ¶40-43	C59.146-149	
. . Catastrophe Losses of Property and Liability Insurance Enterprises	FAS5, ¶4	C59.122	
. . Claims and Assessments	FAS5, ¶4	C59.122	
. . Damage to Property of Others	FAS5, ¶29-30	C59.135-136	
. . Examples	FAS5, ¶16	C59.103	
. . Expropriation of Assets	FAS5, ¶4	C59.122	
	FAS5, ¶32	C59.138	
. . Future Injury to Others	FAS5, ¶29-30	C59.135-136	
. . Guarantees of Indebtedness	FAS5, ¶4	C59.122	
. . Guarantees of Indebtedness to Others	FAS5, ¶12	C59.113	
. . Guarantees to Repurchase Receivables Sold	FAS5, ¶4	C59.122	
. . Hazards Such as Fire or Explosion	FAS5, ¶4	C59.122	
. . Indirect Guarantees of Indebtedness to Others	FIN34, ¶2-3	C59.114	
. . Litigation, Claims, and Assessments	FAS5, ¶33-39	C59.139-145	
. . Litigation, Pending or Threatened	FAS5, ¶4	C59.122	
. . Payments to Insurance Companies That May Not Involve Transfer of Risk	FAS5, ¶44-45	C59.150-151	Q&A.113 #26
	FAS113, ¶18	In6.182	
	FAS113, ¶30		
. . Range of Loss	FIN14, ¶3-7	C59.107	
		C59.124-127	
. . Receivables, Collectibility	FAS5, ¶4	C59.122	EITF.85-44
	FAS5, ¶22-23	C59.128-129	EITF.87-5
	FAS114, ¶21		
. . Relation to Estimates	FAS5, ¶2	C59.121	
. . Relation to Receivables	FAS5, ¶2	C59.121	
. . Return of Restricted Contribution	FAS116, ¶65-66	C67.107	

FAS–FASB Statements   FIN–FASB Interpretations   FTB–FASB Technical Bulletins
APB–APB Opinions   AIN–AICPA Interpretations   ARB–Accounting Research Bulletins
CON–FASB Concepts   EITF–EITF Issues   Q&A–FASB Special Reports

	Original Pronouncements	Current Text	EITF and Other
CONTINGENCIES—continued			
Loss Contingencies—continued			
. . Risk of Loss or Damage of Enterprise Property	FAS5, ¶27-28	C59.133-134	
. . Sale of Marketable Securities with a Put Option			EITF.84-5
. . Standby Letters of Credit	FAS5, ¶4	C59.113	
	FAS5, ¶12	C59.122	
. . Subsequent Events	FAS5, ¶11	C59.112	
. . Warranties and Product Defects	FAS5, ¶4	C59.122	
	FAS5, ¶24-26	C59.130-132	
. . Write-down of Operating Assets	FAS5, ¶31	C59.137	
Loss Contingency Classifications			
. . Probable	FAS5, ¶3	C59.104	
. . Reasonably Possible	FAS5, ¶3	C59.104	
. . Remote	FAS5, ¶3	C59.104	
Loss Contingency on Debt Instruments with Contingent Payments			EITF.86-28
Losses			
. . Appropriations of Retained Earnings	FAS5, ¶15	R70.103	
Measuring Loss Accruals by Transferors for Transfers of Receivables with Recourse			EITF.92-2
Medicare Retroactive Wage Adjustments			EITF.86-2
Other Than Loss Contingencies			
. . Business Combinations	APB16, ¶77	C59.119	
	FAS38, ¶4		
. . Collateral for Loans and Commitments	FAS5, ¶19	C59.120	
. . Letters of Credit	FAS5, ¶18-19	C59.120	
Preacquisition Contingencies	FAS38, ¶4	C59.119	
Real Estate			
. . Future Improvement Costs	FAS66, ¶60	R10.154	
	FAS66, ¶75-76	Re1.173-174	
Recognition of Liabilities in Connection with a Purchase Business Combination			EITF.95-3
Regulated Operations	FAS71, ¶38-39	Re6.143-144	
Relation to Forms of Employee Compensation	FAS5, ¶7	C59.102	
	FAS112, ¶10		
Relation to Postemployment Benefits	FAS112, ¶10	C59.102	
Relation to Pension Costs	FAS5, ¶7	C59.122	
Restrictions on Dividend Distribution	FAS5, ¶18-19	C59.120	
Revenue Recognition When Right of Return Exists	FAS48, ¶7	R75.108	
Scope of Accounting and Reporting Requirements	FAS5, ¶6-7	C59.102	
	FAS5, ¶31		
	FAS5, ¶102		
	FAS112, ¶10		

See "Terminology" for references to defined terms presented in various accounting pronouncements.
See the Introduction to the Topical Index for details on the use of this index.

	Original Pronouncements	Current Text	EITF and Other

CONTINGENCY RESERVES
See Contingencies
See Retained Earnings
CONTINGENT ASSETS/LIABILITIES
See Business Combinations
CONTINGENT CONSIDERATION
See Business Combinations
CONTINGENT LIABILITIES
See Contingencies
CONTINUATION OF BENEFITS
See Postemployment Benefits
CONTINUING OPERATIONS
See Income Statement Presentation:
  Discontinued Operations

Interim Financial Reporting	FAS16, ¶3	A35.109	
	FAS16, ¶15	A35.111	
Relation to Discontinued Operations	APB30, ¶8	I13.105	

CONTRACTOR ACCOUNTING:
  CONSTRUCTION-TYPE
  CONTRACTS
See Disclosure

Accounting Changes	APB20, ¶27	A06.123	
Commitments			
. . Disclosure If Extraordinary	ARB45, ¶16	Co4.113	
Deferred Taxes	FAS37, ¶22	I27.208	
	FAS109, ¶287-288		
Interim Billings	ARB45, ¶2	Co4.102	
Prior-Period Adjustments	APB20, ¶27	A35.114	
Research and Development	FAS2, ¶2	R50.102	
Revenue Recognition Concept	CON5, ¶84		
Revenue Recognition Methods			
. . Completed Contract	ARB45, ¶9-12	Co4.106-109	
. . Percentage-of-Completion	ARB45, ¶4-6	Co4.103-105	
. . Selection of Method	ARB45, ¶15	Co4.110	
Scope of Accounting and Reporting			
Requirements	ARB45, ¶1-2	Co4.101-102	

CONTRACTOR ACCOUNTING:
  GOVERNMENT CONTRACTS
See Disclosure

Cost-Plus-Fixed-Fee Government			
Contracts	ARB43, Ch.11A, ¶10	Co5.101-109	
	ARB43, Ch.11A, ¶15-22		
Deferred Taxes	FAS37, ¶22	I27.208	
	FAS109, ¶287-288		
Price Renegotiation	ARB43, Ch.11A, ¶16	Co5.103	
Research and Development	FAS2, ¶2	R50.102	
Terminated War and Defense Contracts	ARB43, Ch.11C, ¶1-2	Co5.110-129	
	ARB43, Ch.11C, ¶12-13		
	ARB43, Ch.11C, ¶16-25		
	ARB43, Ch.11C, ¶27-32		

FAS–FASB Statements	FIN–FASB Interpretations	FTB–FASB Technical Bulletins
APB–APB Opinions	AIN–AICPA Interpretations	ARB–Accounting Research Bulletins
CON–FASB Concepts	EITF–EITF Issues	Q&A–FASB Special Reports

	Original Pronouncements	Current Text	EITF and Other

CONTRIBUTED CAPITAL (SURPLUS)
See Additional Paid-in Capital
CONTRIBUTED SERVICES
See Contributions
CONTRIBUTIONS
See Disclosure
Collections—Works of Art, Historical
  Treasures, and Similar Assets

	Original Pronouncements	Current Text	EITF and Other
. . Definition	FAS116, ¶128	C67.111	
	FAS116, ¶209	C67.401	
. . Examples of Contributed Collections	FAS116, ¶185-189	C67.137-141	
. . Financial Statement Presentation and			
Disclosure	FAS116, ¶26-27	C67.123-124	
	FAS116, ¶141	No5.142	
. . Optional Recognition and			
Capitalization of Contributed			
Collections	FAS116, ¶11-13	C67.111-113	
	FAS116, ¶135		
Conditional Promises to Give	FAS116, ¶22-23	C67.118-120	Q&A.116/117 #7-9
	FAS116, ¶25	C67.122	
	FAS116, ¶63		
	FAS116, ¶81		
Contributed Services			
. . Criteria for Recognition	FAS116, ¶9	C67.109	Q&A.116/117 #3-4
. . Examples	FAS116, ¶195-206	C67.147-158	
. . Recognition by Donee	FAS116, ¶9-10	C67.109-110	
	FAS116, ¶123		
. . Recognition by Donor	FAS116, ¶18	C67.114	
Definition	FAS116, ¶209	C67.403	
Discounting Receivable and Payable			
. . Unconditional Promise to Give Cash	FAS116, ¶20	C67.116	
Donor-imposed Conditions	FAS116, ¶7	C67.106	
	FAS116, ¶60		
. . Definition	FAS116, ¶209	C67.404	
. . Recognition of Conditional Promises			
to Give	FAS116, ¶22-23	C67.118-120	
	FAS116, ¶63		
	FAS116, ¶81		
. . Transfer of Assets with Conditions	FAS116, ¶22	C67.119	
	FAS116, ¶63		
	FAS116, ¶81		
Donor-imposed Restrictions	FAS116, ¶7	C67.107	
. . As Basis for Classification of			
Contributions	FAS116, ¶14-16	No5.143-145	
	FAS116, ¶146		
. . Definition	FAS116, ¶209	C67.405	Q&A.116/117 #8
. . Failure to Comply with Restrictions	FAS116, ¶65-66	C67.107	
. . Permanent Restrictions	FAS117, ¶168	No5.406	
. . Temporary Restrictions	FAS117, ¶168	No5.410	

See "Terminology" for references to defined terms presented in various accounting pronouncements.
See the Introduction to the Topical Index for details on the use of this index.

	Original Pronouncements	Current Text	EITF and Other

CONTRIBUTIONS—continued

Donor-imposed Restrictions—continued

. . With Donor-imposed Condition............	FAS116, ¶63	C67.119	
....	FAS116, ¶81		
Examples...	FAS116, ¶173-208	C67.125-160	
. . Annuity Trust, Charitable Remainder ...	FAS116, ¶177-178	C67.129-130	
. . Bequest	FAS116, ¶207-208	C67.159-160	
. . Real Estate	FAS116, ¶183-184	C67.135-136	
....	FAS116, ¶192-194	C67.144-146	
Expiration of Donor-imposed Restrictions			
. . Not-for-Profit Organizations	FAS116, ¶17	No5.146-147	
....	FAS116, ¶166		
Gift..			Q&A.116/117 #1
Glossary	FAS116, ¶209	C67.401-411	
Grants, Sponsorships, Memberships...........			Q&A.116/117 #2
Implementation Guidance			Q&A.116/117 #18
Interest Element of Contributions			
Receivable and Payable	FAS116, ¶20	C67.116	
Measurement at Fair Value			
. . Nonmonetary Transactions.....................	FAS116, ¶19-21	C67.115-117	
Nonmonetary Transactions..........................	FAS116, ¶5	C67.104	
....	FAS116, ¶19	C67.115	
Pledges..			Q&A.116/117 #5
			Q&A.116/117 #7
Promises to Give..	FAS116, ¶6	C67.105	Q&A.116/117 #5-6
. . Conditional Promises to Give	FAS116, ¶22-23	C67.118-120	Q&A.116/117 #7-9
. . Disclosures...	FAS116, ¶24-25	C67.121-122	
....	FAS116, ¶117		
. . Legal Enforceability	FAS116, ¶6	C67.105	
....	FAS116, ¶108		
. . Multiyear Promise to Give			Q&A.116/117 #6
. . Present Value of Cash Flows.................	FAS116, ¶20	C67.116	
. . Unconditional Promises to Give	FAS116, ¶5-6	C67.104-105	Q&A.116/117 #6-7
			Q&A.116/117 #9
Recognition by Donee	FAS116, ¶8-11	C67.108-113	
....	FAS116, ¶13-16	No5.143-145	
....	FAS116, ¶123		
Recognition by Donor	FAS116, ¶18	C67.114	
Refundable Advances			Q&A.116/117 #10
Relation to Equity (Net Assets) and			
Liabilities..	CON6, ¶56-59		
Scope of Accounting and Reporting			
Requirements	FAS116, ¶1	C67.101-103	
....	FAS116, ¶3-4		
....	FAS116, ¶49-51		
....	FAS116, ¶53-54		
Transition and Adoption of FASB			
Statements 116 and 117			Q&A.116/117 #13
Unconditional Promises to Give	FAS116, ¶5-6	C67.104-105	Q&A.116/117 #6-7
....	FAS116, ¶24	C67.121	Q&A.116/117 #9

FAS–FASB Statements ·   FIN–FASB Interpretations   FTB–FASB Technical Bulletins
APB–APB Opinions   AIN–AICPA Interpretations   ARB–Accounting Research Bulletins
CON–FASB Concepts   EITF–EITF Issues   Q&A–FASB Special Reports

	Original Pronouncements	Current Text	EITF and Other
CONTROL			
See Consolidation			
See Investments: Equity Method			
By a Particular Enterprise	CON6, ¶183-189		
Definition	FAS57, ¶24	R36.402	
Future Economic Benefits			
. . Relation to Legal Rights	CON6, ¶186-189		
CONVERSION			
See Capital Stock: Capital Transactions			
See Debt: Convertible Debt and Debt with Stock Purchase Warrants			
See Earnings per Share			
See Foreign Currency Translation			
Definition	FAS52, ¶162	F60.402	
CONVERSION FROM MUTUAL OWNERSHIP TO STOCK OWNERSHIP			
Savings and Loan Association			
. . Earnings per Share			EITF.84-22
CONVERSION OF DEBT			
See Debt: Convertible Debt and Debt with Stock Purchase Warrants			
See Earnings per Share			
Accrued Interest upon Conversion			EITF.85-17
Converted under Sweetened Terms			EITF.84-3
Induced Conversions			
. . Recognition of Expense upon Conversion			EITF.84-3
CONVERTIBLE DEBT			
See Capital Stock: Capital Transactions			
See Debt: Convertible Debt and Debt with Stock Purchase Warrants			
See Earnings per Share			
See Financial Instruments			
See Interest: Imputation of an Interest Cost			
Characteristics	CON6, ¶55		
Definition	APB14, ¶3	D10.101	
Recording a Premium Put Option			EITF.85-29
CONVERTIBLE PREFERRED STOCK			
See Capital Stock: Preferred Stock			
See Earnings per Share			
See Financial Instruments			
COOPERATIVES			
See Business Combinations			
Earnings per Share			
. . Exemption from Requirements	APB15, ¶6	E09.102	
CORPORATE JOINT VENTURES			
See Income Taxes			
Definition	APB18, ¶3	I82.401	

See "Terminology" for references to defined terms presented in various accounting pronouncements.
See the Introduction to the Topical Index for details on the use of this index.

	Original Pronouncements	Current Text	EITF and Other

CORPORATE PENSION FUNDS
See Pension Costs
CORPORATE READJUSTMENTS
See Quasi Reorganizations
CORPORATE RETIREMENT PLANS
See Pension Costs
See Postretirement Benefits Other Than
  Pensions
COST
Definition .... CON6, ¶26
COST ALLOCATION
See Business Combinations
See Capital Stock: Stock Dividends and
  Stock Splits
See Intangible Assets
See Interest: Capitalization of Interest
  Costs
See Interim Financial Reporting
See Real Estate: Costs and Initial
  Operations of Real Estate Projects
See Segment of Business Reporting
COST-BENEFIT RELATIONSHIP
Constraint.. CON5, ¶63
In FASB Standards .... CON2, ¶143-144
Not-for-Profit Organizations, Financial
  Information.. CON4, ¶28
Of Providing Information........................... CON2, ¶133-144
COST METHOD OF CARRYING
  INVESTMENTS
See Insurance Industry
See Investments: Equity Method
COST OF GOODS SOLD
See Debt: Product Financing
  Arrangements
See Interim Financial Reporting
COST OF LIVING INDEX (CPI(U))
See Changing Prices: Reporting Their
  Effects in Financial Reports
COST-PLUS-FIXED-FEE
  CONTRACTS
See Contractor Accounting: Construction-
  Type Contracts
See Contractor Accounting: Government
  Contracts
COST RECOVERY METHOD
See Insurance Industry
See Oil and Gas Producing Activities
See Real Estate
See Revenue Recognition
Definition .... FAS60, ¶66   In6.406

FAS–FASB Statements   FIN–FASB Interpretations   FTB–FASB Technical Bulletins
APB–APB Opinions   AIN–AICPA Interpretations   ARB–Accounting Research Bulletins
CON–FASB Concepts   EITF–EITF Issues   Q&A–FASB Special Reports

	Original Pronouncements	Current Text	EITF and Other

COST RECOVERY
METHOD—continued
Franchise Fee Revenue............................. FAS45, ¶6 — Fr3.102
.... FAS45, ¶21 — Fr3.117
Relation to Loss Contingencies.................. FAS5, ¶23 — C59.129
COVENANTS
Grace Period within Which to Cure a
  Violation.. — — EITF.86-30
Material Adverse Change Clause
. . Effect on Accounting for Sale of
      Short-Term Loan Made under a
      Long-Term Commitment.................... — — EITF.87-30
Objective Covenants
. . Effect on Accounting for Sale of
      Short-Term Loan Made under a
      Long-Term Commitment.................... — — EITF.87-30
Subjective Covenants
. . Effect on Accounting for Sale of
      Short-Term Loan Made under a
      Long-Term Commitment.................... — — EITF.87-30
Violation Waived by Creditor...................... — — EITF.86-30
CREDIT CARD FEES
See Lending Activities
CREDIT CARD RECEIVABLES
Classification in Cash Flows Statement...... FAS95, ¶13 — C25.111
Credit Card Portfolio .... — — EITF.88-20
.... — — EITF.88-22
CREDITORS
See Balance Sheet Classification: Current
  Assets and Liabilities
See Debt: Restructurings
See Impairment: Loans
Information Needs..................................... CON1, ¶41
CREDIT RISK
See Financial Instruments
CREDIT UNIONS
See Banking and Thrift Industries
See Earnings per Share
See Financial Instruments
See Impairment: Loans
See Lending Activities
Balance Sheet Presentation of Savings
  Accounts.. — — EITF.89-3
Cash Flows Statement .... FAS104, ¶7 — C25.111A
.... — Bt7.123
CUMULATIVE ACCOUNTING
ADJUSTMENTS
Catch-up Adjustment................................. CON5, ¶34
Definition.. CON5, ¶42
Description.. CON5, ¶43

See "Terminology" for references to defined terms presented in various accounting pronouncements.
See the Introduction to the Topical Index for details on the use of this index.

	Original Pronouncements	Current Text	EITF and Other

CUMULATIVE ACCOUNTING ADJUSTMENTS—continued

Illustration of Relationship to Earnings ...... CON5, ¶44

CURRENCY RESTRICTIONS

See Foreign Currency Translation

See Foreign Operations

CURRENT ASSETS

See Balance Sheet Classification: Current Assets and Liabilities

CURRENT COST ACCOUNTING

See Changing Prices: Reporting Their Effects in Financial Reports

CURRENT LIABILITIES

See Balance Sheet Classification: Current Assets and Liabilities

CURRENT MARKET VALUE

See Fair Value

See Farms

See Futures Contracts

See Inventory

Recognition and Measurement

. . Measurement Attribute .... CON5, ¶67-69

CURRENT OPERATING PERFORMANCE

See Extraordinary Items

See Income Statement Presentation: Discontinued Operations

See Infrequent Items

See Unusual Items

CURRENT RATE METHOD

See Foreign Currency Translation

CURRENT REPLACEMENT COST

See Changing Prices: Reporting Their Effects in Financial Reports

Recognition and Measurement

. . Measurement Attribute .... CON5, ¶67

.... CON5, ¶69

CURTAILMENTS (OF DEFINED BENEFIT PENSION PLANS)

See Pension Costs

CURTAILMENTS (OF DEFINED BENEFIT POSTRETIREMENT PLANS)

See Postretirement Benefits Other Than Pensions

CUSTOMERS

See Major Customers

(The next page is T-97.)

	Original Pronouncements	Current Text	EITF and Other
DAMAGE			
See Contingencies			
See Inventory			
Involuntary Conversions	FIN30, ¶3	N35.117	
DEBT			
See Commitments: Long-Term Obligations			
See Debt: Convertible Debt and Debt with Stock Purchase Warrants			
See Debt: Extinguishments			
See Debt Issue Cost			
See Debt: Product Financing Arrangements			
See Debt: Restructurings			
See Financial Instruments			
See Interest Expense			
See Offsetting			
See Sale vs. Financing			
Accounting for Debt Securities Reported as Loans			EITF.D-39
Accounting for Dual Currency Bonds			EITF.93-10
Accounting for Special Assessments and Tax Increment Financing Entities (TIFEs)			EITF.91-10
Brady Bonds			EITF.D-39
Classification (Current vs. Noncurrent)			
. . Debt When Violation Is Waived by Creditor			EITF.86-30
. . Demand Notes with Repayment Terms			EITF.86-5
. . Increasing-Rate Debt			EITF.86-15
. . Subjective Acceleration Clauses and Debt Classification			EITF.D-23
. . Subsidiary's Loan Payable in Consolidated Balance Sheet When Subsidiary's and Parent's Fiscal Years Differ			EITF.88-15
Classification (Debt vs. Equity)			
. . Debt Repayable by a Capital Stock Transaction			EITF.84-40
. . Put Warrants			EITF.88-9
Classification of Interest-Only Securities as Held-to-Maturity			EITF.94-4
Debt Payable in a Commodity			
. . Accounting for Changes in Commodity Value			EITF.86-28
Debt with Both Guaranteed and Contingent Payments			
. . Allocating Proceeds between Debt and Contingent Right			EITF.86-28

FAS–FASB Statements FIN–FASB Interpretations FTB–FASB Technical Bulletins
APB–APB Opinions AIN–AICPA Interpretations ARB–Accounting Research Bulletins
CON–FASB Concepts EITF–EITF Issues Q&A–FASB Special Reports

	Original Pronouncements	Current Text	EITF and Other
DEBT—continued			
Deferred Interest Rate Setting Arrangements			EITF.84-14
. . Forward Commitments As Surrogate for Deferred Rate Setting			EITF.86-26
Equity Certificates of Deposit			
. . Recognizing Contingent Interest Expense			EITF.84-31
Equity Commitment Notes			
. . Earnings per Share Computations			EITF.85-18
Equity Contract Notes			
. . Earnings per Share Computations			EITF.85-18
Exchangeable for Stock of Unaffiliated Enterprise			EITF.85-9
Foreign Currency Swaps			
. . Offsetting			EITF.86-25
Foreign Debt-for-Equity Swaps			EITF.87-12
Holding Company Debt			
. . Leveraged Buyout Holding Company Debt			EITF.84-23
. . Push-down of Parent Company's Debt to Subsidiary			EITF.84-42
Indexed Debt Instruments			EITF.86-28
. . Convertible Bonds with Issuer Option to Settle for Cash upon Conversion			EITF.90-19
Interest Expense on Increasing-Rate Debt			EITF.86-15
Interest Rate Swap Transactions			EITF.84-7
			EITF.84-36
			EITF.88-8
Leveraged Employee Stock Ownership Plans (ESOPs)			
. . Recognition by Sponsor of ESOP Debt			EITF.89-10
. . Recognition of Compensation Expense When There Is Prepayment of Debt by Sponsor			EITF.89-8
Long-Term Debt			
. . Disclosure Requirements	FAS47, ¶10	C32.105	EITF.86-30
Modification of Debt Terms			EITF.86-18
			EITF.87-18
			EITF.87-19
			EITF.89-15
. . Debtor Experiencing Financial Difficulties			EITF.89-15
Mortgage Swaps			EITF.88-8
Nonrecourse Debt			
. . Debtor's Accounting for Forfeiture of Real Estate Subject to a Nonrecourse Mortgage			EITF.91-2

See "Terminology" for references to defined terms presented in various accounting pronouncements.
See the Introduction to the Topical Index for details on the use of this index.

	Original Pronouncements	Current Text	EITF and Other
DEBT—continued			
Nonrecourse Debt—continued			
. . Grantor Trust...			EITF.84-15
. . Offsetting with Lease Receivables........			EITF.84-25
Offsetting			
. . Asset Puttable to Creditor to Satisfy Debt..			EITF.84-11
. . Nonrecourse Debt with Lease Receivables			EITF.84-25
. . Note Monetization..................................			EITF.84-11
Zero Coupon Bonds			
. . Cash Yield Test for Determining Common Stock Equivalents			EITF.84-16
DEBT: CONVERTIBLE DEBT AND DEBT WITH STOCK PURCHASE WARRANTS			
See Capital Stock: Capital Transactions			
See Earnings per Share			
See Financial Instruments			
Conversion of Debt.....................................	AIN-APB26, #1	D10.501	
Conversion of Debt According to Terms of Issuance	AIN-APB26, #1	D10.103B	
....	FAS84, ¶22-23	D10.501	
Convertible Bonds with Issuer Option to Settle for Cash upon Conversion			EITF.90-19
Convertible Debt...	APB14, ¶3-4	D10.101-103	
....	APB14, ¶7		
....	APB14, ¶12		
. . Accrued Interest upon Conversion........			EITF.85-17
. . Converted under Sweetened Terms			EITF.84-3
. . Definition..	APB14, ¶3	D10.101	
. . Induced Conversions			EITF.84-3
. . Recording a Premium Put Option			EITF.85-29
Debt Exchangeable for Stock of Unaffiliated Enterprise			
. . Accounting for Exchangeability Feature...			EITF.85-9
Debt with Put Warrants...............................			EITF.88-9
Debt with Stock Purchase Warrants	APB14, ¶13	D10.104-106	
....	APB14, ¶16-17		
. . Warrant Includes Put for Stock Purchased			EITF.86-35
Induced Conversions	FAS84, ¶2-4	D10.103A-103D	EITF.84-3
. . Examples of Computing Expense	FAS84, ¶7-13	D10.108-114	
. . Income Statement Display of Expense .	FAS84, ¶3	D10.103C	
. . Measurement Date................................	FAS84, ¶4	D10.103D	
. . Recognition of Expense upon Conversion	FAS84, ¶3	D10.103C	
Other Types of Debt Securities	APB14, ¶18	D10.107	

FAS–FASB Statements	FIN–FASB Interpretations	FTB–FASB Technical Bulletins
APB–APB Opinions	AIN–AICPA Interpretations	ARB–Accounting Research Bulletins
CON–FASB Concepts	EITF–EITF Issues	Q&A–FASB Special Reports

	Original Pronouncements	Current Text	EITF and Other
DEBT: CONVERTIBLE DEBT AND DEBT WITH STOCK PURCHASE WARRANTS—continued			
Scope of Accounting and Reporting Requirements	FAS84, ¶2	D10.103A-103B	
	FAS84, ¶22-23		
	FAS84, ¶29		
	FAS84, ¶33		
DEBT DISCOUNT			
Qualification as an Asset	CON6, ¶235-236		
DEBT: EXTINGUISHMENTS			
See Debt: Convertible Debt and Debt with Stock Purchase Warrants			
See Disclosure			
See Offsetting			
See Troubled Debt Restructuring			
Banker's Acceptances			
. . Risk Participations			EITF.85-34
Capitalized Leases	FAS76, ¶37	D14.102A	
Convertible Bonds with Issuer Option to Settle for Cash upon Conversion			EITF.90-19
Convertible Debentures	FAS76, ¶1	D14.102A	
. . Converted under Sweetened Terms			EITF.84-3
. . Induced Conversions			EITF.84-3
Debt Purchased by Issuer's Agent			EITF.87-20
Debt Tendered to Exercise Warrants	AIN-APB26, #1	D14.505-506	
Defeasance	FAS76, ¶14	D14.102A	
Defeasance and In-Substance Defeasance			
. . Assessing Remoteness of Risk of Trust Assets	FTB84-4, ¶5-9	D14.511-513	
. . Assets Reacquired from Trust by Debtor			EITF.86-36
. . Consolidation of Subsidiary after Instantaneous Defeasance			EITF.84-41
. . Costs Related to Placing Assets in Trust in an In-Substance Defeasance	FAS76, ¶5	D14.102C	
. . Criteria	FAS76, ¶3	D14.102A	
	FAS76, ¶25-26		
	FAS76, ¶37		
. . In-Substance Defeasance of Callable Debt	FTB84-4, ¶10	D14.515-518	
	FTB84-4, ¶12-14		
. . Instantaneous In-Substance Defeasance	FTB84-4, ¶1	D14.507-510	
	FTB84-4, ¶3-5		
. . Invasion of a Defeasance Trust			EITF.86-36
. . Partial Defeasance	FAS76, ¶36	D14.102D	

See "Terminology" for references to defined terms presented in various accounting pronouncements.
See the Introduction to the Topical Index for details on the use of this index.

	Original Pronouncements	Current Text	EITF and Other
DEBT: EXTINGUISHMENTS—continued			
Defeasance and In-Substance Defeasance—continued			
. . Restrictions on the Nature of Assets in Trust in an In-Substance Defeasance .	FAS76, ¶4	D14.102B	
	FAS76, ¶31-32		
	FAS76, ¶35		
. . Special-Purpose Borrowings			EITF.84-26
Definition			
. . Defeasance	FAS76, ¶14	D14.102A	
. . In-Substance Defeasance	FAS76, ¶14	D14.401B	
	FAS76, ¶22		
. . Instantaneous In-Substance Defeasance	FTB84-4, ¶2	D14.401A	
. . Net Carrying Amount	APB26, ¶3	D14.402	
. . Reacquisition Price	APB26, ¶3	D14.403	
Employer's Debt Contributed to ESOP or Defined Contribution Plan			
. . Excess Assets Not Allocated to Participants			EITF.86-27
Exchanges of Debt Instruments			EITF.86-18
Foreclosure on Collateral			EITF.87-18
Gain (Loss) Recognition	APB26, ¶20-21	D14.103-104	
Gain (Loss) Recognition on Special-Purpose Borrowings			EITF.84-26
Income Statement Classification of Gains (Losses)			
. . Extraordinary Items	FAS4, ¶10	D14.105-106	
	FAS64, ¶4	I17.113	
. . Sinking-Fund Requirements	FAS64, ¶4	D14.105	
Liquidation of Collateral			EITF.87-19
Modification of Debt Terms			EITF.86-18
			EITF.87-18
			EITF.87-19
			EITF.89-15
. . Debtor Experiencing Financial Difficulties			EITF.89-15
Reacquired Debt Previously Extinguished in an In-Substance Defeasance	FAS76, ¶33	D14.106A	EITF.86-36
Regulated Operations	FAS71, ¶35-37	Re6.140-142	
Scope of Accounting and Reporting Requirements	APB26, ¶19	D14.101-102	
	FAS76, ¶1		
	FAS76, ¶7		
Substitution of Debtors			EITF.87-19
DEBT ISSUE COST			
Amortization Period for Issue Costs Associated with Increasing-Rate Debt			EITF.86-15
Characteristics	CON6, ¶237		

	Original Pronouncements	Current Text	EITF and Other

DEBT ISSUE COST—continued

Statement Presentation of Discount and
  Premium .... APB21, ¶16   I69.109

DEBT ISSUED WITH STOCK PURCHASE WARRANTS

Imputed Interest
  See Interest: Imputation of an Interest
    Cost

DEBT PREMIUM

Qualification as an Asset .... CON6, ¶238

DEBT: PRODUCT FINANCING ARRANGEMENTS

Accounting by Sponsor .... FAS49, ¶8-9   D18.106-107
. . Capitalization of Interest Cost .... FAS49, ¶9   D18.107
Characteristics .... FAS49, ¶6   D18.104-105
 .... FAS49, ¶22

Definition
. . Product Financing Arrangements .... FAS49, ¶3   D18.401

Different from Long-Term Unconditional
  Purchase Obligations .... FAS49, ¶4   D18.102
 .... FAS49, ¶20   D18.105
 .... FAS49, ¶22

Illustrations .... FAS49, ¶25-31   D18.108-114
Relation to Revenue Recognition .... FAS49, ¶5-6   D18.103-104

Scope of Accounting and Reporting
  Requirements .... FAS49, ¶3   D18.101

DEBT: RESTRUCTURINGS

See Disclosure
See Financial Instruments
See Impairment: Loans
Accounting by Creditors .... FAS15, ¶27-42   D22.123-146
 .... FAS91, ¶14
 .... FAS114, ¶22

. . Accounting for Conversion of a Loan
    into a Debt Security in a Debt
    Restructuring EITF.94-8
. . Combination of Types .... FAS15, ¶33   D22.129
 .... FAS114, ¶22   D22.140
. . Contingent Payments .... FAS15, ¶22   D22.118
. . Contingent Receivables .... FAS15, ¶36   D22.132
. . Estimating Cash Receipts .... FAS15, ¶37   D22.133

See "Terminology" for references to defined terms presented in various accounting pronouncements.
See the Introduction to the Topical Index for details on the use of this index.

	Original Pronouncements	Current Text	EITF and Other
DEBT: RESTRUCTURINGS—continued			
Accounting by Creditors—continued			
. . Gains (Losses)	FAS15, ¶14-15	D22.110-111	
	FAS15, ¶18-19	D22.114-115	
	FAS15, ¶21	D22.117	
	FAS15, ¶32-33	D22.128-129	
	FAS15, ¶35-37	D22.131-133	
	FAS15, ¶39	D22.135	
	FAS114, ¶22	D22.140	
		D22.144	
. . In-Substance Foreclosure on Collateral			EITF.89-9
. . Interest Method	FAS15, ¶16	D22.112	
	FAS15, ¶30	D22.126	
. . Liquidation of Collateral			EITF.87-18
			EITF.87-19
. . Modification of Terms	FAS15, ¶30-32	D22.126-128	EITF.87-19
	FAS114, ¶22	D22.139	
. . Receipt of Assets in Full Satisfaction	FAS15, ¶28-29	D22.124-125	
	FAS121, ¶24		
. . Related Matters	FAS15, ¶34-39	D22.130-135	
	FAS114, ¶22	D22.142-144	
. . Substitution of Debtors			EITF.87-19
. . Use of Zero Coupon Bonds			EITF.87-18
Accounting by Debtors	FAS15, ¶12-24	D22.108-120	
. . Combination of Types	FAS15, ¶19	D22.115	
. . Granting Equity Interest	FAS15, ¶15	D22.111	
. . Modification of Terms	FAS15, ¶16-18	D22.112-114	
. . Related Matters	FAS15, ¶20-24	D22.116-120	
. . Transfer of Assets in Full Settlement	FAS15, ¶13-14	D22.109-110	
Accounting for Conversion of a Loan into a Debt Security in a Debt Restructuring			EITF.94-8
Bankruptcies	FAS15, ¶10	D22.103	
Classification of In-Substance Foreclosed (ISF) Assets by SEC Registrants			EITF.D-37
Debtors in Bankruptcy Situations, Applicability	FTB81-6, ¶1-5	D22.509-513	
Definition			
. . Carrying Amount of the Payable	FAS15, ¶13	D22.401	
. . Debt	FAS15, ¶4	D22.402	
. . Recorded Investment in the Receivable	FAS15, ¶28	D22.403	
. . Time of Restructuring	FAS15, ¶6	D22.404	
. . Troubled Debt Restructuring	FAS15, ¶2	D22.405	
Exchanges of Debt Instruments			EITF.86-18
Leases			
. . Exemption from Requirements	FAS15, ¶8	D22.102	
Loan Fees and Costs	FAS91, ¶12-13	L20.111-112	

FAS–FASB Statements	FIN–FASB Interpretations	FTB–FASB Technical Bulletins
APB–APB Opinions	AIN–AICPA Interpretations	ARB–Accounting Research Bulletins
CON–FASB Concepts	EITF–EITF Issues	Q&A–FASB Special Reports

	Original Pronouncements	Current Text	EITF and Other
DEBT: RESTRUCTURINGS—continued			
Modification of Debt Terms			EITF.86-18
			EITF.89-15
. . Debtor Experiencing Financial Difficulties			EITF.89-15
Parallel Accounting by Creditor and Debtor	FTB80-2, ¶1	D22.506-508	
	FTB80-2, ¶3-4		
Related Parties	FAS15, ¶42	D22.138	
Relationship between Statement 15 and Savings and Loan Audit Guide			
. . Loan Loss Allowances			EITF.87-5
Scope of Accounting and Reporting Requirements	FAS15, ¶1	D22.101-103	
	FAS15, ¶8		
	FAS15, ¶10		
	FAS114, ¶22		
Substituting Debtor	FAS15, ¶42	D22.138	
	FAS114, ¶22	D22.146	
Troubled Debt Restructurings	FAS15, ¶1-2	D22.101-101A	
	FAS15, ¶5	D22.104-105	
	FAS114, ¶22		
. . Accounting for Conversion of a Loan into a Debt Security in a Debt Restructuring			EITF.94-8
. . Comparison with Debt Restructurings	FAS15, ¶7	D22.107	
. . Foreclosure on Collateral			EITF.87-18
			EITF.87-19
. . Loan Fees and Costs	FAS91, ¶14	L20.113	
. . Substitution of Debtors			EITF.87-19
. . Use of Zero Coupon Bonds			EITF.87-18
Valuation Allowances			
. . Following Debt Restructuring			EITF.87-5
DEBT RETIREMENT			
See Debt: Extinguishments			
DEBT SECURITIES			
See Investments: Debt and Equity Securities			
DECISION USEFULNESS			
See Usefulness			
Assessing Services and Ability to Provide Services	CON4, ¶38-39		
Decision Makers and Their Characteristics	CON2, ¶36-39		
Not-for-Profit Organizations, Resource Allocation Decisions	CON4, ¶35-37		
Relation to Qualitative Characteristics	CON2, ¶36-39		
Role of Decision Making	CON2, ¶27-31		
DECLINING-BALANCE METHOD			
Depreciation	FAS109, ¶288	D40.104	

See "Terminology" for references to defined terms presented in various accounting pronouncements.

See the Introduction to the Topical Index for details on the use of this index.

	Original Pronouncements	Current Text	EITF and Other

DEFEASANCE
See Debt: Extinguishments
DEFENSE CONTRACTS
See Contractor Accounting: Government
  Contracts
DEFERRAL
Definition .... CON6, ¶141
DEFERRAL METHOD
See Income Taxes
DEFERRED COMPENSATION
See Compensation to Employees:
  Deferred
See Compensation to Employees: Stock
  Purchase and Stock Option Plans
DEFERRED COSTS
See Capitalized Costs
Accounting for OPEB Costs by Rate-
  Regulated Enterprises EITF.92-12
  ....   EITF.93-4
Asbestos Treatment Costs Incurred in
  Anticipation of Sale of Property EITF.89-13
Costs to Clean Up Environmental
  Contamination to Prepare a Property for
  Sale EITF.90-8
Qualification as Assets................................. CON6, ¶177
  .... CON6, ¶246-250
DEFERRED CREDITS
Qualification as Liabilities........................... CON6, ¶197
DEFERRED INCOME
See Contingencies
See Deferred Revenue
See Revenue Recognition
DEFERRED INCOME TAX CREDITS
Qualification as Liabilities........................... CON6, ¶240-242
DEFERRED INTEREST RATE
Deferred Interest Rate Setting
  Arrangement...   EITF.84-14
DEFERRED REVENUE
Amortization of Amount Received from
  Investor for Future Revenue EITF.88-18
Franchise Fees .... FAS45, ¶7   Fr3.103
  .... FAS45, ¶11   Fr3.107
  .... FAS45, ¶15   Fr3.111
Loan, Commitment, and Syndication Fees. FAS91, ¶5-14   L20.104-113
Motion Picture Industry............................... FAS53, ¶4   Mo6.103
DEFERRED TAXES
See Accounting Changes
See Balance Sheet Classification: Current
  Assets and Liabilities
See Consolidation

FAS–FASB Statements   FIN–FASB Interpretations   FTB–FASB Technical Bulletins
APB–APB Opinions   AIN–AICPA Interpretations   ARB–Accounting Research Bulletins
CON–FASB Concepts   EITF–EITF Issues   Q&A–FASB Special Reports

	Original Pronouncements	Current Text	EITF and Other
DEFERRED TAXES—continued			
See Foreign Currency Translation			
See Income Taxes			
See Insurance Industry			
See Interim Financial Reporting			
See Investments: Equity Method			
Amortization of Acquired Goodwill	APB17, ¶30	I60.111	
	FAS109, ¶288		
Regulated Operations	FAS109, ¶288	Re6.128	
. . Abandonment of Assets	FTB87-2, ¶5	Re6.501-507	
	FTB87-2, ¶14-20		
DEFERRING GAIN AND LOSS RECOGNITION			
See Hedges			
Hedging with Cash Securities			EITF.87-1
DEFINED BENEFIT PENSION PLANS			
See Disclosure			
See Pension Costs			
See Postretirement Health Care and Life Insurance Benefits			
Accounting Policies	FAS35, ¶27	Pe5.126	
Accrual Basis of Accounting	FAS35, ¶9	Pe5.108	
Actuarial Present Value of Accumulated			
Plan Benefits	FAS35, ¶16-21	Pe5.115-120	
	FAS35, ¶134		
	FAS35, ¶153		
	FAS35, ¶156		
	FAS35, ¶184		
	FAS35, ¶198		
. . Changes in	FAS35, ¶23-26	Pe5.122-125	
	FAS35, ¶243		
. . Illustration of Measurement	FAS35, ¶283	Pe5.135	
. . Nonvested Benefits	FAS35, ¶22	Pe5.121	
	FAS35, ¶214		
. . Other Vested Benefits	FAS35, ¶22	Pe5.121	
	FAS35, ¶214		
. . Vested Benefits	FAS35, ¶22	Pe5.121	
	FAS35, ¶214		
Asset Reversions			EITF.84-6
Contribution of Excess Assets to ESOP upon Termination of Plan			EITF.85-10
Contributory Plan	FAS35, ¶28	Pe5.127	
	FAS35, ¶252-253		
	FAS35, ¶262-264		
	FAS35, ¶267		
ERISA	FAS35, ¶28	Pe5.127	

See "Terminology" for references to defined terms presented in various accounting pronouncements.

See the Introduction to the Topical Index for details on the use of this index.

	Original Pronouncements	Current Text	EITF and Other

DEFINED BENEFIT PENSION PLANS—continued

Financial Statement Information	FAS35, ¶5-8	Pe5.104-107A	
	FAS35, ¶50		
	FAS35, ¶60		
	FAS35, ¶208		
	FAS35, ¶232		
. . Accounting Policies	FAS35, ¶27	Pe5.126	
	FAS35, ¶257		
. . Actuarial Present Value of Accumulated Plan Benefits	FAS35, ¶6	Pe5.105	
	FAS35, ¶50	Pe5.121	
	FAS35, ¶60		
	FAS35, ¶214		
. . Benefit Information	FAS35, ¶8	Pe5.107	
	FAS35, ¶232		
. . Benefit Information Date	FAS35, ¶7	Pe5.106	
	FAS35, ¶208		
. . Changes in Actuarial Present Value of Accumulated Plan Benefits	FAS35, ¶25-26	Pe5.124-125	
	FAS35, ¶241		
	FAS35, ¶243		
. . Changes in Net Assets Available for Benefits	FAS35, ¶236	Pe5.114	
	FAS35, ¶238		
	FAS35, ¶260		
. . Claims upon Plan Termination	FAS35, ¶28	Pe5.127	
. . Concentration of Investments	FAS35, ¶28	Pe5.127	
	FAS35, ¶252-253		
. . Contributions Receivable	FAS35, ¶10	Pe5.109	
	FAS35, ¶90-91		
	FAS35, ¶93		
. . Generally Accepted Accounting Principles	FAS35, ¶4	Pe5.103	
. . Illustration	FAS35, ¶281-282	Pe5.129-133	
. . Investments	FAS35, ¶11	Pe5.110-112	
	FAS35, ¶13		
	FAS35, ¶104		
	FAS110, ¶2		
	FAS110, ¶7		
. . Net Assets Available for Benefits	FAS35, ¶6	Pe5.105	
	FAS35, ¶9	Pe5.108	
	FAS35, ¶60		
	FAS35, ¶86		
. . Objectives	FAS35, ¶5	Pe5.104	
. . Operating Assets	FAS35, ¶14	Pe5.113	
	FAS35, ¶128		

FAS–FASB Statements	FIN–FASB Interpretations	FTB–FASB Technical Bulletins
APB–APB Opinions	AIN–AICPA Interpretations	ARB–Accounting Research Bulletins
CON–FASB Concepts	EITF–EITF Issues	Q&A–FASB Special Reports

T-107

	Original Pronouncements	Current Text	EITF and Other
DEFINED BENEFIT PENSION PLANS—continued			
Financial Statement Information—continued			
. . Other	FAS35, ¶27-28	Pe5.126-127	
	FAS35, ¶257		
	FAS35, ¶262-264		
	FAS35, ¶267		
. . Plan Amendments	FAS35, ¶28	Pe5.127	
. . Plan Description	FAS35, ¶28	Pe5.127	
. . Policy Regarding Purchase of Contracts with Insurance Enterprises	FAS35, ¶28	Pe5.127	
. . Real Estate Holdings	FAS35, ¶28	Pe5.127	
. . Related Parties, Transactions with Employer	FAS35, ¶28	Pe5.127	
	FAS57, ¶1	R36.101	
. . Statement of Cash Flows	FAS102, ¶5	C25.135A	
		Pe5.107A	
. . Tax Status	FAS35, ¶28	Pe5.127	
	FAS35, ¶264		
. . Unusual or Infrequent Items	FAS35, ¶28	Pe5.127	
	FAS35, ¶267		
Glossary	FAS35, ¶280	Pe5.401-427	
	FAS110, ¶2		
Guaranteed Investment Contracts (GICs)	FAS110, ¶2	Pe5.110	
Insurance Contracts	FAS110, ¶2	Pe5.110-111	
	FAS110, ¶4		
	FAS110, ¶7		
. . Valuation of	FAS110, ¶28	Pe5.111	
Investment Contracts	FAS110, ¶2	Pe5.110	
	FAS110, ¶4		
Investments in Debt and Equity Securities	FAS115, ¶4	I80.102	
Partial Termination of Plan			EITF.84-44
Scope of Accounting and Reporting Requirements	FAS35, ¶1-2	Pe5.101-102	
	FAS35, ¶50		
	FAS35, ¶71-72		
	FAS35, ¶79		
	FAS35, ¶83		
	FAS35, ¶85		
. . Exclusion from Requirements	FAS110, ¶8	Pe5.101	
	FAS110, ¶24	Pe5.110	
. . Statement of Cash Flows	FAS102, ¶5	Pe5.107A	
Settlement			EITF.84-6
Termination			EITF.84-6
Use of Averages or Reasonable Approximations	FAS35, ¶29	Pe5.128	

See "Terminology" for references to defined terms presented in various accounting pronouncements.

See the Introduction to the Topical Index for details on the use of this index.

	Original Pronouncements	Current Text	EITF and Other
DEFINED BENEFIT POSTRETIREMENT PLAN			
See Postretirement Benefits Other Than Pensions			
DEFINED CONTRIBUTION PENSION PLANS			
See Pension Costs			
DEFINED CONTRIBUTION POSTRETIREMENT PLAN			
See Postretirement Benefits Other Than Pensions			
DEFINITIONS			
See Terminology			
DEFLATION			
See Changing Prices: Reporting Their Effects in Financial Reports			
DELAYED EQUITY CONTRIBUTIONS BY LESSORS			
Leveraged Leases			EITF.85-16
DEMAND OBLIGATIONS			
Balance Sheet Classification	FAS78, ¶5	B05.109A-109B	EITF.86-5
	FAS78, ¶13		
DEPLETION			
See Oil and Gas Producing Activities			
DEPOSIT FLOAT			
See Banking and Thrift Industries			
DEPOSIT METHOD			
See Insurance Costs			
See Insurance Industry			
See Real Estate: Sales			
See Real Estate: Sales Other Than Retail Land Sales			
Definition	FAS60, ¶66	In6.408	
DEPOSITS			
Payment Made to IRS to Retain Fiscal Year			EITF.88-4
Qualification as Liabilities	CON6, ¶197		
DEPRECIATION			
See Disclosure			
Accelerated			
. . Temporary Differences, Regulated Operations	FAS109, ¶288	Re6.128	
Accounting Changes	APB20, ¶23-24	A06.119-120	
Accounting Policy Disclosure	APB22, ¶14	A10.106	
Applicability to Not-for-Profit Organizations	FAS93, ¶5-6	D40.101-101B	
	FAS93, ¶35-36		
Appraisals Not Allowed	APB6, ¶17	D40.102	

FAS–FASB Statements　　　FIN–FASB Interpretations　　　FTB–FASB Technical Bulletins
APB–APB Opinions　　　AIN–AICPA Interpretations　　　ARB–Accounting Research Bulletins
CON–FASB Concepts　　　　EITF–EITF Issues　　　　Q&A–FASB Special Reports

T-109

	Original Pronouncements	Current Text	EITF and Other
DEPRECIATION—continued			
Basic Principle	APB6, ¶17	D40.101-102	
	ARB43, Ch.9C, ¶5	D40.104	
	FAS93, ¶5-6		
	FAS93, ¶35-37		
	FAS109, ¶288		
Deferred Tax Accounting			
. . Revaluation of Assets for Tax Purposes			EITF.84-43
Definition	ARB43, Ch.9C, ¶5	D40.401	
Fixed Assets to Be Recorded at Cost	APB6, ¶17	D40.102	
Historical Treasures	FAS93, ¶6	D40.101A-101C	
	FAS93, ¶35-36		
Idle Facilities			EITF.84-28
Land	FAS93, ¶6	D40.101A	
	FAS93, ¶34		
Method			
. . Annuity	FAS92, ¶37	D40.104	
. . Declining Balance	FAS109, ¶288	D40.104	
. . Sum-of-the-Years' Digits	FAS109, ¶288	D40.104	
. . Units-of-Production			EITF.84-28
Recognition Guidance	CON5, ¶86		
Relation to Contingencies	FAS5, ¶2	C59.121	
Useful Life	ARB43, Ch.9C, ¶5	D40.101	
Works of Art	FAS93, ¶6	D40.101A-101C	
	FAS93, ¶35-36		
DERIVATIVE FINANCIAL INSTRUMENTS			
See Financial Instruments			
DEVALUATION			
See Foreign Currency Translation			
Extraordinary Item	APB30, ¶23	I17.110	
DEVELOPMENT STAGE ENTERPRISES			
See Disclosure			
Cash Inflows and Cash Outflows	FAS7, ¶11	De4.107	
	FAS95, ¶151		
Comparative Financial Statements	FAS7, ¶13	De4.109	
Criteria for Expensing or Capitalization of Costs	FAS7, ¶10	De4.105	
. . When Enterprise Is Consolidated	FIN7, ¶4	De4.106	
Definition	FAS7, ¶8	De4.401	
Dormant Enterprise Reactivated	FAS7, ¶11	De4.107	
End of Development Stage	FAS7, ¶29	De4.104	
Guidelines for Identification	FAS7, ¶8-9	De4.102-104	
	FAS7, ¶29		
Identification of Financial Statements	FAS7, ¶12	De4.108	
Less Than Full Set of Statements	FAS7, ¶11	De4.107	
Nonmonetary Transactions	FAS7, ¶11	De4.107	
Periods Covered	FAS7, ¶11	De4.107	

See "Terminology" for references to defined terms presented in various accounting pronouncements.
See the Introduction to the Topical Index for details on the use of this index.

	Original Pronouncements	Current Text	EITF and Other

DEVELOPMENT STAGE ENTERPRISES—continued

Reporting When No Longer in Development Stage .... FAS7, ¶13 — De4.109

Scope of Accounting and Reporting Requirements .... FAS7, ¶4 — De4.101

Stockholders' Equity Transactions.............. FAS7, ¶11 — De4.107

Typical Activities...................................... FAS7, ¶9 — De4.103

DEVELOPMENT WELLS

Qualification as an Asset .... CON6, ¶247

DILUTION OF EARNINGS PER SHARE

See Earnings per Share

DIRECT FINANCING LEASE

See Leases

DISABILITY BENEFITS

See Postemployment Benefits

DISALLOWANCE OF COSTS

See Regulated Operations

DISC (DOMESTIC INTERNATIONAL SALES CORPORATION)

Effects of the Tax Reform Act of 1984 .... — — EITF.84-2

DISCLOSURE

See Financial Reporting

See Management

Accounting Changes................................... APB20, ¶17 — A06.113

.... APB20, ¶19 — A06.115

.... APB20, ¶21 — A06.117

.... APB20, ¶24-28 — A06.120-124

.... APB20, ¶33 — A06.132-134

.... APB20, ¶38-39

.... FAS73, ¶2

Accounting for Discontinued Operations Subsequently Retained

. . Disclosure by SEC Registrants .... — — EITF.90-16

Accounting for Environmental Liabilities .. — — EITF.93-5

Accounting for Gas-Balancing Arrangements

. . Disclosure by SEC Registrants .... — — EITF.90-22

Accounting for Income Taxes

. . Disclosure by SEC Registrants Prior to Adoption of Standard...................... — — EITF.D-28

Accounting for Postretirement Benefits Other Than Pensions

. . Accounting by Rate-Regulated Enterprises.. — — EITF.92-12

. . Accounting for Estimated Payments in Connection with the Coal Industry Retiree Health Benefit Act of 1992 .... — — EITF.92-13

FAS–FASB Statements   FIN–FASB Interpretations   FTB–FASB Technical Bulletins
APB–APB Opinions   AIN–AICPA Interpretations   ARB–Accounting Research Bulletins
CON–FASB Concepts   EITF–EITF Issues   Q&A–FASB Special Reports

	Original Pronouncements	Current Text	EITF and Other
DISCLOSURE—continued			
Accounting for Postretirement Benefits Other Than Pensions—continued			
. . Disclosure Based on Current Substantive Plan			EITF.D-26
. . Disclosure Based on Probable Plan Amendment			EITF.D-26
. . Disclosure by SEC Registrants Prior to Adoption of Standard			EITF.D-26
Accounting Policies	APB22, ¶6	A10.101-102A	
	APB22, ¶8	A10.105-108	
	APB22, ¶12-15		
	FAS95, ¶152		
	FIN40, ¶5		
Adjustments of Financial Statements for Prior Periods	APB9, ¶18	A35.105-108	EITF.85-35
	APB9, ¶26-27	A35.111	
	APB20, ¶35	A35.113	
	APB20, ¶37	I73.145	
	FAS16, ¶15-16		
Amortization Period for Net Deferred Credit Card Origination Costs			EITF.92-5
Balance Sheet Classification: Current Assets and Liabilities	APB6, ¶14	B05.107	
	FAS6, ¶15	B05.109A	
	FAS78, ¶5	B05.118	
Banking and Thrift Industries	APB23, ¶25	Bt7.115	
	FAS72, ¶11	Bt7.120-121	
	FAS109, ¶288		
Broadcasting Industry	FAS63, ¶3	Br5.104	
	FAS63, ¶10	Br5.111	
Business Combinations	AIN-APB16, #23	B50.115-116	
	APB16, ¶56-57	B50.119-124	
	APB16, ¶60-65	B50.136	
	APB16, ¶78	B50.158F	
	APB16, ¶95-96	B50.164-166	
	FAS38, ¶10	B50.575-579	
	FAS72, ¶11		
	FAS79, ¶6		
Capital Stock: Capital Transactions	APB12, ¶10	C08.102	
Capital Stock: Dividends-in-Kind	APB29, ¶28	C11.102	
Capital Stock: Preferred Stock	APB10, ¶10-11	C16.101-102	
	APB15, ¶50		
Capital Stock: Treasury Stock	APB6, ¶12-13	C23.103-104	
	ARB43, Ch.1A, ¶4	C23.503	
	FTB85-6, ¶3		
Cash Flows Statement	FAS95, ¶25-33	C25.123-135	
	FAS117, ¶30		

See "Terminology" for references to defined terms presented in various accounting pronouncements.
See the Introduction to the Topical Index for details on the use of this index.

	Original Pronouncements	Current Text	EITF and Other
DISCLOSURE—continued			
Changing Prices: Reporting Their Effects in Financial Reports	FAS89, ¶3	C28.101	
	FAS89, ¶7-15	C28.103-111	
	FAS89, ¶20	C28.116	
Classification of In-Substance Foreclosed (ISF) Assets by SEC Registrants			EITF.D-37
Commitments: Long-Term Obligations	FAS47, ¶1	C32.101-102	
	FAS47, ¶6-7	C32.105	
	FAS47, ¶10		
Comparative Financial Statements	ARB43, Ch.2A, ¶2-3	F43.102-103	
Compensated Absences	FAS43, ¶6	C44.104	
Compensation to Employees: Stock Purchase and Stock Option Plans	APB25, ¶8	C47.108	
	APB25, ¶14	C47.114	
	ARB43, Ch.13B, ¶15	C47.123	
Computer Software	FAS2, ¶13	Co2.110-111	Q&A.86#18
	FAS86, ¶11-12	R50.109	
Consolidation	ARB51, ¶4-5	C51.107-108	
	FAS94, ¶14	C51.119	
Contingencies	FAS5, ¶8-12	C59.108-113	
	FAS5, ¶17-19	C59.118	
		C59.120	
Contractor Accounting: Construction-Type Contracts	ARB45, ¶15-16	Co4.112-113	
Contractor Accounting: Government Contracts	ARB43, Ch.11A, ¶21-22	Co5.108-109	
	ARB43, Ch.11C, ¶18-23	Co5.116-121	
	ARB43, Ch.11C, ¶29	Co5.126	
Contributions	FAS116, ¶10	C67.110	
	FAS116, ¶24-25	C67.121-122	
	FAS116, ¶117		
	FAS116, ¶123		
. . Collections—Works of Art, Historical Treasures, and Similar Assets	FAS116, ¶26-27	C67.123-124	
	FAS116, ¶141	No5.142	
Debt: Extinguishments	FAS4, ¶8-9	D14.105	
	FAS64, ¶4	D14.107-108	
	FAS76, ¶6		
Debt: Restructurings	FAS15, ¶21	D22.117	
	FAS15, ¶25-26	D22.121-122	
	FAS15, ¶40-41	D22.136-137	
		D22.145	

FAS–FASB Statements   FIN–FASB Interpretations   FTB–FASB Technical Bulletins
APB–APB Opinions   AIN–AICPA Interpretations   ARB–Accounting Research Bulletins
CON–FASB Concepts   EITF–EITF Issues   Q&A–FASB Special Reports

	Original Pronouncements	Current Text	EITF and Other
DISCLOSURE—continued			
Defined Benefit Pension Plans	FAS35, ¶7	Pe5.106	
	FAS35, ¶13-15	Pe5.112-114	
	FAS35, ¶22	Pe5.121	
	FAS35, ¶25-28	Pe5.124-127	
	FAS35, ¶208		
	FAS35, ¶214		
	FAS35, ¶238		
	FAS35, ¶241		
	FAS35, ¶243		
	FAS35, ¶252-253		
	FAS35, ¶257		
	FAS35, ¶260		
	FAS35, ¶262-264		
	FAS35, ¶267		
Depreciation	APB12, ¶5	D40.105	
Development Stage Enterprises	FAS7, ¶11-13	De4.107-109	
	FAS95, ¶151		
Earnings per Share	APB15, ¶4	E09.104	
	APB15, ¶13	E09.106-107	
	APB15, ¶15-16	E09.109-114	
	APB15, ¶18-23	E09.139	
	APB15, ¶48	E09.141	
	APB15, ¶50	E09.161	
	APB15, ¶70		
	APB20, ¶20		
Employee Stock Ownership Plans (ESOPs)			
. . Disclosures by SEC Registrants			EITF.89-8
Extraordinary Items	APB9, ¶6	I17.101-104	
	APB30, ¶11-12	I17.119	
	APB30, ¶25		
	FAS4, ¶9		
	FAS16, ¶16		
Financial Instruments	FAS105, ¶16	F25.102	
	FAS105, ¶17-20	F25.105I	
	FAS105, ¶43-48	F25.112-115	
	FAS107, ¶9-15	F25.115C-115F	
	FAS107, ¶30-33	F25.115I-115Q	
	FAS119, ¶8-15	F25.135-140	
	FAS119, ¶69	F25.153-156	
. . Implementation of Statement 107			EITF.D-29
Foreign Currency Translation	FAS52, ¶30-32	F60.140-143	
	FAS52, ¶142-144		
Foreign Operations	ARB43, Ch.12, ¶5-6	F65.102-103	
Franchising	FAS45, ¶20-23	Fr3.116-119	
Futures Contracts	FAS80, ¶12	F80.112	Q&A.80 #30
	FAS80, ¶27		Q&A.80 #33
Hedging Anticipated Currency Transactions			EITF.91-4

See "Terminology" for references to defined terms presented in various accounting pronouncements.
See the Introduction to the Topical Index for details on the use of this index.

	Original Pronouncements	Current Text	EITF and Other
DISCLOSURE—continued			
Impairment: Loans	FAS114, ¶74	I08.118-118A	
	FAS118, ¶6		
Impairment: Long-Lived Assets	FAS121, ¶14	I08.133	
	FAS121, ¶19	I08.138	
Income Statement Presentation:			
Discontinued Operations	APB30, ¶8-9	I13.104-109	
	APB30, ¶13		
	APB30, ¶18		
	APB30, ¶25		
	FAS16, ¶16		
Income Taxes	APB4, ¶11	I27.142-148	Q&A.109 #11
	APB23, ¶18	I27.219	Q&A.109 #18
	APB23, ¶25	I27.224	
	FAS109, ¶43-49	I27.229	
Infrequent Items	APB30, ¶26	I22.101	
Insurance Industry	FAS60, ¶19	In6.119	Q&A.113 #41-42
	FAS60, ¶50	In6.156	
	FAS60, ¶54	In6.160	
	FAS60, ¶60	In6.166	
	FAS97, ¶28	In6.191-192	
	FAS113, ¶27-28		
	FAS113, ¶115		
	FAS115, ¶131		
. . Disclosure by SEC Registrants of Multiple-Year Retrospectively Rated Contracts			EITF.93-6
. . Disclosure by SEC Registrants of the Present Value of Future Profits Resulting from the Acquisition of a Life Insurance Company			EITF.92-9
. . Disclosure of Multiple-Year Retrospectively Rated Insurance Contracts by Insurance Enterprises and Other Enterprises			EITF.93-14
. . Mutual Life Insurance Enterprises	FIN40, ¶5-6	In6.166A	
Intangible Assets	APB17, ¶30-31	I60.111-112	
Interest: Capitalization of Interest Costs	FAS34, ¶21	I67.118	
Interim Financial Reporting	APB28, ¶14-15	I73.107-108	EITF.85-35
	APB28, ¶18-19	I73.110	
	APB28, ¶21	I73.112	
	APB28, ¶26	I73.124	
	APB28, ¶29-30	I73.127	
	APB28, ¶33	I73.133	
	FAS3, ¶11-14	I73.137-138	
	FAS16, ¶15	I73.140-141	
	FAS109, ¶288	I73.145-147	
	FIN18, ¶6	I73.149	
	FIN18, ¶8		
	FIN18, ¶17		

	Original Pronouncements	Current Text	EITF and Other

DISCLOSURE—continued

Inventory	ARB43, Ch.3A, ¶9	I78.108	
	ARB43, Ch.4, ¶6	I78.117	
	ARB43, Ch.4, ¶14-17	I78.119-122	
Investments: Debt and Equity Securities	FAS115, ¶19-22	I80.118-121	
Investments: Equity Method	APB18, ¶19-20	I82.109-110	
	FAS58, ¶8		
	FAS94, ¶15		
Leases	FAS13, ¶13	L10.112	
	FAS13, ¶16	L10.119	
	FAS13, ¶23	L10.125	
	FAS13, ¶29	L10.130K-130L	
	FAS13, ¶47	L10.149	
	FAS91, ¶25		
	FAS98, ¶17-18		
Liability Recognition for Costs to Exit an Activity			EITF.94-3
Mortgage Banking Activities	FAS65, ¶29-30	Mo4.130-134	
	FAS122, ¶3		
Motion Picture Industry	FAS53, ¶23	Mo6.122	
Nonmonetary Transactions	APB29, ¶28	N35.120	
Not-for-Profit Organizations	FAS116, ¶14	No5.110	
	FAS116, ¶16	No5.112-113	
	FAS117, ¶12	No5.120-123	
	FAS117, ¶14-15	No5.143	
	FAS117, ¶23-26	No5.145	
. . Collections—Works of Art, Historical Treasures, and Similar Assets	FAS116, ¶26-27	C67.123-124	
	FAS116, ¶141	No5.142	
Oil and Gas Producing Activities	FAS69, ¶6-7	Oi5.156-157	
	FAS69, ¶9-34	Oi5.159-186	
	FAS69, ¶40-41		
	FAS109, ¶288		
Operations Held for Sale after a Business Combination			
. . Disclosure by SEC Registrants			EITF.87-11
			EITF.90-6
Pension Costs	FAS87, ¶54	P16.150	Q&A.87 #4
	FAS87, ¶56	P16.153	Q&A.87 #33
	FAS87, ¶65	P16.162	Q&A.87 #38
	FAS87, ¶69	P16.166	Q&A.87 #70
	FAS88, ¶17	P16.187	Q&A.87 #72-79
Postemployment Benefits	FAS112, ¶7	P32.105	

See "Terminology" for references to defined terms presented in various accounting pronouncements.
See the Introduction to the Topical Index for details on the use of this index.

	Original Pronouncements	Current Text	EITF and Other
DISCLOSURE—continued			
Postretirement Benefits Other Than			
Pensions	FAS106, ¶74	P40.169	Q&A.106 #39-40
	FAS106, ¶77-78	P40.172-173	
	FAS106, ¶82-83	P40.178-179	
	FAS106, ¶106	P40.198	
	FAS106, ¶479-483	P40.276-280	
Postretirement Health Care and Life			
Insurance Benefits	FAS81, ¶6-7	P50.102-103	
	FAS81, ¶28		
Quasi Reorganization	ARB43, Ch.7A, ¶4	Q15.105	
	ARB43, Ch.7A, ¶10	Q15.111	
	ARB46, ¶2		
Real Estate	FAS66, ¶65	R10.159	
Real Estate: Sales	FAS66, ¶50	Re1.150	
	FAS66, ¶65	Re1.163	
Receivables Sold with Recourse	FAS77, ¶9	R20.109	
	FAS77, ¶39		
Record and Music Industry	FAS50, ¶13-14	Re4.108-109	
Regulated Operations	FAS71, ¶15	Re6.114	
	FAS71, ¶19-20	Re6.125	
	FAS71, ¶23	Re6.125F	
	FAS90, ¶13	Re6.127A	
	FAS92, ¶10-12	Re6.128-131B	
	FAS101, ¶8-9	Re6.207-208	
	FIN40, ¶5-6		
. . Accounting for OPEB Costs by Rate-Regulated Enterprises			EITF.92-12
Regulatory-Assisted Acquisitions of Thrifts			EITF.88-19
Related Parties	ARB43, Ch.1A, ¶5	R36.102-105	
	FAS57, ¶2-4		
	FAS109, ¶288		
Research and Development	FAS2, ¶13	R50.109	
Research and Development Arrangements	FAS68, ¶14	R55.112	
Restructuring of Business Operations			EITF.86-22
			EITF.87-4
Retained Earnings	FAS5, ¶15	R70.103	
Segment of Business Reporting	FAS14, ¶7	S20.103	
	FAS14, ¶20	S20.108	
	FAS14, ¶22-27	S20.126	
	FAS14, ¶30	S20.128-133	
	FAS14, ¶35-38	S20.136	
	FAS14, ¶40	S20.141-146	
	FAS21, ¶9		
	FAS30, ¶6		
	FAS95, ¶152		

FAS–FASB Statements   FIN–FASB Interpretations   FTB–FASB Technical Bulletins
APB–APB Opinions   AIN–AICPA Interpretations   ARB–Accounting Research Bulletins
CON–FASB Concepts   EITF–EITF Issues   Q&A–FASB Special Reports

	Original Pronouncements	Current Text	EITF and Other
DISCLOSURE—continued			
Subsidiary's Loan Payable in Consolidated Balance Sheet When Subsidiary's and Parent's Fiscal Years Differ			EITF.88-15
Taxes: Real and Personal Property Taxes	ARB43, Ch.10A, ¶16	T10.106	
Title Plant	FAS61, ¶9	Ti7.109	
Valuation: Use of Valuation Allowances	APB12, ¶3	V18.102	
DISCONTINUED OPERATIONS			
See Income Statement Presentation: Discontinued Operations			
Accounting for Restructuring Charges			EITF.94-3
Exit Costs			EITF.94-3
			EITF.95-3
Liability Recognition for Costs to Exit an Activity			EITF.94-3
			EITF.95-3
Recognition of Deferred Tax Assets for a Parent Company's Excess Tax Basis in the Stock of a Subsidiary That Is Accounted for as a Discontinued Operation			EITF.93-17
DISCOUNTED PRESENT VALUE OF FUTURE CASH FLOWS			
See Present Value			
DISCOUNTING			
See Interest: Imputation of an Interest Cost			
See Present Value			
Accounting for Environmental Liabilities			EITF.93-5
Broadcasting Industry	FAS63, ¶4	Br5.105	
Contributions Receivable and Payable	FAS116, ¶20	C67.116	
Defined Benefit Pension Plans			
. . Actuarial Present Value of Accumulated Plan Benefits	FAS35, ¶16-21	Pe5.115-120	
	FAS35, ¶134		
. . Investment Valuation	FAS35, ¶11	Pe5.110	
	FAS35, ¶104		
Foreign Currency Exchange Contracts			EITF.87-2
Loss Reserves of Insurance Companies			EITF.86-37
Regulated Operations	FAS71, ¶33-34	Re6.127A	
	FAS90, ¶3	Re6.138-139	
DISPLAY			
Financial Statements	CON5, ¶13-14		
Relation to Elements of Financial Statements	CON6, ¶22-23		
Reporting Comprehensive Income	CON6, ¶220		
DISPOSAL OF A PORTION OR SEGMENT OF A BUSINESS			
See Income Statement Presentation: Discontinued Operations			

See "Terminology" for references to defined terms presented in various accounting pronouncements.

See the Introduction to the Topical Index for details on the use of this index.

	Original Pronouncements	Current Text	EITF and Other
DISPOSAL OF A PORTION OR SEGMENT OF A BUSINESS—continued			
Accounting for Discontinued Operations Subsequently Retained			EITF.90-16
. . Disclosure by SEC Registrants			EITF.90-16
Accounting for Restructuring Charges			EITF.94-3
Determination of Gains (Losses)			EITF.85-36
Expected Gain on Disposal with Interim Operating Losses			EITF.85-36
Liability Recognition for Costs to Exit an Activity			EITF.94-3
			EITF.95-3
Operations Held for Sale after a Business Combination			EITF.87-11
			EITF.90-6
Recognition of Liabilities in Connection with a Purchase Business Combination			EITF.95-3
Treatment of Accrual for Future Operating Losses Expected during the Disposal Period under Statement 121			EITF.D-45
DISSENTERS' RIGHTS			
Effect on Pooling-of-Interests Accounting			EITF.87-16
DISTRIBUTIONS TO OWNERS			
See Dividends			
Characteristics	CON6, ¶68-69		
Definition	CON6, ¶67		
Statement of Investments by and	CON5, ¶55-57		
DIVERSIFIED COMPANIES			
See Segment of Business Reporting			
DIVESTITURE			
See Business Combinations			
See Income Statement Presentation: Discontinued Operations			
See Leases			
Business Combinations	APB16, ¶46	B50.105	
DIVIDENDS			
See Capital Stock: Dividends-in-Kind			
See Capital Stock: Stock Dividends and Stock Splits			
Business Combinations	APB16, ¶47	B50.106	
	ARB43, Ch.1A, ¶3	R70.102	
Definition	APB18, ¶3	I82.403	
Disclosure	APB12, ¶10	C08.102	
	FAS5, ¶18-19	C59.120	
Disclosure in Cash Flows Statement	FAS95, ¶20	C25.118	
Per Share	APB15, ¶70	E09.161	
Pooling of Interests			
. . Abnormal	APB16, ¶47	B50.106	

FAS–FASB Statements   FIN–FASB Interpretations   FTB–FASB Technical Bulletins
APB–APB Opinions   AIN–AICPA Interpretations   ARB–Accounting Research Bulletins
CON–FASB Concepts   EITF–EITF Issues   Q&A–FASB Special Reports

	Original Pronouncements	Current Text	EITF and Other
DIVIDENDS—continued			
Preferred Shares			
. . Dividend Rate Initially below Market Rate			EITF.86-45
Preferred Shares, Arrears	APB10, ¶11	C16.102	
	APB15, ¶50		
Prior to Enterprise Being Acquired	ARB43, Ch.1A, ¶3	R70.102	
Restrictions on Distribution	FAS5, ¶18	C59.120	
Treasury Stock	ARB43, Ch.1A, ¶4	C23.101	
DIVIDENDS TO POLICYHOLDERS			
See Insurance Industry			
Definition	FAS60, ¶66	In6.409	
DIVIDENDS-IN-KIND			
See Capital Stock: Dividends-in-Kind			
DOMESTIC SUBSIDIARIES			
See Segment of Business Reporting			
See Subsidiaries			
DONATIONS			
See Capital Stock: Capital Transactions			
See Contributions			
See Not-for-Profit Organizations			
See Real Estate: Costs and Initial Operations of Real Estate Projects			
DORMANT ENTERPRISE			
Accounting and Reporting Requirements	FAS7, ¶11	De4.107	
	FAS95, ¶151		
DOUBTFUL ACCOUNTS			
Valuation Allowances	APB12, ¶3	V18.102	
DOWNSTREAM MERGERS			
See Business Combinations			
DRY HOLE COSTS			
See Oil and Gas Producing Activities			
DUAL CURRENCY BONDS			
Accounting for Dual Currency Bonds			EITF.93-10
DUAL PRESENTATION			
See Earnings per Share			
Definition	APB15, App.D	E09.410	

(The next page is T-129.)

See "Terminology" for references to defined terms presented in various accounting pronouncements.
See the Introduction to the Topical Index for details on the use of this index.

	Original Pronouncements	Current Text	EITF and Other

EARLY EXTINGUISHMENT OF DEBT
See Debt: Extinguishments

Regulated Operations	FAS71, ¶36-37	Re6.141-142	

EARNING POWER

Performance Measurement	CON1, ¶47-48		
	CON1, ¶51		
	CON5, ¶28		

EARNINGS

Change in Use of Term from Concepts Statement 1	CON5, ¶11		
Description and Evolution of Concept	CON5, ¶33-38		
Enterprise Performance	CON1, ¶42-48		
Measurement	CON1, ¶45-48		
Recognition Implications	CON5, ¶49-51		
Relation to Cash Flows	CON1, ¶43-49		
Relation to Comprehensive Income	CON5, ¶42-44		
	CON6, ¶1		
	CON6, ¶72		

EARNINGS OR LOSSES OF AN INVESTEE
See Investments: Equity Method

Definition	APB18, ¶3	I82.404	

EARNINGS PER SHARE
See Disclosure
Accounting Changes

. . Catch-up Adjustment	AIN-APB20, #2	E09.511-514	
. . Restatement	AIN-APB20, #1	E09.503-510	
Adjustment of Income for Interest Expense	APB15, App.C	E09.167	
Antidilutive Securities	AIN-APB15, #5	E09.518	
	AIN-APB15, Part I	E09.533-535	
Brokers and Dealers in Securities	FAS111, ¶8	E09.501-502	
	FTB79-8, ¶1		
	FTB79-8, ¶6		
Classification of Securities	AIN-APB15, Part I	E09.515-517	
Common Stock Contributed to Employee Stock Ownership Plan			
. . Excess Assets Not Allocated to Participants			EITF.86-27
Common Stock Equivalents	AIN-APB15, #2	E09.528	
	FAS111, ¶8		
. . Junior Stock	FIN38, ¶7	E09.130A	
. . Nonrecognition in Financial Statements	APB15, ¶39	E09.132	
Complex Capital Structure	AIN-APB15, #18	E09.164	
	APB15, App.C	E09.168	
	FAS111, ¶8	E09.571-573	
Computational Guidelines	APB15, ¶44	E09.137	
. . Business Combinations and Reorganization	APB15, ¶49	E09.140	EITF.84-22

FAS–FASB Statements   FIN–FASB Interpretations   FTB–FASB Technical Bulletins
APB–APB Opinions   AIN–AICPA Interpretations   ARB–Accounting Research Bulletins
CON–FASB Concepts   EITF–EITF Issues   Q&A–FASB Special Reports

	Original Pronouncements	Current Text	EITF and Other
EARNINGS PER SHARE—continued			
Computational Guidelines—continued			
. . Claims of Senior Securities	APB15, ¶50	E09.141	
. . Conversion from Mutual Ownership to Stock Ownership			EITF.84-22
. . Conversion Rate or Exercise Price to Be Used for Common Stock Equivalents	APB15, ¶57-58	E09.148-149	
. . Convertible Bonds with Issuer Option to Settle for Cash upon Conversion			EITF.90-19
. . Convertible Preferred Stock Held by an Employee Stock Ownership Plan			EITF.89-12
. . Delayed or Changed Conversion Rates or Exercise Prices	APB15, ¶56	E09.147	
. . Dilutive Effect of Outstanding Put Options on Issuer's Stock That Are "In the Money"			EITF.87-31
. . Dividends per Share	APB15, ¶70	E09.161	
. . Earnings Applicable to Common Stock	AIN-APB15, #24	E09.143	
	APB15, ¶52	E09.590-594	
. . Effect on the Calculation of Earnings per Share for the Redemption or Induced Conversion of Preferred Stock			EITF.D-42
. . If-Converted Method of Computation	APB15, ¶51-53	E09.142-144	
. . Issuance Contingent on Certain Conditions	APB15, ¶61-64	E09.152-155	
. . Participating Securities and Two-Class Common	APB15, ¶59-60	E09.150-151	
. . Reverse Treasury Stock Method			EITF.87-31
. . Securities of Subsidiaries	APB15, ¶65-69	E09.156-160	
. . Stock Dividends or Splits	APB15, ¶48	E09.139	
. . Treasury Stock Method	APB15, ¶36	E09.125	
. . Treatment of Tax Benefits for Dividends on Stock Held by an Employee Stock Ownership Plan			EITF.90-4
			EITF.92-3
. . Two-Class Method of Computation	APB15, ¶54-55	E09.145-146	
. . Weighted-Average Number of Common Shares	APB15, ¶47	E09.138	
. . Weighted Average of Shares Outstanding	AIN-APB15, #25	E09.595-601	
Computational Guidelines, Convertible Securities	AIN-APB15, Part I	E09.519-520	
. . Change of Classification	AIN-APB15, #29-30	E09.619-626	
	FAS111, ¶8		
. . Classification and Assumed Conversion	AIN-APB15, #26	E09.602-607	
	FAS111, ¶8		

See "Terminology" for references to defined terms presented in various accounting pronouncements.
See the Introduction to the Topical Index for details on the use of this index.

	Original Pronouncements	Current Text	EITF and Other
EARNINGS PER SHARE—continued			
Computational Guidelines, Convertible Securities—continued			
. . Classification and Computation Not Always the Same	AIN-APB15, #28	E09.613-618	
. . Conversion Assumed for Primary Only	AIN-APB15, #43	E09.652-656	
. . Convertible into Other Convertible Securities	AIN-APB15, #45	E09.661-665	
. . Definition of Same Terms	AIN-APB15, #31	E09.627-628	
. . If-Converted Method at Actual Conversion	AIN-APB15, #44	E09.657-660	
. . Issue Price Is Not a Term	AIN-APB15, #32	E09.629-630	
. . No Antidilution from Convertible Debt	AIN-APB15, #42	E09.649-651	
. . No Antidilution from Convertible Preferred Stock	AIN-APB15, #41	E09.646-648	
. . Original Issue Premium or Discount	AIN-APB15, #40	E09.644-645	
. . Property Included in Yield of Convertible Securities	AIN-APB15, #37	E09.639-641	
	FAS85, ¶3		
. . Put Warrants			EITF.88-9
. . Sold by Issuer from Securities Held as Treasury Securities	AIN-APB15, #33	E09.631-632	
	FAS111, ¶8		
. . Time of Issuance	AIN-APB15, #27	E09.608-612	
. . Yield of Convertible Securities in a Package	AIN-APB15, #36	E09.637-638	
Computations for Warrants Whose Proceeds Are Applied to Retire Debt			
. . Options and Warrants and Their Equivalents	AIN-APB15, #70	E09.786-789	
Contingently Issuable Shares under Equity Commitment and Contract Notes			EITF.85-18
Cooperatives			
. . Exemption from Requirements	FAS21, ¶12	E09.102	
Credit Unions			
. . Exemption from Requirements	FAS21, ¶12	E09.102	
Dilution Less Than Three Percent Test	AIN-APB15, #12	E09.554-559	
Dilutive Security	AIN-APB15, #4	E09.531-532	
Discontinued Operations	APB30, ¶9	I13.107	
Dual Presentation	AIN-APB15, #6	E09.536-538	
. . Dilution Less Than Three Percent	AIN-APB15, #11	E09.550-553	
Effects of Scheduled Changes			
. . Changing Exercise Prices and Conversion Rates	AIN-APB15, #94	E09.889-892	
Election to Classify Outstanding Securities			
. . Effect of New Issues of Common Stock Equivalents	AIN-APB15, #96	E09.893-894	
. . No Change for Options and Warrants	AIN-APB15, #97	F09.895-897	

FAS–FASB Statements   FIN–FASB Interpretations   FTB–FASB Technical Bulletins
APB–APB Opinions   AIN–AICPA Interpretations   ARB–Accounting Research Bulletins
CON–FASB Concepts   EITF–EITF Issues   Q&A–FASB Special Reports

	Original Pronouncements	Current Text	EITF and Other
EARNINGS PER SHARE—continued			
Election to Classify Outstanding Securities —continued			
. . Retroactive Restatement of Prior Periods	AIN-APB15, #99	E09.898-899	
Fully Diluted Earnings per Share	AIN-APB15, #8	E09.541-542	
. . Antidilution	APB15, ¶40	E09.133	
. . When Required	APB15, ¶41-42	E09.134-135	
Glossary	APB15, App. D	E09.401-428	
	FAS21, ¶13		
	FAS85, ¶3		
Government-Owned Enterprises			
. . Exemption from Requirements	FAS21, ¶12	E09.102	
Historical Summaries			
. . Accounting Change	APB20, ¶39	A06.134	
If-Converted Method of Computation	APB15, ¶51-53	E09.142-144	
Illustrative Statements	APB15, App.C	E09.162	
Mutual Savings Bank			
. . Exemption from Requirements	FAS21, ¶12	E09.102	
Not-for-Profit Enterprises			
. . Exemption from Requirements	FAS21, ¶12	E09.102	
Options and Warrants and Their Equivalents	AIN-APB15, Part I	E09.521-524	
. . Antidilutive Exercise	AIN-APB15, #62	E09.745-754	
. . Antidilutive Options and Warrants Included	AIN-APB15, #72	E09.795-796	
. . Applying Ending and Average Market Prices	AIN-APB15, #60	E09.730-736	
. . Classification of	AIN-APB15, #46	E09.666-667	
. . Compensating Balances Excluded	AIN-APB15, #78	E09.815-816	
. . Computations May Differ for Primary and Fully Diluted	AIN-APB15, #81	E09.822-825	
. . Computations for Warrants Allowing Tendering of Debt	AIN-APB15, #69	E09.780-785	
. . Computations for Warrants Requiring the Tendering of Debt	AIN-APB15, #68	E09.778-779	
. . Computations for Warrants Whose Proceeds Are Applied to Retire Debt	AIN-APB15, #70	E09.786-789	
. . Debt Eligible Only While Outstanding	AIN-APB15, #80	E09.820-821	
. . Debt Purchased, Treasury Stock Method	AIN-APB15, #77	E09.812-814	
. . Definition of "Period"	AIN-APB15, #58	E09.723-726	
. . Equivalents of	AIN-APB15, #48	E09.672-673	
. . Explanation of Twenty Percent Provision	AIN-APB15, #74	E09.799-805	
. . Fair Value If No Market Price	AIN-APB15, #56	E09.708-713	
. . Grouping	AIN-APB15, #49	E09.674-678	
. . Investments Assumed Purchased for Treasury Stock Method	AIN-APB15, #79	E09.817-819	

See "Terminology" for references to defined terms presented in various accounting pronouncements.
See the Introduction to the Topical Index for details on the use of this index.

	Original Pronouncements	Current Text	EITF and Other
EARNINGS PER SHARE—continued			
Options and Warrants and Their Equivalents—continued			
. . Junior Stock Option, Purchase and Award Plans	FIN38, ¶7	E09.130A	
. . Market Price to Be Used	AIN-APB15, #54	E09.700-703	
. . Market Prices Used for Treasury-Stock Method	AIN-APB15, #52	E09.689-695	
. . Market Prices Used in Tests to Determine Dilutive or Antidilutive	AIN-APB15, #67	E09.773-777	
. . Methods Used for	AIN-APB15, #50	E09.679-683	
. . No Antidilution	AIN-APB15, #47	E09.668-671	
. . No Order for Exercise	AIN-APB15, #73	E09.797-798	
. . Number of Market Prices to Determine Average	AIN-APB15, #53	E09.696-699	
. . Original Issue Premium or Discount	AIN-APB15, #75	E09.806-807	
. . Outstanding Part of a Period	AIN-APB15, #57	E09.714-722	
. . Over-the-Counter and Listed Stocks Not Traded	AIN-APB15, #55	E09.704-707	
. . Redemption Premium or Discount	AIN-APB15, #76	E09.808-811	
. . Share Averaging	AIN-APB15, #59	E09.727-729	
. . Stock Subscriptions Are Warrants	AIN-APB15, #83	E09.826-829	
. . Tests to Determine whether Securities Are Dilutive or Antidilutive	AIN-APB15, #66	E09.767-772	
. . To Purchase Convertible Securities	AIN-APB15, #84	E09.830-835	
. . Total of Quarters May Not Equal Annual EPS	AIN-APB15, #64	E09.761-764	
. . Treasury Stock Method at Exercise	AIN-APB15, #61	E09.737-744	
. . Treasury Stock Method for Convertibles	AIN-APB15, #71	E09.790-794	
. . Treasury Stock Method Reflects Dilution of	AIN-APB15, #51	E09.684-688	
. . Treasury Stock Method, "Substantially All of Three Months"	AIN-APB15, #63	E09.755-760	
. . Unusual Warrants and Their Equivalents	AIN-APB15, #65	E09.765-766	
Parent Company Only Financial Statements			
. . Exemption from Requirements	FAS21, ¶12	E09.102	
Parent and Consolidated Financial Statements			
. . Securities Issued by Subsidiaries	AIN-APB15, #93	E09.883-888	
Per Share Dividends	APB15, ¶70	E09.161	
Potentially Dilutive Securities	AIN-APB15, #3	E09.529-530	
Primary Earnings per Share	AIN-APB15, #7	E09.115	
	APB15, ¶24	E09.539-540	

FAS–FASB Statements   FIN–FASB Interpretations   FTB–FASB Technical Bulletins
APB–APB Opinions   AIN–AICPA Interpretations   ARB–Accounting Research Bulletins
CON–FASB Concepts   EITF–EITF Issues   Q&A–FASB Special Reports

	Original Pronouncements	Current Text	EITF and Other
EARNINGS PER SHARE—continued			
Primary Earnings per Share, Common			
Stock Equivalents	APB15, ¶25-26	E09.116-117	
	APB15, ¶28-29	E09.119-120	
. . Cash Yield Test for Zero Coupon			
Bonds			EITF.84-16
. . If-Converted Method	APB15, ¶37	E09.126	
. . No Antidilution	APB15, ¶30	E09.121	
. . Test for Convertible Securities	APB15, ¶31	E09.122	EITF.84-16
	APB15, ¶33	E09.123A	
	FAS85, ¶3		
. . Test for Options, Warrants, and Their			
Equivalents	APB15, ¶35-36	E09.124-125	
. . Treasury Stock Method	APB15, ¶38	E09.127	
. . Treatment of Tax Benefits for			
Dividends on Stock Held by an			
Employee Stock Ownership Plan			EITF.90-4
. . Types	APB15, ¶27	E09.118	
Primary and Fully Diluted Earnings per			
Share	AIN-APB15, #21	E09.581-583	
Registered Investment Enterprises			
. . Exemption from Requirements	APB15, ¶6	E09.102	
Restatements of Previously Reported Data.	AIN-APB15, Part I	E09.525-526	
Scope of Accounting and Reporting			
Requirements	AIN-APB15, #9	E09.101-102	
	AIN-APB15, #12	E09.543-547	
	AIN-APB15, #14	E09.554-559	
	APB15, ¶5-6	E09.562-563	
	FAS21, ¶12		
	FAS21, ¶14-15		
Securities Issuable upon Satisfaction of			
Specified Conditions			
. . Contingent Shares	AIN-APB15, #88	E09.852-857	
. . Convertible Securities Contingently			
Issuable	AIN-APB15, #92	E09.878-882	
	FAS111, ¶8		
. . Earnings Conditions	AIN-APB15, #91	E09.869-877	
. . Market Price Conditions	AIN-APB15, #90	E09.860-868	
. . Time of Issuance for Contingent			
Issuances	AIN-APB15, #89	E09.858-859	
Security	AIN-APB15, #1	E09.527	
Simple Capital Structure	APB15, App.C	E09.163	
Situations Not Covered	APB15, ¶43	E09.136	EITF.D-15
Stock Compensation Plans in Earnings per			
Share Computations	FIN31, ¶5	E09.131	
. . Common Stock Equivalents	FIN28, ¶6	E09.128	
	FIN31, ¶2		
	FIN31, ¶6		

See "Terminology" for references to defined terms presented in various accounting pronouncements.
See the Introduction to the Topical Index for details on the use of this index.

	Original Pronouncements	Current Text	EITF and Other
EARNINGS PER SHARE—continued			
Stock Compensation Plans in Earnings per Share Computations—continued			
. . Common Stock Equivalents, Nonrecognition in Financial Statements	APB15, ¶39	E09.132	
. . Dilutive Effect	FIN31, ¶4	E09.130	
. . Junior Stock Option, Purchase and Award Plans	FIN38, ¶7	E09.130A	
. . Treasury Stock Method	FIN31, ¶3	E09.129	
	FIN31, ¶14-21	E09.169-176	
Treasury Stock Method	APB15, ¶36	E09.125	
Treatment of Tax Benefits for Dividends on Stock Held by an Employee Stock Ownership Plan			EITF.90-4
Two-Class Common Stock and Participating Securities			
. . Convertible Securities	AIN-APB15, #87	E09.847-851	
. . Nonconvertible Securities	AIN-APB15, #86	E09.842-846	
. . Treatment	AIN-APB15, #85	E09.836-841	
Two-Class Method for Warrants Issued by REITs	AIN-APB15, #102	E09.911-916	
Unaudited Financial Statements			
. . Applicability of Requirements	AIN-APB15, #14	E09.562-563	
Weighted-Average Number of Shares	APB15, App.C	E09.165-166	
EARNINGS STATEMENTS			
See Income Statement			
See Income Statement Presentation: Discontinued Operations			
EARNINGS SUMMARIES			
Historical Summaries	APB20, ¶39	A06.134	
EARNOUT			
Business Combinations	APB16, ¶80	B50.138	
ECONOMIC LIFE			
See Depreciation			
See Intangible Assets			
Estimated Economic Life of Leased Property			
See Leases			
ECONOMIC RESOURCES			
Allocation in the Economy	CON1, ¶12-16		
Discussion	CON6, ¶11-15		
	CON6, ¶27-31		
Information about	CON1, ¶40-41		
Not-for-Profit Organizations	CON4, ¶43-54		
EFFECTIVE YIELD			
See Earnings per Share			

FAS–FASB Statements	FIN–FASB Interpretations	FTB–FASB Technical Bulletins
APB–APB Opinions	AIN–AICPA Interpretations	ARB–Accounting Research Bulletins
CON–FASB Concepts	EITF–EITF Issues	Q&A–FASB Special Reports

T-135

	Original Pronouncements	Current Text	EITF and Other
ELEMENTS OF FINANCIAL STATEMENTS			
See Assets			
See Expenses			
See Gains			
See Investments by Owners			
See Liabilities			
See Not-for-Profit Organizations			
See Revenues			
Accrual Basis of Accounting	CON6, ¶134-152		
Articulation	CON6, ¶20-21		
Characteristics and Examples	CON6, ¶164-255		
Definition	CON6, ¶5		
Elements			
. . Assets	CON6, ¶25-34		
. . Comprehensive Income	CON6, ¶70-77		
. . Equity or Net Assets	CON6, ¶49-59		
. . Expenses	CON6, ¶80-81		
. . Gains and Losses	CON6, ¶82-89		
. . Investments by and Distributions to Owners	CON6, ¶66-69		
. . Liabilities	CON6, ¶35-43		
. . Revenues	CON6, ¶78-79		
Examples	CON6, ¶229-255		
Financial Representations	CON6, ¶5-7		
Relation to Objectives of Financial Reporting	CON6, ¶9-19		
Relation to Qualitative Characteristics	CON6, ¶9-19		
Relation to Recognition, Measurement, and Display	CON5, ¶64		
	CON6, ¶22-23		
Uncertainty	CON6, ¶44-48		
EMERGING ISSUES TASK FORCE (EITF)			
See FASB Emerging Issues Task Force (EITF)			
EMPLOYEE BENEFIT FUNDS			
See Postretirement Health Care and Life Insurance Benefits			
EMPLOYEE BENEFIT PLANS			
See Pension Costs			
See Postemployment Benefits			
See Postretirement Benefits Other Than Pensions			
See Postretirement Health Care and Life Insurance Benefits			
Accounting for Estimated Payments in Connection with the Coal Industry Retiree Health Benefit Act of 1992			EITF.92-13

See "Terminology" for references to defined terms presented in various accounting pronouncements.

See the Introduction to the Topical Index for details on the use of this index.

	Original Pronouncements	Current Text	EITF and Other
EMPLOYEE BENEFIT PLANS—continued			
Accounting for Involuntary Termination Benefits..			EITF.94-3
Consideration of the Impact of Bankruptcy in Determining Plan Assets under Statement 106......................................			EITF.93-3
Valuations of Investment Contracts with Noninsurance Entities............................			EITF.89-1
EMPLOYEE PENSION FUNDS			
See Defined Benefit Pension Plans			
EMPLOYEE RETIREMENT INCOME SECURITY ACT (ERISA)			
See Defined Benefit Pension Plans			
See ERISA			
EMPLOYEE STOCK OPTIONS			
See Compensation to Employees: Stock Purchase and Stock Option Plans			
See Employee Stock Ownership Plans (ESOPs)			
EMPLOYEE STOCK OWNERSHIP PLANS (ESOPs)			
Accounting for Employer's Contribution			
. . Excess Assets from Terminating Pension Plan......................................			EITF.85-10
Accounting for Treasury Stock in Leveraged Preferred Stock ESOPs...........			EITF.D-19
Compensation Expense			
. . Recognition by Sponsor of Leveraged ESOP When Debt Payments Are Nonlevel..			EITF.89-8
Contributions from Employer			
. . Asset Reversions from Termination of Defined Benefit Pension Plan.............			EITF.86-27
. . Excess Assets Not Allocated to Participants...			EITF.86-27
Convertible Preferred Stock Held by an ESOP			
. . Computation of Sponsor's Earnings per Share			EITF.89-12
. . Earnings per Share Treatment of Tax Benefits from Dividends Distributed .			EITF.92-3
Disclosures by SEC Registrants..................			EITF.89-8
Earnings per Share Treatment of Tax Benefits for Dividends on Stock Held by an ESOP			EITF.90-4
Earnings per Share Treatment of Tax Benefits for Dividends on Unallocated Stock Held by an ESOP...........................			EITF.92-3

FAS–FASB Statements	FIN–FASB Interpretations	FTB–FASB Technical Bulletins
APB–APB Opinions	AIN–AICPA Interpretations	ARB–Accounting Research Bulletins
CON–FASB Concepts	EITF–EITF Issues	Q&A–FASB Special Reports

	Original Pronouncements	Current Text	EITF and Other
EMPLOYEE STOCK OWNERSHIP PLANS (ESOPs)—continued			
Effect of Acquisition of Employer Shares for/by an Employee Benefit Trust on Accounting for Business Combinations...			EITF.93-2
Effect of Unallocated Shares on Applying Pooling-of-Interests Method to a Business Combination			EITF.88-27
Income Tax Benefits from Dividends Distributed			EITF.86-4
. . Earnings per Share Treatment			EITF.90-4
			EITF.92-3
Leveraged ESOPs			
. . Accounting for Treasury Stock in the Context of Pooling-of-Interests Business Combinations			EITF.D-19
. . Recognition by Sponsor of ESOP Debt			EITF.89-10
. . Sponsor's Balance Sheet Classification of Securities with a Put Option Held by an ESOP			EITF.89-11
Sale of Participant's Shares to Employer or to ESOP at Formula Price			EITF.87-23
Sponsor's Balance Sheet Classification of Securities with a Put Option Held by an ESOP			EITF.89-11
Use in a Leveraged Buyout			EITF.85-11
EMPLOYEE STOCK PURCHASE PLANS			
See Compensation to Employees: Stock Purchase and Stock Option Plans			
See Employee Stock Ownership Plans (ESOPs)			
EMPLOYEES			
See Compensation to Employees: Deferred			
See Defined Benefit Pension Plans			
See Pension Costs			
See Termination Benefits			
Definition	FAS35, ¶280	Pe5.410	
Receivables	ARB43, Ch.1A, ¶5	R36.105	
ENTITY			
Description	CON6, ¶24		
ENVIRONMENTAL CONTAMINATION			
Accounting for Environmental Liabilities ..			EITF.93-5
Asbestos Treatment Costs			EITF.89-13
Costs to Clean Up Environmental Contamination			EITF.90-8

See "Terminology" for references to defined terms presented in various accounting pronouncements.
See the Introduction to the Topical Index for details on the use of this index.

	Original Pronouncements	Current Text	EITF and Other

ENVIRONMENTAL LIABILITIES
See Environmental Contamination
EQUIPMENT
See Property, Plant, and Equipment
EQUITABLE OBLIGATIONS

	Original Pronouncements	Current Text	EITF and Other
Description	CON6, ¶202-203		

EQUITY (OR NET ASSETS)
See Shareholders' Equity
See Statement of Investments by and
  Distributions to Owners
Characteristics

	Original Pronouncements	Current Text	EITF and Other
. . Business Enterprises	CON6, ¶50-51		
	CON6, ¶60-63		
	CON6, ¶212-214		
. . Not-for-Profit Organizations	CON6, ¶52		
	CON6, ¶90-102		
	CON6, ¶221-222		
Definition	CON6, ¶49		
Difference between Equity and Liabilities	CON6, ¶55-59		
Elements of Financial Statements	CON6, ¶49-59		
Interrelation with Liabilities	CON6, ¶54-59		
Invested and Earned (Business Enterprises)	CON6, ¶214		
Recognition of Events Affecting	CON5, ¶59-60		
Relation to Assets	CON6, ¶107-108		
Relation to Comprehensive Income	CON6, ¶64-65		
Relation to Residual Interest	CON6, ¶49		
Residual or Ownership Interest	CON6, ¶213		
Sources of Changes in	CON6, ¶64-65		
	CON6, ¶107-108		
Transactions and Events Affecting	CON6, ¶107-110		

EQUITY CAPITAL
See Shareholders' Equity
EQUITY CERTIFICATES OF DEPOSIT
See Financial Instruments

	Original Pronouncements	Current Text	EITF and Other
Recognizing Contingent Interest Expense			EITF.84-31

EQUITY COMMITMENT NOTES
See Financial Instruments

	Original Pronouncements	Current Text	EITF and Other
Earnings per Share Computations			EITF.85-18

EQUITY CONTRACT NOTES
See Financial Instruments

	Original Pronouncements	Current Text	EITF and Other
Earnings per Share Computations			EITF.85-18

EQUITY KICKERS
See Financial Instruments
Acquisition, Development, and

	Original Pronouncements	Current Text	EITF and Other
Construction Loans			EITF.84-4
			EITF.86-21

EQUITY METHOD INVESTMENTS
See Investments: Equity Method

E

	Original Pronouncements	Current Text	EITF and Other

EQUITY METHOD OF ACCOUNTING
See Investments: Equity Method
EQUITY SECURITIES
See Investments: Debt and Equity
 Securities
ERISA
See Defined Benefit Pension Plans
Defined Benefit Pension Plans .... FAS35, ¶28 — Pe5.127
Definition .... FAS35, ¶280 — Pe5.411
ERRORS OR IRREGULARITIES
Affecting Prior Periods .... APB20, ¶13 — A35.103-104
.... FAS109, ¶288
ESTIMATES
Changes in Accounting Estimates .... APB20, ¶10-11 — A06.109-110
.... APB20, ¶31-33 — A06.130-132
Relation to Reliability .... CON2, ¶72-78
Use in Financial Statements .... CON1, ¶21
EVENTS AND TRANSACTIONS
Affecting Assets .... CON6, ¶32-33
Asset and Liability Changes .... CON5, ¶59-60
. . Recognition Criteria .... CON5, ¶88-90
Description .... CON6, ¶135-138
Exchange Transactions .... CON6, ¶137
External Events .... CON6, ¶135
.... CON6, ¶137
Internal Events .... CON6, ¶135
.... CON6, ¶138
Internal Transactions .... CON6, ¶138
Nonreciprocal Transfers .... CON6, ¶137
.... CON6, ¶150-151
EXCHANGE CONTRACT
Definition .... FIN39, ¶3 — B10.104
EXCHANGE RATES
See Foreign Currency Translation
EXCHANGE TRANSACTIONS
See Financial Instruments
Description .... CON6, ¶137
EXCHANGEABLE DEBT
Accounting for Exchangeability Feature .... — — EITF.85-9
EXERCISE OF WARRANTS
See Capital Stock: Capital Transactions
See Earnings per Share
EXPENSES
See Development Stage Enterprises
See Losses
Accruals .... ARB43, Ch.3A, ¶7 — B05.108
Characteristics .... CON6, ¶81
Component of Comprehensive Income ...... CON6, ¶73-77
.... CON6, ¶215-220
Definition .... CON6, ¶80

See "Terminology" for references to defined terms presented in various accounting pronouncements.
See the Introduction to the Topical Index for details on the use of this index.

	Original Pronouncements	Current Text	EITF and Other
EXPENSES—continued			
Elements of Financial Statements	CON6, ¶80-81		
Not-for-Profit Organizations	CON6, ¶111-113	No5.123-125	
	FAS117, ¶26-28		
Recognition Criteria, Guidance in Application			
. . Loss or Lack of Future Benefit	CON5, ¶85-87		
Relation to Losses	CON6, ¶87-89		
EXPLORATION COSTS			
See Oil and Gas Producing Activities			
EXPORT SALES			
See Segment of Business Reporting			
EXPROPRIATION			
See Extraordinary Items			
Loss Contingencies	FAS5, ¶4	C59.122	
Threat of	FAS5, ¶32	C59.138	
EXTENDED WARRANTY CONTRACTS			
See Revenue Recognition			
EXTERNAL EVENTS			
See Events and Transactions			
EXTINGUISHMENT OF DEBT			
See Debt: Extinguishments			
EXTRACTIVE INDUSTRIES			
See Changing Prices: Reporting Their Effects in Financial Reports			
See Oil and Gas Producing Activities			
Accounting Change			
. . From/To Full Cost Method	APB20, ¶27	A06.123	
Advances to Encourage Exploration, Imputed Interest	AIN-APB21, #1	I69.501	
Prior-Period Adjustments			
. . Full Cost Method	APB20, ¶27	A35.114	
EXTRAORDINARY ITEMS			
See Disclosure			
See Income Statement Presentation: Discontinued Operations			
Abnormal Costs	APB30, ¶20-22	I17.108-109	
		I17.401	
Accounting for Estimated Payments in Connection with the Coal Industry Retiree Health Benefit Act of 1992			EITF.92-13
Asbestos Treatment Costs			EITF.89-13
Casualty Loss	APB30, ¶23	I17.111	
Costs Incurred in a Takeover Defense			EITF.85-2
Criteria	AIN-APB30, #1	I17.106-110	
	APB30, ¶19-23	I17.503-504	
. . Costs Incurred in Defending against a Takeover Attempt	FTB85-6, ¶6-7	I17.509-510	EITF.85-2

	Original Pronouncements	Current Text	EITF and Other
EXTRAORDINARY ITEMS—continued			
Criteria—continued			
. . Examples That Do Not Meet Criteria ...	AIN-APB9, #1	I17.501-502	EITF.85-2
....	AIN-APB30, #1	I17.506-507	EITF.89-13
....	FTB85-6, ¶6-7	I17.509-510	
. . Examples That Meet Criteria	AIN-APB30, #1	I17.505	
. . Losses Caused by Bankruptcy	AIN-APB9, #1	I17.501-502	
Debt: Extinguishments	FAS4, ¶8	D14.105-106	
....	FAS4, ¶10		
Debt: Restructurings	FAS15, ¶21	D22.117	
Definition	APB30, ¶20	I17.401	
Devaluation	APB30, ¶23	I17.110	
Equity Method Investments	APB18, ¶19	I82.109	
Expropriation	APB30, ¶23	I17.111	
Extinguishment of Debt	FAS4, ¶8	I17.113	
....	FAS64, ¶4		
Federal Home Loan Mortgage Corporation (FHLMC)			
. . Distribution of FHLMC Participating Preferred Stock	FTB85-1, ¶2	Bt7.502	
Gains (Losses) Not Extraordinary	APB30, ¶23	I17.110	
Induced Conversions			
. . Income Statement Display of Expense .	FAS84, ¶3	D10.103C	
Infrequent Items	APB30, ¶20	I17.107	
....	APB30, ¶22	I17.109	
Interim Financial Reporting	APB28, ¶21	I73.124	
. . Tax Effects	FAS109, ¶288	I73.126-129	
....	FIN18, ¶16-19	I73.182-184	
....	FIN18, ¶56-58	I73.189-195	
....	FIN18, ¶62		
Losses Caused by Bankruptcies	AIN-APB9, #1	I17.501-502	
Materiality	APB30, ¶24	I17.118	
Prior-Period Adjustments	APB30, ¶25	I17.119	
....	FAS16, ¶16		
Receipt of FHLMC Participating Preferred Stock	FTB85-1, ¶1-4	Bt7.501-505	EITF.85-7
....	FTB85-1, ¶14		
Regulated Operations			
. . Discontinuation of Accounting for the Effects of Certain Types of Regulation	FAS101, ¶6	I17.117A	
....	FAS101, ¶9-10	Re6.205	
. . Write-down or Write-off of Abandoned Nuclear Power Plant			EITF.D-5
Scope of Accounting and Reporting Requirements	APB9, ¶6	I17.101	
Significant Asset Disposition after Pooling	APB16, ¶60	I17.117	

See "Terminology" for references to defined terms presented in various accounting pronouncements.
See the Introduction to the Topical Index for details on the use of this index.

	Original Pronouncements	Current Text	EITF and Other
EXTRAORDINARY ITEMS—continued			
Subsequent Realization of Unrecognized Tax Benefits			
. . Sale of Asset Acquired in Purchase Business Combination			EITF.85-3
Takeover Attempt Costs	FTB85-6, ¶6-7	I17.509-510	
Unusual Items	APB30, ¶20-21	I17.107-108	
	APB30, ¶23	I17.111	
Write-down or Write-off of Abandoned Nuclear Power Plant			EITF.D-5
Write-off of Operating Rights of Motor Carriers	FAS44, ¶6-7	I17.114-115	
	FAS44, ¶24		

(The next page is T-151.)

FAS–FASB Statements	FIN–FASB Interpretations	FTB–FASB Technical Bulletins
APB–APB Opinions	AIN–AICPA Interpretations	ARB–Accounting Research Bulletins
CON–FASB Concepts	EITF–EITF Issues	Q&A–FASB Special Reports

	Original Pronouncements	Current Text	EITF and Other
FACTORING			
See Receivables Sold with Recourse			
FAIR VALUE			
See Impairment: Loans			
See Impairment: Long-Lived Assets			
See Investments: Debt and Equity Securities			
See Leases			
See Pension Costs			
Basis in Leveraged Buyout Transactions....			EITF.86-16
			EITF.88-16
Contributions	FAS116, ¶19-21	C67.115-117	
Debt Securities			
. . Determining Fair Value	FAS115, ¶110-111	I80.112	
Defined Benefit Pension Plans	FAS35, ¶11	Pe5.110	
	FAS35, ¶104		
	FAS110, ¶4		
	FAS110, ¶7		
Definition	FAS67, ¶28	P16.422	
	FAS87, ¶264	Re2.405	
Distributions of Loans Receivable to Shareholders			EITF.87-17
Dividends-in-Kind			EITF.87-17
Employee Benefit Plans			
. . Valuation of Investment Contracts with Noninsurance Entities			EITF.89-1
Equity Securities			
. . Determining Fair Value	FAS115, ¶110-111	I80.112	
. . Readily Determinable Fair Value	FAS115, ¶3	I80.101	
Exchange of Interest-Only and Principal-Only Securities for a Mortgage-Backed Security			EITF.90-2
Exchange of Real Estate Involving Boot....			EITF.87-29
Exchanges of Ownership Interests between Entities under Common Control			EITF.90-5
Hedges	FAS80, ¶5	F80.105	
	FAS115, ¶129		
. . Anticipated Transactions			EITF.86-28
. . Consistent Reporting for Hedged Instrument and Hedging Instrument...	FAS115, ¶115	I80.113	
. . Items Reported at Fair Value			EITF.86-28
. . Ongoing Assessment of Correlation			EITF.86-28
Implementation of Statement 107			EITF.D-29
In-Substance Foreclosure on Collateral			EITF.89-9
Liquidation of a Banking Institution			
. . Valuation of Assets and Liabilities by Liquidating Bank			EITF.88-25

	Original Pronouncements	Current Text	EITF and Other
FAIR VALUE—continued			
Nonmonetary Transactions	APB29, ¶20	N35.107	EITF.84-29
	APB29, ¶26	N35.112	EITF.84-39
			EITF.86-29
			EITF.87-17
			EITF.87-29
			EITF.93-11
. . Barter Transactions Involving Barter Credits			EITF.93-11
Quasi Reorganizations			
. . Assets Carried Forward	ARB43, Ch.7A, ¶4	Q15.105	
Transfers between Entities under Common Control			EITF.84-39
Valuation of Repossessed Real Estate			
. . Sale Accounted for under Installment or Cost Recovery Method			EITF.89-14
FARMS			
Inventory of Agricultural Products	ARB43, Ch.4, ¶16	I78.119	
FASB EMERGING ISSUES TASK FORCE (EITF)			
Reporting Accounting Changes	FAS111, ¶10	A06.127	
FEDERAL FINANCIAL INSTITUTIONS EXAMINATION COUNCIL (FFIEC)			
Mortgage Derivative Products			
. . Effect of Potential Designation as a High-Risk Security			EITF.D-39
FEDERAL HOME LOAN MORTGAGE CORPORATION (FHLMC)			
See Banking and Thrift Industries			
See Financial Instruments			
See Mortgage Banking Activities			
Definition	FAS65, ¶34	Mo4.406	
Distribution of FHLMC Participating Preferred Stock	FTB85-1, ¶1-4	Bt7.501-505	EITF.85-7
	FTB85-1, ¶14		
FEDERAL HOUSING ADMINISTRATION (FHA)			
See Financial Instruments			
Mortgage Insurance			
. . Effect on Profit Recognition by Seller			EITF.87-9
FEDERAL INCOME TAXES			
See Income Taxes			
FEDERAL NATIONAL MORTGAGE ASSOCIATION (FNMA)			
See Financial Instruments			
See Mortgage Banking Activities			
Definition	FAS65, ¶34	Mo4.404	

See "Terminology" for references to defined terms presented in various accounting pronouncements.
See the Introduction to the Topical Index for details on the use of this index.

	Original Pronouncements	Current Text	EITF and Other
FEDERAL SAVINGS AND LOAN INSURANCE CORPORATION (FSLIC)			
FSLIC-Assisted Acquisitions of Thrifts......			EITF.88-19
. . Disclosure Requirements.......................			EITF.88-19
Liquidation of a Banking Institution			
. . Valuation of Assets and Liabilities by Liquidating Bank			EITF.88-25
Management Consignment Program			
. . Accounting for Newly Chartered Institutions...			EITF.85-41
Net Worth Certificates			EITF.85-41
Secondary Reserve			
. . Write-off of Prepayments			EITF.87-22
FEEDBACK VALUE			
Component of Relevance	CON2, ¶51-52		
Definition	CON2, Glossary		
FEES			
See Franchising			
See Lending Activities			
See Mortgage Banking Activities			
FHLMC			
See Banking and Thrift Industries			
See Federal Home Loan Mortgage Corporation (FHLMC)			
FIFO (FIRST-IN, FIRST-OUT)			
Inventory Valuation Method			
See Inventory			
FINANCE CHARGES			
Balance Sheet Classification	ARB43, Ch.3A, ¶6	B05.107	
FINANCE COMPANIES			
See Lending Activities			
Nonrefundable Loan Fees and Costs	FAS91, ¶2	Fi4.102	
FINANCIAL CAPITAL MAINTENANCE CONCEPT			
See Capital Maintenance			
FINANCIAL FLEXIBILITY			
Definition	CON5, ¶24		
Use of Statement of Cash Flows in Assessing...	CON5, ¶52		
Use of Statement of Financial Position in Assessing...	CON5, ¶29		
FINANCIAL FUTURES			
See Financial Instruments			
See Futures Contracts			

	Original Pronouncements	Current Text	EITF and Other
FINANCIAL INSTITUTIONS REFORM, RECOVERY, AND ENFORCEMENT ACT OF 1989			
Accounting for Exit and Entrance Fees Incurred in a Conversion from the Savings Association Insurance Fund to the Bank Insurance Fund			EITF.90-11
Divestiture of Certain Investment Securities to an Unregulated Commonly Controlled Entity			EITF.89-18
FINANCIAL INSTRUMENTS			
See Disclosure			
Accounting for Financial Instruments Indexed to, and Potentially Settled in, a Company's Own Stock			EITF.94-7
Collateral	FAS105, ¶18-19	F25.113-114	
Concentrations of Credit Risk			
. . Illustrations	FAS105, ¶43-48	F25.135-140	
. . Illustrations of Disclosures			Q&A.FinDisc Ex. 2-4
. . Operating Leases			EITF.D-22
. . Reporting Requirements	FAS105, ¶20	F25.115	
. . Scope	FAS105, ¶12-14	F25.101-104	
	FAS105, ¶16		
	FAS111, ¶8		
Definitions			
. . Credit Risk	FAS105, ¶7	F25.401	
. . Derivative Financial Instrument	FAS119, ¶5	F25.401B	
. . Fair Value	FAS107, ¶5	F25.401C	
. . Financial Instruments	FAS105, ¶6	F25.402	
	FAS107, ¶3		
. . Market Risk	FAS105, ¶7	F25.403	
. . Risk of Accounting Loss	FAS105, ¶7	F25.404	
Derivative Financial Instruments	FAS119, ¶5-15	F25.105D-105F	
		F25.115I	
		F25.115L-115Q	
. . Encouraged Disclosure	FAS119, ¶10	F25.115N	
	FAS119, ¶12-13	F25.115P-115Q	
	FAS119, ¶69		
	FAS119, ¶73-74		
. . Fair Value	FAS119, ¶15	F25.115I	
	FAS119, ¶90		
. . Hedges of Anticipated Transactions	FAS119, ¶11	F25.115O	
. . Held for Purposes Other Than Trading	FAS119, ¶9	F25.115M	
	FAS119, ¶11	F25.115O	
	FAS119, ¶48		
. . Held for Trading Purposes	FAS119, ¶9-10	F25.115M-115N	
	FAS119, ¶47		
. . Illustrations of Disclosures			Q&A.FinDisc Ex. 1-4
. . Scope	FAS119, ¶5-7	F25.105D-105F	

See "Terminology" for references to defined terms presented in various accounting pronouncements.
See the Introduction to the Topical Index for details on the use of this index.

	Original Pronouncements	Current Text	EITF and Other
FINANCIAL INSTRUMENTS—continued			
Fair Value	FAS107, ¶5-7	F25.105G	
		F25.115A-115B	
. . Core Deposits	FAS107, ¶12	F25.115E	
. . Custom-Tailored Financial Instruments	FAS107, ¶24-25	F25.147-148	
. . Deposit Liabilities	FAS107, ¶12	F25.115E	
	FAS107, ¶29	F25.152	
. . Estimating Fair Value, Examples	FAS107, ¶18-29	F25.141-152	
. . Exemptions from Disclosure Requirements	FAS107, ¶8	F25.105H	
. . Financial Instruments with No Quoted Market Prices	FAS107, ¶22-29	F25.145-152	
. . Financial Instruments with Quoted Market Prices	FAS107, ¶20-21	F25.143-144	
. . Financial Liabilities	FAS107, ¶12	F25.115E	
	FAS107, ¶28	F25.151	
. . Illustrations of Disclosures	FAS107, ¶30-33	F25.153-156	Q&A.FinDisc Ex. 1-4
. . Intangible Assets	FAS107, ¶12	F25.115E	
. . Loans Receivable	FAS107, ¶26-27	F25.149-150	
. . Options	FAS107, ¶25	F25.148	
. . Practicability	FAS107, ¶14-15	F25.115J-115K	
. . Reporting Requirements	FAS107, ¶10-15	F25.115C-115F	
	FAS119, ¶15	F25.115I-115K	
. . Scope	FAS107, ¶7-9	F25.105G-105I	
. . Trade Receivables and Payables	FAS107, ¶13	F25.115F	
Illustrations of Disclosures			Q&A.FinDisc Ex. 1-4
. . Derivative Financial Instruments Held or Issued for Purposes Other Than Trading			Q&A.FinDisc Ex. 1-4
. . Derivative Financial Instruments Held or Issued for Trading Purposes			Q&A.FinDisc Ex. 3-4
. . Domestic Financial Institution			Q&A.FinDisc Ex. 3
. . Entities That Are Limited Users of Derivative Financial Instruments			Q&A.FinDisc Ex. 1
. . International Financial Institution			Q&A.FinDisc Ex. 4
. . Major Corporation			Q&A.FinDisc Ex. 2
Implementation of Statement 105			EITF.D-22
Implementation of Statement 107			EITF.D-29
Off-Balance-Sheet Risk			
. . Illustrations	FAS105, ¶40	F25.133-140	
	FAS105, ¶42-48		
. . Reporting Requirements	FAS105, ¶17-19	F25.112-114	
	FAS119, ¶14		
. . Scope	FAS105, ¶12-16	F25.101-105	
	FAS111, ¶8		
Offsetting of Amounts Related to Certain Contracts	FIN39, ¶8-10	B10.104-106	

	Original Pronouncements	Current Text	EITF and Other

FINANCIAL INSTRUMENTS—continued

Presentation of Market Values Recognized for Off-Balance-Sheet Financial Instruments.. | | | EITF.D-25

FINANCIAL POSITION

See Balance Sheet Classification: Current Assets and Liabilities
See Cash Flows Statement
See Defined Benefit Pension Plans
See Financial Statements: Comparative Financial Statements
See Interim Financial Reporting
See Statement of Financial Position

Definition	APB18, ¶3	I82.404	
....	CON6, ¶20		

FINANCIAL REPORTING

Accrual Basis of Accounting.......................	CON6, ¶134-152	
Character and Limitations of Information Provided	CON1, ¶17-23	
Characteristics...	CON1, ¶5-8	
Compared to Management Reporting.........	CON1, ¶27	
Conservatism	CON2, ¶91-97	
General Purpose External Reporting, Objectives..	CON1, ¶28-31	
Information about Claims on Resources, Changes..	CON1, ¶40-41	
Information about Economic Resources, Changes..	CON1, ¶40-41	
Limitations Due to Nonrecognition	CON6, ¶48	
Limitations of Information..........................	CON1, ¶17-23	
Neutrality of Information	CON1, ¶33	
Nonfinancial Information	CON1, ¶7	
Not-for-Profit Organizations	CON4, ¶43-55	
Not-for-Profit Organizations, Characteristics and Limitations	CON4, ¶23-28	
Objectives...	CON1, ¶32-54	
Relation to Financial Statements................	CON1, ¶5-8	
Relation to Recognition in Financial Statements	CON5, ¶5-9	
Relevant Information....................................	CON1, ¶36	
Role in Decision Making.............................	CON2, ¶27-31	

FINANCIAL STATEMENTS

See Cash Flows Statement
See Disclosure
See Elements of Financial Statements
See Not-for-Profit Organizations
See Recognition and Measurement in Financial Statements
See Statement of Financial Position
See Statement of Income

See "Terminology" for references to defined terms presented in various accounting pronouncements.
See the Introduction to the Topical Index for details on the use of this index.

	Original Pronouncements	Current Text	EITF and Other

FINANCIAL STATEMENTS—continued

Application of Statement 109 in Foreign
Financial Statements Restated for
General Price-Level Changes .... | | | EITF.93-9

Attribute to Be Measured, Definition.......... CON1, ¶2

Characteristics of .... CON1, ¶17-23

Credit Unions
. . Balance Sheet Presentation of Savings
Accounts .... | | | EITF.89-3

General Purpose External............................ CON1, ¶28-30

Historic Reporting Norms .... CON1, ¶6

Limitations.. CON1, ¶17-23

Management Performance, Limitations...... CON1, ¶53-54

New Basis of Accounting Resulting from
Change in Ownership............................. | | | EITF.85-21

Separate Statements of a Subsidiary
. . Push-down Accounting .... | | | EITF.84-23
.... | | | EITF.84-42
.... | | | EITF.85-21

FINANCIAL STATEMENTS: COMPARATIVE FINANCIAL STATEMENTS

See Adjustments of Financial Statements
for Prior Periods
See Disclosure
See Earnings per Share
See Not-for-Profit Organizations
See Segment of Business Reporting

Inconsistencies in Comparative Figures
Disclosed... ARB43, Ch.2A, ¶3   F43.103

Scope of Accounting and Reporting
Requirements .... ARB43, Ch.2A, ¶1-2 F43.101-102

FINANCING

See Balance Sheet Classification: Current
Assets and Liabilities
See Business Combinations
See Capital Stock: Capital Transactions
See Capital Stock: Preferred Stock
See Consolidation
See Debt: Convertible Debt and Debt with
Stock Purchase Warrants
See Debt: Product Financing
Arrangements
See Development Stage Enterprises
See Franchising
See Leases
See Lending Activities
See Quasi Reorganizations
See Real Estate

FAS–FASB Statements   FIN–FASB Interpretations   FTB–FASB Technical Bulletins
APB–APB Opinions   AIN–AICPA Interpretations   ARB–Accounting Research Bulletins
CON–FASB Concepts   EITF–EITF Issues   Q&A–FASB Special Reports

	Original Pronouncements	Current Text	EITF and Other

FINANCING—continued
See Research and Development
  Arrangements
See Retained Earnings
Agreements
    See Balance Sheet Classification:
    Current Assets and Liabilities

FINISHED GOODS
See Inventory

Balance Sheet Classification	ARB43, Ch.3A, ¶4	B05.105	

FIRE AND CASUALTY INSURANCE ENTERPRISES
See Insurance Industry

FISCAL FUNDING, LEASES
See Leases

FIXED ASSETS
See Depreciation

Cash Flows Reporting	FAS95, ¶15-17	C25.113-115	
	FAS95, ¶24	C25.122	

Duplicate Facilities following a Purchase
  Business Combination
. . Costs of Closing Duplicate Facilities

of an Acquirer	FTB85-5, ¶1-2	B50.651-652	EITF.84-35

Environmentally Contaminated Property
. . Costs Incurred to Clean Up

Environmental Contamination			EITF.90-8
Idle Facilities			EITF.84-28

Property with Asbestos
. . Costs Incurred for Asbestos

Treatment			EITF.89-13
Segment of Business Reporting	FAS14, ¶27	S20.133	

Write-downs

. . Operating Assets	FAS5, ¶31	C59.137	EITF.84-28
. . Relation to Contingencies	FAS5, ¶31	C59.102	

FIXED PRICE CONTRACTS
See Contractor Accounting: Construction-
  Type Contracts
See Contractor Accounting: Government
  Contracts

FLOW-THROUGH METHOD
See Income Taxes

FOOTNOTES
See Notes to Financial Statements

FORECASTS
See Development Stage Enterprises

FORECLOSURE
See Debt: Restructurings
See Impairment: Loans

See "Terminology" for references to defined terms presented in various accounting pronouncements.
See the Introduction to the Topical Index for details on the use of this index.

	Original Pronouncements	Current Text	EITF and Other
FORECLOSURE—continued			
Classification of In-Substance Foreclosed (ISF) Assets by SEC Registrants			EITF.D-37
Valuation of Repossessed Real Estate			
. . Sale Accounted for under Installment or Cost Recovery Method...................			EITF.89-14
FOREIGN CURRENCY			
See Foreign Currency Translation			
Accounting for a Change in Functional Currency When an Economy Ceases to Be Considered Highly Inflationary...........			EITF.92-4
. . Income Tax Effects			EITF.92-8
Definition...	FAS52, ¶162	F60.401-423	
Transfer of Receivables in Which Risk of Foreign Currency Fluctuation Is Retained..			EITF.D-13
FOREIGN CURRENCY SWAPS			
See Financial Instruments			
Offsetting			EITF.86-25
FOREIGN CURRENCY TRANSLATION			
See Disclosure			
See Financial Instruments			
Accounting Changes....................................	FAS52, ¶9	F60.113	
....	FAS52, ¶45		
Accounting for a Change in Functional Currency When an Economy Ceases to Be Considered Highly Inffationary............			EITF.92-4
. . Income Tax Effects			EITF.92-8
Accounting for Dual Currency Bonds			EITF.93-10
Currency Swaps...	FAS52, ¶17	F60.124	
Devaluation			
. . Extraordinary Item.................................	APB30, ¶23	I17.110	
Discounting..			EITF.87-2
Exchange Rates..	FAS52, ¶26	F60.136	
. . Criteria for Choice.................................	FAS52, ¶27	F60.137	
. . Different Periods between Entities........	FAS52, ¶28	F60.138	
. . Exchange Rates to Be Used	FAS52, ¶12	F60.118	
. . Lack of Convertibility	FAS52, ¶26	F60.136	
Foreign Currency Swaps			
. . Offsetting			EITF.86-25
Foreign Currency Transactions	FAS52, ¶15-16	F60.122-123	
....	FAS52, ¶96		
....	FAS52, ¶120		
Foreign Debt-for-Equity Swaps			EITF.87-12
Forward Exchange Contracts	FAS52, ¶17	F60.124	EITF.87-2
. . Computation of Gains (Losses).............	FAS52, ¶18	F60.125	
. . Discount or Premium on	FAS52, ¶18	F60.125	

FAS–FASB Statements	FIN–FASB Interpretations	FTB–FASB Technical Bulletins
APB–APB Opinions	AIN–AICPA Interpretations	ARB–Accounting Research Bulletins
CON–FASB Concepts	EITF–EITF Issues	Q&A–FASB Special Reports

	Original Pronouncements	Current Text	EITF and Other
FOREIGN CURRENCY			
TRANSLATION—continued			
Forward Exchange Contracts—continued			
. . Reporting Hedges in Cash Flows			
Statement	FAS104, ¶7	C25.112	
		F60.126A	
. . Speculative Forward Contract	FAS52, ¶19	F60.126	
Functional Currency	FAS52, ¶5	F60.104	
. . Change in and Accounting for That			
Change	FAS52, ¶9	F60.113-114	
	FAS52, ¶46		
. . Classes of Foreign Operations	FAS52, ¶79-81	F60.106-108	
. . Management Judgment in			
Determining	FAS52, ¶8	F60.109	
	FAS52, ¶39		
	FAS52, ¶41		
. . Remeasurement Required If Books			
Not Maintained in Functional			
Currency	FAS52, ¶10	F60.115	
. . Salient Factors in Determining	FAS52, ¶7	F60.110-112	
	FAS52, ¶42-44		
Futures	FAS52, ¶17	F60.124	
	FAS80, ¶1	F80.101	
Gains (Losses) to Be Excluded from Net			
Income	FAS52, ¶20	F60.127-128	
	FAS52, ¶129		
	FAS52, ¶131		
. . Hedge of Net Investment	FAS52, ¶21	F60.129-130	
	FAS52, ¶130		
. . Long-Term Intercompany			
Investments	FAS52, ¶20	F60.127	
	FAS52, ¶131		
Glossary	FAS52, ¶162	F60.401-423	
Hedges	FAS52, ¶21	F60.129-131	
	FAS52, ¶130		
	FAS52, ¶133		
. . Disclosures Required for Hedges of			
Anticipated Currency Transactions			EITF.91-4
. . Hedging Currency Risks with			
Complex Options and Similar			
Transactions			EITF.91-4
. . Hedging Foreign Currency Risks with			
Purchased Options			EITF.90-17
. . Hedging Intercompany Foreign			
Currency Risks			EITF.91-1
			EITF.95-2
. . Hedging with Tandem Currency			EITF.87-26
. . Nonapplicability of Futures Contracts			
Accounting and Reporting			
Requirements	FAS80, ¶7	F80.107	

See "Terminology" for references to defined terms presented in various accounting pronouncements.

See the Introduction to the Topical Index for details on the use of this index.

	Original Pronouncements	Current Text	EITF and Other
FOREIGN CURRENCY TRANSLATION—continued			
Highly Inflationary Economies			
. . Accounting for a Change in Functional Currency When an Economy Ceases to Be Considered Highly Inflationary			EITF.92-4
. . Accounting for the Income Tax Effects under Statement 109 of a Change in Functional Currency When an Economy Ceases to Be Considered Highly Inflationary			EITF.92-8
Income Tax Consequences of Rate Changes			
. . Allocation of Tax Expense	FAS52, ¶24	F60.134	
. . Interperiod Tax Allocation	FAS52, ¶22	F60.132-133	
	FAS52, ¶135		
Intercompany Balances and Transactions	FAS52, ¶25	F60.135	
Inventories			
. . Application of Lower of Cost or Market Rule	FAS52, ¶49-53	F60.148-152	
Objectives of Translation	FAS52, ¶4	F60.103	
Remeasurement of Books of Record into Functional Currency			
. . Items to Be Measured Using Historical Rates	FAS52, ¶48	F60.147	
	FAS109, ¶288		
. . Objectives	FAS52, ¶47	F60.146	
. . Rates to Be Used	FAS52, ¶47	F60.146	
Sale of Future Revenue			
. . Payment to Investor Denominated in Foreign Currency			EITF.88-18
Sale or Liquidation of an Investment in a Foreign Entity	FAS52, ¶14	F60.120	
	FIN37, ¶2		
	FIN37, ¶8		
Scope of Accounting and Reporting Requirements	FAS52, ¶2	F60.101	
. . Consolidation, Equity Investees, and Post-Business Combinations	FAS52, ¶101	F60.102	
Selection of Exchange Rate When Trading Is Temporarily Suspended			EITF.D-12
Statement of Cash Flows			
. . Impact on	FAS95, ¶25	C25.142-152A	
	FAS95, ¶136-146	F60.118A	
Translation Adjustments	FAS52, ¶13-14	F60.119-120	
	FIN37, ¶2		
Translation of Operations in Highly Inflationary Economies	FAS52, ¶11	F60.116-117	
	FAS52, ¶109		

FAS–FASB Statements	FIN–FASB Interpretations	FTB–FASB Technical Bulletins
APB–APB Opinions	AIN–AICPA Interpretations	ARB–Accounting Research Bulletins
CON–FASB Concepts	EITF–EITF Issues	Q&A–FASB Special Reports

	Original Pronouncements	Current Text	EITF and Other
FOREIGN CURRENCY			
TRANSLATION—continued			
Use of Averages or Other Methods of			
Approximation	FAS52, ¶133	F60.139	
FOREIGN ENTITY			
See Foreign Operations			
FOREIGN EXCHANGE			
See Foreign Currency Translation			
FOREIGN EXCHANGE CONTRACTS			
See Financial Instruments			
See Foreign Currency Translation			
FOREIGN EXCHANGE GAINS AND			
LOSSES			
See Foreign Currency Translation			
FOREIGN OPERATIONS			
See Consolidation			
See Disclosure			
See Foreign Currency Translation			
See Income Taxes			
See Oil and Gas Producing Activities			
See Pension Costs			
See Postretirement Benefits Other Than			
Pensions			
See Segment of Business Reporting			
Background to Requirements	ARB43, Ch.12, ¶1-3	F65.100A-100C	
Disclosure	ARB43, Ch.12, ¶5-6	F65.102-103	
Elimination of Write-ups on Depreciable			
Assets	APB6, ¶17	D40.102	
Interest: Capitalization of Interest Costs	FAS34, ¶14	I67.111	
Inventory			
. . Lower of Cost or Market	FAS52, ¶49-53	F60.148-152	
Recognition of Foreign Earnings	ARB43, Ch.12, ¶4	F65.101	
	ARB43, Ch.12, ¶6	F65.103	
. . Deferred Taxes	FAS37, ¶23-25	I27.209-211	
	FAS109, ¶287-288		
. . Earnings in Excess of Amounts			
Received in U.S.	ARB43, Ch.12, ¶5	F65.102	
FOREIGN TAXES			
See Foreign Currency Translation			
See Income Taxes			
FOREST PRODUCTS INDUSTRY			
See Timberlands and Growing Timber			
FORWARD COMMITMENTS			
See Financial Instruments			
See Foreign Currency Translation			
Accounting for Financial Instruments			
Indexed to, and Potentially Settled in, a			
Company's Own Stock			EITF.94-7
Hedges			EITF.86-26
Mortgage Swaps			EITF.88-8

See "Terminology" for references to defined terms presented in various accounting pronouncements.

See the Introduction to the Topical Index for details on the use of this index.

	Original Pronouncements	Current Text	EITF and Other
FORWARD COMMITMENTS—continued			
Surrogate for Deferred Rate Setting............			EITF.86-26
FORWARD CONTRACTS			
See Financial Instruments			
Comparison with Futures Contracts............	FAS80, ¶34	F80.101	
FORWARD EXCHANGE CONTRACTS			
See Foreign Currency Translation			
Accounting for Financial Instruments Indexed to, and Potentially Settled in, a Company's Own Stock			EITF.94-7
FRANCHISE COSTS			
See Cable Television Industry			
FRANCHISING			
See Cable Television Industry			
See Disclosure			
Franchisors			
. . Agency Sales	FAS45, ¶16	Fr3.112	
. . Area Franchise Fees	FAS45, ¶8-9	Fr3.104-105	
. . Commingled Revenue	FAS45, ¶12-13	Fr3.108-109	
. . Continuing Franchise Fees, Revenue Recognition	FAS45, ¶14	Fr3.110	
. . Continuing Product Sales	FAS45, ¶15	Fr3.111	
. . Costs Relating to Franchise Sales	FAS45, ¶17	Fr3.113	
. . Disclosure	FAS45, ¶20-23	Fr3.116-119	
. . Individual Franchise Sales	FAS45, ¶5-7	Fr3.101-103	
. . Individual Franchise Sales, Initial Franchise Fees....................................	FAS45, ¶7	Fr3.103	
. . Option to Repurchase Franchise	FAS45, ¶11	Fr3.107	
. . Repossessed Franchises........................	FAS45, ¶18	Fr3.114	
Franchisors, Franchisees			
. . Business Combinations	FAS45, ¶19	Fr3.115	
. . Relationships	FAS45, ¶10-11	Fr3.106-107	
Glossary	FAS45, ¶26	Fr3.401-408	
Intangible Assets..	APB17, ¶1	I60.101	
FRATERNAL BENEFIT SOCIETIES			
See Insurance Industry			
Definition	FAS60, ¶66	In6.411	
FREIGHT SERVICES			
Revenue and Expense Recognition for Freight Services in Process......................			EITF.91-9
FRINGE BENEFIT PLANS			
See Compensation to Employees: Stock Purchase and Stock Option Plans			
See Defined Benefit Pension Plans			
See Employee Stock Ownership Plans (ESOPs)			
See Pension Costs			
See Postemployment Benefits			

FAS–FASB Statements	FIN–FASB Interpretations	FTB–FASB Technical Bulletins
APB–APB Opinions	AIN–AICPA Interpretations	ARB–Accounting Research Bulletins
CON–FASB Concepts	EITF–EITF Issues	Q&A–FASB Special Reports

	Original Pronouncements	Current Text	EITF and Other

FRINGE BENEFIT PLANS—continued
See Postretirement Health Care and Life
  Insurance Benefits
FULL ACCRUAL METHOD (REAL ESTATE)
See Real Estate: Sales Other Than Retail
  Land Sales
FULL COST METHOD
See Accounting Changes
See Oil and Gas Producing Activities
FULL ELIGIBILITY DATE
See Postretirement Benefits Other Than
  Pensions
FULLY DILUTED EARNINGS PER SHARE
See Earnings per Share
FUNCTIONAL CLASSIFICATION OF EXPENSES
See Not-for-Profit Organizations
FUNCTIONAL CURRENCY
See Foreign Currency Translation

Definition	FAS52, ¶162	F60.415	

FUNDING REQUIREMENTS
See Pension Costs
FUNDS FLOWS
See Cash Flows
FUNDS STATEMENT
See Cash Flows Statement
FUTURE ECONOMIC BENEFITS

Discussion	CON6, ¶26-30		
	CON6, ¶172-182		
Relation to Assets	CON6, ¶190-191		

FUTURES CONTRACTS
See Disclosure
See Financial Instruments
See Foreign Currency Translation

Anticipatory Hedges	FAS80, ¶26	F80.109	
	FAS80, ¶54	F80.112A	
	FAS104, ¶7	F80.123	
Classification			
. . Deferred Future Gains and Losses, Firm Commitments and Anticipated Transactions	FAS80, ¶9-10	F80.109-110	Q&A.80 #16-17
. . Margin Deposits			Q&A.80 #15
Daily Limits on Change in Market Price			Q&A.80 #2
Difference between Options and Futures	FAS80, ¶32	F80.101	
Estimates of Value	FAS80, ¶11	F80.111	Q&A.80 #26
Examples	FAS80, ¶16	F80.113	
. . Hedge of Financial Instruments Held for Sale	FAS80, ¶22-24	F80.119-121	

See "Terminology" for references to defined terms presented in various accounting pronouncements.
See the Introduction to the Topical Index for details on the use of this index.

	Original Pronouncements	Current Text	EITF and Other

FUTURES CONTRACTS—continued

Examples—continued

. . Hedge of an Anticipated Purchase	FAS80, ¶19-21	F80.116-118	
. . Hedge of the Interest Expense Related to Short-Term Deposits.......................	FAS80, ¶25-26	F80.122-123	
. . Nonhedge Contract..............................	FAS80, ¶17-18	F80.114-115	
Exclusion of Forward Contracts, Foreign Currency Futures, and Options.................	FAS80, ¶1	F80.101	Q&A.80 #1
....	FAS80, ¶34		
Glossary...	FAS80, ¶4	F80.401-404	
....	FAS80, ¶15		
Hedges	FAS80, ¶42	F80.103	
. . Amortization of Deferred Gains and Losses	FAS80, ¶7	F80.107	Q&A.80 #18-19
. . Anticipated Liabilities			EITF.86-34
. . Anticipated Transactions......................	FAS80, ¶54	F80.109-110	
....	FAS80, ¶56-57		
. . Classification in Cash Flows Statement..	FAS104, ¶7	C25.112 F80.112A	
. . Commodity Dealers...............................	FAS80, ¶8	F80.108	
. . Criteria	FAS80, ¶4	F80.104	Q&A.80 #3-7
....	FAS80, ¶62		
. . Cross-Hedging with Financial Futures..			EITF.85-6 Q&A.80 #14
. . Designation as a Hedge			EITF.85-6 Q&A.80 #8-11
. . Existing Assets, Liabilities, and Firm Commitments....................................	FAS80, ¶50	F80.106-108	
. . Financial Institutions	FAS80, ¶63	F80.104	
. . Financial Instruments Held to Maturity..	FAS80, ¶4	F80.104	
. . Foreign Currency Exposure and a Tandem Currency................................			EITF.87-26
. . Initial Assessment of Probability of Correlation	FAS80, ¶4	F80.104	Q&A.80 #7
. . Items Reported at Fair Value.................	FAS80, ¶5	F80.105	
....	FAS115, ¶129		
. . Measures of Correlation	FAS80, ¶4	F80.104	Q&A.80 #22-23
. . Of LIFO Inventories	FAS80, ¶8	F80.108	Q&A.80 #13
. . Ongoing Assessment of Correlation	FAS80, ¶11	F80.111	EITF.85-6 Q&A.80 #20-21 Q&A.80 #25
. . Probability of Occurrence of an Anticipated Transaction......................	FAS80, ¶9	F80.109	Q&A.80 #12
. . Reverse Repurchase Agreements..........			EITF.86-34
. . Subsequent to Termination...................			Q&A.80 #31-32
. . Termination of a Hedge........................			EITF.85-6 Q&A.80 #27-30

F   *Topical Index*

	Original Pronouncements	Current Text	EITF and Other

FUTURES CONTRACTS—continued

	Original Pronouncements	Current Text	EITF and Other
Implementation Issues			EITF.85-6
Interest Rate Swap Transactions			EITF.84-7
			EITF.84-36
			EITF.88-8
Mortgage Swaps			EITF.88-8
Recognition of Changes in Market Value	FAS80, ¶3	F80.103	
. . Daily Limits			Q&A.80 #2
Risk Assessment of Items to Be Hedged			
. . Ongoing Assessment	FAS80, ¶11	F80.111	Q&A.80 #24-25
. . Risk of the Business Unit	FAS80, ¶4	F80.104	Q&A.80 #4-5
. . Risk of the Enterprise	FAS80, ¶4	F80.104	Q&A.80 #3
. . Time Frame	FAS80, ¶4	F80.104	Q&A.80 #6
Scope of Accounting and Reporting			
Requirements	FAS80, ¶1-2	F80.101-102	
	FAS80, ¶35		
. . Comparison with Forward Contracts	FAS80, ¶1	F80.101	
	FAS80, ¶34		
. . Comparison with Futures Contracts for			
Foreign Currencies	FAS80, ¶1	F80.101	
. . Comparison with Options	FAS80, ¶32	F80.101	

(The next page is T-171.)

See "Terminology" for references to defined terms presented in various accounting pronouncements.
See the Introduction to the Topical Index for details on the use of this index.

T-166

	Original Pronouncements	Current Text	EITF and Other

GAIN CONTINGENCIES
See Contingencies
GAIN OR LOSS
See Contingencies
See Debt: Extinguishments
See Debt: Restructurings
See Extraordinary Items
See Foreign Currency Translation
See Gains
See Holding Gains (Losses)
See Income Statement Presentation:
  Discontinued Operations
See Income Taxes
See Inventory
See Investments: Debt and Equity
  Securities
See Investments: Equity Method
See Leases
See Losses
See Nonmonetary Transactions
See Pension Costs
See Postretirement Benefits Other Than
  Pensions
See Quasi Reorganizations
See Recognition and Measurement in
  Financial Statements

	Original Pronouncements	Current Text	EITF and Other
Unusual or Infrequent Items	APB30, ¶26	I22.101	

GAINS
See Recognition and Measurement in
  Financial Statements

	Original Pronouncements	Current Text	EITF and Other
Characteristics	CON6, ¶84-89		
Component of Comprehensive Income	CON6, ¶73-77		
Definition	CON6, ¶82		
Elements of Financial Statements	CON6, ¶82-89		
Holding	CON6, ¶71		
Operating vs. Nonoperating			
. . Business Enterprises	CON6, ¶86		
. . Not-for-Profit Organizations	CON6, ¶87-89		
	CON6, ¶111-113		
Recognition Criteria			
. . Guidance in Application	CON5, ¶83-84		
Relation to Revenues	CON6, ¶87-89		
Unrealized	CON6, ¶143		

**GENERAL AND ADMINISTRATIVE
EXPENSES**

	Original Pronouncements	Current Text	EITF and Other
Contractor Accounting	ARB45, ¶10	Co4.107	

**GENERALLY ACCEPTED
ACCOUNTING PRINCIPLES (GAAP)**
See Accounting Changes

FAS–FASB Statements   FIN–FASB Interpretations   FTB–FASB Technical Bulletins
APB–APB Opinions   AIN–AICPA Interpretations   ARB–Accounting Research Bulletins
CON–FASB Concepts   EITF–EITF Issues   Q&A–FASB Special Reports

	Original Pronouncements	Current Text	EITF and Other

GENERALLY ACCEPTED ACCOUNTING PRINCIPLES (GAAP)—continued

Conflict between Principles.........................	FAS111, ¶7	A06.112	
Financial Statements Prepared Based on Statutory Accounting Practices Instead of GAAP..	FIN40, ¶2	In6.106A	
....	FIN40, ¶10		
....	FIN40, ¶18		
Required Change in Accounting Principle..	FAS111, ¶7	A06.112	

GENERAL PRICE-LEVEL ACCOUNTING
See Changing Prices: Reporting Their Effects in Financial Reports
See Price-Level Changes

GENERAL PURPOSE EXTERNAL FINANCIAL REPORTING
See Financial Reporting
See Recognition and Measurement in Financial Statements

GEOGRAPHIC AREAS
See Segment of Business Reporting

GEOLOGICAL AND GEOPHYSICAL COSTS
See Oil and Gas Producing Activities

GIFTS
See Capital Stock: Capital Transactions
See Contributions
See Not-for-Profit Organizations

GNMA DOLLAR ROLLS

Mark-to-Market Accounting			EITF.84-20
Revenue Recognition			EITF.84-20

GOING CONCERN

Description..	ARB43, Ch.3A, ¶2	B05.103	

GOODWILL
See Business Combinations
See Impairment: Long-Lived Assets
See Intangible Assets
See Investments: Equity Method

Definition	APB16, ¶87	B50.403	
....	APB17, ¶1	I60.401	
Recognition and Measurement of the Tax Benefit of Excess Tax-Deductible Goodwill Resulting from a Retroactive Change in Tax Law			EITF.93-12

GOVERNMENT CONTRACTS
See Contractor Accounting: Government Contracts

See "Terminology" for references to defined terms presented in various accounting pronouncements.
See the Introduction to the Topical Index for details on the use of this index.

	Original Pronouncements	Current Text	EITF and Other
GOVERNMENT NATIONAL MORTGAGE ASSOCIATION (GNMA)			
See Financial Instruments			
See Mortgage Banking Activities			
Definition	FAS65, ¶34	Mo4.406	
GNMA Dollar Rolls			
. . Mark-to-Market Accounting			EITF.84-20
. . Revenue Recognition			EITF.84-20
GOVERNMENT-OWNED ENTERPRISES			
See Earnings per Share			
Utilities	FAS71, ¶5	Re6.115	
GOVERNMENTAL UNIT			
See Leases			
Defined Benefit Pension Plans, Application of Accounting Requirements			
. . Effective Date		Pe5.102	
Fiscal Funding Clauses			
. . Leases	FTB79-10, ¶1-5	L10.501-505	
GRACE PERIOD			
Callable Obligations	FAS78, ¶5	B05.109A	
Classifying Obligations (Current vs. Noncurrent)			
. . Covenant Violation Waived by Creditor			EITF.86-30
GRANTOR TRUST			
Consolidation			EITF.84-15
. . Grantor Trusts Owned by a Subsidiary			EITF.84-40
GRANTS			
See Contributions			
GREENMAIL			
See Capital Stock: Capital Transactions			
GROSS PROFIT METHOD			
See Interim Financial Reporting			
GUARANTEED INVESTMENT CONTRACTS (GICs)			
Definition	FAS110, ¶2	Pe5.413B	
Employee Benefit Plans	FAS110, ¶2	Pe5.110	EITF.89-1
GUARANTEES AND WARRANTIES			
See Contingencies			
See Financial Instruments			
See Related Parties			
Business Combinations	APB16, ¶48	B50.107	
Fee Recognition			EITF.85-20
Guaranteed Future Value of Stock Issued by Acquirer in a Business Combination			EITF.87-31
Impact of an Uncollateralized Irrevocable Letter of Credit on a Sale-Leaseback Transaction Involving Real Estate			EITF.90-20
Recognition of Liability			EITF.85-20

FAS–FASB Statements   FIN–FASB Interpretations   FTB–FASB Technical Bulletins
APB–APB Opinions   AIN–AICPA Interpretations   ARB–Accounting Research Bulletins
CON–FASB Concepts   EITF–EITF Issues   Q&A–FASB Special Reports

	Original Pronouncements	Current Text	EITF and Other
GUARANTEES AND WARRANTIES—continued			
Residual Value of Leased Asset	FTB79-14, ¶1-4	L10.514-517	
....	FTB86-2, ¶11-12	L10.538-539	
Revenue Recognition			
. . Sales with a Guaranteed Minimum Resale Value......................................			EITF.95-1
Sponsor's Recognition of Employee Stock Ownership Plan Debt...............................			EITF.89-10
Unsecured Guarantee by Parent of Subsidiary's Lease Payments			EITF.90-14

(The next page is T-179.)

See "Terminology" for references to defined terms presented in various accounting pronouncements.
See the Introduction to the Topical Index for details on the use of this index.

	Original Pronouncements	Current Text	EITF and Other

HEALTH CARE PROVIDERS
See Not-for-Profit Organizations
See Segment of Business Reporting

HEDGES
See Financial Instruments
See Foreign Currency Translation
See Futures Contracts

	Original Pronouncements	Current Text	EITF and Other
Classification in Cash Flows Statement	FAS104, ¶7	C25.112 F80.112A	
Consistent Reporting for Hedged Instrument and Hedging Instrument	FAS115, ¶115	I80.113	
Cross-Hedging with Financial Futures			EITF.85-6
Designation as a Hedge			EITF.85-6
Disclosures Required for Hedges of Anticipated Currency Transactions			EITF.91-4
Foreign Currency Options			EITF.D-16
Futures Contracts Implementation Issues			EITF.85-6
Hedging Currency Risks with Complex Options and Similar Transactions			EITF.91-4
Hedging Foreign Currency Risks of Future Net Income, Revenues, or Costs			EITF.D-16
Hedging Foreign Currency Risks with Purchased Options			EITF.90-17
Hedging Foreign Currency with Tandem Currency			EITF.87-26
Hedging Intercompany Foreign Currency Risks			EITF.91-1 EITF.95-2
Indexed Debt Instruments			EITF.86-28
Interest Costs through Forward Commitments			EITF.86-26
Interest Costs through a Deferred Rate Setting Arrangement			EITF.84-14
Interest Rate Swap Transactions			EITF.84-36 EITF.88-8
. . Termination or Sale			EITF.84-7
Mortgage Swaps			EITF.88-8
Ongoing Assessment of Correlation			EITF.85-6
Termination of a Hedge			EITF.85-6
Using Cash Securities			EITF.87-1

HIGHLY INFLATIONARY ECONOMIES
See Foreign Currency Translation

HISTORICAL COST (HISTORICAL PROCEEDS)

	Original Pronouncements	Current Text	EITF and Other
Recognition and Measurement . . Measurement Attribute	CON5, ¶67-69		

HISTORICAL COST FINANCIAL STATEMENTS

	Original Pronouncements	Current Text	EITF and Other
Conceptual Framework	CON1, ¶2		

FAS–FASB Statements	FIN–FASB Interpretations	FTB–FASB Technical Bulletins
APB–APB Opinions	AIN–AICPA Interpretations	ARB–Accounting Research Bulletins
CON–FASB Concepts	EITF–EITF Issues	Q&A–FASB Special Reports

	Original Pronouncements	Current Text	EITF and Other
HISTORICAL SUMMARIES OF FINANCIAL INFORMATION			
Accounting Changes....................................	APB20, ¶39	A06.134	
HISTORICAL TREASURES			
Depreciation..	FAS93, ¶6	D40.101A-101C	
....	FAS93, ¶35-37		
HOLDING COMPANY			
See Consolidation			
HOLDING GAINS (LOSSES)			
See Changing Prices: Reporting Their Effects in Financial Reports			
Recognition and Measurement in Financial Statements			
. . Financial Capital Maintenance..............	CON5, ¶48		
HOLIDAY PAY			
See Compensation to Employees: Paid Absences			

(The next page is T-185.)

See "Terminology" for references to defined terms presented in various accounting pronouncements.
See the Introduction to the Topical Index for details on the use of this index.

	Original Pronouncements	Current Text	EITF and Other

IDLE FACILITIES
See Impairment: Long-Lived Assets
Depreciation.. | | | EITF.84-28
Impairment of Long-Lived Assets .... | | | EITF.84-28
IF-CONVERTED METHOD
See Earnings per Share
IMPAIRMENT
See Impairment: Loans
See Impairment: Long-Lived Assets
See Lower of Cost or Market (Rule)
Assets Held for Disposal
. . Carrying Amount at Date of Adoption
    of Statement 121 .... | | | EITF.D-45
. . Computation of Cumulative Effect
    of Accounting Change When
    Statement 121 Is Adopted................... | | | EITF.D-45
Debt Securities
. . Recognition of Other-Than-Temporary
    Impairment Due to Planned Sale of
    Debt Security .... | | | EITF.D-44
Equity Method Investments .... APB18, ¶19 | | I82.109 |
Implementation of Statement 121 .... | | | EITF.D-45
Inventory
. . Price Declines during Interim
    Reporting Periods .... | | | EITF.86-13
Long-Lived Assets...................................... | | | EITF.84-28
Marketable Equity Securities
. . Other Than Temporary Decline in
    Market Value...................................... | | | EITF.85-39
Mortgage Obligation Instrument or
  Mortgage-Backed Interest-Only
  Certificate .... | | | EITF.93-18
Regulatory Assets
. . Accounting for OPEB Costs .... | | | EITF.93-4
Title Plant .... FAS61, ¶6 | | Ti7.106 |
IMPAIRMENT: LOANS
See Disclosure
See Financial Instruments
Allowance for Credit Losses .... FAS114, ¶5 | I08.103 |
.... FAS114, ¶7 | I08.105 |
Bad-Debt Expense .... FAS114, ¶13 | I08.111 |
Collateral-Dependent Loan .... FAS114, ¶13 | I08.111 |
Direct Write-Down of Impaired Loans .... FAS114, ¶7 | I08.105 |
Impaired Loan
. . Definition .... FAS114, ¶8 | I08.106 |
.... FAS118, ¶6 |
Income Recognition..................................... FAS118, ¶4 | I08.115 |
.... FAS118, ¶6 |
Insignificant Delay or Shortfall in
  Payment .... FAS114, ¶7 | I08.105 |

FAS–FASB Statements	FIN–FASB Interpretations	FTB–FASB Technical Bulletins
APB–APB Opinions	AIN–AICPA Interpretations	ARB–Accounting Research Bulletins
CON–FASB Concepts	EITF–EITF Issues	Q&A–FASB Special Reports

	Original Pronouncements	Current Text	EITF and Other
IMPAIRMENT: LOANS—continued			
Large Groups of Smaller-Balance Homogeneous Loans That Are Collectively Evaluated for Impairment....	FAS114, ¶6	I08.104	
Loan			
. . Definition	FAS114, ¶4	I08.102	
Measurement of Impairment	FAS114, ¶11-16	I08.109-114	
	FAS114, ¶53		
. . Aggregation of Certain Loans	FAS114, ¶12	I08.110	
. . Change in Measurement	FAS114, ¶16	I08.114	
. . Effective Interest Rate	FAS114, ¶14	I08.112	
. . Estimated Costs to Sell	FAS114, ¶13	I08.111	
	FAS114, ¶15	I08.113	
	FAS114, ¶46		
. . Estimates of Expected Future Cash Flows	FAS114, ¶15	I08.113	
. . Fair Value of the Collateral of a Collateral-Dependent Loan	FAS114, ¶13	I08.111	
. . Observable Market Price	FAS114, ¶13	I08.111	
. . Present Value of Expected Future Cash Flows	FAS114, ¶13	I08.111	
. . Probable Foreclosure	FAS114, ¶13	I08.111	
	FAS114, ¶71		
. . Valuation Allowance	FAS114, ¶7	I08.105	
	FAS114, ¶13	I08.111	
Net Carrying Amount	FAS114, ¶13	I08.111	
Probable Foreclosure	FAS114, ¶13	I08.111	
	FAS114, ¶71		
Recognition of Impairment	FAS114, ¶8-10	I08.106-108	
. . All Amounts Due under Contractual Terms	FAS114, ¶8	I08.106	
	FAS118, ¶6		
. . Loan Review Procedures	FAS114, ¶7-8	I08.105-106	
Recorded Investment	FAS114, ¶13	I08.111	
Scope of Accounting and Reporting Requirements	FAS114, ¶4-7	I08.102-105	
. . Exemption from Requirements	FAS114, ¶6	I08.104	
Subsequent Measurement of Impaired Loans	FAS114, ¶16	I08.114	
Troubled Debt Restructuring	FAS15, ¶2	D22.104	
	FAS114, ¶5	I08.103	
	FAS114, ¶9	I08.107	
	FAS114, ¶14	I08.112	
	FAS118, ¶6	I08.106	
Valuation Allowance	FAS114, ¶13	I08.111	
. . Determining Overall Adequacy of Allowance	FAS114, ¶7	I08.105	
IMPAIRMENT: LONG-LIVED ASSETS			
Assets to Be Disposed Of	FAS121, ¶15-19	I08.134-138	
. . Cost to Sell an Asset	FAS121, ¶16	I08.135	

See "Terminology" for references to defined terms presented in various accounting pronouncements.

See the Introduction to the Topical Index for details on the use of this index.

	Original Pronouncements	Current Text	EITF and Other
IMPAIRMENT: LONG-LIVED ASSETS—continued			
Assets to Be Disposed Of—continued			
. . Recognition and Measurement of Impairment Loss	FAS121, ¶15-17	I08.134-136	
. . Reporting and Disclosure	FAS121, ¶18-19	I08.137-138	
Assets to Be Held and Used	FAS121, ¶4-14	I08.123-133	
. . Goodwill	FAS121, ¶12	I08.131	
. . Recognition and Measurement of Impairment Loss	FAS121, ¶4-12	I08.123-131	
	FAS121, ¶93-94		
. . Reporting and Disclosure	FAS121, ¶13-14	I08.132-133	
Definition	FAS121, ¶65	I08.125	
Goodwill	FAS121, ¶12	I08.131	
Grouping for Measurement and Recognition of Impairment Loss	FAS121, ¶8-10	I08.127-129	
	FAS121, ¶95-97		
	FAS121, ¶99-100		
. . Estimates of Expected Future Cash Flows	FAS121, ¶6	I08.125	
	FAS121, ¶8-10	I08.127-129	
Measurement of Impairment Loss	FAS121, ¶7-11	I08.126-130	
	FAS121, ¶15-16	I08.134-135	
	FAS121, ¶74		
Not-for-Profit Organizations	FAS121, ¶13-14	I08.129	
	FAS121, ¶18-19	I08.132-133	
	FAS121, ¶99	I08.137-138	
Recognition of Impairment Loss	FAS121, ¶6	I08.125	
	FAS121, ¶10-12	I08.129-131	
	FAS121, ¶15-17	I08.134-136	
. . Assessment of Recoverability	FAS121, ¶4-5	I08.123-124	
Restoration of Impairment Losses	FAS121, ¶11	I08.130	
Scope of Accounting and Reporting Requirements	FAS121, ¶3	I08.122	
. . Exemption from Requirements	FAS121, ¶3	I08.122	
IMPLICIT INTEREST RATE			
See Leases			
IMPUTED INTEREST			
See Interest: Imputation of an Interest Cost			
INCENTIVE STOCK OPTIONS			
See Compensation to Employees: Deferred			
See Compensation to Employees: Stock Purchase and Stock Option Plans			
Disqualifying the Plan			EITF.87-6
INCOME			
Measurement	CON1, ¶45-48		

Topical Index

	Original Pronouncements	Current Text	EITF and Other

INCOME FROM CONTINUING OPERATIONS
See Changing Prices: Reporting Their
  Effects in Financial Reports
See Earnings per Share
See Income Statement Presentation:
  Discontinued Operations
See Income Taxes

INCOME RETAINED IN THE BUSINESS
See Retained Earnings

INCOME STATEMENT
See Extraordinary Items
See Financial Statements: Comparative
  Financial Statements
See Income Statement Presentation:
  Discontinued Operations
See Income Taxes

	Original Pronouncements	Current Text	EITF and Other
Application of Statement 109 in Foreign Financial Statements Restated for General Price-Level Changes			EITF.93-9
Costs Incurred in a Takeover Defense			EITF.85-2
Effect of a Retroactive Change in Enacted Tax Rates That Is Included in Income from Continuing Operations			EITF.93-13
Unusual or Infrequent Items			
. . Disclosure	APB30, ¶26	I22.101	
. . Liability Recognition for Costs to Exit an Activity			EITF.94-3
. . Restructuring of Business Operations			EITF.86-22
			EITF.87-4

INCOME STATEMENT PRESENTATION: DISCONTINUED OPERATIONS
See Disclosure

	Original Pronouncements	Current Text	EITF and Other
Accounting for Discontinued Operations Subsequently Retained			EITF.90-16
. . Disclosure by SEC Registrants			EITF.90-16
Allocation of General Corporate Overhead Expense			EITF.87-24
Allocation of Interest Expense			EITF.87-24
Definition			
. . Discontinued Operations	APB30, ¶8	I13.401	
. . Disposal Date	APB30, ¶14	I13.402	
. . Measurement Date of a Disposal	APB30, ¶14	I13.403	
. . Segment of a Business	APB30, ¶13	I13.404	
Disposal of a Portion of a Segment of a Business	AIN-APB30, #1	I22.501-502	EITF.85-36

See "Terminology" for references to defined terms presented in various accounting pronouncements.
See the Introduction to the Topical Index for details on the use of this index.

T-188

	Original Pronouncements	Current Text	EITF and Other
INCOME STATEMENT PRESENTATION: DISCONTINUED OPERATIONS—continued			
Disposal of a Segment of a Business			
. . Adjustments of Amounts Reported in Prior Periods	APB30, ¶25	I13.104	
. . Classification as Extraordinary, Unusual, or Infrequent	AIN-APB30, #1	I13.501-505	
. . Determination of Gains (Losses)	APB30, ¶15-17	I13.101-103	EITF.85-36
. . Expected Gain on Disposal with Interim Operating Losses			EITF.85-36
. . Interim Financial Reporting	FIN18, ¶62	I73.188-195	
. . Pension Costs	FAS88, ¶16	P16.186	
Earnings per Share	APB15, ¶13	E09.104	
	APB30, ¶9	I13.107	
Measurement Date	APB30, ¶15	I13.101	
INCOME TAXES			
See Consolidation			
See Disclosure			
See Foreign Currency Translation			
See Insurance Industry			
See Interim Financial Reporting			
See Oil and Gas Producing Activities			
Accounting Changes	FAS109, ¶35-36	I27.134-135	Q&A.109 #1
	FAS109, ¶228	I27.154	Q&A.109 #20
. . For Tax Purposes	FAS37, ¶19-21	I27.205-207	Q&A.109 #5-6
	FAS109, ¶287-288		
Accounting for Tax Benefits Resulting from Investments in Qualified Affordable Housing Projects			EITF.94-1
Accounting for the Income Tax Effects under Statement 109 of a Change in Functional Currency When an Economy Ceases to Be Considered Highly Inflationary			EITF.92-8
Allocating Consolidated Tax Provision to Subsidiaries	FAS109, ¶40	I27.139	EITF.86-9
	FAS109, ¶49	I27.148	
Allocation of Income Tax Expense or Benefit	FAS109, ¶35-38	I27.134-137	Q&A.109 #19
	FAS109, ¶273-276	I27.200-203	
. . Classification of Income for Which Taxes Were Paid in Prior Years	FAS109, ¶37	I27.136	
. . Cumulative Effect of an Accounting Change	FAS109, ¶36	I27.135	
. . Pretax Income/Loss from Continuing Operations	FAS109, ¶35	I27.134	
. . Shareholders' Equity	FAS109, ¶36	I27.135	
	FAS115, ¶133		

	Original Pronouncements	Current Text	EITF and Other
INCOME TAXES—continued			
Alternative Minimum Tax (AMT)	FAS109, ¶19	I27.118	EITF.87-8
	FAS109, ¶238-239	I27.165-166	
. . Leveraged Leases			EITF.86-43
. . Tax Credit Carryforwards			EITF.86-41
Alternative Tax Systems	FAS109, ¶19	I27.118	
. . AMT	FAS109, ¶238-239	I27.165-166	
Annual Computation of a Deferred Tax			
Asset or Liability	FAS109, ¶17-25	I27.116-124	
	FAS109, ¶224-226	I27.150-152	
	FAS109, ¶233	I27.160	
. . Graduated Tax Rates	FAS109, ¶18	I27.117	
	FAS109, ¶232	I27.158	
	FAS109, ¶236	I27.163	
Applicability of Indefinite Reversal Criteria to Temporary Differences			
. . Inside Basis Differences of Foreign			
Subsidiaries			EITF.93-16
Applicability of Indefinite Reversal Criteria to Timing Differences			
. . Subsidiary Stock Sales			EITF.84-27
Asset/Liability Approach	FAS109, ¶6-8	I27.105-107	
Assets and Liabilities Recorded Net-of-Tax in a Purchase Business Combination			
. . Effect of Change in Tax Rates			EITF.86-42
Balance Sheet Classification of Deferred			
Income Taxes	FAS37, ¶16	I27.204-211	
	FAS37, ¶19-25		
	FAS109, ¶287-288		
Basic Principles	FAS109, ¶6-8	I27.105-107	
Benefit of Net Operating Loss (NOL) Carryforward Realized			
. . Comptroller of the Currency's Rule on			
Deferred Tax Debits			EITF.85-31
. . Recognition of Purchased NOL or			
Own NOL			EITF.86-1
. . Reinstatement of Previously			
Eliminated Deferred Taxes			EITF.85-5
Built-in Gains	FAS109, ¶28	I27.127	Q&A.109 #12
Business Combinations	FAS109, ¶30	I27.129	
. . Acquired Leveraged Leases	FAS109, ¶256-258	I27.183-185	
. . Acquired Operating Loss or Tax Credit			
Carryforward at Transition	FAS109, ¶54-56		Q&A.109 #23-24
. . Acquired Tax Benefits	FAS109, ¶30	I27.129	
	FAS109, ¶264-272	I27.191-199	
. . Carryforwards—Pooling-of-Interests			
Method	FAS109, ¶270-272	I27.197-199	
. . Carryforwards—Purchase Method	FAS109, ¶30	I27.129	
	FAS109, ¶264-269	I27.191-196	

See "Terminology" for references to defined terms presented in various accounting pronouncements.
See the Introduction to the Topical Index for details on the use of this index.

	Original Pronouncements	Current Text	EITF and Other

INCOME TAXES—continued
Business Combinations—continued
. . Depreciable and Amortizable Assets .... FAS109, ¶229 — I27.155
. . Goodwill and Other Intangible Assets .. FAS109, ¶30 — I27.129
.... FAS109, ¶260-269 — I27.187-196
. . Intangible Assets Other Than
    Goodwill .... FAS109, ¶30 — I27.129 — Q&A.109 #16
. . Negative Goodwill .... FAS109, ¶30 — I27.129 — Q&A.109 #13
.... FAS109, ¶259 — I27.186 — Q&A.109 #15
. . Net-of-Tax Balances at Transition .... FAS109, ¶54-56 — — Q&A.109 #22
. . Nontaxable Combinations..................... FAS109, ¶260 — I27.187
.... FAS109, ¶265-267 — I27.192-194
. . Occurring in Years Not Restated for
    Effects of Statement 109..................... FAS109, ¶51 — — Q&A.109 #22-24
.... FAS109, ¶53-56
. . Purchase Price Allocations under IRC
    Section 338 .... — — EITF.86-3
. . Subsequent Realization of
    Unrecognized Tax Benefits................. FAS109, ¶30 — I27.129 — EITF.85-3
.... FAS109, ¶268 — I27.195
. . Subsequent Recognition of an
    Acquired Enterprise's Carryforward.. FAS109, ¶30 — I27.129 — Q&A.109 #13
.... FAS109, ¶268 — I27.195
. . Subsequent Recognition of an
    Acquiring Enterprise's Carryforward.. FAS109, ¶30 — I27.129 — Q&A.109 #14
. . Taxable Combinations........................... FAS109, ¶261-263 — I27.188-190
.... FAS109, ¶272 — I27.199
. . Tax Basis of Acquired Assets and
    Liabilities .... FAS109, ¶30 — I27.129 — Q&A.109 #17
.... FAS109, ¶36 — I27.135
.... FAS109, ¶261 — I27.188
.... FAS109, ¶272 — I27.199
.... FAS109, ¶288
. . Tax Deductible Goodwill .... FAS109, ¶9 — I27.108
.... FAS109, ¶30 — I27.129
.... FAS109, ¶262-263 — I27.189-190
. . "Tax-to-Tax" Differences .... — — EITF.D-31
. . Timing of Recognition of Tax Benefits
    for Pre-reorganization Temporary
    Differences and Carryforwards .... — — EITF.D-33
. . Uncertainties Related to Income Taxes
    in a Purchase Business Combination... — — EITF.93-7
Carrybacks (Operating Losses and
    Tax Credits)... FAS109, ¶21 — I27.120
.... FAS109, ¶37 — I27.136
.... FAS109, ¶240 — I27.167
.... FAS109, ¶245 — I27.172
.... FAS109, ¶289 — I27.401
. . Change in Tax Rates............................. FAS109, ¶233-235 — I27.160-162

FAS–FASB Statements   FIN–FASB Interpretations   FTB–FASB Technical Bulletins
APB–APB Opinions   AIN–AICPA Interpretations   ARB–Accounting Research Bulletins
CON–FASB Concepts   EITF–EITF Issues   Q&A–FASB Special Reports

	Original Pronouncements	Current Text	EITF and Other
INCOME TAXES—continued			
Carryforwards (Operating Losses and Tax Credits)	FAS109, ¶37	I27.136	
	FAS109, ¶240	I27.167	
	FAS109, ¶275	I27.202	
	FAS109, ¶289	I27.402	
. . Acquired in a Business Combination	FAS109, ¶30	I27.129	Q&A.109 #13
. . Assurance beyond Any Reasonable Doubt			EITF.85-15
. . Business Combinations	FAS109, ¶264-272	I27.191-199	
. . Business Combinations That Are Not Remeasured	FAS109, ¶51		Q&A.109 #23-24
	FAS109, ¶53-56		
. . Investment Tax Credit	FAS109, ¶288	I27.230	
. . Purchased in a Business Combination			EITF.84-33
			EITF.85-15
			EITF.86-1
. . Quasi Reorganizations	FAS109, ¶39	I27.138	
. . Recognition of Carryforwards as Offsets to Deferred Tax Credits			EITF.85-5
. . Recognition of Tax Benefits	FAS109, ¶30	I27.129	Q&A.109 #13-14
	FAS109, ¶51	I27.168-171	Q&A.109 #18
	FAS109, ¶241-244	I27.199	
	FAS109, ¶272	I27.202	
	FAS109, ¶275		
. . Reporting of Tax Benefits	FAS109, ¶37	I27.136	
	FAS109, ¶45	I27.144	
	FAS109, ¶245	I27.172	
	FAS109, ¶275	I27.202	
. . Timing of Recognition of Tax Benefits for Pre-reorganization Temporary Differences and Carryforwards			EITF.D-33
Cash Surrender Value of Life Insurance	FAS109, ¶14	I27.113	
	FAS109, ¶251	I27.178	
Change in Tax Laws or Rates	FAS109, ¶27	I27.126	
	FAS109, ¶35	I27.134	
	FAS109, ¶234-235	I27.161-162	
. . Change in Tax Status That Results from Change in Tax Law	FAS109, ¶28	I27.127	Q&A.109 #11
. . Effect of a Retroactive Change in Enacted Tax Rates That Is Included in Income from Continuing Operations			EITF.93-13
. . Effects of the Tax Reform Act of 1986			EITF.86-11
. . Initial Catch-up Adjustment for a Change in Accounting Method for Tax Purposes			Q&A.109 #5-6
. . Phased-in Change in Tax Rates	FAS109, ¶18	I27.117	Q&A.109 #1
	FAS109, ¶233-234	I27.160-161	

See "Terminology" for references to defined terms presented in various accounting pronouncements.

See the Introduction to the Topical Index for details on the use of this index.

	Original Pronouncements	Current Text	EITF and Other
INCOME TAXES—continued			
Change in Tax Laws or Rates—continued			
. . Recognition of Effects of Changes			
Prior to Enactment			EITF.86-11
			EITF.D-7
			EITF.D-30
. . Tax Benefit of Excess Tax-Deductible			
Goodwill Resulting from a			
Retroactive Change in Tax Law			EITF.93-12
Change in Tax Status	FAS109, ¶28	I27.127	Q&A.109 #11-12
	FAS109, ¶35	I27.134	Q&A.109 #28
	FAS109, ¶45	I27.144	
Comprehensive Income Excluded from			
Net Income	FAS109, ¶36	I27.135	
	FAS109, ¶276	I27.203	
	FAS115, ¶133		
Consolidated Tax Return	FAS109, ¶40	I27.139	
	FAS109, ¶49	I27.148	
Construction in Progress			
. . Regulated Operations	FAS109, ¶253-255	I27.180-182	
Corporate Joint Venture Investments			
Accounted for by the Equity Method	APB23, ¶17	I27.130-131	
	FAS109, ¶31-32	I27.133	
	FAS109, ¶34	I27.218	
Debt and Equity Securities	FAS109, ¶36	I27.135	
	FAS115, ¶133		
. . Unrealized Gains (Losses)	FAS115, ¶13	I80.110	
Deferred Tax Assets/Liabilities			
. . Annual Computation	FAS109, ¶17-25	I27.116-124	
	FAS109, ¶224-226	I27.150-152	
	FAS109, ¶233	I27.160	
. . Balance Sheet Classification	FAS37, ¶16	I27.140-141	
	FAS37, ¶19-25	I27.204-211	
	FAS109, ¶41-42		
	FAS109, ¶288		
. . Measurement	FAS109, ¶16-34	I27.115-133	
	FAS109, ¶233-239	I27.160-166	
. . Method of Reporting Construction			
Contracts	FAS37, ¶22	I27.208	
	FAS109, ¶287-288		
. . Offset of Taxable and Deductible			
Amounts	FAS109, ¶42	I27.141	Q&A.109 #1
	FAS109, ¶227	I27.153	
	FAS109, ¶231	I27.157	
. . Operating Loss Carryforwards			
Acquired in Pooling-of-Interests			
Business Combinations	FAS109, ¶270-272	I27.197-199	

FAS–FASB Statements	FIN–FASB Interpretations	FTB–FASB Technical Bulletins
APB–APB Opinions	AIN–AICPA Interpretations	ARB–Accounting Research Bulletins
CON–FASB Concepts	EITF–EITF Issues	Q&A–FASB Special Reports

	Original Pronouncements	Current Text	EITF and Other
INCOME TAXES—continued			
Deferred Tax Assets/Liabilities—continued			
. . Operating Loss Carryforwards Acquired in Purchase Business Combinations	FAS109, ¶30	I27.129	
	FAS109, ¶264-269	I27.191-196	
. . Pattern of Taxable and Deductible Amounts	FAS109, ¶228-229	I27.154-155	Q&A.109 #1
			Q&A.109 #7
. . Recognition	FAS109, ¶16-34	I27.115-133	
	FAS109, ¶224-232	I27.150-158	
Deferred Tax Classification in a Statement of Financial Position	FAS37, ¶16	I27.140-141	Q&A.109 #1
	FAS37, ¶19-25	I27.204-211	Q&A.109 #6
	FAS109, ¶41-42		
	FAS109, ¶288		
Deferred Taxes			
. . Adjustment for Change in State Franchise Tax Statute			EITF.91-8
. . Application of Statement 109 in Foreign Financial Statements Restated for General Price-Level Changes			EITF.93-9
. . Application of Statement 109 to Basis Differences within Foreign Subsidiaries			EITF.93-16
. . Disclosure of Components of Deferred Tax Expense			EITF.D-20
. . Effect of a Retroactive Change in Enacted Tax Rates That Is Included in Income from Continuing Operations			EITF.93-13
. . Increases in Cash Surrender Value of Life Insurance			EITF.87-28
. . Increases in Net Loan Value of Life Insurance			EITF.88-5
. . Recognition of Deferred Tax Assets for a Parent Company's Excess Tax Basis in the Stock of a Subsidiary That Is Accounted for as a Discontinued Operation			EITF.93-17
. . Special Deductions	FAS109, ¶231-232	I27.157-158	
. . Stock Life Insurance Enterprises			EITF.84-1
. . Subsidiary Stock Sales			EITF.84-27
. . Tax Benefit of Excess Tax-Deductible Goodwill Resulting from a Retroactive Change in Tax Law			EITF.93-12
Defined Benefit Pension Plans			
. . Tax Status	FAS35, ¶28	Pe5.127	
	FAS35, ¶264		

See "Terminology" for references to defined terms presented in various accounting pronouncements.
See the Introduction to the Topical Index for details on the use of this index.

	Original Pronouncements	Current Text	EITF and Other
INCOME TAXES—continued			
Definition	FAS109, ¶289	I27.410	
Depreciable and Amortizable Assets	FAS109, ¶229	I27.155	Q&A.109 #2
Different Tax Jurisdictions	FAS109, ¶17	I27.116	Q&A.109 #1
	FAS109, ¶19	I27.118	Q&A.109 #3
	FAS109, ¶21	I27.120	
	FAS109, ¶41-42	I27.140-141	
	FAS109, ¶223	I27.149	
Disallowance of Deduction			
. . Core Deposit Intangibles of Banking or Thrift Institutions			EITF.85-33
. . Liability for			Q&A.109 #4
			Q&A.109 #17
DISC (Domestic International Sales Corporation)			
. . Effects of the Tax Reform Act of 1984			EITF.84-2
Discontinued Operations			
. . Recognition of Deferred Tax Assets for a Parent Company's Excess Tax Basis in the Stock of a Subsidiary That Is Accounted for as a Discontinued Operation			EITF.93-17
Equity Method Investments			
. . Excess of the Tax Basis over the Amount for Financial Reporting	FAS109, ¶34	I27.133	
	FAS109, ¶288	I27.214	
. . Undistributed Earnings	APB18, ¶19	I27.130	
	FAS109, ¶31	I82.109	
ESOP (Employee Stock Ownership Plan)	FAS109, ¶35-36	I27.134-135	
. . Benefit from Distribution of Dividends to Employees			EITF.86-4
Exceptions to Comprehensive Recognition of Deferred Taxes	FAS109, ¶9	I27.108	
. . Goodwill			Q&A.109 #16
. . Tax Bad-Debt Reserves of a Savings and Loan Association			Q&A.109 #8
Extraordinary Items			
. . Tax Benefits of Operating Loss Carryforwards			EITF.86-1
Family-Owned Farms			Q&A.109 #6
Foreign Subsidiaries			
. . Application of Statement 109 to Inside Basis Differences			EITF.93-16
Foreign Tax Assets and Liabilities			
. . Temporary Differences	FAS52, ¶22-24	F60.132-134	
	FAS52, ¶135	I27.108	
	FAS109, ¶9	I27.156	
	FAS109, ¶230		
Franchise Taxes			EITF.91-8

FAS–FASB Statements	FIN–FASB Interpretations	FTB–FASB Technical Bulletins
APB–APB Opinions	AIN–AICPA Interpretations	ARB–Accounting Research Bulletins
CON–FASB Concepts	EITF–EITF Issues	Q&A–FASB Special Reports

	Original Pronouncements	Current Text	EITF and Other

INCOME TAXES—continued

Future Originating and Reversing

Temporary Differences	FAS109, ¶21	I27.120	Q&A.109 #1-2
	FAS109, ¶229	I27.155	
	FAS109, ¶236	I27.163	
	FAS109, ¶244	I27.171	
	FAS109, ¶248	I27.175	
Glossary	FAS109, ¶289	I27.401-420	

Goodwill

. . Recognition and Measurement of the
    Tax Benefit of Excess Tax-Deductible
    Goodwill Resulting from a

Retroactive Change in Tax Law			EITF.93-12
Graduated Tax Rates	FAS109, ¶18	I27.117	Q&A.109 #1
	FAS109, ¶232	I27.158	
	FAS109, ¶236	I27.163	

Income Recognition for Cross Border Tax

Benefit Leases			EITF.89-20

Income Statement

. . Tax Benefits of Operating Loss

Carryforwards			EITF.86-1

Indefinite Reversal Criteria

. . Inapplicability When Savings and
    Loan Association Converts to a

Bank			EITF.86-31

Inside Basis Differences of Foreign

Subsidiaries			EITF.93-16

Insurance Companies

. . Tax Benefits from Discounting Loss

Reserves			EITF.86-37
Intangible Assets	FAS109, ¶30	I27.129	Q&A.109 #16

Intercompany Sale of Inventory or Other

Assets	FAS109, ¶9	I27.108	
Interim Financial Reporting	FAS109, ¶5	I27.104	

Intraperiod Tax Allocation of the Tax
  Effect of Pretax *Income* from Continuing

Operations			EITF.D-32

Inventory

. . Intercompany Sales	FAS109, ¶9	I27.108	
. . Obsolete Inventory	FAS109, ¶248	I27.175	
. . Uniform Cost Capitalization Rules			Q&A.109 #5
Investment in Subsidiaries	APB23, ¶9	I27.130-133	
	APB23, ¶12-13	I27.212-217	
	FAS109, ¶31-34		
	FAS109, ¶288		

Investment Tax Credit (ITC)

. . Alternative Minimum Tax			EITF.87-8
. . Balance Sheet Classification	APB2, ¶14	I27.231	

See "Terminology" for references to defined terms presented in various accounting pronouncements.
See the Introduction to the Topical Index for details on the use of this index.

	Original Pronouncements	Current Text	EITF and Other
INCOME TAXES—continued			
Investment Tax Credit (ITC)—continued			
. . Deferral Method	AIN-APB4, #3	I27.228	
	APB2, ¶13-15	I27.231-232	
		I27.509	
. . Description	APB2, ¶1	I27.227	
. . Effects of the Tax Reform Act of 1986 ..			EITF.86-11
. . Flow-through Method	APB4, ¶10	I27.228	
. . Income Statement Presentation	APB2, ¶15	I27.232	
. . Leased Property	AIN-APB4, #3	I27.507-508	
. . Preferable Accounting	APB2, ¶13	I27.228	
	APB4, ¶10		
Leases	FAS109, ¶9	I27.108	Q&A.109 #1
	FAS109, ¶256-258	I27.183-185	
Leveraged Leases	FAS109, ¶9	I27.108	
	FAS109, ¶257-258	I27.184-185	
. . Change in Tax Rate	FAS109, ¶288	L10.521-524	EITF.86-43
	FTB79-16(R), ¶1-4		
Life Insurance			
. . Deferred Taxes on Increases in Cash Surrender Value of Life Insurance			EITF.87-28
			EITF.88-5
LIFO Adopted Due to Repeal of *Insilco* Tax Court Decision			EITF.84-10
Loss Carryforwards			
. . Assurance beyond Any Reasonable Doubt			EITF.85-15
. . Purchased in Business Combinations ...			EITF.84-33
			EITF.85-15
			EITF.86-1
. . Recognition of Carryforwards as Offsets to Deferred Tax Credits			EITF.85-5
Minority Interest, Settlement of	FAS109, ¶33	I27.132	
Net-of-Tax Reporting			
. . Regulated Operations	FAS109, ¶29	I27.128	
Nonpublic Enterprises	FAS109, ¶4	I27.103	
	FAS109, ¶43	I27.142	
	FAS109, ¶47	I27.146	
	FAS109, ¶289	I27.413	
Offsetting Securities against Taxes Payable	APB10, ¶7	I27.233-235	
Oil and Gas Producing Activities	FAS19, ¶60-62	Oi5.139-141	
	FAS109, ¶231-232	I27.157-158	
Permanent Differences			
. . Different Tax and Accounting Carrying Bases			EITF.84-43
. . Discounting Loss Reserves of Insurance Companies			EITF.86-37
. . Subsidiary Stock Sales			EITF.84-27

FAS–FASB Statements	FIN–FASB Interpretations	FTB–FASB Technical Bulletins
APB–APB Opinions	AIN–AICPA Interpretations	ARB–Accounting Research Bulletins
CON–FASB Concepts	EITF–EITF Issues	Q&A–FASB Special Reports

	Original Pronouncements	Current Text	EITF and Other
INCOME TAXES—continued			
Pooling-of-Interests	FAS109, ¶36	I27.135	
	FAS109, ¶270-272	I27.197-199	
Quasi Reorganizations	FAS109, ¶36	I27.135	Q&A.109 #9-10
	FAS109, ¶39	I27.138	
. . Tax Benefits	FAS109, ¶36	I27.135	
	FAS109, ¶39	I27.138	
Regulated Operations	FAS109, ¶29	I27.128	
	FAS109, ¶252-255	I27.179-182	
	FAS109, ¶288	Re6.128	
. . Abandonments of Assets	FTB87-2, ¶5	Re6.501-507	
	FTB87-2, ¶14-20		
. . Comptroller of the Currency's Rule on Deferred Tax Debits			EITF.85-31
Reorganization Carryforwards			EITF.D-33
Restoration of Deferred Tax Credits Previously Offset by NOL Carryforward...			EITF.85-5
Sale or Purchase of Tax Benefits through Tax Leases	FAS109, ¶288	I27.501-506	
	FTB82-1, ¶1-2		
	FTB82-1, ¶4		
	FTB82-1, ¶6-8		
. . Effect of Change in Tax Law			EITF.86-44
Savings and Loan Associations			
. . Accounting for Income Tax Benefits from Bad Debts of a Savings and Loan Association			EITF.91-3
. . Comptroller of the Currency's Rule on Deferred Tax Debits			EITF.85-31
. . Percentage-of-Taxable-Income Bad-Debt Deduction	FAS109, ¶231-232	I27.157-158	Q&A.109 #8
. . Tax Bad-Debt Reserves	APB23, ¶19-21	I27.220-224	
	APB23, ¶23	I27.130-131	
	APB23, ¶25	I27.133	
	FAS109, ¶31-32	I27.143	
	FAS109, ¶34		
		FAS109, ¶44	
	FAS109, ¶288		
. . Tax Implications of Conversion to Bank			EITF.86-31
Scheduling	FAS109, ¶236	I27.163	Q&A.109 #1
Scope of Accounting and Reporting	FAS109, ¶1	I27.101-104	
	FAS109, ¶3-5		
S Corporations	FAS109, ¶28	I27.127	Q&A.109 #12
			Q&A.109 #28
Separate Financial Statements of a Subsidiary	FAS109, ¶40	I27.139	
	FAS109, ¶49	I27.148	
Special Deductions	FAS109, ¶231-232	I27.157-158	

See "Terminology" for references to defined terms presented in various accounting pronouncements.
See the Introduction to the Topical Index for details on the use of this index.

	Original Pronouncements	Current Text	EITF and Other
INCOME TAXES—continued			
State and Local Income Taxes	FAS109, ¶4	I27.103	Q&A.109 #7
. . Calculation of Deferred Taxes	FAS109, ¶17	I27.116	Q&A.109 #3
. . State Tax Based on the Greater of a Franchise Tax or an Income Tax			EITF.91-8
Statutory Depletion	FAS109, ¶231	I27.157	
Steamship Companies (U.S.)	FAS109, ¶9	I27.108	
	FAS109, ¶32	I27.131	
	FAS109, ¶44	I27.143	
Stock Life Insurance Enterprises			
. . Deferred Taxes	FAS109, ¶288	I27.225	
		In6.161	
. . Effects of the Tax Reform Act of 1984			EITF.84-1
. . Policyholders' Surplus	FAS60, ¶59	I27.226	
	FAS109, ¶8	I27.107	
	FAS109, ¶31	I27.130	
	FAS109, ¶44	I27.143	
	FAS109, ¶288		
Tax Benefits			
. . Investments in Qualified Affordable Housing Projects			EITF.94-1
Tax Holidays	FAS109, ¶183-184	I27.127	
Tax Indemnifications Related to a Change in Tax Law			
. . Leases			EITF.86-33
Tax Leases Used to Transfer Tax Benefits	FAS109, ¶288	I27.501-506	
	FTB82-1, ¶1-2		
	FTB82-1, ¶4		
	FTB82-1, ¶6-8		
. . Effect of Change in Tax Law			EITF.86-44
. . Income Recognition for Cross Border Tax Benefit Leases			EITF.89-20
Tax-Planning Strategies	FAS109, ¶21-22	I27.120-121	
	FAS109, ¶246-251	I27.173-178	
	FAS109, ¶289	I27.418	
. . Criteria	FAS109, ¶22	I27.121	
	FAS109, ¶246	I27.173	
	FAS109, ¶251	I27.178	
. . Deferred Tax Liabilities	FAS109, ¶251	I27.178	
. . Effects of Qualifying Strategies	FAS109, ¶246-248	I27.173-175	
	FAS109, ¶250	I27.177	
. . Elections for Tax Purposes	FAS109, ¶22	I27.121	Q&A.109 #25
	FAS109, ¶246	I27.173	
. . Expense or Loss Associated with Implementing a Strategy	FAS109, ¶22	I27.121	
	FAS109, ¶249-250	I27.176-177	
. . Management Intent to Implement a Strategy	FAS109, ¶246	I27.173	
. . Recognition of Qualifying Strategies Not Elective	FAS109, ¶22	I27.121	Q&A.109 #26

FAS–FASB Statements   FIN–FASB Interpretations   FTB–FASB Technical Bulletins
APB–APB Opinions   AIN–AICPA Interpretations   ARB–Accounting Research Bulletins
CON–FASB Concepts   EITF–EITF Issues   Q&A–FASB Special Reports

I

Topical Index

	Original Pronouncements	Current Text	EITF and Other

INCOME TAXES—continued

Tax-Planning Strategies—continued

	Original Pronouncements	Current Text	EITF and Other
. . S Corporation Status, Not a Strategy	FAS109, ¶28	I27.127	Q&A.109 #28
. . Search for Qualifying Strategies			Q&A.109 #27
. . Valuation Allowance.............................	FAS109, ¶21-22	I27.120-121	Q&A.109 #26
....	FAS109, ¶250-251	I27.177-178	
"Tax-to-Tax" Differences			EITF.D-31
Temporary Differences	FAS109, ¶10-15	I27.109-114	
....	FAS109, ¶289	I27.419	
. . Allocated Negative Goodwill...............	FAS109, ¶30	I27.129	Q&A.109 #15
....	FAS109, ¶259	I27.186	
. . Application of Statement 109 in Foreign Financial Statements Restated for General Price-Level Changes..			EITF.93-9
. . Application of Statement 109 to Inside Basis Differences of Foreign Subsidiaries................................			EITF.93-16
. . Asset Revaluation in Foreign Countries...................................			EITF.84-43
. . Cash Surrender Value of Life Insurance...............................	FAS109, ¶14	I27.113	
....	FAS109, ¶251	I27.178	
. . Comprehensive Income Reported Directly in Stockholders' Equity........	FAS109, ¶35-36	I27.134-135	
....	FAS109, ¶276	I27.203	
....	FAS115, ¶133		
. . Deductible Temporary Differences	FAS109, ¶13	I27.112	
....	FAS109, ¶17	I27.116	
....	FAS109, ¶224-225	I27.150-151	
....	FAS109, ¶248	I27.175	
....	FAS109, ¶289	I27.404	
. . Deferred State Income Tax Asset or Liability...............................	FAS109, ¶17	I27.116	Q&A.109 #3
....			Q&A.109 #7
. . Deferred Taxable Income	FAS109, ¶15	I27.114	Q&A.109 #5-6
. . Depreciable and Amortizable Assets	FAS109, ¶229	I27.155	Q&A.109 #2
. . Disallowance of Tax Deductions			Q&A.109 #4
....			Q&A.109 #17
. . Foreign Tax Assets and Liabilities	FAS109, ¶230	I27.156	
. . Foreign Currency Translation	FAS52, ¶22-24	F60.132-134	
. . Future Originating and Reversing Temporary Differences	FAS109, ¶21	I27.120	Q&A.109 #1-2
....	FAS109, ¶229	I27.155	
....	FAS109, ¶236	I27.163	
....	FAS109, ¶244	I27.171	
....	FAS109, ¶248	I27.175	

See "Terminology" for references to defined terms presented in various accounting pronouncements.
See the Introduction to the Topical Index for details on the use of this index.

	Original Pronouncements	Current Text	EITF and Other

INCOME TAXES—continued
Temporary Differences—continued

	Original Pronouncements	Current Text	EITF and Other
. . Goodwill	FAS109, ¶9	I27.108	
	FAS109, ¶30	I27.129	
	FAS109, ¶259	I27.186	
	FAS109, ¶261-263	I27.188-190	
. . Increase in Cash Surrender Value of Life Insurance			EITF.87-28
			EITF.88-5
. . Intangible Assets	FAS109, ¶30	I27.129	Q&A.109 #16
. . Inventory Costs			EITF.86-46
. . Inventory or Other Assets Transferred between Affiliated Companies	FAS109, ¶9	I27.108	
. . Involuntary Conversions	FIN30, ¶5	N35.119	
. . Leases			Q&A.109 #1
. . LIFO Inventory Differences	FAS109, ¶228	I27.154	EITF.D-31
. . Marketable Securities	FAS109, ¶36	I27.135	
	FAS115, ¶133		
. . Net-of-Tax Assets and Liabilities Acquired in a Business Combination	FAS109, ¶54-56		Q&A.109 #22
. . Nonmonetary Transactions	APB29, ¶27	N35.113	
. . Obsolete Inventory Reserves	FAS109, ¶248	I27.175	
. . Offset of Taxable Deductible Amounts	FAS109, ¶227	I27.153	
. . Regulated Operations	FAS109, ¶29	Re6.128	
	FAS109, ¶252-255	I27.179-182	
	FAS109, ¶288		
. . Reorganization Carryforwards			EITF.D-33
. . Subsidiary Company, Book Basis Exceeds Tax Basis of Parent's Investment	FAS109, ¶31-33	I27.130-132	
	FAS109, ¶251	I27.178	
. . Subsidiary Stock Sales			EITF.84-27
. . Taxable Temporary Difference	FAS109, ¶13	I27.112	
	FAS109, ¶17	I27.116	
	FAS109, ¶289	I27.416	
. . Tax Bad-Debt Reserves of a Savings and Loan Association	APB23, ¶19-21	I27.130-131	Q&A.109 #8
	APB23, ¶23	I27.133	Q&A.109 #12
	APB23, ¶25	I27.143	
	FAS109, ¶31-32	I27.220-224	
	FAS109, ¶34		
	FAS109, ¶44		
	FAS109, ¶288		
. . Tax Benefit of Excess Tax-Deductible Goodwill Resulting from a Retroactive Change in Tax Law			EITF.93-12
Temporary IRS Regulations			
. . Recognizing Effect in Financial Statements			EITF.86-3
Transition	FAS109, ¶50-59		Q&A.109 #20-23

	Original Pronouncements	Current Text	EITF and Other
INCOME TAXES—continued			
Undistributed Earnings of a Subsidiary			
. . Change in Income Tax Rate			EITF.D-7
. . Change in Investment...........................	APB23, ¶13	I27.216	
....	FAS109, ¶33	I27.132	
....	FAS109, ¶288		
. . Indefinite Reversal Criterion	APB23, ¶12	I27.215	
....	FAS109, ¶31	I27.130	
. . Temporary Differences.........................	APB23, ¶9	I27.212-213	
....	FAS109, ¶31-34	I27.130-133	
....	FAS109, ¶251	I27.178	
....	FAS109, ¶287-288		
Uniform Cost Capitalization Rules			Q&A.109 #5
Unremitted Foreign Earnings of			
Subsidiaries.....................................	FAS37, ¶23-25	I27.209-211	
....	FAS109, ¶287-288		
Valuation Allowance....................................	FAS109, ¶17	I27.116	
....	FAS109, ¶20-25	I27.119-124	
....	FAS109, ¶43	I27.142	
....	FAS109, ¶232	I27.158	
....	FAS109, ¶239	I27.166	
....	FAS109, ¶246-251	I27.173-178	
....	FAS109, ¶289	I27.420	
. . Acquired Tax Benefits...........................	FAS109, ¶30	I27.129	Q&A.109 #14
....	FAS109, ¶37	I27.136	Q&A.109 #23
....	FAS109, ¶261	I27.188	
....	FAS109, ¶264-272	I27.191-199	
. . Change in Valuation Allowance	FAS109, ¶26	I27.125	
....	FAS109, ¶35	I27.134	
....	FAS109, ¶226	I27.152	
....	FAS109, ¶245	I27.172	
. . Classification in Statement of			
Financial Position	FAS109, ¶41	I27.140	
. . Controller of the Currency's Rule on			
Deferred Tax Debits............................			EITF.85-31
. . Recognition of Deferred Tax Assets	FAS109, ¶17	I27.116	Q&A.109 #1-2
....	FAS109, ¶34	I27.133	
....	FAS109, ¶224-226	I27.150-152	
....	FAS109, ¶241-244	I27.168-171	
....	FAS109, ¶246	I27.173	
....	FAS109, ¶250	I27.177	
....	FAS109, ¶256	I27.183	
INCREMENTAL BORROWING RATE			
See Leases			
INDEXES			
Consumer Price Index			
See Changing Prices: Reporting Their			
Effects in Financial Reports			
INDIRECT COSTS			
Absorption in Inventory			EITF.86-46

See "Terminology" for references to defined terms presented in various accounting pronouncements.
See the Introduction to the Topical Index for details on the use of this index.

	Original Pronouncements	Current Text	EITF and Other

INDUSTRY GUIDES AND PRACTICES
See Specialized Accounting and Reporting
INFLATION
See Changing Prices: Reporting Their
  Effects in Financial Reporting
Relation to Measurement............................ CON5, ¶72
Relation to Recognition............................... CON5, ¶71
INFLATION ACCOUNTING
See Changing Prices: Reporting Their
  Effects in Financial Reports
INFLATIONARY ECONOMIES
Foreign Earnings and Operations
  See Foreign Currency Translation
INFORMATION BIAS
Relation to Neutrality .... CON2, ¶99-100
INFREQUENT ITEMS
See Disclosure
See Extraordinary Items
See Income Statement Presentation:
  Discontinued Operations
See Interim Financial Reporting Defined
  Benefit Pension Plans............................... FAS35, ¶28   Pe5.127
Scope of Accounting and Reporting
  Requirements .... APB30, ¶26   I22.101
INITIATION DATE
See Business Combinations
INSOLVENCY
See Debt: Restructurings
INSTALLMENT METHOD
See Real Estate: Sales Other Than Retail
  Land Sales
See Revenue Recognition
Franchise Fee Revenue................................ FAS45, ¶6   Fr3.102
.... FAS45, ¶26   Fr3.117
INSTALLMENT RECEIVABLES
Balance Sheet Classification .... ARB43, Ch.3A, ¶4   B05.105
INSTALLMENT SALES
Deferred Gross Profit, Qualification as a
  Liability.. CON6, ¶232-234
IN-SUBSTANCE DEFEASANCE
See Debt: Extinguishments
IN-SUBSTANCE FORECLOSURE
Accounting by Creditor............................... FAS15, ¶34   D22.130   EITF.89-9
.... FAS114, ¶22   D22.142
Accounting by Debtor .... FAS15, ¶20   D22.116
Classification of In-Substance Foreclosed
  (ISF) Assets by SEC Registrants EITF.D-37

	Original Pronouncements	Current Text	EITF and Other
INSURANCE CONTRACTS			
See Postretirement Benefits Other Than Pensions			
INSURANCE COSTS			
See Insurance Industry			
See Life Insurance			
See Postretirement Health Care and Life Insurance Benefits			
Accounting for Multiple-Year Retrospectively Rated Insurance Contracts by Insurance Enterprises and Other Enterprises..			EITF.93-14
Claims-Made Coverage			
. . Accounting by Insureds.........................			EITF.86-12
Payments to Insurance Enterprises That May Not Involve Transfer of Risk			
. . Pooled Risks	FAS5, ¶45	I50.102	
. . Premium Equivalent to a Deposit	FAS5, ¶44	I50.101	
....	FAS113, ¶18	In6.182	
....	FAS113, ¶30		
. . Self-Insurance	FAS5, ¶45	I50.102	
Provision for Deferred Taxes on Increase in Cash Surrender Value of Life Insurance			EITF.87-28
INSURANCE INDUSTRY			
See Contingencies			
See Disclosure			
Accident and Health Insurance Contracts...	FAS60, ¶8	In6.108	
Accounting for Multiple-Year Retrospectively Rated Contracts by Ceding and Assuming Enterprises............			EITF.93-6
....			EITF.D-35
Accounting for Multiple-Year Retrospectively Rated Insurance Contracts by Insurance Enterprises and Other Enterprises..			EITF.93-14
Accounting for the Present Value of Future Profits Resulting from the Acquisition of a Life Insurance Company			EITF.92-9
. . Disclosure by SEC Registrants			EITF.92-9
Acquisition Costs..	FAS60, ¶11	In6.111	
....	FAS60, ¶28-31	In6.134-137D	
....	FAS97, ¶22-25		
. . Illustrations	FAS97, ¶79-82	In6.167	
Adjustments for Holding Gains and Losses as Related to the Implementation of Statement 115			EITF.D-41
Annuity Contracts..	FAS60, ¶8	In6.107B	
....	FAS97, ¶8	In6.108	

See "Terminology" for references to defined terms presented in various accounting pronouncements.
See the Introduction to the Topical Index for details on the use of this index.

	Original Pronouncements	Current Text	EITF and Other

INSURANCE INDUSTRY—continued

Assessment Enterprises

. . Accounting and Reporting

Requirements	FAS120, ¶4-5	In6.106B-106C	
. . Disclosure of Accounting Policies	FIN40, ¶5-6	In6.166	

Catastrophe Losses

. . Property and Liability Insurance

Enterprises	FAS5, ¶4	C59.122	
	FAS5, ¶8	C59.146-149	
	FAS5, ¶40-43	In6.121-126	
	FAS5, ¶96		
Characteristics of Insurance Transactions	FAS60, ¶1	In6.101	
Claims Incurred But Not Reported	FAS60, ¶9	In6.109	
	FAS60, ¶17-18	In6.117-118	

Costs Other Than Those Relating to

Claims and Policy Benefits	FAS60, ¶27	In6.133	
Credit Life Insurance	FAS60, ¶8	In6.108	
Deferred Taxes	FAS60, ¶59	I27.225-226	EITF.84-1
	FAS109, ¶288		EITF.86-37
Endowment Contracts	FAS60, ¶8	In6.108	

Fraternal Benefit Societies

. . Accounting and Reporting

Requirements	FAS120, ¶4-5	In6.106B-106C	
. . Disclosure of Accounting Policies	FIN40, ¶5-6	In6.166	
Glossary	FAS60, ¶66	In6.401-438	
	FAS113, ¶121		
Group Insurance Contracts	FAS60, ¶8	In6.108	
Internal Replacement Transactions	FAS97, ¶26	In6.143A	
Investment Contracts	FAS97, ¶7	In6.107A	
	FAS97, ¶15	In6.107C	
	FAS113, ¶12	In6.176	
Investments	FAS60, ¶12	In6.112	
	FAS60, ¶47-48	In6.151-157	
	FAS60, ¶50-51		
	FAS97, ¶26		
	FAS97, ¶28		
	FAS115, ¶127		
	FAS115, ¶131		
	FAS121, ¶28		
Investments in Debt and Equity Securities	FAS115, ¶4	I80.102	
Life Insurance Contracts	FAS60, ¶4	In6.104	
	FAS60, ¶8	In6.108	

Life Insurance Enterprises

. . Deferred Income Taxes	FAS109, ¶288	In6.161	
. . Deferred Recognition of Realized			
Gains and Losses			EITF.87-1
. . Policyholders' Surplus	FAS60, ¶59	In6.165	
Life-Contingent Payments	FAS97, ¶8	In6.107B	
Limited Payment Contracts	FAS97, ¶9	In6.108A	
. . Liability for Policy Benefits	FAS97, ¶16	In6.132A	

FAS–FASB Statements	FIN–FASB Interpretations	FTB–FASB Technical Bulletins
APB–APB Opinions	AIN–AICPA Interpretations	ARB–Accounting Research Bulletins
CON–FASB Concepts	EITF–EITF Issues	Q&A–FASB Special Reports

	Original Pronouncements	Current Text	EITF and Other

INSURANCE INDUSTRY—continued

Long-Duration Contract Accounting

. . Acquisition Costs .... FAS60, ¶11 — In6.111

.... FAS60, ¶28-29 — In6.134-135

.... FAS60, ¶31 — In6.137

. . Characteristics .... FAS60, ¶4-5 — In6.104-105

.... FAS60, ¶7 — In6.107

. . Examples of Contracts.......................... FAS60, ¶8 — In6.108

. . Liability for Claim Adjustment

    Expenses .... FAS60, ¶10 — In6.110

.... FAS60, ¶20 — In6.120

. . Liability for Future Policy Benefits ...... FAS60, ¶10 — In6.110

.... FAS60, ¶21-26 — In6.127-132C

.... FAS97, ¶16-18

. . Liability for Unpaid Claims .... FAS60, ¶10 — In6.110

.... FAS60, ¶17-18 — In6.117-118

. . Participating Life Insurance Contracts.. FAS120, ¶5-6 — In6.106C-106D

. . Premium Deficiency .... FAS60, ¶32 — In6.138

.... FAS60, ¶35-37 — In6.141-143

. . Premium Revenue Recognition .... FAS60, ¶4-5 — In6.104-105

.... FAS60, ¶10 — In6.110

.... FAS60, ¶16 — In6.115-116

.... FAS97, ¶30

. . Premium Revenue Recognition,

    Description................................. FAS60, ¶2 — In6.102

. . Reinsurance .... FAS113, ¶12-16 — In6.176-180

.... FAS113, ¶19-20 — In6.183-184

.... FAS113, ¶26 — In6.190

.... FAS113, ¶73

.... FAS113, ¶76

.... FAS113, ¶111

Mutual Life Insurance Enterprises

. . Accounting and Reporting

    Requirements .... FAS120, ¶4-5 — In6.106B-106C

. . Accounting for Participating Life

    Insurance Contracts .... FAS120, ¶5 — In6.106C

. . Adjustments for Holding Gains and

    Losses as Related to the

    Implementation of Statement 115 ...... — — EITF.D-41

. . Disclosure of Accounting Policies .... FIN40, ¶5-6 — In6.166

. . Financial Statements Prepared Based

    on Statutory Accounting Practices

    Instead of GAAP.............................. FIN40, ¶2 — In6.106

.... FIN40, ¶5-6 — In6.166

.... FIN40, ¶18

Nonguaranteed Premium Contract............. FAS97, ¶11 — In6.108C

.... FAS97, ¶13 — In6.108E

Participating Contracts .... FAS97, ¶11-12 — In6.108C-108D

Participating Life Insurance Contracts........ FAS120, ¶18 — In6.104B

. . Accounting under AICPA SOP 95-1 ..... FAS120, ¶5-6 — In6.106C-106D

See "Terminology" for references to defined terms presented in various accounting pronouncements.
See the Introduction to the Topical Index for details on the use of this index.

	Original Pronouncements	Current Text	EITF and Other
INSURANCE INDUSTRY—continued			
Policyholder Dividends	FAS60, ¶41-43	In6.147-149	
Policyholders' Surplus			
. . Income Taxes	FAS60, ¶59	I27.226	
	FAS109, ¶288	In6.165	
Premium Deficiency	FAS60, ¶33-37	In6.139-143	
Property and Liability Insurance			
Contracts	FAS60, ¶3	In6.103	
	FAS60, ¶8	In6.108	
Property and Liability Insurance Enterprises			
. . Catastrophe Losses	FAS5, ¶4	C59.122	
	FAS5, ¶8	In6.121-126	
	FAS5, ¶40-43		
	FAS5, ¶96		
Real Estate			
. . Acquired in Settling Claims	FAS60, ¶19	In6.119	
. . Used in the Business	FAS60, ¶52	In6.158	
Reinsurance			EITF.93-6
			EITF.D-35
. . Accounting and Reporting Provisions	FAS113, ¶14-26	In6.178-190	Q&A.113 #25-40
	FAS113, ¶73		
	FAS113, ¶76		
	FAS113, ¶95		
	FAS113, ¶98		
	FAS113, ¶107		
	FAS113, ¶111		
. . Accounting by Assuming Enterprises			EITF.D-35 #2
. . Accounting for Reinsurance of			
Long-Duration Contracts	FAS113, ¶12-16	In6.176-180	
	FAS113, ¶19-20	In6.183-184	
	FAS113, ¶26	In6.190	
	FAS113, ¶73		
	FAS113, ¶76		
	FAS113, ¶111		
. . Accounting for Reinsurance of			
Short-Duration Contracts	FAS113, ¶9-11	In6.172-175	EITF.D-35 #1
	FAS113, ¶14-16	In6.178-180	EITF.D-35 #8-9
	FAS113, ¶19-25	In6.183-189	Q&A.113 #8
	FAS113, ¶62		Q&A.113 #25
	FAS113, ¶64		Q&A.113 #27-40
	FAS113, ¶67		
	FAS113, ¶73		
	FAS113, ¶76		
	FAS113, ¶95		
	FAS113, ¶98		
	FAS113, ¶107		
. . Accumulating Retention			Q&A.113 #21

Note: The Q&A 113 text is reproduced in *EITF Abstracts* as Topic No. D-34.

FAS–FASB Statements	FIN–FASB Interpretations	FTB–FASB Technical Bulletins
APB–APB Opinions	AIN–AICPA Interpretations	ARB–Accounting Research Bulletins
CON–FASB Concepts	EITF–EITF Issues	Q&A–FASB Special Reports

	Original Pronouncements	Current Text	EITF and Other
INSURANCE INDUSTRY—continued			
Reinsurance—continued			
. . Allocation of Premiums to Prospective and Retroactive Portions of a Contract	FAS113, ¶25	In6.189	Q&A.113 #27-33
	FAS113, ¶98		
. . Asset Recognition for Multiple-Year Retrospectively Rated Contracts (RRCs)			EITF.D-35 #23-29
. . Changes in Coverage for RRCs			EITF.D-35 #30-34
. . Concentrations of Credit Risk			Q&A.113 #41-42
. . Conditions for Reporting RRCs as Reinsurance			EITF.D-35 #8-13
. . Contract Amendments			Q&A.113 #6
			Q&A.113 #11-12
. . Definition	FAS60, ¶66	In6.428	EITF.D-35 #3
			Q&A.113 #13
. . Definition of Multiple-Year Retrospectively Rated Contract			EITF.D-35 #4-7
. . Deposit Accounting			EITF.93-6
			EITF.D-35 #8-13
			EITF.D-35 #25-26
			EITF.D-35 #34
. . Funded Catastrophe Covers			EITF.93-6
. . Gain Contingencies			EITF.D-35 #23
. . Illustrations	FAS113, ¶120	In6.193-194	
. . Indemnifications against Loss or Liability Relating to Insurance Risk	FAS113, ¶8-13	In6.171-177	EITF.D-35 #1
	FAS113, ¶58-59		EITF.D-35 #3
	FAS113, ¶62		EITF.D-35 #10-13
	FAS113, ¶64		EITF.D-35 #25
	FAS113, ¶67		EITF.D-35 #34
			Q&A.113 #9-24
. . Liability Recognition for RRCs			EITF.D-35 #14-21
. . Loss Recognition for RRCs			EITF.D-35 #17
. . Multiple Contingent Contractual Features of RRCs			EITF.D-35 #21-22
. . Multiple-Year Retrospectively Rated Contracts (RRCs)			EITF.93-6
. . Obligatory Retrospective Rating Provisions			EITF.D-35 #15-19
. . Ratable Recognition for RRCs Prohibited			EITF.D-35 #16-17
. . Reasonable Possibility of Significant Loss	FAS113, ¶10-11	In6.173-174	EITF.D-35 #12-13
	FAS113, ¶64		Q&A.113 #15-19
			Q&A.113 #24

Note: The Q&A 113 text is reproduced in *EITF Abstracts* as Topic No. D-34.

See "Terminology" for references to defined terms presented in various accounting pronouncements.

See the Introduction to the Topical Index for details on the use of this index.

	Original Pronouncements	Current Text	EITF and Other
INSURANCE INDUSTRY—continued			
Reinsurance—continued			
. . Recognition of Revenues and Costs	FAS113, ¶17-26	In6.181-190	Q&A.113 #33-39
	FAS113, ¶95		
	FAS113, ¶98		
	FAS113, ¶107		
	FAS113, ¶111		
. . Reporting Assets and Liabilities			
Related to Reinsurance Transactions..	FAS113, ¶14-16	In6.178-180	Q&A.113 #35
	FAS113, ¶73		Q&A.113 #39-40
	FAS113, ¶76		
. . Right of Setoff	FAS113, ¶15	In6.179	Q&A.113 #35
			Q&A.113 #40
. . Risk Transfer	FAS113, ¶8-13	In6.171-177	EITF.93-6
	FAS113, ¶58-59		EITF.D-35 #1
	FAS113, ¶62		EITF.D-35 #3
	FAS113, ¶64		EITF.D-35 #10-13
	FAS113, ¶67		EITF.D-35 #25
			EITF.D-35 #34
			Q&A.113 #9-24
. . Scope of Accounting and Reporting Requirements for Reinsurance			
Contracts	FAS113, ¶1	In6.168-170	Q&A.113 #3-8
	FAS113, ¶6-7		
	FAS113, ¶50		
	FAS113, ¶52-53		
	FAS113, ¶119		
	FAS120, ¶9		
. . Scope of Accounting and Reporting Requirements for RRCs			EITF.D-35 #1-7
. . Termination of RRCs			EITF.D-35 #7
			EITF.D-35 #19
			EITF.D-35 #22
. . Timely Reimbursement			Q&A.113 #21-22
. . Transition			Q&A.113 #1-2
			Q&A.113 #4-5
			Q&A.113 #7-9
			Q&A.113 #26
. . Underwriting Risk			EITF.D-35 #11-13

Note: The Q&A 113 text is reproduced in *EITF Abstracts* as Topic No. D-34.

FAS–FASB Statements   FIN–FASB Interpretations   FTB–FASB Technical Bulletins
APB–APB Opinions   AIN–AICPA Interpretations   ARB–Accounting Research Bulletins
CON–FASB Concepts   EITF–EITF Issues   Q&A–FASB Special Reports

	Original Pronouncements	Current Text	EITF and Other
INSURANCE INDUSTRY—continued			
Retrospective and Contingent Commission			
Arrangements	FAS60, ¶44	In6.150	
Scope of Accounting and Reporting			
Requirements	FAS60, ¶6	In6.106	
	FAS120, ¶7		
. . Accounting for Mutual Life Insurance			
Enterprises	FAS120, ¶4-6	In6.106B-106D	
. . Accounting for Reinsurance	FAS113, ¶6-7	In6.169-170	Q&A.113 #3-8
	FAS113, ¶50		
	FAS113, ¶52-53		
	FAS113, ¶119		
	FAS120, ¶9		
Separate Accounts	FAS60, ¶53-54	In6.159-160	
Short-Duration Contract Accounting			
. . Acquisition Costs	FAS60, ¶11	In6.111	
	FAS60, ¶28-30	In6.134-136	
. . Characteristics	FAS60, ¶7	In6.107	
. . Examples of Contracts	FAS60, ¶8	In6.108	
. . Liability for Claim Adjustment			
Expenses	FAS60, ¶9	In6.109	
	FAS60, ¶20	In6.120	
. . Liability for Unpaid Claims	FAS60, ¶9	In6.109	
	FAS60, ¶17-18	In6.117-118	
. . Premium Deficiency	FAS60, ¶32-34	In6.138-140	
. . Premium Revenue Recognition	FAS60, ¶13-14	In6.109	
		In6.113-114	
. . Premium Revenue Recognition,			
Description	FAS60, ¶9	In6.103	
. . Reinsurance	FAS113, ¶9-11	In6.172-175	EITF.D-35 #1
	FAS113, ¶14-16	In6.178-180	EITF.D-35 #8-9
	FAS113, ¶19-25	In6.183-189	Q&A.113 #8
	FAS113, ¶62		Q&A.113 #25
	FAS113, ¶64		Q&A.113 #27-40
	FAS113, ¶67		
	FAS113, ¶73		
	FAS113, ¶76		
	FAS113, ¶95		
	FAS113, ¶98		
	FAS113, ¶107		
Stock Life Insurance Enterprises			
. . Optional Accounting under AICPA			
SOP 95-1	FAS120, ¶6	In6.106D	
Term Life Insurance Contracts	FAS60, ¶8	In6.108	
Title Insurance Contracts	FAS60, ¶5	In6.105	
	FAS60, ¶8	In6.108	
	FAS60, ¶16-20	In6.116-120	

Note: The Q&A 113 text is reproduced in *EITF Abstracts* as Topic No. D-34.

See "Terminology" for references to defined terms presented in various accounting pronouncements.

See the Introduction to the Topical Index for details on the use of this index.

	Original Pronouncements	Current Text	EITF and Other
INSURANCE INDUSTRY—continued			
Universal Life Insurance Contracts	FAS97, ¶4	In6.104A	
	FAS97, ¶10-13	In6.108B-108E	
. . Acquisition Costs	FAS97, ¶22-25	In6.137A-137D	
	FAS97, ¶79-82	In6.167	
. . Initiation Fees	FAS97, ¶20	In6.116B	
. . Liability for Policy Benefits	FAS97, ¶17-18	In6.132B-132C	
. . Revenue and Expense Recognition	FAS97, ¶19-21	In6.116A-116C	
Variable Annuity Contracts	FAS60, ¶53	In6.159	
Whole-Life Insurance Contracts	FAS60, ¶8	In6.108	
INSURED PENSION PLANS			
See Defined Benefit Pension Plans			
See Pension Costs			
See Postretirement Health Care and Life Insurance Benefits			
INTANGIBLE ASSETS			
See Disclosure			
Acquired after October 31, 1970			
. . Acquired from Others	APB17, ¶24	I60.105	
. . Amortization, Maximum Period	APB17, ¶29	I60.110	
. . Amortization, Method and Disclosure	APB17, ¶30-31	I60.111-112	
	FAS109, ¶288		
. . Amortization, Useful Life	APB17, ¶27-28	I60.108-109	
	APB17, ¶31	I60.112	
. . Deferred Taxes	FAS109, ¶30	I27.129	
. . Developed by Enterprise	APB17, ¶24	I60.105	
. . Disposal of Goodwill	APB17, ¶32	I60.113	
. . Measurement	APB17, ¶25-26	I60.106-107	
. . Reevaluation of Useful Life	APB17, ¶31	I60.112	
. . Scope of Accounting Requirements	APB17, ¶5-6	I60.103-104	
Acquired Prior to November 1, 1970			
. . Amortization	APB9, ¶17	I60.118-120	
	ARB43, Ch.5, ¶5-7		
. . Basket Purchase of Assets	ARB43, Ch.5, ¶10	I60.123	
. . Change in Period of Useful Life	ARB43, Ch.5, ¶6-7	I60.119-120	
. . Measurement	ARB43, Ch.5, ¶4	I60.117	
. . Methods of Acquisition	ARB43, Ch.5, ¶1	I60.114	
. . Purchase of Subsidiary's Stock	ARB43, Ch.5, ¶10	I60.123	
. . Types	ARB43, Ch.5, ¶2-3	I60.115-116	
. . Write-off of Intangible Assets	APB9, ¶17	I60.121-122	
	ARB43, Ch.5, ¶8-9		
	FAS44, ¶4		
Acquisition in Process on October 31, 1970	APB17, ¶33	I60.102	
Banking or Thrift Institution Acquisition			
. . Amortization of Intangible Assets	FAS72, ¶5-6	I60.132-134	EITF.85-42
. . Amortization of Unidentifiable Intangible Assets			EITF.85-8
. . Core Deposit Intangibles			EITF.85-33

FAS–FASB Statements   FIN–FASB Interpretations   FTB–FASB Technical Bulletins
APB–APB Opinions   AIN–AICPA Interpretations   ARB–Accounting Research Bulletins
CON–FASB Concepts   EITF–EITF Issues   Q&A–FASB Special Reports

	Original Pronouncements	Current Text	EITF and Other
INTANGIBLE ASSETS—continued			
Banking or Thrift Institution			
Acquisition—continued			
. . FSLIC Management Consignment Program			EITF.85-41
. . Identifiable Intangible Assets			EITF.85-33
. . Identified Intangible Assets	FAS72, ¶4	I60.131	EITF.85-42
. . Reevaluation of Useful Life	FAS72, ¶7	I60.134	
. . Sale of Large Segment of Assets after Business Combination	FAS72, ¶7	I60.135	
. . Scope of Accounting Requirements	FAS72, ¶2	I60.130	
. . Unidentifiable Intangible Assets	FAS72, ¶6-7	I60.132-135	EITF.85-42
	FAS72, ¶12		
	FIN9, ¶9		
Credit Cardholder Relationships			
. . Purchase of Credit Card Portfolio			EITF.88-20
Definition			
. . Goodwill	APB17, ¶1	I60.401	
. . Operating Right	FAS44, ¶3	I60.402	
Developed by Enterprise	AIN-APB17, #1	I60.501-502	
Franchises	APB17, ¶1	I60.101	
Goodwill	APB17, ¶1	I60.101	
. . Adjustments for Uncertainties Related to Income Taxes in a Purchase Business Combination			EITF.93-7
. . Adjustments of Allocation of Original Purchase Price			EITF.85-3
. . Adjustments to Purchase Price Allocations under IRC Section 338			EITF.86-3
. . Amortization			EITF.85-42
. . Arising from Partnership Withdrawals			EITF.85-46
. . Change in Amortization Method for Business Combinations Initiated Prior to the Effective Date of Statement 72			EITF.89-19
. . Deferred Taxes	FAS109, ¶30	I27.129	
. . Recognition of Purchased NOL Carryforwards			EITF.85-15
. . Reduction for Realized Operating Loss Carryforward			EITF.86-1
Impairment	FAS121, ¶21	I60.112	
Motor Carriers			
. . Allocation among Types	FAS44, ¶3-4	I60.125-126	
. . Intangible Assets Other Than Interstate Operating Rights	FAS44, ¶7	I60.129	
. . Interstate Operating Rights	FAS44, ¶5-6	I60.127-128	
. . Motor Carrier Act of 1980	FAS44, ¶1	I60.124	
. . Write-off as Extraordinary Item	FAS44, ¶6	I60.128	
Patents	APB17, ¶1	I60.101	
Regulated Operations	FAS71, ¶29-30	Re6.134-135	

See "Terminology" for references to defined terms presented in various accounting pronouncements.
See the Introduction to the Topical Index for details on the use of this index.

	Original Pronouncements	Current Text	EITF and Other

INTANGIBLE ASSETS—continued

Step Acquisition	AIN-APB17, #2	I60.503-505	
Trademarks	APB17, ¶1	I60.101	
Types	APB17, ¶1	I60.101	

INTANGIBLE DRILLING AND DEVELOPMENT COSTS

See Oil and Gas Producing Activities

INTERCOMPANY BALANCES AND TRANSACTIONS

See Consolidation

See Foreign Operations

See Segment of Business Reporting

Business Combinations	APB16, ¶56	B50.115	
. . Downstream Mergers	AIN-APB16, #26	B50.593-596	EITF.85-4
	FTB85-5, ¶13-14	B50.596E-596F	
. . Stock Transactions between Companies under Common Control	AIN-APB16, #26	B50.596A-596D	
	AIN-APB16, #39	B50.645-648	
	FTB85-5, ¶5-7		
	FTB85-5, ¶12		

Definition

. . Intercompany Profit/Regulated Operations	FAS71, ¶16	Re6.126	
Dividends-in-Kind	APB29, ¶4	C11.101	
Equity Method Investments	AIN-APB18, #1	I82.109	
	APB18, ¶19	I82.501-507	
Foreign Currency Translation	FAS52, ¶20	F60.127	
	FAS52, ¶25	F60.135	
Hedging Intercompany Foreign Currency Risks			EITF.91-1
			EITF.95-2
Interest: Capitalization of Interest Costs	FAS58, ¶6	I67.106	
Regulated Operations	FAS71, ¶16-17	Re6.126-127	
. . Consolidation	ARB51, ¶6	C51.109	

INTEREST

See Interest Expense

See Interest Income

See Interest: Capitalization of Interest Costs

See Interest: Imputation of an Interest Cost

INTEREST-BEARING SECURITIES

See Financial Instruments

Hedging of Interest-Only Strips of Mortgage-Backed Securities			EITF.88-8

INTEREST: CAPITALIZATION OF INTEREST COSTS

See Disclosure

Amount of Interest Cost to Be Capitalized	FAS34, ¶12	I67.109	
. . Basis of Computation	FAS34, ¶13-14	I67.110-111	
. . Expenditures Applicable	FAS34, ¶16	I67.113	

FAS–FASB Statements   FIN–FASB Interpretations   FTB–FASB Technical Bulletins
APB–APB Opinions   AIN–AICPA Interpretations   ARB–Accounting Research Bulletins
CON–FASB Concepts   EITF–EITF Issues   Q&A–FASB Special Reports

	Original Pronouncements	Current Text	EITF and Other

INTEREST: CAPITALIZATION OF INTEREST COSTS—continued

Amount of Interest Cost to Be Capitalized—continued
. . Limitation on Amount ... FAS34, ¶15 — I67.112
Assets Qualifying for Interest
Capitalization ... FAS34, ¶9 — I67.105
... FAS42, ¶4
... FAS58, ¶5
. . Assets Excluded ... FAS34, ¶10 — I67.106
... FAS58, ¶6
... FAS62, ¶5
. . Land ... FAS34, ¶11 — I67.107
. . Oil and Gas Producing Activities
Accounted for by the Full Cost
Method ... FIN33, ¶2 — I67.108
Cable Television Industry ... FAS51, ¶9 — Ca4.107
Capitalization Period
. . Beginning and Ending Criteria ... FAS34, ¶17-19 — I67.114-116
Capitalizing Interest Costs Involving
Certain Tax-Exempt Borrowings ... FAS62, ¶3-4 — I67.116A-116B
. . Example ... FAS62, ¶5 — I67.116C
. . Period of Interest Capitalization ... FAS62, ¶7 — I67.114
Cost/Benefits of Providing Information ... FAS34, ¶8 — I67.104
... FAS42, ¶4
Disposition of the Amount Capitalized ... FAS34, ¶20 — I67.117
... FAS58, ¶7
Equity Method Investments ... FAS34, ¶9 — I67.105
... FAS42, ¶4
... FAS58, ¶5
Foreign Operations ... FAS34, ¶14 — I67.111
Intercompany Transactions ... FAS34, ¶10 — I67.106
... FAS58, ¶6
... FAS62, ¶5
Not to Include Pension Cost Interest ... FAS87, ¶16 — P16.110
Not to Include Postretirement Benefit
Cost ... FAS106, ¶22 — P40.115
Objectives of Capitalization ... FAS34, ¶6-7 — I67.102-103
Oil and Gas Producing Activities ... FIN33, ¶2 — I67.108
Regulated Operations ... FAS34, ¶10 — I67.106
... FAS58, ¶6 — Re6.125
... FAS62, ¶5
... FAS71, ¶15
... FAS90, ¶9
Scope of Accounting and Reporting
Requirements ... FAS34, ¶1 — I67.101

INTEREST EXPENSE
Accounting for Dual Currency Bonds ... EITF.93-10
Accrued Interest Expense upon
Conversion of Convertible Debt ... EITF.85-17

See "Terminology" for references to defined terms presented in various accounting pronouncements.
See the Introduction to the Topical Index for details on the use of this index.

	Original Pronouncements	Current Text	EITF and Other
INTEREST EXPENSE—continued			
Allocation to Assets Held for Sale after Business Combination			EITF.87-11
. . Sale Not Completed within Holding Period			EITF.90-6
Allocation to Discontinued Operations			EITF.87-24
Contingent Interest Expense Recognition			
. . Equity Certificates of Deposit			EITF.84-31
Deferred Interest Rate Setting			EITF.84-14
. . Forward Commitments as a Surrogate for Deferred Rate Setting			EITF.86-15
Increasing-Rate Debt			EITF.86-15
Indexed Debt			EITF.86-28
Interest Rate Swap Transactions			EITF.84-36
			EITF.88-8
. . Termination of Sale			EITF.84-7
Mortgage Swaps			EITF.88-8
Participating Mortgages			EITF.86-28
INTEREST: IMPUTATION OF AN INTEREST COST			
Amortization of Discount and Premium			
. . Interest Method	APB21, ¶15	I69.108	
Contributions Receivable and Payable	FAS116, ¶20	C67.116	
Determining an Appropriate Rate			
. . Considerations	APB21, ¶14	I69.107	
. . Objectives	APB21, ¶13	I69.106	
Disclosure	APB21, ¶16	I69.109	
Eligibility for Interest Capitalization	FAS34, ¶2	I69.110	
Examples of Determining Present Value	APB21, ¶18-20	I69.111-115	
Notes Exchanged for Cash or for Cash and Rights or Privileges	APB21, ¶7	I69.104	
	APB21, ¶11		
Notes Exchanged for Property, Goods, or Services	APB21, ¶12	I69.105	
Pipeline Enterprises			
. . Advances to Encourage Exploration	AIN-APB21, #1	I69.501-502	
Scope of Accounting and Reporting Requirements	APB21, ¶2-4	I69.101-103	
Statement Presentation of Discount and Premium	APB21, ¶16	I69.109	
INTEREST INCOME			
Graduated Payment Mortgages			EITF.85-38
Interest Rate Swap Transactions			EITF.84-36
. . Termination or Sale			EITF.84-7
Negative Amortizing Loan			EITF.85-38
Required Use of the Interest Method			EITF.D-10
Sale of Loan with a Share of Interest Retained			EITF.84-21
Shared Appreciation Mortgages			EITF.86-21

FAS–FASB Statements   FIN–FASB Interpretations   FTB–FASB Technical Bulletins
APB–APB Opinions   AIN–AICPA Interpretations   ARB–Accounting Research Bulletins
CON–FASB Concepts   EITF–EITF Issues   Q&A–FASB Special Reports

	Original Pronouncements	Current Text	EITF and Other
INTEREST METHOD			
Debt: Restructurings	FAS15, ¶26	D22.122	
	FAS15, ¶30	D22.126	
Description	APB21, ¶15	I69.108	
Loan Fees	FAS91, ¶18-20	L20.117-119	
INTEREST-ONLY SECURITIES			
See Financial Instruments			
Classification of Interest-Only Securities as Held-to-Maturity			EITF.94-4
Effect of Unanticipated Mortgage Prepayments			EITF.86-38
Exchange of Interest-Only and Principal-Only Securities for a Mortgage-Backed Security			EITF.90-2
Purchase of Mortgage-Backed Interest-Only Certificates			EITF.89-4
. . Impairment Recognition			EITF.93-18
Sale of Interest-Only Cash Flows from Loans Receivable			
. . Determination of Gain or Loss			EITF.88-11
. . Determination of Remaining Recorded Investment for Portion of Loan Retained			EITF.88-11
INTEREST RATE SWAPS			
See Financial Instruments			
See Hedges			
INTERIM FINANCIAL REPORTING			
See Disclosure			
See Income Taxes			
Accounting Change	APB28, ¶23-26	I73.131-142	
	APB28, ¶28-29	I73.151-164	
	FAS3, ¶9-13		
	FAS3, App.A		
	FAS3, App.B		
	FIN18, ¶21		
	FIN18, ¶40		
. . Change to LIFO Method of Inventory Pricing	APB28, ¶25	I73.140-142	
	FAS3, ¶12-13	I73.158-163	
	FAS3, App.B		
. . Cumulative Effect Type Accounting Changes Other Than Changes to LIFO	APB28, ¶29	I73.135-139	
	FAS3, ¶9-11	I73.196-197	
	FIN18, ¶21		
	FIN18, ¶63-64		
. . Income Taxes, Effect on Prechange Interim Periods of Current Year	FIN18, ¶64	I73.197	
. . Income Taxes, Effect on Retained Earnings at Beginning of Year	FIN18, ¶63	I73.196	

See "Terminology" for references to defined terms presented in various accounting pronouncements.
See the Introduction to the Topical Index for details on the use of this index.

	Original Pronouncements	Current Text	EITF and Other

INTERIM FINANCIAL REPORTING—continued

Accounting Change—continued
. . Reporting a Cumulative Effect Type
(Other Than a Change to LIFO) .... FAS3, App.A | I73.154-157
Accounting Policies .... APB22, ¶10 | A10.104
Accounting for Costs and Expenses Other
Than Product Costs .... APB28, ¶16 | I73.150
Adjustments Related to Prior Interim
Periods of the Current Fiscal Year .... FAS16, ¶13-15 | A35.109-111 | EITF.85-35
.... FAS109, ¶288 | I73.143-145
Application of Statement 105 to Interim
Period Financial Statements .... | EITF.D-22
Contingent Items .... APB28, ¶22 | I73.125
Definition
. . Annual Effective Tax Rate .... APB28, ¶19 | I73.401
. . Ordinary Income or Loss .... FIN18, ¶5 | I73.402
. . Tax (or Benefit) .... FIN18, ¶5 | I73.403
Discontinued Operations
. . Income Taxes Applicable Thereto at an
Interim Date .... FIN18, ¶19 | I73.129
.... FIN18, ¶62 | I73.188-195
Disposal of a Segment .... APB28, ¶21 | I73.124
Extraordinary Items .... APB28, ¶21 | I73.124
Income Tax Provisions
. . Basis of Tax Provision .... FIN18, ¶56 | I73.182
. . Display in Financial Statements .... FIN18, ¶71 | I73.208
. . Effect of New Tax Legislation .... FAS109, ¶288 | I73.114 | EITF.86-3
.... FIN18, ¶68 | I73.203
. . Effect of New Tax Legislation
Effective in Future Interim Period ...... FIN18, ¶69 | I73.204-205
. . Effect of New Tax Legislation
Effective in Previous Interim Period .. FIN18, ¶70
. . Effect of New Tax Legislation,
Effective Date .... FIN18, ¶24 | I73.115
. . Estimated Annual Effective Tax Rate ... APB28, ¶19 | I73.111-112
.... FIN18, ¶6
.... FIN18, ¶8
. . Estimated Annual Effective Tax Rate,
Changes in Estimates .... FIN18, ¶48 | I73.172-173
. . Interim Period Tax (or Benefit) .... FIN18, ¶9 | I73.116
. . Recognition of the Tax Benefit of a
Loss .... APB28, ¶20 | I73.121-123
.... FAS109, ¶288 | I73.170-171
.... FIN18, ¶15 | I73.177-179
.... FIN18, ¶46-47
.... FIN18, ¶52-54
. . Recognizing Changes in Tax Law
Prior to Enactment .... | | EITF.86-11

FAS–FASB Statements   FIN–FASB Interpretations   FTB–FASB Technical Bulletins
APB–APB Opinions   AIN–AICPA Interpretations   ARB–Accounting Research Bulletins
CON–FASB Concepts   EITF–EITF Issues   Q&A–FASB Special Reports

	Original Pronouncements	Current Text	EITF and Other
INTERIM FINANCIAL REPORTING—continued			
Income Tax Provisions—continued			
. . Reduction in Tax Rate Effective for Part of Fiscal Year	FTB79-9, ¶1-3	I73.501-502	
Income Tax Provisions, Changes in Estimates	FIN18, ¶48	I73.172-173	
. . Ordinary Income to Date	FIN18, ¶10	I73.117	
	FIN18, ¶43-44	I73.167-168	
. . Ordinary Losses in Interim Periods, Income to Date	FIN18, ¶45	I73.169	
. . Ordinary Losses to Date	FIN18, ¶11	I73.118	
. . Ordinary Losses to Date, Realization Assured	FAS109, ¶288	I73.170	
	FIN18, ¶46		
. . Ordinary Losses to Date, Realization Not Assured	FAS109, ¶288	I73.171	
	FIN18, ¶47		
Income Tax Provisions, Multiple Jurisdictions			
. . Estimated Annual Effective Tax Rate	FIN18, ¶22	I73.113	
	FIN18, ¶85		
. . Ordinary Income Cannot Be Estimated in One Jurisdiction	FIN18, ¶67	I73.201-202	
. . Ordinary Income in All Jurisdictions	FIN18, ¶65	I73.198-199	
. . Ordinary Loss, Realization Not Assured	FIN18, ¶66	I73.200	
Income Tax Provisions, Ordinary Loss Anticipated for Fiscal Year			
. . Ordinary Income and Losses in Interim Periods	FAS109, ¶288	I73.176	
	FIN18, ¶51	I73.179	
	FIN18, ¶54		
. . Ordinary Income to Date	FAS109, ¶288	I73.119	
	FIN18, ¶12	I73.174	
	FIN18, ¶49		
. . Ordinary Losses to Date	FAS109, ¶288	I73.120	
	FIN18, ¶13	I73.175	
	FIN18, ¶50		
. . Partial Realization of Tax Benefit of Losses Assured	FAS109, ¶288	I73.178-179	
	FIN18, ¶53-54		
. . Realization of Tax Benefit of Losses Not Assured	FAS109, ¶288	I73.177	
	FIN18, ¶52		
Income Tax Provisions, Special Items			
. . Basis of Tax Provision	FIN18, ¶16	I73.126	
	FIN18, ¶57-58	I73.183-184	
. . Discontinued Operations	FIN18, ¶19	I73.129	
	FIN18, ¶62	I73.189-195	

See "Terminology" for references to defined terms presented in various accounting pronouncements.
See the Introduction to the Topical Index for details on the use of this index.

	Original Pronouncements	Current Text	EITF and Other

INTERIM FINANCIAL REPORTING—continued

Income Tax Provisions, Special Items—continued

.. Financial Statement Presentation .... FIN18, ¶17 — I73.127

.. Recognition of the Tax Benefit of a
Loss .... FAS109, ¶288 — I73.128

.... FIN18, ¶18

Infrequent Items.. APB28, ¶21 — I73.124

Inventory

.. Change to LIFO Method of Inventory
Pricing .... FAS3, App.B — I73.158-163

Modifications to Interim Reporting from Annual Reporting

.. All Other Costs and Expenses............... APB28, ¶15 — I73.108-109

.... APB28, ¶17

.. Costs Associated with Revenue .... APB28, ¶13 — I73.106

.. Costs Associated with Revenue, Inventory Method .... APB28, ¶14 — I73.107

.. Costs and Expenses .... APB28, ¶12 — I73.105

.. Revenue .... APB28, ¶11 — I73.104

Motion Picture Industry

.. Inventory Valuation .... FAS53, ¶16 — Mo6.115

Oil and Gas Producing Activities

.. Disclosure of Major Discovery .... FAS69, ¶9 — I73.149A

Price Declines in Inventory below Cost...... — — EITF.86-13

Scope of Accounting and Reporting Requirements .... APB28, ¶3 — I73.101-103

.... APB28, ¶6-7

.... APB28, ¶9-10

Seasonal Price Fluctuations in Inventory.... — — EITF.86-13

Seasonal Revenue, Costs, or Expenses .... APB28, ¶18 — I73.110

Segment of Business Reporting .... FAS18, ¶7 — S20.105

Special Items.. APB28, ¶21 — I73.124

Using a Prior Year Operating Loss Carryforward.. FAS109, ¶288 — I73.130

INTERNAL EVENTS AND TRANSACTIONS

See Events and Transactions

INTERPERIOD TAX ALLOCATION

See Income Taxes

See Interim Financial Reporting

INVENTORY

See Computer Software

See Disclosure

See Interim Financial Reporting

Abnormal Costs.. ARB43, Ch.4, ¶5 — I78.106

.... ARB43, Ch.4, ¶14 — I78.117

Accounting Objective................................. ARB43, Ch.4, ¶4 — I78.104

Agricultural Products................................. ARB43, Ch.4, ¶16 — I78.119

FAS–FASB Statements	FIN–FASB Interpretations	FTB–FASB Technical Bulletins
APB–APB Opinions	AIN–AICPA Interpretations	ARB–Accounting Research Bulletins
CON–FASB Concepts	EITF–EITF Issues	Q&A–FASB Special Reports

	Original Pronouncements	Current Text	EITF and Other
INVENTORY—continued			
Balance Sheet Classification	ARB43, Ch.3A, ¶4	B05.105	
Capitalizing Indirect Costs			EITF.86-46
Cost Basis	ARB43, Ch.4, ¶5-6	I78.105-108	
. . Change in Composition of Cost Elements	FIN1, ¶5	A06.108	
Definition			
. . Cost	ARB43, Ch.4, ¶5	I78.401	
. . Inventory	ARB43, Ch.4, ¶3	I78.402	
. . Lower of Cost or Market	ARB43, Ch.4, ¶9	I78.403	
. . Market	ARB43, Ch.4, ¶9	I78.404	
Description	ARB43, Ch.4, ¶5	I78.102	
Exclusions	ARB43, Ch.4, ¶3	I78.103	
Last-In, First-Out (LIFO)			
. . Change in IRS Conformity Requirement			EITF.84-10
. . Effect of AICPA Issues Paper			EITF.84-24
. . Involuntary Conversion	FIN30, ¶2	N35.115	
. . Prior-Period Adjustment, Change from	APB20, ¶27	A35.114	
. . Prior-Period Adjustment, Change to			EITF.84-10
. . Repeal of *Insilco* Tax Court Decision			EITF.84-10
. . Temporary Differences for Income Tax Purposes			EITF.D-31
Lower of Cost or Market	ARB43, Ch.4, ¶9	I78.110	
	ARB43, Ch.4, ¶11-13	I78.113-116	
. . Damage, Obsolescence, or Deterioration	ARB43, Ch.4, ¶8	I78.109	
. . Foreign Currency Translation	FAS52, ¶49-53	F60.148-152	
. . Net Realizable Value	ARB43, Ch.4, ¶9	I78.110	
. . Price Declines during Interim Reporting Periods			EITF.86-13
. . Replacement Cost	ARB43, Ch.4, ¶9	I78.111	
. . Retail Inventory Method	ARB43, Ch.4, ¶10	I78.112	
. . Seasonal Price Fluctuations during Interim Reporting Periods			EITF.86-13
. . Unusual Losses	ARB43, Ch.4, ¶14	I78.117	
Measurement Attributes Used			
. . Historical Cost, Current Cost, Net Realizable Value	CON5, ¶67		
Motion Picture Industry	FAS53, ¶16	Mo6.115	
Overhead	ARB43, Ch.4, ¶5	I78.106	
Precious Metals	ARB43, Ch.4, ¶16	I78.119	
Purchase Commitments			
. . Losses	ARB43, Ch.4, ¶17	I78.121-122	
Scope of Accounting and Reporting Requirements	ARB43, Ch.4, ¶2	I78.101	
Spoilage	ARB43, Ch.4, ¶5	I78.106	
Standard Costs	ARB43, Ch.4, ¶6	I78.108	
Valuation Methods			
. . Average	ARB43, Ch.4, ¶6	I78.107-108	

See "Terminology" for references to defined terms presented in various accounting pronouncements.
See the Introduction to the Topical Index for details on the use of this index.

	Original Pronouncements	Current Text	EITF and Other
INVENTORY—continued			
Valuation Methods—continued			
. . First-In, First-Out (FIFO)	ARB43, Ch.4, ¶6	I78.107-108	
. . Last-In, First-Out (LIFO)	ARB43, Ch.4, ¶6	I78.107-108	
. . Retail Inventory	ARB43, Ch.4, ¶6	I78.108	
	ARB43, Ch.4, ¶10	I78.112	
INVESTMENT ENTERPRISES			
See Financial Instruments Equity Method			
. . Investment Company Act of 1940	APB18, ¶2	I82.101	
Exemption from the Requirement to			
Provide a Statement of Cash Flows	FAS102, ¶6-7	C25.135B-135C	
		In8.103	
Investments in Debt and Equity			
Securities	FAS115, ¶4	I80.102	
Specialized Accounting and Reporting			
. . Retention in Consolidation			EITF.85-12
INVESTMENT TAX CREDITS			
See Income Taxes			
Deferred, Qualification as a Liability	CON6, ¶243-245		
INVESTMENTS			
See Balance Sheet Classification: Current Assets and Liabilities			
See Financial Instruments			
See Investments: Debt and Equity Securities			
See Investments: Equity Method			
Accounting for Conversion of a Loan into a Debt Security in a Debt Restructuring			EITF.94-8
Classification of Interest-Only Securities as Held-to-Maturity			EITF.94-4
Divestiture of Certain Securities to an Unregulated Commonly Controlled Entity under FIRREA			EITF.89-18
Exchanges of Ownership Interests between Entities under Common Control			EITF.90-5
Investments in Qualified Affordable Housing Projects			
. . Accounting for Tax Benefits			EITF.94-1
Limited Partnership Investments			
. . Cost Method			EITF.D-46
. . Equity Method			EITF.D-46
. . Reporting by SEC Registrants			EITF.D-46
Nonmonetary Exchange of Cost-Method Investments			EITF.91-5

FAS–FASB Statements   FIN–FASB Interpretations   FTB–FASB Technical Bulletins
APB–APB Opinions   AIN–AICPA Interpretations   ARB–Accounting Research Bulletins
CON–FASB Concepts   EITF–EITF Issues   Q&A–FASB Special Reports

	Original Pronouncements	Current Text	EITF and Other

INVESTMENTS—continued
Purchase of Collateralized Mortgage
  Obligation Instruments or
  Mortgage-Backed Interest-Only
  Certificates.. | | | EITF.89-4
. . Impairment Recognition........................ | | | EITF.93-18
Reclassification of Securities in
  Anticipation of Adoption of
  Statement 115 by SEC Registrants........... | | | EITF.D-38
Reverse Repurchase Agreements
. . GNMA Dollar Rolls .... | | | EITF.84-20
Securities Acquired for Cash in a Pooling
  of Interests... | | | EITF.85-14

INVESTMENTS BY OWNERS
See Capital Stock: Capital Transactions
See Capital Stock: Dividends-in-Kind
See Capital Stock: Preferred Stock
See Capital Stock: Treasury Stock
Characteristics....................................... | CON6, ¶68
Definition .... | CON6, ¶66
Element of Financial Statements................ | CON5, ¶13
  .... | CON6, ¶66-69
Partnerships
. . Withdrawals.. | | | EITF.85-46
Statement of... | CON5, ¶55-57

INVESTMENTS: DEBT AND EQUITY SECURITIES
Accounting for... | FAS115, ¶6-18 | I80.103-117
  .... | FAS115, ¶110-111
  .... | FAS115, ¶113
  .... | FAS115, ¶117
Accounting for Conversion of a Loan into
  a Debt Security in a Debt Restructuring... | | | EITF.94-8
Accounting for Debt Securities Reported
  as Loans... | | | EITF.D-39
Adjustments for Holding Gains and
  Losses as Related to the Implementation
  of Statement 115 .... | | | EITF.D-41
Available-for-Sale Securities...................... | FAS115, ¶12-16 | I80.109-111
  | | I80.114-115
Amortized Cost... | FAS115, ¶7 | I80.104
Asset-Liability Management...................... | FAS115, ¶10 | I80.107
Brady Bonds .... | | | EITF.D-39
Carrying Amount....................................... | | | EITF.85-39
  | | | EITF.86-28
. . Effect of Redemption Agreement.......... | | | EITF.85-23
. . Mutual Funds That Invest in U.S.
    Government Securities .... | | | EITF.86-40
Cash Flows Statement .... | FAS115, ¶18 | I80.117
Change in Value of Marketable Securities.. | | | EITF.86-28

See "Terminology" for references to defined terms presented in various accounting pronouncements.
See the Introduction to the Topical Index for details on the use of this index.

	Original Pronouncements	Current Text	EITF and Other
INVESTMENTS: DEBT AND EQUITY SECURITIES—continued			
Classification of	FAS115, ¶6	I80.103	
. . Change in Classification	FAS115, ¶15	I80.114	
	FAS115, ¶22	I80.121	
Classification of Interest-Only Securities as Held-to-Maturity			EITF.94-4
Consolidation			
. . Investee's Unrealized Losses on Marketable Securities	FAS115, ¶135	I80.501-502	
	FTB79-19, ¶1		
Current/Noncurrent, Classified Balance Sheet	FAS115, ¶17	I80.116	
Determining Fair Value	FAS115, ¶110-111	I80.112	
Dividend Income	FAS115, ¶14	I80.111	
Fair Value			
. . Decline in	FAS115, ¶16	I80.115	
	FAS115, ¶113		
. . Readily Determinable	FAS115, ¶3	I80.101	
. . Reporting Changes in	FAS115, ¶13-14	I80.110-111	
Financial Statement Presentation	FAS115, ¶17-18	I80.116-117	
	FAS115, ¶117		
Glossary	FAS115, ¶3	I80.401-406	
	FAS115, ¶137		
Held-to-Maturity Securities	FAS115, ¶7-11	I80.104-108	
	FAS115, ¶14-16	I80.111	
	FAS115, ¶59	I80.114-115	
	FAS115, ¶71-72		
	FAS115, ¶74		
	FAS115, ¶76		
. . Maturities	FAS115, ¶11	I80.108	
	FAS115, ¶66		
. . Sale or Transfer of	FAS115, ¶8-9	I80.105-106	
	FAS115, ¶15	I80.114	
	FAS115, ¶22	I80.121	
	FAS115, ¶59		
	FAS115, ¶71-72		
	FAS115, ¶74		
	FAS115, ¶76		
Hedging of Investments at Fair Value	FAS115, ¶115	I80.113	
Impairment of Securities	FAS115, ¶16	I80.115	
	FAS115, ¶113		
. . Other Than Temporary	FAS115, ¶16	I80.115	
. . Recognition of Other-Than-Temporary Impairment Due to Planned Sale of Debt Security			EITF.D-44
Income Taxes			
. . Unrealized Gains (Losses)	FAS115, ¶13	I80.110	
Interest Income	FAS115, ¶14	I80.111	
Market Value			EITF.86-28

FAS–FASB Statements   FIN–FASB Interpretations   FTB–FASB Technical Bulletins
APB–APB Opinions   AIN–AICPA Interpretations   ARB–Accounting Research Bulletins
CON–FASB Concepts   EITF–EITF Issues   Q&A–FASB Special Reports

I

Topical Index

	Original Pronouncements	Current Text	EITF and Other
INVESTMENTS: DEBT AND EQUITY SECURITIES—continued			
Mortgage-Backed Securities	FAS115, ¶12	I80.109	
Mortgage Derivative Product			
. . Effect of Potential Designation as a High-Risk Security			EITF.D-39
Other Than Temporary Decline in Market Value			EITF.85-39
Realized Gains and Losses	FAS115, ¶14	I80.111	
. . Inclusion in Determination of Earnings	FAS115, ¶14	I80.111	
Receipt of FHLMC Participating Preferred Stock			EITF.85-7
Reclassification of Securities in Anticipation of Adoption of Statement 115 by SEC Registrants			EITF.D-38
Recognition of Other-Than-Temporary Impairment Due to Planned Sale of Debt Security			EITF.D-44
Restricted Stock	FAS115, ¶3	I80.101	
Sale of Marketable Securities with a Put Option			EITF.84-5
			EITF.85-30
			EITF.85-40
Sale of Preferred Stocks with a Put Option			EITF.85-25
Sale of Securities following a Business Combination Expected to Be Accounted for as a Pooling of Interests			EITF.D-40
Scope of Accounting and Reporting Requirements	ARB43, Intro., ¶5	I80.101-102	
	FAS91, ¶3	I80.503-504	
	FAS115, ¶1		
	FAS115, ¶3-4		
	FAS115, ¶115		
	FTB94-1, ¶1		
	FTB94-1, ¶3		
Shareholder's Equity			
. . Separate Component of	FAS115, ¶13	I80.110	
	FAS115, ¶15-16	I80.114-115	
Trading Securities	FAS115, ¶12-15	I80.109-111	
	FAS115, ¶115	I80.113-114	
Transfers between Categories of Investments	FAS115, ¶8	I80.105	
	FAS115, ¶15	I80.114	
	FAS115, ¶71-72		
	FAS115, ¶74		
	FAS115, ¶76		
Troubled Debt Restructuring	FTB94-1, ¶1	I80.503-504	
	FTB94-1, ¶3		

See "Terminology" for references to defined terms presented in various accounting pronouncements.
See the Introduction to the Topical Index for details on the use of this index.

	Original Pronouncements	Current Text	EITF and Other
INVESTMENTS: DEBT AND EQUITY SECURITIES—continued			
Unrealized Holding Gains and Losses	FAS115, ¶13	I80.110	
	FAS115, ¶15	I80.114	
INVESTMENTS: EQUITY METHOD			
See Disclosure			
See Oil and Gas Producing Activities			
Application to			
. . Accounting Changes	APB18, ¶19	I82.109	
. . Capital Transactions by Investee	APB18, ¶19	I82.109	
. . Difference between Cost and Underlying Equity	APB18, ¶19	I82.109	
. . Difference in Year-End from Investor	APB18, ¶19	I82.109	
. . Extraordinary Items	APB18, ¶19	I82.109	
. . Income Taxes on Undistributed Earnings	APB18, ¶19	I82.109	
. . Intercompany Transactions and Balances	AIN-APB18, #1	I82.109	
	APB18, ¶19	I82.501-507	
	FAS94, ¶15		
. . Investees Subject to Repurchase Option			EITF.84-33
. . Losses, Earnings of Investee	APB18, ¶19	I82.109	
. . Partnerships and Unincorporated (Joint) Ventures	AIN-APB18, #2	I82.508-512	
. . Preferred Stock of Investee	APB18, ¶19	I82.109	
. . Prior-Period Adjustments	APB18, ¶19	I82.109	
. . Sale of Investment	APB18, ¶19	I82.109	
. . Subsidiaries under Temporary Control			EITF.84-33
. . Temporary Decline in Value	APB18, ¶19	I82.109	
. . Unconsolidated Subsidiaries		C51.118	
. . Unrealized Losses on Marketable Securities Owned by Investee	FAS115, ¶135	I82.513-514	
	FTB79-19, ¶1		
	FTB79-19, ¶6		
Capitalization of Interest	FAS34, ¶9	I67.105	
Criteria for Applying	APB18, ¶17	I82.104	
. . Basis for Accounting	APB18, ¶18	I82.105	
. . Corporate Joint Ventures	APB18, ¶16	I82.103	
	FAS94, ¶15		
. . Investments in Common Stock, Nonsubsidiaries	APB18, ¶17	I82.104	
. . Parent-Only Financial Statements	FAS94, ¶15	I82.102	
. . Significant Influence	APB18, ¶19	I82.106-109	
	FIN35, ¶2-4		
. . Stand-Still Agreements	FIN35, ¶4	I82.108	
. . Unconsolidated Subsidiaries	FAS94, ¶15	I82.102	
Exchange of Assets for Noncontrolling Equity Interest in New Entity			EITF.89-7

FAS–FASB Statements   FIN–FASB Interpretations   FTB–FASB Technical Bulletins
APB–APB Opinions   AIN–AICPA Interpretations   ARB–Accounting Research Bulletins
CON–FASB Concepts   EITF–EITF Issues   Q&A–FASB Special Reports

T-225

I

Topical Index

	Original Pronouncements	Current Text	EITF and Other
INVESTMENTS: EQUITY METHOD—continued			
Exchange of Interest in Subsidiary for Noncontrolling Equity Interest in New Entity			EITF.89-7
Glossary	APB18, ¶3	I82.401-408	
	APB18, ¶6		
	APB18, ¶11		
Goodwill	APB18, ¶19	I82.109	
Impairment of Value	APB18, ¶19	I82.109	
Income Taxes	APB23, ¶17-18	I27.218-219	
Purchase of Collateralized Mortgage Obligation Instruments or Mortgage-Backed Interest-Only Certificates			EITF.89-4
Real Estate Sales	FAS66, ¶34	R10.137	
		Re1.134	
Sale of Capital Stock by Subsidiary			EITF.84-27
Scope of Accounting and Reporting Requirements	APB18, ¶2	I82.101	
	FAS94, ¶15		
Segment of Business Reporting	FAS14, ¶7	S20.108	
Unconsolidated Subsidiaries	FAS94, ¶15	I82.102	
INVESTORS			
Information Needs	CON1, ¶41		
Interest in Financial Reporting	CON1, ¶32-39		
INVOLUNTARY CONVERSION			
See Nonmonetary Transactions			
IRREGULARITIES			
See Adjustments of Financial Statements for Prior Periods			

(The next page is T-245.)

See "Terminology" for references to defined terms presented in various accounting pronouncements.
See the Introduction to the Topical Index for details on the use of this index.

T-226

	Original Pronouncements	Current Text	EITF and Other
JOINT VENTURES			
See Income Taxes			
See Investments: Equity Method			
JUNIOR STOCK OPTION, PURCHASE AND AWARD PLANS			
See Compensation to Employees: Stock Purchase and Stock Option Plans			
KEY-PERSON LIFE INSURANCE			
See Life Insurance			
Provision for Deferred Taxes on Increases in Cash Surrender Value			EITF.87-28

(The next page is T-247.)

FAS–FASB Statements   FIN–FASB Interpretations   FTB–FASB Technical Bulletins
APB–APB Opinions   AIN–AICPA Interpretations   ARB–Accounting Research Bulletins
CON–FASB Concepts   EITF–EITF Issues   Q&A–FASB Special Reports

T-245

	Original Pronouncements	Current Text	EITF and Other

LAND

Balance Sheet Classification	ARB43, Ch.3A, ¶7	B05.107	
Depreciation	FAS93, ¶6	D40.101A	
	FAS93, ¶34		
Interest: Capitalization of Interest Costs	FAS34, ¶10	I67.106	
Leases	FAS13, ¶25-26	L10.121-122	

LAND SALES (REAL ESTATE)
See Real Estate
See Real Estate: Retail Land Sales

LEASE BROKERS
See Leases

Accreting Lease Residuals			EITF.85-32

LEASES
See Disclosure
See Income Taxes

Accruing Bad-Debt Expense at Inception			EITF.D-8
Allocation of Residual Value or First-Loss Guarantee to Minimum Lease Payments in Leases Involving Land and Building(s)			EITF.92-1

Amortization and Depreciation

. . Capital Leases	FAS13, ¶11-12	L10.107-108	
. . Operating Leases	FAS13, ¶19	L10.115	

Bargain Purchase Option

. . Effect on Classification	FAS13, ¶7	L10.103	
. . Effect on Lease Term	FAS98, ¶22	L10.414	
. . Effect on Minimum Lease Payments	FAS13, ¶5	L10.417	

Bargain Renewal Option

. . Effect on Lease Term	FAS98, ¶22	L10.414	
. . Effect on Minimum Lease Payments	FAS13, ¶5	L10.417	

Business Combinations

. . Accounting When Lease Provisions Are Unchanged	FIN21, ¶12	L10.137	
. . Change in Lease Provisions	FIN21, ¶13	L10.138	
. . Leveraged Leases—Purchase Method	FIN21, ¶16	L10.141	
	FIN21, ¶19	L10.161	
. . Pooling-of-Interests Method	FIN21, ¶14	L10.139	
. . Purchase Method	FIN21, ¶15-16	L10.140-142	

Capital Leases

. . Accounting for Lease Obligation	FAS13, ¶12	L10.108-109	
	FAS13, ¶14		
	FAS22, ¶14		
	FIN26, ¶5		
. . Amortization of Capitalized Asset	FAS13, ¶11-12	L10.107-108	
. . Calculation of Capitalized Amount	FAS13, ¶10	L10.106	
	FIN23, ¶8		
. . Change in Lease Provisions	FAS13, ¶9	L10.105	
	FAS13, ¶14	L10.109	
	FAS22, ¶14		
. . Contingent Rentals	FAS29, ¶13	L10.108	

	Original Pronouncements	Current Text	EITF and Other
LEASES—continued			
Capital Leases—continued			
. . Criteria for Classification	FAS13, ¶7	L10.103	
. . Executory Costs	FAS13, ¶7	L10.103	
. . Extinguishment of Lease Debt	FAS22, ¶12	L10.110	
	FAS22, ¶17	L10.162-163	
. . Gains or Losses	FAS13, ¶14	L10.109-110	
	FAS22, ¶12		
	FAS22, ¶14		
	FIN26, ¶5		
. . Guarantee of Residual Value	FAS13, ¶11-12	L10.107-108	
. . Illustrations for Lessees	FAS13, ¶121-122	L10.150-153	
. . Interest Expense	FAS13, ¶12	L10.108	
. . Purchase of a Leased Asset by Lessee	FIN26, ¶5	L10.109	
. . Refunding of Tax-Exempt Debt	FAS22, ¶12	L10.110	
	FAS22, ¶17	L10.162-163	
. . Renewals or Extensions	FAS13, ¶9	L10.105	
	FAS13, ¶12	L10.108-109	
	FAS13, ¶14		
	FAS22, ¶14		
. . Sale-Leaseback Transactions	FAS28, ¶2-3	L10.128-129	
. . Termination of Capital Lease	FAS13, ¶14	L10.109	
Classifying Leases (Other Than Leveraged Leases)			
. . Changes in Estimates or Provisions for Lessees and Lessors	FAS13, ¶9	L10.105	
. . Illustrations for Lessees and Lessors	FAS13, ¶121-122	L10.150-153	
. . Lessee Criteria	FAS13, ¶6-7	L10.102-103	
. . Lessor Criteria	FAS13, ¶6-8	L10.102-104	
	FAS27, ¶6-7		
	FAS98, ¶22		
Collateral			
. . Money-Over-Money Lease Transactions	FTB88-1, ¶16-17	L10.542-543	
. . Sale of Leased Property	FAS13, ¶22	L10.118	
. . Wrap Lease Transactions	FTB88-1, ¶21-22	L10.544-545	
Computer Software			
. . Cost Incurred to Lease Software	FIN6, ¶5	R50.114	
Concentrations of Credit Risk on Operating Leases			EITF.D-22
Consolidation			
. . Related-Party Leases	FAS13, ¶30	L10.126	
Contingent Rentals			
. . Capital Leases	FAS29, ¶13	L10.108	
. . Direct Financing Leases	FAS98, ¶22	L10.114	
. . Exclusion from Minimum Lease Payments	FAS13, ¶5	L10.417	
	FAS29, ¶10		
. . Illustration of Calculation	FAS29, ¶15-17	L10.164-166	

See "Terminology" for references to defined terms presented in various accounting pronouncements.
See the Introduction to the Topical Index for details on the use of this index.

	Original Pronouncements	Current Text	EITF and Other
LEASES—continued			
Contingent Rentals—continued			
. . Operating Leases with Scheduled Rent Increases	FTB85-3, ¶1-2	L10.525-527B	
	FTB85-3, ¶12-13		
	FTB88-1, ¶1-2		
. . Sales-Type Leases	FAS29, ¶13	L10.113	
Current Value Financial Statements	FTB79-13, ¶1-2	L10.512-513	
Debt: Restructuring			
. . Exemption from Requirements	FAS15, ¶8	D22.102	
Direct Financing Leases			
. . Accounting	FAS13, ¶18	L10.114	
	FAS98, ¶22		
. . Allowance for Doubtful Accounts	FAS98, ¶22	L10.104	
. . Calculation of Gross Investment	FAS98, ¶22	L10.114	
. . Calculation of Net Investment	FAS98, ¶22	L10.114	
. . Change in Lease Provisions	FAS13, ¶9	L10.105	
	FAS22, ¶14		
	FAS27, ¶6-7		
. . Compared with Leveraged Leases	FAS13, ¶42	L10.144	
. . Contingent Rentals	FAS98, ¶22	L10.114	
. . Criteria for Classification	FAS13, ¶6	L10.102	
	FAS13, ¶8	L10.104	
	FAS27, ¶7		
	FAS98, ¶22		
. . Executory Costs	FAS98, ¶22	L10.114	
. . Gains or Losses	FAS13, ¶18	L10.114	
	FAS98, ¶22		
. . Governmental Units	FAS22, ¶12	L10.113	
. . Guarantee of Residual Value	FAS13, ¶18	L10.114	
. . Income Determination	FAS13, ¶18	L10.114	
	FAS98, ¶22		
. . Initial Direct Costs	FAS98, ¶22	L10.114	
. . Involving Real Estate	FAS13, ¶25-26	L10.121-122	
	FAS98, ¶22		
. . Offsetting Nonrecourse Debt with Lease Receivables	FIN39, ¶5-7	B10.101A-101B	EITF.84-25
	FTB88-1, ¶16-17	B10.107	
	FTB88-1, ¶21-22	L10.542-545	
. . Penalty for Failure to Renew Lease	FAS13, ¶18	L10.114	
. . Sale of Leased Property	FAS13, ¶20	L10.116	
. . Sale or Assignment of Lease Receivable with Recourse	FAS13, ¶20	L10.116	
	FAS77, ¶3	R20.102	
	FAS77, ¶10		
. . Subleases	FAS13, ¶36-39	L10.132-135	
. . Termination	FAS13, ¶18	L10.114	
. . Unearned Income	FAS98, ¶22	L10.114	
Discontinued Operations			
. . Subleases	FIN27, ¶2-3	L10.135	
Double-Dip Tax Leases			EITF.89-20

FAS–FASB Statements	FIN–FASB Interpretations	FTB–FASB Technical Bulletins
APB–APB Opinions	AIN–AICPA Interpretations	ARB–Accounting Research Bulletins
CON–FASB Concepts	EITF–EITF Issues	Q&A–FASB Special Reports

	Original Pronouncements	Current Text	EITF and Other
LEASES—continued			
Economic Life			
. . Criteria for Classifying Leases	FAS13, ¶7	L10.103	
Equipment			
. . Revenue Recognition on Equipment Sold and Subsequently Repurchased Subject to an Operating Lease			EITF.95-4
Estimates			
. . Change in Estimates	FAS13, ¶9	L10.105	
. . Executory Costs	FAS13, ¶8	L10.104	
	FAS13, ¶10	L10.106	
. . Lease Term	FAS98, ¶22	L10.414	
. . Leveraged Leases	FAS13, ¶46	L10.148-148B	
	FAS109, ¶256-258		
. . Residual Value	FAS13, ¶5	L10.113-114	
	FAS13, ¶17-18	L10.148	
	FAS13, ¶46	L10.407	
		L10.422	
Executory Costs			
. . Allocation between Land and Buildings	FAS13, ¶26	L10.122	
. . Capital Leases	FAS13, ¶7	L10.103	
. . Consideration in Calculation of Deferred Profit in a Sale-Leaseback Transaction			EITF.89-16
. . Direct Financing Leases	FAS98, ¶22	L10.114	
. . Estimation	FAS13, ¶8	L10.104	
	FAS13, ¶10	L10.106	
. . Excluded from Minimum Lease Payments	FAS13, ¶10	L10.106	
. . Sales-Type Leases	FAS13, ¶17	L10.113	
Expenses			
. . Lease Incentives and Moving Costs	FTB88-1, ¶6-9	L10.527C-527F	EITF.88-3 EITF.88-10
. . Rental Expense on Operating Leases	FAS13, ¶15	L10.111	
	FTB85-3, ¶1-2	L10.525-527F	
	FTB85-3, ¶12-13		
	FTB88-1, ¶1-2		
	FTB88-1, ¶6-9		
Extinguishment of Lease Debt	FAS76, ¶10	L10.110	
. . Change in Provisions because of Refunding of Tax-Exempt Debt	FAS22, ¶12	L10.110	
	FAS22, ¶17	L10.113	
		L10.162-163	
. . Money-Over-Money Lease Transactions	FTB88-1, ¶16-17	L10.542-543	
. . Wrap Lease Transactions	FTB88-1, ¶21-22	L10.544-545	
Fair Value of Leased Property			
. . Appraisal Value	FIN24, ¶4	L10.124	
. . Effect on Lease Classification	FAS13, ¶7	L10.103	
. . Inception of the Lease	FAS23, ¶8	L10.122	

See "Terminology" for references to defined terms presented in various accounting pronouncements.
See the Introduction to the Topical Index for details on the use of this index.

	Original Pronouncements	Current Text	EITF and Other
LEASES—continued			
Fair Value of Leased Property—continued			
. . Leased Property Not Constructed	FAS23, ¶8	L10.106	
		L10.122	
. . Part of a Building	FAS13, ¶28	L10.124	
	FIN24, ¶4		
	FIN24, ¶6		
. . Real Estate	FAS13, ¶28	L10.124	
	FIN24, ¶4		
	FIN24, ¶6		
. . Sale-Leaseback Transactions	FAS28, ¶3	L10.129	
Fiscal Funding Clauses	FTB79-10, ¶1-5	L10.501-505	
Gains or Losses			
. . Capital Leases	FAS13, ¶14	L10.109-110	
	FAS22, ¶12		
	FAS22, ¶14		
	FIN26, ¶5		
. . Direct Financing Leases	FAS13, ¶18	L10.114	
	FAS98, ¶22		
. . Disposal of a Segment	FIN27, ¶2-3	L10.135	
	FTB79-15, ¶1-3	L10.518-520	
. . Illustration	FAS22, ¶17	L10.162-163	
. . Lease Incentives in Operating Leases	FTB88-1, ¶6-9	L10.527C-527F	
. . Leveraged Leases	FAS13, ¶45-46	L10.147-148	
. . Losses Not Involving Disposal of a Segment	FTB79-15, ¶1-3	L10.518-520	
. . Modification or Termination of Operating Leases	FTB79-15, ¶1-3	L10.518-520	EITF.88-10
. . Money-Over-Money Lease Transactions	FTB88-1, ¶16-17	L10.542-543	
. . Operating Leases Involving Real Estate	FAS98, ¶22	L10.115	
. . Refunding of Tax-Exempt Debt	FAS22, ¶12	L10.110	
	FAS22, ¶17	L10.113-114	
. . Related-Party Transactions	FAS13, ¶20-22	L10.116-118	
	FAS13, ¶29-30	L10.125-126	
	FAS77, ¶10		
. . Sale of Property Subject to Seller's Preexisting Lease			EITF.88-21
. . Sale or Assignment to Third Party	FAS13, ¶20-22	L10.116-118	
	FAS77, ¶10		
. . Sale-Leaseback Transactions	FAS28, ¶2-3	L10.128-129	EITF.84-37
. . Sale-Leaseback Transactions Involving Real Estate	FAS98, ¶7-8	L10.130B-130D	
	FAS98, ¶70		
. . Sales-Type Leases	FAS13, ¶17	L10.113	
	FAS22, ¶15		
	FAS27, ¶8		
. . Subleases	FAS13, ¶38-39	L10.134-135	
	FIN27, ¶2-3		
. . Wrap Lease Transactions	FTB88-1, ¶21-22	L10.544-545	

FAS–FASB Statements	FIN–FASB Interpretations	FTB–FASB Technical Bulletins
APB–APB Opinions	AIN–AICPA Interpretations	ARB–Accounting Research Bulletins
CON–FASB Concepts	EITF–EITF Issues	Q&A–FASB Special Reports

	Original Pronouncements	Current Text	EITF and Other
LEASES—continued			
Glossary	FAS13, ¶1	L10.401-424	
	FAS13, ¶5-7		
	FAS13, ¶10		
	FAS23, ¶6		
	FAS29, ¶11		
	FAS91, ¶24		
	FAS98, ¶22		
	FAS98, ¶70		
	FTB88-1, ¶16		
	FTB88-1, ¶21		
Government-Owned Facilities	FAS13, ¶28	L10.124	
	FIN23, ¶6		
	FIN23, ¶8-9		
. . Effect of Fiscal Funding Clauses	FTB79-10, ¶1-5	L10.501-505	
Guarantees			
. . Effect on Capital Lease Asset	FAS13, ¶11-12	L10.107-108	
. . Effect on Minimum Lease Payments	FAS13, ¶5	L10.417	
	FIN19, ¶3-5		
. . Effect on Sale-Leaseback Involving Real Estate	FAS98, ¶11-12	L10.130G-130H	
Impact of Nonsubstantive Lessors, Residual Value Guarantees, and Other Provisions in Leasing Transactions			EITF.90-15
Impairment: Loans			
. . Exemption from Requirements	FAS114, ¶6	I08.104	
Implicit Interest Rate			
. . Illustration of Calculation	FAS13, ¶121	L10.150	
Inception of Lease			
. . Leased Property Not Constructed	FAS23, ¶7-8	L10.104	
		L10.106	
		L10.122	
Income Recognition for Cross Border Tax Benefit Leases			EITF.89-20
Incremental Borrowing Rate			
. . Example of Computation	FAS13, ¶121	L10.150	
. . Use of a Specific Borrowing Rate	FTB79-12, ¶1-3	L10.509-511	
Initial Direct Costs			
. . Direct Financing Leases	FAS98, ¶22	L10.114	
. . Leveraged Leases	FAS13, ¶43	L10.145	
. . Operating Leases	FAS13, ¶19	L10.115	
. . Sales-Type Leases	FAS13, ¶17	L10.113	
Interest Expense and Interest Method			
. . Capital Leases	FAS13, ¶12	L10.108	
. . Direct Financing Leases	FAS13, ¶18	L10.114	
. . Interest Rate Implicit in Lease	FAS13, ¶5	L10.412	
. . Leveraged Leases	FAS13, ¶43-44	L10.145-146	
. . Minimum Lease Payments	FTB79-12, ¶1-3	L10.509-511	

See "Terminology" for references to defined terms presented in various accounting pronouncements.
See the Introduction to the Topical Index for details on the use of this index.

	Original Pronouncements	Current Text	EITF and Other
LEASES—continued			
Interest Expense and Interest Method—continued			
. . Nonapplicability to Operating Leases...	FAS13, ¶15	L10.111	
	FTB85-3, ¶1-2	L10.525-527B	
	FTB85-3, ¶12-13		
	FTB88-1, ¶1-2		
. . Refunding of Tax-Exempt Debt	FAS22, ¶12	L10.110	
		L10.113-114	
. . Sales-Type Leases	FAS13, ¶17	L10.113	
Interest in Residual Value			
. . Acquired by Selling Leased Asset and Retaining Interest in Residual Value ..			EITF.87-7
Investment Tax Credits	AIN-APB4, #3	I27.507-508	
. . Accounting by Lessee or Lessor	AIN-APB4, #3	I27.507-508	
. . Deferral Method of Accounting	AIN-APB4, #3	I27.509	
. . Impact on Implicit Interest Rate	FAS13, ¶5	L10.412	
. . Leveraged Leases	FAS13, ¶42-43	L10.144-145	
Lease Incentives in an Operating Lease	FTB88-1, ¶6-9	L10.527C-527F	
Lease Payments			
. . Allocation between Interest and Principal	FAS13, ¶12	L10.108	
. . Allocation between Land and Buildings	FAS13, ¶26	L10.122	
. . Contingent Rentals	FAS29, ¶13	L10.108	
	FAS91, ¶25		
. . Escalating Rents	FAS13, ¶15	L10.111	
	FAS13, ¶19	L10.115	
	FTB85-3, ¶1-2	L10.525-527B	
	FTB85-3, ¶12-13		
	FTB88-1, ¶1-2		
. . Escalation Clauses	FAS23, ¶8	L10.106	
		L10.122	
. . Executory Costs	FAS13, ¶5	L10.106	
	FAS13, ¶10	L10.417	
. . Lease Incentives	FTB88-1, ¶6-9	L10.527C-527F	EITF.88-3
. . Lease Modification or Termination			EITF.88-10
. . Lessor Estimate of Collectibility	FAS98, ¶22	L10.104	
. . Scheduled Rent Increases (Also Time Pattern of Physical Use of Leased Property)	FAS13, ¶15	L10.111	
	FAS13, ¶19	L10.115	
	FTB85-3, ¶1-2	L10.525-527B	
	FTB85-3, ¶12-13		
	FTB88-1, ¶1-2		
. . Unsecured Guarantee by Parent of Subsidiary's Lease Payments			EITF.90-14
Leased Property Not Constructed			
. . Determining Fair Value	FAS23, ¶8	L10.106	

	Original Pronouncements	Current Text	EITF and Other
LEASES—continued			
Leased Property Not Constructed—continued			
. . Estimated Residual Value	FAS23, ¶9-10	L10.114	
		L10.145	
. . Inception of the Lease	FAS23, ¶7	L10.104	
. . Land and Buildings	FAS23, ¶8	L10.122	
. . Lessor Classification	FAS23, ¶7	L10.104	
Leveraged Leases			
. . Accounting	FAS13, ¶42-47	L10.104	
	FAS23, ¶10	L10.144-149	
	FAS98, ¶22		
. . Alternative Minimum Tax (AMT)			EITF.87-8
. . Applicability to Existing Assets of the Lessor	FTB88-1, ¶11-12	L10.540-541	
. . Business Combination—Purchase Method	FIN21, ¶16	L10.141	
	FIN21, ¶19	L10.161	
. . Changes in Important Assumptions	FAS13, ¶46	L10.148	
. . Compared with Direct Financing Leases	FAS13, ¶42	L10.144	
. . Deferred Taxes	FAS109, ¶256-258	L10.148A-148B	
. . Delayed Equity Contributions by Lessors			EITF.85-16
. . Description	FAS13, ¶6	L10.102	
	FAS13, ¶42	L10.144	
. . Effect of Change in Income Tax Rate	FAS109, ¶288	L10.521-524	EITF.86-43
	FTB79-16(R), ¶1-4		
. . Gains or Losses	FAS13, ¶45-46	L10.147-148B	
	FAS109, ¶256-258		
. . Illustration of Accounting	FAS13, ¶123	L10.154	
. . Initial Direct Costs	FAS13, ¶43	L10.145	
	FAS91, ¶24		
. . Investment Tax Credit	FAS13, ¶42-43	L10.144-145	
. . Involving Real Estate			EITF.85-16
. . Residual Value	FAS13, ¶43	L10.145	
	FAS13, ¶46	L10.148	
	FAS23, ¶10		
. . Sale-Leaseback Transactions			EITF.85-16
. . Unearned Income	FAS13, ¶43	L10.145	
Licensing Agreements	FAS13, ¶1	L10.101	
Loss Contingencies			
. . Lease Incentives	FTB88-1, ¶6-9	L10.527C-527F	
. . Loss on Sublease	FAS13, ¶38	L10.134	EITF.88-10
	FTB79-15, ¶1-3	L10.518-520	
Minimum Lease Payments			
. . Allocation of Residual Value or First-Loss Guarantee in Leases Involving Land and Building(s)			EITF.92-1
. . Effect on Lease Classification	FAS13, ¶7	L10.103	

See "Terminology" for references to defined terms presented in various accounting pronouncements.

See the Introduction to the Topical Index for details on the use of this index.

	Original Pronouncements	Current Text	EITF and Other
LEASES—continued			
Minimum Lease Payments—continued			
. . Illustration of Computation	FAS13, ¶121	L10.150	
. . Interest Rate Used in Calculating			
Present Value	FTB79-12, ¶1-3	L10.509-511	
. . Lease Incentives	FTB88-1, ¶6-9	L10.527C-527F	
Money-Over-Money Lease Transactions	FTB88-1, ¶16-17	L10.542-543	
Moving Costs	FTB88-1, ¶6-9	L10.527C-527F	EITF.88-3
			EITF.88-10
Nonrecourse Debt			
. . Offsetting Nonrecourse Debt			
with Lease Receivables			EITF.84-25
Nonsubstantive Lessors			
. . Impact of Nonsubstantive Lessors,			
Residual Value Guarantees, and			
Other Provisions in Leasing			
Transactions			EITF.90-15
Operating Leases			
. . Accounting for Revenue and Leased			
Asset	FAS13, ¶19	L10.115	
	FAS98, ¶22		
. . Amortization and Depreciation	FAS13, ¶19	L10.115	
. . Change in Lease Provisions	FAS13, ¶9	L10.105	
. . Contingent Rentals—Excluded from			
Minimum Lease Payments	FAS29, ¶10	L10.417	
. . Criteria for Lessee Classification	FAS13, ¶7	L10.103	
. . Criteria for Lessor Classification	FAS13, ¶7-8	L10.103-104	
	FAS98, ¶22		
. . Escalating Rents	FAS13, ¶15	L10.111	
	FAS13, ¶19	L10.115	
	FTB85-3, ¶1-2	L10.525-527B	
	FTB85-3, ¶12-13		
	FTB88-1, ¶1-2		
. . Escalation Clauses	FAS23, ¶8	L10.106	
		L10.122	
. . Gains or Losses from Modification or			
Termination	FTB79-15, ¶1-3	L10.518-520	EITF.88-10
. . Illustrations	FAS13, ¶121-123	L10.150-153	
. . Lease Incentives	FTB88-1, ¶6-9	L10.527C-527F	EITF.88-3
. . Lessee Accounting	FAS13, ¶15	L10.111	
	FTB79-15, ¶1-3	L10.518-520	
	FTB85-3, ¶1-2	L10.525-527F	
	FTB85-3, ¶12-13		
	FTB88-1, ¶1-2		
	FTB88-1, ¶6-9		
. . Lessor Accounting for Initial Direct			
Costs	FAS13, ¶19	L10.115	
. . Losses Involving Real Estate	FAS98, ¶22	L10.115	
. . Minimum Lease Payments	FAS13, ¶5	L10.417	
	FIN19, ¶3-5		

FAS–FASB Statements	FIN–FASB Interpretations	FTB–FASB Technical Bulletins
APB–APB Opinions	AIN–AICPA Interpretations	ARB–Accounting Research Bulletins
CON–FASB Concepts	EITF–EITF Issues	Q&A–FASB Special Reports

T-255

	Original Pronouncements	Current Text	EITF and Other
LEASES—continued			
Operating Leases—continued			
. . Money-Over-Money Lease Transactions	FTB88-1, ¶16-17	L10.542-543	
. . Moving Costs	FTB88-1, ¶6-9	L10.527C-527F	EITF.88-10
. . Participation by Third Parties	FAS13, ¶21-22	L10.117-118	
. . Purchase of Leased Property	FAS13, ¶21-22	L10.117-118	
. . Remaining Rental Payments on Unused Property under Operating Lease	FTB88-1, ¶6-9	L10.527C-527F	EITF.88-10
. . Rental Expense	FAS13, ¶15	L10.111	EITF.88-10
	FTB85-3, ¶1-2	L10.525-527F	
	FTB85-3, ¶12-13		
	FTB88-1, ¶1-2		
	FTB88-1, ¶6-9		
. . Sale and Leaseback of an Asset That Is or Will Be Leased to Another Party			EITF.93-8
. . Sale of an Asset Subject to a Lease and Nonrecourse Debt	FTB88-1, ¶16-17	L10.542-545	EITF.87-7
	FTB88-1, ¶21-22		
. . Sale-Leaseback Transactions	FAS13, ¶34	L10.128-130	
	FAS28, ¶2-3		
. . Scheduled Rent Increases (Also Time Pattern of Physical Use of Leased Property)	FAS13, ¶15	L10.111	
	FAS13, ¶19	L10.115	
	FTB85-3, ¶1-2	L10.525-527B	
	FTB85-3, ¶12-13		
	FTB88-1, ¶1-2		
. . Wrap Lease Transactions	FTB88-1, ¶21-22	L10.544-545	EITF.87-7
Penalty			
. . Accounting for Penalty to Renew a Direct Financing Lease	FAS13, ¶18	L10.114	
. . Accounting for Penalty to Renew a Sales-Type Lease	FAS13, ¶17	L10.113	
. . Effect on Lease Term	FAS98, ¶22	L10.414	
. . Effect on Minimum Lease Payments	FAS13, ¶5	L10.417	
Property			
. . Amortization and Depreciation	FAS13, ¶11	L10.107	
	FAS13, ¶19	L10.115	
. . Calculation of Capitalized Amount	FAS13, ¶10	L10.106	
	FAS23, ¶8		
. . Economic Life	FAS13, ¶5	L10.406	
. . Fair Value	FAS13, ¶5	L10.409	
. . Government-Owned	FAS13, ¶28	L10.124	
	FIN23, ¶6		
	FIN23, ¶8-9		
. . Leased with Land	FAS13, ¶26	L10.122	EITF.85-16
	FAS98, ¶22		

See "Terminology" for references to defined terms presented in various accounting pronouncements.
See the Introduction to the Topical Index for details on the use of this index.

	Original Pronouncements	Current Text	EITF and Other
LEASES—continued			
Property—continued			
. . Money-Over-Money Lease Transactions	FTB88-1, ¶16-17	L10.542-543	
. . Purchase of Leased Property	FIN26, ¶5	L10.109	
. . Sale of Leased Property	FAS13, ¶20-22	L10.116-118	
. . Wrap Lease Transactions	FTB88-1, ¶21-22	L10.544-545	
Purchase of Leased Property			
. . Accounting by Lessee	FIN26, ¶5	L10.109	
. . Accounting by Lessor	FAS13, ¶20-22	L10.116-118	
Real Estate	FAS13, ¶24	L10.120	
. . Allocation of Residual Value or First-Loss Guarantee to Minimum Lease Payments in Leases Involving Land and Building(s)			EITF.92-1
. . Classification as Leveraged Lease			EITF.85-16
. . Delayed Equity Contributions in a Leveraged Lease			EITF.85-16
. . Fair Value Determination	FAS13, ¶28	L10.124	
	FIN24, ¶4		
	FIN24, ¶6		
. . Government-Owned	FAS13, ¶28	L10.124	
	FIN23, ¶6		
	FIN23, ¶8-9		
. . Land and Buildings	FAS13, ¶26	L10.122	
	FAS98, ¶22		
. . Land Only	FAS13, ¶25	L10.121	
	FAS98, ¶22		
. . Part of a Building	FAS13, ¶28	L10.124	
	FIN24, ¶4		
	FIN24, ¶6		
. . Qualifying as a Sales-Type Lease	FAS98, ¶22	L10.102	
		L10.104	
Real Estate and Equipment	FAS13, ¶27	L10.123	
Refunding of Tax-Exempt Debt			
. . Illustration of Accounting	FAS22, ¶17	L10.162-163	
. . Lessee Accounting	FAS22, ¶12	L10.110	
. . Lessor Accounting	FAS22, ¶12	L10.113-114	
Regulated Operations			
. . Accounting for Leases	FAS71, ¶40-43	Re6.145-148	
. . Accounting for Sale-Leaseback Transactions	FAS92, ¶30-35	L10.130J	
	FAS98, ¶14	Re6.188-193	
. . Accounting for Sale-Leaseback Transactions Involving Real Estate	FAS98, ¶14-16	Re6.125H-125J	
Related Parties			
. . Leases between Related Parties	FAS13, ¶29-30	L10.125-126	
. . Transfers between Related Parties	FAS13, ¶20-22	L10.116-118	
	FAS77, ¶10		

	Original Pronouncements	Current Text	EITF and Other

LEASES—continued

Relation to Commitments: Long-Term
Obligations .... FAS47, ¶6 — C32.101

Remarketing Agreements .... FAS13, ¶21-22 — L10.117-118

. . Involving Wrap Lease Transactions ...... — — EITF.87-7

Renewals

. . Bargain Renewal Option .... FAS13, ¶5 — L10.402

. . Capital Leases .... FAS13, ¶9 — L10.105
.... FAS13, ¶12 — L10.108-109
.... FAS13, ¶14
.... FAS22, ¶14

. . Direct Financing Leases .... FAS13, ¶18 — L10.102
.... FAS22, ¶14 — L10.109
.... FAS27, ¶6-7 — L10.114

. . Effect of Penalty .... FAS98, ¶22 — L10.418A

. . Effect on Lease Term .... FAS98, ¶22 — L10.414

. . Sales-Type Leases .... FAS13, ¶6 — L10.102-113
.... FAS13, ¶17
.... FAS22, ¶15
.... FAS27, ¶6-8

Rental Concessions Provided by Lessor

. . Accounting for Lease Incentives .... FTB88-1, ¶6-9 — L10.527C-527F — EITF.88-3

Residual Value

. . Accounting for a Guaranteed
Residual Value .... FTB86-2, ¶11-12 — L10.538-539

. . Accounting for Purchased Leased
Residuals by Lease Brokers .... FTB86-2, ¶7-8 — L10.534-535

. . Accounting for Purchased Leased
Residuals during Lease Term .... FTB86-2, ¶5-6 — L10.532-533

. . Accounting for Retained Residual by
Lessor That Sells Rental Payments .... FTB86-2, ¶9-10 — L10.536-537

. . Accounting for the Purchase of Lease
Residuals .... FTB86-2, ¶1-4 — L10.528-531

. . Allocation of Residual Value or
First-Loss Guarantee to Minimum
Lease Payments in Leases Involving
Land and Building(s) .... — — EITF.92-1

. . Annual Review of Estimate .... FAS13, ¶17-18 — L10.113-114
.... FAS13, ¶46 — L10.148

. . Decline in Estimated Value .... FAS13, ¶17-18 — L10.113-114
.... FAS13, ¶46 — L10.148

. . Direct Financing Leases .... FAS13, ¶18 — L10.114
.... FAS98, ¶22

. . Estimate for Leased Property Not
Constructed .... FAS23, ¶9-10 — L10.114
.... — L10.145

. . Estimated Residual Value of Leased
Property .... FAS13, ¶5 — L10.407

. . Guaranteed by Lessee .... FAS13, ¶5 — L10.417

See "Terminology" for references to defined terms presented in various accounting pronouncements.
See the Introduction to the Topical Index for details on the use of this index.

	Original Pronouncements	Current Text	EITF and Other
LEASES—continued			
Residual Value—continued			
. . Included in Minimum Lease			
Payments	FAS13, ¶5	L10.108	
	FAS13, ¶12	L10.417	
. . Leveraged Leases	FAS13, ¶43	L10.145	
	FAS13, ¶46	L10.148	
	FAS23, ¶10		
. . Sales-Type Leases	FAS13, ¶17	L10.113	
	FAS23, ¶9		
. . Unguaranteed Residual Value	FAS13, ¶5	L10.422	
. . Upward Adjustment of Guaranteed			
Residual Values	FTB79-14, ¶1-4	L10.514-517	
Restrictions of Lease Agreement	FAS13, ¶16	L10.112	
Safe Harbor Leases Used to Transfer Tax Benefits			
. . Disclosure of Sale or Purchase of Tax			
Benefits	FAS109, ¶288	I27.501-506	
	FTB82-1, ¶1-2		
	FTB82-1, ¶4		
	FTB82-1, ¶6-8		
. . Effect of Change in Tax Law			EITF.86-44
Revenue Recognition on Equipment Sold and Subsequently Repurchased Subject to an Operating Lease			EITF.95-4
Sale of an Asset Subject to a Lease and			
Nonrecourse Debt	FTB88-1, ¶16-17	L10.542-545	EITF.87-7
	FTB88-1, ¶21-22		
Sale of Lease Receivable			
. . Direct Financing or Sales-Type Leases.	FAS13, ¶20	L10.116	
	FAS77, ¶3	R20.102	
	FAS77, ¶10		
. . Interest in Residual Value Retained by			
Lessor	FTB86-2, ¶9-10	L10.536-537	
. . Money-Over-Money Lease			
Transactions	FTB88-1, ¶16-17	L10.542-543	
. . Wrap Lease Transactions	FTB88-1, ¶21-22	L10.544-545	
Sale of Leased Property			
. . Collateral	FAS13, ¶22	L10.118	
. . Money-Over-Money Lease			
Transactions	FTB88-1, ¶16-17	L10.542-543	
. . Recognition	FAS13, ¶20-22	L10.116-118	
. . Sale and Leaseback of an Asset That Is or Will Be Leased to Another Party			EITF.93-8
. . Sale of Property Subject to Seller's			
Preexisting Lease			EITF.88-21
. . Wrap Lease Transactions	FTB88-1, ¶21-22	L10.544-545	EITF.87-7
Sale or Purchase of Tax Benefits through Tax Leases			
. . Income Recognition for Cross Border			
Tax Benefit Leases			EITF.89-20

FAS–FASB Statements	FIN–FASB Interpretations	FTB–FASB Technical Bulletins
APB–APB Opinions	AIN–AICPA Interpretations	ARB–Accounting Research Bulletins
CON–FASB Concepts	EITF–EITF Issues	Q&A–FASB Special Reports

	Original Pronouncements	Current Text	EITF and Other
LEASES—continued			
Sale-Leaseback Transactions Involving Real Estate			
. . Consideration of Executory Costs in Calculation of Deferred Profit in a Sale-Leaseback Transaction			EITF.89-16
. . Continuing Involvement	FAS98, ¶10-13	L10.130F-130I	EITF.90-14
			EITF.90-20
			EITF.D-24
. . Criteria for Sale-Leaseback Accounting	FAS98, ¶7-8	L10.130C-130D	
. . Deposit Method with Subsequent Sales Recognition and a Capital Leaseback	FAS98, ¶30-33	L10.160D-160G	
. . Financing Method with Subsequent Sales Recognition	FAS98, ¶38-39	L10.160L-160M	
. . Financing Method with Subsequent Sales Recognition and an Operating Leaseback	FAS98, ¶34-37	L10.160H-160K	
. . Guarantees	FAS66, ¶25-39	L10.130F-130I	
	FAS66, ¶41-43	R10.128-142	
	FAS98, ¶10-13	R10.144-146	
. . Impact of an Uncollateralized Irrevocable Letter of Credit on a Sale-Leaseback Transaction			EITF.90-20
. . Involving Regulated Enterprises	FAS98, ¶14-16	L10.130J	
		Re6.125H-125J	
. . Lessee Participation in Lessor's Interest Savings			EITF.D-24
. . Loans to Buyers by Sellers	FAS98, ¶12	L10.130H	
. . Minor Leaseback	FAS98, ¶8	L10.130D	
. . Normal Leaseback	FAS98, ¶8	L10.130D	
. . Partial Sale-Leaseback			EITF.D-24
. . Recognition of Gain or Loss	FAS98, ¶7-8	L10.130B-130D	
	FAS98, ¶70		
. . Rental Shortfall Agreements and Related Receipts			EITF.84-37
			EITF.85-27
. . Repurchase Options	FAS98, ¶11	L10.130G	EITF.84-37
. . Sale of Property Subject to Seller's Preexisting Lease			EITF.88-21
. . Sale with Gain Recognized under the Installment Method and an Operating Leaseback	FAS98, ¶27-29	L10.160A-160C	
. . Sale-Leaseback Accounting	FAS98, ¶70	L10.130B	
. . Sales Recognition	FAS98, ¶27	L10.160A	
	FAS98, ¶70	L10.420B	
. . Scope	FAS98, ¶6	L10.130A	
. . Short Initial Lease Term with Renewal Options			EITF.84-37

See "Terminology" for references to defined terms presented in various accounting pronouncements.
See the Introduction to the Topical Index for details on the use of this index.

	Original Pronouncements	Current Text	EITF and Other
LEASES—continued			
Sale-Leaseback Transactions Involving Real Estate—continued			
. . Subleases	FAS98, ¶8	L10.130D	
. . Terms of Sale-Leaseback Transaction	FAS98, ¶9	L10.130E	
. . Unsecured Guarantee by Parent of Subsidiary's Lease Payments			EITF.90-14
Sale-Leaseback Transactions Not Involving Real Estate			
. . Accounting by Buyer-Lessor	FAS13, ¶34	L10.128	
	FAS28, ¶2	L10.130	
. . Accounting by Seller-Lessee	FAS28, ¶2-3	L10.128-129	
. . Consideration of Executory Costs in Calculation of Deferred Profit in a Sale-Leaseback Transaction			EITF.89-16
. . Income Recognition for Cross Border Tax Benefit Leases			EITF.89-20
. . Involving Capital Leaseback	FAS28, ¶2-3	L10.128-129	
. . Involving Operating Leaseback	FAS13, ¶34	L10.128-130	
	FAS28, ¶2-3		
. . Involving Regulated Enterprises	FAS92, ¶30-35	Re6.188-193	
. . Leaseback Is a Capital Lease	FAS28, ¶27	L10.160	
. . Leaseback Is More Than Minor but Not a Capital Lease	FAS28, ¶25-26	L10.158-159	
. . Minor Leaseback	FAS28, ¶23-24	L10.156-157	
. . Recognition of Gains or Losses	FAS28, ¶3	L10.129	
. . Remarketing Rights in Wrap Lease Transactions			EITF.87-7
. . Rental Shortfall Agreements and Related Receipts			EITF.84-37
. . Residual Value Guarantee			EITF.86-17
. . Sale and Leaseback of an Asset That Is or Will Be Leased to Another Party			EITF.93-8
. . Sale of Property Subject to Seller's Preexisting Lease			EITF.88-21
. . Short Initial Lease Term with Renewal Options			EITF.84-37
. . Wrap Lease Transactions	FTB88-1, ¶21-22	L10.544-545	
Sales-Type Leases			
. . Accounting	FAS13, ¶17	L10.113	
	FAS22, ¶12		
	FAS22, ¶15		
	FAS23, ¶9		
	FAS27, ¶8		
	FAS29, ¶13		
	FAS98, ¶22		
. . Allowance for Doubtful Accounts	FAS98, ¶22	L10.104	
. . Calculation of Gross Investment	FAS13, ¶17	L10.113	
. . Calculation of Net Investment	FAS13, ¶17	L10.113	
	FAS29, ¶13		

FAS–FASB Statements	FIN–FASB Interpretations	FTB–FASB Technical Bulletins
APB–APB Opinions	AIN–AICPA Interpretations	ARB–Accounting Research Bulletins
CON–FASB Concepts	EITF–EITF Issues	Q&A–FASB Special Reports

	Original Pronouncements	Current Text	EITF and Other

LEASES—continued
Sales-Type Leases—continued

.. Change in Lease Provisions .... FAS13, ¶9   L10.105
.... FAS22, ¶15
.... FAS23, ¶9
.... FAS27, ¶6-8
.. Collectibility .... FAS98, ¶22   L10.104
.. Contingent Rentals .... FAS29, ¶13   L10.113
.. Criteria for Classification .... FAS13, ¶8   L10.102
.... FAS27, ¶7   L10.104
.... FAS98, ¶22
.. Definition .... FAS98, ¶22   L10.102
.. Executory Costs................................. FAS13, ¶17   L10.113
.. Gains or Losses.................................. FAS13, ¶17   L10.113
.... FAS22, ¶15
.... FAS27, ¶8
.. Income Determination........................... FAS13, ¶17   L10.113
.... FAS22, ¶12
.... FAS22, ¶15
.... FAS23, ¶9
.... FAS29, ¶13
.. Initial Direct Costs............................. FAS13, ¶17   L10.113
.. Involving Real Estate .... FAS13, ¶25-26   L10.121-122
.... FAS98, ¶22
.. Lessor Accounting for Initial Direct
   Costs .... FAS13, ¶17   L10.113
.. Offsetting Nonrecourse Debt with
   Lease Receivables.............................   EITF.84-25
.. Penalty for Failure to Renew Lease ...... FAS13, ¶17   L10.113
.. Purchase of Leased Property................. FAS13, ¶20   L10.116
.. Residual Guarantee Contained in
   Lease .... FAS13, ¶17   L10.113
.. Sale of Leased Property......................... FAS13, ¶20   L10.116
.. Sale of Lease Receivable..................... FAS13, ¶20   L10.116
.... FAS77, ¶3   R20.102
.... FAS77, ¶10
.. Termination....................................... FAS13, ¶17   L10.113
.. Unearned Income .... FAS13, ¶17   L10.113
Scheduled Rent Increases Related to
Physical Use...................................... FTB88-1, ¶1-2   L10.527A-527B
Scope of Accounting and Reporting
Requirements .... FAS13, ¶1   L10.101
Special-Purpose Entities
.. Accounting for Lease Transactions.......   EITF.90-15
Subleases and Similar
Transactions
.. Accounting by New Lessee................... FAS13, ¶40   L10.136
.. Accounting by Original Lessee............. FAS13, ¶38-39   L10.134-135
.... FIN27, ¶2-3
.. Accounting by Original Lessor............. FAS13, ¶36-37   L10.132-133

See "Terminology" for references to defined terms presented in various accounting pronouncements.
See the Introduction to the Topical Index for details on the use of this index.

	Original Pronouncements	Current Text	EITF and Other
LEASES—continued			
Subleases and Similar Transactions—continued			
. . Accounting for Losses on Subleases.....	FTB79-15, ¶1-3	L10.518-520	
. . Lease Incentives	FTB88-1, ¶6-9	L10.527C-527F	
. . Recognition of Gain or Loss	FAS13, ¶38-39	L10.134-135	EITF.88-10
....	FIN27, ¶2-3	L10.518-520	
....	FTB79-15, ¶1-3		
. . Sale and Leaseback of an Asset That Is or Will Be Leased to Another Party ...			EITF.93-8
. . Types of Subleases and Similar Transactions	FAS13, ¶35	L10.131	
. . Wrap Lease Transactions........................	FTB88-1, ¶21-22	L10.544-545	
Tax			
. . Sale or Purchase of Tax Benefits...........	FAS109, ¶288	I27.501-506	
....	FTB82-1, ¶1-2		
....	FTB82-1, ¶4		
....	FTB82-1, ¶6-8		
Tax Indemnification Related to a Change in Tax Law..			EITF.86-33
Tax Leases Used to Transfer Tax Benefits			
. . Effect of Change in Tax Law................			EITF.86-44
. . Income Recognition for Cross Border Tax Benefit Leases.............................			EITF.89-20
Termination			
. . Payment to Terminate an Operating Lease	FTB88-1, ¶6-9	L10.527C-527F	EITF.88-10
. . Termination of a Capital Lease	FAS13, ¶14	L10.109	
. . Termination of a Direct Financing Lease	FAS13, ¶18	L10.114	
. . Termination of a Sales-Type Lease.......	FAS13, ¶17	L10.113	
Transactions Involving Special-Purpose Entities...			EITF.90-15
....			EITF.D-14
Uncertainties			
. . Collectibility of Lease Receivables.......	FAS98, ¶22	L10.104	
. . Contingent Rentals	FAS29, ¶11	L10.404	
. . Effect on Lease Classification	FAS13, ¶8	L10.104	
. . Executory Costs...................................	FAS13, ¶8	L10.104	
. . Fair Value Determination	FAS13, ¶5	L10.409	
. . Unreimbursable Costs	FAS13, ¶8	L10.104	
Unearned Income			
. . Direct Financing Lease.........................	FAS98, ¶22	L10.114	
. . Leveraged Leases	FAS13, ¶43	L10.145	
. . Sales-Type Leases	FAS13, ¶17	L10.113	
Unguaranteed Residual Value			
. . Direct Financing Leases........................	FAS98, ¶22	L10.114	
. . Leveraged Leases	FAS13, ¶43	L10.145	
. . Sales-Type Leases	FAS13, ¶17	L10.113	

	Original Pronouncements	Current Text	EITF and Other
LEASES—continued			
Unsecured Guarantee by Parent of Subsidiary's Lease Payments			EITF.90-14
Wrap Lease Transactions...........................	FTB88-1, ¶21-22	L10.544-545	EITF.87-7
....			EITF.93-8
LENDING ACTIVITIES			
See Financial Instruments			
See Impairment: Loans			
Accounting for Individual Credit Card Acquisitions..			EITF.93-1
Acquisition, Development, and Construction Loans....................................			EITF.84-4
....			EITF.86-21
Aggregating Loans or Accounting for Individual Loans	FAS91, ¶4	L20.103	Q&A.91 #8
....	FAS91, ¶19	L20.118	
Amortization of Net Loan Fees or Costs			
. . Estimating Prepayments.......................	FAS91, ¶19	L20.118	Q&A.91 #48-52
....			Q&A.91 #54
. . Interest Method....................................	FAS91, ¶18-19	L20.117-118	Q&A.91 #40-42
....			Q&A.91 #44-47
....			Q&A.91 #53
....			Q&A.91 #65
. . Method for Certain Loan Types			Q&A.91 #43
. . Straight-Line Method	FAS91, ¶20	L20.119	Q&A.91 #55-58
Amortization Period for Net Deferred Credit Card Origination Costs			EITF.92-5
Application of Interest Method and Other Amortization	FAS91, ¶17-20	L20.116-119	
....	FAS91, ¶54		
Classification in Financial Statements	FAS91, ¶21-22	L20.120-121	Q&A.91 #59
....			Q&A.91 #63
Co-branding Arrangements			EITF.93-1
Commitment Fees and Costs.......................	FAS91, ¶8-10	L20.107-109	EITF.85-20
....			EITF.93-1
....			Q&A.91 #25-29
Credit Card Fees	FAS91, ¶10	L20.109	Q&A.91 #31-33
Credit Card Portfolio Securitization...........			EITF.88-22
....			EITF.90-18
Credit Card Portfolio—Purchase			
. . Accounting for Difference between Initial Investment and Principal Amount of Loans..............................			EITF.88-20
. . Accounting for Individual Credit Card Acquisitions			EITF.93-1
. . Amortization of Cardholder Relationships Acquired......................			EITF.88-20
Definition			Q&A.91 #61
Equity Kickers			EITF.84-4
....			EITF.86-21

See "Terminology" for references to defined terms presented in various accounting pronouncements.
See the Introduction to the Topical Index for details on the use of this index.

	Original Pronouncements	Current Text	EITF and Other
LENDING ACTIVITIES—continued			
Examples	FAS91, ¶64-79	L20.123-138	Q&A.91 #54
Fees and Costs in Refinancing or Restructuring	FAS91, ¶12-14	L20.111-113	Q&A.91 #36-38
Glossary	FAS91, ¶80	L20.401-404	
Leasing Activities			
. . Initial Direct Costs	FAS91, ¶23	L20.122	
Loan Acquisitions Involving Table Funding Arrangements			EITF.92-10
Loan Guarantees			
. . Revenue Recognition of Fees			EITF.85-20
Loan Origination Fees and Costs	FAS91, ¶5-7	L20.104-106	Q&A.91 #30
	FAS91, ¶36		Q&A.91 #60
. . Direct Costs	FAS91, ¶6	L20.105	Q&A.91 #12
			Q&A.91 #16-20
			Q&A.91 #24
. . Inclusions in Loans Sold to Affiliated Enterprises			Q&A.91 #60
. . Method of Determining Direct Costs			Q&A.91 #21-23
. . Other Lending Related Costs	FAS91, ¶7	L20.106	Q&A.91 #13-15
. . Third-Party Costs	FAS91, ¶6	L20.105	Q&A.91 #9-11
			Q&A.91 #13
Purchase of Loan or Group of Loans	FAS91, ¶15-16	L20.114-115	Q&A.91 #35
Restatement of Financial Statements			Q&A.91 #62
			Q&A.91 #64
Revenue Recognition			
. . Credit Card Portfolio Securitizations with a "Removal of Accounts" Provision			EITF.90-18
. . Fees Associated with Loan Syndications and Loan Participations			EITF.88-17
. . Sale of Convertible, Adjustable-Rate Mortgages with Contingent Repayment Agreement			EITF.87-25
. . Sale of Short-Term Loan under Long-Term Credit Commitment			EITF.87-30
. . Securitization of Credit Card Portfolio			EITF.88-22
Revolving Credit Agreement	FAS91, ¶20	L20.119	
Scope	FAS91, ¶2-4	L20.101-103	Q&A.91 #1-8
	FAS115, ¶130		
Shared Appreciation Mortgages			EITF.86-21
Syndication Fees	FAS91, ¶11	L20.110	Q&A.91 #34-35
. . Fees Associated with Loan Syndications and Loan Participations			EITF.88-17
LESSEE			
See Leases			
LESSOR			
See Leases			

	Original Pronouncements	Current Text	EITF and Other

LETTERS OF CREDIT
See Contingencies
See Financial Instruments

LEVERAGED BUYOUT

Allocating Basis to Individual Assets and
  Liabilities under Issue No. 88-16 .... | | | EITF.90-12
Carryover of Predecessor Cost................... | | | EITF.86-16
.... | | | EITF.88-16
Financed by Loan to ESOP .... | | | EITF.85-11
Leveraged Buyout Holding Company
  Debt... | | | EITF.84-23
Purchase of Stock Options and SARs by
  Target Company....................................... | | | EITF.84-13
Valuation of Shareholder's Interest............ | | | EITF.86-16
.... | | | EITF.88-16

LEVERAGED LEASES
See Leases

LIABILITIES
See Balance Sheet Classification: Current
  Assets and Liabilities
See Contingencies
See Long-Term Obligations

Characteristics... CON6, ¶36-40
.... CON6, ¶192-211
Criteria for Recognition............................ CON5, ¶58-65
.... CON5, ¶67-69
.... CON5, ¶73-77
Definition .... CON6, ¶35
Elements of Financial Statements .... CON6, ¶35-43
Future Sacrifice of Assets........................... CON6, ¶193-198
Interrelation with Equity............................. CON6, ¶54-59
Items Not Qualified as................................. CON6, ¶169
Measurement of... CON5, ¶67-69
Obligations of a Particular Enterprise .... CON6, ¶199-205
Past Transactions .... CON6, ¶206-211
Proceeds.. CON6, ¶198
Qualification as.. CON6, ¶168
Recognition of Changes in .... CON5, ¶88-90
Relation to Equity (Net Assets) Changes.... CON6, ¶107-108
Transactions and Events Affecting.............. CON6, ¶41-42
Uncertainty of Recognition .... CON6, ¶44-48
Valuation Allowances .... CON6, ¶34   V18.401
.... CON6, ¶43

LICENSES
See Broadcasting Industry
See Motion Picture Industry
See Record and Music Industry
Qualification as Assets................................ CON6, ¶189

LIFE INSURANCE
See Insurance Industry

See "Terminology" for references to defined terms presented in various accounting pronouncements.
See the Introduction to the Topical Index for details on the use of this index.

	Original Pronouncements	Current Text	EITF and Other
LIFE INSURANCE—continued			
See Postretirement Health Care and Life Insurance Benefits			
Cash Surrender Value (CSV)			
. . Balance Sheet Presentation	ARB43, Ch.3A, ¶6	B05.107	
. . Provision for Deferred Taxes on Increases in CSV			EITF.87-28
Company-Owned Life Insurance (COLI) Policies			
. . Recognition of Death Benefits			EITF.88-5
Purchase of Life Insurance	FTB85-4, ¶1-2	I50.504-509	
LIFE INSURANCE ENTERPRISES			
See Income Taxes			
See Insurance Industry			
Definition	FAS60, ¶66	In6.418	
Relation to Contingencies	FAS5, ¶102	C59.102	
LIFO (LAST-IN, FIRST-OUT)			
See Accounting Changes			
See Adjustments of Financial Statements for Prior Periods			
See Interim Financial Reporting			
See Inventory			
Accounting Change Due to Repeal of *Insilco* Decision			EITF.84-10
Change from LIFO Pricing Method	APB20, ¶27	A35.114	
	APB20, ¶29		
	FAS73, ¶2		
Effect of AICPA Issues Paper			EITF.84-24
Inventory Valuation Method			
See Inventory			
Involuntary Conversion	FIN30, ¶2	N35.115	
	FIN30, ¶11		
LIMITED PARTNERSHIPS			
See Partnerships			
LINE OF BUSINESS			
See Segment of Business Reporting			
LINES OF CREDIT			
See Financial Instruments			
See Lending Activities			
See Real Estate			
LIQUIDATION			
See Debt: Restructurings			
See Income Statement Presentation: Discontinued Operations			
Liquidation of a Banking Institution			
. . Valuation of Assets and Liabilities by Liquidating Bank			EITF.88-25
LIQUIDITY			
Definition	CON5, ¶24		
Information about	CON1, ¶49		

FAS–FASB Statements	FIN–FASB Interpretations	FTB–FASB Technical Bulletins
APB–APB Opinions	AIN–AICPA Interpretations	ARB–Accounting Research Bulletins
CON–FASB Concepts	EITF–EITF Issues	Q&A–FASB Special Reports

	Original Pronouncements	Current Text	EITF and Other
LIQUIDITY—continued			
Not-for-Profit Organizations	CON4, ¶54		
Use of Statement of Cash Flow in Assessing	CON5, ¶29		
Use of Statement of Financial Position in Assessing	CON5, ¶29		
LITIGATION			
See Adjustments of Financial Statements for Prior Periods			
See Contingencies			
LOAN AGREEMENTS			
See Balance Sheet Classification: Current Assets and Liabilities			
See Impairment: Loans			
See Lending Activities			
See Loans			
See Offsetting			
LOAN COLLATERAL			
See Financial Instruments			
See Impairment: Loans			
Loss Contingency			
. . Disclosure	FAS5, ¶18	C59.120	
LOAN COVENANT			
See Covenants			
See Financial Instruments			
Restrictions			
. . Disclosure	FIN14, ¶6	C59.126	
LOAN GUARANTEES			
See Financial Instruments			
Business Combinations	APB16, ¶48	B50.107	
Recognition of Liability			EITF.85-20
Revenue Recognition			
. . Fees			EITF.85-20
LOAN LOSS ALLOWANCES			
See Impairment: Loans			
See Valuation Allowances			
LOAN MODIFICATIONS			
Payment Modifications Involving Forgiveness of Principal			EITF.84-19
LOAN ORIGINATION AND COMMITMENT FEES			
See Lending Activities			
See Mortgage Banking Activities			
Accounting for Individual Credit Card Acquisitions			EITF.93-1
Amortization Period for Net Deferred Credit Card Origination Costs			EITF.92-5
Revenue Recognition			EITF.85-20
LOAN PARTICIPATIONS			
See Lending Activities			

See "Terminology" for references to defined terms presented in various accounting pronouncements.
See the Introduction to the Topical Index for details on the use of this index.

	Original Pronouncements	Current Text	EITF and Other

LOANS
See Financial Instruments
See Impairment: Loans
Accounting for Conversion of a Loan into
  a Debt Security in a Debt Restructuring... | | | EITF.94-8
Accounting for Debt Securities Reported
  as Loans................................... | | | EITF.D-39
Acquisition, Development, and
  Construction Loans............................. | | | EITF.84-4
  .... | | | EITF.86-21
Argentine Government Guarantee
. . U.S. Dollar Loans to Argentine
    Private Sector................................ | | | EITF.D-4
Classification of In-Substance Foreclosed
  (ISF) Assets by SEC Registrants............. | | | EITF.D-37
Collateralized Mortgage Obligations
  (CMOs)
. . Consolidation of Issuer with Sponsor... | | | EITF.85-28
Debtor's Accounting for Forfeiture of Real
  Estate Subject to a Nonrecourse
  Mortgage... | | | EITF.91-2
Debt Restructuring
. . Conversion of a Loan into a Debt
    Security..................................... | | | EITF.94-8
Determining a Normal Servicing Fee Rate
  for the Sale of an SBA Loan.................... | | | EITF.94-9
International Loan Swaps
. . Requirements for Loss Recognition...... | | | EITF.D-3
Loan Acquisitions Involving Table
  Funding Arrangements............................. | | | EITF.92-10
Mortgage Loan Payment Modifications ..... | | | EITF.84-19
Negative Amortization of Principal
. . Applying Profit Recognition Criteria
    for Sale of Real Estate .... | | | EITF.84-17
. . Interest Income Recognition .... | | | EITF.85-38
. . Sale of Negative Amortizing Loans...... | | | EITF.85-38
Originating Loans with Intent to Sell.......... | | | EITF.D-2
Participating Mortgage............................... | | | EITF.86-28
Payment Modifications Involving
  Forgiveness of Principal .... | | | EITF.84-19
Sale of Bad-Debt Recovery Rights............. | | | EITF.86-8
Sale of Interest-Only Cash Flows from
  Loans Receivable
. . Determination of Gain or Loss.............. | | | EITF.88-11
. . Determination of Remaining Recorded
    Investment for Portion of Loan
    Retained .... | | | EITF.88-11
Sale of Mortgage Loan by CMO
  Established through Third Party............... | | | EITF.86-24

FAS–FASB Statements   FIN–FASB Interpretations   FTB–FASB Technical Bulletins
APB–APB Opinions   AIN–AICPA Interpretations   ARB–Accounting Research Bulletins
CON–FASB Concepts   EITF–EITF Issues   Q&A–FASB Special Reports

T-269

	Original Pronouncements	Current Text	EITF and Other
LOANS—continued			
Sale of Mortgage Loan with Servicing Rights Retained..			EITF.86-39
Sale of Mortgage Servicing Rights.............			EITF.85-13
Sale of Principal-Only Cash Flows from Loans Receivable			
. . Determination of Gain or Loss..............			EITF.88-11
. . Determination of Remaining Recorded Investment for Portion of Loan Retained			EITF.88-11
Sale of Short-Term Loan under Long-Term Credit Commitment..............			EITF.87-30
Sale to Special-Purpose Entities..................			EITF.84-30
Sale with a Partial Participation Retained...			EITF.84-21
....			EITF.86-38
Small Business Administration Loans			
. . Determining a Normal Servicing Fee Rate for the Sale of an SBA Loan			EITF.94-9
U.S. Dollar Loans to Argentine Private Sector...			EITF.D-4
LOANS RECEIVABLE/PAYABLE			
See Balance Sheet Classification: Current Assets and Liabilities			
See Impairment: Loans			
See Lending Activities			
See Loans			
See Receivables			
LOAN SWAPS			
See Financial Instruments			
See Loans			
LOCAL CURRENCY			
See Foreign Currency Translation			
Definition	FAS52, ¶162	F60.416	
LONG-TERM CONTRACTS			
See Accounting Changes			
See Adjustments of Financial Statements for Prior Periods			
See Commitments: Long-Term Obligations			
See Contractor Accounting: Construction-Type Contracts			
See Contractor Accounting: Government Contracts			
See Debt: Product Financing Arrangements			
See Oil and Gas Producing Activities			
LONG-TERM DEBT			
See Balance Sheet Classification: Current Assets and Liabilities			
See Collateralized Mortgage Obligations			

See "Terminology" for references to defined terms presented in various accounting pronouncements.

See the Introduction to the Topical Index for details on the use of this index.

	Original Pronouncements	Current Text	EITF and Other

LONG-TERM DEBT—continued
See Commitments: Long-Term
  Obligations
See Debt
See Debt Issue Cost
See Debt: Convertible Debt and Debt with
  Stock Purchase Warrants
See Debt: Extinguishments
See Debt: Product Financing
  Arrangements
See Debt: Restructurings
See Disclosure
See Financial Instruments
LONG-TERM INVESTMENTS
See Financial Instruments
See Investments: Debt and Equity
  Securities
See Investments: Equity Method
Balance Sheet Classification .... ARB43, Ch.3A, ¶6   B05.107
LONG-TERM OBLIGATIONS
See Balance Sheet Classification: Current
  Assets and Liabilities
See Balance Sheet Classification: Debt vs.
  Equity
See Commitments: Long-Term
  Obligations
See Debt: Convertible Debt and Debt with
  Stock Purchase Warrants
See Debt: Extinguishments
See Debt: Product Financing
  Arrangements
See Debt: Restructurings
See Financial Instruments
See Long-Term Contracts
Conversion to Capital Stock .... APB12, ¶10   C08.102
Definition
. . Long-Term Obligations .... FAS6, ¶2   B05.403
LOSS CARRYBACKS AND CARRYFORWARDS
See Income Taxes
Benefit of Carryforward Realized
. . Recognition of Purchased NOL or
    Own NOL EITF.86-1
. . Reinstatement of Previously
    Eliminated Deferred Taxes EITF.85-5
Business Combinations
. . Purchased Loss Carryforwards EITF.84-33
    ......   EITF.85-15
    ......   EITF.86-1

FAS–FASB Statements   FIN–FASB Interpretations   FTB–FASB Technical Bulletins
APB–APB Opinions   AIN–AICPA Interpretations   ARB–Accounting Research Bulletins
CON–FASB Concepts   EITF–EITF Issues   Q&A–FASB Special Reports

L   **Topical Index**

	Original Pronouncements	Current Text	EITF and Other
LOSS CONTINGENCIES			
See Contingencies			
LOSS RESERVES			
See Contingencies			
See Insurance Industry			
LOSSES			
See Gain or Loss			
See Income Taxes			
Characteristics	CON6, ¶84-89		
Component of Comprehensive Income	CON6, ¶73-77		
	CON6, ¶215-220		
Definition	CON6, ¶83		
Element of Financial Statements	CON6, ¶83-89		
Holding	CON6, ¶71		
Not-for-Profit Organizations	CON6, ¶111-113		
Operating vs. Nonoperating	CON6, ¶86		
Purchase Commitments			
. . Qualification to Be Included as	CON6, ¶251-253		
Recognition Criteria			
. . Guidance in Application	CON5, ¶85		
. . Guidance in Application, Loss or Lack of Future Benefit	CON5, ¶87		
Relation to Expenses	CON6, ¶87-89		
LOSSES (CATASTROPHE)			
See Insurance Industry			
LOWER OF COST OR MARKET (RULE)			
See Foreign Currency Translation			
See Inventory			
Definition	ARB43, Ch.4, ¶9	I78.403	
Impairment: Loans			
. . Exemption from Requirements	FAS114, ¶6	I08.104	
Inventory			
. . Price Declines during Interim Reporting Periods			EITF.86-13
Investments			
. . Divestiture of Certain Securities to an Unregulated Commonly Controlled Entity under FIRREA			EITF.89-18
Noncurrent Marketable Equity Securities			
. . Other Than Temporary Decline in Market Value			EITF.85-39

(The next page is T-279.)

See "Terminology" for references to defined terms presented in various accounting pronouncements.
See the Introduction to the Topical Index for details on the use of this index.

T-272

	Original Pronouncements	Current Text	EITF and Other

MACHINERY AND EQUIPMENT
See Impairment: Long-Lived Assets
See Property, Plant, and Equipment

MAJOR CUSTOMERS
See Segment of Business Reporting
Concentrations of Credit Risk .... FAS105, ¶20   F25.115

MAJORITY-OWNED SUBSIDIARIES
See Consolidation
See Related Parties
See Subsidiaries

MANAGEMENT
Definition .... FAS57, ¶24   R36.404
Discussion
. . Foreign Currency Translation .... FAS52, ¶144   F60.143
Need for Operational Information.............. CON1, ¶27
Relation to Enterprise Performance .... CON1, ¶50-53
Reporting .... CON1, ¶54
. . Not-for-Profit Organizations .... CON4, ¶55
Representations in Business
   Combinations .... APB16, ¶47   B50.106
Stewardship.. CON1, ¶50-53
. . Not-for-Profit Organizations .... CON4, ¶40-42

MANAGEMENT CONSIGNMENT PROGRAM
Basis of Accounting under FSLIC
Program..   EITF.85-41

MANUFACTURER OR DEALER LESSORS
See Leases

MARKET RISK
See Financial Instruments

MARKET VALUE
See Current Market Value
See Fair Value

MARKETABLE SECURITIES
See Financial Instruments
See Investments: Debt and Equity Securities
Balance Sheet Classification .... ARB43, Ch.3A, ¶4   B05.105

MASTER LIMITED PARTNERSHIPS
Carryover of Predecessor Cost....................   EITF.87-21
Roll-up of Limited Partnerships into an MLP
. . Gain Recognition on MLP Units
    Received in Exchange for Future
    Fees EITF.88-14

MATCHING OF COSTS AND REVENUES
Consumption of Benefits............................. CON5, ¶86

	Original Pronouncements	Current Text	EITF and Other
MATCHING OF COSTS AND REVENUES—continued			
Guidance in Applying Recognition Criteria to Expenses	CON5, ¶85		
Relation to Accrual Basis of Accounting	CON6, ¶145-151		
MATERIALITY			
Accounting Changes	APB20, ¶38	A06.133	
Definition	CON2, Glossary		
Description	CON2, ¶123-132		
Extraordinary Items	APB30, ¶24	I17.118	
Quantitative Considerations	CON2, ¶161-170		
SEC Regulations	CON2, ¶161-162		
Threshold for Recognition	CON5, ¶63		
MEASUREMENT			
See Recognition and Measurement in Financial Statements			
Attributes	CON5, ¶65-70		
. . Current Market Value	CON5, ¶67		
. . Current Replacement Cost	CON5, ¶67		
. . Historical Cost/Historical Proceeds	CON5, ¶67		
. . Net Realizable (Settlement) Value	CON5, ¶67		
. . Present (or Discounted) Value of Future Cash Flows	CON5, ¶67		
Cost-Benefit Constraints	CON5, ¶63		
Criteria			
. . Asset and Liability Changes, Use of Current Prices	CON5, ¶90		
Current (Replacement) Cost	CON5, ¶69		
Current Market Value	CON5, ¶67		
	CON5, ¶69		
Description	CON1, ¶2		
	CON5, ¶65-72		
Elements Definitions	CON5, ¶64		
Materiality Threshold	CON5, ¶63		
Measurability Criterion	CON5, ¶65		
Monetary Unit and Measurement Scale	CON5, ¶71-72		
Relation to Elements of Financial Statements	CON6, ¶22-23		
Relation to Recognition, Measurement, and Display	CON6, ¶23		
MEASUREMENT DATE			
See Compensation to Employees: Stock Purchase and Stock Option Plans			
See Income Statement Presentation: Discontinued Operations			
See Pension Costs			
See Postretirement Benefits Other Than Pensions			
MEAT PACKING OPERATIONS			
Revenue Recognition	ARB43, Ch.1A, ¶1	R75.101	

See "Terminology" for references to defined terms presented in various accounting pronouncements.

See the Introduction to the Topical Index for details on the use of this index.

	Original Pronouncements	Current Text	EITF and Other
MEDICAL INSURANCE			
See Insurance Industry			
See Postretirement Health Care and Life Insurance Benefits			
MEDICARE			
Retroactive Wage Adjustments Affecting Medicare Payments			EITF.86-2
MERGERS			
See Business Combinations			
Accounting for Simultaneous Common Control Mergers			EITF.90-13
Downstream Mergers			EITF.85-4
METHODS OF ACCOUNTING			
See Accounting Changes			
See Business Combinations			
See Contractor Accounting: Construction-Type Contracts			
See Contractor Accounting: Government Contracts			
See Depreciation			
See Earnings per Share			
See Foreign Currency Translation			
See Franchising			
See Income Taxes			
See Interest: Imputation of an Interest Cost			
See Inventory			
See Investments: Equity Method			
See Leases			
See Oil and Gas Producing Activities			
See Pension Costs			
See Postretirement Benefits Other Than Pensions			
See Real Estate			
See Revenue Recognition			
See Specialized Accounting and Reporting			
MINERAL RESERVES			
See Extractive Industries			
Enterprises That Own Mineral Reserves Other Than Oil and Gas			
. . Changing Prices Information	FAS89, ¶14-15	C28.110-111	
	FAS89, ¶23	C28.119	
MINING INDUSTRY			
See Changing Prices: Reporting Their Effects in Financial Reports			
Advances to Encourage Exploration, Imputed Interest	ARB43, Ch.10B, ¶1	I69.501-502	
MINORITY INTERESTS			
See Business Combinations			
See Oil and Gas Producing Activities			

	Original Pronouncements	Current Text	EITF and Other
MINORITY INTERESTS—continued			
Acquisition	AIN-APB16, #26	B50.102	EITF.85-4
	APB16, ¶42	B50.593-596F	
	FTB85-5, ¶5-7	B50.645-648	
	FTB85-5, ¶12		
Adjustments Related to the Implementation of Statement 115			EITF.D-41
Consolidation			
. . Intercompany Profit Elimination	ARB51, ¶14	C51.115	
. . Losses	ARB51, ¶15	C51.116	
Exchanges of Ownership Interests between Entities under Common Control			EITF.90-5
Qualification as a Liability	CON6, ¶254		
Treatment of Minority Interests in Certain Real Estate Investment Trusts			EITF.94-2
MODIFICATION OF DEBT TERMS			
See Debt: Extinguishments			
See Debt: Restructurings			
See Impairment: Loans			
MONETARY ASSETS AND LIABILITIES			
See Nonmonetary Transactions			
Definition	APB29, ¶3	C28.408-409	
	FAS89, ¶44	N35.402	
MONEY			
Medium of Exchange	CON6, ¶29		
MORTGAGE-BACKED SECURITIES			
Classification for Accounting Purposes	FAS115, ¶12	I80.109	
Classification of Interest-Only Securities as Held-to-Maturity			EITF.94-4
Exchange of Interest-Only and Principal-Only Securities for a Mortgage-Backed Security			EITF.90-2
Interest-Only Certificates			
. . Effect of Unanticipated Mortgage Prepayments			EITF.86-38
Mortgage-Backed Interest-Only Certificates			EITF.89-4
. . Impairment Recognition			EITF.93-18
Purchased Investment in Collateralized Mortgage Obligations			EITF.89-4
. . Impairment Recognition			EITF.93-18
MORTGAGE BANKING ACTIVITIES			
See Disclosure			
See Financial Instruments			
See Lending Activities			
Accounting for Debt Securities Reported as Loans			EITF.D-39

See "Terminology" for references to defined terms presented in various accounting pronouncements.
See the Introduction to the Topical Index for details on the use of this index.

	Original Pronouncements	Current Text	EITF and Other
MORTGAGE BANKING ACTIVITIES—continued			
Applicability of Statement 65 to Savings and Loan Associations			EITF.D-2
Balance Sheet Classification			
. . Mortgage Loans	FAS65, ¶28	Mo4.129	
. . Mortgage-Backed Securities	FAS65, ¶28	Mo4.129	
Brady Bonds			EITF.D-39
Classification of Interest-Only Securities as Held-to-Maturity			EITF.94-4
CMOs Established through Third Party			
. . Gain or Loss Recognition by Seller of Mortgages			EITF.86-24
Description	FAS65, ¶1	Mo4.102	
Disclosure	FAS65, ¶29-30	Mo4.130-134	
	FAS122, ¶3		
Exchange of Interest-Only and Principal-Only Securities for a Mortgage-Backed Security			EITF.90-2
Futures Contracts, Hedges	FAS80, ¶63	F80.104	
GNMA Securities			
. . Cost of Issuing	FAS65, ¶15	Mo4.116	
	FAS122, ¶3		
Gain from Sale of Mortgage Loan with Servicing Rights Retained			EITF.86-39
Glossary	FAS65, ¶34	Mo4.401-412	
Loan Acquisitions Involving Table Funding Arrangements			EITF.92-10
Loan and Commitment Fees			
. . Expired Commitments and Prepayment of Loans	FAS65, ¶27	Mo4.128	
. . Fees and Costs for Loans Not Held for Sale	FAS91, ¶27	Mo4.126	
. . Fees for Loans Held for Sale	FAS65, ¶23-24	Mo4.122	
	FAS91, ¶27	Mo4.124-125	
. . Fees for Services Rendered	FAS65, ¶22	Mo4.123	
. . Loan Origination Fees and Costs	FAS91, ¶27	Mo4.122	
. . Types	FAS65, ¶20	Mo4.121	
Mortgage-Backed Securities	FAS65, ¶34	Mo4.408	
. . Classification as Trading Securities	FAS115, ¶12	I80.109	
. . Recovery Doubtful	FAS65, ¶7	Mo4.108	
. . Repurchase Agreements	FAS65, ¶8	Mo4.109	
Mortgage Loans and Mortgage-Backed Securities	FAS65, ¶4-10	Mo4.105-111	
	FAS91, ¶27	I80.109	
	FAS115, ¶12		
	FAS115, ¶128		
. . Carrying Value	FAS65, ¶29	Mo4.130	
. . Determination of Market Value	FAS65, ¶9	Mo4.110	
. . Purchase Discounts	FAS65, ¶5	Mo4.106	

FAS–FASB Statements   FIN–FASB Interpretations   FTB–FASB Technical Bulletins
APB–APB Opinions   AIN–AICPA Interpretations   ARB–Accounting Research Bulletins
CON–FASB Concepts   EITF–EITF Issues   Q&A–FASB Special Reports

	Original Pronouncements	Current Text	EITF and Other
MORTGAGE BANKING			
ACTIVITIES—continued			
Mortgage Loans and Mortgage-Backed Securities—continued			
. . Sold to Affiliated Enterprise	FAS65, ¶12-13	Mo4.113-114	Q&A.91 #60
. . Transfer to Long-Term Classification	FAS65, ¶6	Mo4.107	
	FAS91, ¶27		
	FAS115, ¶128		
. . Valuation Allowances	FAS65, ¶4	Mo4.105	
Normal Servicing Fee Rate	FTB87-3, ¶1-7	Mo4.501-507	
Participation in Future Payment Stream			
. . Sale of Mortgage Servicing Rights			EITF.85-13
. . Unanticipated Mortgage Prepayments			EITF.86-38
Purchase of Collateralized Mortgage Obligation Instruments or Mortgage-Backed Interest-Only Certificates			EITF.89-4
Revenue Recognition			
. . Sale of Convertible, Adjustable-Rate Mortgages with Contingent Repayment Agreement			EITF.87-25
. . Sale of Mortgage Servicing Rights			EITF.89-5
			EITF.94-5
			EITF.95-5
. . Sale of Mortgage Servicing Rights with Subservicing Agreement			EITF.87-34
Rights to Service Mortgage Loans	FAS65, ¶19	Mo4.117-120	
	FAS65, ¶30	Mo4.131	
	FAS122, ¶3	Mo4.508-509	
	FAS122, ¶6		
	FTB87-3, ¶8		
	FTB87-3, ¶10		
. . Balance Sheet Treatment of a Sale of Mortgage Servicing Rights with a Subservicing Agreement			EITF.90-21
. . Determination of Fair Value	FAS122, ¶3	Mo4.119	
. . Normal Servicing Fee	FTB87-3, ¶1-7	Mo4.501-507	EITF.85-26
. . Refinanced Mortgage Loans	FTB87-3, ¶8	Mo4.508-509	
	FTB87-3, ¶10		
. . Sale of Rights with Subservicing Agreement			EITF.87-34
. . Valuation Allowances	FAS122, ¶3	Mo4.118A-118B	
Sale of Loan with a Partial Participation Retained			EITF.84-21
Sale of Mortgage Servicing Rights			
. . Balance Sheet Treatment of a Sale of Mortgage Servicing Rights with a Subservicing Agreement			EITF.90-21
. . Participation in Future Payment Stream			EITF.85-13

See "Terminology" for references to defined terms presented in various accounting pronouncements.
See the Introduction to the Topical Index for details on the use of this index.

	Original Pronouncements	Current Text	EITF and Other
MORTGAGE BANKING ACTIVITIES—continued			
Sale of Mortgage Servicing Rights —continued			
. . Revenue Recognition			EITF.89-5
....			EITF.94-5
....			EITF.95-5
. . With Concurrent Subservicing Agreement..			EITF.87-34
Sales of Loans with Servicing Retained	FTB87-3, ¶1-7	Mo4.501-507	
Scope of Accounting and Reporting Requirements	FAS65, ¶3	Mo4.104	
....	FAS122, ¶13		
Servicing Fees...	FAS65, ¶11	Mo4.112	
. . Collateralized Mortgage Obligations....	FTB85-2, ¶2	C30.502	
. . Loans Sold to Federally Sponsored Agencies..	FTB87-3, ¶1-3	Mo4.501-503	
. . Loans Sold to Private Investors.............	FTB87-3, ¶4-7	Mo4.504-507	
. . Mortgage Loans.....................................	FAS65, ¶2	Mo4.103	
Table Funding Arrangements			EITF.92-10
Unanticipated Mortgage Prepayments			
. . Effect on Amortization of Servicing Rights................................			EITF.86-38
. . Effect on Interest-Only Certificates.......			EITF.86-38
....			EITF.89-4
. . Effect on Purchased Investment in CMO Instruments			EITF.89-4
. . Effect on Receivable for Excess Service Fees			EITF.86-38
MORTGAGE INSURANCE			
Federal Housing Administration (FHA) Insurance			
. . Effect on Profit Recognition by Seller ..			EITF.87-9
Veterans Administration (VA) Mortgage Guarantee			
. . Effect on Profit Recognition by Seller ..			EITF.87-9
MORTGAGES			
See Loans			
MORTGAGE SERVICING RIGHTS			
Balance Sheet Treatment of a Sale of Mortgage Servicing Rights with a Subservicing Agreement............................			EITF.90-21
Gain from Sale of Mortgage Loan with Servicing Rights Retained			EITF.86-39
Loan Acquisitions Involving Table Funding Arrangements.............................			EITF.92-10
Normal Servicing Fee..................................	FTB87-3, ¶1-7	Mo4.501-507	EITF.85-26
Rights Sold But Loan Retained...................			EITF.84-21

FAS–FASB Statements	FIN–FASB Interpretations	FTB–FASB Technical Bulletins
APB–APB Opinions	AIN–AICPA Interpretations	ARB–Accounting Research Bulletins
CON–FASB Concepts	EITF–EITF Issues	Q&A–FASB Special Reports

	Original Pronouncements	Current Text	EITF and Other
MORTGAGE SERVICING			
RIGHTS—continued			
Sale of Rights			
. . Participation in Future Payment			
Stream			EITF.85-13
. . Revenue Recognition			EITF.89-5
			EITF.94-5
			EITF.95-5
. . With Concurrent Subservicing			
Agreement			EITF.87-34
			EITF.90-21
Unanticipated Mortgage Prepayments			
. . Effect on Amortization of			
Servicing Rights			EITF.86-38
MOTION PICTURE INDUSTRY			
See Disclosure			
Balance Sheet Classification			
. . Classified and Unclassified			
Balance Sheets	FAS53, ¶20	Mo6.119	
. . Film Costs to Be Realized from			
Secondary Television and Other			
Exploitations	FAS53, ¶21	Mo6.120	
. . License Agreement for Sale of Film			
Rights for Television Exhibition	FAS53, ¶19	Mo6.118	
Changing Prices Information	FAS89, ¶25	C28.121	
Costs and Expenses			
. . Exploitation Costs	FAS53, ¶15	Mo6.114	
. . Individual Film Forecast Method of			
Amortization	FAS53, ¶11-12	Mo6.110-111	
. . Interim Financial Statements	FAS53, ¶16	Mo6.115	
. . Inventory Valuation	FAS53, ¶16	Mo6.115	
. . Participation	FAS53, ¶14	Mo6.113	
. . Periodic Table Method of			
Amortization	FAS53, ¶13	Mo6.112	
. . Production Costs	FAS53, ¶10	Mo6.109	
. . Story Costs and Scenarios	FAS53, ¶17	Mo6.116	
Disclosure	FAS53, ¶23	Mo6.122	
Films Licensed to Movie Theaters			
. . Deferred Revenue	FAS53, ¶4	Mo6.103	
Glossary	FAS53, ¶26	C28.410	
	FAS89, ¶44	Mo6.401-413	
Home Viewing Market	FAS53, ¶22	Mo6.121	
Investments in Films Produced by			
Independent Producers	FAS53, ¶18	Mo6.117	
Revenue	FAS53, ¶37-39	Mo6.123-125	
. . Films Licensed to Movie Theaters	FAS53, ¶3-4	Mo6.102-103	
. . Films Licensed to Television	FAS53, ¶5-9	Mo6.104-108	
. . Individual Film Forecast Method of			
Amortization	FAS53, ¶40-41	Mo6.126-127	

See "Terminology" for references to defined terms presented in various accounting pronouncements.
See the Introduction to the Topical Index for details on the use of this index.

	Original Pronouncements	Current Text	EITF and Other
MOTION PICTURE INDUSTRY—continued			
Scope of Accounting and Reporting Requirements	FAS53, ¶1	Mo6.101	
MOTOR CARRIERS			
Extraordinary Items	FAS44, ¶7	I17.114-115	
Interstate Operating Rights			
. . Disposition and Amortization	FAS44, ¶1	I60.124-129	
	FAS44, ¶3-7		
Revenue and Expense Recognition for Freight Services in Process			EITF.91-9
MOVING COSTS			
Change from One Leased Property to Another			EITF.88-10
Reimbursements by Lessor			EITF.88-3
MULTIEMPLOYER AND MULTIPLE-EMPLOYER PENSION PLANS			
See Pension Costs			
See Postretirement Benefits Other Than Pensions			
MULTIEMPLOYER BENEFIT PLAN			
Accounting for Estimated Payments in Connection with the Coal Industry Retiree Health Benefit Act of 1992			EITF.92-13
MULTIEMPLOYER PENSION PLAN AMENDMENTS ACT OF 1980			
See Pension Costs			
MULTINATIONAL ENTERPRISES			
See Foreign Currency Translation			
MULTINATIONAL OPERATIONS			
See Foreign Currency Translation			
See Foreign Operations			
See Segment of Business Reporting			
MUNICIPAL BOND FUNDS			
See Investment Enterprises			
MUSIC PUBLISHING			
See Record and Music Industry			
MUTUAL ENTERPRISES (MUTUAL FUNDS)			
See Business Combinations			
See Investment Enterprises			
Fees Paid to Distributors			EITF.85-24
Stock Market Decline			
. . Subsequent Events Disclosure			EITF.D-11
U.S. Government Securities Only Held in Fund			
. . Accounting by Investor in Mutual Fund			EITF.86-40

FAS–FASB Statements   FIN–FASB Interpretations   FTB–FASB Technical Bulletins
APB–APB Opinions   AIN–AICPA Interpretations   ARB–Accounting Research Bulletins
CON–FASB Concepts   EITF–EITF Issues   Q&A–FASB Special Reports

	Original Pronouncements	Current Text	EITF and Other

MUTUAL FUND DISTRIBUTORS
Fees Received from No-Load Funds EITF.85-24

MUTUAL INSURANCE ENTERPRISE
See Insurance Costs

MUTUAL LIFE INSURANCE ENTERPRISES
See Insurance Industry

MUTUAL SAVINGS BANKS
See Banking and Thrift Industries
See Earnings per Share
See Lending Activities
Conversion to Stock Ownership..................   EITF.84-22

(The next page is T-291.)

See "Terminology" for references to defined terms presented in various accounting pronouncements.
See the Introduction to the Topical Index for details on the use of this index.

	Original Pronouncements	Current Text	EITF and Other

NATURAL RESOURCES
See Extractive Industries
Balance Sheet Classification .... ARB43, Ch.3A, ¶6   B05.107
NEGATIVE GOODWILL
See Business Combinations
See Intangible Assets
NET ASSETS
See Equity (or Net Assets)
See Not-for-Profit Organizations
NET INCOME PER SHARE
See Earnings per Share
NET OPERATING LOSS CARRYFORWARDS
See Income Taxes
Allocating Basis to Individual Assets and
  Liabilities under Issue No. 88-16 ....   EITF.90-12
Business Combinations
. . Allocating Cost to Assets to Be Sold EITF.87-11
Loan Loss Allowances
. . Applying Savings and Loan Audit
  Guide......................   EITF.87-5
NET REALIZABLE VALUE
See Inventory
Definition .... FAS53, ¶26   Mo6.410
Recognition and Measurement
. . Measurement Attribute.......................... CON5, ¶67
NET-OF-TAX METHOD
See Income Taxes
NEUTRALITY
Definition .... CON2, Glossary
Financial Reporting .... CON1, ¶33
Relation to Relevance and Reliability......... CON2, ¶98-110
NEW BASIS ACCOUNTING
See Change in Basis of Assets and
  Liabilities
NINETY PERCENT RULE
See Business Combinations
NOMINAL
Definition .... FTB85-2, ¶2   C30.502
NOMINAL DOLLAR ACCOUNTING
Measurement Scale...................................... CON5, ¶71-72
NONBUSINESS ORGANIZATIONS
See Not-for-Profit Organizations
NONCASH TRANSACTIONS
See Cash Flows Statement
See Nonmonetary Transactions
NONCOMPENSATORY PLANS
See Compensation to Employees: Stock
  Purchase and Stock Option Plans

FAS–FASB Statements   FIN–FASB Interpretations   FTB–FASB Technical Bulletins
APB–APB Opinions   AIN–AICPA Interpretations   ARB–Accounting Research Bulletins
CON–FASB Concepts   EITF–EITF Issues   Q&A–FASB Special Reports

	Original Pronouncements	Current Text	EITF and Other

NONCONTRIBUTORY PENSION PLAN
See Defined Benefit Pension Plans
See Pension Costs
NONCURRENT ASSETS AND LIABILITIES
See Balance Sheet Classification: Current Assets and Liabilities
NONDEDUCTIBLE EXPENSES
See Income Taxes
NONMONETARY ASSETS AND LIABILITIES
See Changing Prices: Reporting Their Effects in Financial Reports

Definition	APB29, ¶3	N35.403	
Interest in Lease Residual Value			EITF.85-32

NONMONETARY TRANSACTIONS
See Barter Transactions
See Broadcasting Industry
See Capital Stock: Dividends-in-Kind
See Capital Stock: Treasury Stock
See Compensation to Employees: Stock Purchase and Stock Option Plans
See Contributions
See Disclosure
See Events and Transactions
See Financial Instruments
See Related Parties

Basic Principles	APB29, ¶18	N35.105	
	APB29, ¶25	N35.111	
. . Property Held for Sale or Productive Assets	APB29, ¶7	N35.104	
	APB29, ¶21-22	N35.108-109	
Boot	APB29, ¶4	N35.101	
. . Its Effect			EITF.84-29
			EITF.86-29
			EITF.87-29
Common Stock Contributed to Employee Stock Ownership Plan			
. . Excess Assets Not Allocated to Participants			EITF.86-27
Development Stage Enterprises	FAS7, ¶11	De4.107	
Disclosure	APB29, ¶28	N35.120	
Dividends-in-Kind			
. . Distributions of Loans Receivable to Shareholders			EITF.87-17
Equity Investments			EITF.85-43
			EITF.86-29
Exchange of Assets for Noncontrolling Equity Interest in New Entity			EITF.89-7

See "Terminology" for references to defined terms presented in various accounting pronouncements.
See the Introduction to the Topical Index for details on the use of this index.

Topical Index

	Original Pronouncements	Current Text	EITF and Other
NONMONETARY TRANSACTIONS—continued			
Exchange of Interest in Subsidiary for Noncontrolling Equity Interest in New Entity			EITF.89-7
Exchanges of Real Estate Involving Boot ..			EITF.87-29
Fair Value Not Determinable	APB29, ¶20	N35.107	
	APB29, ¶26	N35.112	
Federal Home Loan Mortgage Corporation (FHLMC)			
. . Distribution of FHLMC Participating Preferred Stock	FTB85-1, ¶2	Bt7.502	EITF.85-7
Glossary	APB29, ¶1	N35.401-407	
	APB29, ¶3		
Guidance in Recognizing Revenues and Gains	CON5, ¶84		
Involuntary Conversions	FIN30, ¶1	N35.114	
. . Gain or Loss	FIN30, ¶4-5	N35.118-119	
. . LIFO Inventories	FIN30, ¶11	N35.115	
. . Nonmonetary Asset Destroyed or Damaged	FIN30, ¶3	N35.117	
. . Temporary Differences	FAS109, ¶287	N35.119	
	FIN30, ¶5		
Joint Ventures			EITF.86-29
Modifications	APB29, ¶19	N35.106	
Nonmonetary Exchange of Cost-Method Investments			EITF.91-5
Nonreciprocal Transfers to Other Than Owners	APB29, ¶6	N35.103	
Nonreciprocal Transfers to Owners	APB29, ¶5	N35.102	
	APB29, ¶23	N35.110	
Property Held for Sale			EITF.86-29
Receipt of FHLMC Participating Preferred Stock			EITF.85-7
Sale of Subsidiary			EITF.85-43
Same Line of Business			EITF.84-29
			EITF.85-43
			EITF.86-29
Scope of Accounting and Reporting Requirements	APB29, ¶4	N35.101	
Similar Productive Assets			EITF.84-29
			EITF.85-43
			EITF.86-29
Temporary Differences	APB29, ¶27	N35.113	
	FAS109, ¶287		
Transfer of Nonmonetary Assets to a New Corporation			EITF.84-39
Transfers between Entities under Common Control			EITF.84-39

FAS–FASB Statements	FIN–FASB Interpretations	FTB–FASB Technical Bulletins
APB–APB Opinions	AIN–AICPA Interpretations	ARB–Accounting Research Bulletins
CON–FASB Concepts	EITF–EITF Issues	Q&A–FASB Special Reports

	Original Pronouncements	Current Text	EITF and Other
NONOWNER CHANGES IN EQUITY			
See Comprehensive Income			
NONPROFIT ENTERPRISES			
See Not-for-Profit Organizations			
NONPUBLIC ENTERPRISE			
Definition	FAS21, ¶8	B50.404A	
	FAS21, ¶13	E09.417	
	FAS79, ¶5	S20.407	
	FAS79, ¶16		
NONRECIPROCAL TRANSFERS			
See Contributions			
See Depreciation			
See Nonmonetary Transactions			
Definition	APB29, ¶3	N35.405	
	CON6, ¶137		
Description	CON6, ¶150-151		
Dividends-in-Kind	APB29, ¶18	C11.101	
NONRECOURSE DEBT			
See Financial Instruments			
Debtor's Accounting for Forfeiture of Real Estate Subject to a Nonrecourse Mortgage			EITF.91-2
Grantor Trust			EITF.84-15
Leases			
. . Delayed Equity Contributions by Leveraged Lessors			EITF.85-16
. . Offsetting Nonrecourse Debt with Lease Receivables			EITF.84-25
NONRECURRING ITEMS			
See Extraordinary Items			
NOT-FOR-PROFIT ORGANIZATIONS			
See Cash Flows Statement			
See Collections—Works of Art, Historical Treasures, and Similar Assets			
See Contributions			
See Disclosure			
Accounting Policies	APB22, ¶9	A10.103	
Accrual vs. Cash Basis of Accounting	CON4, ¶50		
Balance Sheet	FAS117, ¶9-16	No5.107-114	
	FAS117, ¶85-86	No5.131	
	FAS117, ¶93		
	FAS117, ¶156		
. . Classification of Assets and Liabilities	FAS117, ¶11-12	No5.109-110	
. . Endowments and Similar Funds			Q&A.116/117 #12
Budgets	CON4, ¶21-22		
Change in Permanently Restricted Net Assets	CON6, ¶119-122	No5.117	
	FAS117, ¶19		

See "Terminology" for references to defined terms presented in various accounting pronouncements.

See the Introduction to the Topical Index for details on the use of this index.

	Original Pronouncements	Current Text	EITF and Other

NOT-FOR-PROFIT ORGANIZATIONS—continued

	Original Pronouncements	Current Text	EITF and Other
Change in Temporarily Restricted Net Assets	CON6, ¶123-126	No5.117	
	FAS117, ¶19		
Change in Unrestricted Net Assets	CON6, ¶127-133	No5.117	
	FAS117, ¶19		
Changes in Classes of Net Assets	CON6, ¶117-133	No5.116-117	
	CON6, ¶223-227		
	FAS117, ¶18-19		
Characteristics	CON4, ¶6-9		
Characteristics of Information Provided	CON4, ¶23-28		
Characteristics of Net Assets	CON6, ¶90-102		
	CON6, ¶221-222		
Classes of Net Assets	CON6, ¶91-102	No5.111-114	
	FAS117, ¶13-16		
Classification of Revenues, Expenses, Gains, and Losses	FAS116, ¶14-16	No5.118-120	
	FAS117, ¶20	No5.143-145	
	FAS117, ¶22-23		
	FAS117, ¶129		
. . Classification of Endowment Funds			Q&A.116/117 #12
Comparison to Business Enterprise Objectives	CON4, ¶67		
Comparison with Business Enterprises	CON4, ¶6-9		
	CON4, ¶14-22		
Consolidation of Related Entities of Not-for-Profit Organizations			Q&A.116/117 #16
Contributions Received			
. . Required Classification	FAS116, ¶14-16	No5.143-145	
. . Expiration of Donor-imposed Restrictions	FAS116, ¶17	No5.146-147	
	FAS116, ¶166		
Criteria for Consideration as a Not-for-Profit Organization			Q&A.116/117 #15
Deferred Taxes	FAS109, ¶4	I27.103	
Donor-imposed Restrictions	CON6, ¶95-102		
. . As Basis for Classification of Net Assets	CON6, ¶101-102	No5.111-113	
	FAS117, ¶13-15		
. . As Basis for Classification of Revenues	FAS116, ¶14-16	No5.118-119	
	FAS117, ¶20	No5.143-145	
	FAS117, ¶22		
Economic Resources, Obligations, Net Resources, and Changes in Them	CON4, ¶43-54		
Elements of Financial Statements			
. . Applicability	CON6, ¶1-2		
Environmental Context, Objectives	CON4, ¶13-22		

	Original Pronouncements	Current Text	EITF and Other
NOT-FOR-PROFIT ORGANIZATIONS—continued			
Examples of Characteristics of Not-for-Profit Organizations	CON4, ¶7-8		
Exemption from Earnings per Share Requirements	APB15, ¶6	E09.102	
Expiration of Donor-imposed Restrictions	FAS116, ¶17	No5.146-147	
	FAS116, ¶166		
Functional Classification of Expenses	FAS117, ¶26-28	No5.123-125	
General Purpose External Financial Reporting	CON4, ¶10-12		
General Purpose External Financial Statements			Q&A.116/117 #11
. . Comparative Financial Statements	FAS117, ¶70	No5.105	
	FAS117, ¶153	No5.127	
. . Fund Accounting			Q&A.116/117 #11
. . Illustrative Statements and Notes	FAS117, ¶153-167	No5.127-141	
. . Requirements for Complete Set	FAS117, ¶6	No5.104	
. . Statement of Activities	FAS116, ¶14-16	No5.115-125	
	FAS117, ¶17-20	No5.132-134	
	FAS117, ¶22-28	No5.137-141	
	FAS117, ¶129	No5.143-145	
	FAS117, ¶138		
	FAS117, ¶157-159		
	FAS117, ¶163-167		
. . Statement of Cash Flows	FAS117, ¶29	No5.126	
	FAS117, ¶160	No5.135	
. . Statement of Financial Position	FAS117, ¶9-16	No5.107-114	
	FAS117, ¶85-86	No5.131	
	FAS117, ¶93		
	FAS117, ¶100		
	FAS117, ¶156		
. . Statement of Functional Expenses	FAS117, ¶26-28	No5.123-125	
	FAS117, ¶161	No5.136	
Glossary	FAS116, ¶209	No5.402-414	
	FAS117, ¶168		
Illustrations of Financial Statements of Not-for-Profit Organizations	FAS116, ¶141	No5.127-142	
	FAS117, ¶100		
	FAS117, ¶114		
	FAS117, ¶153-167		
Implementation Guidance			Q&A.116/117 #18
Information about Gross Amounts of Revenues and Expenses	FAS117, ¶24-25	No5.121-122	
	FAS117, ¶138		
Information Useful in Assessing Services and Ability to Provide Service	CON4, ¶38-39	No5.123-125	
	FAS117, ¶26-28		
Information Useful in Making Resource Allocation Decisions	CON4, ¶35-37		

See "Terminology" for references to defined terms presented in various accounting pronouncements.
See the Introduction to the Topical Index for details on the use of this index.

	Original Pronouncements	Current Text	EITF and Other

NOT-FOR-PROFIT
ORGANIZATIONS—continued

	Original Pronouncements	Current Text	EITF and Other
Interfund Balances	FAS117, ¶85	No5.109	
Intermediate Measure of Operations	FAS117, ¶23	No5.120	
	FAS117, ¶163-167	No5.137-141	
Investments			Q&A.116/117 #17
Limitations of Information Provided	CON4, ¶23-28		
Liquidity	CON4, ¶54	No5.110	
	FAS117, ¶12		
	FAS117, ¶93		
Management Stewardship	CON4, ¶40-42		
Managers' Explanations and Interpretations	CON4, ¶55		
Nature of Resources	CON4, ¶14-22		
Netting Gains and Losses	FAS117, ¶25	No5.122	
Netting Revenues and Expenses			
. . Investment Revenues and Related Expenses	FAS117, ¶24	No5.121	
. . Special Events	FAS117, ¶138	No5.122	
Nonbusiness Organizations			
. . Change in Terminology	CON6, ¶2		
Objectives of Financial Reporting	CON4, ¶10-12		
	CON4, ¶33-55		
Objectives of Financial Reporting, Nonapplicability	CON1, ¶1		
Objectives, Qualitative Characteristics, and Elements	CON6, ¶9-19		
Organization Performance	CON4, ¶47-53		
Permanently Restricted Net Assets	FAS117, ¶14	No5.112	
Reclassifications of Net Assets	CON6, ¶114-116	No5.117	
	FAS117, ¶19		
. . Expiration of Donor-imposed Restrictions	CON6, ¶152	No5.146-147	
	FAS116, ¶17		
	FAS116, ¶166		
Relation to State and Local Governmental Units	CON4, ¶3-5		
	CON6, ¶2		
Reporting Contributions Received	FAS116, ¶14-16	No5.143-145	
Reporting Revenues, Expenses, Gains, and Losses	FAS117, ¶20	No5.118-125	
	FAS117, ¶22-28		
	FAS117, ¶129		
	FAS117, ¶138		
Resources: Budgetary Appropriations	CON4, ¶21		
Restrictions, Information About	CON6, ¶224-227	No5.111-113	
	FAS117, ¶13-15		
Results of Operations	FAS117, ¶23	No5.120	

	Original Pronouncements	Current Text	EITF and Other
NOT-FOR-PROFIT ORGANIZATIONS—continued			
Revenues, Gains, Expenses, and Losses.....	CON6, ¶111-113	No5.118-125	
....	FAS117, ¶20		
....	FAS117, ¶22-28		
....	FAS117, ¶129		
....	FAS117, ¶138		
Scope..	FAS117, ¶1-2	No5.104-106	
....	FAS117, ¶6-8		
....	FAS117, ¶70		
Service Efforts and Accomplishments	CON4, ¶51-53	No5.123-125	
....	FAS117, ¶26-28		
Special Events..	FAS117, ¶138	No5.122	
State and Local Governmental Units	CON4, ¶65-66		
....	CON6, ¶2		
State and Local Governmental Units, Nonapplicability..	CON4, ¶3-5		
Statement of Activities	FAS116, ¶14-16	No5.115-125	
....	FAS117, ¶17-20	No5.132-134	
....	FAS117, ¶22-28	No5.137-141	
....	FAS117, ¶129	No5.143-145	
....	FAS117, ¶138		
....	FAS117, ¶157-159		
....	FAS117, ¶163-167		
Statement of Cash Flows...............................	FAS117, ¶29	No5.126	
....	FAS117, ¶160	No5.135	
Statement of Financial Position....................	FAS117, ¶9-16	No5.107-114	
....	FAS117, ¶85-86	No5.131	
....	FAS117, ¶93		
....	FAS117, ¶100		
....	FAS117, ¶156		
Statement of Functional Expenses	FAS117, ¶26-28	No5.123-125	
....	FAS117, ¶161	No5.136	
Status of AICPA Audit Guides and SOPs for Not-for-Profit Organizations	FAS117, ¶3	No5.105	Q&A.116/117 #14
Temporarily Restricted Net Assets..............	FAS117, ¶15	No5.113	
Temporary Restrictions	FAS117, ¶14	No5.112	
Transactions and Events That Change Net Assets	CON6, ¶107-116	No5.117-120	
....	FAS117, ¶19-20		
....	FAS117, ¶22-23		
Transition and Adoption of FASB Statements 116 and 117			Q&A.116/117 #13
Types of Users of Financial Reporting........	CON4, ¶29-32		
Unrestricted Net Assets	FAS117, ¶16	No5.114	
Voluntary Health and Welfare Organizations . . Definition..	FAS117, ¶168	No5.414	

See "Terminology" for references to defined terms presented in various accounting pronouncements.
See the Introduction to the Topical Index for details on the use of this index.

	Original Pronouncements	Current Text	EITF and Other
NOT-FOR-PROFIT ORGANIZATIONS—continued			
Voluntary Health and Welfare Organizations—continued			
. . Requirements for Statement of			
Functional Expenses	FAS117, ¶1-2	No5.104	
	FAS117, ¶26	No5.123	
NOTE MONETIZATION			
Offsetting Notes Receivable and Debt			EITF.84-11
NOTES TO FINANCIAL STATEMENTS			
Relation to Recognition in Financial Statements	CON5, ¶7-9		
NOTES, PAYABLE AND RECEIVABLE			
See Debt			
See Financial Instruments			
See Receivables			
Balance Sheet Classification	ARB43, Ch.3A, ¶4	B05.105	
NOTES, SECURED AND UNSECURED			
See Financial Instruments			
See Interest: Imputation of an Interest Cost			

(The next page is T-301.)

FAS–FASB Statements   FIN–FASB Interpretations   FTB–FASB Technical Bulletins
APB–APB Opinions   AIN–AICPA Interpretations   ARB–Accounting Research Bulletins
CON–FASB Concepts   EITF–EITF Issues   Q&A–FASB Special Reports

	Original Pronouncements	Current Text	EITF and Other

OBJECTIVES OF FINANCIAL REPORTING
See Not-for-Profit Organizations
Accrual Accounting and Cash Flows .... CON1, ¶44-49
Amount, Timing, and Uncertainty of Cash
  Receipts .... CON1, ¶37-39
Business Estimates by Users .... CON1, ¶48
Characteristics and Limitations................... CON1, ¶17-23
Comparison between Not-for-Profit and
  Business Enterprises .... CON4, ¶67
Description.. CON1, ¶32-54
Earnings and Enterprise Performance......... CON1, ¶44-48
Environmental Context................................ CON1, ¶9-16
Financial Reporting, General Purpose
  External .... CON1, ¶28-31
Information for Users .... CON1, ¶34-36
Liquidity, Solvency, and Funds Flow.......... CON1, ¶49
Management Performance .... CON1, ¶50-53
Management Reporting .... CON1, ¶54
Not-for-Profit Organizations .... CON4, ¶1
 .... CON4, ¶10-12
 .... CON4, ¶33-55
Relation to Elements of Financial
  Statements .... CON6, ¶9-19
Relation to Qualitative Characteristics........ CON2, ¶21-26
Relation to Recognition and Measurement .. CON5, ¶10-12
Resources, Claims, and Changes in Them.. CON1, ¶40-41
Users, Interests... CON1, ¶24-27
OBLIGATIONS
See Balance Sheet Classification: Current
  Assets and Liabilities
See Commitments: Long-Term
  Obligations
See Contingencies
See Debt
See Debt: Product Financing
  Arrangements
See Financial Instruments
See Franchising
See Leases
Definition... CON6, ¶35
Description.. CON6, ¶200-205
Not-for-Profit Organizations .... CON4, ¶43-54
OBSOLESCENCE
See Contingencies
See Impairment
See Inventory
See Property, Plant, and Equipment

	Original Pronouncements	Current Text	EITF and Other

OFF-BALANCE-SHEET FINANCING
See Commitments: Long-Term Obligations
See Consolidation
See Financial Instruments

OFF-BALANCE-SHEET RIGHTS AND OBLIGATIONS
See Financial Instruments

OFFICERS' AND EMPLOYEES' LOANS AND RECEIVABLES

| Balance Sheet Classification | ARB43, Ch.3A, ¶4 | B05.105 | |

OFFICERS' LIFE INSURANCE
See Cash Surrender Value
See Life Insurance

OFFSETTING
See Hedges

Asset Puttable to Creditor to Satisfy Debt			EITF.84-11
Assurance That a Right of Setoff Is Enforceable in a Bankruptcy under FASB Interpretation 39			EITF.D-43
Balance Sheet Display	FIN39, ¶5-6	B10.101A-101B	
	FIN39, ¶44-45		
	FIN39, ¶47		
Banker's Acceptances and Risk Participations			EITF.85-34
Certificates of Deposit Against Debt			EITF.87-20
Collateralized Mortgage Obligations	FTB85-2, ¶4	C30.504	
Criteria for a Right of Setoff	FIN39, ¶5-6	B10.101A-101B	
	FIN39, ¶44-45		
	FIN39, ¶47		
Deposit Float of Banks			EITF.84-9
Environmental Liabilities . . Inclusion of Potential Recoveries			EITF.93-5
Foreign Currency Swaps			EITF.86-25
Impropriety of, Except Where a Right of Setoff Exists	APB10, ¶7	B10.101-103	EITF.84-11
	FTB85-2, ¶4	C30.504	EITF.84-25
In-Substance Defeasance of Debt . . Defeasance of Special-Purpose Borrowings			EITF.84-26
. . Instantaneous In-Substance Defeasance of Unconsolidated Subsidiary's Debt			EITF.84-41
. . Invasion of a Defeasance Trust			EITF.86-36
Lease Receivables (Sales-Type or Direct Financing) with Nonrecourse Debt			EITF.84-25
Letter of Credit as Guarantee of Lease Payments in a Sale-Leaseback Transaction Involving Real Estate			EITF.90-20

See "Terminology" for references to defined terms presented in various accounting pronouncements.
See the Introduction to the Topical Index for details on the use of this index.

	Original Pronouncements	Current Text	EITF and Other
OFFSETTING—continued			
Netting Gains and Losses			
. . Disposal of Two or More Segments of a Business			EITF.85-36
. . Market Values Recognized for Off-Balance-Sheet Financial Instruments			EITF.D-25
Notes Received for Capital Stock			EITF.85-1
Not-for-Profit Organizations Reporting			
. . Netting Revenues and Expenses and Gains and Losses	FAS117, ¶24-25	No5.121-122	
	FAS117, ¶138		
Offsetting Forward, Interest Rate Swap, Currency Swap, Option, and Other Conditional or Exchange Contracts	FIN39, ¶3	B10.104-106	
	FIN39, ¶8-10		
	FIN39, ¶22		
Offsetting Payables and Receivables under Repurchase and Reverse Repurchase Agreements	FIN41, ¶3-4	B10.106A-106B	
	FIN41, ¶14		
. . Criteria for	FIN41, ¶3	B10.106A	
	FIN41, ¶14		
Offsetting Securities against Taxes Payable	APB10, ¶7	B10.102-103	
Securities Purchased by Third Party with Funds Loaned by Issuer			EITF.86-18
			EITF.87-20
Treatment in Specific Circumstances	FIN39, ¶7	B10.107	
OIL AND GAS PRODUCING ACTIVITIES			
See Disclosure			
See Extractive Industries			
Accounting at Time Costs Are Incurred			
. . Acquisition of Properties	FAS19, ¶15	Oi5.106	
. . Capitalization of Interest	FIN33, ¶2	I67.108	
. . Development	FAS19, ¶21-22	Oi5.112-113	
. . Exploration	FAS19, ¶16-18	Oi5.107-109	
. . Exploratory Wells	FAS19, ¶19	Oi5.110	
. . Geological and Geophysical Costs in Exchange for an Interest	FAS19, ¶20	Oi5.111	
. . Production Costs	FAS19, ¶23-25	Oi5.114-116	
. . Support Equipment and Facilities	FAS19, ¶26	Oi5.117	
Accounting Changes	FAS25, ¶4	Oi5.102	
Accounting for Gas-Balancing Arrangements			EITF.90-22
. . Disclosure by SEC Registrants			EITF.90-22
. . Entitlements Method			EITF.90-22
. . Sales Method			EITF.90-22

	Original Pronouncements	Current Text	EITF and Other

OIL AND GAS PRODUCING
 ACTIVITIES—continued

Capitalizing Interest under Full Cost
 Method .... FIN33, ¶2   I67.108

Definition
. . Complete Set of Financial Statements .. FAS69, ¶1   Oi5.400
 .... FAS95, ¶152
. . Development Well .... FAS19, ¶274   Oi5.401
. . Exploratory Well................................... FAS19, ¶274   Oi5.402
. . Field .... FAS19, ¶272   Oi5.403
. . Foreign Geographic Area .... FAS69, ¶12   Oi5.403A
. . Industry Segment.................................... FAS69, ¶8   Oi5.403B
. . Oil and Gas Producing Activities.......... FAS19, ¶1   Oi5.403C
. . Proved Area .... FAS19, ¶275   Oi5.404
. . Proved Reserves .... FAS25, ¶34   Oi5.405
. . Publicly Traded Enterprise .... FAS69, ¶1   Oi5.405A
. . Reservoir .... FAS19, ¶273   Oi5.406
. . Service Well.. FAS19, ¶274   Oi5.407
. . Stratigraphic Test Well .... FAS19, ¶274   Oi5.408

Disposition of Capitalized Costs .... FAS19, ¶27   Oi5.118
. . Accounting When Drilling of an
 Exploratory Well Is Completed .... FAS19, ¶31-32   Oi5.122-123
. . Accounting When Drilling of an
 Exploratory-Type Stratigraphic Well
 Is Completed .... FAS19, ¶33-34   Oi5.124-125
. . Assessment of Unproved Properties ..... FAS19, ¶28   Oi5.119
. . Costs Relating to Oil and Gas
 Reserves Produced Jointly.................. FAS19, ¶38   Oi5.129
. . Dismantlement Costs and Salvage
 Values .... FAS19, ¶37   Oi5.128
. . Information Available after the
 Balance Sheet Date .... FAS19, ¶39   Oi5.130
 .... FIN36, ¶2
. . Reclassification of an Unproved
 Property.. FAS19, ¶29   Oi5.120
. . Support Equipment and Facilities .... FAS19, ¶36   Oi5.127
. . Surrender or Abandonment of
 Properties .... FAS19, ¶40-41   Oi5.131-132

Full Cost Method
. . Capitalization of Interest .... FIN33, ¶2   I67.108

Impairment Test for Proved Properties and
 Capitalized Exploration and
 Development Cost.................................... FAS121, ¶25   Oi5.141A

Interim Financial Statements
. . Major Discovery..................................... FAS69, ¶9   Oi5.159

Mineral Interests in Properties .... FAS19, ¶11   Oi5.103

Mineral Property Conveyances and
 Related Transactions .... FAS19, ¶42   Oi5.133
. . Accounting for Certain Transactions .... FAS19, ¶47   Oi5.138

See "Terminology" for references to defined terms presented in various accounting pronouncements.

See the Introduction to the Topical Index for details on the use of this index.

	Original Pronouncements	Current Text	EITF and Other

OIL AND GAS PRODUCING ACTIVITIES—continued

Mineral Property Conveyances and Related Transactions—continued

. . Conveyances That Are In-Substance Borrowings	FAS19, ¶43	Oi5.134	
. . Transactions in Which Gain or Loss Shall Not Be Recognized	FAS19, ¶44-46	Oi5.135-137	
Proved Properties	FAS19, ¶11	Oi5.103	
Reserves			
. . Changing Prices Information	FAS89, ¶24	C28.120	
Scope of Accounting and Reporting Requirements	FAS19, ¶1	Oi5.101	
	FAS19, ¶6		
Significant Oil and Gas Producing Activities	FAS69, ¶8	Oi5.158	
Specialized Assets, Capitalization	FAS19, ¶12-13	Oi5.104-105	
Support Equipment and Facilities	FAS19, ¶11	Oi5.103	
Tax Allocation	FAS19, ¶60-62	Oi5.139-141	
	FAS109, ¶288		
Uncompleted Wells, Equipment, and Facilities	FAS19, ¶11	Oi5.103	
Unproved Properties	FAS19, ¶11	Oi5.103	
Wells and Related Equipment and Facilities	FAS19, ¶12	Oi5.104	

OPERATING CYCLE

Definition	ARB43, Ch.3A, ¶5	B05.404	
Description	APB16, ¶49	B05.108	
	CON1, ¶39		

OPERATING INCOME

See Changing Prices: Reporting Their Effects in Financial Reports

See Income Statement Presentation: Discontinued Operations

See Oil and Gas Producing Activities

See Segment of Business Reporting

OPERATING LEASES

See Leases

OPERATING LOSS CARRYBACKS AND CARRYFORWARDS

See Extraordinary Items

See Income Taxes

OPERATING LOSSES

See Income Taxes

OPTIONS

See Compensation to Employees: Stock Purchase and Stock Option Plans

See Earnings per Share

See Financial Instruments

See Stock Options

O   *Topical Index*

	Original Pronouncements	Current Text	EITF and Other

OPTIONS—continued

OPTIONS—continued

Accounting for Financial Instruments Indexed to, and Potentially Settled in, a Company's Own Stock			EITF.94-7
Business Combinations	AIN-APB16, #32	B50.624-626	
Call Options on Debt Securities			
. . Fee for Waiving Call Provision			EITF.86-18
Comparison with Futures Contracts	FAS80, ¶32	F80.101	
Convertible Debt with a Premium Put			EITF.85-29
Currency Options			
. . Hedging Currency Risks with Complex Options and Similar Transactions			EITF.91-4
. . Hedging Foreign Currency Risks of Future Net Income, Revenues, or Costs			EITF.D-16
. . Hedging Foreign Currency Risks with Purchased Options			EITF.90-17
. . Hedging Intercompany Foreign Currency Risks			EITF.91-1
			EITF.95-2
Definition	APB15, App.D	E09.418	
Nonapplicability of Futures Contracts Accounting and Reporting Requirements	FAS80, ¶32	F80.101	
Put Option for Stock Purchased with Warrants			EITF.86-35
Put Option to Satisfy Debt with Asset			EITF.84-11
Real Estate Purchases	FAS66, ¶7	R10.110	
	FAS66, ¶26	R10.128	
	FAS66, ¶32	R10.135	
		Re1.107	
		Re1.126	
		Re1.132	
Real Estate Sales			EITF.86-6
Repurchase Options			
. . Sale-Leaseback Transactions Involving Real Estate	FAS98, ¶11	L10.130G	EITF.84-37
Sale of Put Options on Issuer's Stock			EITF.87-31

ORGANIZATION COSTS
See Development Stage Enterprises
ORIGINATION COSTS
See Mortgage Banking Activities
OTHER MEANS OF FINANCIAL REPORTING

| Relation to Recognition in Financial Statements | CON5, ¶7-9 | | |

OTHER NONOWNER CHANGES IN EQUITY
See Comprehensive Income

See "Terminology" for references to defined terms presented in various accounting pronouncements.
See the Introduction to the Topical Index for details on the use of this index.

	Original Pronouncements	Current Text	EITF and Other

OTHER POSTEMPLOYMENT BENEFITS
See Postemployment Benefits
Not Included in Accounting for
Postretirement Benefits Other Than
Pensions.. FAS106, ¶1   P40.101
.... FAS112, ¶4
OUTSTANDING SHARES
See Capital Stock: Preferred Stock
See Capital Stock: Stock Dividends and
  Stock Splits
See Earnings per Share
OVERFUNDED PENSION PLANS
See Pension Costs
OVERSEAS OPERATIONS
See Foreign Currency Translation
See Foreign Operations
See Segment of Business Reporting
OWNERS' EQUITY
See Shareholders' Equity

(The next page is T-311.)

FAS–FASB Statements   FIN–FASB Interpretations   FTB–FASB Technical Bulletins
APB–APB Opinions   AIN–AICPA Interpretations   ARB–Accounting Research Bulletins
CON–FASB Concepts   EITF–EITF Issues   Q&A–FASB Special Reports

T-307

	Original Pronouncements	Current Text	EITF and Other

PAID ABSENCES
See Compensation to Employees: Paid
   Absences
PAID-IN CAPITAL
See Additional Paid-in Capital
See Capital Stock: Capital Transactions
See Compensation to Employees: Stock
   Purchase and Stock Option Plans
PAID-IN SURPLUS
See Additional Paid-in Capital
See Capital Stock: Capital Transactions
See Compensation to Employees: Stock
   Purchase and Stock Option Plans
PAR VALUE
See Capital Stock: Capital Transactions
See Capital Stock: Preferred Stock
See Capital Stock: Stock Dividends and
   Stock Splits
See Capital Stock: Treasury Stock
PARENT COMPANY
Purchase of Subsidiary's Preferred Stock....   EITF.86-32
Related Parties .... FAS57, ¶1   R36.101
PARENT COMPANY STATEMENTS
See Consolidation
See Earnings per Share
See Investments: Equity Method
PARITY ADJUSTMENT
Changing Prices Information .... FAS89, ¶39   C28.135
.... FAS89, ¶95   C28.190
Definition .... FAS89, ¶44   C28.411
PART PURCHASE/PART POOLING
See Business Combinations
PARTICIPATING SECURITIES
See Earnings per Share
See Financial Instruments
PARTICIPATION LOAN
 AGREEMENTS
See Financial Instruments
See Lending Activities
See Loans
See Mortgage Banking Activities
PARTNERSHIPS
See Investments: Equity Method
Accounting for Limited Partnership
   Investments
 . . Reporting by SEC Registrants EITF.D-46
Accounting for Tax Benefits Resulting
   from Investments in Qualified Affordable
   Housing Projects EITF.94-1

	Original Pronouncements	Current Text	EITF and Other

PARTNERSHIPS—continued

Classification of Payment Made to IRS to Retain Fiscal Year EITF.88-4

Election to Retain Fiscal Year
. . Classification of Payment Made to IRS EITF.88-4

Master Limited Partnerships (MLP)
. . Carryover of Predecessor Cost EITF.87-21
. . Gain Recognition on MLP Units Received in Exchange for Future Fees EITF.88-14
. . Recording Assets Acquired and Liabilities Assumed EITF.87-21

Purchase of Withdrawing Partner's Equity. EITF.85-46

Real Estate Investment Trust (REIT)
. . Accounting for Sponsor's Interest EITF.94-2

Real Estate Syndicators EITF.85-37

Roll-up of Limited Partnership into an MLP
. . Gain Recognition on MLP Units Received in Exchange for Future Fees EITF.88-14

Umbrella Partnership Real Estate Investment Trust (UPREIT) EITF.94-2

Withdrawals EITF.85-46

PAST SERVICE COSTS
See Pension Costs

PATENTS
See Intangible Assets

PAYABLES
See Interest: Imputation of an Interest Cost

PAYING OFF OWN DEBT
See Debt: Extinguishments

PAYMENTS OF CASH
See Cash
See Cash Flows
See Cash Flows Statement

PAYROLL COSTS
See Compensation to Employees: Deferred
See Compensation to Employees: Paid Absences
See Compensation to Employees: Stock Purchase and Stock Option Plans

PENSION COSTS
See Compensation to Employees: Deferred
See Contingencies
See Disclosure

See "Terminology" for references to defined terms presented in various accounting pronouncements.
See the Introduction to the Topical Index for details on the use of this index.

	Original Pronouncements	Current Text	EITF and Other

PENSION COSTS—continued
See Postretirement Health Care and Life
  Insurance Benefits

Accounting Change			Q&A.87 #57
			Q&A.87 #76-77
Accounting for Employers' Obligations for Future Contributions to a Multiemployer Pension Plan			EITF.90-3
Accounting for Pension Benefits Paid by Employers after Insurance Companies Fail to Provide Annuity Benefits			EITF.91-7
Accounting for the Transfer of Excess Pension Assets to a Retiree Health Care Benefits Account			EITF.D-27
Accumulated Benefit Obligation	FAS87, ¶18	P16.112	Q&A.87 #47-49
	FAS87, ¶47-48	P16.143-144	Q&A.87 #59
			Q&A.87 #64
Actuarial Cost Method			
. . Projected-Unit Credit	FAS87, ¶40	P16.134	
. . Unit Credit	FAS87, ¶40	P16.134	
. . Unit Credit with Service Prorate	FAS87, ¶40	P16.134	
Additional Minimum Liability	FAS87, ¶36-38	P16.130-133	Q&A.87 #30
	FAS87, ¶49	P16.145	Q&A.87 #34
	FAS87, ¶52	P16.148	Q&A.87 #36-43
	FAS109, ¶287		Q&A.87 #78
Annuity Contracts	FAS87, ¶54	P16.150	Q&A.87 #82
	FAS87, ¶57-62	P16.154-159	Q&A.88 #6-13
	FAS88, ¶5	P16.178-179	Q&A.88 #16-17
	FAS88, ¶10		Q&A.88 #44
. . Insurance Companies Fail to Provide Annuity Benefits			EITF.91-7
Asset Reversions from Termination of a Defined Benefit Pension Plan			EITF.86-27
Asset Reversions of a Defined Benefit Pension Plan	FAS88, ¶20	P16.188	Q&A.88 #38
			Q&A.88 #65
			Q&A.88 #67-70
Assumptions	FAS87, ¶13-14	P16.107-108	
	FAS87, ¶43-48	P16.137-144	
	FAS87, ¶174		
	FAS87, ¶196		
	FAS87, ¶198-201		
. . Anticipation of Retroactive Plan Amendments	FAS87, ¶41	P16.135	Q&A.87 #13
			Q&A.87 #53
. . Benefit Limitations	FAS87, ¶46-48	P16.142-144	Q&A.87 #63-64
. . Discount Rates	FAS87, ¶44	P16.138	Q&A.87 #55-61
	FAS106, ¶186		Q&A.88 #32-33
	FAS106, ¶188		

FAS–FASB Statements   FIN–FASB Interpretations   FTB–FASB Technical Bulletins
APB–APB Opinions   AIN–AICPA Interpretations   ARB–Accounting Research Bulletins
CON–FASB Concepts   EITF–EITF Issues   Q&A–FASB Special Reports

T-313

	Original Pronouncements	Current Text	EITF and Other
PENSION COSTS—continued			
Assumptions—continued			
. . Expected Long-Term Rate of Return			
on Plan Assets	FAS87, ¶44-45	P16.138	Q&A.87 #60
		P16.141	Q&A.87 #62
. . Future Compensation Levels	FAS87, ¶46	P16.142	Q&A.87 #54
Attribution	FAS87, ¶15	P16.109	
	FAS87, ¶40-42	P16.134-136	
	FAS87, ¶127		
	FAS87, ¶168		
. . Benefit/Years-of-Service Approach	FAS87, ¶40	P16.134	
Automatic Benefit Increases	FAS87, ¶48	P16.144	
Basic Elements of Pension Accounting	FAS87, ¶13-19	P16.106-113	
	FAS87, ¶95		
	FAS87, ¶191		
Business Combinations	FAS87, ¶74-75	B50.146	Q&A.87 #15
			Q&A.87 #35
			Q&A.87 #39-40
			Q&A.87 #74
			Q&A.87 #88-94
Combining/Dividing Pension Plans			Q&A.87 #80-81
Components (of Net Periodic Pension Cost of a Defined Benefit Pension Plan)			
. . Actual Return on Plan Assets	FAS87, ¶16	P16.110	
	FAS87, ¶20	P16.114	
. . Gain or Loss (Component)	FAS87, ¶16	P16.110	
	FAS87, ¶20	P16.114	
. . Interest (Cost)	FAS87, ¶16	P16.110	Q&A.87 #6
	FAS87, ¶20-22	P16.114-116	Q&A.87 #45
	FAS87, ¶54	P16.150	
. . Service Cost (Component)	FAS87, ¶16	P16.110	
	FAS87, ¶20-21	P16.114-115	
	FAS87, ¶54	P16.150	
. . Unrecognized Net Obligation or Net Asset	FAS87, ¶20	P16.114	
. . Unrecognized Prior Service Cost	FAS87, ¶16	P16.110	
	FAS87, ¶20	P16.114	
Contractual Termination Benefits	FAS88, ¶15	P16.185	Q&A.88 #59-60
Curtailment (of a Defined Benefit Pension Plan)			
. . Accounting for	FAS88, ¶6-8	P16.173-175	Q&A.88 #27-29
	FAS88, ¶12-14	P16.182-184	Q&A.88 #39-41
			Q&A.88 #47-58
			Q&A.88 #63-64
. . Occurrence of	FAS88, ¶6-7	P16.173-174	Q&A.88 #14-15
			Q&A.88 #18-24
			Q&A.88 #26
Death and Disability Benefits			Q&A.87 #2
Deferred Compensation Contracts	FAS87, ¶7	P16.101	Q&A.87 #3
Defined Contribution Plan	FAS87, ¶63-66	P16.160-163	EITF.86-27

See "Terminology" for references to defined terms presented in various accounting pronouncements.
See the Introduction to the Topical Index for details on the use of this index.

	Original Pronouncements	Current Text	EITF and Other
PENSION COSTS—continued			
Delayed Vesting	FAS87, ¶42	P16.136	
Discount Rate	FAS87, ¶44	P16.138	
	FAS87, ¶49	P16.145	
	FAS87, ¶54	P16.150	
	FAS106, ¶186		
	FAS106, ¶188		
. . Guidance for SEC Registrants			EITF.D-36
Disposal of a Business Segment			Q&A.87 #100
. . Curtailment			Q&A.88 #15
			Q&A.88 #27-28
			Q&A.88 #39
. . Gain (Loss) from a Settlement or Curtailment of a Defined Benefit Pension Plan	FAS88, ¶16	P16.186	Q&A.88 #25
. . Settlement of a Pension Benefit Obligation			Q&A.88 #15
			Q&A.88 #27-28
			Q&A.88 #37
			Q&A.88 #39
. . Special Termination Benefits			Q&A.88 #61
. . Termination Indemnities			Q&A.88 #60
Early Application of Statement 87			Q&A.87 #60
			Q&A.87 #90-92
			Q&A.87 #94-97
Effective Dates of Statement 87			Q&A.87 #90-92
			Q&A.87 #94
			Q&A.87 #99
			Q&A.87 #101
Employers with Two or More Plans	FAS87, ¶55-56	P16.152-153	Q&A.87 #26
			Q&A.87 #49
			Q&A.87 #70
			Q&A.87 #73
			Q&A.87 #80-81
Excess Benefit (Top-Hat) Pension Plan	FAS87, ¶46	P16.142	Q&A.87 #49
			Q&A.87 #73
Excise Tax			
. . Excess Plan Assets	FAS88, ¶20	P16.188	Q&A.88 #66
Federal Executive Agencies			Q&A.87 #1
Flat-Benefit Pension Plan	FAS87, ¶10	P16.134	Q&A.87 #44
			Q&A.87 #51
Funded Status Reconciliation	FAS87, ¶54	P16.150	
. . (Additional) Minimum Liability	FAS87, ¶54	P16.150	
. . Projected Benefit Obligation	FAS87, ¶54	P16.150	
. . Unrecognized Net Gain or Loss	FAS87, ¶54	P16.150	
. . Unrecognized Net Obligation or Net Asset	FAS87, ¶54	P16.150	
. . Unrecognized Prior Service Cost	FAS87, ¶54	P16.150	
Future Compensation Levels	FAS87, ¶46	P16.142	

	Original Pronouncements	Current Text	EITF and Other
PENSION COSTS—continued			
Gains and Losses	FAS87, ¶29-34	P16.123-128	
. . Immediate Recognition			Q&A.87 #33
. . Minimum Amortization	FAS87, ¶32-33	P16.126-127	Q&A.87 #16-18
			Q&A.87 #31-32
. . Substantive Commitment			Q&A.87 #13
Glossary	FAS87, ¶57	P16.401-466	
	FAS87, ¶264		
	FAS88, ¶3		
	FAS88, ¶5-6		
Illustrations	FAS87, ¶261	P16.189-190	Q&A.87 #43
	FAS88, ¶57		Q&A.88 #13
			Q&A.88 #42-44
Inactive Participants	FAS87, ¶25	P16.114	Q&A.87 #18
	FAS87, ¶32	P16.119	Q&A.87 #31
	FAS87, ¶77	P16.126	Q&A.87 #106-107
Income Tax Considerations	FAS87, ¶37	P16.131	Q&A.87 #9
			Q&A.87 #43
. . Business Combinations			Q&A.87 #40
			Q&A.87 #74
			Q&A.87 #89
			Q&A.87 #93
Insurance Contracts	FAS87, ¶57-62	P16.154-159	Q&A.87 #11
			Q&A.87 #36
			Q&A.87 #82-85
. . Accounting for Pension Benefits Paid by Employers after Insurance Companies Fail to Provide Annuity Benefits			EITF.91-7
. . Nonparticipating Annuity Contracts	FAS87, ¶58	P16.155	
. . Participating Annuity Contracts	FAS87, ¶57	P16.154	
	FAS87, ¶61	P16.158	
Intangible Asset	FAS87, ¶37-38	P16.131-132	Q&A.87 #41-43
	FAS109, ¶287		
Interim Financial Reporting	FAS87, ¶52-54	P16.148-150	Q&A.87 #34
			Q&A.87 #67-68
			Q&A.87 #76-77
			Q&A.87 #98-100
Limited Benefit Accumulation Period			Q&A.87 #45-46
Measurement Date	FAS87, ¶52-53	P16.114	Q&A.87 #37-38
	FAS87, ¶77	P16.148-149	Q&A.87 #65-71
Measurement of Cost and Obligations	FAS87, ¶39	P16.133	
. . Benefit Limitations	FAS87, ¶39	P16.133	Q&A.87 #63-64
. . Career-Average-Pay Pension Plan	FAS87, ¶39-40	P16.133-134	Q&A.87 #44
			Q&A.87 #50-51
. . Combining Pension Plans	FAS87, ¶55	P16.152	Q&A.87 #80
. . Discount Rates	FAS87, ¶39-44	P16.133-138	Q&A.87 #55-61
. . Excess Benefit (Top-Hat) Pension Plan	FAS87, ¶55-56	P16.152-153	Q&A.87 #49
			Q&A.87 #73

See "Terminology" for references to defined terms presented in various accounting pronouncements.
See the Introduction to the Topical Index for details on the use of this index.

	Original Pronouncements	Current Text	EITF and Other
PENSION COSTS—continued			
Measurement of Cost and Obligations—continued			
. . Expected Long-Term Rate of Return on Plan Assets	FAS87, ¶23	P16.117	Q&A.87 #12
	FAS87, ¶30	P16.124	Q&A.87 #24-25
			Q&A.87 #60
			Q&A.87 #62
. . Future Compensation Levels	FAS87, ¶46	P16.142	Q&A.87 #54
. . Limited Benefit Accumulation Period	FAS87, ¶40	P16.134	Q&A.87 #45-46
. . Net Periodic Pension Income	FAS87, ¶16	P16.110	Q&A.87 #7-9
. . Pension Plan with More Than One Benefit Formula	FAS87, ¶40	P16.134	Q&A.87 #47
. . Projected Benefit Obligation Less Than Accumulated Benefit Obligation	FAS87, ¶42	P16.136	Q&A.87 #48
. . Substantive Commitment	FAS87, ¶41	P16.135	Q&A.87 #13
			Q&A.87 #52
Multiemployer Pension Plans	FAS87, ¶67-70	P16.164-167	Q&A.87 #86-87
. . Accounting for Employers' Obligations for Future Contributions			EITF.90-3
. . Withdrawal from			Q&A.88 #26
Multiple-Employer Plans	FAS87, ¶71	P16.168	
Net Periodic Pension Income	FAS87, ¶16	P16.110	Q&A.87 #7-9
	FAS87, ¶20	P16.114	
Non-U.S. Pension Plans	FAS87, ¶56	P16.153	Q&A.87 #2
	FAS87, ¶72-73	P16.169-170	Q&A.87 #94
			Q&A.87 #96
			Q&A.87 #99
Nonbenefit Liabilities	FAS87, ¶54	P16.150	Q&A.87 #72
Nonpublic Enterprise			Q&A.87 #99
Nonqualified Pension Plan			Q&A.87 #11
			Q&A.87 #49
			Q&A.87 #73
Plan Amendments	FAS87, ¶24-28	P16.118-122	Q&A.87 #14-15
			Q&A.87 #44
. . Adding Health Care and Life Insurance Benefits			EITF.86-19
. . Amortization of Prior Service Cost	FAS87, ¶24-26	P16.118-120	Q&A.87 #14
			Q&A.87 #16-21
. . Anticipation of Plan Amendments	FAS87, ¶27	P16.121	Q&A.87 #13
	FAS87, ¶41	P16.135	Q&A.87 #52-53
. . History of Regular Plan Amendments	FAS87, ¶27	P16.121	Q&A.87 #20
. . Negative Amendment (Reduced Benefits)	FAS87, ¶28	P16.122	Q&A.87 #21-23
. . Recognition of Prior Service Cost in a Curtailment	FAS88, ¶3-4	P16.172-174	Q&A.88 #47-48
. . Successor Pension Plan	FAS88, ¶6-7	P16.182	Q&A.88 #14
	FAS88, ¶12		Q&A.88 #23
			Q&A.88 #26

FAS–FASB Statements   FIN–FASB Interpretations   FTB–FASB Technical Bulletins
APB–APB Opinions   AIN–AICPA Interpretations   ARB–Accounting Research Bulletins
CON–FASB Concepts   EITF–EITF Issues   Q&A–FASB Special Reports

	Original Pronouncements	Current Text	EITF and Other
PENSION COSTS—continued			
Plan Assets	FAS87, ¶19	P16.113	
. . Asset Gains and Losses	FAS87, ¶31	P16.125	
	FAS87, ¶54	P16.150	
. . Classes of Assets	FAS87, ¶30	P16.124	Q&A.87 #27
. . Employer-Issued Securities	FAS87, ¶19	P16.113	Q&A.87 #10
. . Employer-Issued Securities Withdrawn from Pension Plan	FAS88, ¶9	P16.187	Q&A.88 #34
. . Expected (Long-Term Rate of) Return on Plan Assets	FAS87, ¶30	P16.124	
	FAS87, ¶45	P16.141	
	FAS87, ¶54	P16.150	
. . Fair Value	FAS87, ¶49	P16.145	
	FAS87, ¶54	P16.150	
. . Fixed-Income Investments	FAS87, ¶49	P16.145	Q&A.87 #36
. . Gains and Losses	FAS87, ¶29-34	P16.123-128	
. . Market-Related Value of Plan Assets	FAS87, ¶30	P16.124	Q&A.87 #25-30
	FAS87, ¶45	P16.141	
	FAS87, ¶50	P16.146	
	FAS87, ¶54	P16.150	
. . Measured at Market-Related Value Other Than Fair Value			Q&A.88 #30
. . Measurement Date	FAS87, ¶49	P16.145	
	FAS87, ¶52	P16.148	
. . Measurement of Plan Assets	FAS87, ¶49-53	P16.145-149	
. . More Than One Pension Plan	FAS87, ¶30	P16.124	Q&A.87 #26
. . Return on Plan Assets	FAS87, ¶23	P16.117	
	FAS87, ¶31	P16.125	
	FAS87, ¶54	P16.150	
. . Used in Plan Operations	FAS87, ¶51	P16.147	
Plan Benefit Formula	FAS87, ¶12	P16.105	
Postemployment Health Care Benefits	FAS87, ¶8	P16.102	Q&A.87 #5
Prepaid Pension Cost	FAS87, ¶35	P16.129	
Presentation			
. . Extraordinary Item	FAS88, ¶48	P16.187	Q&A.88 #63-64
Prior Service Cost	FAS87, ¶24-28	P16.118-122	
. . Amortization Period			EITF.87-13
. . Plan Amendments	FAS87, ¶24	P16.118	
	FAS87, ¶26-28	P16.120-122	
. . Retroactive Benefits	FAS87, ¶24-25	P16.118-119	
. . Retroactive Plan Amendments	FAS87, ¶25	P16.119	
	FAS87, ¶48	P16.144	
. . Unrecognized	FAS87, ¶54	P16.150	Q&A.88 #47-48
	FAS88, ¶12	P16.182	
Projected Benefit Obligation	FAS87, ¶17	P16.111	
	FAS87, ¶54	P16.150	
. . Discount Rate	FAS87, ¶54	P16.150	
. . Mortality	FAS87, ¶17	P16.111	
. . Turnover	FAS87, ¶17	P16.111	

See "Terminology" for references to defined terms presented in various accounting pronouncements.
See the Introduction to the Topical Index for details on the use of this index.

	Original Pronouncements	Current Text	EITF and Other
PENSION COSTS—continued			
Puerto Rican Pension Plans and Pension Plans in Other U.S. Territories			Q&A.87 #101
Rate-Regulated Enterprises	FAS87, ¶210	Re6.155	Q&A.87 #4
Recognition of Assets and Liabilities	FAS87, ¶35-38	P16.129-132	
Related Party Transaction			Q&A.88 #12
			Q&A88 #17
Scope of Accounting and Reporting Requirements	FAS87, ¶7-8	P16.101-104	
	FAS87, ¶10-11	P16.171	
	FAS88, ¶2		
	FAS88, ¶45		
	FAS106, ¶14		
Selection of Discount Rate to Be Used to Measure Obligation			EITF.D-36
Service Cost Component (of Net Periodic Pension Cost)	FAS87, ¶46	P16.142	
Settlement of a Defined Benefit Pension Plan			
. . Accounting for	FAS88, ¶5	P16.177-181	Q&A.88 #17
	FAS88, ¶9-11		Q&A.88 #27-46
	FAS88, ¶21		Q&A.88 #63-64
	FAS88, ¶34		
. . Accounting for Pension Benefits Paid by Employers after Insurance Companies Fail to Provide Annuity Benefits			EITF.91-7
. . Occurrence of	FAS88, ¶3-4	P16.172	Q&A.88 #1-3
			Q&A.88 #6-15
			Q&A.88 #40
Significant Reduction of Expected Years of Future Service of Present Employees			
. . Threshold for	FAS88, ¶6	P16.447	Q&A.88 #18
Spinoff			Q&A.88 #40
State and Local Governmental Units			Q&A.87 #1
Successor Pension Plan	FAS88, ¶7	P16.174	Q&A.88 #14
			Q&A.88 #23-24
			Q&A.88 #26
Temporary Suspension of Pension Benefit Accruals			Q&A.88 #20
			Q&A.88 #49
Termination Benefits of a Defined Benefit Pension Plan			
. . Accounting for	FAS88, ¶15	P16.185	Q&A.88 #54
			Q&A.88 #57-63
Termination Indemnities	FAS87, ¶73	P16.170	Q&A.88 #60
Termination of a Defined Benefit Pension Plan			
. . Asset Reversions Contributed to Defined Contribution Plan			EITF.86-27

	Original Pronouncements	Current Text	EITF and Other
PENSION COSTS—continued			
Termination of a Defined Benefit Pension Plan—continued			
. . Asset Reversions Contributed to ESOP			EITF.86-27
. . Between Measurement Date and Financial Report Date			Q&A.88 #28
. . Contribution of Excess Plan Assets to Defined Contribution Pension Plan			Q&A.88 #29
. . Employees Continue to Work for Employer			Q&A.88 #48
. . Employer-Issued Securities Withdrawn from Pension Plan			Q&A.88 #34
. . Extraordinary Item			Q&A.88 #64
. . Pension Plan Amended to Provide for Its Termination or Suspension			Q&A.88 #56
. . Regulatory Approval			Q&A.88 #1-2
. . Settlement and Curtailment Effects Recognized in Different Periods			Q&A.88 #27
. . Successor Pension Plan			Q&A.88 #14
			Q&A.88 #23-24
			Q&A.88 #26
Transfer of a Pension Benefit Obligation or Plan Assets	FAS88, ¶3-4	P16.172-173	Q&A.88 #15
	FAS88, ¶6		Q&A.88 #40
Transition Requirements	FAS87, ¶20	P16.114	Q&A.88 #58
	FAS87, ¶77	P16.177	Q&A.88 #62
	FAS88, ¶9	P16.188	Q&A.88 #65
	FAS88, ¶20-21		Q&A.88 #67-70
Types of Pension Plans	FAS87, ¶17	P16.111	
. . Career-Average-Pay	FAS87, ¶17	P16.111	
	FAS87, ¶40-41	P16.134-135	
. . Contributory Pension Plan			Q&A.87 #16
. . Final-Average-Pay	FAS87, ¶17	P16.111	
. . Final-Pay	FAS87, ¶17	P16.111	
	FAS87, ¶40	P16.134	
. . Flat-Benefit (Non-Pay-Related)	FAS87, ¶17	P16.111	
	FAS87, ¶40-41	P16.134-135	
. . Pay-Related	FAS87, ¶17	P16.111	
. . Target Benefit	FAS87, ¶66	P16.163	
Unfunded Accrued or Prepaid Pension Costs	FAS87, ¶35	P16.129	Q&A.87 #34
			Q&A.87 #103
Unfunded Accumulated Benefit Obligation	FAS87, ¶36	P16.130	
Unrecognized Net Asset or Net Obligation at Transition to Statement 88	FAS88, ¶9	P16.177	Q&A.88 #35-36
	FAS88, ¶12-13	P16.182-183	Q&A.88 #50-53
	FAS88, ¶20	P16.188	Q&A.88 #68-69

See "Terminology" for references to defined terms presented in various accounting pronouncements.

See the Introduction to the Topical Index for details on the use of this index.

	Original Pronouncements	Current Text	EITF and Other
PENSION COSTS—continued			
Unrecognized Net Asset/Obligation at Date of Initial Application of Statement 87			
. . Amortization	FAS87, ¶24-26	P16.114	Q&A.87 #16-18
	FAS87, ¶32	P16.118-120	Q&A.87 #102
	FAS87, ¶77	P16.126	Q&A.87 #105-107
. . Determination	FAS87, ¶74	B50.146	Q&A.87 #23
	FAS87, ¶77	P16.114	Q&A.87 #38
			Q&A.87 #60
			Q&A.87 #93
			Q&A.87 #103-104
Unrecognized Net Gain or Loss	FAS87, ¶32-34	P16.126-128	
	FAS88, ¶9	P16.177	
	FAS88, ¶21		
Unrecognized Net Obligation or Net Asset	FAS87, ¶20	P16.114	
	FAS87, ¶54	P16.150	
	FAS88, ¶9	P16.177	
	FAS88, ¶21		
. . Transition Requirements	FAS87, ¶77	P16.114	
Vested Benefit Obligation (VBO)	FAS87, ¶18	P16.112	
	FAS87, ¶54	P16.150	
. . Benefits Payable Immediately			EITF.88-1
. . COLA-Adjusted from Termination to Normal Retirement Date			EITF.88-1
. . Effect When VBO Exceeds Accumulated Benefit Obligation			EITF.88-1
Withdrawal Liability	FAS87, ¶70	P16.167	
Withdrawal of Excess Plan Assets	FAS88, ¶20	P16.188	Q&A.88 #4-5
			Q&A.88 #29
			Q&A.88 #34
			Q&A.88 #38
			Q&A.88 #65-70

PENSION FUNDS
See Defined Benefit Pension Plans
PENSION LIABILITIES
See Pension Costs
PENSION PLANS
See Defined Benefit Pension Plans
See Employee Benefit Plans
See Pension Costs
See Postretirement Health Care and Life
  Insurance Benefits
See Related Parties

	Original Pronouncements	Current Text	
Definition	FAS35, ¶280	Pe5.419	

PENSION REFORM ACT OF 1974
See Defined Benefit Pension Plans
See ERISA

	Original Pronouncements	Current Text	EITF and Other

PENSION TRUSTS
See Pension Costs

PERCENTAGE-OF-COMPLETION METHOD
See Contractor Accounting: Construction-
Type Contracts
See Real Estate: Sales Other Than Retail
Land Sales

PERFORMANCE
See Earnings
See Earnings Summaries
See Financial Reporting
See Management
See Return on Investment
Not-for-Profit Organizations .... CON4, ¶47-53

PER SHARE DIVIDENDS
See Capital Stock: Dividends-in-Kind
See Capital Stock: Stock Dividends and
Stock Splits
See Dividends
See Earnings per Share

PER SHARE EARNINGS
See Earnings per Share

PERSONAL HOLDING COMPANY
See Business Combinations

PERSONAL PROPERTY TAXES
See Tax

PERSONNEL COSTS
See Compensation to Employees:
Deferred
See Compensation to Employees: Paid
Absences
See Compensation to Employees: Stock
Purchase and Stock Option Plans

PERSONNEL RETIREMENT PLANS
See Defined Benefit Pension Plans
See Pension Costs

PETROLEUM INDUSTRY
See Oil and Gas Producing Activities

PHANTOM STOCK PLANS
See Compensation to Employees: Stock
Purchase and Stock Option Plans

PHASE-IN PLAN
See Regulated Operations

PHYSICAL CAPITAL MAINTENANCE CONCEPT
See Capital Maintenance

PILOT PLANT
See Research and Development

See "Terminology" for references to defined terms presented in various accounting pronouncements.

See the Introduction to the Topical Index for details on the use of this index.

	Original Pronouncements	Current Text	EITF and Other

PIPELINE ENTERPRISES
See Oil and Gas Producing Activities
Advances to Encourage Exploration
. . Interest: Imputation of an

Interest Cost	AIN-APB21, #1	I69.501	

PLAN
See Compensation to Employees: Stock
 Purchase and Stock Option Plans
See Defined Benefit Pension Plans
PLAN ASSETS
Consideration of the Impact of Bankruptcy
 in Determining Plan Assets under

Statement 106			EITF.93-3

PLAN OF COMBINATION
See Business Combinations
PLANT CLOSINGS
See Business Combinations
Duplicate Facilities following a Purchase
 Business Combination
. . Costs of Closing Duplicate Facilities

of an Acquirer	FTB85-5, ¶1-2	B50.651-652	EITF.84-35

POLICIES, ACCOUNTING
See Accounting Policies
POLICY ACQUISITION COSTS
See Insurance Industry
POLICY RESERVES
See Insurance Industry
POLICYHOLDER DIVIDENDS
See Insurance Industry
POLICYHOLDERS' SURPLUS
See Insurance Industry
POOLED RISKS
See Insurance Costs
POOLING-OF-INTERESTS METHOD
See Business Combinations
POSSIBLE EVENTS
See Contingencies
POST BALANCE SHEET DATE
Refinancings
 See Balance Sheet Classification:
  Current Assets and Liabilities
POSTEMPLOYMENT BENEFITS
See Disclosure
See Postretirement Benefits Other Than
 Pensions
Accounting for Involuntary Termination

Benefits			EITF.94-3
Accounting for Postemployment Benefits	FAS112, ¶6	P32.103-104	
	FAS112, ¶21-23		
Definition	FAS112, ¶1	P32.102	

FAS–FASB Statements   FIN–FASB Interpretations   FTB–FASB Technical Bulletins
APB–APB Opinions   AIN–AICPA Interpretations   ARB–Accounting Research Bulletins
CON–FASB Concepts   EITF–EITF Issues   Q&A–FASB Special Reports

	Original Pronouncements	Current Text	EITF and Other

POSTEMPLOYMENT BENEFITS—continued

Measurement .... FAS112, ¶23   P32.104

Scope of Accounting and Reporting
  Requirements .... FAS112, ¶4-5   P32.101-102

POSTRETIREMENT BENEFIT PLAN

See Postretirement Benefits Other Than Pensions

POSTRETIREMENT BENEFITS OTHER THAN PENSIONS

See Disclosure

Accounting Change

.. Amortization Method .... FAS106, ¶59-60   P40.154-155   Q&A.106 #32

.. Changing from One-Plan Accounting
  to Two-Plan Accounting .... FAS106, ¶76   P40.171   Q&A.106 #42

.. Effect of Implementation Guidance for
  Employers that Previously Adopted
  Statement 106 .... FAS106, ¶108   P40.141   Q&A.106 #55
  .... FAS106, ¶110

.. Transition Method .... FAS106, ¶110   P40.141   Q&A.106 #58

Accounting for Estimated Payments in
Connection with the Coal Industry
Retiree Health Benefit Act of 1992 ....   EITF.92-13

Accounting for OPEB Costs by Rate-
Regulated Enterprises EITF.92-12
....   EITF.93-4

Accounting for the Transfer of Excess
Pension Assets to a Retiree Health Care
Benefits Account EITF.D-27

Accumulated Postretirement Benefit
Obligation... FAS106, ¶21   P40.114
.... FAS106, ¶168

.. Assumed in a Business Combination.... FAS106, ¶86   B50.146

.. Benefits Covered by Insurance
  Contracts .... FAS106, ¶67   P40.162

.. Illustration.. FAS106, ¶392-396   P40.204-208
.... FAS106, ¶418-419   P40.226-227

.. Measurement of................................... FAS106, ¶21   P40.114
.... FAS106, ¶28   P40.121
.... FAS106, ¶30-31   P40.123-126
.... FAS106, ¶33   P40.128
.... FAS106, ¶48   P40.143
.... FAS106, ¶50   P40.145
.... FAS106, ¶174
.... FAS106, ¶194-195

.. Reduction of .... FAS106, ¶55   P40.150   Q&A.106 #24-25
.... FAS106, ¶98-99   P40.190-191

.. Settlement of....................................... FAS106, ¶93   P40.185

Administration Costs............................... FAS106, ¶36   P40.131

See "Terminology" for references to defined terms presented in various accounting pronouncements.
See the Introduction to the Topical Index for details on the use of this index.

	Original Pronouncements	Current Text	EITF and Other
POSTRETIREMENT BENEFITS OTHER THAN PENSIONS—continued			
Aggregating Data for Measurement Purposes	FAS106, ¶75-76	P40.170-171	
	FAS106, ¶357		
Assumptions (Actuarial)	FAS106, ¶19	P40.112	
	FAS106, ¶29-42	P40.122-137	
	FAS106, ¶73	P40.168	
	FAS106, ¶194-195		
. . Active Employee Contributions	FAS106, ¶30	P40.123	Q&A.106 #9
	FAS106, ¶35	P40.130	
. . Administration Costs	FAS106, ¶36	P40.131	
. . (Assumed) Per Capita Claims Cost (by Age)	FAS106, ¶30	P40.123	
	FAS106, ¶34-38	P40.129-133	
	FAS106, ¶41	P40.136	
	FAS106, ¶197		
. . Discount Rates	FAS106, ¶30-31	P16.138	Q&A.106 #8
	FAS106, ¶42	P40.123	Q&A.106 #40
	FAS106, ¶48	P40.126	
	FAS106, ¶186	P40.137	
	FAS106, ¶188	P40.143	
. . Effects of Changes in Assumptions	FAS106, ¶45-46	P40.140-141	
	FAS106, ¶56	P40.151	
	FAS106, ¶59-60	P40.154-155	
. . Expected Long-Term Rate of Return on Plan Assets	FAS106, ¶32	P40.127	
	FAS106, ¶56-58	P40.151-153	
. . Future Compensation Levels	FAS106, ¶30	P40.123	
	FAS106, ¶33	P40.128	
	FAS106, ¶42	P40.137	
. . Health Care Cost Trend Rates	FAS106, ¶30	P40.123	Q&A.106 #11
	FAS106, ¶36-39	P40.131-134	
	FAS106, ¶41-42	P40.136-137	
. . Medicare Reimbursement	FAS106, ¶40	P40.135	Q&A.106 #13
. . Unique to Postretirement Health Care Benefits	FAS106, ¶34-42	P40.129-137	
Attribution	FAS106, ¶19	P40.112	Q&A.106 #14-22
	FAS106, ¶29	P40.122	
	FAS106, ¶43-44	P40.138-139	
	FAS106, ¶47	P40.142	
	FAS106, ¶135		
	FAS106, ¶200		
	FAS106, ¶227		
. . Accrual of Annual Service Cost	FAS106, ¶44	P40.139	Q&A.106 #12
	FAS106, ¶46-47	P40.141-142	Q&A.106 #21
. . Change in Credited Service Period	FAS106, ¶44	P40.139	Q&A.106 #14
	FAS106, ¶55	P40.150	Q&A.106 Ex. 5
	FAS106, ¶96-99	P40.188-191	

FAS–FASB Statements	FIN–FASB Interpretations	FTB–FASB Technical Bulletins
APB–APB Opinions	AIN–AICPA Interpretations	ARB–Accounting Research Bulletins
CON–FASB Concepts	EITF–EITF Issues	Q&A–FASB Special Reports

	Original Pronouncements	Current Text	EITF and Other
POSTRETIREMENT BENEFITS OTHER THAN PENSIONS—continued			
Attribution—continued			
. . Determining the Attribution Period or			
Pattern	FAS106, ¶9	C38.101-101A	Q&A.106 #4-5
	FAS106, ¶13	P40.105	Q&A.106 #14-22
	FAS106, ¶43-44	P40.138-139	
	FAS106, ¶47	P40.142	
	FAS106, ¶411-412	P40.223-224	
. . Determining the Full Eligibility Date	FAS106, ¶21	P40.114	Q&A.106 #15-17
	FAS106, ¶43-44	P40.138-139	
. . Frontloaded Plan	FAS106, ¶21	P40.114	Q&A.106 #17-18
	FAS106, ¶43-44	P40.138-139	
	FAS106, ¶412	P40.224	
. . Effect of Nontrivial Incremental			
Benefits	FAS106, ¶21	P40.114	Q&A.106 #15
	FAS106, ¶43-44	P40.138-139	Q&A.106 #17
	FAS106, ¶398-401	P40.210-213	
. . Illustration	FAS106, ¶409-412	P40.221-228	
. . Nominal Credited Service Period	FAS106, ¶44	P40.139	Q&A.106 #21-22
	FAS106, ¶47	P40.142	Q&A.106 Ex. 5
Automatic Benefit Changes	FAS106, ¶28	P40.121	
Basic Elements of Accounting for			
Postretirement Benefits	FAS106, ¶19-22	P40.112-115	
Basis for Accounting	FAS106, ¶23	P40.118	
Benefit Formula	FAS106, ¶18	P40.111	
	FAS106, ¶43-44	P40.138-139	
Benefits Covered by Insurance Contracts	FAS106, ¶67-71	P40.162-166	
Business Combinations	FAS106, ¶86-88	B50.146	Q&A.106 #45
. . Adjustment of Purchase Price at Date			
of Adoption of Statement 106	FAS106, ¶110-111	P40.141	Q&A.106 #63
. . Unfunded Vested Obligations			EITF.86-20
Change in Accounting Method			EITF.86-19
Collectively Bargained Plan	FAS106, ¶25	P40.118	Q&A.106 #3
Components of Net Periodic			
Postretirement Benefit Cost	FAS106, ¶22	P40.115	
	FAS106, ¶46	P40.141	
. . Actual Return on Plan Assets	FAS106, ¶49	P40.144	
	FAS106, ¶58	P40.153	
	FAS106, ¶295		
. . Amortization of Unrecognized Prior			
Service Cost	FAS106, ¶50-55	P40.145-150	
. . Amortization of Unrecognized Transition Obligation or Transition			
Asset	FAS106, ¶110	P40.141	
	FAS106, ¶112-113	P40.200-201	
. . Gain or Loss	FAS106, ¶56-62	P40.151-157	
. . Interest Cost	FAS106, ¶31	P40.126	
	FAS106, ¶48	P40.143	

See "Terminology" for references to defined terms presented in various accounting pronouncements.
See the Introduction to the Topical Index for details on the use of this index.

	Original Pronouncements	Current Text	EITF and Other
POSTRETIREMENT BENEFITS			
OTHER THAN PENSIONS—continued			
Components of Net Periodic Postretirement			
Benefit Cost—continued			
. . Service Cost	FAS106, ¶28-31	P40.121-123	
	FAS106, ¶47	P40.126	
	FAS106, ¶70	P40.142	
		P40.165	
Consideration of the Impact of Bankruptcy			
in Determining Plan Assets under			
Statement No. 106			EITF.93-3
Consolidated Omnibus Budget			
Reconciliation Act of 1985 (COBRA)			Q&A.106 #2
Contributory Plans			
. . Changing a Plan to Require			
Contribution			Q&A.106 Ex. 1
. . Cost of Retirees' Benefits Reduced by			
Active Employee Contributions	FAS106, ¶35	P40.130	Q&A.106 #9
. . Retiree-Pay-All	FAS106, ¶35	P40.130	Q&A.106 #10
. . Temporary Deviation from the			
Substantive Plan	FAS106, ¶61	P40.156	Q&A.106 #33
			Q&A.106 #35
Cost-Sharing Policy (Provisions)	FAS106, ¶23-25	P40.116-118	Q&A.106 #6-7
	FAS106, ¶35	P40.130	Q&A.106 #9-10
			Q&A.106 #20
			Q&A.106 #33-35
			Q&A.106 Ex. 1
. . Retrospective Adjustment	FAS106, ¶61	P40.156	
Credited Service Period	FAS106, ¶44	P40.139	Q&A.106 #14
	FAS106, ¶50	P40.145	Q&A.106 #19
			Q&A.106 #21-22
			Q&A.106 Ex. 5
. . Frontloaded Plan	FAS106, ¶43-44	P40.138-139	Q&A.106 #18
	FAS106, ¶412	P40.224	
. . Illustration	FAS106, ¶393-395	P40.205-207	
	FAS106, ¶409-412	P40.221-224	
Curtailment of a Plan	FAS106, ¶96	P40.188	
	FAS106, ¶100-101	P40.192-193	
. . Determination of Gain or Loss	FAS106, ¶97-99	P40.189-191	
. . Distinguishing between a Curtailment			
and a Negative Plan Amendment	FAS106, ¶55	P40.150	Q&A.106 #24-25
	FAS106, ¶96-99	P40.188-191	Q&A.106 #30
. . Effect of Implementation Guidance for			
Employers that Previously Adopted			
Statement 106	FAS106, ¶108	P40.141	Q&A.106 #55
	FAS106, ¶110		
. . Events that May Result in a			
Curtailment	FAS106, ¶55	P40.150	Q&A.106 #28
	FAS106, ¶96-99	P40.188-191	Q&A.106 #30
. . Illustration	FAS106, ¶496-501	P40.293-298	

	Original Pronouncements	Current Text	EITF and Other

POSTRETIREMENT BENEFITS
OTHER THAN PENSIONS—continued

Curtailment of a Plan—continued

. . Illustration, with Settlement	FAS106, ¶502-506	P40.299-303	
. . Illustration, with Special Termination Benefits	FAS106, ¶507-511	P40.304-308	
. . Newly Created Negative Prior Service Cost	FAS106, ¶55	P40.150	Q&A.106 #28
	FAS106, ¶96-99	P40.188-191	Q&A.106 Ex. 3
. . Partial Curtailment	FAS106, ¶97	P40.189	
. . Recognition of a Curtailment Gain or Loss	FAS106, ¶55	P40.150	Q&A.106 #26
	FAS106, ¶96-99	P40.188-191	Q&A.106 #28-29
	FAS106, ¶102	P40.194	Q&A.106 #44
. . Requires Remeasurement of Net Periodic Postretirement Benefit Cost	FAS106, ¶73	P40.168	
. . Successor Plan	FAS106, ¶100	P40.192	Q&A.106 Exs. 2-7
. . Unrecognized Negative Prior Service Cost	FAS106, ¶55	P40.150	Q&A.106 #29-30
	FAS106, ¶96-99	P40.188-191	
. . Unrecognized Prior Service Cost	FAS106, ¶55	P40.150	Q&A.106 #27-30
	FAS106, ¶96-99	P40.188-191	
. . Unrecognized Transition Obligation	FAS106, ¶55	P40.150	Q&A.106 #27-28
	FAS106, ¶96-99	P40.188-191	Q&A.106 #30
Deferred Compensation Contracts	FAS106, ¶9	C38.101-101A	Q&A.106 #4-5
	FAS106, ¶13	P40.105	
. . Illustration	FAS106, ¶413-416	C38.103-106	
Defined Benefit Postretirement Plan	FAS106, ¶16-18	P40.109-111	
Defined Contribution Postretirement Plan	FAS106, ¶63	P40.158	Q&A.106 #49-50
	FAS106, ¶104-107	P40.196-199	
	FAS106, ¶382		
Defined-Dollar Capped Plans	FAS106, ¶16-17	P40.109-110	Q&A.106 #6-7 Q&A.106 #33-34
. . Illustration	FAS106, ¶472-478	P40.269-275	
Disability Benefits	FAS106, ¶6	P40.102	Q&A.106 #1
	FAS106, ¶136-137		
. . Illustration	FAS106, ¶406-408	P40.218-220	
Disclosures Prior to Adoption of Standard			Q&A.106 #39
. . SEC Registrants			EITF.D-26
Discount Rate	FAS106, ¶30-31	P16.138	Q&A.106 #8
	FAS106, ¶42	P40.123	
	FAS106, ¶48	P40.126	
	FAS106, ¶186	P40.137	
	FAS106, ¶188	P40.143	
. . Disclosure	FAS106, ¶74	P40.169	Q&A.106 #40
. . Guidance for SEC Registrants			EITF.D-36
Disposal of a Segment	FAS106, ¶103	P40.195	
. . Illustration	FAS106, ¶500-501	P40.297-298	

See "Terminology" for references to defined terms presented in various accounting pronouncements.
See the Introduction to the Topical Index for details on the use of this index.

	Original Pronouncements	Current Text	EITF and Other

**POSTRETIREMENT BENEFITS
OTHER THAN PENSIONS**—continued

	Original Pronouncements	Current Text	EITF and Other
Effective Date of Statement 106	FAS106, ¶108	P40.141	Q&A.106 #51-54
	FAS106, ¶110		
. . Change in Number of Participants			Q&A.106 #52
. . Early Adoption			Q&A.106 #51
			Q&A.106 #54
			Q&A.106 #56-57
. . Effect of Becoming a Public Company.			Q&A.106 #53
. . Employer with More Than One Plan			Q&A.106 #54
. . Equity Method Investment			Q&A.106 #51
. . Subsidiary with Separate Plan			Q&A.106 #56
Employers with Two or More Plans	FAS106, ¶75-78	P40.170-173	Q&A.106 #41-42
	FAS106, ¶357		
Expected Postretirement Benefit Obligation	FAS106, ¶20-21	P40.113-114	
. . Attribution of	FAS106, ¶43-44	P40.138-139	
	FAS106, ¶47	P40.142	
	FAS106, ¶135		
	FAS106, ¶200		
	FAS106, ¶227		
. . Illustration	FAS106, ¶393-396	P40.205-208	
	FAS106, ¶404	P40.216	
	FAS106, ¶406-408	P40.218-220	
. . Measurement of	FAS106, ¶20	P40.113	
	FAS106, ¶25-29	P40.118-122	
	FAS106, ¶31	P40.126	
Floor-Offset Plan	FAS106, ¶104	P40.196	Q&A.106 #49-50
Foreign Plans	FAS106, ¶110	P40.141	Q&A.106 #62
Full Eligibility (for Benefits) Date	FAS106, ¶21	P40.114	Q&A.106 #15-17
	FAS106, ¶43-44	P40.138-139	
. . Attribution Period	FAS106, ¶44	P40.139	
	FAS106, ¶227		
. . Illustration	FAS106, ¶393-408	P40.205-220	
Funded Status Reconciliation	FAS106, ¶74	P40.169	
. . Illustration	FAS106, ¶417-429	P40.225-237	
Future Compensation Levels	FAS106, ¶33	P40.128	
	FAS106, ¶42	P40.137	
. . Illustration	FAS106, ¶399-400	P40.211-212	
Gains and Losses	FAS106, ¶45-46	P40.140-141	Q&A.106 #32-35
	FAS106, ¶56-62	P40.151-157	
. . Change in Amortization Methods	FAS106, ¶59-60	P40.154-155	Q&A.106 #32
. . Constraint on Immediate Recognition	FAS106, ¶60	P40.155	
. . Deviation from Substantive Plan	FAS106, ¶61	P40.156	
. . Effect of Implementation Guidance for Employers that Previously Adopted Statement 106	FAS106, ¶108		Q&A.106 #55
. . Illustration	FAS106, ¶455-471	P40.252-268	
. . Minimum Amortization	FAS106, ¶59-60	P40.154-155	

FAS–FASB Statements	FIN–FASB Interpretations	FTB–FASB Technical Bulletins
APB–APB Opinions	AIN–AICPA Interpretations	ARB–Accounting Research Bulletins
CON–FASB Concepts	EITF–EITF Issues	Q&A–FASB Special Reports

	Original Pronouncements	Current Text	EITF and Other

POSTRETIREMENT BENEFITS OTHER THAN PENSIONS—continued

Gains and Losses—continued

. . Settlements and Curtailments ... FAS106, ¶90-100 ... P40.182-192 ... Q&A.106 #25-26

... Q&A.106 #28-30

... Q&A.106 #46

... Q&A.106 #48

. . Special Termination Benefits ... FAS106, ¶102 ... P40.194 ... Q&A.106 #48

. . Temporary Deviation from the Substantive Plan ... FAS106, ¶61 ... P40.156 ... Q&A.106 #33-35

Glossary ... FAS106, ¶518 ... P40.401-472

Goodwill ... FAS106, ¶110-111 ... P40.141 ... Q&A.106 #63

Health Care Cost Trend Rate ... FAS106, ¶30 ... P40.123

... FAS106, ¶39 ... P40.134

... FAS106, ¶41-42 ... P40.136-137

. . Effect of One Percent Increase ... FAS106, ¶74 ... P40.169

... FAS106, ¶354

Illustrations ... FAS106, ¶391-430 ... P40.202-308

... FAS106, ¶435-437

... FAS106, ¶439-511

Implementation Guidance ... FAS106, ¶11 ... P40.107

Insurance Contracts ... FAS106, ¶67-71 ... P40.162-166

. . Captive Insurance Companies ... FAS106, ¶63-64 ... P40.158-159 ... Q&A.106 #37

... FAS106, ¶67 ... P40.162

. . Investment Contracts ... FAS106, ¶63-64 ... P40.158-159 ... Q&A.106 #37

. . Nonparticipating Insurance Contracts... FAS106, ¶70 ... P40.165

... FAS106, ¶95 ... P40.187

. . Participating Insurance Contracts ... FAS106, ¶68-69 ... P40.163-164

... FAS106, ¶94-95 ... P40.186-187

... FAS106, ¶367

. . Projecting the Cost of Insurance Premiums ... FAS106, ¶36-39 ... P40.131-134 ... Q&A.106 #11-12

Interest Cost Component (of Net Periodic Postretirement Benefit Cost) ... FAS106, ¶22 ... P40.115

... FAS106, ¶31 ... P40.126

... FAS106, ¶46 ... P40.141

... FAS106, ¶48 ... P40.143

Interim Financial Reporting ... FAS106, ¶73 ... P40.168

... FAS106, ¶113 ... P40.201

. . Illustration ... FAS106, ¶442 ... P40.245

Life Insurance Benefits (Outside a Pension Plan) ... FAS106, ¶6 ... P40.102

Measurement Date ... FAS106, ¶31 ... P40.126

... FAS106, ¶39 ... P40.134

... FAS106, ¶65 ... P40.141

... FAS106, ¶72-73 ... P40.160

... FAS106, ¶110 ... P40.167-168

. . Illustration ... FAS106, ¶456 ... P40.253

See "Terminology" for references to defined terms presented in various accounting pronouncements.
See the Introduction to the Topical Index for details on the use of this index.

	Original Pronouncements	Current Text	EITF and Other
POSTRETIREMENT BENEFITS			
OTHER THAN PENSIONS—continued			
Measurement of Cost and Obligations........	FAS106, ¶15	P40.108	
....	FAS106, ¶23-44	P40.116-139	
....	FAS106, ¶183		
....	FAS106, ¶194-195		
. . Accounting for the Substantive Plan.....	FAS106, ¶23-28	P40.116-121	
. . Administration Costs.............................	FAS106, ¶36	P40.131	
. . Aggregating Data..................................	FAS106, ¶75-76	P40.170-171	
....	FAS106, ¶357		
. . Assumptions	FAS106, ¶29-42	P40.122-137	Q&A.106 #8-13
....	FAS106, ¶194-195		
. . Attribution..	FAS106, ¶43-44	P40.138-139	
....	FAS106, ¶135		
....	FAS106, ¶200		
....	FAS106, ¶227		
. . Automatic Benefit Changes...................	FAS106, ¶28	P40.121	
. . Benefit Limitations	FAS106, ¶33	P40.128	
. . Contributions by Active and Retired			
Employees...	FAS106, ¶20	P40.113	Q&A.106 #9-10
....	FAS106, ¶24-25	P40.117-118	
....	FAS106, ¶27	P40.120	
....	FAS106, ¶35	P40.130	
. . Discount Rates.....................................	FAS106, ¶31	P40.126	
....	FAS106, ¶42	P40.137	
....	FAS106, ¶186		
. . Employers with Two or More Plans	FAS106, ¶75-76	P40.170-171	
....	FAS106, ¶357		
. . Expected Long-Term Rate of Return			
on Plan Assets	FAS106, ¶32	P40.127	
....	FAS106, ¶57-58	P40.152-153	
. . Health Care Benefits.............................	FAS106, ¶34-42	P40.129-137	
. . Illustration of Limits on Benefits or			
Obligation	FAS106, ¶472-478	P40.269-275	
. . Limits on Benefits or Obligation...........	FAS106, ¶17	P40.110	
....	FAS106, ¶33	P40.128	
. . Monetary Benefits	FAS106, ¶26	P40.119	
. . Pay-Related Plans.................................	FAS106, ¶33	P40.128	
Medicare Reimbursements.........................	FAS106, ¶40	P40.135	Q&A.106 #13
Monetary Benefits	FAS106, ¶16-17	P40.109-110	Q&A.106 #7
....	FAS106, ¶26	P40.119	
Multiemployer Plans	FAS106, ¶79-83	P40.174-179	Q&A.106 #43-44
....	FAS106, ¶377		
. . Plans Not Considered Multiemployer			
Plans...	FAS106, ¶84	P40.180	
Multiple-Employer Plans	FAS106, ¶84	P40.180	

	Original Pronouncements	Current Text	EITF and Other

POSTRETIREMENT BENEFITS
OTHER THAN PENSIONS—continued

Net Periodic Postretirement Benefit Cost

(for a Defined Benefit Plan)...................... FAS106, ¶22 — P40.115

.... FAS106, ¶45-46 — P40.140-141

. . Accrual of .... FAS106, ¶46-47 — P40.141-142 — Q&A.106 #12

.... — — — Q&A.106 #21

. . Floor-Offset Plan .... FAS106, ¶63 — P40.158 — Q&A.106 #50

.... FAS106, ¶104 — P40.196

. . Measurement Date.................................. FAS106, ¶73 — P40.168

Nonqualifying Assets................................... FAS106, ¶64 — P40.159 — Q&A.106 #36

.... FAS106, ¶67 — P40.162

Non-U.S. Postretirement Benefit Plans........ FAS106, ¶85 — P40.181

Other Welfare Benefits .... FAS106, ¶6 — P40.102

Pay-Related Plans....................................... FAS106, ¶33 — P40.128

. . Illustration... FAS106, ¶399-400 — P40.211-212

Plan Amendments.. FAS106, ¶28 — P40.121

.... FAS106, ¶45 — P40.140

.... FAS106, ¶50-52 — P40.145-147

.... FAS106, ¶54-55 — P40.149-150

.... FAS106, ¶174

. . Amortization of Prior Service Cost....... FAS106, ¶50-55 — P40.145-150

. . History of Regular Plan Amendments .. FAS106, ¶54 — P40.149

. . Illustration... FAS106, ¶423-428 — P40.231-236

.... FAS106, ¶449-454 — P40.246-251

. . Negative Plan Amendment.................... FAS106, ¶55 — P40.150 — Q&A.106 #23-25

.... FAS106, ¶96-99 — P40.188-191 — Q&A.106 #28-30

.... — — — Q&A.106 #57

. . Recognition of Prior Service Cost in a
    Curtailment .... FAS106, ¶97 — P40.189

. . Requires Remeasurement of Net
    Periodic Postretirement Benefit Cost . FAS106, ¶73 — P40.168

. . That Both Increases and Decreases
    Benefits .... FAS106, ¶51-53 — P40.146-148 — Q&A.106 #31

.... FAS106, ¶55 — P40.150

. . That Results in a Curtailment................ FAS106, ¶55 — P40.150 — Q&A.106 #28

.... FAS106, ¶96-99 — P40.188-191 — Q&A.106 #30

. . When Effect of Negative Plan
    Amendments Should Be Recognized.. FAS106, ¶55 — P40.150 — Q&A.106 #23

Plan Assets.. FAS106, ¶63 — P40.158 — Q&A.106 #36-38

.... FAS106, ¶308

. . Actual Return on Plan Assets............... FAS106, ¶22 — P40.115

.... FAS106, ¶46 — P40.141

.... FAS106, ¶49 — P40.144

.... FAS106, ¶58 — P40.153

.... FAS106, ¶295

. . Asset Gains and Losses .... FAS106, ¶58 — P40.153

. . Assets That Do Not Qualify as Plan
    Assets .... FAS106, ¶64 — P40.159

.... FAS106, ¶67 — P40.162

See "Terminology" for references to defined terms presented in various accounting pronouncements.
See the Introduction to the Topical Index for details on the use of this index.

	Original Pronouncements	Current Text	EITF and Other
POSTRETIREMENT BENEFITS OTHER THAN PENSIONS—continued			
Plan Assets—continued			
. . Bankruptcy Proof	FAS106, ¶63-64	P40.158-159	Q&A.106 #36
. . Classes of Assets	FAS106, ¶57	P40.152	
. . Employer-Issued Debt or Equity Securities	FAS106, ¶63-64	P40.158-159	Q&A.106 #37-38
. . Employer-Issued Securities	FAS106, ¶63	P40.158	
. . Expected (Long-Term Rate of) Return on Plan Assets	FAS106, ¶32	P40.127	
	FAS106, ¶57-58	P40.152-153	
. . Fair Value	FAS106, ¶49	P40.144	
	FAS106, ¶57	P40.152	
	FAS106, ¶65-66	P40.160-161	
	FAS106, ¶69	P40.164	
. . Floor-Offset Plan			Q&A.106 #50
. . Gains and Losses	FAS106, ¶56-60	P40.151-155	
	FAS106, ¶62	P40.157	
. . Illustration	FAS106, ¶468	P40.265	
. . Insurance Contracts	FAS106, ¶67-69	P40.162-164	
. . Market-Related Value of Plan Assets	FAS106, ¶32	P40.127	
	FAS106, ¶57-59	P40.152-154	
. . Measurement Date	FAS106, ¶65	P40.160	
	FAS106, ¶72	P40.167	
. . Measurement of Plan Assets	FAS106, ¶63-66	P40.158-161	
	FAS106, ¶308		
. . Participation Rights	FAS106, ¶67-69	P40.162-164	
. . Rabbi Trust	FAS106, ¶63-64	P40.158-159	Q&A.106 #36
. . Tax Implications	FAS106, ¶49	P40.144	
	FAS106, ¶295		
. . Used in Plan Operations	FAS106, ¶66	P40.161	
Plan Benefit Formula	FAS106, ¶18	P40.111	
	FAS106, ¶43-44	P40.138-139	
Plans			
. . Accounting for Two or More Plans	FAS106, ¶21	P40.114	Q&A.106 #16
	FAS106, ¶44	P40.139	Q&A.106 #41-42
	FAS106, ¶76	P40.171	Q&A.106 #54
. . Floor-Offset Plan			Q&A.106 #49-50
. . Multiemployer Plans	FAS106, ¶79-83	P40.174-179	Q&A.106 #43-44
	FAS106, ¶377		
. . Successor Plan	FAS106, ¶100	P40.192	Q&A.106 #44
Plan Termination	FAS106, ¶90	P40.182	Q&A.106 #44
	FAS106, ¶100	P40.192	Q&A.106 #46
Postretirement Benefit Plan	FAS106, ¶6-8	P40.102-104	
	FAS106, ¶10	P40.106	
Postretirement Health Care Benefits	FAS106, ¶6	P40.102	
	FAS106, ¶136-137		
Prior Service Cost	FAS106, ¶30	P40.123	
	FAS106, ¶50-55	P40.145-150	
. . Illustration	FAS106, ¶449-454	P40.246-251	

FAS–FASB Statements   FIN–FASB Interpretations   FTB–FASB Technical Bulletins
APB–APB Opinions   AIN–AICPA Interpretations   ARB–Accounting Research Bulletins
CON–FASB Concepts   EITF–EITF Issues   Q&A–FASB Special Reports

	Original Pronouncements	Current Text	EITF and Other
POSTRETIREMENT BENEFITS			
OTHER THAN PENSIONS—continued			
Prior Service Cost—continued			
. . Newly Created Negative Prior Service			
Cost	FAS106, ¶55	P40.150	Q&A.106 #28
	FAS106, ¶96-99	P40.188-191	Q&A.106 #30
. . Related to a Curtailment	FAS106, ¶97	P40.189	
. . Unrecognized Negative Prior Service			
Cost	FAS106, ¶55	P40.150	Q&A.106 #29-30
	FAS106, ¶96-99	P40.188-191	
. . Unrecognized Prior Service Cost	FAS106, ¶55	P40.150	Q&A.106 #27-30
	FAS106, ¶96-99	P40.188-191	
. . Unrecognized Transition Obligation	FAS106, ¶97	P40.189	Q&A.106 #27
Rate-Regulated Enterprises	FAS106, ¶364	Re6.155	
Scope of Accounting and Reporting			
Requirements	FAS106, ¶6-11	P40.102-107	Q&A.106 #1-3
. . Disabled Employees	FAS106, ¶6	P40.102	Q&A.106 #1
	FAS106, ¶136-137		
Selection of Discount Rate to Be Used to			
Measure Obligation			EITF.D-36
Service Cost Component (of Net Periodic			
Postretirement Benefit Cost)	FAS106, ¶22	P40.115	Q&A.106 #12
	FAS106, ¶28-31	P40.121-123	Q&A.106 #21
	FAS106, ¶70	P40.126	
		P40.165	
. . Measurement of	FAS106, ¶33	P40.128	
	FAS106, ¶47	P40.142	
Settlement of a Plan	FAS106, ¶68	P40.163	
	FAS106, ¶90-95	P40.182-187	
	FAS106, ¶100	P40.192	
. . Additional Recognition of Transition			
Obligation	FAS106, ¶113	P40.201	
. . Illustration	FAS106, ¶484-495	P40.281-292	
. . Illustration, with Curtailment	FAS106, ¶502-506	P40.299-303	
. . Pension Benefits Compensate for the			
Elimination of Postretirement			
Benefits	FAS106, ¶90	P40.182	Q&A.106 #46
	FAS106, ¶93	P40.185	
	FAS106, ¶100	P40.192	
Substantive Plan	FAS106, ¶23-28	P40.116-121	Q&A.106 #6-7
. . Determination of	FAS106, ¶8	P40.104	Q&A.106 #3
	FAS106, ¶16-17	P40.109-110	Q&A.106 #6-7
	FAS106, ¶23-26	P40.116-119	Q&A.106 #23
			Q&A.106 #57
. . Deviation from	FAS106, ¶61	P40.156	
. . Purchase Business Combination	FAS106, ¶86	B50.146	
. . Temporary Deviation from	FAS106, ¶61	P40.156	Q&A.106 #33-35
Successor Plan	FAS106, ¶100	P40.192	Q&A.106 #44

See "Terminology" for references to defined terms presented in various accounting pronouncements.
See the Introduction to the Topical Index for details on the use of this index.

	Original Pronouncements	Current Text	EITF and Other
POSTRETIREMENT BENEFITS			
OTHER THAN PENSIONS—continued			
Termination Benefits	FAS106, ¶6	P40.102	Q&A.106 #47-48
	FAS106, ¶101-102	P40.193-194	
	FAS106, ¶333		
. . Illustration	FAS106, ¶507-511	P40.302-308	
Transition	FAS106, ¶108	P40.141	Q&A.106 #55-64
	FAS106, ¶110-112		
. . Discontinued Operations			Q&A.106 #60-61
. . Effect of Implementation Guidance for Employers that Previously Adopted Statement 106			Q&A.106 #55
. . Effect on Transition Amount of a Negative Plan Amendment in Year of Adoption			Q&A.106 #57
. . Electing a Transition Method			Q&A.106 #56
			Q&A.106 #58-60
			Q&A.106 #62
. . Employer with More Than One Plan			Q&A.106 #56
			Q&A.106 #59
			Q&A.106 #62
. . Financial Statement Presentation of Transition Amount			Q&A.106 #61
. . Foreign Plans			Q&A.106 #62
. . Immediate Recognition of Transition Amount			Q&A.106 #55-56
			Q&A.106 #58-59
			Q&A.106 #62-63
. . Investor and Equity Method Investee Electing Different Transition Methods			Q&A.106 #51
. . Parent and Subsidiary Electing Different Transition Methods			Q&A.106 #56
. . Transition Period			Q&A.106 #64
. . Write-off of Goodwill Included in Cumulative Effect Adjustment			Q&A.106 #63
Transition Obligation or Asset	FAS106, ¶110	P40.141	
. . Illustration	FAS106, ¶418-419	P40.226-227	
	FAS106, ¶430	P40.238-245	
	FAS106, ¶435-437		
	FAS106, ¶439-442		
Unfunded Plans			
. . Aggregating Data for Measurement Purposes	FAS106, ¶75-76	P40.170-171	
	FAS106, ¶357		

FAS–FASB Statements FIN–FASB Interpretations FTB–FASB Technical Bulletins
APB–APB Opinions AIN–AICPA Interpretations ARB–Accounting Research Bulletins
CON–FASB Concepts EITF–EITF Issues Q&A–FASB Special Reports

	Original Pronouncements	Current Text	EITF and Other

POSTRETIREMENT BENEFITS
OTHER THAN PENSIONS—continued

Unrecognized Net Gain or Loss	FAS106, ¶59-60	P40.154-155	Q&A.106 #32
	FAS106, ¶62	P40.157	
	FAS106, ¶92-93	P40.184-185	
	FAS106, ¶98	P40.190	
. . Amortization of	FAS106, ¶22	P40.115	
	FAS106, ¶46	P40.141	
	FAS106, ¶59-60	P40.154-155	
. . Corridor Approach	FAS106, ¶59	P40.154	
. . Illustration	FAS106, ¶455-471	P40.252-268	
Unrecognized Prior Service Cost	FAS106, ¶50-55	P40.145-150	Q&A.106 #27-30
	FAS106, ¶96-99	P40.188-191	
. . Amortization of	FAS106, ¶22	P40.115	
	FAS106, ¶46	P40.141	
	FAS106, ¶52-53	P40.147-148	
. . Illustration	FAS106, ¶449-454	P40.246-251	
Unrecognized Transition Obligation or Transition Asset			
. . Accounting for a Curtailment	FAS106, ¶96-99	P40.188-191	Q&A.106 #27
			Q&A.106 #30
. . Additional Recognition Required	FAS106, ¶55	P40.150	
	FAS106, ¶60	P40.155	
	FAS106, ¶93	P40.185	
	FAS106, ¶97-98	P40.189-190	
	FAS106, ¶113	P40.201	
. . Amortization of	FAS106, ¶22	P40.115	
	FAS106, ¶46	P40.141	
	FAS106, ¶112	P40.200	
. . Illustration	FAS106, ¶430	P40.238-245	
	FAS106, ¶435-437		
	FAS106, ¶439-442		
Unwritten Plans	FAS106, ¶8	P40.104	Q&A.106 #3
Use of Reasonable Approximations	FAS106, ¶15	P40.108	

POSTRETIREMENT HEALTH CARE
AND LIFE INSURANCE BENEFITS

See Disclosure			
See Postretirement Benefits Other Than Pensions			
Business Combinations			
. . Unfunded Vested Obligations			EITF.86-20
Change in Accounting Method			EITF.86-19
Definition			
. . Health Care Benefits	FAS81, ¶5	P50.401	
. . Postemployment	FAS81, ¶1	P50.402	
. . Postretirement	FAS81, ¶1	P50.403	
Illustrations	FAS81, ¶10-12	P50.104-106	
Scope of Accounting and Reporting Requirements	FAS81, ¶5	P50.101	
	FAS81, ¶30		

See "Terminology" for references to defined terms presented in various accounting pronouncements.
See the Introduction to the Topical Index for details on the use of this index.

	Original Pronouncements	Current Text	EITF and Other

POSTRETIREMENT WELFARE BENEFITS
See Postretirement Benefits Other Than Pensions

PRACTICABILITY
See Financial Instruments

PREACQUISTION CONTINGENCIES
See Business Combinations

PRECIOUS METALS
Inventory Valuation .... ARB43, Ch.4, ¶16   I78.119

PRECISION
Relation to Representational Faithfulness... CON2, ¶72-76

PREDICTIVE VALUE
Definition .... CON2, ¶53-55
.... CON2, Glossary

PREFERRED STOCK
See Capital Stock: Capital Transactions
See Capital Stock: Preferred Stock
See Conversion of Debt
See Earnings per Share
See Financial Instruments
Characteristics.. CON6, ¶55
Convertible Preferred Stock Held by an ESOP
. . Computation of Sponsor's Earnings
    per Share EITF.89-12
Effect of a Redemption Agreement on
  Carrying Value of Investment....................   EITF.85-23
Foreign.. FAS52, ¶48   F60.147
Issued to Extinguish Debt Early................. FAS111, ¶8   D14.501-504
.... FTB80-1, ¶1-4
Redeemable Stock .... FAS47, ¶9-10   C32.104-105
.... FAS47, ¶31-32   C32.113-114
. . Purchase by Parent Company EITF.86-32
Redemption or Induced Conversion
. . Calculation of Earnings per Share EITF.D-42
Sale of Preferred Stocks with a Put
  Option...   EITF.85-25

PREMATURITY COSTS AND PERIOD
See Cable Television Industry

PREMIUM ON DEBT
See Interest: Imputation of an Interest Cost

PREOPERATING COSTS
See Development Stage Enterprises

PREPAID EXPENSES
Balance Sheet Classification .... ARB43, Ch.3A, ¶6   B05.107

PREPAYMENT OF DEBT
See Debt: Extinguishments

FAS–FASB Statements   FIN–FASB Interpretations   FTB–FASB Technical Bulletins
APB–APB Opinions   AIN–AICPA Interpretations   ARB–Accounting Research Bulletins
CON–FASB Concepts   EITF–EITF Issues   Q&A–FASB Special Reports

	Original Pronouncements	Current Text	EITF and Other
PREPAYMENTS			
Qualification as Assets	CON6, ¶176		
PREPRODUCTION COSTS			
See Research and Development			
PRESENT VALUE			
See Contributions			
See Defined Benefit Pension Plans			
See Discounting			
See Impairment: Loans			
See Interest: Imputation of an Interest Cost			
See Leases			
Accounting for the Present Value of Future Profits Resulting from the Acquisition of a Life Insurance Company			EITF.92-9
Definition			
. . Actuarially Computed Value	FAS87, ¶264	P16.403	
Foreign Currency Exchange Contracts			EITF.87-2
Recognition and Measurement			
. . Measurement Attribute	CON5, ¶67		
PRETAX ACCOUNTING INCOME			
See Income Taxes			
Definition	APB23, ¶21	Bt7.405	
PRICE CONTROLS			
Regulated Operations	FAS71, ¶8	Re6.118	
PRICE INDEXES			
See Changing Prices: Reporting Their Effects in Financial Reports			
PRICE LEVEL CHANGES			
See Changing Prices: Reporting Their Effects in Financial Reports			
Monetary Unit or Measurement Scale			
. . Effect on	CON5, ¶71-72		
Relation to Capital Maintenance	CON6, ¶71		
Relation to Comprehensive Income	CON6, ¶73-75		
PRICE RENEGOTIATION			
See Contractor Accounting: Government Contracts			
PRIMARY EARNINGS PER SHARE			
See Earnings per Share			
Definition	APB15, App.D	E09.419	
PRINCIPAL-ONLY SECURITIES			
Exchange of Interest-Only and Principal-Only Securities for a Mortgage-Backed Security			EITF.90-2
Sale of Principal-Only Cash Flows from Loans Receivable			
. . Determination of Gain or Loss			EITF.88-11
. . Determination of Remaining Recorded Investment for Portion of Loan Retained			EITF.88-11

See "Terminology" for references to defined terms presented in various accounting pronouncements.
See the Introduction to the Topical Index for details on the use of this index.

	Original Pronouncements	Current Text	EITF and Other

PRINCIPLES OF CONSOLIDATION
See Accounting Policies
See Consolidation
PRIOR-PERIOD ADJUSTMENTS
See Adjustments of Financial Statements
  for Prior Periods
See Earnings per Share
See Extraordinary Items
See Income Statement Presentation:
  Discontinued Operations
See Income Taxes
See Investments: Equity Method
Exclusion from Earnings for the Current
  Period .... CON5, ¶34
PRIVATE FOUNDATIONS
See Not-for-Profit Organizations
**PRO FORMA FINANCIAL
  STATEMENTS**
See Accounting Changes
See Business Combinations
PROBABLE
See Contingencies
Definition .... CON6, ¶25   Re6.405
   .... CON6, ¶35
   .... FAS90, ¶9
PRODUCT DEVELOPMENT COSTS
See Computer Software
See Research and Development
**PRODUCT FINANCING
  ARRANGEMENTS**
See Debt: Product Financing
  Arrangements
PRODUCT GUARANTEES
See Contingencies
See Warranties
**PRODUCT MAINTENANCE
  CONTRACTS**
See Revenue Recognition
PRODUCTION COSTS
See Cable Television Industry
See Computer Software
See Motion Picture Industry
See Oil and Gas Producing Activities
See Record and Music Industry
PROFIT AND LOSS
Definition .... CON6, ¶16
Relation to Comprehensive Income .... CON6, ¶16
PROFIT AND LOSS STATEMENT
See Income Statement

FAS–FASB Statements   FIN–FASB Interpretations   FTB–FASB Technical Bulletins
APB–APB Opinions   AIN–AICPA Interpretations   ARB–Accounting Research Bulletins
CON–FASB Concepts   EITF–EITF Issues   Q&A–FASB Special Reports

	Original Pronouncements	Current Text	EITF and Other
PROFIT AND LOSS STATEMENT—continued			
See Income Statement Presentation: Discontinued Operations			
PROFIT-SHARING PLANS			
See Compensation to Employees: Deferred			
See Earnings per Share			
See Pension Costs			
PROPERTY AND CASUALTY INSURANCE ENTERPRISES			
See Insurance Industry			
PROPERTY DIVIDENDS			
See Capital Stock: Dividends-in-Kind			
PROPERTY, PLANT, AND EQUIPMENT			
See Depreciation			
See Impairment: Long-Lived Assets			
Cash Flows Reporting	FAS95, ¶15-17	C25.113-115	
	FAS95, ¶24	C25.122	
Duplicate Facilities following a Purchase Business Combination			
. . Costs of Closing Duplicate Facilities of an Acquirer	FTB85-5, ¶1-2	B50.651-652	EITF.84-35
Environmentally Contaminated Property			
. . Costs Incurred to Clean Up Environmental Contamination			EITF.90-8
Idle Facilities			EITF.84-28
Property with Asbestos			
. . Costs Incurred for Asbestos Treatment			EITF.89-13
Revenue Recognition on Sales with a Guaranteed Minimum Resale Value			EITF.95-1
Segment of Business Reporting	FAS14, ¶27	S20.133	
Write-downs			
. . Of Operating Assets	FAS5, ¶31	C59.137	EITF.84-28
. . Relation to Contingencies	FAS5, ¶31	C59.102	
PROPERTY TAXES			
Accounting for Special Assessments and Tax Increment Financing Entities (TIFEs)			EITF.91-10
PROPORTIONATE CONSOLIDATION			
See Consolidation			
See Oil and Gas Producing Activities			
PUBLIC UTILITIES			
See Regulated Operations			
PUBLICLY TRADED ENTERPRISE			
See Interim Financial Reporting			
Definition	FAS69, ¶1	Oi5.405A	

See "Terminology" for references to defined terms presented in various accounting pronouncements.
See the Introduction to the Topical Index for details on the use of this index.

	Original Pronouncements	Current Text	EITF and Other
PURCHASE ACCOUNTING (ACQUISITIONS)			
See Business Combinations			
See Earnings per Share			
PURCHASE COMMITMENTS			
See Commitments: Long-Term Obligations			
PURCHASE METHOD			
See Business Combinations			
See Income Taxes			
See Intangible Assets			
Definition	APB16, ¶44	B50.407	
PURCHASE OF OWN CAPITAL STOCK			
See Capital Stock: Treasury Stock			
PURCHASE OF OWN DEBT			
See Debt: Extinguishments			
PURCHASE OF TREASURY STOCK			
See Capital Stock: Treasury Stock			
See Earnings per Share			
PURCHASED RESEARCH AND DEVELOPMENT			
See Research and Development			
PURCHASING POWER GAIN OR LOSS ON NET MONETARY ITEMS			
See Changing Prices: Reporting Their Effects in Financial Reports			
PUSH-DOWN ACCOUNTING			
See Business Combinations			
See Change in Basis of Assets and Liabilities			
Debt of Parent Company			EITF.84-23
			EITF.84-42
IRC Section 338 and Push-Down Accounting			EITF.86-9
Subsidiaries			
. . New Basis of Accounting Resulting from Change in Ownership			EITF.85-21
PUT OPTIONS			
See Financial Instruments			
See Options			
Accounting for Financial Instruments Indexed to, and Potentially Settled in, a Company's Own Stock			EITF.94-7
Convertible Debt with a Premium Put			EITF.85-29
Effect of a Redemption Agreement on Carrying Value of Investment			EITF.85-23
Indexed Debt Instruments			EITF.86-28
Issuance of Debt with Put Warrants			EITF.88-9

	Original Pronouncements	Current Text	EITF and Other
PUT OPTIONS—continued			
Sale of Marketable Securities That Are Puttable to Seller			EITF.84-5
			EITF.85-30
			EITF.85-40
Sale of Preferred Stocks That Are Puttable to Seller			EITF.85-25
Sale of Put Options on Issuer's Stock			EITF.87-31
Securities with a Put Option Held by an ESOP			
. . Sponsor's Balance Sheet Classification			EITF.89-11
Stock Purchased at Discount Puttable to Issuer			EITF.84-34
PUT WARRANTS			
See Financial Instruments			
Balance Sheet Classification			EITF.88-9
Effect on Earnings per Share Calculation			EITF.88-9
PYRAMIDING OF STOCK OPTIONS			
See Compensation to Employees: Stock Purchase and Stock Options Plans			

(The next page is T-345.)

See "Terminology" for references to defined terms presented in various accounting pronouncements.
See the Introduction to the Topical Index for details on the use of this index.

	Original Pronouncements	Current Text	EITF and Other

QUALITATIVE CHARACTERISTICS

Choice between Accounting Methods .... CON2, ¶6-20
Comparability .... CON2, ¶111-122
Conservatism .... CON2, ¶91-97
Costs and Benefits .... CON2, ¶133-144
Decision Making .... CON2, ¶36-39
Exposure Draft Comments and Responses. CON2, ¶152-160
Glossary .... CON2, Glossary
Hierarchy of Accounting Qualities.............. CON2, ¶32-45
Materiality.. CON2, ¶123-132
Nature of Accounting Choices .... CON2, ¶6-20
Neutrality .... CON2, ¶98-110
Recognition Criteria Derived from .... CON5, ¶61
Relation to Elements of Financial
  Statements .... CON6, ¶9-19
Relation to Objectives of Financial
  Reporting... CON2, ¶21-26
Relation to Recognition, Measurement,
  and Display.. CON6, ¶23
Relation to Role of Decision Making .... CON2, ¶27-31
Relative Importance and Trade-offs .... CON2, ¶42-45
Relevance.. CON2, ¶46-57
Reliability... CON2, ¶58-97
Representational Faithfulness .... CON2, ¶63-80
Timeliness... CON2, ¶56-57
Understandability.. CON2, ¶40-41
Verifiability .... CON2, ¶81-89

QUARTERLY FINANCIAL STATEMENTS

See Interim Financial Reporting

QUASI REORGANIZATIONS

See Capital Stock: Capital Transactions
See Debt: Restructurings
See Disclosure
See Income Taxes
Readjustments.. ARB43, Ch.7A, ¶2-3   Q15.102
....   Q15.104
. . Accounting after, Additional Paid-in
    Capital.. ARB43, Ch.7A, ¶11   Q15.112
. . Accounting after, Retained Earnings .... ARB43, Ch.7A, ¶10   Q15.111
                                                                           ARB46, ¶2
. . Accounting after, Similar to New
    Enterprise .... ARB43, Ch.7A, ¶9   Q15.110
. . Charge to Retained Earnings,
    Additional Paid-in Capital.................. ARB43, Ch.7A, ¶6   Q15.107
. . Effective Date of Readjustment .... ARB43, Ch.7A, ¶8   Q15.109
. . Fair Value of Assets Carried Forward ... ARB43, Ch.7A, ¶4   Q15.105
. . Losses, Provision for............................. ARB43, Ch.7A, ¶5   Q15.106
. . Retained Earnings of Subsidiaries .... ARB43, Ch.7A, ¶7   Q15.108

	Original Pronouncements	Current Text	EITF and Other
QUASI REORGANIZATIONS—continued			
Readjustments—continued			
. . Scope of Accounting and Reporting Requirements	ARB43, Ch.7A, ¶12	Q15.103	
Reorganization of Financial Affairs of Enterprise	ARB43, Ch.7A, ¶1	Q15.101	
Tax Benefits	FAS109, ¶39	I27.138	
		Q15.113	

(The next page is T-351.)

See "Terminology" for references to defined terms presented in various accounting pronouncements.
See the Introduction to the Topical Index for details on the use of this index.

	Original Pronouncements	Current Text	EITF and Other

RAILROAD ENTERPRISES
Retirement-Replacement-Betterment
(RRB) Accounting
  See Adjustments of Financial
   Statements for Prior Periods
RATE-MAKING PROCESS
See Regulated Operations
RATE REGULATED INDUSTRIES
See Regulated Operations
RAW MATERIALS
See Inventory
Balance Sheet Classification ...... ARB43, Ch.3A, ¶4   B05.105
REACQUIRED STOCK
See Capital Stock: Treasury Stock
READJUSTMENTS
See Quasi Reorganizations
REAL AND PERSONAL PROPERTY TAXES
See Tax
REAL ESTATE
See Disclosure
See Leases
See Real Estate Enterprises
See Real Estate: Sales Other Than Retail
  Land Sales
Accounting for Limited Partnership
  Investments
. . Reporting by SEC Registrants EITF.D-46
Accounting for Special Assessments and
  Tax Increment Financing Entities
  (TIFEs) EITF.91-10
Accounting for Tax Benefits Resulting
  from Investments in Qualified Affordable
  Housing Projects EITF.94-1
Acquisition, Development and
  Construction Loans EITF.84-4
  ....   EITF.86-21
Basis of Assets
. . Adjustments for Payments during
   Rent-up Period EITF.85-27
Condominium Units .... FAS66, ¶37   R10.140
Cost Recovery Method of Profit
  Recognition .... FAS66, ¶22-24   R10.125-127
  .... FAS66, ¶32   R10.135
  .... FAS66, ¶35   R10.138
  .... FAS66, ¶62-64   R10.156-158
Debtor's Accounting for Forfeiture of Real
  Estate Subject to a Nonrecourse
  Mortgage EITF.91-2
Decision Trees for Accounting and
  Reporting .... FAS66, ¶123   R10.178
  ....   Re1.196

FAS–FASB Statements   FIN–FASB Interpretations   FTB–FASB Technical Bulletins
APB–APB Opinions   AIN–AICPA Interpretations   ARB–Accounting Research Bulletins
CON–FASB Concepts   EITF–EITF Issues   Q&A–FASB Special Reports

	Original Pronouncements	Current Text	EITF and Other
REAL ESTATE—continued			
Deposit Method of Profit Recognition	FAS66, ¶20-22	R10.123-125	EITF.86-7
	FAS66, ¶28	R10.131	
	FAS66, ¶32	R10.135	
	FAS66, ¶37	R10.140	
	FAS66, ¶65-67	R10.159-161	
. . Sale-Leaseback Transaction	FAS98, ¶30-33	L10.160D-160G	
Disclosure	FAS66, ¶65		
Exchanges Involving Boot			EITF.87-29
Financing Method			
. . Sale-Leaseback Transaction	FAS98, ¶34-39	L10.160H-160M	
Financing, Leasing, or Profit-Sharing			
Arrangements	FAS66, ¶26-29	R10.129-132	
Foreclosure			
. . Valuation When Sale Was Accounted for under Installment or Cost Recovery Method			EITF.89-14
Full Accrual Method of Profit Recognition	FAS66, ¶3-18	R10.106-121	
	FAS66, ¶53-54	R10.147-148	
. . Antispeculation Clause			EITF.86-6
. . Buyer's Initial and Continuing Investment			EITF.87-9
			EITF.88-12
. . Graduated Payment Mortgages			EITF.84-17
. . Mortgage Insurance/Guarantee			EITF.87-9
Income-Producing			
. . Changing Prices Information	FAS89, ¶25	C28.121	
Installment Method of Profit Recognition	FAS66, ¶22-23	R10.125-126	
	FAS66, ¶35	R10.138	
	FAS66, ¶56-61	R10.150-155	
	FAS66, ¶90	R10.177	
. . Antispeculation Clause			EITF.86-6
. . Sale-Leaseback Transaction	FAS98, ¶28-29	L10.160B-160C	
Leveraged Leases of Real Estate			EITF.85-16
Lines of Credit	FAS66, ¶9	R10.112	
Management Services			
. . Compensation Imputed	FAS66, ¶31	R10.134	
Partial Sales Transactions	FAS66, ¶33-36	R10.136-139	
Percentage-of-Completion Method of Profit Recognition	FAS66, ¶37	R10.140	EITF.86-7
	FAS66, ¶41-42	R10.144-145	
	FAS66, ¶75	R10.154	
Profit Recognition			
. . Antispeculation Clause			EITF.86-6
. . Collateral Securing Buyer's Note			EITF.88-12
. . Construction of House on Builder's Lot			EITF.86-7
. . Contract Sales for House and Lot			EITF.86-7
. . Illustrations of Calculations	FAS66, ¶69	R10.163	
. . Mortgage Insurance Guarantee			EITF.87-9

See "Terminology" for references to defined terms presented in various accounting pronouncements.
See the Introduction to the Topical Index for details on the use of this index.

	Original Pronouncements	Current Text	EITF and Other
REAL ESTATE—continued			
Profit Recognition—continued			
. . Pledging of Ownership Interest as Part of Down Payment			EITF.88-12
Profit Recognition, Full Accrual Method Inappropriate	FAS66, ¶19-39	R10.122-146	
	FAS66, ¶41-43		
	FAS98, ¶23		
. . Continuing Involvement without Transfer of Risks and Rewards	FAS66, ¶18	R10.121	
Profit Recognition, Illustrations	FAS66, ¶77-90	R10.164-177	
Real Estate Investment Trusts (REITs)			EITF.94-2
Reduced Profit Method of Profit Recognition	FAS66, ¶23	R10.126	
	FAS66, ¶68-69	R10.162-163	
Revenue Recognition			
. . Syndication Fee			EITF.85-37
Sale of Property Improvements Involving Land Lease	FAS66, ¶38-39	R10.141-142	
Sale-Leaseback Transaction	FAS98, ¶6-14	L10.130A-130M	
	FAS98, ¶17-19	L10.155-160M	
	FAS98, ¶23	R10.143	
. . Loans to Buyers by Sellers			EITF.84-37
. . Rental Shortfall Agreements			EITF.84-37
. . Repurchase Options			EITF.84-37
. . Short Initial Lease Term with Renewal Options			EITF.84-37
. . Subleases			EITF.84-37
Scope of Accounting and Reporting Requirements	FAS66, ¶1-2	R10.101-105	
	FAS67, ¶1-2		
Sellers' Continuing Involvement	FAS66, ¶33	R10.146	
. . Antispeculation Clause			EITF.86-6
Support-Operations	FAS66, ¶29	R10.132	
	FAS66, ¶31	R10.134	
	FAS66, ¶33	R10.136	
	FAS66, ¶36	R10.139	
Syndication			
. . Recognition of Receipts from Made-up Rental Shortfalls			EITF.85-27
Time-Sharing Interests	FAS66, ¶37	R10.140	
Transfers between Entities under Common Control			EITF.84-39
Treatment of Minority Interests in Certain Real Estate Investment Trusts			EITF.94-2
Umbrella Partnership Real Estate Investment Trust (UPREIT)			EITF.94-2
REAL ESTATE: COSTS AND INITIAL OPERATIONS OF REAL ESTATE PROJECTS			
Abandonments	FAS67, ¶13-14	Re2.113-114	

FAS–FASB Statements	FIN–FASB Interpretations	FTB–FASB Technical Bulletins
APB–APB Opinions	AIN–AICPA Interpretations	ARB–Accounting Research Bulletins
CON–FASB Concepts	EITF–EITF Issues	Q&A–FASB Special Reports

	Original Pronouncements	Current Text	EITF and Other
REAL ESTATE: COSTS AND INITIAL OPERATIONS OF REAL ESTATE PROJECTS—continued			
Allocation of Capitalized Costs to Components of a Project	FAS67, ¶11	Re2.111	
Amenities	FAS67, ¶8-9	Re2.108-109	
Changes in Use	FAS67, ¶15	Re2.115	
Common Costs	FAS67, ¶8-9	Re2.108-109	
Costs Incurred to Rent Real Estate Projects	FAS67, ¶20-21	Re2.120-121	
Costs Incurred to Sell Real Estate Projects	FAS67, ¶17-19	Re2.117-119	
Donations to Municipalities or Government Agencies	FAS67, ¶14	Re2.114	
Glossary	FAS67, ¶28	Re2.401-414	
Incidental Operations	FAS67, ¶10	Re2.110	
Indirect Project Costs	FAS67, ¶7	Re2.107	
Initial Rental Operations	FAS67, ¶22-23	Re2.122-123	
Preacquisition Costs	FAS67, ¶4-5	Re2.104-105	
Project Costs	FAS67, ¶7	Re2.107	
Recoverability of Costs	FAS67, ¶24	Re2.124	
	FAS121, ¶31		
Revisions of Estimates	FAS67, ¶12	Re2.112	
Scope of Accounting and Reporting Requirements	FAS67, ¶2	Re2.102	
	FAS121, ¶31		
Taxes and Insurance	FAS67, ¶6	Re2.106	
REAL ESTATE DEVELOPMENT			
See Real Estate: Costs and Initial Operations of Real Estate Projects			
REAL ESTATE ENTERPRISES			
See Real Estate: Costs and Initial Operations of Real Estate Projects			
See Real Estate: Retail Land Sales			
Real Estate Syndicators			
. . Recognition of Note Received for Syndication Activities			EITF.85-37
. . Revenue Recognition of Syndication Fees			EITF.85-37
Unclassified Balance Sheet	FAS67, ¶7	B05.102	
REAL ESTATE INVESTMENT TRUST (REIT)			
See Real Estate			
REAL ESTATE MORTGAGE INVESTMENT CONDUITS (REMICs)			
See Financial Instruments			
Purchased Investment			EITF.89-4
. . Impairment Recognition			EITF.93-18
REAL ESTATE: RETAIL LAND SALES			
See Disclosure			
Deposit Method of Profit Recognition	FAS66, ¶48	Re1.148	

See "Terminology" for references to defined terms presented in various accounting pronouncements.
See the Introduction to the Topical Index for details on the use of this index.

	Original Pronouncements	Current Text	EITF and Other

REAL ESTATE: RETAIL LAND SALES—continued

Full Accrual Method of Profit

Recognition	FAS66, ¶45	Rel.145	
	FAS66, ¶70-72	Rel.168-170	
Installment Method of Profit Recognition	FAS66, ¶47	Rel.147	
	FAS66, ¶90	Rel.188	

Percentage-of-Completion Method of

Profit Recognition	FAS66, ¶46	R10.154	
	FAS66, ¶61	Rel.146	
	FAS66, ¶73-75	Rel.171-173	
	FAS66, ¶91-95	Rel.189-193	
Profit Recognition	FAS66, ¶44	Rel.144	
. . Illustrations	FAS66, ¶91-97	Rel.189-195	

Scope of Accounting and Reporting

| Requirements | FAS66, ¶1-2 | Rel.101-102 | |

REAL ESTATE: SALES

Buyer's Initial Investment

| . . Effect of Various Forms of Financing | | | EITF.88-24 |

Cost Recovery Method of Profit Recognition

| . . Effect of Various Forms of Financing | | | EITF.88-24 |

Installment Method of Profit Recognition

| . . Effect of Various Forms of Financing | | | EITF.88-24 |

REAL ESTATE: SALES OTHER THAN RETAIL LAND SALES

See Disclosure

Buyer's Initial Investment

. . Collateral Securing Buyer's Note			EITF.88-12
. . Compliance with FHA or VA Program Requirements			EITF.87-9
. . Effect of Various Forms of Financing			EITF.88-24
. . Mortgage Insurance			EITF.84-17
			EITF.87-9
. . Pledging of Ownership Interest as Part of Down Payment			EITF.88-12
			EITF.87-9
. . Surety Bonds			EITF.87-9
Condominium Units	FAS66, ¶37	Rel.137	

Cost Recovery Method of Profit

Recognition	FAS66, ¶22-24	Rel.122-124	
	FAS66, ¶32	Rel.132	
	FAS66, ¶35	Rel.135	
	FAS66, ¶62-64	Rel.160-162	
. . Effect of Various Forms of Financing			EITF.88-24
Deposit Method of Profit Recognition	FAS66, ¶20-22	Rel.120-122	
	FAS66, ¶28	Rel.128	
	FAS66, ¶32	Rel.132	
	FAS66, ¶37	Rel.137	
	FAS66, ¶65-67	Rel.163-165	
. . Construction of House on Builder's Lot			EITF.86-7

	Original Pronouncements	Current Text	EITF and Other
REAL ESTATE: SALES OTHER THAN RETAIL LAND SALES—continued			
Deposit Method of Profit Recognition—continued			
. . Effect of Various Forms of Financing...			EITF.88-24
. . Sale-Leaseback Transaction	FAS98, ¶30-33	L10.160D-160G	
Description	FAS66, ¶101	Re1.101	
Exchange Involving Boot			EITF.87-29
Financing, Leasing, or Profit-Sharing Arrangements	FAS66, ¶26-29	Re1.126-129	
Financing Method			
. . Sale-Leaseback Transaction	FAS98, ¶34-39	L10.160H-160M	
Full Accrual Method of Profit Recognition	FAS66, ¶3-18	Re1.103-118	
	FAS66, ¶53-54	Re1.151-152	
. . Antispeculation Clause			EITF.86-6
. . Buyer's Initial and Continuing Investment			EITF.87-9
			EITF.88-12
Installment Method of Profit Recognition	FAS66, ¶22-23	Re1.122-123	
	FAS66, ¶35	Re1.135	
	FAS66, ¶56-61	Re1.154-159	
	FAS66, ¶90	Re1.188	
	FAS66, ¶96	Re1.194	
. . Antispeculation Clause			EITF.86-6
. . Effect of Various Forms of Financing...			EITF.88-24
. . Sale-Leaseback Transaction	FAS98, ¶28-29	L10.160B-160C	
Partial Sales Transactions	FAS66, ¶33-36	Re1.133-136	
Percentage-of-Completion Method of Profit Recognition	FAS66, ¶37	Re1.137	EITF.86-7
	FAS66, ¶41	Re1.141	
Profit Recognition			
. . Antispeculation Clause			EITF.86-6
. . Buyer's Initial and Continuing Investment			EITF.87-9
. . Collateral Securing Buyer's Note			EITF.88-12
. . Construction of House on Builder's Lot			EITF.86-7
. . Full Accrual Method Inappropriate	FAS66, ¶19-39	Re1.119-143	
	FAS66, ¶41-43	Re1.175-188	
	FAS98, ¶23		
. . Graduated Payment Mortgages			EITF.84-17
. . Illustrations	FAS66, ¶77-90	Re1.175-188	
. . Mortgage Insurance/Guarantee			EITF.84-17
			EITF.87-9
. . Mortgages with Initial Negative Amortization			EITF.84-17
. . Pledging of Ownership Interest as Part of Down Payment			EITF.88-12
. . Sale of Property Subject to Seller's Preexisting Lease			EITF.88-21

See "Terminology" for references to defined terms presented in various accounting pronouncements.
See the Introduction to the Topical Index for details on the use of this index.

	Original Pronouncements	Current Text	EITF and Other

REAL ESTATE: SALES OTHER THAN RETAIL LAND SALES—continued

Reduced Profit Method of Profit
Recognition .... FAS66, ¶23 — Re1.123
.... FAS66, ¶68-69 — Re1.166-167

Sale of Property Improvements Involves
Land Lease .... FAS66, ¶38-39 — Re1.138-139

Sale-Leaseback Transaction .... FAS98, ¶6-14 — L10.130A-130M
.... FAS98, ¶17-19 — L10.155-160M
.... FAS98, ¶23 — Re1.140

. . Loans to Buyers by Sellers .... — — EITF.84-37
. . Rental Shortfall Agreements .... — — EITF.84-37
. . Repurchase Options .... — — EITF.84-37
. . Residual Value Guarantee .... — — EITF.86-17
. . Sale of Property Subject to Seller's
Preexisting Lease .... — — EITF.88-21
. . Short Initial Lease Term with Renewal
Options .... — — EITF.84-37
. . Subleases .... — — EITF.84-37

Time-Sharing Interests .... FAS66, ¶37 — Re1.137

REALIZATION

Definition .... CON6, ¶143

Revenues and Gains
. . Guidance in Applying Recognition
Criteria .... CON5, ¶83-84

REASONABLY POSSIBLE EVENTS

See Contingencies

RECAPITALIZATION

See Debt: Restructurings
See Quasi Reorganizations
Changes to Fixed Employee Stock Option
Plans as a Result of Equity
Restructuring .... — — EITF.90-9

RECEIVABLES

See Balance Sheet Classification: Current
Assets and Liabilities
See Contingencies
See Financial Instruments
See Impairment: Loans
See Interest: Imputation of an Interest Cost
See Loans
See Receivables Sold with Recourse
See Related Parties
See Valuation Allowances
Acquisition, Development, and
Construction Loans .... — — EITF.84-4
.... — — EITF.86-21

Balance Sheet Classification .... ARB43, Ch.3A, ¶4 — B05.105
.... ARB43, Ch.3A, ¶6 — B05.107
. . Notes Received for Capital Stock .... — — EITF.85-1

	Original Pronouncements	Current Text	EITF and Other
RECEIVABLES—continued			
Credit Card Portfolio Securitizations with a "Removal of Accounts" Provision.........			EITF.90-18
From Officers, Employees, or Affiliates......	ARB43, Ch.1A, ¶5	R36.105	
Graduated Payment Mortgages...................			EITF.84-17
....			EITF.85-38
In-Substance Foreclosure on Collateral			EITF.89-9
Loan Loss Allowances			
. . Applying Savings and Loan Audit Guide..			EITF.87-5
. . Differences between GAAP and RAP ..			EITF.85-44
Loan Payment Modifications			EITF.84-19
Maximum Maturity Guarantees on Transfers with Recourse			EITF.89-2
Measuring Loss Accruals by Transferors for Transfers of Receivables with Recourse			EITF.92-2
Negative Amortizing Loan			EITF.85-38
Offsetting Nonrecourse Debt with Lease Receivables			EITF.84-25
Offsetting Notes Receivables with Debt			
. . Note Puttable to Creditor to Satisfy Debt...................................			EITF.84-11
Operating Real Estate as Collateral............			EITF.86-21
Sale of Bad-Debt Recovery Rights			EITF.86-8
Sale of Credit Card Portfolio with Partial Interest Retained			EITF.88-22
Sale of Interest-Only Cash Flows or Principal-Only Cash Flows from Loans Receivable			
. . Determination of Gain or Loss.............			EITF.88-11
. . Determination of Remaining Recorded Investment for Portion of Loan Retained			EITF.88-11
Sale with a Partial Participation Retained...			EITF.84-21
Sale with Recourse to Special-Purpose Entity			EITF.84-30
Shared Appreciation Mortgages.................			EITF.86-21
Transfer in Which Risk of Foreign Currency Fluctuation Is Retained.............			EITF.D-13
Valuation Allowances	APB12, ¶3	V18.101-103	
RECEIVABLES SOLD WITH RECOURSE			
See Disclosure			
See Financial Instruments			
Description of Types of Transactions..........	FAS77, ¶1	R20.101	
....	FAS77, ¶15		
Glossary	FAS77, ¶12	R20.401-404	
Maximum Maturity Guarantees on Transfers with Recourse			EITF.89-2

See "Terminology" for references to defined terms presented in various accounting pronouncements.

See the Introduction to the Topical Index for details on the use of this index.

	Original Pronouncements	Current Text	EITF and Other

RECEIVABLES SOLD WITH RECOURSE—continued

Measuring Loss Accruals by Transferors for Transfers of Receivables with Recourse .... | | | EITF.92-2

Scope of Accounting and Reporting Requirements .... | FAS77, ¶3-4 | R20.102-104 |
.... | FAS77, ¶20 | |

Transactions Involving Special-Purpose Entities.. | | | EITF.84-30
.... | | | EITF.D-14

Transfer Recognized as a Liability............. | FAS77, ¶8 | R20.108 |

Transfer Recognized as a Sale
. . Criteria for Recognition........................ | FAS77, ¶5-7 | R20.105-107 |
.... | FAS77, ¶22-26 | |
.... | FAS77, ¶28 | |
.... | FAS77, ¶30-31 | |
.... | FAS77, ¶34 | |

RECIPROCAL TRANSFERS

See Nonmonetary Transactions

RECOGNITION

See Recognition and Measurement in Financial Statements

Cost-Benefit Constraints............................. | CON5, ¶63 |
Criteria .... | CON5, ¶62 |
. . Asset and Liability Changes................. | CON5, ¶85-88 |
. . Asset and Liability Changes, Use of Current Prices .... | CON5, ¶90 |
. . Fundamental .... | CON5, ¶63-64 |
. . Guidance in Application to Components of Earnings .... | CON5, ¶79-84 |
. . Guidance in Application to Expenses and Losses.. | CON5, ¶85-87 |
. . Guidance in Application to Revenues and Gains .... | CON5, ¶83-84 |
. . Purposes.. | CON5, ¶59-60 |
. . Relevance.. | CON5, ¶73-74 |
. . Reliability .... | CON5, ¶75-77 |
. . Structure.. | CON5, ¶61-62 |
Definition .... | CON5, ¶6 |
.... | CON6, ¶143 |
Discussion.. | CON5, ¶58 |
Elements Definitions .... | CON5, ¶64 |
Financial Reporting .... | CON5, ¶5-6 |
Limitations .... | CON6, ¶48 |
Purchase Commitments............................. | CON6, ¶251-253 |
Purposes... | CON5, ¶59-61 |
Relation to Elements of Financial Statements .... | CON6, ¶22-23 |
Relation to Measurement and Display .... | CON6, ¶23 |
Relation to Uncertainties........................... | CON6, ¶48 |

	Original Pronouncements	Current Text	EITF and Other

RECOGNITION AND MEASUREMENT IN FINANCIAL STATEMENTS
See Measurement
See Recognition
Articulation of.. CON5, ¶14
Definition
. . Earned.. CON5, ¶83
. . Financial Capital Maintenance
    Concept .... CON5, ¶47
. . Financial Flexibility................................ CON5, ¶24
. . Liquidity .... CON5, ¶24
. . Physical Capital Maintenance
    Concept .... CON5, ¶47
. . Realized or Realizable............................ CON5, ¶83
Financial Statements
. . Articulation... CON5, ¶5
    .... CON5, ¶12
    .... CON5, ¶23
. . Cash Flows during the Period .... CON5, ¶13
. . Classification and Aggregation in .... CON5, ¶20-22
. . Complementary Nature of...................... CON5, ¶23-24
. . Comprehensive Income.......................... CON5, ¶39-41
. . Comprehensive Income (Total
    Nonowner Changes in Equity) for
    the Period .... CON5, ¶13
. . Cumulative Accounting Adjustments ... CON5, ¶42-44
. . Details of Display Not Addressed .... CON5, ¶14
. . Earnings.. CON5, ¶33-38
. . Earnings (Net Income) for the Period... CON5, ¶13
. . Financial Capital Maintenance.............. CON5, ¶45-48
. . Financial Position .... CON5, ¶13
. . Full Set of .... CON5, ¶13-14
. . Gains and Losses.................................... CON5, ¶43
. . General Purpose Financial Statements
    and Individual Users.......................... CON5, ¶15-16
. . Individual.. CON5, ¶25
. . Investments by and Distributions to
    Owners during the Period.................... CON5, ¶13
. . Net Income, Relation to Earnings .... CON5, ¶33-35
. . Notes to Financial Statements and
    Supplementary Information................ CON5, ¶7-9
. . Other Nonowner Changes in Equity ..... CON5, ¶43
. . Recognition Implications of Earnings .. CON5, ¶49-51
. . Relation to Other Means of Financial
    Reporting.. CON5, ¶7-9
. . Statement of Cash Flows, Nature and
    Recognition Considerations................ CON5, ¶52-54
. . Statement of Financial Position,
    Nature and Recognition
    Considerations .... CON5, ¶26-29

See "Terminology" for references to defined terms presented in various accounting pronouncements.
See the Introduction to the Topical Index for details on the use of this index.

	Original Pronouncements	Current Text	EITF and Other

RECOGNITION AND MEASUREMENT IN FINANCIAL STATEMENTS—continued

Financial Statements—continued

. . Statement of Investments by and Distributions to Owners: Nature, Recognition .... CON5, ¶55-57

. . Statements of Earnings and Comprehensive Income: Nature, Recognition .... CON5, ¶30-51

. . Usefulness of Financial Statements, Individually and Collectively .... CON5, ¶17-19

Gains and Losses .... CON5, ¶42

Not-for-Profit Organizations
. . Nonapplicability to .... CON5, ¶4

Objectives of Financial Reporting
. . Relationship .... CON5, ¶10-12

Other Nonowner Changes in Equity
. . Description.. CON5, ¶43

RECORD AND MUSIC INDUSTRY

See Disclosure

Advance Royalty .... FAS50, ¶10 ... Re4.105
.... FAS50, ¶12 ... Re4.107

Artist Compensation Cost .... FAS50, ¶10 ... Re4.105

Glossary .... FAS50, ¶18 ... Re4.401-405

Licensee Accounting .... FAS50, ¶15 ... Re4.110

Record Masters
. . Cost.. FAS50, ¶11 ... Re4.106
. . Valuation... FAS50, ¶11 ... Re4.106

Revenue Recognition
. . Licensor Accounting.............................. FAS50, ¶8 ... Re4.103

RECOURSE ARRANGEMENTS

See Receivables Sold with Recourse

REDEEMABLE STOCK

See Financial Instruments

Accounting.. FAS47, ¶9 ... C32.104

Disclosure
. . Unconditional Purchase Obligations..... FAS47, ¶10 ... C32.105

Early Extinguishment EITF.86-32

Effect of a Redemption Agreement on Carrying Value of Investment.................... EITF.85-23

Illustration.. FAS47, ¶31-32 ... C32.113-114

Redemption Requirements .... FAS47, ¶10 ... C32.105

Sale of Put Options on Issuer's Stock
. . Classification in Issuer's Balance Sheet...................................... EITF.87-31

Unconditional Purchase Obligations........... FAS47, ¶9-10 ... C32.104-105

REDEMPTION OF DEBT

See Debt: Extinguishments

	Original Pronouncements	Current Text	EITF and Other
REDUCED PROFIT METHOD			
See Real Estate			
See Real Estate: Sales Other Than Retail Land Sales			
REFINANCING			
See Balance Sheet Classification: Current Assets and Liabilities			
See Debt: Restructurings			
REFUNDING OF DEBT			
See Balance Sheet Classification: Current Assets and Liabilities			
See Debt: Extinguishments			
See Interest: Capitalization of Interest Costs			
See Leases			
REFUNDS			
Prior Interim Period Adjustments	FAS16, ¶13	A35.109	
Regulated Operations	FAS71, ¶11	Re6.121	
	FAS71, ¶19	Re6.130	
	FAS71, ¶44-47	Re6.149-152	
Revenue Recognition	FAS48, ¶3	R75.105	
REGISTERED INVESTMENT ENTERPRISES			
See Earnings per Share			
See Investment Enterprises			
REGISTERED STOCK			
Business Combinations	AIN-APB16, #6	B50.519-520	
	AIN-APB16, #11	B50.530-533	
REGISTRATION COSTS			
Business Combinations	AIN-APB16, #35	B50.632-634	
REGULATED OPERATIONS			
See Consolidation			
See Depreciation			
See Disclosure			
See Insurance Costs			
Abandonments of Assets	FAS90, ¶3-6	Re6.127A-127D	
. . Adjustment of Carrying Value	FAS90, ¶4	Re6.127B	
. . Amortization during Recovery Period	FAS90, ¶6	Re6.127D	
. . Before Recovery Begins	FAS90, ¶5	Re6.127C	
. . Carrying Charges	FAS90, ¶5	Re6.127C	
. . Computation of a Loss	FTB87-2, ¶5	Re6.501-507	
	FTB87-2, ¶14-20		
. . Deferred Income Taxes	FTB87-2, ¶5	Re6.501-507	
	FTB87-2, ¶14-20		
. . Discount Rate Used	FAS90, ¶3	Re6.127A	
. . Full Return on Investment Expected	FAS90, ¶3-6	Re6.127A-127D	
. . Illustrations	FTB87-2, ¶34-47	Re6.508-521	
. . Partial or No Return on Investment Expected	FAS90, ¶3-6	Re6.127A-127D	
	FTB87-2, ¶15-20	Re6.503-507	

See "Terminology" for references to defined terms presented in various accounting pronouncements.
See the Introduction to the Topical Index for details on the use of this index.

	Original Pronouncements	Current Text	EITF and Other
REGULATED OPERATIONS—continued			
Accounting by Rate-Regulated Utilities for the Effects of Certain Alternative Revenue Programs			EITF.92-7
Accounting Changes	FAS71, ¶31-32	Re6.136-137	
Accounting for OPEB Costs by Rate-Regulated Enterprises			EITF.92-12
			EITF.93-4
Allowable Costs	FAS71, ¶1-3	Re6.111-113	
Allowance for Earnings on Shareholders' Investment Capitalized for Rate-Making Purposes Only	FAS92, ¶5	Re6.125B	
	FAS92, ¶8-9	Re6.125G	
	FAS92, ¶40-41	Re6.198-199	
. . As Related to Disallowance	FAS92, ¶42-43	Re6.200-201	
. . As Related to Phase-in Plan	FAS92, ¶44-45	Re6.202-203	
Allowance for Funds Used during Construction	FAS71, ¶15	Re6.125	
. . Capitalization Criteria	FAS90, ¶9	Re6.125	
	FAS90, ¶66-68		
. . Prudence Investigation	FAS90, ¶68	Re6.125	
Application of Authoritative Accounting Pronouncements	FAS71, ¶7	Re6.117	
Asset			
. . Impairment by Actions of Regulator	FAS71, ¶10	Re6.120	
	FAS90, ¶9		
	FAS121, ¶32		
. . Reasonable Assurance of Existence	FAS71, ¶9	Re6.119	
	FAS90, ¶9		
	FAS121, ¶32		
Capitalization of Cost	FAS71, ¶4	Re6.114	
	FAS71, ¶9	Re6.119	
	FAS90, ¶9		
. . Allowance for Earnings on Shareholders' Investment	FAS92, ¶8-9	Re6.125G	
. . Phase-in Plan	FAS92, ¶4-5	Re6.125B-125C	
Capitalization of Interest	FAS34, ¶10	I67.106	
. . Allowance for Funds Used during Construction	FAS71, ¶15	Re6.125	
	FAS90, ¶9		
	FAS90, ¶66-68		
Changing Prices Information	FAS89, ¶31	C28.127	
Compensated Absences	FAS71, ¶48-49	Re6.153-154	
Contingencies	FAS71, ¶38-39	Re6.143-144	
Deferred Cost	FAS71, ¶4	Re6.114	
. . Allowance for Earnings on Shareholders' Investment	FAS92, ¶8-9	Re6.125G	
. . Phase-in Plan	FAS92, ¶4-5	Re6.125B-125C	
Deferred Taxes	FAS109, ¶29	I27.128	
	FAS109, ¶252-255	I27.179-182	

FAS–FASB Statements	FIN–FASB Interpretations	FTB–FASB Technical Bulletins
APB–APB Opinions	AIN–AICPA Interpretations	ARB–Accounting Research Bulletins
CON–FASB Concepts	EITF–EITF Issues	Q&A–FASB Special Reports

	Original Pronouncements	Current Text	EITF and Other
REGULATED OPERATIONS—continued			
Definition			
. . Allowable Costs	FAS71, ¶1	Re6.401	
. . Capitalize	FAS71, ¶4	Re6.402	
. . Incurred Cost	FAS71, ¶9	Re6.403	
. . Intercompany Profit	FAS71, ¶16	Re6.404	
. . Phase-in Plan	FAS92, ¶2	Re6.404A	
. . Probable	FAS90, ¶9	Re6.405	
. . Regulatory Lag	FAS92, ¶39	Re6.406	
Differences between GAAP and RAP			EITF.85-44
Disallowance of Costs of Recently Completed Plants	FAS90, ¶7	Re6.127E	
	FAS90, ¶60-62	Re6.176-178	
. . Excess Capacity	FAS90, ¶60	Re6.176	
. . Hidden, Indirect Disallowance	FAS90, ¶62	Re6.178	
. . Illustrations of Disallowance Due to "Cost Cap"	FAS90, ¶28-31	Re6.169-172	
. . Illustrations of Disallowance of Plant Costs	FAS90, ¶26-27	Re6.167-168	
. . Illustrations of Explicit, but Indirect, Disallowance	FAS90, ¶32-34	Re6.173-175	
. . Value-Based Ratemaking	FAS90, ¶61	Re6.177	
Disallowance of Plant Cost			
. . As Related to Allowance for Earnings on Shareholders' Investment Capitalized for Rate-Making Purposes Only	FAS92, ¶42-43	Re6.200-201	
. . As Related to Phase-in Plan	FAS92, ¶7	Re6.125E	
. . Capitalized for Rate-Making Purposes Only	FAS92, ¶42-43	Re6.200-201	
Discontinuation of Accounting for the Effects of Certain Types of Regulation	FAS101, ¶5-7	Re6.204-206	
. . Illustrations of Specific Situations	FAS101, ¶13-20	Re6.209-216	
. . Income Statement Presentation of Net Effect	FAS101, ¶6	Re6.205	
	FAS101, ¶9-10	Re6.208	
Divestiture of Certain Investment Securities to an Unregulated Commonly Controlled Entity under FIRREA			EITF.89-18
Early Extinguishment of Debt	FAS71, ¶35-37	Re6.140-142	
Financial Statements Prepared Based on Statutory Accounting Practices Instead of GAAP	FIN40, ¶5-6	Re6.114	
	FIN40, ¶18		
Impairment of Assets	FAS71, ¶10	Re6.120	
	FAS101, ¶6	Re6.205	
	FAS121, ¶32-33		

See "Terminology" for references to defined terms presented in various accounting pronouncements.
See the Introduction to the Topical Index for details on the use of this index.

	Original Pronouncements	Current Text	EITF and Other
REGULATED OPERATIONS—continued			
Income Taxes	FAS109, ¶29	I27.128	
	FAS109, ¶252-255	I27.179-182	
	FAS109, ¶288	Re6.128	
	FTB87-2, ¶5	Re6.501-507	
	FTB87-2, ¶14-20		
Intangible Assets	FAS71, ¶29-30	Re6.134-135	
Intercompany Profit	FAS71, ¶16-17	Re6.126-127	
Leases	FAS71, ¶40-43	Re6.145-148	
Liability			
. . Eliminated by Regulator	FAS71, ¶12	Re6.122	
. . Imposed by Regulator	FAS71, ¶11	Re6.121	
Modification of Debt Terms When Debtor Is Experiencing Financial Difficulties			EITF.89-15
Nonutility Generators (NUGs)			EITF.91-6
Pension Costs	FAS87, ¶210	Re6.155	
Phase-in Plan			
. . As Related to Disallowance	FAS92, ¶7	Re6.125E	
. . Background	FAS92, ¶48-50	Re6.114A-114B	
. . Criteria	FAS92, ¶5	Re6.125C	
. . Definition	FAS92, ¶3	Re6.125A	
. . Illustrations of Specific Situations	FAS92, ¶21-45	Re6.179-203	
. . Modifications of/Supplement to	FAS92, ¶6	Re6.125D	
. . Plants Completed at Different Times and Sharing Facilities			EITF.D-21
Postretirement Benefits Other Than Pensions	FAS106, ¶364	Re6.155	EITF.92-12 EITF.93-4
Price Controls	FAS71, ¶8	Re6.118	
Recovery of Costs with Return on Investment			
. . Abandoned Assets	FAS90, ¶3-6	Re6.127A-127D	
Recovery of Costs without Return on Investment	FAS71, ¶20	Re6.131	
	FAS71, ¶33-34	Re6.138-139	
. . Abandoned Assets	FAS90, ¶3-6	Re6.127A-127D	
	FTB87-2, ¶15-20	Re6.503-507	
. . Phase-in Plan	FAS92, ¶9	Re6.125G	
Reduced Rates	FAS71, ¶11	Re6.121	
Refunds to Customers	FAS71, ¶11	Re6.121	
	FAS71, ¶19	Re6.130	
	FAS71, ¶44-47	Re6.149-152	
Regulatory Accounting	FAS71, ¶5	Re6.115	
Regulatory-Assisted Acquisitions of Thrifts			EITF.88-19
. . Disclosure Requirements			EITF.88-19
Revenue Collected Subject to Refund	FAS71, ¶44-45	Re6.149-150	
Revenue Recognition of Long-Term Power Sales Contracts of Nonutility Generators (NUGs)			EITF.91-6

FAS–FASB Statements	FIN–FASB Interpretations	FTB–FASB Technical Bulletins
APB–APB Opinions	AIN–AICPA Interpretations	ARB–Accounting Research Bulletins
CON–FASB Concepts	EITF–EITF Issues	Q&A–FASB Special Reports

	Original Pronouncements	Current Text	EITF and Other
REGULATED OPERATIONS—continued			
Sale-Leaseback Transactions	FAS98, ¶14-16	Re6.125H-125J	
Scope of Accounting and Reporting Requirements	FAS71, ¶5-8	Re6.115-118A	
	FAS90, ¶2		
	FAS92, ¶2		
. . Discontinuation of Accounting for the Effects of Certain Types of Regulation	FAS101, ¶1	Re6.117A-117B	
	FAS101, ¶4		
Write-down or Write-off of Abandoned Nuclear Power Plant			EITF.D-5
REGULATORY ACCOUNTING PRINCIPLES			
Differences between GAAP and RAP			
. . Loan Loss Allowances			EITF.85-44
REINSURANCE			
See Insurance Industry			
Definition	FAS60, ¶66	In6.428	
Funded Catastrophe Covers			EITF.93-6
Multiple-Year Retrospectively Rated Contracts (RRCs)			EITF.93-6
			EITF.D-35
See Insurance Industry			
RELATED PARTIES			
See Disclosure			
See Interest: Imputation of an Interest Cost			
See Investments: Equity Method			
See Leases			
See Research and Development Arrangements			
Arm's-Length Basis Transactions	FAS57, ¶3	R36.103	
Common Control	FAS57, ¶4	R36.104	EITF.86-16
			EITF.88-16
Consolidation of Special-Purpose Entity without Equity Ownership			EITF.84-30
Defined Benefit Pension Plan and Employer	FAS35, ¶28	Pe5.127	
	FAS57, ¶1	R36.101	
Glossary	FAS57, ¶24	R36.401-406	
Leases	FAS13, ¶29-30	L10.125-126	
Receivables from Employees, Officers, or Affiliated Enterprises	ARB43, Ch.1A, ¶5	R36.105	
Scope of Accounting and Reporting Requirements	FAS57, ¶1	R36.101	
RELEVANCE			
Criterion for Recognition	CON5, ¶74		
Definition	CON2, Glossary		
Feedback Value	CON2, ¶51-52		
Predictive Value	CON2, ¶53-55		
Primary Qualitative Characteristic	CON2, ¶46-57		

See "Terminology" for references to defined terms presented in various accounting pronouncements.
See the Introduction to the Topical Index for details on the use of this index.

	Original Pronouncements	Current Text	EITF and Other
RELEVANCE—continued			
Relation to Neutrality	CON2, ¶98-110		
Relation to Reliability	CON2, ¶90		
Relation to Timeliness	CON2, ¶56-57		
Role in Financial Reporting	CON1, ¶36		
RELIABILITY			
Criterion for Recognition	CON5, ¶75-77		
Definition	CON2, Glossary		
Degree of	CON2, ¶65-71		
Financial Statements, Nature of Audit	CON1, ¶8		
Precision and Uncertainty	CON2, ¶72-76		
Primary Qualitative Characteristic	CON2, ¶58-97		
Relation to Conservatism	CON2, ¶91-97		
Relation to Neutrality	CON2, ¶98-110		
Relation to Relevance	CON2, ¶90		
Relation to Representational Faithfulness	CON2, ¶63-80		
Relation to Substance vs. Form	CON2, ¶160		
Relation to Uncertainty	CON6, ¶45-48		
Relation to Verifiability	CON2, ¶81-89		
RELIGIOUS ORGANIZATIONS			
See Not-for-Profit Organizations			
RELOCATION COSTS			
See Moving Costs			
REMOTELY POSSIBLE EVENTS			
See Contingencies			
RENEGOTIATION			
See Contractor Accounting: Construction-Type Contracts			
RENEWAL OPTIONS			
See Leases			
RENTAL CONCESSIONS			
Accounting by Tenant (Lessee)			EITF.88-3
RENTALS			
See Leases			
REORGANIZATIONS			
See Debt: Restructurings			
See Quasi Reorganizations			
Accounting for Restructuring Charges			EITF.94-3
Classification of Restructuring Gain or Loss			EITF.86-22
			EITF.87-4
Exit Costs			EITF.94-3
Income Taxes			
. . Carryforwards			EITF.D-33
. . Temporary Differences			EITF.D-33
Liability Recognition for Costs to Exit an Activity			EITF.94-3
REPLACEMENT COST			
See Changing Prices: Reporting Their Effects in Financial Reports			

FAS–FASB Statements   FIN–FASB Interpretations   FTB–FASB Technical Bulletins
APB–APB Opinions   AIN–AICPA Interpretations   ARB–Accounting Research Bulletins
CON–FASB Concepts   EITF–EITF Issues   Q&A–FASB Special Reports

	Original Pronouncements	Current Text	EITF and Other

REPLACEMENT COST—continued
See Measurement

REPORTING ENTITY CHANGES
See Adjustments of Financial Statements
for Prior Periods

REPRESENTATIONAL FAITHFULNESS

	Original Pronouncements	Current Text	EITF and Other
Definition	CON2, Glossary		
Relation to Bias	CON2, ¶77-78		
Relation to Completeness	CON2, ¶79-80		
Relation to Precision	CON2, ¶72-76		
Relation to Reliability	CON2, ¶63-80		
Relation to Uncertainties	CON2, ¶72-76		

REPURCHASE AGREEMENTS
See Financial Instruments

	Original Pronouncements	Current Text	EITF and Other
GNMA Dollar Rolls			EITF.84-20
Offsetting Payables and Receivables under Repurchase and Reverse Repurchase Agreements	FIN41, ¶3-4	B10.106A-106B	
	FIN41, ¶14		

REPURCHASED STOCK
See Capital Stock: Treasury Stock

RESEARCH AND DEVELOPMENT
See Computer Software
See Disclosure

	Original Pronouncements	Current Text	EITF and Other
Accounting	FAS2, ¶12	R50.108	
Acquired in Business Combination	FAS2, ¶34	B50.151-152	
	FIN4, ¶4-5		
Elements of Costs to Be Identified with	FAS2, ¶11	R50.107	
Examples of Activities Typically Excluded	FAS2, ¶10	R50.112	
Examples of Activities Typically Included	FAS2, ¶9	R50.111	
Glossary	FAS2, ¶8	R50.401-402	
Performed by Venture Capital Subsidiaries			EITF.85-12
Process	FIN6, ¶4	R50.105	
Purchased in a Business Combination			EITF.86-14
Qualification as an Asset	CON6, ¶176		
Scope of Accounting and Reporting Requirements	FAS2, ¶1-3	R50.101-103	

RESEARCH AND DEVELOPMENT ARRANGEMENTS
See Disclosure

	Original Pronouncements	Current Text	EITF and Other
Loan or Advance to Other Parties	FAS68, ¶12	R55.110	
Obligation Is a Liability	FAS68, ¶4-9	R55.102-107	
Obligation Is to a Person			
. . Contractual Services	FAS68, ¶10-11	R55.108-109	
Related Parties	FAS68, ¶8	R55.106	
Scope of Accounting and Reporting Requirements	FAS68, ¶3	R55.101	

See "Terminology" for references to defined terms presented in various accounting pronouncements.
See the Introduction to the Topical Index for details on the use of this index.

	Original Pronouncements	Current Text	EITF and Other

RESEARCH AND DEVELOPMENT ARRANGEMENTS—continued
Stock Issued to Acquire Results of a Research and Development
Arrangement.. FTB84-1, ¶1-2   R55.501-504
.... FTB84-1, ¶6-7
Warrants or Similar Instruments Issued ...... FAS68, ¶13   R55.111
RESERVE FOR BAD DEBTS
Valuation Allowance.................................... APB12, ¶2   V18.102
RESERVES
See Contingencies
See Extractive Industries
Qualification as Liabilities........................... CON6, ¶197
RESIDUAL INTEREST
See Equity (or Net Assets)
Characteristics.. CON6, ¶49-53
.... CON6, ¶213
.... CON6, ¶222
RESIDUAL VALUE
See Leases
RESOURCES
See Economic Resources
RESTATEMENTS
See Adjustments of Financial Statements for Prior Periods
RESTATE-TRANSLATE METHOD
See Changing Prices: Reporting Their Effects in Financial Reports
RESTRICTED FUNDS
See Not-for-Profit Organizations
Not-for-Profit Organizations .... CON4, ¶21
.... CON4, ¶46
Relation to Net Assets .... CON6, ¶191
RESTRUCTURING OF BUSINESS OPERATIONS
Accounting for Restructuring Charges EITF.94-3
Changes to Fixed Employee Stock Option Plans as a Result of Equity
Restructuring...   EITF.90-9
Classification of Resulting Gain or Loss.....   EITF.86-22
....   EITF.87-4
Exit Costs...   EITF.94-3
Liability Recognition for Costs to Exit an
Activity..   EITF.94-3
RESTRUCTURING OF DEBT
See Debt: Restructurings

FAS–FASB Statements   FIN–FASB Interpretations   FTB–FASB Technical Bulletins
APB–APB Opinions   AIN–AICPA Interpretations   ARB–Accounting Research Bulletins
CON–FASB Concepts   EITF–EITF Issues   Q&A–FASB Special Reports

	Original Pronouncements	Current Text	EITF and Other

RESULTS OF OPERATIONS
See Adjustments of Financial Statements
  for Prior Periods
See Extraordinary Items
See Income Statement
See Income Statement Presentation:
  Discontinued Operations
See Interim Financial Reporting
See Not-for-Profit Organizations
See Oil and Gas Producing Activities

RETAILERS

	Original Pronouncements	Current Text
Inventory Valuation	ARB43, Ch.4, ¶6	I78.108
	ARB43, Ch.4, ¶10	I78.112

RETAIL LAND SALES
See Real Estate: Retail Land Sales

RETAINED EARNINGS
See Disclosure
See Financial Statements: Comparative
  Financial Statements
See Quasi Reorganizations
See Statement of Investments by and
  Distributions to Owners

	Original Pronouncements	Current Text
Appropriations	APB9, ¶28	C08.101
Appropriations for Loss Contingencies	FAS5, ¶15	C59.117
		R70.103
Charges against	FAS5, ¶15	R70.103
Preacquisition Dividends of Purchased Subsidiary	ARB43, Ch.1A, ¶3	R70.102
Preacquisition Earnings of Purchased Subsidiary	ARB51, ¶9	R70.101
Prior-Period Adjustments	APB9, ¶26	A35.106-107
	FAS16, ¶16	

RETIREE HEALTH CARE COSTS
See Postretirement Benefits Other Than
  Pensions

RETIREE MEDICAL BENEFITS
See Postretirement Benefits Other Than
  Pensions

RETIREMENT OF DEBT
See Debt: Extinguishments

RETIREMENT OF STOCK
See Capital Stock: Capital Transactions

RETIREMENT PLANS
See Defined Benefit Pension Plans
See Pension Costs
See Postretirement Benefits Other Than
  Pensions
See Postretirement Health Care and Life
  Insurance Benefits

See "Terminology" for references to defined terms presented in various accounting pronouncements.
See the Introduction to the Topical Index for details on the use of this index.

	Original Pronouncements	Current Text	EITF and Other

RETIREMENT-REPLACEMENT-BETTERMENT (RRB) ACCOUNTING
See Adjustments of Financial Statements for Prior Periods

RETURN ON INVESTMENT
Accrual vs. Cash Basis of Accounting .... CON1, ¶45-48
Prospects for .... CON1, ¶37-39
Relation to Capital Maintenance .... CON6, ¶71

RETURNS
See Revenue Recognition

REVENUE AND EXPENSE MATCHING
See Matching of Costs and Revenues

REVENUE RECOGNITION
See Interest Income
See Leases
See Real Estate: Sales Other Than Retail Land Sales
See Sales
Accounting for Barter Transactions
  Involving Barter Credits .... | | | EITF.93-11
Amortization of Amount Received from
  Investor for Future Revenue .... | | | EITF.88-18
Banking and Thrift Industries
. . Sale of Convertible, Adjustable-Rate
      Mortgages with Contingent
      Repayment Agreement .... | | | EITF.87-25
. . Sale of Mortgage Loan with Servicing
      Rights Retained................................. | | | EITF.86-39
. . Sale of Servicing Rights on Mortgages
      Owned by Others .... | | | EITF.85-13
. . Sale with a Partial Participation
      Retained .... | | | EITF.84-21
Credit Card Portfolio Securitization........... | | | EITF.88-22
  .... | | | EITF.90-18
Defeasance of Special-Purpose
  Borrowings... | | | EITF.84-26
Definition
. . Revenues... FAS14, ¶10 | S20.411 |
Equipment Sold and Subsequently
  Repurchased Subject to an Operating
  Lease.. | | | EITF.95-4
Extended Warranty and Product
  Maintenance Contracts
. . Definitions .... FTB90-1, ¶2 | R75.502 |
  .... FTB90-1, ¶4 | R75.504 |
. . Incremental Direct Acquisition Costs ... FTB90-1, ¶4 | R75.504 |
  .... FTB90-1, ¶12 | |
. . Loss Recognition .... FTB90-1, ¶5 | R75.505 |

FAS–FASB Statements	FIN–FASB Interpretations	FTB–FASB Technical Bulletins
APB–APB Opinions	AIN–AICPA Interpretations	ARB–Accounting Research Bulletins
CON–FASB Concepts	EITF–EITF Issues	Q&A–FASB Special Reports

T-371

	Original Pronouncements	Current Text	EITF and Other
REVENUE RECOGNITION—continued			
Extended Warranty and Product Maintenance Contracts—continued			
. . Recognition of Revenues and Costs	FTB90-1, ¶1-5	R75.501-505	EITF.89-17
Franchisors			
. . Cost Recovery Method	FAS45, ¶6	Fr3.102	
. . Installment Recovery Method	FAS45, ¶6	Fr3.102	
GNMA Dollar Rolls			EITF.84-20
Grantor Trust			
. . Sales between Trust and Company			EITF.84-15
Guidance for Applying Recognition Criteria	CON5, ¶84		
Installment Method of Accounting	APB10, ¶12	R75.103	
Invasion of a Defeasance Trust			EITF.86-36
Leases			
. . Offsetting Nonrecourse Debt with Lease Receivables			EITF.84-25
. . Recognition of Receipts from Made-up Rental Shortfalls			EITF.85-27
. . Sale-Leaseback with Guaranteed Residuals			EITF.86-17
. . Sale-Leaseback with Repurchase Option			EITF.84-37
Loan, Commitment, and Syndication Fees			
. . Fees Associated with Loan Syndications and Loan Participations			EITF.88-17
. . Interest Method	FAS91, ¶17-20	L20.116-119	
Loan Guarantee Fees			EITF.85-20
Loan Sales			
. . Sale of Bad-Debt Recovery Rights			EITF.86-8
. . Sale of Convertible, Adjustable-Rate Mortgages with Contingent Repayment Agreement			EITF.87-25
. . Sale of Loan to Special-Purpose Entity			EITF.84-30
. . Sale of Loan with a Partial Participation Retained			EITF.84-21
. . Sale of Mortgage Loan with Servicing Rights Retained			EITF.86-39
. . Third-Party Establishment of CMOs			EITF.86-24
Long-Term Power Sales Contracts of Nonutility Generators (NUGs)			EITF.91-6
Master Limited Partnership (MLP)			
. . Gain Recognition on MLP Units Received in Exchange for Future Fees			EITF.88-14
Mutual Fund Distributors			
. . Fees Received from No-Load Funds			EITF.85-24

See "Terminology" for references to defined terms presented in various accounting pronouncements.
See the Introduction to the Topical Index for details on the use of this index.

	Original Pronouncements	Current Text	EITF and Other
REVENUE RECOGNITION—continued			
Nonmonetary Transactions			
. . Exchange of Assets for Noncontrolling Equity Interest in New Entity.............			EITF.89-7
. . Use of Fair Value..................................			EITF.86-29
Options			
. . Options to Purchase Stock of Another Entity......................................			EITF.85-9
. . Repurchase Option in Sale-Leaseback Transaction..			EITF.84-37
Preferred Stock			
. . Acquisition of a Subsidiary's Mandatorily Redeemable Stock			EITF.86-32
Product Financing Arrangements................	FAS49, ¶6	D18.104	
Profit Recognition......................................	ARB43, Ch.1A, ¶1	R75.101	
....	APB10, ¶12		
....	FAS111, ¶8		
Real Estate			
. . Antispeculation Clause in Sales Contract.......................................			EITF.86-6
. . Construction of House on Builder's Lot..			EITF.86-7
. . Recognition of Receipts from Made-up Rental Shortfalls			EITF.85-27
. . Sale of Builder's Land and Related Construction Contract.........................			EITF.86-7
. . Sale with Graduated Payment Mortgage or Insured Mortgage...........			EITF.84-17
. . Sale-Leaseback with Repurchase Option			EITF.84-37
. . Syndication Fees....................................			EITF.85-37
Relation to Contractor Accounting: Construction-Type Contracts	ARB45, ¶4-6	Co4.103-110	
....	ARB45, ¶9-12		
....	ARB45, ¶15		
Relation to Contractor Accounting: Government Contracts	ARB43, Ch.11A, ¶19-20	Co5.106-107	
Relation to Franchising: Accounting by Franchisors	FAS45, ¶12-14	Fr3.108-110	
Revenue and Expense Recognition for Freight Services in Process.....................			EITF.91-9
Sale of Marketable Securities with a Put Option...			EITF.84-5
....			EITF.85-30
....			EITF.85-40
Sale of Mortgage Servicing Rights.............			EITF.89-5
....			EITF.94-5
....			EITF.95-5
Sale of Preferred Stocks with a Put Option...			EITF.85-25

	Original Pronouncements	Current Text	EITF and Other
REVENUE RECOGNITION—continued			
Sale of Real Estate			
. . Antispeculation Clause in Sales Contract			EITF.86-6
. . Negative Amortization			EITF.84-17
			EITF.85-38
Sale of Servicing Rights on Mortgages Owned by Others			EITF.85-13
Sale of Subsidiary for Equity Interest in Buyer			EITF.85-43
Sales with a Guaranteed Minimum Resale Value			EITF.95-1
Seasonal Revenue			
. . Interim Financial Reporting	APB28, ¶18	I73.110	
Television Barter Syndicators			
. . Advertising Time for Television Programming			EITF.87-10
Unrealized Profits			
. . Nonrecognition	ARB43, Ch.1A, ¶1	R75.102	
When Right of Return Exists	FAS48, ¶6-8	R75.107-109	
. . Scope of Accounting and Reporting Requirements	FAS48, ¶3-4	R75.105-106	
REVENUES			
See Revenue Recognition			
Characteristics	CON6, ¶79		
Component of Comprehensive Income	CON6, ¶73-77		
Definition	CON6, ¶78		
Element of Financial Statements	CON6, ¶78-81		
Guidance in Applying Recognition Criteria	CON6, ¶87-89		
Not-for-Profit Organizations	CON6, ¶111-113		
Relation to Gains	CON6, ¶87-89		
REVERSE REPURCHASE AGREEMENTS			
See Financial Instruments			
GNMA Dollar Rolls			EITF.84-20
Hedging with Futures Contracts			EITF.86-34
Offsetting Payables and Receivables under Repurchase and Reverse Repurchase Agreements	FIN41, ¶3-4	B10.106A-106B	
	FIN41, ¶14		
REVERSE STOCK SPLIT			
See Earnings per Share			
REVOLVING CREDIT AGREEMENT			
See Balance Sheet Classification: Current Assets and Liabilities			
See Lending Activities			
RIGHT OF RETURN			
See Revenue Recognition			

See "Terminology" for references to defined terms presented in various accounting pronouncements.
See the Introduction to the Topical Index for details on the use of this index.

	Original Pronouncements	Current Text	EITF and Other

RIGHT OF SETOFF
See Offsetting
Definition .... FIN39, ¶5   B10.101A

RIGHTS
See Debt: Convertible Debt and Debt with
  Stock Purchase Warrants
See Debt: Extinguishments
See Earnings per Share
See Franchising
See Leases
See Mortgage Servicing Rights
See Oil and Gas Producing Activities
See Options
Conversion
  See Debt: Convertible Debt and Debt
    with Stock Purchase Warrants
  See Debt: Extinguishments
  See Earnings per Share
Debt with Both Guaranteed and
  Contingent Payments
. . Allocating Proceeds between Debt and
    Contingent Right................................ EITF.86-28
Employee Purchases Capital Stock at a
  Discount
. . Issuer Has Right of First Refusal EITF.84-34
Pooling-of-Interests Method for Business
  Combinations
. . Right of First Refusal EITF.84-38
Right of Setoff
. . Impropriety of Offsetting Except
    Where Right of Setoff Exists.............. EITF.84-11
    .... EITF.84-25
Sale of Bad-Debt Recovery Rights EITF.86-8
Stock Appreciation Rights
. . Purchase by Target Company in
    Leveraged Buyout.............................. EITF.84-13
. . Pyramid Stock Option Plans EITF.84-18
Stock Depreciation Rights.......................... EITF.87-33
Stock Indemnification Rights..................... EITF.87-33

RISK
See Contingencies
See Financial Instruments

RISK PARTICIPATIONS
See Financial Instruments
Banker's Acceptances.................................. EITF.85-34

ROYALTIES
See Oil and Gas Producing Activities
Definition ,................................... FAS50, ¶18   Re4.405

(The next page is T-393.)

FAS–FASB Statements   FIN–FASB Interpretations   FTB–FASB Technical Bulletins
APB–APB Opinions   AIN–AICPA Interpretations   ARB–Accounting Research Bulletins
CON–FASB Concepts   EITF–EITF Issues   Q&A–FASB Special Reports

	Original Pronouncements	Current Text	EITF and Other

S CORPORATIONS
See Income Taxes
Classification of Payment Made to IRS to
  Retain Fiscal Year EITF.88-4
Election to Retain Fiscal Year
. . Classification of Payment Made to
  IRS EITF.88-4
SABBATICAL LEAVE
See Compensation to Employees: Paid
  Absences
SAFE HARBOR LEASES
See Leases
SALE
Loan with a Partial Participation Retained
. . Income Recognition EITF.84-21
SALE-LEASEBACK TRANSACTIONS
See Leases
See Real Estate: Sales Other Than Retail
  Land Sales
SALE VS. FINANCING
Collateralized Mortgage Obligations
  Established through a Third Party
. . Gain or Loss Recognition by Seller of
    Mortgages EITF.86-24
Effect of a "Removal of Accounts"
  Provision on the Accounting for a Credit
  Card Securitization.................................... EITF.90-18
GNMA Dollar Rolls
. . Reverse Repurchase Agreements EITF.84-20
Sale of Bad-Debt Recovery Rights EITF.86-8
Sale of Convertible, Adjustable-Rate
  Mortgages with Contingent Repayment
  Agreement.. EITF.87-25
Sale of Credit Card Portfolio with Partial
  Interest Retained EITF.88-22
Sale of Future Revenue EITF.88-18
Sale of Marketable Securities with a Put
  Option... EITF.84-5
  .... EITF.85-30
  .... EITF.85-40
Sale of Mortgage Servicing Rights with
  Subservicing Agreement........................... EITF.87-34
. . Balance Sheet Treatment....................... EITF.90-21
Sale of Preferred Stocks with a Put
  Option.. EITF.85-25
Sale of Short-Term Loan under
  Long-Term Credit Commitment............... EITF.87-30
SALES
See Contractor Accounting: Government
  Contracts

FAS–FASB Statements   FIN–FASB Interpretations   FTB–FASB Technical Bulletins
APB–APB Opinions   AIN–AICPA Interpretations   ARB–Accounting Research Bulletins
CON–FASB Concepts   EITF–EITF Issues   Q&A–FASB Special Reports

	Original Pronouncements	Current Text	EITF and Other
SALES—continued			
See Leases			
See Nonmonetary Transactions			
See Receivables Sold with Recourse			
See Revenue Recognition			
See Revenues			
SALES OF BUSINESS			
See Business Combinations			
See Income Statement Presentation: Discontinued Operations			
SALES RETURNS			
See Revenue Recognition			
SALES-TYPE LEASE			
See Leases			
SAVINGS AND LOAN ASSOCIATIONS			
See Banking and Thrift Industries			
See Financial Instruments			
See Impairment: Loans			
See Lending Activities			
Accounting for Income Tax Benefits from Bad Debts			EITF.91-3
Acquisition of a Savings and Loan Association by a Bank			
. . Accounting for Exit and Entrance Fees Incurred in a Conversion from the Savings Association Insurance Fund to the Bank Insurance Fund			EITF.90-11
. . Tax Implications of Excess Bad-Debt Reserves			EITF.86-31
Activities Similar to Mortgage Banking Enterprise	FAS65, ¶3	Mo4.104	
Bad-Debt Reserves			
. . Income Taxes	APB23, ¶23	Bt7.119	
	FAS109, ¶31-33	I27.130-132	
	FAS109, ¶44	I27.143	
	FAS109, ¶288		
Cash Flows Statement	FAS104, ¶7	C25.111A	
		Bt7.123	
Collateralized Mortgage Obligations (CMOs)			
. . Impairment Recognition			EITF.93-18
. . Purchased Investment			EITF.89-4
Conversion from Mutual Ownership to Stock Ownership			
. . Earnings per Share			EITF.84-22

See "Terminology" for references to defined terms presented in various accounting pronouncements.
See the Introduction to the Topical Index for details on the use of this index.

	Original Pronouncements	Current Text	EITF and Other
SAVINGS AND LOAN ASSOCIATIONS—continued			
Conversion of Savings and Loan Association to a Bank			
.. Accounting for Exit and Entrance Fees Incurred in a Conversion from the Savings Association Insurance Fund to the Bank Insurance Fund...............			EITF.90-11
.. Tax Imposed on Excess Bad-Debt Reserves......................................			EITF.86-31
Divestiture of Certain Investment Securities under FIRREA			EITF.89-18
Implementation of Statement 107			EITF.D-29
Intangible Assets			
.. Adjustments of Allocation of Original Purchase Price			EITF.85-3
.. Amortization of Unidentifiable Intangible Assets................................			EITF.85-8
.. Core Deposit Intangibles........................			EITF.85-33
.. Identifiable Intangible Assets			EITF.85-42
.. Unidentifiable Intangible Assets			EITF.85-8
....			EITF.85-42
Investments			
.. Classification of Interest-Only Securities as Held-to-Maturity			EITF.94-4
.. Purchase of Collateralized Mortgage Obligation Instruments or Mortgage-Backed Interest-Only Certificates			EITF.89-4
....			EITF.93-18
Modification of Debt Terms When Debtor Is Experiencing Financial Difficulties			EITF.89-15
Mortgage Banking Activities			
.. Applicability of Statement 65			EITF.D-2
.. Loan Acquisitions Involving Table Funding Arrangements			EITF.92-10
.. Sale of Mortgage Servicing Rights			EITF.89-5
....			EITF.94-5
....			EITF.95-5
Relationship between Statement 15 and Savings and Loan Audit Guide			
.. Loan Loss Allowances			EITF.87-5
Reorganization of a Savings and Loan Association			
.. Regulatory-Assisted Combinations			EITF.85-41
Write-off of Prepayments to the Secondary Reserve of the FSLIC			EITF.87-22
SCHOOLS			
See Not-for-Profit Organizations			
SCIENTIFIC RESEARCH COSTS			
See Research and Development			

	Original Pronouncements	Current Text	EITF and Other
SCRAP			
See Inventory			
SEASONAL BUSINESSES			
See Interim Financial Reporting			
See Revenue Recognition			
See Segment of Business Reporting			
SECURITIES			
See Earnings per Share			
See Financial Instruments			
See Investments			
See Investments: Debt and Equity Securities			
See Investments: Equity Method			
Definition	APB15, App.D	E09.421	
SEGMENT OF BUSINESS REPORTING			
See Disclosure			
See Earnings per Share			
See Income Statement Presentation: Discontinued Operations			
Accounting Changes	FAS14, ¶27	S20.133	
Accounting Principles to Be Used	FAS14, ¶5	S20.106	
. . Equity Method Investments	FAS14, ¶7	S20.108	
. . Foreign Investee That Is Not a Subsidiary of the Primary Reporting Enterprise	FAS24, ¶5	S20.109	
. . Foreign Operations	FAS14, ¶7	S20.108	
. . If Segment Information Provided in Another Enterprise's Financial Statements	FAS24, ¶5	S20.110	
. . Intercompany Balances and Transactions	FAS14, ¶8	S20.111	
. . Intersegment Transactions	FAS14, ¶6	S20.107	
. . Nonconsolidated Subsidiaries	FAS14, ¶7	S20.108	
. . Significant Equity Method Investments	FAS24, ¶5	S20.110	
Brokers and Dealers in Securities			
. . Applicability of Accounting and Reporting Requirements	FAS111, ¶8	S20.505-507	
	FTB79-8, ¶1		
	FTB79-8, ¶5-6		
Customers, Health Care Facilities	FTB79-5, ¶1	S20.503-504	
	FTB79-5, ¶3		
Definition			
. . Complete Set of Financial Statements	FAS24, ¶1	S20.401	
	FAS95, ¶152		
. . Consolidated Financial Information	FAS14, ¶6	S20.402	
. . Financial Report	FAS24, ¶1	S20.403	

See "Terminology" for references to defined terms presented in various accounting pronouncements.
See the Introduction to the Topical Index for details on the use of this index.

	Original Pronouncements	Current Text	EITF and Other

SEGMENT OF BUSINESS REPORTING—continued

Definition—continued

. . Foreign Investee That Is Not a Subsidiary of the Primary Reporting Enterprise .... FAS24, ¶5 — S20.404

. . Identifiable Assets................................. FAS14, ¶10 — S20.405

. . Industry Segment.................................... FAS14, ¶10 — S20.406

. . Nonpublic Enterprise............................. FAS21, ¶8 — S20.407
.... FAS21, ¶13

. . Operating Profit or Loss .... FAS14, ¶10 — S20.408

. . Profit Center.. FAS14, ¶13 — S20.409

. . Reportable Segment .... FAS14, ¶10 — S20.410

. . Revenue .... FAS14, ¶10 — S20.411

Depreciation, Depletion, and Amortization .... FAS14, ¶27 — S20.133

Disposal of a Portion of a Segment of a Business.. AIN-APB30, #1 — I22.501-502

. . Expected Gain on Disposal with Interim Operating Losses .... — — EITF.85-36

Disposal of a Segment of a Business

. . Expected Gain on Disposal with Interim Operating Losses .... — — EITF.85-36

. . Gain (Loss) from Settlement/ Curtailment of Pension Plan............... FAS88, ¶16 — P16.186

. . Prior-Period Adjustments .... APB30, ¶25 — I13.104

Domestic Operations

. . Sales to Unaffiliated Customers .... FAS14, ¶35-36 — S20.141-142

Equity Method Investments .... FAS14, ¶27 — S20.133

Export Sales.. FAS14, ¶31-32 — S20.142-143

Foreign Operations .... FAS14, ¶31-35 — S20.137-141
.... FTB79-4, ¶1 — S20.501-502
.... FTB79-4, ¶3

. . Disclosures Reconciled to Consolidated Information................... FAS14, ¶38 — S20.144

Grouping Products and Services by Industry Lines .... FAS14, ¶12-14 — S20.114-118
.... FAS14, ¶100-101

Inclusion in Complete Set of Financial Statements

. . Comparative Statements........................ FAS14, ¶3 — S20.104
.... FAS95, ¶152

. . Interim Period Statements .... FAS18, ¶8 — S20.105

Industry Segments .... FAS14, ¶9 — S20.112

Information about Major Customers........... FAS30, ¶6 — S20.145

Property, Plant, and Equipment................... FAS14, ¶27 — S20.133

Publicly Traded Enterprises Having Significant Oil and Gas Activities .... FAS69, ¶24 — S20.133A

Purpose... FAS14, ¶5 — S20.106

	Original Pronouncements	Current Text	EITF and Other
SEGMENT OF BUSINESS REPORTING—continued			
Reportable Segments			
. . Criteria for Determining	FAS14, ¶11	S20.113	
. . Data to Be Presented in Dollars	FAS14, ¶29	S20.135	
. . Dominant Segment	FAS14, ¶20	S20.126	
. . Information to Be Presented	FAS14, ¶22-27	S20.128-133	
. . Methods of Presentation	FAS14, ¶28	S20.134	
. . Practical Limit on Number	FAS14, ¶19	S20.125	
. . Reconciliation to Consolidated Information	FAS14, ¶30	S20.136	
. . Selection Criteria	FAS14, ¶15-18	S20.119-124	
	FAS14, ¶103-104		
. . Voluntary Disclosure of Detailed Information	FAS14, ¶21	S20.127	
Restatement of Previously Reported Information	FAS14, ¶40	S20.146	
Scope of Accounting and Reporting Requirements	FAS14, ¶4	S20.101-103	
	FAS21, ¶9		
	FAS21, ¶12		
	FAS21, ¶14-15		
SIC Codes	FAS14, ¶91-98	S20.149-156	
SELF-INSURANCE			
See Contingencies			
See Insurance Costs			
SELLING, GENERAL AND ADMINISTRATIVE EXPENSES			
See Interim Financial Reporting			
SENIOR SECURITIES			
See Earnings per Share			
SERVICE CONTRACTS			
See Revenue Recognition			
SERVICE EFFORTS AND ACCOMPLISHMENTS			
Not-for-Profit Organizations	CON4, ¶51-53		
SERVICE INDUSTRIES			
Revenue Recognition	FAS48, ¶4	R75.106	
SERVICE POTENTIAL			
Definition	CON6, ¶28		
Discussion	CON6, ¶26-30		
	CON6, ¶172-173		
SERVICING FEES			
See Mortgage Banking Activities			
See Mortgage Servicing Rights			
See Receivables Sold with Recourse			
Determining a Normal Servicing Fee Rate for the Sale of an SBA Loan			EITF.94-9

See "Terminology" for references to defined terms presented in various accounting pronouncements.
See the Introduction to the Topical Index for details on the use of this index.

	Original Pronouncements	Current Text	EITF and Other

SETOFF
See Offsetting
SETTLEMENTS (OF DEFINED BENEFIT PENSION PLANS)
See Pension Costs
SETTLEMENTS (OF POST-RETIREMENT BENEFIT PLANS)
See Postretirement Benefits Other Than Pensions
SEVERANCE PAY
See Income Statement Presentation: Discontinued Operations
See Postemployment Benefits
Accounting for Involuntary Termination Benefits...................................... EITF.94-3
SHADOW STOCK PLANS
See Compensation to Employees: Stock Purchase and Stock Option Plans
SHAREHOLDERS' EQUITY
See Additional Paid-in Capital
See Business Combinations
See Capital Stock: Capital Transactions
See Capital Stock: Dividends-in-Kind
See Capital Stock: Preferred Stock
See Capital Stock: Stock Dividends and Stock Splits
See Capital Stock: Treasury Stock
See Foreign Currency Translation
See Retained Earnings
See Statement of Investments by and Distributions to Owners
Development Stage Enterprises .... FAS7, ¶11   De4.107
Nonreciprocal Transfers .... APB29, ¶5   N35.102
Separate Component for Unrealized Gains (Losses) of Investments in Debt and Equity Securities .... FAS115, ¶13   I80.110
SHAREHOLDERS/OWNERS
See Shareholders' Equity
SHARES OUTSTANDING
See Capital Stock: Preferred Stock
See Capital Stock: Stock Dividends and Stock Splits
See Earnings per Share
SHORT-TERM DEBT
Balance Sheet Classification .... ARB43, Ch.3A, ¶7   B05.108
SICK PAY
See Compensation to Employees: Paid Absences

FAS–FASB Statements   FIN–FASB Interpretations   FTB–FASB Technical Bulletins
APB–APB Opinions   AIN–AICPA Interpretations   ARB–Accounting Research Bulletins
CON–FASB Concepts   EITF–EITF Issues   Q&A–FASB Special Reports

	Original Pronouncements	Current Text	EITF and Other
SIGNIFICANT INFLUENCE			
See Investments: Equity Method			
SINKING FUNDS			
See Capital Stock: Preferred Stock			
See Commitments: Long-Term Obligations			
See Debt: Extinguishments			
Balance Sheet Classification	ARB43, Ch.3A, ¶6	B05.107	
Redeemable Stock	FAS47, ¶10	C32.105	
SMALL BUSINESS ADMINISTRATION (SBA)			
Determining a Normal Servicing Fee Rate for the Sale of an SBA Loan			EITF.94-9
SOFTWARE			
See Computer Software			
SOLVENCY			
Information about	CON1, ¶49		
SPECIAL ASSESSMENTS			
Accounting for Special Assessments and Tax Increment Financing Entities (TIFEs)			EITF.91-10
SPECIALIZED ACCOUNTING AND REPORTING			
See Accounting Changes			
See AICPA Statements of Position (SOPs)			
See Banking and Thrift Industries			
See Broadcasting Industry			
See Cable Television Industry			
See Contractor Accounting: Construction-Type Contracts			
See Contractor Accounting: Government Contracts			
See Defined Benefit Pension Plans			
See Development Stage Enterprises			
See Employee Benefit Funds			
See Finance Companies			
See Franchising			
See Insurance Industry			
See Investment Enterprises			
See Mineral Reserves			
See Mortgage Banking Activities			
See Motion Picture Industry			
See Not-for-Profit Organizations			
See Oil and Gas Producing Activities			
See Real Estate Enterprises			
See Record and Music Industry			
See Regulated Operations			
See Title Plant			
Retention in Consolidation			EITF.85-12

See "Terminology" for references to defined terms presented in various accounting pronouncements.
See the Introduction to the Topical Index for details on the use of this index.

	Original Pronouncements	Current Text	EITF and Other
SPECIAL-PURPOSE BORROWINGS			
Gain or Loss Recognition on Defeasance...			EITF.84-26
SPECIAL-PURPOSE ENTITIES			
Accounting for Special Assessments and Tax Increment Financing Entities (TIFEs)			EITF.91-10
Consolidation without Equity Ownership...			EITF.84-30
Impact of Nonsubstantive Lessors, Residual Value Guarantees, and Other Provisions in Leasing Transactions			EITF.90-15
Receivables Sold with Recourse . . Sales to Special-Purpose Entity			EITF.84-30
Sales Recognition on Transfers of Assets by Sponsor................................			EITF.84-30
Transactions Involving Special-Purpose Entities................................			EITF.D-14
SPECIAL TERMINATION BENEFITS PAID TO EMPLOYEES			
See Pension Costs			
See Postretirement Benefits Other Than Pensions			
SPINOFF			
Changes to Fixed Employee Stock Option Plans as a Result of Equity Restructuring			EITF.90-9
Description..	APB29, ¶5	N35.102	
Distributions of Loans Receivable to Shareholders..			EITF.87-17
SPOILAGE			
Inventory..	ARB43, Ch.4, ¶5	I78.106	
SPOT RATE			
See Foreign Currency Translation			
Definition..	FAS52, ¶162	F60.419	
STANDARD COSTS			
See Inventory			
STANDARD INDUSTRIAL CLASSIFICATION (SIC) CODES			
See Segment of Business Reporting			
STANDARDIZED MEASURE OF DISCOUNTED FUTURE NET CASH FLOWS			
See Oil and Gas Producing Activities			
STANDARDS, FINANCIAL ACCOUNTING			
Relation to Concepts....................................	CON1, ¶3		
STANDSTILL AGREEMENTS			
Costs Incurred in a Takeover Defense			EITF.85-2
Effect on Subsequent Pooling of Interests ..			EITF.87-15
Limit on Investors............	FIN35, ¶9	I82.108	

FAS–FASB Statements	FIN–FASB Interpretations	FTB–FASB Technical Bulletins
APB–APB Opinions	AIN–AICPA Interpretations	ARB–Accounting Research Bulletins
CON–FASB Concepts	EITF–EITF Issues	Q&A–FASB Special Reports

	Original Pronouncements	Current Text	EITF and Other
STANDSTILL			
AGREEMENTS—continued			
Takeover Attempts	FTB85-6, ¶4-7	I17.509-510	
		I60.507-508	
. . Costs Incurred in a Takeover Defense ..			EITF.85-2
START-UP COSTS			
See Development Stage Enterprises			
STATE AND LOCAL			
GOVERNMENTAL UNITS			
Application of Conceptual Framework	CON4, ¶65-66		
	CON6, ¶2		
Compensated Absences			
. . Limitation of Accounting and			
Reporting Requirements	FAS43, ¶2	C44.102	
Contributions	CON4, ¶6		
Defined Benefit Pension Plans			
. . Application of Accounting			
Requirements	FAS35, ¶1	Pe5.101	
Relation to Not-for-Profit Organizations	CON4, ¶3-5		
	CON6, ¶2		
Utilities	FAS71, ¶5	Re6.115	
STATEMENT OF ACCUMULATED			
PLAN BENEFITS			
See Defined Benefit Pension Plans			
STATEMENT OF ACTIVITIES			
See Not-for-Profit Organizations			
STATEMENT OF CASH FLOWS			
See Cash Flows Statement			
STATEMENT OF CHANGES IN			
ACCUMULATED PLAN BENEFITS			
See Defined Benefit Pension Plans			
STATEMENT OF CHANGES IN			
NET ASSETS AVAILABLE FOR			
BENEFITS			
See Defined Benefit Pension Plans			
STATEMENT OF FINANCIAL			
POSITION			
See Balance Sheet Classification: Current			
Assets and Liabilities			
See Financial Position			
See Financial Statements: Comparative			
Financial Statements			
See Not-for-Profit Organizations			
See Offsetting			
Component of Full Set of Financial			
Statements	CON5, ¶13		
Definition	APB18, ¶3		
	CON6, ¶20		
Description, Nature, and Recognition			
Considerations	CON5, ¶26-29		

See "Terminology" for references to defined terms presented in various accounting pronouncements.

See the Introduction to the Topical Index for details on the use of this index.

	Original Pronouncements	Current Text	EITF and Other

STATEMENT OF FUNCTIONAL EXPENSES
See Not-for-Profit Organizations
STATEMENT OF INCOME
See Earnings per Share
See Extraordinary Items
See Financial Statements: Comparative
  Financial Statements
See Income Statement Presentation:
  Discontinued Operations
See Income Taxes
STATEMENT OF INVESTMENTS BY AND DISTRIBUTIONS TO OWNERS
See Shareholders' Equity
Component of Full Set of Financial
  Statements .... CON5, ¶13
Description, Nature, and Recognition
  Considerations... CON5, ¶55-57
STATEMENT OF RETAINED EARNINGS
See Retained Earnings
STATEMENT OF STOCKHOLDERS' EQUITY
See Shareholders' Equity
See Statement of Investments by and
  Distributions to Owners
STATEMENTS OF EARNINGS AND COMPREHENSIVE INCOME
See Comprehensive Income
See Earnings
Components of Full Set of Financial
  Statements .... CON5, ¶13
Description, Nature, and Recognition
  Considerations... CON5, ¶30-41
Relationship between Earnings and
  Comprehensive Income .... CON5, ¶42-44
STATEMENTS OF NET ASSETS AVAILABLE FOR BENEFITS
See Defined Benefit Pension Plans
STATEMENTS OF POSITION (SOPs)
Accounting Changes.................................... FAS111, ¶10   A06.127
.... FIN20, ¶5
STEAMSHIP COMPANIES (U.S.)
Income Taxes .... FAS109, ¶9   I27.108
.... FAS109, ¶32   I27.131
STEP ACQUISITIONS
See Consolidation
See Intangible Assets

FAS–FASB Statements	FIN–FASB Interpretations	FTB–FASB Technical Bulletins
APB–APB Opinions	AIN–AICPA Interpretations	ARB–Accounting Research Bulletins
CON–FASB Concepts	EITF–EITF Issues	Q&A–FASB Special Reports

	Original Pronouncements	Current Text	EITF and Other

STEP ACQUISITIONS—continued

Basis in Leveraged Buyout Transactions EITF.86-16

....   EITF.88-16

. . Allocating Basis to Individual Assets and Liabilities under Issue No. 88-16 ....   EITF.90-12

STOCK APPRECIATION RIGHTS

Compensation Expense Relating to Cancellation..   EITF.D-18

Definition .... FIN28, ¶9   C47.403

Description................................... FIN28, ¶2-5   C47.119-122

.... FIN28, ¶19-27   C47.138-146

Purchase by Target Company in Leveraged Buyout.....................................   EITF.84-13

Pyramid Stock Option Plans EITF.84-18

STOCK BONUS OR AWARD PLANS

See Compensation to Employees: Stock Purchase and Stock Option Plans

STOCK DEPRECIATION RIGHTS

See Compensation to Employees: Stock Purchase and Stock Option Plans

See Stock Options

STOCK DIVIDENDS

See Capital Stock: Capital Transactions

See Capital Stock: Dividends-in-Kind

See Capital Stock: Stock Dividends and Stock Splits

See Consolidation

See Earnings per Share

Definition .... ARB43, Ch.7B, ¶1   C20.401

STOCK DIVIDENDS SUBSIDIARIES

See Consolidation

STOCK INDEMNIFICATION RIGHTS

See Compensation to Employees: Stock Purchase and Stock Option Plans

See Stock Options

STOCK ISSUED TO EMPLOYEES

See Compensation to Employees: Stock Purchase and Stock Option Plans

See Earnings per Share

STOCK LIFE INSURANCE ENTERPRISES

See Insurance Industry

STOCK OPTION AND STOCK PURCHASE PLANS

See Compensation to Employees: Stock Purchase and Stock Option Plans

See Earnings per Share

See "Terminology" for references to defined terms presented in various accounting pronouncements.

See the Introduction to the Topical Index for details on the use of this index.

	Original Pronouncements	Current Text	EITF and Other

STOCK OPTIONS

See Compensation to Employees: Stock Purchase and Stock Option Plans

See Employee Stock Ownership Plans (ESOPs)

See Financial Instruments

Accounting for a Reload Stock Option EITF.90-7

Acquired in a Business Combination EITF.85-45

Book Value Stock Option Plans

. . Effect of Initial Public Offering on Compensation Expense EITF.88-6

Book Value Stock Purchase Plans

. . Accounting by a Privately Held Company EITF.87-23

. . Accounting by a Publicly Held Company EITF.88-6

. . Effect of Initial Public Offering on Compensation Expense EITF.88-6

. . Measurement of Compensation Cost....   EITF.87-23

Buyout of Compensatory Stock Options EITF.94-6

Cancellation and Reissuance of Options.....   EITF.87-33

Changes to Fixed Employee Stock Option Plans as a Result of Equity Restructuring...   EITF.90-9

Exchange of Options EITF.90-9

Options to Purchase Stock of Another Entity EITF.85-9

Permanent Discount Restricted Stock Purchase Plans.......................................   EITF.84-34

Purchase by Target Company in Leveraged Buyout.....................................   EITF.84-13

Pyramid Stock Option Plans EITF.84-18

Repricing of Options ....   EITF.87-33 / EITF.90-9

Repurchase of Options ....   EITF.87-33 / EITF.94-6

Settlement of Stock Options and Awards in a Business Combination EITF.85-45

Stapled Options...   EITF.90-9

. . Nonstapled Options EITF.90-9

Stock Depreciation Rights...........................   EITF.87-33

Stock Indemnification Rights......................   EITF.87-33

STOCK PURCHASE PLANS

See Compensation to Employees: Stock Purchase and Stock Option Plans

STOCK PURCHASE WARRANTS

See Capital Stock: Capital Transactions

See Debt: Convertible Debt and Debt with Stock Purchase Warrants

See Earnings per Share

FAS–FASB Statements   FIN–FASB Interpretations   FTB–FASB Technical Bulletins
APB–APB Opinions   AIN–AICPA Interpretations   ARB–Accounting Research Bulletins
CON–FASB Concepts   EITF–EITF Issues   Q&A–FASB Special Reports

	Original Pronouncements	Current Text	EITF and Other
STOCK PURCHASE WARRANTS—continued			
See Financial Instruments			
Debt Tendered to Exercise Warrants	AIN-APB26, #1	D14.505-506	
Debt with Stock Purchase Warrants	APB14, ¶13	D10.104-106	
	APB14, ¶16-17		
Includes Put for Stock Purchased			EITF.86-35
Qualification as a Liability	CON6, ¶254		
STOCK SPLITS			
See Capital Stock: Capital Transactions			
See Capital Stock: Stock Dividends and Stock Splits			
Definition	ARB43, Ch.7B, ¶2	C20.402	
STOCKBROKERAGE INDUSTRY			
See Earnings per Share			
See Investments: Debt and Equity Securities			
See Segment of Business Reporting			
Unclassified Balance Sheet	FAS6, ¶7	B05.102	
STOCKHOLDERS' EQUITY			
See Shareholders' Equity			
STOCKHOLDERS/OWNERS			
See Shareholders' Equity			
SUBCHAPTER S CORPORATIONS			
See Earnings per Share			
SUBCONTRACTORS			
See Contractor Accounting: Construction-Type Contracts			
See Contractor Accounting: Government Contracts			
SUBJECTIVE ACCELERATION CLAUSE			
See Balance Sheet Classification: Current Assets and Liabilities			
SUBLEASE			
See Leases			
SUBSCRIPTIONS			
Qualification as Liabilities	CON6, ¶197		
SUBSEQUENT EVENTS			
See Contingencies			
See Foreign Currency Translation			
See Nonmonetary Transactions			
SUBSIDIARIES			
See Consolidation			
See Discontinued Operations			

See "Terminology" for references to defined terms presented in various accounting pronouncements.
See the Introduction to the Topical Index for details on the use of this index.

	Original Pronouncements	Current Text	EITF and Other
SUBSIDIARIES—continued			
See Earnings per Share			
See Foreign Currency Translation			
See Income Taxes			
Business Combinations	AIN-APB16, #18	B50.556-559	
	AIN-APB16, #36	B50.635-637	
Definition	APB18, ¶3	I82.408	
Exchanges of Ownership Interests between Entities under Common Control			EITF.90-5
Fiscal Year of Parent and Subsidiary Differs			
. . Classification of Subsidiary's Loan Payable in Consolidated Balance Sheet			EITF.88-15
Income Tax Provision			
. . Allocating Consolidated Tax Provision			EITF.86-9
Preacquisition Earnings	ARB51, ¶9	R70.101	
Push-down Accounting			EITF.86-9
Push-down of Parent Company Debt			EITF.84-42
Related Parties	FAS57, ¶1	R36.101	
Sale of Capital Stock by Subsidiary			
. . Recognizing Income Tax Effect			EITF.84-27
Separate Financial Statements			
. . Push-down Accounting			EITF.85-21
. . Push-down of Parent Company Debt			EITF.84-23
Unconsolidated	FAS14, ¶27	C51.102-103	
	FAS94, ¶13	I82.102	
	FAS94, ¶15	S20.133	
SUBSTANCE VS. FORM			
Relation to Reliability	CON2, ¶160		
SUCCESSFUL EFFORTS METHOD			
See Oil and Gas Producing Activities			
SUMMARY OF ACCOUNTING POLICIES			
See Accounting Policies			
SUM-OF-THE-YEARS DIGITS METHOD			
Depreciation	FAS109, ¶288	D40.104	
SUPPLEMENTAL FINANCIAL INFORMATION			
See Changing Prices: Reporting Their Effects in Financial Reports			
See Earnings per Share			
See Oil and Gas Producing Activities			
See Segment of Business Reporting			
Relation to Recognition in Financial Statements	CON5, ¶7-9		

	Original Pronouncements	Current Text	EITF and Other
SUPPLEMENTAL UNEMPLOYMENT BENEFITS			
See Postemployment Benefits			
SURPLUS (CAPITAL/ CONTRIBUTED/PAID-IN)			
See Additional Paid-in Capital			
See Capital Stock: Capital Transactions			
See Statement of Investments by and Distributions to Owners			
SWAPS			
See Financial Instruments			
Foreign Currency Swaps			
. . Offsetting			EITF.86-25
Foreign Debt-for-Equity (Investor's Perspective)			EITF.87-12
Hedged by Cash Security			EITF.87-1
Interest Rate Swap Transactions			EITF.84-36
			EITF.88-8
. . Termination or Sale			EITF.84-7
Mortgage Swaps			EITF.88-8
SYNDICATION FEES			
Fees Associated with Loan Syndications			EITF.88-17
Real Estate Syndicators			
. . Revenue Recognition of Syndication Fees			EITF.85-37
SYNDICATION OF REAL ESTATE			
Recognition of Receipts from Made-up Rental Shortfalls			EITF.85-27

(The next page is T-421.)

See "Terminology" for references to defined terms presented in various accounting pronouncements.
See the Introduction to the Topical Index for details on the use of this index.

	Original Pronouncements	Current Text	EITF and Other
TAKE-OR-PAY CONTRACTS			
Definition	FAS47, ¶23	C32.403	
Illustration	FAS47, ¶29-32	C32.111-114	
TAKEOVER ATTEMPTS			
Costs Incurred in a Takeover Defense			EITF.85-2
Issues Relating to	FTB85-6, ¶1-7	C23.501-503	
		I17.509-510	
		I60.507-508	
TANDEM PLANS			
See Compensation to Employees: Stock Purchase and Stock Option Plans			
TAX			
See Income Taxes			
See Interim Financial Reporting			
Definition	FIN18, ¶5	I73.403	
Real and Personal Property	ARB43, Ch.10A, ¶10-14	T10.101-108	
. . Balance Sheet and Income Statement			
Disclosure	ARB43, Ch.10A, ¶16-18	T10.106-108	
TAXABLE INCOME			
See Income Taxes			
Definition	APB23, ¶21	Bt7.408	
	FAS109, ¶289	I27.415	
TAX-EXEMPT BORROWINGS			
See Interest: Capitalization of Interest Costs			
TAX-EXEMPT SECURITIES			
See Leases			
TAX INCREMENT FINANCING ENTITIES (TIFEs)			
Accounting for Special Assessments and Tax Increment Financing Entities (TIFEs)			EITF.91-10
TAX INDEMNIFICATIONS			
Leases			EITF.86-33
TAX LEASES			
See Income Taxes			
TAX REFORM ACT OF 1984			
Deferred Taxes			
. . DISC (Domestic International Sales Corporation)			EITF.84-2
Leases			
. . Delayed Equity Contributions by Leveraged Lessors			EITF.85-16
Stock Life Insurance Companies			
. . Policy Reserves Recomputed			EITF.84-1
TAX REFORM ACT OF 1986			
Alternative Minimum Tax			EITF.87-8
. . Tax Credit Carryforwards			EITF.86-41

FAS–FASB Statements　　　FIN–FASB Interpretations　　　FTB–FASB Technical Bulletins
APB–APB Opinions　　　AIN–AICPA Interpretations　　　ARB–Accounting Research Bulletins
CON–FASB Concepts　　　EITF–EITF Issues　　　Q&A–FASB Special Reports

	Original Pronouncements	Current Text	EITF and Other

TAX REFORM ACT OF 1986—continued
Change in Tax Rate
. . Effect on Assets and Liabilities
    Acquired in a Business Combination ..   EITF.86-42
Discounting Loss Reserves of Insurance
  Companies...   EITF.86-37
Effect on Income Tax Provision EITF.86-11
Inventory Cost Capitalization Rules EITF.86-46
Lease Agreements
. . Tax Indemnifications EITF.86-33
Master Limited Partnerships
. . Carryover of Predecessor Cost..............   EITF.87-21
Recognition Prior to Enactment EITF.86-11

TAX REFORM ACT OF 1993
Accounting for Tax Benefits Resulting
  from Investments in Qualified Affordable
  Housing Projects EITF.94-1
Effect of a Retroactive Change in Enacted
  Tax Rates That Is Included in Income
  from Continuing Operations EITF.93-13
Recognition and Measurement of the Tax
  Benefit of Excess Tax-Deductible
  Goodwill Resulting from a Retroactive
  Change in Tax Law EITF.93-12

TAX REGULATIONS
See Income Taxes
See Interim Financial Reporting
See Leases

TELEVISION BARTER SYNDICATORS
Revenue Recognition
. . Advertising Time for Television
    Programming EITF.87-10

TEMPORARY DIFFERENCES
See Income Taxes

TERMINATION BENEFITS
See Pension Costs
See Postemployment Benefits
See Postretirement Benefits Other Than
  Pensions
See Special Termination Benefits Paid to
  Employees
Accounting for Involuntary Termination
  Benefits..   EITF.94-3

TERMINATION OF PENSION PLAN
See Pension Costs

TERMINATION RATE
See Insurance Industry
Definition .... FAS60, ¶66   In6.435

See "Terminology" for references to defined terms presented in various accounting pronouncements.
See the Introduction to the Topical Index for details on the use of this index.

	Original Pronouncements	Current Text	EITF and Other
TERMINOLOGY			
Accounting Changes	APB20, ¶6	A06.401	
Accounting Policies	APB22, ¶6	A10.401	
Accounting Principle	APB20, ¶7	A06.402	
Accrual	CON6, ¶139-141		
Accumulated Benefit Obligation	FAS87, ¶264	P16.401	
Accumulated Plan Benefits	FAS35, ¶280	Pe5.401	
Accumulated Postretirement Benefit Obligation	FAS106, ¶518	P40.401	
Acquisition Costs	FAS60, ¶66	In6.401	
Active Plan Participant	FAS106, ¶518	P40.402	
Actual Return on Plan Assets Component (of Net Periodic Pension Cost)	FAS87, ¶264	P16.402	
Actual Return on Plan Assets Component (of Net Periodic Postretirement Benefit Cost)	FAS106, ¶518	P40.403	
Actuarial Present Value	FAS87, ¶264	P16.403	
	FAS106, ¶518	P40.404	
Actuarial Present Value of Accumulated Plan Benefits	FAS35, ¶280	Pe5.403	
Advance Royalty	FAS50, ¶18	Re4.401	
Affiliated Enterprise	FAS65, ¶34	Mo4.401	
Affiliates	FAS57, ¶24	R36.401	
Allocated Contract	FAS87, ¶264	P16.404	
Allocation	CON6, ¶142		
Allocation Period	FAS38, ¶4	B50.401	
Allowable Costs	FAS71, ¶1	Re6.401	
Amenities	FAS67, ¶28	Re2.401	
Amortization	CON6, ¶142	P16.405	
	FAS87, ¶264		
	FAS106, ¶518	P40.405	
Annual Effective Tax Rate	APB28, ¶19	I73.401	
Annuity Contract	FAS60, ¶66	In6.402	
	FAS87, ¶57	P16.406	
	FAS87, ¶264		
	FAS88, ¶5		
Area Franchise	FAS45, ¶26	Fr3.401	
Articulation	CON6, ¶20-21		
Assessment Enterprise	FAS60, ¶66	In6.403	
Assets	CON6, ¶25		
Assumed Per Capita Claims Cost (By Age)	FAS106, ¶518	P40.406	
Assuming Enterprise	FAS113, ¶121	In6.403A	
Assumptions	FAS87, ¶264	P16.407	
	FAS106, ¶518	P40.407	
Attribute	CON6, ¶65-67	F60.401	
	FAS52, ¶162		
Attribution	FAS87, ¶264	P16.408	
	FAS106, ¶518	P40.408	
Attribution Period	FAS106, ¶518	P40.409	

	Original Pronouncements	Current Text	EITF and Other
TERMINOLOGY—continued			
Bargain Purchase	FAS45, ¶26	Fr3.402	
Bargain Purchase Option	FAS13, ¶5	L10.401	
Bargain Renewal Option	FAS13, ¶5	L10.402	
Barter	FAS63, ¶14	Br5.401	
Benefit	FIN18, ¶5	I73.403	
Benefit Formula	FAS87, ¶264	P16.409	
	FAS106, ¶518	P40.410	
Benefit Information	FAS35, ¶280	Pe5.404	
Benefit Information Date	FAS35, ¶280	Pe5.405	
Benefit Security	FAS35, ¶280	Pe5.406	
Benefit/Years-of-Service Approach	FAS87, ¶264	P16.411	
Benefits	FAS35, ¶280	P16.410	
	FAS87, ¶264	Pe5.407	
	FAS106, ¶518	P40.411	
Bias	CON2, Glossary		
"Book Entry" Securities	FIN41, ¶3	B10.401	
Broadcaster	FAS63, ¶14	Br5.402	
Cable Television Plant	FAS51, ¶17	Ca4.401	
Call Price	APB15, App.D	E09.401	
Callable Obligations	FAS78, ¶1	B05.400	
Capital Leases	FAS13, ¶7	L10.403	
Capital Maintenance	CON6, ¶71		
Capitalize	FAS71, ¶4	Re6.402	
Captive Insurer	FAS87, ¶264	P16.412	
	FAS106, ¶518	P40.412	
Career-Average-Pay Formula (Career-Average-Pay Plan)	FAS87, ¶264	P16.413	
Carrybacks	FAS109, ¶289	I27.401	
Carryforwards	FAS109, ¶289	I27.402	
Carrying Amount	FAS72, ¶5	Bt7.401	
Carrying Amount of the Payable	FAS15, ¶13	D22.401	
Cash Equivalents	FAS95, ¶8	C25.106	
Ceding Enterprise	FAS113, ¶121	In6.403B	
Change in Permanently Restricted Net Assets	CON6, ¶119		
Change in Temporarily Restricted Net Assets	CON6, ¶123		
Change in Unrestricted Net Assets	CON6, ¶127		
Changes in Financial Position	CON6, ¶20		
Circumstances (Affecting an Entity)	CON6, ¶136		
Claim Adjustment Expenses	FAS60, ¶66	In6.405	
Claims	FAS60, ¶66	In6.404	
Coding	FAS86, ¶52	Co2.401	
Collateralized Mortgage Obligations	FTB85-2, ¶1	C30.501	
Collections	FAS116, ¶209	C67.401	
Commitment Fees	FAS91, ¶80	L20.401	
Common Costs	FAS67, ¶28	Re2.402	
Common Stock	APB15, App.D	E09.403	
Common Stock Equivalent	APB15, App.D	E09.404	

See "Terminology" for references to defined terms presented in various accounting pronouncements.
See the Introduction to the Topical Index for details on the use of this index.

	Original Pronouncements	Current Text	EITF and Other

TERMINOLOGY—continued

Comparability	CON2, Glossary		
Compensated Absences	FAS43, ¶1	C44.401	
Complete Set of Financial Statements	FAS24, ¶1	Oi5.400	
	FAS24, ¶5	S20.401	
	FAS69, ¶1		
	FAS95, ¶152		
Completeness	CON2, Glossary		
Comprehensive Income	CON6, ¶70		
Conditional Contract	FIN39, ¶3	B10.402	
Conditional Promise to Give	FAS116, ¶209	C67.402	
Conservatism	CON2, Glossary		
Consistency	CON2, Glossary		
Consolidated Financial Information	FAS14, ¶6	S20.402	
Consolidated Statements	ARB51, ¶1	C51.401	
Constructive Obligations	CON6, ¶40		
Contingencies	FAS5, ¶1	C59.401	
Contingency Consideration	APB16, ¶78	B50.402	
Contingent Issuance	APB15, App.D	E09.405	
Contingent Rentals	FAS29, ¶11	L10.404	
Continuing Franchise Fee	FAS45, ¶26	Fr3.403	
Contribution	FAS116, ¶209	C67.403	
Contributory Plan	FAS35, ¶280	P16.414	
	FAS87, ¶264	Pe5.408	
	FAS106, ¶518	P40.413	
Control	FAS57, ¶24	R36.402	
Conversion	FAS52, ¶162	F60.402	
Conversion Price	APB15, App.D	E09.406	
Conversion Rate	APB15, App.D	E09.407	
Conversion Value	APB15, App.D	E09.408	
Conversion of Debt	FAS84, ¶3	D10.103C	
Convertible Debt	APB14, ¶3	D10.101	
Corporate Joint Ventures	APB18, ¶3	I82.401	
Cost	ARB43, Ch.4, ¶5	I78.401	
	CON6, ¶26		
Cost Method	APB18, ¶6	I82.402	
Cost Recovery Method	FAS60, ¶66	In6.406	
Cost-Sharing (Provisions of the Plan)	FAS106, ¶518	P40.414	
Costs Incurred to Rent Real Estate Projects	FAS67, ¶28	Re2.403	
Costs Incurred to Sell Real Estate Projects	FAS67, ¶28	Re2.404	
Credit Card Fees	FAS91, ¶80	L20.402	
Credited Service Period	FAS106, ¶518	P40.415	
Credit Life Insurance	FAS60, ¶66	In6.407	
Credit Risk	FAS105, ¶7	F25.401	
Cumulative Accounting Adjustments	CON5, ¶42		
Currency Swaps	FAS52, ¶162	F60.403	
Current (Normal) Servicing Fee Rate	FAS65, ¶34	Mo4.402	
	FAS77, ¶12	R20.401	
Current Assets	ARB43, Ch.3A, ¶4	B05.401	

FAS–FASB Statements   FIN–FASB Interpretations   FTB–FASB Technical Bulletins
APB–APB Opinions   AIN–AICPA Interpretations   ARB–Accounting Research Bulletins
CON–FASB Concepts   EITF–EITF Issues   Q&A–FASB Special Reports

T-425

	Original Pronouncements	Current Text	EITF and Other
TERMINOLOGY—continued			
Current Cost/Constant Purchasing Power...	FAS89, ¶44	C28.401	
Current Exchange Rate	FAS52, ¶162	F60.404	
Current Liabilities	ARB43, Ch.3A, ¶7	B05.402	
Current Market Value	FAS89, ¶44	C28.402	
Current Tax Expense or Benefit	FAS109, ¶289	I27.403	
Curtailment	FAS87, ¶264	P16.415	
	FAS88, ¶6	P16.447	
Curtailment (of a Postretirement Benefit Plan)	FAS106, ¶518	P40.416	
Customer Support	FAS86, ¶52	Co2.402	
Daylight Overdraft or Other Intraday Credit	FIN41, ¶3	B10.403	
Daypart	FAS63, ¶14	Br5.403	
Debt	FAS15, ¶4	D22.402	
Debt Security	FAS115, ¶137	I80.401	
Deductible Temporary Difference	FAS109, ¶289	I27.404	
Defeasance	FAS76, ¶14	D14.102A	
Deferral	CON6, ¶141		
Deferred Tax Asset	FAS109, ¶289	I27.405	
Deferred Tax Expense or Benefit	FAS109, ¶289	I27.406	
Deferred Tax Liability	FAS109, ¶289	I27.407	
Defined Benefit Pension Plan	FAS35, ¶280	P16.416	
	FAS87, ¶264	Pe5.409	
Defined Benefit Postretirement Plan	FAS106, ¶518	P40.417	
Defined Contribution Pension Plan	FAS87, ¶264	P16.417	
Defined Contribution Postretirement Plan	FAS106, ¶518	P40.418	
Dependency Status	FAS106, ¶518	P40.419	
Deposit Method	FAS60, ¶66	In6.408	
Depreciation Accounting	ARB43, Ch.9C, ¶5	D40.401	
Derivative Financial Instrument	FAS119, ¶5	F25.401B	
Detail Program Design	FAS86, ¶52	Co2.403	
Development	FAS2, ¶8	R50.401	
Development Stage Enterprises	FAS7, ¶8	De4.401	
Development Well	FAS19, ¶274	Oi5.401	
Dilution (Dilutive)	APB15, App.D	E09.409	
Direct Financing Leases	FAS13, ¶6	L10.405	
Direct Selling Costs	FAS51, ¶17	Ca4.402	
Discontinued Operations	APB30, ¶8	I13.401	
Discount Rate	FAS87, ¶264	P16.418	
	FAS106, ¶518	P40.420	
Discount or Premium on a Forward Contract	FAS52, ¶162	F60.405	
Disposal Date	APB30, ¶14	I13.402	
Distributions to Owners	CON6, ¶67		
Distributor	FAS53, ¶26	Mo6.401	
Dividends	APB18, ¶3	I82.403	
Dividends to Policyholders	FAS60, ¶66	In6.409	
Donor-imposed Condition	FAS116, ¶209	C67.404	

See "Terminology" for references to defined terms presented in various accounting pronouncements.
See the Introduction to the Topical Index for details on the use of this index.

	Original Pronouncements	Current Text	EITF and Other
TERMINOLOGY—continued			
Donor-imposed Restriction	FAS116, ¶209	C67.405	
	FAS117, ¶168	No5.402	
Dual Presentation	APB15, App.D	E09.410	
Earned	CON5, ¶83		
Earnings	CON5, ¶33		
Earnings or Losses of an Investee	APB18, ¶3	I82.404	
Earnings per Share	APB15, App.D	E09.411	
Economic Resources	CON6, ¶27		
Effective Yield	FAS85, ¶3	E09.123A	
Elements of Financial Statements	CON6, ¶5		
Employee	FAS35, ¶280	Pe5.410	
Endowment Contract	FAS60, ¶66	In6.410	
Endowment Fund	FAS117, ¶168	No5.403	
Enterprise	FAS52, ¶162	F60.406	
Entity	CON6, ¶24	F60.407	
	FAS52, ¶162		
Equitable Obligations	CON6, ¶40		
Equity	CON6, ¶49-50		
Equity Method Investments	APB18, ¶6	I82.405	
	APB18, ¶11		
Equity Security	FAS115, ¶137	I80.402	
ERISA	FAS35, ¶280	Pe5.411	
	FAS87, ¶264		
Estimated Economic Life of Leased Property	FAS13, ¶5	L10.406	
Estimated Residual Value of Leased Property	FAS13, ¶5	L10.407	
Event	FAS109, ¶289	I27.408	
Events	CON6, ¶135		
Exchange Contract	FIN39, ¶3	B10.404	
Exchange (Exchange Transactions)	APB29, ¶3	N35.401	
	CON6, ¶137		
Executory Costs	FAS13, ¶7	L10.408	
	FAS13, ¶10		
Exercise Price	APB15, App.D	E09.412	
Expected Long-Term Rate of Return on Plan Assets	FAS87, ¶264	P16.419	
	FAS106, ¶518	P40.421	
Expected Postretirement Benefit Obligation	FAS106, ¶518	P40.422	
Expected Return on Plan Assets	FAS87, ¶264	P16.420	
	FAS106, ¶518	P40.423	
Expenses	CON6, ¶80		
Explicit (Approach to) Assumptions	FAS87, ¶264	P16.421	
	FAS106, ¶518	P40.424	
Exploitation Costs	FAS53, ¶26	Mo6.402	
Exploratory Well	FAS19, ¶274	Oi5.402	
Extended Warranty Contracts	FTB90-1, ¶2	R75.502	
Extraordinary Items	APB30, ¶20	I17.401	

FAS–FASB Statements   FIN–FASB Interpretations   FTB–FASB Technical Bulletins
APB–APB Opinions   AIN–AICPA Interpretations   ARB–Accounting Research Bulletins
CON–FASB Concepts   EITF–EITF Issues   Q&A–FASB Special Reports

	Original Pronouncements	Current Text	EITF and Other

TERMINOLOGY—continued

	Original Pronouncements	Current Text	EITF and Other
Fair Value	FAS67, ¶28	P16.422	
	FAS87, ¶264	Re2.405	
	FAS106, ¶518	P40.425	
	FAS107, ¶5	F25.401C	
	FAS115, ¶137	I80.403	
Fair Value of the Leased Property	FAS13, ¶5	L10.409	
Federal Home Loan Mortgage Corporation (FHLMC)	FAS65, ¶34	Mo4.403	
Federal National Mortgage Association (FNMA)	FAS65, ¶34	Mo4.404	
Feedback Value	CON2, Glossary		
Field	FAS19, ¶272	Oi5.403	
Film	FAS53, ¶26	Mo6.403	
Film Distributor	FAS53, ¶26	Mo6.404	
Final-Pay Formula (Final-Pay Plan)	FAS87, ¶264	P16.423	
Financial Capital Maintenance Concept	CON5, ¶47		
	CON6, ¶71-72		
Financial Flexibility	CON5, ¶24		
Financial Instrument	FAS80, ¶15	F25.402	
	FAS105, ¶6	F80.401	
	FAS107, ¶3		
Financial Position	CON6, ¶20		
Financial Position of an Investee	APB18, ¶3	I82.404	
Financial Report	FAS24, ¶1	S20.403	
Firm Commitment	FAS80, ¶15	F80.402	
Flat-Benefit Formula (Flat-Benefit Plan)	FAS87, ¶264	P16.424	
Foreign Currency	FAS52, ¶162	F60.408	
Foreign Currency Financial Statements	FAS52, ¶162	F60.409	
Foreign Currency Transactions	FAS52, ¶162	F60.410	
Foreign Currency Translation	FAS52, ¶162	F60.411	
Foreign Entity	FAS52, ¶162	F60.412	
Foreign Geographic Area	FAS69, ¶12	Oi5.403A	
Foreign Investee That Is Not a Subsidiary	FAS24, ¶5	S20.404	
Forward Exchange Contracts	FAS52, ¶162	F60.413	
Forward Rate	FAS52, ¶162	F60.414	
Franchise Agreement	FAS45, ¶26	Fr3.404	
Franchisee	FAS45, ¶26	Fr3.405	
Franchisor	FAS45, ¶26	Fr3.406	
Fraternal Benefit Society	FAS60, ¶66	In6.411	
Fronting Arrangements	FAS113, ¶121	In6.411A	
Full Eligibility Date	FAS106, ¶518	P40.427	
Full Eligibility (for Benefits)	FAS106, ¶518	P40.426	
Full Set of Financial Statements	FAS24, ¶1	Oi5.400	
	FAS24, ¶5	S20.401	
	FAS69, ¶1		
	FAS95, ¶152		
Fully Diluted Earnings per Share	APB15, App.D	E09.413	
Fully Eligible Plan Participants	FAS106, ¶518	P40.428	
Functional Classification	FAS117, ¶168	No5.404	

See "Terminology" for references to defined terms presented in various accounting pronouncements.

See the Introduction to the Topical Index for details on the use of this index.

	Original Pronouncements	Current Text	EITF and Other
TERMINOLOGY—continued			
License Agreement for Television Program Material	FAS53, ¶26	Mo6.407	
License Agreements	FAS50, ¶18	Re4.402	
Life Insurance Enterprises	FAS60, ¶66	In6.418	
Liquidity	CON5, ¶24		
Local Currency	FAS52, ¶162	F60.416	
Long-Term Interest-Bearing Assets	FAS72, ¶5	Bt7.403	
Long-Term Obligations	FAS6, ¶2	B05.403	
Loss	CON6, ¶16	P16.431	
	FAS87, ¶264		
Losses	CON6, ¶83		
Lower of Cost or Market (Rule)	ARB43, Ch.4, ¶9	I78.403	
Maintenance	FAS86, ¶52	Co2.404	
Maintenance Costs	FAS60, ¶66	In6.419	
Maintenance of Net Assets	CON6, ¶105		
Management	FAS57, ¶24	R36.404	
Market	ARB43, Ch.4, ¶9	I78.404	
	FAS53, ¶26	Mo6.408	
Market Parity	APB15, App.D	E09.416	
Market-Related Value of Plan Assets	FAS87, ¶264	P16.432	
	FAS106, ¶518	P40.437	
Market Risk	FAS105, ¶7	F25.403	
Master Netting Arrangement	FIN39, ¶10	B10.405	
Materiality	CON2, Glossary		
Measurement Date	APB25, ¶10	C47.401	
	FAS87, ¶264	P16.433	
	FAS106, ¶518	P40.438	
Measurement Date of a Disposal	APB30, ¶14	I13.403	
Medicare Reimbursement Rates	FAS106, ¶518	P40.439	
Mineral Resource Assets	FAS89, ¶44	C28.407	
Minimum Guarantee	FAS50, ¶18	Re4.403	
Minimum Lease Payments	FAS13, ¶5	L10.417	
	FAS29, ¶10		
Monetary Assets	APB29, ¶3	C28.408	
	FAS89, ¶44	N35.402	
Monetary Liabilities	APB29, ¶3	C28.409	
	FAS89, ¶44	N35.402	
Money-Over-Money Lease Transactions	FTB88-1, ¶16	L10.417B	
Morbidity	FAS60, ¶66	In6.420	
Mortality	FAS60, ¶66	In6.421	
Mortality Rate	FAS87, ¶264	P16.434	
Mortgage Banking Enterprise	FAS65, ¶34	Mo4.409	
Mortgage Guaranty Insurance Enterprise	FAS60, ¶66	In6.422	
Mortgage-Backed Securities	FAS65, ¶34	Mo4.408	
Motion Picture Films	FAS53, ¶26	C28.410	
	FAS89, ¶44	Mo6.409	
	FAS87, ¶264	P16.435	
Multiemployer Plan	FAS87, ¶264	P16.435	
	FAS106, ¶518	P40.440	

	Original Pronouncements	Current Text	EITF and Other

TERMINOLOGY—continued

Multiple-Employer Plan	FAS87, ¶264	P16.436	
	FAS106, ¶518	P40.441	
Negaive Goodwill	APB16, ¶87	B50.404	
Net Asset Information	FAS35, ¶280	Pe5.414	
Net Assets	CON6, ¶49-50		
Net Assets Available for Benefits	FAS35, ¶280	Pe5.415	
Net Carrying Amount	APB26, ¶3	D14.402	
Net Incurred Claims Cost (by Age)	FAS106, ¶518	P40.442	
Net Periodic Pension Cost	FAS87, ¶264	P16.437	
Net Periodic Postretirement Benefit Cost	FAS106, ¶518	P40.443	
Net Premium	FAS60, ¶66	In6.423	
Net Realizable Value	FAS53, ¶26	Co2.405	
	FAS86, ¶10	Mo6.410	
Net Receivables	FAS77, ¶12	R20.402	
Net-Spread Method	FIN9, ¶2	Bt7.404	
Network Affiliation Agreement	FAS63, ¶14	Br5.405	
Neutrality	CON2, Glossary		
Nominal	FTB85-2, ¶2	C30.502	
Nonforfeiture Benefits	FAS60, ¶66	In6.424	
Nonmonetary Assets	APB29, ¶3	N35.403	
Nonmonetary Liabilities	APB29, ¶3	N35.403	
Nonmonetary Transactions	APB29, ¶1	N35.404	
Nonparticipating Annuity Contracts	FAS87, ¶264	P16.438	
Nonparticipating Insurance Contract	FAS106, ¶518	P40.444	
Nonpublic Enterprise	FAS21, ¶13	B50.404A	
	FAS79, ¶5	E09.417	
	FAS79, ¶16	S20.407	
	FAS87, ¶264	I27.413	
	FAS109, ¶289		
Nonreciprocal Transfer	APB29, ¶3	C67.406	
	CON6, ¶137	N35.405	
	FAS116, ¶209		
Nonrecourse Financing	FAS98, ¶70	L10.417C	
Normal Servicing Fee Rate	FAS65, ¶34	Mo4.402	
	FAS77, ¶12	R20.401	
Not-for-Profit Organizations	FAS116, ¶209	C67.407	
	FAS117, ¶168	No5.405	
Obligations	CON6, ¶35		
Oil and Gas Producing Activities	FAS19, ¶1	Oi5.403C	
Operating Cycle	ARB43, Ch.3A, ¶5	B05.404	
Operating Lease	FAS13, ¶6	L10.418	
Operating Profit or Loss	FAS14, ¶10	S20.408	
Operating Right	FAS44, ¶3	I60.402	
Option	APB15, App.D	E09.418	
Ordinary Income or Loss	FIN18, ¶5	I73.402	
Origination Fees	FAS91, ¶80	L20.404	
PBGC (Pension Benefit Guaranty Corporation)	FAS35, ¶280	Pe5.417	
	FAS87, ¶264		

See "Terminology" for references to defined terms presented in various accounting pronouncements.
See the Introduction to the Topical Index for details on the use of this index.

	Original Pronouncements	Current Text	EITF and Other

TERMINOLOGY—continued

	Original Pronouncements	Current Text
Parity Adjustment	FAS89, ¶44	C28.411
Participant	FAS35, ¶280	P16.439
	FAS87, ¶264	Pe5.416
Participating Annuity Contract	FAS87, ¶264	P16.440
Participating Insurance	FAS60, ¶66	In6.425
Participating Insurance Contract	FAS106, ¶518	P40.445
Participating Life Insurance Contract	FAS120, ¶18	In6.425A
Participation	FAS53, ¶26	Mo6.411
Participation Right	FAS87, ¶264	P16.441
	FAS106, ¶518	P40.446
Pay-Related Plan	FAS106, ¶518	P40.447
Penalty in Lease Arrangement	FAS98, ¶22	L10.418A
Pension Benefit Formula (Plan's Benefit Formula or Benefit Formula)	FAS87, ¶264	P16.442
Pension Benefits	FAS35, ¶280	P16.443
	FAS87, ¶264	Pe5.418
Pension Plans	FAS35, ¶280	Pe5.419
Per Capita Claims Cost by Age	FAS106, ¶518	P40.448
Permanent Investor	FAS65, ¶34	Mo4.410
Permanent Restriction	FAS117, ¶168	No5.406
Permanently Restricted Net Assets	CON6, ¶92	No5.407
	FAS117, ¶168	
Phase	FAS67, ¶28	Re2.411
Phase-in Plan	FAS92, ¶3	Re6.404A
Physical Capital Maintenance Concept	CON5, ¶47	
Plan	APB25, ¶4	C47.402
	FAS35, ¶280	Pe5.420
	FAS106, ¶518	P40.449
Plan Administrator	FAS35, ¶280	Pe5.421
Plan Amendment	FAS87, ¶264	P16.444
	FAS106, ¶518	P40.450
Plan Assets	FAS87, ¶264	P16.445
	FAS106, ¶518	P40.451
Plan Assets Available for Benefits	FAS87, ¶264	P16.446
Plan Curtailment	FAS87, ¶264	P16.447
	FAS88, ¶6	
Plan Demographics	FAS106, ¶518	P40.452
Plan Participant	FAS106, ¶518	P40.453
Plan Termination	FAS106, ¶518	P40.454
Plan Termination/Reestablishment	FAS87, ¶264	P16.449
Plan's Benefit Formula	FAS87, ¶264	P16.448
Pooling-of-Interests Method	APB16, ¶45	B50.405
Postemployment	FAS81, ¶1	P50:402
Postemployment Benefits	FAS112, ¶1	P32.402
Postretirement	FAS81, ¶1	P50.403
Postretirement Benefit Plan	FAS106, ¶518	P40.455
Postretirement Benefits	FAS106, ¶518	P40.456
Postretirement Benefits Other Than Pensions	FAS106, ¶518	P40.457

	Original Pronouncements	Current Text	EITF and Other
TERMINOLOGY—continued			
Postretirement Health Care Benefits	FAS106, ¶518	P40.458	
Preacquisition Contingencies	FAS38, ¶4	B50.406	
Preacquisition Costs	FAS67, ¶28	Re2.412	
Predictive Value	CON2, Glossary		
Prematurity Period	FAS51, ¶17	Ca4.403	
Prepaid Pension Cost	FAS87, ¶264	P16.450	
Pretax Accounting Income	APB23, ¶21	Bt7.405	
Primary Earnings per Share	APB15, App.D	E09.419	
Principal Owners	FAS57, ¶24	R36.405	
Prior Service Cost	FAS87, ¶264	P16.451	
	FAS106, ¶518	P40.459	
Probable	CON6, ¶25	C59.403	
	CON6, ¶35	Re6.405	
	FAS5, ¶3		
	FAS90, ¶9		
Probable Adjustments	FAS77, ¶12	R20.403	
Probable Mineral Reserves in Extractive Industries Other Than Oil and Gas	FAS89, ¶44	C28.412	
Producer	FAS53, ¶26	Mo6.412	
Product Design	FAS86, ¶52	Co2.406	
Product Enhancement	FAS86, ¶52	Co2.407	
Product Financing Arrangements	FAS49, ¶3	D18.401	
Product Maintenance Contracts	FTB90-1, ¶2	R75.502	
Product Masters	FAS86, ¶52	Co2.408	
Production Costs	FAS53, ¶26	Mo6.413	
Productive Assets	APB29, ¶3	N35.406	
Profit	CON6, ¶16		
Project Costs	FAS67, ¶28	Re2.413	
Project Financing Arrangements	FAS47, ¶23	C32.401	
Projected Benefit Obligation	FAS87, ¶264	P16.452	
Promise to Give	FAS116, ¶209	C67.408	
Property and Liability Insurance Enterprise	FAS60, ¶66	In6.426	
Prospective Reinsurance	FAS113, ¶121	In6.426A	
Proved Area	FAS19, ¶275	Oi5.404	
Proved Mineral Reserves in Extractive Industries Other Than Oil and Gas	FAS89, ¶44	C28.413	
Proved Reserves	FAS25, ¶34	Oi5.405	
Public Enterprise	FAS109, ¶289	I27.414	
Publicly Traded Enterprise	FAS69, ¶1	Oi5.405A	
Purchase Method	APB16, ¶44	B50.407	
Purchaser's Incremental Borrowing Rate	FAS47, ¶23	C32.402	
Purchasing Power Gain or Loss	FAS89, ¶44	C28.414	
Reacquisition Price of Debt	APB26, ¶3	D14.403	
Realization	CON6, ¶143		
Realized, Realizable	CON5, ¶83		
	CON6, ¶143		
Reasonably Possible	FAS5, ¶3	C59.404	
Reciprocal or Interinsurance Exchange	FAS60, ¶66	In6.427	

See "Terminology" for references to defined terms presented in various accounting pronouncements.
See the Introduction to the Topical Index for details on the use of this index.

	Original Pronouncements	Current Text	EITF and Other
TERMINOLOGY—continued			
Recognition	CON5, ¶6		
	CON6, ¶143		
Record Master	FAS50, ¶18	Re4.404	
Recorded Investment in the Receivable	FAS15, ¶28	D22.403	
Recourse	FAS77, ¶12-14	R20.404	
Recoverable Amount	FAS89, ¶44	C28.415	
Redemption Price	APB15, App.D	E09.420	
Regulatory Lag	FAS92, ¶39	Re6.406	
Reinsurance	FAS60, ¶66	In6.428	
Reinsurance Receivables	FAS113, ¶121	In6.428A	
Reinsurer	FAS113, ¶121	In6.428B	
Related Parties	FAS13, ¶5	L10.419	
	FAS57, ¶24	R36.406	
Relative Fair Value before Construction	FAS67, ¶28	Re2.414	
Relevance	CON2, Glossary		
Reliability	CON2, Glossary		
Remote	FAS5, ¶3	C59.405	
Renewal or Extension of a Lease	FAS13, ¶6	L10.420	
Reporting Currency	FAS52, ¶162	F60.417	
Reporting Date	FAS35, ¶280	Pe5.423	
Reporting Enterprise	FAS52, ¶162	F60.418	
Representational Faithfulness	CON2, Glossary		
Repurchase Agreement (Repo)	FIN41, ¶1	B10.406	
Research	FAS2, ¶8	R50.402	
Reserve for Bad Debts	APB23, ¶19	Bt7.406	
Reservoir	FAS19, ¶273	Oi5.406	
Restate-Translate	FAS89, ¶44	C28.416	
Restricted Stock	FAS115, ¶3	I80.405	
Restricted Support	FAS116, ¶209	C67.409	
		No5.408	
Retirees	FAS106, ¶518	P40.460	
Retroactive Benefits	FAS87, ¶264	P16.453	
Retroactive Reinsurance	FAS113, ¶121	In6.428C	
Return on Plan Assets	FAS87, ¶264	P16.454	
Revenue	CON6, ¶78		
Reverse Repurchase Agreement (Reverse Repo)	FIN41, ¶1	B10.407	
Right of Setoff	FIN39, ¶5	B10.408	
Risk	FAS80, ¶4	F80.404	
Risk of Accounting Loss	FAS105, ¶7	F25.404	
Risk of Adverse Deviation	FAS60, ¶66	In6.429	
Royalties	FAS50, ¶18	Re4.405	
Sale-Leaseback Accounting	FAS98, ¶70	L10.420A	
Sales Recognition	FAS98, ¶70	L10.420B	
Sales-Type Lease	FAS13, ¶6	L10.421	
Salvage	FAS60, ¶66	In6.430	
Security	APB15, App.D	E09.421	
	FAS115, ¶137	I80.406	
Segment of a Business	APB30, ¶13	I13.404	

FAS–FASB Statements	FIN–FASB Interpretations	FTB–FASB Technical Bulletins
APB–APB Opinions	AIN–AICPA Interpretations	ARB–Accounting Research Bulletins
CON–FASB Concepts	EITF–EITF Issues	Q&A–FASB Special Reports

	Original Pronouncements	Current Text	EITF and Other
TERMINOLOGY—continued			
Senior Security	APB15, App.D	E09.422	
Separately Priced Contracts	FTB90-1, ¶2	R75.502	
Separate-Valuation Method	FIN9, ¶3	Bt7.407	
Service	FAS35, ¶280	P16.455	
	FAS87, ¶264	Pe5.424	
Service Cost Component (of Net Periodic Pension Cost)	FAS87, ¶264	P16.456	
Service Cost Component (of Net Periodic Postretirement Benefit Cost)	FAS106, ¶518	P40.461	
Service Period	FIN28, ¶3	C47.402A	
Service Potential	CON6, ¶28		
Service Providing Efforts	CON6, ¶112		
Service Well	FAS19, ¶274	Oi5.407	
Servicing	FAS65, ¶34	Mo4.411	
Setoff	FIN39, ¶5	B10.408	
Settlement (of a Postretirement Benefit Plan)	FAS106, ¶518	P40.462	
Settlement Period	FAS113, ¶121	In6.430A	
Settlements	FAS87, ¶264	P16.457	
	FAS88, ¶3		
Short-Term Obligations	FAS6, ¶2	B05.405	
Similar Productive Assets	APB29, ¶3	N35.407	
Single-Employer Plan	FAS87, ¶264	P16.458	
	FAS106, ¶518	P40.463	
Sponsor	FAS35, ¶280	Pe5.425	
Spot Rate	FAS52, ¶162	F60.419	
Standby Commitment	FAS65, ¶34		
Statutory Accounting Practices	FAS60, ¶66	In6.431	
Stock Appreciation Rights	FIN28, ¶9	C47.403	
Stock Dividend	ARB43, Ch.7B, ¶1	C20.401	
Stock Split	ARB43, Ch.7B, ¶2	C20.402	
Stratigraphic Test Well	FAS19, ¶274	Oi5.408	
Subjective Acceleration Clause	FAS78, ¶10	B05.405A	
Subrogation	FAS60, ¶66	In6.432	
Subscriber Related Costs	FAS51, ¶17	Ca4.404	
Subsidiary	APB18, ¶3	I82.408	
Substantive Plan	FAS106, ¶518	P40.464	
Supplemental Actuarial Value	FAS35, ¶280	Pe5.426	
Supplementary Earnings per Share	APB15, App.D	E09.423	
Suspension	FAS87, ¶264	P16.459	
Take-or-Pay Contract	FAS47, ¶23	C32.403	
Tax	FIN18, ¶5	I73.403	
Taxable Income	APB23, ¶21	Bt7.408	
	FAS109, ¶289	I27.415	
Taxable Temporary Difference	FAS109, ¶289	I27.416	
Tax Consequences	FAS109, ¶289	I27.417	
Tax-Planning Strategy	FAS109, ¶289	I27.418	
Temporarily Restricted Net Assets	CON6, ¶93	No5.409	
	FAS117, ¶168		

See "Terminology" for references to defined terms presented in various accounting pronouncements.
See the Introduction to the Topical Index for details on the use of this index.

	Original Pronouncements	Current Text	EITF and Other
TERMINOLOGY—continued			
Temporary Difference	FAS109, ¶289	I27.419	
Temporary Restriction	FAS117, ¶168	No5.410	
Termination	FAS60, ¶66	In6.434	
Termination Benefits	FAS106, ¶518	P40.465	
Termination Rate	FAS60, ¶66	In6.435	
Term Life Insurance	FAS60, ¶66	In6.433	
Testing	FAS86, ¶52	Co2.409	
Throughput Contract	FAS47, ¶23	C32.404	
Time of Issuance	APB15, App.D	E09.424	
Time of Restructuring	FAS15, ¶6	D22.404	
Timeliness	CON2, Glossary		
Title Insurance Enterprise	FAS60, ¶66	In6.436	
Title Plant	FAS61, ¶1	Ti7.401	
Transaction	CON6, ¶137		
Transaction Date	FAS52, ¶162	F60.420	
Transaction Gain (Loss)	FAS52, ¶162	F60.421	
Transition Asset	FAS106, ¶518	P40.466	
Transition Obligation	FAS106, ¶518	P40.467	
Translate-Restate	FAS89, ¶44	C28.417	
Translation	FAS52, ¶162	F60.422	
Translation Adjustment	FAS52, ¶162	C28.418	
	FAS89, ¶44	F60.423	
Treasury Stock Method	APB15, App.D	E09.425	
Troubled Debt Restructuring	FAS15, ¶2	D22.405	
Turnover	FAS87, ¶264	P16.460	
Two-Class Method	APB15, App.D	E09.426	
Uncertainty	CON6, ¶44		
Unconditional Promise to Give	FAS116, ¶209	C67.410 No5.411	
Understandability	CON2, Glossary		
Unfunded Accrued Pension Cost	FAS87, ¶264	P16.461	
Unfunded Accumulated Benefit Obligation	FAS87, ¶264	P16.462	
Unfunded Accumulated Postretirement Benefit Obligation	FAS106, ¶518	P40.468	
Unguaranteed Residual Value	FAS13, ¶5	L10.422	
Unrealized	CON6, ¶43		
Unrecognized Net Gain or Loss	FAS87, ¶264	P16.463	
	FAS106, ¶518	P40.469	
Unrecognized Prior Service Cost	FAS87, ¶264	P16.464	
	FAS106, ¶518	P40.470	
Unrecognized Transition Asset	FAS106, ¶518	P40.471	
Unrecognized Transition Obligation	FAS106, ¶518	P40.472	
Unrelated Parties	FAS13, ¶5	L10.423	
Unrestricted Net Assets	CON6, ¶94	No5.412	
	FAS117, ¶168		
Unrestricted Support	FAS116, ¶209	C67.411 No5.413	

FAS–FASB Statements   FIN–FASB Interpretations   FTB–FASB Technical Bulletins
APB–APB Opinions   AIN–AICPA Interpretations   ARB–Accounting Research Bulletins
CON–FASB Concepts   EITF–EITF Issues   Q&A–FASB Special Reports

	Original Pronouncements	Current Text	EITF and Other

TERMINOLOGY—continued
Valuation Allowance .... FAS109, ¶289 — I27.420
.... CON6, ¶34 — V18.401
Value in Use .... FAS89, ¶44 — C28.419
Variable Annuity Contract .... FAS60, ¶66 — In6.437
Variable Stock Option, Purchase and
  Award Plans .... APB25, ¶29 — C47.405
Verifiability .... CON2, Glossary
Vested Benefit Obligation .... FAS87, ¶264 — P16.465
Vested Benefits .... FAS35, ¶280 — P16.466
.... FAS87, ¶264 — Pe5.427
Voluntary Health and Welfare
  Organizations .... FAS117, ¶168 — No5.414
Warrant .... APB15, App.D — E09.427
Weighted-Average Number of Shares .... APB15, App.D — E09.428
Whole-Life Contract .... FAS60, ¶66 — In6.438
Working Capital .... ARB43, Ch.3A, ¶3 — B05.406
Working Model .... FAS86, ¶52 — Co2.410
Wrap Lease Transactions .... FTB88-1, ¶21 — L10.424
THREE PERCENT RULE
See Earnings per Share
THRIFT INDUSTRY
See Banking and Thrift Industries
THROUGHPUT CONTRACTS
See Financial Instruments
Definition .... FAS47, ¶23 — C32.404
Illustration .... FAS47, ¶24-28 — C32.106-110
TIMBERLANDS AND GROWING TIMBER
Changing Prices Information .... FAS89, ¶25-26 — C28.121-122
TIMELINESS
Definition .... CON2, Glossary
Relation to Usefulness and Relevance .... CON2, ¶56-57
TIME-SHARING INTERESTS (REAL ESTATE)
See Real Estate: Sales Other Than Retail Land Sales
TITLE INSURANCE ENTERPRISE
See Insurance Industry
See Title Plant
Definition .... FAS60, ¶66 — In6.436
TITLE PLANT
See Disclosure
Capitalization .... FAS61, ¶3-6 — Ti7.103-106
Definition .... FAS61, ¶1 — Ti7.401
Description .... FAS61, ¶1 — Ti7.101
Impairment of Value .... FAS61, ¶6 — Ti7.106
.... FAS121, ¶29
Maintenance and Title Searches .... FAS61, ¶7 — Ti7.107
Sale of Asset .... FAS61, ¶9 — Ti7.109

See "Terminology" for references to defined terms presented in various accounting pronouncements.
See the Introduction to the Topical Index for details on the use of this index.

	Original Pronouncements	Current Text	EITF and Other
TITLE PLANT—continued			
Scope of Accounting and Reporting Requirements	FAS61, ¶2	Ti7.102	
Storage and Retrieval	FAS61, ¶8	Ti7.108	
TOTAL NONOWNER CHANGES IN EQUITY			
See Comprehensive Income			
TRADEMARKS			
Intangible Assets	APB17, ¶1	I60.101	
TRADE PAYABLES/RECEIVABLES			
See Balance Sheet Classification: Current Assets and Liabilities			
See Financial Instruments			
TRANSACTIONS			
See Events and Transactions			
TRANSACTIONS WITH AFFILIATES			
See Related Parties			
TRANSFERS, NONRECIPROCAL AND RECIPROCAL			
See Nonmonetary Transactions			
TRANSLATE-RESTATE METHOD			
See Changing Prices: Reporting Their Effects in Financial Reports			
TRANSLATION			
See Foreign Currency Translation			
Definition	FAS52, ¶162	F60.422	
TRANSLATION ADJUSTMENTS			
See Changing Prices: Reporting Their Effects in Financial Reports			
See Foreign Currency Translation			
Definition	FAS52, ¶162	F60.423	
TREASURY BONDS			
See Debt: Extinguishments			
TREASURY STOCK			
See Capital Stock: Treasury Stock			
TREASURY STOCK METHOD			
See Earnings per Share			
Definition	APB15, App.D	E09.425	
TROUBLED DEBT RESTRUCTURING			
See Debt: Restructurings			
See Impairment: Loans			
Definition	FAS15, ¶2	D22.405	
TRUSTS			
Acquisition of Employer Shares for/by an Employee Benefit Trust			EITF.93-2
Assets in Defeasance Trust Reacquired			EITF.86-36
Consideration of the Impact of Bankruptcy in Determining Plan Assets under Statement 106			EITF.93-3

FAS–FASB Statements	FIN–FASB Interpretations	FTB–FASB Technical Bulletins
APB–APB Opinions	AIN–AICPA Interpretations	ARB–Accounting Research Bulletins
CON–FASB Concepts	EITF–EITF Issues	Q&A–FASB Special Reports

T-439

	Original Pronouncements	Current Text	EITF and Other

TRUSTS—continued
Financial Statements of Common Trust
  Funds
. . Exemption from the Requirement to
     Provide a Statement of Cash Flows.... FAS102, ¶6-7   C25.135B-135C
Related Parties .... FAS57, ¶1   R36.101
TWENTY PERCENT RULE
See Earnings per Share
TWO-CLASS COMMON STOCK
See Earnings per Share

(The next page is T-453.)

See "Terminology" for references to defined terms presented in various accounting pronouncements.
See the Introduction to the Topical Index for details on the use of this index.

	Original Pronouncements	Current Text	EITF and Other

UMBRELLA PARTNERSHIP REAL ESTATE INVESTMENT TRUST (UPREIT)
See Real Estate

UNAMORTIZED DISCOUNT
See Debt: Extinguishments
See Debt: Restructurings
See Interest: Imputation of an Interest Cost

UNASSERTED CLAIMS
See Insurance Industry

UNAUDITED FINANCIAL STATEMENTS

Accounting Policies	APB22, ¶10	A10.104	
Earnings per Share	AIN-APB15, #14	E09.562-563	

UNBILLED RECEIVABLES
See Contractor Accounting: Government Contracts

UNCERTAINTIES
See Accounting Changes
See Adjustments of Financial Statements for Prior Periods
See Contingencies
See Franchising
See Pension Costs
Actuarial Assumptions
  See Defined Benefit Pension Plans

Effects of	CON6, ¶44-48	
Relation to Assets	CON6, ¶175	
Relation to Recognition of Assets and Liabilities	CON6, ¶48	
Relation to Reliability	CON6, ¶45-48	
Relation to Representational Faithfulness	CON2, ¶72-76	

UNCONSOLIDATED SUBSIDIARIES
See Consolidation
See Investments: Equity Method
See Segment of Business Reporting

UNDERSTANDABILITY

Definition	CON2, Glossary	
User-Specific Characteristic	CON2, ¶40-41	

UNDEVELOPED PROPERTIES
See Oil and Gas Producing Activities

UNDISTRIBUTED EARNINGS OF SUBSIDIARIES
See Income Taxes

UNEARNED DISCOUNTS

Balance Sheet Classification	ARB43, Ch.3A, ¶4	B05.105

UNEARNED REVENUES
See Revenue Recognition

Qualification as Liabilities	CON6, ¶197	

	Original Pronouncements	Current Text	EITF and Other
UNFUNDED PAST (PRIOR) SERVICE COST			
See Pension Costs			
UNFUNDED PENSION PLANS			
See Defined Benefit Pension Plans			
See Pension Costs			
UNINCORPORATED VENTURES			
See Investments: Equity Method			
UNINSURED RISKS			
See Contingencies			
Accounting by Insureds for Claims-Made Insurance Policies			EITF.86-12
UNIT OF PRODUCTION METHOD			
See Oil and Gas Producing Activities			
Depreciation			EITF.84-28
UNIVERSITIES AND COLLEGES			
See Not-for-Profit Organizations			
UNPROVED PROPERTIES			
See Oil and Gas Producing Activities			
UNREALIZED			
Definition	CON6, ¶143		
UNREALIZED PROFITS			
See Inventory			
See Revenue Recognition			
UNSTATED RIGHTS OR PRIVILEGES			
That Affect Interest Rate on a Note	APB21, ¶7	I69.104	
UNUSUAL ITEMS			
See Defined Benefit Pension Plans			
See Extraordinary Items			
See Income Statement			
See Income Statement Presentation: Discontinued Operations			
See Interim Financial Reporting			
Disclosure	APB30, ¶26	I22.101	
Scope of Accounting and Reporting Requirements	APB30, ¶26	I22.101	
USEFUL LIFE			
See Depreciation			
See Intangible Assets			
USEFULNESS			
Choice between Accounting Methods	CON2, ¶10-11		
	CON2, ¶14-15		
	CON2, ¶17		
Financial Statements			
. . Classification and Aggregation in	CON5, ¶20-22		
. . Individually and Collectively	CON5, ¶17-19		
Information for Assessing Cash Flow Prospects	CON1, ¶37-39		
Information for Investment and Credit Decisions	CON1, ¶34-36		

See "Terminology" for references to defined terms presented in various accounting pronouncements.
See the Introduction to the Topical Index for details on the use of this index.

	Original Pronouncements	Current Text	EITF and Other

USEFULNESS—continued

Relation to Timeliness .... CON2, ¶56-57

USERS OF FINANCIAL INFORMATION

Description .... CON1, ¶24-27

External Users .... CON1, ¶25-27

General Purpose Financial Statements .... CON5, ¶15-16

.... CON5, ¶28-30

Management .... CON1, ¶27

Not-for-Profit Organizations .... CON4, ¶29-32

Understanding Financial Accounting .... CON2, ¶36-41

UTILITIES

See Insurance Costs

See Regulated Operations

(The next page is T-461.)

FAS–FASB Statements	FIN–FASB Interpretations	FTB–FASB Technical Bulletins
APB–APB Opinions	AIN–AICPA Interpretations	ARB–Accounting Research Bulletins
CON–FASB Concepts	EITF–EITF Issues	Q&A–FASB Special Reports

	Original Pronouncements	Current Text	EITF and Other
VACATION PAY			
See Compensation to Employees: Paid Absences			
VALUATION ALLOWANCES			
See Bad-Debt Allowances			
See Disclosure			
See Impairment: Loans			
See Income Taxes			
Deferred Profit on Repossessed Real Estate			EITF.89-14
Definition	CON6, ¶34	V18.401	
	CON6, ¶43		
Examples			
. . Bad Debts	APB12, ¶2	V18.102	
. . Depreciation, Depletion	APB12, ¶2-3	V18.102	
. . Losses on Investments	APB12, ¶2-3	V18.102	
Following Conversion of a Loan into a Security			EITF.94-8
Following Debt Restructurings			EITF.87-5
Loan Loss Allowances			
. . Applying Savings and Loan Audit Guide			EITF.87-5
. . Differences between GAAP and RAP			EITF.85-44
Mortgage Loans, Mortgage-Backed Securities	FAS65, ¶4	Mo4.105	
	FAS115, ¶128		
Mortgage Servicing Rights	FAS122, ¶3	Mo4.118A-118B	
VALUATION METHODS			
Last-In, First-Out (LIFO)			EITF.84-24
VARIABLE STOCK OPTION PLANS			
See Compensation to Employees: Stock Purchase and Stock Option Plans			
VENTURE CAPITAL COMPANY			
Accounting for a Business Combination Involving a Majority-Owned Investee of a Venture Capital Company			EITF.90-10
VERIFIABILITY			
Component to Reliability	CON2, ¶81-89		
Definition	CON2, Glossary		
VESTED BENEFIT OBLIGATION (VBO)			
See Pension Costs			
Benefits Payable Immediately			EITF.88-1
COLA-Adjusted from Termination to Normal Retirement Date			EITF.88-1
Effect When VBO Exceeds Accumulated Benefit Obligation			EITF.88-1
VETERANS ADMINISTRATION (VA)			
Mortgage Guarantee			
. . Effect on Profit Recognition by Seller			EITF.87-9

FAS–FASB Statements   FIN–FASB Interpretations   FTB–FASB Technical Bulletins
APB–APB Opinions   AIN–AICPA Interpretations   ARB–Accounting Research Bulletins
CON–FASB Concepts   EITF–EITF Issues   Q&A–FASB Special Reports

	Original Pronouncements	Current Text	EITF and Other
VOLUNTARY HEALTH AND WELFARE ORGANIZATIONS See Not-for-Profit Organizations			
Definition	FAS117, ¶168	No5.414	
VOTING STOCK See Capital Stock: Capital Transactions			

(The next page is T-465.)

See "Terminology" for references to defined terms presented in various accounting pronouncements.
See the Introduction to the Topical Index for details on the use of this index.

	Original Pronouncements	Current Text	EITF and Other

WAGES
See Compensation to Employees: Deferred
See Compensation to Employees: Paid Absences

WAR CONTRACTS
See Contractor Accounting: Government Contracts

WARRANTIES
See Contingencies
See Related Parties
Extended Warranty and Product Maintenance Contracts

. . Recognition of Revenues and Costs	FTB90-1, ¶1-5	R75.501-505	EITF.89-17
....	FTB90-1, ¶8-9		
....	FTB90-1, ¶12		
Recognition of Revenues and Costs Associated with Extended Warranty Contracts			EITF.89-17
Revenue Recognition	FAS48, ¶4	R75.106	

WARRANTS
See Debt: Convertible Debt and Debt with Stock Purchase Warrants
See Financial Instruments

Business Combinations	AIN-APB16, #12	B50.534-538	
Contingent Stock Purchase Warrants			EITF.84-8
Exchangeable Debt......................................			EITF.85-9
Issued in Connection with Research and Development Costs	FAS68, ¶13	R55.111	
Issued in Connection with Sales Agreements			EITF.84-8
Issued with Debt	APB14, ¶16	C08.104	EITF.85-9
....			EITF.86-35
Put Warrants			
. . Balance Sheet Classification			EITF.88-9
. . Effect on Earnings-per-Share Calculation			EITF.88-9

WHOLLY OWNED SUBSIDIARIES
See Consolidation
See Related Parties

WORK-IN-PROCESS
See Inventory

Balance Sheet Classification	ARB43, Ch.3A, ¶4	B05.105	

WORKERS' COMPENSATION
See Compensation to Employees: Deferred
See Compensation to Employees: Paid Absences
See Contingencies
See Postemployment Benefits

	Original Pronouncements	Current Text	EITF and Other

WORKING CAPITAL
Definition .... ARB43, Ch.3A, ¶3   B05.406
WORKS OF ART
Depreciation.. FAS93, ¶6   D40.101A-101C
.... FAS93, ¶35-37
WRAP LEASE TRANSACTIONS
See Leases
WRITE-DOWNS
See Contingencies
See Debt: Restructurings
See Fixed Assets
See Impairment
See Impairment: Loans
See Lower of Cost or Market
See Property, Plant, and Equipment
See Write-offs
Operating Assets... FAS5, ¶31   C59.137
WRITE-OFFS
See Extraordinary Items
See Write-downs
Intangible Assets... ARB43, Ch.5, ¶8-9   I60.121-122
.... FAS44, ¶4
WRITE-UPS
See Depreciation
Foreign Assets... APB6, ¶17   D40.102

(The next page is T-471.)

See "Terminology" for references to defined terms presented in various accounting pronouncements.
See the Introduction to the Topical Index for details on the use of this index.

	Original Pronouncements	Current Text	EITF and Other

YIELD
See Earnings per Share
ZERO COUPON BONDS
See Financial Instruments
Cash Yield Test for Determining Common
  Stock Equivalents.....................................   EITF.84-16
Use in a Troubled Debt Restructuring.........   EITF.87-18

(Cut along this line.)

TO USERS OF THE *ORIGINAL PRONOUNCEMENTS/CURRENT TEXT* (1995/1996 EDITION)

To assist us in improving the quality of the topical index, please complete this form and return it to the Financial Accounting Standards Board. Thank you.

• If you have had difficulty locating a particular topic in the index, please indicate that topic below.

_____

• List the paragraph(s) in the source material that cover(s) this topic.

_____

• Please indicate your suggested reference terms for locating this topic in the index.

(Primary heading) _____

(First subheading) _____

(Second subheading) _____

• If you think the topic should be listed under more than one primary heading, please indicate where.

_____

• Please list any other suggestions for changes that would make this volume more useful to you.

_____

(Optional information):

Name _____

Firm/Organization _____

Address _____

( ) _____
City/State/Zip   Telephone

Send the completed form to:

Financial Accounting Standards Board
Attn: Judith A. Noë
401 Merritt 7
P.O. Box 5116
Norwalk, CT 06856-5116